The Handbook of Child Language

Edited by

*Paul Fletcher and
Brian MacWhinney*

Blackwell
Publishing

BLACKWELL PUBLISHING
350 Main Street, Malden, MA 02148-5020, USA
108 Cowley Road, Oxford OX4 1JF, UK
550 Swanston Street, Carlton, Victoria 3053, Australia

First published 1995
First published in paperback 1996
Reprinted 2000, 2004 (twice)

Library of Congress Cataloging-in-Publication Data

The Handbook of Child Language / edited by Paul Fletcher and Brian MacWhinney
    p. cm.
  Includes bibliographical references and index.
  ISBN 0–631–18405–8 — ISBN 0–631–20312–5 (pbk)
  1. Language acquisition. 2. Language disorders in children.
  I. Fletcher, Paul. II. MacWhinney, Brian
P118.H347 1995
401'.93—dc20
                        94–15066
                        CIP

A catalogue record for this title is available from the British Library.

Set in 10 on 12 pt Palatino
by Graphicraft Typesetters Ltd, Hong Kong
Printed and bound in India
by Replika Press Pvt Ltd, Kundli

The publisher's policy is to use permanent paper from mills that operate a sustainable forestry policy, and which has been manufactured from pulp processed using acid-free and elementary chlorine-free practices. Furthermore, the publisher ensures that the text paper and cover board used have met acceptable environmental accreditation standards.

For further information on
Blackwell Publishing, visit our website:
www.blackwellpublishing.com

Contents

Contributors

Dorothy M. Aram
Emerson College

Martyn Barrett
University of Surrey

Elizabeth Bates
University of California at San Diego

Robin S. Chapman
University of Wisconsin-Madison

Eve V. Clark
Stanford University

Holly K. Craig
University of Michigan

Philip S. Dale
University of Washington

Annick de Houwer
Belgian National Science Foundation and University of Antwerp

Jill de Villiers
Smith College

Julie A. Eisele
Skidmore College

Richard Ely
Boston University

Paul Fletcher
Reading University

Jane Gillette
University of Pennsylvania

Jean Berko Gleason
Boston University

Lila R. Gleitman
University of Pennsylvania

Roberta Michnick Golinkoff
University of Delaware

Maya Hickmann
Université René Descartes, Paris Centre National de la Recherche
Scientifique, EPHE

Kathy Hirsh-Pasek
Temple University

Richard Ingham
University of Reading

Raymond D. Kent
University of Wisconsin-Madison

Thomas Klee
University of Newcastle upon Tyne

Laurence B. Leonard
Purdue University

John L. Locke
Massachusetts General Hospital and Harvard Medical School

Brian MacWhinney
Carnegie Mellon University

Jürgen M. Meisel
University of Hamburg

Lise Menn
University of Colorado

Jon F. Miller
University of Wisconsin-Madison

Giuliana Miolo
University of Wisconsin-Madison

Elinor Ochs
University of California at Los Angeles

Ann M. Peters
University of Hawai'i

Kim Plunkett
Oxford University

Andrew Radford
University of Essex

Bambi Schieffelin
New York University

Catherine E. Snow
Harvard University Graduate School of Education

Carol Stoel-Gammon
University of Washington

Donna Thal
San Diego State University

Acknowledgments

Editorial duties for this volume were rendered less onerous by the cooperation of our contributors in meeting deadlines and in speedy responses to editorial requests. The emergence of the book was ably overseen by our publishers, particularly Steve Smith; and our copy-editor, Jack Messenger, dealt efficiently with a particularly complex manuscript. Our thanks go to all of them.

Paul Fletcher
Brian MacWhinney

Part I Theory, Method, and Context

Introduction

Theoretical Approaches (Chapters 1–3)

The study of child language acquisition is alive and well. The chapters in this volume portray a field that is awake, energetic, and open to a wide variety of new ideas. While maintaining the hard-won methods and insights developed over the last 30 years, language acquisition researchers continue to explore the implications of new models, techniques, and data from linguistics, psychology, cognitive neuroscience, artificial intelligence, philosophy, and socialization theory. The thirst of language acquisition researchers for new data and new data analysis procedures has been further whetted by developments in computer technology and data storage. The store of crosslinguistic samples and transcript comparisons continues to grow month to month, as does the richness of theory, observation, and experimentation with both normal and disordered children.

Not surprisingly, this energy and activity is also accompanied by lively theoretical and methodological debates, many of which are represented in this volume. Chomskyans emphasize the extent to which children are guided by innate linguistic knowledge. Connectionists emphasize the ways in which cognitive structure, general learning mechanisms, and the structure of cues in the environment can facilitate a flexible approach to language learning. Socialization theorists focus particularly on the ways in which children pick up language in social contexts with the help of caregivers and peers, under the guidance of the structure of social meanings. No one doubts the eventual importance of all three of these perspectives. However, detailed proposals regarding the ways in which children acquire particular target structures are inevitably subject to dispute, as each of the major paradigms attempts to maximize the extent to which it can account for important phenomena in language acquisition.

This first section of our handbook presents three chapters specifically designed to explicate each of these major perspectives. Generative grammar is represented by Jürgen Meisel, connectionist learning theory by Kim Plunkett, and socialization theory by Elinor Ochs and Bambi Schieffelin.

Parameter theory

Meisel presents a lucid summary of the approach to language development currently being developed within generative grammar. This approach is grounded on the now classic "poverty of stimulus" argument. Citing evidence from retracings, ellipses, and slips of the tongue, Chomsky has claimed that the verbal input to the child is degenerate, deficient, and impoverished. He argues that no learner can build an adult language out of such degenerate input, unless closely guided by a rich set of species-specific innate hypotheses coded in the genetic determinants of the language organ. However, any attempt to set these innate hypotheses in too rigid a way would run afoul of the obvious fact that languages differ markedly in the ways in which they structure words and sentences. In order to allow for flexibility, while still preserving innate guidance, Mcisel recommends an approach to language acquisition based on the theory of "parameter setting." According to this model, children's basic task in language learning is to set values on each of these parameters that correspond to those required by their native language. Not all aspects of language need to be determined through parameters, only those which show actual variation across languages. In order to set the correct value for a parameter, the child needs to be able to detect the presence in the input of the specific "trigger" for that value of the parameter.

The parameter setting approach to language acquisition needs to address three difficult issues. First, linguists must succeed in isolating a set of parameters that correctly define the class of possible human languages. It is much too early to say whether this can be done in a descriptively adequate and theoretically satisfying way. Second, language acquisition researchers must be able to specify a series of triggers or procedures for converting input data into triggers that can work to set the right values of each parameter for each language without reliance on techniques for subsequent resetting and retuning. In this regard, there has been progress in terms of limiting the degree of sentential embeddedness required for detecting parameters to main clauses and certain limited aspects of subordinate clauses. However, the actual specifications for trigger identification and usage are still extremely unclear. Third, once proposals regarding trigger identification have been formalized, a procedure must be developed for testing the empirical adequacy of these proposals. Until these matters are resolved, it will be difficult to evaluate the eventual possible contribution of parameter setting as an articulation of the generative vision of language acquisition.

Connectionism

Plunkett reviews recent progress in associationist models of language learning. These models are developed within the framework of the Parallel Distributed Processing (PDP) neural network models of Rumelhart and McClelland (1986). The neural network simulation of the learning of the English past tense developed by Rumelhart and McClelland presents a radical alternative to the rule-based and category-based symbols of generative grammar (MacWhinney, 1994). Plunkett reviews the debate between the connectionist and the symbolists in regard to the learning of inflectional marking. He shows that, under certain conditions, connectionist models can capture the basic overgeneralization phenomena that have been used to argue for a separation between "rote" and "rule." It seems to me that connectionist models have succeeded reasonably well in accounting for some of the basic facts of inflectional learning. However, the models for concept formation, vocabulary development, and syntactic learning that Plunkett presents seem to be rather too limited to capture even the core range of phenomena in each of these areas. It is certainly too early to declare that connectionism should be written off as a possible approach to language learning. However, it will be important for workers in this area to focus on the conversion of small-scale models to full models that can be directly tested against the full set of facts about language learning currently available.

Socialization theory

Ochs and Schieffelin underscore the extent to which cultural factors have been neglected in current descriptions of grammatical learning. Although cultures appear to differ markedly in the extent to which they support language learning through grammatical simplification, children all begin to master the core aspects of linguistic structure during their third year. Thus, it is not spoon-feeding of particular forms that children need to pick up language, but rather direct engagement in socially meaningful and appropriate activities. If a grammatical form is a part of a socially valued activity and if children are encouraged to learn that form, it will inevitably be learned. If a form is not a part of an activity in which the child is encouraged to become a full participant, it will not be learned. Thus, mere exposure is not a sufficient condition for learning. It is unclear whether the emphasis that Ochs and Schieffelin place upon the social dimension in language learning should be viewed as a challenge to other major views of grammatical learning. At a minimum, it would force connectionists to implement a social attention focusing mechanism and generativists to factor in social structures into any predictions regarding the course of maturation of grammatical knowledge. On a deeper level, models may need to treat social information as strongly competitive with other percepts. Some steps in that direction can be found in chapters 6–9.

Methods (Chapters 4 and 5)

Theories and models are crucial to every science. They provide a way of organizing findings and orienting thinking. But science does not live on theory alone. Theory must be accompanied by a powerful and solid methodology. In large measure, child language research has depended upon methodologies developed within linguistics and psychology. From linguistics, it has borrowed the techniques of field work, distributional analysis, and the comparative method. From psychology, it has borrowed basic experimental technique, applications of statistics, and computational modeling. More recently, advances in computational power have made available a wide range of data organization techniques through text editors, digitization methods, databases, morphological analyzers, and parsers. This section comprises two chapters exemplifying some of the most recent advances in child language methodology.

Individual differences

Bates, Dale, and Thal present some of the most recent results of a general research program pursued by Bates and her colleagues since the early 1970s. Stimulated initially by proposals from Nelson (1973) and Bloom et al. (1975), Bates developed a technique for studying individual differences based on correlations between measures from maternal interview, symbolic play, gesture, lexical development, phonology, and early syntax. The patterns of individual differences delineated by Bates and her colleagues have had major theoretical consequences for the study of innate contributions to language development, modularity, and the biological bases of language disorders. In the current chapter, Bates, Dale, and Thal report on applications of the MacArthur Communicative Development Inventory (CDI). Using the CDI, they document certain patterns of variability and dissociations between comprehension, production, and the use of word combinations. They use these data to argue against modular views of language development, and also apply the techniques of individual differences analysis to shed new light on the contrast between analytic and holistic learning styles, as well as on the status of language disorders such as Williams and Down Syndrome. Throughout, the authors emphasize that the dissociations they have observed between comprehension and production are complemented by strong positive associations between lexical and grammatical development. It is safe to say that our theories of language learning have not yet succeeded in accounting for these major new findings.

Transcript technology

Just as the CDI has emerged as the major research tool for studying patterns of early language learning, the CHILDES tools developed by MacWhinney, Snow, and colleagues have become the procedures of choice for the study of language development in the third year and beyond. The CHILDES Project has set as its goal the establishment of a uniform database of naturalistic data on language learning. This database is supplemented by a consistent system for transcription and a set of analysis programs that run on all the major computer platforms. Since their introduction in 1986, these tools have had a major impact on the way in which child language research is conducted. It would be safe to say that the majority of new empirical studies of spontaneous language production are now making use of the CHILDES transcript format and data analysis programs. At the same time, the database has been used in hundreds of studies as a way of testing hypotheses and directing the collection of new data. Despite these successes of the CHILDES Project, there are many clear limitations, including an overreliance on coded text, problems with consistent use of certain transcription categories, and difficulties in using the more complex aspects of some of the programs. To address these problems, MacWhinney and colleagues have begun to focus on links between transcripts and actual digitized sound, new computer interfaces promoting increased user-friendliness, and automatic tools for conducting structural analyses.

Social and Contextual Influences (Chapters 6–9)

Ochs and Schieffelin (chapter 3) have pointed out the degree to which theories of language learning need to assign a role to social and contextual factors. For theories to do this successfully, we need to have increasingly clear data on exactly how social forces impact upon the child. The four chapters in this section document the considerable progress that has been made in this area across four very different fronts. Together, these new analyses provide a substantive groundwork for reevaluating the role of the social context in language learning.

The role of the input

Snow directly challenges the Chomskyan emphasis on the "poverty of the stimulus," pointing to a wide array of forces that underscore the subtlety and the complexity of social impacts on language learning. Much of her argument rests upon recent work demonstrating a remarkable "finetuning" of the parent's input to the child. The initial studies in this area often used coarse and global measures of language learning and skill. Looking at the process of acquisition with finer measures more attuned to individual aspects of learning across a wider range of communicative abilities has provided stronger evidence for a direct role of the input on language learning. By intensifying our focus on individual difference, cultural differences, and differences caused by developmental delay, we can gain still further insights regarding the effects of input on the learning process. It may turn out that parental input has relatively more impact on learning of the lexicon and discourse than on the core features of grammatical knowledge. But it seems likely that the study of detailed features of parental input will be a topic of ongoing interest for all students of language acquisition.

Discourse organization

The learning of discourse skills involves a complex interplay of social, contextual, cognitive, lexical, and grammatical functions. Although the child learns the core grammatical and phonological aspects of the native language by age three, there is a great deal of discourse learning that continues well into the school years. At the same time, there are many ways in which the referential skills underlying discourse function develop even before the use of the first words. Hickmann surveys the wide range of this important field, examining important functions such as given–new organization, foregrounding, and the various types of anaphoric reference. She paints a picture of certain universal patterns in discourse development, such as the shift from exophoric to anaphoric reference, or the increased structure of texts and scripts. At the same time, she emphasizes the importance of the devices provided by individual languages in determining the exact nature of the contrasts expressed by children at a given point in development.

Early bilingualism

De Houwer reviews a wide range of recent literature on the learning of two or more languages during early childhood. A core question that motivates much of this literature is the interest in determining whether the child treats the two different languages as grammatically separate from the beginning or whether there might be a period of time during which the two languages are functionally merged. Focusing primarily on evidence from her own Dutch–English bilingual subject, De Houwer concludes that there is little strong evidence for early language mixing. Of course, this conclusion needs to be qualified in a variety of ways. First, one needs to characterize the many different social configurations in which two languages can be learned. Second, one has to carefully sort out data in which overt code switching occurs within utterances. Third, one needs to collect very large amounts of data from a long age range including some of the earliest sentences in order to provide a careful test of language merger. Finally, one has to realize that languages as close as Dutch and English may not provide the most stringent test of the early separation hypothesis. Having made these various provisos, one must agree with De Houwer, that evidence currently available provides little or no support for the hypothesis of early bilingual language merger.

Contextual influences

Ely and Gleason examine the issue of the influence of language and context on the process of socialization. Even though they confine themselves to data on language socialization contexts in the English-speaking world, the literature they are examining is truly vast. Much of this work emphasizes the ways in which the community socializes the child not just through overt verbal formulations, but also indirectly through example and assumption. For the first few years, the parent is the chief bearer of the child's "social marching orders." However, as the child grows older, the school, other caregivers, the peer group, and the mass media each play important and nonoverlapping roles in the process of language socialization. By understanding the ways in which children are socialized through language, we come to learn more about language, social structure, and fundamental aspects of human nature.

Theoretical Approaches

1 Parameters in Acquisition

JÜRGEN M. MEISEL

1 Introduction

Parameter theory, a version of a theory of universal grammar (UG), has been developed to account for universal as well as particular aspects of grammars. The latter point, the fact that it is designed to explain language variation, makes it particularly attractive for research concerned with the development of grammar in children, for it offers theoretical concepts and mechanisms designed to deal not only with diversity among languages but also with variation across the range of possible interim grammars in language acquisition. The present chapter introduces and discusses crucial notions of parameter theory and outlines current developments. It thus focuses on variable properties of child grammars.

It should be noted that, in spite of the fact that this theory has been received very positively by many researchers, a fair number of the issues addressed in this chapter are far from being settled. In fact, even a number of rather fundamental questions about the epistemological status of parameters, as well as about how exactly one should imagine them actually operating, remain unanswered. In what follows, I will summarize, in each case, what is generally agreed upon and what I believe to be the crucial arguments in the ongoing debate; whenever possible, I will suggest solutions for controversial issues, even though, in more than one case, these may not represent the most widely accepted opinion.

2 Principles and Parameters of Universal Grammar

According to Chomsky (1986a, b), the goal of the theory of UG is to model the specific mental capacity which enables humans to process the highly complex structures of language. The kind of knowledge involved seems to be largely underdetermined by the data, i.e. humans apparently have access to a substantial body of knowledge about language which cannot be "learned," since the relevant information is not present in the empirical basis for such learning, neither in the primary linguistic data nor in the context. Because of this discrepancy between experience and knowledge, termed "Plato's problem," the implicit knowledge constituting the initial state of the language faculty is claimed to be genetically transmitted. The theory of UG formulates this *a priori* knowledge in terms of principles and parameters which determine the set of possible human languages.

This approach represents an important difference, when compared to earlier versions of generative grammar. In the "Standard Theory" (Chomsky, 1965), for example, the initial state had been assigned the task of defining possible rules, as well as providing for an evaluation procedure selecting the optimal rule system. In the "Principles and Parameters Theory," as developed by Chomsky (1981) and others, however, UG is not conceived of as a set of rules. In fact, the notion that independent "rules" can be stipulated has been entirely eliminated. The reason is that it became increasingly obvious, as pointed out by Williams (1987), that even if one were to succeed in writing descriptively adequate grammars consisting of sets of rules, no progress would be made towards explanatory adequacy unless the evaluation metric was discovered which enables the child to choose between the (possibly very large number) of grammars which account equally well for the given data. Yet little progress had been made with regard to insights concerning this evaluation metric. Rather, the more elaborate the rules – transformations and others – became, the less obvious it was how children could acquire such rule systems and how they would evaluate them in comparison to descriptively equally adequate ones. Reflections of this kind, in addition to empirical observations indicating that language development proceeds quite uniformly even under very different input conditions (e.g. multilingual environment, blindness, deafness) and with severe neurological deficits, led to the conclusion that UG is part of the genetically endowed knowledge of humans.

The well-foundedness of this assumption cannot be discussed here. What matters for the present purpose is that the principles of UG are not rules comparable to relatively unconstrained rewriting rules of phrase structure grammar or to transformations, as familiar from earlier versions of generative theory. Phrase structure rules of the type $S \rightarrow NP + VP$, for example, have been replaced by the X-bar principle. It states that the internal structures of sentential constituents (phrases) is identical in many ways. There is always a head (X^0, or "zero projection"), and one finds in all phrases the same number of structural layers[1] (projections), probably two, i.e. X^1 and X^2; the latter is, thus, the maximal projection (XP). X^0 combines with a complement, itself a maximal projection, to form an X^1, and X^1 combines with a specifier, again an XP, to form the maximal projection of the head. X-bar theory claims that not only do all categories of a particular grammar conform to this schema, but it applies universally, across the languages of the world.

In certain respects, however, some principles of UG do not account exhaustively for properties of grammars; they are "under-specified" (Williams, 1987), offering several options, i.e. parameters are left unspecified. These parameters not only account for the obvious differences between grammars of different languages; they also allow for variation in a more general fashion, including variation in language development. Note that instead of opening an infinite space of variation, parameter theory restricts variation across grammars in a rather tight way: the principle in question is given by UG, and the parameterized options are limited. Take the example of phrase structure, again. X-bar theory provides the general format of a syntactic phrase, the internal structure of which, however, may vary crosslinguistically. One such point of variability is the position of the head of an XP; it may appear to the left or to the right of its complement, e.g. as VO or OV in a VP. Note that, in this case, the parameter offers just two options, head-initial or head-final. But this is not a theoretically necessary restriction. It is, instead, quite likely that, in other instances, a choice may be given between more than two possible parameter settings; see, for example, Manzini and Wexler (1987), who discuss a multivalued parameter concerning the binding domain for anaphors in a given language. Most parameters suggested so far, however, offer a choice between only two values.

One important aspect of parameter theory which does not become apparent by our example of head direction is that the setting of a parameter value may cause a cluster of superficially unrelated grammatical properties to appear in the language; see Chomsky (1981: 6). This can be illustrated by means of the "null-subject" or "pro-drop" parameter, perhaps the most extensively studied case. Whereas some languages allow empty subjects in tensed clauses, e.g. Spanish, others normally require this position to be filled lexically, e.g. English. The null-subject parameter specifies the grammatical conditions which must be met for this empty category "pro" to be allowed to occur. What exactly these conditions are is the object of quite some controversy; see Jaeggli and Safir (1989) for a discussion of such problems. All authors seem to agree, however, that the nature of the inflectional system of the verb agreeing with the subject plays a decisive role. Now, with respect to the issue discussed here, the clustering of superficially unrelated phenomena, it has been suggested that this parameter relates not only to null-subjects but to a number of other syntactic properties as well. One is that null-subject languages do not exhibit expletive elements, such as English *it* and *there* in "it seems" or "there is"; on the other hand, these languages allow "free inversion" of subjects in simple sentences, as in Italian "ha mangiato Giovanni," "Giovanni ate." Other properties which have been claimed to be related to the null-subject parameter are (a) "long wh-movement" of subjects, (b) empty resumptive pronouns in embedded clauses, and (c) apparent violations of the [that-trace] filter (Chomsky, 1981: 240ff). A more comprehensive account of these issues is not necessary for the present purpose. The crucial point is that, according to parameter theory, a number of surface phenomena may depend on the setting of a single parameter, thus lending this concept considerable explanatory force. It is of secondary importance whether the various properties just mentioned are indeed all related to the null-subject parameter; in fact, "free inversion" has been called into question. Only if one had to conclude that, in general, parameters each determine individual properties of grammars, would the entire concept lose much of its theoretical attractiveness, and parameters would merely be descriptive devices. Recent developments, indeed, give reason for apprehension of this kind since one finds a certain inflation of new parameters which are proposed whenever a generalization about grammar does not hold universally. In view of this, it should be stated unequivocally that parameter theory as an explanatory framework for language acquisition depends to a large extent on the assumption that parameterized options are defined on an abstract level of grammar, typically triggering a number of apparently unrelated surface effects.

These as well as a number of other issues concerning parameter theory need to be further investigated in order to reach broader consensus than is currently the case. I will address some of them during the ensuing presentation, in as far as they relate to acquisition problems. This discussion will show that, most importantly, parameter theory needs to be more strictly constrained. Various constraints have, indeed, been suggested as a result of analyses of developing grammars, thus demonstrating that language acquisition studies can contribute to grammatical theory.

3 Parameters of UG in Language Development

Since UG, in generative theory, is conceived of as a set of principles and parameters representing the innately specified initial state of the language faculty, it is also understood as a crucial component of the language acquisition device. This implies, most importantly, that a developing grammatical system, at each stage of the process of change, only contains structures and mechanisms which do not violate the principles of UG. In other words, the relevance of grammatical theory for language acquisition studies – and vice versa – depends on the continuity assumption. This is to say that "the child's grammatical rules should be drawn from the same basic rule types, and be composed of primitive symbols from the same class, as the grammatical rules attributed to adults in standard linguistic investigations" (Pinker, 1984: 7).

The continuity assumption, however, leads to an apparent paradox: children's grammars differ from adult grammars but they are of the same type as mature grammars. This is where parameter theory becomes relevant. It offers a solution for this puzzle and it helps to explain the incomplete knowledge about language one must attribute to children. Recall that grammatical theory distinguishes between phenomena related to nonparameterized universal principles and those that depend on parameters of UG or on language-specific properties of grammar. Only in the case of nonparameterized principles will the continuity assumption predict that they are invariably present in child as well as in adult grammars. Concerning phenomena that depend on language-specific properties, UG and the continuity assumption quite obviously have nothing to say. The most interesting properties of grammar, from an acquisitional perspective, are the parameterized principles of UG, for children need to find out how the values of the parameters are set in the language(s) they are acquiring. Since UG allows for different solutions in these cases, one can, in fact, expect children to explore[2] the range of variation defined by parameterized options of UG, precisely because these choices are not determined *a priori* but have to be made on the basis of information available in the input.

A number of consequences follow from these assumptions and make it possible to test them empirically. One claim, implicit in these hypotheses, is that nonparameterized properties of grammar should exhibit no variation, neither in the course of development nor interindividually, for they are not learned, in the usual sense of the term; see Atkinson (1992) for an in-depth discussion. With respect to the X-bar principle, for example, the claim is that the child does not have to learn about the internal structure of the various syntactic phrases; since this principle is part of UG, it belongs to the child's implicit knowledge right from the start. Variation comes in with language-specific learning or as the result of parametric choice. The latter determines, for example, the particular set of categories which are instantiated in a specific grammar, e.g. whether or not there are prepositions. Once this has been decided, the internal structure of a PP is given. Language-specific learning, in this case, involves, among other things, putting together the list of lexical items representing prepositions in the language, e.g. adding the equivalent of English "for," French "de," or German "für" to it and/or to the list of complementizers. Thus, although parameterized properties of grammar, just like other principles of UG, are part of the knowledge present prior to experience, the appropriate setting of parameters needs to be triggered by experience, and it is conceivable that a child chooses the wrong option.

The distinction between learning and triggering of knowledge is, nevertheless, an essential one; see Carroll (1989). Learning requires more frequent exposure to the input, possibly also over a longer period of time, and it probably needs salient and unambiguous input data; but it will nevertheless exhibit more intra- and interindividual variation due to trial and error procedures, and it may still lead to inadequate preliminary hypotheses. Triggering differs from learning in each of these points; it is predicted to happen faster, requiring less frequent and less simple input data, and the developmental pattern is expected to be much more uniform across individuals.

Another consequence of parameter theory follows from what has been said about the clustering effect of different surface properties of a single parameter setting. The obvious implication is that the child needs to discover only one of the properties indicating the correct setting of the parameter for the particular language, and all others will be automatically available. The empirical prediction is that the various phenomena will appear within a short period of time. The null-subject parameter can serve as an example, again. The discovery of one of its properties, e.g. the existence of expletives, is predicted to suffice to set the parameter to the correct value – in this case to [-null-subject]; all other phenomena should emerge more or less simultaneously.

4 The Initial State of Parameters

An essential, in fact the defining property of a grammatical parameter, is that it needs to be specified for the adequate value required by the particular language. This raises the question about its initial state. Asked differently: what does a grammar look like before the parameter values have been set correctly? There seem to be two possibilities, and both have indeed been suggested in the literature:

1 The parameter is set on a default value provided by UG; this need not be the correct option in terms of the target system but it can be found in some adult grammar; in this case, parameters will have to be reset in some languages.

2 Both (or all) values are accessible simultaneously; this can be interpreted as meaning that the parameter is not set, at first, but the various options are, for a limited time, simultaneously present in the developing grammar.

Let us briefly look at both of these possibilities. Option (1) is probably the best known and perhaps also the most widely accepted one. Hyams (1986), for example, argued that the null-subject parameter is initially set on the [+null-subject] (or [+pro-drop]) value as the default specification, early grammars thus generating null-subject languages (the "early English as Italian" hypothesis). It is a well-known fact that children, during early phases of language acquisition, tend to omit elements which are obligatory in adult grammar. According to this analysis, at least some of these cases of subject omission are grammatically licensed rather than being motivated by the context or by performance limitations. This version of the default assumption raises, however, a number of questions. Leaving aside specific problems of this particular analysis,[3] there still remain some more general, theoretical and empirical issues. The most far-reaching one concerns the problem of whether and how the parameter can be reset, for it has, indeed, been argued (Clahsen, 1991b; Müller, 1994) that parameters cannot be reset; this will be discussed in more detail in section 8, below.

Another problematic issue is how to determine the default value among the various options offered. Note that there exist at least two types of parameters, one with nested values, the other with disjoint ones. As for the former (nested), fixing the parameter on one value yields a grammar which generates a larger set of structures, as compared to the grammar which results from setting the parameter on the other value. The option [+pro-drop], for example, allows for sentences with or without overt subjects, since, in null-subject languages, subjects may also be lexically realized. The [-pro-drop] option, on the other hand, does not, normally, tolerate subjects to be lexically empty. The set of structures generated by the latter option thus seems to be a subset of the one generated by the former. The "subset principle," as first suggested by Berwick (1985) for language acquisition, states that the learner, as a first choice, must select the narrowest possible language consistent with the data. In fact, ordering "parameter values according to the subset relations of the languages that the values generate" (Manzini and Wexler, 1987: 414) has been claimed to be "the one fundamental principle of learnability" (ibid.: 425). The argument contained in the subset principle, therefore, is that the default value of the parameter should be the one generating the smaller set of structures. This will enable the child, on the basis of positive evidence alone, to realize that the parameter needs to be reset. To illustrate this point, if the pro-drop parameter is set on the negative option as the default value, a child acquiring Spanish should merely have to realize that sentences lacking overt subjects are used in his or her environment to be able to reset the parameter. In the reverse case, i.e. with the parameter set on [+pro-drop], a child learning English cannot easily arrive at the same conclusion. Only negative evidence, i.e. information indicating that lexically empty subjects are not tolerated, could enable the learner to do so. Yet negative evidence is normally not available, for children's grammatical errors are usually not corrected (see Brown and Hanlon, 1970), and corrections, even if given, are not easily understood and used (see Pinker, 1989). In the absence of negative evidence and if positive evidence is not sufficient, the child would have to become aware of the fact that one of the options offered by the grammar actually never appears in the input. This kind of evidence has been referred to as "indirect negative evidence" (Chomsky, 1981). As Valian (1988, 1990a) points out, however, the problem with indirect negative evidence is that there is no principled way of knowing how long one should wait before concluding that a specific structure will never emerge in the data. Therefore, the learner can never be sure that the corresponding parameter option may indeed be ruled out as a possibility for the grammar being acquired.

As for parameters with disjoint values, like the head-direction parameter, similar problems do not arise, for no subset relationship holds. The two possible grammars generate two disjoint sets of structures, e.g. with head-initial or head-final categories. This, however, leads to the consequence that one does not have principled reasons for deciding which value represents the default setting. Whether or not a default option for parameters with disjoint values is at all necessary is indeed not obvious, since learnability considerations of the sort discussed for nested parameters do not apply. In order to achieve a uniform treatment of all parameters, one might nevertheless opt for this solution pending further empirical scrutiny.

Let us now consider option (2), where all values are accessible simultaneously.

Figure 1.1

$$G_0: (X), Y \begin{cases} Y: G_1 \\ X, Y: G_2 \end{cases}$$

This is not to say that multiple settings are possible; rather, as suggested by Lebeaux (1988: 179ff; 1990), the initial grammar, G_0, allows access to the default as well as to alternative values provided by UG before the parameter is actually set on a specific value. This amounts to saying that G_0 preserves the initial state in which a value (X) is ordered before the default value Y.[4] In the setting G_1, option X is erased, leaving only the default value Y. In the setting G_2, the brackets indicating optionality are erased, X applies and overrides Y; see figure 1.1.

In other words, parameter setting leads to the elimination of alternative options. But as long as the child has not yet set the parameter, the child "falls into" the default grammar, i.e. value Y is active as a default, rather than G_0 being specified for Y, and alternative options remain available. Note that, even though UG principles are not violated, the early system G_0 is not a possible final grammar because the parameter has not been set; this has been pointed out by Lebeaux (1988) himself and also by Roeper (1992). What is attractive about this approach, however, is that it can do without the rather problematic notion of parameter "resetting." It furthermore predicts that initial grammars make available all values of a parameter, a solution which seems to be required for other reasons as well.

This becomes evident from work by Valian (1988: 12ff; 1990a: 122ff), although her proposal is not identical to that of Lebeaux. Expanding on a suggestion by Berwick and Weinberg (1984), she argues that all parametric options need to be available in early grammar for parsing considerations. Her arguments are based on the idea that the child, right from the earliest point of grammatical development, has to be able to parse and assign a structure to a sentence he or she hears. Since the parser is fed by the grammar it is also limited by the grammar. Thus, if parameters are initially set on one of the possible values, the parser cannot process structures generated by grammars set on the other value. If, for example, a child acquiring Spanish has first set the null-subject parameter on the [-null-subject] value, potentially disconfirming data cannot actually disconfirm the option to be changed, since the child's current grammar does not provide the parser with the necessary information. "Only if we give the parser access to the missing, correct, value, can the datum serve the function of contradicting the incorrect value" (Valian, 1988: 14).

In sum, the assumption that default options exist for at least some parameters appears to be plausible, but it is problematic to conclude that parameters are already set on the default value at the initial state of language development. Rather, first grammars need to allow for the possibility of accessing all options before fixing one value.

5   Triggering Parameter Setting

The triggering of parameter setting is perhaps the most difficult issue to be dealt with here, for it requires an assessment of the role of the input – a delicate problem for a theory of language acquisition which holds as one of its fundamental hypotheses that much of the relevant information is not contained in the primary linguistic data. Remember the distinction made in section 3, above, between different acquisitional mechanisms: instantiation of UG principles, learning of language-specific features, and triggering of parameters. Only in the latter do we find the subtle interplay between knowledge available prior to experience and information contained in the data. Yet many accounts attribute properties of inductive learning to triggering (see Atkinson, 1992, chapters 8–10) – probably a residue of trial and error learning, as pointed out by Haider (1993). But it is quite likely that, in contrast to this, triggering involves parametric choices leading to consequences from which the learner may not be able to retreat. Importantly, the standard assumption is that triggering this knowledge, as opposed to learning, requires less robust data and less exposure to the input. This raises the question of what exactly is needed to serve as triggering information.

One point has already been raised in section 4, namely that it may plausibly be assumed that primary linguistic data only contain positive evidence. Negative evidence and indirect negative evidence, to the extent that they are at all present in a child's linguistic environment, are apparently not used in a systematic fashion.

A second point concerns the reliability of the input data. There are, in fact, reasons to suspect that their reliability is flawed. First of all, it has been argued that surface properties of sentences can be ambiguous in terms of parameter values and therefore misleading with respect to the correct setting. This is the case when specific lexical items give rise to exceptions to syntactic generalizations; see Truscott and Wexler (1989). Another example is that of the omission of subjects in some languages. English and German, for example, tolerate null subjects in certain contexts although they do not exhibit grammatical properties of pro-drop languages. This can be interpreted as ambiguous evidence for the null-subject parameter; see Weissenborn (1992: 286). Secondly, and more seriously perhaps, adult language even when used with children is not always grammatical. It is not only that performance errors occur; adults use utterances which they themselves judge as nongrammatical. Furthermore, some types of ungrammatical sentences are perfectly acceptable in specific contexts, just as certain types of grammatical sentences are not always acceptable for native speakers. Valian (1990a: 120ff), for example, found in a survey of her data from American English children and parents that 4 percent of parental replies to children were ungrammatical, and 16 percent were acceptable but not fully grammatical, i.e. parents say things like "Want your lunch now?," "Raining hard," etc. Now, for linguistic analyses of adult language it may or may not be acceptable to simply ignore the nongrammatical utterances as irrelevant. In the present context, these facts are of utmost importance. The very notion of triggering implies that, in principle, an extremely small number of examples should suffice to set the parameter on a specific value; see section 3, above. Consequently, 20 percent or even 4 percent of ungrammatical sentences are likely to make the child's task impossible; he or she has to find out whether a given sentence to which he or she cannot assign a grammatical structure is indeed ungrammatical or whether the grammar or the parser is inadequate. Valian (1988), discussing this issue in some detail, concludes that parameter setting theory, if it cannot handle this problem, will be "0 percent accurate."

Valian (1988; 1990a) argues that the child needs to be equipped with a mechanism evaluating the significance of parser failure or parser success. The solution she advocates consists in attributing to the child the ability to (unconsciously) "run experiments" by "floating an utterance" and subsequently comparing it with the adult's reply. This hypothesis gains in plausibility by the observation that adults tend to reply to children using an utterance which is lexically and structurally similar to the child's sentence, and they seem to do so more frequently than when responding to other adults. Valian (1990a: 135) found that, in addition to 5 percent verbatim replies, approximately 30 percent of the adults' replies are similar to the child's previous utterances, and about two thirds of these included an implicit correction of the child's error. The idea is that the comparison process will enable the child to identify ungrammatical input, and it avoids the problem normally tied to the use of indirect negative input, i.e. that there is no way to tell when to stop searching for evidence. Assuming a comparison process, the child may reasonably expect the phenomenon under consideration to emerge within a short time period.

Another solution to the problem of how to deal with ambiguous and partly ungrammatical data is to assume that parameter setting is triggered only by narrowly defined properties of the data, not by all features which are possibly relatable to a given parameter value. Roeper and Weissenborn (1990: 151), for example, make the following claim: "If a given parameter is marked by several features, then there will be one unique trigger specified in UG"; see also Roeper and de Villiers (1992), who discuss the existence of such a unique trigger (or "telltale"; Valian, 1990b). According to this hypothesis, the presence of a specific feature in the data indicates unambiguously that the parameter has to be set on a given value. The pro-drop parameter can serve as an example again. We have seen that overtly missing subjects do not unambiguously point to the [+pro-drop] value. The use of expletive subjects, on the other hand, seems to provide more reliable information to the effect that the language is not a null-subject language; see Hyams (1986, 1989). It remains to be seen whether a unique trigger can indeed be identified for each parameter.[5] I will return below to the question of what the structural properties of the trigger should be expected to be.

How, then, can we decide between the two solutions? The use of indirect negative evidence, as advocated by Valian, implies that there is hypothesis testing involved, after all. Although this is certainly a possibility, it is one which weakens the theoretical position taken by parameter theory, shifting from a grammatical explanation to one based on strategies of language use. The unique trigger solution is not only more in tune with the spirit of parameter theory as a grammar-based explanation; it also seems to be the more parsimonious approach, not having to rely on the existence of poorly understood additional procedures of hypothesis testing. Ultimately, however, we may hope to be able to decide on empirical grounds between the two possibilities, for they make rather different empirical predictions. If hypothesis testing is involved, one should expect to find interindividual variation; children may also go wrong, initially, before setting a parameter correctly, and this leads to intraindividual variation. The unique trigger solution does not predict variation of this sort, even though one cannot exclude, at this point, the possibility that due to data ambiguity a feature might be identified erroneously as the "unique trigger." Yet even in this case, one does not expect to find oscillation between different parameter values but rather than the learner retreats via lexical learning; see section 8 on parameter "resetting."

The third point to be raised here concerns the frequency of occurrence of a feature and the length of exposure of the learner to the relevant data. As mentioned above, the theory claims that minimal exposure to the data should be sufficient for parameter setting. Ideally, a single example encountered in the input could indeed suffice. While it is obvious that this strong idealization cannot be maintained under realistic conditions, not much is known as to how much exactly is necessary. Clahsen (1991b), for example, simply observes that the child "seems to require a certain amount of positive evidence to fix a parameter at a particular value." Randall (1992: 100) goes one step further and postulates the existence of a "trigger threshold," i.e. that a "sufficient number of tokens" need to occur, admitting, however, that "we know surprisingly little about it." Lightfoot (1991) even goes so far as to claim that data must be salient and frequent in order to be able to act as triggers. Two sorts of concerns apparently lead to this or similar conclusions. The first is related to what has been said above about ambiguous and ungrammatical data. As Lightfoot (1991: 14) phrases it, the trigger should be "something less than the total linguistic experience," since occasional exposure to divergent forms, e.g. a different dialect spoken by a houseguest, or the language use of a second language learner, "normally has no noticeable effect on a child's linguistic development."

Note, however, that these are merely empirical observations to the effect that not every form present in the input automatically triggers the parameter for which it is apparently relevant, that there is no evidence for constant switching of parameter settings, and that parameterized acquisition, although faster than inductive learning, does take some time, after all. Notice further that no empirical or theoretical criteria are presented identifying the threshold level. In fact, nothing obliges us to accept a solution based on quantitative criteria at all. In view of this, I find it preferable to stick to my suggestion to first attempt to solve the problem in a way consistent with grammatical theory. This amounts to saying that further grammatical constraints should be imposed on what may act as a trigger. Adopting the "unique trigger" proposal has been a first step in this direction; eliminating the possibility of parameter resetting (Clahsen, 1991b) leads us further down this way. In what follows, a number of suggestions will be presented which drastically limit the range of possible triggers in terms of their grammatical properties; see section 8. Further restrictions are derived from the assumption that a particular feature can only act as a trigger if certain prerequisites are already met by other parts of the developing grammar; see section 6.

Yet the better we succeed in more strictly defining possible triggers, the more acute becomes the second concern, i.e. the question whether these items will be accessible to all learners. Truscott and Wexler (1989: 160), for example, object that if one were to assume that a specific phenomenon reliably indicates the correct setting of a parameter, "this unknown phenomenon would have to occur with a fairly high frequency (high enough that all learners of the language would encounter it)." The latter point seems to be well taken: triggering data must be of a sort which may plausibly be expected to be accessible to every child. But this has little to do with frequency. Rather, what matters is that triggering elements should not appear only in what Lightfoot (1991) calls "exotic" contexts. In this sense it is reasonable to ask for "robust" data; frequency of occurrence, however, does not appear to be relevant. The question thus remains, what may contribute to "robustness."

This leads to the fourth and last point. Summarizing what has been discussed so far, one can say that triggering data must materialize as positive evidence easily accessible to the child. In the current theoretical framework, their deficiency with regard to reliability cannot be amended in a satisfactory way by frequency requirements. A more promising approach is to define accessibility in structural terms. Structural properties of the data have only been mentioned in passing, up to now. It should be obvious, however, that this is what this discussion is all about. Only to the extent that the child is capable of assigning a structure to an element encountered in the input can this feature be integrated into the grammar of the learner. Yet it is most likely that during the period of linguistic development when parameter values are set, the child's capacity to (implicitly) perform such an analysis is restricted to a certain type of data, not only in terms of reliability, etc., but also with regard to grammatical complexity. This is suggested by Lightfoot (1989, 1991); he proposes that degree-0 learnability is sufficient for parameter setting, picking up on the learnability proof by Wexler and Culicover (1980), who demonstrated that it is possible, in principle, for a child to identify the grammar of a language if it is exposed to sentences with at most two levels of embedding (degree-2 learnability). Morgan (1986), based on different assumptions about what constitutes the child's input, succeeded in giving proof for degree-1 learnability. Lightfoot does not aim at an improvement of the learnability proof (see

Williams, 1989). Rather, he attempts to show that in order to discover the positive evidence necessary to decide on the settings of a number of parameters, it is sufficient to have access to degree-0 "plus a little," i.e. only main clause structures plus the front of the lower clause need to be accessible. The reason why Lightfoot (1989, 1991) arrives at this somewhat peculiar "zero-plus" formula is that he defines structural range not in terms of clauses but of binding domains. For the present purposes, however, it is possible to retain a definition based on clauses. It has, in fact, been argued by several authors, e.g. Baker (1989), Wasow (1989), Wilkins (1989), that degree-1 is more adequate, and that adopting it does not, in fact, weaken or strengthen Lightfoot's hypothesis.

This brings us to another proposal concerning the structural range within which triggers are to be found, the "subordinate clause strategy" suggested by Roeper (1973), according to which children pay particular attention to subordinate clauses. The idea was inspired by Emonds' (1970) finding that structure preservation is strictly adhered to in subordinate clauses. Note that this strategy represents a more radical version of the Degree-1 Hypothesis, for it claims that certain clues about how to set a parameter are to be encountered in subordinate clauses, exclusively. Roeper and Weissenborn (1990) elaborate on this; they advocate the Unique Trigger Hypothesis, but specify that it applies in subordinate clauses, at least as far as some parameters are concerned. An example of this is the null-subject parameter, again. Arguing that all the potential triggers proposed, including the presence of expletives, are not reliable, they attempt to show that unambiguous information can indeed be detected in embedded clauses where the occurrence of null-subjects is restricted to true pro-drop languages. Another example is the underlying clause-final position of verbs in languages like Dutch and German where finite verbs surface in final position in subordinates, but in second position in root sentences. From these observations one might conclude that the language learner must be sensitive to the root/nonroot distinction right from the start of grammatical development.[6] Unfortunately, however, the evidence is not entirely convincing in either case. Lightfoot (1991: 52ff.) demonstrates that a number of unembedded indicators appear in so-called verb-second languages, enough for the child to be able to discover underlying OV order. As for zero subjects, Rothweiler (1989) has found a number of lexically empty referential subjects in subordinate clauses of German children. Following Roeper and Weissenborn (1990: 156), this should not be possible, since the null-subject parameter must have been set correctly once the children are able to use embedded clauses.

In sum, then, information contained in subordinate clauses is clearly necessary for at least some parameters to be set on the correct value. It is, however, doubtful whether children are able to exploit the matrix. v. embedded clause distinction from very early on, and it also remains a controversial issue whether the child really focuses on subordinate clauses in cases of ambiguous data with respect to potential triggers. Information beyond the degree-1 complexity, on the other hand, is certainly not required for parameter setting.

6 A Developmental Schedule: Maturation or Ordering of Parameters?

The preceding section dealt with difficulties in determining what kind of evidence is required for a parameter to be set to the correct value. Surprisingly, perhaps, an equally puzzling problem emerges when one adopts the opposite perspective. Assuming we are able to identify the elements which can act as triggers, the question arises why the triggering does not happen immediately, as soon as the relevant piece of evidence appears in the child's input. This is Borer and Wexler's (1987: 128) "triggering problem." The crucial issue here is to account for the fact that the data required to trigger the setting of parameter values are, presumably, present in the child's linguistic environment from early on; yet many structural properties appear in a sequential order which is uniform across individuals and, in many respects, even crosslinguistically. Why, then, do triggers operate at a given point, why not earlier or later? The obvious answer seems to be that language development follows a specific underlying logic. The nature of this logic, however, is quite controversial. Whereas some authors believe that neurological maturation is the underlying cause, others contend that it is a grammar-internal phenomenon by which parameters are ordered.

The Maturation Hypothesis was first developed by Felix (1984), but similar ideas had already been proposed by Gleitman (1981) and White (1982). Felix (1984, 1987, 1992) claims that UG principles emerge according to an innately specified maturational schedule. Under his account, early grammars will, in contradiction to the continuity assumption (see section 3), exhibit properties which are in conflict with the as yet latent UG principles (Felix, 1987: 115) before biological maturation makes the relevant principles accessible to the child. This, then, leads to a reorganization of the interim grammar in such a way as to make it conform to the newly developed principles. Another version of the Maturation Hypothesis has been suggested by Wexler and his associates. Borer and Wexler (1987: 124) state that "certain principles mature. The principles are not available at certain stages of the child's development, and they are available at a later stage." The example they discuss is the formation of A-chains; informally speaking, this refers to the mechanism necessary for assigning a thematic role to a moved NP. It should, therefore, be impossible for the child to assign thematic roles nonlocally if A-chain formation is not available; as a consequence, child grammars at this point of development should not be able to analyze constructions which depend on this mechanism, e.g. passives. Note that it is not clear whether this example really illustrates a case of nonavailability of UG principles. Subsequent work clarifies, in fact, that it should not be interpreted as meaning that UG principles themselves are subject to maturation. Instead, Wexler (1990: 105) suggests a "UG-Constrained Maturation" hypothesis according to which "UG constrains every stage of child development, but certain constructs may not be available at certain ages." Under this hypothesis, learning constraints are responsible for restricting the availability of UG principles; these restrictions are successively removed as a result of physical maturation, thus giving the child access to more principles. The major difference between this weak version of the Maturation Hypothesis and its stronger counterpart is that the former predicts intermediate grammars to be consistent with UG at every point of development.

Nonmaturational accounts of the developmental schedule look for grammar-internal ordering principles rather than referring to physical maturation. In this vein, a number of authors, notably Lebeaux (1987), Roeper and Weissenborn (1990), Roeper and de Villiers (1992), and Weissenborn (1992), have suggested that parameter settings are interdependent, i.e. the value on which one parameter is set depends on the setting of another one. Ordering here means that "A decision in Parameter B is not executed until Parameter A is fixed . . . In effect, this constitutes an input filter: a sentence that involves Parameter B will simply not receive a full grammatical analysis until the acquisition system is ready for revision (after Parameter A has been set)" (Roeper and de Villiers, 1992: 193). This can be illustrated by an example discussed by Roeper and Weissenborn (1990); they claim that the correct setting of the pro-drop parameter depends on the parameter determining whether or not there is overt wh-movement. Weissenborn (1992) specifies that the crucial fact here is whether COMP is filled lexically, either by a complementizer in the head position of CP or by a wh-phrase in SpecCP. The line of reasoning then runs roughly as follows: the presence of complementizer phrases is itself parameterized; children's initial sentence structures, like adult Chinese or Japanese, lack CPs; overt complementizers or wh-movement trigger the implementation of a CP system in the child's grammar, and only in structures of this kind does one find a unique trigger for the pro-drop parameter; see the preceding section.

Note that in all these cases ordering is defined as intrinsic order,[7] and this is not restricted to parameterized properties of grammars. New grammatical features need to be integrated into the existing system, and unless this is possible, i.e. the new feature fits into the system, the learner is "blind" towards what the input offers. With respect to parameters again, the situation is quite similar, for triggering depends on previously acquired grammatical knowledge, as well, for possible triggers cannot be recognized as such unless they can be assigned a grammatical structure. Intrinsic ordering of this type appears to be uncontroversial.

Strictly speaking, however, we have introduced at least one case of extrinsic ordering, namely default settings of parameters. The nondefault option can be interpreted as the marked setting, yet markedness (or what counts as unmarked, i.e. the default case) is not defined by grammar-internal but by some external criteria. At best, it is justified by the subset principle (see section 4), but this too is a principle of learnability, not of grammar. Indeed, Wexler and Manzini (1987) view the theory of markedness which they outline as part of a "learning module." Markedness here applies to the possible values of a parameter, and the subset principle specifies the markedness hierarchy for these values. They further propose the "Subset Condition" (see also Manzini and Wexler, 1987), which ensures that the languages generated by two or more values of a parameter are ordered by proper inclusion. Yet although this, together with the subset principle, imposes a strict order on the choice of values of a specific parameter, they strongly reject the idea of ordered parameters, i.e. of interdependence of parameters.

At this point, in may be useful to pause briefly and to attempt a contrasting evaluation of maturation and grammatical ordering hypotheses. The first point to observe is that no one is able to offer independent evidence for the respective mechanisms invoked as explanatory factors. In other words, we are left where we started from: grammatical development is observed to follow a uniform sequential pattern which asks for an explanation. The second step could thus be to ask whether the various approaches attain descriptive adequacy. Leaving details aside, they do seem to succeed here equally well. Critics of maturational approaches, for example, generally concede that maturation might explain the properties of child grammar discussed by the authors under review – objecting at the same time that maturation is not needed as an explanation; see Weinberg (1987), Guilfoyle and Noonan (1988), and Clahsen (1991, 1992), among others. As far as I can see there is only one major point where empirically distinguishable claims are made, namely with respect to possible violations of principles of UG. Under the strong Maturational Hypothesis, they are expected to happen, whereas everybody else denies their existence. The aforementioned critics, for example, claim that the apparent violations can all be accounted for in a UG-conforming fashion. For the time being, I suggest we accept this as a temporary solution although some doubts remain, particularly with respect to child language at the so-called two word stage; see Felix (1987, 1992). Given this state of affairs, I suggest proceeding in the, by now, customary way, resorting to Occam's razor, i.e. to evaluate those candidates most highly which can do without an additional apparatus. According to this logic, the least desirable approaches are those requiring extrinsic ordering and those postulating learning principles whose sole function is to block access to grammatical knowledge which is supposedly present but cannot be used. The solution to be preferred, then, is the one which attempts to explain the observed sequences in terms of grammatical properties without having recourse to extrinsic ordering, maturation schedules, or markedness hierarchies. Note that this verdict is tentative and will be withdrawn as soon as one can (a) give compelling empirical evidence to the contrary, and/or (b) independently motivate the additional mechanisms.

It should be pointed out, in this connection, that assuming maturation is, of course, by no means an implausible hypothesis, given that our theory emphasizes strongly the biological basis of language, and biological maturation is quite uncontroversial in other areas for children of this age (Borer and Wexler, 1987; Felix, 1987). It is, nevertheless, necessary to indicate what the physiological basis (neurological or other) for these claims might be. In fact, one such piece of evidence may have been found by Greenfield (1991). Discussing findings from neurophysiological and neuroanatomical research, she concludes that the development of brain connections provides the foundation for structural development in language. A crucial point is that this research focuses on neural circuits, not on brain areas alone. Specific circuits connecting various cortical areas develop as a result of gradual differentiation by which "multiple short-range connections are 'pruned' to fewer, more specific and longer-range connections" (Greenfield, 1991: 544). In the case of Broca's area, dendritic growth leads to a differentiation of two functionally distinct neighboring areas, and this happens precisely during the period when complex grammatical structures emerge in child language, beginning at around age two. Broca's area is now starting to receive input from the anterior prefrontal area. "If this is confirmed by further research, then language is not modular at birth or even at the beginning of language development; it becomes increasingly modular with age and neural differentiation" (Greenfield, 1991: 550). One way to interpret this is to say that UG becomes available at around age 2;0 as a result of maturation. Such a view is in accordance with the theory developed by Bickerton (1990b), who distinguishes between protolanguage and language, only the latter being the product of grammatical knowledge, with language proper emerging at about age two.[8] Assuming, then, that the findings reported by Greenfield justify the claim that biological maturation makes UG accessible to the child at approximately age 2;0, this provides independent evidence for the Maturation Hypothesis. Notice, however, that it only explains why early language uses are not constrained by UG, as claimed by Felix (1987) and Bickerton (1990b). In order to justify the hypothesis that principles within UG mature successively, as suggested by Felix, evidence of a different kind is required.

Our discussion has thus led to the conclusion that the best candidate for an adequate explanation of acquisitional sequences is an approach which relies primarily on intrinsic ordering. As a consequence, one might opt for what Guilfoyle and Noonan (1988) termed the "Structure Building Hypothesis"; see also Radford (1986, 1990). It is based on the hypothesis that early grammars only contain projections of referential categories, most importantly verbs and nouns. Functional categories, on the other hand, are implemented in the course of further acquisition. This means, for example, that early grammars lack CP and possibly also IP. Grammatical properties related to these categories, like certain word order phenomena resulting from movement to IP or CP, the finite/infinitive distinction handled by INFL, case assignment depending on properties of INFL, and so forth, will therefore also be absent during early phases, and parameters related to functional categories obviously cannot be set until these elements are instantiated in the developing grammar. Moreover, since in most or all cases functional categories are interdependent in the way they are implemented in the grammar of a specific language, tying parameter setting to the emergence of these elements provides us with an intrinsically motivated developmental schedule. I will return to this issue below, in section 8.1. Let me merely add at this point that, in this framework, lexical learning is claimed to solve the triggering problem (see Clahsen, 1991b), i.e. increases in the learner's lexicon (including morphological items) are said to induce restructuring of intermediate grammars.

7 Setting Parameter Values

In the preceding sections, the initial state of parameters and the nature of triggering data have been discussed in some detail, as well as the question of why the presence of potential triggers in the input does not lead to instantaneous fixing of all relevant parameters simultaneously. What remains to be asked is how triggering can be thought to actually operate. It has been argued that parameters determine knowledge which cannot be learned inductively; several options are latently present, one of which must be chosen. This choice, it has been claimed, is triggered when an analysis of the data reveals the presence of a triggering element. I furthermore argued that assuming the existence of a unique trigger for each parameter appears to be the most promising solution for the intricate triggering problem. But the role of the data emerges once more as a potential problem, this time with respect to the question of whether the relationship between the input data and the setting of the parameter value is deterministic in nature or not.

Surprisingly enough, only a few studies address these issues explicitly, notably Valian (1988, 1990a), Haider (1993: 13), and Atkinson (1992: 206ff), and I will therefore only mention some basic points. Haider, for example, makes some interesting observations which may help to clarify the problem under scrutiny, even though he wants to eliminate the notion of parameter fixing altogether, for reasons beyond the scope of this chapter.[9] He points out that fixing a parameter requires three distinct acts: "A particular property in the input data must be identified, the property recognized in the data must be identified as relevant for setting the parameter of a specific principle, and, eventually, the parameter of the principle must be set to the value corresponding to the input data property" (Haider, 1993: 5). This amounts to saying that, as a first step, the utterance will have to be parsed, and a structural representation must be constructed, independently of the fixing of parameters. It is this structure to which the parameter setting mechanism can apply. Since the parser can be assumed to be fed by the grammar, it should be obvious that the first step already requires grammatical knowledge. The more controversial point here is whether steps two and three will indeed have to be distinguished. One way to view this is to imagine that parameters function like switches, metaphorically speaking, tripped by incoming data which, thereby, set them properly in a quasiautomatic fashion. If this is correct, the child does not play an active part in this process. An alternative view would be to attribute to the child a more active role. Valian (1988), for example, argues that simple exposure to the language is insufficient and that learning is required, where learning is understood as nonconscious hypothesis testing.

In my understanding, there are a number of reasons, already alluded to in section, to prefer the solution claiming that parameter setting is deductive learning, i.e. it happens in a quasiautomatic fashion. In fact, this seems to follow logically from adopting the notion of a unique trigger. It also appears to be more in line with the theoretical framework of parameter theory, given that it strictly reduces the role of inductive learning. Remember that the insight that learning as hypothesis testing cannot account for crucial aspects of language development was one of the major reasons for adopting the Principles and Parameters Theory. Consequently, a deterministic approach to parameter setting is to be preferred, unless compelling evidence to the contrary is found. Note that it also seems to be the more commonly held view to assume that setting the values of a parameter is a causal effect of properly analyzed and recognized incoming data.

To offer another metaphor, one may think of each parameter value as a lock into which only one key fits, i.e. the specific grammatical feature emerging from an analysis of the data functioning as the telltale trigger. How can this be reconciled with the important role of variation, not only in language acquisition but also in historical change? A theory of grammar failing to assign an adequate status to variability cannot hope to account satisfactorily for grammatical development. The notion of parameter has been introduced to explain crosslinguistic variation, and it is obviously also the locus where the possibility of ontogenetic and historic development should be explained. Yet variability need not be a property of the parameter itself nor of the parameter setting mechanism. Instead, variability exists in language use and therefore also in the potential triggering data. As has been discussed at some length in section, this may even lead to ambiguity with respect to the correct choice of parameter values. As opposed to most authors who believe that the notion of a "telltale" or "unique" trigger is incompatible with the idea of incorrect settings, e.g. Roeper and Weissenborn (1990), I want to argue that telltale triggers do not exclude the possibility of setting parameters incorrectly. The reason is that although a particular structural property may indicate unambiguously that a specific value must be chosen, the data may very well be structurally ambiguous, and this may lead, in exceptional cases, to wrong analyses and consequently also to wrong settings. I will return to this point in section 8.2. This is not all: we even have to allow for the possibility that the input data may contain conflicting evidence, i.e. that they can be analyzed by the child in a way leading to the conclusion that there exists a telltale trigger for both parameter values. What, at first sight, appears to be selfcontradicting is in fact a welcome result, I believe. To illustrate this point, let me mention French as an example. Old French was a null-subject language, but Modern Standard French has lost this syntactic property. During an extended period of time, however, French exhibited characteristics of both [+pro-drop] and [-pro-drop] languages. In other words, language change shows that different grammars or subgrammars can coexist simultaneously, and it is plausible to assume that this has also been the case within the grammatical competence of individuals, not only across the linguistic community, for this is what we find in bilinguals as well, and even in bidialectal speakers. In fact, the individual's ability to set one parameter on contradictory values may very well be a necessary condition for becoming a multilingual. In other words, it is precisely this type of evidence for conflicting parameter settings which enables the bilingual child to conclude that separate grammatical systems are underlying the incoming data.

In conclusion, then, the view advocated here interprets parameter setting as a quasiautomatic process triggered by a telltale trigger detected in the grammatical structure which has been assigned to the data. In exceptional cases, this does not exclude the possibility of incorrect decisions, and it predicts that conflicting evidence concerning the value to be chosen will serve as a trigger to differentiate two grammatical systems.

8 Constraints on Parameter Theory

It should have become apparent by now that parameter theory, in spite of its success in explaining important aspects of grammatical development, still needs to be elaborated in more detail with respect to a number of crucial theoretical assumptions. Most importantly, tighter constraints have to be imposed in order to make all of the major claims of the theory amenable to empirical scrutiny. In the remainder of this contribution, I will discuss briefly two important constraints proposed recently, namely that only functional heads should be parameterized and that resetting should be excluded.

8.1 Parameterization of (functional) heads

The first proposal concerns the issue of what parts of grammar can be parameterized. It appears to be desirable to restrict parameterization to a strictly limited domain of UG. Initially, it had been hypothesized that universal principles themselves are parameterized; see Chomsky (1981, 1986a). Take the principle of subjacency[10] as an example; informally speaking, it states that an element, e.g. a wh-phrase, may not be moved over more than one bounding node. Whereas the principle as such seemed to hold universally, what would count as a bounding node in the grammar of a specific language had been argued to be subject to parameterization. In English grammar, for example, NP and IP are bounding nodes, whereas in Italian CP, but not IP, functions as such. Yet in a number of studies, Wexler and others, e.g. Wexler and Manzini (1987), Truscott and Wexler (1989), demonstrated that the value of a parameter "cannot be associated with grammars as a whole but rather must be associated with single lexical items" (Manzini and Wexler, 1987: 424). It was Borer (1984) who first suggested moving the burden of parametric choice from the computational component to the lexicon. Picking up on this, Manzini and Wexler (1987) proposed their "Lexical Parameterization Hypothesis." Note, however, that although this means that the value of a parameter is associated with properties of individual lexical items, rather than being defined over the entire grammar, it still implies that the principle itself is subject to parametric variation.

A more radical change has been introduced by Chomsky (1989), also taking up the suggestions by Borer (1984). He proposes that parameters of UG should only relate to the lexicon, not to the computational system, thus restricting the class of possible parameters to categories of lexical items or to properties of lexical items (e.g. canonical government). This excludes, for example, parameterization of subjacency. Chomsky (1989) goes, in fact, a step further, stating "If substantive elements (verbs, nouns, etc.) are drawn from an invariant universal vocabulary, then only functional elements will be parameterized." This amounts to saying that parameterization should be restricted to a closed class of functional heads like COMP, INFL, and DET. Interestingly, this Functional Parameterization Hypothesis is in line with hypotheses based on acquisition data like the Structure Building Hypothesis by Guilfoyle and Noonan (1988), mentioned above in section 6, and similar approaches by Radford (1986, 1990) and Lebeaux (1988); see the contributions in Meisel (1992), for some recent discussions of this issue.

The most consistent attempt to pursue the research program outlined by Chomsky (1989), according to which functional heads are the prime *locus* of parameterization, can be found in the work by Ouhalla (1990, 1991). He claims that grammatical properties of a language are all due to the set of functional categories implemented in its grammar, and all parameters reflect properties of functional categories. One of the merits of Ouhalla's proposal is that it offers an explicit definition of functional categories which distinguishes them from their substantive counterparts, resulting in a set comprising some categories normally not classified as functional elements, e.g. pronouns and certain prepositions. Ouhalla (1991) succeeds in giving a unified treatment to a variety of phenomena. Word order patterns, for example, can be related to properties of functional categories. Take the position of the verb. Rather than having the head-direction parameter apply to the VP, verb placement depends on the internal structure and on the position of the functional category to which the verb is moved; in fact, the order of V in VP is not fixed at all. This has interesting consequences for language development. Assuming that first grammars lack functional categories, early child utterances are correctly predicted to exhibit variable verb placement patterns. It is only when AGRP or some other functional phrase of this type has been implemented that the verb will assume a fixed position corresponding to the position of the functional head. Note that under this approach word order is partly accounted for as resulting from variable order of functional categories in clause structure. In other words, at least for some of these categories, namely AGR, TNS, and NEG, it is claimed that grammars of various languages differ with respect to whether AGR appears above TNS or vice versa. This contradicts the widely held belief in studies on UG that clause structure is identical for all languages at an abstract level. The implications for language acquisition are obvious. According to the Structure Building Hypothesis, the child has to discover which functional categories, out of a limited set offered by UG, are instantiated in the particular grammar to be acquired. If Ouhalla's claim can be maintained, it follows that the child faces the additional task of determining the hierarchical order of these elements in the clause structure of the language he or she is acquiring using information contained in the data, most importantly by making inferences based on the surface order of morphemes realizing these functional categories. It remains to be seen whether this is theoretically viable and whether it represents indeed a feasible task for the learner.

8.2 Can parameters be reset?

The second proposal concerns the possibility of parameter resetting, until recently an uncontroversial assumption. Under several scenarios this issue becomes crucial. One example is the above mentioned case (section 4) of default settings of parameters (see Hyams, 1986, 1989). If this is correct, it is necessary to allow the possibility of switching from one setting to another, and this again means that the respective other option must remain accessible to the learner. One way to avoid the necessity of resetting is to follow the suggestion by Lebeaux (1988) according to which the child "falls into" the default grammar without actively setting the parameter on one of its values. But the problem remains in view of the expected ambiguity of the data, discussed in section 5, above; if one cannot rule out the possibility that the child initially chooses the wrong option, one will have to explain how the correct choice can eventually be made and, perhaps even more difficult, make sure that the parameter is not constantly set and reset.

An explicit account of this "pendulum problem" and of how it might perhaps be solved is given by Randall (1990, 1992). She proposes the Catapult Hypothesis, based on the assumption that there exists, indeed, a unique trigger for each parameter. The "catapult" is a mechanism enabling the child to retreat from a false choice. It consists of a principle of grammar and a piece of primary data. The logic underlying the catapult is the *modus ponendo tollens*, i.e. "Either A or B. A, therefore: not B." A is a phenomenon encountered in the data which can serve as a trigger, B is a particular setting of the parameter, e.g. A = there exist expletives, B = [+pro-drop]. The either/or logic of the catapult forces the learner to eliminate possibility B if fact A is found in the data. Yet the second question remains: what prevents the child from resetting the parameter at every instance when it encounters data which appear to be in conflict with an earlier decision? Randall believes that because of unique triggers the pendulum problem will not arise in syntax but only in the lexicon, the case discussed by her (1990, 1992). Here, the child can assume a conservative strategy, i.e. retreat item by item.

It is, however, by no means obvious that the pendulum effect should not be a problem for syntax, given the repeatedly mentioned ambiguity of the data; see section 7. And yet, one first important observation (Clahsen, 1992) is that one does not find evidence for the pendulum effect; children do not switch back and forth between different parameter values. Clahsen (1991b), therefore, proposes the Parameter Setting Constraint, according to which parameters cannot be reset. He then proceeds to show that certain word order phenomena in the acquisition of German can be accounted for without resorting to parameter setting; see below. But if this is correct, does it mean that the settings must be correct in the first place, or are there other means to retreat from the error?

An interesting case is discussed by Müller (1993, 1994). As has been mentioned before in connection with the Structure Building Hypothesis, a number of studies indicate that early grammars lack CP. This creates a problem in explaining certain verb placement phenomena with children acquiring German, since they do use SVO, during this period, and occasionally also apparent V2 structures, with some element preceding the finite verb and the subject following it (e.g. OVS, AdvVS). For adult German, a verb-second language, the usual analysis argues that finite verbs move to the head of CP, and a maximal projection (e.g. the subject or some other topicalized constituent) appears in the specifier position of CP. Both these positions are, however, not available as long as the child does not have access to CP; assuming that VP is head-final, the child should therefore only use verb-final constructions. One solution could be that, in these cases, the verb appears in a head-initial functional category other than CP, i.e. IP or some variant thereof (e.g. FP, AGRP); see Clahsen (1991), Meisel and Müller (1992). This is in accordance with the verb-second parameter proposed by Platzack and Holmberg (1989), according to which the finiteness operator is placed either in IP (Romance languages, English, etc.) or in CP (V2 languages). Eventually, however, the child needs to revise his or her grammar in order to make it conform to the adult version. Meisel and Müller (1992) suggest that the verb-second parameter is reset, once CP has been implemented in the grammar, triggered by the acquisition of complementizers. A functional category thus has to be added. Yet if resetting of parameters is excluded, this solution has to be ruled out. As a consequence, one would have to predict that if the parameter has indeed been set on an incorrect value, the corresponding properties of the target grammar which the correct parameter value would have yielded automatically will have to be acquired by inductive learning. Analyzing the language development of bilingual (French and German) children, Müller (1993, 1994) demonstrates that this is indeed what happens. Leaving details aside, one can summarize her findings by stating that functional categories in early grammars tend to be underspecified in terms of their featural composition, as suggested by Clahsen (1991b); these intermediate grammars can thus be restructured without having to reset parameters. For one child, however, Müller finds that he has indeed set the finiteness parameter on the wrong value, in the fashion described above. As a consequence, once subordinate clauses appear, he uses verb-second patterns and verb-third constructions with the finite verb immediately following the complementizer as well as the subject or the topicalized nonsubject. The reason for the erroneous setting apparently is that for this child complementizers evolve out of prepositions instantiated initially by *für*, "for." Given patterns of historic change of a similar sort, this is by no means an implausible hypothesis, but it results in a misanalysis of COMP as a substantive rather than a functional category. The most fascinating point, however, is what happens subsequently. Once the boy starts using items representing the functional category COMP, this does not entail adultlike use of word order in subordinate clauses. In other words, no clustering of syntactic phenomena related to one parameter can be observed. Rather, he learns the correct ordering, separately for each complementizer, in an item-by-item process extending over a considerable period of time (approximately two years).

To conclude then, not only has Clahsen (1991b) demonstrated that certain phenomena for which parameter resetting had been suggested as an explanation can be accounted for adhering to the Parameter Setting Constraint, Müller (1993) offers empirical evidence indicating that erroneous settings need to be remedied by a long drawn-out process of inductive learning, thus lending strong support to the proposed constraint.

9   Conclusions

The objective of this chapter ahs been to present a critical discussion of the contribution of parameter theory to explanations of language development. Focusing on two examples, the null-subject and the head-direction parameter, its fundamental theoretical concepts were introduced and a number of empirical consequences were outlined. I hope to have shown that this theory is potentially of great interest for language acquisition studies. At the same time, however, it should also have become clear that the theory still needs to be elaborated in more detail. Most importantly, it is too powerful in some respects and needs to be constrained more tightly. Several such proposals have been discussed here. In the current state of our knowledge, it seems to be possible to restrict parameterization to lexical heads, probably even to functional heads. It furthermore appears to be preferable to exclude the possibility of resetting parameters, once they have been set to a specific value; this also constrains the use of default options.

The specific interest of parameter theory is in great deal due to the fact that it defines the role of the input data for grammatical development, a rather sensitive issue within a theoretical framework which has virtually eliminated inductive learning as a means to acquire abstract grammatical knowledge. It is, nevertheless, crucial not to confound issues related to parameters as elements of a theory of UG and those concerning the way they are put to use. The subset principle, to mention one example, defines an important learnability condition, but it is not part of parameter theory proper, i.e. of UG. A number of requirements concerning the data have been dealt with at some length during this chapter, e.g. that parameters should not require anything other than positive evidence, probably of a structurally simple nature. The claim, however, that for each parameter there should be a telltale or unique trigger, defines the nature of parameters and is therefore part of the theory, notwithstanding the fact that the learner may go wrong in identifying this trigger. It must be kept in mind that triggers do not appear labeled as such in the data; rather, they need to be identified by means of a grammatical analysis.

I believe that parameter theory has become popular because the notion of parameter has been understood as offering a particularly useful metaphor for an as yet poorly understood mechanism of the language-specific mental capacity. In my view, it is quite legitimate to proceed in this way and to operate temporarily with a vaguely defined concept, for this enables one to reflect upon issues of which one only has a vague understanding. It should be obvious, however, that during the course of further research one must make every effort to arrive at more precise definitions. At the same time, the epistemological implications should be spelled out, and the neurobiological basis for these assumptions will have to be clarified. In this way, one may hope to gain profound insights into the human linguistic capacities. Although the enterprise may still fail, I believe that it is worthwhile pursuing.

NOTES

I am grateful to Susanne E. Carroll and Jürgen Weissenborn, as well as to Andolin Eguzkitza, Lynn Eubank, Georg Kaiser, Helen Leuninger, Natascha Müller, Zvi Penner, and Achim Stenzel, for reading and commenting on an earlier version of this chapter.

1 There has been some discussion, recently, as to whether all maximal projections have the same internal structure, e.g. whether they all require a Spec position; see Speas (1990).

2 Verbs like "explore," "choose," etc. are used metaphorically in this context. I do not mean to imply intentionality on behalf of the child or that this is a case of hypothesis testing.

3 See Meisel (1990c), Valian (1990b), and Weissenborn (1992), among others, who argue against this hypothesis.

4 Lebeaux (1988: 184ff) actually revises this approach in order to make it compatible with his General Congruence Principle.

5 Roeper and Weissenborn (1990), for example, mention a number of studies which apparently provide evidence against each telltale suggested for the null-subject parameter so far. They claim that

unambiguous information can only be found in subordinate clauses; see below.

6   I want to thank Jürgen Weissenborn (pers. comm.) for clarifications on this point.

7   Roeper and de Villiers (1992), however, also discuss the possibility of extrinsic ordering.

8   Although protolanguage is not constrained by UG, it does not seem to be adequate to talk of violations of UG principles, in this case, for UG has not yet been activated. Strictly speaking, this is not even in contradiction with the continuity assumption, although Bickerton argues for discontinuity. Discontinuity, as defined by Pinker (1984), refers to the claim that adult grammars evolve out of earlier systems consisting of categories and rules which are not defined in terms of abstract grammatical principles, as mature grammars, but are motivated differently, e.g. in terms of semantic and pragmatic functions. If these distinctions are kept in mind (see Meisel, 1994), it is of only marginal interest which terminology is used.

9   Haider (1993) argues that fixing parameters presupposes the existence of an interpreting interface between UG and the general cognitive mechanisms for which there is no evidence. In his view, "The UG-potential is a cognitive co-processor. It is activated whenever there is a data structure that suits the capacity . . . Under this perspective, the processing potential amounts to a filtering and reinforcement device. It will channel the processing of the language data into UG-conformable channels, and it will do so inevitably" (Haider, 1993: 13).

10 For technical details, see any of the recent introductions to generative syntax, e.g. Freidin (1992: 110ff).

2 Connectionist Approaches to Language Acquisition

KIM PLUNKETT

1 Introduction

During the past three decades, language acquisition research has pendulumed between nativist and empiricist approaches to development. In the sixties, Chomsky proposed the existence of a language acquisition device that encapsulated knowledge of a universal grammar, in order to resolve problems associated with the impoverished nature of the input stimulus. In the seventies, cognitive and social knowledge was introduced as a support system to the language acquisition process in order to take the strain from the overloaded formal learning machine. Finally, the eighties saw the maturation of concern in individual differences and crosslinguistic approaches to acquisition but the problem of learnability still loomed large.

The naive observer of these events may be forgiven for wondering whether a theoretical resolution will ever emerge. My best guess is that they are likely to be disappointed, at least in the short term. The story about to be told might best be described as a summary of a recent version of the empiricist/nativist debate – or, at least, one side of the debate. The goal of this chapter is to convince you that connectionist approaches to understanding language acquisition offer a useful new tool for pushing the debate further, hopefully in a constructive fashion.

Tools like observers are not theoretically neutral. In the field of language acquisition, connectionism is best known in the context of discussions of the acquisition of English verb morphology. The Rumelhart and McClelland (1986) verb learning model offered an alternative to rule-based accounts of the inflectional system. Furthermore, they implemented a learning device that honored the supposed facts of acquisition in a manner that was primarily data driven. The initial impact of Rumelhart and McClelland's (R&M) model resulted from the manner in which it handled the regular past tense verb inflection in English without recourse to a symbolic rule system. The more fundamental shift in thinking, however, concerned the input sensitivity of the learning device in the R&M model. Nativist accounts of language acquisition have consistently staked their theoretical claims on the grounds that the input stimulus is too impoverished to account for the specific knowledge structures associated with the mature language user. Supplementary information in the form of innate structures and processes are indispensable in guiding the learner to an appropriate end state. The data-driven, emergent representation of the R&M verb learning model conflicted fundamentally with this rationalist view of the source of cognitive and linguistic structure.

The input sensitivity of connectionist systems makes them obvious tools for exploring empiricist accounts of language acquisition. However, it should be emphasized that connectionism and empiricism are not necessary bedfellows. I will try to show in this chapter that connectionism offers a tool for examining the tradeoff between the role of the input and the role of preadapted structures and processes in development. Although the representations formed by connectionist systems are indeed highly sensitive to input parameters, it is the architectures and learning algorithms of connectionist systems themselves that afford this sensitivity. Since connectionist architectures differ in terms of their network structures and learning algorithms, they will also differ in the manner in which they respond to the same inputs. Network architectures offer an additional source of hypotheses as to the initial state of the learning device before it is exposed to any input. Consequently, connectionism is also a useful tool for exploring interactionist and nativist accounts of language acquisition.

This chapter contains three main sections. In the first section, I will provide a brief overview of some connectionist models of the English past tense and elaborate on the principles of network dynamics that are responsible for producing the patterns of behavior observed. In addition, I will point out the essential differences between connectionist accounts of the past tense and their symbolic counterparts, and suggest what kinds of evidence are likely to enable us to choose between the two approaches.

In the second section, I will describe a connectionist model of concept formation and vocabulary growth. Although this model should not be interpreted as a literal account of concept formation and vocabulary growth in young children (the visual and auditory stimuli used are quite artificial), the model does have the dual utility of showing how:

1 Phenomena which have formerly been given disparate accounts in the literature can be integrated within a single explanatory framework.
2 The interaction of different modalities (in this case, vision and audition) can give rise to developmental phenomena that would not emerge if treated separately.

The model also has the virtue of making some new predictions about children's behavior.

In the final main section of the chapter, I will review some exploratory work that attempts to discover how connectionist networks might be used for under-standing children's acquisition of syntactic knowledge. So-called Simple Re-current Networks (Elman, 1990) have proved surprisingly adept at learning grammatical categories and dependencies and the conditions under which they do so are particularly illuminating for developmentalists.

2   Learning Inflectional Morphology

The central issues at stake in the past tense debate are concerned with the argument from the "poverty of the stimulus" (in this case, that the apparent qualitative distinction between regular and irregular verbs in the mature cog-nitive system cannot be derived from the input) and the consequent need for a dual route mechanism (in this case, the need for a rule-governed device supplemented with a rote look-up table or associative memory). However, the implications of this debate extend beyond the particular details of inflectional morphology. For example, much of current linguistic theory in the tradition of transformational generative grammar attempts to postulate highly general rules, such as "Move alpha" (move anything anywhere), in order to reduce the number of rules needed to characterize universal grammar. In order to pre-vent these highly general rules from overgenerating and producing sentences outside the target grammar, linguists propose the existence of specific linguis-tic constraints that constitute exceptions to the general rules. Linguistic con-straints are also taken to be part of the apparatus that implements universal grammar. Appeals to dual mechanisms thus proliferate through much of cur-rent linguistic theory. Furthermore, it is typically argued that the origins of these dual architectures are innate. Connectionist approaches to the past tense problem suggest, on the contrary, that qualitative distinctions between highly regular and exceptional patterns of behavior can emerge within the confines of a single mechanism.

2.1   *The dual route model*

Traditional rule-based accounts assume that two mechanisms are needed to explain the profile of development associated with children's acquisition of the English past tense (see Pinker and Prince, 1988). First, a memory storage device contains the past tense of highly frequent and irregular forms in the language. Second, a rule-based system appends the appropriate allomorph of /ed/ to the stem of the verb to form the past tense. Early correct usage of past tense forms is explained by the operation of the first memory storage device. The onset of overgeneralization errors is explained by the interference of the two mechanisms. Specifically, the memory storage device fails to block the application of the regular rule to an irregular stem. Finally, mature

Figure 2.1 Dual route model for the English past tense. The model inv
route that is insensitive to the phonological form of the stem and a route
capable of blocking the output from the regular route.

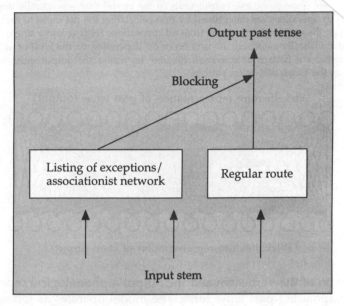

competence is explained by the two mechanisms discovering the correct division of verbs into regulars and irregulars. In terms of the operation of the dual route mechanism, this is achieved by a strengthening of the representations of the irregular verbs in the memory storage device so that blocking of the application of the regular rule to irregular forms becomes more effective. It is important to note that rule-governed mechanism is insensitive to the phonological form of the verb (except for the need to append the appropriate allomorph). In effect, the input stem is replaced by an arbitrary symbol V. Hence, the rule-governed mechanism treats all stems as equivalent. Figure 2.1 provides a schematic for this model.[1]

2.2 The single route model

In contrast, the Rumelhart and McClelland (1986) model assumes only a single mechanism to do the job of learning both regular and irregular forms of the past tense. This mechanism takes the form of a single layered neural network, i.e. it has a set of input units connected directly in a simple feedforward fashion to a set of output units. The general form of such networks is shown in figure 2.2. Like the dual route model, it assumes that one of the problems facing the child in learning the past tense of English is to relate the stem of the verb to its past tense form. Therefore, the input to the model is a phonological

Figure 2.2 The learning network in the Rumelhart and McClelland (1986) model of the acquisition of the English past tense. The input is a distributed representation of the stem of the verb and output a distributed representation of the appropriate past tense. The network is not drawn to scale, i.e. there are more input and output units in the model than are actually depicted in the diagram. Output activations are determined by first calculating the net input to each output unit (net input is just the weighted activations from all connections feeding into a single output node) and then probabilistically switching the unit on or off depending on the level of activation. This procedure produces a pattern of activation (0s and 1s) across the output units which can be compared with the target activation pattern.

Wickelfeature representation of past tense (output)

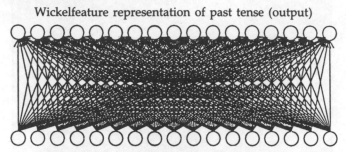

Wickelfeature representation of stem (input)

representation of the verb stem and the output a phonological representation of the corresponding past tense form. The model operates as follows. A verb stem representation is presented to the input units. Activation passes along the connections to produce a pattern of activation on the output units. The activation pattern on the output units is compared to the target activation pattern, i.e. the correct phonological representation of the past tense of the verb. Any discrepancy between the actual output pattern and the target output is used as an error signal to a learning algorithm that makes small adjustments to the connections in the network. If the same stem were presented to the network again, then the output error will be smaller. Repeated presentations of the stem will eventually eliminate the output error, i.e. the network will have learned to produce the correct past tense form of the verb given its stem. It is also possible to evaluate the network's performance at various training by determining it's current best guess as to what the past tense form of the stem is supposed to be. Initially, the output will not make any sense since the network knows nothing about the relation between the stem and past tense forms of verbs. However, as training proceeds the network's attempt to construct the correct form can result in a variety of intermediary forms that can be compared to the forms that children produce en route to learning the English past tense.

Of course, the network has to learn more than just one stem/past tense pair. In fact, R&M trained their model on 420 verbs. The set of verbs chosen was selected as a representative sample of regular and irregular verbs in English. Thus, most of the verbs chosen were regular verbs and the exceptions included an assortment of the irregular types found in English, e.g. go/went, hit/hit, see/saw, sleep/slept. On successive training trials, the network was presented with different verb stems. It was thereby required to learn many verbs at the same time, since it was not permitted to completely learn a single stem/past tense pair before proceeding to the next. This type of training regime has important consequences for the behavioral characteristics of the network.

Consider a training cycle in which a regular verb is presented to the network. In order to produce the correct past tense form, the connections in the network must be adjusted so that the activity on the output units corresponds to a stem plus an /ed/ suffix. Suppose on the next training trial another regular verb is presented to the network. Although a different stem should be activated on the output units, the network still has to activate the /ed/ suffix. Hence, the strengthening of the connections on the previous learning trial will facilitate the correct suffixing response on the current learning trial. And the learning that occurs as a result of the presentation of the new regular verb will strengthen the /ed/ response still further. In essence, verbs that belong to the same class will cause similar changes in the weight matrix of the network and so contribute to the learning of other verbs in the same class.

A critical feature of the English past tense is that not all verbs undergo the same type of transformation from stem to past tense form. As noted above, the irregular verbs undergo a variety of changes, e.g. arbitrary change, no change, vowel suppletion, blending. Let us suppose then that on the third hypothetical learning trial, the verb that is selected for learning is an irregular verb, say hit/hit. In this case, the network is once again supposed to activate the stem on the output units but this time the /ed/ suffix should not be active. Since the network has only seen regular verbs so far, there will already be a slight tendency to turn on the /ed/ suffix. This tendency will be apparent on the output pattern for hit, i.e. there is likely to be quite a large discrepancy between the actual output on the suffix units and the target output. Importantly, this error signal will then be exploited by the learning algorithm to adjust the weights in the network so that the suffix units are turned off. If the regular verbs were presented again, the recent presentation of hit will have decreased the probability of the suffix units turning on. In other words, the adjustments to the connections in the network that arise as the result of presenting an irregular verb interfere directly with the configuration of connections constructed to deal with the regular verbs.

It is worth emphasizing here that these interference effects result from the fact that a single set of connections is being used to represent the stem/past tense relations of many verbs and that in English the regular and irregular verbs are in direct competition with each other in the manner in which they attempt to adjust connection strengths of the network.

The general level of performance of the R&M model at different points in training is shown in figure 2.3. The graph distinguishes performance on regular and irregular verbs. During the first few epochs[2] of training, performance on regular and irregular verbs increases rapidly. During this period the network

Figure 2.3   Performance of the Rumelhart and McClelland (1986) verb learning model. The graph plots success rate on regular and irregular verbs separately. Irregular verbs experience a decrement in performance around the tenth training epoch.

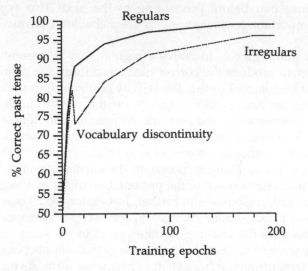

unravels the general nature of the problem it has to solve and learns about the phonological representations used at the input and output level. After ten epochs of training, performance on the irregular verbs deteriorates. A qualitative analysis of network performance reveals that overgeneralization errors are occurring, i.e. the network begins to produce past tense output errors such as "go-ed" and "hit-ed." Just a few epochs earlier the network had produced the correct past tense forms for these verbs. Further training on the verbs gradually eliminates the errors on irregular verbs though other types of overgeneralizations appear at sporadic intervals. For example, the network might judge the past tense of "eat" to be "ated" or the past tense of "go" to be "wented." These blending errors typically occur late in the training of the network. After several hundred epochs of training the network had mastered the overwhelming majority of verbs in the training set.

R&M noted that this profile of learning in the network was reminiscent of the developmental profile of children learning the English past tense. In particular, a stage of learning occurs where irregular verbs that earlier have been correctly produced are overgeneralized. Furthermore, the timing of certain kinds of errors (such as the late appearance of blending errors) reflects the timing of such errors in young children. These findings supported R&M's conclusion that a single network device could encode the relationship between the stem and past tense forms of regular and irregular verbs without recourse to the representational notion of a rule. Furthermore, their work suggested that the pattern of overgeneralization errors observed in young children can be explained purely in terms of a device that extracts the patterns of regularity and subregularity from a data set without reference to a pre-structured architecture that distinguishes regular from irregular forms, as is the case in the traditional symbolic account. In effect, their model seemed to offer the beginnings of a solution to Plato's problem or the "poverty of the stimulus" argument.

2.3 Problems with the verb learning model

The R&M verb learning model offered the prospect of a radically different approach to our understanding of language acquisition – an approach that suggested a different balance between the role of innate structure and linguistic experience in the developmental process than previously supposed by mainstream theorists. However, the R&M model suffered from a number of drawbacks.[3] For example, Pinker and Prince (1988) argued that the phonological representation used for the stem and past tense of the verb in the R&M model did not provide unambiguous representations of verb forms, nor could it deal with the representation of forms where syllables are repeated. Pinker and Prince also pointed out that the type of network architecture used by R&M was in principle capable of producing reverse transformations such as /hit/→/tih/, a type of mapping not observed in the languages of the world. Hence, the model was overpowerful and underconstrained. Furthermore, the network was observed to produce past tense errors of a type not observed in young children, e.g. membled as the past tense of mail. More importantly from a developmental perspective, Pinker and Prince pointed out that R&M manipulated the training set in an unrealistic fashion. When R&M trained their network on the past tense problem they did not use the full set of 420 verbs during the early stages of training. They chose just ten verbs, eight irregular and two regular, and trained the network on just those ten verbs for ten epochs. After ten epochs, they introduced the remaining 410 verbs and continued training. Since their final vocabulary was intended as a representative sample of English verbs, the overwhelming majority of new verbs added into the training set after ten epochs were regular verbs.

Now reconsider the performance profile of irregular verbs depicted in figure 2.3. Note that the first decrement in performance on the irregular verbs occurs exactly at the ten epoch mark – the point in training where vocabulary size is suddenly increased. Since the learning algorithm is now exposed to a large number of verbs which require a suffix, it will strengthen the connections in the network that produce a suffix on the output units. Consequently, the suffixation process for regular verbs in the initial training set of ten verbs will be facilitated by the change in vocabulary composition, whereas the irregular verbs will suffer. In particular, the network will tend to treat the irregular verbs as though they are regular and add a suffix to them, i.e. overgeneralize. Hence the decrement in performance on irregular verbs.

The justification for the vocabulary discontinuity in R&M's training set was twofold: first, they wanted the training set to reflect the fact that certain verbs in the language are more frequent than others. Hence, the initial set of ten verbs was just those verbs which are highly frequent in the language. Early training on these forms resulted in the network processing them a greater number of times than verbs introduced after the vocabulary continuity. Second, R&M were aware that many children pass through a period of vocabulary development known as the vocabulary spurt, where the rate of increase of vocabulary size accelerates suddenly. Superficially then R&M's manipulation of the training set seems to be reasonably justified. However, two facts undermine their assumptions:

1   The vocabulary spurt is generally recognized as representing a sudden increase in the number of nouns (not verbs) in children's vocabularies (McShane, 1979).

2   The onset of overgeneralization of the /ed/ morpheme does not usually occur until towards the end of the child's third year, whereas the vocabulary spurt occurs during the latter half of the child's second year.

Thus, the input assumptions R&M make do not seem to be justified by the facts of language acquisition. Indeed, Pinker and Prince reported the results of a count of regular and irregular verbs produced by children in the Brown (1973) study and showed that regular and irregular verbs were present in roughly equal proportions throughout the period analyzed. For many developmentalists, these discrepancies undermined the force of R&M's claim to have provided an alternative account of the mechanisms underlying children's acquisition of the English past tense and the notion that a symbolic rule system could be dispensed with as an explanatory tool for linguistic behavior.

2.4   *Alternative past tense models*

Several groups of researchers attempted to show that the shortcomings of the R&M model were not an inevitable consequence of connectionist models *per se* but rather were associated with the particular implementation that R&M employed. For example, MacWhinney and Leinbach (1991) used a multilayered network and a training set of over 2,000 verbs. The verb forms were encoded in a standard phonological representation (as opposed to the Wickelphone representation used by R&M). The phonological representation provided an unambiguous representation of individual verbs. MacWhinney and Leinbach also incorporated a set of "copy connections" in their network, enabling it to pass information directly from the input units to the output units without passing through the intermediate layers of the network. These architectural and representational manipulations enabled the network to avoid a number of the problems raised by Pinker and Prince, such as stem reversal, syllable repetition, and improbable past tense errors.

Similarly, Plunkett and Marchman (1991) employed a multilayered network (though without copy connections) and a standard phonological representation on a training set of 500 verbs. In addition, they introduced two further modifications to the training environment:

1 A distinction between the *type* and *token* frequency of the verbs in the training set permitted input characteristics of the target language to be modeled more closely. Type frequency refers to the number of verbs that undergo the same kind of change from stem to past tense form (say "add an /-ed/"). Thus, irregular verbs tend to have a *low* type frequency whereas regular verbs have a very *high* type frequency. Token frequency refers to the number of instances of a particular verb that will, on average, be presented to the network during a given epoch of training. Thus, irregular verbs tend to have a *high* token frequency whereas regular verbs vary considerably in their token frequency.

2 The network was trained on a constant diet of verbs, i.e. there are no discontinuities in the training set.

As in the R&M model, the network had to resolve the competition between conflicting verb types. Plunkett and Marchman predicted that U-shaped errors would arise from this competition within the weight matrix *even though no discontinuity in the training set was introduced*. The profile of performance of the network confirmed that *all* verb types underwent U-shaped development.

It is important to note that successful network performance was only achieved by systematically exploring a variety of type and token frequencies for the different verb types. For example, Plunkett and Marchman observed that if the vocabulary set contained a large number of irregular verb types that underwent an arbitrary mapping (e.g. go → went) and/or the token frequency of the arbitrary verbs was low, then the network had considerable difficulty learning these forms. Similarly, if the vocabulary contained a disproportionately large number of vowel change verbs (e.g. see → saw), then the network had difficulty mastering the regular types. In general, the frequency conditions that seemed to support optimal learning in the network were those that most closely resembled the type and token frequency of the corresponding verb types in English. For example, the arbitrary verbs were learned best by the network when their type frequencies were low and their token frequencies high. This is also true of the two examples of arbitrary verbs in English (/go/→/went/ and /am/→/was/).

Several other important results appeared in the developmental profiles for the regular and irregular verbs in the simulations. First, the regular verb types underwent U-shaped error profiles. These include errors in which subregularities of the irregular classes leaked to the regular class. For example, the regular verb /fit/ might be mapped as /fit/ or /pick/ might be mapped as /puck/. These *irregularization* errors have also been noted in the literature, especially in studies that involve elicitation tasks (Bybee and Slobin 1982). However, they have not been reported as part of children's spontaneous speech errors. Second, the profile of errors observed in the Plunkett and Marchman simulations does not follow a simple stagelike pattern. U-shaped errors on irregular verbs are observed from the third epoch of training up to the twelfth epoch of training. During this period, individual verbs may be overregularized, then recover from error only to be overregularized again. Plunkett and Marchman (1991) refer to this characteristic profile of U-shaped curves as *micro U-shaped* development, to distinguish it from the *macro U-shape* that characterizes a stagelike process. Finally, the simulation did not produce a period of performance where no errors are observed. In particular, the simulation did not exhibit an initial period of error-free performance which is thought to characterize children's early usage of past tense forms. Of course, it is not surprising that the network performs badly during the initial phases of training. It starts out with a randomized weight matrix and is confronted with the task of learning 500 stem/past tense mappings, many of which are in conflict with each other.

2.5   The past tense revisited

A recent study by Marcus, Ullman, Pinker, Hollander, Rosen and Xu (1992) has provided a detailed analysis of the overregularization errors in the spontaneous speech of 83 English children. The data were taken from the CHILDES archive of computerized child language transcriptions (MacWhinney and Snow, 1985) and automatically searched for overregularization errors. Profiles of development for four of the children in the database are reproduced in figure 2.4. Adam, Eve, and Sarah (taken from the Brown (1973) corpus) are fairly typical of the other children whose data were analyzed. Abe (from the Kuczaj (1977) corpus) is an atypical outlier in the overall profile of children in that he produces the highest rate of overregularization errors. Marcus et al. provide a picture of development that can be briefly summarized as follows:

- Early acquisition is characterized by a period of error-free performance.
- The overall rate of overregularization errors is usually quite low – typically between 5 percent and 10 percent.
- Overregularization errors are not restricted to a circumscribed stage of development. Once errors begin to appear, they recur throughout the period studied.
- Irregular verbs with a high token frequency tend to be robust to overregularization errors. Thus, errors like /goed/ are particularly rare.
- Errors are phonologically conditioned. For example, irregular "no change" verbs which end in a dental consonant (/t/ or /d/) are robust to overregularization. Thus, errors like /hitted/ are particularly rare.

Figure 2.4 Overregularization errors produced by four of the 83 children analyzed by Marcus, Ullman et al. (1992). Percent correct of irregular verbs is plotted against age. Adam, Eve, and Sarah (the children from the Brown, 1973, corpus) are fairly typical in the overregularization profiles, whereas Abe (Kuczaj, 1977, corpus) represents an outlier.

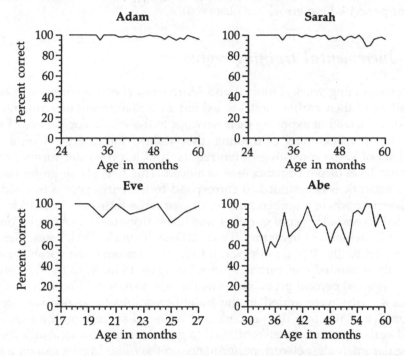

- A very small number of irregularization errors are observed. For example, Adam produces /bat/ for the past tense of /bite/.[4]

This picture of development is quite different from the view that there is a stage of development where overregularization errors occur, or that over-regularization errors are a common phenomenon in child language. Errors occur intermittently throughout much of children's language development and on particular types of verbs, i.e. low frequency irregular verbs and irregular verbs which do not belong to strong family resemblance classes.

Now compare this profile of development to that produced by the Plunkett and Marchman simulation. Both error profiles share the characteristics of micro U-shaped development over a protracted period of development. Furthermore, the simulation, like the children, tended not to produce many over-regularization errors on high frequency irregular verbs or irregular verbs which belong to a phonologically coherent subclass. Irregularization errors are most prominent on low frequency irregulars and/or the Vowel Change verbs. Finally, the simulation produced irregularizations of both regular and irregular verbs. In contrast to the children analyzed by Marcus et al., the simulation does not exhibit an initial period of error-free performance. In this respect, the simulation failed to capture an important feature associated with children's acquisition of inflectional morphology which has traditionally been used to argue for the view that language acquisition is a process of learning a system of rules, i.e. the transition from a period of entirely correct behavior to a *subsequent* period where errors are observed.

2.6 *Incremental training regimes*

In later modeling work, Plunkett and Marchman (1993) attempted to rectify the failure of their earlier model to exhibit an initial period of error-free performance. Instead of exposing their network to the whole vocabulary of verbs from the very beginning of training, they trained their network on a small initial set of verbs consisting of ten regular and ten irregular forms until an optimum level of performance was achieved. This first phase in the training of the network was assumed to correspond to the early period in children's verb learning where a limited number of past tense forms are learned by rote. The initial vocabulary configuration was taken from the MacArthur Communicative Development Inventory (Fenson, Dale, Reznick, Thal, Bates, Hartung, Pethick and Reilly, 1993). In the second phase of training, the vocabulary was gradually expanded one verb at a time. For each addition to the training set, there was an 80 percent probability that the new verb would be a regular verb. The new verbs were added to the training vocabulary at regular intervals irrespective of whether the network had achieved success on the previously added verb. Vocabulary size continued to grow steadily to a total of 500 verbs. At regular intervals, network performance on the *trained* verbs and on a set of novel verbs was evaluated. Performance on the novel verbs permitted an evaluation of the extent to which the network had extracted a general pattern for the past tense. Testing on novel verbs can be regarded as an artificial equivalent to carrying out a "wug" test (Berko, 1958).

The profile of overregularization errors produced by the network during training is compared to the profile of overregularization errors produced by Adam in figure 2.5. Note that the rate of overregularization errors produced by the network is very low (typically less than 10 percent). Furthermore, the network exhibits an initial period where no overregularization errors on irregular verbs are observed. This period extends well into the period of vocabulary expansion. In fact, overregularization errors are not observed until the vocabulary size reaches around 120 verbs. It is useful to compare the network's profile of overregularization errors with the manner in which it responds to novel verbs. Figure 2.6 depicts the likelihood of the network adding a suffix to the stem of a novel verb at different points in training. During the earliest phases of training (up to around 50 verbs), novel stems are treated in an unsystematic fashion by the network. No suffix is added to the stem and the output cannot be classified in a straightforward manner. This indicates that the network has not extracted a *systematic* representation of the training

Figure 2.5 Network overregularization errors from the Plunkett and Marchman (1993) simulation compared to those of Adam (Marcus et al. 1992). The thick line indicates the percentage of regular verbs in the child's/network's vocabulary at various points in learning.

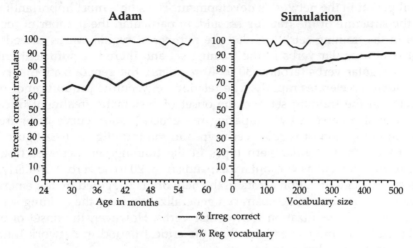

— % Irreg correct

— % Reg vocabulary

Figure 2.6 Network performance on novel verbs as a function of vocabulary size. The graph plots the tendency to add a suffix to the novel stem (from Plunkett and Marchman, 1993).

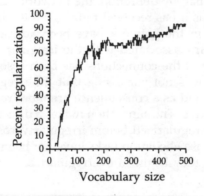

patterns and that successful performance on the trained verbs has been achieved via a process of rote learning. However, as the vocabulary expands from 50 verbs to 120 verbs the likelihood of adding a suffix to novel verbs increases from 2 percent to around 70 percent. This result indicates that the network has abstracted a generalization concerning the manner in which past tense forms are generated from stems in the training set.

The tendency to add a suffix to novel verb stems continues to increase as vocabulary size expands beyond 120 verbs. However, the rate of increase is much lower than in the period when vocabulary expands from 50 to 120 verbs. There would thus appear to be a critical period in the training of the network where it acquires the ability to add appropriate suffixes to novel stems and thereby reorganize itself from a mode of rote representation to one of systematic representation. Plunkett and Marchman (1993) carried out a number of control simulations in order to identify the determinants of this critical period in the network's development. The single most important factor was the structure of the training set and, in particular, the number of regular verbs in the training set.[5] Provided the number of regular verbs exceeds the number of irregular verbs in the training set and there is a sufficient critical mass of regular verbs (around 30 to 40 regulars), the generalization curve to novel stems accelerates rapidly. The relation between the proportion of regular verbs in the training set and the onset of systematic treatment of novel stems can also be seen by comparing the generalization curve in figure 2.6 with the proportion of regular verb types in the training set (see figure 2.5). The proportion of regular verb types in the training set increases from 50 percent to 76 percent as vocabulary expands from 20 to 80 verbs. Similarly, the onset of overregularization errors in the network is triggered by the emerging tendency of the network to abstract a generalization from the training set and overapply the generalization to irregular verbs. However, the onset of overregularization errors comes later than the critical period in network training where novel stems begin to be suffixed.

At first blush, one might expect that the tendency of the network to regularize novel stems and irregular verbs should occur simultaneously. However, it should be recalled that, by definition, the network has received no training on novel verbs whereas it has received training on the irregular verbs. Therefore, the connections in the network have been adjusted to respond to the particular input patterns associated with the irregular verbs. In contrast, no such direct finetuning of the connections has been associated with the novel verbs. Consequently, it is not surprising that the irregular verbs are recognized by the network and as a consequence are more robust to regularization than the novel verb forms. The simulation makes a direct prediction that novel verb forms should be regularized before irregular verbs are overregularized. Unfortunately, past tense elicitation tasks have not been carried out with children at an age before they begin to overregularize.

2.7   Vocabulary size and the onset of overregularization errors

Marcus et al. (1992), in their analysis of 83 English children's overregularization errors, found no evidence for a correlation between children's vocabulary composition and the onset of overregularization errors. The essence of their finding can be seen in figure 2.5. Note that the variations in the proportion of regular verbs in Adam's regular verb vocabulary exhibits no relation to the pattern of his overregularization errors. This result would appear to contradict the predictions of the Plunkett and Marchman simulation which maintains that there should be a very close relation between vocabulary composition and the onset of overregularization errors. Notice, however, that the overregularization errors in the simulation occur during a period in which the percentage regular verb types in the training vocabulary varies between 70 percent and 77 percent. For Adam the overregularization errors occur while the percentage of regular verbs varies between 68 percent and 77 percent. Furthermore, in the simulation there is no significant correlation between overregularization errors and percentage regular during the period immediately prior to the onset of overregularizations and beyond (i.e. while percent regular verb types is in the same range as observed for Adam). Yet we know from a purely mechanistic analysis of the network's behavior that an appropriately rich regular verb vocabulary is a necessary condition for the onset of overregularization errors in the simulation. One might suppose therefore that a similar vocabulary composition precondition might hold for the children. However, this hypothesis was not explored by Marcus et al. because the material on which their findings are based do not cover a sufficiently wide range of verb vocabulary sizes.

Marchman and Bates (1994) have used the MacArthur Communicative Development Inventory (Fenson et al., 1993) to explore the relation between the rate of overregularization errors in children and their regular verb vocabulary size. In contrast to the Marcus, Ullman et al. study which is based primarily on 83 children's spontaneous utterances, the Marchman and Bates study uses parental report measures for over 1,000 children. The most important finding in the present context is the discovery of a nonlinear relation between regular verb vocabulary size and the rate of overregularization errors. In particular, overregularization errors do not occur with small regular verb vocabularies and the onset of overregularization errors seems to exhibit a critical mass effect, i.e. overregularization errors do not occur until regular verb vocabularies have achieved a criterial size. Furthermore, once the critical mass of verbs is a achieved the rate of overregularization errors does not correlate in a simple linear fashion with the proportion of regular verbs in children's vocabularies. These results are entirely compatible with the predictions from the Plunkett and Marchman simulations. Marcus et al.'s failure to find a relationship between the size of verb vocabulary and the onset of overregularization errors would thus appear to be an artefact of their data sampling, i.e. they did not analyze data from children with very small verb vocabularies – preventing them from discovering a critical mass effect.

The evidence available, therefore, is consistent with the view that the onset of overregularization errors in children is related to the number of regular verbs in their vocabularies. Note, however, that although vocabulary composition is a necessary condition for the onset of overregularization errors, it is not a sufficient condition. Extended training must occur before the mass effect of regular verbs in the child's vocabulary can impinge upon irregular verb performance. Even after extensive training, the pattern of overregularization errors will depend on the strength of the irregular verb representations in the child's mental lexicon. The strength of the representation will itself depend on a number of other factors such as type and token frequencies and phonological coherence of the irregular verb subclass (see Plunkett and Marchman, 1991).

2.8   Beyond phonological representations

Children know more about the past tense than the relationship between phonological representations of the stem and past tense forms. Indeed, the psychological plausibility of the past tense models rely on the existence of additional past tense knowledge. For example, they assume that the child is able to recognize the past tense forms of verbs in the linguistic environment (the teacher signal in the model) in order to access a lexical representation of the verb which provides the child with the phonological representation of the corresponding stem. The stem, thus procurred, is then fed into the network system to ascertain the child's own current hypothesis as to the past tense form of the verb. The output of the network can then be compared to a phonological trace of the teacher signal to determine any discrepancy which can be used by the learning algorithm to adjust the current hypothesis (the weight matrix of the network) as to the appropriate past tense form. So the model assumes the existence of a great deal of past tense machinery which it nevertheless leaves unspecified.

Of course, one of the strengths of the past tense models is their ability to account for the range of errors produced by children by reference to such a limited part of the overall system. However, this parsimony of explanation is undermined by a number of simple facts about the English past tense. For example, Pinker and Prince (1988) point out that a system that exploits a purely phonological representation at the input will not be able to learn the past tense variants of homophonic verb stems. The phonological stem /ring/ takes on three different past tense forms (/rang/, /wrung/, and /ringed/) depending on the intended meaning associated with /ring/. It is possible to adapt the past tense model to capture these different responses to identical input: introduce an additional set of input units that disambiguates the phonological representation so that a different output pattern is produced depending on the state of the additional input units. We might imagine these additional input units to represent the semantics of the verb. However, Pinker and Prince point out that this type of solution is in danger of running into other difficulties. To appreciate why, it is necessary first to know that networks tend to respond in accordance with the similarity structure of the input patterns. That is, similar input patterns tend to produce similar outputs. Thus, if you train a network to produce /walked/ as the past tense of /walk/ then it will benefit from this training in learning that the past tense of /talk/ is /talked/. The homophonic verb stem problem is an extreme case of this property of networks: identical inputs will produce identical outputs. Now consider the verbs "hit," "strike," and "slap." In terms of their semantic features they are all closely related, dealing with some form of sudden contact.

Yet they each form their past tenses in very different ways – "hit," "struck," and "slapped" – no change, vowel change, and suffixation. Clearly, it is not possible to use the semantics of the verb to predict the past tense class membership. Hence, the connectionist who attempts to resolve the homophonic verb stem problem by simply adding in extra "semantic" units is in danger of falling afoul of the semantic similarity effect. For example, two forms of /ring/ involve a circular feature in their semantic representations. This similarity may interfere with the network's ability to produce distinct types of past tense forms for the homophonic verb stems.

A related problem concerns the fate of denominal verbs in the process of past tense formation. Denominal verbs are verbs that are derived from nouns. These may be verbs that are permanently resident in the English speaker's mental lexicon or nouns which are converted to verbs "on the fly" ("He captained the ship"). Kim, Pinker, Prince, and Prasada (1991) note that denominal verbs are invariably inflected as regular verbs. This is a curious result especially considering that some denominal verbs sound very similar (and a number identical) to irregular verbs (see Kim et al., 1991: 179–80 for a list of such forms). From the perspective of the past tense model which only processes phonological information, the past tense forms of denominal verbs should follow the pattern for other similar sounding verbs in the language. In other words, many denominal verbs should be inflected in an irregular fashion. The fact that relatively few denominals are inflected in an irregular manner again points to the inadequacy of the past tense model as a complete account (and perhaps a misguided account) of how children acquire the English past tense.

Several attempts to construct connectionist models that address these issues have already appeared in the literature, though it should be noted that, to date, their success has been somewhat limited. For example, Cottrell and Plunkett (in press) and Hoeffner (1992) have constructed models that take semantic input representations of verbs and map them to various phonological output representations associated with the verb, e.g. the present and past tense forms. Additional input units indicate to the network whether the present or past tense form of the verb is required on a particular presentation. The additional units may be interpreted as representing the output of other linguistic modules concerned with sentence production that guide the choice of verb form in the utterance.

These connectionist models demonstrate that Pinker and Prince's observation that semantically similar verbs may undergo quite dissimilar mapping processes need not be a cause for concern. Multilayered networks which are able to construct their own internal representations of verb semantics are capable of learning quite distinct inflectional processes even for verbs that are semantically very similar. En route to learning the distinct inflectional processes for semantically associated verbs, however, the network may confuse the relevant inflections in a semantically driven overregularization error. For example, "hit" might be overregularized as "hitted" because it is semantically similar to "slap." To date, the relevant analyses of the acquisition data have not been performed to permit an evaluation of this type of prediction. Nevertheless, this type of model emphasizes the fact that connectionist models need not rely exclusively on the phonological information in making predictions concerning the acquisition of the English past tense. In fact, the modeler is at liberty to exploit any information which might be thought to play a role in the developmental process. A sensible strategy is to keep the model simple by restricting access to limited sources of information, thereby permitting a careful evaluation of the potential contribution of individual information types for the developmental process. However, when the facts of development seem to implicate the role of multiple data sources, the simulation should also be offered access to this information.

2.9   *The case of the minority default mapping*

The number of verbs in English that take an irregular past tense form constitute a small minority of the total number of verbs in English. This was not always the case. Strong verbs used to be in the majority in English (see Hare and Elman, 1993). Today, there are about 150–80 irregular past tense verbs in English. Most of the irregular verbs produce past tense forms that are quite predictable from the phonological form of the stem. For example, all of the "no change" verbs in English end in a dental consonant (a /t/ or a /d/): other irregular verbs form family resemblance clusters in which vowel–consonant codas predict the vowel suppletion that relates the stem to its past tense form (/cling/→/clung/, /sling/→/slung/, /sting/→/stung/, /string/→/strung/ /swing/→/swung/, /wring/→/wrung/). These transformations are perfectly well formed. The reason that they are called irregular verbs is that there are only a few of them in the language and that their phonological forms do not define the mapping class, i.e. verbs with the same characteristics can undergo different types of past tense formation (/bring/→/brought/, /fit/→/fitted/).

The overwhelming majority of verbs in English take the /ed/ ending in the past tense. Furthermore, there are no phonological properties which seem to define the regular class (Pinker and Prince, 1988; Prasada and Pinker, 1993), i.e. regular verbs are as similar to irregular verbs as they are to each other. The connectionist models described in this chapter exploit the relative size of the regular class in developing a default mapping for novel verbs and in producing overregularization errors on the irregular verbs. The simulations also produced irregularization errors in which the subregularities of the irregular classes leaked to other classes (/pick/→/puck/). But these are much less frequent than overregularization errors. The size of the regular class in English plays a dominant role in the pattern of behavior produced by the connectionist models.

It is relatively straightforward to understand why the large class size of the regular verbs in English promotes /ed/ as the default mapping and forces the errors on irregular verbs. Recall that the type of feedforward networks that have been employed in the modeling of the English past tense are sensitive to the similarity structure of the training set to which they are exposed. Hence, when a novel form is presented to the network, the response will tend to reflect the relative similarity of the novel form to the other forms on which the network has been trained. If the novel form resembles an irregular verb, then the novel form may inherit the subregularity associated with the irregular verb. If the novel form resembles a regular verb, it will inherit the /ed/ suffix. We may consider the phonological properties of English verbs to define a space such that each verb stem corresponds to a point in this space. Naturally, this phonological space is highly dimensional – the number of dimensions corresponding to the number of phonological properties that are required to uniquely identify all the verb stems in English. In this space, irregular verbs will tend to cluster together in groups like galaxies of stars in space, whereas regular verbs will populate the space at relatively random points, both within the "galaxies" themselves but also in "intergalactic" space. The number of irregular verb clusters is small and the number of verbs within any cluster is also small. So the space is sparsely populated as far as irregular verbs are concerned. In contrast, the space contains many regular verbs. When we present a novel verb stem to the network we are, in effect, identifying a specific point in this multidimensional space. The chances of a randomly selected point being close to a regular verb are much higher than the chances of the novel verb being close to an irregular verb – not only are there more regular than irregular verbs in the space but the regular verbs fill the space more homogeneously. In this space, closeness is synonymous with similarity. So the relative closeness of the novel verb in the phonological space to a trained form will be a good predictor of the type of mapping that the novel form will experience. The distribution of regular verbs in the space clearly predicts that the regular mapping – add an /ed/ – will be the most likely mapping process for randomly selected novel verbs.

Now let us consider several other types of inflectional systems that differ from English in at least one important respect, in that there is not a single mapping type (inflectional class) which applies to a majority of the forms in the language. For example, the majority of plurals in Arabic are characterized by a system of subregularities conditioned by phonological characteristics of the noun stem – the so-called Arabic broken plural (McCarthy and Prince, 1990). Knowing the phonological shape of a noun in Arabic tells you how to form its plural. A small minority of nouns take the sound plural. Sound plural nouns have no phonological characteristics that make them cohere as a class and do not possess the phonological template associated with the broken plural. The sound plural constitutes a default mapping process that is distinct from the irregular broken plural forms in the language. Although we don't have any direct evidence on the matter, one might speculate that novel nouns in Arabic which don't conform to any of the phonological templates associated with the broken plural will be assimilated to the sound plural (Prince, personal communication). The question arises as to whether a connectionist network could learn both types of plural in Arabic and generalize the sound plural to novel nouns that don't resemble the broken plural nouns. Given the discussion in the previous paragraph, it may seem unlikely that a single network could succeed in learning the Arabic plural system: for example, given a randomly selected novel noun stem, the chances of that stem resembling a broken plural stem are greater than it resembling a sound plural stem (there are many more broken plural stems than sound plural stems). Hence, a novel stem presented to a network is more likely to behave like a broken plural rather than a sound plural – the supposed default mapping.

This picture of network behavior is essentially correct for single layered networks which can only solve linearly separable problems. The response of a single layered network to a novel input is subject to the linear predictability constraint (Minsky and Papert, 1969). In effect, this means that the network will respond to a novel stimulus in a manner that reflects its weighted similarity to all the patterns on which the network has been trained. Thus, the most similar training pattern has the greatest effect on the novel stimulus and the least similar training pattern has the least effect. However, this constraint can be overcome by the use of multilayered networks with intermediate hidden units that form internal representations of the input patterns. The internal representations of the input stems can have a very different similarity structure to that of their literal input forms. For example, we saw above that the phonological space occupied by the regular and irregular verbs in English is populated in such a fashion that irregular verbs cluster in "galaxies" whereas regular verbs are distributed throughout the space. Hidden unit representations of the verb stems can be interpreted as a transformation of this space. For example, the English irregular clusters could be folded into very small regions such that they occupied an even smaller region of the space while regular verbs expanded to occupy almost the entire space. Under these conditions, the chances of the internal representation of a novel verb stem resembling an irregular verb would be diminished still further and the likelihood of it receiving a default /ed/ mapping increased accordingly. The ability of multilayered networks to transform the similarity structure of the input space is facilitated by the presence of subregularities in the input. If the set of input stems that undergo a particular type of mapping all share an invariant feature (such as no-change verbs in English all ending in a dental consonant), then the network can exploit this regularity by mapping all such verbs onto the same point in the internal representation of phonological space so that they are treated in an identical fashion. Effectively, the network creates an internal category representation.

Now reconsider the Arabic plural system. We can now see that a multilayered perceptron is, in principle, capable of solving a problem of this type. Since the broken plurals consist of phonological subregularities that are definitional of the plural mapping type, the network can form an internal representation that collapses all the members of a subregularity onto a very small region of transformed phonological space. This leaves the sound plural to occupy the rest of the space. If a novel stem presented to the network does not possess a phonological feature that is definitional of the broken plural, then it will be mapped into the region of transformed phonological space that is populated by sound plurals and treated accordingly. Hence, it is possible in principle for a network to mimic the behavior of an inflectional system where the default mapping is associated with a minority of the forms in the language. It should be pointed out, however, that a working connectionist model of the Arabic plural system has not yet been constructed.

In contrast to the Arabic broken plural, the German plural system does not seem to be characterized by a set of phonological subregularities that might enable a connectionist network to collapse classes of noun stems onto internal category representations (Clahsen, Rothweiler, Woest, and Marcus, 1992; Marcus, Brinkmann, Clahsen, Wiese, Woest, and Pinker, 1993). German possesses half a dozen or so different ways of forming the plural where no one class comes close to constituting a majority of the forms in the language. Yet Clahsen et al. (1992) and Marcus et al. (1993) provide evidence that it is primarily one class – the /s/ class or *emergency plural* – that children overregularize to other classes and use as a default mapping for novel forms (though Clahsen et al. also note limited overregularization of the/-en/ plural). The /s/ class, like the sound plural in Arabic, covers a relatively small number of forms in the language. Marcus et al. (1993) argue that German children form a default rule that adds /s/ to the stem of the noun when other mappings do not apply. The status of this default "add /s/" rule is entirely parallel to the symbolic status of the "add /ed/" rule in the dual route model of the English past tense (Pinker and Prince, 1988). The difference between the default mapping in the English past tense and that of the German plural is that the former constitutes a majority of forms in the language whereas the latter a minority of forms. Marcus et al. (1993) question the capacity of a connectionist network to learn such a minority default mapping in the absence of phonological subregularities to help the network discover features to predict class membership.

The case of the German plural does seem to offer a challenge to the standard connectionist account of how children might acquire inflectional morphology. At the very least, it suggests that phonological information may be inadequate for conceptualizing the mapping problem. However, it is still possible that weak distributional tendencies associating phonological features within a class and across classes might act in consortium to support learning and representation of a minority default process by a neural network. For example, MacWhinney, Leinbach, Taraban, and McDonald (1989) showed how a neural network could exploit such weak distributional information in its categorization of German nouns according to gender. Even if such weak phonological information proves inadequate to achieve appropriate inflectional categorization, other sources of information might substitute or supplement the categorization of the German plural. Clahsen et al. (1992) note that the class of nouns which form the plural by adding /-en/ is predominantly restricted to the female gender nouns. This subregularity may serve to encourage overregularization errors of the /-en/ type and/or act in consortium with other nondefinitional features to help partition the inflectional space of the German plural. Indeed, Wurzel (1990) points to a complex interaction between gender and phonological characteristics for the determination of class membership in the German plural system.

3   Concept Formation and Vocabulary Development

The past tense model described in the previous section provides an example of reorganizational processes within a given representational domain (in this case, inflectional morphology). In general, representational domains interact with each other at the same time as they perform their own specific task. Furthermore, the dynamics of intradomain processes may be influenced by interdomain interactions. A classic example of these interactive processes can be found in the interface between vocabulary growth and concept formation. The Cognition Hypothesis (Cromer, 1974) claims that "We are able to understand and productively to use particular linguistic structures only when our cognitive abilities enable us to do so." Thus, in the domain of vocabulary development, the referential use of words depends upon the formation of nonlinguistic categories. However, the structure of the vocabulary of the language being acquired plays the role of highlighting which categories should be semantically represented. For the individual learner, the lexical items used frequently by the caregiver provide a scaffold for organizing his or her semantic knowledge.

In this section, I describe a connectionist model of concept formation and vocabulary growth that attempts to capture the dynamics of intra- and interdomain processes. (See Chauvin, 1988 and Plunkett, Sinha, Moller, and Strandsby, 1992 for a fuller account). The model has four main behavioral properties:

1   The model exhibits a prototype effect.
2   The model reveals a comprehension/production asymmetry.
3   The model undergoes a vocabulary spurt.
4   The model manifests under- and overextension errors.

The main purpose in describing this model is to show how a connectionist system can encompass a variety of phenomena which have otherwise been explained in diverse ways. The model offers a coherent, integrated account of the phenomena, demonstrating how they are closely linked together. It also provides a concrete example of how distinct domains (in this case, visual and auditory) can interact to produce structures that would not emerge given intradomain processes alone.

Figure 2.7 Network architecture used in Plunkett et al. (1992). Note that there are 32 labels and 171 image units. The image is filtered through a retinal preprocessor prior to presentation to the network.

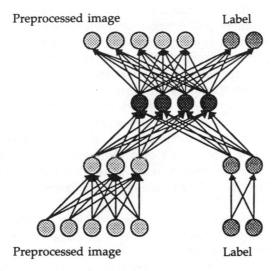

3.1 The model

The network's task is to associate images with labels. The images are random dot patterns similar to those used by Posner and Keele (1970) in assessing human subjects' sensitivity to nonnatural categories. The images are clustered in categories which have an internal prototype structure. Each image is generated from one of 32 prototype random dot patterns by displacing each of nine dots by a specified length in a random direction. Prespecified displacement lengths provide three different distortion levels corresponding to the distance between the image and its prototype. For each prototype pattern, two distortions at each distortion level are generated giving a total of six distortions per prototype. 32 clusters of patterns are generated in this manner, giving a total of 192 distortions plus 32 prototype patterns. No prototype pattern has more than two dots in common with any other prototype pattern. However, a small degree of overlap between high level distortions of one prototype and that of another prototype is permitted.

Each cluster of images is associated with a discrete label. Labels consist of 32 bit patterns in which only a single bit is active for each label. All label patterns are orthogonal to each other. In other words, there is no internal categorial structure to the set of labels and there is an arbitrary relationship between a label and its associated cluster of images.

The network architecture is shown in figure 2.7. Several aspects of this architecture are worth noting. First, the task of the network is simply to reproduce the distinct images and label representations that are presented to the network, on the output units. This type of task is called autoassociative learning and is considered a form of unsupervised learning. In other words, there is no teacher signal that can be considered distinct from the input signal. The task is nontrivial in the sense that input representations are translated to other representational formats before being converted back to the original image and label representations. Second, the penultimate layer of hidden units forms a composite representation of both the image and label patterns such that the presentation of an image alone will elicit a label (production) and presentation of a label alone will elicit an image (comprehension). Third, separate channels are reserved for the preprocessed random dot patterns and the label patterns respectively. Each modality projects to a separate bank of hidden units before converging on the common set of hidden units. The first banks of hidden units permit the network to organize its own representation of the input patterns. For example, the bank of hidden units associated with the image modality carries out a further fine tuning of the clustering process initiated by the retinal preprocessor.

The network is trained in a three phase cycle. First, an image representation is presented at the input units and activity is propagated through the network to the output units. The activity on the retinal output units is compared to the initial image representation. Any discrepancy is recorded as an error signal. A back propagation learning algorithm then adjusts the weights on the "image side" of the network only. A similar learning trial is conducted for the label associated with the previously presented image, except that weight adjustment now occurs only on the "label side" of the network. Finally, both image and label are presented simultaneously and error signals are used to adjust weights on both sides of the network. This three phase learning sequence is successively and repeatedly applied to all image/label pairs in the training set. Image/label pairs are selected randomly. In training the network only distorted images and their associated labels are used. The network is never trained on a prototype image. A useful mnemonic interpretation of the three phase training cycle is as an attention switching process. First, the network attends to the image, then to the label, and finally associations between the two are constructed.

The performance of the network in producing output labels and image representations is evaluated at various points in training. Performance is evaluated in terms of a "comprehension" and a "production" measure. "Production" is here defined as the capacity of the network to activate the appropriate output label in response to the presentation of an image representation at the input. In other words, production measures the ability of the network to name images correctly in the absence of a label input. In a similar fashion, "comprehension" is defined as the ability of the network to activate the appropriate retinal representations in response to the presentation of a label at the input. However, since there are many image representations consistent with a single label (image to label mappings are many to one while label to image mappings are one to many), comprehension is evaluated in a slightly different way to production. For each output image representation elicited by a given label, we calculate the number of image distortions captured by that retinal output. An image distortion is captured by a retinal output if the retinal representation of the distortion is sufficiently close to the retinal output.[6] In some cases, an image distortion may be captured by more than one image output. Under these circumstances, the image output closest to the distortion wins that distortion. If an appropriate distortion is captured by the retinal output, then the network is judged to successfully comprehend the label with respect to that distortion. For each label, a comprehension score from zero to six is computed. Comprehension and production scores are evaluated for all labels and all image distortions after each three phase training cycle throughout the training period.

Two other types of measure are used to evaluate the network's performance throughout the training period. First, the network's comprehension and production of trained patterns is compared with its performance on the prototype patterns. Remember that the network has never seen a prototype during the course of training. Performance on prototypes can thus be interpreted as an evaluation of the network's generalization characteristics. Correct production for a prototype corresponds to the activation of the appropriate label units on the output. Correct comprehension for a prototype corresponds to the retinal output of the label capturing the retinal representation of the appropriate prototype random dot image.

Second, overextension and underextension phenomena are examined in the performance of the network. We calculate the total number of distortions that elicit a given label, irrespective of the label's appropriateness, and the total number of distortions that are captured by the retinal output of a given label, again irrespective of the images' appropriateness. Next, we evaluate the number of output labels which are correct with respect to a given image input and the number of retinal outputs which are correct with respect to a given label input. A comparison of these two measures enables us to determine when a label is over- or underextended in production, and when the set of image distortions captured by a label is over- or underextended in comprehension.

Figure 2.8 (a) provides a summary of the comprehension/production scores for the image distortions and distortion labels during the first 100 epochs of training. Three aspects of these learning curves are noteworthy. First, both the comprehension and production measures manifest a growth spurt. For comprehension, the spurt occurs after a few training epochs. The production spurt occurs after a more prolonged period of training during which the proportion of distortions that are correctly named remains at a relatively low level. Second, comprehension scores exceed production scores throughout the period of training. This asymmetry is particularly noteworthy during the early and middle phases of training. Figure 2.8 (b) plots the comprehension and production scores for the prototypes. Note that the production measure for the prototypes reflects the tendency of the network to label correctly an image to which it has never been exposed.

Figure 2.8   Performance on distorted and prototype images in comprehension and production.

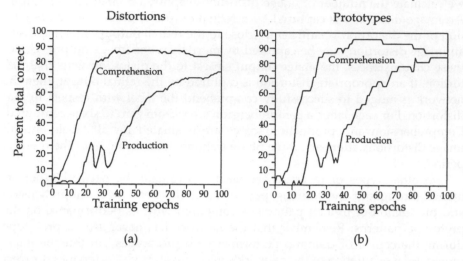

(a)   (b)

Figure 2.8 (b) can therefore be interpreted as an assessment of the extent to which the network generalizes to novel patterns. The prototype measures closely parallel those reported for the distortions. Both comprehension and production of prototypes reveal a spurt period of growth and comprehension precedes production at all points in training. The most noteworthy result is yielded by a comparison between the prototype and distortion measures. For both the comprehension and production measures, the performance on the prototypes exceeds performance on the distortion throughout the training period, despite the fact that the network has never been trained on prototype image/label pairs.

Analysis of the network's performance in naming distortions (production) from each of the 32 categories of random dot figures reveals a number of pure underextensions (application of a label to some but not all the category images with no false positives) in production – 11 categories in all. Pure overextensions (application of a label to inappropriate images once all the images within a category are appropriately labeled) are also observed though less frequently than pure underextensions – only two categories. Pure overextensions in production occur late in training while pure underextensions in production occur early in training.

Analysis of the network's performance in comprehending labels associated with each of the 32 categories of random dot figures reveals that there are only a few examples of pure underextension (the label results in a retinal output which captures only a subset of the appropriate images and no others) – just four categories. There are a larger number of pure overextensions in comprehension – 13 categories. As with the production measure, pure overextensions occur later in training while pure underextensions occur earlier in training.

A number of these network performance characteristics resemble properties of the processes of human concept formation and children's vocabulary growth. For example, the original experimental studies of concept formation with random dot figures (e.g. Posner and Keele, 1970) report a prototype effect in which subjects respond with high level confidence ratings to their categorization of prototype figures even though the prototypes have never been observed by the subjects during the training session. This result is explained in terms of a concept formation process which extracts central tendencies from the constellations of patterns that subjects are given to categorize. The network in these simulations is also extracting a central tendency from the constellations of training patterns, grouping them together in clusters, and responding most accurately to the central tendency of the cluster which, given the method of pattern generation, is likely to be close to the prototype pattern. Interestingly, the network takes longer to discover the appropriate clusterings when labels are not included as input in the training regime. This finding indicates that the network exploits the predictive power of the label in identifying category membership, as well as the natural clustering of the distortions in the image plane. In this respect, the findings do not support a pure cognitive prerequisite account of semantic development but an interactional account of the kind advanced by Vygotsky (1986).

A second result from these simulations, also well documented in the child language literature, is the finding that the network undergoes a vocabulary spurt. It is commonly observed that children's vocabulary growth is relatively slow during the first half of the second year. Later in the second year, however, expressive vocabulary typically increases dramatically (Bates, Bretherton, and Snyder, 1988; McShane, 1979; Plunkett, 1986, 1993). This finding is paralleled by the results from the production profiles in the simulations where production scores remain low for the first 20 to 30 epochs of training, but subsequently increase dramatically. Furthermore, the timing of pure over- and underextension phenomena observed in production in these simulations closely parallels that observed in young children. Underextensions are characteristic of the early stages of semantic development in young children while overextensions are typically observed after the vocabulary spurt (Barrett, 1986). There is also empirical evidence for a comprehension spurt in some young children – particularly those that tend to demonstrate a production spurt (Reznick and Goldfield, 1992).

Thirdly, these simulations demonstrate a higher comprehension score than production score throughout the period of training reported. The asymmetry between comprehension and production is well documented in the child language literature (Clark, 1983) and also in evaluations of adults' active and passive vocabularies. In network terms, the comprehension advantage during the early stages of training is relatively easy to explain: label patterns are far better predictors of category membership than image patterns which can be characterized as fuzzy and, for the high level distortions, sometimes equivocal in terms of their category membership. Until the network has established an accurate representation of the clustering of the images, labels provide more reliable cues to category membership. Indeed, this interpretation of network dynamics also explains why the comprehension/production asymmetry is greatest during the early phases of training. The partitioning of the image space is more difficult to achieve (similar input patterns may map onto dissimilar categories) than the partitioning of the label space (all label patterns are orthogonal so label partitioning is linearly separable). Unfortunately, we lack the necessary evidence from naturalistic and experimental studies to evaluate the prediction from these simulations that the comprehension/production asymmetry in young children acquiring language is greater prior to the vocabulary spurt than after the vocabulary spurt.

4   The Acquisition of Syntax

One of the most persuasive arguments provided by Chomsky (1959), in his attack on behaviorist accounts of language, focused on the observation that grammatical agreement phenomena in sentences are honored for constituent elements that are structurally related but temporally distant from one another. He showed how sentence processing mechanisms based on computing transitional probabilities between adjacent pairs in a string (such as Markov grammars) are insufficiently powerful to capture long-distance agreement phenomena. In this section, we examine the capacity of *recurrent* networks to extract structural information from sequentially ordered elements. It will be shown that structure dependent representations need not be defined in terms of hierarchical nestings in which all elements are explicitly preserved in their rerepresentations at higher levels. This claim addresses one of the central assumptions of the symbolic position; namely, the *Principle of Compositionality*, which postulates that ordered sequences have to be structure-preserved as explicit substructures in order for their associated truth values to be recoverable in processing (Fodor and Pylyshyn, 1988). Furthermore, we shall examine the conditions under which recurrent networks are capable of extracting sequential structure from an ordered input and the manner in which such information is represented in connectionist networks.

Elman (1990) describes a *recurrent* network that succeeds in assigning words to grammatical categories (such as noun and verb) on the basis of distributional evidence extracted from strings of grammatically well-formed sentences. In later work (Elman, 1992), he demonstrates that recurrent networks are able to learn long-distance grammatical dependencies. Because language is a behavior which unfolds over time, we require a network architecture which has dynamical qualities and which itself "lives in time." Recurrent networks involve the use of recurrent connections from the hidden units back to themselves. In standard feedforward networks these recurrent connections are lacking. Hidden units develop internal representations of inputs which are functionally fixed by the current input alone. In the simple recurrent network

Figure 2.9 A simple recurrent network.

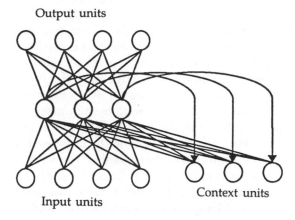

architecture that Elman employs for language processing, the hidden units take on the additional task of representing the sequential structure of a time series, and do so in surprisingly subtle ways. The state representations which encode temporal information are also able to represent, in a distributed fashion, hierarchical organization.

Figure 2.9 depicts a *recurrent* network in which *context* units provide feedback connections to a layer of hidden units. The activations to the context units are direct copies of the hidden unit activations on the previous time step. Connections from the hidden units to the context units are fixed while connections from the context units to the hidden units are adjustable, in the same manner as all the other connections in the network. Context units can be thought of as providing the network with a dynamic memory, such that identical input signals may be treated differently depending on the current status of the context units. Note that the distributional properties of the stimuli, and the structural relations governing these, are not represented in the architecture of the network; this is precisely what the network has to discover.

The task involves presenting the network with successive words in a sentence, one at a time, and training it to output a prediction of the next word. Thus, the training involves only stimuli which are directly observable in the world and do not presuppose an intelligent teacher. The training corpus consists of thousands of different sentences covering a range of structural types (see Elman (1992) for details). Consequently, the network cannot learn to predict without learning the abstract grammatical patterns which govern word order.

In fact, Elman's network was not particularly successful at predicting the next word in the input sequence, even after considerable training. This result is not particularly surprising given that there are more often than not a wide variety of possible next candidates in a sentence string. In this sense, the problem confronting the network is indeterminate and so it is bound to fail often. What is illuminating from this simulation concerns the type of predictions the network ended up making. The network invariably partially activated a range of possible candidates at its output layer all of which belonged to the appropriate grammatical category for the current position in the sentence. In other words, the network seemed to be capable of inducing the grammatical structure of the input sentences from the input strings themselves, and this without any prior knowledge as to the type of grammar that was initially used to generate the training set. It is important to note that the training sentences included verbs that varied in their argument structure, contained nouns that could occur in the singular and plural and which licensed number agreement on the verbs and, importantly, possessed embedded clauses that required the network to remember whether the subject of the sentence was singular or plural so as to predict the correct form of the verb in the main clause occurring after a potential embedded clause. In other words, the network had to keep track of long-distance agreement as well as varied sentence structures.

Training a network to produce a complex behavior, no matter how difficult, tells us little about how the network actually solves the task. Artificial neural networks offer insights into possible mechanisms underlying human language only to the extent that we understand how the networks function. A useful technique for analysing the internal organization of a trained network is to examine the hidden unit activation values in response to individual input patterns and how the hidden unit activations change over time as a sentence is processed. Because the internal hidden unit representations are of a distributed multidimensional form, a principal components analysis is used to find dimensions of variation which are more easily interpretable. It is then possible to construct state space trajectories of the network's internal representations as it processes sentences. For example, figure 2.10 (a) shows state space trajectories for the network while it is processing the two sentences:

Boys who boys chase chase boy.
Boy who boys chase chases boy.

These two sentences contain identical embedded clauses. The network is able to maintain a memory trace of the subject while processing the embedded clause and predict the correct form of the verb when it exits the embedded structure. The memory trace is manifest in the slighty different trajectories for the network through the two sentences. Figure 2.10 (b) shows state space trajectories for verbs with different argument structures. The regions of state space occupied by verbs differ considerably depending on their argument structure. The representation of constituent syntactic structure is reflected by the shape of the network's trajectory through state space. Grammatical boundaries are reflected in characteristic turns in the trajectory, and verb argument structure is reflected by the regions in state space to which trajectories are attracted. Grammatical agreement phenomena are also honored by the model,

Figure 2.10 State space trajectories recorded from hidden unit activations while processing individual words. Axes are two of the principal components taken from the variations in hidden unit activations (see Elman, 1992).

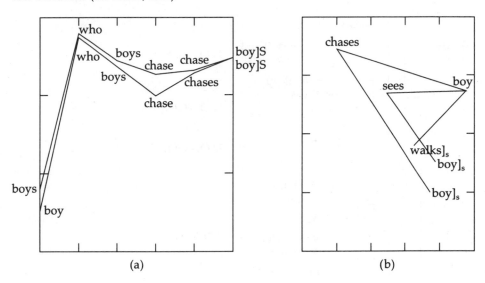

(a)   (b)

even when the structurally related items are separated by several clause boundaries. For example, in the sentence,

The boys who chase the boy who chases the dog chase the girl.

the network succeeds in selecting the third person plural form of the verb "chase" in the main clause.

Although the network's approach to representing constituent structure accomplishes many of the same things which can be easily done in a symbolic approach employing a push-down stack, there are significant differences. The network representations of any given sentential element degrade gradually during the processing of subsequent parts of the sentence. The result is that different grammatical structures are affected in different ways. For instance, centre embedded sentences, "The boy the cat the dog saw chased likes" are more difficult for the network to process than right branching sentences, "The boy likes the cat that saw the dog that chased the rat" – as is also true of humans.

Cluster analyses of the hidden unit activations permit identification of the similarity structure of the constituent words as perceived by the network. Figure 2.11 depicts the results of a cluster analysis of hidden unit activations in the network, in response to presentations of single words. These analyses of the hidden unit activations reveal that the network's internal representations are highly structured. The representations of individual lexical items in the sentences are clustered in a manner that reflects both the unique identity

Figure 2.11   A cluster analysis of hidden unit activations.

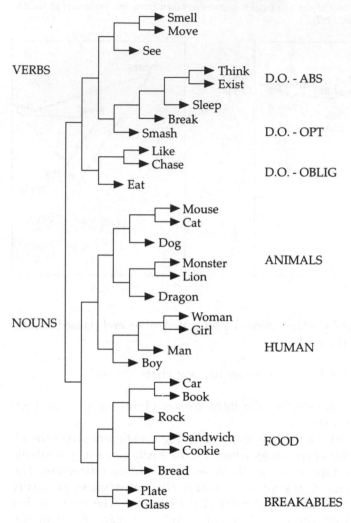

of the word, and the grammatical role of that word in the sentence. Thus, verbs are clustered together, as are nouns: hidden unit activations corresponding to different token presentations of the same word will reflect whether the word plays the role of subject or verb in the current sentence.

The success of simple recurrent networks in extracting the constituent structure of complex embedded sentences turns out to be contingent on the manner in which system is trained. Elman (1992) found that exposing the network to the complete range of structures (simple and complex) represented in the corpus from the very beginning of training, resulted in poor performance on the complex forms, e.g. it failed to master verb agreement across clause boundaries.

However, application of an incremental training technique resulted in success. If the network is exposed at the start of training only to the simple syntactic forms and then gradually exposed to an increasing proportion of complex structures, then final performance on complex forms improves dramatically. The simple forms provide the network with an opportunity to discover the basic building blocks of the sentence constituents. Once the network has derived these components from the training corpus and encoded them in the weight matrix, the more complex sentences, which otherwise present themselves as structurally opaque, become amenable to analysis.

Elman's result is highly suggestive of a language learning strategy much discussed in the child language literature in the late seventies that relied on a simplified input to the child (see Snow and Ferguson, 1977). However, it is by no means clear that all children are exposed to simplified input or that such an input is beneficial to the child (Newport, Gleitman, and Gleitman, 1977). Therefore, Elman (1992) investigated a more plausible procedure that might benefit the network in its efforts at syntactic discovery. Instead of manipulating the training set, Elman manipulated the memory span of the network for previously processed words. More specifically, he flushed the activations of the context units after every third or fourth word by resetting their activations to zero. This removed any memory for words occurring more than four items earlier in the sentence. As far as the detection of structure is concerned, this procedure is clearly deleterious for long sentences and most often those sentences that have complex constituent structures. As training proceeded, Elman gradually increased the memory span until there was unlimited feedback. In early training, this had the effect of limiting the network to discovering short-distance dependencies such as canonical sentence structure. Once the network discovered these simple dimensions of structural variation, it exploited them to discover the more complex dependencies as memory span was increased. Eventually the network was able to master the training corpus to a level comparable to that achieved by the data manipulation procedure. In this manner, Elman was able to demonstrate an actual advantage of limited memory span in simple recurrent networks for the initial extraction of syntactic structure and suggested that the importance of starting small may also impinge on children's syntax acquisition.

Elman's work represents an important first step in understanding how compositional lexical structure and hierarchical syntactic constituency might be represented in an artificial neural network. This is not to suggest that the problem of learning syntactic structure has been solved. It has not. For example, artificial neural networks have still not succeeded in resolving the subjacency problem (which refers to the linguistic fact that in many languages noun phrases can be extracted from subordinate clauses but not from relative clauses). However, this work does demonstrate that much of the initial pessimism concerning the ability of artificial neural networks to deal with hierarchical constituent structure in cognition in general and in language in particular is ill-founded.

5   Conclusions

The domain of language acquisition has played host to a heated debate in recent years concerning issues that are at the very heart of cognitive science. Researchers seek an explanatory framework most appropriate to describe the nature of cognitive and linguistic representations in the adult and the nature of the start state of human infants embarking on their linguistic and cognitive apprenticeships. Broadly speaking, we may identify two major protagonists – the symbolic approach and the subsymbolic (connectionist) approach. Traditionally (though not of necessity), these theoretical positions have faced each other across a nativist/empiricist divide with symbolic approaches taking a nativist stance. In this chapter, I have attempted to demonstrate how connectionist networks can extract rich representations of linguistic structure from input data which is normally described as impoverished by the symbolic theorist. In some cases, these models have provided elegant simulations of human behavior. In other cases, they provide useful sources for developmental explanation. However, connectionist models do not refute the symbolic accounts. More often than not, they provoke symbolic theorists to refine their own hypotheses and seek out new data. Are the protagonists ever likely to resolve their differences?

Connectionist models clearly have a neurological appeal. Parallel computations by units connected in a web of weighted lines provides a crude but effective abstraction of the central nervous system. Indeed, connectionists have themselves anointed their approach "brain-style processing" (Rumelhart, McClelland, and the PDP Research Group, 1986). Neural net simulations are indeed providing neurophysiologists with insights into the dynamics of massively parallel systems. But are connectionists' systems constrained to providing models at the neurological level of explanation? The testimony of research reported in this chapter indicates that connectionist models have a role to play at higher, functional levels of description and explanation. This is a controversial claim. Many researchers working within the classical symbol manipulation approach to cognitive science argue that functional accounts of the cognitive level must be couched in terms of discrete, categorical symbol processing systems. Furthermore, they argue that current connectionist models do not behave in the necessary symbolic fashion. According to this argument, connectionist models will not be able to provide explanations and descriptions at the cognitive level. It is conceded, however, that connectionist models, appropriately hardwired, may be able to implement the foundations of a cognitive system in much the same way that the hardware of a computer provides the necessary working environment for symbolic programs (Pinker and Prince, 1988). Indeed, it is widely acknowledged that something like a connectionist system must provide the neurological foundations for the apparent symbolic mind. In this view, a symbol processing machine sits on top of a connectionist implementation of the neurological system. It makes sense to talk about a two-level system because the symbolic machine operates according to its own autonomous set of principles.

Many developmental connectionists resist this relegation of their domain of explanation to the implementational level. One of the primary motivations for building connectionist models of cognitive processes is that symbolic approaches seem to lack certain characteristics that are needed at precisely the cognitive level of functioning (parallel processing, graceful degradation, learning). A compromise solution in which connectionist mechanisms and symbol manipulating devices work side-by-side in a harmonious cognitive system, is currently fashionable – so-called hybrid systems. However, there is a danger in this approach. An advantage of connectionist systems is that they can learn while symbolic systems are notoriously impenetrable and static. They typically embody universal principles which cannot be extracted unaided from the stimuli to which they are exposed. In accepting a tandem architecture of connectionist and symbolic systems we are in danger of accepting an adevelopmental approach to human cognition in general and language acquisition in particular. To be sure, the newborn mind comes equipped with a sophisticated set of constraints for processing its environment. Indeed, all of the connectionist models described earlier in this chapter exploit quite distinct neural architectures to achieve their results. Developmental connectionists are no more *tabula rasa* empiricists than symbolic theorists. However, we must be careful to ensure that the competences attributed to the newborn mind by a symbol processing device or a connectionist network do not exceed what we can glean from the facts of human development. Given that we are only just beginning to scratch the surface of the potential learning capacities of connectionist systems, it would seem premature to compromise in favor of a more heterogeneous account. Parsimony requires a far more thorough investigation of the limits of the connectionist approach to cognition and language acquisition.

NOTES

1 Later in this section we shall observe that the traditional symbolic model is now thought to be a probabilistic hybrid model possessing both a symbolic and a connectionist route. The connectionist route replaces the old unstructured listing of exceptions and is introduced to account for the observation of *irregularization* errors (see below).

2 An epoch consists of one complete presentation of all the verbs in the training set, usually selected at random.

3 See Pinker and Prince (1988) for a detailed discussion of the failings of the model and MacWhinney and Leinbach (1991) for a detailed response.

4 Bybee and Slobin (1982) also report a small number of irregularizations of irregular verbs. Bowerman (personal

communication) reports both the irregularization of regular and irregular verbs. For example, Christy produces /puck/ as the past tense of /pick/.

5 The number of hidden units, learning rate, and length of training also have an effect but do not alter the timing of the critical period over a fairly wide range of variation in these parameters. See Plunkett and Marchman (1993) for details.

6 The proximity metric used is defined as proportional to the average Euclidean distance between the 32 prototype patterns that are used to generate the distortions. See Plunkett et al. (1992) for more details.

3 The Impact of Language Socialization on Grammatical Development

ELINOR OCHS AND BAMBI SCHIEFFELIN

1 An Offer

The architecture of grammatical development in the talk of young children is the central concern of language acquisition research. The critical task of language acquisition scholarship over the last several decades has been to account for when, how, and why children use and understand grammatical forms over the course of the early period of their lives. Language socialization – the process in which children are socialized both through language and to use language within a community (Ochs and Schieffelin, 1984) – has been largely examined without regard to the dynamics of grammatical development, focusing, rather, on culturally relevant communicative practices and activities. In this discussion, we reverse this orientation and focus directly on the role of language socialization in the acquisition of grammatical competence.

What can a language socialization perspective offer to scholarship on grammatical development? A language socialization perspective yields a more sophisticated model of grammatical development, that is, one tuned into certain cultural realities that influence when, how, and why young children use and understand grammatical forms. Such a model of grammatical development takes an informed look at ideology and social order as forces that organize children's use and comprehension of grammatical forms. A language socialization enriched model decries reductionistic visions that view the sociocultural context as "input" to be quantified and correlated with children's grammatical patterns. Rather than reducing the context of grammatical development to frequencies of grammatical forms in the child's linguistic environment, our socialization enriched model accounts for children's grammatical development in terms of the *indexical* meanings of grammatical forms. This approach rests on the assumption that, in every community, grammatical forms are inextricably tied to, and hence index, culturally organized situations of use and that the indexical meanings of grammatical forms influence children's production and understanding of these forms.[1] In this approach, the frequency with which a grammatical form is used in the child's environment may or may not have very much to do with a child's handling of grammatical forms. As we will discuss later, a grammatical construction may be ubiquitous in the child's hearing environment and yet the child may not use the construction until quite late in his or her development. And conversely, a form may be used relatively rarely by adults and others in the child's surroundings and yet be ubiquitous in the child's speech.

In a language socialization enriched model of grammatical development, children are viewed as tuned into certain indexical meanings of grammatical forms that link those forms to, for example, social identities of interlocutors; they may not use a form they frequently hear because it is indexically inappropriate for them to do so, and they may use a form they don't often hear because it is indexically appropriate for them to do so. Children's nonuse of grammatical forms may be a reflection of their indexical sensitivities (Ochs, 1988; Peirce, 1931–58; Silverstein, 1993) and not a reflection of their lack of grammatical competence or awareness. Counting and correlations can't differentiate between nonuse that is socially and culturally competent and nonuse that is incompetent. Only an informed understanding of the indexical scope of grammatical forms can provide this information.

What makes a language socialization approach different from existing functionalist approaches to grammatical development? Functionalist approaches to grammatical development tend to end their inquiry at the level of the immediate informational or actional context of grammatical forms, relating children's use and understanding of grammatical forms to, for example, foregrounding and backgrounding of information on the one hand, and/or to speech acts on the other. A language socialization approach relates children's use and understanding of grammatical forms to complex yet orderly and recurrent dispositions, preferences, beliefs, and bodies of knowledge that organize how information is linguistically packaged and how speech acts are performed within and across socially recognized situations.

A language socialization approach promotes an updated version of linguistic relativity and asserts that children's use and understanding of grammatical forms is culturally reflexive – tied in manifold ways to local views of how to think, feel, know, (inter)act, or otherwise project a social persona or construct a relationship. At the same time, a language socialization approach promotes the notion that certain relations between grammatical forms and sociocultural order have universal scope (Ochs, 1990; 1993). Language socialization involves children in language and cultural competencies that span the boundaries of local communities. That is, children are being socialized the world over to draw on similar grammatical resources to index thoughts, feelings, knowledge, identities, acts, and activities not only because of biological and cognitive patterning but also because of universal characteristics of culture as a common artefact of humankind.

In the remainder of this discussion, we articulate ways in which a language socialization approach can enrich existing accounts of the phenomena of child language acquisition. Although this approach is orthogonal to the controversies surrounding learnability and innateness mechanisms underlying grammatical competence (in the sense that it does not take sides), it is highly relevant to all theories relating grammatical development to mind, brain, and experience. Our discussion opens the discourse of grammatical development to a domain of orderliness that exists beyond the person, indeed, that exists *between* persons who interact on a regular basis and who belong to a community with a history and a future.

The language socialization approach advocated in this chapter integrates universal and local properties of language-in-culture. In particular, it provides a *culturally organized means–ends model* of grammatical development. Informally, this model provides for the possibility that across many cultures, members rely on certain similar linguistic means to accomplish certain similar social ends, such as the use of quantifiers to index affective intensity (e.g. "He spilled it all over the place," Labov, 1984; Ochs and Schieffelin, 1989). However, at the same time these ends are culturally organized in terms of their situational scope – who appropriately attempts to accomplish this end, when, where, how often, etc. – and their significance *vis-à-vis* local ideologies about emotion, person, language, and the like. Communities thus are both alike and different in the ways in which they rely on grammatical resources, and as such, children's understandings of grammatical forms are accordingly both alike and different as one traverses the boundaries of language communities. Similar linguistic realizations of social goals across communities enable communication within our species; different cultural organizations of social goals, however, throw a monkey wrench into crosscultural exchanges and make the task of acquiring second languages in different communities all the more difficult.[2]

This culturally organized means–ends perspective will be applied to three questions relevant to accounting for grammatical development in early childhood:

1 Does grammatical development depend upon children's participation in a simplified speech environment?
2 Can cultural systems of belief, knowledge, and social order partially account for young children's acquisition of particular grammatical constructions?

3   Can cultural systems of belief, knowledge, and social order partially account for young children's acquisition (and nonacquisition) of particular languages in linguistically heterogeneous communities?

We turn now to address each of these questions.

2   The Cultural Milieu of Language Acquirers

A critical question addressed in acquisition research is whether or not children's grammatical competence is an outcome of children's participation in simplified communicative exchanges designed to facilitate language use and comprehension. Our response to this question is a qualified "no." This conclusion is based on the observation that all normal children acquire a measured degree of competence in producing and understanding grammatical constructions in the early years of their lives, yet the ways in which cultures organize communicative exchanges with children varies widely from community to community (see especially Clancy, 1985, 1986; Crago, 1988; Heath, 1982; Miller, P., 1982; Ochs, 1985, 1988; Ochs and Schieffelin, 1984; Philips, 1983; Schieffelin and Ochs, 1986a, 1986b; Schieffelin, 1986, 1990; Scollon, 1982). To explore this phenomenon in a culturally illuminative fashion, we focus on how cultures organize communication directed *to* children (children as addressees) and *by* children (children as speakers).

2.1   *Cultural organizations of talk to children (addressees)*

In all societies, members want to get their intentions across to children. This is a universal propensity of human culture, a prerequisite for the transmission of cultural orientations from one generation to the next. Furthermore, when members set the goal of getting their intentions across to children, they tend to modify their language in similar ways across the world's communities. Adults, older siblings, and others wanting to communicate to infants and small children in many cultures tend to simplify the form and content of their talk to achieve that end. Common simplifications characteristic of speech addressed to children include consonant cluster reduction, reduplication, exaggerated prosodic contours, slowed pace, shorter sentences, syntactically less complex sentences, temporal and spatial orientation to the here-and-now, and repetition and paraphrasing of sentences (Ferguson, 1964, 1977, 1982).

If we are promoting the notion that communicating intentions to children as addressees is a universal end and that simplification is a widespread if not universal means to achieve that end, how do we justify the conclusion that grammatical development does not depend on children's exposure to simpli-fied speech? A culturally organized means–ends approach to the question of simplified speech urges us to examine further the goal of communicating intentions to children and the kinds of simplifications made once this goal is set in motion within particular communities. Ethnographic observations sug-gest that cultures differ widely in the *contextual pervasiveness of setting this goal and in the extensiveness of simplification processes* when speakers do set this goal, and that these differences are integrally linked to cultural views of children, social order, and the path to grammatical competence.

How, then, is the goal of communicating intentions to children realized across different communities? While in all communities, children participate as addressees in interactions with others, the developmental point at which they take on this role varies from community to community. In some commu-nities, such as white middle class communities in the United States and Canada, children are given this role starting at birth, when mothers begin to greet and otherwise attempt to converse with their infants (Bates, Camaioni, and Volterra, 1979; Bloom, K., 1990; Ochs and Schieffelin, 1984; Stern, 1977). Once the goal of communicating intentions to small infants is put into effect, speakers have quite a job on their hands if they hope to be understood and responded to (see Brown, 1977). Indeed, in the case of communicating intentions to newly born infants, caregivers may not only go to great lengths to gain and sustain their attention (e.g. via high pitch, exaggerated intonation), they also may have to voice or do the child's response themselves (Lock, 1981; Stern, 1977; Trevarthen, 1979). In other communities, members do not generally set the goal of com-municating intentions to children (i.e. wanting children to understand and respond) at quite such an early point in their lives. In a number of societies, infants are not engaged as addressees until they evidence that they can pro-duce recognizable words in the language. For example, among the K'iche' Mayan, "vocal interaction between infants and parents is minimal, although there is some variation between parents in this regard, particularly among different economic classes . . . K'iche' parents treat their toddlers as conversa-tional partners after they learn to speak" (Pye, 1992: 242–3). Similarly, African–American working class families in the town of "Trackton" in the Piedmont South Carolina region of the United States "do not see babies or young chil-dren as suitable partners for regular conversations. For an adult to choose a preverbal infant over an adult as a conversational partner would be consid-ered an affront and a strange behavior as well" (Heath, 1983: 86). In rural and urban Javanese communities, adults also address babies infrequently. Smith-Hefner (1988: 172–3) notes:

> Javanese children are clearly the objects of great pride and affection, and yet what is striking to the western observer is that Javanese do not talk to babies very much. In response to my initial questions concerning talking to babies, Javanese caregivers frequently commented that little babies (and even young children for that matter) *durung ngerti* or "do not yet understand" . . . the most common way

of holding young babies is on the hip with the child naturally facing outwards or half hidden under the mother's arm. We never recorded in all of our observations a mother holding her young baby in the face to face position facilitating dialogue.

These descriptions are also paralleled in accounts of talking to infants in traditional Western Samoan communities (Ochs and Schieffelin 1984; Ochs, 1982, 1988) and among the Kaluli of Papua New Guinea (Ochs and Schieffelin, 1984; Schieffelin, 1990).

In societies such as these, infants are not singled out as preferred addressees. Rather, they tend to participate in communicative interactions in the role of *overhearers* of nonsimplified conversations between others. This assumes that small children are being socialized in the context of multiparty interactions, the unmarked condition in traditional and many other societies. In many upper middle class households of the United States and Europe, however, small children may pass the day primarily in the presence of a single adult (e.g. mother) and thus may not have the situational opportunity to take on the role of overhearers of nonsimplified conversations. Indeed, the communicative ecology of upper middle class households may be an important factor in organizing young children in the role of addressees. The sole adult in the household is not likely to talk to herself/himself all day long and thus may be situationally predisposed to attempt to recruit a child of whatever age as a communicative partner in meaningful, albeit highly simplified, exchanges.

In those communities where infants and small children are generally not recruited as conversational partners, they still become grammatically competent speakers–hearers, developing linguistic knowledge in a communicative environment full of grammatical complexity and oriented towards competent interlocutors. Some communities have an explicit ideology of language acquisition centered on precisely the idea that children need to hear linguistically *complex* and not simplified speech to become grammatically competent. Kaluli adults were surprised that American parents produced baby talk in the presence of young children and wondered how the children learned to speak proper language (Schieffelin, 1990).

In addition to differences in goal setting, cultures also differ in the extent to which they simplify when they do address children. In some communities, such as among the Tamil (Williamson, 1979), Inuit (Crago, 1988), and working and middle class Americans and Europeans (Cross, 1977; Newport, Gleitman, and Gleitman, 1977), simplification involves phonological, morphosyntactic, and discourse modifications. In other communities, such as among Samoans (Ochs, 1988), working class African–Americans of Trackton (Heath, 1983) and Louisiana (Ward, 1971), Javanese (Smith-Hefner, 1988) and Kaluli (Schieffelin, 1990), simplification may be primarily *restricted* to the domain of discourse, and in particular, to self-repetition of an earlier utterance. An important difference between simplification through repetition and simplification through phonological and grammatical adjustments is that the former tends to preserve the integrity of the adult form of the utterance whereas the latter does not. To understand this difference, think of setting the goal of getting a young child to participate in a traditional dance. One way of getting the child to understand what she or he is supposed to do is to let the child see repeated uninterrupted performances of the dance. In this way, the integrity of the dance is preserved, and the simplification primarily consists of showing it over and over again. Another way of achieving competence is to break down the dance into components and to repeatedly present one component at a time until the child evidences that she or he understands the steps. This simplification strategy deforms the conventional shape and execution of the dance in an effort to guide children's participation in the dance (Rogoff, 1990).[3]

An interesting possibility is that cultures that simplify at all levels of linguistic structure in talking to children may put children in the role of conversational partners, i.e. as addressees expected to actively and centrally participate in communicative exchanges, more often than in cultures that simplify primarily through repetition. A similar point was made by Brown (1977: 12) when he argued that baby talk is not used by caregivers to teach their children how to speak but rather to communicate with them: "What I think adults are chiefly trying to do, when they use BT with children, is to communicate, to understand and to be understood, to keep two minds focussed on the same topic." Brown's conclusion was influenced by the research of Cross (1977: 166–7), who captures the effects of 62 parameters of mothers' speech on children's language in the comment

> Few researchers in the area of mothers' speech would argue that the provision of language lessons to the language-learning child is the primary motivation for mothers' speech adjustments. Rather, they appear to be the incidental outcome of trying to converse with a listener capable of expressing and receiving meaning in verbal form, but with very undeveloped linguistic skills.

A corollary of the possibility that cultures with a highly simplified baby talk register may treat children as conversational partners relatively often is that cultures that rely on such widespread simplification may expect children to be active and central participants in conversational exchanges at an earlier age than children growing up in cultures where simplification is primarily through repetition. More empirical evidence is needed to substantiate these possibilities; however, in cultures where speakers addressing children simplify infrequently and primarily through repetition, there appears to be little interest in engaging young infants in extended conversational exchanges. For example, Heath (1983) and Ward (1971) describe working class African–American adult family members in rural South Carolina and Louisiana not only as dispreferring infants as conversational partners but also as hardly simplifying their speech to young children. And the same is true for traditional Samoan (Ochs, 1988), Kaluli (Schieffelin, 1990), and Javanese (Smith-Hefner, 1988) family members. From the perspective of the working class African–American, Samoans, Kaluli, and Javanese communities studied, members of cultures that rely on wide-spread simplification are more eager (or perhaps even anxious) for children early in their lives to take on central communicative roles. In these African–American communities and among the Samoans, Javanese, and Kaluli, how-ever, there seems to be less pressure for very young children to assume an active, central role in the social exchanges at hand, but rather a preference for children at this early stage to stay on the sidelines – on the backs of caregivers, or nestled on their laps or hips or alongside – as observers and overhearers.[4]

In summary, if we look across cultures, children who are expected to be active communicators early in life are often likely to be addressed with highly simplified speech and put in the position of conversational partner. On the other hand, children who are expected to actively participate in communi-cative exchanges somewhat later in their childhood hear predominantly unsimplified speech and are treated as conversational partners less frequently. The upshot of this discussion, however, is that while these children are social-ized into different expectations concerning their social role *vis-à-vis* other par-ticipants in a social situation and perhaps as well into different cognitive skills (e.g. the role of overhearer may enhance observational skills), *the outcome in terms of the ultimate acquisition of grammatical competence is not substantially dif-ferent across these two cultural strategies*. In both cases, most children growing up in these cultures are producing and understanding grammatical construc-tions before their second birthday. In Western Samoa, for example, a child of 19 months was not only producing multimorphemic utterances but using with some skill two phonological registers (Ochs, 1985). Kaluli children between 20 and 24 months use imperative and declarative verb forms, first and second person pronouns, locatives, possessives, several forms of negation, and dis-course particles (Schieffelin, 1986).

2.2   Cultural organizations of talk by children (speakers)

An important focus in the controversy over effects of the communicative en-vironment on language acquisition is the extent to which grammatical compe-tence is facilitated by the practice of caregivers verbally reformulating a child's intended message in grammatically correct adult form. This practice is known as *expansion* (Brown et al., 1968). Typically expansions are caregivers' responses to a young child's relatively ambiguous message and function as requests for confirmation or repair initiations (Schegloff, Jefferson, and Sacks, 1977). The facilitating effect of expansions is posited on the assumption that children will match an intention that is currently in their consciousness with the adult for-mulation of the intended message (Brown et al., 1968; McNeill, 1970).

The effects of expansions on the acquisition of particular grammatical con-structions have been widely discussed in the psycholinguistics literature, and the results are at best mixed (see, for example, Cazden, 1965; Cross, 1977; Newport et al., 1977; Shatz, 1983). Our focus here is on the cultural organization and import of expansions, a discussion which situates expansions in cultural ideologies and systems of social order which organize how members of societies respond to ambiguous or partially unintelligible utterances of interlocutors, whether adult or child. Within a culturally organized means–ends approach, we explore the extent to which the goal of trying to formulate the ambiguous intentions of others is culturally viable. We also explore how cultures organize children of different ages as *speakers*, particularly as authors of utterances.

Infants and small children universally produce utterances whose sense is not transparent to those present, and universally those copresent respond using one or more of the following strategies: (1) ignore the utterance; (2) indicate to the child that the utterance is unclear (e.g. by claiming nonunderstanding, by directing the child to resay the utterance, by teasing the child for being unclear); (3) present to the child a candidate understanding or reformulation of the utterance (i.e. make a guess). However, while children's unintelligibility and responses to it are universal, the preference for strategy (1), (2), or (3) varies across communities for reasons of ideology and social order. Specifically, communities organize the goal of decoding the intentions of children in different ways. In some communities, members are keen to disambiguate aloud what infants and young children might be intending across a wide range of situations, and in other communities the situations in which members take on this goal are highly restricted.

To pursue the cultural organization of decoding the intentions of children it is necessary to unpack some of the assumptions of this end. One assumption that underlies this end is that children are indeed acting intentionally, the children are the authors of their utterances. One variable of crosscultural import is the developmental point at which children are treated as intentional beings who not only vocalize and gesture but do so to make a communicative point. Another way of considering this aspect of crosscultural variation is to see cultures as varying in their view of children as *authors* of messages. In some communities, children are treated as if their gestures and vocalizations are meaningful and communicative from a very early point in their infancy (see especially Trevarthen's (1979) analysis of middle class British caregivers interpreting small infants in this manner). Caregivers in these communities will respond to the actions of tiny infants as if they were intentionally directed towards them, and in this way establish the child as an interlocutor (Lock, 1981). In middle class American and European communities, this practice of treating the infant as an author is the counterpart to treating the infant as addressee in that both roles combined constitute the infant as conversational partner.

Many of us may take for granted that caregivers and infants interact in this manner and may find it surprising that in many communities infants are not considered as authors. Their gestures and vocalizations are not considered by others as intentional communicative acts. For example, among the Walpiri, before the age of two, " 'talk' by the child is not interpreted as language, and there are no expansions and recasts of the child's early words" (Bavin, 1992: 327). Similarly, among the Inuit, caregivers rarely responded to the vocal and nonvocal actions of very young children. Crago (1988: 210–11) describes Inuit interactions with two children under the age of two years:

> Suusi and Jini were the youngest of the four children at the outset the videotaping. In several of the tapes that were made of them, they frequently made unintelligible vocalizations. The majority of these vocalizations went unheeded. Many times their parents did not respond, not even by looking up at the children . . . Clarification of unintelligible vocalizations did not take place on any of the videotapes. Intentions, then, were not imputed to these early unintelligible utterances nor did they elicit a communicative response from the caregivers in most instances.

Even if, within a community, an infant's or young child's vocalizations are constructed as intentional by a copresent adult or older sibling, there may still be a strong dispreference for attempting to clarify intentions through candidate expansions of the child's intended message. In both Kaluli (Schieffelin, 1990) and Western Samoan (Ochs, 1988) communities, for example, caregivers rarely clarify children's utterances because there is a strong dispreference generally towards guessing at the unarticulated psychological states of others. Kaluli say that one cannot know what is in another's head. Samoans not only rarely expand an unclear utterance of a child, they also rarely conjecture about possible motivations for an action undertaken, or disambiguate riddles, or try to figure out test questions, where there is some notion in the mind of another that has to be discovered (Ochs, 1982).

In traditional Western Samoan communities, issues of social order also impact the dispreference for expanding children's ambiguous vocalizations and gestures. In particular, if we compare the three alternative responses to a child's unclear action – ignore, indicate unclarity, and provide candidate understanding of child's intended meaning (expansion / guess) – the responses differ in the extent to which they require an interlocutor to take the perspective of the child. Ignoring requires almost no perspective-taking whatsoever, and the various means of indicating unclarity (e.g. by requesting a repetition, teasing) also demand little decentering by others. Proferring a candidate understanding of the child's message through an expansion, on the other hand, involves other interlocutors in searching for clues as to what the child could be intending – looking at what the child is doing, where the child is gazing, what the child was just doing or saying, and other situational leads to arriving at intentionality. The extensiveness of this cognitive accommodation runs counter to Samoan notions of the caregiver–child relationship, which is grounded in social asymmetry. As in other societies, sibling and adult caregivers in traditional Samoan communities expect and socialize the children in their charge to accommodate to them. Both siblings and adult family members are keen to socialize children at a very early age to decenter and take the perspective of more mature interlocutors in their presence. For these reasons and others, Samoan caregivers tend to respond to children's unclear messages in ways that force children to make a greater effort to meet the communicative needs of those around them. They are far more likely to ignore or say "What?" or tease than to attempt to formulate what the child could be intending and offer it up to the child to confirm or disconfirm.

Finally, in some communities, members allow for the possibility that children are speaking intentionally but rather than trying to establish what these intentions might be, members assign a socially normative meaning to the child's utterance. As noted earlier, a psycholinguistic argument is that expansions facilitate language acquisition because they build on a child's personal intentions, matching the child's meaning to adult message form. In contrast, there is evidence that, in certain communities, children's personal intentions sometimes take second place to the members' notions of what is socially appropriate to a situation at hand. For example, Scollon (1982) reports that Athapaskan adults provide a cultural "gloss" for the child's unclear utterance, that is, a socially appropriate rendering that is situationally sensitive, disregarding what the child might be intending to express.

The use of cultural glosses is far more widespread than might be assumed, in that adults may impose a cultural gloss on children's gestures and utterances without recognizing that they are doing so. First words, for example, may reflect and construct cultural expectations concerning what children want to communicate. In many communities, first words are highly conventionalized. For example, among the Kaluli, the words for "mother" and "breast" are recognized as everyone's first words. In traditional Samoan communities, the child's first word is part of the curse "Eat shit!" Among the Gapun people of Papua New Guinea,

> a child's very first word is generally held to be *ki* (go+IRREAL STATUS). This is a Taiap vernacular word meaning, approximately, "I'm getting out of here." Attributed to infants as young as two months, this word encapsulates the adult belief that babies will "do what they want" . . . and go where they will regardless of the wishes of others. (Kulick, 1992: 101–2)

It can also be argued that although caregivers in white middle class American, European, and Japanese households are acting on the belief that their expansions capture the intended meaning of the child's utterance, their expansions may similarly reflect their cultural understandings of what children want. Clancy (1986) and Cook, H. M. (1988), for example, argue that middle class Japanese mothers often reformulate children's utterances to be culturally acceptable.

These practices from diverse communities suggest that a primary goal of members is to socialize infants into culturally appropriate persons and this goal may override any goal relating to drawing out and validating the child as an author of a unique personal message. In these situations, other members actively participate in the authorship of messages. Other-authorship of children's utterances is also manifest in prompting practices, wherein members author a culturally appropriate message for the child to repeat back to the author (dyadic interaction) or to a third party (triadic interactions). Extended prompting of this sort is practiced in a wide range of societies, including Kaluli (Schieffelin, 1990), Samoan (Ochs, 1988), Mexican–American (Eisenberg, 1986), white working class American (Miller, 1982), Basotho (Demuth, 1986), Javanese (Smith-Hefner, 1988), and Kwara'ae (Watson-Gegeo and Gegeo, 1986). A more extreme version of cultural prevoicing is found in the practice of ventriloquating for preverbal infants, wherein a member speaks as if the infant were speaking and others respond as if this were the case. Kaluli caregivers, for example, hold small infants facing a third party addressee and speak to that addressee in a high pitch nasalized register (without grammatically simplifying utterances). Here the infant is presented as a speaker without being presented as an author.

The many practices that are alternatives to expansions of personalized messages – either ignoring the utterance, indicating unclarity, providing a cultural gloss, prompting, or ventriloquating – socialize the child to accommodate to the social situation at hand. In contrast, attempts to expand the child's intended meaning evidence an accommodation by others to the child. That is, expansions of the sort discussed by psycholinguists reflect a child centered style of socialization (characteristic of the communities of the psycholinguists), whereas the alternative practices reflect a situation centered style of socialization (Ochs and Schieffelin, 1984; Schieffelin and Ochs, 1986a). Similarly, pervasive use of grammatically simplified speech directed to children as addressees reflects a child centered orientation, whereas more restricted use of simplification reflects a situation centered orientation. Because children living in communities falling along the continuum of child and situation centered communicative practices acquire grammar, grammatical development *per se* can not be accounted for in terms of any single set of speech practices involving children.

3   The Cultural Milieu of Children's Grammatical Forms

While the achievement of grammatical competence in itself cannnot be said to depend on any particular cultural circumstances, the acquisition of specific grammatical constructions can be profoundly impacted by the cultural organization of language. Children produce certain constructions and not others and come to an understanding of constructions in part because of their cultural significance. As noted earlier, grammatical constructions are intricately linked to norms, preferences, and expectations that organize how members are to act, think, and feel in social situations. Children's acquisition of grammatical constructions in this sense is partly the acquisition of language competence and partly the acquisition of cultural competence. Further, because grammatical constructions are systematically and profoundly associated with social order and cultural beliefs, values, and knowledge, they carry sociocultural meanings, which are acquired along with their formal features. In the following discussion, we consider three circumstances in which sociocultural organization impacts the production and comprehension of particular grammatical forms:

1   Where a grammatical form is widely used in the child's verbal environment, but is not produced by the child in the early stages of language acquisition because it is socially inappropriate.
2   Where a grammatical form is infrequently used in the child's verbal environment, but none the less becomes part of the child's earliest linguistic repertoire because it is socially appropriate.
3   Where a grammatical form used to express specific stances and speech acts in the child's verbal environment is acquired early as part of the acquisition of those stances and speech acts.

3.1   Grammatical form as frequent but inappropriate for child use

While perceptual salience, frequency, and conceptual complexity of forms in the verbal environment of the child can affect when children acquire particular grammatical constructions, these variables need to be evaluated *vis-à-vis* the social and cultural matrix of each construction. It may well be the case, for example, that a form that is perceptually salient, highly frequent, and conceptually relatively simple may not appear in the child's linguistic repertoire until rather late. In these cases, children's nonproduction of a particular form may reflect their understanding of that form as a sociocultural resource for displaying social statuses, social relationships, stances, actions, and other situational dimensions, and in particular, reflect their understandings of that form as inappropriate for child use.

An example of a widely used, relatively simple grammatical form that is not produced by children early in their language development is the Samoan deictic verb *sau*, "come." Among the set of deictic verbs in a language, "come" is considered to be conceptually less complex than verbs such as "give" and "bring" (Clark and Garnica, 1974) and tends to be produced and understood by young children before these more complex forms. While Samoan children evidence understanding of the verb *sau*, "come," early in their development (by 19 months), they tend to produce the deictic verb *'aumai* before they produce *sau*, and they produce *'aumai* far more frequently than *sau* (Platt, 1986). What can account for this acquisition order? Why don't Samoan children produce a form that they routinely hear and appropriately respond to?

In traditional Samoan communities, physical movement is associated with relatively lower status persons; higher status persons tend to position themselves and direct lower status persons to carry out actions that require movement. Young children, for example, are bombarded with imperative forms of *sau*. When these children begin to use language, they appear to be aware of the social indexicality of this verb. As they are usually the lowest status persons in the household, there are few opportunities to use the verb appropriately. When the children do use *sau*, they use it in imperative form to direct the movements of lower ranking entities, such as animals and younger infant siblings. In some cases, the children will use the form at the prompting of an older person to call out to an older child to come to that still older person (e.g. Mother: *Vala'au Iuliaga e sau*, "Call Iuliana to come" ... Child: *Ana sau*, "Iuliana come!"). In contrast, children are widely encouraged to beg for food and other items. The verb *'aumai*, "give/bring," is the conventional grammatical structure (imperative form) for carrying out the act of begging. This imperative form of the verb appeared prevalently in children's speech from 19 months of age on (Platt, 1986; Ochs, 1988).

Another example of a construction that is widely used by adults in the child's verbal environment and is relatively simple is the Kaluli imperative verb of saying, *elema*, "say like that." While pervasive in the verbal environment of all children, this construction is produced only by a subset of young, language acquiring Kaluli children (Schieffelin, 1990). *Elema* is used in prompting sequences in which an older child caregiver or adult tells the young language learning child what to say to a third party, followed by the imperative *elema*. As noted earlier, all Kaluli children actively participate in extensive prompting sequences.

When we look at children's own use of *elema*, there is a marked gender difference: only young girls (two to four years) produce this form to direct even younger children to "say like that." When they do so, it is with the appropriate demeanor of an assertive voice, and an appropriate message form, followed by the imperative verb of saying. Furthermore, young girls will also engage their mothers in playful routines, getting them to respond (dyadically) to their requests to "say like that." Boys, who were also addressees and respondents repeatedly in such socializing interactions, never produced *elema*. They associated this form with the talk of women and older sisters, who were responsible for all of the caregiving. Indeed, fathers very rarely used *elema* with children. The absence of *elema* in boy's verbal repertoire in this sense is a reflection of their understanding of gender appropriate behavior, a form of social knowledge never made explicit. It should be noted that adult men do use *elema* in social activities in which young children are not participants. Hence, boys eventually come to use *elema* in these activity settings.

It should also be noted that young children's understandings of the relation between gender and *elema* is finely tuned, in the sense that it is only the imperative form of the verb "to say like that" that is gender associated. Other forms of this verb are used widely by both men and women in the verbal environment of the child, and both boys and girls use the verb in a variety of inflections and moods – for example, to report others' speech as well as their own. Children's understandings of gender and other social roles are clearly indexed in a language like Kaluli where each verb stem is morphologically differentiated for tense and mood and where specific morphological forms such as the imperative (*elema*) may carry social meanings, e.g. gender-marked language instruction.

The point that we are trying to make is that children are sensitized to the social and cultural indexicality of particular morphosyntactic encodings of verbal forms. The social and cultural contexts of imperative forms seem especially salient as they are exploited in a variety of speech acts, such as requesting, begging, and prompting. This may be because these acts involve issues of desire, control, and most importantly, require some type of action uptake on the part of another member of the community. These action uptakes provide immediate and salient social and cultural validation or sanctioning of the child's and other's use of that form.

This degree of finetuned sensitivity to how different forms of the same verb encode social information is also evident in Kaluli children's acquisition of the compound verb *omina*, "having chewed, give." Children hear this verb often and in a variety of inflected forms, such as first person present interrogative, "Having chewed it, do I give it to you?" (*ge omiyolo?*). The children themselves, however, use the compound verb only in its present imperative form (*ge)omina*, "You, having chewed, give," as a request to a parent or older sibling to chew food (for the child) and then give it to the child (Schieffelin, 1986). In so doing, young Kaluli children are acting in a role-appropriate manner. They are expected to ask for food to be chewed and given to them but are not expected to chew and give food to others.

3.2 Grammatical form as infrequent but appropriate for child use

A language socialization approach to grammatical development can also help to account for why young children produce forms that are relatively rare in their verbal environment. For example, as noted above, young Kaluli children produce the imperative form of the Kaluli compound verb "having chewed, give." What was not noted, however, is that this form of the verb is almost never used by others in the child's environment, as adults and older children have no need to request that someone else chew food for them. This phenomenon should sensitize us to the fact that children's linguistic repertoire is not a simple reflection of what they do or do not hear in their surroundings,[5] but rather that children are taking an active role in constructing language that is most useful to their needs and appropriate to their social status.

Another interesting example of children's productive use of a grammatical form that appears relatively infrequently in their verbal environment is Samoan children's use of the first person affect-marked pronoun *ta ita*, "poor I/poor me." This form is morphologically productive and can appear in a variety of cases and be inflected for number and specific/nonspecific as well as for alienable/inalienable possession when used as a genitive constituent. That is to say, this form is not a frozen or idiomatic lexical form. It appears far less often in household interactions involving children (as overhearers, and perhaps in other roles) than the more neutral first person pronoun *a'u*, "I," yet young children produce the affective pronoun earlier (19 months) and more often than the neutral form (Ochs, 1988). In particular, young children use the affective pronoun as a benefactive (*ia te ita* "for poor me"). This form is the linguistic core of the speech act of begging, which, as noted in section 2, is expected of and appropriate for young children. Samoan children, thus, appear to pull from their linguistic environment and deploy strategically those linguistic structures that help them to satisfy their desire for food and other objects.

We have seen in sections 3.1 and 3.2 relatively marked circumstances in which children's grammatical repertoire cannot be easily predicted from either the rate of use or relative complexity of grammatical forms in the child's verbal environment. Rather, children's use of particular grammatical forms at particular moments of their language development is profoundly linked to social and cultural norms, expectations, and preferences which may not be explicit and are not easily detected or counted. Children acquire grammatical forms as part of becoming a person in society; they use grammatical forms as communicative resources to participate in social situations, express their ideas and feelings, and otherwise accomplish social and individual goals. Language socialization theory provides a framework for how children use such forms for sociocultural ends. One notion within language socialization research is that members of communities (including language acquiring children) use grammatical forms to build speech acts and express stances which, in turn, are part of more complex social identities and social activities (Ochs, 1993). Thus, in Kaluli a grammatical form such as *elema* is used to build the speech act of prompting and this act in turn is used to help establish the gender identity of girls; and *omina* is used to build the speech act of requesting and this act in turn is used to help establish the generational identity of young children. Similarly, in Samoan *sau* is used to build the directive to come and this act in turn helps to establish the identity of the speaker as relatively higher status than the addressee. Other examples of the interface of culture and the acquisition of particular grammatical forms remain to be described by other researchers.

4   The Cultural Milieu of Children's Code Choice

Thus far we have focused on the impact of culture on the acquisition of one particular language and have not attended to acquisition of more than one language in linguistically heterogeneous communities. A language socialization perspective can account for code acquisition in such communities by examining the social distribution and social meanings of code choice within communities and households and constructing a model of language ideology that informs patterns of code selection and acquisition. Just as children's acquisition of a particular grammatical form cannot be accounted for simply in terms of rate of that form in the child's verbal environment, so children's acquisition of a particular code cannot be accounted for simply in terms of the presence of that code in the child's intimate environment. A language socialization perspective can account for why and how children may not be acquiring the languages in their multilingual environment in spite of the fact that their parents say that they want their children to speak these languages. What is missing from the majority of psycholinguistic studies of simultaneous bilingual acquisition is in-depth ethnographic analysis of the complex language ideologies, i.e. the values attached to the different codes, that are characteristic of multilingual communities and their relation to language practices in those communities (Kulick, 1992; Schieffelin, 1994).

Psycholinguistic studies of the simultaneous acquisition of two languages (i.e. bilingualism under the age of five years) have focused on the question of whether young children develop a unitary, undifferentiated language system (integrating features of both languages) or whether they develop two differentiated systems used in contextually sensitive ways (see reviews in Genesee, 1989; Romaine, 1989; De Houwer, 1990). In pursuing this question, many psycholinguists have assumed a notion of bilingualism similar to that articulated by Weinrich (1953: 73): "The ideal bilingual switches from one language to the other, according to appropriate changes in the speech situation, but not in unchanged speech situations and certainly not in a single sentence." It is widely assumed that the "ideal" bilingual situation (wherein the speaker associates particular codes with particular situations) facilitates bilingual acquisition, whereas code mixing in a single situation, especially by a single speaker, inhibits bilingual acquisition (McLaughlin, 1984a).

Two types of studies address the issue of code differentiation in the course of bilingual acquisition. The first set of studies examine bilingual acquisition among children from bilingual Spanish–English-speaking communities in the United States (e.g. the Southwest). Most used an experimental design where child speakers were told that an investigator only understood one language, thus inhibiting the use of the other language. The second set of studies examine bilingual acquisition among children who have at least one bilingual parent but who reside otherwise in a monolingual community (e.g. children with a German–Italian bilingual parent residing in Italy (Volterra and Taeschner, 1978). Investigators taperecorded adult–child speech in the home.

To ascertain the norms of bilingual code use in particular households, most researchers rely exclusively on parental reports of their speech practices with young children.[6] In parental reports from both sets of studies, parents insisted that they followed the one person–one language rule ("rule of Grammont" (Ronjat, 1913)), that is, they did not mix languages when speaking to the child. From a language socialization perspective, this response reflects a widespread belief across many societies that mixing two languages lexically and/or grammatically is indicative of confusion and lack of education, and is generally stigmatized as impure language. When researchers employed more ethnographic methods of investigating bilingualism by looking at naturalistic speech to and in the hearing environment of the child, they found that, despite parental reports of "one person–one language," their language practices showed a significant amount of code switching (Goodz, 1989; De Houwer, 1990). Because these naturalistic studies do not anlayze the effects of code mixing on bilingual acquisition and because other psycholinguistic studies do not examine bilingual practices in the home, the question of what type of bilingual language practices (one person–one language versus language mixing) facilitates the acquisition of separate codes cannot be adequately answered at this time.

One consequence of pursuing the question of unitary or differentiated bilingual acquisition is that researchers have neglected a very important acquisition phenomenon, namely the acquisition of code switching itself in early childhood. While there are numerous sociolinguistic studies of school-age children code switching behavior (Auer, 1988; Genishi, 1981; McClure, 1977; Zentella, 1990), there are no studies of the acquisition processes that lead to this competence in later life. Questions that might illuminate grammatical development include: how does code switching change over developmental time? Do young children's code switching practicing follow the same lexical and grammatical constraints as that of the adults in their speech communities? How do young children use code switching to achieve pragmatic ends?

Another neglected but crucial question in understanding the processes and outcomes of bilingual acquisition is how local language ideologies underlying the languages in particular communities affects young children's acquisition of these languages. Not all languages are valued equally; some may be viewed as prestige forms whereas others may be disvalued or even stigmatized by the community and/or by members of a child's family. The prestige forms are often associated with educational achievement and social and economic mobility, while the nonprestigious forms are often associated with traditional values. These ideologies surrounding particular languages are socialized along with the codes themselves, sometimes in extremely subtle ways. Where there is high value placed on a particular code over another, the highly valued code has a better chance of survival as part of a young child's individual linguistic repertoire as well as part of the community's repertoire over historical time.

A dramatic example of the role of ideology in causing a shift from multilingual to monolingual acquisition is found in Kulick's language socialization study of the Gapun community of Papua New Guinea, where Taiap and the lingual franca Tok Pisin as well as the vernaculars of other villages are actively used (Kulick, 1992). In this community, the local vernacular Taiap is rapidly disappearing from the linguistic repertoire of language acquiring children, not because of an explicit devaluation of Taiap but because of implicit devaluation through language socialization practices. Taiap adults insist that they want children to acquire the local vernacular, and place the blame for its loss on the will of the children to reject Taiap in favor of Tok Pisin. However, their language socialization practices indicate that caregivers code switch into Tok Pisin far more than they realize and that they socialize young children into associating Tok Pisin with modernity, Christianity, and education and Taiap with backwardness and paganism. The result is that "although no village child under 10 actively commands the vernacular language, most children between 5 and 10 possess a good passive understanding of Taiap" (Kulick, 1992: 217).

Another example of how ideology affects bilingual acquisition come from Schieffelin's language socialization study of Haitian families in New York City (Schieffelin, 1994). Young children in these families participate in Haitian Creole, English, and sometimes French conversational exchanges, but for the most part are using English. Adults assume that all Haitian children learn to speak Creole; it is integral with their Haitian identity. English, on the other hand, is seen as essential for success in school and for successful participation in American society. In contrast to Creole, English is viewed as requiring attention and explicit instruction. This ideology can be seen in the language socialization practices with children, wherein adults will themselves use Creole to praise children when the children speak in English. In addition, adults convey this ideology through recurrent code switching in which they paraphrase their own and children's Creole utterances in English.[7]

5 Steps to a Cultural Ecology of Grammatical Development

A consistent message throughout this chapter is that grammatical development cannot be adequately accounted for without serious analysis of the social and cultural milieu of the language acquiring child. We have seen that grammatical development is an outcome of two primary sociocultural contexts: (1) where children participate regularly in socially and culturally organized activities, and (2) where the language(s) being acquired is/are highly valued and children are encouraged to learn it/them.

The first point implies that no special form of language, such as simplified grammar, is necessary for children's grammatical development; the only requirement is that children are involved routinely in a community's social network and in the everyday activities that hold that community together. We have suggested that certain linguistic accommodations may be an outcome of cultural conceptions of the child, including expectations about the communicative roles of young children from birth onward. In communities where infants and young children are frequently expected to take on *central* communicative roles such as addressee or speaker, members provide a great deal of social, cognitive, and linguistic support. For example, in selecting an infant or young child as addressee, members may simplify their grammar, as a means of getting the child to respond. Or, in selecting a child as speaker, members may simplify the child's task by, for example, ventriloquating, prompting, or expanding the message. On the other hand, in communities where infants and young children are often assigned the more *peripheral* role (Lave and Wenger, 1991) of overhearers, they are participants in linguistically complex activities. In all communities, children take on a range of communicative roles but *when* in their development, in *which* social situations, and *how often* they do so varies from community to community. A culturally organized means–ends model accounts for this pattern in that it allows for crosscultural similarity in the linguistic means employed to accomplish social ends (such as talking to a child), but allows for the possibility that there will be cultural variation in the situational manifestation of a particular social end (e.g. the developmental point at which members start treating children as addressees who are to respond in culturally appropriate ways.)

The second point implies that mere exposure to a language is not sufficient to account for its acquisition. Analyses of grammatical development in linguistically heterogeneous communities need to be culturally contextualized by including the language ideologies prevalent in those communities. Further, as noted earlier, analysts can not rely exclusively on members' reports of their own and others' speech behavior to assess these ideologies; ideologies are often below the level of awareness and must be investigated through the systematic analysis of speech practices. For example, in multilingual communities, the practice of code switching reveals values attached to each code that members do not articulate through structured interviews. Depending on historical and cultural contexts, codes may be differently valued, and members may display ambivalent feelings towards one or more of these codes in their everyday speech practices. Our point is that language acquiring children acquire values associated with each code through participation in social activities involving code selection and this cultural knowledge impacts their acquisition of codes. With the increasing number of diaspora communities worldwide and the spread of international languages and literacies, the acquisition and maintenance of minority and indigenous languages is becoming increasingly problematic (Dorian, 1989). Psycholinguistic studies of children's bilingual acquisition need to attend to the fact that grammatical development takes place in a world market of languages, where different languages, like other cultural commodities, carry different economic and political values.

In summary, while grammatical development does not depend upon a simplified speech environment, cultural values attached to particular codes do impact the acquisition (or nonacquisition) of those codes. Furthermore, cultural systems of belief, knowledge, and social order profoundly affect the acquisition of particular grammatical constructions. In section 3, we suggested that even very young children appear to be sensitive to the ways in which grammatical constructions within a code index social identity, in that they select forms that appropriately constitute their identity as "child" or as "male" or "female," or as one who is carrying out an appropriate role, such as "one who begs for food or things." A language socialization approach provides an analytic framework for assessing the social activities and identities that grammar indexes as well as the cultural norms, preferences, and expectations that define those activities and identities.

In this analysis, we have drawn primarily on ethnographic studies to make the point that culture affects grammatical development in surprising and subtle yet systematic ways. Culture is still missing from most accounts of grammatical development, and until more culturally sensitive accounts are available, we will only be guessing about the extent to which culture organizes the linguistic forms and practices of young children as speakers, addressees, and audiences over developmental time.[8] Until the cultural ecology of grammar is better understood, grammatical development will continue to be viewed predominantly as an acultural process. Since language is a universal resource for constituting social life and cultural knowledge, and since members are deeply concerned with children's able participation in social life and command of cultural knowledge, then it makes good sense that analyses of children's production and comprehension of grammar seriously take these sociocultural universals into account and incorporate ethnographic methodology to capture the complexities of the social life of language (Sankoff, 1980).

NOTES

Our thanks to Lois Bloom, Patrick Gonzalez and Brian MacWhinney for comments on an earlier draft of this chapter.

1 Research on children's understanding of word meanings in terms of event structures (Nelson, 1986; Sell, 1992) indicates that early in their lives, young children develop conceptual structures that link language systematically to situational contexts.

2 The work of John Gumperz (1982a, 1982b) and his collaborators investigating interethnic communication, or "cross-talk," amply demonstrates many of these difficulties.

3 We are not suggesting that these are the only strategies for simplifying the dance to novices. As the work of Lave and Wenger (1991) and Rogoff (1990) suggest, the child could, for

example, be assigned a limited role in the dance and not have to master the entire routine. In language, this might correspond to expecting the child to understand and respond to/display only a portion of a message.

4 Rogoff (1990) presents the interesting hypothesis that children and caregivers who are in body contact with one another for most of the day have the opportunity to communicate nonvocally through body movements. Infants can signal discomfort and caregivers can manipulate the infant entirely through somatic means.

5 This point was emphatically made by Bloom (1970) regarding the absence of the instrumental and dative in children's early utterances in spite of their pervasiveness in adult speech.

6 Two exceptions are De Houwer (1990) and Goodz (1989), both of whom relied not on parental report but also examined speech practices in the home.

7 Focusing on young adults and children, Schmidt (1985) and Bavin (1989) have related language ideology to language shift among the Djirbal and Walpiri peoples of Australia respectively. For studies of language shift more generally, see Dorian (1989), Gal (1979), and Hill and Hill (1986).

8 Slobin (1992: 6) comments in his crosslinguistic study of language acquisition: "This may be time to remember – as Ochs and Schieffelin (1984) have incisively argued – that language acquisition ALWAYS takes place in cultural and interpersonal contexts. The ethnographic content of chapters on 'exotic' languages shows how much ethnography is MISSING from our accounts of the acquisition of languages in more familiar settings."

Methods

4 Individual Differences and their Implications for Theories of Language Development

ELIZABETH BATES, PHILIP S. DALE, AND DONNA THAL

Introduction

Like every other aspect of human development, language development is characterized by variation. Historically this variation has been largely ignored by students of child language, who have concentrated on the remarkable similarities in sequence of development that are usually observed across children acquiring a given language. Individual differences in rate of development and individual differences in learning style have been left to applied practitioners such as speech pathologists and special educators. We believe it is no accident that these professionals, concerned with such important questions as the definition of abnormality, the relationship of language to nonverbal cognition, and the role of environmental variables, have found it essential to focus on variation.

It is our contention that quantitative and qualitative variations within and across components of early language are also relevant, indeed essential, if we want to understand the mechanisms that underlie normal language development. Far from simply reflecting noise in our measuring instruments or variability in low-level aspects of physiological maturation, the variations that we will document here are *substantial, stable*, and have their own *developmental course*. Because this variation is substantial, it is critical for defining the boundary between normal and abnormal development; because it is stable, it provides a window onto the correlates and (by inference) the causes of developmental change; and because it has its own developmental course, it can be used to pinpoint critical developmental transitions that form the basis for theories of learning and change.

Although we are well aware of the clinical applications that hinge on an adequate assessment of normal variation (i.e. one cannot define "abnormal" without an adequate definition of "normal"), our primary goal here will be an exploration of the implications of individual differences for theories of normal language. We will concentrate on the early stages of language learning, from the onset of word comprehension (around eight to ten months of age) to the onset of grammar (from 20–36 months). This is the period in which the most dramatic changes in language ability are observed, phenomena which have been amply documented in small and large sample studies. It is also a period characterized by dramatic events in postnatal brain development (e.g. synaptogenesis), which means that biological factors may play a particularly important role in those aspects of language that change at the same time (Bates, Thal, and Janowsky, 1992). For these reasons, we stand a good chance of discovering something interesting about the interplay of biology and environment. The chapter is divided into four parts, as follows:

1   *Variations in rate within components of early language*   In this section we will review evidence for variations in speed of development in word comprehension, word production, first word combinations, and the first stages of grammar. As we shall see, there are enormous individual differences in onset time and rate of growth in each of these components, variations large enough to challenge and constrain the notion of a universal bioprogram (Bickerton, 1984) or a universal maturational timetable for early language development (Lenneberg, 1967). Such maturational accounts are insufficient, because the linguistic variations that we observe in perfectly healthy children are so much larger than the variations that are usually observed in other maturational milestones like crawling or walking. At the same time, environmental variables (at least those that have been examined to date) appear to account for only a modest proportion of the variance observed in early comprehension and production of language. At the risk of inviting accusations of radical centrism, we conclude that the variations observed in early language development are so large that they require substantial contributions from *both* genetic and environmental factors, with special emphasis on their interaction.

2   *Dissociations between components of early language*   Having demonstrated large-scale variation in rate of development *within* individual components, we can go on to ask about the degree of association or dissociation in rate of development that is observed *between* those components. In this section, we will look for evidence of developmental asynchrony between comprehension and production, and between lexical production and grammar. The purpose of this investigation is to locate the seams and joints of the language processor, i.e. components that can develop at different rates because they depend on different cognitive and/or neural mechanisms. Hence, this section has implications for the hotly contested issues of modularity and the autonomy or interdependence of linguistic and cognitive systems (Fodor, 1983).

3   *Variations in learning style*   Continuing our search for the seams and joints of the language processor, we will move on in this section to a brief

review of evidence for qualitative variations in learning style (aka "referential v. expressive style," "nominal v. pronominal style," "analytic v. holistic style"). We end by concluding that stylistic variation is the emergent property of quantitative variations in the information processing mechanisms that all children must have for successful language learning.

4   *Atypical populations: variation at the extremes of the normal range*   Finally, we will review evidence on the same three themes (rate, dissociations, and style) in the early stages of development of several quite different atypical populations: early talkers (a nonclinical but very unusual group), late talkers (many of whom go on to qualify for a diagnosis of specific language impairment), children with focal brain injury (to provide insights into the neural mechanisms that underlie individual differences in early language), and children with contrasting forms of mental retardation (i.e. Williams Syndrome, where language eventually moves ahead of many other cognitive domains; Down Syndrome, where language levels often fall behind mental as well as chronological age). This will be a very brief review of a large topic, but it will help to round out our understanding of the mechanisms involved in early language development, across the period from first words to grammar (Bates, Bretherton, and Snyder, 1988). We will conclude that most of the variations observed in atypical populations represent extensions of the variations that are also observed in the normal range.

1   Variations in Rate

We will start with variations in rate of development within individual components, a form of variation that is (at least in principle) easy to define and quantify. In fact, this apparently simple form of measurement poses a substantial methodological problem. Estimations of variability, even more than estimations of central tendency, require a substantial sample size. For obvious reasons, this is generally not possible for studies of child language, which are exceptionally time and labor intensive. The great majority of research studies have included fewer than 25 subjects; and many of the most influential have been far smaller, i.e. single case studies (e.g. Leopold, 1949) or studies of three or four children (e.g. Bloom, 1970; Brown, 1973). Even studies nominally focused on individual differences have continued the tradition of small samples or single case studies (e.g. Peters, 1983). As illuminating as these studies have been in defining those patterns of individual variation that are *possible*, the extent and nature of such variation will remain controversial until large samples are available. For this reason, we will concentrate here on a single study with a uniquely large sample of more than 1,800 children: the norming study for the MacArthur Communicative Development Inventories (Fenson, Dale, Reznick, Thal, Bates, Hartung, Pethick, and Reilly, 1993; Bates, Marchman, Thal, Fenson, Dale, Reznick, Reilly, and Hartung, 1994; Marchman and Bates,

1994; Fenson, Dale, Reznick, Bates, and Thal, in press). These results are based on two parental report instruments (CDI: Infants, for children 8–16 months, and CDI: Toddlers, for children 16–30 months) that have been developed over a period of more than 15 years. A variety of studies have demonstrated the reliability and validity of this instrument and its immediate predecessors (Dale, Bates, Reznick, and Morisset, 1989; Dale 1991; Camaioni, Caselli, Longobardi, and Volterra, 1991). For example, the vocabulary checklists correlate positively and significantly with laboratory assessments (both standard tests and free speech) with coefficients ranging from +0.40 to +0.80; the grammatical complexity scale correlates with laboratory measures of Mean Length of Utterance at +0.88 at 20 months and +0.76 at 24 months. In hindsight, this high validity is hardly surprising. Parents have a far larger dataset than researchers or clinicians can ever hope to assemble; it is also far more *representative* of the child's ability, as it is based on the child's behavior in a wide range of situations which call for an equally wide range of language skills.

There are, of course, limitations to the kind of information that can be obtained with parental report. As Bates et al. (1994) acknowledge,

> We can say nothing here about phonological development (e.g. segmental v. suprasegmental approaches to the analysis of speech), nor about the frequency with which children use particular vocabulary types (i.e. type/token relations). We cannot distinguish between imitations and spontaneous speech, nor can we specify the range of contexts in which individual lexical items are used (e.g. flexible and productive use v. memorized frames). However, we can provide an exceptionally clear view of developmental changes from 8 to 30 months of age, and we can establish the boundaries of variation . . . within and across levels of development.

As long as we keep these variations firmly in mind, and make no attempts to generalize beyond the factors that can be studied reliably and accurately with parental report, a database of this kind can be extraordinarily useful.

Methodology

Parents of 1,803 children between eight and 30 months participated in a norming study for these inventories, conducted in San Diego, Seattle, and New Haven (Fenson et al., 1993). Parents of 673 children between 8–16 months completed the CDI: Infants; parents of another 1,130 children, between 16–30 months, completed CDI: Toddlers. A minimum of 30 males and 30 females are represented at each age level. Children with serious health problems or extensive exposure to a language other than English were excluded from the study, and are not included in the numbers just listed. The sample includes a wide socioeconomic range, although it is heavily weighted toward families in the middle class (e.g. parents with at least a high school education). For the present discussion, we focus on two core subscales from the CDI: Infants (word comprehension, word production) and three subscales from the CDI: Toddlers (word production, onset of word combinations, and grammatical complexity).

Parents of 500 children in the original sample also completed a second inventory approximately six weeks later. Parents of another 503 children completed a second inventory approximately 6.5 months later. Of this latter group, 62 parents of children in the Infant sample completed the CDI: Infants a second time; parents of 217 children in the Infant sample completed the CDI: Toddlers; and parents of 224 children in the Toddler sample completed the CDI: Toddlers a second time. This information was used to assess the cross-age stability of parental report.

The CDI: Infants includes a 396-item vocabulary checklist organized into 19 semantic categories. Ten of these categories comprise nouns (animal names, vehicles, toys, food and drink, clothing, body parts, furniture and rooms, small household items, outside things and places to go, and people). Additional categories are included for sound effects and animal sounds, games and routines, verbs, adjectives, pronouns, question words, prepositions and locations, quantifiers, and words about time. Parents are asked to indicate which words the child *understands* (comprehension) and which words the child *says and understands* (production). Note that we have excluded a third theoretically plausible category, i.e. words that the child says but does not understand. This decision reflects our discovery and acknowledgment of an important limitation of parental report. In earlier versions of the CDI, we asked parents to distinguish between words that the child imitates without comprehension, and words that are produced spontaneously and productively. Our results made it clear that parents find it difficult to make a distinction of this kind; indeed, most parents operate under the assumption that production reflects understanding. We have built that parental assumption into the final version of the CDI, but we realize that there is no way to win on this matter. Degree of productivity is a subtle dimension that must be studied with a different methodology, including in-depth observations of language use and context and detailed interviews with parents that elicit information about the contexts in which words are used (see Snyder, Bates, and Bretherton, 1981, and Bates et al., 1988, for results using the interview technique).

The CDI: Toddlers includes a 680-word vocabulary checklist, organized into 22 semantic categories. The larger number of categories on the toddler form is a result of two sections (helping verbs, and connecting words) and the division of outside things and places into separate sections. As vocabulary becomes larger, it is no longer possible for parents to monitor comprehension vocabulary; they are asked only to indicate use (production). The second part of the toddler form is designed to assess morphological and syntactic development. Only two measures from this part will be discussed here. Parents are asked if their child is combining words; they can respond "not yet," "sometimes," and "often." If they respond "sometimes" or "often," they proceed to a set of 37 forced-choice recognition items in which they choose the member of each pair that best reflects their child's current level of language use ("In each of the following pairs, please mark the one that sounds MOST like the way your child talks right now"). The 37 items include contrasts in the use of bound morphemes (e.g. "Daddy car" v. "Daddy's car"), functors (e.g. "Kitty sleeping" v. "Kitty is sleeping"), and early-emerging complex sentence forms (e.g. "Baby crying" v. "Baby crying cuz she's sad").

Stability of individual differences

Before turning to evidence for the substantial variation in rate of development observed in early child language, we should review evidence for the stability/ reliability of this variation from the six-month longitudinal data collected in the norming study. To evaluate continuity, we applied a very stringent multiple regression analysis, controlling age (a rough index of maturational status), gender (reflecting a combination of biological and cultural factors), and six family and social class variables (birth order, SES, mother's education, father's education, mother's occupation, and father's occupation), before the Time 1 measure was entered as a predictor of the corresponding Time 2 measure. Five such analyses were performed: Infant–Infant Comprehension; Infant–Infant Production; Infant–Toddler Production; Toddler–Toddler Production; and Toddler–Toddler Sentence Complexity. In every case the earlier measure was a highly significant ($p < 0.001$) predictor of the later measure, accounting for an additional 16.6 percent to 31.1 percent of the variance on the final step. Thus, the individual differences discussed below are unusually robust, compare with other psychometric studies in the same age range (McCall, Eichorn, and Hogarty, 1977). It also follows from these analyses that a substantial portion of the variation described below cannot be explained by such traditional factors as age, gender, and social class.

Vocabulary comprehension

Figure 4.1 shows the mean developmental function for word comprehension between eight and 16 months, together with functions that describe children who are 1.28 standard deviations above or below the mean. This contrast (which we will use in most of the graphs that follow) illustrates the developmental zone occupied by approximately 80 percent of the sample (so that the probability of falling outside this region is $p < 0.10$ at either tail of the distribution).

For most children, robust evidence of word comprehension first appears between eight and ten months of age. At the eight month entry point, the mean number of words that parents report in comprehension is 36, although the median (a more conservative measure) is only 17. At ten months of age the mean has surged to 67 words, with a median of 41. By the 16 month exit point for the CDI: Infants scale, children have a mean receptive vocabulary of 191,

Figure 4.1   Word comprehension on the MacArthur CDI Infant Scale.

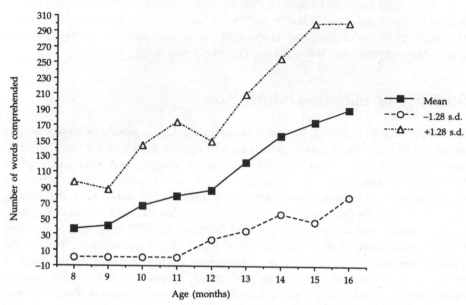

with a median of 169. These median scores are consistent with other estimates of the onset of word comprehension and its early growth (Benedict, 1979; Rescorla, 1981; Bates et al., 1988). However, the means are relatively high, reflecting much more variability in the onset and rate of receptive vocabulary growth than might have been expected from previous research. For example, the 1.28 standard deviation range at ten months of age goes from a low of zero words to a high of 144. By 16 months the corresponding range is from 78 to 303 words. An indication of the magnitude of individual differences is the fact that the overall correlation between word comprehension and age is positive and significant ($r = 0.60$, $p < 0.001$), but accounts for only 36 percent of the variance. The remainder of the variance must be a combination (exact recipe unknown) of true individual variation and the noise and error of parental report.

Some evidence for the reality of this variation comes from recent electrophysiological studies of comprehension. Mills, Coffey, and Neville (1993) tested a group of ten-month-old children, half of them "early comprehenders" reported to understand at least five to ten words from a short laboratory checklist, and half "early noncomprehenders" reported as not understanding these common words. Event-related brain potentials (ERPs) were recorded while the children listened to familiar and unfamiliar words. Significant differences between familiar and unfamiliar words were observed for children in the "early comprehenders" group, but not for children in the "noncomprehenders" group. Thus, the parental report of comprehension was correlated with an electrophysiological measure of recognition. Of course, this does not mean

Figure 4.2 Word production on the MacArthur CDI Infant Scale.

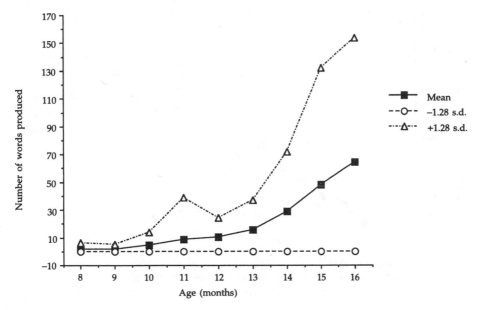

that high-performing ten-month-olds understand the meaning of familiar words. The ERP in this experiment is an index of recognition, nothing more. However, it does suggest that parents who report high comprehension are aware of their child's selective sensitivity to speech.

The very high levels of word comprehension reported for children at the upper end of the distribution at eight to ten months may also reflect a much less interesting factor. In particular, some parents may adopt a different and more liberal definition of "understands" than we had in mind, inferring comprehension from nothing more than evidence for high attention and positive effect. There is some evidence that this overestimation may be more characteristic of parents with low education (see Fenson et al., in press). Nevertheless, taken together, the Mills et al. (1993) electrophysiological data and the cross-age stability cited earlier demonstrate that a high proportion of the variance in early word comprehension is authentic.

Vocabulary production

Figures 4.2 and 4.3 show the mean developmental function and range of variation (1.28 standard deviations in either direction) for word production between eight and 16 months (on the CDI: Infants), and between 16–30 months (on the CDI: Toddlers). The mean and median functions are consistent with previous small-sample studies, showing that expressive language does not get off the ground for most children before 12 months of age. For most children,

Figure 4.3   Word production on the MacArthur CDI Toddler Scale.

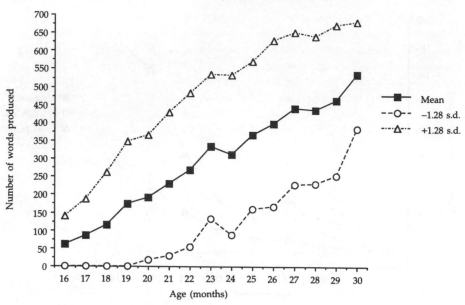

there is slow growth in vocabulary production from a mean of 1.8 words at eight months (with a median of 0), to a mean of ten words at 12 months (with a median of 6), to a mean of 64 words at 16 months (and a median of 40).[1] By 30 months, the mean score has increased to 534 words, with a median of 573 (notice that the median is now lower than the mean, indicating that the distribution is now skewed by "late talkers" at the low end of the distribution – see section 4). The overall correlation between age and vocabulary is 0.47 (p < 0.001) for the Infant data, accounting for just 22 percent of the variance. For the Toddler data, the age correlation is 0.68 (p < 0.001), accounting for 46 percent of the variance. Thus, there is a substantial amount of age-independent variation.

Around these central tendencies, variation in vocabulary production has a complex and interesting time course. There is relatively little individual variance at or before 12 months. The 1.28 standard deviation window at one year of age extends from a low of zero words to a high of 24. However, after 13 months there is a dramatic increase in variability, due primarily to rapid growth in children at the high end of the distribution. At 16 months, for example, children in the top tenth percentile have reported productive vocabularies of at least 154 words, while children in the lowest tenth percentile are still producing no words at all. This highly skewed distribution continues to characterize variation in expressive vocabularies throughout the 16–30-month range, until ceiling effects are operative. For example, at the two-year point (24 months), the mean for reported expressive vocabulary on this measure is 312 words, but the 1.28 standard deviation range goes from a low of 89 to a high of 534 (see also Huttenlocher, Haight, Bryk, Seltzer, and Lyons, 1991).

It seems likely that the nonlinearities in figures 4.2 and 4.3 have something to do with a controversial phenomenon called the "vocabulary burst." Some time during the second year of life, many children experience a marked acceleration in rate of word learning (Nelson, 1973; Dromi, 1987; Gopnik and Meltzoff, 1987; Goldfield and Reznick, 1990). For most of the children that have been studied to date, the growth curve starts to rise somewhere between 50–100 words. The single best example in the literature comes from Dromi's detailed and exhaustive longitudinal study of vocabulary development in a single child (see also Van Geert, 1991). A number of contrasting proposals have been offered to account for this nonlinear shift. For example, it has been argued that children achieve a sudden insight into the ideal that things have names (Dore, 1974), or alternatively, that all objects ought to have a name (Baldwin and Markman, 1989). Others have attributed this shift to a more general change in cognition, including developmental changes in the ability to categorize objects (Gopnik and Meltzoff, 1978) and/or developmental shifts in representational capacity (Shore, 1986; Brownell, 1988). Yet another class of explanations revolve around reorganizations in the phonetic segmentation (Plunkett, 1993) and/or articulatory ability (Menn, 1976). All of these accounts are interesting, but they suffer from two related problems: lack of universality, and absence of an inflection point. Let us address each of these in turn, and then see what we can glean from the large cross-sectional database currently at our disposal.

The first problem with the various explanations of the vocabulary burst cited above revolves around the fact that not all children display a growth spurt of this kind. Reznick and Goldfield, among others, have argued from longitudinal data that the burst is not universal. In some children, vocabulary grows so continuously that it is difficult to identify a single point or narrow region of acceleration (see below). In other cases, vocabulary development is characterized by a series of small bursts, a stairstep pattern that is difficult reconcile with most single factor theories of "the burst."

A second problem comes from the discontinuity implied by the word "burst," and by most of the theories that seek to explain accelerations in word learning. Van Geert (1991) and Bates and Carnevale (1993) have noted that individual growth curves described in longitudinal studies of vocabulary development during the second year (see especially Dromi, 1987) are best fit by a smoothly accelerating exponential function, or by related nonlinear functions such as the quadratic or the logistic. By appropriate variation in their parameters, such nonlinear models could lead to growth curves marked by apparently intense bursts, weaker bursts, or no significant acceleration at all. The key insight here is that there is no inflection point in the exponential portion of the so-called vocabulary burst, i.e. no single "take-off point" of the kind assumed by most of the theories cited above. And yet there does appear to be a region of acceleration during the second year that cries out for explanation.

Because the CDI database is essentially cross-sectional (one cannot construct a growth curve from two points), it cannot provide direct information about the existence, incidence, or prevalence of the legendary burst. If there are a large number of individual stepwise functions, they are masked by summation across individual children. However, these data can provide two indirect sources of information about the timing and nature of nonlinear changes in rate of development.

First, let us assume that accelerations in rate of development become most evident between 50–100 words. If this is the case, then some children in our sample are on their way to a vocabulary burst between 14–16 months of age (see figure 4.3) – well before the 17–19 month transition predicted by many theories. By the same argument, the data in figure 4.3 suggest that some children in the third year of life are still well below the 50–100 word boundary where the putative burst typically appears. Thus, if a vocabulary burst does occur, its timing is characterized by wide individual variation. For some children, it may occur as early as 14 months, for some as late as 24–6 months.

A second set of facts derives from analyses of stability over time in the MacArthur Norming Study. Reznick and Goldfield (1992) have reported longitudinal data from the 500 parents who completed a second inventory approximately six weeks after the initial questionnaire. Correlations between initial and later scores were computed separately for each age group, based on the child's age at first administration. Correlations for the CDI: Todders exceeded r = 0.90 at every age. Correlations for the CDI: Infants were in the 0.8–0.9 range for both comprehension and production, with a single exception: at 12 months, the test–retest correlation for infant vocabulary production dropped to r = 0.60. Analyses of our six-month longitudinal data were consistent with these results, suggesting a discontinuity in individual differences occurring at approximately one year of age. The lower reliability coefficient at 12 months may reflect a general reorganization of infant cognition at the 12-month boundary (see McCall, Eichorn, and Hogarty (1977) for a similar 12-month discontinuity in longitudinal studies using the Bayley Scales of Infant Development). Alternatively, it may reflect a discontinuity in parental perceptions of infant language. That is, the emergence of meaningful speech at 12 months may cause some parents to reevaluate the criteria that they used before this point to define a "real word" (e.g. "I thought he said 'mama' before, but what he is doing now is really different"). If this observation is correct, then the most important discontinuity in early word production is the one that occurs between 12–13 months of age – and not the one that is supposed to occur later in the second year. The putative vocabulary burst from 16–20 months may be the inevitable product of a growth function that is set in motion at the end of the first year, i.e. from 10–12 months.

These statistical observations are consistent with some informal observations of Dale and Thal (personal communication), both of whom have studied early talkers. It is difficult to locate children below the age of 12 months with a demonstrable productive vocabulary of, say, ten or more words. It is much

Figure 4.4 Percent children combining words as a function of age on the MacArthur CDI Toddler Scale.

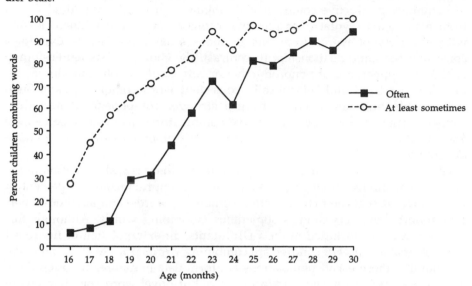

easier to identify children at 14–16 months with very large vocabularies of 100 words or more. We suspect that there may be a "bottleneck" or "gate" into referential vocabulary which cannot be substantially accelerated. Once that milestone is passed, however, exceptional ability may lead to a flowering of vocabulary. It is an intriguing, but speculative, hypothesis that this phenomenon may be biologically specified.

Combining words

For English, with its relatively modest inflectional morphology and general absence of case markings, the initial step in grammatical development for most children is combining words (this generalization is not entirely accurate even for English, and is of course highly inaccurate for languages such as Japanese and Hungarian). In the MacArthur study, parents were given three options for describing their child's combinatorial language: "not yet," "sometimes," and "often." Parents appeared to interpret these terms quite consistently, even though they were given without precise quantitative specification. Figure 4.4 shows the regular progression in parents' response to this question. There is a gap of approximately three to four months between the two criteria. It might have been expected that "sometimes" would be more easily quantified by parents ("greater than zero") than "often," and hence more reliably judged. Contrary to this expectation, the "often" criterion was more highly correlated with both age (0.58) and total vocabulary size (0.73) than was "sometimes"

(0.47 and 0.57 for age and vocabulary, respectively). Fenson et al. (1993) have suggested that parents choose "often" in response to their children's first use of genuinely productive combinatorial language, in which individual words from a particular syntactic or semantic category may be combined flexibly with a variety of words from one or more other categories to express a consistent semantic relationship. In contrast, the choice of "sometimes" may reflect the appearance of nonproductive or rote combinations that do not reflect a generalized and semantically consistent word combining skill. Such rote combinations are likely to have a stronger component of individual stylistic variation than does productive combinatorial language (see below), and are therefore less strongly correlated with other measures of language development.

Whichever criterion is used, it is apparent that there is wide variation in the onset of combinatorial language. At 18 months, approximately 11 percent of parents report that their child is often combining words, and another 46 percent report that their child is sometimes combining words. Although this question was not included in the CDI: Infants, an extrapolation of figure 4.4 suggests that a subset of children are combining words prior to 16 months. We assume that these early combinations are formulaic in nature, although there are sporadic reports in the literature of rare but novel word combinations in children as young as 14 months (e.g. the expression "Wadoo baba – Water bottle" – uttered by a 14-month-old child after throwing a playmate's bottle in a wading pool: Bates et al., 1988). By 25 months, nearly all parents report some combinations, but 19 percent are still not reporting combinations "often." Thus, the much used clinical criterion of failure to combine words by age two years (e.g. Rescorla, 1989) corresponds roughly to the lowest 10 percent of the CDI distribution.

Sentence complexity

Finally, we turn to grammatical development, as indexed by parental response to the 37 forced-choice recognition items. Figure 4.5 illustrates the developmental function and standard deviations for this scale. The 37 items include bound morphemes, functor words, and early-emerging complex sentence forms. The mean developmental function of figure 4.5 is concordant with observational studies of early grammatical developmental, but there is (once again) substantial variation from the earliest period. Children functioning 1.28 standard deviations above the mean at 16 months are at a level which will not be achieved by children one standard deviation below the mean until 28 months. In other words, there is a full calendar year separating children at the high v. low end of the distribution for sentence complexity.

To clarify the range of variation, and make it more meaningful, we can convert this scale to a more familiar one, namely, Mean Length of Utterance (MLU). MLU is widely used as a measure of early grammatical development,

Figure 4.5 Grammatical complexity scores on the MacArthur CDI Toddler Scale.

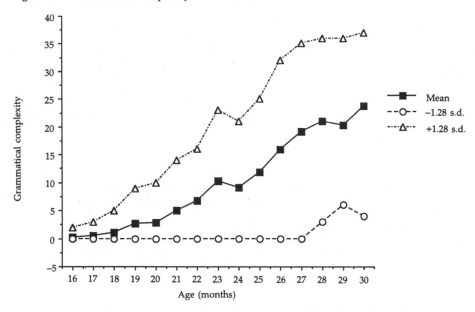

despite a number of limitations (Crystal, 1974; Klee and Fitzgerald, 1985). For purposes of characterizing variation, the two most significant limitations of MLU are the absence of good normative data, and the potential for achieving similar MLU values with quite different syntactic abilities (and conversely, achieving different MLU values with similar syntactic abilities). Here we attempt to characterize variation in MLU with a much larger sample than has been previously available, taking advantage of the high correlation between sentence complexity and MLU. A correlation of 0.84 (p < 0.001) between sentence complexity and observed MLU was obtained by Dale for a sample of 44 children at 20–24 months (Fenson et al., in press). Based on this high correlation, a linear regression formula for estimating MLU can be derived from the parent measure:[2]

$$MLU = e^{(.174*(\ln(C + 1)) + .7299)^{-1}}.$$

This estimation formula was then applied to sentence complexity normative data (n = 1,130) from the CDI: Toddlers, yielding the developmental function for estimated MLU illustrated in figure 4.6. The mean growth in MLU produced with this method is startlingly close to the estimated norms provided by Miller and Chapman (1981) on the basis of a much smaller sample of 123 children. And, like figures 4.4 and 4.5, it indicates that normal children of the same chronological age can vary from six months to a year in their "grammatical age."

To summarize so far, substantial variation is observed in early vocabulary

Figure 4.6   MacArthur CDI Toddler form estimated MLU (observed).

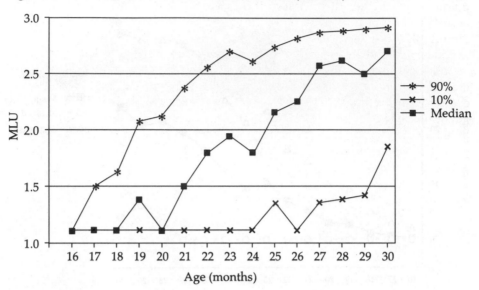

comprehension. Equivalent variability does not emerge in vocabulary production until after 12 months, an age which appears to mark a discontinuity. Vocabulary growth is positively accelerated after this point, although it is not yet clear whether this is best characterized as a "burst" or a smoothly accelerating curve. If it is the latter, then it is safe to say that the "true discontinuity" in vocabulary development is the one that starts around 12 months of age. The nonlinearities that are observed after this point represent nothing more (or less) than the predictable course of growth along an exponential function that was set in place around the 12 month mark. There is also a great deal of variability in the onset of word combinations, and the growth of MLU following the transition to grammar. To determine whether this later "burst" in grammar is a true discontinuity, or a continuation of the earlier "burst" in vocabulary, we turn to the analyses of associations and dissociations between components of early language.

2 Finding the Fault Lines: Dissociations Between Components of Early Language

In the previous section, we presented evidence showing massive variation in rate of development for healthy, normal children, in every area of early communication and language from 8–30 months of age. The existence of such variation leads to another question: are these variations in rate consistent across all areas of development, or can we document significant dissociations in rate of development between the major components of early language? As we pointed out in the introduction, the existence and nature of dissociations between components of early language is relevant to the vexed issue of modularity.

Fodor (1983) has proposed a distinction between *vertical modules* that operate on a particular information type and respect the boundaries between domains (e.g. a putative module for face perception), and *horizontal modules* that cut across information types (e.g. short-term memory, or particular forms of attention). In Fodor's view, the human language faculty is an excellent candidate for vertical modularity, i.e. an innate, encapsulated, special-purpose processor that operates on language and language alone. Fodor makes no claims about further modular subdivisions within this language faculty, although he acknowledges Noam Chomsky's proposal (e.g. Chomsky, 1986a, b, 1988) that language itself is made up of distinct subdivisions that fit the criteria for vertical modules (e.g. phonology v. grammar, grammar v. the lexicon – see also Pinker, 1991). In testing for the fault lines of early language development we will examine the case for and against one potential set of horizontal modules (comprehension v. production) and another potential set of vertical modules (grammar v. vocabulary). We note that Fodor might view both of these as instances of vertical modularity, since they deal primarily with the processing of language. However, we will review limited evidence to suggest that the comprehension/production dissociation implicates abilities outside the boundaries of language proper.

Comprehension v. production

Every pediatrician has had worried inquiries about children who have barely started to talk, even though they appear to understand much of the speech that is addressed to them. Cases of this sort are also well attested in the child language literature, in virtually every study that has investigated comprehension and production in the same set of children (Goldin-Meadow, Seligman, and Gelman, 1976; Bates, Benigni, Bretherton, Camaioni, and Volterra, 1979; Benedict, 1979; Oviatt, 1980; Snyder, Bates, and Bretherton, 1981; Mills, Coffey, and Neville, 1993, and in press).

Most of these studies have concentrated on comprehension and production of single words, but studies that have investigated comprehension and production of grammatical forms in the same set of children yield a similar conclusion. In a few cases that dissociation actually seems to run in the opposite direction, with children demonstrating poor comprehension of sentence forms that are present in their own spontaneous speech. However, most researchers agree that dissociations of the latter sort reflect cases in which (a) the comprehension test itself involves complex task demands that obscure the child's actual knowledge of grammatical structure (Chapman and Miller, 1975; Crain, 1992), and/or (b) children appear to display production of grammar in

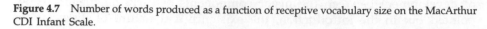

Figure 4.7   Number of words produced as a function of receptive vocabulary size on the MacArthur CDI Infant Scale.

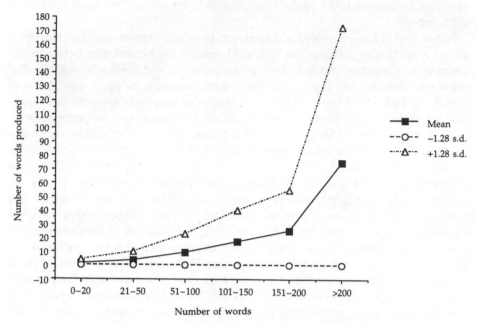

advance of comprehension because they are using the grammatical forms in question in unanalyzed formulae that have been acquired through rote memory (Bates et al., 1988). When these confounds are eliminated, then the comprehension/production profiles observed for early grammar match those that have been reported for comprehension and production of single words. That is, some children appear to understand far more than they are able to say (Hirsh-Pasek and Golinkoff, 1991). Furthermore, these profiles appear to be relatively stable over time. In a longitudinal study tracking development from first words to grammar, Bates et al. (1988) report significant correlations between the comprehension/production profiles that children display at the lexical level from 13–20 months, and the comprehension/production profiles that the same children display at the grammatical level at 28 months of age.

The incidence and magnitude of the dissociation between comprehension and production has been demonstrated at the lexical level in two successive large-sample studies within the MacArthur CDI project described above. Figure 4.7 illustrates the relationship between number of words in comprehension (horizontal axis) and number of words in production (vertical axis) for children between eight and 16 months of age in the CDI norming study. This graph shows a characteristic fan effect, created by a substantial number of children in each sample who seem to understand far more words than they produce – including some children who are producing no words at all despite receptive vocabularies of more than 200 words! Hence, the comprehension/

production dissociation appears to be a robust and pervasive phenomenon in the early stages of language development. But it is a phenomenon that is still in search of an explanation. To find that explanation, we need to consider some of the cognitive and neural correlates of this profile.

First, let us consider the limited evidence that is currently available on the nonlinguistic measures that correlate with comprehension and production, respectively. Since the 1970s, a large number of studies have investigated the cognitive predecessors and correlates of early language milestones, with a particular focus on the correlates of first words and first word combinations in production. Candidates include aspects of tool use and causality (Bates, Camaioni, and Volterra, 1975; Bates, Benigni, Bretherton, Camaioni, and Volterra, 1979; Harding and Golinkoff, 1979), categorization (Sugarman, 1983; Gopnik and Meltzoff, 1986a, 1987; Mervis and Bertrand, 1993), block construction (Shore, 1986), and symbolic play (Nicolich, 1977; Snyder, 1978; McCune-Nicolich, 1981a; McCune-Nicolich and Bruskin, 1982; Shore, O'Connell, and Bates, 1984; Kelly and Dale, 1989; Shore, Bates, Bretherton, Beeghly, and O'Connell, 1990; Rescorla and Goossens, 1992). In most of these studies, on effort was made to parcel out the contributions of comprehension v. production to the observed correlations. However, as we shall see in more detail in section 4 on abnormal variations, comprehension and production map onto different aspects of nonlinguistic development. In particular, when there is a dissociation between these two modalities of language, comprehension appears to "win custody" of most of the cognitive correlates of early language. For example, Bates, Thal, Whitesell, Fenson, and Oakes (1989) have shown that variation at 14 months in communicative and symbolic gesture correlates more strongly with lexical comprehension than it does with lexical production. A similar pattern appears in the MacArthur CDI parental report data for children from 8–16 months of age. The finding that nonlinguistic measures correlate better with comprehension than they do with production can be paraphrased as follows:

Most cognitive variables correlate with what the child *knows* about language (indexed by comprehension), as opposed to what the child *does* (indexed by production).

A different kind of evidence about the correlates and fellow travelers of comprehension and production comes from recent electrophysiological studies of normally developing children. Mills, Coffey, and Neville (1993, and in press) have examined the the event-related brain potentials elicited by auditorily presented words in children between 13 and 20 months of age. Although this is clearly a test of receptive processing (i.e. passive reaction to familiar words), Mills et al. report specific patterns of brain activity that distinguish between the child's current level of comprehension (indexed by bilateral waves over posterior cortex) and the same child's current level of production (indexed by waves that are larger over left anterior cortex). Hence, even though these event-related potentials are all elicited in the receptive modality, they suggest that different neural systems mediate comprehension and (latent) production.

To summarize this section, there are robust dissociations between comprehension and production in the early stages of language learning. These dissociations are observed across the transition from first words to grammar, and the profiles of individual children tend to be preserved at both the lexical and the grammatical level. Studies with normally developing children also suggest that comprehension and production draw on different cognitive resources, and are mediated by different neural systems. In particular, rate of progress in comprehension appears to be associated with a wide range of nonlinguistic measures, mediated (at least in the early stages) by bilateral brain mechanisms. By contrast, variations in production have fewer nonlinguistic correlates (when levels of comprehension are controlled), and may involve a special form of mediation by anterior regions of the left hemisphere. We suggest than this dissociation between comprehension and production constitutes a form of horizontal modularity, i.e. a dissociation that cuts across linguistic and (perhaps) nonlinguistic information types.

Grammar v. the lexicon

In contrast with the comprehension/production profiles described above, any dissociations that we might observe between grammatical and lexical development could be used to argue in favor of vertical modularity, i.e. a dissociation that respects the boundaries between well specified linguistic domains. However, in our investigation of the relationship between grammar and the lexicon in the first stages of language learning, we have to distinguish between two forms of dissociation: temporal asynchrony *within* individual children, and dissociations in rate of development *across* individual children. As we shall see, there is solid evidence for the former but very little evidence for the latter.

The temporal asynchrony between grammatical and lexical development is one of the best established facts in developmental psycholinguistics. In every language that has been studied to date, children do not combine or inflect words productively until they have passed through a prolonged single word stage, where content words are used with few (if any) inflectional contrasts. Even in languages such as Turkish and Japanese, in which some inflections appear in the one word stage, this development occurs after a prolonged noninflected stage. During the one word stage, there are also significant changes in the composition of the lexicon, changes that signal a shift from reference, to predication, to grammar. Figure 4.8 from Bates et al. (1994) illustrates this change in vocabulary composition from 16–30 months of age, based on cross-sectional results from the MacArthur norming study. In this figure, children are divided by vocabulary level rather than age, as follows: 0–50 words, 51–100 words, 101–200, 201–300, 301–400, 401–500, 501–600, and > 600. Although these 100-word groupings are rather arbitrary, figure 4.8 shows a systematic

Figure 4.8 Vocabulary Composition as a function of vocabulary size on the MacArthur CDI Toddler Scale.

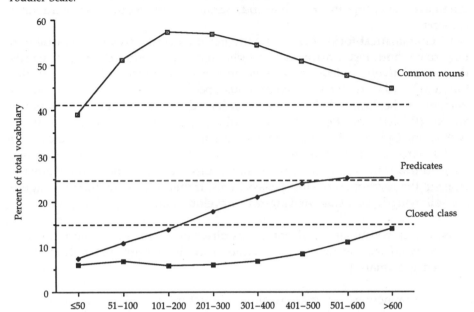

and elegant relationship between vocabulary size and vocabulary composition. Figure 4.8 illustrates the average *proportion* of total vocabulary made up of common nouns (i.e. names for common objects), predicates (verbs and adjectives), and function words (pronouns, prepositions, articles, quantifiers, conjunctions, modal and auxiliary verbs) at each vocabulary level. The horizontal lines on the graph represent the total proportion of common nouns, predicates, and function words on the list as a whole (i.e. the checklist ceiling for each vocabulary type). If vocabulary development drew randomly (or evenly) from each of these lexical categories, then the average proportion scores at each vocabulary level should follow these horizontal lines. Clearly, this is not the case. Common nouns predominate in the first stages of language learning, reaching a peak around 100 words and then dropping down sharply to the checklist ceiling. Predicates show a slow but steady proportional increase across the entire period of development. Function words show no proportional growth at all, averaging approximately 6 percent of total vocabulary until somewhere around the 400-word mark; after that point, function words increase rapidly until they reach the 14 percent checklist ceiling. In other words, each of these vocabulary types shows a different growth function, and each one has its own season.

These temporal asynchronies suggest that different mechanisms may be involved in lexical and grammatical development. But is this necessarily the case? Temporal asynchronies of this kind can also be observed when a single learning device is applied to a complex task with several levels of difficulty. That is, grammatical function words, grammatical inflections and word combinations may come in later than individual content words, for two related reasons:

1   Grammatical forms may come in later than content words because they tend to be short, fast, unstressed, and phonologically reduced. In other words, they are relatively difficult to perceive. In fact, several studies have shown that function words excised from continuous speech are recognized less than 30 percent of the time when they are presented out of context to competent adults (Pickett and Pollack, 1963; Pollack and Pickett, 1963; Goodman, Nusbaum, Lee, and Broihier, 1990), compared with recognition rates from 50–80 percent for content words (see also Gerken, 1994; Goodman and Nusbaum, 1994). Hence, it appears that adults have to depend on context to assist in the perception of closed-class items. If this is the case, then it suggests the following hypothesis for language development:

Closed-class vocabulary will not be acquired until children have built up a content word lexicon that is large enough to "bootstrap" perception of unstressed grammatical forms.

2   Most function words are relational in nature, i.e. their purpose is to set up a relationship between other items in the sentence. O'Grady (1987) has proposed a formal taxonomy of lexical items into three logical types, based on the number of elements and relationships that must be presupposed for that item to work in its intended fashion. Primaries are elements with a "stand alone" function or meaning. Secondaries are items that depend upon a relation with at least one primary. Tertiaries are items that presuppose or depend upon at least one secondary relationship. Within O'Grady's system, most nouns are primaries, most verbs and adjectives are classified as secondaries, and most (though not all) function words are classified as tertiaries. The developmental results outlined in figure 4.8 are quite consonant with O'Grady's theory: nouns are acquired first because they must be acquired first (although they may coexist with routines like "bye-bye" that also stand alone), verbs and adjectives tend to come in later because they presuppose the prior existence of nouns, and closed-class elements cannot be acquired until some requisite number of primary and secondary elements are in place.

In short, the temporal asynchrony that is invariably observed in the acquisition of lexical and grammatical functions may be an inevitable by product of phonetic and semantic differences among these linguistic types. Indeed, if proposals by Goodman et al. (1990) and O'Grady (1987) are correct, this temporal asynchrony may reflect a powerful cause and effect relationship. To the extent that this is true, we should expect to find robust correlations between lexical and grammatical development across individual children. That is, in fact, exactly what we find (Bates et al., 1988; Bates et al., 1994; Dale, 1991; Marchman and Bates, 1994). In their longitudinal study of 27 children from

Figure 4.9   Percent of subjects producing word combinations as a function of vocabulary size on the MacArthur CDI Toddler Scale.

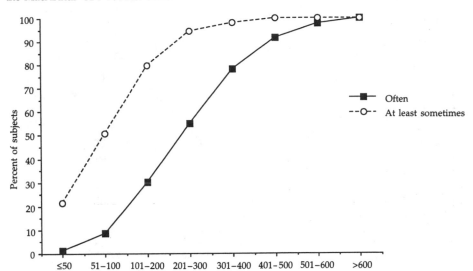

10–28 months of age, Bates et al. (1988) report a correlation of +0.83 between vocabulary size at 20 months (determined by parental report) and mean length of utterance at 28 months (based on videotapes of free speech in home and laboratory settings). This correlation falls at the reliability ceiling for MLU (i.e. split-half and test-retest correlations for samples of MLU do not exceed +0.83). Because no measure can correlate any higher with another variable than it correlates with itself (i.e. "Spearman's Law"), we can conclude that the relationship between 20-month vocabulary and 28-month MLU is one that approaches statistical identity.

The developmental nature of this relationship between vocabulary size and grammar is illustrated in figures 4.9 and 4.10 from the MacArthur CDI norming study. Figure 4.9 shows the number of children who are reported by their parents to produce at least some word combinations, as a function of the same eight vocabulary groupings described above (figure 4.8). Figure 4.9 shows that there is a strong correlational relationship between vocabulary size and the appearance of multiword speech. For most children, word combinations start to appear when vocabularies fall between 50 and 200 words. Figure 4.10 displays an equally strong but later-emerging relationship between vocabulary size and sentence complexity (a parent report measure that, as we noted earlier, correlated around +0.84 with mean length of utterance based on laboratory observations). For most children, sentence complexity accelerates markedly (following a smooth exponential function) when total vocabulary exceeds 400 words. Note that there is a significant nonlinear component to the

Figure 4.10   Grammatical complexity score as a function of vocabulary size on the MacArthur CDI Toddler Scale.

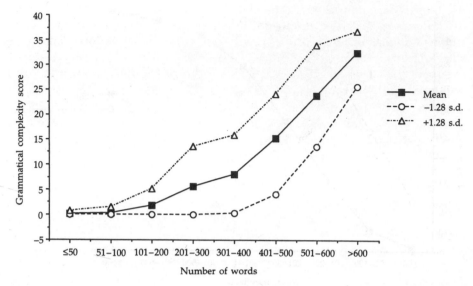

grammar/vocabulary relationship in both these graphs. Marchman and Bates report similar but more specific nonlinear relationships between verb vocabulary (i.e. the number of specific regular and irregular verbs reported on the vocabulary checklist) and the emergence of verb morphology (including correct regulars, correct irregulars, and the appearance of overgeneralizations like "falled").

As described in more detail by Plunkett (this volume; see also Plunkett and Marchman, 1991, 1993; Marchman, 1993) and MacWhinney (1989, 1991a, b), these functions are quite similar to the nonlinear "mass action" effects reported in studies of language learning in neural networks. In these connectionist models, the same learning mechanism is responsible for acquisition of vocabulary items and acquisition of the past tense markings for specific present tense forms. In other words, there is no modular distinction between lexical and grammatical learning. Nevertheless, the models display a temporal asynchrony between lexical development and the subsequent emergence of grammatical marking. To illustrate, consider the incremental learning of past tense marking in a recent simulation by Plunkett and Marchman (1993; cf. Plunkett, this volume). In the early stages of learning, the system appears to learn each mapping from present to past tense by rote, with no generalization to novel lexical forms (i.e. it flunks the wug test) and no overgeneralization errors. As instances of present/past tense mapping accumulate, some dramatic nonlinear changes are observed: the rate of learning accelerates markedly, overgeneralization errors start to appear, and the system starts to provide a default mapping to novel items (i.e. it passes the wug test). Superficially, the network behaves as though it has switched from one mode of learning (rote) to another (rule). And yet there are no structural discontinuities in the system itself, or in the one-verb-at-a-time nature of the input. Instead, the behavioral discontinuities observed in these simulations result from the operation of a single nonlinear learning device. Simply put, grammatical generalizations (i.e. rulelike behaviors) do not arise until the system has acquired enough instances to support those generalizations. When the requisite number of items has been acquired, dramatic changes can take place, even within a single system.

These neural network simulations provide a possible explanation for the strong nonlinear correlations between lexical and grammatical development observed in human children from 16–30 months of age. Indeed, it could be argued that lexical and grammatical development are paced by the same learning mechanisms – at least within this age range. However, before we accept such a strong conclusion we need to ask whether dissociations between grammar and vocabulary are *ever* observed. Recall the fan effect observed in figure 4.7, which illustrates the relation between comprehension and production. Figure 4.10 presents comparable information on individual variability in the relationship between vocabulary size and sentence complexity. Note that there is no fan effect at all in Figure 4.10, i.e. no children with very large expressive vocabularies but no evidence of grammar. In other words, *there are no lexical/grammatical dissociations in normally developing children from 16–30 months of age*. We will return to this point later, in section 4 on variations outside the normal range.

However, this does not mean that grammar and semantics are "the same thing." As Gerken (in press) and O'Grady (1987) have pointed out, function words and content words have different perceptual, semantic, and logical properties. Hence, they cannot be *processed* in exactly the same way, even though they may be *acquired* by the same kind of learning device. In fact, new electrophysiological studies by Mills, Neville, and colleagues suggest that content words and function words are mediated by different areas of cortex (Mills, 1993). By the time normally developing children are three years of age, grammatical function words elicit specific patterns of activity over left anterior cortex that are not observed in response to content words (see also Greenfield, 1991). These patterns may be the hallmark of fluent, connected speech, a skill that requires forms of information processing that are not required for the comprehension or production of single words.

To summarize so far, studies of normal children provide robust evidence for a dissociation between comprehension and production. By contrast, there is very little evidence for a dissociation between lexical and grammatical development for children who fall within the normal range. To be sure, temporal asynchronies are reliably observed in the passage from first words to grammar. However, these temporal asynchronies may reflect a powerful cause and effect relationship between grammar and the lexicon, reflected in the strong nonlinear correlations illustrated in figures 4.9 and 4.10. We suggest that grammatical development depends upon the establishment of a critical lexical base.

Indeed, *different* grammatical events may each depend upon a *different* lexical base (e.g. word combinations emerge in the 50–100 word range; verb morphology emerges in the 400–600 word range – see Marchman and Bates, 1994). These mass-action effects are consonant with simulations of grammatical learning in neural networks, which suggests in turn that grammatical and lexical development may be achieved with the same kind of learning device (Plunkett, this volume). Nevertheless, there are clearcut semantic and perceptual differences between grammatical and lexical forms, which may require a different mix of processors for rapid and efficient language use.

3   Individual Differences in Style

Both the previous sections, which have focused on rate differences among children in specific components of language, and on potential dissociations, or asynchronies, among those components, have implicitly assumed a uniform sequence of acquisition within each of these components. The credibility of this assumption is the fruit of several decades of research on child language. It is not the whole story, however. An appreciation of stylistic variation, encompassing differences in sequence and in qualitative aspects of language development, was delayed for many years by a focus on universal sequences of acquisition – especially in grammar – as a window onto innate structures and processes, and by an apparently innocent methodological decision to select relatively talkative, intelligible, and nonimitative children for early studies (Goldfield and Snow, 1985). As the domain of child language studies expanded to include semantic and pragmatic development, and a wider range of children were observed, the universal fact of stylistic variation has become obvious.

Three phases in the study of stylistic variation

At a highly oversimplified level of abstraction, we may distinguish three phases in the study of qualitative variation in early child language. The first might be captured with the phrase "gee whiz." Following Nelson's (1973) seminal monograph on the composition of early vocabulary, a stream of research projects attempted to document variation in specific aspects of language development. Nearly all of them were successful. Comprehensive reviews of this research are available in Wells (1985), Goldfield and Snow (1985), and Bates et al. (1988). Here we note only that whether the components of language are conceived as horizontal or vertical (cf. previous section), variation may be observed within each of them. We list just a few examples organized by linguistic content area. Within phonology, differences have been noted in emphasis on segmental v.

suprasegmental features, and in the consistency of pronunciation across word tokens. Within semantics, there are differences in the proportions of nouns in early vocabularies, and in the use of semantically empty "dummy" words. Within grammar, there are differences in use of nouns v. pronouns in early sentences, and in degree of overgeneralization of morphological rules. And within pragmatics, children differ in their variety of speech acts, and in the balance of declarative and imperative utterances. Alternatively, differences may be organized by processing modules. Children differ in the degree to which comprehension is superior to production, in their rate of imitation and whether it is ahead of or behind spontaneous speech, and whether early utterances are limited to single words or are reproductions of longer phrases and sentences.

The general argument in most of these studies has been to draw inferences from product to process. For example, the higher proportion of nouns in children with referential vocabularies has been interpreted as evidence for an interest in language as a tool for talking about objects and categorizing them, whereas children with expressive vocabularies are assumed to be more socially oriented, and to be acquiring language to talk about themselves and others. Bloom, Lightbown, and Hood's (1975) observation of variability in the use of nouns v. pronouns in early word combinations was interpreted as evidence for two qualitatively distinct strategies, one more "pivot-like" (Braine, 1963) in using all-purpose pronouns in combination with lexical items, the other based on combining content words from large categories. These process differences in turn were often attributed to differences among children specific to the domain of language. For example, Nelson (1981) proposed that children have different hypotheses as to the essential function of language. Bloom et al. (1975) suggested that nominal and pronominal children were distinguished by a concentration on the word-order properties of language or on morphology (i.e. closed-class items), respectively.

A second phase of study of language acquisition styles may be viewed as the "grand synthesis" phase. This phase began with Nelson's (1973, 1981) reanalysis of her own data, which showed a substantial correlation between her original classification of children as referential or expressive based on their early vocabularies, and Bloom et al.'s (1975) distinction between nominal and pronominal basis of early syntax. This report was followed by a flurry of studies, some data-based and some more purely speculative, arguing for a cohesion of the various dimensions of stylistic variation. Table 4.1, from Bates et al. (1988), represents a synthesis of these arguments, attempting to combine virtually all of the reported dimensions. In this "unitary dimension" or "two strand" theory of individual differences, infants who are word oriented during the babbling period grow into children with referential vocabularies at the first word level, and into children who display nominal style in their first word combinations, followed by high rates of morphological overgeneralization during the acquisition of grammar. Conversely, children who are intonation oriented during the babbling period grow into children with expressive

Table 4.1   Individual differences in language development: summary of claims in the literature

Strand 1	Strand 2
Semantics	
High proportion of nouns in first 50 words	Low proportion of nouns in first 50 words
Single words in early speech	Formulae in early speech
Imitates object names	Unselective imitation
Greater variety within lexical categories	Less variety within lexical categories
	Use of "dummy" words
Meaningful elements only	Low adjective use
High adjective use	Context-bound use of names
Context-flexible use of names	Slower vocabulary growth
Rapid vocabulary growth	
Grammar	
Telegraphic in Stage I	Inflections and function words in Stage I
Refers to self and others by name in Stage I	Refers to self and others by pronoun in Stage I
Noun phrase expansion	Verb phrase expansion
Morphological overgeneralization	Morphological undergeneralization
Consistent application of rules	Inconsistent application of rules
Novel combinations	Frozen forms
Imitation is behind spontaneous speech	Imitation is ahead of spontaneous speech
Fast learner	Slow learner
Pragmatics	
Object oriented	Person oriented
Declarative	Imperative
Low variety in speech acts	High variety in speech acts
Phonology	
Word oriented	Intonation oriented
High intelligibility	Low intelligibility
Segmental emphasis	Suprasegmental emphasis
Consistent pronunciation across word tokens	Variable pronunciation across word tokens
Demographic variables	
Female	Male
Firstborn	Laterborn
Higher SES	Lower SES

vocabularies in the one word stage, and then show a formulaic, pronominal style in first word combinations, followed by a pattern of grammatical learning characterized by undergeneralization and inconsistent application of rules. At the highest level of generality, these styles have been labelled "analytic" v. "holistic" or "rote," respectively.

Perhaps not surprisingly, given the psychologically loaded terminology of "analytic" v. "rote," the first strand usually included the descriptor "fast learner." And indeed, it also included certain demographic variables – female, firstborn, high SES – assumed to be associated with more rapid language learning. In fact, the primary evidence for this claim was restricted to just two of the aspects of style listed in table 4.1: proportion of nouns, and error rate. Several studies, such as that of Horgan (1981), observed a positive relationship between the use of nouns and the overall rate of language development, a finding to which we return below. In the second set of studies, Horgan (1981) and Ramer (1976) demonstrated a positive relationship between rate of errors, including word order errors, and overall rate of development.

As the dimensions of stylistic difference were reduced in number, but broadened in scope, it became increasingly appropriate to look for explanations outside of language proper: the nature of maternal input, the child's temperament, global (IQ) or specific (play, information-processing style, etc.) aspects of cognitive functioning, neurological differences, and others. In addition, new versions of language-based explanations were offered, such as the proposal of Gleitman and Wanner (1982) that learners differ significantly in their emphasis on the open-class lexicon (nouns, verbs, adjectives) and closed-class lexicon (function words). Some of these alternative accounts are summarized in table 4.2 (adapted from Bates et al., 1988).

It is essential here to distinguish processing mechanisms, such as analysis, or rote memory, from more distal factors, such as gender or maternal input, which may lead to differences in the degree to which children rely on one or the other of these mechanisms. These constitute two qualitatively different levels of explanatory factors. We suggest that it may be a more fruitful research program to characterize first the processing differences, and then seek the more distal explanations. It is too easy to be guided (or misguided!) by implicit or explicit stereotypes about these external factors to inferences about mechanisms which may not be valid, e.g. that higher SES children have larger vocabularies, that girls have more precise pronunciation, or that the left hemisphere superiority for analytic processing will lead to a fundamental difference among children in degree of analysis. For this reason, we will have little to say in the present chapter about the exogenous factors that push processing mechanisms apart. Our focus will be on the nature of the mechanisms that underlie a dissociation in styles.

The third phase of the study of stylistic variation may be dubbed "sober reconsideration." It is characterized by a critical examination, on empirical, conceptual, and methodological grounds, of the grand synthesis. Evaluation of a theory of individual differences necessarily requires a substantial number of

Table 4.2   Individual differences in language development: alternative explanations

Social explanations	
Exogenous	Maternal style and input
	• Object v. person focus
	• Does or does not imitate the child
	Social class
	• Elaborated v. restricted code
Endogenous	Temperament
	• Object v. person orientation
	• Reflective v. impulsive approach to problems
Linguistic explanations	
Within language proper	• Language function v. language form
	• Open v. closed-class lexicon or semantics v. grammar
	• Word order v. morphology
Between language and cognition	• Environmentally sensitive and insensitive processes
Neurological explanations	
Interhemispheric	• Right v. left hemisphere emphasis
Intrahemispheric	• Anterior v. posterior emphasis within the dominant hemisphere
Cognitive explanations	
Unidimensional	• General intelligence
	• Field dependence – independence
Multidimensional	• Analytic v. Gestalt/holistic processing
	• Analytic v. imitative learning mechanisms
	• Patterners v. dramatists
	• Information sensitive v. frequency sensitive
	• Comprehension driven v. production driven
	• Analysis for understanding v. analysis for reproduction

subjects, measures, and time points. For example, Bloom et al. (1975) noted that their two "nominal" children were both girls, whereas the two "pronominal" children were both boys. This is an intriguing observation, but assuming a null hypothesis that any single child has a 50/50 chance of developing either style, there is a 1 in 8 probability that a group of four children would divide in a gender consistent fashion. A few studies are appearing which at least approximate the requirements above, and the results are generally more complex than the grand synthesis would predict. Bates et al. (1988) followed a group of 27 children through four age levels: 10, 13, 20, and 28 months. Correlational and factor analyses based on the full longitudinal dataset were most consistent with a model consisting of *three* language acquisition mechanisms, not two: comprehension, analyzed production, and rote production, with a complex relationship over time between comprehension and analyzed production. For example, MLU at 28 months was predicted by early measures of comprehension and analyzed production, not by MLU at 20 months, which was associated instead with earlier measures of rote production (for further evidence supporting this partitioning, see Shore, 1986; Dixon and Shore, 1992, 1993). In other words, the simple two strand account (figure 4.11a, from Bates et al., 1988) must give way to a more complex, dynamic account of associations and dissociations over time (figure 4.11b, from Bates et al., 1988).

Even more important than the accumulation of larger datasets on individual variation is the need to embed characterizations of individual variation into a larger model of developmental change. Stylistic variables are not nearly as distinct from developmental ones as the literature would lead one to believe. Children differ in their use of nouns and pronouns in early sentences, as Bloom et al. (1975) demonstrated; but children also generally increase their use of pronouns during this period. Children vary in their rate of spontaneous imitation, but there is also an inverted U-shaped developmental trend for imitation, first rising and then declining. And so on down the line. Paradoxically, only if we can separate these two types of variance can we hope to understand their relationship. Otherwise we may only be demonstrating one more time that "good things go together."

The validation of stylistic differences

What constitutes adequate evidence for the characterization of a dimension of stylistic variation? We suggest there are at least three necessary criteria: the first is the requirement of *synchronic generality and discrimination*. There are two parts to this requirement, sometimes called convergent and discriminant validity in the psychometric literature. The first is based on the view that a single measure of variability is unlikely to be interpretable or interesting on its own. It might simply be error variance; alternatively, it might be genuine, but so limited in scope as to have few implications. Stylistic dimensions which have multiple measures, especially measures based on different types of linguistic performance or content, provide a more substantial basis for interpretation.

Figure 4.11   (a) Two-strand design: ideal patterns; (b) Pattern of best fit to the observed longitudinal data.

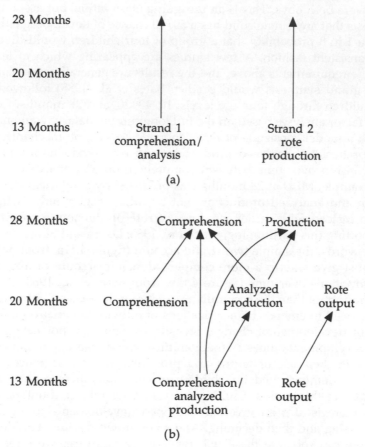

The second requirement, of discrimination, simply reflects the observation that when everything is changing at the same time, correlations are not interesting. Methodologically, this first criterion requires correlations among the proposed system of variables, contrasting with smaller correlations between the stylistic variables and other measures. In practice, the demonstration of these correlations and their interpretation is far more difficult than it sounds. There are three recurring substantial difficulties with the correlational approach. One is that the size of a correlation is not determined solely by the relationship between the underlying constructs, but also by the inherent reliability of the measures. As Spearman first noted, measures cannot correlate more highly with each other than they do with themselves. Many child language measures, especially stylistic ones, have only modest reliabilities, which will depress correlations among them. A second difficulty is that the relationships among stylistic measures may not be linear, as assumed by the test of significance of the ubiquitous Pearson coefficient. The relationship may be nonlinear, e.g. a discontinuity or step function, or even nonmonotonic, as when the extremes of a measure have more in common with each other than with the middle of the distribution. The third difficulty concerns the underlying nature of the variables, which may have different meaning at differing time points. As will be discussed below, the frequency of closed-class words in a child's vocabulary has quite a different meaning at 20 months than at 28 months. Hence, evaluation of a dimension of stylistic variation that includes closed-class word usage must consider carefully the most appropriate age for assessment.

The second criterion for identification of a stylistic dimension is *longitudinal continuity*. No matter how substantial a dimension of variability may be at a single moment in time, if it has no enduring predictive significance, it is unlikely to play a major role in understanding language development. This is *not* a requirement for "dimension permanence." Early use of nominals and pronominals in word combinations appears to be a stable characteristic, associated with other aspects of style, though eventually it fades as children become fluent with both approaches to sentence construction. It appears to reflect a genuine difference in first approach to syntax. The three strands identified by Bates et al. (1988) discussed above were supported by synchronic generality and longitudinal continuity. Demonstrating longitudinal continuity is subject to the same difficulties as those listed above under synchronic generality. The third difficulty, the changing meaning of measures, is particularly challenging and important. Kagan (1971) and others have pointed out that there are two types of longitudinal continuity: homotypic continuity (cross-age correlations within the same content domain, such as vocabulary totals) and heterotypic continuity (e.g. correlations between early measures of vocabulary and later measures of grammar). Heterotypic continuity may be more common, and more interesting theoretically, than homotypic continuity, as it suggests more abstract, underlying explanatory mechanisms. Conversely, what appears to be the *same* measure at two ages may not be correlated, i.e. a homotypic discontinuity. For example, proximity seeking in a two-year-old is a good measure of attachment to a parent, and is positively correlated with other measures of social and emotional development; proximity seeking in a four-year-old is more likely to be a sign of dependency, with negative correlations to other measures. Thus proximity seeking at the two ages is either uncorrelated or negatively correlated. A similar conclusion holds for closed-class usage: this measure at 20 months correlates significantly and *negatively* with the "same" measure of closed-class use at 28 months (Bates et al., 1988). Homotypic discontinuity does not eliminate the significance of such measures for understanding individual differences in children; it suggests only that the measures have a qualitatively different relationship to stylistic variation at the two different times.

The third criterion for establishing a dimension of stylistic variation concerns the nature of the measure which is evaluated for synchronic and longitudinal generality. In particular, stylistic variables must be *unconfounded with developmental rate*, in order to be interpretable. We exemplify both the need for this unconfounding and one approach for doing so with a recent study by Bates et al. (1994). As discussed earlier, a number of studies have reported that referential style, that is, a high proportion of common nouns early in development, is associated with faster rates of development. However, the percentage of nouns in total vocabulary itself shows a monotonic increase longitudinally during the period of acquisition of the first 50 or 100 words. Hence, the correlation between rate of development and referential vocabulary observed at a given age style may simply reflect the developmental change in noun use. Those children with larger vocabularies will have a higher proportion of nouns as a consequence of developmental change. As Pine and Lieven (1990) have pointed out, age-based measure and correlations based on them are not appropriate for evaluating stylistic variation.

To address this issue, Bates et al. (1994) used the large norming sample from the MacArthur Communicative Development Inventories discussed earlier in this chapter. Their first goal was to identify developmental changes in vocabulary composition across the 8–30 month period. As noted in section 2, they identified three "waves of reorganization": (1) an initial increase in percent common nouns between 1–100 words, followed by a slow proportional decrease; (2) a slow linear increase in predicates, i.e. verbs and adjectives, with the largest gains occurring between 100–400 words; (3) no proportional change in closed-class vocabulary (pronouns, prepositions, question words, quantifiers, articles, auxiliary verbs, and connectives) between 1–400 words, followed by a sharp increase after 400 words. These changes were summarized as "a shift in emphasis from reference, to predication, to grammar."

The second goal of their project was to characterize stylistic variation in vocabulary composition independent of these developmental changes. Figure 4.12 plots the observed changes in percent common nouns as a function of the vocabulary levels adopted in figures 4.8–4.10. In addition to values for children at the mean, figure 4.12 also includes referential-style scores for children who are 1.28 standard deviations above or below the mean at each vocabulary level. It is clear that there is very substantial variation in "nouniness," even when total size is held (approximately) constant. This variation is greatest for children with vocabularies below 50 words, replicating the original observation in Nelson (1973). At this vocabulary level, children who are 1.28 standard deviations above the mean (i.e. "referential style") have vocabularies that comprise more than 58.5 percent common nouns; children who are 1.28 standard deviations below the mean (i.e. "expressive style") have fewer than 18 percent common nouns.

Variation in closed-class vocabulary showed a different pattern, illustrated in figure 4.13. As noted earlier, there is little developmental change in these proportion scores before 400 words, although there is still some variation around the mean (ranging from no closed-class words at all to more than 15 percent). After vocabularies pass the 400 word point, there are increases in the relative size of the closed class for all children, including those at the low end of

Figure 4.12 Percent common nouns as a function of vocabulary size on the MacArthur CDI Toddler Scale.

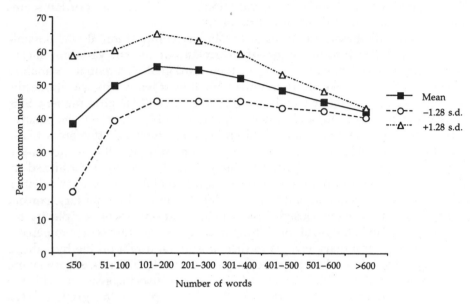

Figure 4.13 Percent closed class as a function of vocabulary size on the MacArthur CDI Toddler Scale.

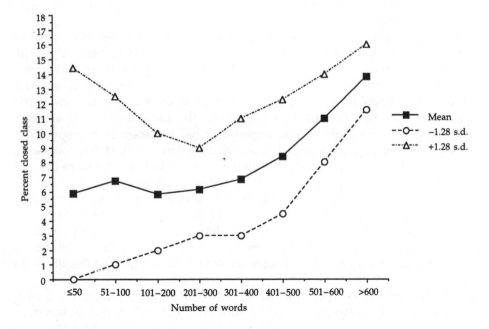

the distribution. In other words, everybody has to get around to learning those little words eventually, regardless of style (see also Bloom et al., 1975). Hence, developmental and stylistic variation in closed-class proportion scores are confounded after the 400 word point.

With percentile-based measures of vocabulary composition, it was possible for Bates et al. (1994) to investigate the correlates of stylistic variation unconfounded with developmental variation, their third goal. Referential vocabulary style for children between 8–16 months with at least ten words was modestly, but significantly, correlated with age (0.15), gender (0.11, girls higher), SES, mother's education (0.18) and father's education (0.19). Note that the positive correlation with age means that children high in referential style are actually *older* than those with proportionally fewer common nouns, that is, not precocious in overall vocabulary growth. This finding is strikingly confirmed by studies of the longitudinal predictiveness of referential style. Referential style at 8–16 months was not significantly correlated with total vocabulary, percent common nouns, percent closed-class words, or grammatical complexity 6.5 months later. Thus, the result of shifting from age-based raw scores to percentiles based on vocabulary level is to cast substantial doubt on the hypothesis that referential style is a harbinger of language precocity. The lack of correlation, positive *or* negative, with later closed-class use is also inconsistent with the view that referential children are more likely to display a "telegraphic" style in early word combinations, while expressive children are more likely to adopt a pronominal/holistic style. The modest correlations of referential style with social class and maternal education suggest that environmental factors may contribute some of the variance in early "nouniness."

A second set of analyses investigated the correlates of closed-class proportion scores. As should be clear from figure 4.13, variation in closed-class use appears to change in nature when vocabulary reaches approximately 400 words. Prior to this point there is no increase in closed-class proportion scores as a function of vocabulary size, suggesting that variation is due to stylistic rather than developmental factors; after this point, the same measure is strongly correlated with vocabulary size, suggesting that variation is strongly influenced by developmental status. For this reason, Bates et al. (1994) conducted correlational analyses separately for these two periods. Children were divided into three groups: (1) children who were below that 400 word level at both time points (i.e. continuity in closed-class style during the nonproductive phase), (2) children who were above 400 words at both ages (i.e. continuity in closed-class development within the productive phase), and (3) the largest and most informative group, children who were below 400 words at Time 1 but above 400 words at Time 2 (to test for continuity or lack thereof around the 400 word border).

For children below the 400 word level at both time periods, early closed-class usage was negatively associated with later vocabulary (−0.19) but positively associated with later closed-class usage (0.46). This suggests some continuity in style within this early period, but it also suggests that the style dimension is unrelated to other aspects of progress in language. For children above the 400 word level at both time periods, closed-class scores were strongly correlated with one another *and* with progress in vocabulary. This suggests that variance in closed-class use after the 400 word mark is a stable index of productive grammar, and it also shows (from another perspective) that the emergence of productive grammar is paced by lexical growth (see section 2).

A more striking finding comes from the largest group of children, those below 400 words at Time 1 and above 400 words at Time 2. In this group, there was no relationship between early closed-class use and the emergence of productive grammar. This is an excellent example of *homotypic discontinuity*, i.e. a measure that looks like the same thing has a very different meaning at Time 1 and Time 2. There was also no continuity between early closed-class usage and later vocabulary scores.

So what exactly is the basis of early closed-class use? Bates et al. do report positive correlations below the 400 word point between closed-class proportion scores and age. That is, children who use a relatively high proportion of "little words" at an early stage of development tend to be somewhat older than children who avoid those words at a comparable vocabulary level. Hence, their superior ability to detect and reproduce function words may be due to their more mature memories and/or perceptual abilities. As Bates et al. (1994) conclude:

> We need not assume that early use of function words is "bad for children." Instead, we suggest that children who are developing slowly (for reasons we do not yet understand) arrive at the "same" stage of lexical development with an information-processing system that is somewhat more mature in other respects from that of younger lexically matched controls. (Bates et al., 1994.)

These longitudinal findings provide still more evidence for the point made earlier, that the same measure may have quite different meaning at different points in development. Closed-class use after 400 words is an excellent indicator of grammatical development, but in early development it reflects a particular stylistic approach.

A supplementary, but potentially very valuable, approach for evaluating dimensions of stylistic variation is the training study. By introducing novel concepts and words in a controlled fashion, we can observe the acquisition of a piece of language in "real time" (Nelson and Bonvillian, 1978), and test our hypotheses concerning processing differences in language acquisition. Bates et al. (1988), for example, introduced a novel object ("fiffin") and action ("glooping") to 20-month-old children at home, and also administered several tests two to three days later in the laboratory. Of particular interest was the tendency to imitate the label or the action when it was first presented, and the child's later comprehension in the laboratory. These measures were then related to a two strand model of individual differences posited for early development: comprehension + analyzed production (something like referential style), and rote production (something like expressive/holistic style). Comprehension of the new label was predicted by other measures of the first strand, e.g. comprehension, whereas imitation was predicted by the second strand. (As Bates et al. (1988) point out, the link to imitation here is limited to imitation of a new label when it is first presented.) Thus, the hypothesized differences extended to novel concepts and labels. Interpretation of their results and those of others, such as Nelson, Baker, Denninger, Bonvillian, and Kaplan (1985), is made more problematic because of the curvilinear relationship of imitation to development, observed in many domains. It is likely that the phenomenon of imitation itself would also benefit from an analysis which separates developmental from individual variation. In any case, training studies can provide some of the most direct evidence for both the nature and generality of stylistic dimensions.

Rethinking "analytic" and "holistic"

The most sweeping characterization of individual differences in early language remains the pair of terms "analytic" v. "holistic." We conclude with a suggestion that the equation of holistic with rote may be a substantial oversimplification. Children who differ along this dimension might better be characterized as differing in the size of the unit they are able or prefer to manage (Peters, 1977). Plunkett (1993) has pointed out that articulatory fluency and articulatory precision may be inversely related, and that a learner who has extracted a longer expression as a chunk may produce it fluently, at the expense of precision. There is an analogy between this inverse variation and the speed–accuracy tradeoffs so often seen in cognitive performance. What appear to be qualitative differences among subjects may simply reflect selection of a different point along the speed–accuracy continuum. A holistic strategy corresponds to emphasizing speed by selecting a larger unit for processing; an analytic strategy corresponds to emphasizing accuracy, by selecting a smaller unit. Such a distinction is consonant with the observation of Vihman (1981b) and others that some children utilize a small but consistent repertoire of segmental phonemes in prespeech and early meaningful speech, while others use a larger but less consistent repertoire.

There are, in fact, at least two hypotheses here about the relationship of analytic processes and the preferred size of units, to be distinguished and evaluated in future research. First, it is possible that all children are essentially analytic in their approach to language, but the preferred size of units varies, so some children appear more holistic than others. Alternatively, the dimensions of analysis v. rote processes, and of size of unit, are distinct dimensions of individual differences. Some children have good enough memories, and are sufficiently analytic in approach, that they can pick up larger units and combine them productively, as well as later analyzing them into their subparts. Wong-Fillmore's (1979) well-known observations of differences among child second language learners are relevant here. Her most successful learners began by acquiring phrases and sentences of immediate functional use, and then systematically analyzed them into parts for recombination. The two precocious children M and S, to be discussed in the next section , also exemplify highly analytic children with different preferred size of units. Differences in preferred size of units might have continuing consequences for language development. Plunkett suggests that the lack of articulatory precision associated with larger, i.e. formulaic, units might lead to impoverished representations for these longer units, which in turn might hinder the recognition of new linguistic units in the speech signal. He predicts that the vocabulary spurt will be relatively delayed for these children (but cf. previous section on the vocabulary spurt).

To summarize, we have learned some sobering lessons about individual differences in style of language learning, especially with regard to the confound between developmental and stylistic aspects of vocabulary composition (i.e. referential style; closed-class usage). It is increasingly clear that these dimensions of variation cut across different aspects of language processing (i.e. heterotypic continuity), and it is also clear that the "same" measure means different things at different points in time (i.e. homotypic discontinuity). The relevant underlying dimension may involve factors like the size of the unit that children prefer to use at a given point in time, the tradeoff between speed and accuracy in linguistic performance, variations in perceptual acuity and/ or variations in memory capacity within a given language level. For all these reasons, it is likely that no single measure will suffice of we want to divide children into meaningful groups. It may also be the case that no single language will suffice if we really want to understand the causal mechanisms responsible for stylistic variation. The dimensions of variation that have proven relevant in the acquisition of English might be quite different in another language, e.g. a language like Turkish with a regular and perceptually salient set of inflectional markers (Slobin, 1985a), or a language like Greenlandic Eskimo where a complete sentence may consist of nothing more than a single word with six or eight grammatical inflections (Fortescue and Lennert Olsen, 1992). There is still a great deal to be learned about the nature and meaning of stylistic variation in early language, but we are in a much better position to meet this challenge than we were 20 years ago.

4   Atypical Children: Variation at the Extremes

Up to this point, we have focused on variation in normal language development. We have described differences in rate of development, dissociations between comprehension and production (but not between lexical and grammatical aspects of language), and differences in cognitive style that are reflected in language learning in normal children between eight and 30 months of age. In the final section we turn to studies of a number of atypical populations that have added useful data to the investigation of language acquisition. These include children with delayed onset of expressive vocabulary (late talkers), children with precocious onset of expressive vocabulary (early talkers), children with pre- or perinatal focal brain injury, and children with cognitive deficits resulting from Williams and Down Syndrome. Within each subgroup, our discussion is organized into the same three divisions that we used to describe variation in normal children: variations in rate, dissociations between components, and variations in style. As we shall see, the available data on children at the extremes adds significantly to our understanding of the nature and causes of normal variation.

Late talkers

Only recently have researchers begun to focus on toddlers with delayed onset of language. Because there is a great deal of variability in early language development, and many of these children will appear normal within a year or so, researchers have been hesitant to call these children language impaired. Thus, they have come to be called "late talkers" by most of the researchers who are studying them (Thal and Bates, 1988a; Caulfield, Fischel, DeBaryshe, and Whitehurst, 1989; Fischel, Whitehurst, Caulfield, and DeBaryshe, 1989; Rescorla and Schwartz, 1990; Paul, 1991; Whitehurst, Fischel, Arnold, and Lonigan, 1992). However, in many samples there is a disturbing continuity in language delay for a substantial proportion of these toddlers (Rescorla and Schwartz, 1990; Scarborough and Dobrich, 1990; Paul, Spangle-Looney, and Dahm, 1991; Thal, Tobias, and Morrison, 1991).

Variations in rate

By definition, late talkers are delayed in rate of expressive language development. Researchers have shown that rate of development remains delayed in approximately 40 to 50 percent of their late-talking subjects, and that other factors are correlated with continued delay. Paul et al. (1991), for example, reported that children from families with lower socioeconomic status were most likely to remain delayed. Rescorla and Schwartz (1990) noted that those children who were older when initially identified as late talkers, and those with the largest lag in expressive vocabulary, were most likely to remain delayed. Fischel, Whitehurst, and Connors (1987) reported that the factors identified by Rescorla and Schwartz were correlated with short-term outcome. However, in a follow-up one year later they reported that all children had caught up in expressive vocabulary (Whitehurst et al., 1992).

Our own studies of three different groups of children also have varying results. In all cases late talkers were defined as children who were in the lowest 10 percent for vocabulary production on the MacArthur Communicative Development Inventory (CDI). In our first cohort, 40 percent (four out of ten) of the children were delayed in vocabulary production and MLU one year after being identified (Thal, Marchman, Stiles, Aram, Trauner, Nass, and Bates, 1991). All of those children had been delayed in vocabulary comprehension as well as vocabulary production. Children who had normal comprehension at the first time point had normal production vocabulary and MLU one year later. In the second cohort, nine of 17 children with specific expressive language delay were compared to age and language matched controls on MLU and IPSyn (Scarborough, 1990) scores one year later (Thal, Cleveland, and Oroz, in preparation). Late talkers remained delayed in MLU (i.e. they were significantly lower than age matched controls) but had normal IPSyn scores (i.e. they were significantly higher than language matched controls and no different from age matched controls). This suggests that their continued delay may have more to do with fluency (i.e. utterance length) than complexity (i.e. diversity of morphosyntactic structures). In a third cohort, children who served in the longitudinal validation of the CDI in the norming study were used (Thal, Bates, and Fenson, in preparation). Of 33 toddlers in the lowest 10 percent for vocabulary production who received the CDI again six to eight months later, 19 (or 57 percent) were still delayed in vocabulary production at the second assessment.

Although the data vary to some extent, the majority of the studies indicate continuity in the delayed rate of language development in a large proportion of late talkers over a six month to two year period. We are aware of only one study in which the development of children identified as delayed in expressive language at 24 months of age has been followed for a longer period of time (Rescorla, 1993). Data from that study demonstrated normal vocabulary development by age three or four years, but continued delays in subtle aspects of language use for many children through age five. At ages six, seven, and eight most of the specific expressive language delayed children in this study performed normally on standardized tests of language development. However, they were still significantly different from age matched controls in a number of areas including verbal short-term memory, sentence formulation, word retrieval, auditory processing of complex information, and elaborated verbal expression. It is also worth noting that although the late talkers did perform in the average range on most of these measures (at or near the 50th percentile), their age, sex and SES matched controls were performing significantly above the national average (in the 70–80th percentile). In short, the jury is still out on the long-range consequences of an initial delay in word production. Some children do qualify for a diagnosis of specific language impairment, but a majority (of still unspecified size) go on to perform within the normal range.

Dissociation between comprehension and production

The most striking dissociation in our studies of late talkers has been the dissociation between comprehension and production in those late talkers with specific expressive language delay. The mean production vocabulary (based on the CDI) for normal comprehenders in the first group noted above was 23.33 (range 2–64), whereas the mean comprehension vocabulary was 285.8 (range 224–371). In the second cohort the mean for production was 25.1 (1–59) and comprehension was 268.5 (182–405). In both samples comprehension vocabulary (even the lowest end of the range) was well above the average comprehension expected for children with production vocabularies in that range. Hence, the late talker population provides an extreme variant of the comprehension/production dissociations that we described for children in the normal range. The fact that so many of our late talkers do catch up further down the line may be related to their unimpaired receptive language skills. Conversely, their initial delays in expressive language could reflect a temporary bottleneck in processing that can be overcome further down the line.

Dissociation between lexicon and grammar

Vocabulary and grammar appear to be strongly associated in our studies of late talkers. In the first cohort, subjects with normal comprehension had normal vocabulary production and MLU one year later. Those with delayed comprehension had delayed vocabulary production and MLU one year later. In our second cohort, late talkers were significantly below age matched controls on MLU, but they performed within the normal range on a measure of syntactic diversity.

Although these results may be typical of late talkers in the earliest stages of language acquisition, we know that some language impaired children with normal expressive vocabulary have particular difficulty with grammatical morphology. Johnston and Kamhi (1984), for example, found that language impaired five-year-olds had more difficulty with auxiliary, catenative, and infinitive verb structures than MLU matched controls. Others have noted that many children with specific language impairment are especially weak in use of grammatical morphology, with grammatical morphology lagging behind other areas of language (Johnston and Schery, 1976; Steckol and Leonard, 1979; Kahn and James, 1983; Bliss, 1989; Leonard, Bortolini, Caselli, McGregor, and Sabbadini, 1992b). Thus, with prolonged delay it appears that dissociations within language itself can and do develop. It may be the case that early grammatical learning is inextricably tied to lexical level, but dissociations develop later at the point where normal children develop a more fluent and automatized ability to use grammar in real time – in line with our conclusions for variability in the normal range at the end of section 2.

Variations in style

Earlier studies have suggested that the so-called "holistic style" may be more common in children who are developing on a slow schedule (Horgan, 1981; Bates et al., 1988), perhaps because these children have more mature perceptual systems and/or better memory for longer strings of sound compared with younger children at the same level of language development. When vocabulary composition was examined in the cohorts described above, no differences were found between late talkers and vocabulary matched controls in proportion of open- and/or closed-class words, suggesting that late talkers are not atypical on these dimensions. Hence, the correlation that has been observed between age and "holistic style" may be restricted to children within the normal range of language development.

Early talkers

Rate of development

Linguistic precocity has been the focus of only a few studies (Robinson, Dale, and Landesman, 1990; Crain-Thoreson and Dale, 1992; Dale, Robinson, and Crain-Thoreson, 1992; Thal and Bates, 1988b; Thal, Bates, Zappia, and Oroz, 1994). In our studies, we have defined early talkers as children between the ages of 11 and 21 months of age who are in the top 10 percent for vocabulary production for their age on the CDI. By definition, they are ahead of their peers, demonstrating considerable variability in the rate of language development in this early period.

We know relatively little about the long-term stability of early precocity in language. However, at least one study suggests that early talkers tend to stay ahead of their peers. Robinson, Dale, and Landesman (1990) identified children as precocious at 20 months on the basis of vocabulary, MLU, or verbal reasoning (language items on the Bayley Scales of Infant Development) at a level two standard deviations above the mean. Their precocity was maintained for the five years of the project. For example, at 24 months the mean MLU for this group was 3.14, equivalent to that of average children at 36 months; at 30 months the mean PPVT-R vocabulary age equivalent was 42.6 months; and at age 6½, their Stanford-Binet IV Vocabulary age equivalent was nine years, ten months. Each of these scores is approximately two standards deviations above the mean, suggesting that early talkers maintain a significant advantage throughout early childhood.

Dissociations between comprehension and production

Many of these early talkers appear to be equally precocious in comprehension and production. However, as in the late talkers described above, there are also a number of children who display a dissociation between comprehension and production. In this case, the dissociation takes a different form: production does not *exceed* comprehension, but the disparity between receptive and expressive vocabulary displayed by most normal children (and adults) is markedly reduced. In essence, these early talkers might be described as "saying everything they know." As a result they are normal in comprehension (i.e. around the 50th percentile for their age) but abnormally high in production (in the upper 10th percentile for their age). Hence, there is strong evidence for a dissociation between comprehension and production at both extremes of the normal distribution.

Dissociations between lexicon and grammar

Some interesting relationships between grammar and the lexicon have been observed in some of our early talkers. We have studied four of the children with extremely precocious language development in some detail (Thal and Bates, 1988b; Thal, Bates, Zappia, and Oroz, 1994). In two of these children, grammar did appear to lag behind lexicon, suggesting some degree of dissociation, at least in extreme cases. However, detailed examination of the data reveals an unexpected association between vocabulary development and inflectional morphology in these two single-word-stage children. Table 4.3 (from Thal, Bates, Zappia, and Oroz, 1994) provides examples of the utterances produced by two of the children who form a contrasting pair, S (17 months old with an expressive vocabulary of 603 words on the CDI) and M (21 months old with an expressive vocabulary of 696 words on the CDI). With an MLU of 2.13, S demonstrates the correlation between grammar and vocabulary that we have come to expect. M, on the other hand, has just begun to combine words (MLU 1.12). At first glance it appears that grammar and vocabulary are dissociated in this child. However, M does produce contrasting grammatical inflections in her single-word speech. This is a very odd phenomenon for children acquiring English, but typical of children acquiring a highly inflected lanuage such as Turkish (Slobin, 1985a). In fact, the amount and type of grammatical morphology observed in M's speech falls well within the range that we would expect for children with more than 500 words (Marchman and Bates, 1994). Thus, the seeming dissociation between lexicon and grammar does not exist. The difference between these children must be sought elsewhere, which brings us to the next point.

Variations in style

In the early talker group identified within the CDI norming study, we found the same range of variation in referential and/or closed-class style evidenced by children further down in the distribution. This mirrors our results (or lack thereof) for late talkers, suggesting that vocabulary style is not uniquely associated with slow or fast rates of language learning.

However, we did find some interesting evidence for stylistic variation in the case studies of very early talkers described above. Whereas M produced carefully articulated single words, S was observed to use longer utterances that often appeared formulaic in nature. Her parents indicated that she could remember and produce a number of songs and idiomatic expressions (e.g. "No way, José," or "You little monkey!"). An examination of the sample utterances for S in table 4.3 supports this idea. She appears to make use of partially analyzed formulae and "frame-slot" structures in her spontaneous speech (e.g.

Table 4.3   Examples of language production by two very early talkers

Sarah		*Maryann*	
Age	17 months	Age	21 months
Vocabulary	596 words	Vocabulary	627 words
Vocabulary age	30 months	Vocabulary age	>30 months
MLU	2.13	MLU	1.19
MLU age	28 months	MLU age	20 months

Where cup went?	Pretty.
Where chair went?	Cute.
Teddy bear went?	Big.
Baby doing?	Round.
	Dry.
Wanna walk e baby.	Hungry.
Wanna put it on.	Wet.
Wanna go ride it.	Different.
Want mom get off.	Enough.
	Else.
Daddy take her. (referring to self)	More.
Help with the apple.	Minute.
Can't get the teddy bear.	Brushing.
Teddy bear the bath.	Hiding.
	Baby crying.
Too much carrots on the dish.	
	Hold.
Move it around.	Hold it.
Clean e bottom.	Dropped it.
	Bring it.
Put ne sofa.	
Put in eye.	Falling.
	Fell.
Mommy wear hat.	
Mommy smell it.	Talk.
Mommy read the book.	Talking.
Mommy sit down.	
	Wash 'em.
Find Becky.	Shirt on.
See Becky in the morning.	Teddy up.
Becky is nice.	Mommy shoe.
Saw Becky and goats.	

Source: Thal and Bates, "Relationships between language and cognition" (1988b)

"Where — went?"). In fact, to the surprise and amusement of her mother and the experimenter, S produced a novel juxtaposition of two established formulae during one of the experimental sessions: "No way, you monkey!" Thal et al. tentatively conclude that the apparent dissociation between grammar and lexicon illustrated by M and S actually reflects a style dimension based on the length of the unit that can be retained in memory. Both M and S appear to produce analyzed utterances, and both seem to use a slot-filler approach to combining words. Examples of S's formulaic combinations were noted above. M's few two-word utterances were typical pivot-style utterances made with two pronouns (see table 4.3), including "hold it," "keep it," "pour it," and "hide it." What was different between the two children was not so much analytic versus holistic processing but, rather, the size of the units which they were able to combine.

Children with focal brain injury

For a number of years, we have studied the first stages of language development in children with unilateral damage to the right or left hemisphere, injuries that were acquired prenatally or before six months of age (i.e. before the onset of meaningful speech). It has been known for some time that children with this etiology go on (more often than not) to achieve normal or near-normal levels of language ability, despite damage to areas that often result in irreversible aphasia when they occur in an adult (Lenneberg, 1967; Hecaen, 1967; Rasmussen and Milner, 1977; Woods and Teuber, 1978). Hence, this group of children provides compelling evidence for the plasticity of neural organization for language in our species. However, this does not mean that the newborn brain is equipotential for language (for reviews, see Satz, Strauss, and Whitaker, 1990; Stiles and Thal, 1993; Eisele and Aram, this volume). Current evidence suggests a compromise between two theoretical extremes (i.e. irreversible determinism v. total equipotentiality). There are initial biases, which affect the timing and nature of early language, but eventually most of these children find alternative modes of behavioral and / or neural organization that are sufficient to sustain adequate (if not optimal) language development.

In this section, we will review evidence on the early stages of language in children with focal brain injury with two purposes in mind: (1) to uncover further evidence for variations in rate and style and dissociations between components, at the extremes of normal development, and (2) to provides some insights into the neural bases of the patterns that have been observed in other populations.

Rate of development

As a group, children with focal brain injury are delayed in phonology (Marchman, Miller, and Bates, 1991), and in lexical development (Thal et al.,

1991) and MLU (research in progress). These group delays have been found to continue through 44 months of age (our most recent data point). However, there are exceptions among individual children, including some who fall within the normal range from the very beginning. In the largest sample that we have studied to date, 38 children between 16–31 months of age have been assessed with the vocabulary scale of the CDI: Toddlers. For the group as a whole, including those with left and right hemisphere damage, 16 out of 38 children (approximately one third of the sample) have vocabulary scores in the bottom 10th percentile. Although this is far more than we would expect by chance (p < 0.001), it also means that most children with focal brain injury fail to meet the criterion used to define late talkers. When attention is restricted only to the children with left hemisphere damage, 13 out of 25 children (one half of the ample) fall in the bottom 10th percentile. Obviously left hemisphere damage is a serious risk factor for early language delay, but it is also true that half of even this "high risk" sample falls within the normal range, including a substantial number of children with scores well above the median.

We are now trying to determine those sites within the left hemisphere that are most often associated with a serious initial language delay, to determine whether and to what extent the "risk sites" map onto findings from brain behavior mapping in adult aphasics. So far it is clear that these results will be approximate at best. Some sites may be more important than others (e.g. sites surrounding Broca's and Wernicke's areas). However, we have seen individual cases of children with injuries that involve all of the tissue in and around the classical language areas, who nevertheless display normal levels of language comprehension and production (see also Dall'Oglio, Bates, Volterra, Di Capua, and Pezzini, 1992; Feldman, Holland, Kemp, and Janosky, 1992; Vargha-Khadem, Isaacs, Van der Werf, Robb, and Wilson, 1992). These findings on the earliest stages of development in children with focal brain injury fit with a well-established finding on the long-term sequelae in this population: more often than not, these children go on to develop language skills that are well within the normal range, testimony to the extraordinary plasticity of the human brain for its most important cognitive skill.

Dissociations between comprehension and production

Within the focal lesion population, we find some of the same strong dissociations between comprehension and production reported for the late talker sample. At the same time, we also find children who are impaired in both modalities, and children who appear to have escaped unimpaired in both receptive and expressive language.

One of the first questions that we have asked of this population pertains to the neural sites associated with deficits in comprehension v. production. The answers to date are mixed (Thal et al., 1991; Wulfeck, Trauner, and Tallal, 1991), but they do suggest some differentiation in the neural mechanisms that underlie development in these two modalities. Comprehension deficits occur with damage to either hemisphere, and are (if anything) somewhat more common in children with unilateral right hemisphere damage. Hence, we tentatively conclude that early comprehension is a "whole-brain activity," i.e. a bilaterally distributed process that may require more right hemisphere mediation during the early stages of learning than we see in adults with equivalent forms of brain injury. This is, in fact, quite compatible with the electrophysiological studies of comprehension and production in normal children that we reported in section 2 (Mills et al., 1991, and in press).

Production deficits do appear to be somewhat more likely with damage to the left hemisphere, although the intrahemispheric sites associated with initial delays are variable from one study to another. In the study by Thal et al., (1991) delays in expressive vocabulary were equally likely between 12–16 months with left or right hemisphere damage, and with damage to both anterior and posterior sites on the left. In other words, brain damage is certainly not a good thing to have, and it is hard to get expressive language off the ground with any form of cortical or subcortical damage. By contrast, between 16–36 months, there was a clear association between continued expressive delays and damage to left hemisphere sites. In the Thal et al. sample, these delays in recovery of expressive language were greater in children with left posterior damage – a peculiar reversal of the usual story for adult aphasics (where damage to frontal sites around Broca's area tends to result in nonfluent aphasia). However, in our more recent studies with an expanded sample, delays in recovery from expressive deficits are associated with specific sites in both the anterior and posterior quadrants of the left hemisphere.

These results are complicated by a number of factors, including (a) the absence of a solid database on normal brain development to anchor analyses of damage to specific lesion sites (see Bates et al., 1992, for a discussion of this point), and (b) confounding factors like seizure activity and seizure medications that plague research on children with focal brain injury. For the moment, we must be content with only one tentative conclusion: dissociations between comprehension and production do occur in the focal lesion sample, and they appear to be associated with different patterns of focal brain injury. However, the brain–behavior correlations observed in early language development do not map consistently onto the correlations that are observed in adults with analogous lesions.

Dissociations between lexicon and grammar

In contrast with the strong dissociations between comprehension and production that appear in the focal lesion population, we find (once again) virtually no evidence for a dissociation between grammar and the lexicon – at least not within the period from 20–36 months when the foundations of grammar are laid down. Indeed, within our latest sample of toddlers with focal brain injury, the correlation between vocabulary and grammar scores falls between +0.70– +0.92, depending on the subset of children who are included or excluded from the sample. Thus, we may conclude that early grammatical development is lexically driven in this population as well. However, we leave open the possibility that a dissociation may appear at later stages of development, when grammar must become a fluent and automatized skill.

Variations in style

One of the first questions that we are often asked when we lecture on individual variations in style revolves around the potential neural bases of the analytic/holistic contrast. For example, it has been argued that the right hemisphere of the normal adult brain plays an important role in the integration of perceptual information (including but not restricted to visual–spatial patterns) into a global configuration, while the left hemisphere plays a more important role in the extraction of perceptual detail (Robertson and Delis, 1986; Lamb, Robertson, and Knight, 1990; Dukette and Stiles, 1991). By analogy to this analytic/holistic division in perceptual analysis, it has been suggested to us that children who evidence a holistic approach to language may make greater use of right hemisphere processes, while children who adopt an analytic style rely to a greater extent on left hemisphere processes.

A different neural basis for stylistic variation has been suggested for children with left hemisphere damage. In particular, it has been pointed out that children at the extreme analytic end of the normal distribution produce telegraphic speech with a high proportion of content words and very few function words (e.g. "Mommy sock") – very much like the speech that is characteristic of adult patients with Broca's aphasia. By the same token, children at the extreme holistic end of the normal distribution tend to produce utterances with a relatively high ratio of function words to content words (e.g. "I wan' dat") – very much like the speech that is characteristic of adult patients with Wernicke's aphasia. To the extent that (a) Broca's aphasia is correlated with left frontal injury, and (b) Wernicke's aphasia is correlated with left posterior injury, it has been proposed that the analytic/holistic dimension in early language learning could reflect differential use or rate of maturation in anterior v. posterior regions of the left hemisphere, with "little words" handled by the regions around Broca's area and content words mediated by left posterior cortex.

Our evidence on this point is meager and inconclusive on both these points, but to the extent that it can be used at all, it suggests exactly the opposite conclusion on both counts. In general, we find the same mix of vocabulary composition scores in our focal lesion population that we find in the normal range, and in both our late talker and early talker groups. Nor do we find a strong association between language style and lesion type, organized by side (left v. right) or site (left anterior v. left posterior). However, the study by Thal et al. found significantly less use of closed-class morphemes in children with injuries involving left posterior cortex – in direct contradiction to both the interhemispheric hypothesis (right hemisphere = holistic; left hemisphere =

analytic) and the intrahemispheric hypothesis (left anterior = function words; left posteriors = content words). A more definitive answer regarding the cortical basis of analytic v. holistic style will await studies that use a broader range of measures, including laboratory analyses of imitativeness, phonological precision, and speech rate.

Williams Syndrome and Down Syndrome

A final source of information on the extremes of variation comes from children with two dramatically different forms of mental retardation, Williams Syndrome and Down Syndrome. Children with Down Syndrome are markedly delayed in the acquisition of language, but more importantly, their language abilities at virtually every stage (including the adult steady state) fall below the levels that we would expect based upon their mental age (Miller, 1987b; Bellugi, Marks, Bihrle, and Sabo, 1988; Bellugi, Sabo, and Vaid, 1988; Miller, 1988; Bellugi, Bihrle, Jernigan, Trauner, and Doherty, 1990; Jernigan and Bellugi, 1990; Reilly, Klima, and Bellugi, 1991; Bellugi, Bihrle, Neville, Jernigan, and Doherty, 1992; Wang, Doherty, Hesselink, and Bellugi, 1992; Wang, Hesselink, Jernigan, Doherty, and Bellugi, 1992; Mervis and Bertrand, 1993; Bellugi, Wang, and Jernigan, in press; Miller, in press a & b). Furthermore, they appear to be especially impaired in the use of bound and free grammatical morphemes, constituting a form of congenital agrammatism that is even more severe than the selective impairments in grammatical morphology reported for children with Specific Language Impairment (see above). By contrast, older children and adults with Williams Syndrome display levels of linguistic knowledge and language use that are surprisingly good when they are compared with the low levels of performance that the same individuals show on most measures of visual–spatial cognition, problem solving, and reasoning (Bihrle, Bellugi, Delis, and Marks, 1989; Bellugi et al., 1992; Karmiloff-Smith and Grant, 1993; Carey, Johnson, and Levine, 1993; Mervis and Bertrand, 1993).

Before we go into details on the early stages of language learning in these two groups, we should point out that older children and adults with Williams Syndrome cannot be characterized as "language savants," where savants are defined as retarded individuals who show skills far above normal in a single domain. Indeed, those studies that have used normal controls have shown that the linguistic performance of Williams subjects is invariably below their *chronological age* – which is, of course, not surprising for subjects with an IQ score around 50. When they are compared with younger normals matched for *mental age*, the picture is mixed: they perform above mental age controls on some measures (e.g. the Peabody Picture Vocabulary Test, word fluency, and a number of measures of grammar), while they look very much like mental age controls on others (e.g. the Wisc R). The excitement that research on Williams Syndrome has engendered in recent years hinges not on their absolute levels of performance, but on the striking profiles of sparing, deviance, and delay that they display across different linguistic and nonlinguistic tasks

– a profile that challenges many existing theories of the relationship between language and cognition. On some linguistic measures their performance is not only superior to mental age controls, but qualitatively different from normal of any age. For example, on word fluency tasks (e.g. "Name all the animals you can think of") they tend to produce low-frequency items like "ibex" and "brontosaurus" that are never produced by normals or by other individuals with mental retardation. Even more compelling evidence for qualitative variation comes from a story telling task (Reilly, Klima, and Bellugi, 1991), where Williams Syndrome children and adolescents were compared with normal controls and with IQ matched subjects with Down Syndrome. In retelling the same story to the same audience, normal children and Down Syndrome individuals tend to produce succinct stories with relatively flat affect, stories that get shorter and less interesting with every retelling. By contrast, the Williams Syndrome subjects produce novel, colorful, and emotional descriptions on every trial, with no loss of enthusiasm. Aside from their command of the grammar, their stories abound with rich prosody and "audience hookers" like "You know what?" or "And then guess what happened!" This level and style of performance has not been observed in any other normal or clinical group. The peculiar patterns of sparing and impairment that are observed within the language domain in Williams Syndrome are complemented by equally interesting patterns of sparing and impairment outside of language. For example, although they show severe impairments on most visual–spatial tasks, they are remarkably good at face recognition (Bellugi, Wang, and Jernigan, in press; see also Bertrand, Mervis, Rice, and Adamson, 1993), surpassing their age matched controls on some measures. And although they perform poorly on virtually all reasoning and problem solving tasks, they are far less impaired on so-called "theory of mind" tasks that requite an ability to reason about the intentions and plans of other human beings (Karmiloff-Smith and Grant, 1993).

Taken together, these contrasts between Down Syndrome and Williams Syndrome provide an important challenge to interactive theories of language and cognition, and appear at first glance to provide considerable support for the autonomy of language from other cognitive systems (Karmiloff-Smith, 1992; Bellugi, Wang, and Jernigan, in press). However, when we compare the early stages of language development in these two clinical groups, a somewhat more subtle picture emerges.

Rate of development

A number of studies have begun to explore the early stages of language development in children with Williams Syndrome. In every case these children are significantly delayed and the developmental period is prolonged (Thal, Bates, and Bellugi, 1989; Mervis and Bertrand, 1993). In other words, despite their ultimate proficiency with language, children with Williams Syndrome are late talkers. This has become exceedingly clear in a recent study by Bellugi, Bates, and colleagues (research in progress), who have used the MacArthur

CDI to obtain early language data from more than 130 children with Williams and Down Syndrome, between one and six years of age.

In the period of development covered by the CDI: Infants (equivalent to normal children between 8–16 months), both the Williams and the Down samples are delayed by many months or years on both word comprehension and word production. The predicted separation between the two clinical groups does not emerge until the period of development covered by the CDI: Toddlers (equivalent to normal children between 16–30 months), around the time when grammar begins (see below). At this point, both groups are approximately two years older than normal language matched controls.

The late appearance of language in Williams Syndrome sets interesting limits on the degree of dissociation that can be observed between linguistic and nonlinguistic skills. We tentatively suggest that the similarities between Williams and Down Syndrome in the first stages of language development, and the late onset of language (both vocabulary and grammar) in both these groups, are evidence in favor of a revised version of the cognitive prerequisites to language view proposed in the 1970s (for reviews, see Bates and Snyder, 1987; Bates and Thal, 1991; Bates, Thal, and Marchman, 1991). Specifically, we propose the following hypothesis:

Language cannot get off the ground until some minimal set of cognitive infrastructures are finally in place, including cognitive structures that are necessary though (perhaps) not sufficient for the establishment of reference and predication.

Dissociations between comprehension and production

Although there is considerable variability within both these clinical groups, we do not find more comprehension/production dissociations in either group than we would expect by chance (i.e. no more than we would expect if these children were drawn from the normal population). Furthermore, there are no significant differences between the two groups in comprehension/production profiles. The general picture appears to be one of delay rather than deviance, at least along this dimension.

Dissociations between grammar and the lexicon

In contrast with their findings for the Infant scale, Bellugi and colleagues report a sharp divergence between Williams Syndrome and Down Syndrome children during the period in which grammar is finally under way. However, the direction of this disparity is interesting, and perhaps somewhat surprising. Within the Williams group, grammatical development appears to be paced by vocabulary size, in the normal fashion. In fact, when these children are compared with lexically matched normal controls from the CDI sample, the relationship between grammar and vocabulary size is identical, following the nonlinear accelerating function described in section 2 (see figure 4.10). In short, there is no evidence for a dissociation between grammatical and lexical development in the Williams group – at least not in this early phase of grammatical development.

By contrast, data for the Down Syndrome sample provide our first evidence to date for a significant dissociation between grammar and the lexicon. In particular, Down Syndrome children score significantly *below* the grammatical levels displayed by normal children (or Williams Syndrome children) matched for vocabulary size. We tentatively conclude that lexical size is a *necessary but not sufficient* condition for the acquisition of grammatical function words, the onset of word combinations, and growth in sentence complexity. This finding is compatible with reports on the selective impairment of grammar displayed by older Down Syndrome children, although the basis of the impairment is still unknown. It could be due to impairment of some domain-specific grammatical processor (e.g. Pinker, 1991), or, alternatively, it may derive from aspects of information processing that are only indirectly related to grammar. For example, Wang and Bellugi (1993) have presented evidence from older Williams and Down Syndrome individuals suggesting that there may be a double dissociation in the two groups between auditory digit span (significantly better in Williams Syndrome) and visual short-term memory on the Corsi sequential block touching task (significantly better in Down Syndrome). If Down Syndrome individuals suffer from a selective impairment in aspects of auditory processing (superimposed on their more general cognitive deficits), then it is not unreasonable to infer that they may be selectively impaired in the ability to detect, store, and/or retrieve aspects of the auditory input that are low in phonological salience or stress (Leonard et al., 1992) and low in visual imagery (Goodglass and Menn, 1985).

It would be premature to conclude from these data that grammar is perfectly normal in Williams Syndrome but impaired in Down Syndrome. Studies of older Williams Syndrome individuals have uncovered subtle but significant deficits in certain aspects of grammatical morphology, including prepositions (Rubba and Klima, 1991) and grammatical gender (a study of French-speaking Williams Syndrome individuals by Karmiloff-Smith and Grant, 1993). There is still a great deal to be learned about the patterns of sparing and impairment that occur inside and outside of language in this puzzling syndrome (Carey and Grant, 1993; Mervis and Bertrand, 1993; Bellugi, Wang, and Jernigan, in press). For our purposes here, we may conclude that grammar does not develop ahead of the lexicon in the early phases of development, in any of the syndromes that we studied to date including Williams Syndrome. However, the Down Syndrome data show that dissociations in the opposite direction can and do occur, with grammar falling behind vocabulary growth.

Variations in style

Older children and adults with Williams Syndrome produce language that is novel and creative, although it is occasionally bizarre or inappropriate from a pragmatic point of view. They also show better receptive language skills (including judgments of grammaticality and interpretation of reversible passives) than we would expect on a formulaic/echolalic interpretation of their spontaneous speech. We can, therefore, reject the hypothesis that Williams Syndrome children are little taperecorders, spewing back sentences that they heard the day before (i.e. "cocktail party syndrome" – Tew, 1975). In other words, Williams Syndrome does not constitute an extreme variant of holistic/formulaic style as it was originally conceived.

On the other hand, it should be clear from our review in section 3 that the formulaic/echolalic view also fails to capture the speech produced by normal children at the holistic end of the analytic/holistic distribution. To be sure, there was an initial effort to characterize this dimension as a continuum from spontaneous production to imitative speech, and there is a small amount of evidence suggesting that holistic-style children imitate more often than children at the analytic/telegraphic end of the distribution (e.g. immediate imitation of nonsense words at 20 months of age in Bates et al., 1988). However, other studies have shown that children who are high in referential style imitate more often when they are presented with a series of new names for novel objects (Leonard et al., 1991). In short, imitativeness may be a correlate or fellow traveler along this mysterious dimension, but it does not define the set of distinctions reviewed in section 3. We have proposed instead that the distinction between analytic and holistic style has more to do with factors like auditory short-term memory and the size of the unit a child can manage at a given point in time, degree of perceptual acuity (which help some children to tune into inflections and function words at a relatively early point in lexical development), and/or a tradeoff between speed and accuracy in early speech production. Armed with this refinement of the analytic/holistic dimension, let us reconsider the applicability of this dimension to language development in children with Williams and Down Syndrome.

In an ongoing study by Ursula Bellugi and colleagues of William and Down Syndromes using the MacArthur CDI, parental reports have been analyzed to determine whether the two groups differ significantly in vocabulary composition, including referential style (controlling for vocabulary level) and closed-class style (in the period before 400 words, i.e. before the emergence of productive grammar). Results suggest that there is considerable variability within *both* groups along *both* of these dimensions, but no more than we would expect if children were drawn from the normal population (i.e. no more than we find in language matched controls), and there were no significant differences between the two groups. In other words, there is no evidence in support of the idea that Down Syndrome children display a variant of analytic style while Williams Syndrome children display an extreme version of holistic style. On the other hand, as we pointed out in section 3, vocabulary composition scores offer an indirect and inadequate view of this important dimension of variation. More interesting information would come from studies that include repetition/imitation of nonsense words, phonological precision and consistency, frequency of certain construction types in spontaneous speech, auditory short-term memory, and so forth. In these respects, the predicted analogy may still hold (see also Thal, Bates, and Bellugi, 1989). As we noted above, Williams Syndrome individuals perform significantly better than Down Syndrome children in an auditory memory task. Karmiloff-Smith and Grant (1993) have also shown that older individuals with Williams Syndrome are actually more proficient than age matched normal controls in a task that requires immediate repetition of novel words – even though they perform more poorly than controls in the assignment of grammatical gender for the same new words. In other words, we think the analytic/holistic dissociation may be fruitfully pursued in research on Williams and Down Syndrome, but only with the caveats that we have described here.

There is, of course, another possibility: the peculiar profiles of linguistic and nonlinguistic ability displayed by older children and adults with Williams Syndrome may reflect a qualitatively different form of brain organization for language, unlike anything that we have seen in any other normal or abnormal population (Jernigan and Bellugi, 1990; Jernigan, Bellugi, Sowell, Doherty, and Hesselink, 1993). If this proves to be the case, then evidence from Williams Syndrome will have greatly expanded our understanding of variation and plasticity in language development.

Conclusion

We have reviewed evidence for individual differences in early language development in normal children, and in several contrasting clinical populations. Some consistent themes emerge from this survey.

First, there is enormous variability in rate of development during the passage from first words to grammar, in each and every one of our measures. These variations are so stable that they cannot be ascribed to noise, and so large that they are hard to explain with any single causal factor, maturational or environmental. We do not pretend to have exhausted the universe of possible biological and/or demographic causes for this variation, but we think it likely that a combination of factors will be required to explain individual differences of this magnitude (see also Huttenlocher et al., 1991; Hampson and Nelson, 1993). This includes a need for crosslinguistic studies of developmental variation, to complement crosslinguistic studies that compare the sequences and central tendencies that are observed in different language families (Slobin, 1985b, vols 1 and 2; Slobin, 1992 vol. 3).

Second, we find robust evidence for a dissociation between comprehension and production in several normal and abnormal populations. A possible explanation for this dissociation comes from independent evidence suggesting that the two modalities are correlated with different nonlinguistic factors (in particular, comprehension is strongly associated with several different measures of cognitive development during the first and second year), and may be mediated by different neural systems (bilateral mechanisms for word comprehension, specialized left hemisphere mechanisms for word production).

By contrast, we find a remarkably strong association between lexical and grammatical development in the period from 16–30 months of age (or its developmental equivalent in clinical populations). For example, there is a powerful nonlinear relationship between vocabulary size and the appearance of word combinations (usually between 50–100 words), and an equally strong exponential relationship between vocabulary size and increases in utterance length and sentence complexity (with a "take-off point" somewhere between 300–600 words). This relationship is also observed in late talkers, early talkers, children with focal brain injury, and children with Williams Syndrome. The robust nonlinear association between grammar and vocabulary size is predicted by recent connectionist models of morphological development (Plunkett and Marchman, 1993), and it is consistent with theories that underscore the role of perceptual and/or semantic bootstrapping or mass-action effects (Goodman and Nusbaum, 1994; O'Grady, 1987). We should point out, however, that this finding does not preclude the possibility of a grammar/semantics dissociation at some later point in development, when grammar achieves the status of a fluent, automatic skill (e.g. Marchman, Bates, Burkhardt, and Good, 1991).

Down Syndrome children are the only group that we have seen so far in which there is a clear dissociation between grammar and vocabulary during this stage of language learning. For these children, early grammar falls far behind vocabulary growth, suggesting that lexical size is a necessary but not sufficient condition for the extraction of grammatical regularities. The nature of the limiting factor that creates the grammatical deficit in Down Syndrome is still unknown, but it may be related to limitations in auditory short-term memory (Wang and Bellugi, 1993).

We also reviewed the history and current status of a peculiar dimension of qualitative or stylistic variation that travels under many names. The most common name for this dimension of variation is "analytic v. holistic style," although our review suggests that this may be an unfortunate choice of terms. To be sure, this dimension of individual differences cuts across specific ages and content domains (i.e. phonology, vocabulary, grammar), and it does seem to have something to do with the size and precision of the unit that children can handle (or prefer to use). But it has proven frustratingly difficult to operationalize this dimension (if it is indeed a single dimension). There are some serious confounds between developmental and stylistic variance in the vocabulary composition scores that have been used to assess language styles in previous studies. Propensity for imitation is clearly an associate of the style dimension, but it does not define that dimension. Furthermore, as several studies have shown (Thal and Bates, 1988b; Pine and Lieven, 1990; Thal, Bates, Zappia, and Oroz, 1994), holistic style is not the same thing as frozen or formulaic speech, and can be a route into grammatical productivity. Our findings for children with focal brain injury offer little help in uncovering the neural bases of this dimension. The most obvious neural hypotheses receive on support in our results to date (e.g. identification of holistic style with the right hemisphere; identification of telegraphic style with limitations in Broca's area). The contrasting profiles presented by Williams Syndrome and Down Syndrome hold some promise in unravelling the basis of this mysterious contrast in learning styles, but most of the important work still lies before us. We have proposed that future work in this direction should focus not on simple measures of vocabulary composition, but on processing dimensions like auditory short-term memory, perceptual acuity, unit size, and a speed–accuracy tradeoff in real-time language use. Needless to say, these are difficult variables to study in children under three years of age.

One conclusion seems uncontroversial: the Average Child is a fiction, a descriptive convenience like the Average Man or the Average Woman. Theories of language development can no longer rely on this mythical being. Any theory worth the name will have to account for the variations that are reliably observed in early language learning.

NOTES

1 Although the mean is higher at 16 months for the CDI: Toddlers list than for the same age on the CDI: Infants list, the medians are quite similar: 44 and 40 words, respectively. The skewed nature of the distribution is responsible for the differences in means.

2 To ensure normality and linearity of relationship, both complexity and MLU were log-transformed. Note also that the intercept in this formula is greater than 1.0, due to the fact that a child may receive a complexity score of zero because the child is still in the single word stage, or because the child is combining words, but still producing the less advanced form in each sentence pair.

5 Computational Analysis of Interactions

BRIAN MACWHINNEY

Child language research thrives on naturalistic data – data collected from spontaneous interactions in naturally occurring situations. However, the process of collecting, transcribing, and analyzing naturalistic data is extremely time consuming and often quite unreliable. One of the major methodological developments in the field of child language research over the past decade has been the introduction of computerized systems for dealing with the transcription, coding, and analysis of spontaneous production data. One such system – the Child Language Data Exchange System (CHILDES) – will be our focus in this chapter. We will begin by reviewing the background to the formation of the CHILDES system. Next, we will examine the basic CHILDES tools, and the ways these tools can be used to address particular research goals. The chapter will then explore a new range of analytic capabilities planned for the next few years.

1 Background

The dream of establishing an archive of child language transcript data has a long history, and there were several individual efforts along such lines early on. For example, Roger Brown's (1973) transcripts from the children called Adam, Eve, and Sarah were typed onto stencils from which multiple copies were duplicated. The extra copies have been lent to and analyzed by a wide variety of researchers – some of them (Moerk, 1983) attempting to disprove the conclusions drawn from those data by Brown himself! In addition, of course, to the copies lent out or given away for use by other researchers, a master copy – never lent and in principle never marked on – has been retained in Roger Brown's files as the ultimate historical archive. In this traditional model, everyone took his copy of the transcript home, developed his/her own coding scheme, marked codes and tallies directly on the transcript, wrote a paper about the results and, if very polite, sent a copy to Roger. The original database remained untouched. The nature of each individual's coding scheme and the relationship among any set of different coding schemes could never be fully plumbed.

The dissemination of mimeographed and photocopied transcript data cast a spotlight on the weak underbelly of our analytic techniques in language acquisition research. As we began to compare handwritten and typewritten transcripts, problems in transcription methodology, coding schemes, and cross-investigator reliability became more apparent. But, just as these new problems were coming to light, a major technological opportunity was emerging in the shape of the powerful, affordable microcomputer. Microcomputer word-processing systems and database programs allowed researchers to enter transcript data into computer files which could then be easily duplicated, edited, and analyzed by standard data-processing techniques. The possibility of utilizing shared transcription formats, shared codes, and shared analysis programs shone at first like a faint glimmer on the horizon, against the fog and gloom of handwritten tallies, fuzzy dittoes, and idiosyncratic coding schemes. Slowly, against this backdrop, the idea of a computerized data exchange system for the study of child language development began to emerge.

In 1984 a meeting of 16 child language researchers formally launched the CHILDES system with Brian MacWhinney and Catherine Snow as co-directors. The initial focus on the CHILDES project was on the collection of a nonstandardized database of computerized corpora. Between 1984 and 1986, our work focused on the assembly of a large computerized database of transcripts. As the database grew, it soon became apparent that researchers needed more than a disparate set of corpora transcribed in a confusing diversity of styles. They needed a consistent set of standards both for the analysis of old data and for the collection and transcription of new corpora. During the period from 1986 to 1991, the CHILDES system addressed these needs by developing three separate, but integrated, tools. The first tool is the database itself, the second tool is the CHAT transcription and coding format, and the third tool is the CLAN package of analysis programs. These three tools are presented in detail in MacWhinney (1991a) and illustrated through practical examples in Sokolov and Snow (1994). Researchers who plan to make use of the CHILDES tools will want to consult both of these resources.

The three major components of the CHILDES system are the database, the CHAT transcription systems, and the CLAN programs. The next three sections describe these three basic tools.

2 The Database

The first major tool in the CHILDES workbench is the database itself. Researchers across the globe can now reach the CHILDES database through the

InterNet, retrieving huge amounts of consistently coded child language transcript data. In effect, researchers now have access to the results of nearly a
hundred major research projects in over a dozen languages across the last 25
years. Using the CHILDES database, a researcher can directly test a vast range
of empirical hypotheses against either this whole database or some logically
defined subset.

The database includes a wide variety of language samples from a wide
range of ages and situations. Learners include children with language impairments, adults with aphasia, second language learners, and bilingual children.
Most importantly, almost all of the data represent real spontaneous interactions
in natural contexts, rather than some simple list of sentences or test results.
Although more than half of the data come from English speakers, there is also
a significant component of non-English data. All of the major corpora have
been formatted into the CHAT standard and have been checked for syntactic
accuracy. The total size of the database is now approximately 160 million
characters (160 MB). The corpora are divided into six major directories: English,
non-English, narratives, books, language impairments, and bilingual acquisition.
In addition to the basic texts on language acquisition, there is a database from
the Communicative Development Inventory (Dale, 1990) and a bibliographic
database for child language studies (Higginson and MacWhinney, 1990).

2.1   Access to the database

Membership in CHILDES is open. However, members are asked to abide by
the rules of the system. In particular, users should not distribute copies of
programs or files without permission; they should abide by the stated wishes
of the contributors of the data; and they should acknowledge properly all uses
of the data and the programs. Any article that uses the data from a particular
corpus must cite a reference from the contributor of that corpus. The exact
reference is given in a file called *00readme.doc* which is distributed along with
each data set. On the top level of the database is the general 00readme.doc file
that requests that users also cite MacWhinney (1991) and MacWhinney and
Snow (1985) when using the programs and data in published work.

All of the CHILDES materials can be obtained without charge by anonymous FTP to poppy.psy.cmu.edu. InterNet connections that can reach
poppy.psy.cmu.edu in Pittsburgh or atila-ftp.uia.be in Antwerp are now widely
available at universities both in the United States and abroad. The procedure
for transferring files depends on the type of machine you are using and the
type of files you wish to retrieve. However, in all cases, you first need to
follow certain basic rules for anonymous FTP connections:

1   Connect to poppy.psy.cmu.edu (128.2.248.42) using anonymous FTP.
    If you get an answer from poppy, then you know that you have
    InterNet access. If you do not get an answer, you may not have access
    or access may be temporarily broken.

2   When you receive the request for a username, enter "anonymous." Type in your name as a password.

3   If you want to retrieve data files, type "cd childes" to move to the /childes directory. If you want to retrieve the CLAN programs, type "cd clan" to move to the /clan directory.

4   Type "ls" to view the directory structure and use "cd" again as needed. It is easy to confuse directories with files. When in doubt type "cd filename." If that works, it was a directory. If not, it was a file.

5   Type "binary" to set the transfer type. Although some of the files you wish to retrieve may be text files, the binary mode will work across all file types and it is safest to use it as your default transfer type.

6   Use the "get" command to pull files onto your machine.

7   When you are finished, type "bye" or "quit" to close the connection.

In some cases the machine that is running FTP is not the final destination for the files. For example, some users run a program like Kermit from a DOS machine to connect to a UNIX machine and then use the UNIX machine to reach poppy.psy.cmu.edu. Although the FTP transfer is usually reliable, the second transfer through Kermit is more often error prone and slow. It is better if you can run FTP from the machine that will be the final destination for the files.

Once the files are on your local machine, you must untar them. This means that before you can look at the data, you will need to get a copy of the TAR program. TAR is always available on UNIX systems. If you are running FTP from a Macintosh or a DOS machine, you can retrieve a copy of the TAR program from poppy.psy.cmu.edu. The DOS tar.exe program can be found in the /clan/msdos directory and the Macintosh tar.hqx file can be found in the /clan/macintosh directory. The Macintosh version of TAR must be decoded using binhex 4.0 before it can be used. Once the TAR application is debinhexed, it functions as a normal Macintosh application with menus that are fairly easy to follow. There is also a file called "tar.doc" describing TAR in greater detail.

Once you have retrieved and installed a copy of TAR, you are ready to untar the CHILDES files you have retrieved. The UNIX or DOS TAR command you need to issue is something like this:

tar -xvf eng.tar

Untarring the files will recreate the original directory structure. Each corpus has been placed into a separate tar file.

In addition to the tar files for the database, you can retrieve the CLAN programs and the CHILDES/BIB database from poppy.psy.cmu.edu also through anonymous FTP. If you are running FTP from a Macintosh, you can retrieve the most recent version of CLAN along with certain Macintosh utilities. You should connect to poppy.psy.cmu.edu and use cd clan/macintosh to move into the directory with Macintosh programs and utilities. These files are all in binhexed format, as indicated by the .hqx extension. The basic CLAN program is clan.hqx. The file manual.hqx has the CHILDES manual in MS-Word format. The Macintosh tar program is in tar.hqx. Once the files are on your machine, use binhex 4.0 to decode them. Do not use binhex 5.0. When transferring CLAN, also remember to transfer the text files in /clan/lib. DOS users can also use FTP to retrieve the most recent version of CLAN from poppy.psy.cmu.edu. Get all the clan.tar file from the /clan/msdos directory and untar the file.

For users without access to the InterNet, as well as for those who want a convenient way of storing the database, we have published (MacWhinney, 1994) a CD-ROM in High Sierra format which can be read by Macintosh, UNIX, and MS-DOS machines which have a CD-ROM reader. The disk contains the whole database, the programs, and the CHILDES/BIB system. One directory contains the materials in Macintosh format and the other contains the materials in UNIX/DOS format. If you have been thinking about adding CD-ROM capabilities to your system, the availability of this CD-ROM will provide you with an excellent excuse to make the addition. There is no charge for the CD-ROM, but you will have to spend $400 or so for a CD-ROM reader. This unit fits directly into the SCSI port on the Mac. For the IBM-PC, it requires an adaptor card that will provide a SCSI port. Often these are sold along with the CD-ROM reader. CD-ROM access is relatively slow and you cannot write CLAN output files to the CD-ROM, so you may want to copy over particular CHILDES corpora to your hard drive. However, it is possible to run CLAN programs on files on the CD-ROM and to then direct the output to your hard disk. A major advantage of the CD-ROM is that the entire database can be stored on a single stable disk.

For further information on changes to the database and programs, researchers can subscribe to the info-childes@andrew.cmu.edu electronic bulletin board.

2.2   *Reformatting of the database*

All of the current corpora are in good CHAT format. This means that they can pass through the CLAN program called CHECK without producing any errors. However, only a few of the most recent corpora were entered directly into CHAT. The process of converting the older corpora into CHAT required years of careful work. Some corpora had to be scanned into computer files from typewritten sheets. Other corpora were already computerized, but in a wide variety of transcription systems. For each of these datasets, we had to translate the project-specific codes and formats into CHAT. Several sets of files were translated from SALT (Miller and Chapman, 1982–93) using the SALTIN program. For other corpora, special purpose reformatting programs had to be written. The fact that these transcripts now all pass through CHECK without error means that all of the files now have correct headers, correct listings of participants, and correct matches of coding tiers to main lines. Each main line has only one utterance and every utterance ends with a legal terminator. There are no incorrect symbols in the middle of words and all paired delimiters are correctly matched. However, we cannot yet guarantee that the files are consistently coded on the level of individual words. This level of consistency checking requires processing through the MOR program which will be discussed later.

3 CHAT

The most conceptually difficult task we faced in developing the CHILDES system was the formulation of the CHAT transcription system. From 1984 to 1990, during the period which we now refer to as the period of protoCHAT, we explored a variety of transcription forms. In 1990 we began to finalize the shape of CHAT until it reached the more stable form published in the manual in 1991 (MacWhinney, 1991). Users have expressed happiness with the current status of CHAT and the fact that virtually no changes have been made to the basic conventions since 1990. The finalization of CHAT allowed us to sharpen the workings of the CLAN CHECK program so that it now constitutes a computational implementation of the whole CHAT system.

No coding or transcription system can ever fully satisfy all the needs of all researchers. Nor can any transcription system ever hope to fully capture the richness of interactional behavior. Despite its inevitable limitations, the availability of CHAT as a lingua franca for transcription both within the Program Project and within the general field of child language research has already led to solid improvements in data exchange, data analysis, and scientific precision.

3.1 Key features of CHAT

The CHAT system is designed to function on at least two levels. The simplest form of CHAT is called minCHAT. Use of minCHAT requires a minimum of coding decisions. This type of transcription looks very much like the intuitive types of transcription generally in use in child language and discourse analysis. A fragment of a file in minCHAT looks like this:

```
@Begin
@Participants:   ROS Ross Child BRI Brian Father
*ROS:            why isn't Mommy coming?
%com:            Mother usually picks Ross up around 4 PM.
*BRI:            don't worry.
*BRI:            she'll be here soon.
```

```
*ROS:          good.
@End
```

There are several points to note about this fragment. First, all of the characters in this fragment are ASCII characters. The @Begin and @End lines are used to guarantee that the file was not destroyed or shortened during copying between systems. Each line begins with a three-letter speaker code, a colon, and then a tab. Each line has only one utterance. However, if the utterance is longer than one line, it may continue onto the next line. A new utterance must be given a new speaker code. Commentary lines and other coding lines are indicated by the % symbol.

Beyond the level of minCHAT, there are a variety of advanced options that allow the user to attain increasing levels of precision in transcription and coding. Some of the major specifications available in the full CHAT system are:

1   *File headers.* The system specifies standard file headers such as "Age of Child," "Birth of Child," "Participants," "Location," and "Date" that document a variety of facts about the participants and the recording.

2   *Word forms.* CHAT specifies particular ways of transcribing learner forms, unidentifiable material, and incomplete words. It also provides conventions for standardizing spellings of shortenings, assimilations, interactional markers, colloquial forms, baby talk, and certain dialectal variants.

3   *Morphemes.* There is a system for morphemicization of complex words. Without such morphemicization, mean length of utterance is computer based on words, as defined orthographically.

4   *Tone units.* There is a system for marking tone units, pauses, and contours.

5   *Terminators.* There are symbols for marking utterance terminations and conversational linkings.

6   *Scoping.* CHAT uses a scoping convention to indicate stretches of overlaps, metalinguistic reference, retracings, and other complex patterns.

7   *Dependent tiers.* There are definitions for 14 coding tiers. Coding for three of these dependent tiers has been worked out in detail:
   (a)   *Phonological coding.* CHAT provides a single-character phonemic transcription system for English and several other languages called UNIBET. It also provides an ASCII translation for the extended IPA symbol şet called PHONASCII.
   (b)   *Error coding.* CHAT provides a full system for coding speech errors.

(c) *Morphemic coding.* CHAT provides a system for morphemic and syntactic coding or interlinear glossing.

The full CHAT system is covered in MacWhinney (1991).

3.2 How much CHAT does a user need to know?

CHILDES users fall into two groups. One group of researchers wants to examine corpora, but has little interest in collecting and transcribing new data. Another group of researchers wants to collect and transcribe new data and may be only marginally interested in analyzing old data. Typically, linguists and computer scientists fall into the first category and developmental psychologists and students of language disorders fall into the second category. Researchers in the second group who are using CHAT to transcribe new data soon come to realize that they need to learn all of the core CHAT conventions. Although these users may begin by using minCHAT, they will eventually gain familiarity with all of the conventions used on the main line, as well as with those dependent tier codes relevant to their particular research goals.

Users who are focusing on the analysis of old data may think that they do not need to master all of CHAT. For example, if a researcher wants to track the development of personal pronouns in the Brown corpora, they may think it sufficient to simply look for strings such as "he" and "it." However, this type of casual use of the database is potentially dangerous. For example, users need to understand that, in the Brown corpora, the forms "dem" and "dese" are often used as spelling variants for "them" and "these." Failure to track such variants could lead to underestimates of early pronoun usage. There are dozens of correspondences of this type that researchers need to understand if they are to make accurate use of the database.

When users start to use more detailed analysis programs such as MLU or DSS, the need to understand symbols for omitted elements and repetitions becomes increasingly important. For example, users need to understand that some corpora have been morphemicized in accord with the standards of chapter 6 and that others have not. Users also need to understand how symbols for missing elements or retracings can affect both lexical and syntactic analyses. It is possible that, in many cases, users could reach correct conclusions without a full understanding of the core features of CHAT. However, it is impossible to guarantee that this will happen. It is clear that the best recommendation to CHILDES users is to try to learn as much of CHAT as possible. If a researcher makes erroneous use of the database, these errors cannot be attributed to the CHILDES system, but only to the researcher who has failed to fully learn the system. Reviewers of articles based on the use of CHILDES data need to make sure that the researcher fully understood the shape of the database and the inevitable limitations of any empirical dataset.

3.3 *The importance of dry runs and* CHECK

Before a new user of CHAT and the CLAN programs spends hundreds of hours transcribing data, it is important to spend a few hours conducting small analytic "dry runs." This involves using your favorite editor to create a simple test file with some of the target forms that you plan to track in your larger analysis. Then you should make sure that this file passes cleanly through the CHECK program. It is difficult to overemphasize the importance of learning to use CHECK.

After running CHECK, you should apply those CLAN programs that will track the forms you wish to analyze. If you can demonstrate to yourself that the entire process of data entry and analysis will go through successfully from start to finish for some small sample file, then you can be relatively certain that expansion of the database and addition of further research questions will go smoothly. Failures to follow this simply advice have led to hundreds of wasted hours. *Verbum sapientibus sat.*

3.4 *Beyond CHAT*

The basic desiderata motivating all transcription systems include: readability, computational consistency, high retrievability, category expressivity, and precision. Unfortunately, these goals are often incompatible. In particular, it is often the case that codes which are important for some analysis are ones that we don't even want to look at for another analysis. Moreover, the need to retrieve categories will often require us to transcribe utterances in terms of standard words, phonemes, speech acts, or syntactic categories, despite the fact that often the standard categories do not apply.

These conflicting pressures on transcription systems can only be relieved by allowing the analyst a closer contact to the reality underlying the transcript. One way of providing this is to construct a complete phonological transcription, together with prosodic and intonational markings, as suggested by Peters, Fahn, Glover, Harley, Sawyer, and Shimura (1990). However, the work involved in producing a %pho line is so enormous that only two of the nearly 70 current corpora have full phonological transcripts. A major current goal of the CHILDES project is the creation of a linkage between the transcript and the underlying audiovisual reality that will minimize reliance on particular coding decisions and maximize the analyst's ability to explore the reality of the interaction.

4 CLAN

The third major tool in the CHILDES workbench is the CLAN package of analysis programs. The CLAN (Child Language Analysis) programs were written in the C programming language by Leonid Spektor at Carnegie Mellon University. The programs benefitted from work done by Jeffrey Sokolov, Bill Tuthill, and Mitzi Morris, as well as from the SALT systematization developed by Jon Miller and Robin Chapman (Miller and Chapman, 1982–93).

The CLAN programs can be compiled to run under MS-DOS, UNIX, VMS, XENIX, or Macintosh operating systems. The Center at Carnegie Mellon provides contributing members with executable versions of CLAN on floppies, technical assistance, and a manual for the programs. Researchers who are not planning on contributing to the database can purchase these materials from Lawrence Erlbaum Associates. Most users install the programs on a hard disk along with CHAT files either from their own research projects or from the CHILDES database.

CLAN commands include the program name, as set of options, and the names of the files being analyzed. For example the command

freq + f*.cha

runs the FREQ program on all the files in a given directory with the ".cha" extension. The "+f" switch indicates that the output of each analysis should be written to a file on the disk. Unless specifically given a file extension name, the FREQ program will figure out names for the new files. Many of the programs have quite a few possible options. Each option is explained in detail in the manual.

The programs have been designed to support five basic types of linguistic analysis (Crystal, 1982; Crystal, Fletcher, and Garman, 1976/89); lexical analysis, morphological analysis, syntactic analysis, discourse analysis, and phonological analysis. Let us look at how CLAN can be used to test hypotheses in each of these four areas.

4.1 CLAN for lexical analysis

The easiest types of CLAN analyses are those which look at the frequencies and distributions of particular word forms. for example, it is a simple matter to trace the use of a word like "under" or a group of words such as the locative prepositions. The analysis can be done on either a single file or a group of files. For example, let us suppose that we want to trace the use of personal pronouns in the three children studied by Roger Brown. We would construct a file including all of the personal pronouns with one pronoun on each line and call this file "pronouns." We would then use the FREQ command to count the occurrences of the pronouns in a file with a command like this:

freq + spronouns + t*ADA adam01.cha

The switch +t*ADA is included in order to limit the tally to only the utterances spoken by the child. If we also want the frequencies of the words spoken by the mother, we would use this command:

freq + spronouns + t*MOT adam01.cha

If we want to extend our analysis to all of the files in the directory, we can use the wild card:

freq + spronouns + t*ADA adam*.cha

If we want the collection of files to be treated as a single large file, we can add another switch:

freq + spronouns + t*ADA + u adam*.cha

The FREQ command is powerful and quite flexible, permitting a large number of possible analyses. The outputs of these analyses can be sent to either the screen or to files. The names of the output files can be controlled. For example, one might want to maintain a group of output files with the extension ".mot" for the frequencies of the mother's speech. These can be kept in a separate directory for further analysis.

The second major tool for conducting lexical analyses is the KWAL program which outputs not merely the frequencies of matching items, but also the full context of the item. For example, the KWAL command that searches for the word "chalk" in the sample.cha file will produce this type of output:

kwal + schalk sample.cha
kwal is conducting analyses on:
ALL speaker tiers
****
From file <sample.cha>

***File sample.cha. Line 39. Keyword: chalk
*MOT: is there any delicious chalk?

It is possible to include still further previous and following context using additional switches.

Frequency analyses

With tools like FREQ and KWAL, one can easily construct frequency analyses for individual children at specified ages. Many such counts have been produced. However, it is more difficult to move up to the next level of generalization on which a frequency count is constructed across children and ages. First, one would want to tabulate frequency data for the speech of children separately from the speech of adults. And one would not want to automatically combine data from children of different ages. Moreover, we would not want to merge data from children with language disorders together with data from normally developing children. Differences in social class, gender, and educational level may lead one to make further separations. And it is important to distinguish language used in different situational contexts. When one finishes looking at all the distinctions that could potentially be made, it becomes clear that one needs to think of the construction of a lexical database in very dynamic terms.

Such a database could be constructed using FREQ and other CLAN tools, but this work would be fairly tedious and slow. What we plan to do to address this problem is to build a file with every lexical item in the entire database and attach to each item a set of pointers to the position of the item in every file in which it occurs. These key files and pointer files will be stored along with the database on a CD-ROM. Using the pointers from the master word list to the individual occurrences of words, the user can construct specific probes of this database configured both on facts about the child and facts about the words being searched. The program that matches these searches to the pointer file will be called LEX. Using LEX, it will be possible, for example, to track the frequency of a group of "evaluative" words contained in a separate file in two-year-olds separated into males and females. And the same search can also yield the frequency values for these words in the adult input. Although we may want to publish hard-copy frequency counts based on some searches through this database, the definitive form of the lexical frequency analysis will be contained in the program itself.

Once the LEX tool is completed, the path will be open to the construction of three additional tools. The first of these is a simple extension of the current KWAL program. Currently, researchers who want to track down the exact occurrences of particular words must rely on the use of the +d option in FREQ or must make repeated analyses using KWAL and keep separate track of line numbers. With the new LEX system, instead of running through files sequentially, KWAL will be able to rely on the pointers in the master file to make direct access to items in the database.

Lexical field analyses

A second type of lexical research focuses attention not on the entire lexicon, but on particular lexical fields. Using the +s@file switch with FREQ and KWAL, such analyses can already be computed with the current version of CLAN. Completion of the LEX facility will further facilitate the analysis of lexical fields. For example, using the lexical database, we will be able to examine the development of selected lexical fields in the style of the PRISM analysis of Crystal (1982) and Crystal, Fletcher, and Garman (1976/89). This analysis tracks the child's developing use of content words in 239 lexical subfields. Examples of these fields include farm tools, units of weight measurement, and musical instruments. These 239 fields can be merged into a set of 61 categories which can, in turn, be merged into nine high level fields. Bodin and Snow (1993) show how analyses of this type can be conducted on the CHLDES database. Likely candidates for intensive examination include mental verbs, morality words, temporal adverbs, subordinating conjunctions, and complex verbs.

Other important semantic fields include closed-class items such as pronouns, determiners, quantifiers, and modals. As Brown (1973), Lahey (1988) and many others have noted, these high frequency closed-class items each express important semantic and pragmatic functions that provide us with separate information about the state of the child's language and cognitive functioning. For example, Antinucci and Miller (1976), Cromer (1991), Slobin (1986), and Weist et al. (1984) argue that tense markings and temporal adverbs are not controlled until the child first masters the relevant conceptual categories.

It is also possible to track basic semantic relations (Bloom, 1975; Lahey, 1988; Leonard, 1976; Retherford, Schwartz, and Chapman, 1981) by studying the closed-class lexical items that mark these relations. In particular, one can follow these correspondences between semantic relations and lexical expressions:

Relation	*Lexical expressions*
Locative	in, on, under, through, by, at
Negation	can't, no, not, won't, none
Demonstrative	this, that
Recurrence	more, again, another
Possession	possessive suffix, of, mine, hers, her
Adverbial	-ly
Quantifier	one, two, more, some
Recipient	to
Beneficiary	for
Comitative	with
Instrument	with, by

Lexical rarity index

A third measure that can be developed through use of the LEX facility is the Lexical Rarity Index or LRI. Currently, the major index of lexical diversity is the type–token ratio (TTR) of Templin (1957). A more interesting measure would focus on the relative dispersion in a transcript of words that are generally rare in some comparison dataset. The more than a child uses "rare" words, the higher the Lexical Rarity Index. If most of the words are common and frequent, the LRI will be low. In order to compute various forms of this index, the LRI program would rely on values provided by LEX.

Another easy way of tracking the emergence of "long" words is to use the WDLEN program which provides a simple histogram of word lengths in a file along with the location of the longest words.

4.2 CLAN for morphological analysis

Many of the most important questions in child language require the detailed study of specific morphosyntactic constructions. For example, the debate on the role of connectionist simulations of language learning (MacWhinney and Leinbach, 1991; MacWhinney, Leinbach, Taraban, and McDonald, 1989; Marcus et al., 1991; Pinker and Prince, 1988; Plunkett and Sinha, 1992) has focused attention on early uses and overregularizations of the regular and irregular past tense markings in English. A full resolution of this debate will require intensive study of the acquisition of these markings not just in English, but in a wide variety of languages at a wide sampling of ages. Similarly, the testing of hypotheses about parameter setting within G-B theory (Hyams, 1986; Pizzuto and Caselli, 1993; Valian, 1991; Wexler, 1986) often depends upon a careful study of pronominal markings, reflexives, and wh-words.

During the earliest stages of language learning, the most obvious developments are those involving the acquisition of particular grammatical markings. The study of the acquisition of grammatical markers in English has been heavily shaped by Brown's (1973) intensive study of the acquisition of 14 grammatical morphemes in Adam, Eve, and Sarah and the cross-sectional follow-up by de Villiers and de Villiers (1973a). Since Brown's original analysis, there have been scores of studies tracking these same morphemes in second language learners, normally developing children, and children with language disorders. There have also been many studies of comparable sets of morphemes in other languages.

The 14 morphemes studied by Brown include the progressive, the plural, the regular past, the irregular past, *in, on,* the regular third person singular, the irregular third person singular, articles, the uncontracted copula, the contracted copula, the possessive, the contracted auxiliary, and the uncontracted auxiliary. Brown's framework for morpheme analysis has been extended in systems such as the LARSP procedure by Crystal, Fletcher, and Garman (1976), the DSS procedure by Lee (1974), the ASS procedure of Miller (1981), and the IPSyn procedure of Scarborough et al. (1991). Other markers tracked in LARSP, ASS, and DSS include the superlative, the comparative, the adverbial ending -ly, the uncontracted negative, the contracted negative, the regular past participle, the irregular past participle, and various nominalizing suffixes. Within the CHILDES framework, de Acedo (de Acedo, 1993) shows how CHAT and CLAN can be used to study the Spanish child's learning of grammatical markers. In the next two sections, we discuss several CLAN tools for the study of morphological structure.

Morphological analysis from the main line

Chapter 6 of the CHILDES manual describes a system for coding the presence of grammatical markers on the main line. For example, the word "jumped" can be coded as "jump-ed." Words that cannot be analyzed into simple combinations of morphemes can be represented using the replacement option as in:

went [: go-ed]

These two forms of coding allow users to search for all instances of the past "-ed." The basic lexical tools of FREQ and KWAL can be used to do this. In a more complex language, such as Italian or Hungarian, main line coding of morphemes tends to become cumbersome and hard to read. To address this problem, we have written a program for the automatic extraction of codes on a secondary %mor tier.

MOR – *Automatic morphological anlaysis*

The more extensive coding needed for many projects requires a complete construction of a part-of-speech analysis for each word on the main line. This analysis is placed on a separate tier called the %mor tier. The coding of the %mor tier is done in accord with the guidelines specified in chapter 14 of the CHILDES manual. Once a complete %mor tier is available, a vast range of morphological and syntactic analyses become possible. However, hand coding of a %mor tier for the entire CHILDES database would require perhaps 20 years of work and would be extremely error-prone and noncorrectable. If the standards for morphological coding changed in the middle of this project, the coder would have to start over again from the beginning. It would be difficult to imagine a more tedious and frustrating task – the hand coder's equivalent of Sisyphus and his stone.

The alternative to hand coding is automatic coding. Over the last three years, we have worked on the construction of an automatic coding program for CHAT files, called MOR. Although the MOR system is designed to be transportable to all languages, it is currently only fully elaborated for English and German. The language-independent part of MOR is the core processing engine. All of the language-specific aspects of the systems are built into files which can be modified by the user. In the remarks that follow, we will first focus on ways in which a user can apply the MOR system for English.

How to run MOR

The MOR program takes a CHAT main line and automatically inserts a %mor line together with the appropriate morphological codes for each word on the main line. The basic MOR command is much like the other commands in CLAN. For example, you can run MOR in its default configuration with this type of command:

mor sample.cha

However, MOR is unlike the other CLAN programs in one crucial regard. Although you can run MOR on any CLAN file, in order to get a well-formed

%mor line, you often need to engage in significant *extra work*. We have tried to minimize the additional work you need to do when working with MOR, but it would be misleading for us to suggest that no additional work is required. In particular, users of MOR will often need to spend a great deal of time engaging in the processes of (1) lexicon building and (2) ambiguity resolution.

Lexicon building. In order to determine whether MOR correctly recognizes all of the words in your transcripts, you can first run MOR on all of your files and then run this KWAL command on the .mor files you have produced:

kwal + t%mor + s"?|*" *.mor

If KWAL finds no question marks on the %mor line, then you know that all the words have been recognized by MOR. If there are question marks in you *.mor output files, you will probably want to correct this problem by running MOR in the interactive update mode. You can then either add the new words to you main lexicon or else create a secondary, corpus-specific lexicon with the missing words needed for this corpus.

Ambiguity resolution. MOR automatically generates a %mor tier of the type described in chapter 14. As stipulated in chapter 14, retraced material, comments, and excluded words are not coded on the %mor line produced by MOR. Words are labeled by their syntactic category, followed by the separator " | ," followed by the word itself, broken down into its constituent morphemes.

*CHI: the people are making cakes.
%mor: det|the n|people v:aux|be&PRES v|make-ING n|cake-PL.

In this particular example, none of the words have ambiguous forms. However, it is often the case that some of the basic words in English have two or more part-of-speech readings. For example, the word "back" can be a noun, a verb, a preposition, an adjective, or an adverb. The "^" character denotes the alternative readings for each word on the main tier:

*CHI: I want to go back.
%mor: pro|I v|want inf|to^prep|to
         v|go adv|back^n|back^v|back.

The entries in the eng.clo file maintain these ambiguities. However, open-class words in the eng.lex file are only coded in their most common part-of-speech form. The problem of noun–verb ambiguity will eventually be addressed through use of the PARS program, which is currently under development. Those ambiguities which remain in a MOR transcript after the drules and the PARS program has operated can be removed by using MOR in its ambiguity resolution mode. The program locates each of the various ambiguous words one by one and asks the user to select one of the possible meanings.

MOR *for other languages*

In order to maximize the portability of the MOR system to other languages, we have developed a general scheme for representing allomorphic rules and combination rules. This means that a researcher can adapt MOR for a new language without doing any programming at all. However, the researcher/linguist needs to construct: (1) a list of the stems of the language with their parts-of-speech, (2) a set of "arules" for allomorphic variations in spelling, and (3) a set of "crules" for possible combinations of stems with affixes. Building these files will require a major one-time dedication of effort from at least one researcher for every language. Once the basic work of constructing the rules files and the core lexicon files is done, then further work with MOR in that language will be no more difficult that it currently is for English. However, construction of new rules files is an extremely complex process. And construction of a closed-class and open-class lexicon will also take a great deal of time. Although no programming is required, the linguist building these files must have a thorough understanding of the MOR program and the morphology of the language involved. Complete documentation for the construction of the rules files is available from Carnegie Mellon and will also be included in the next edition of the CHILDES manual.

4.3   CLAN *for syntactic analysis*

Once a %mor line has been constructed, either through use of MOR or through hand coding, a variety of additional morphosyntactic analyses are then available. Instead of analyzing the lexical items on the main line, programs can now analyze the fuller morphosyntactic representation on the %mor line. The simpler forms of analysis can still be done using FREQ and KWAL. However, several other programs add additional power for morphosyntactic analysis. The MLU program can compute the basic Mean Length of Utterance index in a variety of ways (Rollins, 1993). COMBO extends the power of FREQ and KWAL by permitting more complete Boolean string matching. For example, if the user wants to search for all instances of a relative pronoun followed eventually by an auxiliary verb, it is possible to compose this search string in COMBO. Certain types of matching between the main line and the %mor line can be achieved using the +s switch in the MODREP program. In addition, the COOCCUR program can be used to tabulate sequences of syntactic structures appearing on the %mor line.

More complex analyses of syntactic development require us to deal with structures defined in terms of traditional syntactic categories such as Subject, Object, and Main Verb. Among the most important syntactic structures examined by procedures such as LARSP, ASS, IPSyn, and DSS are these:

Structure	Example
Art + N	the dog
Adj + N	good boy
Adj + Adj + N	my new car
Art + Adj + N	the new car
Adj/Art + N + V	my bike fall
V + Adj/Art + N	want more cookie
N + poss + N	John's wallet
Adv + Adj	too hot
Prep + NP	at the school
N + Cop + PredAdj	we are nice
N + Cop + PredN	we are monsters
Aux + V	is coming
Aux + Aux + V	will be coming
Mod + V	can come
Q + V	who ate it?
Q + Aux + V	who is coming?
tag	isn't it?
aux + N	are you going?
S + V	baby fall
V + O	drink coffee
S + V + O	you play this
X + conj + X	boy and girl, red and blue
V + to + V	want to swim
let/help + V	let's play
V + Comp	I know you want it
Sent + Conj + Sent	I'll push and you row
V + I + O	read me the book
N + SRel	the one you have in the bag
N + ORel	the one that eats corn
S + Rel + V	the one I like best is the monster
passive	he is kicked by the raccoon
Neg + N	no dog
Neg + V	can't come
PP + PP	under the bridge by the river
comparative	better than Bill

Several of these structures also define some of the semantic relations that have been emphasized in previous literature. These include recipient (direct object), agent (subject in actives), verb, and object.

The discussion in this section has focused on the construction of indicators for development in English. However, these same tools can also be usefully applied to basic issues in crosslinguistic analysis. Once we have collected a large database of transcripts in other languages and created a full %mor tier encoding, we can ask some of the basic questions in crosslinguistic analyses. Are there underlying similarities in the distribution of semantic relations and grammatical markings used by children at the beginning of language learning? Exactly which markings show the greatest language-specific divergences from the general pattern? How are grammatical relations marked as ergative in one language handled in another language? Under what circumstances do children tend to omit subject pronouns, articles, and other grammatical markers?

4.4   *CLAN for discourse and interactional analyses*

Many researchers want to track the ways in which discourse influences the expression of topic, anaphora, tense, mood, narrative voice, ellipsis, embedding, and word order (Halliday and Hasan, 1976; MacWhinney, 1985b). To do this, researchers need to track shifts in narrative voice, transitions between discourse blocks, and foreground–background relations in discourse. They are also interested in the ways in which particular speech acts from one participant give rise to responsive or nonresponsive speech acts in the other participant. CLAN provides several powerful tools for examining the structures of interactions and narrations.

Coder's Editor

The most important CLAN tool for data coding is the CED Coder's Editor, which is a new program in CLAN 2.0. CED can lead to remarkable improvements in the accuracy, reliability, and efficiency of transcript coding. If you have ever spent a significant amount of time coding transcripts or if you plan to do such coding in the future, you should definitely consider using CED. More importantly, CED is at the core of our plans for an integrated exploratory workbench, to be discussed in the next section.

CED provides the user with not only a complete text editor, but also a systematic way of entering user-determined codes into dependent tiers in CHAT files. The program works in two modes: coder mode and editor mode. Initially, you are in editor mode, and you can stay in this mode until you learn the basic editing commands. The basic commands have been configured so that both Word Perfect and EMACS keystroke equivalents are available. If you prefer some other set of keystrokes, the commands can be rebound.

In the coding mode, CED relies on a codes.lst file created by the user to set up a hierarchical coding menu. It then moves through the file line by line asking the coder to select a set of codes for each utterance. For example, a codes.lst list such as

```
$MOT
:POS
    :Que
    :Res
:NEG
$CHI
```

would be a shorter way of specifying the following codes:

```
$MOT:POS:Que
$MOT:POS:Res
$MOT:NEG:Que
$MOT:NEG:Res
$CHI:POS:Que
$CHI:POS:Res
$CHI:NEG:Que
$CHI:NEG:Res
```

This coding system would require the coder to make three quick cursor movements for each utterance in order to compose a code such as $CHI:NEG:Res.

Chains and sequences

Once a file has been fully coded in CED, a variety of additional analyses become possible. The standard tools of FREQ, KWAL, and COMBO can be used to trace frequencies of particular codes. However, it is also possible to use the CHAINS, DIST, and KEYMAP programs to track sequences of particular codes. For example, KEYMAP will create a contingency table for all the types of codes that follow some specified code or group of codes. It can be used, for example, to trace the extent to which a mother's question is followed by an answer from the child, as opposed to some irrelevant utterance or no response at all. DIST lists the average distances between words or codes. CHAINS looks at sequences of codes across utterance. Typically, the chains being tracked are between and within speaker sequences of speech acts, reference types, or topics. The output is a table which maps, for example, chains in which there is no shift of topic and places where the topic shifts. Wolf, Moreton, and Camp (1993) apply CHAINS to transcripts that have been coded for discourse units. Yet another perspective on the shape of the discourse can be computed by using the MLT program which computes the mean length of the turn for each speaker.

Recasts

Currently there is only one CLAN program that focuses on the lexical and syntactic match between successive utterances. The is the CHIP program developed by Jeffrey Sokolov and Leonid Spektor. CHIP is useful for tracking the extent to which one speaker repeats, corrects, or expands upon the speech of the previous speaker. Sokolov and Moreton (1993) and Post (1993) have used it successfully to demonstrate the finetuning of instructional feedback to the language learning child.

Discourse display

There is more to a transcript than a series of codes and symbols. The superficial form of a transcript can also lead us to adopt a particular perspective on an interaction and to entertain particular hypotheses regarding developments in communicative strategies. For example, if we code our data in columns with the child on the left, we come to think of the child as driving or directing the conversation. If we decide instead to place the parents' utterances in the left column, we then tend to view the child as more reactive or scaffolded. Ochs (1979) noted that such apparently simple decisions as the placement of a speaker into a particular column can both reflect and shape the nature of our theories of language development. Because it is important for the analyst to be able to see a single transcript in many different ways, we have written three new CLAN programs that provide alternative views onto the data. The basic principle underlying these data display programs is the motto of "different files for different styles." The display programs – COLUMNS, LINES, and SLIDE – are designed to facilitate the alternative ways of viewing turns and overlaps.

The COLUMNS program produces CHAT files in a multicolumn form that is useful for explorations of turn-taking, scaffolding, and sequencing. COLUMNS allows the user to break up the one-column format of standard CHAT into several smaller columns. For example, the standard 80 character column could be broken up into four columns of 20 characters each. One column could be used for the child, one for the parent, one for situational descriptions, and one for coding. The user has control over the assignment of tiers to columns, the placement of the columns, and the width of each separate column. As in the case of files produced by SLIDE, files produced by COLUMNS are useful for exploratory purposes, but are no longer legal CHAT files and cannot be reliably used with the CLAN programs.

Yet another form of CLAN display provides a focus on overlaps and cross-tier correspondences. Using SLIDE, a CHAT file can be displayed as a single unbroken stretch of speech across an "infinite" left-to-right time line. Whereas standard CHAT files use carriage returns to break up files into lines, a file displayed in SLIDE has all carriage returns removed. The SLIDE program converts a CHAT file into a set of single long lines for each speaker. These lines can be scrolled across the computer screen from left to right. At any point in time, only 80 columns are displayed, but the user can rapidly scroll to any other point in this single left–right line by using the cursor keys. When two speakers overlap in a conversation, SLIDE displays the overlapped portions on top of each other. SLIDE can also be used to display accurate placement of material otherwise indicated by <aft> and <bef> and to provide correct display of the match between morphemes on a %mor line with corresponding words on the main line as required in many systems of interlinear morphemicization. This form of display provides far better time–space iconicity than any previous form of display. Of course, this display cannot be captured on the printed page; it is only available on the computer screen because of its capacity to scroll almost limitlessly left to right. An earlier noncomputerized prototype for SLIDE can be found in Ervin-Tripp (1979).

Finally, CED itself is now capable of varying the way in which transcripts are viewed by allowing the user to suppress display of particular tiers or even data from particular speakers right in the CED window while coding and editing the transcript.

4.5 *CLAN for phonological analyses*

Despite all the care that has gone into the formulation of CHAT, transcription of child language data remains a fairly imprecise business. No matter how carefully one tries to capture the child's utterances in a standardized transcription system, something is always missing. The CHAT main line induces the transcriber to view utterances in terms of standard lexical items. However, this emphasis tends to force the interpretation of nonstandard child-based forms in terms of standard adult lexical items. This morphemic emphasis on the main line can be counterbalanced by including a rich phonological transcript on the %pho line. As Peters, Fahn, Glover, Harley, Sawyer, and Shimura (1990) have argued, the inclusion of a complete CHAT %pho line is the best way to convey the actual content of the child's utterances, particularly at the youngest ages. CHAT provides two systems for transcribing utterances on the %pho tier. For coarse transcription, researchers can use the UNIBET systems that have been developed for English and several other languages. For a finer level of phonetic transcription, researchers can use the PHONASCII rendition of IPA notation.

Analysis of the %pho line

The construction of a complete %pho tier for even a few hours of data is a formidable task. Verification of the reliability of that transcription is an even bigger problem. However, once this tier is produced, CLAN provides several programs to facilitate analysis. The two programs that are most adapted to this analysis are PHONFREQ, which computes the frequencies of various segments, separating out consonants and vowels by their various syllable positions, and MODREP, which matches %pho tier symbols with the corresponding main line text. For more precise control of MODREP, it is possible to create a separate %mod line in which each segment on the %pho corresponds to exactly one segment on the %mod line.

Linking to a digitized record

Although inclusion of a complete %pho line is a powerful tool, even this form of two-tier transcription misrepresents the full dynamics of the actual audio record. If the original audiotapes are still in good condition, one can use them to continue to verify utterances. But there is no way to quickly access a particular point on an audiotape for a particular utterance. Instead, one has to either listen through a whole tape from beginning to end or else try to use tape markings and fastforward buttons to track down an utterance. The same situation arises when the interaction is on videotape.

Computer technology now provides us with a dramatic new way of creating a direct, immediately accessible link between the audio recording and the CHAT transcript. The system we have developed at Carnegie Mellon, called Talking Transcripts, uses fast optical erasable disks, a 16-bit digitizer board, and the Macintosh operating system to forge these direct links. Once a large sound file has been written to disk, the transcriber can use CED to control access to the file during the coding of a new transcript. Although this process requires some additional time setting up the basic digitization, this investment pays for itself in facilitating high-quality transcription. Each utterance can be played back exactly and immediately without having to use a reverse button or foot pedal.

As a user of this new system, I have found that having the actual audio record directly available gave me a much enhanced sense of an immediate relation between the transcript and the actual interaction. The impact on the transcriber is quite dramatic. Having the actual sound directly available does not diminish the importance of accurate transcription, because the CLAN programs must still continue to rely on the CHAT transcript. However, the immediate availability of the sound frees the transcriber from the fear of making irrevocable mistakes, since the ongoing availability of the audio record means that codes can always be rechecked for reliability.

Phonological analysis with a digitized record

Using this new link between the CHAT %pho line and digitized speech, the way is now open for us to design an entire Phonologist's Workbench grounded on the immediate availability of actual sound. The new programs for phonological analysis that we now plan to write include:

1   *Inventory analysis.* We will extend the PHONFREQ program, so that it can compute the numbers of uses of a segment across either types or tokens of strings on the %pho line. The program will also be structured so that the inventories can be grouped by distinctive features such as place or manner or articulation or by groups such as consonants versus vowels. The ratio of consonants to vowels will be computed. Summary statistics will include raw frequencies and

percentage frequency of occurrence for individual segments. Non-occurrences in a transcript of any of the standard segments of English will be flagged.

2 *Length.* The MLU program will be used to compute mean length of utterance in syllables. This can be done from the %pho line, using syllable boundaries as delimiters.

3 *Variability.* The MODREP program will be made to compute the types and tokens of the various phonetic realizations for a single target word, a single target phoneme, or a single target cluster. For example, for all the target words with the segment /p/, the program will list the corresponding child forms. Conversely, the researcher can look at all the child forms containing a /p/ and find the target forms from which they derive.

4 *Homonymy.* Homonymy refers to a child's use of a single phonetic string to refer to a large number of target words. For example, the child may say "bo" for *bow, boat, boy, bone,* etc. The MODREP program will calculate the degree of homonymy observed by comparing the child's string types coded on the %pho tier with the corresponding target forms coded on the %mod tier.

5 *Correctness.* In order to determine correctness, the child pronunciation (%pho line) must be compared with the target (%mod line). The MODREP program will be modified to compute the number of correct productions of the adult target word, segment, or cluster. For example, the percentage consonants correct (PCC) will be computed in this way.

6 *Phonetic product per utterance.* This index (Bauer, 1988; Nelson and Bauer, 1991) will be computed by a new CLAN program called PHOPRO. The index computes the phonetic complexity of the utterance as a function of the number of place of articulation contrasts realized. This index is low if everything is at one place of articulation; it is high if all points of articulation are used.

7 *Phonological process analysis.* Phonological process analyses search for systematic patterns of sound omission, substitution, and word formation that children make in their simplified productions of adult speech. Thus, such processes refer to classes of sounds rather than individual sounds. Process analysis must be based upon the comparison of the %pho and %mod tiers. The Clan Analysis of Phonology, or CAP, will examine rates of consonant deletion, voicing changes, gliding, stopping, cluster simplification, and syllable deletion. In addition, nondevelopmental error will be identified an calculated (Shriberg, 1990).

8 *PHONASCII and UNIBET code modifications.* PHONASCII and UNIBET codes will be modified and/or elaborated to enable cross-tier analysis.

9 *Automatic phonetic transcription of high-frequency words.* To facilitate phonetic and phonological transcription of corpora, we will develop an on-line users reference to provide automatic phonological coding

of the 2,000 most frequently used words in the English language to facilitate phonetic transcription of naturalistic speech data (e.g. words such as "and" and "the" will not have to be redundantly transcribed each time they occur).

10   *Phonologist's reference.* To help beginning phonologists and to stabilize reliability for trained phonologists, we will have available a complete set of digitized speech samples for each phonological symbol used in either UNIBET or PHONASCII.

11   *Transcription playback.* The same phonological database used by the Phonologist's reference can also be used to playback the sounds of candidate transcriptions.

Alongside the development of programs to support these analyses, we will also be working to broaden the CHILDES database of phonological transcripts. There are very few computerized transcripts currently available, so we can reasonably start from scratch in this area. Because we are starting from scratch, we can require that all transcripts in the CHILDES phonological database be accompanied by good quality tape recordings which will be digitized at CMU and then distributed through CD-ROM.

4.6 Utilities

CLAN also includes a variety of features to make life easier when manipulating files and transcripts. The CHSTRING program can be used to make simple string replacements across collections of files. The CAPWD program prints all capitalized words. The GEM program is designed to allow the user to place important passages into a file for later analysis. Using a text editor, the user marks the passages to be stored. GEM then uses these marks to determine what should be excised and placed in the "gems" file. A good example of the use of GEM with FREQ can be found in Post (1993). For users working with files from SALT, the SALTIN program helps in the conversion to CHAT. The LINES program allows users to mark their CHAT files with line numbers. DATES can be used to compute a child's age, given the current date and the child's birthdate. The BIBFIND program is used to access the CHILDES/BIB database. In addition to these utility programs, the CLAN interface includes a keystroke editing function, some help facilities, and a program for displaying text files called PAGE. The Macintosh version of CLAN also has pulldown menus that can be used to construct CLAN commands.

5   The Future

If the CHILDES database is to continue to grow, we must continue to receive extensive cooperation from individual scientists. Researchers who use the

CHILDES tools to collect new data have the responsibility to contribute these new data to the database. In particular, researchers whose work has benefitted from government support have an obligation to contribute to scientific progress by adding their data to the database. In fields such as the sequencing of proteins in DNA, researchers, journals, and the government have set the requirement that only data which are publicly available in the Human Genome database can be published. A similar policy for language development studies would ensure the stable and continued development of the CHILDES database. Until such a policy is developed, voluntary acceptance of these responsibilities will guarantee continued growth of the database.

We expect that new additions to the CHILDES database will no longer require reformatting, since they will be transcribed in CHAT from the start. Already, we are starting to receive most new data files in CHAT format. Soon we expect this to become the norm. The database will also continue to grow beyond its original scope. The first corpora included in the database were on first language acquisition by normal English-speaking children. In the future, the database will grow to include large components of second language acquisition data, adult interactional data, and a variety of data from children with language disorders. The numbers of languages represented will continue to grow. As the database grows, it will be important to distinguish between the CHILDES system, the Aphasia Language Data Exchange System (ALDES), the Second Language Acquisition Data Exchange System (SLADES), and the overall Language Data Exchange System (LANDES).

As multimedia computational resources become increasingly available, and as fractal video compression methodology becomes more widely distributed, the CHILDES database will shift from its current concentration on ASCII transcripts to a focus on transcripts accompanied by digitized audio and video. Using the CED editor, links between events in the audio and video records will be tied to an increasingly rich set of links in the transcript. These links will be increasingly dynamic, allowing the user to move around through the audio and video records using the transcript as the navigational map. The full digitization of the interaction will allow the observer to enter into the interaction as an explorer. This is not the virtual reality of video adventures. The scientist is not seeking to change reality or to interact with reality. Instead, the goal is to explore reality by viewing an interaction repeatedly from many different perspectives. These new ways of viewing a transcript will be important for phonological and grammatical analyses, but their most important impact will be on the analysis of interactional structure and discourse. Having full video and audio immediately available from the transcript will draw increased attention to codes for marking synchronies between intonational patterns, gestural markings, and lexical expressions in ongoing interactional relations.

The construction of this new multimedia transcript world would allow us to begin work on the successor to the CHILDES Project. This is the Human Speech Genome Project. One of the first goals of the Speech Genome Project would be the collection, digitization, transcription, parsing, and coding of complete speech records for all the verbal interaction of a set of perhaps a dozen young children from differing language backgrounds. They might include, for example, a child learning ASL, a child with early focal lesions, a child growing up bilingual, and children with varying family situations. The multimedia records will allow us to fully characterize and explore all of the linguistic input to these children during the crucial years for language learning. We will then be in a position to know exactly what happens during the normal course of language acquisition. We can examine exactly how differences in the input to the child lead to differences in the patterns of language development. We will have precise data on the first uses of forms and how those first uses blend into regular control. We will be able to track all types of errors and first usages with great precision.

Alongside this rich new observational database, the increased power of computational simulations will allow us to construct computational models of the language learning process that embody a variety of theoretical ideas. By testing these models against the facts of language learning embodied in the Speech Genome, we can both refine the models and guide the search for new empirical data to be included in the multimedia database of the future.

ACKNOWLEDGMENTS

This work was supported from 1984 to 1988 by grants from the John D. and Catherine T. MacArthur Foundation, the National Science Foundation, and the National Institutes of Health. Since 1987, the CHILDES Project has been supported by grants from the National Insitutes of Health (NICHHD). For full acknowledgments and thanks to the dozens of researchers who have helped on this project, please consult pages viii and ix of the manual (MacWhinney, 1991). The CLAN programs were developed by Leonid Spektor. Mitzi Morris wrote the DSS and MOR programs with extensive help from Julia Evans, Leonid Spektor, Roland Hausser, Carolyn Ellis, and Kim Plunkett. Nan Bernstein-Ratner collaborated in the development of guidelines for the creation of a phonological analysis system. Ideas regarding the Talking Transcripts project came from Helmut Feldweg and Sven Strömqvist. Joy Moreton, Catherine Snow, Barbara Pan, and Lowry Hemphill helped test and design the CHAINS and CED programs. Important suggestions for modifications of CHAT coding came from Judi Fenson, Frank Wijnen, Giuseppe Cappelli, Mary MacWhinney, Shanley Allen, and Julia Evans. Roy Higginson was the chief compiler of the CHILDES/BIB system. Steve Pinker suggested a name for the Human Speech Genome Project. George Allen designed the UNIBET and PHONASCII systems.

Social and Contextual
Influences

6 Issues in the Study of Input: Finetuning, Universality, Individual and Developmental Differences, and Necessary Causes

CATHERINE E. SNOW

History of Research on Input

Claims about the nature of input to language-learning children are central to formulations about any theory of language acquisition. The contention that input was ill-formed, incoherent, and complex constituted a critical argument in Chomsky's original formulation of the nature of LAD (Chomsky, 1965): the poverty of the input had to be compensated for by the innate structure available to the language learner. Chomsky's anecdotal evidence for the poverty and degeneracy of the input was quickly challenged by a series of studies designed to provide quantified descriptions of the kinds of speech addressed to young children (see Snow, 1977, 1986 for reviews). The results of those studies are now generally accepted in support of the notion that the speech directed to young children (child directed speech, CDS), whether by adults or older siblings, differs from speech among peers on a variety of dimensions. It is syntactically simpler, more limited in vocabulary and in propositional complexity, more correct, and more fluent. At the formal level, then, such speech can be seen as a simpler, cleaner corpus from which to learn language. In other ways, though, CDS is still quite complex; it displays the full range of conventional indirectness, for example, without the simplification of form–function mapping one might expect (Shatz, 1978). While in general CDS is constrained to the here-and-now and related to the child's focus of attention or ongoing activity, a high proportion of at least some mothers' CDS redirects children's attention and activity, introduces nonpresent referents, and in other ways seems to complicate the task of learning language.

After the first demonstration that CDS constituted a "register" distinguishable from adult–adult talk, new research questions emerged. Those which have stimulated the greatest amount of work can be categorized as follows:

1   How does CDS vary as a function of the child's age, language age, or interactive behaviors? In other words, is CDS finetuned to the child's ability to understand or produce language? Is it regulated by the child's signals of (non)comprehension or response, and if so on what dimensions? This set of questions can be subsumed under the general heading of attention to issues of *finetuning*.

2   How does CDS vary as a function of other child characteristics? Does CDS differ in ways that are helpful or harmful when the addressee has impairments in hearing, vision, or cognitive development, or language-specific impairments? Research related to this question will be reviewed below in the section entitled *effects of developmental problems*.

3   How does CDS vary as a function of language, culture, and social class? Is it universal? Are there specific types of adaptations that are culturally prescribed rather than regulated by the interactants? Is CDS itself a cultural artefact, the product of a particular Western, Anglo-American view of how children should be treated? Research and thinking about this topic are treated under the rubric *universality*.

4   Does amount or type of CDS relate to differences in child outcome? For example, is CDS the source of individual differences in style of language development (e.g. the difference between expressive and referential children)? Does it explain differences in speed of acquisition? These questions will be discussed in the section on *individual differences*.

5   Are the adaptations of CDS prerequisite to normal language acquisition? What are the limits on the nature and amount of CDS that support normal acquisition? Above those threshold limits, do particular aspects of CDS facilitate children's acquisition of language, and if so how? In short, are the adjustments widely seen within CDS *essential, facilitative, or irrelevant* to normal language development?

In this chapter, these questions will be used as a basis for organizing what has become an enormous literature on CDS; the work done on these questions is so extensive that a complete review would go far beyond the limits of this chapter. However, an extensive, up to date review of this literature is available in Gallaway and Richards (1994); in this chapter, then, I will rely on that review as background and attempt to synthesize the research to provide the best current answers to the five sets of questions within the constraints of the research that has been done.

Finetuning

Finetuning of CDS begins in infancy. An early and oft-noted characteristic of CDS is its high pitch and exaggerated intonation pattern. First analyzed by Garnica (1977), the presence of this characteristic of CDS has been confirmed for Chinese (Grieser and Kuhl, 1988), Japanese (Masataka, 1992), and various European languages (Fernald, Taeschner, Dunn, Papousek, Boysson-Bardies, and Fukui, 1989). It has also been widely suggested that use of high pitch and lively intonation represents a response to infants' attentional patterns. Infants demonstrate a preference for higher pitched over lower pitched voices (Fernald, 1985; Werker and McLeod, 1989), and are more likely to respond to higher pitched utterances with vocalizations and smiles (Masataka, 1992). Manipulation of these prosodic characteristics is very high at precisely the age when infants are most responsive (Stern, Spieker, Barnett, and MacKain, 1983), and by age five children receive almost no prosodic adjustments (Garnica, 1977). Thus, it seems clear that prosody is tuned to child responsiveness or attentiveness, at least somewhat finely. Research and thinking on this topic has been reviewed by Sachs (1977) and Cruttenden (1994).

The phonetics of CDS seem also to be adjusted, such that both enhanced clarity of vowels (as reflected in the F1–F2 spread; Bernstein Ratner, 1984a) and full production of often-reduced consonants (Bernstein Ratner, 1984b) is characteristic in speech addressed to children at the one word stage. These phonetic clarifications seem to occur during a relatively brief period just as children are struggling with establishing their initial lexicon, and to be abandoned by about the time of the vocabulary spurt.

Most of the discussion of finetuning has related to the level of syntax. We know that speech to young language learners is syntactically relatively simple, but does it approach the levels of complexity in adult directed speech in a gradual way that is responsive to child growth? The first attempts to demonstrate that it did were discouraging; Newport, Gleitman, and Gleitman (1977), for example, concluded "there is no compelling evidence in our data that mothers tune their syntactic complexity to the growing language competence of their children through this crucial age of syntax acquisition" (p. 124). Cross (1977, 1978) countered that CDS adjustments might reflect child comprehension more than child production levels – preserving the viability of a finetuning hypothesis, but failing to support it in any concrete way. Furthermore, the research models typically used in the early studies – simple correlations between, for example, maternal and child MLU – have been criticized on methodological and conceptual grounds (see Snow, Perlmann, and Nathan, 1987); they do not take into account that different adults may be finetuning their speech quite carefully to child growth, but with different baselines. Nor do they consider the possibility that aspects of CDS are finetuned that are not reflected in global measures like MLU.

An alternative approach is exemplified in the recent work of Sokolov (1993), who analyzed the relations between adjacent parent and child utterances to determine whether particular classes of lexical items were deleted or added. He found, in an automated analysis of the entire corpora from Abe, Adam, and Sarah, close to perfect correlations between the frequency with which parents added and children deleted modals, nouns, and pronouns; in other words, the more "telegraphic" the child speech, the more likely the parent was to fill in the missing item. Parental additions also showed a main effect of child age, decreasing linearly as children's language grew more complex. It is important to note that the extreme finetuning Sokolov demonstrated required analyses of interutterance relationships and targeting analyses at specific lexical classes.

An alternative approach to demonstrating finetuning exploits the availability of longitudinal data to model growth in crucial characteristics of both child and parent speech. For example, Pan, Feldman, and Snow (1993) found that parental measures such as MLU, MLU of the five longest utterances in ten minutes, and number of different word types produced in ten minutes showed significant growth over time (child age was 14 months at the first session, 32 months at the final session). Furthermore, growth in the same measure of the child's language was a significant predictor of parental growth rate – suggesting rather specific parent-to-child tuning as well as global tuning to developmental level of the child.

While these new methods enable us to demonstrate finetuning in CDS, it must also be noted that a relative absence of finetuning from some interlocutors may have developmental advantages. Considerable work (see Mannle and Tomasello, 1987; Barton and Tomasello, 1994, for extensive reviews) suggests that fathers (or secondary caregivers) and older siblings produce CDS that is less finely tuned to the child's developmental level than do mothers; these less familiar interlocutors are in general less responsive to immature child utterances and less likely to continue child topics. Perhaps as a result, they experience more failures of understanding and repair those failures less effectively. Fathers are also more likely to use unusual vocabulary items than are mothers. While the immediate effect of this poorly tuned speech may be conversational disruption, it is possible that fathers and other less familiar interlocutors provide children with important opportunities to learn skills needed for communication to more distant or unknown audiences, without the contextual and conversational support very young children enjoy in interaction with mothers. These distanced communication skills typically develop after age three, and are not reflected in developmental indices like MLU. If we had reliable ways of reflecting children's abilities to produce coherent, comprehensible narratives, reports, explanations, and arguments, we might be able to track long-term positive consequences of access to CDS which is challenging rather than finely tuned.

Effects of Development Delays

Input to children with developmental delays has been extensively studied for a number of reasons: (1) hypotheses about characteristics of the child that control the input received can be tested in populations where language abilities and cognitive capacities are less tightly linked than in normally developing children; (2) understanding the linguistic environment of children with various sorts of disabilities may contribute to improved intervention or prevention of language sequelae; and (3) children with developmental delays or disabilities may constitute a powerful case for testing the facilitative or prerequisite effects of input on normal language development. Aspects of CDS that are prerequisite to language development may be invisible in input to normally developing children, whose robust language acquisition capacities may establish such a low threshold for effects that every child has adequate access. The developmentally delayed or disabled child is more vulnerable to the effects of suboptimal input, and may enable us to identify effects otherwise swamped by robust language learning capacities.

Of course, research on CDS to groups of atypical children might be expected to generate highly variable findings, depending on the nature and severity of the child's disability. It was striking, then, that early research efforts almost all converged on the conclusion that speech to atypical children was more directive and less semantically contingent than speech to normally developing children – findings confirmed for children with hearing impairments, visual disabilities, Down Syndrome, specific language impairments, and learning disabilities (see Gallaway and Woll, 1994; Conti-Ramsden, 1994, for reviews). These findings were interpreted as suggesting that the language environment of atypical children may compound their difficulties in learning language, since directives were generally associated with slower progress in normally developing children, while rapid progress was associated with the rich availability of semantically contingent speech. However, it was also noted that the children in these various atypical groups were, for a variety of reasons, less active and effective spontaneous communicators, thus that parental directiveness may be an inevitable compensation for child passivity, incomprehensibility, or low responsiveness.

A recent review of the role of input in the development of language by children with visual impairments is instructive (Andersen, Dunlea, and Kekelis, 1993). Andersen et al. report a very high reliance on labeling and on object related directives in speech to their blind subjects, not just by mothers but by researchers as well. Though the blind children presumably needed descriptions and explanations more than sighted children, they received much less. The difficulty of reading cues from blind children about their targets of attention or their levels of comprehension no doubt led in part to these counterproductive interactive strategies.

Nelson, Welsh, Camarata, Butkovsky and Camarata (1993) reported a similar impoverishment of CDS to children with specific language impairment (SLI); they focused particularly on recasts, or responses to children's utterances that included most of the content words but added or rearranged the material. Nelson and colleagues had shown in previous work that recasts are effective in teaching targeted syntactic structures in training sessions with normal language learners (e.g. Nelson, 1987). Thus, their relative absence in speech to slow language learners might be a factor compounding the effects of the specific language impairment. Furthermore, Nelson, Camarata, Welsh, Butkovsky, and Camarata (1993) provided recasts in planned intervention sessions to a group of children with SLI and younger, language-age matched controls, to test if the children with SLI could make equally efficient use of the information available from the recasts. They found that both groups acquired the targeted structures rapidly, but that the children with SLI were more efficient learners than the younger children. These findings suggest that the rich availability of those input features shown to promote acquisition for normally developing children to children with language delay would constitute effective therapeutic intervention.

Universality

A full review of crosscultural and cross-social class differences in degree and type of modification in CDS would constitute a chapter in itself (see Lieven, 1994, for a recent review). Clearly, arguments about the value of CDS to the language learner would be compromised if there were children who learned language perfectly well despite an absence of any modification in their input. Of course, specific aspects of middle class Anglo-American CDS may well be absent from CDS in Samoan, Qui'che Mayan, Kaluli, or any of the more than 5,000 language communities yet to be studied. However, no one has seriously made the claim that CDS is indistinguishable from adult directed speech in any culture, nor has anyone argued that precisely the adjustments documented for middle class Anglo-American CDS are the only facilitators of language development. CDS has been widely reported to differ from adult directed speech wherever it has been studied; given the enormous cultural and linguistic differences among the groups studied, there is a remarkable convergence in types of modifications noted in lexicon and phonology (Ferguson, 1977), phonetics and prosody (Cruttenden, 1994) – the domains most widely studied. Of course, culture can always override linguistics, turning universals into extremely high probabilities. Thus, for example, the Qu'iche Mayan cultural prescription that high pitch be used to persons of high status conflicts with the otherwise universal use of high pitch to (low status) infants (Ratner and Pye, 1984), and wins out. The Kaluli cultural proscription on "birdtalk" (which recalls the mythic identification of birds with the souls of dead children) conflicts with the use of nonsense or babytalk words with infants (Schieffelin,

1983), and wins out. Rural African–American cultural preference for talk for social purposes conflicts with mathetically oriented naming during picturebook reading (Heath, 1983) and wins out. Language input is first and foremost for its producers a form of socialization (see Ely and Berko Gleason, this volume), and a culturally prescribed activity. That it also conforms to fairly universal tendencies toward phonological simplification, prosodic exaggeration, lexical and grammatical reduction, and communicative clarity even despite the cultural differences is impressive. We have not even begun to analyze whether variation within the culturally prescribed forms of CDS in every society relate to differences in speed or ease of language development by the children in that society. It has been suggested (Snow and Gilbreath, 1983) that a wide variety of mechanisms for language acquisition (e.g. hypothesizing salient lexical items name salient objects, rote learning recurrent phrases, segmenting recurrent initial and final syllables and calculating their cooccurrences, comparing adjacent utterances to identify additions and rearrangements, to name just a few) must be available to every language learner, and that every social environment must facilitate the action of some but not necessarily all of these.

Individual Differences

The major dimension of individual differences which has been related to aspects of CDS is the expressive/referential distinction (Nelson, 1973). Children typically fall along a continuum in terms of the kinds of words they first tend to acquire, with referential children preferring common nouns or general nominals, and expressive children preferring words that mark actions, social interactions, or individuals. Though it is important not to confound referential style with rapid lexical acquisition (a danger in cross-sectional analyses because an increasing proportion of later learned words are likely to be nouns for all children; Pine and Lieven, 1990), it is possible to relate children's relative early preference for nouns to characteristics of the input. Nelson's original study suggested a relation between expressiveness and maternal directiveness, a relationship that was confirmed in later studies (e.g. Della Corte, Benedict, and Klein, 1983). Child factors also played a role, though; Goldfield (1986, 1987, 1990) could predict degree of referentiality in 20-month-olds quite effectively in two different studies from child tendency to point to or use objects in social interaction, combined with maternal tendency to name objects. Even children who showed a lot of interest in objects at 14 months, for example, did not end up highly referential if their mothers responded to their showing or pointing with social rather than nominal speech. Goldfield's findings were supported by findings that maternal naming and object description related to referentiality (Della Corte et al., 1983; Hampson, 1989). Goldfield (1993) reported that number of maternal noun types and tokens in 12 minutes of toy play correlated with percent of nouns in children's first 50 words, perhaps in part because nouns in toy play contexts tended to occur in short

maternal utterances or in final position in longer utterances – perceptually salient positions.

Lieven, Pine, and Dresner-Barnes (1992) have argued that the distinction
between referential and expressive children can better be expressed as a distinction between children who prefer common nouns versus frozen phrases
(see also Peters, 1983). The tendency to acquire and use frozen phrases has not
been related to specific aspects of the input in large-scale studies, though it has
been noted as a characteristic of blind children (Andersen et al., 1993), and it
clearly relates to certain interactive contexts – routinized games, recurrent
interaction frames, and speech that is difficult to map onto external referents
(see Snow, Perlmann, and Nathan, 1987). Finding relationships between characteristics of CDS and language learning style probably will require, as Pine
(1994) argues, a set of methods targeted to finding specific mechanisms by
which children make use of various sorts of input. Traditional methods in this
field have tended to use relatively global indicators of input and output, such
that emergent correlations between input and output are hard to relate to any
convincing mechanism of acquisition and can only be explained in a post hoc
manner.

Essential, Facilitative, or Irrelevant?

We know that children need some linguistic input in order to learn language.
The questions of interest circle around the ways in which the crucial language
exposure works – whether as a trigger (Lightfoot, 1989) or catapult (Randall,
1990) launching the child into the language system with a single nudge, or as
a source of opportunities for incremental learning. Some lower limit can be
placed on the degree to which the input functions as a trigger by examining
impoverished linguistic environments. For example, hearing children of deaf
parents fail to learn language from television and casual encounters with hearing
adults (Sachs, Bard, and Johnson, 1981), and in one study three-and-a-half
year old children from families in which neglect had been confirmed showed
language delays of six months (Culp, Watkins, Lawrence, Letts, Kelly, and
Rice, 1991). On the other hand, most children clearly receive more input than
is strictly necessary to support normal language acquisition, as shown by the
fact that input can be distributed over two or three languages with the result
that the child is a fully bilingual or trilingual speaker. We will consider the
evidence on how the input works and how crucial it is to normal acquisition
for a number of domains separately.

The lexicon

No one would argue with the claim that vocabulary acquisition must depend
on vocabulary input. None the less, it has been suggested that vocabulary

acquisition is constrained by innate principles that are crucial to enabling the child make sense of the input, and map word meanings onto word forms correctly (e.g. Markman, 1989). The empiricist position on word learning is espoused by those who argue that it is possible to identify the conditions of exposure to new words that will facilitate or even ensure correct learning, without recourse to specific constraints on the nature of lexical representation or lexical acquisition strategies.

Two factors which have been clearly implicated in vocabulary acquisition are (1) density of maternal speech (Huttenlocher, Haight, Bryk, Seltzer, and Lyons, 1991) or frequency of exposure to words, and (2) situation of exposure to the novel word. The evidence is quite clear that the first words children learn are those they are most frequently exposed to (Hart, 1991; Harris, Barrett, Jones, and Brookes, 1988). Furthermore, children whose mothers talk more per unit time show more rapid growth of vocabulary (Huttenlocher, et al., 1991).

Nouns are most likely to be learned by young children during episodes of joint attention (Tomasello and Todd, 1983; Tomasello and Farrar, 1986b). Tomasello and Todd reported that nouns used during joint attentional focus between adult and child in naturally occurring interactions were the most likely to be acquired, and Tomasello and Farrar confirmed this experimentally. These findings recall some of those noted above, suggesting that highly nominal children are those whose mothers respond to social initiatives by naming objects the child is attending to (Goldfield, 1990). Huttenlocher, et al.'s findings (1991) complement this picture by showing that children who hear more maternal speech, other things being equal, learn vocabulary faster. Thus, we can extrapolate to the conclusion that absolute frequency rather than just percent of joint attentional episodes promotes lexical acquisition – at least for nouns.

Verbs, though, do not seem to be learned from being used during joint mother–child attention to the action they name. Tomasello and Kruger (1992) report that verbs used to name *impending* actions are better learned than those used to name ongoing action. The facilitative effect of impending action contexts for verb display might seem to contradict the findings that highly directive mothers have children who learn language more slowly (e.g. Della Corte, Benedict, and Klein, 1983; Tomasello and Todd, 1983), since directives typically include the impending action verbs; however, more careful analysis of directive mothers' talk suggests that "responsively directive" mothers, those who issue directives that do not shift the child's attentional focus but follow on from the current activity, actually facilitate vocabulary acquisition (r = 0.78 in a study by Akhtar, Dunham, and Dunham, 1991).

While early-learned nouns and verbs can be acquired from exposure through contexts of ostensive definition (Ninio and Bruner, 1978), joint attention (Tomasello and Todd, 1983), or impending action (Tomasello and Kruger, 1992), many later-learned nouns, verbs, and other words cannot. Mental state terms, for example, do not lend themselves to such contexts for acquisition, nor do abstract nouns like superordinates. Furrow, Moore, Davidge, and Chiasson (1992) found that maternal use of cognitive verbs (e.g. know, think, remember) increased by a factor of more than two between age 2;0 and 3;0, suggesting some finetuning in use of this lexical class. In addition, though, maternal use of these terms at 2;0 in two particular situations – to refer to someone's mental activities, or to encourage child reflection – predicted child use at 3;0, whereas maternal use of the cognitive terms in utterances designed to direct child activity or interaction (do you think that's a garage?) did not relate to child acquisition. Bodin and Snow (1994) found that one mother's use of superordinates often occurred in implicitly or explicitly tutorial interactions, e.g. in conjunction with mention of class members, and Nelson, Hampson and Kessler Shaw (1993) report that maternal use of nouns for other than basic object terms often occurred in predictable action contexts that supported correct interpretation.

Communicative intents

Acquisition of the lexicon can only with difficulty in the earliest stages of language development be distinguished from acquisition of the language system as a whole. As children acquire new words during the one word stage, they typically also acquire expanded capacities to express themselves. There is considerable controversy over the degree to which children's early meanings and the means for expressing them derive directly from input. For example, Ninio (1992) demonstrates that over 90 percent of 18-month-olds' single word utterances are used to express the same communicative intents as the single word utterances of mothers addressing them, and futhermore that the children typically selected the most frequent form used by the mothers to express any particular speech act. She argues that this is possible because the children have an adultlike system for analyzing communicative intent, but rely on predictable form–function mappings in the input when seeking ways of expressing those intents. Barrett, Harris, and Chasin (1991) agree that initial word uses are closely tied to maternal use, but argue that subsequent uses by the child are less predictable from high frequency maternal use. Note that Barrett et al. were analyzing use in terms of situation, whereas Ninio analyzed communicative intent rather than situational meaning as the basis for matching mother to child use. Also, Barrett et al. considered any maternal use of children's early acquired words, whereas Ninio's analysis was limited to maternal single word utterances.

Syntax

In the domain of grammatical acquisition, most of the attention has been directed to establishing the existence and role of negative evidence. The argument for the central importance of negative evidence goes like this: given children's will attested tendencies to hypothesize, generalize, and extrapolate from the available information, negative evidence is crucial to help them restrict the overly general rules they are likely to formulate. Oddly, much of the argumentation related to negative evidence has circled around a problem of morphology – strong versus regular past tense forms in English – not a problem of syntax at all. A recent review of work on negative evidence (Sokolov and Snow, 1994) concludes that the claim that negative evidence is unavailable to the language learning child has been greatly exaggerated. In addition, though, the claim that children generalize and extrapolate, thus generating the need for negative evidence, is somewhat overstated. While there are domains (e.g. pockets of irregularity in otherwise regular morphological systems) which induce overgeneralization by some children, most children fail to exploit most opportunities for potential error, operating in a way that can only be described as conservative and highly respectful of lexical limits.

Extended discourse

Snow (1989) noted that the aspects of language development that might be most susceptible to input effects were the then still relatively little studied skills associated with producing extended discourse. Since then, considerable data have accumulated suggesting that extended discourse skills are, indeed, quite vulnerable to differences in interaction style and characteristics of CDS. A first confirmation of these effects derives, of course, from the widely attested cultural and social class differences in narrative style, control over classroom discourse rules, and style of self presentation (e.g. Heath, 1983). However, more recently actual interactive analyses have suggested some of the mechanisms by which children come to acquire the characteristics of their own culture and social group in producing extended discourse, as well as mechanisms by which some children come to be highly skilled at extended discourse production.

Peterson and McCabe (1992), for example, report that the kinds of questions asked by mothers during children's personal event narrations predicted the kinds of information the children came to include in their narratives – much contextual and orienting information in one case, and much event elaboration in the other. McCabe and Peterson subsequently replicated these findings in a larger group of children (1991b), and showed that children whose parents asked topic extending questions ended up producing longer and more coherent narratives than children whose parents asked diverting or detail questions.

Though they did not have later outcome measures on children's language, Sorsby and Martlew (1991) report that four-year-olds responded more accurately to high level requests for information and that their mothers engaged in more abstract during book reading than during a play-doh modeling task. This study represents an early attempt to analyze CDS for cognitive challenge and support to more complex language, going beyond the traditional emphasis on purely lexical or grammatical acquisition. Watson (1989) showed effects of parental use of cognitive verbs and superordinate labels while reading books with two-year-olds on the sophistication of children's definitions and understanding of taxonomic relationships a year later. The kinds of relatively sophisticated, abstract, and decontextualized talk possible during book reading with even quite young children may promote both linguistic and cognitive sophistication.

In a longitudinal study of CDS as related to language outcomes of low income children, amount of talk during book reading that went beyond the immediate content of text and pictures at three and four related to skill at extended discourse when children were five (De Temple and Beals, 1991). In the same study, additional powerful predictors of language outcomes included percent of talk during mealtimes that was explanatory (De Temple and Beals, 1991), and use of rare vocabulary items (i.e. words that fell neither within the most common 3,000 words nor were derived from local, familial, or popular culture referents) by family members (Snow and Tabors, 1993).

Conclusion

A number of general themes emerge from the many studies of CDS and its effects. One is the need to differentiate CDS much more carefully than early studies did. The first studies in this field were fairly cavalier about the ages and language levels of the children being addressed, assuming evidently that the same features of CDS would facilitate growth at any age, and that growth could be represented rather globally. More recent work has made clear that what might facilitate the acquisition of a common noun for a 14-month-old in the context of toy play might not work in a different activity with the same child, nor would it necessarily be helpful to an older child working on quite a different set of problems.

Another issue which has emerged is the role of frequency or density of certain events in CDS (see Hoff-Ginsberg, 1992). Because they were sampling only a small amount of mother–child interaction, researchers in this field have almost universally used proportions of various categories of utterances in their descriptions and predictive models. Thus, directive mothers were those who produced a high proportion of directives, independent of the number of directives they produced. If we assume, though, that each occurrence of certain events (e.g. recasts) provides a child with opportunities to learn, then the raw frequency of such events might be more important than their proportions. Furthermore, as Nelson (1987) has pointed out, such events might be irrelevant until the child has attained a certain developmental readiness, at which point they become crucial, so some absolute though perhaps low frequency is more meaningful than proportional use. Hoff-Ginsberg has argued that we misrepresent the degree of difference between the experience of children growing up in working class versus educated, middle class households by using proportions, which tend to make the two groups of mothers appear rather similar. In fact, though, the middle class mothers talk much more, and thus provide their children with much higher frequencies of exposure to lexical items, to recasts and clarification questions, and of course also to directives and prohibitions. We possess remarkably little basis for extrapolating from what we can record of CDS or child language in an hour's observation to an estimate of the child's total linguistic experience. But it is clearly the child's total experience, not the possibly somewhat unnatural interaction during the observation, that we would like to capture for descriptive and predictive purposes.

The study of input to children has started to emerge from the methodological barbarities that characterized its early years. We now recognize that measuring change by partialling out scores at Time 1 from outcomes taken at Time 2 violates both statistical and developmental common sense. The best developmental measures are based on estimates of growth, which in turn should be based on multiple waves of data – the recent study by Huttenlocher et al. (1991) is a healthy example of the value of growth rather than level as an outcome. Furthermore, we have gone beyond expecting global measures of language development to reflect global characteristics of "quality" in the input, focusing instead on very specific input–output relations, e.g. number of words heard to vocabulary growth (Huttenlocher et al., 1991), exposure to specific morphological markers to control over those markers (Farrar, 1990), exposure to nouns under conditions of joint attention to learning nouns (Tomasello and Farrar, 1986b; Goldfield, 1993), exposure to recasts of particular syntactic structures to acquisition of those particular structures (Nelson, 1987), and so on. Given that some of the predictors and outcomes of interest are relatively infrequent, only the availability of archived transcript data and automated search and analysis procedures (MacWhinney, 1991) makes promising analyses of phenomena that would otherwise be too time consuming or unproductive to pursue (e.g. work by Sokolov, in press). Furthermore, a few of the hypotheses derived from correlations in observational data have been tested in experimental designs (Tomasello and Farrar, 1986b; Nelson, 1987), clearly a direction in which the field has moved too slowly.

Finally, work is starting to emerge which confirms the effects of input on language acquisition at a level not yet seriously focused on in CDS – the level of the language system itself. Goldin-Meadow and Mylander (1990) wrote, "Linguistic input has an obvious impact on the child's acquisition of language – a child who hears Swahili learns Swahili, not French or Polish" (p. 3,232). This statement was presumably an identification of what is relatively *uninteresting* about the effects input. It turns out, though, that language typological effects on acquisition can be documented, effects not of variation within a language community in types of input offered, but of variation between language communities. Ultimately, of course, it is not surprising that children in Israel end up speaking Hebrew while children in Korea end up speaking Korean. What is surprising is how early they *start out* speaking their own languages. The universal biases and strategies that we once assumed drove language acquisition, and ultimately succumbed to the idiosyncrasies of specific languages, have been very hard to find. Children in Israel do not persist very long in thinking they are learning words as isolable units – they start out almost immediately exploiting the complex morphological possibilities a Semitic language offers, in which word forms are marvellously variable (Berman, 1988a). Children in Japan do not start out learning nouns, sharing with English-speaking children the unquestioned conviction that nouns are cognitively more accessible, easier to map onto referents, and simpler in form; they prefer to learn verbs, just as their language prefers to retain verbs and delete nouns in conversational ellipsis (Clancy, 1985). Children in Korea do not start out assuming that the crucial distinction relevant to expressing location is containment versus support; they seem from the start content with the distinction marked in Korean between tight and loose attachment (Choi and Bowerman, 1991). These effects of language structure on children's language systems suggest an enormous susceptibility on the part of language learners to the effects of input, only a tiny portion of which have we yet documented.

7 Discourse Organization and the Development of Reference to Person, Space, and Time

MAYA HICKMANN

1 Introduction

The ability to organize discourse is a necessary component of children's developing knowledge during first language acquisition. Reaching mature communicative competence requires that children learn the pragmatic principles that govern how information is organized across utterances and that allow the construction of cohesive discourse. As a result, children become able to rely maximally on linguistic context when talking about entities and events that are not in the immediate speech situation. Among the different devices that must be mastered are those that contribute to two aspects of discourse organization: (1) the relative givenness or newness of information, i.e. information status must be marked as a function of available mutual background knowledge; (2) the foregrounding or backgrounding of information, i.e. the flow of information must be regulated as a function of communicative focus.

Recent psycholinguistic research has begun to show the importance of discourse organizing principles for children's language acquisition. This chapter provides an overview of studies pertaining to three domains in child language: person, space, and time. The focus is on oral speech, leaving aside important aspects that might be specific to written language or to nonverbal behavior. Particular attention is placed on the interrelations between functional factors operating at the discourse level and syntactic–semantic factors operating at the sentence level. In all three domains considered below, it is typically the same devices that must be acquired at the discourse and sentence levels, because they contribute both to the organization of information in discourse and to the expression of propositional information in the sentence. Mastering this multifunctionality, it is argued, is a central part of children's task during the acquisition process, regardless of what language they are acquiring.

There are, however, some variations in the particular devices that are available to speakers across languages for the expression of relations within and across utterances, e.g. for noun phrase roles (case inflections, word order, verbal morphology), temporal–aspectual distinctions (verbal inflections, particles, adverbials, connectives), and spatial relations (verb and satellites such as particles, prepositional phrases, adverbials). Thus, even though all children must acquire the devices necessary for the construction of cohesive discourse, they have different problems to solve during the course of acquisition depending on the particular way in which subsystems in their native language are organized. Determining the role of general v. language-specific factors during language acquisition has become an essential issue, which is still relatively unexplored in the domain of discourse organization. As discussed below, formal and functional differences across languages also raise specific questions concerning the rate and course of the development of discourse cohesion.

2   Discourse Functional Aspects of Reference

2.1   *Multifunctionality, context dependence, and units of analysis*

An essential property of all linguistic systems is their inherent multifunctionality: language consists of multiple relations among forms and functions at different levels (cf. Halliday, 1975; Jakobson, 1971; Silverstein, 1987a). Thus, Halliday characterizes language in terms of three macrofunctions: the *ideational* function, dependent on the fact that language is a system encoding propositional information; the *social* function, related to interpersonal aspects of language use; and the *textual* function, pertaining to the interrelations among utterances in discourse context (central to our discussion below). One implication of multifunctionality is the need for two distinct units of analysis: the sentence and discourse. The properties of reflexive v. nonreflexive pronouns illustrate this distinction (*bound* v. *free anaphora*, cf. Deutsch and Koster, 1982; Deutsch, Koster, and Koster, 1986; Lust, 1986): roughly, reflexives are highly constrained grammatically to particular coreferential relations within the clause, e.g. *himself* can only refer to John in (1), whereas nonreflexives are not as constrained, e.g. *him* in (2) can refer to the boy or to some other referent previously mentioned and/or in nonlinguistic context (but not to John):

(1)   The boy said that John washed himself.
(2)   The boy said that John washed him.

A number of theoretical questions arose in linguistics and philosophy as a result of considering units of analysis that are larger than the sentence. Traditional functional approaches argued that the organization of the sentence is (at least partly) determined by context, e.g. sentences establish a certain *perspective*, which depends partly on the extent to which elements are salient and communicative, given variouś aspects of the context (e.g. Daneš, 1974; Firbas, 1964, 1966, 1971; Foley and van Valin, 1985; Halliday and Hasan, 1976). New types of models have also been proposed for logical analyses of texts in which a *discourse representation structure* is first constructed on the basis of the sequences of sentences in narratives before texts are interpreted (Kamp, 1979).

Such notions have had direct consequences for the psycholinguistic study of language behavior (e.g. Chafe, 1976, 1979; MacWhinney, 1977). From a developmental point of view, it has become clear that we must account for how children master the uses of devices at both the sentence and discourse levels. At the sentence level they must learn to express semantic and syntactic relations in grammatically well-formed sentences in which they refer to entities, predicate states, or events about them, and situate them in time and space. In addition, we must account for how children relate utterances to their contexts of use. In this respect, the discourse unit of analysis necessarily involves a relation between speech and context. As shown below, context dependence consists of two types of *anchoring*: anchoring in the nonlinguistic context and/or in the surrounding linguistic context. In addition, intersentential links can be *local*, i.e. across adjacent utterances, or more *global*, i.e. at the level of whole texts. The gradual mastery of all types of context dependence is central to children's development: children at first anchor speech in the immediate here-and-now and it becomes essential for them to anchor speech locally and globally in discourse when they begin to displace reference away from the speech situation.

2.2   *Exophora, endophora, and discourse cohesion*

Anchoring in nonlinguistic v. linguistic context places different constraints on language use and acquisition. These two types of context dependence have been designated with various terms, such as *exophora* v. *endophora, deixis* v. *anaphora* or *cataphora, deictic* v. *intralinguistic* uses, or *speaker* v. *discourse deixis* (cf. Anderson and Keenan, 1985; Fillmore, 1982; Halliday and Hasan, 1976; Hickmann, 1982, 1987b, 1991a; Jarvella and Klein, 1982; Lyons, 1975, 1977; Silverstein, 1976; Wales, 1986; Weissenborn and Klein, 1982). In all languages both types involve indexical devices that *point* to something in the context, thereby anchoring speech to the personal, spatial, and temporal parameters of the speech situation. Exophoric uses typically point to and presuppose some parameter of the immediate nonlinguistic situation, endophoric ones some discourse-internal aspect of the context.[1]

In the domain of person, exophoric devices denote entities that are physically present in the context, e.g. first and second person pronouns (*I, you*) denote the immediate interlocutors, third person pronouns (*he, she*), definite nominals (*the book*), or demonstratives (*that*) denote other entities in the situation. Demonstratives are also among the devices used for spatial deixis, e.g. they can encode distance through a relation to the speaker or listener (e.g. *here/there, this/that book*). Other spatial deictics include verbs of motion (e.g. *come/go*) expressing a displacement towards or away from a presupposed point (the *origo*), typically taken to be the immediate speech situation, unless otherwise specified. In the domain of temporality, deictic devices locate the time of denoted situations in relation to the speech situation. Thus, in *Yesterday I checked John's homework*, the past inflection *-ed* marks that my checking occurred before the moment at which I am speaking and the adverb *yesterday* further specifies that this moment occurred at some point within the previous 24 hours.

In contrast, endophoric uses relate utterances to the linguistic context of speech as speakers establish various types of links between the ongoing utterance and the preceding or subsequent utterances (within and across speaking turns). Such uses are necessary when the interlocutors cannot rely on much background mutual knowledge and they can be of different kinds. Connectives constitute obvious local ways of linking successive clauses, e.g. temporally or causally (e.g. *then, while, when, because*). Endophoric links also include other tense-aspect markings (verbal inflections, particles, adverbials) that serve to organize information in discourse, as well as the use of referring expressions that presuppose in various degrees the existence and identity of referents in discourse (e.g. English third person pronouns).

Proposals have been made to relate the two kinds of indexical uses in various ways and it has been hypothesized that endophoric uses evolve out of exophoric ones in acquisition (e.g. Ehlich, 1982; Jakobson, 1971; Jarvella and Klein, 1982; Fillmore, 1982; Hickmann, 1982, 1987b, 1991a; Halliday and Hasan, 1976; Hinrichs, 1986; Karmiloff-Smith, 1979; Levinson, 1983; Lyons, 1975, 1977; Schiffrin, 1990; Silverstein, 1976). This distinction, however, is not always easy to make, particularly in child language. Typically, indexical devices pertaining to person, space, and time can be either exophoric or endophoric: some are primarily exophoric, but they can be endophoric; others are primarily endophoric, but they can be exophoric; yet others are primarily nonindexical, but they can be indexical. For example, in reported speech, first and second person pronouns, as well as spatiotemporal devices, refer to the parameters defining the reported situation, rather than the immediate one (*John said, "I saw you here yesterday"*). Conversely, third person pronouns typically refer in entities previously mentioned in discourse, but they can be used to denote referents that are present and in attention focus. In addition, some spatial prepositions are primarily independent of context (e.g. *X is in front of the truck*, given that trucks have an inherent front), but they can be interpreted deictically in relation to the speaker's location (e.g. *X is in front of the tree*).

Endophoric uses are intrinsic to the construction of *discourse cohesion*, in particular when speakers must rely maximally on language use in the absence of relevant mutual background knowledge. As summarized by Halliday and Hasan (1976: 4), cohesion consists of various types of dependence relations within linguistic context:

> Cohesion occurs where the interpretation of some element in the discourse is dependent on that of another [across clauses]. The one presupposes the other in the sense that it cannot be effectively [or can only be partially] decoded, except by recourse to it. When this happens, a relation of cohesion is set up and the elements, the presupposing and the presupposed, are thereby at least potentially integrated into a text.

Two related aspects of discourse cohesion must be learned by children during language acquisition. Both involve a variety of linguistic devices which regulate the information flow across utterances in discourse: the *marking of information status*, whereby speakers indicate the degree to which different components of the information in their utterances are presupposed; the *grounding of information*, whereby they indicate what is the main information in focus and what is secondary. We briefly turn to each one below.

2.3 Given and new information

Any stretch of discourse requires that speakers indicate whether the denoted information is relatively *given* or *new*, particularly in the absence of relevant nonlinguistic context (cf. Chafe, 1976; Clark and Haviland, 1976; Haviland and Clark, 1974; Halliday and Hasan, 1976). When speakers cannot assume that their interlocutors know about a particular referent, they must first introduce this entity in discourse by means of linguistic devices that do not presuppose existence and identity, e.g. English indefinite nominal determiners (*a car*) mark that the denoted information is brand new. In contrast, definite noun phrases (*the car, it*) maintain reference after entities have been introduced, presupposing their identity to different degrees, e.g. depending on potential ambiguities due to competing candidates in surrounding discourse. Similarly, verbal anaphora and ellipsis also presuppose states and events already mentioned (e.g. *John went home and so did Mary* or *Where did John go? Home*).

In addition, any stretch of discourse requires that speakers share a common spatiotemporal frame of reference. When interlocutors talk about entities that are present in the immediate speech situation and about events that are happening in that situation, they can simply assume that this spatiotemporal frame is the here-and-now, thereby taking the speech situation as their *origo*. However, when the denoted entities and events are displaced, they must provide a minimal amount of information allowing the interlocutor to locate them in space and time. Thus, consider (3), in which the interlocutors are speaking of a common friend John:

(3) Yesterday John found a beautiful painting in an antique furniture store near his house. He liked it so much that he went back there today and bought it cash.

The speaker introduces a new referent (*a beautiful painting*), while providing information about time (*yesterday*) and place (*an antique furniture store near his house*). Reference can then be maintained to John (*he*), to the painting (*it*), and to the spatial frame (*there*) in an utterance that contains a deictic motion verb and particle (*went back*) presupposing that John left the spatial frame between the initial time frame (*yesterday*) and a new subsequent one (*today*).

2.4   Foreground and background

In addition to marking information status, speakers must *ground information*, i.e. present it as belonging to the *foreground* v. *background* of discourse. Roughly, utterances in the foreground correspond to the skeleton of the narrative, i.e. to the chronologically ordered main events that constitute the time line and make the plot line move forward, whereas backgrounded ones need not be chronologically ordered (simultaneity or overlap) and they tend to correspond to secondary information surrounding the foreground (cf. Dry, 1981, 1983; Ehrlich, 1987, 1988; Hopper, 1979a, 1979b, 1982; Givón, 1987; Reinhart, 1984; Tomlin, 1987).[2]

A number of devices contribute to the presentation of backgrounded v. foregrounded situations: aspect, subordination, word order, and voice (Hopper, 1979a, 1979b; 1982; Hopper and Thompson, 1980; Kamp, 1979; Li, Thompson, and Thompson, 1982; Reinhart, 1984; Schiffrin, 1981; Thompson, 1987; Tomlin, 1987; cf. interesting counterexamples in Chvany, 1985). For example, grammaticalized aspect (verbal inflections, particles), sometimes in conjunction with other aspectual devices (adverbials, connectives) marks different *perspectives* in relation to the temporal structure of situations: the perspective of the *imperfective* is located within the internal structure of ongoing situations, whereas *perfective* aspect marks an external perspective which represents situations as points after they have stopped and/or are completed and independently of their internal structure. For example, in (4) the inflections (perfective *arrived*, imperfective *was eating*) represent Mary's arrival as a point which occurs after John began eating the apple and before he finished it: Mary's arrival is a foregrounded event moving the plot line forward, John's eating a backgrounded event overlapping with the foreground. Similarly, (5) shows how imperfective aspect and subordination can coincide as backgrounding devices: the perfective past (*sat down, started to read, rang*) marks foregrounded events, the subordinated progressive (*while he was reading*) a backgrounded event:

(4) John was eating an apple. Mary arrived.
(5) John sat down and started to read a book. While he was reading, the door bell rang.

Information status and grounding interact in discourse. Referential links (referent introductions, reference maintenance) and temporal–aspectual markings can be combined as indications of episode boundaries (Ehrlich, 1987, 1988). Backgrounding information can occur throughout narratives, including in the initial setting, where the spatial, temporal, and personal parameters of the plot are established. Conversely, there is a strong tendency for highly presupposed information to occur in foregrounded clauses, e.g. human main protagonists mentioned with pronominal forms in highly transitive clauses (cf. Hopper, 1979a, 1979b, 1982; Hopper and Thompson, 1980).

2.5 *Universal and language-specific functional aspects of acquisition*

Crosslinguistic research is crucial for evaluating the impact of language-independent cognitive determinants, the role of language-specific factors, and the place of Universal Grammar in acquisition. Until recently, however, few have considered the implications of universal and language-specific aspects of discourse cohesion for acquisition (cf. Berman and Slobin, 1994; Hendriks, 1993; Hickmann, 1991a; Hickman, Kaiser, and Roland, 1991; Hickmann and Liang, 1990; Slobin, 1991). Although information status and grounding are universal principles of discourse organization that must be acquired by all children, languages provide different systems of devices, presenting children with different problems to solve.

Such crosslinguistic differences are both formal and functional. The richness and type of morphology exhibited by different languages vary a great deal (Bybee, 1985): languages can be highly inflected (tense, aspect, number, gender, case) in various ways (prefixes, suffixes, infixes), or have no morphology at all. As a consequence, variations are found in the available devices expressing relations within and across clauses, as well as in the functional load carried by any one of them. Such differences have been claimed to cause relative ease or difficulty during the acquisition process. For example, *local* markings affect one particular element in the clause (e.g. inflections) and have been claimed to be easier to acquire than *global* ones which affect the entire clause (e.g. word order), particularly when they are placed at the end of lexical items[3] (cf. Ammon and Slobin, 1979; Slobin, 1973, 1982, 1985; Johnston and Slobin, 1979; Slobin and Bever, 1982; but cf. counterarguments in Bowerman, 1985; Weist and Konieczna, 1985). Indeed, it is easier for children to interpret sentences when their language has a rich and transparent morphology (e.g. Turkish) than when it depends more on word order to express grammatical relations (e.g. English). Studies of sentence comprehension across languages also show that adults and children (as young as two years) use the cues that are the most available and reliable in their language, e.g. word order in English and lexical or morphological cues in Italian, suggesting a model in which children must learn how functions compete and coalesce in relation to available forms (Bates and MacWhinney, 1982, 1987; MacWhinney and Bates, 1989).

3 The Development of Discourse Organization

3.1 Scripts, structural coherence, and textual cohesion

The development of discourse organization has been studied within at least two main theoretical frameworks, focusing on two aspects of discourse: *coherence*, which corresponds to the structure of discourse content, and *cohesion*, which pertains to the linguistic devices providing the links whereby this content is organized.[4] Some researchers within the first type of framework have provided a general account of verbal and nonverbal knowledge in the form of *macrostructures* or *scripts* guiding how we organize complex event sequences (e.g. French and Nelson, 1985; Hudson and Nelson, 1983; McCartney and Nelson, 1981; Nelson, 1986; Nelson and Gruendel, 1979, 1981; Shank and Abelson, 1977; Van Dijk, 1980). Others have examined our knowledge of particular discourse types, proposing general principles or even *story grammars* to capture the properties of structurally well-formed stories (e.g. Applebee, 1978; Fayol, 1985; Labov and Waletzky, 1967; Mandler, 1978; Mandler and DeForest, 1979; Mandler and Johnson, 1977; Quasthoff and Nikolaus, 1982; Stein, 1982; Stein and Glenn, 1979, 1982; Stein and Nezworski, 1978; Stein and Trabasso, 1981). Despite some inherent properties differentiating story schemata from scripts, both approaches postulate the existence of *cognitive schemata* that underly our representations of complex event structures. Structural properties of narratives include the types of units and relations necessary for the construction of a well-formed story. For example, Stein's story grammar contains a *Setting* and an *Episode* consisting of the following sequence of units: an *Initiating Event* triggering subsequent events, i.e. an *Internal Response* on the part of the main protagonist, motivating an *Attempt* to reach a goal, with some *Consequence* resulting in a *Reaction*. On the basis of experimental evidence, story grammars have been claimed to be psychologically real and to guide the processing and production of stories by adults and children. For example, when subjects are asked to recall anomalous stories (missing or displaced units), their recall decreases and they modify the texts in such a way as to make them more compatible with well-formed texts.

Exceptions to this pattern occur, showing a relation between story schemata and textual markers. For example, children's free recall of anomalous stories actually increases when the displacements of some units are marked by linguistic devices (e.g. *this happened because*, Stein and Nezworski, 1978). More generally, a number of studies have begun to examine the relation between the development of the cognitive schemata underlying coherence and of the linguistic devices necessary for cohesion. It can be argued that some structural anomalies cooccur with textual ones and that discourse cohesion may even be partially constitutive of effects attributed to schemata, e.g. deleting or displacing units that contain referent introductions results in subsequent anomalies in reference maintenance (cf. a discussion in Hickmann, 1982). Furthermore, adults' and seven to eight-year-olds' recall of structurally anomalous stories (randomized sentences) is improved when referring expressions are changed to restore cohesive continuity (Garnham, Oakhill, and Johnson-Laird, 1982). Indeed, children are sensitive not only to structural anomalies (e.g. Espéret, 1991), but also to anomalies in cohesion (Hickmann and Schneider, 1993): from five years onward they can correct discourse cohesion when they have to process structurally well-formed stories that contain anomalous referring expressions (e.g. definite forms introducing referents indefinite ones maintaining reference), as long as the task does not require conscious awareness. Finally, children do use cohesive devices to integrate information during on-line text processing from seven years onwards (e.g. Tyler, 1984).

The need to relate structural coherence and textual cohesion in discourse organization has been stressed in recent research focusing on children's narrative productions (e.g. discussions in Fayol, 1985, 1991). Some studies have shown similar developmental progressions in both aspects of children's narrative organization (Shapiro and Hudson, 1991). Others have argued that scripts or story grammars are major determinants of the use and acquisition of cohesive devices, such as referring expressions (e.g. Orsolini, 1990) or connectives (e.g. French and Nelson, 1985). Yet others find in children's productions some linguistic correlates of their ability to comprehend story content (e.g. Stenning and Michell, 1985). As shown below, more research is needed to relate coherence and cohesion, given how children mark information flow in discourse across languages.

3.2   Emergence of the textual function

A number of studies show that children as young as two years display the ability to sustain conversation, to participate in successful joint referential activities, and to mark links across speaker turns in various ways, e.g. by repetition, juxtaposition, sequencing (Bruner, 1983; Keenan, 1974, 1977; Keenan and Klein, 1975; Keenan and Schieffelin, 1976; Sachs, 1979, 1983). These results have been taken as evidence that young children can organize discourse at some level, despite their need to rely on adult scaffolding and despite claims that they are unable to *decenter* in communication. From about two years on children also begin to recall, report, and discuss past events, i.e. to displace reference from the *here-and-now* to the *there-and-then* (e.g. Eisenberg, 1985; Fivush, Gray, and Fromhoff, 1987; French and Nelson, 1985; Kemper, 1984; McCabe and Peterson, 1991a; McCartney and Nelson, 1981; Menig-Peterson,

1975; Menig-Peterson and McCabe, 1978; Miller and Sperry, 1988; Nelson, 1986; Peterson, 1990; Peterson and Dodsworth, 1991; Peterson and McCabe, 1983; Preece, 1987; Sachs, 1979, 1983; Todd and Perlmutter, 1980; Umiker-Sebeok, 1979). For example, Sachs (1983) finds that children under three years begin to displace reference, even in a limited way: conversations are brief, not always successful and/or focused, dependent on adult initiation or scaffolding, and they lack the necessary linguistic devices. Early displaced reference is also highly dependent on routines and scripts, i.e. children first talk about situation types frequently encountered, rather than about specific events. After about 29 months children spontaneously initiate less general and longer stretches of speech. These stretches, however, are still relatively disorganized.

In general, results diverge with respect to how early children master devices when displacing reference. On the one hand, some have challenged the idea that children are unable to use devices appropriately because of their cognitive immaturity: when asked to speak about familiar scripted events, children as young as two to three years use connectives and adverbials (e.g. *before, after, so*), inflections (timeless present), nominal determiners ("intrinsic" use in *the teacher* v. *a noise*, cf. French and Nelson, 1985). On the other hand, it has been shown that displaced reference is characterized by a gradual increase in both coherence and cohesion. With respect to coherence, young children fail to produce particular units, for example, settings (e.g. Eisenberg, 1985; Menig-Peterson and McCabe, 1978; Fayol, 1985), which are central for the introduction of initial parameters in narratives: one finds some spatial orientation with events that took place away from home, but practically no orientation concerning the participants, and none concerning time (e.g. Gopnik, 1989; Sachs, 1983; Peterson, 1990).

With respect to cohesion, the emergence of intersentential links has been reported to emerge at two to three years, although deictic and intralinguistic uses are rarely distinguished (e.g. Peterson and Dodsworth, 1991). Such utterances contain relatively few ties at first, the most common one being lexical cohesion (talking about the same thing), while pronouns and connectives are also frequent and increase with age. In an analysis distinguishing endophora and exophora, Pellegrini (1984) reports that children from six years on use endophora in some situation types (absence of mutual knowledge, dramatic play), exophora in others (discussion, drawing). More detailed analyses of early spontaneous discourse show that children's uses of linguistic devices evolve gradually. Thus, pronouns emerge at around two years, then develop gradually through longer cohesive chains, through function shifts (e.g. from verb phrase to subject), and more generally through the child's ability to grasp formal contrasts in prior discourse (e.g. Levy, 1989; Nelson and Levy, 1987). Temporal terms also evolve gradually in discourse: adverbials (Levy and Nelson, in press), connectives (e.g. Bennett-Kastor, 1986; Jisa, 1984/5, 1987), and verbal inflections (e.g. fletcher, 1979, 1981). As shown below, it has been actually argued that children do not master adult functional properties of these devices until late, despite their frequent early uses of "correct" forms.

3.3   *Referent introductions and reference maintenance*

Crosslinguistic variation

In all languages oppositions among NP types provide local markings allow-ing speakers to presuppose referents in different degrees. In addition, there is a universal principle, according to which relatively given information is placed towards the beginning of the sentence, including highly presupposed topical information in sentence-initial position, and relatively new (or less presupposable) information towards the end (Chafe, 1976; Firbas, 1964, 1966; MacWhinney, 1977). The degree of reliance on one or the other type of devices varies across languages. For example, English provides a continuum of NP types (e.g. *a book < the book < it < 0*), among which indefinite forms presuppose entities the least, zero elements the most (cf. also Givón, 1983; Silverstein, 1987b). Zero elements are more or less constrained across languages, e.g. despite related syntactic and semantic constraints, they are more frequent in Chinese than in English when the identity of referents can be retrieved from context (cf. Huang, 1984; Li and Thompson, 1976, 1979, 1981). In some inflected languages explicit pronominal forms are so rare that the study of young children's person distinctions cannot be based on them (e.g. Portuguese, cf. Simoes and Stoel-Gammon, 1979). In some languages nominal determiners are obligatory and the distinction between indefinite and definite ones marks information status, along with gender, number, and case, predication (e.g. *This is a car*), nonspecific reference (e.g. *I want a car*) or counting (e.g. French *un* and German *ein* mark newness and counting, as opposed to English *a/one*). In contrast, determiners do not exist or are not obligatory in other languages (e.g. Polish, Hungarian, Chinese). Speakers of these languages can indicate infor-mation status with other local markings, e.g. newness with numerals (*one N*) and givenness with demonstratives (*this N*), but clause-structure variations are more common, e.g. existentials (*There is a X*) or subject–verb inversions such as (6) to (9) can serve to mark newness by placing a referent introduction in postverbal position (out of sentence-initial position). Such (X)SV constructions are typical in some languages, e.g. Chinese (6) (Hickmann and Liang, 1990; Li and Thompson, 1981; Sridhar, 1989) and Polish (7) (from Smoczynska, 1992), whereas they constitute optional stylistic variants in others, e.g. in English (8) and French (9) (also cf. examples in Hebrew and Spanish in Berman and Slobin, 1994):

(6)   laíle māo ("come+perfective cat")
(7)   Przyszed? kot ("com+past+perfective cat+nominative")
(8)   Along came a cat.
(9)   Derrière le chat apparut un chien. ("Behind the cat appeared a dog.")

Such formal differences have implications for the functional load carried by any one device. For example, in addition to marking information status, position contributes to sentence-internal distinctions, especially in the absence of morphology as in Chinese, or with reduced morphology as in English, where sentential subjects are marked by few verbal inflections (e.g. present *hit/hits*) and pronominal case distinctions (e.g. *he/him*): in these languages sentence-initial position is essential for the marking of subjecthood (*John hit Fred*).[5] Therefore, speakers of these languages should rely more on word order for the expression of grammatical relations than for discourse organization, in comparison to speakers of languages with numerous local markings (e.g. German).

Developmental studies

Among the many developmental studies of referring expressions, a large number focused on sentence-internal determinants of these devices (cf. reviews in Hickmann, 1982, 1987b, 1991a). Some focusing on syntactic determinants of pronoun acquisition find that reflexives are acquired earlier than non-reflexives, but there is some divergence concerning the more or less gradual acquisition of related grammatical principles (e.g. Berkovits and Wigodsky, 1979; Chomsky, 1969; Deutsch and Koster, 1982; Deutsch et al., 1986; Ingram and Shaw, 1988; Lust, 1986; Solan, 1983; Stevenson and Pickering, 1987). Semantic factors have been shown to affect children's use of pronouns, e.g. gender (Kail and Léveillé, 1977), number and count/mass distinctions (e.g. Chipman and de Dardel, 1974; Tanz, 1976), animacy, case and/or agency (e.g. Baron and Kaiser, 1975; Kaper, 1976; Tanz, 1974, 1980), role relations (cf. a review in Kail, 1983). The pragmatic effects of intentions on seemingly sentence-bound alternations (*I/my*) have also been explored (Budwig, 1990a).

Studies focusing on nominal determiners show that children have acquired some sentence-internal functions of these devices relatively early, e.g. the expression of specific v. nonspecific reference (Brown, 1973; Cziko, 1986a; Maratsos, 1974, 1976; Thomas, 1989). It has been argued that children and adult second language learners initially associate indefinite–definite forms with specific–nonspecific reference, thereby first extending definite ones to new specific referents, and only later differentiating forms as a function of mutual knowledge (e.g. Cziko, 1986a; Thomas, 1989). Such findings go against the view that young children fail to use indefinite forms appropriately because of their cognitive immaturity and they have even been taken as evidence for the existence of an innate language *bioprogram*.

Whatever the case may be, prior questions must be addressed before reaching such a conclusion. For example, it has been claimed that the functions of referring forms change from being primarily exophoric at first to endophoric later. Thus, young children use frequent deictic means to draw their listeners' attention (Atkinson, 1979; Hickmann, 1982, 1987b; Keenan and Schieffelin, 1976; Karmiloff-Smith, 1979; Wales, 1986; Warden, 1976, 1981), but the acquisition of the discourse-internal functions of referring expressions is more controversial, being reported to occur either relatively early (e.g. Bamberg, 1986, 1987; Bennett-Kastor, 1983, 1986; Brown, 1973; Charney, 1978; Emslie and Stevenson, 1981;

Huxley, 1970; Maratsos, 1974, 1976; Power and Dal Martello, 1986) or relatively late (e.g. De Weck, 1991; Gopnik, 1989; Hickmann, 1980, 1982, 1991a,
1991b; Hickmann and Liang, 1990; Kail and Hickmann, 1992; Karmiloff-Smith,
1981, 1985, 1987; Vion and Colas, 1987; Sauvaire and Vion, 1989; Warden,
1976, 1981; Wigglesworth, 1990, 1993).

For example, Karmiloff-Smith (1981, 1985, 1987) shows developmental
progressions in (French and English) children's uses of referring expressions
in narratives. At first, children's uses are exophoric and their narratives lack
an overall organization, being determined by bottom-up processes. During a
second late phase, children rely on top-down processes, using a *thematic subject strategy*, whereby they systematically reserve subject pronouns for the main
protagonist and organize the entire discourse around this *discourse theme*. The
oldest children and adults integrate bottom-up and top-down processes, producing more flexible narratives. In comparison, Bamberg (1987) reports that
young (German) children use the thematic subject strategy from three years
on, thereby organizing discourse around a global discourse theme, while the
older children and adults also follow an *anaphoric* strategy, using pronouns
where there is local coreference (*reference maintenance*) and nominals otherwise
(*swith reference*).

Such diverging findings highlight the importance of adequate control in
studies of children's discourse organization (cf. reviews in Hickmann, 1982,
1991a, 1991b; Kail and Hickmann, 1992). Studies vary with respect to a considerable number of variables, such as children's prior familiarity with the story,
the type and complexity of this story, the form in which it is presented, and
whether mutual knowledge is built into the situation. With respect to the last
variable, for example, the interlocutor is either naive (e.g. far away, blindfolded,
separated by a screen) or not (leafing through a picture book with the child).
Clearly, in order to determine if children are able to mark information status,
it is necessary to examine situations in which referents are not mutually known.
Indeed, most studies focusing on referent introductions in controlled contexts
conclude that young children do not master the marking of new information
in the absence of mutual knowledge. For example, a direct comparison of narratives produced in the presence v. absence of mutual knowledge shows that
only nine-year-old children differentiate the two situations systematically, while
younger children use deixis in both (Kail and Hickmann, 1992).

Additional factors have been shown to affect referent introductions, including those that also determine the likelihood of thematic status in reference maintenance, such as referential content (e.g. animacy, humanness), agency, and
status as main protagonist (Bamberg, 1987; Bennett-Kastor, 1983; Hickmann,
1980, 1982; Kail and Hickmann, 1992; McGann and Schwartz, 1988; Sauvaire
and Vion, 1989; cf. also Silverstein, 1987b). Several studies also suggest that
endophoric uses of referring forms become automatized. For example, whereas
nine-year-olds distinguish their referent introductions as a function of mutual
knowledge (definite when knowledge is mutual, indefinite otherwise), 11-year-
olds use indefinite ones, regardless of mutual knowledge (Kail and Hickmann,

1992). Similarly, the narratives of four to seven-year-olds contain increasingly more formal beginnings (but fewer formal endings), as well as increasingly more indefinite introductions, regardless of mutual knowledge, suggesting that they gradually learn conventions for marking a story stance (Gopnik, 1989) and, more generally, to differentiate discourse types (cf. Bronckart and Schneuwly, 1991; De Weck, 1991; De Weck and Schneuwly, in press). Finally, older children use indefinite forms in reported speech when the mutual knowledge conditions of the quoted speaker v. narrator differ (Hickmann, 1993a). In sum, children gradually learn to use these devices in narratives to mark information status, discourse genres, and speaker perspective.

Relatively little is known about children's discourse uses of referring expressions and of clause structure across languages. Some evidence indicates that they use word order to mark discourse pragmatic distinctions in different ways during the course of development (cf. a review in Slobin, 1985b). For example, in contrast to adults, children acquiring a considerable number of languages seem to place new information at the beginning of their utterances, at least during the initial phases of development. Such a phenomenon, however, might be strongly related to the fact that young children presuppose information from nonlinguistic context. It is in fact likely that the acquisition of adult pragmatic uses of word order is correlated with the development of intralinguistic discourse cohesion. MacWhinney and Bates (1978) compare children's marking of information status across languages (English, Italian, and Hungarian) with different local markings (e.g. no obligatory nominal determiners in Hungarian) and word-order uses (e.g. more variation in Italian than in English). Children seem to acquire the opposition between indefinite and definite forms quite early (three to four years, except in Hungarian), but there is no clear relation between word order and information status. A replication of this study (Vion and Colas, 1987) shows that (French) children's uses are frequently deictic before six years, as might be expected given that they had to provide descriptions of three pictures which did not form stories and which were mutually known.

Some recent crosslinguistic analyses focus on how children organize discourse in controlled situations, where pictures formed a story and mutual knowledge could not be assumed, with particular attention to NP types and clause structure in a database including French, English, German, Dutch, Chinese (Hickmann, 1991a; Hickmann and Liang, 1990; Hendriks, 1993) and Polish (Smoczynska, 1992). With respect to the introduction of the protagonists, these analyses show that in all languages children do not use appropriate referent introductions until relatively late (six to seven years), frequently using deictic ones before this point. Regardless of language, then, children do not mark the distinction between first and subsequent mentions *within* discourse.

Some crosslinguistic differences can also be observed. Chinese children begin to mark newness locally before they master global markings, even though local markings are not obligatory and are combined with global ones by adults.

In comparison, neither the adults nor the children use local markings in Polish. In addition, children do not use global markings for referent introductions to the same degree and with the same functions across languages. Most NPs (first and subsequent mentions) are postverbal in German, especially in the narratives of the young children, as a result of their frequent use of utterance-initial elements providing spatiotemporal anchors in discourse (e.g. *da* "there," *dann* "then," causing obligatory subject–verb inversions), for example, (10). In English position is rarely determined by discourse, but rather by sentential factors, e.g. the verb–argument structures of (11), even at a late age. Discourse factors have the most direct effect on the positions of first mentions in Chinese, French, and Polish: children gradually learn to mark newness by means of postverbal introductions in various utterance types, e.g. existentials, as well as SVO and XSV structures such as (6) to (9) (above).[6] This process includes learning to avoid some structures, e.g. French left-dislocations such as (12), which are inappropriate for new information according to adult norm (cf. Lambrecht, 1981): children produce them until seven years to introduce referents, thereafter reserving them for *topic promotion* either in reference maintenance (in the absence of immediate coreference) or in presentative sequences such as (13.1) and (13.2):

(10)   Dann kommt ein Hund und da zieht der Hund die Katze runter. ("Then comes a dog and there pulls the dog the cat down.")
(11)   A horse comes and he sees a cow.
(12)   Le chat il arrive. ("The cat he comes.")
(13)   1 Et y'a un chat qui arrive. ("And there's a cat who comes.")
      2 Alors le chat i regarde le nid. ("So the cat he looks at the nest.")
      3 Il voit les oiseaux . . . ("He sees the birds . . .")

These results suggest that children's marking of newness is affected by the particular system of devices available in their language. For example, young children acquiring English and Chinese avoid pragmatic variations in word order, relying on this device for the expression of sentence-internal relations, given the reduced set of available morphological markings. However, after an initial phase, the Chinese children diverge from the English-speaking ones: since Chinese numeral determiners are functionally less complex than word order, they prefer to rely on (optional) local markings, rather than on (obligatory) global ones at first, later gradually adopting the pattern that is typical of the adults.

3.4   Motion and location in discourse

Crosslinguistic variation

Children must acquire a number of linguistic devices in order to mark spatial relations, e.g. static locations such as (14), motion within general locations such as (15), or changes of location such as (16). The necessary local or global devices vary across languages (e.g. Talmy, 1983, 1985; Weissenborn and Klein, 1982). Local devices include motion and posture verbs (e.g. *go, run, sit (down)*), prepositions (*in, on, into*), adjectives and adverbials (*far, nearby*), particles (*up, away, back*), additional deictics (*here/there*), case markings, e.g. the German dative (general location) v. accusative (change of location) in (17). Global devices include word order, e.g. general locations are preverbal and changes of location postverbal in Chinese. In addition, *event conflation* in the clause varies (Talmy, 1983, 1985; see qualifications in Choi and Bowerman, 1991; Levinson, 1990): some languages combine *motion* with *manner* in the verb, others with *path*. For example, in (16) motion and manner are encoded in the verbs (*crawl, run*), the path in the verb satellite (preposition *into*). In contrast, in the French equivalent (18), the main verb (*est entré*) combines motion with path, while manner is expressed by other means (*en rampant* "by crawling," *courant* "by running"):

(14) The baby is (sitting) on/in/under the bed.
(15) The baby is running/crawling (around) in the kitchen.
(16) The baby ran/crawled into the kitchen.
(17) Das Baby krappelte in der/die Küche. (The baby crawled in/into the kitchen.)
(18) Le bébé est entré dans la cuisine en rampant/courant. (The baby entered in(to) the kitchen by crawling/running.)

Developmental studies

A number of studies have examined children's acquisition of spatial terms, focusing on various linguistic, cognitive, and perceptual determinants in the development of spatial reference (Charney, 1979; Clark, E. V., 1972b, 1978b; Clark and Garnica, 1974; Clark, H., 1973; Clark and Sengul, 1978; Cox and Isard, 1990; de Villiers and de Villiers, 1974; Johnston, 1984, 1988a; Kuczaj and Maratsos, 1975; Piaget and Inhelder, 1956; Tanz, 1980; Wales, 1986; Webb and Abrahamson, 1976; Weist, 1991). Much attention has been placed on children's uses of deictic terms (e.g. *here/there, this/that, come/go*), with some controversy with respect to how early children use these terms in a nonegocentric way. Other studies have focused on sentential aspects of children's spatial terms across languages (Bowerman, 1985, 1989; Choi and Bowerman, 1991; Johnston, 1988a; Johnston and Slobin, 1979). Children's production of locative expressions follows a similar sequence across a large number of languages, which could be determined by cognitive complexity: (1) *in, on, under, beside;* (2) *between, back, front* with featured objects; (3) *back* and *front* with nonfeatured objects. However, crosslinguistic differences occur, e.g. children have less difficulty in Italian and Turkish than in English and Serbocroatian as a result of language-specific factors (pre- v. postpositions, morphological complexity, lexical diversity, synonymity). Choi and Bowerman show that English and

Korean-speaking children under two years already produce the devices that are most typical in their language: in English they use path particles, e.g. *out* (wanting to go out), *up* (wanting to be picked up), *down* (sitting down), whereas in Korean they learn first some forms of caused motion and use the equivalents of path particles for spontaneous motion only later. Thus, initial acquisition is not only based on universal sensorimotor concepts, as previously predicted (e.g. Miller and Johnson-Laird, 1976; Piaget and Inhelder, 1956; Slobin, 1970, 1973, 1985), but also on the language being acquired.

Developmental studies of spatial reference in discourse show that children have difficulties establishing and maintaining spatial frames in discourse until a late age. Analyses of room descriptions (Ehrich, 1982; Ehrich and Koster, 1983) show that (Dutch) children do not use adult discourse strategies systematically until ten or 12 years. They do not segment discourse by means of *frame anchoring* strategies (e.g. with segment-initial clauses such as *Onder het raam staat een bank*, "Under the window there is a sofa"). In addition, although they rely on some *linearization* strategies, e.g. using some objects as reference points for other objects across clauses, they produce inadequate linguistic devices, such as ambiguous deictic expressions (e.g. *daarnast* "there-beside"). Similarly, a study of route directions (Weissenborn, 1986) finds that (German) children up to at least ten years do not use the same devices as adults in the absence of mutual knowledge: under eight to ten years they are not able to depend maximally on discourse, e.g. they use ambiguous adverbials (*da durch laufen* "run through there"), rather than adequate devices (*vor* "in front of," *hinter* "behind," *neben* "near," *rechts* "right") and a discourse-internal strategy.

Recent research has begun to examine children's uses of spatial devices in discourse across languages. Some have shown that typological differences such as those described by Talmy affect what spatial information adults and children focus upon and how they organize the flow of information in discourse (Berman and Slobin, 1994; Slobin, 1991). That is, the packaging of information varies not only within the sentence, but also in discourse, both at the local level of successive clauses and at a more global textual level. Thus, whereas English or German speakers elaborate the trajectories followed by protagonists in their displacement through space, Spanish speakers provide simpler displacements with less elaborate paths and more static information situating protagonists and scenes. For example, static locations must be inferred from paths in English, e.g. (19), whereas paths must be inferred from path verbs and static locations in Spanish, e.g. (20):

(19) The boy put the frog down into a jar.
(20) El niño metió la rana en el frasco que había abajo. (The boy inserted the frog in/on the jar that was below.)

Other analyses focus more specifically on how children mark the status of spatial information in discourse across languages (e.g. Hendriks, 1993; Hickmann, 1993b). These analyses compare children's narratives in several languages (Chinese, French, English, German, Dutch), focusing on how they set spatial frames, on how explicit and useful these frames are in the story context, and on the extent to which they specify relevant spatial information thereafter in the story. The results show first a general developmental progression: with increasing age children become gradually able to set spatial frames and to maintain reference to them by means of appropriate devices. However, important crosslinguistic differences can also be observed during the course of development, both across and within the typological groups outlined by Talmy. For example, at all ages children choose more general and elaborate grounds in Chinese than in Dutch (same group in Talmy's typology) when setting the spatial origo of their stories, but they provide less explicit grounds subsequently, relying on previous discourse and on temporal–aspectual markers (e.g. perfective particle) to indicate changes of locations.

3.5 Temporality in discourse

Crosslinguistic variation

The tightly related categories of tense and aspect play an important role in the organization of discourse. As noted above, tense establishes temporal relations between denoted situations and some reference points, while aspect marks different *perspectives* in relation to the temporal structure of situations: internal imperfective v. external perfective perspectives (e.g. among others, Comrie, 1976a, 1985; Dahl, 1985; Dowty, 1982, 1986; Foley and Van Valin, 1985; Klein, in press; Lyons, 1977; Smith, 1980, 1983, 1986). The devices available to express tense–aspect and the particular distinctions encoded by them vary across languages. For example, in the absence of verbal morphology, Chinese expresses aspect by means of particles and tense by various means such as adverbials (e.g. Li and Thompson, 1981; Li Ping, 1990). Inflected languages also vary in many ways: some mark tense by means of inflections and aspect in other ways (Hebrew, e.g. Berman and Neeman, 1994); some have a progressive inflection (e.g. English *ate/was eating*), others optional periphrastic constructions (e.g. French *être en train de* + *INF*); some mark aspect only in the past, e.g. the French *imparfait* (*mangeait*) v. *passé composé* (*est arrivée*) in (21) (equivalent to (4) above). In many languages some inflections are multifunctional, e.g. the perfective past and present are habituals in (22) and *historical tenses* in (23), denoting successive past events in a narrative (e.g. Dry, 1981, 1983; Kamp, 1979; Schiffrin, 1981; Silva-Corvalán, 1983; Wolfson, 1979):

(21) Jean mangeait une pomme. Marie est arrivée.
(22) Everyday John ate/eats an apple.
(23) John ate/eats an apple, then left/leaves.

As suggested above, temporal relations can be deictic and/or anaphoric. Thus, the pluperfect tense in (24) is *relative* rather than *absolute*, i.e. it takes as reference point the time of an event mentioned in discourse (Comrie, 1976a, 1985). In addition, it has been argued that even the simple past or temporal adverbials such as *then* can involve some binding across sentences in discourse (cf. Partee, 1973; Schiffrin, 1990). More generally, different types of temporal anaphora combining tense morphemes, conjunctions, and adverbials have been distinguished, e.g. (25) to (27) (from Hinrichs, 1986: 63), where the interpretation of the second temporal element is dependent upon the first one:

(24)   John had eaten an apple. Mary arrived.
(25)   Adverb + Tense: Sheila had a party last Friday and Sam got drunk.
(26)   Conjunction + Tense: When Susan walked in, Peter left.
(27)   Tense + Tense: He took off his clothes, went into the bathroom, took a shower, and went to bed.

Finally, there is a tight relation in all languages between the semantic properties of the verbs and temporal–aspectual markings. Some have even argued that these properties constitute a kind of aspect, *situation aspect*, to be distinguished from the *viewpoint aspect* discussed above (e.g. Smith, 1983, 1986). One of these properties is *boundedness*, i.e. the presence v. absence of inherent endpoints (e.g. *run to school, die* v. *be home, run around*) (cf. Comrie, 1976a; Dahl, 1985; Dowty, 1986; Smith, 1983, 1986; Vendler, 1967; for related terms, such as *telicity, resultativity, one-* v. *two-state* verbs, cf. Klein, in press; Lyons, 1977). In this respect, spatial relations interact with the inherent temporal properties of verbs: e.g. boundaries often result from the addition of elements to the verb, among which are spatial prepositions expressing changes of location (e.g. *run into* is bounded in (16)) as opposed to general locations (*run around*) is unbounded in (15)).

Some of the consequences of boundedness for the uses of temporal–aspectual markers apply to the sentence, others to discourse. For example, at the sentence level, past perfective inflections imply that the process is completed with bounded verbs, whereas they only indicate that it has stopped with unbounded ones. Thus, the predicate in (28) (*run a mile*) is bounded and it is therefore understood that John ran an entire mile before leaving, whereas the one in (29) (*run around*) is unbounded, i.e John simply stopped running before leaving:

(28)   John ran a mile and then he left.
(29)   John ran around and then he left.

Verb semantics have also been claimed to be central for discourse organization (e.g. Dry, 1981, 1983; Kamp, 1979; but cf. counterarguments in Comrie, 1976b; Dowty, 1986). For example, consider (31a, b) as possible continuations of (30). All verbs are in the perfective past. Like (30), (31a) contains a bounded and foregrounded predicate, understood to happen right after (30). In contrast, (31b) represents a state that is understood to overlap with (30) and is therefore backgrounded:

(30)   Mary walked into the room.
(31)   a John greeted her.
       b John sat in the rocking chair.

Developmental studies

A large number of developmental studies of temporal–aspectual devices have been concerned with local markings within the sentence or across adjacent sentences, e.g. with connectives (Amidon and Carey, 1972; Clark, E. 1973b; Coker, 1977; French and Brown, 1977; Johnson, 1975; Stevenson and Pollitt, 1987; Trosborg, 1982), adverbials (e.g. Crain, 1982; Di Paolo and Smith, 1978; Scott, 1984; Weist and Buczowska, 1987; Youssef, 1990), aspect particles (Li Ping, 1990), and/or verbal inflections (particularly since Bronckart and Sinclair, 1973). Recent diverging claims have been made, particularly with respect to the impact of verb semantics on children's acquisition of verbal inflections. On the basis of a considerable number of languages, a *defective tense hypothesis* has been proposed, according to which children's inflections at first do not encode tense, but rather viewpoint aspect (perfectivity) and/or situation aspect (results)[7] (Aksu-Koç, 1988; Antinucci and Miller, 1976; Bronckart and Sinclair, 1973; Cromer, 1974, 1988; Cziko, 1986b; de Villiers and de Villiers, 1979; Meisel, 1985; Stephany, 1981). This claim has been qualified or disputed on the basis of findings showing the effects of various factors, such as age, language, situation, and discourse (e.g. Bamberg, 1987; Bloom, Lifter, and Hafitz, 1980; De Lemos, 1981; Fayol, Abdi, and Gombert, 1989; Harner, 1976, 1980, 1981, 1982; Johnson, 1985; Li Ping, 1990; McShane and Wittacker, 1988; McShane, Wittacker, and Dockwell, 1986; Mapstone and Harris, 1985; Smith, 1980; Szagun, 1978; Weist, 1986, 1989; Weist, Wysocka, and Lyytinen, 1991; Weist, Wysocka, Witkowska-Stadnik, Buczowska, and Konieczna, 1984). Thus, children's acquisition of distinctions such as past–nonpast, perfective–imperfective, and bounded–unbounded seems to differ across languages, e.g. children acquiring a transparently inflected language such as Polish do mark tense with all verb types, regardless of whether these inflections constitute prefixes or suffixes (Weist and Konieczna, 1985; Weist et al., 1984).

With respect to discourse factors, some evidence shows that adults often use perfective aspect with resultative verbs to draw children's attention to the results of everyday events, suggesting that interpersonal processes might affect children's uses and/or be affected by the same factors (e.g. De Lemos, 1981). In addition, some uses of verbal inflections are modal, rather than only temporal–aspectual (Gerhardt and Savasir, 1986): English-speaking three-year-olds use the simple present in the context of ongoing activities (where the present progressive is also frequent) to indicate that these activities conform to a norm. Tense and aspect also come to play a role in the development of children's discourse cohesion (Bamberg, 1987, 1990; Bamberg and Marchman, 1990; Bazzanella and Calleri, 1991; Hickmann, Kaiser, and Roland, 1991). Bamberg (1987) shows that German adults shift to the *Perfekt* (past perfective)

to mark a *retrospective assessment* of preceding discourse or to highlight information which is *prospectively relevant* for subsequent discourse, indicating
whether information is locally backgrounded or foregrounded in discourse
and simultaneously chunking discourse into units (scenes and episodes). Such
shifts occur late (nine to ten years), while younger children use the *Perfekt* to
mark *completion* (three to four years) or to *readjust* events that are out of chronological order in relation to previous discourse. For Bamberg these results show
that development goes from early global strategies to the gradual integration
of local and global concerns in discourse organization.

Few have compared how children use temporal–aspectual devices to organize discourse across languages (cf. Bamberg and Marchman, 1990; Berman,
1988b; Berman and Slobin, 1987, 1994; Slobin, 1991). Analyses of German and
English narratives show that adults and children make differential use of devices
to mark episodic structure, e.g. they produce more overt inceptive aspect in
English (e.g. *he started to*) to mark the instantiation of event sequences (Bamberg
and Marchman, 1990). Furthermore, adults and children from three years on
focus on different aspects of the temporal structure of narratives across languages, e.g. English ones tend to assert actions and imply results, whereas the
reverse is true in Spanish (Slobin, 1991). Children use the obligatory markings
available in their language right away. In order to express that punctual and
durative events are simultaneous, children contrast aspectually neutral forms
v. progressive ones in English (32), perfective v. imperfective forms in Spanish
(33). In Hebrew (which has no aspect) the adults – but not the children –
switch present and past tenses with discourse functions, e.g. marking perfective aspect with crucial events (34) (Berman and Neeman, 1994). Finally, German has a relatively simple aspectual system and children therefore adhere to
one anchor tense from there to four years on (as in Hebrew), young children
produce more tense shifts in more complex systems such as Spanish, Turkish,
and English (Aksu-Koç and Stutterheim, 1994):

(32) The boy fell out and the dog was being chased by the bees.
(33) Se cayó el niño y le perseguían al perro las avispas. (The boy fell-PFV
      and the bees chased-IPFV the dog.)
(34) And the bees pursue him, the owl threatens the boy, and the boy climbed
      onto a large rock, and looks for his frog.

Some further evidence indicates that verb semantics have an impact on children's use of tense–aspect in English, French, and German, but that language-
specific and discourse factors also affect the developmental process (Hickmann,
Kaiser, and Roland, 1991). The overall use of the past v. nonpast as an anchor
tense varies across these languages, the past being less frequent in French and
German than in English. In addition, although the past perfective is related to
boundedness, this relation varies with language and age. Thus, in all languages
the past perfective is more frequent with bounded verbs than with unbounded
ones. However, the English-speaking four-year-olds differentiate bounded and

unbounded verbs the most, using mainly the simple past with bounded verbs and the present with unbounded ones, while the older children use both inflections with all verbs. In French and German the present is more frequent with all verbs at all ages and therefore the association between boundedness and perfective past is less evident. Heavy reliance on the present may reflect the high frequency of the historical present in French and German[8] and/or the greater ease with which narratives can be told in the present, given that this tense neutralizes aspect. Finally, regardless of language, switches from the nonpast to the perfective past mark specific discourse relations from six to seven years on: they establish the setting, background some events in relation to other overlapping events, and indicate narrators' comments. Example (35) shows a seven-year-old's uses of past perfective forms, connectives, and adverbials indicating the setting (*just got born*) and an overlap (*when the cat just about got up there*), whereas the four-year-old in (36) describes a result (*flew away*):

(35)   It starts out like one day some birds just got born and the bird's starting to fly off to get some worms. The cat comes to the tree, sits down and starts to climb. And the dog's just walking along and the dog bites the cat's tail when the cat just about got up there and the bird's coming. And then the dog chases away the cat and the bird's . . . has the worm at the nest.

(36)   The birds are in the nest. The big daddy and the mommy is standing up on the nest. Mommy and daddy flew away. And the birds are still in the nest. The cat is on the ground and it's looking at the birds in the nest.

4   Concluding Remarks

This chapter examined a large range of studies pertaining to how children learn to organize discourse, with particular attention to the acquisition of the linguistic devices in the domains of person, space, and time. Two aspects of the organization of information in these domains were considered: the marking of information status and the grounding of information in discourse. In all domains the following three recurrent observations are reported: relatively late developmental progressions in discourse organization, interrelations among the utterance and discourse levels of analysis, and a combination of general developmental patterns and of language-specific ones. All three conclusions must be taken into account in any model of first language acquisition.

With respect to the timing of acquisition, discourse organization seems to be a late development in all languages considered, despite some evidence that very young children begin to differentiate given v. new information or foregrounded v. backgrounded information in discourse, at least partially and/or with primitive means. Although some studies claimed that young children master the uses of various devices, few focused on pragmatic determinants which are specific to discourse-internal functions. It is precisely such uses that are acquired late and they seem to evolve out of earlier deictic uses anchored in the here-and-now of the immediate speech situation. The shift from exophora to endophora seems to be the main process whereby children become able to displace reference successfully and, more generally, to use discourse as a new kind of context in which to anchor their utterances when necessary (Hickmann, 1986).

The remaining two conclusions are related. The ways in which form–function relations are systemically organized in different subdomains of reference vary across languages. Languages distribute differently sets of functions onto sets of forms, including not only sentence-internal functions, but also discourse-internal ones. As a result, the functional load, and therefore the cognitive complexity involved in acquiring any one device, may vary from language to language. For example, in the domain of referent introductions, children's pragmatic use of position depends on the extent to which they rely on word order for the expression of sentence-internal relations: the English-speaking children rely little on word order for discourse, a result which is consistent with the fact that they rely heavily on it during sentence comprehension (cf. MacWhinney and Bates, 1989). The Chinese children behave like the English-speaking ones initially, choosing local and unifunctional devices, but then follow a different developmental course, as they learn the specificities of their language.

Similarly, the expression of spatiotemporal relations within the clause and across discourse are interrelated. Thus, given the different ways in which spatial information is packaged in the clause across languages, adults and relatively young children assert and presuppose different aspects of the narrative, e.g. the protagonists' motion through space (processes) or the locations at which events happen and results of these events (states). In addition, given the ways in which languages manage information status in discourse, they introduce and presuppose spatial information in different ways, e.g. focusing on general v. specific spatial frames in more or less explicit ways. Finally, the rate at which temporal–aspectual distinctions are acquired at the sentence level (pastness, perfectivity) and at the discourse level (grounding) varies across languages depending on the richness and transparency of their morphology, as shown by children's uses of verbal inflections (main anchor tenses and tense shifting) in conjunction with temporal–aspectual adverbials and connectives.

Further research is necessary to specify more precisely how the sentence and discourse levels interact during the acquisition process. On the one hand, some discourse factors in all domains can influence the ways in which elements are organized within the sentence, e.g. children's explorations with verb argument structures, word order, and other types of clause structure variations are often motivated by discourse organizing principles. On the other hand, some grammatical factors in all domains also influence how the information is organized across clauses in discourse, e.g. the ways in which spatial information is packaged in the clause has an impact on what children foreground or background in discourse.

This review of the literature in the area of discourse development provides a different perspective on previous writings in developmental theory. Thus, according to the traditional Piagetian view, young children's underlying cognitive immaturity prevents them from decentering and therefore they are unable to organize personal, spatial, and temporal parameters in such a way as to produce coherent and cohesive discourse (cf. Piaget, 1959; see also reviews in Hickmann, 1986, 1987b). However, more recent research with young children reveals more capacities than had been expected. For example, children under two years include information about temporal order in their initial representations of event sequences that have been acted out in front of them (e.g. Bauer and Mandler, 1989; O'Connell and Gerard, 1985). In addition, from about two years on they show concern for drawing their interlocutor's attention verbally and nonverbally, using linguistic devices deictically, until they are able to use them endophorically.

In addition, comparative research shows that, despite the similarities that can be observed during the acquisition process in all languages, children may follow different developmental courses from an early age onward, depending on the particular properties of the language they are acquiring. Similarities and differences have been reported by a number of studies focusing on children's use and interpretation of linguistic devices in different domains for the expression of semantic and syntactic relations at the sentence level. Recent interest in crosslinguistic research has now also extended to discourse processes, yielding similar results in all of these domains. On the one hand, all children learn to master whatever devices are available in their native language to organize discourse. On the other hand, from very early stages of development, they rely on the means that are most typical for this purpose in their native language.

More studies are necessary to specify the relation between cognitive and linguistic aspects of children's discourse abilities. For example, it would be informative to understand on a crosslinguistic basis the relation between children's ability to organize events linguistically into a cohesive narrative and their ability to order events nonverbally (e.g. Fivush and Mandler, 1985). More generally, further research should be devoted to a thorough understanding of the interrelations among three aspects of children's development: (1) general cognitive aspects, e.g. spatial and temporal concepts, object permanence, scripts for general event structures, narrative schemata; (2) general discourse development, including the acquisition of global and local principles guiding discourse organization, such as the marking of information status and the grounding of information; (3) language-specific aspects of acquisition, including the impact of formal and functional variations on the rate and course of acquisition in specific subdomains of discourse organization.

NOTES

1   Not all indices presuppose entities that exit independently (see Silverstein, 1976, for a discussion of *presupposing* v. *creative* indices).

2   The notion of *grounding* is borrowed from Gestalt psychology, where one finds the concepts of *figure* and *ground*. There is some ambiguity in the criteria defining this notion and/ or on whether these criteria are independent from language (cf. also Givón, 1987; Tomlin, 1985).

3   This distinction between local and global markings is oversimplified: a continuum might provide a better account of intermediary devices, such as case markings, which affect one element locally, but establish relations across elements in the clause.

4   The notions of cohesion and coherence are frequently confused, e.g. the term *coherence* has been used to refer to links among cohesive devices.

5   Semantic information of course frequently plays a role in relating NPs within the verbal network. For example, given an agentivity and transitivity continuum (cf. Silverstein, 1987b; Hopper and Thompson, 1980), agents and subjects coincide in highly transitive clauses at one extreme (e.g. *John fed the cat, the lion ate up the mouse in one bite*), not necessarily at the other extreme (e.g. *John sat next to Fred*). Some optional local devices in Chinese can mark role relations in the clause, e.g. *bǎ* marks definite patients affected by agents in highly transitive SOV clauses.

6   In about 20 percent of the cases, the Polish adults use neither local nor global markings for referent introductions (preverbal bare nominals), suggesting that word order may have a different primary function, such as marking focus (cf. Smoczynska, 1992).

7   Not all studies make a clear distinction between predicate types (linguistic property) and situation types (nonlinguistic reality).

8   The historical present is more frequent in French and German than in English.

8 Bilingual Language Acquisition

ANNICK DE HOUWER

1 Introduction

Lately, there has been a great surge of interest in the study of young bilingual children's language development. This increase can be related to two major factors: first, a growing awareness of the importance of bi- and multilingualism in our increasingly internationally oriented world today, and second, the increased interest in crosslinguistic studies of language acquisition in general. The aim of the present chapter is to review the most significant findings on bilingual language acquisition emerging from the last 12 years of research. For overviews of work on bilingual children done primarily prior to 1980, the reader is referred to Lindholm (1980), McLaughlin (1984b), and Redlinger (1979). The reader interested in early second language acquisition is referred to chapter 2 of Wode (1981), which provides a clear overview covering the main theoretical issues. An excellent discussion of the early and classic work on bilingual children by Werner Leopold and Madorah Smith can be found in chapter 3 of Hakuta (1986).

Section two of this chapter discusses the relevance of the study of bilingual children both to the field of child language research and the actual practice of raising children bilingually. Section three deals with issues involved in characterizing variations in the bilingual acquisition situation. Section four will look at the role of variations in the shape of the input, including parental discourse strategies. In section five the formal relationship between a bilingual child's two languages will be discussed. The primary focus here is to what extent the bilingual child develops two separate linguistic systems. Section six reviews what is known about young bilingual children's language choice both within and across utterances, before the concluding remarks and suggestions for future research in section seven.

2   Why Study Bilingual Children?

As García (1983: 62) points out, early childhood bilingualism is a very wide-spread phenomenon. It is estimated that nearly half of the world's population is functionally bilingual, and that most of these bilinguals are "native speakers" of their two languages (Wölck, 1987/8). In this context, it is only fitting that studies of child language should not focus primarily on the world's monolingual children, but on the "multilingual majority" (Snow, 1985b: 197) as well (see also De Houwer, 1992; García, 1983). Developmental psycholinguistics as a field of scientific enterprise should not be satisfied with offering only explanations of a subtype of acquisition but must try to encompass all types of language acquisition in early childhood.

The study of bilingual children can greatly contribute to theories of acquisition, since bilingual acquisition can show us more clearly the limits of language acquisition or, more positively, it can teach us much more about the potential for language learning in early childhood. As Levy (1985: 552) has suggested,

> the strengths and weaknesses that bilingual children manifest may prove revealing with respect to the issue of establishing the limitations upon the potential linguistic abilities of children at a given phase in development. This may help establish the boundaries within which the process of language acquisition must unfold and thus be, theoretically, extremely informative.

More specifically, Hakuta and Diaz (1985: 325–6) write that "because bilingualism induces an early separation of word and referent, it is possible that bilingual children also develop an early capacity to focus on and analyze the structural properties of language." Pléh et al. (1987) have made a similar suggestion on the basis of their sentence comprehension experiments with young Hungarian/Russian preschoolers. They propose that their subjects' exposure to two languages "encourages them to focus on the formal properties of each" (Pléh et al., 1987: 596). Meisel has put forward the intriguing hypothesis that "bilinguals tend to focus more on formal aspects of language and are therefore able to acquire certain grammatical constructions faster and with fewer errors than many or most monolinguals" (1990b: 18; as Meisel readily admits, though, his hypothesis "is still rather speculative"). Goodz et al. (1987) also claim that early bilingualism leads to a "more finely tuned understanding of the rules of each language" than is the case in monolingual development.

There is some evidence, however, that bilingual experience helps in developing an early awareness of language: Levy's (1985) study of a Hebrew-speaking child exposed to English from 1;7 onwards shows this child to have a high level of linguistic awareness already by the age of two. Levy suggests that this awareness, which appeared unusually early in comparison with monolingual children, is a direct result of the bilingual environment. Similarly, Clyne (1987:

85) has argued that "children being brought up bilingually within the home ... have more opportunity than their monolingual counterparts to develop from an early age ... an awareness about language." Clyne substantiates his claim on the basis of a wide variety of comments on structural and functional aspects of language uttered by his German/English bilingual daughter Joanna between the ages of two and five, and contrasts his findings with some claims made for monolingual children.

The importance of studies on bilingual acquisition for approaching general problems within child language research has also been mentioned by, amongst others, Hayashi (1992a) and Vila (1984). Meisel (1990b: 17) is "particularly interested in the role of grammar in [early] grammatical development." Here lies his motivation for carrying out studies of bilingual children's early language development rather than monolingual children's, since, as Meisel writes, various factors that may affect the acquisition of a particular language, such as cognitive development and personality, are controlled in a bilingual population. Similarly, I have argued that the bilingual child, as "the perfect matched pair," is the ideal subject for crosslinguistic research investigating the relative impact of language-specific v. more universal factors in acquisition (De Houwer, 1987a: 53).

The latter issue has so far been addressed most clearly by Ingram (1981a). Ingram draws a link between the results of analyses of the phonological forms used by a two-year-old English/Italian bilingual and issues in phonological development in general. Ingram's subject showed evidence of two separate phonological systems that were each relatable to the phonological systems of the child's input languages, and, furthermore, that consisted of very different phonological characteristics. This led Ingram to question the position that a child's individual phonological strategy preferences are stronger determinants in acquisition than the phonological shapes of the input languages. Since he found two opposed strategies (or preferences) in one child that were each relatable to a different input language, Ingram suggests that the role played by the input language is very great.

Indeed, when one studies bilingual children it is almost inevitable to come eventually to the insight that the nature of the input plays a very important role in the bilingual acquisition process (De Houwer, 1990: 342; Deuchar and Clark, 1988, 1992, Lanza, 1990: 447). This in turn raises questions concerning acquisition in general. The role of the input in monolingual children is probably almost just as important as it seems to be for bilingual children, but because the input to monolingual children may be more homogeneous – in comparison with a bilingual input condition it certainly is much less varied – the precise nature of its influence is much less obvious and can easily be overlooked in the search for explanations of monolingual acquisition data (though see Snow, chapter 6, this volume). Studies of bilingual children can thus "contribute to the debate within monolingual acquisition as to the role of the input" (Lanza, 1990: 447).

Finally, the study of bilingual children is directly relevant to many families living in a bilingual situation. These families unfortunately encounter many prejudices against early bilingualism (Kielhöfer and Jonekeit, 1983; Koehn and Müller, 1990). Many of these prejudices can be explained by ignorance about bilingual development in particular and bilingualism in general. An especially sad symptom of this is that "many professionals such as speech therapists view normal language mixing as harmful and are therefore liable to give advice to parents which is not in keeping with the realities of normal bilingual development" (Romaine, 1989: 213). Bilingual families have been known to give up being bilingual, much to their social, cultural, and emotional detriment, as a result of worries caused by uninformed warnings by people in authority concerning the supposed negative effects of a bilingual upbringing (see in particular Saunders, 1988: 100–5 for a frank and very valuable discussion of this problem). If ignorance about early bilingualism can cause problems for normal bilingual development it can only be imagined what it will do in the case of language-impaired bilingual children.

Studying bilingual children, then, is important because of the theoretical insights it can bring to the field of developmental psycholinguistics. Moreover, a better knowledge of how children successfully acquire two languages from early on may greatly help more children on their way to speaking the languages of their environment.

3   Bilingual Language Acquisition: A Characterization

Quite a large number of children are probably exposed to two varieties of what is commonly seen as the same language. Depending on the extent of the structural differences between the two varieties in question, such situations might well be termed bilingual or diglossic. However, in what follows I shall concentrate solely on those situations in which a child comes into early contact with varieties of two distinct spoken languages. Since hardly any work has been done on trilingual children (but see Hoffmann, 1985; Mikes, 1990; Stavans, 1990), the main focus in this chapter is on the acquisition of just two languages from infancy.

Ambiguous terms that could indicate language, ethnicity, or nationality, unless otherwise specified, will be used to refer to language only. Thus, for instance, "Finnish" stands for "Finnish-speaking."

The present chapter concerns investigations of the bilingual language acquisition of preschool children. My particular focus is on children who are regularly addressed in two spoken languages from before the age of two and who continue to be regularly addressed in those languages up until the final stages of data collection.

Bilingual language acquisition, then, refers to the result of the very early, simultaneous, regular, and continued exposure to more than one language.

Within bilingual language acquisition, it is important to distinguish between Bilingual First Language Acquisition (BFLA, a term introduced by Meisel, 1989) and what I will call Bilingual Second Language Acquisition (BSLA). BFLA refers to the acquisition of two or more languages from birth or at most a month after birth (De Houwer, 1987b: 5), and BSLA refers to those cases of bilingual language acquisition that are not cases of BFLA. In other words, first regular exposure to a second language starts no earlier than one month after birth, but before the age of two.

At first sight, the distinction between BFLA and BSLA may seem unimportant. Yet the distinction may eventually turn out to be quite significant: in the case of BFLA, exposure to each language begins shortly after birth. Thus, comparisons between monolingual children and children bilingual from birth can be carried out without the possibly confounding variable "time of first exposure." As will be discussed later in this chapter, such comparisons are of great theoretical importance in the field of bilingual language acquisition. Furthermore, it is yet to be investigated to what extent differences between the times of first regular exposure to two languages for one individual have an effect on acquisition patterns.

To what extent the theoretical distinction between BFLA and BSLA is in fact relevant cannot be determined at this point. Because of its possible significance, however, I would like to argue that it is important for researchers to specify exactly when their bilingual subjects were first regularly exposed to more than one language. Without this detailed information, we cannot even start to investigate the role played by time of initial exposure, and comparisons with monolingual children become problematic, since the main variable is no longer just "exposure to more than one language" but possibly also "time of first exposure" (De Houwer, 1990: 4).

4 The Role of the Input in Bilingual Acquisition

4.1 General exposure conditions

In bilingual language acquisition the time of first regular exposure to two languages may vary from child to child, as may the way in which the languages are presented to the child. Romaine (1989: 166–8) emphasizes the importance of three dimensions of the bilingual learning situation: (1) the language(s) the parents speak with their child(ren); (2) the language(s) the parents have as their native language(s), and (3) the extent to which the parents' language(s) reflect the dominant language(s) of the community at large. The importance of the first factor is obvious. However, it is less clear whether the other two factors play a major role in the process of acquisition as it evolves in the bilingual child. First, it is doubtful that whether a parent uses his or her native language in addressing the child or not has a direct effect on the child's bilingual development. Although an understanding of the parent's private language history is an aspect that may affect certain language attitudes at a much later age, such an understanding is simply not accessible to the preschool child, and hence cannot affect the early bilingual acquisition process in any major way.

Second, language usage patterns existing in the community at large are only relevant to the extent that they form part of the bilingual child's microcosm in early childhood. For instance, the region of Flanders in Belgium is generally regarded as a Dutch-speaking community. Nevertheless, many children from upper middle class families in Flemish cities such as Antwerp and Ghent grow up bilingually in French and Dutch. Although the mainstream Flemish education system uses only Dutch as a means of instruction in preschool, and although all administrative business and most other aspects of public life are carried out in Dutch, it can be questioned whether preschool children from French-speaking or bilingual French–Dutch families in Antwerp or Ghent (clearly Dutch-dominant cities) actually experience their community as being Dutch dominant. On closer scrutiny, one may find that the particular bilingual child one is studying goes to a French-medium music school on Wednesday afternoons and a Dutch-medium preschool on weekday mornings. One may further find that the paternal grandparents address the child in Dutch, while the maternal grandparents use French. However, the child sees the maternal grandparents every weekday afternoon, and the paternal grandparents only on Sundays. The child's babysitters, who spend approximately three waking hours a week with the child, use exclusively French, and the children that the child regularly plays with also only speak French. The child's parents have mostly French-speaking friends. Television programs are usually watched in French. The family always goes to the south of France for holidays, and does to for a total of two months a year.

In this situation, the child's community at large is Dutch-dominant, but the actual day-to-day reality for the child shows the child's immediate environment outside the family to be French-dominant. In this case, then, to claim that the child is growing up in a Dutch-dominant environment is misleading. It is the language use within the child's individual social network that must be taken into account to determine input patterns, rather than the dominance configuration in the community at large that the child's family happens to live in.

In most cases researchers will have to rely on parental reports to determine the nature of early exposure patterns. It is imperative that researchers obtain estimates from parents about the actual opportunities for early child–environment interaction in the two languages concerned ("environment" here refers to parents, other caregivers, siblings, friends, relatives – in short, any person directly addressing he bilingual-child-to-be). It is not enough to know what language each person used with the child, but in addition it is important to find out approximately how much time the main input carriers each spent with the child. If, for instance, in a claimed one parent/one language situation the child's father hardly ever spent any time with his young baby, and if the father was the sole input carrier of his language, then it is doubtful that the child actually regularly heard two languages spoken from an early age onwards (Elizabeth Lanza, personal communication).

4.2   *Language separation in the input*

An input continuum can be envisaged with one extreme end characterized by the total separation of two languages by person, and the other by the total lack of separation of the two languages by person. On the basis of detailed information of who addresses which language(s) to the bilingual child and in what circumstances, it should be possible to decide which end of the continuum best characterizes the global bilingual language input situation that a particular child finds itself in.

Most actual input conditions will, of course, fall somewhere in between the two endpoints of the continuum. Idiazábal (1984) even goes so far as to claim that the absolute and total separation of languages in the input and the total identification of one person with one language is an impossibility. There is some evidence that she might have a point. Goodz et al. (1988) and Goodz (1989) report on studies of parental input to bilingual children that they carried out on the basis of recorded spontaneous conversations between parents in bilingual families and their offspring. It was found that even parents who claimed to be using only one language (A) in addressing their children actually used utterances containing elements from two languages (A and B), as well as utterances entirely in the other language (B) once their children had started to talk.

The focus here on input patterns in terms of their being separate or not for each language has its reasons. Indeed, the degree of language separation in the input has often been seen as a major determinant in early bilingual acquisition in general. Traditionally, the "one person/one language" input condition (or the "interlocutor principle," as Clyne (1987) calls it) has been hailed as the best method for ensuring problem-free (read "mixing-free") bilingual development. Already in 1937, Maximilian Braun suggested that what he called "Partnerzwang" or partner pressure was at the root of language separation in bilinguals. More recently, advocates of the "one person/one language" input pattern have included, amongst others, Bain and Yu (1980) and Kielhöfer and Jonekeit (1983: 19).

Clyne (1987) sees as a particular advantage of the one person/one language input condition the early development of a high degree of metalinguistic awareness, which in turn he sees as a good basis for developing translation skills. Bain and Yu (1980: 313) claim that if the languages "are kept distinctly apart by the parents over approximately the first three and a half years of the child's life, nativelike control of both languages tends to accrue." Strong advocates of the interlocutor principle, such as Lebrun and Paradis (1984: 13), even warn that the occurrence of mixed utterances in the input may contribute to the development of a stutter disorder in bilingual children with an existing tendency twoards stuttering.

On the other hand, García (1983) shows that the lack of complete adherence to a one person/one language input condition does not necessarily lead to the child's failure to communicate effectively using two linguistic systems. Although the Spanish/English preschoolers that García studied heard both English and Spanish from their mothers in speech addressed to them, the incidence of mixed utterances used by the children was quite low (range: 1–15 percent), and the children were able to use both Spanish and English as separate systems.

Lately, the issue of the degree of language separation in the input has more specifically been explored in relation to the extent to which bilingual children "mix" their languages or not (Genesee, 1989; Meisel, 1989). Genesee (1989) states that there is no reason for bilingual children to know that their languages ought not to be mixed if they are exposed to frequent mixing in the input (see also Goodz et al., 1990). Both Genesee (1989) and De Houwer (1990: 54) note, however, that the relationship between input and mixing cannot be properly addressed at this time, since most descriptions of language input conditions in the literature on bilingual children are insufficiently informative to approach the issue.

Although the separation of the two languages by person has received the most attention so far, the separation of the two languages in the input may also be effected by situation-bound factors (for instance, Finnish spoken by all family members inside the home, but Swedish once they are outside). To my knowledge there has again been no research investigating the effect of this type of input situation v. others on young bilingual children's language development.

Finally, many of the world's bilingual children grow up in "native bilingual communities," in which monolingual norms may be unavailable or nonexistent (Wölck, 1987/8). As far as I am aware, the effect of the virtually complete lack of separation of the two input languages here on the development process has not been studied.

At this time, then, the relation between the shape of the input and acquisition patterns remains unclear, but since there might well be an important connection between them, studies of bilingual children should clearly describe the linguistic environment in which these children became bilingual, and should give an informed estimate of the degree of language separation in the input.

4.3　Changes in input conditions

Since a bilingual child's linguistic environment is potentially very changeable (Romaine, 1989: 173), and since input in one of a bilingual child's two languages may suddenly cease for prolonged periods of time, it is inevitable that many young bilingual children will experience some kind of language loss or attrition (Kessler, 1984: 42). Very little work has been done in this area, although the study of early language loss phenomena as related to the degree of the lack of input could furnish important information about the minimal input requirements for sustaining active use potential in a particular language, whether in bilingual or monolingual children. A recent study in the area of early language loss in bilingual children by Hansen-Strain (1990) suggests that both the degree of competence in both languages before a changed input condition, as well as age, play a role in the extent to which productive control over one of the languages continues.

Researchers have often noted in passing that active use of one of a bilingual child's languages decreases as a result of the temporary lack or decrease of input in one of the languages concerned, or, alternatively, that active use and level of one of a bilingual child's languages increases as a result of increased input in one of the languages concerned (Idiazábal, 1984; Schlyter, 1993). It is thus not surprising that not only the type but also the amount of input in a particular language is seen as being of importance in the developmental process (Hoffmann, 1985; Lanza, 1990: 441; Romaine, 1989: 169; Schlyter and Westholm, 1991). Kessler (1984: 35) even goes as far as to claim that "children develop faster in the language which is used most in their environment." This claim may indeed go too far, since, as Saunders (1982: 162) has suggested, the unequal amount of input in each language may affect only part of children's language learning. It does not, for instance, as Saunders found for his two sons, seem to affect receptive vocabulary. Döpke (1988: 103), on the other hand, believes that "the quality of input takes precedence over the quantity." Unfortunately, Döpke gives no independent criteria that further characterize the notion of "quality."

Although the exact role played by the amount of input in a bilingual child's language development remains unknown, one can agree with Kessler (1984: 35) that in order to be maintained, "bilingualism requires the continued use of both languages in communicative naturalistic settings."

4.4 *Parental discourse strategies*

Besides input patterns proper, the role played by parental discourse strategies has lately attracted particular attention. Researchers have suggested a variety of discourse-related influences on the bilingual acquisition process.

A decade go, Kielhöfer and Jonekeit (1983: 16) proposed that parents' interactional styles may affect the bilingual acquisition process. More recently, Romaine (1989: 193) has claimed that in a bilingual situation "interaction patterns can affect the development of individual structures," and that "parents' consistency in language choice" (p. 169) is a possible factor affecting bilingual development. Saunders (1982: 195) suggests as a possible reason for his German/English sons' infrequent use of lexical transfers the fact that these were not encouraged. Lanza (1988) suggests that metalinguistic input by parents may contribute to their children's awareness of bilingualism.

Hardly any work has been done on the exact relationship between parental discourse strategies and aspects of acquisition (but see section six, below). However, it appears that in a bilingual family situation, parents develop various specific strategies to respond to their children's use of mixed utterances and "wrong" choice of language. There also appear to be specific functions attached to parents' use of mixed utterances and language choice regardless of children's preceding utterances.

Idiazábal (1984) has noted in her study of Spanish/Basque BSLA that the parents of the child she was studying regularly and explicitly corrected their daughter's utterances if they contained elements from both languages. Other parental strategies observed by the same author consisted of the repetition and subsequent translation (with or without expansion) of (parts of) a Spanish child utterance that the parent was responding to (the parents spoke to the child in Basque and apparently expected her to address them in Basque, too). In his report on two French/German boys Kielhöfer (1987) mentions that their French-speaking mother would regularly use correction strategies if her sons addressed her in German, thus signalling to them her nonacceptance of the "wrong" language choice. Goodz (1989: 38) found that the four sets of parents of English/French bilingual children that she studied in naturalistic conversations tended to respond to their children's (few) mixed utterances "with mixed utterances of their own."

The two English-dominant mothers in Lanza's (1990) study each reacted differently when their Norwegian/English bilingual children used lexically mixed utterances in addressing their mothers, who mainly used English with the children. One mother would use discourse strategies that discouraged the use of lexically mixed utterances, while the other mother's discourse strategies were more accepting of the child's use of these. As Lanza (1990: 375) suggests, "the parent's more or less conventionalized manner of responding to the child's mixing, and indeed whether or not the parent actually mixes languages with the child, forms an interactional style concerning mixing. This interactional style will inevitably have an impact on the child's perception of and expectations concerning the appropriateness of the mixing." The child's parent is thus giving negative feedback about (in)appropriate language use.

García (1983: 143) notes that the Spanish-dominant mothers in his study used mixed utterances addressed to their Spanish/English children "as a clarification device or a teaching aide." Mothers would, for instance, use translations within a mixed utterance. In this particular setting, mothers apparently perceived Spanish as the weaker language for their children, a state of affairs confirmed by García's (1983) independent comparative analyses of the children's verbal production in both Spanish and English.

In Goodz et al.'s (1988) study of 13 English/French children and their parents, parental language switching was used to attract children's attention, in order to discipline, and for emphasis. Goodz et al. also found a very strong tendency on the parents' part to repeat sections of their children's utterances even if they were not in the parent's native language, thus resulting in parental code switching. There is also some evidence that in a bilingual situation mothers use different strategies from fathers, In addition, Goodz et al. (1988) noted a stronger actual adherence to the claimed one person/one language input condition in fathers than in mothers. The fathers in Goodz et al.'s (1989) study were in general "more demanding and somewhat less supportive of their children's early linguistic efforts than mothers" (p. 3 in ms.).

That fathers need not always be fairly unaccommodating is shown by Evans (1987), who writes that the Welsh-speaking father in the Welsh/English family she is reporting on in fact went as far as to adapt his use of Welsh in speaking to his child and wife, who are both learners of Welsh, to the extent that he himself started to produce learner-type errors in Welsh.

In a rare study focusing entirely on parental communication strategies in bilingual families, Döpke (1986) puts forward the hypothesis that parental communication styles that have been found to possibly facilitate monolingual development are also a major variable in determining the final success of a bilingual upbringing. As Lanza (1990: 366–7) notes, however, the analyses do not differentiate between parental responses to mixed v. nonmixed child utterances, hence glossing over aspects that might well be of great importance in a bilingual setting. Furthermore, parental discourse structures are not explicitly related to child utterances (cf. Lanza, 1990: 349). In addition, the lack of information on the sociolinguistic setting of the data recordings make it difficult to unambiguously interpret the findings. As such, Döpke's interesting hypothesis remains to be further explored.

Although actual studies of parental strategies in a bilingual situation are few and far between, the investigation of those strategies, combined with detailed analyses of the language use by the children of these parents, offers an excellent, realistic basis on which to approach the issue of the relationship between input and acquisition.

4.5 Other factors relating to the input

It is not my intention to list here all possible factors influencing bilingual development (that would be impossible anyhow). Rather, I would just like to stress a few that, I believe, are particularly important.

According to Saunders (1982: 22), "if children's bilingualism . . . were viewed favorably both by their families and by the population in general, few problems would exist." Similarly, Romaine (1989: 213) writes: "Attitudes of extended family and friends can . . . affect the development of children's bilingualism."

Parents' own attitudes towards their role and linguistic choices *vis-à-vis* their potentially bilingual children are of great significance as well. Whether a parent chooses to use his or her native language or not may have an effect on how the parent comes to regard whatever language chosen. Any moderately negative feelings might affect parental discourse strategies, for instance. Whatever decision parents take regarding the language(s) they will be using with their children, it is important, I think, that the bilingual child should receive what Deuchar (1988: 461) calls "sociolinguistically authentic" input, and that if the one person/one language situation is unnatural for parents they should not use it.

In a report on bilingual English/Welsh mothers in Wales, it was noted that mothers of various backgrounds, but especially lower class mothers, believed that bilingual children's language is likely to be deficient (Harrison et al., 1981). According to the same authors, this ignorance about early bilingual development was one factor in the general failure of the English/Welsh mothers to raise their children bilingually. Döpke (1988: 102) makes a similar observation, namely that in German families in Australia young parents anticipate that raising children bilingually "is doomed to failure." As a result of this attitude, young parents "give up speaking German to their children if success is not immediate" (ibid., 102), hence, of course, failing to actually raise bilingual children.

It would seem, then, that a very important factor in bilingual acquisition (i.e. in whether it is going to take place at all) is parents' expectations and knowledge about children's language development and what to expect in a bilingual situation. These expectations and knowledge are, in turn, related to general attitudes towards bilingualism.

5 The Formal Relationship Between a Bilingual Child's Two Languages

5.1 Introduction

The central issue in the field of bilingual language acquisition so far has been the question of to what extent a young bilingual child develops two separate linguistic systems from the very beginnings of speech production. It is this issue that has inspired much of the work done in the field in the 1980s.

The single most influential publication regarding this issue has been the *Journal of Child Language* article by Volterra and Taeschner (1978). In this thought provoking article, the authors present a three stage model of early bilingual development which basically sees that development as going from a lexically mixed stage to a lexical and structural separation (or differentiation) of the two languages.

Nearly 15 years later, there seems to be a consensus in the field that the three stage model of early bilingual development as first proposed by Volterra and Taeschner (1978) and later partially elaborated by Taeschner (1983) does not accurately describe or explain the bilingual acquisition process. It is clear that anyone still wishing to pursue the model at this time must take into account the many pertinent criticisms that have been levelled at the three stage model and its corollary, the initial single system hypothesis.

5.2 The single system hypothesis

The criticisms directed at the three stage model have mainly concentrated on its first two central components, namely (1) the claim that bilingual children start out with a single system, "Stage I," containing words from both languages (Taeschner, 1983: 28), and (2) the claim that in "Stage II" bilingual children apply "the same syntactic rules to both languages" (Volterra and Taeschner, 1978: 312). Both claims together constitute what is known as the "single system hypothesis." Claims of an initial single system (but not necessarily in the framework of a stage model) have also been made by authors other than Volterra and Taeschner (Klausen and Hayashi, 1990; Redlinger and Park, 1980; Vihman, 1985).

The scanty evidence given by Volterra and Taeschner (1978) for the hypothesized "Stage I" basically relates to the child's linguistic productions in the second year of life. More precisely, the evidence consists of one list of words for each of Volterra and Taeschner's two bilingual subjects at the ages of 1;10 and 1;6 (the total body of data adds up to a list of 137 words). It is claimed that in "Stage I" the terms used in one language have no equivalent meaning that correspond to the terms in the other (Taeschner, 1983: 24), i.e. lexically, the bilingual child is claimed to "have" a single, undifferentiated system.

On purely methodological grounds having to do with data collection procedures and transcription practice,[1] it is doubtful that the corpus gathered by Volterra and Taeschner furnishes a sufficient basis to address the issue of whether their one-year-old subjects used words in a similar meaning or not (De Houwer, 1990: 31–2). For example, it is hard to see how just on the basis of audiotapes informed decisions could be taken as to whether a particular term was being used as a translation equivalent of another term or not. Another methodological problem is that the purported evidence for "Stage I" ultimately depends on the absence of certain forms rather than their presence (De Houwer, 1987b: 88). Related to this is the fact that the data are not presented or analyzed in relation to the sociolinguistic contexts in which they occurred (Genesee, 1989; Mikes, 1990; Quay, 1993), though the data seem to be limited primarily to recordings of the children in interaction with their main German-speaking interlocutor. Even if we accept that no or few translation equivalents occurred in this setting (Taeschner is not very clear on this point), it is still possible that such equivalents might have turned up in recorded conversations with the children's main Italian-speaking interlocutor.

The empirical claim that very young bilingual children use no translation equivalents stands on very shaky ground indeed. Volterra and Taeschner's (1978) and Taeschner's (1983) purported evidence, besides having major methodological drawbacks, in fact goes against this claim. A reanalysis of the data in Taeschner (1983: 25–6) by Quay (1993) shows that in "Stage I" Volterra and

Taeschner's subjects actually did use quite a few equivalent pairs (six out of 64 words for subject Lisa, 14 out of 73 words for subject Giulia).

The fact that express efforts to find more evidence against the existence of early equivalent pairs have failed also indicates that empirically there is little reason to accept that early equivalent pairs do not occur in early bilingual development. In an attempt to replicate Taeschner's (1983) study, Jekat (1985) was unable to decide whether her young German/French subjects used equivalent pairs or not, even though detailed protocols from videorecordings were used. In a similar attempt to find more evidence for "Stage I," Hayashi (1992b) also failed to find support for it. In fact, her two Danish/English subjects appear to have used equivalents from early on. Mikes (1990) reports similar findings for her three trilingual subjects acquiring Serbocroatian, Hungarian, and German.

The most convincing evidence so far against the claim that early equivalent pairs do not occur in early bilingual child language comes from a well-designed study by Quay (1993). Quay clearly shows that her Spanish/English bilingual subject used crosslinguistic equivalents from the beginning of interpretable speech on wards (18 out of 47 word types at age 1;5, 13 formed nine translation pairs). One of the keys to this finding undoubtedly is the fact that the data collection procedure took into account sociolinguistic factors, i.e. data were gathered in two different contexts, namely in the presence of a Spanish interlocutor and in the presence of an English interlocutor. Another important methodological point is that the activities, toys, and books used in the recording sessions were very similar across linguistic contexts, thus ensuring that if translation equivalents actually were available to the child the setting made it possible for them to be used.

It has been questioned whether the purported nonuse of equivalents in early bilingual acquisition must necessarily be interpreted in the sense that the child speaks only "one language which is a language system of his own" (Volterra and Taeschner, 1978: 317). As Hayashi (1992b) has pointed out, the occurrence of only one member of an equivalent pair in early child productions could, for instance, be relatable to a gap in the input (and subsequent intake), and as such does not tell us anything about whether the child is approaching his or her two input systems as a single system or not. Another point is that it is not clear how Volterra and Taeschner can make any claims about the general nature of the young bilingual child's language system based on a purported finding relating to only the lexicon (De Houwer, 1987b: 92–3).

Vihman (1985) has put forward evidence that she claims also supports the initial undifferentiated system hypothesis. Her study is based on the early language productions of her son Raivo, who was first exposed to Estonian, but from the age of six months started to have regular exposure to English as well. According to Vihman, Raivo also went through "Stage I" in Volterra and Taeschner's (1978) sense.

Pye (1986) gives a detailed critique of Vihman's (1985) paper. He reanalyzes Vihman's data in a different fashion and finds that in fact there can be no question of a "mixed language" stage as Vihman suggests; rather, "R[aivo] gives every indication of distinguishing between the English and Estonian vocabulary from the beginning of his lexical development . . . and . . . it is premature to conclude that R had only a single lexicon in the early stages of language acquisition" (Pye, 1986: 593). Genesee (1989: 166) labels Vihman's analyses "incomplete or questionable". To say the least, then, "the claim that bilingual children initially use only one lexicon is by no means non-controversial" (Meisel, 1989: 14).

This brings us to "Stage II" or the initial single grammatical system hypothesis. When morphosyntax first appears in a bilingual child, it is claimed, morphosyntactic rules are "not yet bound to their respective languages" (Taeschner, 1983: 167).[2] This claim is tantamount to arguing for an "inability to separate two grammatical systems" (Meisel, 1989: 37), a phenomenon which in the literature on bilingualism has been called "fusion" (Wölck, 1984). The most outspoken criticism on the initial single grammatical system hypothesis has come from Meisel and Mahlau (1988) and Meisel (1989). Meisel and Mahlau (1988) even go as far as to propose that, in fact, the evidence given by Volterra and Taeschner (1978), rather than a single system interpretation, actually supports language-specific claims for early grammatical bilingual development. As was the case for "Stage I," the criticism leveled at he fusion interpretation for early grammatical bilingual development concerns both methodological/ analytical and theoretical issues.

The methodological points raised by Meisel and Mahlau (1988) and Meisel (1989) mainly revolve around the independent criteria used to define "Stage II" and internal contradictions in Volterra and Taeschner's discussion of their data.[3] For instance, Volterra and Taeschner (1978) claim that in the positioning of adjectives their subject(s) initially used the same syntactic rules. However, Volterra and Taeschner's subjects did not use Italian adjectives until quite late. If this is so, Meisel and Mahlau (1988) wonder, how can the early absence of Italian adjectives be used as a basis for the claim that adjective position in Italian and German shows the existence of similar rules applied to both languages? On a more analytical level, Meisel (1989) criticizes Volterra and Taeschner (1978) for using interference phenomena as a basis for their fusion claim. Interference phenomena cannot be used as a basis for a single grammatical system claim, since in order to speak of interference, there must be two systems that can interfere with each other (cf. also Meisel and Mahlau, 1988). In a similar vein, Huerta-Macías (1981: 168) has suggested that the alternate use of two languages "depends on the separateness of the languages . . . so that the tendency might . . . be for codeswitching itself to perpetuate two distinct languages as such, rather than to bring about their convergence."

Volterra and Taeschner (1978: 324) further present evidence that their subject Lisa used the same negative structures as monolingual children in each language separately at a time when she was still claimed to be in "Stage II." Meisel and Mahlau (1988) protest that these data cannot be used in support of Volterra and Taeschner's claim that Lisa used the same syntactic rules in her two languages. Similarly, Taeschner (1983: 155) claims that her bilingual subjects' word order patterns in early two word utterances show the application of a single grammatical system, while at the same time she notes that the girls' word order patterns closely resemble the orders used by monolingual children in each of the two languages. Again, it can be doubted here that there is sufficient evidence for Taeschner's fusion interpretation. After all, when similarities are found between bilingual and monolingual data it is possible that what might at first sight look like the application of the same "rule" to two languages by the bilingual child is in fact the result of general acquisition principles related to the acquisition of each language separately (see 5.3.3, below).

In her rebuttal to Pye (1986), Vihman (1986) writes that in her 1985 article the assumption was, as for Volterra and Taeschner (1978), "that the child could not at first be aware of the dual origin of the linguistic input provided by his or her particular social context and could thus be expected to begin with an undifferentiated lexicon, with words deriving from either language but not yet identified as such by the child" (Vihman, 1986: 595). It is very important, I believe, that this assumption is made explicit, since it lays bare the existence of fundamentally different perspectives on bilingualism and language acquisition in general that exist within the community of researchers dealing with young bilingual children. Since this is not the appropriate place to go into this issue in any depth, I would like to limit myself to a short response to Vihman's explanation quoted above: is there any preconceived reason why a newborn should expect to be confronted with only one linguistic system? If from the earliest days of life a baby hears distinct sound patterns from different speakers, he or she is in a position to start associating certain sounds with certain speakers. And if perception and comprehension in language acquisition are in fact at least partially related to language production, the differential association in perception of a particular set of sounds with a particular speaker furnishes a very good basis, it would seem, for the eventual production of two fundamentally separate sets of sounds.

There is some evidence that young bilingual children do develop two separate sets of sounds from early on. In a carefully planned study of early phonological acquisition by Deuchar (1989) that was specifically set up to find evidence for an initial "single system" in bilingual acquisition, no proof was found for the existence of such a system. Although Deuchar (1989) is not ready to claim a "dual system" for her Spanish/English subject Manuela, who was studied between the ages of 1;7 and 2;3, Deuchar and Clark (1992: 18) conclude that Manuela "developed separate voicing systems for the two languages." Ingram (1981a) has also specifically addressed the single system hypothesis in the early stages of bilingual phonological development. Ingram's careful and well-considered analyses of phonological forms in a set of speech productions by an Italian/English girl at age two lead him to argue against a single system hypothesis for early phonology; instead, Ingram claims, "there is evidence for two phonological systems in the sense that there are specific tendencies in the output that help identify words as belonging to one lexicon or another" (1981a: 103).

So far, it is not clear whether infant bilinguals in their earliest language production process two linguistic systems or one. As Romaine (1989: 186) writes, "it is often difficult to decide what counts as evidence for differentiation." It seems to be equally hard to see what would count as evidence for the lack of language separation.

More fundamentally, it has been questioned whether it is appropriate to discuss bilingual development before about two years of age in terms of an initial single system or a dual systems hypothesis. Klausen et al. (1992) suggest it is not, and that it is more important to study the possible determining factors in bilingual development (see also Lanza, 1990: 436, 448). Furthermore, as Wode (1990: 43) writes, "much of the debate on whether or not L1 bilinguals can or do keep the systems of their languages apart [from the start] is pointless unless the notion of system is made clear."

5.3 Morphosyntactic development in bilingual preschoolers

5.3.1 Introduction

In the last half a dozen yeas or so, some major studies have emerged that aim to trace the development of morphosyntax in bilingual children. Besides furnishing direly needed empirical data that were not available before, these studies have carved out novel analytical methods that, amongst others, allow the formulation of hypotheses concerning the relationship between a bilingual preschooler's two language.

Ingram (1981a: 105) argues that the separation question "can be resolved by observing [bilingual] children who are learning highly different languages." A major methodological insight in the field of bilingual acquisition related to this is that in order to investigate the question to what extent bilingual children acquire two separate grammatical systems, the main focus should be on structural aspects where the two languages involved differ (De Houwer, 1987b: 141; Koehn and Müller, 1990; Meisel and Mahlau, 1988). Data purportedly showing the existence of a single underlying rule system should be taken only from comparable areas of grammar that differ across the adult target systems or, even better, from related structural areas which show a different developmental path in monolingual children acquiring each of the two languages (Meisel, 1989). After all, it is only these types of data that can potentially show up either differences or similarities in bilingual development. In cases where bilingual children use similar forms in either of their two languages that relate to structurally similar adult forms in the two target systems, it is simply impossible to ascertain whether the child is processing the two languages as one or two systems.

Furthermore, as I have argued elsewhere (De Houwer, 1990: 68–9), and as has been implicitly accepted in most recent studies of bilingual morphosyntactic development, the database for probing the structural relationship between a young bilingual child's two languages should ideally consist of utterances with lexical elements from one language only. After all, in analyzing the data, comparisons need to be made with each of the input languages, and only single lexicon utterances can be unambiguously related to either one of those input systems.

Even if one is analyzing a corpus of single lexicon utterances for usage areas that clearly differ in the child's two input languages, it is often hard to determine whether a particular nonadultlike form is developmental in nature or not (De Houwer, 1994; Romaine, 1989: 195). In my own Dutch–English corpus, for instance, I found that my three-year-old bilingual subject Kate produced the English sentences "I want an other" and "You try and put the big one in there xx the big fat there!" From an adult point of view, the pronominalizer ONE would have been expected here after "other" and "fat." In Dutch, adjectives are used as heads of a noun phrase without a pronominalizer (e.g. "Ik [I] wil [want] een [an] ander [other]"). Can we interpret Kate's omission of ONE in the two examples above as being the result of influence from the Dutch system (transfer interpretation)? Or are the errors a result of Kate's as yet insufficient control over the English system in itself (developmental stage interpretation)? The choice is an impossible one. The errors are equivocal and their occurrence cannot be used as evidence for or against either interpretation.

5.3.2   Two grammatical systems from the start

Somewhat as a reaction to Volterra and Taeschner's (1978) fusion proposal (see 5.2), but primarily as a result of detailed empirical research based on important methodological insights like the ones pointed out in 5.3.1 above, it has lately been suggested that bilingual morphosyntactic development proceeds along separate lines for each language from early on. Koehn and Müller (1990) claim that an early structural separation of a bilingual child's two languages is quite possible, at least if the child grows up in a one person/one language situation and if the children are balanced bilinguals. The possible role of the nature of the input is also reflected in the Separate Development Hypothesis (SDH), which claims that "the morphosyntactic development of a preschool child regularly exposed to two languages from birth which are presented in a separate manner proceeds in a separate fashion for both languages" (De Houwer, 1990: 339; the SDH is not to be confused with the Independent Development Hypothesis as defined by Bergman, 1976).[4] Meisel and Mahlau (1988) equally claim that from early on bilingual children use two separate grammatical systems.

The most convincing evidence so far for the hypothesis that on the morphosyntactic level young bilingual children develop their two languages independently from one another comes from a variety of longitudinal case

Table 8.1 Case studies of BFLA giving evidence of separate morphosyntactic development

Subject	Languages	Age range	Sources
1 Caroline	German/French	1;6–3;6	Berkele (1983)
		1;11–4;6	Klinge (1990)
		1;0–3;6	Meisel (1985)
		1;10–3;10	Meisel (1986, 1989)
		1;0–3;1	Meisel (1990c)
		1;6–5;0	Meisel and Müller (1992); Müller (1990a)
2 Christoph	German/French	2;3–3;8	Klinge (1990)
		1;1–3;8	Parodi (1990)
		1;11–3;5	Schlyter (1990b)
3 François	German/French	2;4–3;4	Schlyter (1990b)
4 Ivar	German/French	2;2–3;5	Klinge (1990)
		1;9–3;5	Koehn (1989)
		1;4–2;9	Meisel (1990b)
		1;5–4;3	Meisel and Müller (1992); Müller (1990b)
		1;10–3;5	Schlyter (1990b)
5 Kate	Dutch/English	2;7–3;4	De Houwer (1987a, 1987b, 1988, 1990)
6 Manuela	Spanish/English	1;7–2;3	Deuchar (1989, 1992)
7 Pascal	German/French	1;5–4;0	Meisel and Müller (1992); Müller (1990b)
8 Pierre	German/French	1;0–3;6	Meisel (1985)
		2;7–3;8	Meisel (1986)
		2;6–4;0	Meisel (1989)
		1;0–4;0	Meisel (1990c)
9 Peru	Basque/Spanish	1;11–3;2	Idiazábal (1988, 1991)

studies explicitly addressing the separation issue. Below, I will present a selective overview of the relevant findings. All the children reported on here grew up in a claimed one person/one language environment.[5] Except for the work done by Deuchar, Idiazábal, and myself all the case studies referred to in the following overview were carried out in the framework of the Hamburg DUFDE project ("Deutsch und Französisch – Doppelter Erstspracherwerb" [German and French – Double First Language Acquisition]) led by Jürgen Meisel.[6]

For easy reference, table 8.1 gives a succinct overview of all the case studies mentioned in the present subsection.

From the earliest appearance of bound morphology, it has been found that forms are used in a language-specific manner. Idiazábal (1988, 1991) found this to be the case for noun phrases and Deuchar (1992) for verb phrases. As the bilingual child starts to use multiword utterances, bound morphology continues to be used in a language-specific manner (Deuchar, 1992), and this pattern has been found to persist until the bilingual child produced complex sentences around age three (De Houwer 1987b, 1990).

Subject–verb agreement has also received quite a bit of attention in the child bilingualism literature. Again, repeated evidence has been found for the hypothesis that structural developments take place within each input system, without the need for reference to the other one. Deuchar's (1992) Spanish/English subject marked subject–verb agreement in language-specific ways from the very beginning, as did Meisel's (1989) French/German subjects. As the bilingual child begins to use many more multiword and also complex sentences, subject–verb agreement within each language continues to be used independently of the child's other language (De Houwer, 1987b, 1990).

As soon as they begin to produce two and multiword utterances, bilingual children have been found to use clearly language-specific orderings (Deuchar, 1989; Meisel, 1989). The situation remains the same as children approach the stage at which they are about ready to use complex sentences (De Houwer, 1988; Müller, 1990b; Parodi, 1990). Also in their use of complex sentences bilingual children use word orders in a language-specific manner (De Houwer, 1988; Müller, 1990b).

In a variety of other areas bilingual children have been found to follow two separate developmental paths in their acquisition of each language as well. This is the case for the development of tense and aspect (Schlyter, 1990b), the functional use of gender (De Houwer, 1987a), and the use of tag questions and indirect objects (De Houwer, 1987b, 1990).

Even in case studies of bilingual children that have not specifically focused on the bilingual aspect of the data, or on the relationship between the subjects' two languages, occasional comments appear that give further evidence for the SDH.

Berkele (1983: 85), for instance, notes a different development for her subject's two languages as far as the first frequent occurrence of the definite article goes (it first appears strongly in French, and only later in German). Koehn (1989) traces the development of the formal expression of number distinctions in her subject Ivar. Although the focus is not on the relationship between Ivar's two languages, Koehn (1989) claims that the forms expressing plurality are language-specific from very early on, and that the functions of the various plural forms are language-specific as well. Meisel (1990c: 279), in his investigation of the +/− finite distinction and grammatical agreement, claims that his three bilingual subjects "have available different underlying systems in German and in French" as far as their use of clitics is concerned. Meisel's (1985) aim is to trace the development of the TMA system in his two subjects. His finding that the children used different formal means in the two languages to express a similar meaning can be interpreted as constituting further evidence for the early separate development of morphosyntax in bilingual children. Meisel's (1986) article is mainly geared towards showing that children have available a grammatical mode of processing from an early age onwards. Within this context, however, Meisel presents evidence that as soon as his two German/French subjects produce multiword utterances, they "use certain word-order patterns only in one or the other language, depending on the presence of this pattern in the target grammar" (1986: 124).

Although Meisel's (1986) analyses of his subjects' use of case marking does not specifically focus on the relationship between their two languages, the very fact that he deemed it unproblematic to discuss developments in German and French separately suggests that the German and French data could be interpreted as constituting two distinct, closed systems (a similar argument can be made for the work by Berkele, 1983; Koehn, 1989; and Meisel, 1985, 1990c). Indeed, in any study of bilingual children that treats morphosyntactic data for each language as separate systems and analyzes the data for each language without reference to the child's knowledge of the other language, the assumption must be that in developing two languages simultaneously there is little or no influence from the one language on the other. Only with this assumption as background can researchers start to work on data from bilingual children to address more general issues in the study of child language, as is recently being done by researchers associated with the DUFDE project in Hamburg.

A prime example of this new trend is Meisel and Müller's (1992) work, in which data from bilingual children are used solely to approach theoretical issues in child language research in general: Meisel and Müller's emphasis is on finding evidence for the claim that a complementizer system is lacking at a time that the structural prerequisites for such a system are available to the child. Klinge's (1990) study consists of a general analysis of the semantic functions of prepositions as they are used by three children who happen to be bilingual. Müller (1990a) has looked at the development of formal means to express gender in a French/German girl. None of the studies mentioned in this paragraph, however, address issues specifically related to bilingual development, but they do treat the data from one bilingual child as if they were produced by two monolingual children, without any discussion of possible influence from one language on the other. Obviously this can only be done if indeed the bilingual child's two morphosyntactic systems have previously been shown to fundamentally develop separately from each other.

The children reported on so far in this subsection were all brought up in a claimed one person/one language environment. If one accepts that children try as much as possible to speak like the people around them, it should really come as no surprise that they develop two separate morphosyntactic systems in a separate input condition.

There may be more to the separate development claim for morphosyntax, however, than a simple input–output relationship. Reports on children whose input conditions were not necessarily of the one person/one language kind still speak of separate development. Nwokah (1984), for instance, reports that her data on three-year-old children learning English and the non-Indo European language Igbo from infancy on, show syntactic structures, lexical items, and certain sounds to be used in a language-specific way. Unfortunately, more details are lacking. Similarly, García (1983: 39–40) notes that his subjects developed their two languages separately from each other on the morphosyntactic level (age range: 3;0 to 4;2). Intriguingly, García's subjects had not as a rule heard their two languages spoken mostly by distinct people in their environment: all of the subjects' parents would use both English and Spanish, as well as mixed utterances, in addressing their children. The fact that García's bilingual subjects did not have comparable productive control over their two languages gives further rise to the assumption that separate development is a processing strategy with a wide application in early bilingual development.

Many of the Turkish/German children that Pfaff and her associates studied in the KITA project did not necessarily hear their languages separated in the input either. Nevertheless, Pfaff (1990: 126) reports that the findings of previous studies that form part of the KITA project show that "the grammars of early bilinguals' languages are separate from the outset." The areas investigated are case marking, subject–verb agreement, and pro-drop phenomena. Kardam and Pfaff (to appear) also claim that in the early bilingual acquisition of Turkish and German the two languages develop separately as far as morphosyntax goes. Finally, Pfaff (1992) writes that in the acquisition of German by two Turkish-dominant German/Turkish bilingual preschoolers with Turkish as L1, the grammatical categories of Turkish are hardly ever transferred to German.

Contrary to what some authors believe, then, it may not be absolutely necessary that a bilingual child's two languages are separated in the input for the separate development of two grammatical systems to take place.

To my knowledge, there are no methodologically sound studies of morphosyntactic development in young bilingual children that have found any evidence against the separate development hypothesis. This is not to say that the issue has been settled: the limited number of studies actually addressing the separate development issue precludes any generalizing statements. Although currently the hypothesis that young bilingual children develop their two languages independently from one another as far as morphosyntax goes remains unchallenged, many more investigations are needed to further substantiate it.

5.3.3   Comparisons with monolingual children

Closely connected with the issue of what is the relationship between the bilingual child's two languages is the question of how bilingual development in each language compares to the development of either language in monolingual children (see also Meisel and Mahlau, 1988). Obviously, separate bilingual development is theoretically possible without there being any similarity with monolingual acquisition. Thus, even if bilingual children's errors are different from monolingual children's, it is possible for bilingual children's errors not to be due to interlinguistic influence. On the other hand, however, if it can be proved that for each language a bilingual child follows the course of development taken by a comparable monolingual child of around the same age, there is strengthened evidence that the bilingual child is developing two separate morphosyntactic systems.

Before I present some findings related to comparisons between monolingual and bilingual children, it must be pointed out that for many languages there are still only few data available on monolingual acquisition. Furthermore, those that we have may not be representative for the child population as a whole. For this reason alone, features of development in bilingual children that have not been reported on for comparable monolingual children do not necessarily reflect basic, general differences between monolingual and bilingual children.

Related to the scarcity of comparison material is the point that any apparent differences between monolingual and bilingual children may be manifestations of normal interindividual variation existing in both the bilingual and the monolingual child population (see also Koehn and Müller, 1990). In addition, the monolingual literature in itself may yield contradictory evidence as well, again pointing to the wide range of variation in acquisition. Furthermore, as Hakuta and Diaz (1985: 329) put point, "there will be a large number of variables that differentiate the bilingual from the monolingual other than simply that the bilingual speaks two languages and the monolingual one." Code switching, lexical borrowings, and possibly increased metalinguistic awareness (see section 3) are obvious examples. This again may make comparison data very difficult to interpret.

In the most general of terms, it does seem to be the case that "the development of a bilingual system taps the same basic developmental processes utilized in monolingual development" (Kessler, 1984: 38), and that "bilingual first language acquisition does not differ in substantial ways from monolingual development" (Meisel, 1990c: 17). Taeschner (1987) has also claimed that the bilingual acquisition process is essentially the same as the monolingual one.

Given that "there is no reason to believe that the underlying principles and mechanisms of language development [in bilinguals] are qualitatively different from those used by monolinguals" (Meisel, 1986: 64), it comes as no surprise that, like monolingual children, bilingual children go through an initial babbling stage, followed by the one word stage, the two word stage, the multiword stage, and the multiclause stage. There are no reports, for instance, of bilingual children whose first vocalizations consist of fully adultlike complex sentences. Neither have major delays been reported concerning the ages at which bilingual children start using two word utterances (to list but one possibility) as compared to monolingual children.

More detailed and precise comparisons of bilingual and monolingual children's language development are unfortunately few and far between. Part of the reason for this is the lack of comparable data for monolingual and bilingual acquisition. After all, one must be sure to compare like with like.

Ideally, bilingual and monolingual children should be studied within the same research project using data collection and analysis methods that are as closely similar as possible. There has, to my knowledge, been only one study so far that has attempted to do this in a methodologically sound manner: within the framework of a much larger research project, García (1983) collected data for English-speaking monolingual and Spanish/English bilingual children that he then compared to each other. He found no systematic differences between the English monolingual and bilingual data in the use of English morpheme categories (García, 1983: 49).

Second best are analyses or reanalyses of third party corpora that are then compared to the bilingual data. Such data may be available from colleagues informally, or through publications or public data exchange systems such as CHILDES (MacWhinney and Snow, 1990).[7] Using French comparison material available through CHILDES, Müller (1990b) found that French finite verb placement as used by her two French/German subjects was identical in nature to that used by the French monolingual child Philippe as recorded by M. Leveillé (Suppes et al., 1973). After an analysis of a set of data from a Dutch monolingual child appearing in the Appendix to Leemans and Ramaekers (1982) I was able to make a close comparison between those data and my own for my Dutch/English subject, Kate, as far as the use of Dutch sentential word order goes (De Houwer, 1990: 247–59). I found that my bilingual subject used exactly the same word orders as the monolingual child, both as far as types and proportional use was concerned.

Besides using a coherent body of raw data, it is also possible to draw on excerpts of data appearing in published articles and books. Drawing on data for Stern and Stern's (1928) monolingual German son Günther, Müller (1990b) found that her two French/German subjects' use of German finite verb placement was very similar to that of Günther's, at least before the appearance of complementizers. Comparing my longitudinal data for bilingual Kate with excerpts of transcripts for a three-year-old English subject studied by Fletcher (1985) I found that English natural gender pronouns were used with referential appropriateness by both the bilingual and the monolingual girls (De Houwer, 1990: 144). Various examples in Schaerlaekens and Gillis (1987) for Dutch monolingual children show that before age three the definite article DE is used appropriately in front of nonneuter nouns. A similar result was found for the Dutch data from bilingual Kate (De Houwer, 1990: 142). Examples of utterances produced by a three-year-old Dutch monolingual child (Tinbergen, 1919) show the use of a finite verb without an overt subject. Such Dutch utterances were found in the data from bilingual Kate as well (De Houwer, 1990: 192). I also used Dutch examples from Schaerlaekens (1977) for comparisons of subject–verb agreement and again found great similarities between my data from bilingual Kate and utterances produced by monolingual children (De Houwer, 1990: 199).

Another possibility is to work from analyzed data in third party sources. For quite a number of topics I have used the wealth of material available in the various tables in Wells (1985) as a basis for comparing aspects of the English data from bilingual Kate with data for monolingual English children (De Houwer, 1990). Using this method, I have been able to find very strong similarities between the monolingual and bilingual data for the use of plural v. singular nouns, the internal structure of NPs with a noun as head, the incidence and types of elements occurring between finite and nonfinite verbs in clauses with a multicomponent verb phrase, the incidence of negative interrogatives, interrogative pronoun usage, and the comparative usage of declaratives v. interrogatives.

The least satisfying source for comparison material, but often unfortunately the only one available, consists of disparate reports in the literature on various monolingual children. In order to compare their word order data for two French/German subjects after the advent of complementizers, Müller (1990b) and Meisel and Müller (1992) took reports in the literature on German monolingual acquisition as a basis and found that their bilingual subjects used finite verb placement in German that was reported for at least one monolingual German child as well. As far as subject–verb agreement goes, Meisel (1989: 31) states that his German/French subjects "acquire *each* of the two languages very much like monolingual children." Parodi (1990) found that her French/German bilingual subject used the same word order in his German subclauses as German monolingual children reportedly do. Schlyter (1990b) suggests that the verb forms used by her three French/German subjects are similar to those reportedly used by monolingual French and German children as evident from the literature. Pfaff and Savas (1988) state that in the use of Turkish case marking, their four-year-old Turkish/German subjects made the same errors of commission as reported in the literature on monolingual Turkish children. In my study of English/Dutch Kate I also found many areas where there existed clear parallels between the bilingual data and various reports in the literature on monolingual English and Dutch children (De Houwer 1987b, 1990). For both English and Dutch, I was able to find such parallels for the following aspects: most structural aspects of verb usage, the types of preposed elements in affirmative sentences, the incidence of nonadultlike word order, nonfinite verb placement, clause types, sentence types, conjunctions, the incidence of subclauses, the number and type of clause constituents, and question inversion. For Dutch I found further similarities between the Dutch portion of my bilingual data and reports on Dutch monolingual children for the use of personal pronouns and the incidence of plurals. *Mutatis mutandis*, the same was found for English for auxiliary usage in questions, the use of tags, interrogative pronoun usage, the use of the pronoun *it*, the variety of structural patterns, and the use of indirect v. direct objects.

Summing up, then, whenever comparisons have been attempted between

monolingual children and children growing up bilingually from birth, researchers have found similarities rather than differences. The only "dissonant" finding here is one by Meisel (1989), who found less variability in the use of word
order in his bilingual subjects than in monolingual French and German children as evidenced by the literature. However, as Koehn and Müller (1990)
have pointed out, it cannot be excluded that Meisel's findings reflect individual differences, particularly since the literature on German and especially
French children is quite small.

The very fact that in virtually all the comparisons between monolingual and
bilingual children the methodologies used are very disparate can be interpreted as lending even more support to the generalization that bilingual and
monolingual development are highly similar: apparently, we are here dealing
with a very robust finding. For each of their languages respectively, bilingual
children make the same types of errors as their monolingual peers and use
similar structures at similar stages in development.

In this context, it is not surprising that occasionally the metaphor crops up
of the young bilingual child as being two monolingual children in one. This
metaphor, however, strongly abstracts from the bilingual child's daily reality,
which involves a constant interplay between the two languages that the child
needs to communicate satisfactorily. This interplay is the subject of the next
section.

6   Language Contact Phenomena in Young Bilingual Children

Typical adult bilingual behavior involves the use of code switching i.e. the
alternate use of two linguistic codes within a stretch of discourse (Baetens
Beardsmore, 1982; Grosjean, 1982; Gumperz, 1982a). A variety of different
factors have been isolated as potential determinants of whether, when, and
how adults will engage in code switching behavior. Most researchers agree
that the communicative context in which language use takes place lies at the
basis of whether and to what extent code switching occurs. As speakers select
a particular code in order to negotiate interpersonal relationships (Myers-
Scotton, 1990), they exhibit behavior that is socially highly significant.

In order to learn how to code switch as it is deemed appropriate within a
particular context, then, the bilingual child's socialization process is of central
importance (Kwan-Terry, 1992; Lanza, 1992). One suggestion has been, for
instance, that bilingual children's use of mixed utterances may be modeled on
mixed utterances provided in the input (Bentahila and Davies, 1992; Genesee
1989; Goodz, 1989; Saunders, 1988: 181–6). Another suggestion is that parents'
discourse strategies may encourage or discourage particular choices in code
selection (Lanza, 1990, 1992).

Very little is actually known about how the bilingual child is socialized into code switching behavior. Although researchers studying bilingual children agree that they regularly use elements from two languages within one utterance, conversational turn, or longer stretch of discourse, a theory of how code switching develops has yet to be formulated (Lanza, 1992). One reason for this rather large gap in the body of knowledge about bilingual acquisition is that until very recently little attention was paid to the contexts in which children grow up bilingually (Genesee, 1989; Lanza, 1990). A second reason is that bilingual children's speech productions have often been studied without reference to the sociolinguistic situations in which they occurred, hence making it impossible to analyze the possible factors underlying any code switching behavior (De Houwer, 1987b; Gal, 1985; Goodz et al., 1990; Meisel, 1990a; Meisel and Mahlau, 1988).

As studies of adult bilinguals have shown, the sociolinguistic context is paramount in finding explanations for code switching. Poplack (1981), for instance, lists the norms or perceived norms of the speech situation and the bilingual ability or perceived bilingual ability of the speaker and the hearer as elements that play a decisive role in predicting the occurrence of code switching. The studies of early bilingual acquisition that have actually taken into account the sociolinguistic contexts in which bilingual children produce speech show that the factors listed by Poplack for adult bilinguals also lie at the root of code switching behavior and language choice in very young bilingual children. A study by Quay (1992) demonstrates very clearly that code switching as a function both of the interlocutor and the language norms established by a bilingual interlocutor can already occur at the age of 1;8. Lanza's (1990) two-year-old Norwegian/English subjects Siri and Tomas also exhibited contextually sensitive code switching behavior. In speaking to monolingual interlocutors, Lanza's subjects used only one language. In speaking to bilingual interlocutors, the children behaved differently. Lanza shows that her subjects' code selection hinged on whether their interlocutor negotiated what Lanza calls "a monolingual context" v. "a bilingual context." In the former, the bilingual interlocutor tends to use only one language in interactions with the child and through various discourse strategies shows the child that she is expected to do the same. In the latter, the bilingual interlocutor tends to use a lot of code switching in interactions with the child and makes no demands on the child's language selection. Siri's mother used a basically monolingual English context, and Siri addressed her mother mainly in English. Tomas' mother, on the other hand, negotiated a bilingual context, and Tomas tended to use mainly Norwegian and only occasionally English in interactions with his mother. Both children thus seemed to be quite sensitive to the norms for language selection as established by their mothers.

Kielhöfer (1987) found a similar sensitivity in his two French/German bilingual subjects, who were addressed in French by their mother and in German by their father from birth. From the beginnings of their third year of life, Kielhöfer's subjects addressed their mother in French and their father in

German. The children went out of their way to avoid the use of mixed utterances (i.e. utterances that combine morphemes belonging to both languages) and utterances in the "wrong" language (see also Saunders, 1988: 181). At around age two years and three months, Kielhöfer's subjects would show dissatisfaction when either of their parents inadvertently addressed them in other than the usual language. Thus, Kielhöfer claims, his subjects had a normative attitude towards language choice from very early on. A main factor leading to this normative attitude, Kielhöfer argues, is that his subjects' French-speaking mother used correction strategies that clearly showed her nonacceptance of her sons' occasional use of German or mixed utterances with her. Other factors that contributed to his subjects' normative attitude, Kielhöfer writes, are the rather strict adherence to a one person/one language situation and the general language attitudes existing in the monolingual German environment in which the children grew up. These attitudes strongly discouraged the use of mixed utterances.

The importance of perceived bilingual ability is further shown in an inventive experimental study by Marcon and Coon (1983) using fairly balanced Spanish/English bilingual preschoolers as subjects. In the children's natural environment, most Spanish speakers would normally have passive and productive capabilities in English as well, but most English speakers would not know any Spanish. When addressed in English during the experiment, the bilingual subjects tended to consistently respond in English. When addressed in Spanish, the subjects used both Spanish and English. Thus, expectations of the addressee's language capabilities played a major part in the children's language selection.

Such expectations of the addressee's language capabilities were also found to be at the root of three-year-old Dutch/English Kate's code selection patterns (De Houwer, 1987b, 1990). In speaking to basically monolingual interlocutors, Kate tended to use her conversation partner's only language. With people she knew to be fluent bilinguals, however, she was much more ready to use either of her languages both within and across utterances. At the same time, though, Kate still followed the norms for language use laid down by these bilinguals in selecting primarily one language for interacting with them. An older preschool child, Elvoo, who acquired Singapore Colloquial English and Cantonese-Chinese simultaneously (Kwan-Terry, 1992), shows a similar tendency to distinguish between speakers he characterized as monolingual v. bilingual. With people he characterized as monolingual who might in fact be bilingual, but who limited themselves to the use of only one language with the child, Elvoo limited himself to that one language as well. Elvoo's mother, however, used both English and Cantonese-Chinese with him, and negotiated what Lanza would call a bilingual context. In interactions with his mother, Elvoo used a great deal of code switching. The adult norms for language choice were also applied by two children between the ages of 4;5 and 5;0 who were exposed to Moroccan Arabic, French, and a variety involving frequent code switching between Arabic and French (Bentahila and Davies, 1992). Even in this rather complex situation, the children studied were found to alternate their three varieties in the same ways as their parents and other adults.

In an analysis of code switching by young Turkish/German preschoolers, Kardam and Pfaff (to appear) found that Turkish lexical elements occurred very rarely in the children's German discourse, whereas German lexical elements in their Turkish discourse occurred more often as the children grew older. The authors claim this shows that the bilingual children were adapting to community norms, which disallow the use of Turkish in German, but do allow the use of German in Turkish (see also Pfaff, 1991). Finally, Saunders (1982: 92) states that language choice by his German/English children throughout their early childhood is "predominantly dependent on who the person being addressed is and which language has been established as being appropriate to speak to that person in."

The evidence so far concerning the development of code switching behavior consistently shows, then, that both knowledge of the interlocutor's linguistic capabilities and sensitivity to the norms for code choice upheld by their interlocutors are the major factors determining language choice in bilingual children even before the age of two. Once it is established that code switching with a particular interlocutor is allowable a plethora of other factors may help determine when code switching will actually occur. Some of the determinants that have been identified for young bilingual children include: semantic domain (De Houwer, 1990: 95; Kwan-Terry, 1992), different ability in the two languages (Bentahila and Davies, 1992; García, 1983), switches by the interacting bilingual interlocutor (De Houwer, 1990: 94; Marcon and Coon, 1983), and even personality (Hoffmann, 1985; McClure, 1981; Romaine, 1989).

As indicated before, code switching involves the use of elements from two languages within one utterance, conversational turn, or longer stretch of discourse. In the child bilingualism literature, it is particularly the first type here, namely the use of two languages within a single utterance, also known as "intrasentential code switching" (Poplack, 1980) or "code mixing" (Sridhar and Sridhar, 1980), which has attracted attention. For clarity's sake I shall use the term "mixed utterances" to refer to utterances in which elements from two languages cooccur.

While the context-appropriate occurrence of mixed utterances has been explained by some as the fairly random result of "relaxed" speech production processes (De Houwer, 1983; Vihman, 1981a), the following have been proposed as determining factors as well: the existence of a lexical gap in B; the influence of a previous mention of a lexical item in A in the ongoing discourse; the initial learning of a concept in the context of A; the greater frequency of the inserted item in A; the possibility of making a semantic distinction in A that is not available in B; the greater saliency of the item in A as compared to B, and so on (see, for example, Saunders, 1988: 181–6). Taeschner et al. (1982: 32) have made the original suggestion that "bilingual children, when they do not know enough words in one of the two languages . . . prefer to insert lexical items from the other language in their sentences rather than produce incomplete sentences or nuclear structures."

It has been noted repeatedly that bilingual children do not usually use mixed utterances when addressing monolinguals (Kielhöfer, 1987; Stavans, 1990; Vihman 1981a). However, there have been some reports of young bilingual children who do occasionally use mixed utterances with speakers they know to be monolingual. Vihman (1982) notes that at the age of 2;6 her English/ Estonian subject occasionally used Estonian words when addressing English monolingual speakers. Similarly, I found that even after her third birthday, my English/Dutch subject occasionally used a mixed utterance when addressing her monolingual English-speaking mother (De Houwer, 1990: 112–13). Such contextually inappropriate mixed utterances have been explained as unrepaired slips of the tongue (De Houwer, 1987b: 186; Kielhöfer and Jonekeit, 1983: 43).

Finally, researchers have also looked at the structural features of young bilingual children's mixed utterances. Quite a robust finding here is that for mixed utterances clearly involving the insertion of guest language elements into the host language, the guest language elements have been found to minimally consist of one free morpheme. Most frequently, the guest insertion consists of a single noun (De Houwer, 1987b: 178; García, 1983: 142; Kwan-Terry, 1992; Vihman, 1981a; but see Bentahila and Davies, 1992).

7   Final Remarks and Suggestions for Further Research

The initial single system hypothesis describes the bilingual child as beginning with the creation of a system that is quite different from each of the child's input systems. As such, the bilingual child is implicitly seen as following a different route to acquisition from monolingual children, whose early lexicons are commonly seen as approximations of, and in fact related to, their input system. This view of early bilingual development has been discredited. Instead, more and more evidence suggests that bilingual children do not differ much from monolingual children in their approach to the language learning task. Like monolingual children, bilingual children pay a lot of attention to the input they receive. They soon notice that this input differs depending on who is talking or where and in what situation someone is talking. Just like monolingual children, bilingual children attempt to talk like the people around them. Because of the bilingual situation, however, the bilingual child has more options than the monolingual one: from very early on, the bilingual child makes contextually sensitive linguistic choices that draw on a developing knowledge of two separate language systems. Bilingual children's earliest use of morphosyntax appears to be language-specific from the start, and already at a very young age bilingual children are skilled conversationalists who easily switch languages according to interlocutor.

These insights about bilingual children's language development have come to the fore only within the last decade, and they derive from studies of bilingual children that are firmly rooted in the tradition of developmental psycholinguistics, giving due attention to methodological modifications and complications necessitated by the bilingual situation. Indeed, a major step forward in the field of bilingual language acquisition has been the realization of the immense complexity involved in studying bilingual children, and the need to take that complexity fully into account in the development of appropriate methodologies. Earlier, major conclusions were all too often drawn on the basis of anecdotal data only, and although earlier studies were interested in addressing the question of separate v. nonseparate development, they left out of consideration a major insight that, although it is a very obvious point, has emerged only recently: in order to answer the question whether the bilingual child uses language-specific rules or not one can only take as a basis for analysis related constructions which differ in the input languages. A second major step forward in the field of bilingual language acquisition is the recent realization that the sociolinguistic situation is a great contributor to the actual language production of the bilingual child, as well as the fact that this realization is starting to be taken into account in both the organizing of data collection settings and in the analyses and interpretations of the data.

Despite these obvious advancements in the field of bilingual acquisition, much remains to be discovered. As has become clear from the survey presented in this chapter, the "baseline" of normal bilingual development has not yet been established. Equally unresolved is the issue of what is part of "normal" development in bilingual children and what can be considered as deviant, and we are far from establishing any norms for bilingual development, although such norms are sorely needed (Ball, 1984). After all, bilingual children have as much of a right as monolingual children to be helped in their language development if they are experiencing any problems. Such help geared specifically towards a bilingual situation, unfortunately, is not sufficiently available at this time. One way of making a start towards remedying this situation is by setting up many large-scale crosslinguistic studies comparing children from various bilingual backgrounds. Another major gap in the field is that notwithstanding the generally accepted importance of input factors in bilingual acquisition, most explanations of the bilingual acquisition process so far have tended to neglect the role of the input. Without a clear understanding of the particular input situation the bilingual child is in many aspects of the child's linguistic productions cannot be satisfactorily explained.

Since a young bilingual's language usage is at least partially sociolinguistically determined, this must be taken into account in attempts at psycholinguistic explanations of the bilingual development process. The development of this sociolinguistic behavior *per se* is to be explained as well. As these insights have now been made explicit and suitable methodologies have been developed to approach them, the field of bilingual language acquisition has grown out of its infancy. It is now ready to tackle in an informed and well considered manner the challenge of further exploring how young children may become bilingual.

ACKNOWLEDGMENTS

I am greatly indebted to all the many colleagues who have contributed to this chapter (1) by referring me to work done on bilingual children that I was not aware of before, (2) by sending me otherwise inaccessible copies of publications and manuscripts, and (3) by offering helpful comments and suggestions at all stages of writing. In particular, however, I would like to thank Margaret Deuchar, Liz Lanza, Brian MacWhinney, Natascha Müller, and Wolfgang Wölck.

NOTES

1 Volterra and Taeschner (1978) and Taeschner (1983) claim that the data are based on bimonthly recordings. In Taeschner (1987) it is stated, however, that recordings (of the same data) were made monthly. Obviously, the information given is inconsistent here.

2 This statement is quite curious in the light of Taeschner et al.'s (1982: 34) claim that "in the development of the sentence, as far as the fundamental structures are concerned, the bilingual child acquires two quite distinct linguistic systems."

3 According to Meisel and Mahlau (1988), Volterra and Taeschner's (1978) article suffers from methodological problems which raise serious doubts about the general value of the investigation.

4 How important exactly the separate input factor is in the development of two separate morphosyntactic systems, however, needs yet to be determined (cf. De Houwer, 1994).

5 Deuchar's subject Manuela was exposed to English from her monolingual grandmother, and to Spanish from both her parents. Manuela's parents did occasionally address her in English rather than Spanish when monolingual English speakers were present. Apart from this exception, though, Manuela can be said to have become bilingual in a one person/one language situation.

6 For a clear overview of the DUFDE project, see Schlyter (1990a); all the findings in the present chapter related to the acquisition of German and French are part of the DUFDE project.

7 At the time of final preparation of this chapter, three sets of corpora containing transcriptions of data from young bilingual children were available through CHILDES: (1) the English/Spanish corpus for Manuela (contributed by Margaret Deuchar), (2) the Japanese/Danish corpus for Anders (contributed by Mariko Hayashi), and (3) the Dutch/English corpus for Kate (contributed by Annick de Houwer).

9 Socialization across Contexts

RICHARD ELY AND JEAN BERKO GLEASON

Through the process of socialization, children take on the beliefs, feelings, and behaviors appropriate to their particular role in their own culture. Much socialization is effected explicitly through language, in the verbal instructions parents direct to their children during everyday activities, as well as through stories and aphorisms that express cultural values. In addition, children are socialized in the use of language itself: parents and others give explicit directions to children about what to say, and how and when they should say it. Finally, children are socialized indirectly through participation in verbal interactions that are subtly marked for role, status, and other aspects of their society's structure.

This chapter will explore some of the contexts for socialization that are part of the common experience of English-speaking children in the Western world. We begin with a brief general discussion of the nature of socialization and of the concept of *context*. We then move to empirical studies of linguistic socialization in a variety of contexts, broadly grouped by setting: home, school, and the wider world. In each of these settings, children experience a small number of typical socializing experiences. We conclude with some inferences that may be drawn from these studies, comments about their limitations, and recommendations for future research.

Processes of Socialization: Theories

How socialization, in its broader sense, is defined and effected is a matter of some contention among researchers. Historically, either behavioral or psychodynamic approaches dominated early work on socialization (Maccoby, 1992). Behaviorists view the parent as active and the child as passive (Skinner, 1957). According to behaviorist theory, adults shape children's behavior through selective reinforcement – by rewarding desired responses, gradually shaping the child's behavior. Social learning theorists (Bandura, 1977) add modeling and imitation to the repertoire of tools believed to influence socialization. Thus, adults selectively reinforce the child's behaviors, and they provide models for the child to imitate, as illustrated in the example below (from Gleason, Perlmann, and Greif, 1984: 500–1), in which the parent explicitly models what the child is expected to say:

Child: Mommy, I want more milk.
Mother: Is that the way to ask?
Child: Please.
Mother: Please what?
Child: Please gimme milky.
Mother: No.
Child: Please gimme milk.
Mother: No.
Child: Please . . .
Mother: Please, may I have more milk?
Child: Please, may I have more milk?

In contrast to behaviorist theory, the psychodynamic model of socialization emphasizes conflict (Freud, 1924/1952). According to psychoanalytic theory, the child has intrinsic motivations and behavioral dispositions (drives) that are contrary to those of the parents and of society. Parents and other adults are responsible for curbing the child's natural tendencies while concurrently instilling behaviors and values that are compatible with those of the community. For instance, in the example cited above, the child might be seen as driven by her immediate want for milk; the mother's behavior might be interpreted as directing the child to express her need in a socially acceptable manner. Basic aspects of socialization are completed when the child resolves his or her Oedipal conflict and identifies with the same-sex parent. The child internalizes the parent's value system, taking on an appropriate gender role and moral system. The "internal parent" becomes the child's superego, which thenceforth assures that socialized behavior takes place, or punishes the child with feelings of guilt.

In recent years, sociocultural theories of socialization have challenged the traditional behavioral and psychodynamic assumptions. Unlike the psychodynamic and behavioral approaches, which focus on universal psychological processes that are found in all families, these approaches highlight social, cultural, and historical forces and their varying effects on individual development (Vygotsky, 1978, 1986; Rogoff, 1990; Wertsch, 1985, 1991). In a Vygotskian, sociocultural approach, the emphasis is on social exchange: the higher mental functions, such as thinking, speech, and consciousness, all become intrapsychic phenomena only after they have existed between the child and adults. Children's mental processes are formed under the influence of the adults around them (Wertsch, 1991). Vygotsky (1986) viewed language as a social tool, drawn from the child's social milieu. In his explanation of the use of "private speech" (speaking aloud to oneself), for instance, he claimed that children use private speech not as a manifestation of egocentricism (Piaget, 1959) but as a means of understanding, planning, and guiding their own behavior. As we have noted elsewhere (Gleason, 1988), some of the language that the child uses in private speech is actually a repetition of what the parent has said. For example, in Ruth Weir's (1962) study of her son Anthony's crib talk (a monologue delivered by the child before going to sleep) she noted many utterances such as "Don't go on the desk," and "Don't take Daddy's glasses," that clearly originated with one of his parents. According to Vygotskian theory, as children grow older, private speech becomes internalized speech, or verbal thought. A social rule that is first uttered by the parent (e.g. "Don't take Daddy's glasses") later becomes something the child says aloud in private speech, and ultimately becomes something that she thinks to herself silently.

In this chapter, we will approach linguistic socialization from a social interactionist perspective (Bruner, 1983; Snow, 1986). This perspective recognizes the contributions of both learning theory and the sociocultural model described above. At the same time it emphasizes individual development as it evolves through interaction; adults and children calibrate their language and other behaviors in response to subtle cues from one another. Reciprocal roles are played by both children and adults in the socialization process (Trevarthen, 1988). Children actively seek social exchanges, and parents are sensitive social partners. For instance, beginning in the prelinguistic period, mothers and infants employ a sophisticated repertoire of social skills and communicative processes, including turn-taking, social referencing, and affect attunement (Bruner, 1983; Campos and Sternberg, 1981; Kaye, 1982; Sorce, Emde, Campos and Klinnert, 1985; Stern, 1985).

Language and Socialization

Although the process of socialization is universal, the content of socialization varies widely, though systematically, across cultures. Every society develops an approach to child rearing that reflects its indigenous cultural values (LeVine, 1988). In this chapter our focus is on linguistic socialization in Western society and, more specifically, on the variation in linguistic socialization that appears across different contexts in Western society. Regardless of the particular context, however, the goal of linguistic socialization is always to promote communicative competence (Hymes, 1972) – the ability to use language appropriately in the community.

Language intersects with socialization in three distinct domains (Gleason, 1988). First, parents and other caregivers use language to instruct the child about what to do, feel, and think – essentially the child's "marching orders."

Here, the social and moral rules of conduct are the topic, and language is the medium. A variety of linguistic forms, including commands, explanations, and anecdotes, can be used to convey these social and moral rules (Shweder and Much, 1987). For example, a teacher defines the social rules for her classroom by explaining to a child that "All the children are friends in school" and by directing the child "to make them [unfriendly children] your friend" (Shweder and Much, 1987). At American dinner tables, parents explicitly tell children how to sit and what to eat (Blum-Kulka, 1990). Although parents and other caregivers sometimes dictate the topics and form of socialization unilaterally, direct socialization through language also occurs in response to children's initiations, through questions about or challenges to rules and standards of conduct.

The second domain in which socialization occurs is explicitly linguistic; parents teach children what to say (or not to say) on various occasions. From an early age children are instructed to produce particular speech forms, including politeness routines, greetings, and religious and holiday performatives (e.g. saying "thank you," saying "hi," saying grace, and saying "trick or treat"). These instructions may take a variety of forms. Children may be told to say one thing, teased to say another, or forbidden to speak at all.

The third and final domain in which linguistic socialization occurs is in the subtle and indirect aspects of the linguistic interaction itself. Certain features of interaction vary systematically and are correlated with individual or group variables. A dramatic example of this was cited in a recent report entitled "How Schools Shortchange Girls" (American Association of University Women, 1992). The report summarized one study (Sadker, Sadker, and Thomas, 1981, cited in American Association of University Women, 1992) in which it was found that boys in elementary and middle school called out answers (e.g. interrupted) eight times more frequently than girls. Furthermore, boys' remarks were treated as legitimate and appropriate, whereas girls were chided for speaking without having been called upon. In another study by these same researchers (Sadker and Sadker, 1984), teachers were observed to comment on boys' classroom contributions more frequently than on those of girls. Teachers also provided boys with feedback that was more pedagogically useful (e.g. praise, criticism, and remediation) than the "acceptance" response that girls disproportionately received. Thus, the socialization of gender specific speech roles is accomplished at least in part through differential verbal interactions with boys and girls.

Similar phenomena occur at home. For example, parents interrupt girls more than boys (Greif, 1980) and direct more diminutives and terms of endearment to girls than to boys (Gleason, Perlmann, Ely and Evans, 1994; Warren-Leubecker, 1982). Through interactions such as these, parents express and perpetuate specific cultural and gender-based standards. Such standards are not typically recognizable to either participants or researchers in any single observation, but become apparent only over time and only when the particular behaviors (e.g. interrupting, praising) are noted to vary according to the child's gender. Implicit social rules for language use underlie many observed differences related to gender, age, and social class.

Common Contexts in Western Society

Having explicated our use of the term socialization, it is important to discuss briefly our definition of the term *context*. Context is a complex and, at times, elusive concept that incorporates a wide range of components (Duranti and Goodwin, 1992). In its broadest sense, context refers to the background or frame (Goffman, 1974) in which a particular event takes place. Keller-Cohen (1978) has identified a number of distinct aspects of context relevant to language use. For example, social context encompasses several subcomponents: the *setting* (e.g. at home, at school), the *relationship* between the speaker and the addressee (e.g. parent–child, student–teacher), and the *interactional rules* (e.g. Grice's (1975) maxims) that govern a particular conversation. In Western society, children learn to use language in a small number of typical situational and interpersonal contexts.

In the sections that follow, we review some of the processes of linguistic socialization that have been described in the literature and in our own work. Given the complex nature of the topic, our approach is more illustrative than comprehensive. We have organized our presentation under two broad headings based on one aspect of context – the setting. Thus, we look first at socialization practices that are found in the home in interactions with parents and siblings. Within this setting, there are a variety of contexts that are considered. The second major setting that we consider encompasses a range of out-of-home settings, with special attention to the school setting. Also included in this section is a consideration of the socializing influences of television.

Not every aspect of linguistic socialization can be considered, nor can we systematically include every context (Keller-Cohen, 1978). Rather, our selection of material is guided by a wish to illustrate the most salient and significant processes and contexts.

Home contexts

Behavioral and cognitive socialization in the home

All theories of language acquisition acknowledge the necessity of *input*. When the focus of theorizing shifts beyond the acquisition of utterance-level structural aspects of the linguistic system, theorists readily acknowledge that children are acquiring the indigenous social knowledge of their culture when they acquire the language of their community (Dunn, 1988; Ochs, 1988; Schieffelin and Ochs, 1986b). As Judy Dunn has written (Dunn, 1988: 4–5):

> People do not simply cue each other into propositional exchanges: they communicate their moods and desires, their sense of absurdity and amusement, disapproval, pride or shame. They communicate shared beliefs about the way life should be lived and about relationships between the members of their world in a variety of subtle and not-so-subtle ways.

As Dunn suggests, the social order of a community can be transmitted in a variety of ways. Whatever the form of transmission, much of the child's earliest socialization experiences take place in the home and through language.

In many Western societies, parents, and especially mothers, are the primary caretakers of young children. Despite the increase in out-of-home care, the nuclear family remains the standard social unit of most communities. Although a child may attend daycare, such care is generally conceptualized as supplementing at-home care. Systematic access to care by older siblings or relatives, a common feature of non-Western childrearing (Whiting and Edwards, 1988), is relatively uncommon in Western households. Since parents in these households are the primary source of care and nurturance, parental input across a variety of domains has a particularly privileged influence.

There exists a large body of research that describes the effects parental, mostly maternal, input has on children's language development (Rice, 1984; Snow, 1986: Snow and Ferguson, 1977). Although this influence has been noted to vary across features of language (Hoff-Ginsberg, 1985; Shatz, 1982), some robust findings remain unchallenged. For example, mothers who talk more to their children have children with larger vocabularies (Hoff-Ginsberg, 1991; Huttenlocher, Haight, Bryk, Seltzer, and Lyons, 1991) and more complex sentence structure (Barnes, Gutfreund, Satterly, and Wells, 1983). Thus, the effects of specific aspects of home environment on core aspects of language development are well substantiated.

Parents also use language to tell children about social knowledge and cultural norms, and young children are likely to absorb much of this knowledge *in toto*. A number of researchers have developed comprehensive developmental accounts of this general process of socialization (Dunn, 1988; Rogoff, 1990; Schaffer, 1984). Because a review of this literature is beyond the scope of this chapter, we will briefly illustrate the process of socialization through language by examining two processes: (1) how parents direct children's ongoing behavior through the use of prohibitives, and (2) how parents use and encourage "abstract" or decontextualized language.

Prohibitives. One important aspect of socialization through language is the pervasive use of language to mediate the child's ongoing activity. Prior to the child's acquisition of language, both parents and children appear to be attuned to certain prosodic aspects of language. Mothers use variations in pitch to praise and prohibit behaviors when speaking to infants as young as two months of age, and infants are responsive to these paralinguistic features (Fernald, 1984). As children's language development unfolds, parents control their behavior with explicit linguistic directives such as prohibitives (e.g. *no*, *don't*). In a study of 32 mothers and children in semistructured laboratory play sessions at two ages, 14 and 20 months, Perlmann and Gleason (1990) found that prohibitives were pervasive and common, with more than 500 occurrences appearing in the speech of mothers of 14-month-olds alone. More prohibitives were directed to boys than to girls, and there was a trend toward a social class difference in girls, with lower middle class girls hearing more prohibitives than middle and upper middle class girls. An examination of the form of prohibitives revealed a wide range of variation, with some prohibitives mitigated by the use of tag questions (e.g. "Don't touch, okay?") or diminutives (e.g. "Don't touch, sweetie"). Furthermore, in looking at a portion of the laboratory session in which mothers were instructed to prevent their children from touching an attractive toy, we found a number of attention-diverting utterances used by some mothers in instances where other mothers used only prohibitives. The mothers who avoided explicit prohibitions tended to use comments or questions that focused on featural aspects or the attractiveness of the forbidden toy (e.g. "Is it pretty?" "Do you like it?"). Thus, mothers may achieve the same behavioral goals through qualitatively different means, some of which may be more cognitively enhancing than others.

Decontextualized language. A more complex form of socialization through language is found in parents' use and encouragement of decontextualized language. Two distinct examples illustrate this phenomenon: parents' use of abstract and metaphorical language, and parental involvement in children's emergent literacy. In a study of variations in socialization styles, Perlmann (1984) analyzed dinnertime conversations from 16 middle class families. One socialization coding category, termed *world*, defined utterances that elicited or conveyed knowledge about how the world works. Although these utterances were often preceded by utterances that focused on the immediate context, utterances coded as *world* made reference to phenomena beyond the immediate context (Perlmann, 1984).

> Child: Who's that spoon?
> Father: That is the gravy spoon. All the juice from the meat runs into that little hole, you spoon it out.
> Child: Isn't that running in?
> Father: Well, it was running in. See all these little holes in the tracks down here.
> Child: Yes.
> Father: When you cut the meat, the juice runs out of the meat into that little track there. Runs down till it gets to that hole. Blu-up! Fills it right up. [Pause] That's the way rivers and lakes work.

In this example, the father has treated the child's questions as opportunities to impart knowledge about the world, about how juice flows from cooked meat, as well as how this process can metaphorically be interpreted as representing geological processes (e.g. the formation of rivers and lakes).

In this study, utterances coded as *world* represented 7 percent of all utterances across families (Perlmann, 1984). However, in five of the 16 families, the use of this abstract category of language was more frequent, accounting for more than one quarter of all utterances in one family. In addition, there was an inverse relationship between parental utterances designed to control immediate behavior and utterances that imparted knowledge. For whatever reasons, families that were able to talk about events removed from the immediate context were families in which there were fewer verbal directives, broadly defined. Attention to immediate behavior appeared to come at the expense of decontextualized conversation. This finding extends our understanding of the dynamics of the relationship between home experiences and children's academic performance. For example, one study (Anderson, Wilson, and Fielding, 1988) found that the length of family mealtimes positively predicted children's literacy scores, an association that was felt to reflect children's exposure to decontextualized language. Together, these studies suggest that families that spend more time together at dinner are providing their young children with more opportunities to engage in talk beyond the here and now.

Parental use and encouragement of decontextualized language can also be seen in how some parents encourage early literacy. There is a large and growing literature that examines the processes of emergent literacy that take place in the home. We now know something about how parental behaviors can influence children's early abilities to decipher and use printed language (Chall, Jacobs, and Baldwin, 1990; Heath, 1983; Snow, Barnes, Chandler, Goodman, and Hemphill, 1991; Teale and Sulzby, 1986). Jim Gee (1992: 120) eloquently describes how some middle class parents have become the "*best* teachers of school based literacy" (emphasis in original) without the benefit of any formal training in educational practices:

> They [parents] engage their children in conversations and keep them on a single topic even when the children can hardly talk at all. They play alphabet games, recite nursery rhymes, read books along with great affect. They ask their children "What's that?" and "What's that say?" of pictures in a book they've seen a hundred times. They encourage children to pretend they can read when they can't; they let them manipulate magnetic letters on a refrigerator; and they get them to watch "Sesame Street" for hours on end. They send them to preschool and constantly relate what the children have seen or heard in books to the children's daily experience of the world. (Gee, 1992: 123, reference citations in original deleted)

Thus, parents who themselves have been exposed to and value literacy and other forms of decontextualized language transmit these practices to their children. In Gee's (1992: 123) words, parents mentor or apprentice children into the discourses of literacy. Although the implementation of preliteracy mentoring involves a range of linguistic socialization processes, middle class parents' selective focus on literacy practices communicates explicitly that competence in reading, writing, and decontextualized talk are socially and culturally valued activities. Children growing up in these households are at a distinct advantage upon entering school, where there is continuity between the focus on decontextualized talk at home and the dominant and valued decontextualized discourse of the classroom (Gee, 1992). Alternatively, children who are not exposed to these preliteracy experiences are often at a severe disadvantage (Heath, 1983; Michaels, 1991). These examples of behavioral and cognitive socialization through language provide a small window into a much larger arena of socialization that is beyond the scope of this chapter.

Explicit linguistic socialization: what to say

We turn now to an examination of explicit linguistic socialization – instances where parents and other adults specifically provide instruction in the use of language. We, along with others, have noted that parents begin to urge children to use designated forms at a very early age (Gleason and Weintraub, 1976; Greif and Gleason, 1980). Preverbal infants are initiated into games of peekaboo (Bruner and Sherwood, 1976), encouraged to make sounds approximating *What the birdie says*, and urged to say *bye-bye*. In other words, explicit linguistic socialization begins before the child has begun to speak.

As children begin to acquire a rudimentary command of the language, parents begin to pay particular attention to pragmatic competencies (Becker, 1990). The successful performance of a variety of routines, particularly politeness routines, acquires particular significance (Snow, Perlmann, Gleason, and Hooshyar, 1990). In some instances, parents make extended efforts to obtain pragmatically appropriate speech, as the following example from our dinner data (Gleason, 1980) illustrates:

Child:	I want some ketchup!
Mother:	That's not the way you ask for it.
Child:	Please.
Father:	Say: "Please could I have some ketchup."
Child:	Please.
Father:	Please may I have some ketchup.
Child:	Please.
Father:	Just say the whole sentence for a change.
Child:	Please.
Father:	No. We're gonna wait til you say: "Please may I have some ketchup."
Child:	Please can I have the ketchup.

The acquisition of pragmatic skills is a deceptively complex task (Becker, 1990; Gleason and Weintraub, 1976; Snow et al., 1990). In the case of many performatives, directives, and expressives (e.g. greetings, requests, thanks) children must learn to utter a variety of terms (e.g. *hi, please, thank you*) that have no specific referent at a particular point within an interaction. The high frequency with which some routines occur undoubtedly makes their acquisition easier; for instance, children make frequent requests and thus have many opportunities to learn the politeness forms that are part of pragmatically correct requests. However, in the case of holiday performatives (e.g. *Trick or treat* and *Happy New Year*), exposure is temporally limited and situationally circumscribed (Gleason and Weintraub, 1976).

Judith Becker (1990) has examined the speech behaviors of children that are subject to socialization by middle class parents. When parents concentrated on the contents of children's speech, *address terms* and *slang* received the greatest amount of attention across the five families she studied. The single most frequently socialized behavior was in the category *How to say it* and involved volume – instructing children to lower their voices. An analysis of the teaching techniques used by parents indicated that parents overwhelmingly relied on prompts, usually in the form of indirect comments on errors (e.g. "Who's leaving?" in response to a child who inappropriately said "Goodbye") or to omissions (e.g. a parent saying "You're welcome" in the response to the child's failure to express thanks) (Becker, 1990).

More recently, we have been examining how parents use speech verbs (e.g. *to say, to tell*) in directing the speech behavior of their children (Gleason, Ely, and Perlmann, 1992). In our earlier work on politeness routines (Greif and Gleason, 1980), we had noted that 95 percent of parental prompts for politeness routines employed the speech verb *say* in formulations such as "Say thank you, " "Can you say thank you?" or "What do you say?" In our current work, we examined the dinnertime conversations of 22 middle class parents and children between the ages of two and a half and five years. The most frequent category of speech prompts directed by parents to their children was a request for narratives or for propositional information:

Mother: Did you tell Dad what we did today?
Mother: Can you tell Daddy about the doll that Denise had?

The second most frequent category of prompts that employed a speech verb was elicitation of politeness terms (e.g. "Say: 'Please could I have some ketchup' ") and other specified routines, as in directing children to say "Happy Birthday" or to utter their own names. In this category, mothers prompted their children significantly more frequently than fathers. The other categories of prompts that employed speech verbs, including requests for clarification and controlling speech itself by telling children *when* to talk, occurred much less frequently.

These studies have shown that parents play an active role in the linguistic socialization of their children, particularly in the socialization of pragmatics: children receive explicit instruction in politeness routines and other linguistic behaviors related to appropriate interpersonal discourse.

mothers and fathers are very similar in the structural–linguistic features of the speech they direct to their young children (Mannle and Tomasello, 1987), but that they have different interactive and communicative styles. These stylistic differences become especially apparent when the pragmatic aspects of their child directed speech are examined.

Beginning in infancy, mothers and fathers provide qualitatively different interactional experiences for their children. In traditional middle class families in which mothers are the primary caretakers, fathers engage in more physically stimulating and playful interactions than mothers (Clarke-Stewart, 1978). Fathers converse with children less frequently than mothers do (Stoneman and Brody, 1981), and, perhaps as a consequence, are somewhat less familiar with their children's linguistic abilities. Fathers are more likely than mothers to have difficulty understanding their children (Weist and Kruppe, 1977), and consequently make more requests for clarification than mothers (Rondal, 1980). Fathers' speech also contains rarer words. Fathers use terms like "construction site," "carburetor," "rachet wrench," and "focus knob" to preschoolers (Gleason, 1987; Ratner, 1988) and fathers' conversations often focus on complex concepts (Gleason, 1975). Finally, fathers are more liable to use both an authoritarian as well as a playful style of communication (Bellinger and Gleason, 1982): their speech contains many direct imperatives as well as more word play. Fathers are thus more likely than mothers to speak in a way that is linguistically and pragmatically challenging for children. These special aspects of fathers' speech may, in turn, have a unique impact on children's linguistic and social development.

Perhaps the best known theoretical claim about the role of fathers' speech is that it serves as a bridge to the larger world (Gleason, 1975; Mannle and Tomasello, 1987). Children who converse with fathers are speaking with a familiar but communicatively more demanding adult. In this sense, fathers serve in an intermediate role between mothers and the less familiar discourse partners the child encounters outside the home – hence the notion of bridge. Recent research (Pratt, Kerig, Cowan, and Cowan, 1992) has found that fathers are not as well attuned to their children's levels of syntactic development as are mothers. This finding suggests that, for children, fathers' discourse is more complex and, presumably, more demanding. And the proposal that interactions with fathers enhance and enrich children's linguistic development has also been demonstrated: fathers' (but not mothers') didactic style, including verbal encouragement of their children, when children were 13 months old predicted the children's lexical development at 20 months (Bornstein, Vibbert, Tall, and O'Donnell, 1992).

Sibling speech

To this point, we have been treating linguistic socialization as it takes place in the home as if the key interactions occurred exclusively between parents and children. However, researchers have recently begun to recognize the important role siblings play in children's linguistic and social development (Brown and Dunn, 1992; Dunn and Kendrick, 1982; Howe, 1991; Howe and Ross, 1990; Mannle and Tomasello, 1987; Wellen, 1985). The work of these researchers provides empirical support for longstanding theoretical speculations (cf. Piaget, 1932/1965) about the influence sibling relationships have on the development of social understanding (Brown and Dunn, 1992).

The work of Judy Dunn and her colleagues has been especially illuminating of a number of important aspects of sibling relationships. In a study that examined children's talk about inner states with their siblings and with their mothers, Brown and Dunn (1992) found that as children get older, they spend increasingly more time with one another, in conversation as well as a variety of other activities. These mother-absent interactions present the children with opportunities to assume roles they rarely assume when talking with adult partners. In conversations with mothers, the focus is frequently on how inner states (e.g. sorrow, pain) are corollaries or consequences of behavioral activities (e.g. "It hurts to get soap in your eye"). Mothers act as caretakers and teachers, guiding the children's interpretation of their own and others' expressed feelings. By contrast, in sibling-to-sibling exchanges the conversation is more reciprocal, with siblings talking more about their own feelings than they do in conversations with their mothers. Siblings' talk about feeling states was also characterized as more playful (e.g. "You like Barbie dolls!") and more self-serving (e.g. "I like her puppets!") than talk that occurred with their mothers (Brown and Dunn, 1992).

Similar qualitative differences between mother–child and sibling–sibling interactions were found in children's arguments (Dunn and Munn, 1987). In a study of family interactions at home, the frequency and type of disputes was documented. Although nondisputatious talk about feeling states among siblings tended to be playful, children also expressed more anger and distress toward their siblings than toward their mothers when they engaged in disputes. In addition, disputes with siblings were more focused on concerns with rights and ownership and were more prolonged than those with mothers. Finally, children used social rules as justifications more often in arguments with siblings than with mothers, although references to social rules were relatively infrequent overall (Dunn and Munn, 1987).

Much of the work reported above has been on siblings who are fairly close in age. It remains to be seen whether the same types of exchanges extend to wider sibling-to-sibling age differentials. Nevertheless, these findings are illustrative of how important sibling relationships, where present, can be in the socialization of children, and how, in a sense, children themselves act as socializing agents. Valued aspects of social and economic life (e.g. property rights) are more likely to be discussed and fought over among peers than with a parent. Children in the same family are learning the ways of the greater world in their daily conversations and squabbles with one another.

School and beyond

Language socialization in the school

When children enter school, they enter a new environment with new rules for social and verbal interaction. As we noted earlier, for some children there is continuity between home and school, whereas for others the transition marks a dramatic departure from their preschool social and linguistic experiences (Heath, 1983). As an institution, school is the epitome of socialization. Schools transmit important social and cultural knowledge and practices. Recent disputes over curriculum content make it clear that no subject matter is culture free (Gee, 1990). In this section, we do not focus on how socialization occurs through language, since the topic encompasses areas of educational research and theory too broad to be discussed here. Rather, we illustrate here how linguistic socialization takes place in certain pedagogical classroom practices, both directly, in instructions on what to say, as well as indirectly, in how teachers interact with students.

Direct socialization: what to say in school. Earlier, we described how de-contextualized language was "taught" by middle class parents (Gee, 1992). Middle class parents engage their children in verbal interactions that prepare and encourage literacy. For example, parents often elicit personal narratives, the informal telling of anecdotes about oneself or the world at large, from their children (McCabe and Peterson, 1991b). There is currently much theoretical and empirical support for viewing narratives as important social and cognitive tools for understanding and defining one's culture and one's world (Bruner, 1986; Hymes and Cazden, 1980; Gee, 1992). Children typically adopt the narrative style of their own community. However, all narrative styles are not valued equally, as some children quickly realize upon entering school (Hymes and Cazden, 1980; Michaels, 1981, 1991; Michaels and Cazden, 1986). Middle class white children generally tell *topic-centered* narratives, stories about a single person or event, that have clear beginnings, middles, and ends. In contrast, children from other cultures, African–American children for example, often tell what are termed *topic-associating* narratives. Topic-associating narratives link several episodes thematically. These episodes may involve several principal characters and shifts in time and setting, and the narratives themselves are usually longer than topic-centered narratives.

Sara Michaels has persuasively described what she terms the "dismantling" of topic-associating narratives that takes place in preschool classrooms (Michaels, 1981, 1991; Michaels and Cazden, 1986). She documents what happens when children tell stories that do not follow the conventional topic-centered formula because they employ the topic-associating approach they learned in their own community: a topic-associating first-grade African–American girl was instructed by her teacher to tell "about things that are really

really very important" and "to stick with one thing" (Michaels, 1991: 316, 320). The way this girl made sense of her world through her personal narratives was explicitly challenged. She was urged to adopt a narrative style that conformed to the genre of the teacher and the dominant community and culture.

Although there is nothing intrinsically wrong with instructing students in the practice of different speaking genres, the effects of teachers' implicitly devaluing the speaking genres of children's indigenous cultures may be far reaching. In a follow-up interview one year later, the African–American child described above angrily portrayed her first-grade teacher as having been uninterested in what she had to say. Because this experience occurred early in her educational experience, its influence on her attitude toward teachers, school, and literacy was potentially profound. In a positive way, it may have helped her to recognize and value her own culture's narrative style. In a negative way, it may have led her to view the dominant genre as oppressive (DeVos, 1967; Ogbu, 1990). Many researchers now see a need for schools to recognize these potential conflicts and to provide educational environments that can nurture both cultural diversity and academic achievement (Gee, 1992; Michaels, 1991; Ogbu, 1990).

Indirect socialization: variation in interaction. In addition to children being told what to say (and later what to write) in the classroom, they are socialized indirectly in ongoing verbal interactions with teachers. We have already cited the American Association of University Women's (1992) report that documented the pervasiveness of teachers' gender typing. Michaels (1991) presents similar findings. For example, she reported that at the beginning of the school year, classroom sharing-time consisted of equal numbers of contributions by African–American and white school children. However, by the end of the year, children whose sharing-time accounts most closely conformed to a topic-focused structure spoke more often. Not surprisingly, these children were predominately white (Michaels, 1981, 1991). Furthermore, the topic-associating children (predominately African–American) continued to experience high rates of interruptions. These interruptions were part of the dismantling process, in that they were designed to keep the child on a single topic. However, to the African–American narrators, the interruptions were experienced as intrusive and frustrating rather than as helpful (Michaels, 1991: 321).

Peers as conversational partners

The attention researchers have paid to socialization that takes place within family interactions has tended to overshadow the role that others, including peers, may play in children's socialization. Family relationships have traditionally been viewed as precursors to relationships with the larger world (e.g. with peers, teachers, other adults). Like relationships with siblings, relationships with peers become increasingly important as children grow older. These interactions frequently exclude adults and are some of the earliest child discourse that is not structured by an adult caregiver (Rice, 1992). In time, the importance of peer interaction can exceed that of parent interaction (Richards and Light, 1986; Whiting and Edwards, 1988).

We have assumed that children acquire the basic aspects of communicative competence in early interactions with their parents and other familiar caretakers. Once children move outside the home, their ability to express themselves and respond to others plays a very important role in their social performance (Black and Hazen, 1990; Rice, 1992). However, some aspects of peer talk are uncommon in parent–child talk, particularly in the areas of verbal play and verbal disputes (Dunn, 1988; Martlew, Connolly, and McCleod, 1978). Although children use humor, verbal wit, and argument to establish, maintain, and reorder social hierarchies with other children, little attention has focused on how they develop initial expertise in these genres. Clearly, some family interactions, especially those involving siblings or fathers, may foster or model language that is both playful and mocking – for instance, fathers may call their children names like "Dingaling" and "Wise guy" (Gleason, 1975). Miller and Sperry (1987) have also documented how working class mothers purposely tease their very young daughters in order to instruct them in the community's modes of dealing with anger and aggression. Although these data show that children's home experiences may provide a basic foundation or early start, we still need more information on both the pervasiveness of such experiences and their actual effect on children's peer interactions.

Once among their peers, children engage in much language play and verbal humor (Ely and McCabe, 1993). Some types of language games represent forms of play fighting, for example playing the dozens (Labov, 1972), wherein verbal wit and agility are prized as much as physical prowess. Verbal aggression is also a common part of children's discourse and has been found in more than one fourth of all children's classroom utterances (McCabe and Lipscomb, 1988). Thus, a child who cannot share jokes with other children or does not know how to tease and be teased is a child who lacks important aspects of communicative competence (Carson, Skarpness, Schultz, and McGhee, 1986; Masten, 1986).

It is also likely that children directly socialize one another, though data on this practice is sparse. A child who is teased for having said something "silly" is probably less likely to repeat the silly utterance. Children sometimes highlight other children's pragmatic errors, as this example from a kindergarten classroom illustrates (Ely and McCabe, 1993):

Mark: Can I pick up the turtle, John.
Teacher: Not right now.
Mark: Please, John.
Allison: No nagging. When, when he [Mark] keep telling him [the teacher] and telling him, that's nagging.

Preece (1992) has described how children act as critics and correctors of peers' narratives, making lexical corrections (e.g. *septic tank* for *subject tank, ear muffs* for *ear mufflers*) and objecting to story content (e.g. "Saint Nicholas went back to his self! What's that mean? That doesn't make sense."). Included in her corpus of narratives were some that focused explicitly on politeness routines (Preece, 1992: 288):

> Bronwyn: (to Kepmen) Did you say, "Thank you very much"?
> Kepmen: Yes I did . . . but I said it quietly . . . Cuz if you said, (loud) "THANK YOU! (he and Bronwyn giggle) what would happen? They'd say, "Get outta here right now!! Say thank you better next time!"

This example demonstrates that young children monitor and make relatively sophisticated judgments about their own and other children's linguistic performance. Through the process of sharing these judgments with peers, children are acting as socializing agents of one another.

To the degree that origins of communicative competence are to be found in the home, researchers will need to pay close attention to how particular parent–child and sibling–sibling conversational styles contribute to children's optimal communicative competence for independent interactions with their peers. As Rice (1992) has remarked, the "ultimate testing ground" of a children's communicative competence occurs in peer interactions. Peer interactions both test the child's initial preparedness and, at the same time, provide a variety of "crash courses" for developing competence in peer discourse.

Television as a model

In our society, children spend an extraordinary amount of their out-of-school time watching television (Anderson, Wilson, and Fielding, 1988; Williams, Haertel, Haertel, and Walberg, 1982). Some observers claim that the influence such viewing has on many aspects of children's lives is profound (Singer and Singer, 1990: 177):

> television pervades the consciousness of children. It is manifest in the clothes they wear, the toys and games they play with, the characters with whom they identify, and the cereals and candy they eat. No other extraparental influence has penetrated the lives of children as television has.

Recent data indicate that in the US preschoolers average 26 hours per week of television viewing (Nielsen, 1987). Ironically, television's effect on children's language development has, until recently, been ignored (Rice and Woodsmall, 1988). It was long believed that television was an incomprehensible, and consequently insignificant, source of linguistic input, especially for the young child (e.g. Clark and Clark, 1977). Even studies examining the role of television on the development of literacy in preschool and school-age children (e.g. Neuman, 1991) have devoted little attention to television's effects on language development. Finally, although television has often been seen as a powerful socializing influence, especially in behaviors like aggression and gender-role stereotyping, there are currently little data on how television might contribute to (or impede) children's evolving communicative competence.

Despite claims that dismiss television's role in language development, there are some theoretical and empirical grounds for considering that television may have an important effect on children's language development. Television is an attractive medium that has intrinsic appeal to young children (Singer and Singer, 1981). Some television shows, especially educational shows like *Mr. Rogers*, have language that approximates that of child directed speech (Rice and Haight, 1986). The language on these shows is often simple, redundant, rarely disfluent, and usually focused on objects or events in the immediate (televised) context. Furthermore, television viewing is not always a passive and solitary experience. When parents view television with young children, there is frequently much conversation about what is being viewed (Bryce, 1987). These conversations are sometimes analogous to those that occur in shared book reading (Lemish and Rice, 1986). Thus, at least some television provides children with input of a type that is known to affect language development in other contexts.

Empirical research has clearly demonstrated that children can and do learn language, especially vocabulary, from television viewing (Rice and Woodsmall, 1988). Although early studies (e.g. Schramm, Lyle, and Parker, 1961) found that children in communities with television had larger vocabularies than children living in communities without television, more recent work (Williams, 1986) has found little relation between children's overall exposure to television and their lexical development. Rather, the actual programs that children watch appear to determine the degree to which they learn new words. Children who watch more educational television have larger vocabularies than children who watch cartoons and situation comedies (Rice, Huston, Truglio, and Wright, 1990). Of course, these correlations may be influenced by factors that include self-selection on the part of the children's television viewing practice.

The socializing effects of television on children's linguistic behavior may be even more pervasive. Rice (1983: 220) has noted that television presents "a wider variety of social contexts and their associated language than is available to young children within their immediate environment." Noble (1983) found that Australian youth learned how to be "cool" by watching reruns of American sitcoms like *Happy Days*. Television (and the other popular media) provide, often stereotypical, models of conversations we rarely have in real life; for instance, children (and adults) who have never encountered cowboys or surfers know how to greet them (e.g. *Howdy partner* and *Hey, dude*). Many researchers now believe that television is a powerful influence on children's development, but beyond incidental information contained in research addressing gender and culture stereotyping, there are few data that address how television affects children's language use. There are anecdotal accounts that children talk about television and adopt the voices of television characters in their play and in their narratives (e.g. Watson-Gegeo and Boggs, 1977), although such talk is not likely to be extensive. For example, the Singers (Singer and Singer, 1981) reported the number of young children's utterances in free play that referred specifically to television rarely exceeded 1 percent of their total utterance count.

Finally, the technology of television and related media like video games and video cassette recorders have generated a rich and generally understudied lexicon of words and metaphors (Provenzo, 1991). We have heard children speak of wanting to "fastforward" to their birthdays, of gray winter days that look "time-stopped," and of asking if they could "pause" the ongoing conversation while they use the bathroom. As these examples show, terms relating to time are especially prevalent. Their use suggests that children readily extend the language of a specialized domain (e.g. video technology) to all aspects of their life.

Television in all its forms is an inextricable part of most children's development. To date, research on television and language development has been largely limited to studies of vocabulary growth and literacy. This work suggests that children's television viewing has both positive and negative effects on these domains. However, television's impact on children's linguistic socialization has been little studied. Clearly, television provides a rich source of verbal information about the world, replete with the intrinsic biases of those producing and disseminating such information. Television, particularly educational programs for very young viewers, occasionally provides children with explicit instruction in language behaviors. And finally, television presents portraits of how people (and a variety of animals and fantastic creatures) talk to one another. The degree to which children absorb what they hear and see, the manner in which children's absorption is affected by parental coviewing, and the long-term effects television viewing has on children's language are largely uncharted. Given that young children may spend more time watching television than interacting directly with their parents, it is important that we understand how the context of television viewing socializes children's language use.

Conclusion

In this chapter we have attempted to illustrate the ways in which language and socialization intersect. Socialization through language is ubiquitous. In verbal interactions with parents, siblings, teachers, and peers, and through observing media such as television, children are exposed to and absorb many of the important values and beliefs of their communities. We have also described and illustrated instances in which children are explicitly taught how to use language appropriately, and how, in some cases, this instruction may create conflicts between indigenous language practices and those of the dominant culture.

Part II The Emergence and Consolidation of Linguistic Abilities

Introduction

This section reflects a number of dimensions of current interest in research into the growth of the child's language abilities. For the child, learning language is an integrated process not generally available for conscious reflection. For the analyst, on the trail of understanding, language development is analyzed into its component parts, and separated into receptive and expressive abilities, and earlier and later phases. Chapters in this section supply accounts of the child's learning of English organized under the traditional linguistic headings of phonetics, phonology, grammar, and lexis. The two aspects of an individual's language competence, comprehension and production, are considered separately, though as always unequally: the ready availability of production data, and the methodological problems of addressing receptive abilities, have ensured an imbalance in our knowledge of the two systems. It is however encouraging that the chapter in this section that is devoted to comprehension should go some way to redressing the balance by dealing with novel methods for assessing receptive ability. Early and later development is addressed for vocabulary and syntax independently, though one chapter brings them closer towards integration by considering the role of syntax in the learning of verbs. And within and across chapters, parallel or distinct perspectives on the same developmental transitions are revealed. So there are alternative but complementary versions of the underpinnings of speech and language as they develop during the first year of life. And the transition to grammar is seen as constrained on the one hand by abstract syntactic categories, and on the other by the phonetic nature of the exponents of these categories in input to the child. While the chapters in this section cannot add up to a unified account of the developmental process of language acquisition, they are nevertheless instructive on many aspects of the precursors, the emergence, and the consolidation of linguistic abilities.

The infrastructure for spoken language

The major part of child language research, from Brown's pioneering work onwards (see Brown, 1973), has taken as its starting point the emergence of the first recognizable words, or even the earliest combinations of those words. The theoretical importance of the transition to grammar cannot be underestimated, it is true: grammar is a major hurdle for the child. Yet the skills that converge, in the child's second year, on the understanding and production of recognizable words in the target language, and then combinations of those words, must have a history. Of course, the child's first year of life has not gone uncharted. What Locke's chapter seeks to do (in common with Locke, 1993b) is to work out how children's development in their first year on a number of fronts – emotional, social, perceptual, motoric, neural, cognitive, and linguistic – brings them to the brink of language by the first birthday. This is a tall order. Locke's strategy is to adopt an ethological approach, answering a series of questions concerning children's attentional biases, vocal capabilities, and neural specializations in terms of their development in the context of infants' affective relations and interactions with caregivers. The child's specialization in social cognition is one aspect of a species-specific infrastructure for language learning.

Kent and Miolo fill in the details of the infant's phonetic abilities, and integrating a great deal of research of their own and others, provide an up-to-date account of the child's perception and production abilities during the crucial first year. Reviews of infants' developing vowel (vocant) and consonant (closant) sounds facilitate the discussion of current views on the relationship between babbling and the child's target language. Crosslinguistic studies (e.g. Boysson-Bardies et al., 1986, 1992) reveal that the influence of the target language can be identified in the babbling of children at ten months of age. Kent and Miolo also review measurement and procedural issues in phonetic research on infant voacalizations.

The development of the phonological system

One of the procedural issues raised by Kent and Miolo concerns the appropriate level of transcription for representing infant sounds. The reliability and validity of auditory impressionistic transcription are also matters for concern in tracking the later development of the child's pronunciation ability (Weismer, 1984). Accounts of phonological development are based almost exclusively on such data, which may be unreliable in certain areas (voicing, vowel length) at certain points in the child's development (Macken and Barton, 1980). A point stressed by Menn and Stoel-Gammon is that the segmental character of the transcription system does not attest to the child's awareness of segments at an early stage. The earliest words are variable in their pronunciation, may not stand in a clear phonological relation to adult targets, and are limited in number. As Locke also suggests, the phonological system may emerge out of the earliest pronunciations of words rather than underpin them.

Menn and Stoel-Gammon emphasize that to try to determine the order of acquisition of phonological elements is to ask the wrong question. The child's early pronunciation reflects the interplay of a variety of influences: perceptual abilities (not dealt with in detail in the chapter – see Barton, 1980); words the child knows, and is prepared to try to pronounce; preferred schemas for the production of these words; rules or processes (e.g. final devoicing, stopping) that systematically map adult targets onto child forms, and that are commonly found across numbers of children; nonsystematic reduction schemas that a particular child has developed, for easing the problems of pronouncing words. A successful developmental phonological theory will need to encompass both general tendencies in children, and individual differences.

Learning words

The three chapters here, by Barrett, Clark, and Gleitman and Gillette, deal respectively with early and late vocabulary development, and the learning of verbs. Early studies of vocabulary development in this century tended to concentrate on the size of a child's vocabulary. More recently, the concerns of researchers in relation to early and later word learning have broadened. An enduring theme has been the child's semantic representations ans how to conceive of them and find evidence for them. The first modern studies centered on the extension of nominals, and the role of nonadult extension (overextension, e.g. Clark, 1973a, and underextension, e.g. Reich, 1976) in our understanding of young children's intensions, originally interpreted in terms of semantic features. Subsequently, constructs such as prototypes, scripts, and event representations have been invoked to account for children's word meanings. The relationship between cognition and lexical learning, for example in the relation between stages of sensorimotor development and the onset of naming, has been examined. So too has the role of input, and the interaction between input and the child's own word learning abilities. One view of what the child brings to the task of word learning argues for the existence of (presumably innate) constraints on children's inferences about word meaning. Markman (1990) discusses the "whole object" assumption, and the "taxonomic" assumption, which are argued to encourage children to interpret new object names that they hear as referring to whole objects rather than parts of those objects. A further constraint, labeled "contrast" by Clark (who refers to it as a "pragmatic principle") leads children to the assumption that different forms do not have overlapping extensions. Some scholars (and Barrett would agree, as would Nelson (e.g. Nelson, 1988)) do not see the need for constraints and would rely on the child's general cognitive principles to get the job done.

These important themes are among those reflected in the first two chapters in the section, in relation to earlier and later word learning. The final chapter dealing with vocabulary reflects a concern with what is referred to as the "mapping problem." The requirement that a child match a concept with a phonological shape is fundamental to all vocabulary learning. Here Gleitman and Gillette consider the issue only in relation to verbs, and to the role a verb's complementation may play in their learning. Pinker (1984, 1989) has drawn our attention to the role the learning of verbs may play in the child's transition to syntax. Knowing something about the meaning of a verb (e.g. that *give* involves a giver, a gift, and a recipient) can assist the child to map these semantic roles for the verb onto their syntactic realizations. Learning a verb's meaning may therefore help the child to "bootstrap" into syntax. Gleitman and Gillette turn this notion on its head, arguing that learning the semantics of a verb "requires access to the phrase structure of the exposure language." To learn the meanings of novel verbs, children require structural information.

Learning grammar

The early phase of modern research into the acquisition of morphology and syntax – up to the end of the 1970s, say – concentrated on English, and on description. From Brown's pioneering study we knew a good deal about the order of acquisition of 14 grammatical morphemes, for example, in the three children he studied. The last 15 years have seen developments on two fronts. First, our knowledge is no longer confined to English, and second, there is a renewed interest in explanation, especially though not exclusively by linking acquisition with linguistic theory. The one chapter in this subsection that eschews a Chomskyan framework for an alternative perspective on the development of morphosyntax is also the only chapter to pay more than lip-service to other languages. Although the emphases in the other three differ, the chapters by Golinkoff and Hirsh-Pasek, Radford, and de Villiers all depend at least descriptively on Chomsky's Government and Binding (GB) framework, though the extent of their commitment to nativist claims is not always clear.

Phase III of Golinkoff and Hirsh-Pasek's model of comprehension development, dealing with complex syntactic analysis, is, they say, prompted by Bloom's "principle of elaboration." Bloom (no Chomskyan) sees the development of more complex syntax between two and three as related to the child's increasingly elaborate (presumably nonlinguistic) mental representations. Golinkoff and Hirsh-Pasek, however, couch their discussion of Phase III largely in GB terms, though they do point out that one important area for them, binding theory, does respond to accounts other than Chomsky's. They select the Chomskyan framework because it is the one that has generated most psycholinguistic research. Radford's chapter on the ontogenesis of phrase structure again appeals to the GB framework, and exploits its categories wholeheartedly in characterizing children's early sentences. The purpose of the chapter is to demonstrate how early sentence development can be explained by taking the current X-bar configuration literally. The earliest verbal clauses are claimed to be lexical-thematic VPs, without functional projections of VP into IP and CP. Functional categories are a later development. In a section on explanation Radford does consider, as one possibility, that functional categories may be later acquired because they are subject to parameterization (see part one, introduction and chapter 1). The final chapter in this subsection, by de Villiers, deals with complex syntax and in particular the acquisition of one kind of empty category, the one left behind when a question word is "moved to the front of the sentence." De Villiers also accepts the relevant aspects of the GB framework as given for the purpose of addressing the developmental issues, and does not discuss possible explanations, except in terms of the specificity and character of the grammatical knowledge the child brings to the task of acquiring empty categories in the first place.

Ann Peters takes a very different approach to the issue of morphosyntactic acquisition than is represented in the other three chapters. In the development of abstract syntactic categories as viewed via GB no attention is paid to the way in which exponents of (particularly functional) categories may be realized in the stream of speech. Peters takes the prosodic structure of a language, especially the role of stress in the saliency or otherwise of an exponent of a particular grammatical paradigm, as an independent variable in the child's acquisition of a category. The prosodic structure of a language, in relation to morphosyntactic categories, interacts with semantic transparency and form–content mappings to facilitate (or otherwise) the acquisition of functional categories. So the acquisitional problem may be simplified if morphemes are phonologically salient, with clear semantic roles, limited allomorphy, and non-homonymy. Peters cites the passive in Turkish and Sesotho as examples. By contrast English plural, possessive, and third person agreement all share the same exponent, which is an unstressed suffixed element arguably of limited phonetic salience. And we know from Brown's results that the acquisition sequence for these morphemes is long drawn-out, with plural reaching the 90 percent appearance in obligatory contexts criterion first, with possessive next, and third person agreement trailing some way behind.

Peter's crosslinguistic review of the acquisition of bound and free morphemes is informed by some detailed examples from detailed longitudinal case studies, and ends with a list of strategies that children appear to be following in trying to make sense of these aspects of the structure of their language. Hugging the phonetic ground, and scrutinizing the facts of development with extreme care, Peters makes a compelling case for the relevance of the phonology of the input language, as well as its syntax and semantics, to the course of the child's development.

Early Speech Development

10 Development of the Capacity for Spoken Language

JOHN L. LOCKE

To understand the child's development of spoken language we must come to grips with a great many things. We must figure out how children develop the emotional, social, perceptual, motoric, neural, cognitive, and linguistic capabilities required for the efficient use of language. As a result, the several disciplines claiming some responsibility for language development collectively have a great many theoretical burdens. Linguistic theories must explain the emergence of linguistic forms and operating principles. Psycholinguistic theories must explain the emergence of cognitive mechanisms needed for language, and they must account for variations in the developmental path taken by particular infants. Neurolinguistic theories must be able to relate the developmental processes that facilitate and enable language mastery to a variety of neuroanatomical and neurophysiological developments, and to correlate mental operations needed for language with brain structures and activities.

Unfortunately, these theories leave a lot of theoretical terrain uncharted. Here I will attempt to map out some of this terrain, discussing elements of a biolinguistic theory that is presented in greater detail elsewhere (Locke, 1993b). The theory addresses the infant's development of linguistic capacity, and therefore should be seen as complementary to other types of developmental linguistic theories.

Of Hominids and Human Infants

For centuries, scholars have debated the question of how hominids evolved the capacity for spoken language. Throughout this time, for unknown reasons, the ontogenetic equivalent of this question was never asked. And for the most part, the infant's development of linguistic capacity still is not recognized as a problem area by linguistics and psychology.

Perhaps the reason for this transdisciplinary neglect is the recognition that human infants, as *Homo sapiens*, belong to a species that has linguistic capacity. But how infants come to possess and use their own copy of this capacity is another matter. And since it is an empirical matter, one hopes that someday we will have a satisfactory account of the infant's development of spoken language.

If we are to achieve this outcome, however, we may need to let go of some biases that have been unhelpful in the past. One of these is our tendency to ask how language develops, when in reality it is developing children that increasingly manifest the capacity for language. Another is to assume that language is acquired, when it is not obvious that acquisition is the sole process by which infants come to produce behaviors that are taken by others to be linguistic. Indeed, it is not clear that young infants are aware of anything linguistic that is "out there" to be acquired. As Studdert-Kennedy (1991) has declared, "language is not an object, or even a skill, that lies outside the child and has somehow to be acquired or internalized. Rather it is a mode of action into which the child grows because the mode is implicit in the human developmental system"(p. 10).

Another of our unhelpful biases is the tendency to look at language from the top, to "see the end in the beginning" as some have put it. This "adultocentric" practice is not surprising – we theorists are also facile users of language, and it is natural to view the infant's situation from our own vantage point. But it is not our behavior that needs to be understood, it is the infant's. Even the biologically oriented must continually guard against this; Bullowa (1979) once admitted that "knowing that an infant is destined to become a speaker, it is hard not to anticipate" (p. 15). And yet, if we are to understand language development, we may need to perform an act of mental rotation, turning language over in our minds and imagining how talkers must look and sound to those who view it from the underside. We can then begin to evaluate the development of linguistic behaviors in their own right, without measuring them against the yardsticks of mature language usage.

The human infant travels along a developmental growth path, a canalization of behavior (Holt, 1931; Kuo, 1976; Waddington, 1940) that is not itself linguistic but naturally leads to spoken language. We now know that in other animals, canalizations for vocal behavior are heavily influenced by early experience in ways that might only have been imagined a dozen years ago (Gottlieb, 1991a, b). Infants are thus deposited on, and held to, the path leading to language by a unified force set up jointly by the human genome and perceptual experiences that characterize our species.

On the Path to Spoken Language: Eight Questions

If successful in our efforts to view language learning from its inferior surface, we will see the need to address several questions about the developmental growth path that leads to spoken language. I list below eight of these questions, and then proceed to take them up one by one, in varying degrees of detail.

1   What do people do when talking?
2   What do infants attend to when people talk?
3   Where do infants' attentional biases come from?
4   How do the infant's vocal capabilities emerge?
5   What developmental conditions favor language learning?
6   How does the overall process of language learning occur?
7   What kind of neural specializations produce linguistic capacity?
8   How do our neural specializations configure the development of language?

One sees immediately that most of these questions reflect an ethological or a neuroethological approach. As put, they allow us to ask what information about language is displayed and picked up by the observing infant, thereby requiring few assumptions about the infant's appreciation of the symbolic value or social significance of behaviors that have not yet entered its repertoire. And these questions encourage us to ask about the neural correlates of emergent linguistic capabilities (Camhi, 1984).

What do people do when talking?

Like Studdert-Kennedy, I start with the presumption that language is not an object, nor is it some opaque form of knowledge. The developmentally significant things that the infant needs to learn about spoken language are written on the faces, voices, and gestures of those who talk. When we think of language in this context, we come to see it as a *display*.

A major set of cues displayed by talking people includes the visible structure and movement patterns of the face. The human face represents an exceedingly active channel when individuals engage in *en face* spoken communications. The structure of the face provides indexical information, that is, identifies sender and receiver, thus supplying each participant with what is arguably the single most important piece of information in a social interaction. Where the individuals are unknown to each other, facial structure none the less supplies information about age, sex, health, and other personal attributes.

The activities of the face, particularly the eyes, also may convey some indexical information. But the primary contribution of the face to communication is affective or illocutionary in that it (a) reveals the speaker's emotional state and appraisal of his or her interlocutor; (b) reinforces, augments, or unintentionally contradicts the nominal message; (c) conveys information about aspects of the environment that command the speaker's attention; (d) signals the desire to take or yield the floor; and (e) conveys by nods, winks, smiles, frowns, yawns, glances, and other activity both parties' reactions to spoken messages. Additionally, orofacial activity supplies information about intended phonemes, particularly their place of articulation. In parallel with facial displays, the structure and activities of the voice convey redundant information about personal identity and emotionality, and additionally include information on social dialect and level of education. Indeed, the collaboration of facial and vocal activities is so coordinate and redundant as to represent a unified system (Locke, 1993a).

What do infants attend to when people talk?

How did the face and voice come to take on the behaviors that they display during the act of speaking? If words have the potency with which that have been credited, why do we entrust so much social communication to ocular activities that have no direct responsibilities for lexical transmission? These issues have an evolutionary feel to them, but they are inextricably linked to development matters, for in pursuing these issues we have an opportunity to see how linguistic form emerges from ontogenetic function. And this brings me to my second question – what do infants attend to when people talk?

The infant is developmentally incomplete, but it is fully competent to deal with cue displays that are of biological significance. Newborns prefer facelike to nonfacelike stimuli (Goren, Sarty, and Wu, 1975), and quickly learn to recognize their mother's face (Bushnell, Sai, and Mullen, 1989; Field, Cohen, Garcia, and Greenberg, 1984) as well as her voice (DeCasper and Fifer, 1980) and smell (Porter, Makin, Davis, and Christensen, 1992). They are also aware of facial movements, particularly mouth posturings of various kinds (Meltzoff and Moore, 1977). Early in their infancy, young humans express an interest in the eyes more than any other region of the face (Haith, Bergman, and Moore, 1977). This is adaptive, as the eyes are vital components of our social signaling system, revealing much about the objects of our attention, as well as our emotions and social intentions. Infants are aware of the correspondence between certain kinds of facial and vocal activity by at least three to four months, when they still have achieved little articulatory experience on their own (Dodd, 1979; Kuhl and Meltzoff, 1982; MacKain, Studdert-Kennedy, Spieker, and Stern, 1983).

The human infant is more inclined to look at a pleasantly moving face than one that is still (Tronick, Als, Adamson, Wise, and Brazleton, 1978), just as it prefers a voice with large rises and falls to one with little frequency variation (Fernald, 1985). We know from several decades of perception research that the infant is also likely to notice a variety of discontinuities in the speech stream, many of which correspond to phonetic categories that are used in speech.

The infant's interest in the structure and activities of the face and voice is not a passive one. Indeed, infants are willing to expend a great deal of energy to gain access to precisely this type of information. The human infant, like the

young of other species, is a stimulus-seeking animal. The reason experimenters are able to use head turning and nonnutritive sucking as dependent measures of discrimination is that infants readily, even eagerly, do these things to
get the stimulation they want. Under naturalistic circumstances, the infant is
adept at influencing, through its own actions, the stream of prosodic and
facially expressive behavior produced by caretakers. The infant is motorically
limited, but its "social muscles" are under excellent control, and with a smile,
a coo, or a glance it can move others to raise their eyebrows, smile, and vocalize in uncharacteristically variegated ways.

The stimulation that infants obtain for themselves influences their neural
and, therefore, conceptual and perceptuomotor development. How others
choose to address the infant is greatly influenced by its own behavior – how
the infant looks at caregivers, what noises it makes, what it does with its face,
eyes, and hands. While the infant's brain is preconfigured to take on behaviors
that lead to spoken language, neural development also depends on stimulation, much of which is elicited, or supplied directly, by the infant itself.

How do the infant's vocal capabilities emerge?

While the infant continues to monitor the social channel that informs it about
the nature of spoken forms and their referents, there are concurrent advances
in its capabilities to respond in kind. These advances are manifested in the
infant's intended or unintended use of voice to signal or to convey, and in the
differentiation of vocal behavior into controllable and recombinable units.

Vocal signalling

Let us look at the initial use of vocalizations that convey, whether or not they
are launched with the utilitarian objective of imparting information. Most
primates communicate affective states by voice, often in conjunction with
movements of the face and other parts of the body. This is readily achievable
because mechanisms that control expression of vocal affect are capable of
doing so in degrees, therefore humans and some nonhuman primates are
able to signal *degrees of feeling* vocally (Green, 1975; Malatesta, 1981; Moynihan,
1964). This provides primates with a vocal mechanism that can be used to
convey degrees of meaning or to intensify messages whose referential content
is otherwise carried by discrete vocal signals or nonvocal cues.

In human infants, the affect conveyed by vocalization is grossly discriminable
and separately classifiable from the start. Babies in pain sound different from
angry infants (Wolff, 1969), a distinction reflecting variations in frequency,
duration, and a host of other vocal parameters. Initial distinctions of this sort
also appear to be possible in nonhuman primates (Malatesta, 1981; Newman,
1985).

We may assume that, initially, distinctive signalling of this sort occurs without communicative intent, presumably as a form of irrepressible "leakage" analogous to the unconscious facial display of one's true feelings (Ekman and Friesen, 1969). But some infants may begin to *use their voice* at some point before the middle of their first year. D'Odorico (1984) followed four Italian infants from the age of four months to the age of eight months. Recordings were made in four naturalistic circumstances in which the mother or experimenter played with the infant in a normal fashion, with or without a toy, or the infant was observed alone with a toy.

D'Odorico obtained evidence for three sound categories. Discomfort sounds, which included cries, whimpers, and moans, occurred mainly when the infant was bored, having lost interest in a toy. Call sounds occurred when the infant, left alone, was no longer interested in a toy and began to look for his mother. Request sounds included noncry vocalizations that in other respects resembled discomfort sounds but lacked the facial expressions associated with crying. Both discomfort and request sounds ceased when the mother entered the room. There was, then, some vocal differentiation according to pragmatic context. Additionally, D'Odorico found that within infants there was some internal consistency in the "call structure" of her subjects according to acoustic analyses of fundamental frequency, melodic contour, and duration, and perceptual analyses of phonetic length.

Vocal differentiation and control

At about seven months, infants begin to chop up their vocalizations with oral articulations, a process that presumably is abetted by elevation of the mandible. This produces activity known as babbling, the production of syllables that are typically of the consonant–vowel shape (e.g. ba, da). These syllables are frequently produced repetitively and with a certain rhythmicity (Bickley, Lindblom, and Roug, 1986). The small set of consonantlike sounds that are heard by listeners typically fall into a few phonetic categories, mainly stops, nasals, and glides. Fricatives, affricates, and liquids are extremely rare, as are clusters (Locke, 1983a). Less is known about vocalic sounds, but vowels initially tend to be low and open.

No other animal does anything quite like babbling. The lipsmacking of monkeys is not really close, since the sounds appear to be produced without phonatory support, and the activity tends to occur only as a display in certain social contexts. Nonhuman primates evidence a limited amount of vocal control in experiments (Trachy, Sutton, and Lindeman, 1981), but not more than that, and are far less inclined than humans to vocalize at all in the wild (Gardner, Gardner, and Drumm, 1989) – a major difference between human and nonhuman primates.

There are several reasons why babbling might directly or indirectly facilitate development of spoken language. First, there is substantive continuity between babbling and speaking. In normally developing infants, Vihman (1986) found size of consonant inventory in the initial lexicon of 12-month-olds to correlate positively with phonololgical development at the age of three years. Similarly, Menyuk, Liebergott, and Schultz (1986) found positive correlations between degree degree of syllabicity in vocal play at 12 months and the production of word-final consonants at 29 months. Second, there may be a connection between the age of babbling onset (or the quantity and quality of babbling) and later progress in lexical development (Stoel-Gammon, 1989). Third, infants who have been denied the opportunity to babble audibly appear to vocalize in a less complex fashion than would otherwise be expected (Locke and Pearson, 1990).

Just how babbling exerts its facilitative effects is a separate question. It has been argued that when babbling commences, social caregivers are able to respond contingently, producing like forms themselves and encouraging expansions of wordlike behaviors into words (Locke, 1986). This seems to be an important effect in speech learning, and I will say more about contingent vocal responding below. It also seems likely that through the activity of babbling the infant develops, and familiarizes itself with, its own unique repertoire of speech sounds and syllable shapes (Locke, 1983a). The infant then is able to draw on this repertoire when attempting words, a practice that is revealed when it selectively targets words whose constituent sounds are concurrently being played with in the infant's babbling (Messick, 1984).

Babbling may also finetune the infant's vocal guidance system. Rudiments of this system are present very early on – infants are aware of auditory–motor correspondences well before the babbling stage begins (Kuhl and Meltzoff, 1982). This early knowledge appears to be traceable to a preadapted, "experience-expectant" neural capability that, like other such capabilities, is activated by no more than token exposure to ambient stimulation (Greenough, Black, and Wallace, 1987). Such a vocal guidance system would enable infants to imitate the speech articulations they see and hear without a great deal of prior articulatory practice. To become fully operational, however, the system may need to engage in certain kinds of activity. This is suggested by several different types of studies. First, Thelen's (1981) work on motor development has found that stereotypes such as rhythmic manual activity tend to begin abruptly and to fade out as motor control increases. That the repetitive and rhythmic activity of babbling tends to begin abruptly, and to fade during a period in which articulatory control increases, suggests that babbling may have a facilitative effect at the strictly motoric level.

Babbling may facilitate speech by increasing the infant's ability to process and adjust its behavior in accordance with feedback by way of a second modality. Studies of self-locomotion reveal that when infants begin to crawl they also become better able at negotiating precarious situations, such as the visual cliff task (Bertenthal, Campos, and Barrett, 1984), and locating objects that are placed in certain locations (Telzrow, Campos, Shepherd, Bertenthal, and Atwater, 1987). These studies suggest that the salience of environmental cues is increased once they become relevant to the infant.

Self-guidance systems also become more accurate in processing the cues that are known to be salient. In the studies of Richard Held and his associates (e.g. Hein and Held, 1967; Held and Hein, 1963), it was found that denying animals access to sensory feedback from their motor activity reduces their ability to use such information in guiding movement, and by inference, prevents the establishment of long-term storage of motor–sensory correlations. Our vocal guidance system may require the action of two processes. One process is experience-expectant and requires very little articulatory experience. The other is babbling dependent.

There also appear to be two epiphenomenal relationships between babbling and speaking. One relationship derives from the possibility that babbling signals advances in the neuromotor control capabilities that are needed for speaking (Locke, Bekken, Wein, and McMinn-Larson, 1991). If they have a common control system, babbling may appear to facilitate speaking when it is merely subject to some of the same constraints. In the other relationship, babbling is seen as a form of play (Locke, 1993b), a labile behavior (Martin and Caro, 1985) that is impaired by illness, hunger, fatigue, and fear. Since these conditions could retard the development of language, any delays in babbling may appear to be associated with delayed language, and masquerade as its cause.

Where do infants' attentional biases and motor dispositions come from?

Infants begin postnatal life with a stock of perceptual biases already operating. The neonate is obviously oriented to human voice, since it reveals awareness of the indexical properties of its own voice and that of its mother within the first several days of life (DeCasper and Fifer, 1980; Martin and Clark, 1982) and seems already to prefer prosodic patterns associated with the language spoken by its mother in utero (Bertoncini, Morais, Bijeljac-Babic, McAdams, Peretz, and Mehler, 1989; Mehler, Jusczyk, Lambertz, Halsted, Bertoncini, and Amiel-Tison, 1988).

These early postnatal effects probably reflect prior learning in the uterus. In the final trimester of gestation, the normally developing fetus hears frequencies (Birnholz and Benacerraf, 1983) in the range of maternal voice, and maternal voice rises above background intrauterine noise at precisely those frequencies (Benzaquen, Gagnon, Hunse, and Foreman, 1990; Querleu, Renard, and Crepin 1981). Moreover, intrauterine learning of vocal patterns has been demonstrated with tests performed prior to birth for externally presented materials (Zimmer, Fifer, Kim, Rey, Chao, and Myers, 1993) and several days after birth for maternally presented utterances (DeCasper and Spence, 1986). In composite, this research suggests that the infant prefers the "language" spoken by its mother because it prefers familiar patterns – in this case, what for all intents and purposes are the mother's patterns. The mother's tongue thus becomes the child's mother tongue.

Where the motoric biases of babbling originate is difficult to say with any precision. Indeed, this subject – for me at least – is practically like the black hole of developmental vocal physiology. But the question is no less important than its perceptual analog, and it seems possible to say a few fairly general things. First, the vocal-movement repertoire revealed by human infants seems to share some properties with modal action patterns described in other animals. These early movement patterns emerge with a small amount of prior experience. As a class, they are not greatly affected by ambient influence, and change little over the lifetime of the animal. These are to be contrasted with movement patterns that appear later, are more susceptible to alterations in response to environmental stimulation, and assume more different forms in the behavior of mature animals (for further detail on these distinctions, as they apply to speech, see Locke and Pearson, 1992).

But the real issues here are more specific than the general ones discussed above. For example, the first syllables produced by the typically developing infant are likely to begin with a voiced anterior stop such as [d] and end with a voiceless velar stop such as [k]. What is the prior experience that produces these patterns? To what developmental processes do we owe these movements? And here we come up with less than one would like. On the experiential side, the tendency is to appeal vaguely to vegetative patterns of movement associated with feeding, and I noted some years ago that front-to-back articulatory progressions appear to prevail both in language and in swallowing (Locke, 1983a). This might explain movement patterns but it cannot handle voicing patterns. For these, we must appeal to the design of the vocal tract or to an ease of production principle, e.g. that voiced sounds in prevocalic position do not require a slightly unnatural act – suppression of phonation until the stop is released. Thus, converging explanations may be needed from early experience on the one hand, and vocal tract anatomy and physiology on the other, but we have a long way to go before we are able to specify the nature of these interdependencies.

What developmental conditions favor language learning?

The literature contains documentations of successful language development in children whose environmental or physical circumstances threaten the developmental course that normally leads to language. This includes infants who heard little of their own voice or that of their parents (Locke and Pearson, 1990; Sachs, Bard, and Johnson, 1981), blind children (Mulford, 1988), the neglected and the abused (Koluchova, 1972, 1976), and infants with aglossia or focal brain lesions (MacKain, 1984; Marchman, Miller, and Bates, 1991). These individuals developed spoken language in spite of their abnormalities because, as humans, they had the gross capacity for spoken language.

That children are able to develop their species-specific capacity for language in spite of various accidents of nature speaks to the robustness of this capacity. But there are some "macrolevel" things that cannot be interfered with if language is to develop. Infants' capacity for spoken language emerges in a biological context whose general character favors the development of complex social behaviors. Two important aspects of this biosocial context – helplessness and maternal attachment – foster sustained and intimate interactions that permit development of vocal and referential learning as required by the construction of a lexicon.

Helplessness

An inspection of the correlations between brain weight and evolutionary advancement suggests that brain size is important to the development of complex behaviors. But from an ontogenetic viewpoint, the size of the mature brain may be less important than when it is that the brain assumes its ultimate proportions, i.e. how prepared it is to respond to, and to be reshaped by, early experience. Hominid mothers had a very narrow birth canal, relative to other primates, an evolutionary development that is attributable to changing torques associated with bipedal locomotion (LeBarre, 1973; Leutenegger, 1980; McHenry, 1975).

Since the head of the human fetus enlarges dramatically just before birth (Dobbing and Sands, 1979), procreation presented our ancestors with an "obstetrical dilemma" of monumental proportions (Washburn, 1960). If the fetus was not delivered during a time when the cephalopelvic relationship was favorable, birth complications were certain to occur. The solution was premature birth: to be born at all, the infant had to be delivered early in the gestational game. This has produced two characteristics that singly, and especially in their interaction, favor the development of linguistic capability.

The first is that very little of our species' brain growth takes place "on the inside." The human newborn's brain is only about 26 percent of what it will weigh in maturity (Harvey and Clutton-Brock, 1985; Lindburg, 1982). The second is that our young are born helpless, and remain that way for a long period of time. As mammals, they must be kept near and be held by their mother. The human infant's brain therefore does most of its forming during a protracted interval of intense social stimulation. It is hard to think of a developmental circumstance that would more favorably affect development of linguistic capacity.

Maternal attachment

Helplessness, mediated by attachment (Bowlby, 1969; see also Bretherton, 1992), favors social circumstances which promote development of language. Attachment critically depends on the ability of caregivers and receivers to recognize each other and interpret each other's emotions. The voice and face are routinely and almost exclusively used for these purposes. The infant's helplessness is thus indirectly responsible for the creation of a communication channel.

This channel that carries information about personal identity and social intentions can be used to convey other kinds of information, too, and it is the channel used for communication by way of spoken language. The face is the source of speech, and since neonates naturally turn toward the source of environmental sound, when individuals speak infants naturally get free information about the sender of the message. Visible movements of the face also contribute to phonetic identification and message interpretation.

As mentioned earlier, newborns respond preferentially to the sight of their mother's face and spend hours looking at faces. This interest in the face escalates further over the first few years of life (Farran and Kasari, 1990). Clearly, such an investment of energy must be sustained by emotional payoffs. There is a suggestion of this in infants' responses to inexpressive faces. In one experiment where mothers were instructed to look at their baby with a "poker face" (Tronick et al., 1978), the infants smiled less, slumped down in their seats, and looked away. The mothers reported that "they found it very difficult to sit still-faced in front of the infant and resist his powerful sallies and bids to interaction" (p. 10). In another study, maternal poker face significantly reduced three and four-month-old's eye gaze at their mother (Berger and Cunningham, 1981). In other research, simulated maternal depression caused three and four-month-olds to produce many more sober or negative facial expressions, which continued for at least the first minute after the mother had switched into her normal mode of relating (Cohn and Tronick, 1983).[1]

The voice plays a similar role. Bowlby (1969) suggested that vocalization is the infant's instrument for maintaining maternal contact. He commented that "babbling . . . has the function of maintaining a mother-figure in proximity to an infant by promoting social interchange between them" (p. 289). In turn, it appears that vocal and referential learning are encouraged by the social and emotional ties between the infant and its mother or other caretakers. In the first several days of life, infants also reveal a listening preference for their mother's voice (DeCasper and Fifer, 1980; Mehler, Bertoncini, Barriere, and Jassik-Gerschenfeld, 1978), seemingly a preference for familiar stimulation owing to prenatal learning.

Using an operant head-turning technique, Fernald and Kuhl (1987) found that four-month-olds prefer to hear the higher fundamental frequency and more exaggerated frequency variations associated with infant directed speech. They speculated that this listening preference might be due to the perceptual salience of radical frequency sweeps associated with inherent design features of the auditory system. Exaggerations of pitch seem to hold a certain universal appeal, presumably as a result of underlying biological mechanisms that have evolved to serve ontogenetic functions (Fernald, 1992). Crosslinguistic studies indicate that large variations in vocal pitch are a key feature of motherese and occurred in a number of disparate languages and cultures (Fernald and Simon,

1984; Fernald, Taeschner, Dunn, Papousek, Boysson-Bardies, and Fikui, 1989; Grieser and Kuhl, 1988). Extreme pitch variations also evoke pleasant emotions in adult subjects, who associate them with happiness, interest, and surprise (Scherer, 1979).

Fernald (1992b) sees a parallel between the human mother's use of intonation to transmit affect to her infant and nonhuman primates' use of pitch, intensity, rhythm, and other "graded" vocal parameters to convey information about intentions and motivational states. This parallel, and some interesting crosscultural research, speak to a biological basis for mothers' manipulation of, and infants responses to, nonarbitrary relationships between intonation and affective meaning. These early sound–meaning correspondences include mothers' use of falling frequency contours when attempting to soothe a distressed infant, rising contours when attempting to engage attention or elicit a response, and rising–falling contours when seeking to maintain attention. Fernald has reported that infants react to these manipulations as their mothers intend; regardless of the language spoken or the infants' understanding of the words, they pick up and reproduce in their own facial activity the affect that mothers intend to convey in their statements of approval and prohibition.

In addition to its indexical and affective value, the voice is of course the major carrier of information needed to recognize spoken words and vocal prosody. That the voice is a major point of attachment is therefore directly relevant to our species-specific capacity for linguistic communication that travels over the same wires.

The universal bias toward vocal languages may be due to the fact that the voice and vocalizing faces already contain the information that babies naturally attend to and are prepared to process. To be assured of a measure of success from the start, it would have made excellent biological sense for any new communicative displays to "piggy back" onto this open channel – to take advantage of a long-standing human commitment to maternal–infant attachment by embedding new information in the same stream of cues. Elsewhere (Locke, 1993b), I have speculated that this is what our ancestors did when they invented spoken language. This adaptation would have posed no threat to either the extant attachment system or the new code, since voice quality and prosody can be manipulated independent of articulatory activity. In principle, this feature gives phonological languages a "naturalness" not shared by systems of encoding in which information about the speaker – age, sex, identity, mood, credibility, intentions – are conveyed via wholly different muscles and perceptual mechanisms.

In contemporary parlance, this facial–vocal channel "buys" theorists a great deal, for it has the infant paying attention to the things people do when they talk. It has the mother remaining at close range, and providing her infant with facial and vocal behaviors that cement and sustain emotional attachment. Because she happens to use *speech* as the primary vehicle for this affective communication, rather than merely vocalizing nonverbally, we have both parties acting as they should if spoken language is to be a result.

How does the process of language learning occur?

When the infant and its caregivers behave playfully, their faces and voices become toys that are passed back and forth like brightly colored rubber balls. A natural outgrowth of these playful dispositions are specific modes of interactions, including turn taking, vocal accommodation, and contingent vocal responding. These behaviors ate strong features of our species-characteristic capability in social cognition. This capability is also manifested in two other linguistically relevant developments. One of these is shared gaze, or the tendency for mothers and infants to conjointly attend to the same aspects of their environment. The other is the infant's discovery that other people have their own unique mental lives.

Turn taking

In nurturant cultures, mothers pay close attention to the voices of their infants from the first postnatal moments. Like other primate mothers, they use vocal information to identify their infants, and to gain information about their health and emotional state. Infants also pay close attention to their mother's voice. But even though nonvocal rhythmicities are evident soon after birth, there is initially a great deal of vocal clashing between mothers and their infants.

Since infants freely expend energy to gain access to their mother's familiar voice, as discussed earlier, we should expect them to cease expending energy, i.e. to suspend or withhold vocalization when their mothers are talking. And typically the clashing subsides when the infant is about three or four months old. Then, both parties conspicuously begin to take turns while vocalizing, and thus lay down the interactive framework for vocal learning and dialogue (Berger and Cunningham, 1983; Ginsburg and Kilbourne, 1988).

Vocal accommodation

Vocal accommodation is the process whereby infants assimilate aspects of speakers' voices, speech sounds, and speaking style (Locke, 1993b). This assimilative process has little to do with any efforts to learn language, or even to communicate. Rather, it appears to be motivated by a desire to incorporate superficial characteristics of individuals to whom infants are emotionally attached, and since we constantly speak to and in the presence of babies, they incorporate speaking behaviors too. Oller (1981) has suggested that once an infant understands "that talking is a natural aspect of being human, he may act like a human being talking."

Examples of vocal accommodation are ubiquitous. At one time or another, most of us have seen a preverbal child "talking" on a toy telephone with the superficial vocal characteristics of a conversing person. There are also facial and manual accommodations, e.g. the changing smile of the sighted child relative to blind peers (Freedman, 1964), and prelexical increases in manual activity among infants reared in signing homes (Petitto and Marentette, 1991). At about eight months, both mothers and their infants significantly increase the amount of vocal, facial, and manual imitation (Uzgiris, Benson, Kruper, and Vasek, 1989). Vocal accommodation is, then, a subdivision of a larger category of socially accommodative behaviors that includes gestures in various modalities.

At this point, the evidence for vocal accommodation is still emerging. Kessen, Levine, and Wendrich (1979) asked a "tutor" to sing an open vowel on three different pitches to five and six-month-olds. Frequently, the infants responded with vowels of their own. The proportion of correct perceptual matches, as evaluated by trained musicians, significantly exceeded chance. The authors commented that "the babies worked hard at their assignment. They watched the experimenter closely and they vocalized to her often and energetically" (p. 96).

Recently, vocal accommodation was demonstrated in even younger infants in a completely naturalistic circumstance. Masataka (1992) observed six Japanese infants at three to four months, interacting with their mother or other caregiver as they normally would. The joint occurrence of four intonation patterns (rising, falling, bell-shaped, and flat or complex) in the utterances of mothers and their infants were tabulated. Masataka found that when the mothers produced more than two utterances before their infants responded, the infants' reproduction of all four maternal vocal contours increased to a significant degree.

As we will see later, vocal accommodation may be responsible for the first vocal behaviors that *seem to be linguistic*. These false positives – words that have no meaning, phrases that contain no words – are developmentally positive, for they encourage the infant along a path that leads to linguistic mastery. The developmental linguistic significance of this process is that vocal accommodation gives the infant an immediate repertoire of word and phraselike vocal patterns. During the next few months of development, many of these forms may be analyzed further, revised, and retained in more adultlike form.

But some things may not change. The rhythmicity of speech that is traceable to very early experience, and the patterning in a child's utterances that reflects exposure to the peculiar affectations of its caregivers' speech, may not be readily altered by subsequent experience. Vocal accommodation, in the sense that I mean it here, is affect-driven language. Perhaps one very special feature of the sensitive period for language learning is that during this (and only this) time the infant is maternally attached, and its utterances ate therefore formed under the influence of affective factors that subside with growing independence and autonomy. This is speculative, of course, but it is speculation that deserves consideration.

Contingent vocal responding

Turn taking appears to facilitate vocal imitation by encouraging infants to attend to and reproduce model utterances. It also provides mothers with the opportunity to monitor their utterances and respond contingently. That is, as the infants' vocalizations become more playful and speechlike, mothers increasingly reconfigure their own utterances to complement those of the infants.

Pawlby (1977) looked at the incidence of mother-to-infant and infant-to-mother imitation in eight mother–infant dyads followed longitudinally from 17 to 24 weeks (Period I) to 26 to 33 weeks (Period II) to 35 to 42 weeks (Period III). She found that over 90 percent of the total imitation that occurred involved the mother imitating the child. Her data also revealed a dramatic increase in mothers' imitation of speech sounds from the second to the third period, when there was a large decrease in mothers' imitation of infants' nonspeech sounds. This could be because infants make relatively fewer nonspeech sounds, since this period is associated with variegated babbling, in which infants may produce a wider variety of speechlike sounds (Oller, 1980). It could also be because of preferential reproduction of speech sounds by mothers, who recognize that words are just around the corner. This latter possibility is suggested by Pawlby's observation that "almost from the time of birth there seems to be a marked tendency for mothers to reflect back to their infants certain gestures which occur spontaneously within their baby's natural repertoire of activities. She appears, however, to select actions which she can endow with communicative significance, especially vocalizations" (pp. 219–20).

As for the nature of its developmental effects, it has been suggested that phonetically contingent responding increases infants' receptivity or attention to adult speech (Papousek and Papousek, 1975: 249). Pawlby (1977) interpreted the effects of phonetically contingent responding in this way, commenting that "babies do pay special attention (in that they laugh and smile and appear to be pleased) when the mothers themselves imitate an action which the child has just performed. The infant's action is thus 'highlighted' or 'marked out' as something special" (p. 220). She also thought that "in kind" maternal responses "may be what leads to the infant's more deliberate production of the action. Because the mother has repeatedly reflected back an event which he himself has just performed and since he finds this pleasing and attractive, the same action is produced by the child on a different occasion *in order that* his mother does likewise" (p. 220, her italics).

Contingent responding also may make infants' vocal output more speechlike. Bloom, Russell, and Wassenberg (1987) found that contingent responding by adults increased the ratio of syllabic to vocalic sounds in three-month-olds. Veneziano (1988) found that when mothers produced the closest lexical equivalent to their infants' wordlike forms, the infants reproduced the original utterances or accommodated to the mother's pronunciation. Hardy-Brown, Plomin, and DeFries (1981) found a significant correlation between the frequency of mothers' contingent responding and the communicative development of their infant at one year. If contingent responding has these beneficial effects, reduced contingent responding could retard the rate of (early) language development, and there is evidence that this is so (Tomasello, Mannle, and Kruger, 1986).

Shared gaze

Studies indicate that shared gaze between mothers and their infants contributes to the establishment of object reference. Babies spend a great deal of time looking at their mother's head orientation and eye gaze, seemingly attempting to find out what she might be thinking about. As early as two to four months, but rising sharply by eight to ten months, infants tend to follow an adult's line of regard (Scaife and Bruner, 1975). This would not be particularly helpful if they were unable to appreciate an important concept: the object of a mother's attention while vocalizing is probably the subject of her reference. Though rarely mentioned, this may be one of the more important conceptual precursors to lexical acquisition.

Mothers also spend a great deal of time looking at the things to which their infants attend. If an infant points or gazes at an object while vocalizing, the mother frequently infers that the object is central to the child's attention. This is a valid inference; Golinkoff, Hirsh-Pasek, Cauley, and Gordon (1987) found that 16-month-olds tend to look longer at objects and actions that have just been named for them. Following a simultaneous gaze and vocalization, mothers also tend to name or talk about the object of their infant's attention, impute referential intent to their infant, and expand upon incomplete utterances that accompany these nonverbal gestures.

Collis (1977) studied the eye gaze and labeling behavior of nine mothers interacting with their 43-week-old infants. He found that mothers named toys in the room at precisely those moments when they could see that their children were looking at the toys. Exactly half of the toy namings occurred when the infant was looking at the toy that was named. In 98 percent of the cases in which mothers uttered a name while looking at a toy, the mothers were looking at the same toy they named. Head and eye movements thus served as reliable referential cues.

Tomasello and his colleagues (Tomasello et al., 1986; Tomasello and Farrar, 1986b) estimated the vocabulary development of children from whom they also obtained a measure of joint attention – the amount of time spent by mother and infant looking at the same object or event. They obtained a positive correlation between the amount of time spent in joint attention episodes at 15 months and the size of the children's expressive vocabulary at 21 months. They also found that words referring to objects at which the child was already looking were learned between than words that were presented in an attempt to refocus the child's attention.

The processes of social cognition described above are all conspicuously operative in the first half year of life. These processes are sufficient to account for the formulaic words and stereotyped phrases of the 18 to 24-month-old child, and the referential and contextual information needed to deploy that material appropriately. Nonhuman primates have specialized social cognition systems that resemble our own in relevant respects, which is why they, like our own young, seem to be almost linguistic.

Unshared mental activity

Whatever the similarities, there is a major difference between the social cognition of humans and nonhuman primates, and between the human infant and the young child. This difference relates to the theory of other minds, a concept that emerges between two and four years of age when children reveal an awareness that other people have thoughts and knowledge that differ from their own (Bretherton, McNew, and Beeghly-Smith, 1981; MacNamara, Baker, and Olson, 1976; Sodian, Taylor, Harris, and Perner, 1991).

Autistic children, by contrast, appear to be deficient in the capacity to sense or act on the inferred mental states of others, or even to talk about mental states (Tager-Flusberg, 1992). In one study (Baron-Cohen, Leslie, and Frith, 1985), autistic, Down Syndrome, and normally developing young children were shown a girl doll putting a marble in a basket. Then, when the doll walked off, the child was allowed to see the experimenter transfer the marble to another location. When the doll was brought back, children were asked where she would look for her marble. The retarded subjects and the young normals pointed to the basket, which is where the doll had last seen it, but the autistic children indicated the place where they (but not the doll) had seen the marble go. In other words, the autistic children seemed unable to dissociate their own knowledge from that of the doll. In effect, they failed to apply a theory of mind.

When the human child acquires the concept of other minds, it realizes that other people are unaware of its thoughts and feelings and that it is unaware of theirs. This is the first time that intentional transmission of novel (unshared) information is logically possible, a condition that is assumed to underlie the human child's strong urge to communicate and, in succession, the expansion of its capability for reference.[2] It is after the age of two years, then, that linguistic communication begins in earnest – both for these reasons pertaining to communicative motivation and, as we will see later, for reasons pertaining to grammatical facility.

What kind of neural specializations produce linguistic capacity?

All the interactive behaviors mentioned above – sending and interpreting vocal affect, vocal turn taking and accommodation, contingent vocal responding, mutual gaze, and the emergent concept of other minds – belong to our species-characteristic endowment in social cognition (Brothers, 1990). This endowment may well reflect phylogenetic histories (Andrew, 1963, 1964) that have converged to produce unitary neural mechanisms for the processing of facial and vocal activity. In human and nonhuman primates, face and voice processing capabilities appear to be heavily preconfigured by genetic factors, activation requiring no more than a minimal amount of stimulation. In nonhuman primates, there are dedicated cells that fire either to faces or to facial activity (see review in Desimone, 1991), and similar cells have been reported in humans (Holmes, Ojemann, Cawthon, and Lettich, 1991). In humans, clinical, electrophysiological, and experimental studies all suggest that face identification and interpretation of facial affect are accomplished by different brain mechanisms, as are voice identification and interpretation of vocal affect as well. Face and voice identification also appear to follow a similar developmental course (see Locke, 1993b, for a current review of supporting research).

Young children can achieve a fair amount of referential vocal behavior with this highly specialized social communication system. Add to this a capacious memory for vocal sounds (Gathercole, Willis, Emslie, and Baddeley, 1992) and children have most of what they need to achieve a receptive lexicon. These resources also allow children to deal with irregular verb forms such as *run-ran* through strictly associative processes (Pinker, 1991). Learners seem to commit these forms to memory by rote. For this reason, it is possible for "came" to precede, and inconsistently to be replaced by, "comed" in the utterances of a grammatically developing child.

This specialization in social cognition (SSC) allows children to achieve a working vocabulary, but this specialization is insufficient for an elaborate linguistic system. For this, we need a second specialization, a coldly analytical and computational system of the type proposed by Fodor (1983). As modular as it may be, though, this second specialization is not *the* language module. Rather, it is, in effect, a grammatical analysis module (or GAM). The GAM deals in rules and representations. Among other things, in English it computes regular past tense verb forms by application of a rule which concatenates affixes with stem endings (such as *walk-walked*). It is only this computational part of morphology that requires the operations of a specialized linguistic system, and the neural systems subserving this component are mostly distinct from the hardware underlying the associative memory system and whichever of our neural resources deal with irregular forms (Locke, 1992; Pinker, 1991).

If the SSC cannot accomplish all that language requires without the GAM, the reverse is also true. The warmly interactive SSC supplies the coldly analytical GAM with an enormous sample of linguistically relevant data, without which there would be nothing to analyze and no forms to reconfigure by application of computational rules.

If the SSC operates from the infant's earliest opportunities to experience social stimulation, when does the GAM begin to operate? Morphological evidence suggests that this takes place sometime between 20 and 30 months (Marcus, Pinker, Ullman, Hollander, Rosen, and Xu, 1992), depending on prior success in utterance acquisition (Locke, in press, a, b). It is during this interval that the utterances of human children diverge from those of nonhuman primates trained in sign language (Bickerton, 1990a).

How do our neural specializations configure the development of language?

The dual specialization hypothesis accounts for a range of currently unexplained psycholinguistic phenomena, and the operation of both a socially cognitive and a grammatically analytical system give language development many of the properties that we have come to recognize. These phenomena include (1) a previously unrecognized aspect of language that may be considered a variant of so-called duplex perception; (2) young children's frequent and heavily context-bound use of formulaic phrases; (3) qualitative differences in lexical development between children; (4) recidivism – an effect of componential analysis of holistically stored linguistic forms; (5) differences in the rate of lexical development in signed and spoken languages; and (6) the nature of language delay in otherwise normally developing children.

Duplex perception

The intriguing phenomenon known as duplex perception (Liberman and Mattingly, 1985) is produced dichotically by presenting the critical cue to consonantal place of articulation, a formant transition, to one ear and the remaining portion of the syllable to the other ear. For computer synthesized syllables such as [da] and [ga], the isolated transition normally resembles a "chirp" and the remaining portion is heard as a syllable initiated by a consonant of ambiguous place of articulation. But in the dichotic mode, listeners tend to hear both a chirp *and* an intact syllable with clear consonantal place cues, hence the term duplex perception. The reason for this phenomenon, according to Liberman and Mattingly (1991), is that the "closed module" that handles speech perception is preemptive, taking the chirp for its own segmental purposes and denying an "open module" that is concerned with prosody the chance to process this sound for its pitch, loudness, and timbre.

My reason for bringing this up here is that if duplex perception argues for a speech perception module, there must be another type of duplex perception that argues for the converging but distinct contributions of socially cognitive and grammatical operations. We process the segmental stream and the emotionality of spoken language in parallel, and we are simultaneously mindful of the lexical and the emotional content of speech. Listeners can hear words that, by themselves, would suggest a particular meaning, but simultaneously they pick up a tone of voice that implies a different interpretation altogether. And these cues seem to be prioritized differently than the consonantal place cues discussed earlier.

Developmentally, the additivity of language becomes conspicuous when the GAM turns on, for it is then that a multiplicity of categorial phonetic cues are piled on top of the prosodic, affective, and speaker-identifying cues that infants already value and process. In the real speech of sophisticated speakers, where both linguistic content and vocal affect are present, one type of cue does not preempt the other, and for speech to work this must be the case. Listeners must know both what the speaker is saying *and* what he or she intends by saying it. We duplexly pick up information about linguistic content and speaker affect because the cues to these things are of different sorts and are processed by different brain mechanisms. The listener is thus able to hear conflicts between "the words" and "the music" of spoken language.

To some degree, the dual specializations of language seem to map onto hemispheric functions as currently understood. If the left hemisphere is disproportionately responsible for phonetic processing, we may assume it is coldly and asocially analytical. The right hemisphere, on the other hand, is warmly social and emotional, and is seemingly dominant for the processing of personally relevant information, no matter the modality (Van Lancker, 1991).

Formulaicity

As indicated earlier, the SSC does more than feed utterance data to the GAM. By itself, it is responsible for a great deal of behavior that is communicative and taken to be linguistic. The principle intake mechanisms of the SSC absorb a great many utterances, and with them, a variety of high-frequency words and phrases. This specialization is slavishly vocal and socially sensitive. That is why it, like the vocal mimicry system of talking birds, can reproduce words and stereotyped phrases. It is obvious that some nonhuman primates (Savage-Rumbaugh, 1990) have this specialization but lack the vocal control needed for production of speechlike sounds.

A decade ago, Peters (1983) documented that "the first units of language acquired by children do not necessarily correspond to the minimal units (morphemes) of language described by conventional linguistics. They frequently consist of more than one (adult) word or morpheme." It is now widely accepted that the earliest utterances of children are *formulaic*. They are, to use Pinker's (1991) terms, associative, noncomputational, and nonrule governed. Formulaic utterances are thought to be holistically perceived and stored, and irreducible to their syllabic or segmental parts. Presumably, formulas reflect the infant's prosodic orientation, perhaps combined with its inability to analyze speech into segment-sized elements. If irreducible to discrete sound elements, the infant's utterances lack any possibility of recombination – a defining attribute of linguistic phonologies.

On a functional level, formulas are legitimately a part of spoken language. First, listeners naturally recognize them as phrases and sentences, so they do linguistic work. Second, formulas are not at all rare: recent research (Lieven, Pine, and Dresner Barnes, 1992) suggests that children's first 50 words usually include about nine formulas, on average; their first hundred words typically contain about 20 formulas. For some children, nearly half the items in their lexicon are these frozen phrases. Third, we have no reason to assume that children acquire and reproduce formulaic units with anything but the perceptual and speech-motor systems that are invoked in word production. Indeed, Lieven et al. (1992) have speculated that phrases provide children with templates which, following analysis, are converted into lexically based patterns.

Qualitative differences in lexical development

The vocally accommodative ways of the SSC explain several known developmental trajectories. Young children in the first 50 word stage (approximately 18 to 20 months of age) seem to have two different language learning styles. These children have been called, variously, analytical and holistic (Peters, 1977), noun lovers and leavers (Horgan, 1980), and referential and expressive (Nelson, 1973, 1981).

Nelson's data reveal that the initial lexicons of referential children contain a large number of object oriented words. The early vocabularies of expressive children, on the other hand, are more self oriented. In place of object words in the lexicons of expressive children is a supply of personal–social terms for expressing feelings, needs, and social forms. At an early age, these children produce a number of socially conventional phrases such as "go away," "stop it," "thank you," and "I want it." Referential children produce shorter phrases than expressive children, and they tend to say fewer function words and personal–social terms.

Expressive children are heavily formulaic; at an early age they appear to produce phrases and sentences as single units, and their speech contains functors and pronouns as well as nouns. According to Nelson (1981), these gestalts "have the characteristic of being wholistically produced without pauses between words, with reduced phonemic articulation, and with the effect of slurred or mumbled speech but with a clear intonation pattern" (p. 174).

Because little more than vocal accommodation and shared gaze are needed for the production of situation-appropriate words and phrases, and social terms are the currency of interpersonal commerce, it seems likely that expressive children's utterances are due primarily to their SSC. The differences between them and referential children may be due, at least in part, to the age of the child when the GAM is fully activated.

Development of phonological operations

Something that may have obscured the dual existence of conjoint specializations in the past is the presumption that phonology precedes the lexicon, and that first words imply the prior existence of a phonological system. Because phonology is a part of language, first words, in this view, would signify that language had already developed, even though the child had not yet advanced to morphology, syntax, and more complex form–meaning relationships. However, the proper question is not whether phonology is a component of language but whether the child's first words and stereotyped phrases are evidence of phonology. In my opinion, they are not.

Studdert-Kennedy (1991) shares this position. He believes that phonemes, like other differentiations, fall out of lexical behavior rather than precede it. Phonology tends not to develop until a moderate inventory of words is stored and used. If the initial lexicon has no phonology, there is no reason to interpret first words as the onset of the GAM. This makes it logical to suppose that phonology, morphology, and syntax are all a function of the GAM. The immediate theoretical benefit of this supposition is that phonology, which frequently gets short shrift, is now reintegrated with the other grammars of language (Liberman, 1970).

The earliest utterances are prephonological – products of the processes of vocal accommodation that are heavily influenced by the infant's relationship with speakers and familiarity with social contexts. Very little of this activity deserves phonological credit because there is little evidence of systemic behavior; few utterances, if any, are transformed by the application of acquired phonological principles.

Some of the phonetic evidence for activation of the GAM comes from studies of consonant–vowel interactions. Several phonologists (Davis and MacNeilage, 1990; Stoel-Gammon, 1983) have reported adjacency effects in young children's early words. For example, a particular consonantal closure may never occur before particular vowels that other closures frequently precede. The movements travel together, as though indivisible and not, therefore, combinable. Nittrouer, Studdert-Kennedy, and McGowan (1989) observed two parallel trends in the production of fricative-vowel syllables by three to seven-year-old children. As the spectral energy in [s] and [ʃ] became increasingly distinct, the degree of their coarticulation with following vowels decreased. At the production level, this would seem operationally to define the discovery of the phonemic principle, or at least a productive application of that principle.

Nittrouer et al. (1989) also speculated about how this process occurs. At first, they said, the young child has a few meaningful phonetic sequences that have an acoustically coherent structure. One assumes these items have been submitted to analyses that emphasize prosodic contour and skip over constituent parts. But

> as the number and diversity of the words in a child's lexicon increase, words with similar acoustic and articulatory patterns begin to cluster. From these clusters there ultimately precipitate the coherent units of sounds and gesture that we know as phonetic segments. Precipitation is probably a gradual process perhaps beginning as early as the second to third year of life when the child's lexicon has no more than 50–100 words. But the process is evidently still going on in at least some regions of the child's lexicon and phonological system as late as 7 years of age. (p. 131).

Recidivism

In the developmental phonology literature various observers have commented on the existence of progressive idioms in children's speech. These words, like formulas, are more advanced than would be expected from contemporaneous analyses of the child's phonological system. Examples include an eight-month-old boy who said "clock" and "truck" correctly. Six months later, because of a phenomenon sometimes called recidivism, the boy had revised this pronunciation to [kak]. Similarly, a girl who expressed the word "pretty" with an adultlike [pr] cluster at eight months had transformed this to [pIti] by 20 months (Moskowitz, 1980).

Moskowitz (1980) noted that when a phonologically developing child begins to revise word pronunciations, the alterations tend to spread rapidly through his or her lexicon, leaving behind "two separate lexical encodings" for all items in the process of change. One presumes this dual registration ultimately reduces to a single (standard) form. Dual representation of early word forms is exactly what we would predict if infants' earliest speech is done by processes of the SSC and then taken over by the GAM.

Of course, morphological regressions also occur. In English, these include "correction" of plural and past tense forms in which, for example, *feet* may be changed to *foots, mice* to *mouses*, and *went* to *goed*. More extensive accounts of these errors of overregularization are available elsewhere (Bowerman, 1982a; Marcus et al., 1992). I would argue that regressions index the activation of the GAM. They do not represent a fall back of any kind but the beginning of a new way of doing linguistic business.

It is possible that formulaic phrases and idiomatic words are processed and stored differently than fully analyzed forms. The most appropriate developmental psycholinguistic data are unavailable, but there is some evidence in adults that "automatic speech" is more likely to be represented in the brain bilaterally (Van Lancker, 1991). If true in children as well, we might be even more confident that early formulas and idioms are a function of the SSC, for socially cognitive operations tend to be bilaterally distributed, whereas segmental phonetic analysis is performed primarily by the left cerebral hemisphere.

Nonproductive utterances

If formulaic phrases function as minimal units, many of young children's phrases will be unproductive. That is, the morphemic elements in their phrases will not be freely recombinable if their existence is unknown to the children who produce them. Using observation and interviews, Kelly and Dale (1989) classified two-year-olds with an MLU above 1.0 as Productive or Nonproductive Syntax Users. Utterances were considered productive if each word was grammatically free, that is, if it occurred in at least two utterances and carried the same semantic associations and occupied the same position within the utterance. In nonproductive utterances, there was no indication that the child knew that the constituent words could be combined in different ways and thus were separable from the utterance.

Children were given a symbolic play task and an imitation task using nonce words made up of sounds that either were in their lexicon at that time or not present in their lexical inventory. Kelly and Dale commented that many children demonstrated language skills that exceeded expectations based on cognitive measures. Overall, their data reveal no striking relationship between children's linguistic stage and their performance on object permanence and means–end tasks. There was, however, a tendency for productive syntax users to outperform those with nonproductive syntax on the means–end measure. If there was to be a difference between any nonlinguistic cognitive measure and a language measure, this is exactly where one would expect to find it, since the other subjects provide no evidence in their utterances that they know anything about linguistic principles of organization.

Signed and spoken languages

Comparative studies by John Bonvillian and his colleagues (Bonvillian and Folven, 1987; Bonvillian, Orlansky, and Novack, 1983; Orlansky and Bonvillian, 1984) suggest that in manual languages, first signs may appear several months before first words, but that morphology and syntax tend to appear at about the same ages in speakers and signers. Semantic relations, verb agreement, deictic pronouns, and morphologically complex verbs of motion and location all seem to develop at the same rate in both speech and sign.

It does not surprise me that there would be one "age" for the onset of spoken words as phonetically sensitive components of language, and another for linguistic elements that are sensitive to other considerations, since the production of words depends heavily upon mechanisms of perception and production. Productive control emerges according to a biological schedule that could easily differ for visual–manual and auditory–vocal systems of communication. Once these perceptuomotor mechanisms are functioning, it becomes possible to say words but inflected material must await activation of the GAM.

The "two age" situation outlined above suggested to Meier and Newport (1990) the possibility of "two (or more) largely independent timing mechanisms . . . one controlling the onset of lexical acquisition and another controlling the acquisition of grammar (that is, syntax and morphology)" (p. 13). I take this observation as support for dual specialization.

If human infants acquire syntax and morphology at about the same age in manual as well as spoken languages, the GAM may be amodal, as Meier and Newport suggest. Many of the subsystems of the SSC are amodal, too, but this specialization places a very high value on facial–vocal activity (Locke, 1993a). We may assume that it also values movements of the hands. Manual activity can signal intentions (including threat), and there is evidence that nonhuman primates have cells that are attuned to hand movements. There is also evidence that human infants are aware of finger movements (Meltzoff and Moore, 1977).

Because the SSC operates on physical cues, it is not unlikely that components of a language in one modality might be expressed earlier or later than the corresponding structures in languages occupying other modalities. In humans, the first specialization to develop, the SSC, also enables and activates the second specialization, the GAM, which handles phonology, morphology, and syntax. Because the first specialization feeds the second, the timing of the two (in the form of developmental "milestones") tend to be coordinated.

Concluding Remarks

In this chapter I have presented what I believe to be a biologically responsible and psycholinguistically useful perspective on the infant's development of linguistic capacity. According to this perspective, the human infant does not, and cannot, acquire languages as such, but instead travels along a developmental growth path that leads to linguistic capacity. Infants are kept on this path by various factors, including endogenous orienting and attentional mechanisms that are tuned to facial and vocal activity, and caregivers who respond appropriately to the infant's vocally affective signals.

The coordinated exchange of affective messages between infants and caregivers increases during a period in which the brain rapidly organizes. One assumes this encourages elaboration of species-typical neural systems that are preadapted for language. This preadaptation includes a specialization for social cognition that acquires utterance material and feeds it to a mechanism that is specialized for analysis and computation. Humans have, thus, a dual specialization for language with processors that are sited separately in the two cerebral hemispheres.

Duality of specialization accounts for a number of disparate and incompletely explained phenomena. Here I have drawn attention to formulaic utterances and the discontinuities that arise as grammatical capabilities activate and all levels of language reorganize. In future work, I hope to demonstrate that the sequential activation of linguistic systems is relevant to, and can enrich our understanding of, children's developmental language disorders (Locke, in press, b).

NOTES

1   Something of the reverse also occurs. In her studies of the blind, Fraiberg (1979) noted that "when the eyes do not meet ours in acknowledgment of our presence, it feels curiously like a rebuff" (p. 155).

2   There is much more to be said about the child's motivation to communicate, and I go into this in some depth elsewhere (Locke, 1993b).

11 Phonetic Abilities in the First Year of Life

RAY D. KENT AND GIULIANA MIOLO

1 Introduction

The answer to the question, "What are the phonetic abilities of infants in the first year?" requires first an answer to another question, "What are the *possible* phonetic abilities at this age?" Many authorities throughout the years have regarded the infant as *prelinguistic*. Indeed, the word *infant* means "incapable of speech." If the infant is truly prelinguistic (incapable), then what could be said about phonetic capabilities? Could they exist at all, and if they do, how can one describe them? One possibility is simply to apply phonetic methods developed for the study of adult speech to the sounds produced by the infant, whatever these sounds may be. This approach begs the question that these methods are suitable to infants' sounds in the first place. But another possibility is that the infant is not prelinguistic in the strictest sense, but possesses – at the least – certain predispositions that are continuous with, and perhaps supportive of, later linguistic development. The latter perspective is the one taken in this chapter. It is assumed that the infant has certain phonetic abilities that are relevant to the processes of language learning and that can be studied with the methods of phonetic science and perhaps even phonology.

The task then is to describe the nature of the infant's phonetic abilities and to demonstrate their potential role in language development. The infant may be regarded as a "spontaneous apprentice" (to borrow George Miller's (1977) title). The infant comes to the task of language development with certain biological, cognitive, and emotional resources. When placed in an appropriate environment that affords language exposure, the infant spontaneously apprentices to the task of becoming a language user. But the young apprentice may be specially equipped by genetic endowment for the challenge. As Miller (1977) wrote, "Young children have an unusual faculty for learning language, and it is well that they do, for we expect them to learn far more than we could self-consciously teach them" (p. xxvii). The position in the present chapter is not that language is genetically determined, but rather that certain capacities that enable language acquisition are genetically determined. We might say that some apprenticeship talents are common to the human genome. The infant applies these talents to the task of learning to speak.

Phonetic abilities can be defined in both the perceptual and productive domains. This chapter will emphasize the latter but will consider the former at least briefly. A proper treatment of infants' phonetic ability necessarily involves a discussion of the perceptual and productive aspects of this ability. In very early infancy, these two aspects may have somewhat different courses of development, but they are ultimately integrated in spoken language competence. A major challenge to developmental theory is to show how perceptual and productive abilities are combined as the infant acquires a particular language.

A reasonable argument can be made that perception is the best place to begin. The argument is encapsulated in the common wisdom that comprehension (or perception) precedes production. Generally, a child demonstrates a particular language competence first in comprehension and later in production. This is not to suggest that all of the sounds an infant produces are a necessary and direct consequence of the infant's auditory experience (this does not seem to be true), but rather to say that the typical infant has substantial auditory experience with language within a few days after birth, and probably even prenatally. This auditory exposure to a particular language, or languages, should be kept in mind in any consideration of how infants gain linguistic competence.

2   Speech Perception in Infants

The study of infants' speech perception has been a fruitful area of research. The following review can mention only the highlights of the burgeoning literature on the perception of speech by infants. The review is directed to answer one fundamental question: when do infants show the capability to discriminate and recognize speech sounds and how does this capability develop in the face of exposure to a particular language?

In the interests of conciseness, this section will be presented as a chronological review, proceeding in intervals of one, two, or three months. The review begins arbitrarily with birth, but it should be recognized that the fetus already may have been exposed to the human voice and to some characteristics of the ambient language (Lecanuet and Granier-Deferre, 1993). The cochlear appears to be sufficiently well developed that the fetus could hear sounds transmitted to the intrauterine environment. Prenatal exposure to the maternal voice may be the basis for the infant's early preference for the mother's voice over another woman's voice.

(For additional references and expanded discussion of points summarized below, see Jusczyk, 1992; Kuhl, 1987, 1988; Werker and Pegg, 1992).

Birth to one month. In about the first 30 days of life, infants already demonstrate considerable ability to discriminate acoustic contrasts that are phonetically relevant. Since the seminal paper by Eimas et al. (1971), a large number of studies have made it very clear that infants can discriminate many of the phonetic contrasts used by the world's languages. The studies on English fall just short of allowing the conclusion that infants can discriminate *every* phonetic contrast in the language. However, this discriminative ability does not constitute evidence that the infants possess segmental recognition, or the ability to identify the phonetic elements of the language. If nothing else, infants can discriminate the acoustic contrasts that are fundamental to segmental recognition. Infants at this young age also can discriminate (a) their own mother's voice from the voices of other women (DeCasper and Fifer, 1980), (b) some foreign utterances from utterances in the parent language (Mehler et al. 1988), and (c) forward and backward played versions of a native or nonnative vowel sound (Weintraub, Walton, and Bower, 1992). In short, there is a sensitivity to the speech patterns of individuals, to the ambient language, and to the general acoustic properties of natural speech.

One to four months. Infants within this interval can normalize for different talkers (Jusczyk, Pisoni, and Mullennix, in press) and for different speaking rates. That is, they can detect the same vowel when spoken by different talkers (who produce the vowel with different acoustic properties), and can recognize the same element when spoken at different rates of speech. Infants of about this age also can detect variations in intonational patterns and can recognize the same syllable in different utterances.

Four to six months. The infant can detect prosodic markers for clausal units and has a preference for infant directed over adult directed speech (Fernald, 1985; Fernald and Kuhl, 1987). There is also some ability to match vocalizations with appropriate facial shapes, especially for vowels (Kuhl and Meltzoff, 1982).

Six to eight months. Infants demonstrate the use of prosodic features to distinguish foreign words from words in the parent language.

Seven to ten months. There is now a decline in the ability to detect certain foreign contrasts, perhaps indicating that the infant has developed some aspects of a language-specific phonetic recognition (Werker and Pegg, 1992; Werker and Tees, 1984). Support for this conclusion comes from evidence that infants at this age have some ability to distinguish foreign from native words on the basis of phonetic cues. And, significantly, it is in this period that the first systematic evidence appears for the comprehension of some words – usually specific, context-supported words such as *no no, bye bye,* or the child's name (Bates, Thal, and Janowsky, 1992). Nine-month-olds also respond differentially to utterances that are artificially segmented at linguistically coincident, as opposed to noncoincident, boundaries (Jusczyk et al., in press).

Ten to twelve months. By this age, the child may have reorganized the perceptual categories to match the phonetic structure of the native language (Werker and Pegg, 1992). Evidence for this conclusion is that the infant of this age appears to have lost the ability to discriminate some acoustic contrasts

Figure 11.1 Comparison of the vocal tract anatomy for infants and adults.

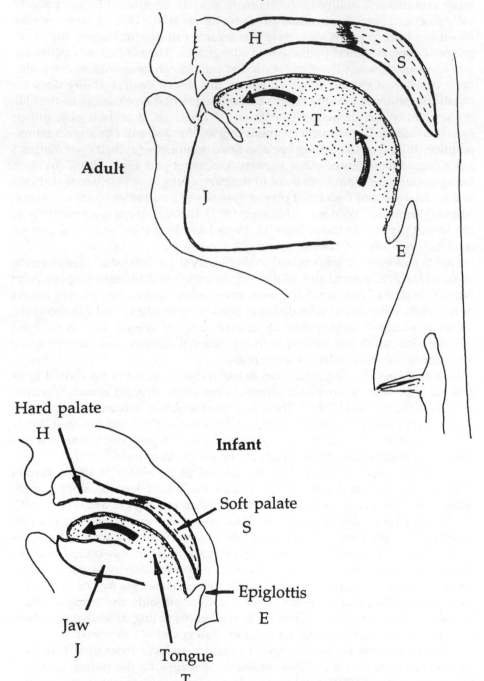

that are not used in the ambient language. An early capacity to discriminate the acoustic contrasts appropriate for a variety of phonetic distinctions in different languages seems to be replaced by discriminatory abilities that are attuned to experience in a particular language.

3 Speech Production in Infants

Phonetic abilities of production are defined broadly to include speechlike vocalizations uttered by infants within the first year of life. Among the sounds excluded from the present discussion are vegetative sounds (burps, hiccoughs, and the like), fuss and cry, and laughter. Also excluded are nonaudible movements of the speech organs. The exclusion is not meant to imply that these sounds and oral behaviors lack communicative value or are irrelevant to the development of language. Fuss, cry, laughter, and even nonvocalized oral movements may figure prominently in an infant's early communicative experience. They may well be central to early emotional interactions between infant and caregiver (Kent, Mitchell, and Sancier, 1991; Trevarthen and Marwick, 1986). The exclusion of these sounds from the present review is not because they are unimportant but only because space limitations demand that boundaries of some kind be drawn. The boundaries in effect here determine a class of sounds that are arguably *speechlike* in character. Grunts are a special challenge to phonetic studies. Although these sounds have been neglected in some studies, their high frequency of occurrence, interaction with other vocal types, and possible communicative significance are reasons for careful investigation of their production (Kent and Bauer, 1985; McCune, 1992).

3.1 Developmental anatomy of the vocal tract

Phonetic studies of infant sounds often assume implicitly or explicitly that infants and adults share a similar sound production mechanism. However, anatomical evidence belies this assumption (Bosma, 1975; Kent, 1992a, b; Lieberman, Harris, Wolff, and Russel, 1971; Lieberman, Crelin, and Klatt, 1971). Until the age of about three months, the infant has a vocal tract configuration that is more like that of nonhuman primates than the adult human. Some differences between infant and adult vocal tracts are shown in figure 11.1. Specifically, the infant's larynx has an elevated position, so that the epiglottis nearly touches the velum (an arrangement called engagement of the larynx and velopharynx). The pharyngeal cavity is very short compared to that of the adult, and the infant's oral cavity is relatively broader. The infant's tongue nearly fills the oral cavity and is biomechanically suited to back-and-forth piston-like movements. It is only by about four months that the infant's vocal tract is remodeled to resemble that of the adult human. But developmental changes continue in a number of respiratory, laryngeal, and supralaryngeal structures. The full significance of these changes for phonation and articulation is not well understood, but it is likely that at least some of them are relevant in evaluating the phonetic capabilities of infants.

Unfortunately, only limited data are available on the relative rates of development of the various structures that are involved in speech production. However, from the evidence that has been published, it is reasonable to conclude that the various tissues (muscle, bone, cartilage, and other tissues in different parts of the vocal tract) do not have a linear rate of growth, nor do all tissues grow at the same rates (Hirano, Kurita, and Nakachima, 1983; Kent, 1984; Polger and Weng, 1979; Stark, 1979). This situation is typical of ontogeny. As Gollin (1981) remarked, "Because the various structures and functions change at different rates during ontogenesis, the configurational character of the system is different at successive periods in the life sequence of an organism" (p. 239).

3.2   Neural maturation associated with vocal development

In addition to the major changes that occur in the musculoskeletal system that supports vocalization, infancy is marked by rapid and impressive changes in the nervous system. Myelogenetic cycles have been cited as important correlates of vocal development in infants (Lecours, 1975). Netsell (1981) pointed out that neural maturation occurring in the three to nine month period of infancy includes myelination of the pyramidal tract, postthalamic somatosensory pathways, and corpus striatum. Major developmental changes also occur in the middle cerebellar peduncle. Netsell explains the significance of these changes: "Taken together, these motor corticifugal–striatal–cerebellar–thalamic sensorimotor cortical connections are forming a network of loops or circuits that are most strongly implicated in more recent theories of fine motor control" (p. 140).

Of course, the cerebral cortex is preeminent in many discussions of the neural maturation needed to support language development. Milner (1976) proposed that mere vocalization could be subcortically controlled, but that preverbal babbling requires the functioning of the lower three layers of the cortex. Whitaker (1976) speculated that babbling reflects both the maturation of Broca's area and an increasing interaction between Broca's area and Wernicke's area via the arcuate fasciculus. Scheibel (1993) examined brain tissue from children ranging in age from three months to 72 months using a quantitative Golgi method. He observed that dendritic development was initially greater in the cortical areas subserving orofacial and laryngopharyngeal motor control than in the cortical areas that correspond to Broca's (motor speech) area and its homologous area on the contralateral hemisphere. One interpretation of these data is that babbling reflects maturation of the motor cortex more than of Broca's area. Scheibel also noted better development of dendritic systems initially in the language related areas of the right hemisphere, but this trend began to be reversed after the first year of life.

Scheibel's data indicate that near the end of the first year, the infant has relatively advanced development of the motor regions of the cortex associated with vocalization and a relatively advanced development of the right as opposed to the left language area. This cortical development seems appropriate to support the motor activity in first-year vocalizations such as cooing and babbling. The significance of the earlier cortical development in the right hemisphere is uncertain, particularly given that infants as young as three months of age demonstrate a left hemisphere bias in the auditory processing of some speech sounds (Molfese and Segalowitz, 1988). Perhaps perceptual mechanisms are drawn to the left hemisphere early in infancy, while the motor systems that serve vocalization develop earlier in the right. The right hemisphere in adults is often associated with holistic processing, such as the processing of melody or rhythm (Ross and Mesulam, 1979). A relatively mature right hemisphere may support the rhythmic processes that many ascribe to babbling in the second half-year of life (Kent, Mitchell, and Sancier, 1991). The development asynchrony between the two hemispheres would ensure some independence of development of these cortical regions while allowing for an eventual integration of the sensory and motoric aspects of speech behavior. Bates, Thal, and Janowsky (1992) also describe possible correlates of early language development. They suggest that regional connectivity established by nine to ten months correlates with the first evidence of word comprehension. More specifically, Bates et al. point to the establishment of long-range connections among brain regions and to the establishment of adultlike patterns of metabolism (Cheguni, Phelps, and Mazziota, 1987) as important neural correlates of language behavior in the first year of life. Combining Schiebel's observations with the pattern of neural development described by Bates et al., one might think of the one-year-old as having a roughly adultlike metabolic pattern, extensive corticocortical connections, and a fairly well-developed cortex for motor control of the structures of vocalization. This neural groundwork is the essential base for the development of language. Another important ingredient is the rich variety of sensory information available to the infant engaged in vocalization and in the routines of mother–infant interaction. This plurimodal sensory information enables the infant to correlate different types of afference (auditory, visual, tactile, kinesthetic) and to associate sensory effects with motor initiatives (Kent, 1992c).

3.3 Syllables in infant vocalizations

What is it that makes a vocalization speechlike? Apparently, the single best criterion may be syllabicity. Bloom (1988) concluded that the "speechiness" of an infant's vocalization is related to the perception of syllables and has its

Table 11.1   Acoustic features of the canonical syllable, as defined by Oller (1986)

Feature	Description
Power envelope	Peaks and valleys differ by at least 10dB
Syllable duration	In the range of 100–500 ms
Syllable nucleus	Has a periodic source and a relatively open vocal tract
Syllable shape	Has at least one margin of low resonance with a relatively obstructed vocal tract
Formant pattern	Smooth formant transitions between the margin(s) and nucleus; transition duration falls in the range of 25–120 ms
Intensity range	Less than about 30dB
Vocal frequency	Fundamental frequency range of less than about one octave

beginnings in about the third month of life. Definitional problems notwith-standing, the syllable appears to be a unit that can be usefully applied to the vocalizations of infants.

It is one thing to assert that syllables are useful and quite another to define what they are. We may well heed the cautions from phonology and phonetics. Haugen (1956) stated, "The syllable has become something of a stepchild in linguistic description. While sooner or later everyone finds it convenient to use, no one does much about defining it." Goldsmith (1990) noted that the syllable has been the subject of persistent discussions in the phonological literature of this century and that it is now clear to "even the most skeptical observers that the syllable could not be overlooked by phonological theory" (p. 104). If syllables define "speechiness" (the essential auditory quality of human speech) and if syllables are a potent construct in phonological theory, then there is sufficient motivation to learn more about syllables in infant vocalizations. It has been suggested that syllables may be important units by which infants learn the basic phonological structure of English and perhaps all languages (Kent, 1992c).

Oller (1978) also drew attention to the syllable, particularly the *canonical syllable*, which he related to a concept of "the minimal rhythmic unit of natural languages, the syllable, and its components, the nucleus, the margin(s), and the formant transition(s)" (p. 24). Oller (1986) regarded this unit as a means of bridging the "methodological chasm" between acoustic and phonetic approaches to the study of infant vocalizations. The canonical syllable was proposed as a construct that could be defined both phonetically and acoustically (in terms of a number of measures dealing primarily with power envelope, duration, formant structure, and prosodic range; see table 11.1). The canonical syllable is the basic constituent of *canonical babbling*, which typically first appears at about the seventh month of life. This form of babbling is significant both for its apparent reliance on a unit similar to the syllables in adult speech and for its productivity of repetitive and variegated babbling strings. Oller recognized an earlier and more primitive type of syllable, the *marginal syllable*, which may be a precursor of the canonical syllable.

More conventionally, syllables have been defined in terms of phonetic description, such as a sequence of consonantlike and vowellike sounds apparently produced as an articulatory or prosodic unit. For example, Kent and Bauer (1985) analyzed the vocalizations of five 13-month-olds with respect to the syllable types used in phonetic transcriptions of the infants' utterances. The syllable structures were, in order of decreasing frequency of occurrence:

V (60%)   CV (19%)   CVCV (8%)   VCV (7%)   VC (2%)   CVC (2%)

The listed syllable types accounted for about 98 percent of the syllable structures produced by the infants. The V and CV categories alone accounted for 79 percent of the patterns. Bisyllabic utterances tended to be either CVCV or VCV in form.

Vihman (1992) analyzed the types of syllables produced by children in different language environments, with particular emphasis on "practiced" syllables, or syllables that appeared frequently in the infants' utterances. She concluded that the six top ranked of the practiced syllables were, in decreasing order of frequency:

[da], [ba], [wa], [də], [ha], and [hə].

These six syllables alone accounted for half (50.3 percent) of the practiced syllables. In terms of their phonetic constituents, these syllables conform to the following patterns: (1) vocants (the vocalic portions) tend to be low-back or central; (2) closants (consonantal portions) tend to be bilabial, apical, or glottal; and (3) closants made with a supraglottal constriction are voiced. Apparently, these phonetic characteristics are largely independent of the phonology of the parental language. For example, [h] occurs frequently not only for English infants but also for French infants (French does not have the /h/ phoneme). Vihman's analyses conform to a frequently reported conclusion: infants' syllables are largely of CV or V structure.

(It is interesting that at least three of the practiced syllables may not qualify as a canonical syllable by Ollers' (1986) definition. Because [wa] has prolonged formant transitions, it very likely would be excluded from canonical syllables. Because [h] does not typically have well defined formant transitions, it also would be excluded. Hence, strict conformance to Oller's definition may exclude from canonical babbling some frequently occurring syllables.)

Whether or not the syllable proves to be the unit of choice in analyzing infant vocalizations, it is a convenient pivot for discussion. Internal examination of the syllable reveals the phonetic elements of the infant's vocalizations, and external examination discloses the position of a given syllable in larger prosodic contexts, such as rhythmic babbling sequences, or dyadic exchanges between mother and infant. MacNeilage and Davis (1990) believed that the motoric capability to produce alternating sequences of louder sounds (vowels) and weaker sounds (consonants) is an important step in vocal development. They further proposed that canonical syllables in early babbling could be produced almost entirely by mandibular movement. Hodge (1989) reached a similar conclusion from acoustic studies of infant babbling which showed that jaw movement is a primary factor underlying early syllable sequences, even some sequences involving a lingual articulation for the consonant. Hodge explained that as the tongue passively moves along with the jaw, the infant can produce articulations that are perceived as alveolar stop + vowel sequences.

MacNeilage and Davis (1990) proposed a frame/content hypothesis for early babbling behavior that is based on a syllable construct. This hypothesis holds that the prosodic form of early babbling constitutes a "frame" within which later segmental components (the "content") could be inserted. Alternating loudness patterns associated with consonantlike and vowellike sounds is the prosodic frame. Subsequent experience enables the infant to learn how to insert various phonetic elements (content) into the frame.

We turn next to phonetic analyses, or what MacNeilage and Davis might refer to as the "content" of infant utterances.

3.4   *Phonetic elements of infants' vocalizations*

Phonetic description has been the traditional method of studying infant vocalizations. The intent has been to identify the phonetic segments that correspond to those in adult languages. Irwin, in particular, published a series of studies that described infant utterances in terms of the phonetic elements judged to constitute them. This work relates primarily to the question: what phonetic segments do adults hear in infant vocalizations? The question probably should be expressed in a more refined form as follows: what phonetic segments do adults with a particular language background hear in infant vocalizations? That is, adult listeners tend to hear segments relevant to their own linguistic experience. Two polar hypotheses have been considered. The first hypothesis is that infant vocalizations contain virtually all of the sounds from the world's languages. With this hypothesis, the process of mastering a particular phonetic system is mainly one of contraction, or selecting the desired phonetic elements from a larger set. The second hypothesis is that infant vocalizations begin with a restricted set of sounds that is augmented with exposure to a language. These two hypotheses, contraction and expansion, motivated some of the early research on the phonetic characteristics of infant babbling.

3.5   *Vowel (vocant) sounds*

Irwin and his associates (Chen and Irwin, 1946; Irwin, 1947a, b, 1948; Irwin and Chen, 1946) conducted a series of studies that provide phonetic descriptions of infant vocalizations. In these studies, the vocalizations of 95 infants were phonetically transcribed once every two months over two and one-half years. Sounds produced by each child during 30 noncrying breath exhalations over a 30-minute period were transcribed by two observers using a sound classification system consisting of 28 consonant phonemes (all but two of which occur in American English), 11 vowels, and five diphthongs (Irwin and Chen, 1946).

Mowrer (1980) summarized the work of Irwin and associates with respect to four stages of development: (1) 0–2 months, (2) 2–4 months, (3) 4–8 months, and (4) 8–12 months. A major change that occurs over these stages is the vowel-to-consonant (V/C) ratio, which assumed the following values for the four stages: (1) 4.5, (2) 3.6, (3) 2.8, and (4) 2.0. The overwhelming predominance of vowels in the first stage gradually gives way to a 2 : 1 ratio, which is still more vowel dominated than adult speech. The vowels identified in phonetic transcription varied relatively little with respect to their frequency of occurrence at a given stage. The rank order of frequency of occurrence for Stage 1 was: /ɛ/ (43 percent), /I/ (27.4 percent), /ʌ/ (25.2 percent), and all other vowels combined (4.4 percent). At Stage 2, /ɛ ʌ I/ continued to constitute the great majority of vowel productions (for a total of 81.5 percent), but the remaining vowels were produced with a somewhat greater frequency of occurrence than at Stage 1. Patterns of vowel production at Stages 3 and 4 were similar to those at Stage 2, although the proportion of vowels other than /ɛ ʌ I/ increased to just over 30 percent at Stage 4. It appears from these results that although the V/C ratio diminishes considerably over the four stages of development, the nature of vowel articulation is altered relatively little during this period. For the most part, the infants produce vowels with midfront or central tongue carriage.

Kent and Bauer's (1985) analyses of vocant (V) and vocant + vocant (VV) sounds in one-year-old infants showed marked inequalities in frequency of occurrence. By far the most frequently occurring vocant was the central /ʌ/ or /ə/ (partly because of its frequent appearance in gruntlike vocalizations). These two central vowels (which will be considered as a single vowel because of the perceptual difficulty of assigning stress to distinguish them) accounted for nearly half (46 percent) of the total vocant production. The next most frequently occurring vocants were /ɑ/ (22 percent), /æ/ (8 percent), and /v/ (6 percent). These four most frequently occurring vocants accounted for 82 percent of the vocants in V and VV utterances.

Individual differences in vocant production are noteworthy. Table 11.2 shows the rank order for frequency of occurrence of vocants produced in V and VV utterances in Kent and Bauer's analyses. Table 11.3 presents the rank orders for vocants in CV syllables. The most frequently occurring vocants in V, VV, or CV utterances (first or second rank) were /ʌ/, /ɛ/, or /ɑ/. But the vocants in the third through fifth ranks were quite variable, including, for one infant's CV syllables, even the vowel /i/, which tends to be infrequently recorded in first-year vocalizations. Although general statements can be made about vocants

Table 11.2 Rank order for frequency of occurrence of vocants produced by one-year-olds in Vocant or Vocant + Vocant utterances. The number in parentheses is the number of utterances on which the ranks are based for each infant.

| | Rank order | | | | |
	1	2	3	4	5
Infant 1 (152)	ʌ	ɛ	æ	ʊ	e
Infant 2 (269)	ʌ	ɛ	ʊ	æ	ɑ
Infant 3 (141)	ɛ	ʌ	æ	e	ʊ
Infant 4 (295)	ʌ	ɛ	e	ʊ	æ
Infant 5 (313)	ʌ	ɛ	o	æ	ʊ

Source: Based on data from Kent and Bauer (1985)

Table 11.3 Rank order for frequency of occurrence of vocants produced by one-year-olds in CV utterances

| | Rank order | | | | |
	1	2	3	4	5
Infant 1 (27)	ɛ	ɑ	ə/ʌ	ɛ =	æ
Infant 2 (82)	ɑ	ɛ	ʌ	æ	i
Infant 3 (76)	ɛ	ʌ	æ	ɪ	ʊ
Infant 4 (142)	ʌ	ɑ	i	e	o = ʊ
Infant 5 (42)	ɑ	ɛ	ʌ	o	a

Source: Based on data from Kent and Bauer (1985)

favored in infant vocalizations, considerable allowance must be made for individual patterns. One difference between the data in tables 11.2 and 11.3 deserves comment: vocant /ɑ/ tended to occur with very high frequency in CV syllables but appeared in the top five ranks for only one infant's V or VV utterances. Perhaps vocant /ɑ/ has a natural advantage in combining with consonants in CV-syllable production. Vihman's (1992) data for highly practiced syllables show a similar preference. In her data, the six most frequently occurring "practiced" syllables were formed of either /a/ or /ə/ vocants.

In summary, vocants produced in the first year of life tend to be heard by adult observers predominantly as mid to lowfront, central, or mid to lowback. High vowels such as /i/ and /u/ are rather infrequently heard, although individual infants may produce these vocants fairly often. Interestingly, the high vowels /i/ and /u/, which are not frequent in babbling, are among the most accurately produced vowels in later speech development (Davis and MacNeilage, 1990; Hare, 1983; Hodge, 1989; Otomo, 1988; Paschell, 1983).

Possibly, the near absence of high vowels reflects anatomical constraints. Lieberman (1975, 1977) believed that the right-angled craniovertebral relationship with two distinct vocal tract cavities (oral and pharyngeal) was necessary for production of /i/ and /u/. As noted above, this vocal tract configuration is a developmental accomplishment within the first year of life. Anatomic–physiological factors also were considered by Kent (1992a) as possible determinants of vowel mastery in infants and young children. Davis and MacNeilage (1990) concluded from their analysis of the vowel development of one infant that, "None of the vowels favored in prespeech babbling were both strongly favored and usually correctly produced in words, independent of context, in this subject" (p. 25). This observation, if verified for a large number of subjects, would point to a discontinuity of vowel production between babbling and later phonetic development. Such a discontinuity would be an important exception to a growing literature that indicates a considerable degree of phonetic continuity between babbling and early words (Oller, Wieman, Doyle, and Ross, 1976; Vihman, Ferguson, and Elbert, 1986).

A growing number of acoustic studies help to define some of the acoustic properties associated with phonetic events in infant vocalizations. Most of the acoustic work has focused on vowellike sounds which are usually easier to analyze than consonantlike sounds. Formant-frequency determination is the favored acoustic analysis for vowels. Some procedural limitations should be noted. In particular, analysis is complicated by high fundamental frequencies (resulting in formant–harmonic interaction), large formant bandwidths, nasalization, and variations in phonation (Kent and Read, 1992).

Acoustic measurements have been used to derive quantitative data on the durations of vowel sounds, which, by virtue of their relatively high intensity, readily lend themselves to temporal analysis. Increasing durations of vocalization have been reported in longitudinal studies of infants in the first few months of life (Papousek and Papousek, 1981; Zlatin-Laufer and Horii, 1977) and over the range of three to nine months in a cross-sectional study by Kent and Murray (1982). Papousek and Papousek (1981) noted that vowel sounds in the infant they studied frequently were produced in rhythmic sequences of four to eight units per expiration, with vowel duration ranging from 150–1,100 mseconds. A faster articulatory rhythm appeared at about the third month. Stark (1978), in a study of coo vocalizations, reported that these sounds occurred as single units upon first emergence at 8–12 weeks but shortly afterward tended to be produced in a series, with pauses of no greater than 1-second duration between successive coos. Vocal sequences were observed in somewhat older infants (4–8 months) by D'Odorico, Franco, and Vidotto (1985). Vocalizations were segmented into vocal sequences in which each sequence was separated from temporally adjacent utterances by a pause of at least two seconds. Then a further segmentation was made for Units of Vocalization (UVs), which were defined as vocalizations separated by an interruption of phonation that lasted at least 50 mseconds. The number of UVs per sequence varied from 1–16 with a mean of 1.56 for noncry calls. The pause durations between noncry UVs were in the range of 627–93 mseconds. These studies on the temporal patterns of vocalizations in the first few months indicate a developmental change toward longer vocalizations and vocalizations occurring in series rather than in isolation. Pauses of varying lengths define the temporal structure of these early sounds, but a pause duration in the range of 0.5–1 second appears to be particularly frequent.

Formant structure is an attractive tool for the study of vowellike sounds, given that a relatively small set of measures (the first two or three formant frequencies) may suffice as an acoustic description of vowel production. However, relatively few data on formant frequencies have been reported for the first year of life. In a cross-sectional study involving infants aged three, six, and nine months, Kent and Murray (1982) observed a gradual increase in the F1–F2 regions for sampled vocant productions. The ranges for the first two formant frequencies were as follows for each age group: three-month-olds, 0.5–1.5 kHz for F1 and 1.8–3.8 kHz for F2; six-month-olds, 0.5–1.7 kHz for F1 and 1.6–3.89 kHz for F2; nine-month-olds, 0.5–1.8 kHz for F1 and 1.4–4.1 kHz for F2. These ranges are illustrated in figure 11.2. Roughly comparable ranges were reported by Buhr (1980) in a longitudinal study of one infant and by Kent et al. (1986) in a longitudinal study of monozygotic twins who differed in auditory function.

Hodge (1989) studied vowel production in infants, children, and adults, using perceptually validated vowel tokens. The criterion for perceptual validation was that four of five listeners had to identify the vowel. The perceptual accuracy varied across vowels in a way that was largely independent of age. For all subjects, /i/ and /u/ had the highest accuracy, /ae/ had an intermediate accuracy, and /ɑ/ and /ʌ/ had the lowest accuracy. Hodge evaluated a Bark-difference transformation as a means of normalizing acoustic data on vowel formant frequencies across the various age groups. Speaker normalization is an important issue in infant–adult comparisons because of the large differences between these groups when linear frequency is used to express acoustic measures of formant values. Bark-difference values have been proposed as a partial solution to the speaker normalization problem. The Bark scale, or critical band scale, was derived from a variety of psychoacoustic studies. It serves as a nonlinear tonality scale for human audition. Hodge calculated Bark differences for F2–F1 and F3–F2 as recommended by Syrdal and Gopal (1986). These transformations accomplished normalization quite well for the point vowels /i u a ae/, achieving nearly complete separation of the data clusters for the different vowels. Hodge's results demonstrate the applicability of the Bark-difference measure to infant vocants, and it is likely that the Bark-difference transformation or other normalization procedures will be increasingly applied in acoustic studies of infant vocalizations.

By virtue of their frequent production and perceptual salience, vocants are of special interest in crosslanguage studies. In a series of investigations, Boysson-Bardies and associates have sought to determine the age at which an infant begins to adjust vocant production in accord with the vowel patterns of the

Figure 11.2 First and second formant frequency ranges for the vocant sounds produced by an infant at the ages of 8, 12, and 15 months. Reprinted from Kent et al. (1986) with permission from the American Speech–Language–Hearing Association.

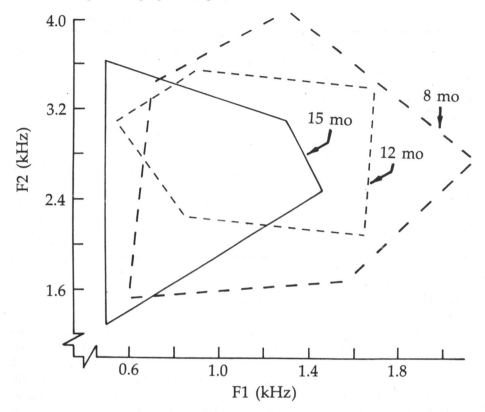

ambient language. In an acoustic study by Boysson-Bardies, Sagart, Halle, and Durand (1986), Long Term Spectrum (LTS) analysis was used to compare the vocant spectra of ten-month-old infants with reference vowel spectra for adult speakers representing the infants' language groups (French, Algerian, Arabic, and Cantonese). The LTS results were interpreted as evidence of general spectral similarities among adult males, adult females, and infants within a language group. For example, French and Cantonese infants had an LTS with a dominant peak, but the peak was higher in frequency for the Cantonese subjects (about 1200 Hz) compared to the French infants (about 825 Hz). The LTS for Algerian infants had two peaks, one about 830 Hz and the other at about 1600 Hz. In a related study, crosslinguistic adjustments for vowel formant frequencies were described by Boysson-Bardies, Halle, Sagart, and Durand (1989). These studies, together with other acoustic and perceptual studies by Boysson-Bardies and her colleagues, indicates that babbling takes on certain characteristics of the parent language in a kind of attunement process.

Table 11.4 Frequency of occurrence of closants in babbling for 15 different languages as summarized by Locke (1983a)

Repertoire		Nonrepertoire	
Consonant	Frequency	Consonant	Frequency
b	100	v	39
m	100	l	36
p	87	ŋ	27
d	80	r	13
h	73	θ	7
n	73	z	7
t	67	f	7
g	60	ʃ	7
k	60	ð	7
j	47	ʒ	0
w	47	ʧ	0
s	20	ʤ	0

3.6 Consonant (closant) sounds

Locke (1983a) summarized phonetic patterns in infant babbling for a number of different language backgrounds. These analyses indicate a striking similarity across languages in the sounds most frequently produced by infants. Locke interpreted this crosslanguage congruence as evidence for biological determinants, given that the infants shared biological factors but not language background. The most frequently occurring and least frequently occurring closant sounds recorded by Locke are shown in table 11.4.

Irwin and colleagues conducted a series of studies that included the classification of consonants produced by infants (see section 3.4 for a summary description of procedures, but note in particular that the classification system for consonants included 28 phonemes, only two of which – /χ/ and /ç/ – are not part of the phonetic inventory of American English). It was concluded that consonant production changed in two major ways over the four stages of development (0–2, 2–4, 4–8, 8–12 months). First, as noted earlier, the vowel-to-consonant ratio declined from 4.5 at Stage 1 to 2.0 at Stage 4. By the end of their first year, the infants greatly increased the proportion of consonants in their vocalizations. The second major change is in the repertoire of consonants. At Stage 1, the majority (87 percent) of consonants were /h/ and /ʔ/, followed by /k/ and /g/ (for a combined 11.6 percent). The remaining 4.4 percent included /m ç b t ʃ n p w/ (listed in decreasing order of occurrence). A similar pattern of consonant production was noted at Stage 2. The glottal fricative /h/ was still the most prominent consonant, accounting for 59.8 percent of the consonants produced. It was followed by /ʔ/ at 15.5 percent and /g/ at 11.7 percent. The remaining consonants, listed in order of most to least frequent, were: /k d b w l j m θ t ð n ŋ p v ç z ʃ s χ/ (Irwin, 1947b). According to Irwin's data, /ʍ f z/ were the only consonant sounds not produced by infants at four months of age. The glottal /h/ retained its dominance at Stage 3, accounting for 59.9 percent of the consonants tallied. Somewhat reduced frequencies (compared to Stage 2) were seen for the consonants /ʔ/ (10.5 percent), /g/ (6.4 percent). Slight increases were observed for /m b k/. Marked changes occurred at Stage 4, with /d/ increasing 45-fold to 18.1 percent, and a doubling of frequency for /m/ and /b/ (to 16 percent), while /h/ was reduced in frequency by nearly half (36.5 percent). The glottal stop /ʔ/, which occurred at high frequency at earlier stages, now joined the ranks of infrequently occurring consonants with a percentage of only 4.8.

One way of characterizing changes in consonant production is by noting a change from predominantly laryngeal to predominantly supralaryngeal stricture. The laryngeal sounds /h ʔ/ are overwhelmingly dominant at Stage 1 but fall to less than 50 percent in their combined total by Stage 4. Accompanying the decline in the occurrence of laryngeal consonants is an increase in lingual and labial consonants, especially /d/ and /m b/.

Smith and Oller (1981) reported a longitudinal study of the relative frequency of place of consonant production in nine typically developing infants from birth through 12–15 months of life. The only remarkable change occurred between their first age sample (birth to six months) and their second age sample (six to nine months). The change was a marked drop in the frequency of occurrence of the velar place of production and an increase in the number of consonants with an alveolar place of production. Consonant production patterns for place of articulation were virtually unchanged for the age span from the six to nine month sample to the 15–21 month sample, despite the fact that the early sample was judged to contain virtually no meaningful speech whereas the later sample contained meaningful speech productions. In evaluating this conclusion, Smith (1988) wrote,

> it is logical to conclude that physical and biological characteristics of their speech-production mechanisms were the primary factors responsible for the premeaningful sound patterns observed during this age range [and] that intrinsic properties of the speech-production system continued to significantly influence the types of consonants produced in these children's meaningful lexical items from 15–21 months of age. (p. 84)

After much neglect, crosslanguage studies of infant sound patterns are being pursued with great interest. Work by Boysson-Bardies and associates has spurred much of this interest. A fundamental objective is to determine the age at which infants' babbling assumes some of the phonetic qualities of the ambient language. Boysson-Bardies et al. (1986) demonstrated with acoustic analyses (reviewed earlier in this chapter) that the vocalic spaces of ten-month-old infants reflected crosslinguistic differences for adults from different language groups. Boysson-Bardies et al. (1992) pursued this question with respect to the consonant inventories of infant vocalizations, concluding that some crosslinguistic differences were present at the earliest age examined (9–13 months). For example, with respect to manner of production, French infants produced more nasals but fewer stops than Swedish infants. With respect to place of production, French and English infants produced more labials than Japanese and Swedish infants, but Japanese infants produced more velars than English or French infants. In several of the comparisons, the distribution of the target consonants in the adult languages predicted the pattern for the infants' consonants. Thus, the patterns summarized above for labials and velars reflect the fact that French has a high frequency of labials but a low frequency of velars.

Vocant and closant results are similar in that although certain sounds of each type tend to occur with very high frequencies of occurrence in group data, individual infants may show production patterns that do not conform to group trends. Sound inventories are probabilistic rather than highly determined.

There have been very few acoustic studies of consonant sounds in infant utterances, but the published reports demonstrate that acoustic methods can be informative. However, special considerations pertain to this kind of study applied to the sounds of infants. Bauer and Kent (1987) reported data on the spectral content of fricative and trill sounds produced in the first year of life. The data indicate that these infant sounds contain significant energy that runs to 16 kHz or higher, which extends considerably beyond the 8 kHz limit conventionally used in spectrography. Some [s]-like fricatives judged to be produced with an apical articulation had their primary energy between about 5–14 kHz. In comparison, apical fricatives in adult speech have their primary energy in the frequency range of 3.5–8 kHz (Strevens, 1960). Trills resembled fricatives in their spectral content but often were produced with longer durations, especially in their isolated forms. Trill rates for infants varied from 16–180 closures/s, compared with rates of 26–32 closures/s for adult speakers (Disner and Ladefoged, 1976). Trill rate varies little with place of articulation for both infants and adults.

The developmental pattern by which acoustic cues come to serve phonetic function may vary with acoustic–phonetic classes, but one pattern that has important implications was described for the word-initial voicing contrast. Macken and Barton (1980) reported a three stage pattern for voice onset time (VOT) for word-initial stop consonants. Initially, children make no acoustic distinction between voiced and voiceless cognates. At a second stage, the children make a consistent contrast, but the acoustic contrast is made with VOT values that fall within the VOT range for one of the adult categories. For example, the children may produce reliable differences for /p/ and /b/, but both sets of values fall within the adult range of VOT values for /b/. Accordingly, adults will hear both sound classes as a /b/. At the third stage, the children produce the cognates with VOT values that conform to the adult pattern. The results of the Macken and Barton study are important because they (1) indicate one pattern of acoustic–phonetic development for speech sounds, and (2) demonstrate the sensitivity of acoustic methods to developmental changes that may be missed by perceptual evaluation alone.

In the phonetic studies of infant vocalization reviewed in this section, the emphasis has been placed on the use of phonetic methods to record infant sounds. But the use of phonetic methods to represent infant utterances does not necessarily mean that the infant in fact uses phonetic segments or phonemes to control vocalizations (Kent and Bauer, 1985). Lindblom (1992) proposed that phonetic gestures are *emergents*. He wrote, "children end up with phonemes for two reasons. They possess the necessary conceptual capacity and the communicative need to develop large lexicons" (p. 158). It is not clear to what extent infants in the first year of life have converged on phonemic organization. It appears reasonably certain that the infant makes some adjustments in the direction of the parent language, but these adjustments may not qualify as phonemic organization. It is well to heed the caution that just because phonetic (or phonemic) transcriptions can be made of infant utterances, it is not necessarily the case that the infants have phonetic systems congruent with those of their adult caregivers.

3.7 *Prosodic features of infants' vocalizations*

Prosodic analysis has been suggested either as a primary aspect of infant vocalizations or as a complementary aspect to phonetic (segmental) analysis. In one of the largest studies of prosodic characteristics (in terms of numbers of subjects and vocalizations recorded), Delack and Fowlow (1978) made biweekly recordings of 19 infants over the age range of one to 12 months. The following patterns emerged from their analyses of over 11,000 vocalizations:

1 The mean f0 is stable over the first year of life (with an overall mean of 355 Hz).
2 The mean duration increases by about 50 percent over the 12-month period.
3 The range of f0 increases by about 20 percent during the first six months, then increases further for the girls but decreases for the boys.
4 The rise–fall f0 contour occurred the most frequently and also showed the largest developmental change in frequency of occurrence (increasing from 40 to 55 percent during the first year).
5 The rank order of frequency of occurrence of f0 contours was similar for boys and girls. The order for females was (R = rise; F = fall; L = level): RF, F, FRF, RFR and R, FR, L. The order for males was: RF, FRF, F and RFR, R, FR, L.

6   In addition to an increase in the frequency of occurrence of the RF contour, the group data show a decline followed by an increase in the R contour, an overall decline in F and L contours, and an overall increase (but mostly in the early periods) in RFF contours.

A nutshell summary of these results is that during the first year of life, vocalizations get longer, the f0 range increases, and the RF f0 contour becomes increasingly common. Subsequent studies are in general agreement with Delack and Fowlow's prosodic analyses. Kent and Bauer (1985) reported the following rank order of frequency of occurrence for f0 contours in the vocalizations of one-year-olds:

RF (55%)   F (22%)   R(10%)   RLF and LF (3% each)   L (2%)

Contours with a falling termination accounted for about 80 percent of the total. Unlike Delack and Fowlow, Kent and Bauer reported a very small usage of FRF and RFR contours. Possibly, differences in instrumentation and criterion may explain the different results for these contours.

Multisyllabic rhythmic patterns also have been described in infant vocalizations (Kent, Mitchell, and Sancier, 1991; Oller and Lynch, 1992). Evidence of such patterns comes from observations of temporal structure, fundamental frequency contour, or intensity envelope that are manifest over two or more syllables. Branigan (1979) drew attention to prosodic variables in deciding whether two or more utterances are simply successive single-word productions or multiword combinations. Prosodic coherence across utterances was seen in fundamental frequency contours that bridge the utterances or in durational adjustments, such as lengthening of the final utterance relative to an earlier utterance. Fundamental frequency contours that span several syllables appear to be ritualized, may be universal, and could have functional significance (Oller and Lynch, 1992). Multisyllabic patterns have particular interest because they may be a bridge between early monosyllabic utterances and the complex syllabic patterns of later babbling and running speech.

Oller and Lynch (1992) defined a unit that they called a "canonical utterance" as follows. First, the canonical utterance consists of at least one syllable (the minimal rhythmic unit). Second, prosodic coherence of the canonical utterance is evidenced by an integrity of amplitude and pitch contours occurring between breaths. Third, canonical utterances are separated by silent intervals (pauses) longer in duration than the 100–400 msec usually allowed for a syllable margin. These criteria accord closely with the concept of a breath group and identify a potentially multisyllable utterance that has a prosodic coherence. With these criteria, Oller and Lynch asked observers to identify "utterance clusters" in infant vocalizations. The authors concluded that, "when dealing with babbled utterances that are relatively easy to count, UC [utterance cluster] determination can be extremely reliable across difference judges working with nothing more than their own intuitions about which utterances go together" (p. 527). From an examination of the clustering of utterances, Oller and Lynch proposed that a canonical utterance cluster is a unitary grouping of a number of utterances (typically in the range of two to six) that tend to be produced in a time of one to eight seconds, with an optimal duration of about three seconds. Adult listeners attribute coherence to the utterance cluster on the bases of phonetic and/or suprasegmental similarities among the constituents of the cluster. Consecutive clusters tend to be separated by intervals longer than 1.5 seconds.

Another prosodic feature that has been investigated in infant vocalizations is Final Syllable Lengthening (FSL), or the lengthening of syllables that occur at the end of utterances or breath groups. FSL (also called prepausal lengthening) occurs in many adult languages at major syntactic boundaries. Given the generality and robustness of this phenomenon, some investigators thought it likely that FSL would emerge early in vocal development. The phenomenon is relatively easy to measure in infant vocalizations, requiring only segmentation of syllables.

Oller and Smith (1977) concluded that FSL did emerge early in infancy. They studied six infants (aged 8–12 months) and compared the durations of final v. nonfinal syllables in reduplicated babbling. Oller and Smith also compared the syllable durations of the infant vocalizations to those of adults who imitated the infants' babbling. Final syllables had longer durations than nonfinal syllables for both groups of subjects, but the adults had greater FSL effects. In view of the differences between infants and adults, Oller and Smith concluded that FSL is a learned behavior. In a study of four infants over the first six months of life, Laufer (1980) observed that in bisyllable utterances, final syllables were about half again as long as nonfinal syllables. Her data indicate that FSL precedes the onset of single words and continues as the infant acquires language. Laufer's interpretation was that FSL reflects an inherent temporal organization in which articulatory activity is linked to the breath cycle. Mitchell (1988) also found evidence of FSL in a study of bisyllabic utterances in infants at seven, nine, and 11 months. Finally, Robb and Saxman (1990), who studied seven infants from preword to multiword stages, observed FSL in "nearly every recording session for all children" (p. 591). They reported that final syllables were longer than nonfinal syllables in several types of bisyllable utterances (word v. nonword, open v. closed final syllable).

As noted by Kent, Mitchell, and Sancier (1991), the discrepancies between the results of Oller and Smith (1977) and those of Laufer (1980), Mitchell (1988), and Robb and Saxman (1990) may be partly attributable to the fact that Oller and Smith studied multisyllabic babbling, whereas the other investigators restricted their analyses to bisyllable utterances. Generally, FSL in adult speech is less pronounced in longer utterances or in connected discourse (Klatt, 1976; Umeda, 1975). It seems reasonable to conclude that FSL is apparent early in infancy, well before word production, but that its magnitude is governed by utterance properties, especially number of syllables.

Figure 11.3 Several stage descriptions of infant phonetic development in the first year of life. The approximate durations of the individual stages is shown for each system.

AGE (Months)	0	1	2	3	4	5	6	7	8	9	10	11	12
STARK (1979)	Reflexive crying and vegetative sounds			Cooing and laughter				Vocal play			Reduplicated babble			Nonreduplicated babble and expressive jargon
OLLER (1978)	Phonation			GOOing		Expansion		Canonical babble			Variegated babble		
HOLMGREN et al. (1986)	Cont. phon. with no artic.		Interr. phon. with no artic.	Continuous or interrupted phonation with no articulation		Continuous or interrupted phonation with one articulation		Phonatory variants with or without articulation		Continuous or interrupted phonation and reduplicated articulation			
ELBERS (1982)	Vocalizing								Repetitive	Concatenating			Mixing
KENT (1990)	Early phonation		Late phonation		Simple articulation with phonatory variants			Repetitive babbling		Multisyllabic babbling (Reduplicated and variegated babbling developing in parallel)			
NAKAZIMA (1980)	Reflexive crying		Development of phonatory-articulatory-auditory mechanisms of babbling							Reorganization of phonatory-articulatory-auditory mechanisms			

3.8 Implications of phonetic studies for stage models

It is helpful to chart the infant's progress with a developmental calendar of some kind. Phonetic abilities have been summarized with a number of stage descriptions. Although stage descriptions may not apply uniformly to all infants, they capture certain regularities and give some order to the events that mark the first year of life. Several stage descriptions are summarized in figure 11.3, which shows the stage chronology for the systems proposed by Elbers (1982), Holmgren et al. (1986), Oller (1978, 1980), Stark (1979, 1980), and Nakazima (1980).

The stages of development may overlap, and probably do. It should be noted that infants continue to babble even as they begin to utter their first words. The transition between stages is not necessarily abrupt, but the developmental sequence has been sufficiently compelling that stage descriptions have dominated the literature. It should be noted that stage descriptions have been a convenient way of charting changes in some patterns of infant vocalization, but the various stage models have not been rigorously tested.

Phonetic observations such as those in the foregoing sections have been a primary source of evidence for the postulation of stages of vocal development in infancy. The stage systems summarized in figure 11.3 derive in part from general phonetic properties ascribed to infant vocalizations. Although the different proposals of vocal stages are dissimilar in some respects, certain general features of commonality can be identified. The proposals typically recognize an early stage, from birth to one month, that is associated with cry and "reflexive" vocalizations such as grunts, belches, and coughs. Between about one and two months, the different stage systems tend to mark a developmental advance called vocal play, cooing, or phonation. A subsequent stage common to many of the systems is one that begins at about three months and extends to about six months. This stage is associated with an increasing degree of supralaryngeal articulatory behavior. Phonetically, this change is defined by a marked increase in the number of supraglottal constrictions compared with glottal strictures. At about six months, the various stage systems usually describe the emergence of multisyllabic babbling, known variously as repetitive, reduplicative, or canonical babbling. Toward the end of the first year, from about nine to twelve months, the stage systems typically agree on a further advance in the form of jargon babble or other labels denoting complex vocalizations.

Stage models are being examined more critically as the data on first-year vocalizations have become more abundant. Recent studies have not confirmed some aspects of individual stage models. Both the Stark and Elbers models propose that a repetitive (or reduplicated) babbling stage emerges at about six to seven months, to be followed by a stage in which repetitive patterns give way to nonrepetitive or concatening patterns. Failure to confirm this expectation was reported by Smith, Brown-Sweeney, and Stoel-Gammon (1989) and by Mitchell and Kent (1990). In both of these studies, reduplicated babbling was accompanied by variegated babbling even at the earliest appearance of multisyllabic patterns of babble. For example, Smith et al. reported that for the internal of six to nine months, reduplicated and variegated babble occurred at rates of 57 percent and 43 percent, respectively.

4   Analytic and Quantitative Methods

The scientific study of infant vocalizations has been marked by a growing set of analytic approaches. There has been considerable interest in developing quantitative indices of productivity and diversity. Productivity refers to the quantity or number of vocalizations. Diversity refers to contrastivity or variety among vocalizations. Phonetic development can be described both in terms of the amount of vocalization and the variety of types of vocalization. Tables 11.5 and 11.6 outline the major approaches to the quantitative study of infant vocalizations. Table 11.5 is a summary of perceptual methods used for inventories and quantitative indices. Table 11.6 is a summary of acoustic measures used in the study of infant vocalizations.

Limitations of perceptual and acoustic methods of analysis have been described in a number of papers, including Bauer and Kent (1987); Huggins (1980); Kent and Bauer (1985); Miller, Roussel, Daniloff, and Hoffman (1991); Oller and Eilers (1975); and Stockman, Woods, and Tishman (1981). A basic issue is determining which phonetic categories or acoustic measures are appropriate. Investigators have used a variety of categories and measures, and this variance in method can confound comparisons among various published studies. As noted earlier in this chapter, several stage descriptions of phonetic development have been proposed, so that even stage classification is not uniform.

Despite considerable progress in the development and refinement of research methods, several fundamental questions remain to be answered. Consider, for example, the very fundamental question: how many utterances should be sampled from one infant in order to obtain a reliable estimate of phonetic patterns? To give at least a preliminary answer to this question, a reanalysis was performed on the data from Kent and Bauer (1985) with respect to the measure, Mean Level of Babbling (MLB), as defined by Stoel-Gammon (1989). MLB was calculated for cumulative sets of 50 utterances; that is, MLB was calculated for the first 50 utterances, for the first 100, for the first 150, and so on. The results are graphed in figure 11.4, which shows how MLB varied for five infants for samples of increasing length. As sample length increases, the MLBs for all subjects converge. Apparently, a relatively large sample of utterances is needed to ensure a stable estimate of babbling complexity using the

Figure 11.4   Mean Level of Babbling (MLB) calculated for cumulative sets of 50 utterances produced by five one-year-olds. The patterns show the effect of calculating MLB on progressively larger utterance sets.

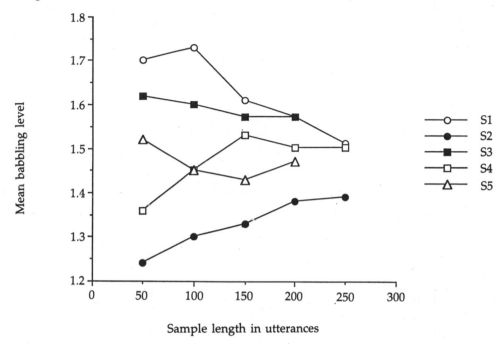

MLB measure. Unfortunately, clinicians and researchers often report data based on as few as 50 utterances.

Another basic issue pertains to phonetic transcription. What phonetic symbol system should be used? To begin with, there is no guarantee that infants will produce only those sounds that are found in adult languages. Indeed, given the anatomic differences between infant and adult vocal tracts, it is conceivable that infants can produce some sounds that would be difficult or impossible for an adult. The converse may also be true. But beyond this issue, there is the general question about the level of transcription that is most appropriate for describing infant sounds. For example, should the transcription be broad (roughly phonemic in the adult system) or narrow (to capture allophonic variations)? Presumably, the narrower the transcription, the more the information it provides. However, attempts to transcribe narrowly may be confounded by poor reliability within or across transcribers. And, if narrow transcription is used, what types of diacritics are needed? Stark (1979) lists various auditory or phonetic features that have been proposed for the study of infant sounds. The lists include features such as "saliva constrictive," "dysphonation," "egressive v. ingressive," and "subharmonic break."

Table 11.5 Summary of perceptual methods used for inventories and quantitative indices

Method	Comments	References
Utterance counts	The number of vocalizations based on utterances separated by a pause, utterances produced in one breath group or some other criterion	D'Odorico, Franco, and Vidotto (1985) Oller and Lynch (1992)
Inventory of syllable shapes	(V, CV, VC, CVC, etc.)	Kent and Bauer (1985)
Inventory of vowels (vocants) and consonants (closants)	Inventory may be categorized by: 1 vowel chart or consonant place/ manner 2 distinctive features	Davis and MacNeilage (1990) Dyson (1988) Kent and Bauer (1985) Irwin (1947) Lieberman (1980) Locke (1983) Mowrer (1980) Stoel-Gammon (1985) Vihman, Ferguson, and Elbert (1986)
Vowel and consonant affiliations	1 Identification of frequently occurring combinations 2 Randomness tests on transition probabilities	Davis and MacNeilage (1990) Martin (1981) Vihman (1992) Stasny and Bauer (1990)
Phonetic Record	A time history of utterances classified in terms of place and/or manner of production	Bauer (1988) Kent and Bauer (1985) Sancier (1989)

Measure	Description	References
Phonetic Product	An index of phonetic diversity derived from the phonetic record	Bauer (1988)
Information Theory of Diversity		Baylis (1974) Marler (1982)
Closant Curve (C/V Ratio)	Ratio of closants to vocants	Bauer (1988) Mowrer (1980) Robb and Bauer (1991)
Babbling Ratio	Ratio of canonical syllables to total utterances	Oller and Eilers (1988) Oller and Seibert (1988)
Mean Babbling Level	Individual vocalizations weighted differently depending on phonetic constituents of syllables	Stoel-Gammon (1989)
Inventory of multisyllabic sequences	Repetitive, variegated, or mixed	Elbers (1982) Mitchell and Kent (1990) Smith, Brown-Sweeney and Stoel-Gammon (1989) Oller and Lynch (1992)
Inventory of vocalization types according to a widely used stage description	Canonical utterance clusters	Oller (1978, 1980) Roug, Landberg, and Lundberg (1989)
Descriptive feature systems		Holmgren et al. (1986) Stark (1979)
Description of prosodically contrastive Utterances to define infant's prosodic units or features		Delack and Fowlow (1978) Vihman and Miller (1988) Waterson (1971)

Table 11.6 Summary of acoustic measures used in study of infant vocalizations

Method	Comments	References
Fundamental frequency	Mean or median, distribution of instantaneous values, range or other measure of variability, frequency of occurrence for intonation contours	Delack and Fowlow (1978) Keating and Buhr (1978) Kent and Bauer (1985) Laufer (1976) Murry and Murry (1980) Robb and Saxman (1985) Robb and Saxman (1988) Robb, Saxman, and Grant (1989) Zlatin-Laufer and Horii (1977)
Phonation types	1 Normal, hypophonation, hyperphonation 2 "Cry" score 3 Occurrence of phonation subtypes: harmonic doubling, noise components or noise intervals, abrupt frequency shift, biphonation, roll, tremor, changes in spectral balance, etc. 4 Perturbation measures (jitter, shimmer) 5 Noise measures (S/N or H/N ratio)	Kent and Murray (1982) Laufer (1976) Murry and Murry (1980) Robb and Saxman (1988)

Measure	Description	References
"Infant phonetogram" or "voice field"	Intensity by fundamental frequency portraits of phonation (based on long-term recordings of spontaneous vocalizations)	Apparently not part of the published literature but well within technological capability
Durations of cries, utterances syllables, pauses, or phonetic segments	Special case of final syllable lengthening	Kent, Mitchell, and Sancier (1991) Laufer (1976) Mitchell (1988) Oller and Smith (1977) Robb and Saxman (1990)
Rhythmic structure	Syllable crests, long-term fundamental frequency patterns, vocalization intervals, measures of repetitive acoustic structure such as stop bursts and formant shifts in repetitive babbling	Kent, Mitchell, and Sancier (1991)
Formant frequencies	F1–F2 plot of vowel formants	Buhr (1980) Hodge (1989) Kent and Murray (1982) Kent et al (1986) Sancier (1989)
Spectra of frication or plosive burst		Bauer and Kent (1987)
Dynamic measures (C/V Ratio)	Rise time of the amplitude envelope, formant transitions	Hodge (1989) Oller (1986) Robb and Bauer (1991)
Measures of laryngeal stridor		Cohen and Lieberman (1986) Hirschberg (1980)

5   The Role of Infants' Phonetic Abilities in Early Language Development

It is quite clear that infant vocalizations are continuous with later development of spoken language. The bulk of recent evidence supports the continuity hypothesis, although counterevidence has been reported for vowels in one infant (Davis and MacNeilage, 1990). Developmental continuity is contrary to Jakobson's proposal that babbling is an isolated system that has little or no relevance to the acquisition of language. However, to say that babbling is phonetically continuous with spoken language acquisition does not mean that babbling is *necessary* for acquisition of language. This issue is open to interpretation. It appears that for most typically developing infants, the phonetic characteristics of babbling persist into early word production and may have a selective influence on early words. Moreover, sounds that have been classified as babbling may in fact have sound–meaning correspondences. Blake and Fink (1987) analyzed the babbling of five infants in their second year with respect to cooccurrences of phonetic patterns and contexts of vocalization. Their crossinfant data showed that 14–40 percent of the utterances recurred in specific contexts with a frequency greater than expected by chance.

It is also clear that individual differences are considerable (Vihman, Ferguson, and Elbert, 1986). Despite these differences, it is hard to ignore the evidence for biological determination of phonetic tendencies in first-year vocalizations. Sounds do not appear in early babbling with uniform frequencies of occurrence. Certain sounds are much more likely to appear than others, and it is these same sounds that tend to occur most frequently in early lexicons. Nonuniformities in frequency of occurrence that are independent of language exposure often are interpreted as evidence of biological disposition (Locke, 1983a). Nonuniformities that vary with the language background of the infant are taken to reflect the infant's sensitivity to language exposure. Both influences appear to be at work during much, if not all, of infancy. There is reason to believe that language exposure has some prenatal effects (Lecanuet and Granier-Deferre, 1993), which means that the newborn is to a certain degree already biased toward a particular linguistic system, or at least a linguistic family. But biology also enters the developmental equation, not as a constant but as a developmental variable in its own right. The vocal and articulatory apparatus is subject to considerable modification during the first few years of life. The infant learns to use an instrument that is gradually remodeled in a striking evolutionary progression.

Before infants utter sounds that are readily identified as words by their parents, they may begin to use vocalization for communicative functions. Nakazima (1980) described nine-month-olds as "developing prelinguistic communication in sounds" (p. 274). Examples of this capability are the utterance of "simple meaningless sounds" such as isolated vowels in response to the communicative behaviors of familiar persons. At about the same time, infants may begin to utter vowel sounds that are at least grossly adjusted to the vowel repertoire of the ambient language (Boysson-Bardies et al., 1986). This initial evidence of congruence of vowel patterns is consistent with the idea that infants are beginning to use vocalization in a communicative fashion.

The common wisdom is that infants learn speech in large part through imitating adult speech patterns. Successful imitation requires that the infant produce a satisfactory replica of patterns produced by the adult. Imitation therefore requires both perceptual and productive capability. Common wisdom about the importance of imitation notwithstanding, imitation in infants has had relatively little scientific examination. Nakazima (1980) reported that infants begin to imitate speech sounds at about ten months of age. However, recent studies demonstrate that infants can imitate speech sounds at even earlier ages. The work of Kuhl and Meltzoff (1982) is instructive. They reported two important characteristics of four-month-olds' vocal imitation:

1   The infants differentially responded to speech v. nonspeech sounds. Speech sounds were imitated with speechlike vocalizations. Nonspeech sounds tended to elicit squeals and squeaks.
2   Infants imitated phonetic qualities of the sounds presented to them. Infants who heard /a/ vowels responded with /a/-like sounds, whereas infants who heard /i/ vowels produced /i/-like sounds.

These imitative behaviors and related evidence of crossmodal mapping in infants were discussed extensively by Kuhl and Meltzoff (1988) and Meltzoff (1990), who suggested that speech is a multimodal event even in infancy. In this view, the study of infant experiences with speech should include visual, tactile, and auditory sensory modalities interacting with emerging motor capabilities.

Toward the end of the first year of life, infants often are credited with the production of complex patterns of babbling that may prefigure intonational structures in adult speech. Terms such as *jargon* babbling are used to refer to these late-babbling utterances that resemble adult speech in at least certain characteristics. These utterances can be highly complex in their phonetic and acoustic structure and can present difficulties to both perceptual and instrumental analysis (Kent and Bauer, 1985). However, these vocalizations are particularly interesting, given their apparent role in the infant's transition from babbling to speech.

Shortly after imitation and jargon babbling are clearly in evidence, infants begin to produce early words. First words typically are observed at about 11–12 months, and their appearance thus marks the developmental boundary of this chapter. But the age at which an individual infant's first words appear is quite variable, falling somewhere in the range of 9–15 months on the average (Capute et al., 1986; Largo et al., 1986).

Careful observation of infants in the first year of life has resulted in several surprising discoveries within the last two decades. Infants possess a remarkable capability to discriminate acoustic contrasts that are phonetically relevant to language learning. Furthermore, some investigators believe that by the end of the first year, infants have lost the ability to discriminate some acoustic contrasts that are not used in the parent language. Infants also can imitate facial expressions and some speech sounds, at very early ages. And even though strong crosslanguage commonalities have been observed in the types of sounds that infants produce within their first year of life, there is also evidence that infants younger than one year begin to adjust their sound patterns to reflect characteristics of the ambient language. These discoveries hold important implications for the development of language. It does not appear that the first year of life is merely a time of physical maturation that must be undergone before language development can commence. There is very good reason to seek early mechanisms of language development in the infant who has yet to see a full year of postnatal life.

12 Phonological Development

LISE MENN AND CAROL STOEL-GAMMON

1 Introduction

1.1 Babytalk and popular knowledge

Most cultures have a speech register known as "babytalk," which contains special words for concepts used in the daily lives of small children (family members, food, personal hygiene, familiar animals). It is also distinguished by certain phonological patterns (in English, use of alveolars for initial velars), and perhaps by morphological regularizations (e.g. "comed, goed") (Ferguson, 1978a; Haynes and Cooper, 1986). The lexical items are taught to children, and the babytalk register is popularly considered to be "how children talk." Folklore characters (e.g. the Hausa trickster figure (Dresel, 1977), or the Warner Bros cartoon canary "Tweety Pie") may be represented as speaking "in babytalk."

In English, where some preliminary work has been done on the question (Menn and Gleason, 1986), the phonological patterns of this stereotyped babytalk do appear to represent a few of the commonest features of children's early pronunciation, but a stereotype of course cannot represent the very notable individual variation across or within children (Ferguson, 1986).

1.2 History of the field and sources of information

Since the study of child language entered its modern era, our sources for the study of phonological acquisition come from three types of data, each contributing a different perspective.

Diary studies

Diary studies were the initial major source: detailed notes taken by parents interested in language development, who were often linguists. Such studies first appeared over a century ago (e.g. Humphreys, 1880) and are still being carried out. Those by linguists, such as W. Leopold's four volume account of his daughter's language development (1939–49), H. V. Velten's article (1943) and N. V. Smith's detailed study of his son's speech patterns from ages two to four (1973) are still frequently cited. Portions of diary data are reported to address particular questions, e.g. Menn (1971) on her son's early constraints on sound sequences, Stoel-Gammon and Cooper's (1984) study of individual differences in their children, and Donahue's (1986) and Stemberger's (1988) accounts of children's error patterns within and across phrases. Diary studies have both strengths and weaknesses: if the parent is a trained observer, they can provide unique insights into developmental phenomena which experimenters can never capture, and they can trace developmental patterns and give detail on variation within the individual's production which are not available from group studies. However, the lack of structure in data collection and small numbers of subjects make it difficult to compare diaries across children and make generalizations; the parent as researcher introduces the strong possibility of observer bias; and on-line transcriptions make it impossible to determine transcription reliability unless supplementary tape recordings are available. (Most current individual developmental studies rely on audio and video recordings at weekly or more frequent intervals.)

Cross-sectional studies

A second type of study, begun in the 1930s, is based on cross-sectional data from large numbers of subjects. In these, productions of a predetermined set of words are elicited, usually through picture naming. The purpose of this type of investigation was not to document developmental patterns in young children, but to establish a set of "norms" for the ages at which the various phonemes of English were mastered. The researchers, primarily educators and speech pathologists, could then use these norms to identify children who were delayed or deviant in their phonological development. The findings of Wellman and colleagues (1931) and Poole (1934) are still used as the basis for determining normal performance. The largest of these is Templin's (1957) study of 480 children. More recent large sample studies include Prather, Hedrick, and Kern (1975) and Smit et al. (1990).

Norming studies and diary accounts yield very different types of data. Diary studies provide longitudinal data on a single child and typically trace development until the age of three or four years; the productions are entirely unstructured, those that occur in everyday interactions. In contrast, the norming studies provide information only on a restricted set of words or phrases and no data on longitudinal patterns of a particular child. Taken together, they complement one another and provide a fuller picture of the phenomena at hand.

Small group experimental and naturalistic studies

The most recently developed approach to studying phonological acquisition has been referred to as "linguistic" study (Ingram, 1976). These investigations are informed by linguistic theory and utilize phonological analyses. In most cases they are small group studies in which data are collected in a semistructured fashion and are designed to answer a single question or set of related questions. The purpose is not simply to document children's speech productions, but to determine the linguistic underpinnings of the patterns observed. Data are recorded and carefully transcribed; in some cases, acoustic analyses are also performed. The majority of child phonology studies since 1960 are of this type, including the often cited work of Charles Ferguson and his colleagues and students at Stanford University (e.g. Edwards, Ingram, Macken, Stoel-Gammon, Vihman). In recent years, the naturalistic approach adopted by the "linguistic" studies has been supplemented by a series of experimental investigations designed to control particular variables. For example, Ferguson and colleagues noted the phenomenon of "lexical selection" whereby children chose to include certain words in their early vocabularies on the basis of phonological features of the target word (Ferguson, Peizer, and Weeks, 1973; Ferguson and Farwell, 1975). It appeared that words which were selected for inclusion in the production lexicon contained sound classes or syllable structures that the child could produce fairly accurately, and that words beyond the child's pronunciation ability were deliberately avoided. However, the alternative explanation, that differences in early vocabulary were related to differences in input, could not be ruled out. Schwartz and Leonard (1982) provided definitive support for the notion of lexical selection by designing an experiment in which frequency of input of sound classes and syllable shapes was strictly controlled by teaching children made-up "names" for novel objects. Thus, the use of experimental procedures in the study of child phonology permits researchers to test hypotheses in ways that are not possible using naturalistic paradigms. Together, naturalistic and experimental approaches provide data essential for hypothesis testing and theory construction.

2 The Prelinguistic Period and the Relation of Babble to Speech

2.1 Universals

Research on prelinguistic vocal development over the past two decades has two recurring themes. First, regardless of language community in which they are raised, infants pass through an ordered sequence of stages in terms of

vocal development. Initially, their vocalizations are reflexive vegetative productions, but by the second month, some comfort state "coos" and "goos"
emerge; at the onset of canonical babbling, their utterances become increasingly adultlike with identifiable CV syllables and clear intonation patterns (see
Kent and Miolo, this volume, for a complete description of vocal development
in the first year). The second major theme is that the sound classes and syllable
structures characteristic of the later babbling period (10–12 months) are highly
similar across subjects and across languages. For example, in all studies to
date, the consonantal repertoires of infants in the later babbling period typically include a high proportion of front (i.e. labial and dental/alveolar) consonants, of stops and nasals, and of CV syllables. The finding that these
characteristics also obtain in early meaningful speech has led to a new view
of the relationship between babbling and speech.

The discontinuity/continuity controversy

In his influential monograph on phonological acquisition, Jakobson (1968)
claimed that infants' vocalizations prior to the first words were not related to
subsequent phonological development. He described babbling as "the pur-
poseless egocentric soliloquy of the child ... biologically oriented 'tongue
delirium' " (1968: 22) and stated that "the appearance of phonemes in a linguistic system has nothing in common with the ephemeral sound productions
of the babbling period" (ibid., p. 28). Although many of Jakobson's claims
regarking phonological acquisition have subsequently been supported, his views
on the relationship between babbling and speech have not. The first major
refutation of Jakobson's position was Oller (1976), which showed that the
sounds and syllable structures characteristic of the canonical babbling period
closely resembled those of early meaningful speech. This finding has since
been replicated by several researchers. Although infants may indeed produce
a wide array of sound types during the prelinguistic period, only a small
subset of these occur frequently. Locke's review (1983c) of three separate investigations of American infants showed that 12 consonants: [p, t, k, b, d, g,
m, n, w, j, h, s] accounted for 92–5 percent of the consonantal phones produced at 11–12 months. This set of consonants is the same set that predomi-
nates in early word productions in English (Stoel-Gammon, 1985). Moreover,
the CV syllable structure characteristic of the canonical babbling period is also
the most frequent in early word productions. Thus, babbling and early speech
share the same phonetic properties in terms of sound types and syllable shapes.

2.2   Individual and crosslinguistic variation

Further support for continuity between babbling and speech comes from
longitudinal investigations of individual children. Detailed analyses of data
from individual subjects show, first, that there is interchild variability in place
and manner of articulation, syllable shape, and vocalization length, and

second, that such differences are often "carried forward" from the prelinguistic period to the first words (Stoel-Gammon and Cooper, 1984; Vihman, Macken, Miller, Simmons, and Miller, 1985; Vihman, Ferguson, and Elbert, 1987). Vihman (1992) documents individual differences in the occurrence of "practiced syllables" in babbling and then shows that these same syllables form the foundation of children's first words.

Crosslinguistic research has yielded a small but growing body of evidence that prelinguistic vocalizations show effects of the ambient language as early as ten months. Work by Boysson-Bardies and colleagues (1989, 1992) has showed language-specific effects in both the consonantal and vocalic system. Effects of the ambient language appear to be clearest in the frequency of occurrence of particular types (i.e. in the number of tokens), rather than in the repertoire of types of sounds and syllable structures produced.

2.3   The role of practice and feedback

Speech has a skill component and, as with any skilled activity, practice increases the control and precision with which a movement is performed. Thus, the more often a baby produces the movements which shape the vocal tract to produce particular sounds and sound sequences, the more automatic those movements become and ultimately the easier it is to execute them in producing meaningful speech. As mentioned, Vihman (1992) identified a set of frequently occurring CV syllables ("practiced" syllables) for each subject and reported that the syllables used in early words were "primarily drawn from the repertoire of practiced syllables." Given this finding, babies who have a large stock of practiced CV syllables in babbling might have an advantage in early word acquisition because of having a larger repertoire of forms to which meaning can be attached. Vihman (1992) noted that subjects with slower vocabulary acquisition were those who failed to use their "practiced syllables" in meaningful speech production. Similarly, Stoel-Gammon (1989) reported that one of the two "late talkers" she studied produced many CV syllables, mostly velar-onset, in his nonmeaningful productions, but did not use these forms in his attempts at real words, which were mostly labial-onset.

Practice in the production of speechlike vocalizations is also important for feedback. Infants are exposed to two types of vocal input, the speech of others and their own productions. In addition to improving the motor skill component of speech production, practice allows infants to hear their own vocalizations. The feedback loop has been described by Fry (1966: 189): "As sound producing movements are repeated and repeated, a strong link is forged between tactual and kinesthetic impressions and auditory sensations that the child receives from his own utterances."

Awareness of the links between one's own oral–motor movements and the acoustic signal which results is a prerequisite to auditory–vocal matching which underlies word production. The more a child babbles, the greater the opportunity to establish the feedback loops necessary for producing and monitoring their own speech. Moreover, the feedback loop may help infants recognize words in the adult language that resemble their own babbled forms. Thus, for example, a baby who frequently produces [ba] or [baba] might be likely to acquire the word "ball" or "bottle" because these words are similar to the forms for which auditory and kinesthetic feedback patterns have been established.

Practice and feedback are not independent aspects of early vocal development. Practice involves the repeated production of sounds; feedback involves hearing and monitoring these practiced productions. Both are crucial for the acquisition of adult language: studies of prelinguistic vocalizations of deaf babies demonstrate that the effects of a lack of auditory input can be detected at seven to eight months. Hearing impaired babies have a normally developing vocal apparatus which would allow them to practice the movements associated with the production of CV syllables, and they would have tactile and kinesthetic feedback from oral movements; however, hearing impaired babies are significantly delayed in the onset of the Canonical Stage (Oller and Eilers, 1988) and in the frequency and diversity of supraglottal consonants in their vocalizations (Stoel-Gammon and Otomo, 1986; Stoel-Gammon, 1988). Presumably, this failure is linked to the lack of auditory input, which precludes both forming auditory feedback loops and hearing the speech of adults.

It appears that lack of motor practice also affects development. Locke and Pearson (1990) examined the linguistic development of a cognitively normal baby girl who was tracheostomized and "generally aphonic" from 5–20 months. During this period, she vocalized infrequently, producing utterances which usually consisted of "a single vocalic sound of approximately syllable length" (p. 7). Although exposed to speech from adults, she was unable to produce canonical babbles and had little opportunity to form auditory or tactile feedback loops based on her own vocalizations. Following removal of the tube which had prevented normal respiration, just prior to 21 months, she showed a marked increase in the frequency of vocal output. Of the 909 utterances produced in several weeks after the tube was removed, however, only six met the criteria for canonical syllables. In addition to the lack of well formed syllables, she had a limited repertoire of consonantal types. The authors noted that her speech was similar to that of deaf infants studied by Stoel-Gammon and Otomo (1986) and by Oller and Eilers (1988). Thus, the findings of this case study of a single child support the essential role of practice and of hearing one's own vocalizations in normal vocal development.

3 Production of Early Words

3.1 *Characteristics of early words*

Children's earliest attempts at words often are sporadic, unsystematic in their phonological relation to the adult target word, and extremely variable in pronunciation, and there may be many homonyms. As their words become more identifiable, numerous, systematic, and stable over the first few months of speaking, the following basic properties become more and more evident.

Loss of information

In several ways, children's words carry less phonological information (i.e. are more redundant) than the corresponding abult targets. Children's total recognition vocabulary is small, and production vocabulary is even smaller; they also cannot maintain all the adult phonetic contrasts that would be needed to produce their words accurately. Furthermore, the total set of output forms consists largely – but not entirely – of clusters of closely related forms, which can be described formally in terms of prosodies or canonical forms in autosegmental representation (see property 6 below, and section one). These forms individually also tend to contain fewer independently specified elements (less information) than the corresponding adult forms.

Systematicity of mappings and natural processes

Children usually have systematic ways of reducing adult words to forms which fit within their production capacities. Most children's words bear regular mapping relations to their adult targets; these rules or regularities can be described formally with standard phonological notation if desired. Rules reduce the information contained in each word, yielding the overall picture described in section one, above. Some of these regularities, such as final devoicing (i.e. failure to continue vocal cord vibration during the production of a consonant such as /b, d, g, v, z/ at the end of a word) are widespread and appear to have phonetic motor control explanations; the term "natural process" has been applied to such regularities by Stampe (1969) and others (e.g. Edwards and Shriberg, 1983). Other natural processes include substitution of stops for fricatives ([ti] for "see"), reduction of consonant clusters to a singleton consonant ([pat] for "spot"), deletion of initial [h], and deletion of initial and medial unstressed syllables ([næ] or ['nænæ] for "banana"). However, it has been noted that a child may fail to use such processes on his or her earliest words and then start to use them somewhat later; this leads us to regard these processes as natural faiure or default modes rather than as hardwired "innate rules." Other common rules for English-acquiring children which are not prominent (or in some cases, even attested) in adult language include deaspiration of voiceless initial stop consonants ([do] for "toe," heard as "voicing" by native English speakers), and various partial assimilation rules that ensure whole-word consonant harmonies, especially place assimilation ([gak] for "sock") and nasal assimilation ([minz] for "beans").

Some rules used by children are not "natural" in the sense of having plausible explanations which are solely motor based. For English, it has been observed that an unstressed syllable in a word may be replaced by a "dummy syllable" (either a stereotyped near-constant shape or a copy of the stressed syllable) instead of being deleted ([rita:] for "guitar"; Smith, 1973). Consonant cluster simplification, usually accomplished by preservation of the most obstruent element, may instead be done by combining features from the several segments (e.g. /s+nasal/ rendered as voiceless nasal, /sk/ rendered as the velar fricative [x]), even when the adult language does not possess the resulting feature combination.

Context-dependent rules/processes and their psycholinguistic implications

Rules/processes may be context free – that is, they may apply to a given sound or class of sounds in all cases – for example, all adult /l/'s being replaced by /w/, or all velar consonants (k, g, ŋ) being replaced by corresponding alveolar consonants (t, d, n). However, most rules/processes are context dependent: the fate of the target sound depends on its position in the word or syllable and/or on other sounds in the word. For example, word-initial velars may be replaced by alveolars while other velars are produced accurately, yielding, for example, [tUki] for "cookie." In one form of consonant harmony indicated above, the initial consonant of a consonant–vowel–consonant word is changed to match the position of articulation of the final consonant, yielding [gʌk] for "duck." In addition to context-free and context-dependent substitution rules, children also may have context-free or context-dependent omission rules (e.g. omitting all liquids; omitting the liquids only in stop-liquid clusters, such as the /r/ in "truck").

Because context-dependent rules are so prominent, we consider children as learning to master adult sound sequences as well as adult sounds; a child may well be able to make all the individual sounds in a sequence, yet be unable to combine them and produce the sequence itself.

Nonsystematic reductions

Not all ways of producing adult sounds are systematic. There are also nonsystematic, "unruly" reductions. One kind of nonsystematic mapping is typically found among the very early words: a few of these may be produced more accurately than later words and contain relatively complex sequences of segments. These are called "progressive phonological idioms" (Moskowitz, 1970); the term "idiom" is used because the knack of producing such sequences does not generalize to other similar words. Such phonological idioms may be stable over a long period of time, or may disappear early.

Some nonsystematic reductions are unstable; that is, they give variable outputs. They may apply to word sequences: for example, there are children who map entire multiword phrases onto loosely articulated sequences (e.g. "I don't want it" rendered as a nasal vocalic sequence [ãõã:]; Peters, 1977). Other nonsystematic reductions reorder the sounds of adult words in variable ways to fit into the child's own restricted output templates (Priestly, 1977). The child in this famous study seemed to have a several different ways of mapping certain adult words into a [CVjVC] canonical form, e.g. [majos] and [mɛjan] for "monster," [tajak] and [tajaŋ] for "tiger." Examination of the range of forms he produced do not encourage one to think in terms of well-defined selection rules at all. It looks as though many of the output forms were made by taking the stable [CVjVC] skeleton from the "output lexicon" and then adding in the unstable consonant specifications on line from the "input lexicon."

Some nonsystematic reductions are relatively stable over time. Output templates for words may include "melodic" patterns like "first vowel higher than second vowel," "medial consonant = glottal stop," "first consonant labial, second alveolar" (Macken, 1993). Stable mappings onto templates may be specific to a given word or two; if one writes rules or lists processes for them, the result is a very odd collection of ad hoc statements.

Rule changes, "inertia," and their psycholinguistic implications

Children's word production systems have considerable "inertia." When children do display regularities of information reduction, the rules which describe those regularities may be stable for long periods. Changes in these rules frequently are seen first in new lexical items, and spread only slowly to established words.

A rule may have originated as a way of changing or omitting an adult sound or sequence of sounds that the child could not yet produce, but it may continue in force after the child has started to produce the needed sound pattern in new words. This slow change is sometimes due to misperception of the adult target word (Macken, 1992), but often it is not; there is typically a true lag in the application of new rules to existing words.

A frequently used example of a rule which cannot be attributed to misperception, and which originated in spite of the child's early correct or near-correct production, comes from Daniel (Menn, 1971). Daniel at about two years of age produced "down" correctly as [dæUn] and "stone" as [don]. These were both very frequent words. Sometime later, he began to show a nasal assimilation rule: in new words containing both a nasal consonant and a nonnasal stop consonant, he regularly changed the nonnasal stop to the corresponding nasal stop, producing "dance" with initial [n] and "beans" with initial [m]. For some weeks after this, "down" and "stone" were maintained in their nonassimilated forms, but then the forms [næUn] and [non] began to appear as variant pronunciations. Finally, the early forms [dæUn] and [don] disappeared, and [næUn] and [non] became the only forms for these words.

Such instances of "inertia" indicate that a child has stored something about the way to say at least some of his/her words; in other words, children's rules do not work exclusively "on-line," as some accounts imply. This example also illustrates regression of a correct to an incorrect form as a rule generalizes, a phenomenon familiar from other aspects of linguistic and cognitive development.

Canonical forms

Children's words tend to group into phonologically based sets; the sound pattern describing such a set is usually called a "canonical form " or a "template." As mentioned under property 1, the earliest kind of systematicity in children's words is the organization of their output vocabulary into words of similar syllable shape – and often, similar phonetic content as well. For example, a child may have a group of /CVCV/ words with the same stop consonant repeated, a group of /CVs/ words with low vowels, and a group of words that begin with nasals and have no final consonant. These abstractions of the patterns of groups of words are called "canonical forms," "templates,"or "prosodies" (Waterson, 1971); as mentioned, this organizational pattern clearly can be seen even in babbling as "vocal motor schemes" (Vihman, 1992), and understanding why such an organization should exist is one of the goals of current model building in child phonology.

Summary

Fitting these observations together, we may summarize the data presented so far as follows: a young child having a use for an adult target word has limited means at his or her disposal. If the target word matches one of the canonical forms exactly, it is likely to be produced correctly, but only a few adult words will fall into this category. If the target word falls outside the set of canonical forms which the child has already mastered, it may be attempted or avoided. If it is attempted, the child may reach beyond the repertoire and try the new sound sequence, or may adapt the word by omitting, changing, or rearranging some of its sounds so that it fits an available canonical form. (For example, a child with a /CVs/ canonical form who cannot yet produce two adjacent consonants may render "snow" as [nos].) In many cases, this adaptation can and will be done by using an existing regular mapping pattern (rule), but sometimes no rule has been established.

Many kinds of individual differences are found within this general framework. For example, it is common for children not to be able to say CVC words where the initial and final consonants have different positions of articulation – in phonological terms, we may say that young children cannot violate a restriction of "consonant harmony." Some children may avoid such words, but they are too common in English for this strategy to be used for long. Most children deal with them by modifying them in some way – by omitting the final consonant, reducing them to CV; by changing one of the consonants to be more like the other (assimilation), as mentioned above; by replacing one of the consonants with a glottal stop; or by other idiosyncratic regular or irregular devices. The art of producing words that violate consonant harmony may be learned piecemeal – for example, the child may develop a "melodic" canonical form such as [bVk] or [gVt] well before becoming able to execute all the CVC sequences of the ambient language. Similar constraints may hold for CVCV words (Macken, 1992) in English and other languages; see below.

3.2   Units of early production

The word as the earliest unit

Children's earliest phonological "units" appear to be whole words. Although several authors have treated the syllable as a subword unit of construction, a syllable-based approach has very limited applicability. The appropriate subword unit of analysis is the canonical form or template of the word, which can be treated as corresponding to the skeleton "tier" of adult autosegmental phonology (Macken, 1992).

An early and long discredited view of children's words is that they were built up as sequences of isolated phoneme units. The abundant data showing that learning to produce a new sound sequence is as much a challenge as learning to produce a new sound quickly made this idea untenable. The hypothesis that the syllable is a unit of word construction has had some currency, because many constraints on sound sequences can be stated in terms of syllables in adult language and in child language as well (e.g. English has /h/ only in syllable-initial position). However, the syllable is not an early unit in any strong sense, because young children cannot freely combine syllables to produce words; early CV-CV words have restrictions on the possible pairs of consonants just as early CVC words do. In addition, they may have restrictions on the possible pairs of vowels. So, for example, children who have mastered the two different syllables that would be needed for an adult word like "kitty" may still be unable to combine them to produce the word. Macken (1992) classifies these sound-sequence restrictions into "harmony" patterns (requiring the consonants/vowels to be identical or similar) and "melody" patterns (requiring specified dissimilar sequences of consonants or vowels).

Multiword utterances

Production constraints may extend across word boundaries (Donahue, 1986; Matthei, 1989; Stemberger, 1988). Early attempts to produce two-word phrases may show reduction in the accuracy of the production of the individual words, and these cannot in general be explained as regression to an earlier pronunciation.

Donahue (1986) showed consonant assimilation across word boundaries, and Matthei (1989) demonstrated that the forms in another child's early word combinations were more appropriately described as truncations of existing forms. In Matthei's study, even forms which had always had the shape CVCV, e.g. "mama" [mɔmɔ], were truncated: "mama's key" was produced as [mɔ ki].

Therefore, rules/constraints must also operate "on line" – they cannot merely be statements of constraints on stored word forms.

3.3   Strategy variations and metalinguistic awareness in the early period

Instead of replacing adult sounds or sound sequences with ones within their repertoires, children (especially those who still have fewer than about 50 words in their productive vocabulary) may refuse to say them. Experimental work (Schwartz and Leonard, 1982; Schwartz, Leonard, Loeb, and Swanson, 1987) suggests that such avoidance is especially likely to be found in children who have acquired less than about 25–75 words of output vocabulary. Children may also appear to seek out adult words which have sounds that do lie within their repertoires, even when such words are not very frequent or of high evident utility; this is referred to as a "favorite sounds" or "exploitation" strategy.

Individual children vary in the extent to which they prefer to avoid adult words which they cannot yet render accurately. Children's avoidance of words outside their existing production repertoire (shown as young as 15 months in diary studies) indicates an unexpected degree of metalinguistic ability. There is much other evidence (e.g. repeated attempts at self-correction) to indicate that very young children are often aware of inadequacies in their renditions of adult words.

On the other hand, children are often apparently unaware of the inaccuracy of their attempts. With respect to any given adult target which a child does attempt to match, there appears generally to be a progression. First, there may be an initial stage at which the child seems unable to become aware that his/her rendition is not the same as the adult's, despite perhaps strenuous efforts to get the child to attend to the disparity: numerous studies have reported interchanges in which a child misprounounces a word (e.g. [fIs] for "fish"), an adult requests the child to "say [fIʃ]" (emphasizing the final [ʃ], and the child responds "I did say [fIs]" (with similar emphasis). Given the experimental evidence that young infants can make discriminations such as this between auditory stimuli, perhaps in these cases the child is attending only to the meaning of the word that the adult is repeating and not to how it sounds.

At a later time the child attends to the difference but cannot manage any change in production (and now may be able to comment on his/her inability; see Smith, 1973); later, correction can be approximated in imitation but not maintained in spontaneous speech; still later, a more correct form and the earlier form appear variably in production, and finally the more correct form is maintained. Progress through these phases may be slow or rapid, and a child may be at an advanced stage with respect to an early-acquired sound or sound sequence while at a beginning stage with respect to a more difficult target.

3.4   Order of acquisition

The age and also the order of mastery of phones, phonemes, and phonemic contrasts is variable across children; only probabilistic statements can be made. A traditional question for child phonology is: "In what order do children acquire the phonemes of their native language?" Speech pathologists would like to determine a normal order of acquisition so that they can recognize abnormality and target remedial intervention towards the"earlier" phonemes first. Linguists, beginning with Jakobson (1941/1968), ask the related question, "In what order do children acquire the phonemic contrasts of their native language?" so that they can test predictions of various phonological theories against data from child phonology.

However, there are serious problems with either of these questions as formulated. First, they assume that there is a typical or perhaps universal order of acquisition for children learning a given language (or all languages). Second, they fail to allow for the fact that some of the phones (contextually determined variant pronunciations) belonging to a phoneme may be acquired much earlier than others. Third, some investigators fail to distinguish carefully between the first question (when do children master appropriate pronunciations of the phones belonging to the phonemes of a language) and the second question (when do children give evidence of acquiring the phonemic contrasts of the language). Fourth, investigators addressing the "appropriate pronunciations" issue who do take the time lag problem into account appear to consider "acquisition" to have occurred when a child produces an acceptable allophone of a consonant phoneme in singleton initial, intervocalic, and final positions, but other variables besides initial–medial–final position also affect pronunciation and are often overlooked in the construction of elicitation stimuli. For example, the importance of consonant harmony has been emphasized above, yet "yellow" is frequently used as the test item for initial /j/; as would be expected, the /j/–/l/ sequence is more difficult for most children than the /j/ in a monosyllable like "you." Irwin and Wong's (1983) study of acquisition of phonemes in conversational speech for 100 children from ages 1.5 to 10 also ignored the possible effects of other sounds in a word or position in a word. (Criteria for acquisition of vowels are rarely defined at all.) Fifth, different studies use different elicitation methods (e.g. single word imitation, spontaneous running speech). And finally, sixth, dialect differences, such as the acceptability of alveolar flap for medial /t/ or of glottal stop for final /t/, have generally been ignored, as have other types of variation.

As mentioned in the introduction, the standard references on the development of American English consonants (Wellman et al., 1931; Templin, 1957) were large group studies which utilized single-word elicited and imitated productions. Sander (1972) reanalyzed these data to show the ages at which 50 percent and 90 percent of the children tested produced "acceptable"allophones of American English consonants when data for initial, medial, and final positions were combined. For labials /p/, /b/, /m/, and /w/, and also for /h/ and /n/, the 50 percent mark was reached before age two on their test materials. Except for /b/, these reached 90 percent by age three. The velars /k/, /g/, /ŋ/, and the alveolar stops /t/ and /d/ reached 50 percent correct production at age two; /b/, /k/, /g/, and /d/ reached 90 percent by age four, but /t/ and /ŋ/ did not do so until age six. The greatest lag between the 50 percent and the 90 percent criteria was shown by /s/, which resched 50 percent at age three but did not reach 90 percent until age eight. Thus, even with these simplified, averaged data, the "order of acquisition" is not well defined.

Furthermore, longitudinal small group studies of pronunciation have found considerable individual differences in the order of acquisition of stops (Macken, 1980) and fricatives (Edwards, 1978, 1979; Ingram et al., 1980). Stoel-Gammon and Herrington (1990) showed that the American English vowel system is generally completed before the consonantal system is complete, and that the vowels acquired early are /i/, /u/, /a/, /o/, and /ʌ/; but again, no finer-grained generalization can be maintained.

General statements for the pronunciation of English can at most be sustained at the level of phoneme classes: stops in general precede fricatives and affricates; glides precede liquids. Individuals may show exceptions; some children learn to produce some fricatives in particular word positions relatively early. For languages which employ more complex articulations, it appears that simply articulated consonants such as [k] are mastered before glottalized [k'] or other more marked phones (Pye, Ingram, and List, 1987). A phoneme may be mastered earlier in a language in which it is more frequent (ibid.; Ingram, 1992), but the very late mastery of /ð/, the most frequent consonant in English, makes it clear that frequency cannot be a determining factor.

The order and age of mastery of phonemic contrasts is likewise variable across children within a given language. The order of contrast acquisition which was proposed by Jakobson (1941/1968) on the basis of general phonological markedness is quite a good fit probabilistically, but many exceptions have been reported in the literature. Therefore, his famous description is terms of "laws of irreversible solidarity" cannot be considered appropriate. It does seem that phones which are dependent on precise relative timing of glottal and supralaryngeal events (e.g. aspirated or glottalized stops) are generally acquired later than those which are not so dependent, other things being equal; also, phones which seem to require more precise positioning without tactile feedback (fricatives and liquids as opposed to stops) are acquired relatively late.

No general theory is yet able to account both for the degree of observed variation and the degree of observed commonality of acquisition of phones and of phonemic contrasts across children. Dinnsen (1992) has attempted to construct a phonological hierarchy, but once again, individual differences in early phonological acquisition make this model probabilistic rather than universal. Starting from a different perspective, Lindblom et al. (1983, 1992) have proposed a promising model of early phonemic development in terms of self-organizing systems.

4 Later Phonological Development: Acquisition of Morphology and Morphophonemic Rules

Before children finish mastering the phonetic details of the ambient language, they have begun to acquire its morphology (rules of word formation) and morphophonemics (the contextual variations in shapes of morphemes which are not due to general phonological rules).

Phonological rules with a heavy natural component (e.g. voicing assimilation) appear to be acquired early, with the correct output form always present; forms in which an ending happens to be very similar to a final stem syllable or consonant (e.g. the plural of sibilant final nouns in English) tend to be aquired late (Menn and MacWhinney, 1984). Frequency and many other factors interact in the acquisition of rules which apply to particular classes of morphemes (MacWhinney, 1978; Slobin, 1989), including the transparency and reliability of any semantic and/or phonological conditioning factors. Rote application of a rule to a few frequent words precedes general application of a rule.

Overgeneralization of a rule to cases where it should not apply is taken (here as elsewhere) as the hallmark of actual rule learning (e.g. past tense formations such as "hitted," "bited"), where phonology interacts with the learning of subregularities that are conditioned by morphological factors such as membership in gender classes and conjugational or declensional classes (see Slobin, 1985a, 1993). Some nonproductive but well-evidenced morphophonological rules, such as the stem-final palatalizations in the Romance stratum of English (correct/correction; invade/invasion), are apparently not learned until mid or late adolescence (Myerson, 1975).

Little is known about the acquisition of segmental or of tonal sandhi rules that apply across word boundaries or of rules that apply in rapid speech, in spite of their evident productivity. The ability to understand and produce the fine details of English stress and intonation patterns is developed gradually during the elementary school years (Atkinson-King, 1973; Cruttenden, 1974, 1985).

5 Metalinguistic Awareness

Metalinguistic awareness, i.e. the ability to think about language as an object, develops gradually during childhood and is not fully in place until the age of eight or nine years. Young children generally tend to view language as a means of communication, with primary focus on content and use rather than the form of an utterance.

5.1   Early signs of metalinguistic awareness

Although conscious metalinguistic awareness is not fully in place until the primary school years, rudimentary aspects of such awareness appear in the earliest stages of language learning, as discussed above. For example, children with productive vocabularies of 50 words or less often adopt patterns of "lexical selection and avoidance"; that is, they select words with phonemes or syllabic structures that they can produce accurately for inclusion in their productive lexicon, while avoiding words with phonemes and structures they cannot render accurately (Ferguson and Farwell, 1975; Schwartz and Leonard, 1982). These selection and avoidance behaviors indicate that children as young as 12–15 months old are, at some level, aware of their own phonetic output and how well it matches the target phonemes of the adult word.

Additional evidence of early awareness comes from spontaneous self-corrections and repairs following a failure to communicate (Clark, 1978c) and the phenomena of "practice" sessions in which the children drill themselves on grammatical or phonological patterns of the language. Weir (1962, 1965) provides a clear example of practice on the part of her son David, aged two years, seven months, while he was alone in his crib. In his "crib monlologue," David produced various pronunciations of the word "orange," a form which he had mispronounced earlier in the day in a conversation with an older brother.

5.2   Conscious awareness

Even though young children are capable of some metalinguistic activities, the level of awareness needed for behaviors such as those described above may be minimal. Metalinguistic tasks which require an explicit awareness of linguistic structures have proven to be more difficult. In the phonological domain, assessment of conscious awareness typically centers around tasks involving segmentation of words into syllables and phonemes; success on some of these tasks is not achieved until the age of six or seven. For example, Liberman and colleagues (1974) found that even at age six, only 70 percent of the subjects were able to tap out the number of phonemes in a word. Since most children are engaged in reading activities by age six to seven years, some researchers have hypothesized that the increase in metalinguistic abilities is a consequence rather than a precursor of learning to read. However, failure on some metalinguistic test tasks may be also due to difficulties with understanding the task itself. In a study by Fox and Routh (1975), the subjects were asked to "say just a little bit" of a word produced by the experimenter. In this relatively simple task, three-year-olds and four-year-olds were indeed capable of segmenting some words into syllables and then dividing syllables into phonemes.

Rhyming tasks also provide evidence of a level of conscious phonological awareness in children as young as four years. Detection or creation of rhyming words involves two skills: the child must be able to divide a word into subunits of "onset" and "rime," and to recognize that the rime unit is the same; in other words, to recognize that the words "day" and "play" rhyme, a child must be aware that they have different onsets ("d-" and "pl-," respectively), but the same rime ("-ay").

5.3   *Phonological awareness and reading*

Language awareness plays an important role in language arts curriculum at the primary school level, particularly in learning to read, and performance on phonological awareness tasks is one the best predictors of success or failure in learning to read. To examine the relationship between awareness and reading, Bradley and Bryant (1983, 1985) tested more than 400 children, aged four to five years, on rhyming and other phonological awareness tasks before the children had learned to read. After tracking the educational performance of their subjects for a three year period, they assessed reading. They also assessed spelling and mathematical abilities at age eight to nine years, and found that performance on onset-rime tasks in the prereading period was related to subsequent reading and spelling abilities, but not to mathematical skills. The link between phonological awareness and reading is also supported by research showing that children with reading problems evidence difficulties with phonological awareness tasks (e.g. Bradley and Bryant, 1978; Webster and Plante, 1992).

6   Phonological Models and Theories

6.1   *Child v. adult phonology*

Standard phonological theories are designed to account for the skilled speaker; so, in accounting for the phonology of the unskilled child, it is not unreasonable to have to add new theoretical ideas. To quote Ferguson and Farwell (1975): "Our approach is to try to understand children's phonological development in itself in order to improve our phonological theory, even if this requires new constructs for the latter." The proper developmental constraint on models is just this: that the child's system should evolve towards the adult endstate through demonstrable effects of the environment and maturation. Also, given the extent of individual variation emphasized above, a model must provide a temporal *probability envelope* for the events of phonological development, rather than an absolute temporal sequence.

The models of child phonology we are concerned with here are psycholinguistic models, in which psychological considerations are more important than descriptive elegance (in contrast with the priorities of linguistic theories of adult phonology). Each child must construct his/her own version of the adult system for word production, for there is no way to "internalize" the adult system without this; in this sense, the child has his/her own system, which must eventually come to approximate the adult system.

The most obvious difference between child phonology and adult phonology is the huge gap between what children understand and what they can produce. Originally, this gap was bridged by describing rules or processes that would describe children's approximations to adult words; the rules/processes were considered to operate on an adult target form, or on the child's hypothesized perceptual representation of the adult target, and to produce the child's form as output. However, this approach is not adequate. As indicated above, some outputs are "unruly" – that is, not derived by well defined rules. Furthermore, some rule-governed derivations do not work in "real time," for words that a child has learned to say at a later date may be subject to different rules than words that she/he learned to say at an earlier time. Therefore, the output forms of the older rules, at least, must be in some sense stored. Models of child phonology differ from standard theories of adult phonology because of attempting to deal with such facts.

6.2   Frequency effects

A major characteristic of the progressive idioms, discussed above, is that they are used very frequently by the child; it seems that they resist assimilation into the child's general patterns or rule system because they are used often, and become well established. It is generally the newer and less frequently produced forms which undergo immediate change when new rules are added (see the "down"/"stone" example above). A theory of child phonology cannot ignore word frequency, although current adult phonological theory has no place for this notion.

6.3   Specific theories, models, and formalisms

"Pure" linguistic theories

Some researchers (e.g. Dinnsen, 1992; cf. section 3.4 above) have followed the lead of Roman Jakobson, attempting to develop a hierarchical theory of the order of development of phonemic contrasts that will describe observed regularities. It has, however, proved difficult to sustain many substantive claims because of the amount of individual and crosslanguage variation. Ingram (1992) uses a modified version of this approach which includes the factor of "functional load," noting that certain phonemes which are usually late in English (e.g. /v/ and /l/) are earlier in languages where they are used in more words.

Cognitive approaches

Another group of researchers, following Charles A. Ferguson and including the present authors, have taken what Ferguson and Macken have called a "cognitive" approach to child phonology, viewing the child as actively attempting to solve the problem of "learning to pronounce" with initially limited articulatory resources (Ferguson, 1978b; Macken and Ferguson, 1983). Avoidance, selection, and overgeneralization were taken as hallmarks of this activity. Menn (Kiparsky and Menn, 1977; Menn, 1983) proposed a psycholinguistic model with an input or recognition lexicon and a separate output or production lexicon to account for the facts indicating that children's output forms often appear to be stored. This terminology has been somewhat problematic, as essentially the same semantic information is connected to the input and output phonological representations; Matthei's (1989) reformulation of the model as having a single lexicon with input and output "phonological registers" is an improvement.

Connectionist models and self-organizing/dynamic systems approaches

Recent cognitive models have had a major impact on psycholinguistic theories of phonological development (e.g. see chapters by Lindblom, McCune, Mohanan, Menn and Matthei, and Stemberger in Ferguson et al., 1992).

The child clearly has both internal and external feedback loops for learning sequential (e.g. phonotactic) and simultaneous (e.g. crossmodal) associations; these can be used in simulating a self-organizing model. Internal loops (those loops which do not require responses from another person) include those activated during babble and other sound production: as indicated above (section 3.3), in the normal child, these production experiences link simultaneous and sequential motor commands, the child's percept of his/her own sounds, and kinesthetic information across and within these three (motor, auditory, and kinesthetic) modalities. Simply listening to ambient language also creates auditory sound-to-sound associative links between features that cooccur (building the knowledge of the phones of the language) and between phones that occur in sequence (building phonotactic expectations); Jusczyk (1992) shows that some of this phonotactic knowledge is in place by about ten months of age.

When the child is capable of imitation, this behavior links some perceived adult sound patterns with the child's own motor patterns. Imitation also links the child's own sounds with adult sounds, within the auditory modality. Comprehension links sound patterns with recurrent real-world states, so creating and depending upon links between the auditory modality and the full variety of sensory modalities by which the child experiences the world (taste, smell, tactile, motor, etc.).

The child's external loop feedback types (i.e. those which are dependent on responses of another person) can be described in a similar way. Adult imitation of the child's sounds intensifies the linkage between the adult-produced and child-produced sound patterns, and because the adult's imitation will be filtered through the adult's perception and production, it should produce some feedback about the difference between the child's output and the repertory of adult phones in the given language. Meltzoff (1990) indicates that children are highly attentive to adults whom they perceive as imitating them.

Semantically contingent imitation by the adult – that is, adult production of what she/he takes to be the child's intended semantic target – intensifies the linkages between real-world events and the sound patterns referring to them; it also produces considerable feedback about the difference between the child's output and the target word. Perceived communicative success or failure in obtaining the desired response from the adult gives feedback, but if there is no adult imitation of the target word, this type of feedback – e.g. getting a smile, a different word, or a cookie – can only reinforce globally. The poverty of information in such responses – the fact that they can only tell the child that she/he did or did not get close to the target word – reminds us that the primitive notion of reinforcement by obtaining a desired real-word objective is a rather blunt instrument for teaching. Nevertheless, its contribution may be nonnegligible, as communicative failure may lead the child to monitor the quality of his/her output more closely.

Connectionist models for child phonology have attracted several researchers, as they inherently have many of the properties described in section two: "fuzzy" boundaries, interactions among forms, frequency effects, and storage of both input and output forms in some linked way. Nevertheless, implementation of models is proceding slowly, and many problems remain to be solved.

Autosegmental phonology as formalism and theory

Prosodic and, more recently, autosegmental methods have been successfully applied to the description of child phonology for many years (Waterson, 1971; Menn, 1977; Spencer, 1986) and have given many insights (Macken, 1993). Autosegmental notation is quite felicitous for describing young children's severe syllable-based and word-based limitations on output sound sequences (consonant harmony, canonical forms). Furthermore, the conceptual approach which underlies both autosegmental and prosodic phonology is useful because it can be closely linked with the psychophysiological demands of sequential articulatory motor control and of decoding the rapidly varying incoming speech

Table 12.1   Gestural score representation for "duck" (timing details omitted)

	d	ʌ	*k*
Jaw	Up	Down	Up
Lips	Open		
Tongue front	Up	Down	Down
Tongue back	Down	Down	Up
Velum	Raised		
Glottis	Vibrating		Not vibrating

signal; these presumably are the causes of the observed limitations on output sound sequences. The gestural phonology of Goldstein and Browman (Browman and Goldstein, 1989) is even more closely attuned to articulatory control; MacNeilage and Davis (1990) and Nittrouer, Studdert-Kennedy, and McGowan (1989) exemplify gesture oriented approaches to child phonology (see also Kent, 1992).

All of these approaches, despite their many disagreements, consider a word as a complex of simultaneously occurring events. As in the standard (segmental) phonological theory, each phoneme of a word is seen as consisting of a set of features describing how it is articulated and/or how it sounds. However, the segmental approach considers "duck," for example, as fundamentally consisting of discrete segments {[d], [ʌ], [k]}; each segment is like a "chord," a vertical column of features. Prosodic, autosegmental, and gestural approaches, conversely, consider the word "horizontally," as several simultaneous "melodies." Each melody is essentially the sequence of events relating to one (or a small group) of the features or articulators – for example, in gestural terms, the jaw is high during the initial [d], lowers for the [ʌ], and is raised again for the [k] (table 12.1).

Autosegmental phonology provides a widely accepted formalism (Goldsmith, 1990, is the standard reference; see especially chapter six): each "melody" is notated on a separate horizontal level, called a "tier." A segment is represented by linking all the simultaneous events that characterize it to a single "node" on a basic tier, the "root" tier. For describing most phenomena of early child phonology, a simplified autosegmental notation is adequate: the root tier, a skeletal (CV) tier giving the syllable structure of the word, a place (= place-of-articulation) tier for the consonants, a nasality tier, a laryngeal tier (for vocal cord activity) and a vocalic tier (figure 12.1).

We can then describe consonant harmony (e.g. the production of "duck" as [gʌk]) by limiting the child's place tier to one entry per word (velar, in the example). Most other child phonology phenomena can be handled by imposing similar complexity limitations.

Figure 12.1 (a) Two-dimensional cross-section of possible 3D planar representation at a consonant node, showing hierarchical grouping of feature tiers (adapted from Goldsmith, 1990); (b)
simplified autosegmental representation for the word "duck" (nasality tier omitted; adapted from
Goldsmith, 1990). Features which tend to show cooccurence restrictions are placed on the same
tier; features which interact less are shown on separate tiers.

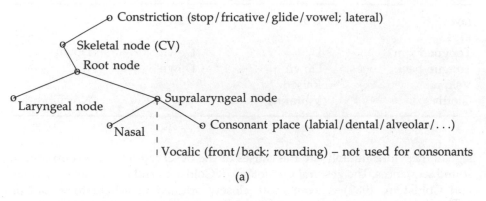

(a)

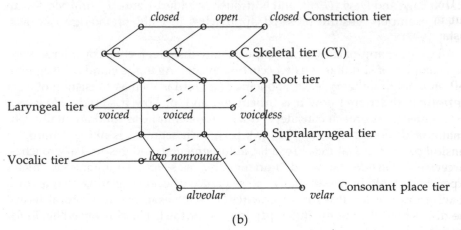

(b)

6.4 *Internal representation in theories of*
phonological development

Linguists have tended to assume internal representation in terms of phonemes
or phonological features, but since Eimas et al. in 1971 showed infants'
sensitivity to fine phonetic details (a tradition of work continued and elaborated by Kuhl, Jusczyk, Werker, and others; see Jusczyk, 1992, 1993; Werker
and Pegg, 1992; Best, 1993; Kuhl, 1993; Werker, 1993, for reviews), child phonologists have had to confront the disparity between these findings, on the
one hand, and children's apparent near-inability to distinguish minimal pairs
of words (e.g. "coat" v. "goat") in experimental situations before the age of
about two and a half years (Barton, 1980). One must also take into account that

the child who has a productive vocabulary of more than, say, 15 words, is sure to have some minimal pairs distinguished in her productions. Ferguson and Farwell (1975: 36)

> assume that a phonic core of remembered lexical items and articulations that produce them is the foundation of an individual's phonology and remains so throughout his linguistic lifetime. Lexical items of particular phonetic shapes are acquired together with notions of appropriateness of use in particular social frames, and changes in the phonic core are to be understood and accounted for in terms of at least lexical, phonetic, and social parameters. Thus we assume the primacy of lexical learning in phonological development, even though it may be heavily overlaid or even largely replaced by phonologically organized acquisition processes in later stages. . . . since children have different inputs and utilize different strategies, the gradual development of phonological organization and phonological awareness may proceed by different routes and at different paces so that adult phonologies may differ from one another just as the lexical stocks of individuals may differ.

This point of view was difficult to assimilate into models for many years, but it is highly compatible with connectionist approaches, which assume instance-based learning.

6.5 *Innateness in theories of phonological development*

Anatomical maturation, developing abilities of fine motor control, auditory sensitivities, potential auditory categorizing abilities, preferences for attending to certain kinds of stimuli, general learning abilities, and specific language experience play obvious roles in phonological development, but the question of whether there is a further, specifically phonological innate component to the discovery of phonological patterning (and if so, what its nature might be) continues to be difficult to address. For example, the phoneme is not definable in phonetic terms, but only in terms of *contrast*: which alterations in sound could differentiate one word from another in a particular language (phonemic differences, as in "cat" v. "bat"), and which alterations could only be considered as possible different ways of saying the same word (phonetic differences, as in the pronunciation of "cat" by speakers of slightly differing dialects). Is the ability to recognize these kinds of differences a linguistically specialized ability or is the "emic"/"etic" distinction one we make in exactly the same way across many realms of cognition? One might go on at some length listing other universal properties of phonology and posing "the innateness question" for each of them. Rather than do so, we will conclude by describing a clear example of "innate knowledge" from Marler's (1984) work on birdsong, as an indication that this category does appear to exist in some species which demonstrate learning.

Most birds produce species-appropriate songs with no exposure to adult songs as models. Their ability to produce their songs is as therefore innate as their feathers. Marler (1984) claims that there are also at least two types of innate components for the many species of birds that do require exposure to models in order to learn to sing. His data show a rudimentary level of species-specific song patterning, which might be termed a "motor" level, even in deafened birds of these species. A richer, but still deficient, level of species-specific song patterning, which we might term a "motor + feedback" level, occurs in normal birds reared in isolation (normal song occurs only in hearing birds exposed to appropriate adult model songs). The large incremental gain between the "motor" and the "motor + feedback" levels of abnormal song indicates that the untutored but normal-hearing birds improve their singing by hearing themselves sing. Therefore, they have an innate knowledge or preference for what sounds "good" v. "bad" in their attempts to sing, which takes them far beyond the output of the "motor" mechanism which is all that is available to the deafened birds. Marler (1984: 291) describes this information as contained in "central auditory templates guiding vocal development by feedback control." We can take these birds to represent the category of innate auditory/vocal knowledge, and then ask ourselves what, if anything, in human behavior might be like it in some measure.

7 Summary

Principal sources for the study of children's early language are diary records, cross-sectional large-group norming studies, and small-group short-term longitudinal studies; experimental studies have also been done. Over the past two decades, research has shown that infants pass through an ordered sequence of stages of prelinguistic vocal development, and that their productions are initially quite similar across languages. Within this broad pattern of similarities, effects of both the ambient language and individual differences in babbling become prominent late in the first year of life. These individual differences usually carry over into the first months of the production of identifiable words. This demonstrable continuity of late babble and early speech is a major finding and is contrary to earlier accepted claims.

Feedback from hearing oneself talk is a major and essential contributor to the mastery of speech sounds; while deaf babies babble, their progress through the usual phases of babble development is delayed and their variety of sounds is impoverished.

Children's early words may be attempts to match single adult words or to match the overall characteristics of longer phrases. The attempts to match adult words with articulatory sequences that are within the child's repertoire (i.e. to output articulatory "templates") may yield systematic relations between child and adult words which can be described in terms of "rules" or "processes," but many child words are not related to their adult targets in ways that can be captured so neatly. Children may also refuse to attempt words that they cannot say accurately; there is much individual variation in all these matters. A very few child pronunciation errors can be ascribed to misperceptions of the adult target.

Children's earliest phonological units appear to be whole words; the appropriate subword unit of analysis is the canonical form or template of the word, which can be treated as corresponding to the skeleton "tier" of adult autosegmental phonology. The age and also the order of mastery of phones, phonemes, and phonemic contrasts is variable across children; only loose probabilistic statements can be made.

Children's metalinguistic awareness develops slowly, from the minimal sense of whether or not they have approximated an adult word adequately, through finer and finer segmentation as literacy is acquired; prereading rhyming ability is correlated with later reading and spelling ability. Failures on some experimental metalinguistic word dividing tasks may be due to failure to understand the task, however.

Phonological theories based on adult language need to be augmented in order to account for the behavior of the unskilled speaker, and each child must construct his/her own version of the adult system for word production. Autosegmental phonology provides a helpful formalism; in addition, however, a theory of child phonology must deal with frequency effects, with individual differences, with "fuzzy boundaries" of rule domains, with nonrule-governed behavior, and with the large gap between what a child can understand and what she/he can produce. Cognitive models, and more recently, connectionist models are being explored; the latter incorporate the "instance-based" nature of early phonological representation.

Learning Words

13 Early Lexical Development

MARTYN BARRETT

This chapter has as its principal focus the early acquisition of words and word meanings by young children. Young children typically acquire their first words round about nine to 12 months of age; by the time that they are two or two and a half years old, they may have acquired up to 500 words or more. This chapter describes the principal phenomena which characterize this early period of lexical development, and also examines some of the main theoretical frameworks which have been used in attempts to explain these phenomena.

The Principal Phenomena Characterizing Early Lexical Development

Quantitative aspects of early lexical development

Many studies which have documented the early growth of children's vocabularies have relied upon measures of the number of words which children spontaneously produce. For example, Nelson (1973) conducted a longitudinal study in which the mothers of 18 children were asked to keep regular records of their children's spontaneous production of words. Nelson found that the average age at which these children had acquired ten words was 15 months (with a range of 13–19 months), the average age at which they had acquired 50 words was 20 months (range 14–24 months), and the average vocabulary size at 24 months of age was 186 words (range 28–436 words). Comparable figures for the number of words which are spontaneously produced at different ages are reported by Benedict (1979), who also relied upon maternal diary records for documenting the early word productions of the eight children in her sample. An alternative to maternal diary records is to ask mothers to select from checklists of words those particular words which their children produce.

This method has been used by Fenson et al. (1993) in a large-scale cross-sectional norming study of 1,789 children ranging in age from eight to 30 months of age. They found that these children had typically acquired ten words by 13 months of age (range eight to 16 months), 50 words by 17 months (range ten to 24 months), and at 24 months they had acquired 310 words (range 41–668 words).

However, measures of spontaneous word production almost certainly underestimate the rate of early vocabulary growth; a more accurate picture can be obtained from measures of children's word comprehension. This conclusion emerges from several studies which have compared production with comprehension. For example, Benedict (1979) not only asked her mothers to record their children's spontaneous word productions; she also asked them to keep a diary of all the words which their children could comprehend. In addition, she gave the mothers regular checklists to check off all the words which were understood by their children. These methods revealed that, at the time when these children could produce ten words, they could understand 60 words on average (the rage being 30–182 words). There was also an average gap of about five months between the attainment of the 50 word level in comprehension and the attainment of the same level in production. A similar picture emerges from the study by Fenson et al. (1993), who relied upon just the checklist method to measure word comprehension. They found that when their children could produce ten words (at 13 months of age), they could comprehend about 110 words on average; and when they were 16 months old, they could produce 45 words but could comprehend an average of over 180 words.

Longitudinal studies documenting early vocabulary growth have also revealed that young children often exhibit a sudden upturn in the rate of acquisition of new words during the course of the second year of life (see, for example, Bloom, 1973; Nelson, 1973; Halliday, 1975; Dromi, 1987). First words are typically acquired at a comparatively slow rate, with only one, two, or three new words being acquired each week. However, round about the time when the vocabulary has grown to about 20–40 words, there is often a vocabulary explosion or spurt in which the rate of word acquisition suddenly begins to accelerate, and within two to three weeks the child may be acquiring eight or more new words per week (all figures here are derived from production measures).

However, it is important to take proper note of the fact that there is considerable individual variation in patterns of early vocabulary growth. The degree of individual variation is apparent from the magnitude of all the ranges cited above. There is a tendency for girls to acquire words at a slightly faster rate than boys overall (Fenson et al., 1993), but the magnitude of this gender difference is small in comparison to the sheer range of variation which is exhibited within each gender. In addition, Goldfield and Reznick (1990) have shown that not all children display a vocabulary spurt. They examined the vocabulary growth of 18 children, using both maternal diaries and word checklists to measure production, and found that five of these 18 children did not display a suddenly accelerating rate of acquisition. These five children instead acquired words at a much steadier rate throughout the second year of life, and this rate of acquisition was only occasionally punctuated by modest upward and downward fluctuations and plateaus in the number of new words acquired.

The types of words acquired during early lexical development

During the course of their early lexical development, children acquire many different types of words. Some early vocalizations seem to function as direct expressions of the child's internal affect states. These particular vocalizations are often nonconventional and idiosyncratic, but insofar as they display relatively consistent phonetic forms which are used for specific communicative functions, they may be classified as words. For example, Halliday (1975) reports that his son produced the sound [uæyi] to express pleasure, while Dore (1985) reports that his son produced the vocalization [məməmə] to signal his distress or discomfort.

Other early words may be heavily context bound; that is, they may be produced by the child only in very limited and specific situations or contexts in which particular actions or events occur. Some examples of context-bound word use are shown in table 13.1 Notice that, in all of these examples, the child failed to use the word in the full range of situations in which an adult might use that word, and instead only used it in a single, highly restricted context. Context-bound word use has now been reported in many different studies investigating early lexical development, including those by Bloom (1973), Bates, Benigni et al. (1979), Lock (1980), Gopnik (1981, 1982), Barrett (1983a, 1986), Dore (1985), Dromi (1987), Harris et al. (1988), Smith and Sachs (1990), and Tomasello (1992).

As can be seen from table 13.1, there are various kinds of context to which this type of word may be bound. In some cases, the context simply consists of a specific action which the child regularly produces in the course of free play with a particular object (e.g. *duck*, *bye*, and *sweep*). In other cases, the context consists of a specific action which frequently occurs within a specific social-interactional routine such as picturebook reading or peekaboo, etc. (e.g. *see* and *boo*). However, the context does not necessarily involve overt motor activity by the child; in some instances, the word is instead produced by the child in response to a perceptually salient event which the child frequently experiences (e.g. *car* and *papa*). Notice, though, that in all cases the context is characterized by an event which occurs with some regularity for the child (see Barrett 1986, 1989, for further discussions of this phenomenon).

However, not all early words are context bound; instead, many early words are used in a range of different behavioral contexts (see table 13.2). Some

Table 13.1 Examples of context-bound word use

Word	Contexts of use	Source
duck	While the child hits a toy duck off the edge of the bath.	Barrett (1986)
bye	While the child puts a telephone receiver down.	Bates et al. (1979)
sweep	While the child sweeps with a broom.	Tomasello (1992)
see	While the child points and turns to the listener for eye contact.	Bates et al. (1979)
boo	While the child hides behind a curtain.	Harris et al. (1988)
car	While the child looks out of the living room window at cars moving on the street below.	Bloom (1973)
papa	When the child hears the doorbell.	Bates et al. (1979)

of these contextually flexible words may be used referentially as the names for classes of objects (e.g. *ball*, *doggy*, *chair*); others may be used as the proper names of individual objects, people, or animals (e.g. *teddy*, *mommy*, *Spot*); while others may be used to refer to particular actions (e.g. *open*, *wash*, *tickle*). Numerous examples of these various referential word types have now been reported in a large number of different studies, including those by Bloom (1973), Gruendel (1977), Bowerman (1978), Rescorla (1980), Barrett (1986), Dromi (1987), Harris et al. (1988), and Tomasello (1992).

In addition, some of the referential words which children acquire during the second year of life are used for referring to the properties, qualities, or states of objects and events. For example, some words are used for referring to the recurrence of objects and actions (e.g. *more*); others are used for referring to the disappearance of objects (e.g. *gone*); some may be used to refer to the spatial location of objects (e.g. *in*, *on*, *up*, *down*); while others may be used for referring to the attributes and states of objects or people (e.g. *big*, *dirty*, *nice*). Various examples of these different word types are reported by Bloom (1973), Gopnik (1982), Barrett (1983a), Dromi (1987), Harris et al. (1988) and Tomasello (1992).

Table 13.2   Examples of contextually flexible word use

Word	Contexts of use	Source
ball	While the child looks at, plays with, or requests: tennis balls, large colorful play balls, a beach ball.	Barrett (1986)
teddy	While the child looks at a teddy; while the child touches the same teddy; while the child points to the same teddy; while the child plays with the same teddy.	Harris et al. (1988)
open	As a request by the child for: a door to be opened; a jar of jelly to be opened; a box of cookies to be opened; her mother's hand to be opened.	Tomasello (1992)
more	While the child holds out an empty bowl; while the child brings an empty bottle to her mother; while the child reaches for a drinking cup before having another drink; while the child reaches into a toybox and takes out more bricks.	Harris et al. (1988)

Finally, in addition to affect expressions, context-bound words, and these various types of referential words, children usually acquire some social–pragmatic words during this early period of lexical development. Social–pragmatic words are words which are used to fulfill specific pragmatic functions within the context of particular interactional exchanges with other people. Common examples are the word *no*, which is often used by very young children in a range of situations to oppose the actions of other people; *please*, which is often used for requesting objects from other people; and *look*, which is often used to direct the attention of other people to a particular object. Some social–pragmatic words may actually consist of formulaic phrases which are useful for directing the behavior of others, e.g. *you do it*, *here you are*, *go away*, etc. Various examples of social–pragmatic words are reported by Bloom (1973), Barrett (1981), Dromi (1987), and Tomasello (1992), amongst others.

It has been suggested by some authors that the different word types are acquired at different points in the child's development. For example, Dore (1978, 1985), McShane (1979, 1980), Nelson (1983), Nelson and Lucariello (1985), and Kamhi (1986) have all suggested that, prior to the vocabulary explosion, children only acquire context-bound words, social–pragmatic words, and affect expressions, and that the acquisition of referential words does not take place until after the vocabulary explosion has occurred. These authors have argued that children only acquire the insight that words can be used symbolically to represent referents *after* they have already acquired some of their earliest words; the acquisition of this insight then leads to the sudden acquisition of large numbers of referential words, and hence to the vocabulary explosion. Probably the strongest evidence in support of this suggestion is that reported by Dore (1985) and Kamhi (1986), each of whom report a single case study of an individual child whose early lexical development did indeed conform to this general pattern. However, it is clear from the evidence which has been obtained in many other studies (e.g. Bates et al., 1979; Harris et al., 1988; Goldfield and Reznick, 1990) that this is by no means the only pattern of development which can occur. For example, Harris et al. (1988) examined the early lexical development of four children, and found that all four children had acquired some referential words amongst their very first words (out of the first ten words acquired by each child, the number which were referential ranged from two to seven). Thus, if the acquisition of referential words is dependent upon some kind of insight into the symbolic nature of language, then these children must have acquired this insight at a much earlier point in their development, before they had acquired any words.

In addition, Dore (1985) has suggested that idiosyncratic affect expressions are acquired before any other word type. However, once again, although the evidence from Dore's own case study is consistent with this hypothesis, the evidence from other studies (e.g. Bates et al., 1979; Barrett, (1986; Dromi, 1987; Harris et al., 1988) indicates that this is not a typical pattern of development, and that idiosyncratic affect expressions may not even be acquired by some children.

Consequently, considerable caution needs to be exercised when it comes to some of the stronger claims which have been made about the order of acquisition of the various word types. However, this caution noted, Fenson et al. (1993) have found three general trends which seem to characterize early lexical development. The first trend is for the proportion of common nouns in children's vocabularies to increase as total vocabulary size grows from zero to 100 words, to level out at this point in development, and then to decrease as children's vocabularies grow larger than 200 words. The second general trend is for the proportion of verbs in children's vocabularies to begin increasing as total vocabulary size grows from 50–100 words, and then to continue increasing as vocabularies grow to about 400–500 words, at which point the increase in the proportion of verbs finally begins to level out. Thirdly, the proportion of adjectives in children's vocabularies also begins to increase as total vocabulary size grows from 50–100 words, and continues to increase up until the time that children's total vocabularies contain 500 words or more. Putting these three trends together, it would appear that, during the earliest phase of lexical development (up until about 50–100 words), children tend to predominantly acquire common nouns, but after this earliest phase, they also come to acquire larger numbers of verbs and adjectives as well. It should, incidentally, be noted that all figures here are derived from measures of word production, not comprehension. Also, it should be noted that, although Fenson et al. refer to "nouns," "verbs," and "adjectives" in their report of these findings, there is no evidence that children themselves, at the beginning of their lexical development, group the words which they are acquiring into these grammatical categories (which are defined by reference to the way in which the words will function within the grammatical system which will eventually be acquired by the child).

Around these general trends, however, there are considerable individual differences in terms of the proportions of the different word types which make up children's early vocabularies. Nelson (1973) was the first to observe that children could be distinguished in terms of whether, at the 50 word, productive vocabulary level, more or less than 50 percent of the words which have been acquired consist of general object names. "Referential" children have 50 word vocabularies which contain more than 50 percent of object names; these children acquire a large number of object names as well as some action names, proper names, state names, etc. By contrast, "expressive" children have 50 word vocabularies which contain fewer than 50 percent of object names; these children have a tendency to acquire larger numbers of personal names, action names, state names, and social–pragmatic words (including formulaic phrases), as well as general object names. There is evidence that referential children lexicalize their object orientated speech acts (such as requesting objects, drawing attention to objects, commenting on objects, etc.) in relatively elaborate and diverse ways, whereas expressive children lexicalize their socially orientated speech acts (such as commenting upon people, manipulating the behavior of other people, playing games with people, etc.) in more elaborate and diverse ways (Barrett, 1981). This finding is not surprising, given the differing contents of the children's vocabularies. However, the proportions in which the different speech acts occur in the total language output of referential and expressive children may not be related to the proportions of the different types of words which make up their vocabularies (Pine, 1992). Also, it ought to be noted that many children are neither extreme referential nor extreme expressive types, but instead fall between the two end points of what should really be construed as a continuum (see Bretherton et al., 1983; Fenson et al., 1993; Lieven et al., 1992).

Phenomena characterizing the use of individual words during the period of early lexical development

During the period of early lexical development, individual words exhibit various phenomena and patterns of developmental change. As has already been noted, some words, when they are first acquired, are used only in a context-bound manner. In the case of some of these context-bound words,

Table 13.3 Examples of the modification of context-bound word use

Word	Contexts of use	Source
catch	Initial use: while the child throws an object to another person. Subsequent use: while either the child or someone else throws an object to another person.	Barrett (1983a)
dog	Initial use: while another person points to one specific picture of a dog. Subsequent use: while either the child or another person points to the same specific picture of a dog.	Barrett (1986)
boo	Initial use: while the child hides behind a curtain. Subsequent use: while the child hides behind either a curtain or a large floor cushion.	Barrett et al. (1991)
brush	Initial use: while the child brushes with a hairbrush. Subsequent use: while the child brushes with either a hairbrush or other types of brushes.	Tomasello (1992)

subtle changes subsequently occur to the way in which these words are used, even though they nevertheless remain context bound. Examples of this type of change in word use have been reported by Barrett (1983a, 1986), Dromi (1987), Barrett et al. (1991), and Tomasello (1992) amongst others; some examples are shown in table 13.3. In each case, the word remained context bound after the change had occurred, but either there was an extension of the range of agents who could perform the action defining the context that elicited the use of the word, or there was an extension of the range of objects which could appear in the eliciting context.

As the child's lexical development proceeds, many context-bound words (although not necessarily all) are subsequently decontextualized (see Bates, Benigni et al., 1979; Lock, 1980; Gopnik, 1981, 1982; Barrett, 1983a, 1986; Dore, 1985; Smith and Sachs, 1990; Barrett et al., 1991, and Tomasello, 1992, for documentations of this phenomenon). Some examples of decontextualization are shown in table 13.4. In each instance, the word was initially acquired and

Table 13.4   Examples of the decontextualization of context-bound words

Word	Contexts of use	Source
off	Context-bound use: while the child removes an item of clothing from either her own or another person's body. Subsequent uses: when the child sees another person remove an item of clothing; while the child tries to pull away from her mother; while the child pulls a toy cat out of a carrycot; to refer to getting off a train. (Common reference: the separation of objects which have previously been in contact.)	Barrett (1983a)
duck	Context-bound use: while the child hits a toy duck off the edge of the bath. Subsequent uses: while the child plays with a toy duck in any situation; after the child is asked "What's that?" in reference to a toy duck; when the child sees a toy duck lying on the floor. (Common reference: a toy duck.)	Barrett (1986)
choo-choo	Context-bound use: while the child pushes a toy train along the floor. Subsequent uses: while the child looks at a picture of a train in a book; while the child puts a teddy into a carriage of a toy train; while the child pulls a toy steamroller out of a toy box; while the child pushes a toy steamroller along the floor. (Common reference: a wheeled vehicle.)	Barrett et al. (1991)
down	Context-bound use: while the child is in a parent's arms, requesting to be put down. Subsequent uses: as a comment on her own activity of getting down; as a request for others to put objects down; as a comment on her own and other people's actions of putting an object down. (Common reference: the putting down of a person or object.)	Tomasello (1992)

used by the child in just one particular context, but at a subsequent point in time, the word began to be used by the child in a much wider range of situations. As can be seen from table 13.4, decontextualization seems to involve a shift away from using the word in a context-bound manner to using the word referentially. Furthermore, the reference of the word after decontextualization seems to be derived from one of the core aspects of the event which previously elicited the context-bound use of the word.

Other phenomena characterizing young children's use of referential words are underextension, overextension, overlap, and mismatch. Many different studies have now documented in considerable detail these four types of extensional error which are often made by young children (see, for example, Clark, 1973a; Reich, 1976; Anglin, 1977, 1983, 1986; Gruendel, 1977; Barrett, 1978, 1982; Bowerman, 1978; Rescorla, 1980; Dromi, 1987; Tomasello, 1992). Underextension consists of the child using a referential word in a range of different situations to refer to only a subset of the full range of objects, actions, states, or properties which are properly labeled with that word in the adult language. Overextension, by contrast, consists of the child using a referential word to refer not only to all of the objects, actions, states, or properties which are properly labeled with that word in the adult language, but also to refer to some further inappropriate objects, actions, states, or properties as well. In the case of overlap, a word is overextended to refer to inappropriate referents but is only used to refer to *some* and not all of the appropriate adult referents. As Anglin (1983) has noted, it is actually very difficult in practice to distinguish clearly between such cases and cases of true overextension. In addition to underextension, overextension, and overlap, young children's words may occasionally display a complete mismatch with the adult word, where there is no overlap at all between the referential scope of the child's word and the referential scope of the adult word. Some examples of underextension, overextension, overlap, and mismatch are shown in table 13.5.

Of these four phenomena, it is the phenomena of underextension and overextension which have received the most attention, particularly in connection with children's acquisition of object names. It has been estimated that between 12 percent and 29 percent of a young child's object names may be underextended during the course of early lexical development, the precise figure depending upon the particular method which is used to test the child's vocabulary (Anglin, 1977). Estimates of the proportion of young children's total vocabulary which is overextended also vary somewhat from study to study, but usually fall within the range of 7 percent to 33 percent, (see Anglin, 1977; Gruendel, 1977; Barrett, 1978; Rescorla, 1980; Nelson, 1982).

In addition, analyses of the full set of referents which are labeled by means of an overextended word have revealed that all of these referents do not necessarily have any features in common with each other; however, each referent does usually have at least one feature in common with the particular object, action, property, or state which originally functioned as the initial referent for the word (see Bowerman, 1978; Barrett, 1982; Nelson, 1982). For

Table 13.5   Examples of overextension, underextension, overlap, and mismatch

Word	Referents	Source
1 Overextension		
dog	Dogs, lambs, cats, wolves, cows.	Anglin (1983)
kick	The kicking of a ball, a fluttering moth, cartoon turtles doing the can-can, making a ball roll by bumping it with the front wheel of a kiddicar, pushing a teddy bear's stomach against the chest of another child, pushing own stomach against a mirror, pushing own chest against a sink.	Bowerman (1978)
tick-tock	Clocks, both analog and digital watches, wallpaper circles with radiating spikes, a circular roadsign, a barometer with a circular dial.	Barrett (1986)
2 Underextension		
bottle	Plastic baby bottles only.	Anglin (1983)
cut	The action of cutting, but only when performed with a knife.	Barrett (1986)
teddy	One particular teddy bear only.	Harris et al. (1988)
3 Overlap		
umbrella	Open umbrellas, a large green leaf, kites (but *not* closed umbrellas).	Anglin (1983)
4 Mismatch		Reich (1976)
TV guide	Television sets (but *not* the program guide).	

example, one child used the word *clock* to refer to clocks, a circular bracelet, and the sound of dripping water, amongst other things (Rescorla, 1976). While the bracelet and the sound of dripping water do not have any features in common with each other, both objects share a common feature with a clock, which was the initial referent for this word.

In this example, the overextended referents shared perceptual features with the initial referent (either a visual feature or an auditory one). However, some overextensions are based upon shared functional features, rather than shared perceptual features. Anglin (1983), for example, reports the case of one child who used the word *hat* or refer to all objects which she put on her head, irrespective of their perceptual form (these included a plastic bowl, a washcloth, a juice can, and a sneaker). Overextensions can be based either upon perceptual features which are shared with the initial referent of the word, or upon functional features which are shared with that referent, although the majority of object name overextensions seem to be perceptually based and only a minority seem to be functionally based (Clark, 1975; Barrett, 1978; Bowerman, 1978; Rescorla, 1980; Anglin, 1983).

It has now become clear from various studies, however, that not all overextensions are caused by categorical errors by the child (i.e. by the child classifying the overextended referent as a genuine member of the category denoted by the word). Bloom (1973), Grieve and Hoogenraad (1977), Barrett (1978, 1982, 1986), Anglin (1983), and Hoek et al. (1986) have all drawn attention to the fact that overextension can result from a variety of other factors as well. These include the child deliberately stretching the use of an acquired word in order to fulfill a communicative purpose for which the child has not yet acquired a more appropriate word; the child accidentally retrieving the wrong word from memory when labeling a referent (e.g. retrieving the word *horse* instead of *donkey*); the child making an object recognition error by mistaking one object for another, and hence referring to that object by means of an incorrect word (e.g. mistaking a donkey for a horse by not paying sufficient attention to it); the child misapplying a word deliberately, either for the humorous effect or for the purposes of symbolic play; the child using the word in a metaphorical manner in order to draw attention to a perceived similarity or analogical relationship between two referents; the child, having formed an association between two objects (e.g. between trains and railway bridges), producing the name of one of the two objects (*train*) when perceiving the other object (the bridge); the child mispronouncing a word (due either to an articulatory slip or to a systematic phonological transformation of that word) such that in its child-produced form it sounds similar to another word which therefore appears to be overextended (e.g. producing the name *Martyn* as *Mama*); substituting a phonologically simple word for a phonologically complex one which the child has difficulty in producing; the child producing a word with a displaced reference to an absent object but with another object contingently present which the observer misinterprets as the intended referent. Thus, overextension may actually result from any one of a large number of different factors.

In addition, longitudinal studies which have traced the use of individual referential words by young children over a period of time have also revealed that the extensional ranges of referential words do not always remain constant after their initial acquisition; instead, the extensional ranges of referential words

Table 13.6   Examples of words which were initially underextended but subsequently overextended

Word	Extensional scope	Source
close	Initially: for closing gates, doors, and drawers only. Subsequently: also for closing boxes and other containers; while pushing handles of scissors, tongs, and tweezers together; for getting people to put their arms or legs together; for folding up a towelette; while fitting a piece into a jigsaw puzzle.	Bowerman (1978)
ball	Initially: a blue beach ball only. Subsequently: also oranges, pumpkins, peas, round beads on a necklace, pompoms on a sweater, beads on a chain, polkadots on her dress, spherical earrings.	Anglin (1983)
duck	Initially: toy yellow ducks only. Subsequently: also real ducks, pictures of ducks, swans, geese, a picture of a quail.	Barrett (1986)

often either expand or contract as the child's lexical development proceeds. The expansion of referential scope has been described by Bowerman (1978), Barrett (1986), Dromi (1987), Barrett et al. (1991), and Tomasello (1992), amongst others. Some examples of words which were initially underextended but whose referential scope subsequently expanded so that they were eventually overextended are shown in table 13.6.

The opposite phenomenon, the contraction of referential scope, has also been noted by Barrett (1978, 1982), Rescorla (1981), Mervis (1984), and Dromi (1987). For example, using word production data, Barrett (1978, 1982) has shown how the referential scopes of categorically overextended words often contract when new words, which are more appropriate for labeling the overextended domains, are acquired by the child. In addition, Mervis (1983, 1984) has used systematic longitudinal testing of children's comprehension of object names to obtain further evidence concerning this process. She has shown that object names which are categorically overextended when they are first acquired (e.g. *car*) are typically used to refer to objects in the overextended domain for which the child has not yet acquired more appropriate names (e.g. *trucks*). When the more appropriate name for an object in the overextended domain is subsequently acquired (e.g. *truck*), both the old overextended name and the new name are typically applied to the overextended domain interchangeably for a period of time; that is, there is often a transitional period in which the extensions of the two words overlap. Finally, the extensions of the two words eventually become mutually exclusive, with the new word capturing the domain of overlap from the old word, and with the referential scope of the old word consequently contracting (i.e. the overextension of *car* to label trucks is finally rescinded).

Thus, we now have a great deal of information about the various phenomena which characterize children's early use of words, including context-bound word use, the modification of context-bound word use, decontextualization, underextension, overextension, overlap, mismatch, and the expansion and contraction of referential scope. In addition, several studies have now demonstrated that individual words can exhibit several of these phenomena in succession during the course of their development. This point has become very clear from longitudinal studies which have traced the ontogenesis of individual words (e.g. Barrett, 1986; Dromi, 1987; Tomasello, 1992); these studies have revealed that children's early words can exhibit an enormous variety of different developmental profiles.

Probably the most exhaustive study of these developmental profiles is that carried out by Dromi (1987), who examined the early lexical development of one child between the ages of ten and 18 months. Dromi analyzed the developmental profiles which were exhibited by every one of the 276 words on which she collected longitudinal data. She found that, within the sample of 276 words, there were many different developmental profiles. Context-bound word use and underextension tended to be phenomena which occurred early on in the developmental history of individual words, whereas overextension tended to be a phenomenon which occurred relatively late in the history of individual words (although there were a few words which were overextended at the time of their initial acquisition). Nevertheless, there were nearly as many words (136 in total) in Dromi's sample that showed no changes across the study period as there were words which did exhibit changes (which numbered 140). Similar findings emerge from other studies (e.g. Barrett, 1986; Tomasello, 1992). A selection of just some of the developmental profiles which have now been documented in these various studies are shown in table 13.7.

Theoretical Explanations of Early Lexical Development

Semantic feature theory and lexical contrast theory

Over the last two decades, many different theoretical frameworks have been advanced in attempts to explain the various phenomena which characterize

Table 13.7   Examples of the developmental profiles exhibited by individual words

Profile	Sources
ACBW	Barrett (1983), Dromi (1987)
ACBW > MCBWU	Barrett (1986), Tomasello (1992)
ACBW > MCBWU > D > RE	Barrett (1983, 1986)
ACBW > MCBWU > D > U > ERS > RE	Barrett (1983)
ACBW > D > RE	Barrett (1986), Dromi (1987)
ACBW > D > U > ERS > RE	Barrett (1983)
ACBW > D > U > ERS > O > CRS > RE	Barrett (1986)
AU	Barrett (1986), Dromi (1987)
AU > ERS > RE	Dromi (1987), Tomasello (1992)
AU > ERS > O > CRS > RE	Dromi (1987)
AO	Barrett (1986), Dromi (1987)
AO > CRS > RE	Dromi (1987), Mervis (1983)
ARE	Barrett (1986), Dromi (1987)
ARE > ERS > O > CRS > RE	Dromi (1987)

ACBW = acquisition of context-bound word; MCBWU = modification of context-bound word use; D = decontextualization; RE = regular extension; U = underextension; O = overextension; ERS = expansion of referential scope; CRS = contraction of referential scope; AU = acquisition of underextended word; AO = acquisition of overextended word; ARE = acquisition of regularly extended word

early lexical development. Clark (1973, 1975) put forward one of the earliest of these frameworks, semantic feature theory. According to this theory, the meanings of words consist of smaller, more primitive, units called "semantic features." The meaning of the word *cat*, for example, would be said to consist of a set of semantic features [+object, +animate, +four-legged, +furry, +whiskers, +miaows]. These features are criterial for the application of the word; that is, a referent must be characterized by all of these features in order for the word to be applicable to it. Semantic features vary according to their level of generality, with some being very general (e.g. [+object] and [+animate]) and others being more specific (e.g. [+whiskers] and [+miaows]).

Clark (1973) hypothesized that, during the course of their early lexical development, children acquire the semantic features for any given word one at a time, over an extended period. In addition, she postulated that these features are acquired in the order from the most general down to the most specific. As a consequence, the meaning of the word *cat*, for example, might only consist, midway through its acquisition, of the subset of features [+object, +animate, +four-legged]. As these features are criterial for the application of the word to individual objects, the word would be used by the child to refer to any four-legged animate object (i.e. the word would be overextended to label dogs, sheep, horses, cows, etc.), not just to refer to cats. And this overextension would be rescinded only when the child finally acquires the more specific semantic features for the word. Thus, the major prediction of this theory is that words will be overextended when they are first acquired, and that these overextensions will only be gradually narrowed down (through the addition of increasingly specific semantic features) until the correct adult extension of the word is eventually achieved.

Clark (1973) presents a wealth of evidence, extracted from early diary studies, to support the prediction that overextension is a very pervasive phenomenon in early lexical development. However, more recent findings have served to cast some doubt upon the empirical adequacy of this theory. Firstly, as we have already seen, overextension is not such a common phenomenon as the semantic feature theory predicts: estimates of the proportion of children's total set of words which are overextended only fall within the range from 7 percent to 33 percent (see, for example, Anglin, 1977; Barrett, 1978; Rescorla, 1980). Secondly, when overextension does occur, it is more likely to occur comparatively late in the developmental history of a word (Dromi 1987), rather than immediately after the initial acquisition of the word (in fact, underextension is more likely to occur than overextension at this early point in the development of the meaning of a word). Thirdly, it has actually proved impossible in practice to identify the relevant sets of semantic features which make up the meanings of the vast majority of words (see Greenberg and Kuczaj, 1982, for a discussion of this problem, which seriously undermines the credibility of semantic feature theory). Fourthly, as we have seen earlier in this chapter, the full range of referents of individual words do not necessarily have any invariant features in common with one another (and which could therefore be interpreted as being the criterial features for the application of the word). Instead, each of these referents often shares common features with just the initial referent of the word (recall the example of the word *clock*, which was used by the child to refer both to a bracelet and to the sound of dripping water, two referents which do not have any features in common with each other but each of which shares a common feature with a clock). That is, the extensions of referential words exhibit a family resemblance structure, rather than a structure which is characterized by an invariant set of common features as predicted by semantic feature theory.

More recently, Clark (1983, 1987, 1990a) herself has abandoned semantic feature theory, largely for the reasons just given. In its place, she has instead proposed a different theoretical framework, namely lexical contrast theory. In this theory, the basic building blocks of the meanings of words are lexical contrasts rather than semantic features: these are representations of the contrasts which exist between the meanings of different words. According to this theory, the process of lexical development is driven by two dominant operating principles which are followed by the child: the principle of contrast and the principle of conventionality. The principle of contrast means that the child assumes that any new word which is encountered must contrast in its meaning with other words which are already known to the child; this principle therefore leads the child to search for possible lexical contrasts for that word. The principle of conventionality, on the other hand, means that the child assumes that there are always conventional linguistic forms which can be used for referring to particular entities; this principle leads the child to search for conventional means for referring to entities.

Thus, according to this theory, overextensions in early lexical development are due to the child stretching the use of a conventional word in order to refer to something for which the more appropriate word, and its attendant lexical contrasts, has yet to be acquired. But when that more appropriate word is eventually acquired, the child searches for the appropriate lexical contrasts and, when they are finally identified, rescinds that overextension. This interpretation is consistent with the evidence reported by Barrett (1978, 1982) and Mervis (1983, 1984) discussed above, on the rescission of overextensions. However, lexical contrast theory has never really been fully developed as an explanation of any of the other major phenomena which characterize early lexical development (such as context-bound word use, decontextualization, the range of developmental profiles exhibited by different words, etc.). Instead, Clark, in most of her recent work, has explored this theory in relationship to the processes of later (rather than early) lexical development (see chapter 14, this volume).

Prototype theory

Another theory which has been extremely influential in the study of children's early acquisition of referential words is prototype theory. According to this theory, the meaning of a referential word is initially acquired, not in the form of either semantic features or lexical contrasts, but in the form of a prototypical referent for that word. This prototypical referent effectively functions for the child as a specification of the clearest and most typical referent of that word. The child then generalizes the word to other referents on the basis that they share common features with this prototype. Referents which have many features in common with the prototype are highly typical referents of the word, while referents which have relatively few features in common with the prototype are atypical or peripheral referents of the word.

This theory readily accounts for the finding that the full set of referents which are included within the extension of a word are not always linked by an invariant set of common features, but are sometimes only linked by a family resemblance instead. This is because, although all the referents must share common features with the prototypical referent, they do not have to share the same common features as each other. Prototype theory can also explain the finding that, when young children underextend words, it is usually the more peripheral referents which are excluded from the extension of the word, and not the more typical referents (Kay and Anglin, 1982). This is because the probability of a referent being included within the extension of a word is determined by the number of features which that referent shares with the prototypical referent, and so typical referents are more likely to be included in a word's extension than peripheral referents.

In addition, prototype theory can explain the results which have been obtained in studies of word comprehension by young children. These studies have shown that, when children are tested for their comprehension of words which they spontaneously overextend in production by asking them to "show me the X" or "give me the X" (where X is the overextended word), they usually begin by choosing a central typical referent rather than an atypical overextended referent; this is because the child chooses that referent which has the most features in common with the prototypical referent which has been acquired for that word. Consequently, if comprehension testing is terminated at this point, then the child appears not to be overextending the word in comprehension (Thomson and Chapman, 1977; Fremgen and Fay, 1980). However, if the child is allowed to continue choosing further referents, then with each successive choice, progressively less typical referents are chosen until, eventually, overextended referents are selected by the child (Kuczaj, 1982). This sequence of choosing referents is precisely what would be pre dicted by prototype theory, with the most typical referents (i.e. those which have the most features in common with the prototype) being chosen first, and the least typical referents (i.e. those which have the fewest features in common with the prototype) being chosen last. (It should be noted, however, that although many words do indeed display a similar extensional scope both in production and in comprehension, this is not the case for all words; see, for example, Kay and Anglin, 1982, and Kuczaj, 1986, both of whom have reported evidence suggesting that various types of asymmetries between the extensions of words in comprehension and in production can occur.)

Thus, prototype theory is able to account for a wide variety of different phenomena. For this reason, it currently commands very wide support amongst researchers in this field: see, for example, the various papers in Kuczaj and Barrett (1986). Nevertheless, there are some serious problems with this theory. Firstly, there is a distinct lack of consensus in the literature as to what precisely is meant by the term "prototype." For example, Anglin (1977, 1979) has argued that a prototype is a generalized abstract schema which represents the central tendency of a set of specific referential instances that have been experienced by the child. By contrast, Kuczaj (1982; Greenberg and Kuczaj, 1982) has argued that prototypes are holistic mental representations of individual referential exemplars that the child has encountered. A third position, advocated by Bowerman (1978, 1980) and Barrett (1982, 1986, 1987), is that, although prototypes may first be acquired as mental representations of individual referential exemplars, these representations are subsequently analyzed by the child into their constituent features, with the result that these prototypes eventually come to consist of correlational clusters of perceptual and functional features.

In addition to this lack of consensus about what a prototype actually consists of, there are also several phenomena characterizing early lexical development which prototype theory does not address. Prototype theory is essentially a theory about the meanings of referential words, and as such it draws its principal strength from its ability to explain: (1) why referential words are often underextended early on in their developmental history (because initially words may only be used to refer to referents which bear a high degree of similarity to the prototype); (2) why referential words sometimes become overextended subsequently (because words are subsequently generalized to novel referents on the basis of the perceptual or functional features which they share with the prototype); (3) why the extensions of referential words exhibit a family resemblance structure (because the extensions of referential words are defined by reference to a central prototypical referent); and (4) why there are typicality effects in children's production and comprehension of referential words (again, because the extensions of referential words are defined by reference to a prototypical referent). However, prototype theory does not explain (or even address) children's acquisition of context-bound and social–pragmatic words, or the process of decontextualization. Also, without further theoretical constructs such as lexical contrasts being introduced, prototype theory offers no explanation of how the child's overextensions are rescinded (see Barrett, 1982).

Event representation theory

The acquisition of context-bound and social–pragmatic words, and the process of decontextualization, have, however, been directly addressed by another theory of early lexical development, namely event representation theory, put forward by Nelson (1983, 1985, 1986; Nelson and Lucariello, 1985). This theory postulates that, before they acquire their first words, young children build up a knowledge of the frequently recurring events that take place in their everyday environments. For example, they would acquire mental representations of the events which occur regularly in their free play with objects, of the events which occur in the social-interactive routines and exchanges in which they regularly participate, and of other perceptually salient events which are regularly experienced by the child.

According to this theory, the mental representations of these events which the child acquires contain four different types of information. Firstly, they specify the sequence of constituent acts which are lined together temporally (and possibly causally as well) to form the represented event. Secondly, they specify the people who are involved in these constituent acts, and the roles which these people occupy in those acts (including the child's own roles as well). Thirdly, they specify the objects which may be involved in the constituent acts. And finally, the specifications of people and objects may be represented as slots, which can be variably filled by different people or objects in different instantiations of the represented event. In addition to these character-istics, Nelson also postulates that one-year-old children's event representa-tions are holistic in nature; that is, the constituent components and relations of these event representations have not yet been analyzed or separately iden-tified by children of this age.

These holistic event representations which are acquired during infancy there-fore enable the prelinguistic child to participate in regularly occurring events, and to anticipate and to make predictions about the future course of these events. Nelson further postulates that, when the first words are subsequently acquired, they are either built into or mapped onto these event representa-tions. Thus, the first words are either produced by the child embedded within the enactment of a particular event representation, or are produced by the child as a response to the global instantiation of an event representation. Thus, the child's first words are typically tied either to the events which occur regu-larly in free play or in social-interactive routines and exchanges, or they are produced in response to perceptually salient events which regularly occur in the environment of the child; that is, the child's first words are either context bound or social–pragmatic in their nature.

Nelson further postulates that, during the course of the second year of life, the child finally begins to analyze these event representations into their con-stituent components and relations, which then become available as separate units in the child's system of mental representations, forming concepts of individual people, objects, actions, relations, etc. These are two linguistic phe-nomena which occur as a consequence of this process of partitioning event representations into their constituent concepts. Firstly, words which were previously embedded within event representations become mapped onto just one of the derived concepts. This results in the decontextualization of previ-ously context-bound words, and the subsequent use of these words to refer to people, objects, actions, or relations falling within the extensions of these con-cepts. Secondly, the partitioning of event representations leads to the sudden proliferation of concepts. Consequently, the child now has available a large number of additional concepts onto which new words can be mapped. Thus, there is a vocabulary explosion in which large numbers of new referential words are suddenly acquired.

The particular strengths of event representation theory are that it explains several of the phenomena characterizing early lexical development: the acqui-sition of context-bound and social–pragmatic words, decontextualization, the initially slow growth of the lexicon, and the acquisition of referential words in very large numbers once the vocabulary explosion has taken place. However, there are certain lines of evidence which this theory has some difficulty in accommodating. Firstly, as we saw earlier, it is now known that the child's first words are not always either context bound or social–pragmatic in nature, and there are no consistent orders of acquisition of the various word types in early lexical development. In fact, the very first words of some children may be used referentially, right from the outset (Harris et al., 1988), even though other children do indeed display the pattern predicted by Nelson (Dore, 1985; Kamhi, 1986). Secondly, not all children exhibit the vocabulary explosion predicted by the theory; instead, some children exhibit a much steadier rate of acquisition of new words throughout the second year of life (Goldfield and Reznick, 1990). Thirdly, decontextualization is not a sudden phenomenon which occurs midway through the second year of life, simultaneously affecting all of the context-bound words which are in the child's vocabulary. Instead, the decontextualization of context-bound words can begin at a very early age, just after the acquisition of the first words, and may then continue gradually, word by word, throughout the second year of life and even later (see Barrett, 1986, 1989; Barrett et al., 1991). Fourthly, some words which could potentially be used referentially may be acquired and used initially only as context-bound words well after the vocabulary explosion has already occurred (Barrett, 1983a, 1986). Thus, although event representation theory is indeed able to explain the acquisition of context-bound words and social–pragmatic words, and the process of decontextualization, this theory is not consistent with much of the more detailed empirical data which is now available concerning these particular phenomena.

The multiroute model of early lexical development

The multiroute model was formulated in order to explain the development of the meanings of context-bound, social–pragmatic, and referential words (Barrett 1983b, 1986, 1991). According to this model, early lexical development proceeds on a local word-by-word basis, rather than proceeding via global systematic changes which simultaneously affect large numbers of different words. The model postulates that there are two principal routes in early lexical development, one of which is followed by context-bound and social–pragmatic words, the other of which is followed by referential words (see figure 13.1). The model proposes that these two routes differ in terms of the nature of the mental representations onto which the words are initially mapped. Context-bound and social–pragmatic words are initially mapped onto event representations; the child then uses these words in the contexts of these represented events. By contrast, referential words are initially mapped onto mental representations of prototypical referents; the child then uses these words to refer to objects, actions, properties, or states which closely resemble these prototypes. Thus, according to this model, children utilize *two* different kinds of internal representation when they first begin to acquire words: event representations *and* prototypes (Mandler, 1983; Barrett, 1987). Nelson (1985, 1986) presents good evidence for postulating that children have indeed built up event representations by the time that they begin to acquire words. But, in addition, there is very good evidence that children have also acquired prototypically structured concepts before they have acquired any words (indeed, there is good evidence that prototypically structured object categories are acquired before

Figure 13.1   A diagrammatic summary of the multiroute model (adapted from Barrett, 1986).

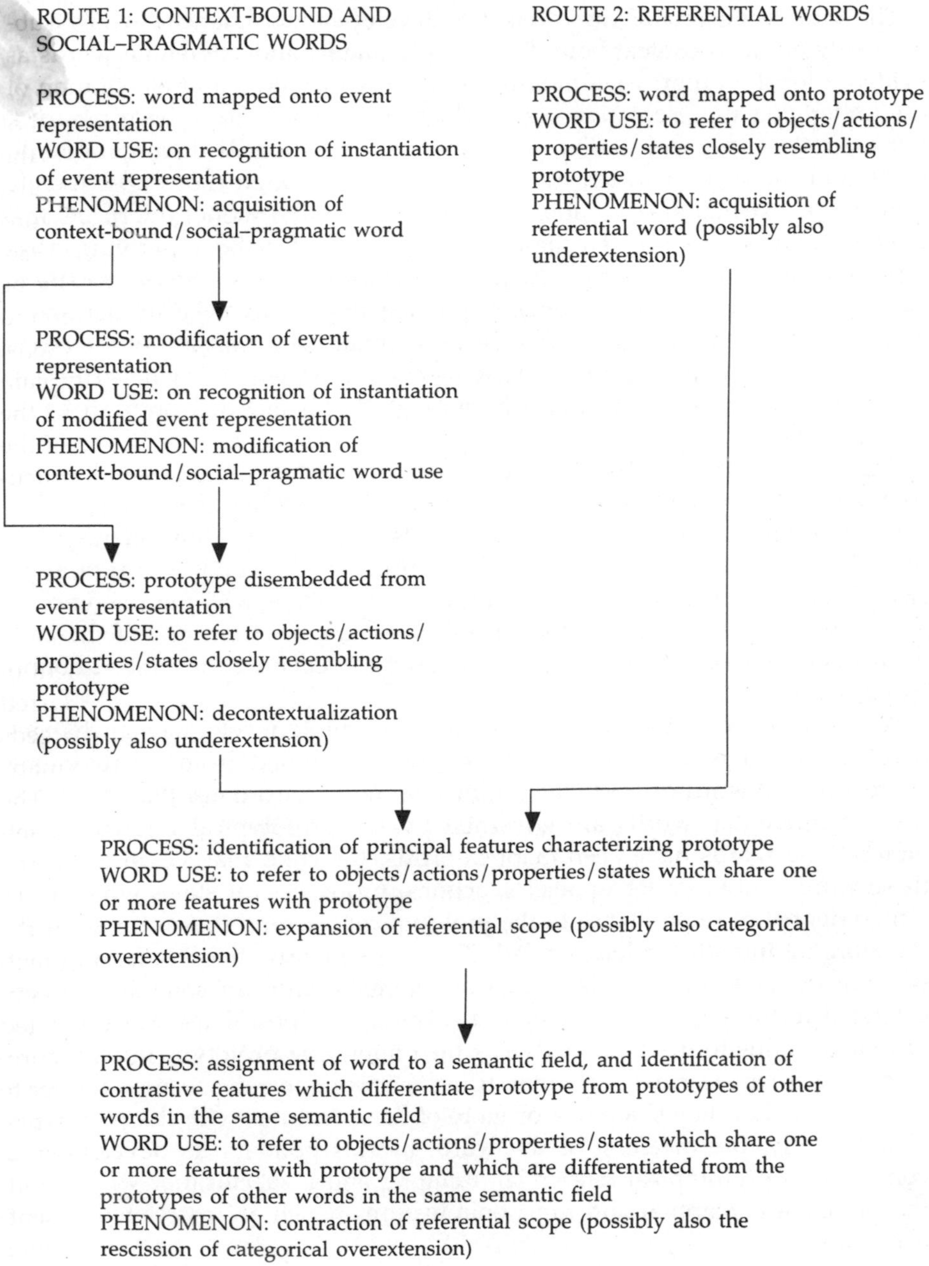

ROUTE 1: CONTEXT-BOUND AND
SOCIAL–PRAGMATIC WORDS

ROUTE 2: REFERENTIAL WORDS

PROCESS: word mapped onto event
representation
WORD USE: on recognition of instantiation
of event representation
PHENOMENON: acquisition of
context-bound/social–pragmatic word

PROCESS: word mapped onto prototype
WORD USE: to refer to objects/actions/
properties/states closely resembling
prototype
PHENOMENON: acquisition of
referential word (possibly also
underextension)

PROCESS: modification of event
representation
WORD USE: on recognition of instantiation
of modified event representation
PHENOMENON: modification of
context-bound/social–pragmatic word use

PROCESS: prototype disembedded from
event representation
WORD USE: to refer to objects/actions/
properties/states closely resembling
prototype
PHENOMENON: decontextualization
(possibly also underextension)

PROCESS: identification of principal features characterizing prototype
WORD USE: to refer to objects/actions/properties/states which share one
or more features with prototype
PHENOMENON: expansion of referential scope (possibly also categorical
overextension)

PROCESS: assignment of word to a semantic field, and identification of
contrastive features which differentiate prototype from prototypes of other
words in the same semantic field
WORD USE: to refer to objects/actions/properties/states which share one
or more features with prototype and which are differentiated from the
prototypes of other words in the same semantic field
PHENOMENON: contraction of referential scope (possibly also the
rescission of categorical overextension)

infants are even six months old: see, for example, Roberts and Horowitz, 1986; Colombo et al., 1987).

The multiroute model interprets the developmental changes which subsequently occur to context-bound, social–pragmatic, and referential words as evidence for the progressive modification, reorganization, and elaboration of the underlying representations onto which these words have been mapped. For example, as we saw earlier, some context-bound words undergo a modification of the way in which they are used, even though they subsequently remain context bound (see table 13.3). The multiroute model interprets this phenomenon as evidence of a change having occurred to the underlying event representation, such that either the range of possible actors who participate in the represented event, or the range of possible objects involved in that event, is altered (such modifications often seem to entail the expansion of the range of alternative slot fillers in the underlying event representation); nevertheless, the word remains context bound because it is still mapped onto an event representation.

According to this model, the decontextualization of context-bound words (see table 13.4) is due to the partitioning of the underlying event representation, and the disembedding of one of its constituent components; this disembedded component is subsequently used by the child as a prototypical referent for the word. This model therefore explains why the reference of such a word after decontextualization derives directly from one of the core elements in the event which had previously been eliciting the context-bound use of the word.

As we have seen, referential words can also exhibit developmental changes (irrespective of whether these words have developed from a previously context-bound word or not). The multiroute model postulates that the initial uses of referential words are governed by the prototypical referents onto which these words have been mapped. Thus, the child may begin by using these words only to refer to objects, actions, properties, or states which bear a high degree of resemblance to the prototypical referent; these words might therefore be initially underextended. But, subsequently, the words are often generalized to a much wider range of referents, and are sometimes overextended in the process (see table 13.6). The model postulates that this type of change is due to the child analyzing the underlying prototype into its principal constituent features, and then using the word to refer to new referents on the basis that they share one or more of these features with the prototype. Consequently, the meaning of the word, by this point in its development, consists of a prototypical referential exemplar and a specification of some of the principal perceptual and functional features which are correlated in that exemplar.

It should be noted that, if a word is overextended at this point in its development as a result of its meaning being determined by reference to the features of a prototype, then the overextension is likely to be exhibited not only in the child's production of that word, but also in the child's comprehension of the word (as it derives from an underlying semantic representation, which is hypothesized to guide both the production and the comprehension of the word). Thus, categorical overextensions need to be distinguished from all the other types of overextension which may occur, for example, from overextensions which are caused by the child making either accidental lexical retrieval or object recognition errors, by the child deliberately misapplying the word for humorous or playful purposes, etc. The distinction between categorical overextensions and all these other types of overextension needs to be emphasized because, with all these other types, there is no reason to expect that the child will exhibit the overextension in both production and comprehension (see Barrett, 1986; see also Kay and Anglin, 1982, and Kuczaj, 1986, who provide evidence that both symmetrical and asymmetrical patterns do indeed occur).

When a categorical overextension does occur, the multiroute model postulates that the overextension will eventually be rescinded when the child finally identifies the features which differentiate the prototype of the word from the prototypes of the other categories which fall within the same semantic domain. For example, if the word *cat* is overextended to label other animals, then that overextension will be rescinded when the child identifies those features which differentiate the prototype of the word *cat* from dogs, sheep, cows, etc. Notice that there is no reason to suppose that the child will identify these features immediately; for example, it may take the child some time after acquiring both the word *cat* and the word *dog* (together with their respective prototypes) before the child finally identifies the contrasting features which differentiate cats from dogs. Thus, prior to the identification of these contrasting features, there may be a transitional period during which the child uses either of these two words (the application of each being governed by its own prototype) to refer to objects which have features in common with both prototypes; that is, the two words may exhibit overlapping extensions prior to the identification of the relevant contrasts. However, once the relevant contrasts have been identified, then the extensions of the two words should separate out and become mutually exclusive. Notice that this developmental sequence is precisely that which has been reported by Mervis (1983, 1984) in her studies of the rescission of overextensions. Thus, according to the multiroute model, the meanings of referential words eventually come to contain three different forms of information: a prototypical referential exemplar, a specification of some of the principal perceptual and functional features which are correlated in that exemplar, and a specification of the contrasting features which differentiate the prototypical referent from the prototypical referents of other words which fall within the same semantic domain.

In the original formulation of the multiroute model (Barrett 1983b, 1986), it was also noted that some words do not exhibit any developmental changes during the course of early lexical development; this observation has since received further support from the studies by Dromi (1987) and Barrett et al. (1991). For example, some context-bound and social–pragmatic words may continue to be used in exactly the same unchanging manner throughout the second year of life. Thus, with some of these words, there may be no modification to, or partitioning of, the event representation which underlies the use of the word.

It was also noted in the original formulation of this model that some referential words appear to be used by the child in an entirely appropriate manner right from the outset; this finding has also received additional confirmation from Dromi (1987). These words appear to be mapped onto an accurate category structure right from the outset. But, as we have already seen, there is evidence that infants acquire some prototypically structured categories well before they have acquired any words. Consequently, the acquisition of the accurate use of a referential word right from the outset is readily explicable by postulating that such words are mapped immediately onto a comparatively mature category structure which has already been acquired by the child before the acquisition of the word itself.

In addition, some words may be mapped onto underlying category structures which are still in the process of their formation by the child. For example, the child may have acquired a prototype for a particular category, and may have already identified the principal features of that prototype, but might not yet have identified the contrasting features which differentiate that prototype from the prototypes of other semantically related categories. If a word were to be mapped onto such a category which is still in the middle of its formation, then we might expect such a word to be overextended on its initial acquisition; this overextension would then be rescinded later on, when the child finally identifies the relevant contrasting features.

Consequently, the multiroute model accounts for a very wide range of different phenomena (e.g. context-bound word use, decontextualization, underextension, overextension, etc.). It also accounts for the various sequences in which these phenomena occur when the child's use of individual words is traced over an extended period of time (see table 13.7). Furthermore, because the model postulates that some words may be mapped onto fully developed category structures, while others may be mapped onto category structures which are only partially developed, it also accounts for the fact that not all words display the full sequences of developmental phenomena. But although this model predicts that many different developmental profiles can occur, it also predicts that there are certain constraints on these profiles, not in terms of the individual phenomena which will be displayed in the development of any given word, but in terms of the sequences in which the phenomena should occur if they are displayed in the development of any particular word.

The multiroute model is therefore able to account for a much wider range of the phenomena which characterize early lexical development than any of the other available theoretical accounts. However, this model is also incomplete in its current formulation. For example, it does not incorporate any explicit account of the child's acquisition and use of affect expressions (although these could quite easily be incorporated by postulating that such words are not mapped onto a representation of an external event or a prototypical referent, but onto an internal affect state of the child: see Barrett, 1989). It is also unclear at the present time (for reasons of insufficient data) whether all referential words fit the developmental patterns predicted by the multiroute model, or whether some words (particularly certain words which refer to the properties, qualities, and states of objects, actions, and events) fall outside the explanatory scope of this model. Nevertheless, although this model is almost certainly incomplete at the present time and will no doubt require expansion and modification as further data come to light, it does serve to illustrate the much more flexible kind of theoretical modeling which seems to be required if we are to explain any more than just a selected subset of the phenomena characterizing early lexical development.

The Relationship Between Early Lexical Development and Children's Cognitive Development

During the 1970s, it was commonly maintained that there was a very close relationship between the cognitive development of the child and the child's early lexical development. For example, Brown (1973) and Bloom (1973) both argued that in order for the child to acquire object names, the child first had to attain stage six of sensorimotor intelligence (Piaget, 1953, 1955, 1962); more specifically, it was argued that the child's acquisition of object names and the vocabulary spurt were both dependent upon the child's prior acquisition of stage six object permanence and the emergence of the capacity for mental representation. However, the empirical studies which were conducted to examine these claims found very little evidence for this relationship between level of object permanence and children's acquisition of object names (see Corrigan, 1979; Bates et al., 1979; Miller et al., 1980; Bloom et al., 1985).

However, Bates et al. (1979) did find that the acquisition of first words was correlated with the child's attainment of stage five means–ends behavior. This behavior consists of the ability to use tools in order to achieve particular goals (e.g. using a string or a cloth in order to obtain an object); as the child's first words are similarly used as a means to an end (i.e. as a means to communicate with other people), this correlation between the emergence of first words and the achievement of means–ends behavior is not surprising. In order to explain this correlation, Bates et al. themselves proposed that performance on means–ends tasks and the use of first words are both based upon the same underlying cognitive structure which is then manifested in both of these two domains.

More recent studies, however, have moved away from examining such global relationships between cognitive and linguistic development, and have instead focused upon the possible relationships between specific cognitive achievements and the acquisition of particular lexical items. For example, Gopnik (1984) and Tomasello and Farrar (1984) have examined words which specifically refer to the visible movements of objects (such as *move, fall down, up,* etc.); they found that these words tend to emerge during stage five of object permanence, which entails performing successfully on object hiding tasks which involve the visible displacement of objects. By contrast, they found that words which refer to object movements at least part of which are not visible (such as *away, gone, find,* etc.) are not acquired until stage six of object permanence; stage six entails successful performance on object hiding tasks which involve the conceptualization of invisible displacements. Furthermore, Tomasello and Farrar (1986a) found that they could teach visible displacement words to both stage five and stage six children (i.e. to children who had mastered concepts of both visible and invisible displacements), but they could teach invisible displacement words only to stage six children, and not to stage five children who had not yet mastered the concept of invisible displacement. These finding suggest that, in order for young children to learn these kinds of words, it is necessary for them to have first acquired the underlying concepts onto which these words can then be mapped.

Similarly, Gopnik and Meltzoff (1984, 1986a, 1986b) have found that the acquisition of words which express success and failure (such as *hooray, uh-oh, oh dear,* etc.) are related to the development of stage six means–ends performance which involves the ability to reflect on and to compare plans in order to solve tasks. Gopnik and Meltzoff (1986a) also found that the acquisition of success and failure words is not related to the attainment of stage six object permanence, and that the acquisition of invisible displacement words is not related to the attainment of stage six means–ends performance. This suggests that the links between linguistic and cognitive development can be highly specific.

Thus, it appears that when some early words are acquired, they are mapped onto cognitive structures which have already been acquired by the child. In addition, as we have seen earlier, there is evidence that children acquire both prototypically structured object categories (Roberts and Horowitz, 1986; Colombo et al., 1987) and event representations (Nelson, 1985, 1986) prior to the acquisition of words, and that some early words are probably mapped onto these existing cognitive structures when they are first acquired (with object names being mapped onto natural object categories, and context-bound and social–pragmatic words being mapped onto event representations). However, in addition, the child's acquisition of a new word may itself sometimes precipitate the formation of a new concept or category by the child. In several experimental studies (for example, those conducted by Nelson, 1982; Schwartz and Terrell, 1983; Hoek et al., 1986), young children have been taught nonsense words to refer to artificial referents for which it is extremely unlikely that they had previously formed any categorical structure. In these studies, the children often acquire the artificial words along with a knowledge of their appropriate referents. Furthermore, the children subsequently generalize these words to novel referents, in a way which suggests that they are using the original artificial referents as prototypes, and have constructed a new category around these prototypes (Nelson, 1982). Thus, the relationship between early lexical development and cognitive development is almost certainly complex and bidirectional, with new words in some cases being mapped onto existing cognitive structures, but in other cases the acquisition of new words precipitating the formation of new categorical structures.

Finally, there is some evidence suggesting that there may be a link between the vocabulary explosion and the way in which children categorize objects. Gopnik and Meltzoff (1987) examined young children's physical sortings of groups of objects into different categories, and they found that these children had always acquired the ability to sort different types of objects into categorically clear groups or piles *before* they exhibited what was termed the "naming explosion" (operationally defined as the first time that the child acquired ten or more general object names within a three week period). Furthermore, Gopnik and Meltzoff found a strong positive correlation between the age at which this naming explosion occurred, and the age at which this type of sorting behavior emerged. Gopnik and Meltzoff suggest that both developments may be based upon the acquisition of the understanding that objects belong in categories, and that in world can be divided into natural kinds, an understanding which first emerges in children's sorting behavior and then in their language. However, it ought to be borne in mind that not all children exhibit a naming explosion (Goldfield and Reznick, 1990), that children can already categorize objects well before any language is acquired (Roberts and Horowitz, 1986; Colombo et al., 1987), and that many children use words to refer to categories of objects well before the naming explosion takes place (Harris et al., 1988). But, whatever the correct explanation of Gopnik and Meltzoff's finding may be, it nevertheless represents another example of how the links between early lexical and cognitive development tend to be highly specific and localized rather than global (see also Bloom et al., 1985).

The Relationship Between Early Lexical Development and the Linguistic Input Received by the Child

Children's early lexical development clearly does not take place in isolation from their social-interactional experiences; instead, it is precisely these experiences which provide them with the conventional lexical forms which they acquire during the course of their early lexical development. Bruner (1983; Ninio and Bruner, 1978; Ratner and Bruner, 1978) and Ferrier (1978) have examined some of the social-interactional routines in which prelinguistic children regularly participate (such as picturebook reading, peekaboo, build-and-bash games, and routine caregiving activities such as feeding, bathing, diaper changing and dressing). These studies have revealed how these regularly occurring social-interactional routines typically consist of highly structured and standardized formats which contain clearly demarcated roles for both the adult and the child participant. Furthermore, particular linguistic forms tend to be produced by the adult at predictable points in the sequences of actions which make up these interactional formats. Such a consistent experience of individual lexical forms embedded at specific points in regularly occurring and ritualized events clearly provides the child with an optimal situation for acquiring not only event representations but also context-bound and social–pragmatic words. It is therefore not surprising to find that many of the child's early words are produced in the context of precisely these types of social-interactional routines.

In addition, other studies (e.g. Schaffer et al., 1983; Harris et al., 1983, 1984) have revealed that, during social-interactive episodes involving mother and young child, the mother tends to monitor the child's focus of attention very carefully, and to time her utterances to coincide with moments in the interaction when the relevant referent (either an object or an action) already occupies the child's focus of attention. Tomasello and Todd (1983) and Tomasello et al. (1986a) found evidence that the amount of time which mother–child dyads spend in this kind of joint attentional episode is directly and positively related to the child's later vocabulary size. In addition, Tomasello and Farrar (1986b) found that the use of object names by mothers to refer to objects which are already at the child's focus of attention is also positively correlated with later vocabulary size. However, Tomasello's studies reveal that attempts by the mother to actively redirect the child's attention (rather than to monitor and to follow it) is negatively correlated with the proportion of object names in the child's vocabulary. Also, these studies have revealed that the use of referential words by mothers outside episodes of joint attention do not correlate with measures of the subsequent lexical development of the child.

However, there are factors other than joint attention, maternal responsiveness, and the presence of social-interactional formats which also influence what the child picks up from the linguistic input. For example, Leonard et al. (1981) have shown that young children are more likely to acquire new words from the linguistic input if the phonological characteristics of those words are consistent with the children's own existing phonological systems (rather than if the sounds which make up the words are not part of the children's existing phonological systems), while Schwartz and Terrell (1983) have shown that young children are more likely to acquire words which occur frequently rather than infrequently in the linguistic input (and also that the distributed rather than the massed occurrence of a word in the input leads to a greater uptake of that word by children).

Harris et al. (1988) found, however, that individual words (including not only referential words but also context-bound and social–pragmatic words) are rarely modeled for children in the input which they receive in a consistent and clearcut fashion across all the separate incidences of each individual word;

instead, mothers typically use each individual word in a wide range of varied and diverse situations and behavioral contexts while they are interacting with their children. Harris et al. examined which of these various maternal uses of a word is subsequently picked up by the child; they found that, in the overwhelming majority of cases (83 percent), it is the most frequently occurring use of a word by the child's mother which is subsequently acquired by the child as the child's own initial use for that word (irrespective of whether the word is acquired as a referential, context-bound, or social–pragmatic word).

In a follow-up study, Barrett et al. (1991) examined the subsequent developmental history of each individual word which had been examined by Harris et al. (1988). The aims of this follow-up study were threefold: to ascertain whether the subsequent changes in the children's uses of these words were consistent with the predictions of the multiroute model; to ascertain whether the mothers finetuned their modeling of lexical forms in the children's linguistic input in order to pace the lexical progress of their children; and to examine the nature of the relationship between the subsequent changes which occurred in the children's uses of these words and the maternal uses of the same words. It was found that all of the patterns of change which were exhibited by the children's words were compatible with those predicted by the multiroute model, but there was little evidence for much finetuning by the mothers. It was also found that a large proportion of the children's subsequent uses of these words bore no relationship at all to any of the maternal uses of these words; thus, the children did not appear to be deriving their subsequent uses of these words from any of the models of lexical usage which were available to them in their mothers' speech. These findings, when considered in conjunction with those obtained by Harris et al. (1988), suggest that, although the linguistic input may play a crucial role in helping the child to establish initial uses for words, the influence of the child's speech environment may decline quite rapidly thereafter, with the child coming to rely upon the endogenous cognitive processing of internal representations (in the ways indicated in figure 13.1), as much as the exogenous linguistic input, for establishing the subsequent uses of words.

Conclusion

The early acquisition of words and word meanings by young children is clearly an immensely complicated process. This process is heavily constrained by the child's existing cognitive representations (although, as we have seen, the acquisition of words can also precipitate the formation of new cognitive structures), by the child's capacity for analyzing, modifying, and elaborating internal representations, and by the linguistic input which is received by the child. It is also clear that there are considerable individual differences in the patterns of early lexical development which are displayed by different children (for example, in terms of the contents of their vocabularies, and in terms of the quantitative growth of the early lexicon).

As we saw at the beginning of this chapter, by the time that children are aged two to two and a half years old, they have usually managed to acquire modest vocabularies containing perhaps 500 words or more. However, this is still nowhere near the size of an adult's lexicon, which has been estimated to contain between 50,000 and 250,000 words (Seashore and Eckerson, 1940; Aitchison, 1987). The subsequent developments which enable children to go on to achieve this prodigious number of words form the focus of chapter 14 by Clark in the present volume.

14 Later Lexical Development and Word Formation

EVE V. CLARK

Words are indispensable. Without words, speakers are tongue-tied. Without them, they can't exemplify syntactic patterns, morphological structure, or even the sound patterns of their language. Words, in short, offer the primary linguistic means for conveying meaning. English-speaking adults, for example, make use of a production lexicon of anywhere from 20,000 to 50,000 wordforms; their comprehension lexicon is even larger. Learning words, then, is a major part of learning language, and it is inextricably linked to the acquisition of syntax, of morphology, and of phonology. By age two, children may be able to produce anywhere from 50 to 500 or 600 words. They add steadily to this stock at a rate estimated at around ten words a day, to reach a vocabulary of some 14,000 by age six (Carey, 1978; Templin, 1957). From then on, children average at least 3,000 new words a year through age 17. It has also been estimated that, from about age ten on, schoolchildren are exposed to about 10,000 new words a year; so by age 15, they have been exposed to some 85,000 word roots and as many as 100,000 distinct word meanings in school texts alone (Nagy and Anderson, 1984; Nagy and Herman, 1987).

How do children acquire new words? How do they store them? What kinds of information must children represent about each word so they can identify and understand it when they hear it from someone else, and so they can retrieve and produce it when they speak? In this chapter, I focus on lexical development in children from about age two on, after the initial steps in word learning have occurred (Barrett, chapter 13, this volume). First, I consider some pragmatic principles that guide children's acquisition as they map meanings onto forms, and consider the speed with which children assign *some* meaning to an unfamiliar word. I then look at the kinds of semantic domains children have by age two, and how they elaborate these as they add more words to their vocabularies. I turn next to children's exploitation of word formation – their analysis of words into parts (roots and affixes), and their coining of words for objects, actions, and properties. I look at the means children rely on in their coinages, at the circumstances under which they create new words to convey their meanings, and how these uses compare to adult usage and adult creativity in the lexicon. I then take up children's appreciation of how lexical choices reflect the speaker's perspective on the events being talked about. And I end by looking at children's growing grasp of idioms and figurative uses of language.

Conventionality and Contrast

What must children do when they learn the words of a language? First, they must learn to isolate words from the stream of speech so they can identify words when they hear them on other occasions, and they must also begin to analyze parts of words so they can identify roots, inflections, and eventually other affixes. Second, they must identify potential meanings, and here they appear to draw on the kinds of ontological categories they have already set up in representing the world around them – categories of objects, of actions and events, of relations, and of properties (e.g. Clark, 1993). Third, they must map possible meanings onto the forms they have identified. Their initial mappings may overlap only slightly with the adult mapping and so require considerable adjustment. These adjustments, in fact, are what result in the patterns of early word usage, with over- and underextensions, partial overlaps, and even, on occasion, total mismatches (see chapter 13).

In mapping meanings onto forms, children appear to be guided by pragmatic principles. Two in particular play a major role for child and adult speakers alike – conventionality and contrast. These two principles capture two essential design features of languages. First, speakers must agree on which forms convey which meanings. Without such agreements or conventions, it would be much harder for addressees to work out what a speaker meant on any particular occasion. Conventionality offers a shortcut in the form of consistency over time: "For certain meanings, there is a form that speakers expect to be used in the language community." Second, speakers practice a certain economy in their assumptions about forms and meanings. The assumption here is one of contrast: "Speakers take every difference in form to mark a difference in meaning." That is, if speakers use a form different from the one that might have been expected, they must mean something different.

Conventionality and contrast together place certain constraints on speakers' uses of the lexicon. First, established words – those with a conventional meaning – take priority. If what a speaker means is already captured by a conventional form–meaning combination, that is the form that must be used. Conventional words therefore preempt other forms with the same meaning that might have been used in their place but that are not conventional for the meaning intended. Conventionality and contrast together capture the fact that speakers do not tolerate full synonyms in a language. If two expressions would have exactly the same meaning, speakers always give preference to the conventional one over any innovation. If one of the two terms has been borrowed from another language or dialect, its meaning is then typically differentiated in some way from the other established term so as to avoid synonymy (e.g. Bolinger, 1977; Bréal, 1897).

For children, conventionality and contrast have essentially the same consequences as for adults, but since children start out with a much more limited conventional lexicon, they do not always apply these pragmatic principles with the same effects as adult speakers (Clark, 1990a, 1993). Children begin by taking as their targets the conventional words they hear in the input around them. But as they talk more and more about what is happening around them, they become more likely to encounter gaps where they lack conventional words for what they want to talk about. At this point, children may stretch the resources available, and extend a word they already know. Or they may coin a new word for that occasion to carry the necessary meaning.

Rapid Mapping and Bootstrapping

Children need only minimal exposure to a new form, it appears, before they assign *some* meaning to it. This rapid mapping may follow as little as one exposure to the unfamiliar word. For example, when three-year-olds heard an unfamiliar word form, *chromium*, alongside other words for color, only once or twice, they assumed that it too picked out a color (Carey, 1978; Heibeck and Markman, 1987). That is, children appear to map some meaning almost immediately onto any form they isolate. It is possible that any meaning associated with a form helps to make that form more memorable. That in turn should make it easier to recognize the next time it's heard in adult input.

Rapid mapping may capture only a fraction of the conventional meaning of a form. And working out the full meaning may take years. Yet children often manage to overlap with enough of the adult meaning both for some uses to seem appropriate, and for them to recognize the same form on subsequent occasions. in fact, rapid mapping lets children set up large numbers of lexical entries in memory, with partial meanings, in a short time. Once children have some form in memory, they can gradually adjust the information associated with it – its meaning – as they find out more about how it is used. This more detailed mapping of meaning onto form may take months or even years.

Words once identified must also be assigned to the relevant syntactic category. How do children discover grammatical entities like "Noun" or "Verb"? Although such entities do not have semantic definitions, nouns and verbs do typically refer to distinct, identifiable semantic classes in parental speech. Notions like physical object, agent, and action are thereby made available to children in the input language they hear. Adults talk about things, actions, properties, and relations. When they use a noun or a verb, they do so with the relevant formal information that goes with each syntactic word class – noun inflections, on the one hand (*a cat, two cats, the cat's ear*), and verb inflections, on the other (*we push, he pushes, they are pushing, you pushed, they have pushed*). Adult usage, then, presents a strong correlation of category type and word class. This input offers children a potential route into syntax.

If they assume different word classes for their mappings of different ontological types, children should be able to bootstrap themselves into the syntactic categories such as "Noun" and "Verb." Once they make a preliminary assignment of words to word classes, they can then start to make use of inflectional details to assign unfamiliar words to a grammatical type. Such semantic bootstrapping would offer a *way in* to the syntactic categories needed for the acquisition of syntax (see Pinker, 1984, 1989).

Could children start from syntactic information instead, and use it to make inferences about certain aspects of meaning? For example, once they have registered that *hat* takes the plural ending, and that *pull* takes past tense *-ed*, can they use inflectional information to decide that a new word is a verb or a noun? Although syntactic class cannot yield specific noun or verb meanings, it can offer hints about the general type of meaning – action, object, or substance (Brown, 1957). And young children can use inflectional clues to distinguish words by syntactic type. Reliance on such syntactic bootstrapping could be important in assigning preliminary meanings to unfamiliar words. For example, they could use information about word order and arguments to decide whether a new verb was transitive or not: compare *The boy chased the cat* and *The boy sat down*. In fact, three-year-olds seem to do just this when dealing with unfamiliar words from a "puppet language": they treat terms with two noun phrases as transitive verbs, and terms with one noun phrase as intransitives (see Gleitman, 1990; Naigles, 1990).

Children surely take advantage of any and all available clues to meaning. Structural clues from inflections, word order, and argument structure should complement children's reliance on conceptual categories as they map meanings onto word forms. But the extent to which they can bootstrap their way into syntax as a whole is not yet clear (see chapter 15).

Adding Words to One's Vocabulary

I will look first at children's elaboration of semantic domains as they add more words to their lexicon, and then turn to the kinds of coinages they favor as they fill semantic gaps.

Elaborating semantic domains

By age two to two and a half, children can typically produce somewhere between 50 and 600 words. In their first few months of speaking, children talk

Table 14.1 Animal terms in D's speech

A Initial repertoire (1;0,29–1;11,30)

1;0,29 doggie, 1;1,15 dog, 1;3,3 mouse, 1;3,23 cat, 1;4,28 horse, 1;6,13 cow, 1;6,28 rabbit, 1;11,30 goat

1;1,26 bear, 1;7,19 lion, 1;8,8 alligator, 1;11,16 gorilla, 1;10,24 seal

1;2,0 bird, 1;3,0 duck, –1;4 chicken, 1;7,2 goose

1;5,6 turtle, 1;6,4 fish, 1;8,7 frog, 1;8,8 snake, 1;8,22 crab, 1;10,19 ladybug

1;7,20 animal

B Elaborating the repertoire (2;0–3;0)

2;0,8 puppy-dog <toy dog>, 2;2,24 baby-rabbit, 2;5,21 mummy-bunny <toy rabbit>, 2;7,27 sheep, 2;11,1 cattle, 2;11,1 baby-cattle, 2;11,1 daddy-cattles, 2;11,3 bronco-horse, 2;11,10 bucking-horse

2;0,11 hippo, 2;1,7 camel, 2;4,10 baboon, 2;4,16 tiger, 2;5,21 monkey, 2;7,15 wolf, 2;7,15 raccoon, 2;8,8 armadillo, 2;8,8 fox, 2;8,17 beaver

2;3,21 stork, 2;3,21 ostrich, 2;4,6 robin, 2;4,17 sparrow, 2;4,19 flamingo, 2;4,20 dove, 2;5,10 grouse, 2;5,14 woodpecker, 2;8,6 owl

2;5,1 trout, 2;5,4 flounder, 2;5,6 spider, 2;5,6 grasshopper, 2;7,2 fly, 2;7,2 bee, 2;8,14 butterfly, 2;9,21 lizard-animal <live>, 2;9,21 frog-animal <live>

Source: Clark, diary data

about people and animals, toys and household utensils, food and eating, everyday routines and activities (e.g. Clark, 1979; Dromi, 1987; Nelson, 1973). As they add further words to their vocabularies, they elaborate each semantic domain, subdividing some and reorganizing others as they add superordinate and subordinate terms in production. Let's take animal terms: by age 2;0, one child, D, produced some 24 terms, starting with *doggie*, his first one (later *dog*), at 1;0,29. In the next year, between age 2;0 and 3;0, he added a further 38 terms, as shown in table 14.1 (see also Clark, 1978a; Smith, 1973). The animal terms he produced in the first year (1;0,29 to 1;11,30) fall into several clusters: words for domestic animals and pets, for wild animals, for birds, and for fish, reptiles, and insects. At 1;7,20 D produced his first use of *animal*. This term was used from then on in two ways: as a superordinate, especially when

Table 14.2   Food terms in D's speech

A Initial repertoire (1;1,10–1;11,27)

1;1,10 bottle, 1;1,17 cup, 1;2,0 [meme] <food>

1;2,17 banana, 1;3,1 cheese, 1;3,18 nut, 1;3,23 cracker, 1;6,9 bread, 1;6,13 egg, 1;6,4 pea, 1;7,1 cereal, 1;7,4 carrot, 1;7,6 cookie, 1;7,8 apple, 1;7,21 ring <cheerio>, 1;7,15 raisin, 1;7,22 orange, 1;7,26 jam, 1;8,23 rhubarb, 1;8,29 crumb, 1;9,1 yoghurt, 1;9,23 sugar, 1;10,14 flake, 1;10,15 salt, 1;10,16 graham-cracker, 1;11,13 toast, 1;11,27 cornflakes

1;2,23 juice, (1;4,6 water), 1;4,20 tea, 1;6,9 milk, 1;5,25 [meme] <medicine>, 1;8,1 orange-juice, 1;11,3 apple-juice

1;7,0 food, 1;7,6 drink [verb], 1;7,21 eat [verb], 1;10,12 taste [verb]

B Elaborating the repertoire (2;0–3;0)

2;0,18 strawberry, 2;2,28 tangerine, 2;6,5 nuts

2;0,29 chicken, 2;4,19 soup, 2;4,28 shredded-wheat things, 2;6,19 soufflé, 2;6,19 (la)sagna, 2;6,24 blackbean-soup, 2;7,14 blue cheese, 2;7,14 kwaark, 2;7,17 barley, 2;7,25 meat, 2;9,26 potato, 2;10,21 potato-sticks <French fries>, 2;11,26 corn

2;1,25 cake, 2;1,27 oatmeal, 2;2,5 spaghetti, 2;2,17 sandwich, 2;3,3 pie, 2;5,17 pancakes, 2;8,13 birthday-cake, 2;9,14 brioche, 2;9,19 ice-cream, 2;9,2 finger-breads <strips>, 2;9,24 lavendar-pastry <fantasy food>, 2;10,5 crumb-cookie <hazel cookie>, 2;10,18 ices <cubes>, 2;10,29 licker-pop <lollipop>

2;4,5 candy, 2;6,19 popcorn, 2;8,4 pretsel, 2;8,11 peanuts 2;9,20 chocolate

2;1,30 butter, 2;4,0 sauce, 2;6,2 cream, 2;7,0 marmalade, 2;8,11 peanut-butter, 2;8,18 pickle, 2;9,2 pepper, 2;9,2 honey

2;3,1 milk-shake, 2;4,12 wines <bottles of>, 2;6,19 coffee, 2;6,20 grapefruit-juice, 2;6,24 hot chocolate, 2;8,1 beer, 2;11,6 tomato-juice, 2;11,9 iced-tea

2;2,23 breakfast, 2;6,21 supper, 2;9,25 picnic

Words in angle brackets identify the referent of the term
Source: Clark, diary data

talking about several different kinds at the same time, and also, for several weeks, as a general-purpose term for any animals where, as yet, he had no other label.

In his second year of production (2;0–3;0), D added terms to each of the earlier groupings. For example, he added 10 terms for wild animals to the five from his first year; he added nine terms for birds to the four already known; and he added nine more fish, reptile, and insect terms (see table 14.1).

Other domains are elaborated in much the same way: children begin with just one or two terms, add two or three more, and then elaborate each part of the overall domain still further, using newly added words to mark finer and finer distinctions. This holds just as much for other domains, as can be seen in table 14.2 for food terms, and table 14.3 for vehicle terms.

With food terms, D initially relied on a general request for food, /meme/, and on *bottle* and *cup*, used as requests for milk or juice. He then added more specific terms for different kinds of food, for a total of 38 food words by age two. By age 1;8, these included two superordinate terms, *food* – used for bananas, rings [cheerios], cereal, cheese, jelly, bread, oranges – and *juice* – used for juice, water, milk, and tea. In the next year, D added a further 51 terms for kinds of food, plus three meal terms (*breakfast, supper, picnic*) (see table 14.2).

The domain of vehicle terms grew at a similar pace. In his first year of talking, D acquired some 25 terms for vehicles, including two part terms (*wheel, steering-wheel*). In the next year, he added another 58 terms, mainly for subtypes of vehicle, and also a variety of words for parts of vehicles (e.g. *mast, engine, pedals, tooter, oars*), as shown in table 14.3. These three domains – animals, food, and vehicles – are representative of how children add to and elaborate their vocabulary after they learn to produce their first words.

This general pattern of elaboration appears to hold as much for relational terms as for object labels. In talking about location, for example, English-speaking children may at first produce only a neutral vowel sound (a schwa) to mark the position in their utterance of a missing locative preposition. They then gradually adjust their pronunciation towards a syllabic /n/ sound, and only some months later begin to produce distinct forms for prepositions like *in, on, near, above, or under* (e.g. Clark, 1993b; Peters and Menn, 1993). Children follow much the same path when they talk about dimensionality. At first, they use only the relational terms *big* or *little* (*tiny, wee*); then they add other terms like *high* and *long*, then *tall, wide*, and *deep* over the course of two or more years (see Clark, 1972a; Donaldson and Wales, 1970). But despite the rapid addition of so many conventional terms in each domain, children often try to talk about things, actions, and qualities for which they lack the conventional words.

Filling semantic gaps

Children have a much smaller vocabulary than the adults around them, so they are often faced with semantic gaps and have to find some means to fill

Table 14.3 Vehicle terms in D's speech

A Initial repertoire (1;3,11–1;11,30)

–1;4,0 car, 1;5,10 (air)plane, 1;6,8 truck, 1;6,8 train, 1;6,9 bicycle, 1;6,23 airplane, 1;7,0 (motor)bike, 1;7,10 bike <motorbikes, child bikes>, 1;7,24 cart, 1;8,7 helicopter, 1;8,22 sled, 1;8,31 fire-truck, 1;9,17 bus, 1;10,8 garbage-truck, 1;10,14 motorcycle-car <3-wheeler>, 1;10,20 fire-engine, 1;10,29 boat, 1;10,30 choo-choo train, 1;11,16 BIRTHDAY-you-you car <toy RollsRoyce>, 1;11,17 race-car, 1;11,30 push-chair, 1;11,30 baby-bus

1;3,11 wheel, 1;8,27 steering-wheel

1;10,23 drive [verb]

B Elaborating the repertoire (2;0–3;0)

2;0,9 cickycle <baby bicycle>, motocickycle <motorbike>, 2;2,15 rolls-royce <toy>, 2;2,16 fire-truck, 2;3,22 tractor, 2;4,3 motor-car, 2;4,5 ferry-boat, 2;4,10 jet-plane, 2;4,18 snow-car <white car>, 2;4,24 bike <baby bicycle>, 2;4,24 bicycle <adult bicycle>, 2;5,1 light-cars <with headlights on>, 2;5,11 school-bus, 2;5,11 car-truck <transporter>, 2;5,11 cow-truck <animal-transport>, 2;5,11 shovel-truck <earth-mover>, 2;5,11 flying fortress, 2;5,13 airplane-spaceship, 2;5,13 pillow-spaceship, 2;6,10 house-truck <truck with high cab>, 2;6,20 snow-plough, 2;6,20 farmyard-truck <with animals in>, 2;7,2 farmyard-wagon <cart with animals>, 2;7,4 street-sweepers, 2;7,5 building-ship <large liner>, 2;7,25 police-boat <destroyer with turrets>, 2;8,22 police-garbage-truck <with siren>, 2;9,3 volvo-car, 2;9,11 taxi, 2;9,17 London-bus <red>, 2;9,18 mixing-truck <cement-mixer>, 2;9,23 upstairs-bus <double-decker>, 2;9,24 digger-shovel <earth-mover>, 2;10,22 bump-car <bumper-car>, 2;10,26 logger-truck <with logs>, 2;10,28 ambulances, 2;11,3 police-car, 2;11,4 motor-boat, 2;11,21 puller <tow-truck>, 2;11,28 fighter-cars <as crashed them>

2;0,25 mast, 2;4,3 motor, 2;4,5 smoke-stack, 2;4,18 engine, 2;4,24 pedals, 2;5,6 brakers <brakes>, 2;6,22 seat, 2;6,27 drivers, 2;7,22 peep <car horn>, 2;7,25 siren, 2;7,27 tooter, 2;8,1 clean-wipers <windshield-wipers>, 2;8,7 pilot, 2;8,11 gas, 2;9,10 oars, 2;10,28 steers <steering-wheels>, 2;11,2 windshield, 2;11,4 car-seat

Words in angle brackets identify the referent of the term
Source: Clark, diary data

Table 14.4 Some novel nouns coined by two to five-year-olds

(1) GR (1;7, of a picture in a book): *There crow-bird.*

(2) HL (1;11, spoon for her cod-liver oil): *Oil-spoon.*

(3) EP (2;0, seeing her father's colleague who worked in the rat lab): *There comes the rat-man.*

(4) EP (2;0, seeing a coffee-grinder): *Coffee-churn.*

(5) GR (2;1, torn picture of a jungle tribe holding spears): *Mommy just fixed this spear-page.*

(6) GR (2;4): *You're the sworder and I'm the gunner.*

(7) SC (2;5,14): *I want a butterfly-shirt.*

(8) MW (2;5,24, talking about a ladder): *That is a climber against the wall.*

(9) AG (2;6,20, having fixed a raisin box onto a red pen): *Candycane-flag!*

(10) SC (2;8, of a bean-bag chair): *Dat's a ball-chair.*

(11) FR (2;8, pretending): *I was being the firetruck-man.*

(12) CC (2;11,21, talking about one of her books): *That's a duck-story.*

(13) CR (3;6): *You be the storyer, daddy*

(14) DS (3;9, putting a feather in the screen door): *Look at this door-feather.*

(15) BS (3;11, hanging a drawing with scotch-tape): *Am I a good hanger?*

(16) JP (4;4, of a model pump): *It's supposed to be a pumper. You pump it.*

(17) BS (4;7): *You're a copy-catter, daddy. You say what I say.*

(18) BS (4;8, watching the parakeet climbing the bars of its cage): *He is like a tight-roper.*

(19) CS (4;8, after complaining about a playmate): *I didn't show my angriness.*

Source: Clark, collection of spontaneous child coinages

them. The first recourse may be to rely on known lexical options. Children can make use of deictic terms like *this* or *that* to pick out as-yet unlabeled objects. They can also use a general purpose noun like *thing*. When they lack words for particular actions, they can rely on general purpose verbs like *do, make, go,* or *put* (Clark, 1983). But on many occasions, they instead coin their own words – new nouns for objects, new verbs for actions, and new adjectives for states or qualities. Some representative examples of such spontaneous child coinages are given in tables 14.4, 14.5, and 14.6.

From as young as age two, children coin novel nouns when they need them. The earliest such coinages in a language like English are typically root compounds, formed from two nouns, as in *crow-bird* or *taxi-car* (both from two-year-olds). Note that many such compound nouns in fact identify subkinds of a kind already known and labeled by the child, as in *crow-bird* used of a kind of bird (see Berman and Clark, 1989; Clark, Gelman, and Lane, 1985). Soon after age two, children start to use some derivational suffixes as well when they construct new nouns. The first noun suffix used in English is generally the agentive *-er*, as in *sworder* (for someone who uses a sword) or *hanger* (for

Table 14.5   Some novel verbs coined by two to five-year-olds

(1) SC (2;4, as his mother prepared to brush his hair): *Don't hair me.*
(2) JA (2;6, seated in a rocking chair): *Rocker me, mommy.*
(3) SC (2;7, hitting baby sister with toy-broom): *I broomed her.*
(4) SC (2;9, playing with a toy lawnmower): *I'm lawning.*
(5) RG (3;0, of a bell): *Make it bell.*
(6) DM (3;0, pretending to be Superman): *I'm supermanning.*
(7) SC (3;1, watching a cement truck revolving, not pouring): *That truck is cementing.*
(8) SC (3;2, putting on his cowboy hat with a string-and-bead fastening): *String me up, mommy.*
(9) JM (3;2, realizing his father was teasing): *Daddy, you joked me.*
(10) FR (3;3, of a doll that disappeared): *I guess she magicked.*
(11) AG (3;7, of food on his plate): *I'm gonna fork this.*
(12) KA (4;0, pretending to be a doctor fixing a broken arm): *We're gonna cast that.*
(13) BS (4;0): *Maybe it rained or it fogged yesterday.*
(14) RT (4;0): *Is Anna going to babysitter me?*
(15) CE (4;11): *We already decorationed our tree.*
(16) KA (5;0): *Will you chocolate my milk?*

Source: Clark, collection of spontaneous child coinages

someone who hangs pictures). By age four, children readily coin new agent nouns with *-er* when asked what they could call someone who Xs, where X is the term for some activity (Clark and Hecht, 1982). Use of *-er* for instrument nouns tends to emerge a little later. Also later are other agentive suffixes like *-ist* (Clark and Cohen, 1984), and nominal suffixes like *-ness* used to form nouns from adjectives (see table 14.4).

Children also coin new verbs for talking about actions. In English, they rely on zero derivation for this, and spontaneously make nouns into verbs from age two on. This way of forming new verbs is particularly productive in English, and it is acquired very early (Bowerman, 1982a; Clark, 1982; Clark and Clark, 1979). The noun chosen designates one of the participants in the event, most often the object affected (as in *to hair*, for brushing hair, or *to lawn*, for mowing the lawn), or the instrument used (as in *to broom*, for hitting with a broom, or *to fork*, for eating or picking up with a fork). See table 14.5.

Finally, children also coin new adjectives for talking about qualities and states. The earliest option they use is the *-y* suffix for deriving an adjective from a noun or verb, as in *growly* ("likely to growl"), or *pointy* ("with a point"). From about age four on, they also begin to use suffixes like *-al*, *-ful*, and *-able*, as in *changeable* ("able to change into Batman and back again") (see table 14.6). Novel adjectives, though, are less common among children's coinages than novel nouns and verbs.

Table 14.6   Some novel adjectives coined by two to five-year-olds

(1) EL (2;2, for "too damp"): *Too dampy.*

(2) MB (2;6, of a door that was banging): *It's bumpy.*

(3) GR (3;5, of a dinosaur he'd just drawn): *That looks growly, doesn't it?*

(4) DM (4;0, for something with a point on it): *It's pointy.*

(5) GS (4;0, of a parasol blown by the wind): . . . *a windy parasol.*

(6) GE (4;8, of a dog running round and round the room): *What a runny dog!*

(7) DM (4;0,7, when asked how he felt one morning): *Toothachey.*

(8) SB (4;0+, to his mother): *Try to be more rememberful, mom.*

(9) SB (4;2): *I am a sciential boy.*

(10) CG (c. 4;0, of a box of cocoons): *And about what time will they be flyable?*

(11) JW (5;9, of a model Batman dressed as Batman): *I wish he was changeable.*
RW (9;6): What do you mean?
JW: *I wish he could change into Bruce Wayne and back again.*

(12) YV (5;9, of a tree she had seen a boy climbing): . . . *an unsafeable tree.*

Source: Clark, collection of spontaneous child coinages

How do children choose which word forms to use in constructing new words? Why do they acquire some affixes and compounding patterns before others? As children analyze the internal structure of conventional words, they learn to identify roots and affixes, and to attend to how these are combined. At times, they comment spontaneously on their analyses of word parts, even as young as age two. Their comments reveal that transparency of meaning is one important dimension in their analyses. For example, they offer explanations of word meanings based on their identification of specific roots. Some examples of spontaneous analyses from one child are given in table 14.7.

Children also depend in their coinages on simplicity of form. That is, it is easier for them to discern a root in a complex word form if its shape remains unchanged by affixation or any adjacent roots. In their construction of new word forms, children observe both transparency and simplicity. They build with already familiar elements – roots and affixes – when they coin words. And they make the least possible change in any roots being used. They are also sensitive to the relative productivity of each option in the adult language around them. The first affixes they produce are the most productive ones available for expressing the pertinent meaning. For example, English-speaking children produce agentive -*er* in innovative agent nouns long before agentive -*ist* or -*ian*, and they produce root compounds formed from two nouns before they progress to any synthetic compounds where the constituent noun or verb roots are combined with affixes. In short, when children coin new words, they attend not only to conventionality and contrast, but also to transparency, simplicity, and productivity (see Clark, 1993).

Table 14.7   Some explicit analyses of word forms from D

---

(1) Mo (pointing at a picture of a ladybug): What's that?
   D (2;4,13): *A ladybug! That like "lady."*
(2) D (2;6,20, to Fa, about a stick): *This is a running-stick.*
   Fa: A running-stick?
   D: *Yes, because I run with it.*
(3) D (2;9,10): *You know why this is a HIGH-chair? Because it is high.*
(4) D (2;9,24) *Eve, you know what you do on runways? You run on them because they start with "run."*
(5) Mo: We're going to a place called Sundance.
   D (2;11,0): *And you dance there. If there is music, we will dance there.*
(6) D (2;11,2): *Windshield! Wind goes on it. That's why it's called a windshield.*
(7) D (2;11,25, asking about a road): *What's it called?*
   Mo: King's Mountain Road.
   D: *Do kings live in it?*
(8) D (2;11,28, looking at flowering ice-plants): *What's that called?*
   Mo: That's ice-plant.
   D: *Does it grow ice?*
(9) D (3;2,15): *Egg-nog comes from egg!*
(10) D (3;2,20, as he climbed into the car, holding both index fingers up to his head): *D'you know what headlights are?*
   Mo: No.
   D: *They're lights that go on in your head!*

Source: Clark, diary data

Children's reliance on such factors allows for some general predictions about the kinds of word forms they will construct when they fill semantic gaps. For example, in a language that allows verb formation either with or without affixation, children should opt for the simplest form type first. And they do: young English-speaking children rely only on zero derivation to form new verbs from nouns. And in a language that allows both compounding and derivation with affixes, children should prefer some compounding patterns before any affixes in their coinages. And they do: English-speaking rely on root compounds from age two or younger, and only rather later begin to use some derivational affixes. The patterns observable in child and adult coinages depend critically on what is available and productive in each language. For example, compounding is not productive in Hebrew, and children rarely produce novel compounds before age six or seven. The same holds for French, where again compounding in general is not a productive option. This contrasts with Germanic languages where compounding is highly productive. There, children consistently begin to exploit this option from around age two (see further Clark, 1993; Clark and Berman, 1984; Chmura-Klekotowa, 1971;

MacWhinney, 1976). The typology of each language and the nature of the input children hear, then, interacts with transparency, simplicity, and productivity, to produce particular developmental patterns in children's coinage types at different ages.

Children's coinages appear to have a function similar to that of adult coinages. They fill lexical gaps, gaps where children know no conventional word for just the meaning they wish to express. Coinage offers a valuable resource for extending the lexicon whenever necessary. This resource is available to adults too, but the greater size of the adult lexicon tempers the degree to which speakers need to construct new words.

Taking a Perspective

As children add to their lexical repertoires, they also come to realize that one can convey much the same information from a variety of perspectives. The particular words chosen convey what the speaker wants to pick out about each entity or each event. One can pick out an entity, for example, as *the dog, the family pet, the hunter, the hearth-rug,* or *the boxer.* Each set of choices represents a different perspective on the animal in question. One can also present actions from different perspectives, as in *The door opened* (with the object affected being of main interest), *The key opened the door* (with the mediating instrument identified), or *Rod opened the door with the key* (with the agent and instrument explicitly identified as participants in the action). Here, the transitivity of the verb and the number of arguments allow the speaker to present the same event from different perspectives by picking out particular participants or combinations of participants. Speakers can also make use of voice in the verb to present different perspectives on an event, as in *Kate lit the fire* versus *The fire was lit by Kate,* or *They washed the shirts* versus *The shirts washed well* (Clark, 1990b).

Children learn that the same referent may be talked about in a number of ways, depending on the perspective chosen by the speaker. And they begin to learn this very early during acquisition. For example, two-year-olds can categorize objects at at least two levels: basic and subordinate. That is, they can refer to something with a basic-level term, as in *the tree* or *the dog,* and they can refer to the same entities with more specific, subordinate terms, such as *the snow-tree* (for a fir tree) or *the Dalmatian-dog.* When they need to distinguish subcategories of a familiar category, children as young as two are able to shift perspective and produce subordinate labels such as *the spear-page* versus the *duck-page* (pages in a book designated by the relevant illustrations), or *the snow-car* versus *the race-car* (two toy cars, one with whited-out windows, the other a convertible). When two and three-year-olds need subordinate labels for subcategories, they typically identify the basic category and add some modifying noun to it in a novel compound such as *car-smoke* (smoke from cars, exhaust), *key-pants* (pants with a keyring attached), or *fire-dog* (stray dog found at the site of a fire) (all from two-year-olds). They coin numerous subordinate terms like this, and by two and a half to three, have already two and sometimes three hierarchical levels represented in their words for many domains (see Clark et al., 1985; Gelman, Wilcox, and Clark, 1989; Waxman and Hatch, 1992).

This finding appears to go counter to the view that children initially opt for only one label per referent, and reject other unfamiliar labels offered. This, it has been proposed, is a way of simplifying, temporarily, how much they have to deal with as they learn word meanings (e.g. Markman, 1987). But close examination of rejections reveals that most of the labels children spurn are terms already known to them, so their rejections appear to be more a matter of choosing the best word for something than of rejecting a second label (Clark, 1993). In fact, when two and three-year-olds are asked questions that assume different perspectives, they readily accept and use alternative labels for the same entity: they can move from *bear* to *animal* and back, and also from *bear* to *sailor* and back (Clark and Svaib, 1991). This strongly suggests that children are attentive to input that tells them very early that multiple labels are commonplace. They hear themselves referred to as *the baby, my son, her grandson, the boy*, plus proper names and a variety of endearments uses as address terms (*pumpkin, sweetheart, love*). They hear two or more labels for other family members, for family pets, animals, cars, plants, food, and for many household items. They also hear different descriptions offered for the same event. In effect, the input tells them very early on that there is not just one way to label an object or an action: speakers have choices, and the words they choose present differing perspectives on the events they talk about.

At the same time, languages do not all offer the same range of perspectives in their conventional vocabulary. They differ in which semantic domains contain hierarchically structured taxonomies, and they differ in the range of options available for describing kinds of activities. Some languages have elaborate taxonomies for types of containers; others do not. Some have elaborate taxonomies for kinds of vehicles; others do not. Some have highly regular verb paradigms that offer transitive and intransitive forms for each verb; others do not. Part of later lexical acquisition consists in learning not only what the range of conventional options is in each domain and but also the range across the lexicon in general, and hence how to mark one's perspective on the activities and participants in each event.

Many locative verbs in English, for example, allow two perspectives on the relation between a container and its contents, as in *He stuffed the clothes into the bag* versus *He stuffed the bag with clothes*, but others allow only one, as in *She filled the box with apples* (but not **She filled apples into the box*) or *They pour water into the hole* (but not **They poured the hole with water*). Among early uses of verbs like *touch, cover,* and *fill* where the "container" should be the direct object, children may choose the "contents" as direct object instead, as in utterances like *I'm gonna touch it on your pants* (3;0), *I'm gonna cover a screen over me* (4;5), *She's gonna pinch it on my foot* (4;9), or *Can I fill some salt into the bear?* (5;0). They make the opposite error too, when they choose the "container" as the direct object with verbs like *spill*, as in *I don't want it* [toast] *because I spilled it of orange-juice* (4;11) (Bowerman 1982b). Learning which verb exemplifies which perspective, and which verbs allow both perspectives (where the direct object can be realized as either the "contents" or the "container") takes time (Gropen, Pinker, Hollander, and Goldberg, 1991).

Children must also learn which verbs allow two or only one perspective in other domains too. In English, for example, the verb *to give* allows the speaker to focus on the recipient, as in *Jan gave the boy a doughnut*, or on the object being transferred, as in *Jan gave the doughnut to the boy*. But close relatives of *give* may allow only one perspective, as in *He donated the sculpture to the gallery* (but not *He donated the gallery the sculpture*). Similar differences hold for benefactive verbs: compare *They baked a cake for her/baked her a cake* with *She designed a house for them/*designed them a house*. Although children begin to produce verbs like *give, show, read,* and *buy* as early as age two, they typically use only one of two possible forms for each verb for several months. And they make errors of perspective by producing alternations that are not conventional, as in *Don't say me that or you'll make me cry* (3;6, "to me"), *You ate me my cracker* (3;3, "for me"), *Button me the rest* (3;4, "for me"), and *Pick me up all those things* (5;2, "for me") (Bowerman, 1987; Gropen, Pinker, Hollander, Goldberg, and Wilson 1989). They continue to make errors as they get older, notably with Latinate verbs that do not allow alternation, as in *Mattia demonstrated me that yesterday* (8;0, "to me"). Learning which verbs can and can't alternate takes a long time: many 12-year-olds still judge nonconventional alternations to be acceptable (Mazurkewicz and White, 1984).

Perspective can also be marked by voice. In English, this is usually realized in the contrast between active and passive forms of the verb, as in *The child threw the ball* versus *The ball was thrown by the child*. The passive voice here serves to shift the perspective away from the prototypical transitive event described with the active voice, by making the object affected, instead of the agent, the topic of the utterance. Children begin to produce passive verb forms soon after age two, and by three produce both *get* and *be* passives. These seem to differ in that *get* passives, as in *We will get striked by lightning* (3;6), are more likely to have animate subjects than *be* passives (59 percent versus 32 percent). They are also more likely to express some adverse consequence for the entity affected; 65 percent versus 18 percent for *be* passives. In fact, *be* passives are much more likely to be neutral in the effect they describe; 74 percent versus 26 percent for *get* passives. This contrast can be seen in utterances like *Does the cream of wheat need to be cooled?* (2;8) or *I want these pancakes to be sugared* (4;2) compared to *I just got pinched from these pointed stuff* (3;3). Because of this difference (adverse versus neutral), there is little overlap between the verbs that appear in *get* passives and those in *be* passives. Children not only use two forms of passive to focus on the patient or object affected of the action, they also distinguish kinds of entity affected – animate versus inanimate – and kinds of outcome – adverse versus neutral (see Budwig, 1990b).

Children exploit syntax to indicate their perspective on an event from an early age. When they wish to talk about the object affected by an action, they either omit the agent altogether or they demote it from the subject slot while promoting the phrase for the entity affected. But two-year-olds often lack the conventional syntactic means (a *by* phrase) to do this, so they have to find some consistent way to mark such demoted entities. They typically treat demoted agents as sources of actions and, like sources of motion, they mark them with the preposition *from*, as in *I took my temperature from the doctor* (2;2, meaning "had my temperature taken by") or *These fall down from me* (2;2,3, meaning "were knocked down by"). Demoted possessors, causes, and stand-ards of comparison are also marked as sources in the same way, as in *That's a finger from him* (3;0,13, "belonging to"), *Then I cried a bit from you go get him* (2;6,12, "cried because you went"), and *See? This ear is longer from the other ear* (3;1,15, "longer than") (see Clark and Carpenter, 1989).

Children attend, from early on, to the perspective marked both lexically and syntactically in the utterances of others. They are consistent, for example, in choosing different pictures in response to active versus passive utterances when they are asked to show what the speaker is talking about. With *The boy is riding the bicycle*, they choose a picture of a boy over that of a bicycle, but for *The bicycle's being ridden by the boy*, they choose the picture of the bicycle (see Hornby, 1971; Turner and Rommetveit, 1967). Their decision about the topic of an utterance is a critical ingredient in their identification of the per-spective being taken by the speaker.

Finally, perspective is also marked by the different deictic devices in a lan-guage. Speakers can use pronouns to mark whether an action is attributable to the speaker (*I*), the addressee (*you*), or to a third person (*he, she, they*). While children begin early on the perspective shifts inherent in the *I/you* contrast (Loveland, 1984), they take time to master the details of perspective marking in locative, demonstrative, and verbal forms. For example, it is only around age four that English-speaking children consistently take *here*, roughly "where the speaker is," to contrast deictically with *there*, roughly "somewhere where the speaker is not." The analogous deictic contrast between *this* and *that* is mastered even later, and the contrast between verbs in pairs like *come/go* and *bring/take* in English, later still (Clark, 1978b). In each case, children must learn the many conditions for using proximal versus distal terms to mark particular perspectives.

In summary, much of later lexical learning involves the acquisition of lexical relations among word meanings, and how specific meanings mark one or an-other perspective on an activity or on the participants in an event. Shifts in perspective may involve both lexical choice and constructional shifts that exploit word order as well as morphological changes in word forms. Later lexical acquisition is inseparable from the acquisition of both syntax and morphology.

Idioms and Figurative Language

Learning the lexicon involves more than learning words. The lexicon also contains numerous idioms. Some of these typically appear in just one syntactic form (e.g. *sitting on pins and needles*, while others can appear in a variety of syntactic forms (e.g. *make up your mind*). The fixed or frozen form idioms might be easier to learn initially just because they remain in a single chunk or phrase when they appear. Flexible idioms may be harder to discern as idioms just because they can appear in a variety of syntactic forms, e.g. *make up my/your/his mind, are their minds made up, did she make up her mind*, and so on. Some idioms have meanings that are relatively close to the literal meanings of the relevant phrase, as in *hold your tongues*; others are much less close and the connection between the literal and idiomatic interpretations may have become opaque, as in *beat around the bush*.

Both syntax and transparency have an effect on acquisition: when five and six-year-olds are asked to explain the meanings of idioms or choose the intended interpretation from several alternatives, they consistently do better on fixed than on flexible idioms (Gibbs, 1987). But as they get older, there is little difference between the two types, whether in stories or in isolation. And, at all ages (from five to ten), they do better on phrases whose idiomatic and literal interpretations are closely related (as in *hold your tongues*) than on idioms where the two are not close (as in *beat around the bush*). Overall, children (like adults) have a harder time glossing opaque idioms than relatively transparent ones. Finally, children do better at interpreting idioms as they get older, and they do better on idioms in stories than on idioms presented in isolation.

Idioms span a continuum from opaque (where the motivation for the original idiom has been lost) to transparent where modern-day speakers can still relate the idiomatic and nonidiomatic senses of the relevant phrases. One result is that frequency of exposure to idioms appears to have little effect on acquisition. But exposure to idioms in rich contexts – stories that offer multiple clues to the meaning of an idiom – facilitate idiom comprehension at all ages. In production, children use few idioms and, at age seven, offer completions only for highly familiar ones (Levorato and Cacciari, 1992). In short, children appear to understand and produce few idioms before age five or six. But by age nine to ten, they understand a number of idioms and can come up with interpretations for idioms heard in contexts that provide them with clues. They probably find syntactically frozen idioms easier to interpret because these are identified as idioms (lexical chunks with a single meaning) earlier than idioms with greater syntactic flexibility.

Children also have to learn that language can be used figuratively, that expressions may be intended as metaphors rather than as literal descriptions. But for a child use to be identified as metaphorical, one needs to be able to distinguish conventional uses of languages from metaphorical ones. For example, a child should be able to apply the conventional label for a category before being given credit for figurative usage in the application of a nonconventional label, e.g. as when a child uses *my tail* for a piece of string earlier called *string*. "Renaming" like this is common in symbolic play and is often accompanied by gestures that redefine the object in question, as when a child put his foot into a wastebasket and said *boot*. One child, A, produced 185 such renamings in 112 hours of tape transcripts (Winner, 1988). What is striking here is that figurative uses typically require a shift in perspective: the object or activity is presented from a new point of view, as a member of a different category. Such symbolic play metaphors have been distinguished from sensory metaphors, which are based on physical similarities, as when A called a big pencil *needle* or a red balloon attached to a green tube *apple on a tree*. At age two, A produced more symbolic than sensory metaphors (62 percent to 25 percent), but by age four, these proportions had reversed, and he produced sensory metaphors more often than symbolic ones (76 percent to 10 percent). Data from two other children, though, suggest that some children may produce more sensory than symbolic metaphors from the start (Winner, 1988).

To produce either type of metaphor, children must be able to perceive similarities and map the relevant properties from one object to another. In symbolic play metaphors, there is little emphasis on physical similarities so almost any object can stand in for another: a ladder for a pair of scissors, as the child pretends to cut his mother's hair and says *scissors*, or a blanket for ice-cream as the child "dipped" his spoon in and raised it to his mouth saying *ice-cream*. At what point can children map one domain onto another, while preserving the pertinent properties and relations? In one study, four-year-olds and adults were asked to map the human body, while preserving the relations among body parts, onto such objects as trees and mountains. They answered questions like "If a tree had a knee, where would it be?" about both body parts and facial features. Four-year-olds did very well and were equally good at mapping onto trees and mountains. In another task, four and six-year-olds were presented with trees that were upright, horizontal, or inverted, and again asked about body parts, and again they did very well. They were also asked about facial features for mountains drawn with local details that were compatible or not with the features being asked about. Here children were better than adults at ignoring the local detail when they answered questions about where the mouth or eyes would be (Gentner, 1977). In short, the basic analogical ability needed for simile and metaphor appears to be well established for this domain by age four. Familiarity with the domain to be mapped is, of course, a prerequisite for any figurative uses.

In summary, children must learn not only the meanings of individual words but also the meanings of idioms. And building up a repertoire of idioms takes time. Children produce few idioms before age six, but begin to show some comprehension of them earlier than that. But this aspect of lexical acquisition is one that probably lasts through adulthood. We continually encounter new idioms, from different registers, different dialects, and from different eras. And the acquisition of idioms appears more complicated when the nonidiomatic

15 The Role of Syntax in Verb Learning

LILA R. GLEITMAN AND JANE GILLETTE

We discuss here the mapping problem for vocabulary acquisition: how word-level concepts are matched with their phonological realizations in the target language. Traditional approaches to this problem assume that, at least at early stages in the acquisition process, children try to line up the utterance of single words with their contingencies in the world. Thus, their task would be to discover that *elephant* is most often said in the presence of elephants and rarely said in their absence (Locke, 1690, and many modern sources).

Our recent investigations (Gillette and Gleitman, forthcoming) show how well such a procedure could work in practice for the case of concrete nouns. Adult subjects are shown videotapes of mothers playing with their infants (aged about 18 months, MLU < 2;0) but with the audio turned off. These film clips are long enough for subjects to pick up the pragmatics of the conversation, e.g. of a mother showing and describing an elephant puppet to the child, who then takes it and manipulates it. The subjects are told that whenever the mother is uttering the target noun, a beep will sound; their task is to identify the word that she uttered. Subjects have no trouble with this task, guessing correctly about 50 percent of the time even on the first video-beep exposure, and improving with the addition of more instances. And if any of the maternal usages are deictic, the subjects are even better in guessing what noun she was saying.

This laboratory situation is radically reduced from the problem that infants face in assigning interpretations to novel words. The subjects are made aware in advance that the target is a noun. These nouns all describe concrete objects that are present in the videotaped scenario, and are foci of the mother–child conversation.[1] In light of the task as set for them, the subjects also know that there exists in English a single common word that will fit their observations of these objects in these scenes. Moreover, they are solving for one target noun at a time; their exposures to this item are not complicated by the intervention of any other novel items, so they have no memory problem. In contrast, a child learner might reencounter the new item only after the passage of considerable time, and mingled with other new words.

One further proviso is even more controversial. No doubt arises that the adult subjects can conceptualize the objects in the scenes (e.g. they can represent the concept "elephant") and can interpret the pragmatics of the mother–child conversation. So built into the claim that these findings are informative for understanding the mapping problem is our assumption that adults and young children are much the same not only in their data-handling procedures, but also in the ways they interpret the everyday world of things, actions, causes, intentions, and so forth (for a recent discussion of this "rationalist perspective," see Bloom, P., in press, a).

Overall, then, the Gillette and Gleitman experiment models the child's vocabulary learning situation in at best a highly idealized fashion. But it does add to a literature demonstrating that maternal usage, at least of highly frequent nouns, is sufficiently faithful to the "here and now" to support learning by inspecting how the sounds of words match up with present scenes (Bruner, 1974/75; Ninio, 1980).

This apparent simplicity of the mapping problem for vocabulary acquisition – once purged of the "concept learning" issues – accounts for why it has been something of a stepchild in recent linguistic inquiry into language learning. The task has seemed devoid of any interesting internal structure: merely a matter of associating single words (*qua* phonological objects) with their standard contexts of use, as in the experiment just described.

The burden of the present discussion is to show that, over the vocabulary at large, this word-to-world pairing procedure is too weak to account fully for mapping. Our claim is that word learning is in general performed by pairing a *sentence* (*qua* syntactic object) with the observed world.

Insufficiency of Observation for Verb Learning

As a first demonstration of the structural requirement in word learning, we now reconsider the Gillette and Gleitman experiment as it pertains to the acquisition of verbs. The manipulation is the same. The subjects are shown silent videotapes of mother–infant interactions, long enough to reveal the pragmatic contexts for the verbs' use. At the moment that the mother was really uttering some target verb, the beep sounds. Again, only the mothers' most frequent child directed verbs are tested, and again the subject receives several beep-scenario pairs (that is, pairings of the utterance of the target verb with its observational contingencies) as the basis for his or her guess. Now the results are entirely different from those of the noun experiments. The subjects correctly identify the verb the mother was actually saying less than 15 percent of the time.[2]

Once again the experiment has various unrealistic elements, notably that the subjects know all these English verbs in advance, and have been told that it is a verb that they are seeking. But this should make their task· easier, not harder. One could also object, alluding to the results from a generation of developmental psycholinguists, that children are better language learners (including vocabulary learners) than adults and would therefore do better in this task.

Despite these real contaminants, one effect stands firm: this is the massive *difference* for verbs and nouns in their tractability to this procedure. While the nouns were easily identified from their word (beep) to world (video) contingencies, the verbs were not.

How can we explain the special difficulty of verbs in this manipulation? One factor is that some of the verbs that mothers use *most frequently* to their babies represent concepts that are not straightforwardly observable: *want, know,* and *think* are in the top group in usage frequency. Even some of the "more concrete" frequent verbs encode some intentional content rather than solely a property of the perceived world, e.g. *show, see,* and *give*. Another factor, evident upon inspection of these videotapes, is the temporal precision with which the environment matches the utterance. When *elephant* is uttered, overwhelmingly often the elephant is being held, waved, even pointed at. But "push" is usually said well before or after the pushing event takes place (Lederer, Gleitman, and Gleitman, forthcoming; Tomasello and Kruger, 1992). The verb uses do not line up transparently with their situational contexts, a problem we have called *interleaving*: by the time the mother says *push* ("You pushed the poor elephant down!"), the child is usually *looking* and *smiling* at the consequences of his or her prior pushing action (or the reverse, as when the mother says "Go push the truck"). This makes it hard for the subjects to guess that the beep referred to the pushing act.

If young children are like our adult subjects, they too should have more trouble learning verbs than nouns. And indeed they do. A robust generalization from the vocabulary learning literature is that early vocabularies (the first 50 words) contain few – often no – verbs; and nouns continue to outnumber verbs in productive vocabularies beyond their frequency distribution in maternal speech until the child is past three years of age (Gentner, 1978; 1982).

We have mentioned two usage distinctions that can help explain this learning oddity. The first is merely a pragmatic fact of usage with nothing essential to do with the formal or substantive universals of the word classes: caretakers' most frequent nouns to babies in our corpus are predominantly items that describe observeable objects while their verbs are often abstract: they often say "I think . . ." to their babies, but they rarely say "The thought . . ." A second and more important factor is that verb use, as opposed to noun use, is not tightly timelocked with the extralinguistic contexts, and more often refers to the nonpresent. (In fact, in Beckwith, Tinker, and Bloom's (1989) corpus of speech to babies, verbs are used out of context more than a quarter of the time – this includes physical action verbs like *open*).

But there is a third factor – one that we believe holds the primary key to this lexical-class order effect in vocabulary acquisition: verb acquisition requires access to the phrase structure of the exposure language, and it takes the infant some time to get the structural properties under control.[3]

More Power to Verb Learning

Eric Lenneberg (1967) provided the first evidence suggesting a structure-sensitive model for the learning of verbs (and perhaps all classes of words which do not typically express concrete object concepts): the "explosion" of spoken vocabulary, including sudden increase in the range of lexical types, coincides with the appearance of rudimentary (two word) sentences at approximately the 24th month of life. Perhaps an ability to comprehend the spoken sentence is a requirement for efficient verb learning. It may be that once the child has learned some nouns, she can ask not only "What are the environmental contingencies for the use of this word?" but "What are its environmental contingencies, *as constrained by the structural positions in which it appears* in adult speech?"

For short-term reasons that have no present relevance, this approach to vocabulary acquisition has been called "syntactic bootstrapping" (Gleitman, 1990). But since the term itself is something of a misnomer, let us discard it. The idea is that structural information is required by learners – along with the scenario information – to fix the meaning of novel verbs.

Origins and motivation

The first direct demonstration that vocabulary acquisition is sensitive to linguistic context was from Brown (1957), who showed that children would interpret the relation of a novel word to a scene (in this case, a picture) differently depending on available morphological cues: if they heard "the gorp," they pointed to a visible novel object, but if they heard "gorping" they pointed to the implied action, and so forth. The linguistic cues affected the interpretation of the scene in view, to some extent reversing the causal chain suggested by common sense (namely, that the scene in view determines the interpretation of the linguistic object). The findings hint that learners expect there to be a link between formal properties of language (lexical class membership in this case) and semantic interpretation.

Landau and Gleitman (1985) carried this line further, positing that children use linguistic cues in identifying novel word meanings within as well as across the major lexical classes. Their immediate impetus was a quite startling finding: the first verb in a congenitally blind learner's spoken vocabulary was *see*. Although the exposure conditions for learning this word necessarily differ for blind and sighted, both populations acquire the word as a term of achieved perception, and do so at the same developmental moment.

But such exotica are not really required to show that children acquire aspects of word meaning that do not seem to be warranted by perception and pragmatic inference. Consider a sighted child hearing her mother say "I see a bird over there." Often there will be an occluding object between child and bird. Children come to know that *see* means "see" despite the fact that maternal speech is not a faithful running commentary on events in view.

Related problems in learning from observation alone abound. One is that the listener's focus of attention may differ from that of the speaker, as when the adult says "Come take your nap" while the child inspects a cat on a mat. Another is that the scene that accompanies utterance of a verb includes many events, only one of which is encoded by that verb. Consider the plight of the child to whom an adult says "Do you want some ice-cream?" The adult is speaking, smiling, holding, and waving the cone, and perhaps pointing to it; it is observably something good to eat, dripping, pink, an object of present desire, and so forth. It requires no empiricist bias (e.g. Quine, 1960) to believe that these interpretive complexities create practical problems in vocabulary learning. None of the aspects of the scene just described is irrelevant to the conversational intent, as this might be reconstructed by a sophisticated observer (which we assume the youngster to be). Yet only one of them is correct to map onto the item *want*. A picture is worth a thousand words, but that's the problem: a thousand words describe the varying aspects of any one picture.

Attempts to circumvent these difficulties involve a probabilistic procedure in which the mapping choice is based on the most frequent word–world match across situations (see Pinker, 1984, for discussion). No one can doubt that cross-situational observation plays a role in vocabulary acquisition, but taken alone it seems to be insufficient. One difficulty has to do with the observed rapidity and relative errorlessness of child vocabulary learning. Children are apparently acquiring five or more new words a day beginning at about the fifteenth month of life (Carey, 1978). It strains credulity to suppose that they are lucky enough to hear – within a very short time interval – most such words in the variety of information environments that would be required to parse out the right interpretation.

Form–meaning interactions in verb learning

Inspection of any corpus of natural speech shows that different verbs characteristically occur with different complements, in accord with their differing argument structures. Thus, inalienable actions typically are encoded with intransitive structures (*Pinnochio dances*), acts that affect another's state with transitive structures (*Gepetto kisses the puppet*), and so forth. This form–meaning correlation is usually described by saying that the structure is a projection from (aspects of) the verb's meaning; that is, the surface structures are mapped from the argument structure of the verb. Two complementary views of verb learning have recently been put forward, both taking advantage of such relations between verb meaning and sentence structure.

Bootstrapping complementation privileges from knowledge of verb meaning

If form–meaning correlations are systematic across the languages of the world (quirks aside), we should expect that children can project the complement structures for a verb whose meaning they have acquired via event observation, rather than having to memorize the structures independently (Grimshaw, 1981; Pinker, 1984). One kind of evidence in support of this hypothesis comes from studies of the invention of language by linguistically deprived youngsters (deaf children of hearing parents who are not exposed to sign language; Goldin-Meadow and Feldman, 1977; Feldman, Goldin-Meadow, and Gleitman, 1978). The self-invented gesture systems of these children appear to conform to the theta-criterion (Chomsky, 1981): they gesture one noun in construction with their invented gesture for *dance*, two in construction with *hit*, and three with *give*.[4] Another kind of evidence comes from child errors in complementation; these appear to occur primarily where there are quirks and subtleties in the way the exposure language maps from argument structure to surface structure (Bowerman, 1982a). In short, children use their knowledge of a verb's meaning as a basis for projecting the phrase structure of sentences in which it appears.

Bootstrapping verb meaning from knowledge of verb complementations

A second learning hypothesis also is consistent with the view that verb clause structure is a projection from verb argument structure: hearing some new verb in a particular structural environment should constrain its interpretation (Landau and Gleitman, 1985; Gleitman and Gleitman, 1992). Thus, hearing *John gorps* increases the likelihood that *gorp* means "smile" and decreases the likelihood that it means "hit." And hearing *John gorps Bill* should imply the reverse. Thus, knowledge of the semantic implications of the sentence structure in which a novel verb appears can narrow the search-space for its identification. It is this structurally derived narrowing of the hypothesis space for verb meaning on which we now concentrate.

The zoom lens hypothesis

According to our hypothesis, the first use of structural information is as an online procedure for interpreting a novel verb. Though there may be quite a few salient interpretations of the scene, the learner "zooms in" on one (or at least fewer) of these by demanding congruence also with the semantic implications of the sentence form. Thus, the input is

1   the extralinguistic event, as represented by a perceptually and pragmatically sophisticated observer,

paired with

2   the linguistic event, represented as a novel verb positioned within the
parse tree constructed from the adult utterance.

The learner exploits the semantically relevant structural information in (2) to
choose among the several interpretations that may be warranted by (1).

An early demonstration is from Naigles (1990). She investigated responses
to novel verbs as a function of linguistic-introducing circumstances in children
under two years of age, who had no or few verbs in their spoken vocabularies.
In the learning phase of the experiment, the children were shown videotaped
action scenes that had two novel salient interpretations. For example, they saw
a rabbit pushing down on a duck's head, thus forcing the duck to bend over;
simultaneously, both the duck and the rabbit were wheeling their free arm in
a broad circle. While watching this scene, half the babies heard "The rabbit is
gorping the duck" while the other half heard "The rabbit and the duck are
gorping." Then "gorping" might plausibly refer to forcing-to-bend or to arm-
wheeling. Subsequently, the scene disappeared and a voice said "Find gorping
now! Where's gorping?" At this point, new action scenes appeared, one on a
videoscreen to the child's left, the other on a screen to her right. The one on
the left showed the rabbit forcing the duck to bend, but with no arm wheeling.
The one on the right showed rabbit and duck wheeling their arms, but with
no forcing to bend. The measure of learning was the child's visual fixation
time on one or the other screen during a six second interval. Twenty-three of
24 infants tested looked longest at the videoscreen that matched their syntactic
introducing circumstances. Evidently the transitive input biased subjects toward something like the cause-to-bend interpretation, while the intransitive
input biased them toward arm wheeling. Though we cannot know from this
manipulation exactly what the children learned about "the meaning of gorp,"
their interpretation of what they were (relevantly) perceiving during the training phase was clearly affected by the syntax, for the subjects' situations differed in no other way.

More direct evidence of the effect of syntactic context on verb identification
comes from studies with three-year-old learners. This age group is the one in
which the verb vocabulary (and complex sentence structure) burgeons. These
relatively elderly subjects are also useful because they can answer questions
about the meanings of novel verbs that they encounter. Fisher, Hall, Rakowitz,
and Gleitman (1994) investigated the acquisition of perspective verbs (e.g.
chase/flee, lead/follow) with children of this age.

Principled difficulties for observation-based learning arise for these verbs,
for they come in pairs that vary primarily in the speaker perspective on a
single action or event, and thus their situational concommitants are virtually

always the same. This makes them a good testing ground for proposed learning procedures that rely on word-to-world contingencies only. Consider *give* and *get*.[5] Both these verbs describe the same intentional transfer of possession of an object between two individuals. Disentangling them based on the pragmatics of the conversation would require the listener to gain access to the mental perspective of the speaker – whether she is likely referring to Mary's volitional act of passing the book to John or John's consequent act of getting the book from Mary. Children perhaps can do some mind reading of just this sort by attending to the gist of conversation.

But additional information can come from inspecting the structural positioning of (known) nouns in the sentence heard and comparing these against the scene in view, providing that the learner determines the semantic implications of the sentence structure itself. If that scene shows the book moving from Mary to John, then an adult utterance like

(1)   Look! Ziking!

provides no differentiating information, but if she says

(2)   Mary zikes the ball to John

zike likely means *give* (or *throw*, etc.). In contrast, if the sentence is

(3)   John zikes the ball from Mary

then *zike* likely means *get* (or *take, receive, catch*, etc.). The potential clues for disentangling this pair are the choice of nominal in subject position, and the choice of a goal (*to*) v. source (*from*) preposition.

Fisher et al. (1994) showed such scenes/sentences to young children, in a context where a puppet was uttering the sentence: the children were asked to help the experimenter understand some "puppet words" (e.g. *zike*). The structure of the findings was this: if the input sentence to the child was uninformative of the *give/get* distinction (e.g. example sentence (1)), then child and adult subjects showed a bias in interpreting the scene: they were likely to say that it described something like giving rather than getting. This "agency bias" (whoever was subject of the transitive verb was agent of the action) characterized the set of five scenarios tested, including also chasing in preference to fleeing (running away), and so forth.[6] If the input sentence was (2), which matches the bias as to how to interpret the scene, the tendency to respond with a verb that meant something like *give* was further enhanced; in fact, almost categorical. But if the input sentence was (3), which mismatches the perceptual/conceptual bias toward *give*, subjects' modal response became *get* (or one of its relatives, e.g. *take*).

In sum, structural properties of the sentence heard influence the perception of a single scene even in cases where the bias in event representation, taken alone, leads in the opposite direction. Such findings begin to explain why children rarely confuse the perspective verbs despite the fact that they occur in very similar extralinguistic contexts.

The multiple frames hypothesis

In many cases, a surface-structure/situation pair is insufficient or even misleading about a verb's interpretation. For instance, the phrase structure and the typical situation in adult–child discourse are often the same when the adult says "Did you eat your cookie?" as when he says "Do you want a cookie?" In principle, examination of the further syntactic privileges of *eat* and *want* can cue distinctions in their interpretations. For example, *want* occurs with (tenseless) sentence complements, suggesting a mental component of its meaning.

More generally, the range of syntactic frames can provide convergent evidence on the meaning of a verb. "John is ziking the book to Bill" suggests an active verb of transfer (progressive, ditransitive). This would include a broad range of verbs such as *bring, throw, explain*, etc. But then "John is ziking that the book is boring" narrows the interpretive range to mental verbs. Taken together – and examined against the accompanying scenes – these structural properties suggest mental transfer, whose local interpretation is communication (e.g. *explain*; Zwicky, 1971; Fisher, Gleitman, and Gleitman, 1991).

There is evidence that the linguistic information provided by mothers to their young children is refined enough to support learning from frame ranges. Lederer, Gleitman, and Gleitman (in press) examined lengthy conversations of mothers with babies (MLU < 2). For the 24 most common verbs in these mothers' speech, a verb by syntactic-environment matrix was developed. Within and across mothers, each verb was found to be unique in its syntactic range. Using a procedure devised by Fisher et al. (1991), it was shown that degree of overlap in syntactic range predicted the verbs' semantic overlap to a striking extent.

The potency of various evidentiary sources

So far we have shown some demonstrations with children and adults suggesting that they can use syntactic evidence to aid in the mastery of new verbs. The question remains how much of the burden of verb identification the structure bears; particularly the multiple-frame evidence. After all, even if syntactic constraints will affect the observer's interpretation in some carefully constructed laboratory situations, in real life the evidence from extralinguistic and other cues may be so decisive that syntactic deductions rarely if ever come into play.

One indirect but suggestive kind of evidence that multiple-frame information is exploited by learners comes from correlational studies (Naigles and Hoff-Ginsberg, 1993). The idea behind such studies is to inquire how well maternal usage at some point in learning ("Time 1") predicts learning, by testing the child's progress after some suitable interval ("Time 2"). Specifically, they investigated the use of common verbs in the speech of mothers to one and two-year olds, and then their children's subsequent use of these verbs. The *diversity of syntactic frames* in which verbs appeared in maternal speech at Time 1, with verb frequency in maternal speech partialled out, significantly predicted the frequency with which these verbs appeared in child speech ten weeks later.

Lederer, Gleitman, and Gleitman (forthcoming) have examined the potential information value of various properties of mothers' speech to infants: its (multiple) extralinguistic contexts, nominal cooccurrences, selectional and syntactic properties. Which of these attributes of adult speech, taken singly or in various combinations, provide enough information for solving the mapping problem for verbs?

The method was to provide (adult) subjects with large numbers of instances (usually, about 50) of the use of some target verb by mothers to 18-month-olds, but blocking out one or another potential source of information. For example, some subjects saw 50 or so videotape clips of mothers uttering a single common verb but without audio; the procedure was repeated for the 24 most common verbs in these mothers' child directed speech. Other subjects were told the nouns that occurred with the target verb in each of the 50 maternal sentences. A third group was shown the list of 50 sentences that the mother actually uttered but with all nouns as well as the verb converted to nonsense (e.g. *Rom GORPS that the rivenflak is grum, Can vany GORP the blick?*)

The first finding was that, just as in the Gillette and Gleitman experiment cited earlier, subjects systematically failed to guess the verb from observing its real-world contexts of use (7 percent correct identification).[7] In the second condition, subjects did not see the video but were told the cooccurring nouns for each sentence in which the mother uttered that verb: after all, if a verb regularly occurs with nouns describing edibles, maybe it means *eat*. Subjects identified the verb from this kind of information in about 13 percent of instances.

It is surprising that subjects' mapping performance was so dismal in both the scene and noun conditions. And when new subjects were given both these kinds of information (that is, shown the videos *and* told the cooccurring nouns) they still hit upon the target verbs only 28 percent of the time.

But when subjects were provided with frame-range information – no scenes, no real nouns or verbs, just the set of syntactic structures that the mothers used, with all their content-bearing words converted to nonsense – the subjects identified 52 percent of the verbs correctly. It appears that syntactic range information is highly informative.

A difficulty with interpreting these results onto the child learning situation is that these subjects (when correct) by definition were identifying old verbs that they knew: perhaps they just looked up the frame-ranges for these known verbs in their mental lexicons rather than using the frames to make semantic deductions. Because of this possibility, the pertinence of the findings to the real learning situation is more easily evaluated by inspecting the 48 percent of instances where subjects *failed* in this condition (and the 93 percent of cases where they failed in the scene condition, etc.). The finding is that false guesses given in response to frame-range information were semantically close to the actual verb that the mother had said (as assessed by the Fisher et al. (1991) semantic-similarity procedure), e.g. for *think*, the only false guess was *believe*. In contrast, the false guesses offered in response to looking at the scenes in which *think* was actually said were semantically unrelated to this verb (including *run, catch, go, look*, etc.). The frame-range information put the subjects into the "semantic neighborhood" of the target verb. In contrast, false interpretations of scenes don't get the subject close to the mark at all. This latter result raises puzzles for how a cross-situational learning scheme that is blind to syntax might work in practice.

Note that 52 percent correct identification in the presence of syntactic frame-range information only, while a significant improvement over 7 percent, is not good enough if we want to model the fact that verb learning by three-year-olds is a snap. They do not make 48 percent errors so far as we know, even errors close to the semantic mark. But as we have stressed, our hypothesis is not about a procedure in which the child ignores the scene, or the cooccurring nominals, and attends to syntax alone (as Lederer et al. forced their subjects to do in the experiment just described). We have hypothesized a sentence-to-world pairing procedure for verb vocabulary acquisition. Indeed, adding the real nouns to the frames without video in this experiment led to over 80 percent verb identification; adding back the scene yielded almost perfect performance.

Summarizing these results, scene information and noun contextual information taken alone are quite uninformative (7 percent and 13 percent correct identification, respectively) while frame-range information is highly informative (52 percent correct identification). But when we combine the information sources, the results look quite different. Once the observer is given access to the structure, he or she makes highly efficient use of frame and noun-context information. The reasons why are easy to see. Consider the noun contexts: it doesn't much help to know that one of the words in an utterance was *hamburger*. But if this word is known to surface as direct object, the meaning of the verb might well be "eat." (That is, the structural information converts cooccurrence information to selectional information.) Similarly for the video-tapes: once the structure of the sentences uttered in their presence is known, the subject can zoom in on fewer interpretations of the events and states that might be pertinent for the mother to have said of them. So if the child has available – as she does in real life – multiple paired scenes and sentences, we can at last understand why verb learning is easy.

How the structures of sentences can aid vocabulary acquisition

We have suggested that the formal medium of phrase structure constrains the semantic content that the sentence is expressing, thus providing clues to the meaning of its verb. One such clue resides in the number of arguments: a noun-phrase position is assigned to each verb argument; this will differentiate *push* from *fall* when viewing a scene where both actions are taking place. Another concerns the positioning of the arguments: the subject of transitives is the agent, differentiating *chase* from *flee*. The case marking and type of the argument also matters, e.g. spatial verbs which allow expression of paths and locations typically accept prepositional phrases, and verbs that express mental acts and states appear with sentence complements.

Of course, one cannot converge on the unique construal of a verb from syntactic properties alone. Because the subcategorization properties are the syntactic expressions of their arguments, it is only those aspects of a verb's meaning that have consequences for its argument structure that could be represented syntactically. Many – most – semantic distinctions are not formally expressed with this machinery. The role of the syntax is only to narrow the search-space for the meaning, as this latter is revealed by extralinguistic context.

What our experimentation suggests is that this initial narrowing of the hypothesis space by attention to structure is the precondition for using the scene information efficiently to derive the verb's meaning. When babies do not appear to know the phrase structure, they learn few if any verbs (Lenneberg, 1967). When adults and young children are required to identify verbs without phrase structure cues (as when told "Look! Ziking!" or when presented with silent videos of mother–child conversations) again they do not identify target verbs. But the observation of scenes taken together with observation of the structures is sufficient to the task.

Relation of surface syntax to semantics

A well-known view is that there are cross-cutting "verb classes," each defined over some abstract semantic domain (e.g. "mental" or "spatial") and – therefore – licensing certain structural formats, or frames (see Levin, 1993). We suggest instead that verb frames have semantic implications, and verbs have meanings. Neither the frames nor their semantic implications are part of lexical information: any verb can appear grammatically in any structural environment. But owing to the meaning of the verb, it may be semantically implausible, and thus rarely or never uttered, in some syntactic contexts. For example, we do not typically say things like "Barbara looked the ball on the table." Arguably, we do not forebear from such utterances because that verb in that sentence would be ungrammatical. Rather, the interpretation of the sentence structure would imply that some external agent (Barbara) caused the ball to go on the table just by looking at it. The improbability of psychokinesis is what makes this verb in this syntactic context rare. This is shown by the fact that if the rare circumstances do occur, *look* can be used unexceptionally in this structure: the rules of baseball make it possible to say (and sports announcers do say) "The shortstop looked the runner back to third base." In this case, moving is immediately caused by the threatening glance, rendering the sentence plausible.

If the view just sketched is correct, verbs have no "subcategorization privileges." To take one more example, one doesn't usually say *Mary danced John* because dancing is ordinarily not externally caused, rather the act of a volitional agent, and this structure implies direct causation of John's dancing by Mary. But one does comfortably say *Gepetto danced Pinnochio* just because here the dancer is a nonvolitional puppet. If there are no subcategorization privileges for individual verbs, then the child never has to learn them.[8]

What the child *must* know are the semantic implications of these structures. There is considerable evidence from the work of a generation of linguists that these semantic–syntactic linkages are to a useful degree universal (see Grimshaw, 1990, for a review and theoretical perspective) and given by nature to the learner (e.g. the evidence from the isolated deaf that we have cited).

Our suggestion is that learners note the frame environments in which verbs characteristically occur, thus deducing the argument structures with which their meanings typically comport. These ranges of "typical structures" are compatible with only small sets of verb meanings. The phrase structures in turn provide constraints on the interpretation of extralinguistic information, increasing the efficiency of observational learning.

NOTES

We thank a grant from Steven and Marcia Roth to Lila Gleitman and an NSF Science and Technology Center Grant to the University of Pennsylvania, Institute for Research in Cognitive Science, for supporting this work.

1 This is because only the words the mothers uttered most frefrequently were used as targets. Because in real life the child is sporadically confronted with the utterance of words in the absence of their referents, the word-to-world matching procedure would necessarily be probabilistic, gaining its power from cross-situational observation (Pinker, 1984).

2 Further analyses are even more revealing of the noun–verb difference. All test nouns are identified by most subjects, but fully one third of verbs are misidentified by every subject. Moreover, for verbs there is no cross-subject agreement on the misidentifications (virtually every subject makes a different false guess) while for nouns there is.

3 The requirement for knowledge of phrase structure in vocabulary learning also should hold for nouns

beyond the simplest object terms. A number of authors have recently described the use of syntax–semantics links in the acquisition of abstract nominal categories, e.g. mass versus count nouns and proper names. See particularly Bloom, P., (in press, b).

4   Actually, the inferential line that leads to this generalization concerning the isolated deaf children is quite complex. The bulk of data come from two and three-gesture sentences produced by the children. The number of arguments that show up in the utterance is constrained heavily by this, as has been shown also for young hearing speakers by Bloom (1970), and documented again and again. The number of underlying argument positions in the deaf children's sentences therefore was assessed by a measure that took into account the selective omission of different argument types (in more recent parlance, pro-drop); for this analysis, see Feldman, Goldin-Meadow, and Gleitman (1978).

5   Dissociating events where one of these verbs is sensible and the other is not are hard to find, though there are some, e.g. while Mary can get a coke from the vending machine, that machine does not "give" it (Pinker, personal communication). But the usefulness of these rare dissociating events for these verbs has to be considered against two facts we just mentioned: (1) children often learn from a very few exposures, and (2) verbs are often uttered in the absence of their referents and often are not uttered in the presence of their referents. Taken together, these factors imply that (a) a child is unlikely to hear *give* in a usefully dissociating context during the very brief learning interval for this word; (b) for the same reason, the child couldn't make much of the absence

of *give* from conversations about vending machines; and (c) if she has happened to conjecture falsely from prior exposures that *give* means "get," the single mismatching word-event observation, should this occur, can hardly dissuade her, and would likely be interpreted as an instance of noise in the database.

6   As we will discuss further, the syntactic environment, while narrowing the hypothesis space, still supports a variety of pertinent interpretations, even in the brief videos that these children were shown. Thus, one can't tell whether the rate or trajectory of the ball's motion is encoded in the new verb (as *throw*) or not (as *give*). Therefore, subjects might conjecture either of these as the meaning of *zike*. Moreover, the child subjects seemed loathe to conjecture that this new item was identical to some verb in their vocabulary, perhaps because they believe that there are no synonyms (see, for discussion, Clark, 1987; Markman and Wachtel, in press). Thus, they were more likely to respond "making him eat out of a spoon" than "feed," and so forth.

7   This compares with 15 percent correct in the Gillette and Gleitman manipulation. The difference in performance levels is largely a consequence of how the stimulus materials were constructed for the two experiments. Lederer et al. used very brief film clips. This surely blocked subjects from some pragmatic information. But it served an important purpose because the short clips solve the interleaving problem (artificially). They display only the action pertinent to utterance of the verb even though this action hadn't really occurred simultaneously with the verb utterance by the mother. But the important point is

that even this unrealistic aid to subjects pumped up their performance only to a pathetic 7 percent correct.

8 We do not deny that there are some quirks in language design – some facts about the complements typical for the use of certain verbs seem arbitrary rather than semantically conditioned. Learners appear to conform to such exceptional usage patterns in the linguistic community fairly well. But the more important facts are that errors by young children are predominantly returns to canonical syntax–semantics complementation (Bowerman, 1982a), that sentences containing verbs in disfavored syntactic environments are understood consensually (for some experimental evidence with young children, see Naigles, Gleitman, and Gleitman, 1993), and that novel syntactic environments are often exploited as a device to express irony and the like (e.g. *The general volunteered the private*). If subcategorization frames are rigidly specified in the verb lexicon, there is an awful lot of ungrammaticality in everyday speech, and it is suspiciously understandable.

Learning Grammar

16 Reinterpreting Children's Sentence Comprehension: Toward a New Framework

ROBERTA MICHNICK GOLINKOFF AND KATHY HIRSH-PASEK

John (around 18 months of age) is standing in the living room. His father asks, "Do you need a dry diaper?" John feels his diapers and hurries into his bedroom where the diapers are kept, returning with a diaper [much laughter]. His father changes him, stands him up, pats him on the seat and says "There! Now you have a dry diaper." John feels his diapers and hurries into his bedroom, returning with two diapers. (Chapman, 1978: 313)

What appears to be sentence comprehension may be the comprehension of much less! We start with an anecdote to introduce a number of substantive and methodological questions surrounding children's comprehension of sentences. First, why bother with comprehension when the child's productions provide such rich data and when the interpretation of comprehension data appears so problematic? Second, given the problem revealed in the anecdote, can sentence comprehension be reliably assessed? Are there ways to "trick" the young child into showing competencies that are not necessarily revealed in language production? Third, and finally, what exactly is "sentence comprehension?" How shall we conceptualize a process which occurs (at least, in adults) with the sensation of instantaneity? In attempting to address this last question, we present the rudiments of a new model of language comprehension (see Hirsh-Pasek and Golinkoff, 1993b), one that helps explain why the comprehension of linguistic structures appears to precede its production. After briefly presenting this framework, we review what is known about children's sentence comprehension capabilities in terms of the model's three phases.

This chapter will explore all the above questions and offer some tentative answers. What this chapter will not do is exhaustively review the studies that have used sentence comprehension as a window on children's developing language skill. Instead, we sample from the literature and use it to direct us to new questions. We begin, then, with the obvious question raised by the anecdote: if comprehension data appear to be so equivocal, why rely on them?

Why Not Wait for Children to Show Evidence of their Abilities in Language Production?

There can be little doubt that studies on children's language production have provided a rich source for language acquisition theories. Language production, the observable half of the child's language performance, however, is only part of the story. Just as astronomers were not satisfied to study only the light side of the moon, researchers have long recognized that data from the "dark" side, namely language comprehension, illuminates the language acquisition process far more than the study of production alone. In particular, language comprehension data serve three useful purposes. First, comprehension data can yield a more accurate picture of the content of the child's emerging language system. This is because it is not necessarily true that any structure that *can* be produced *will* be produced. Without comprehension assessments, the researcher is forced to wait for the child to spontaneously produce the structure of interest.[1] In comprehension experiments, one can test for a wide range of syntactic sensitivities whether they have been produced or not. The resulting data, then, provide a base for developing more complete theories of acquisition.

A case in point on how comprehension data may be indispensable in falsifying theoretical assertions about the young child's linguistic competence comes from work by Radford (1990; chapter 18, this volume). Radford stated that young children's language productions provide no evidence of a determiner system or an inflectional system. One possibility is that Radford is correct: the absence of these linguistic elements is what gives early speech its telegraphic character. On the other hand, Radford may be wrong. Although these elements do not appear in *speech*, perhaps the child is sensitive to and aware of these systems in comprehension. Shipley, Smith, and Gleitman (1969) and Gerken, Landau, and Remez (1990) showed that children who do not use function words in their own speech none the less seem to expect them. When they are missing or altered, sentence comprehension and memory suffers. In other words, if the child's sentence comprehension is adversely affected by the absence or mutilation of some linguistic feature, can it be said that the child operates completely without such a system? In this way, studies on sentence comprehension can be used to decide between various theoretical accounts of early acquisition.

A second reason for focusing on comprehension is that it may provide a window onto the *process* of language acquisition. Arguably, by the time a child is producing a particular structure, the child has already acquired it. Yet, the steps leading up to the analysis and mastery of that structure would be closed to inspection without studies of sentence comprehension.

The third and last reason why comprehension data are useful has to do with the issue of *methodological control*. In the real world there may be circumstances (as in the opening anecdote) in which children appear to comprehend certain structures when in fact they do not. With comprehension experiments, researchers interested in a certain structure and the circumstances under which it is used, can create situations that control for extraneous variables, such as children's bias to respond with action (Shatz, 1978).

In sum, studies of language comprehension are useful for three reasons: they permit us to (a) probe for structures which are not yet produced; (b) study the process of acquisition; and (c) gain methodological control. The benefits of comprehension research were noted almost 30 years ago when Chomsky (1964: 36) appealed to researchers to go beyond "direct description of the child's verbal output" to develop "devious and clever ways" of assessing linguistic performance. "Going beyond" verbal output with young children meant the development of methods to assess language comprehension. Yet, this challenge posed its own set of difficulties as the next section makes clear. Assessing language comprehension is fraught with difficulties.

Can Young Children's Sentence Comprehension be Reliably Assessed?

The short answer to the question is "yes–but." Including variations, several procedures have dominated comprehension assessment. First, researchers have used "enactment tasks" such as providing children with miniature objects and asking them to "Make the boy kiss the girl!" Second, children have been asked to carry out actions themselves such as, for example, "Kick the ball!" Third, presented with a choice of pictures, children have been asked to point to the picture a test sentence describes. For example, Fraser, Bellugi, and Brown (1963) asked children to "Point to the picture that shows 'The deer are jumping.' " The pictures showed a single or multiple deer jumping, making discrimination hinge on the number specified by the auxiliary verb (i.e. "is" v. "are"). A brief review of these methods and their limitations will be followed by a description of new methods which hold promise for assessing comprehension more sensitively.

Enactment and acting out tasks

These tasks may underestimate linguistic knowledge because children's predisposition to "act like x" may override the instruction to "act like y," even if the information in the sentence has been understood. This problem was acknowledged by Shipley, et al. (1969), de Villiers and de Villiers (1973b), and especially in Shatz (1978). Alternatively, young children may simply refuse to act on command. Yet, a failure to respond is not evidence of noncomprehension; rather only of noncompliance.

Picture pointing tasks

In addition to requiring action (see above), pictorial displays may fail (a) to provide young children with sufficient motivational incentive; and (b) to make sought-after distinctions – such as those involving action – salient and unambiguous. Friedman and Stevenson (1975) and Cocking and McHale (1981), for example, have shown that young children do not understand artistic conventions such as curved lines around joints to indicate movement.

Golinkoff, Hirsh-Pasek, Cauley, and Gordon (1987) claimed that studies of sentence comprehension have been biased *toward* nouns, *against* an understanding of action terms, and *against* the relationships embedded in grammatical constructions. This claim does *not* dismiss the great deal the field has already gained from research on language comprehension. It does, however, highlight the need for methods which (a) do not require action, and (b) represent dynamic events in a more natural way.

New methods

Several methods have emerged which appear to answer these needs. One involves the assessment of cortical event-related potentials (ERPs). When electrodes are placed on subjects' scalps, it is possible to record the ongoing electrical activity of the brain (Molfese, 1983) under various stimulus presentations. ERPs establish strict temporal relationships between the onset of a discrete stimulus event and changes in the resulting ERP pattern in different regions of the brain. ERPs have been used to study the infant's grasp of word meanings (e.g. Molfese, Morse, and Peters, 1990; Molfese, Burger-Judisch, Gill, Golinkoff, and Hirsh-Pasek, in press) as well as children's sentence processing (e.g. Holcomb, Coffey, and Neville, 1992). The main virtue of this method is that it requires neither speech nor action.

Another method, the "preferential looking paradigm" (Golinkoff and Hirsh-Pasek, 1981; Golinkoff et al., 1987; Hirsh-Pasek and Golinkoff, 1991, 1993a, b), presents children with two videotapes of objects or dynamic events and a single linguistic stimulus that matches or "goes with" only one of the video displays. Figure 16.1 depicts the layout of the experimental setting. The hypothesis is that if children understand the linguistic structure under test, they will prefer to watch the screen that matches the linguistic stimulus more than

Figure 16.1 Experimental set-up of the preferential looking paradigm.

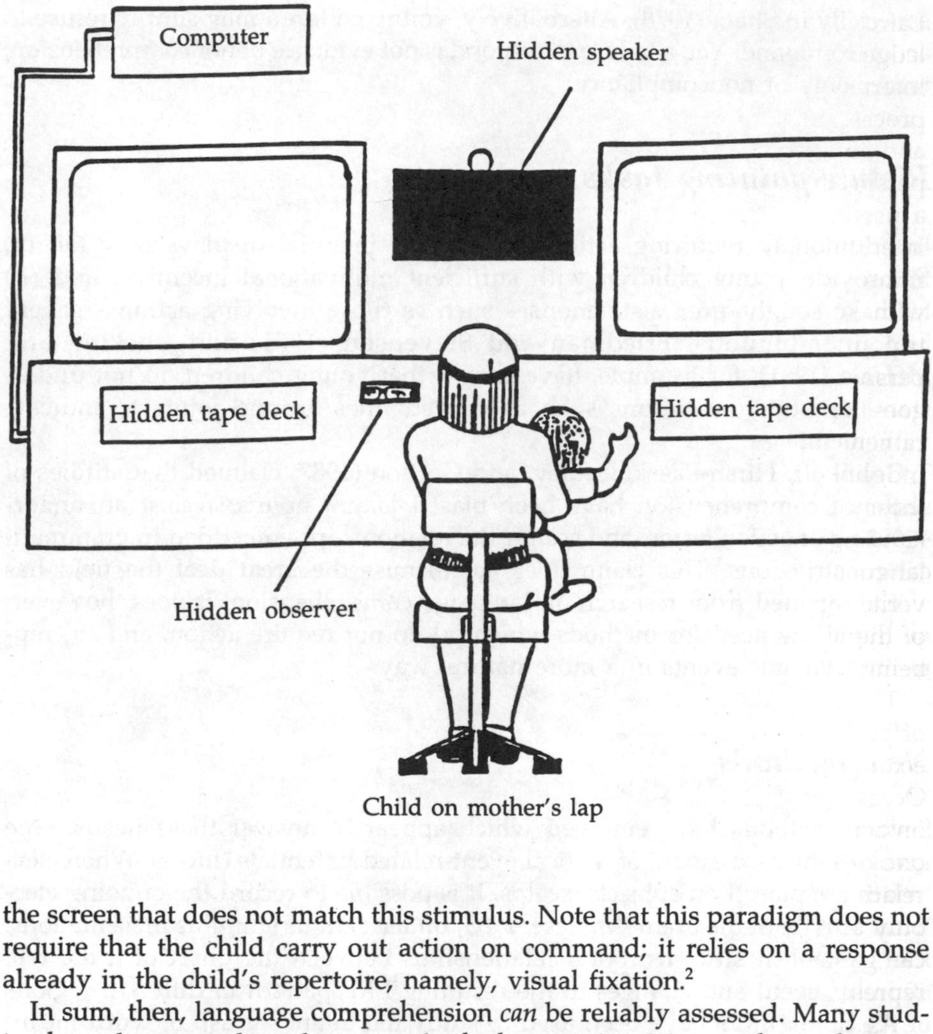

Child on mother's lap

the screen that does not match this stimulus. Note that this paradigm does not require that the child carry out action on command; it relies on a response already in the child's repertoire, namely, visual fixation.[2]

In sum, then, language comprehension *can* be reliably assessed. Many studies have been conducted, some of which capitalized better than others on young children's natural response repertoires. Given that comprehension can be reliably assessed and provide important data, it becomes imperative to understand more about the process itself.

What Exactly is Sentence Comprehension?

The working definition of language comprehension that we have adopted is one that sublimates the goal of language comprehension to the broader end of cognitive development. Language comprehension is viewed as the process of using linguistic input to assist in the building of mental models (Johnson-Laird, 1983; Gernsbacher, 1990; Kintsch, 1988). One of the widely acknowledged hallmarks of human development is children's increasing ability to internally represent their external world – to construct mental models. This process involves both an *internalization* of the events that children witness and an *interpretation* of these events in ways that incorporate past experience, perspective, affect, etc. An analogy from the field of film making provides a useful way of conceptualizing the difference between internalization and interpretation as they are used here. The internalization process is like the film genre called "cinema vérité": ongoing events are captured as they occur, with little or no interpretation by the director. The camera is simply set on a tripod to record the movements and relationships in view and no directorial perspective is added. While this analogy feels starkly perceptual, our view goes beyond perception. Cinema vérité incorporates objects and animate beings rather than mere shapes. It also shows more than vectors and trajectories. Indeed, the child in cinema vérité is equipped with primitive meanings like those of causality, animacy, and containment that emerge in what Mandler (1992) called the "image schematic" format. The earliest characterization of language comprehension, then, is one in which the child operates like a cinema vérité director, using the language (or more specifically the surface properties of the language) as an accompaniment to representations of objects, animate beings, and relations in the world.

The *interpretation* component of language adds yet another dimension – that of perspective. Utilizing the techniques of a skilled cinematographer, the director guides viewers towards a particular focus or interpretation of events. Occasionally, for example, the director may employ a zoom lens, zeroing in on actors' faces to suggest how they feel.[3] Or the director may focus on only one of the actors in an event, foregrounding his or her actions and emotions relative to the others. Language comprehension comes to serve this function only after the child has engaged in much internalization. That is, before one can gain a perspective on the world's events, one must be able to analyze and represent those events.

As children create a mental analogue of the world, they move away from cinema vérité and more toward becoming talented film interpreters who bring with them past knowledge of how to "read" the angles and how to "feel" the scenes. The mental model becomes annotated with personal experience. Thus, quite early in development, each person's model has some "family resemblance" to, but is not a carbon copy of, the events that were witnessed (Bloom, 1993b, 1994).

Some have argued that this move towards sophisticated mental models that involve both internalization and interpretation of physical events was one of the evolutionary forces behind the creation of language itself. For example, Miller (1990) contends that language evolved from the twin pressures for efficient communication about the world and for sophisticated representation of that world. Bloom (1993b) suggests that for the child, the drive toward more sophisticated mental representations and for communication about them provides the incentive for language growth. As mental models become more discrepant from children's representation of the perceptual world (more interpreted in our terminology), they seek to share the contents of their minds with others. Communication, first through affect and then through the propositions of language, is therefore born from the need to talk about the increasingly complex contents of the mind (Bloom, 1993b: 14):

> Children will acquire the grammar of a language as the contents of intentional states become increasingly discrepant from the data of perception. In earliest infancy, mental contents are constrained to the data of perception. What young infants are seeing is, to a large extent, what they are thinking. With developments in the capacity for representation and in the procedures for retrieval and recall, infants come to access objects and events from memory that do not match the data of perception. This recall of past events is needed for interpreting what others do and, eventually, what they say.

Where does language comprehension, *per se*, fit into the larger context of mental model building? Following Gernsbacher (1988, 1990), and others (e.g. MacWhinney, 1977; Johnson-Laird, 1983; Kintsch, 1988), we propose that language is an abstract and concise way to both internalize and interpret the world's events. By using language, we codify events in an abstract way, not only affording a way of quickly internalizing what was witnessed (as in "Oh, the *dog* was jumping!"), but also adding perspective or interpretation (as in "The dog is chasing the cat" rather than "The cat is fleeing from the dog") (Gleitman and Wanner, 1988; Fischer, Gleitman, and Gleitman, 1991).

Overview of a model of the development of language comprehension

How might language comprehension assist the young child in internalizing and interpreting events? We propose that the development of language comprehension goes through the following three phases. First, language assists the child in segmenting the *nonlinguistic events* to be internalized and roughly interpreted. At this point, language may not even be processed *qua* language. That is, language may be processed more acoustically (or visually for signers) than linguistically. This first "internalization" phase (lasting roughly from four to nine months) involves Peters' (1985; chapter 17, this volume) process of *extraction* but goes much beyond it to involve what we call *acoustic packaging*. That is, children use extracted (or perceived) acoustic units as a guide to segmenting and processing nonlinguistic events. In the second, interpretation phase (from approximately nine to 24 months), children begin to analyze *within* the acoustic units extracted in phase I and to map the resulting products (words and phrases) onto their corresponding representations of objects and events. Children make these mappings in ways compatible with the semantics of their native language. When the cues from the semantic, prosodic, contextual, and syntactic systems are redundantly correlated, children can show evidence of multiword sentence comprehension (Hirsh-Pasek and Golinkoff, 1991) even before they produce two-word utterances. For phase III children (about 24–36 months), reliance on correlated cues in the input declines as their ability to perform relatively unsupported syntactic analyses increases. Now sentence comprehension can occur in the absence of the events being described and children can perform interclausal linguistic analysis to gain meaning. Hence, phase III is referred to as "complex syntactic analysis" – an advanced phase of language interpretation.

We offer this framework for three reasons. First, it is a new way of organizing the existing data; second, it takes seriously the oft-stated, but rarely researched, claim that different language systems (prosody, semantics, and syntax) and environmental influences (e.g. social interaction) interact; and third, it views language comprehension as a tool for studying cognitive development in the context of mental model building.

For this speculative framework of comprehension to succeed it must be the case that children (a) attempt to construct mental models and (b) use language as a vehicle to assist in the construction of these models. Thus, children must recognize that language maps onto perceived relationships else they would have no obvious motivation to access the information available (at a number of levels) in the input. The rest of this chapter reviews selected literature on language comprehension from the vantage point of the three phases described above. Table 16.1 summarizes our claims about these phases.

Phase I: Internalization: Acoustic packaging of nonlinguistic events (around four to nine months)

Imagine if you will, that you are watching a movie made in Japan and have no knowledge of Japanese. Would you gain a firmer grasp of the significant events in the movie if you watched it with the accompanying language rather than in silence? We contend that you would. Beyond affording information on the emotional tone of a scene, the narrative assists us in "packaging" or segmenting the flow of events and in focusing our attention. For one thing, you assume that the language you hear somehow relates to the events you observe. In addition, the language helps you to unitize what might be separate events. For example, you may see someone performing multiple actions (opening a closet, removing a coat, putting it on, and leaving). If you hear what sounds like a sentence over the part where the person put on the coat, you will subsequently remember that event better than the other events which did not have a linguistic overlay. Furthermore, if language had overlapped the entire event, you would probably think of the subparts as a single event,

Table 16.1   A three-phase model of language comprehension

Dominant process	Form of representation		Language Comprehension	Production
Phase I: Extraction and acoustic packaging (4–9 months)				
Internalization	Acoustic correlates of linguistic structure	Image-schemas (not propositional)	Some words	Few, if any, words
Phase II: Segmentation and linguistic mapping (9–24 months)				
Internalization and interpretation	Words, some early grammar	Propositions; cuts becoming language dependent	Syntactic, when redundant cues from context, semantics, and prosody coincide	Prototypical transitive and intransitive sentences; often incomplete
Phase III: Complex syntactic analysis (24–36 months)				
Interpretation	Hierarchical representation of linguistic structure	Propositions; language dependent in nature	Syntactic, even when redundant cues fail to coincide; can compute interclausal relations	Complete sentences, variety of structures

rather than as four separate events, when you remembered it later. Thus, without knowing Japanese, you would have used the language to help you focus and unitize the observed events.

Now imagine that you are an infant and bring no preconceived notions about events like "leave-taking" to your observation of the world. Acoustic accompaniments to events should influence infants' perception even more profoundly than it does for adults watching a foreign film. At this level, language (or the acoustic equivalent from the infant's point of view) sets up the boundaries for real world events. To use acoustic packaging, phase I infants need two prerequisite abilities. First, they must refine their analysis of the world's *nonlinguistic* events. Second, infants must attend to the acoustic information in the incoming language stream. Acoustic packaging, therefore, is a precursor to linguistic mapping. Infants use acoustic information to help them segment complex, nonlinguistic events into what will be linguistically relevant units at the next phase. Below we review some evidence for infants' possession of these prerequisites.

Prerequisite 1: Forming image schemas of the world's events

Infants construct mental models based on their representations of the perceived world of objects, actions, and events; they are not merely reactive to the flow of sensory input. Indeed, even infrahuman species must have this capability to function in the world. Mandler (1992) proposed that infants parse the events in their world into a set of "image schemas" such as PATH, LINK, CONTAINMENT, ANIMACY, CAUSALITY, and AGENCY. These are constructed from infants' analysis of movement trajectories and self-initiated and contingent movement. Work on infants' ability to find hidden objects provides one piece of evidence for these image schemas. By nine months of age, infants can use spatiotemporal cues along with perceptual cues to find a hidden object when their own perspective has been shifted (Acredolo, 1980, 1978; Acredolo and Evans, 1980). To do this, infants must develop an internal working model of the spatial environment that is transformable.

Prerequisite 2: Extracting acoustic correlates of linguistic units from the speech stream

As Peters (1985: 1,033) wrote, "The child's first problem is to get hold of something to work with linguistically." A new line of research suggests that even before infants understand the semantics of sentences – let alone their syntactic composition – they reveal an ability to locate the acoustic correlates of phrasal and clausal units (see Fernald, 1991; Hirsh-Pasek and Golinkoff, 1993a, for reviews). Hirsh-Pasek, Jusczyk, Kemler Nelson, and their colleagues (Hirsh-Pasek, Kemler Nelson, Jusczyk, Cassidy, Druss, and Kennedy, 1987; Jusczyk, Hirsh-Pasek, Kemler Nelson, Kennedy, Woodward, and Piwoz, 1992; Kemler Nelson, Hirsh-Pasek, Jusczyk, and Wright Cassidy, 1989) have found that six-month-old infants prefer to listen to speech in which the integrity of the clausal boundaries has been maintained rather than to speech in which the integrity of these boundaries has been disturbed. That is, natural, infant directed speech contains pauses of approximately one second's duration between clauses. Infants prefer to listen to speech when the pauses are kept at the boundaries as opposed to speech in which the pauses are artificially inserted *inside* the units. A little later in development (by nine months) infants seem to be sensitive to the acoustic markers that segment major phrasal units such as noun phrases and verb phrases (Jusczyk, et al., 1992) while shortly after that at 11 months, they show awareness of word units (Woodward, 1987). Thus, with increasing age, infants become capable of discriminating between smaller and smaller constituents. Peters (1985) likens this to a "figure-ground" phenomenon: after a unit (e.g. the phrase, "Shut the door") has been extracted as a single unit, the phrase which stood out as the figure in the speech stream now comes to serve as the ground within which a new figure (e.g. a single word, "door") emerges.

Once children have formed image-schematic representations of events and can isolate acoustic chunks in the language stream, they are ready to form "acoustic packages." Eventually some acoustic chunks will be repeated often enough that the infant will begin to map these onto the same sort of events, often called "routines" (Peters, 1985). The child has not analyzed the interior of the particular acoustic chunk and just responds (somewhat like a trained seal) when told, "Blow your nose, Irving!" Thus, before the child possesses the wherewithal to analyze these language chunks, "sentence" comprehension occurs when children respond to these well-worn routines.

Of course, if the three phase framework we offer here is to be upheld, research must examine how language (as say, compared to music or silence) influences four to nine-month-olds' perception and memory for events. Because mothers of first year infants (at least Western ones) *do* talk about objects, actions, and events that are in the infant's focus, there is reason to believe that infants' event perception may be influenced by the acoustic stream (Harris, Jones, Brookes, and Grant, 1986). At present, little evidence exists on how acoustic packaging works in detail.

Summary of phase I

Before infants can engage in linguistic analysis and try to understand the mappings between language and events, they must recognize the link between elements of the acoustic stream and events. This prerequisite to language acquisition has, by and large, been presupposed in prior treatments of language acquisition. In phase I, then, infants use the acoustic aspects of language to direct their attention and to "package" nonlinguistic events. These acoustically framed units allow the infant to *internalize* information about events, building the foundation for future interpretations. The boundaries that result from the parsing of events constrain the linguistic mapping task to follow. Segmenting events into language-relevant units delimits the window within which infants will look for finer, linguistic correlations between events and clauses. This reduces the potentially overwhelming number of degrees of freedom in the linguistic mapping task.

Development from phase I to phase II is prompted by a mechanism that Bloom (in press) describes as the Principle of Discrepancy (quoted above). As the contents of consciousness become different from the data of perception, Bloom argues that infants are motivated to discover more about the grammar of their language so they can express their more complex ideas.

In short, infants' incentive for continued progress in language learning is to express and enrich their mental models. If infants only internalized what they saw, they could never comprehend novel relations between objects nor could they create and communicate about novel combinations of objects or scenes from their mental world. As infants leave phase I and enter phase II, they have internalized some of the basic units of event structure and of language. The job now turns to one of preliminary linguistic mapping at the level of individual words and grammar.

Phase II: Segmentation and linguistic mapping (around nine to 24 months)

In phase II infants move beyond acoustic packaging to linguistic mapping. In phase I *any* extracted acoustic chunk could map to some aspect of an event. In phase II, infants begin with some acoustic chunks that are reliably paired with some particular objects, events, or actions in the world. Thus, the products of phase I become the input to phase II as infants begin to segment these chunks, performing more find grained linguistic analysis (Peters, 1985; chapter 17, this volume). In this phase, the child begins to map individual words to their referents (be they actions, objects, or properties of objects and events). By the end of the latter part of this phase (between about 16 to about 24 months) linguistic mappings will occur at the level of *relations* as the child comprehends and produces strings of utterances.

From the start in phase II children are influenced by the particular language they are learning. As Slobin (1985: 1176) wrote,

> I propose the OP:Functors begins by mapping acoustically salient, uninterpreted speech segments onto Scenes as a whole, or onto focused elements of Scenes. Using such preliminary mappings as an anchor, Scenes can gradually be analyzed into those particular Notions which are grammaticized in the parental language.

Slobin (1985) claims that children first map language onto prototypical transitive activity scenes (as when an animate being acts on an inanimate object). In contrast, Bowerman (1985) and Choi and Bowerman (1991) argue that children are less rigidly constrained about what they will choose to talk about and even *more* influenced by their particular language than Slobin believes. In either events, during phase II, the child's task is to carve acoustic units into linguistic ones and to learn the relationships that map sound to meaning. This occurs at many levels – from the word to sentential relations.

Linguistic mapping: Individual words

Some researchers have suggested that there may be a set of principles that guide the mapping of individual words to their referents. While outside the scope of this chapter, this has become an active research area. Suffice it to say that children may approach the word learning task with some heuristics or principles that can be used in forming the mappings between isolatable words and their referents (Markman, 1989; Merriman and Bowman, 1989; Waxman and Kosowski, 1990; Golinkoff, Mervis, and Hirsh-Pasek, 1993, for reviews).

Linguistic mapping: Beyond the individual word

One could imagine that an infant might know a few words that map to objects or events, but still not realize that *strings* of words, in sentences, map to events in the world. When do infants realize that strings of words come in "packages" or constituents that "go together" or form a unit in some way to comment on witnessed events?

Hirsh-Pasek and Golinkoff (1991, 1993a) have shown that by 13 or 14 months, even before infants have 25 words in their productive vocabularies, they expect strings of words to map to complex events. Utilizing the preferential looking paradigm described above (Golinkoff and Hirsh-Pasek, 1981) (see figure 16.1), infants saw on one screen, for example, a woman kissing a set of keys and holding a ball in the foreground. On the other screen, the infant saw just the opposite: a woman kissing the ball and holding the keys in the foreground. The linguistic stimulus was, "She's kissing the keys! Where's she kissing the keys?" (It was ascertained from maternal report that infants comprehended the nouns used.) The hypothesis was that subjects would prefer to watch the screen which matched these sentences over the nonmatching screen. However, other outcomes were possible. On one view (Slobin, 1985), infants might prefer to watch the last-named noun ("keys") on the screen where they dangled in the foreground (the nonmatch). Alternatively, infants might watch both screens to the same degree: after all, each screen contained a "she,", a set of keys, and the act of kissing. In fact, infants preferred to watch the screen which matched what they heard rather than the screen which did not match the test sentence. Thus, infants preferred to watch the screen where the woman was kissing the keys rather than the ball. A subsequent control experiment was conducted to rule out the alternative explanation that infants were simply noting the last word they heard (i.e. "keys") and then looking for the screen where the keys were the focus of the interaction. The linguistic stimulus in the control experiment, therefore, omitted the verb (e.g. "Where are the keys?"). All other details were kept identical. In this control experiment, the previous result was not obtained. Thus, infants recognize that language comes in "packages" which map to events. In general, the very fact that linguistic stimuli drive looking preferences (measured in visual fixation times) to particular events, suggests that infants assume specific mappings between what they hear and what they see. The ability to recognize that language units map complexly to events must surely rest on the prior stage of acoustic packaging when infants discern that elements in the acoustic stream punctuate and highlight different parts of events.

Having shown that infants by 13 or 14 months know that strings of words form units, the child is poised to engage in more detailed, clause-internal analyses. Prior to addressing children's comprehension of various sentential relations in phase II, the question of what a sentence is must be addressed.

The components of the "sentence"

While Miller (1981) urged his colleagues to "hang loose" with respect to commitments to a particular grammar, there are facts about language which every theory of grammar incorporates. Among these is the idea that languages are comprised of (1) units at a number of levels, e.g. words, phrases, and clauses; (2) relations or ways of arranging these units to express meanings; and (3) hierarchical organization – units at one level comprise the units at the next higher level, e.g. words comprise phrases which in turn comprise clauses. Any account of children's sentence comprehension must describe how children become sensitive to the types of units and relations sentences contain.

Finding units within the clause

Once infants find the words in sentences, they must distinguish between "open" and "closed" class words, or words which bear content (e.g. "chair") and words such as "with" and "by" which, while semantically rich, carry more abstract, grammatically informative meanings. These word classes are distinguished by around two years of age (but see Radford, 1990; chapter 18, this volume) since children's sentence comprehension and sentence memory is adversely affected when closed class items are omitted (Shipley et al., 1969; Gerken et al., 1990; Hirsh-Pasek, Naigles, Golinkoff, Gleitman, and Gleitman, 1988).

Children must also be able to assign novel words to the correct open word class. Valian (1986) found that by 2.5 children operate with all the standard form classes. To assign a word to a form class, children have a variety of information at their disposal. For example, they may rely on inflectional endings (as in "ing" or "ed" on verbs), cooccurring closed class words (e.g. the articles which almost invariably precede nouns), or perhaps, acoustic markers such as syllable number and stress (Morgan, in press; Kelly, 1992). In English, nouns have more syllables on average than verbs and nouns receive first syllable stress (e.g. REcord is the noun; reCORD, the verb). Research suggests that some combination of these cues – especially closed class items – contributes to the 24-month-old's ability to identify a novel word as a noun versus a verb (Golinkoff, Diznoff, Yasik, and Hirsh-Pasek, 1992) and a noun versus an adjective (Golinkoff, Menutti, Lengle, and Hermon, 1992).

In sum, to comprehend novel sentences, children must first find the units that compose these sentences. In the first year of life, infants appear to be sensitive to the acoustic correlates of some syntactic units. By the second year, children can figure out the part of speech novel words belong to and, judging from their production, use the traditional lexical categories. Sentence comprehension involves more than finding the units, however. It involves finding which units are interdependent even though they may be physically discontinuous.

Finding sentential relations

The single most important feature which all languages share is that they are "structure-dependent" (Chomsky, 1972) rather than "serial-order dependent." The ability to comprehend sentences implies that children are able to understand links between words which are not physically contiguous. Sentence agreement offers a good example. Despite the separation of the subject of the sentence from the verb (as in the sentence, *"John*, the boy next door, works for the University"), the subject "John" determines the ending of the verb "work." To appreciate these dependencies, children must detect which units are structurally dependent on which other units. This in turn involves an implicit appreciation of language's hierarchical structure and the abstract relational elements which comprise that structure. In the case of agreement, children need to discover relations such as "subject" and "object" of the sentence. Knowing that subjects and objects are types of nouns goes only part of the way; the same noun can often play either grammatical role. Further, grammatical relations such as subject of the sentence allow even nominalized verbs, as in "The flying of the airplane was dangerous." Thus, one cannot rely on simple semantic definitions (e.g. animate beings) to determine what kinds of things may play the role of subject. Another example of a dependency between physically disparate elements comes from pronominalization (see phase III, below). If children are to comprehend sentences containing pronouns, they must be able to link the pronoun to the correct referent. For a sentence such as "After he hugged Mark, John left," the child must sort out which of the two possible referents for the pronoun "he" is the correct referent.

In sum, comprehending sentences involves finding the sentential units (at a number of levels) as well as the relations between those units. Length limitations prevent us from treating young children's sensitivity to these relations in any depth. Controversies about the developmental course of this sensitivity, however, have been a topic of debate since the 1970s (e.g. see Bloom, 1970; Bowerman, 1973; Braine, 1976; Pinker, 1984; Hirsh-Pasek and Golinkoff, 1993a, b). We next review the comprehension of word order and of passive sentences.

The comprehension of word order

Word order, in addition to inflections and tones, is one way in which the world's languages convey meaning relations (Greenberg, 1963; Comrie, 1981). For example, in English, the statement "Brutus killed Caesar" captures history while "Caesar killed Brutus" violates it. The other end of the continuum from English is exemplified by languages like Walpiri or Turkish, which have much freer word order but which use strong inflectional systems. Children acquiring Turkish learn to rely on the endings that are appended to nouns to figure out "who-did-what-to-whom" in the event being described. Italian children use animacy whenever possible as their main cue for sentence comprehension (Bates, MacWhinney, Caselli, Devescovi, Natale, and Venza, 1984).

Why would it be important to know when and whether young children can comprehend differential word order, holding other factors constant? For those languages that rely heavily on word order, this becomes the main vehicle providing some perspective on events. By way of example, the sentence "The cat chases the dog" provides the listener with a different focus than does the sentence "The dog flees from the cat" (Gleitman and Wanner, 1988). Thus, children who are attentive to word order probably construct different mental models of events than do children who are insensitive to word order.

Word order comprehension is also important in deciding what children bring to the acquisition process. Hirsh-Pasek and Golinkoff (1993a, b) have distinguished between two types of theories of language acquisition: "inside-out" and "outside-in." On inside-out theories, the child comes to the task of acquisition armed in advance with considerable linguistic knowledge. Input is needed merely to discover how the particular language the child is acquiring instantiates this knowledge. If the child comprehends word order, it is because the child recognizes grammatical relations such as subject–verb–object from the beginning. Thus, in the context of Chomsky's 1981 theory, attention to word order is required to determine how to set some of the parameters with which the child arrives at the scene. For example, Atkinson (1987) and Berwick (1986) both point out that children must determine whether they are learning a "head-initial" or a "head-final" language. That is, does the lexical item which gives the phrase its name (viz. the verb in a verb phrase) go first or last in the phrase?

On the outside-in view of acquisition, children "arrive" with little explicit linguistic knowledge. They proceed to construct grammar from the bottom up, forming ever broader semantic categories (Bloom, in press; Schlesinger, 1971; Tomasello, 1992) which eventually become syntactic categories such as subject of the sentence (see Bowerman, 1973; Pinker, 1984, for opposite perspectives on this issue). On the outside-in view, word order comprehension reveals the ability of the child to apply rules such as, "the first noun mentioned is the agent, the second the patient of the action." While these two types of theories differ, both share the fundamental assumption that learners are predisposed to notice word (or particle) order in the input language.

Given the importance of word order cues, then, to mental model building and to both inside-out and outside-in theories, it is little wonder that questions concerning the young child's sensitivity to word order have occupied a prominent position in debates of syntactic competence. Furthermore, one can identify all possible positions on the relationship between the comprehension and production of word order: either the comprehension of word order precedes its production (Hirsh-Pasek and Golinkoff, 1991); the production of word order precedes its comprehension (Chapman and Kohn, 1978; Chapman and Miller, 1975); or both appear contemporaneously (Bloom, 1978). Below the age of two, when MLU is about 2.00, the data have proven equivocal. Some studies find that toddlers are not even sensitive to whether a sentence contains scrambled or normal word order (Wetstone and Friedlander, 1973). Other studies suggest that children – at least by 24 months – show the ability to distinguish among word orders (Roberts, 1983; Golinkoff and Markessini, 1980).

To resolve the issue of when young children are able to use word order to derive meaning relations, Hirsh-Pasek and Golinkoff (1991, 1993a, b) used Golinkoff and Hirsh-Pasek's (1981) preferential looking paradigm (see above). Golinkoff et al. (1987) had already demonstrated in this paradigm that 28-month-old children, producing two and three-word sentences, could use word order to distinguish between sentences such as "Where is Big Bird washing Cookie Monster?" versus "Where is Cookie Monster washing Big Bird?" Would children not yet producing multiword speech show comprehension of word order? Infants (mean age, 17 months), most of whom were producing only single words, demonstrated a significant looking preference for the screen which matched the linguistic stimulus than for the screen that did not match it. Precocious word order comprehension was revealed because first, the paradigm requires only a visual fixation response, and second, sentential syntax is *not* put into conflict with semantic cues. Thus, in this paradigm, even fragile knowledge of word order is exposed.

The finding that word order is comprehended early is interesting from the perspective of both outside-in and inside-out theories (Hirsh-Pasek and Golinkoff, 1993a). However, these results cannot address the question of whether the child solves the word order problem by accessing either a syntactic or a semantic system. That is, it is not clear whether the child is doing a subject–verb–object or an agent–action–patient analysis.

Under our story, the child in phase II can comprehend word order relations only when the prosodic, semantic, and syntactic systems act in parallel. That is, the phase II child, with fragile syntax, relies on the redundant cues available in the prosodic, semantic, and social domains. "Redundant" is the operative word here, for if any of these systems are disrupted in some way, sentence comprehension will suffer. There is evidence that the phase II child needs to have the "moons in alignment" as it were, to comprehend sentences. For example, Strohner and Nelson (1974) disrupted the comprehension of active declarative sentences at 36 months when they gave children sentences such as "The mouse chased the elephant." Rather than rely exclusively on syntax, children at this age seem to place great weight on the semantic system, relying instead on event probability to act out this sentence.

In general, the child moves from a period (phase II) of relying heavily on redundant semantic, prosodic, and social information to a time (phase III) when the child can comprehend sentences using syntactic structures in the face of conflicting cues from these other systems. That is, the comprehension system in phase II requires support from multiple sources of input to form a coalition of cues. It is "fragile" rather than resilient comprehension. By phase III, the child's syntactic knowledge is strong enough such that comprehension

in theories of grammar. The passive is important to assess since children who can comprehend the passive in reversible[5] sentences are using a syntactic, as opposed to a semantic, grammar. This is because passive sentences violate the agent–action–patient sequence of English's subject–verb–object pattern. To comprehend passives, the child must be operating with the syntactic relations of subject and object. Comprehension of the passive also requires that the child notice and understand the function of the closed class word "by" (as in "The dog is being chased by the girl"). Since early speech is notorious for the absence of closed class items, and since theories of adult parsing (e.g. Wanner and Maratsos, 1978; Marcus, 1980) require the exploitation of the closed class, comprehension of the passive becomes of great interest. On this score, Maratsos and Abramovitch (1975) showed that children are sensitive to markers for the passive. Children's comprehension was disrupted when they were given sentences without the "by" (as in "The cat is licked the dog") or with a nonsense syllable inserted into the position occupied by the "by" (as in "The cat is licked po the dog") (see also Stromswold, Pinker, and Kaplan, 1985, for children's use of different cues for the passive).

In the standard linguistic account, the passive (under Chomsky, 1957, 1965) was created by a transformation that moved the logical object to what was ordinarily the logical subject's position. In addition, a past participle was added to the verb, an auxiliary verb inserted, and the "by-phrase" introduced. On the derivational complexity theory of sentence processing (see Hayes, 1970), sentences like the passive with transformations should be more difficult to comprehend than sentences (like the active declarative) without transformations. This prediction received ample confirmation (e.g. Bever, 1970; Strohner and Nelson, 1974; Beilin, 1975) in studies of children's comprehension of passive versus active sentences.

Under the Government and Binding analysis (Chomsky, 1981; Jaeggli, 1986), passives result in an "argument-chain" (A-chain), since a coindexed trace of the object NP remains after the NP is moved to the subject position. This is seen in sentences (1) and (2) below:

(1)   Josh chased Allison.
(2)   Allison$_i$ was chased e$_i$ by Josh.

The passive morpheme absorbs the external theta role, which can be assigned to the oblique object. The subject of the sentences now receives nominative case. Because of the movement and the case changes, the passive should also be a difficult construction to acquire. Indeed, it emerges in English-speaking children's sentences around late age three (Bowerman, 1973).

Borer and Wexler (1987) argue for a maturational explanation of the late appearance of this construction. Children should not be able to acquire the passive until the principle for A-chain formation is available. To make their case, Borer and Wexler argue that early appearing truncated passives are not verbal passives but adjectival passives. For example, a truncated passive sentence such as "The doll was broken," has a structure parallel to the sentence "The doll was green," and not to the full passive "The doll was broken by Mary." There is no movement required to create the adjectival passive; only the verbal passive requires the movement of the object to the subject position. This argument would be seriously weakened, however, if crosslinguistic research suggested that adjectives and truncated passives were dissassociated in some languages having the following consequences: (a) the two forms appeared at radically different developmental times; or (b) one of the constructions appeared in the absence of the other, i.e. a language in which there was no adjectival form. Sesotho, a southern Bantu language in which the passive is more central to the grammar, is just such a language. Children acquiring Sesotho produce passives, albeit not at high rates, in their second year of life (Demuth, 1989, 1990). Thus, early appearing passives in a language which does not contain adjectival passives, weakens the maturational account because children who use those languages could not be producing passives based on analogy with adjectival passives. Additional evidence against the adjectival interpretation of the passive form is provided by the Maratsos and Abramovitch (1975) study described above. If children assume that passives are adjectival forms, then their comprehension of passives should not have suffered when the "by" was either removed or substituted by a nonsense syllable.

Demuth's data do not sufficiently address, however, another important issue in the acquisition of the passive – an issue which begs for comprehension tests of various kinds of passives by Sesotho children. Does the child generate a class-based rule for which verbs can passivize or does the child form verb-based rules, one at a time, as they are witnessed in the input (see Tomasello, 1992)? Since not all verbs can passivize (e.g. *"The shampoo was contained by the bottle"), how does the child learn which verbs can and which cannot passivize? The issue of whether the passive is rule-generated or lexically based (or possibly some combination) was first raised by Maratsos, Kuczaj, Fox, and Chalkley (1979) (see replications by de Villiers, Phinney, and Avery, 1982; Pinker, Lebeaux, and Frost, 1987) when they found that four and five-year olds' comprehension of passives was not equally good for all kinds of verbs. Passives containing prototypic actional verbs (such as "The boy was hit by the girl") were comprehended more readily than sentences containing nonactional verbs (such as "The boy was liked by the girl").[6] Even in Sesotho, children's spontaneous passives contain primarily action verbs. One of Demuth's (1990) subjects was observed to have difficulty with a noncanonical, nonagentive verb ("surpass"). Why should children understand and produce actional passives more readily than nonactional passives? And more broadly, how do children learn that only some verbs can be passivized?

Several explanations have been offered, ranging from the frequency of the different types of passives in the input (Gordon and Chafetz, 1990); to a semantic rule for passivization, allowing only subjects and objects that are agents and patients, respectively, to undergo passivization (Maratsos et al., 1979); to children functioning with Hopper and Thompson's (1980) transitivity hierarchy (Maratsos, Fox, Becker, and Chalkley, 1985); to children operating with a form of Jackendoff's (1972) Thematic Hierarchy Condition as a constraint on passive production (Pinker et al., 1987). Whatever the ultimate explanation of these phenomena, the larger question which structures like the passive may illuminate, is how children generalize from such limited exposure to the passive in such consistent ways. That is, the passive is a prototypical example of how children come to be able to produce a linguistic structure based on limited input.

In English, where the passive is an infrequent structure in speech to children (Wells, 1978), it is a difficult construction to master. The first thing children do when presented with passive sentences is to treat them as though they were active declaratives, apparently ignoring the elements which signal the existence of a different kind of sentence structure. For example, deVilliers and de Villiers (1972) asked two and three-year-old children (MLUs were 2.87–4.67) to act out reversible active and passive sentences. The younger the child (and the lower the MLU) the more the child reversed the meaning of the passive, treating the first mentioned noun as though it was the subject (or agent) of the verb. At the same time, these children had virtually reached ceiling level performance on their comprehension of active sentences. Bever (1970) claimed that children begin by interpreting all N–V–N sequences as if they were agent–action–patient sentences.

Strohner and Nelson (1974) found that two and three-year-olds' passive sentence comprehension was also heavily influenced by event probability, as phase II of the present mental model framework would predict. Past the time when children comprehend reversible passives (four and five years old), performance is disrupted by using sentences which contain unlikely events, such as "The elephant was chased by the mouse." These results, like the results discussed above on the differential success children have with actional and nonactional passives, suggest that when semantic cues are put in *conflict* with syntactic cues, children cannot rely exclusively on syntactic cues until they are about five years of age. When passive comprehension emerges for English-speaking children around late age three, they appear to prefer passives which describe highly probable events, contain prototypically transitive verbs, and have inanimate patients being acted on by animate agents. However, data are needed on children's passive comprehension in languages such as Sesotho in which passives are more frequent in the input and more central to the grammar (Demuth, 1990) than in English in order to evaluate whether children are capable of functioning with syntactic and not exclusively semantic categories from very early in the acquisition process. Such data might eventually be available for English speakers using a methodology like the preferential looking paradigm (Golinkoff et al., 1987) which makes minimal demands on infant subjects. None the less, given that the passive construction plays a less central role in English grammar than the grammar of other languages (like Sesotho), it is unlikely that the English passive will be the best route for diagnosing early syntactic competence.

To summarize, the comprehension of passive sentences has proven useful for understanding when children (a) seem to possess abstract syntactic categories; (b) movement capabilities; and (c) the interaction of semantic and syntactic variables. The passive helps us to begin to get a handle on Baker's (1979) paradox, or how, from extremely limited positive data, the child formulates correct generalizations about the language. Further, it appears that children's comprehension of passive sentences is in advance of their production of those sentences (at least in English) and that passives are seen as a unique structure by the child as opposed to an adjectival variant.

Recapitulating the story thus far, the phase II child has discovered linguistic units (not just acoustic units as in phase I) in the input and is able to roughly map those units onto event structure. Whether by using semantic or syntactic rules, the budding linguist of phase II can comprehend strings of words. This child, however, is at a disadvantage when the linguistic units do not correspond one-to-one with the semantics of the event and when nonwitnessed events are described. For example, passives are sometimes misinterpreted as active sentences. The phase III child, in contrast, recognizes that sentential relations are mapped complexly to events and are governed by structure-dependent rules. In phase III the child recognizes that the first mentioned noun need not be the actor, but that, given a set of linguistic rules, it can serve as the patient of the sentence. A further example of this growing linguistic knowledge comes from examination of the constructs found in binding theory. Here we will see that children have internalized the fact that language has a complex, hierarchical structure.

The comprehension of sentences with pronouns and anaphor: Tests of the binding principles

Among the modules proposed in Chomsky's 1981 government and binding work, is "binding theory."[7] This theory deals with restrictions on the coreference of elements such as pronouns and anaphors and the traces left by movement. Thus, in order to understand binding, children must know about movement (as with passive sentences) and they must also know about relationships within the hierarchical structure of sentences. Binding theory will cover cases such as the following:

(3)   After Josh$_i$ arrived, Benjie hugged him$_i$.
(4)   After Josh arrived, Benjie$_i$ hugged himself$_i$.

In sentence (3) the pronoun "him" refers to Josh – hence the subscript on "Josh" and "him" matches to indicate coreference. Note, however, that it can also refer to an as yet unnamed person, in which case the subscripts would be as follows:

(5)   After Josh$_i$ arrived, Benjie hugged him$_j$.

As will be shown, a reading of the sentence in which "Benjie" and "him" coreferred is ruled out on binding theory. In sentence (4), the anaphor "himself" can only refer to Benjie. Binding theory once again rules out a reading in which "Josh" and "himself" corefer. These alternative readings of sentences (3) and (4) are ruled out because of the way in which the hierarchical structure of the sentence lays out. Briefly, "him" (in sentence (3)) can only refer to Josh but not to Benjie because in the sentence tree (or phrase marker), "him" is found to have no particular relationship to "Josh" in the hierarchy. On the other hand, "Benjie" is higher than "him" in the hierarchy and these lexical items share a common mother node. That is, "Benjie" and "him" are in a relation referred to as "c-command" (short for constituent-command). Pronouns may not share coreference with a noun that is structurally superior (or c-commands) to them. Of course, "him" may refer outside of the sentence altogether to some third male person who is present in the context. What we have just been discussing is one of the binding principles, namely Principle B. Binding theory reduces to three principles:

Principle A: An anaphor must be bound in its local domain.
Principle B: A pronominal must be free in its local domain.
Principle C: An R-expression must be free.

Before discussing what we know of how children comprehend sentences which exemplify these principles, we must give some technical definitions for the terms mentioned. "Anaphors" are reflexive words like "himself" or "themselves." Pronouns are words like "he" and "her." "R-expressions" are referring expressions like "John" or noun phrases like "the state government." A "domain" is the space in which the principles operate, namely the S (sentence) node immediately above the pronoun or anaphor. If an element is "bound," it means that that element is coindexed (has the same subscript numbers in linguistic notation) with another element in the sentence. Binding can only occur between elements which are at the same height or higher in the sentence tree. That is, binding can only occur when one element c-commands another element. A relation of "c-command" exists between two nodes in the sentence tree if and only if the first branching node above A dominates B and neither A nor B dominate each other. In other words, if A and B occur on the same level of the sentence hierarchy they are called sisters. A node c-commands its sister nodes and all its sister's descendants (or nieces, if you will). The best way to understand c-command is to see an example:

Here, by our definition, Q c-commands R (its sister) since they share a common "mother" in the P node and since neither dominates the other. Q also c-commands nodes S and T, the daughters of R who are nieces to Q. The relationship, as in families, is reciprocal – R c-commands Q (that is, R is also Q's sister) but Q has no other descendants. It is this relationship of c-command which is essential for understanding binding. Let us return now to the first binding principle, Principle A.

Figure 16.2   Sentence diagrams.

Tree 1   Principle A

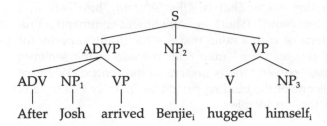

After Josh arrived Benjie$_i$ hugged himself$_i$

Tree 2   Principle B

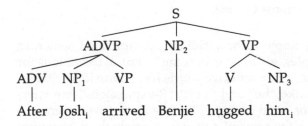

After Josh$_i$ arrived Benjie hugged him$_i$

The trees in figure 16.2 show the hierarchical structures of sentences (3) and (4) above; tree 1 shows the operation of Principle A while tree 2 shows the operation of Principle B. Recall that Principle A requires that an anaphor be bound in its local domain. This is in fact the case since in tree 1, the NP$_2$ (the second noun phrase) node c-commands the NP$_3$ node since NP$_3$ is a niece of NP$_2$. Notice that NP$_1$ could not be coreferenced with NP$_3$ since NP$_1$ does not c-command NP$_3$ by virtue of the fact that these nodes do not share the same branching node as the first node above them. On the other hand, Principle B requires that a pronoun be free (that is, not bound) in its domain. In tree 2 it can be seen that the same c-commanding relation exists between NP$_2$ and NP$_3$. Therefore, NP$_3$ cannot, by the definition of Principle B, corefer with NP$_2$. This leaves either NP$_1$ (or, on another reading, some other person not mentioned in the sentence) to corefer with NP$_3$.

What do children around the world understand of these sentence-internal hierarchical relationships? While the binding theory analysis is a part of

Chomsky's Universal Grammar, there are variations, for example, in the c-command relations which exist in different languages' grammars. This variation is a function of the size of the domain in which c-command is computed. Whether children begin the task of language acquisition, on the UG account, in possession of parameters which capture the variation in the domain over which c-command applies, or whether the properties of UG interact with learning, is a topic of debate. Whatever the ultimate answer, the comprehension of sentences which conform to binding theory reveals children's appreciation of language's hierarchical structure. To construct mental models which are accurate representations of reality, phase III children must be able to interpret sentences containing pronouns, anaphors, and referring expressions.

Due to space constraints, we next review only the research on Principles A and B; for Principle C, the reader might consult Goodluck (1991) and Atkinson (1992) for reviews.

Principles A and B

Jakubowicz (1984) used an acting-out procedure to test children's comprehension of pronouns and anaphors. She gave three to five-year-old children sentences such as

(6) John said that Peter washed him.
(7) John said that Peter washed himself.

Children got many more anaphor (7) than pronoun (6) sentences correct. Interestingly, when children erred on sentences like (6) they tended to treat the pronoun as if it were an anaphor, and showed Peter washing himself. Results like these led Jakubowicz to conclude that children cannot distinguish between pronouns and anaphors and treat pronouns like anaphors. However, Wexler and Chien (1985) disagree. Children distinguish between pronouns and anaphors since they rarely use the latter deictically. That is, in response to a question such as "Who did that?" children use a pronoun "Him!" and never an anaphor, "Himself!"

When studies have manipulated the internal structure of the sentences in which anaphors occur, correct comprehension is sometimes as late as age eight. One way to complicate a sentence which includes an anaphor is to have it mention other potential referents for the anaphor. Deutsch, Koster, and Koster (1986) tested Dutch children with sentences such as the following:

(8) The brother of Piet washes himself.
(9) The brother of Piet washes him.

Children appeared to reach asymptote on sentences like (8) by the age of eight. At the age of six, they were still only getting around 50 percent correct – too close to chance to consider reliable. Yet, the pronoun sentences such as (9) were even more difficult: even by age ten, children only got around 80 percent correct.

Chien and Wexler (1987) also find that anaphors are easier than pronouns. Children from young twos to middle sixes were told they were playing a party game and should act out what the characters at the party told them to do. Children were given sentences such as:

(10)   Kitty says that Sarah should give herself a car.
(11)   Kitty says that Sarah should give her a popsicle.

With sentences like (10) children could have selected Kitty as the car recipient if they were not in command of Principle A. Children reached 80 percent correct on reflexives between the ages of 3.5 and 4 and continued to improve with age. On pronoun sentences, even at the upper age group (6.5), children only got about 60 percent correct. Further, when they erred, children again treated pronouns as if they were anaphors.

What have we learned so far about children's appreciation of the hierarchical structure of sentences containing pronouns and anaphors? In some studies, children as young as three show sensitivity to the c-commanding relation of reflexives (Deutsch et al., 1986; Jakubowicz, 1984; Wexler and Chien, 1985; Chien and Wexler, 1987). That is, children appear to bind the reflexive to the noun phrase which c-commands it (see figure 16.2). That children will do this, even when there are other potential referents for the reflexive in the same sentence – and as in sentence (7), the potential referent is physically closer to the reflexive – suggests that children are not conducting a simple linear analysis of the sentence. Instead, children appear to be sensitive to the way in which meaning is encoded in the hierarchical structure of the sentence.

The story with pronouns, however, is a bit murkier. Children apparently can distinguish between pronouns and anaphors although when they err, they treat pronouns as if they were anaphors and bound (rather than free) in their local domain. Why should this be so? Kaufman (1987) and Grimshaw and Rosen (1990) suggest that children only *appear* to violate Principle B. This is because the tests designed to assess Principle B have put it in conflict with two factors: (a) children's ability to process complex sentences; and (b) children's expectation that a pronoun must have an antecedent. While this solution still remains controversial (Chien and Wexler, 1991), Kaufman's data demonstrates children's adherence to Principle B of binding theory.

Kaufman acted out events with objects as she presented children (two to three; five to six years of age) with sentences. This procedure was designed to minimize children's difficulties with figuring out the intended referent of object pronominals. For example, she acted out scenes in which hippos chased elephants. Either the hippos then bumped the elephant causing it to fall down, or each hippo fell down and hurt himself. Following a procedure used by Crain and McKee (1986), children were asked to judge whether a puppet (Kermit the frog) describing the scene just enacted, told what *really* happened.

If the child thought Kermit's description was accurate, she fed Kermit a cookie; if she thought Kermit's description was inaccurate, she fed Kermit a rag. One clear virtue of a judgment task is that no action is required; children had merely to decide whether the sentence they heard matched the event they had just seen. Another important element Kaufman included was a prior context sentence in which both potential antecedents for the pronominal were mentioned. From pretesting, Kaufman had observed that watching the event being performed was insufficient for children to establish the intended referent. Children apparently needed a discoursal antecedent for the pronoun as well. From a mental model perspective, the prior sentence allowed the child to lay the foundation for the sentence to follow. So, for example, the sentences – both correct and incorrect – used to accompany the scenes with the elephant and hippos described above were:

(12) Preliminary sentence: The hippos chase the elephant. [Said as the hippos caused the elephant to fall down.]
Test: Every hippo hurt him.
OR
The hippos hurt him. [These are correct and deserve a cookie.]

(13) Preliminary sentence: The hippos chase the elephant. [Said as the hippos themselves fell down.]
Test: Every hippo hurt him.
OR
The hippos hurt him. [These are incorrect since the event was a reflexive.]

The reason Kaufman used sentences with and without quantifiers is that Wexler and Chien (1985) had argued that children should do better with quantified antecedents than with pronouns coreferent with a referential antecedent. They believed that children have a more restricted version of Principle B than do adults and first employ Principle B only with "bound" pronouns like the quantifiers. Kaufman also varied sentence complexity. The examples above are simple sentences. Complex sentences included tacked on temporal adverbials, as in "Every/the horse hurt him, when the pig came to visit."

Kaufman's results indicated that sentences with and without quantifiers were just as easy for children in both age groups. In the younger group, children were well above chance in accepting as accurate both simple and complex sentences (mean = 88 percent correct). Children were also very good at rejecting the simple incorrect sentences (mean = 84 percent correct); the rejection of complex sentences was more difficult (mean = 62 percent correct).

What do these results show? Children as young as 2.5 appear to follow Principle B to the same degree in simple and complex sentences and in sentences containing quantifiers or referential pronouns. Thus, these results suggest that when other factors impinging on children's performance are minimized, children are capable of showing highly developed syntactic knowledge before they reach their third year.

In sum then, phase III marks a grammatical breakthrough in language comprehension; the child is now using language-specific constructs to interpret meaning and relations. No longer is the child bound to the surface structural features of the input for internalization. The phase III child can gain perspective on events – what we called interpretation – by relying on deep grammatical knowledge. For example, this child appreciates that word order does not signal event relationships in the passive and that the hierarchical organization of sentence structure determines coreference. This child is now on the doorstep of discourse analysis.

Overall Summary and Conclusions

We began with an anecdote to show how simple it would be to overinterpret children's performance as reflective of the comprehension of sentence structure. This led us to question whether sentence comprehension could be reliably assessed in young children. After a discussion of some of the methods used to assess comprehension, we concluded that comprehension can be reliably assessed. In fact, data from language comprehension can and have been used to falsify various theoretical hypotheses about what children know about language structure and when they know it. Indeed, comprehension data has provided the field with information about the process of language acquisition which cannot be garnered from an exclusive focus on language production. With the case secure for the accessibility and utility of data from language comprehension, we next tackled the question, "What is language comprehension?" Inspired by the work of Gernsbacher (1988, 1990) and Bloom (1993b), we provided a new framework for thinking about the development of language comprehension. This framework defines comprehension as a way to build mental models of the world. This view further presumes (and the evidence supports) that young children attend to the acoustic information in the input and hypothesize that it somehow relates to the events they witness in the world. Fully recognizing that this framework is in its infancy, we offer it as a way to think about how children's increasing ability to comprehend language feeds into their increasingly elaborate representations of the world.

The child goes through three phases during the course of language acquisition. First, language is used for its acoustic properties to accomplish two purposes: to find the acoustic correlates of the units of language (the process of extraction) and to define the boundaries of events (the process of acoustic packaging). Acoustic events then come to be linked with environmental events, assisting the child in internalizing events for their mental models. The child was likened to a film maker employing the technique called cinema vérité.

In the second phase, children begin to segment the units they have extracted into clause-internal propositions and to engage in linguistic mapping onto objects, actions, and events. Children use language not just for the internalization of their mental models but for perspective or interpretation as well. Phase II children already have the capability to parse the speech signal into phrasal and clausal-type units and to carve up the observed world into event sequences. They rely heavily on redundant cues (within language systems and outside language) as they learn the linguistic tools that will enable them to interpret the world from the perspective of the skilled cinematographer. In the third and final phase, children learn to comprehend complex sentences which contain multipropositional crossclause constructions in order to represent more complex events that they may not have witnessed. With the increased capacity to hold more than one event in mind, they are motivated to learn about linguistic tools that expand their power to express and comprehend. By phase III, the child is constructing complex meanings from even longer stretches of text; comprehending stories and conversations that often presuppose a great deal of knowledge, knowledge partly gained from the continual refinement of the mental models constructed through language.

Where do we go from here?

The framework gives increased prominence to research using language comprehension. This is because the model asserts that sentence comprehension is the *product* of children's attempt to weave together information from a variety of sources. That is, to construct a mental model, children must use information from their perception and representation of events in the world, from social interaction, from the prosodic envelope in which sentences are spoken, and from the propositions which comprise sentences. This approach leads to a number of obvious questions about the process of language comprehension. What information in the sentence and the world does the young child integrate to construct these models? How does the child weight the various sources of information which are concurrent (and often redundant) with language to form a mental model? In other words, what are the "rules" the child uses to link events to language and how do these change with development? How does the child lay a foundation for further incoming language input? Questions like these do not have simple answers.

It may be that sentence comprehension is best explained within the framework of "dynamical systems theory" (Thelen and Smith, 1994; Tucker and Hirsh-Pasek, 1993), an old theory newly imported into psychology which can accommodate the complexity of the different systems which contribute to the development of language comprehension. Dynamic systems theory "expressly seeks to integrate information from multiple interacting subsystems with asynchronous developmental pathways [such as the prosodic, semantic, and syntactic system] which cooperate to engender qualitative developmental shifts (Thelen and Smith, in press: 24). The use of a dynamic systems model for language acquisition, therefore, may enable us to move away from "smoking gun" models of acquisition which emphasize a single type of "bootstrapping" into the linguistic system. As Hirsh-Pasek, Tucker, and Golinkoff (in press: ms. 22) argued, systems theory can provide a way of rethinking the process of language acquisition. As they wrote,

> The crux of the story is this: Rather than characterizing the different language inputs as always being in some hierarchic relation to each other, it is much more useful to think of these inputs as systems of developing knowledge that are mutually informing and always available, but with differing weights at different developmental points. Such a vision provides us with a non-linear framework for development.

This view impels us to continue to study language comprehension in order to uncover how this coalition of redundant sources of information feeds into the child's burgeoning language processing. To conclude, then, through a focus on language comprehension we have found capabilities in the young child which are not manifest in language production and which are capable of illuminating the process of acquisition itself. This is because language comprehension is at the cutting edge of language acquisition.

NOTES

The research described herein was supported by grants HD-5964 and HD-19568 from NICHHD to both authors and grants from the Pew Foundation and from Temple University's Biomedical Funds to Hirsh-Pasek. Golinkoff also received UNIDEL and Biomedical grants from the University of Delaware, a John Simon Guggenheim Foundation Fellowship, and a James McKeen Cattell Sabbatical Award. We wish to thank all the students who have helped us over the years and are too numerous to mention by name. Also, comments on a draft of this chapter by Paul Fletcher, Brian MacWhinney, and Nora Newcombe were greatly appreciated.

1 Crain (1989) has developed a method which elicits the production of sentences children do not appear to spontaneously produce. Crain's findings suggest – as will the literature on comprehension to be reviewed later in this chapter – that children do not produce a good bit of what they are clearly capable of syntactically.

2 Thomas, Campos, Shucard, Ransay, and Shucard (1981) developed a signal detection procedure to test for lexical comprehension which also relies on differential visual fixation responses.

3 The metaphor of language functioning as a "zoom lens," which gives a particular perspective on an event, was suggested by Gleitman (1990). Whether she would have carried the analogy to the lengths we did is another matter!

4 It is interesting to note that many

Brocas aphasics can master phase II syntax in comprehension, but cannot deal with many of the relational constructs that emerge in phase III (Schwartz et al., personal communication).

5 Reversible sentences are those in which the subject (in this case, the dog) could serve as the object (in this case, the girl) and vice versa without creating a semantic anomaly.

6 This fact is incidentally another datum against the maturational view – actional passives should be more difficult than nonactional passives if the child is treating the verb as an adjective.

7 It is important to note that there are alternative accounts of binding theory in the literature, e.g. Sag and Hankamer (1984). Since Chomsky's account has generated most of the psycholinguistic research in acquisition, we restrict our discussion to his theory.

17 Strategies in the Acquisition of Syntax

ANN M. PETERS

1 Overview[1]

The *morphosyntax* of any language is the totality of those devices which can be used to express grammatical relations. These include not only word order ("syntax") but also all of the language's grammatical morphemes, whether they be free-standing particles or bound affixes. It is with the acquisition of morphosyntax that a child's language progresses from mere concatenation of lexical items to true "language." In this chapter I will only consider segmentable morphemes, primarily free morphemes and affixed inflections, but with some discussion of derivational morphemes. I am excluding morphemes that are represented by processes such as the internal vowel changes of the English irregular plural and irregular past. (See, for example, Bybee and Slobin, 1982, for discussion of the latter.)[2]

Although a good deal is known about children's acquisition of open-class vocabulary and word order, much less is known about how they acquire the closed-class morphemes which are also important for the expression of syntactic functions. These bits of language, whether free or bound, pose a particularly interesting problem to the learner of any language, because in many languages they have a tendency to be both short and unstressed, falling in the cracks between stressed syllables, which are both louder and carry fuller, more distinctive vowels. For these reasons many of them are among the least salient components of a language – certainly less salient than open-class stems. How, then, are children able to learn them?[3]

Gaining full control of a grammatical morpheme entails mastering it both perceptually and productively. Thus, children must learn at least three different kinds of perceptual information: what it sounds like, including the permissible range of its forms (its allomorphs); where in a sentence it is likely to occur (its distribution); and what it is used for, marking e.g. the object of a verb, the tense of a verb, that a noun is a possessor, etc. (its syntactic function(s)). From the point of view of production children must learn which forms to use to achieve which functions.

By 20–24 months, when children are becoming aware of grammatical functors, they are well along in developing two major kinds of knowledge which will help them in this task. First, their familiarity with the prosodic structure of the language they have been hearing, particularly with the likely placement within an utterance of open-class items, combined with their ability to recognize a growing number of open-class items even when embedded in a stream of speech, now allows them to begin to focus on what occurs *between* these open-class items. Second, their expanding awareness of the sorts of functions language can accomplish leads them to look for the linguistic means to express these functions; cf. Slobin (1982, 1985b) for elaboration. Exactly how a given learner proceeds seems to vary, depending on an interaction between the kinds of linguistic information the child is predisposed to pay attention to, and the prosodic and morphosyntactic characteristics of the language being learned.

One proposal that we will be particularly concerned with in this chapter is that prosodic and/or segmental awareness of an otherwise unidentified chunk of language can serve to alert the learner to the presence of a form to learn more about. In other words, at times and for some children phonology acts as a kind of "handle" for getting hold of grammatical morphemes.[4] At other times and/or for other children it is the function or 'meaning" of the morpheme that serves as the initial nucleus for collecting information about a particular functor. Our attention will be on the earlier stages of the acquisition process – early enough that gaps in the learner's grasp of the morphosyntactic structure of her language are likely to be filled with fuzzily perceived, prosodically defined place-holders. In general, learners at this stage have not yet progressed to a syntax with fully recursive embedding. Section two will present an overview of what is known about the learning of inflectional, derivational, and free grammatical morphemes. Although the focus will primarily be on English, we will also look at how other languages differ. In section three we will consider how children's acquisition strategies might interact with the prosodic and morphosyntactic structure of the language being learned.

2   The Acquisition of Grammatical Morphemes

Making no claims to be exhaustive, let us briefly review what is known about the acquisition of both bound and free grammatical morphemes. For ease of discussion, let us further divide the bound morphemes into two classes: inflectional, which children begin to learn fairly early, and derivational, which are acquired later.

As compared with such other language as Turkish, Finnish, or Eskimo, English has relatively few bound morphemes because most of its functors are free-standing particles. And because most of the early work on language acquisition was done on English, it was long thought that children's first productive combinations were of two words rather than two morphemes. We now know that this is not the case, particularly in agglutinative languages such as Turkish (Aksu-Koç and Slobin, 1985) or West Greenlandic Eskimo (Fortescue and Lennert Olsen, 1992). Even in less heavily morphological languages such as Japanese (Clancy, 1985: 481–6), early combinations may consist of an open-class word or stem plus either an inflection or a free particle. And I have argued elsewhere (Peters, to appear) that the so-called "pivot constructions" in English tend to be combinations of a closed-class item with an open-class one.

Crosslinguistically, derivational morphemes tend to occur closer to the root to which they are attached than do inflectional morphemes (e.g. Bybee, 1985). Schematically this can be represented as in (1).

(1)   Inflections–derivations–root–derivations–inflections

Moreover, researchers have found that the grammatical morphemes that children are first likely to combine productively are the more salient ones in the sense that they are (a) located in a prominent place such as the end of a word, (b) can sometimes carry stress, or (c) have more easily identifiable semantic content. These early productive morphemes often include the equivalents of English pronouns and prepositions. Since the earliest productive bound morphemes tend to be those that occur on the ends (rather than in the middles) of words, we find inflections being combined before derivations. This has been found, for example, for Turkish (Aksu-Koç and Slobin, 1985), West Greenlandic Eskimo (Fortescue and Lennert Olsen, 1992), and Mohawk (Mithun, 1989). The location of derivational affixes in the interior of a word, nearer the stem, is likely to render it harder to perceive and hence to segment. One result of this can be that derivational affixes may actually be produced as early, if not earlier than inflectional ones, but only because they have been learned by rote as if they were part of the stem. This happens, for instance, in Hungarian (MacWhinney, 1975a).

2.1   Inflectional morphemes

The first systematic studies of the acquisition of inflectional morphemes in English were carried out by Roger Brown and his students (e.g. Berko, 1958; Cazden, 1968; Brown, 1973). Using nonce-word probes of four to seven-year-olds (Berko's "wug-test") and naturalistic data from three much younger children (Brown's Adam, Eve, and Sarah), they studied children's production of plural, possessive, third person singular, progressive, and regular and irregular past tense. They found that, while the first productions of progressive, plural, and possessive inflections appear fairly early, it may be many months before full control is achieved, in terms either of consistent insertion where required or of production of the less common allomorphs. Moreover, the other target inflections, third person singular and past tense, are acquired much more slowly. Although other researchers have further investigated the acquisition of specific English inflections (e.g. Kuczaj, 1977, regular and irregular past; Kuczaj, 1978, progressive; Mervis and Johnson, 1991, plural), the findings of Brown and his colleagues remain the definitive ones.

An interesting, and perhaps important characteristic of the set of inflectional morphemes in English is the amount of homonymy that exists. Not only do the plural, possessive, and third person singular all utilize an identical set of allomorphs {z/s/əz},[5] the contracted forms of copular *is* and the auxiliaries *is* and *has* also have the same phonological forms. This means that, except for the difference in the first word of the last line, there is no phonological distinction between the forms in each column of (2).

(2) Homonymous English suffixes

PLURAL:	the boys (came early)	the plays (were outstanding)
POSS:	the boy's (book)	the play's (director)
AUX*is*:	the boy's (coming)	the play's (the thing)
COP*is*:	the boy's (here)	the play's (a triumph)
AUX*has*:	the boy's (come already)	the play's (succeeded)
3SING:		she plays (the trumpet)

Such homonymy has two potential effects for the learner, one facilitative, the other not. On the one hand it increases the frequency with which a given phonological sequence occurs.[6] This may increase its perceptibility to the learner and lead to early segmentation. On the other hand, having several morphemes "contained" within a single phonological sequence may make it difficult for the learner to realize that it does not function in a unitary way. This may lead to delays in getting the form–function mappings sorted out.

Menn (Peters and Menn, 1993) has given us the first fine-grained look at how these {Z}-morphemes can emerge, showing that, at least for her single subject, there was a strong interaction between phonology and morphology. Her analysis was based on nearly daily phonetic diary entries for her son Daniel between 2;0 and 2;10. She finds that at first Daniel acted as if the addition of {Z} at the end of a word was *phonologically* rather than *morphologically* conditioned, i.e. as if it was required by the phonological shape of the word it was added to rather than by any meaning it might convey.[7] As Daniel developed the *cognitive* notions of possession and plurality, which he first expressed by other means, as hypothesized by Slobin (1973, 1982), he discovered that the *linguistic* means for their expression was through suffixation of {Z}. This resulted in a gradual shift to a semantic basis for inclusion of {Z}, and a successive withdrawal of possessive and plural from the phonological rule. Surely the homonymy of these morphemes played an important role in Daniel's initial treatment of them as a single phonological category.

Homonymy among grammatical morphemes is not unique to English. Hanne

Gram Simonsen informs me that a similar situation occurs in Norwegian, which has a set of -*r* suffixes which mark (1) the regular plural on nouns, (2) the present tense on verbs, and (3) the agentive on nouns. Moreover, (4) the copula *er* and the auxiliaries (5) *er*, and (6) *har* are quite similar in phonological form. An investigation of the role of homonymy in children's acquisition and adults' perception of grammatical morphemes could shed interesting new light on the psycholinguistic characteristics of these forms.

2.2   *Derivational morphemes*

The function of derivational morphology is to enable speakers to build words from other words or stems, e.g. nouns from verbs, adjectives from nouns, or verbs from verbs (where the new verb expresses a related notion such as the undoing or the causing of an activity). While the class of English derivational morphemes is much larger than the set of inflections, none of its members is nearly so frequent. It includes prefixes that are both fully productive (*un*-, *non*-) and less fully so (*pre*-, *con*-), as well as suffixes, which also vary in frequency (e.g. diminutive -*ie*, agentive -*er*, nominalizers -*ness* and -*ity*, causative -*ize*, comparative -*er*, superlative -*est*, adverbializer -*ly*). With linguistic, cognitive, and social development, children come to want to express these sorts of notions and begin actively looking for how their language does this. While less is known about the acquisition of derivational than inflectional morphemes, it does seem that children first produce and then come to fully control the former much later than the latter. Let us consider four indicative studies.

Berko's (1958) pioneering research in this area used nonsense words to test the ability of four to seven-year-olds to form a diminutive of a noun, derive an adjective from a noun (-*y*), form the comparative (-*er*) and superlative (-*est*) of an adjective, derive an agentive from a verb (-*er*), and form a compound (the house a wug lives in). Since she used only one probe for each kind of derivation, her results were only suggestive. Even for the older children, the only one of these suffixes that they produced was the agentive (11 percent), although, when prompted with the comparative form, 35 percent could form the superlative. Compounding was greatly preferred over derivation.

Derwing and Baker (1986) have extended Berko's research to include more derivational morphemes and to follow the acquisition process longer, with subjects ranging from preschoolers to adolescents. They found that the first word-formational process to be used productively in English is noun-compounding (by seven of their 15 preschool subjects). The first productive derivational affix is the agentive suffix -*er* (by 25 of their 40 six to eight-year-olds). The homonymous instrumental suffix -*er* did not become productive until the next age group (for 18 of the 40 nine to 11-year-olds); the adjectival -*y* was also beginning to be mastered at this same age (by 22 of the subjects).

Finally, the adverbial *-ly* was only productive in the 12–17-year-old group (for 32 of 40 subjects).

Two researchers who have taken a more semantic approach by looking at the development of children's abilities to create words are Eve Clark and Melissa Bowerman. The former has studied what children do to fill gaps in their lexicons, while the latter has focused on the bidirectional interaction of meaning with linguistic form, i.e. how children construct new forms to express the meanings they want to convey and as well as how they build meanings to fit the forms they hear.

Among her extensive studies of children's word-making abilities, Clark (1982) looked at children's strategies (simple transfer, compounding, or derivational morphology) for changing nouns into verbs in English, French, and German. Since English nouns can rather commonly be used directly as verbs, her examples from English-speaking three-year-olds show rather little utilization of derivational morphemes (although inflections are added as appropriate): e.g. *I'm crackering my soup; It was Band-Aided* (p. 406). In French and German, however, three-year-olds have begun to actively use prefixes to express notions such as location; e.g. French *en-*: *pain en-oeufflé* "egged bread (with egg on)" or *pain en-confituré* "jammed bread (with jam on)" (p. 406), *emboîter* "in-boxed (put in a box)" (p. 409); German *be-*: *der Löffel ist be-suppt* "the spoon is souped (has soup on it)" (p. 407), *der Stock soll be-wassert sein* "the stick is supposed to be watered (in the water)" (p. 409).

One of Bowerman's interests has been in how children come to express particular notions such as reversal and causation. Her diary data show that her daughters began to use the reversative prefix *un-* productively, generalizing it to new verbs (as in *un-straighten* or *un-hate*) sometime after their third birthday (Bowerman, 1982b: 326). For several years the girls overused the morpheme *un-*, adding it to more verbs than an adult would as they homed in on the appropriate classes of verbs to which it applies. It is noteworthy that for *un-* the mapping between form and function is fairly easy for learners to identify. In contrast, English provides no such easy mapping for cause/effect relations, which are expressed rather idiosyncratically, depending on the verb. Bowerman's girls tended to express such relations syntactically rather than morphologically, producing sentences such as *I'm patting her wet* (patting her sister's arm after dipping her hand into water) (1982: 330). It is not surprising that, in the absence of clear morpheme–function mappings, children would be slow in acquiring derivational morphemes. Moreover, in the absence of such clear mappings, syntax will tend to dominate in a syntax-heavy language such as English.

In many other languages derivational morphology plays a much greater role than it does in English. And children learning these languages acquire derivational processes correspondingly earlier. For instance, a child learning West Greenlandic (Eskimo) is reported to have been using 13 inflectional endings and eight derivational affixes, each with some degree of productivity by 2;2 (Fortescue and Lennert Olsen, 1992: 140). Descriptions of acquisition of a number of morphologically complex languages support the generalization that children first produce morphemes occurring at the outer edges of words, gradually moving to those nearer the stem (e.g. Mohawk: Mithun, 1989; Turkish: Aksu-Koç and Slobin, 1985; West Greenlandic: Fortescue and Lennert Olsen, 1992). In languages in which all affixal morphemes have approximately equal phonolgical salience it looks as though children tend first to acquire the morphemes which occur in the perceptually salient positions at the ends of words; these are the inflections (see (1) above), which also tend to be obligatory and therefore frequent. Learners then focus on and acquire the next most salient morphemes, which tend to be those occurring just next to the outer layer of inflections. They then move to the morphemes next to these, working ever nearer the stem and acquiring derivational morphemes as they go.

The acquisition problem is rendered more complex when some morphemes are more salient than others, e.g. some are full syllables while others are single vowels or consonants (as in Georgian: Imedadze and Tuite, 1992), or when morphemes straddle syllable boundaries (K'iché Maya: Pye 1992). But when a language offers its learners derivational morphemes that have sufficient phonological content to be easily perceivable, sufficiently clear semantic roles, and one-to-one mappings between form and content, children are capable of extracting and producing them very early. For instance, agentless passives appear by 2;4 in Turkish (Aksu-Koç and Slobin, 1985: 846), and by 2;8 in Sesotho (Demuth, 1992).

One impediment to acquiring derivational morphology arises when the morphemes are infixed rather than affixed, as in the Semitic languages. In Hebrew, for instance, many derivational morphemes have the form of patterns of vowels that are interdigitated into the roots, which have the form of sequence of consonants. Sometimes the derivational morphemes include prefixes or suffixes as well. Typical morphemes are illustrated in (3) (from Berman, 1985: 259–60).

(3)   The interdigitation of morphemes in Hebrew

Root	Morpheme	Morph-gloss	Derived form	Gloss
k–t–b	–a–u–	noun	katuv	written (not oral)
	–a–a–	agent	katav	reporter
	–a–a–	verb	katav	write
	ni–a–	passive	niktav	be written
	hit–a–e–	reciprocal	hitkatev	write each other
	hi–i–	causative	hixtiv[8]	dictate (writing)

In such circumstances, children have little choice other than to learn morphologically complex words as unanalyzed wholes at first. By three to four years of age, however, they begin to perceive the patterns of infixation and to start using them productively. Close to full productivity is achieved by five to six years of age (Berman, 1985: 276–7).

In general then, when derivational morphemes are salient and unambiguous it is possible for them to be acquired so early as to surprise an English speaker. On the other hand, when they are hard to disentangle from the stems to which they attach, or when a given notion can be expressed in a number of ways, or when their function is relatively obscure, the may not be fully acquired until learners are eight to ten years or even older.

2.3 Free-standing grammatical morphemes

What difference does it make to acquisition if grammatical morphemes are free rather than bound? For instance, are the phonological shapes of freely movable words generally easier to perceive and segment than those of affixes? Are their patterns of occurrence easier or harder to discover?

In syllable-timed languages[9] open and closed-class morphemes may be prosodically less differentiated from each other than in stress-timed languages. In the latter, open-class morphemes tend to carry stress whereas closed-class ones ordinarily do not.[10] Unfortunately, we still know too little about how stress v. syllable-timing affects perceptibility of functors. In stress-timed languages such as English, were we to compare bound and free morphemes that had been equated for syllabicity and number of phonemes, it is likely that their lack of stress would render them equally nonsalient. This perceptual effect would be augmented by the fact that, in pronunciation, unstressed syllables, including free morphemes, are vulnerable to elision that either reduces their vowels to schwa or eliminates them entirely, as in (4).

(4) Elision of grammatical morphemes in English

	Morpheme	Full-form	Reduced-form(s)
Be	am	æm	m
	is	Iz	s/z
	are	ar	r
Aux	have	hæv	v/f
	will	wIl	1
	would	wUd	d
Pronouns	you	ju	j/jə
	them	ðɛm	əm
	him	hIm	Im/əm/m
	her	hɚ	ə/r
Prepositions	to	tu	t/tə/nə
	of	əv	v

An example of an English-learning child's difficulty in disentangling two regularly elided free morphemes is found in the data from a child named Seth (Wilson, 1986; Peters, 1987). The caregiver speech he heard contained many questions of the form *Did you [do X]?*, in which *did you* was pronounced

/dɪǰə/ or /dɪǰu/. For several months Seth seems to have analyzed *didja* as a single unit that marked action just completed by himself – he used this unit productively in sentences such as those in (5).

(5)   Seth's use of *didja* as a single unit
         24.0 months:
            Didja hear car   = I heard a car
         25.2 months:
            Didja help you drive   = I helped Daddy drive
            Didja throw little blocks   = I threw little blocks
         26.3 months:
            Didja break ya face   = I bumped my face
            Didja find it   = I found it
         28.0 months:
            Didja dump it out   = I dumped it out
            Didja throw everything out   = I threw everything out
         29.0 months:
            Didja burp   = I burped
         30.3 months:
            Di'ya knock that tube down   = I knocked . . . [immediate past]
            Did you go to Mommy's new house = I went . . . [longer ago]

Seth had similar problems disentangling *what* from *are, do, did,* and *a* – all free grammatical morphemes that often follow it (*what're you doing, what'da you want to do, what'd they say, what a big bird*) but which all tend to be elided into something like /wətə/ (see Peters, 1987, for discussion and examples).

All this suggests that free morphemes are often no more phonologically salient than bound ones. (Exceptions in English include verbal particles, as in *Pick it up*, which often carry at least secondary stress.) On the other hand, in stress-timed languages, the near universal lack of stress on functors may actually help learners distinguish open-class from closed-class items (see below). This particular contrast is not available in syllable-timed languages.

An important property of free morphemes is that they can occur in more than one position in a sentence. Does the resulting variation in ordering make it harder or easier for the learner? This question has yet to be systematically investigated. It is possible that predictability of place could make it easier for learners to anticipate just where a "new" functor will appear next time so she can try to perceive its form and/or function more clearly. But freedom in the combinatorial sense does not necessarily cooccur with freedom of positioning with respect to other constituents. While in many languages (particularly those for which "slot" or "item and arrangement" descriptions seem well suited), bound morphemes are quite rigidly ordered (and hence very predictable as to location), this is not always the case. In languages such as West Greenlandic (Fortescue and Lennert Olsen, 1992), words do not have clear "slots" because it is possible for a given derivational process to apply more than once within a single word; this gives the morpheme involved concomitantly less predictability of position.

On the other hand, in languages such as English which have many free functors, many of these both are stressless and have positions that are fixed at least within phrases (determiners at the beginnings of noun phrases, prepositions at the beginnings of prepositional phrases, and auxiliaries, modals, or cliticizable subject pronouns at the beginnings of verb phrases). It seems possible that such morphemes could begin to carry the functional load of signalling head-of-phrase quite early. This is supported by the findings of LouAnn Gerken, who has been investigating the interaction of perception and production of unstressed syllables in children's acquisition of English. Focusing on grammatical morphemes, Gerken and McIntosh (1992) found that even children who were as yet *producing* extremely few functors (MLUs < 1.50) responded significantly better in a *comprehension* task when the correct functors were included in the stimuli. (The stimuli contrasted the correct functor with: no functor, the wrong functor, and an unstressed nonsense syllable.)

The first results concerning the acquisition of free grammatical morphemes again come from the work of Roger Brown (1973). Using the criterion of production in 90 percent of situations where required in adult speech, he found that in English the acquisition orders of bound and free morphemes were interdigitated. Thus, his three subjects gained control of two (free) prepositions (*in* and *on*) earlier than any other morphemes except the (bound) present progressive. The (free) uncontractible copula (*is*) and articles (*a, the*) then followed the (bound) plural and possessive. Finally, the (free) auxiliaries and contractible copula were acquired after the (bound) regular past and third singular present. Brown's longitudinal results have been replicated cross-sectionally by deVilliers and deVilliers (1973a).

But what happens before Brown's 90 percent criterion is reached? A number of children have been observed to produce schwa-like "filler syllables" in positions where free grammatical morphemes would be expected in the adult language. For instance, Bloom (1970) reports such syllables for all three of the children she observed. Simonsen (1990) reports a similar phenomenon for a Norwegian child, as do Bottari et al. (1991) for Italian children. Seth, too, produced many of these fillers.

Using biweekly tapes from Seth when he was between 20 and 30 months, I have traced the development of pronouns, prepositions, articles, auxiliaries, and modals. (Peters and Menn, 1993, contains some of the results on prepositions and pronouns.) I found that by 20 months, while still in the one-word stage (or more accurately the "one-open-class-item stage"), Seth seems already to be aware of free morphemes. Evidence is that he produces phonologically vague "filler syllables" in positions where such a morpheme is expected in the adult language.[11] The examples in (6) show that these fillers (glossed as "F") are realized with a range of vocalic and nasal forms.

(6)   Seth's filler syllables (F) at 1;8.16
    /ə   shú:/   "F shoe."
    /i   ká:/   "F car."
    /a   gÚdki/   "F cookie."   /ɔ̃ kUki./   "F cookie."
    /a   hǽt/   "F horse."   /n has./   "F horse."
    /n   báp/   "F bump."
    /Um pwá:j/   "F play?"

Although it is difficult to identify specific targets for these syllables, they seem to reflect the above-noted prosodic characteristic of English that open-class words are often preceded by unstressed syllabic functors. Moreover, it is possible to trace the evolution of Seth's fillers into grammatical morphemes in two ways: distributionally and phonologically.

The distributional evidence is that these syllables are located in positions where free functors could be expected in adult productions. Moreover, as Seth's utterances expand to include two open-class words, he produces fillers in more positions per utterance. This suggests that he has become aware of more "functor-slots" although, as can be seen in the examples in (7), he is not at first consistent about filling in a particular slot in any given utterance.

(7)   Increases in production of Seth's filler syllables
    at 1;10.16:

/	tsí		hæts/	"	see		hedge."
/ n	si	zə	hǽč/	"F	see	the?	hedge?"
/ən	si		sóns/	"F	see		stones?/"
/n	si	ə	bák/	"F	see	F	bark (of tree)?"
/m	pɪk	ə	fáwis/	"F	pick	F	flowers?"

    at 1;11.6:

/n	brəš	ə	tíf/	"F	brush	F	teeth?"
/ə	bəš	ə	tíf/	"F	brush	F	teeth?"
/ɔ̃	tek	ə	bǽf/	"F	take	F	bath?"
/m	pU?	ə	ér-/	"F	put	F	there-"
/m	pu?	ə	ɔn táj/	"F	put	F	on tight?"

At the same time as they are appearing in more positions, Seth's fillers also gain phonological substance, making it possible to identify their adult targets with increasing certainty. The sentences in (8) present an illustrative sequence of Seth's approximations to *it* following a verb, then table 17.1 quantitatively traces the development of his approximations to *it* in three different environments (before verbs, after verbs with another element following, utterance-finally). Note that Seth achieves adult pronunciation relatively early with utterance-final *it*, while his productions in the sentence-internal positions remain hard to identify for much longer.[12]

Table 17.1 Phonetic development of *it* for Seth

Age	Variants/__V					Variants/V__X#							Variants/V__#										Total
	ə	j	jI	I	t	Clt	It	ə	j	C	1	U	I	It	E	I	C	t	Ut	Et	Clt	It	
1;10.16	1	1																2		1	3	7	15
1;11.06	1	1	1	1		3	5					3	3				1	3	1	1		25	49
1;11.14	1	1	1	1		2	1						1		1	1	2	7				6	25
2;00.00								1	1	2			1	1		1						2	9
2;00.16	1										1		5	2	1	2				1		25	38
2;01.03				3			4				3	1	3	4		1						14	33
2;01.13				5			1				1	1	8			3	1	1		6	1	35	63
2;02.01	2			1			2				1			1	1	2		1		1		10	22
2;02.22	1			5	2	2	8						2			1	1	1				18	41
2;03.11				3	2	2	2				4	1	2	15	1	1	1	2				42	78

(8) Developmental sequence of utterances with *it*

1;10.16		te	ə	án		"	turn	it? on"
1;11.06	m	pU	ə	án	taj	"F	put	it? on tight"
1;11.14	õ	pU	pə		táp	"F	put	F top"
2;00.00	ə̃	pUd	æ	Én		"F	put	it? in"
2;00.16	o	pUd	ə	ən	nÉk	"F	put	it? on neck"
2;01.03	ə	pUd	I	fo	wəbĬš	"F	put	it? throw rubbish"
2;01.13	ʔm	pU	U	Un	kǽwnr	"F	put	it? on counter"
2;02.01		fŕo	t	In	də wŕabəš	"	throw	it in the rubbish"
2;02.22	ə̃ču	pU	ʔI	an	də káwnnr-	"F you	put	it on the counter"

The kind of gradual emergence seen here shows that the acquisition of grammatical morphemes, whether bound or free, often does not progress simply or smoothly towards the adult target. Upon reflection, this is not surprising because what is involved is the simultaneous working out of three "dimensions" of attributes: phonological shape, distribution, and function. The very complexity of this process can lead to a long period of variation in the child's productions of a particular morpheme.[13] Like the other kinds of morphemes we have looked at, when free morphemes are salient and unambiguous it is possible for them to be acquired very early, but when they present difficulties in one or more of the three dimensions their acquisition can be protracted.

3   Strategies for the Acquisition of Grammatical Morphemes

We have already mentioned some of the strategies used by learners in the process of acquiring grammatical morphemes. Let us now take a closer look at this topic, first focusing on English and then considering how the prosodic and morphosyntactic structure of the language being learned might affect acquisition strategies.

3.1   Bridging from one word to several in English

Children learning English are generally considered to go through three major stages of productive ability: the one unit stage in which productions are limited to single lexicalized chunks, the several unit stage in which productions are expanded to include multiple units although still limited to single clauses, and fully recursive syntax that includes embedding of clauses. Although, as we have seen, children continue to acquire full competence with the more difficult grammatical morphemes for a long time, the major period during which such morphemes blossom is in the transition from single units to single clauses. What do learners seem to be doing at this time?

Let us first note that children's early one unit productions rarely coincide exactly with adult words: they may be close to their target (/dada/ for *Daddy*), but they often either are too small (/fənt/ for *elephant*), or consist of a whole adult phrase (/aga/ for *all gone*, /əsæt/ for *what's-that*, /dUkə dæ/ for *look-at-that*; see Peters 1983, 1986, for discussion). Brown (1973) has noted that, as children move into the multiunit stage, they seem to be motivated to talk about a relatively small set (he identified 11) of semantically based relationships. Some of these (NOMINATION, RECURRENCE, NONEXISTENCE) tend to be expressed by means of frames with a fixed, functorlike element plus a slot for a single open-class item (*this/that/here* + N, *more/'nother/again* + N, *no/all-gone/no-more* + N, N + *away/gone*). Although some of the other relations, such as AGENT+ACTION, ACTION+OBJECT, or ENTITY+LOCATION, may be expressed as concatenations of two open-class items (*car go, hit ball, sweater chair*), often with a slight pause between items at first, this is not uniformly the case. Children such as those that Nelson (1973) classified as "expressive" or "pronominal" use frames with functoids here, too, as in *I/my/you* + V, V + *it*, N + *here/there* (see also Braine, 1976). One could argue that two major strategies seem to be operating here, often simultaneously: a juxtapositional strategy in which open-class lexical items are concatenated, and a holistic strategy in which single open-class items are inserted into formulaic frames containing functorlike elements. Juxtaposers will need to learn to fill in the missing grammatical morphemes, while holists must learn to expand their frames and make them more flexible. How do they accomplish this?

Filling in the gaps

Children whose focus seems to be on learning names for objects (Nelson's "referential" or "nominal" children) tend to produce their first combinations in the form of a succession of semantically related single word utterances, each with its own intonation contour and separated by pauses. As fluency improves the pauses become shorter and the words are integrated into a single contour (Branigan, 1979; Bloom, 1973). Scollon (1976) calls this the move from "vertical" to "horizontal" construction. The next step is often to concatenate two-word productions in a similar way; Scollon (1976: 172–3) reports that his subject Brenda produced "vertical" sequences at 1;10 such as those in (9).

(9) *Brenda.*⎫
    see that.⎭
    tape corder.⎫
    in there. ⎭
    my turn.⎫
    do it. ⎭

While children like Brenda seem already to be including identifiable functors at this stage, children like Seth use filler syllables to mark locations where they are aware a functor belongs but which they are not yet ready to produce in full.

Generalizing frames

Turning now to children who rely on formulaic frames, we first note that in English closed-class morphemes tend to be (parts of) unstressed syllables whereas open-class words generally contain at least one stressed syllable (Cutler, 1993). These two kinds of constituents therefore participate in complementary ways in the rhythm of the language, with the open-class items providing the strong beats and the closed-class items contributing to the weak ones. Formulaic children seem to be sensitive to both rhythm and intonation, making noticeable efforts to reproduce them even in their early utterances. These tend to contain multisyllabic chunks composed of unsegmented combinations of adult words.[14] As learners become able to segment these chunks, they find structure in the form of "frames with open slots" (Peters 1983, 1986) or "positional patterns" (Braine, 1976, 1987; MacWhinney 1975b). The fixed elements of many of these frames are grammatical morphemes such as pronouns or demonstratives. The next step for these children is to combine and expand these patterns. Ewing (1982) shows how his son combined pairs of positional patterns, first to form two-unit patterns with more general slots in one or both positions, and then to form multiunit patterns.

(10)　(a) Integration of two 2-unit constructions resulting in a frame with a slot:

$$\left.\begin{matrix} \text{want + change} \\ \text{want + see} \\ \text{want + skate} \\ \text{want + turn} \end{matrix}\right\} \quad > \quad \text{want + V}$$

(b) Integration of a 2-unit construction with an overlapping 2-unit frame-and-slot, resulting in a 3-unit combination with a slot:

$$\text{I} + \left.\begin{matrix} \text{want} \\ \text{want + V} \end{matrix}\right\} \quad > \quad \text{1 + want + V}$$

(c) Integration of a set of 2-unit constructions resulting in a more general frame with two slots:

I	do		Experiencer + Experience

$$\begin{matrix} \text{I} & \text{do} \\ \text{me} & \text{walk} \\ \text{Guy} & \text{play} \\ \text{me} & \text{fish} \\ \text{me} & \text{laugh} \\ \text{doggy} & \text{see} \\ \text{I} & \text{drive} \\ \text{Daddy} & \text{do} \\ \text{Guy} & \text{watch} \end{matrix} \quad > \quad \left.\begin{matrix} \text{I} \\ \text{me} \\ \text{Guy} \\ \text{Daddy} \\ \text{doggy} \end{matrix}\right\} \quad + \quad \left.\begin{matrix} \text{do} \\ \text{walk} \\ \text{play} \\ \text{fish} \\ \text{laugh} \\ \text{see} \\ \text{drive} \\ \text{watch} \end{matrix}\right\}$$

Depending on the child, filler syllables and other protomorphs do or do not appear in such constructions. We saw in (7) that Seth developed a frame of the form *(NF) see (F) NOUN*, where NF was an optional nasal filler (which eventually developed into the quasimodal *wanna*) and F was an optional nonnasal filler (which eventually developed into a determiner/demonstrative).

In sum, we can identify two major, often simultaneous, strategies for acquisition of grammatical morphemes in English: discovering and filling in the gaps between open-class items, and generalizing the fixed part of a frame to include other members of a class of words or grammatical morphemes that can occur there.

3.2 A crosslinguistic look at strategies

Since languages differ in how easy it is to perceive and segment their grammatical morphemes, they set somewhat different problems for their learners. This in turn can be expected to influence the strategies most likely to be employed in learning a particular language. Before we can consider how segmentability might affect acquisition we need a brief review of three possible influences of morphological typology: how easy grammatical morphemes are to segment phonologically, how predictable their positions are, and how easy their functions are to identify.

A common scheme for classifying languages on the basis of their morphological structure takes into account both the numbers of morphemes that can be aggregated into words and how easy it is to decompose the morphemes semantically. In rough order of increasing word size, the four groups of this scheme are: isolating, inflecting, agglutinative, and polysynthetic.

The ideal isolating language has no bound morphemes: words consist either of single free morphemes or of compounds. Although the Chinese languages are usually cited as prototypical examples, languages such as Beijing Mandarin do have bimorphemic words with a functorlike second element that is bleached of meaning and carries neutral tone.[15] Many free grammatical morphemes also have this neutral tone which renders the syllables it falls on both shorter and less tonally distinctive than syllables with full tones. This is quite analogous to lack of stress on English functors. *A priori*, free-morpheme status for functors could be expected to render isolating languages easy to segment. Certainly, a Chinese-learning child does not go far wrong if she hypothesizes that any syllable is a potential word. On the other hand, phonological processes can interfere with this ideal picture. For instance, as we saw in (4), in English the various forms of *be* and *have* tend to be reduced so that they lose their syllabicity and become phonologically incorporated into neighboring words (*I am > I'm, you are > you're, he has > he's*). Moreover, the fact that functors are *free* means that they can, in principle, occur in a range of locations with respect to the constituents they are functionally associated with. Although this suggests that positional information may be less available to the learner as a segmentation aid, we note that in English, which is a reasonably isolating language, the appearance of a determiner (or an auxiliary) is a reliable indication of a noun (or verb) to come. As to how easy functions are to identify, there is no easy generalization that can be made for these languages.

Inflecting languages, which include many of the Indo-European family, have both free functors and bound morphemes (as well as compounding of free morphemes into single words). Nonfunctor words tend to consist of fewer than four or five morphemes (although they can be longer). Phonologically, bound morphemes can consist of single segments or of full syllables or even of vowel patterns interdigitated into consonantal roots, as we saw for Hebrew. It is likely that full-syllable morphemes would be easier to segment than those of other shapes, although phonological processes such as resyllabification or elision may obscure boundaries. Positionally, bound morphemes can be expected to be more consistent than free ones. An important characteristic of these languages is that their inflections are often "portmanteau morphs" in which two or more functions are inextricably bound into an unsegmentable phonological form rendering them semantically hard to disentagle, even though they may not be phonologically hard to segment. Examples are shown in (10):

(11)   Italian verb endings: $-o$ = Present + Singular + 1st-Person
$-i$ = Present + Singular + 2nd-Person
$-a$ = Present + Singular + 3rd-Person

In agglutinative languages, although there may be some free functors, words are likely to contain fairly long strings of bound morphemes. Segmentability of affixes depends partly on whether they consist of full syllables, as do most in Turkish (Aksu-Koç and Slobin, 1985) or Japanese (Clancy, 1985), of single segments, as do many in Georgian (Imedadze and Tuite, 1992), or of –VC– sequences that straddle syllable boundaries, as in K'iché (Pye, 1992). Positionally, bound morphemes can be primarily suffixes (Turkish) or be both prefixes and suffixes (Bantu, Georgian). In general, they have fairly fixed positions within words, providing the learner with clear positional guidelines. Finally, their morphosyntactic functions are not fused, making them easier to identify than in inflecting languages.

Finally, polysynthetic languages have the fewest free morphemes, with sentences often consisting of a single word. This word contains an open-class stem in combination with all the derivational and inflectional affixes needed to specify the syntactic and thematic relations between the constituents. In languages that allow noun incorporation, such as Mohawk, there may be more than one open-class stem in such a single-word construction (Mithun, 1989). Affixes may be primarily suffixes (Eskimo: Fortescue and Lennert Olsen, 1992), primarily prefixes (Navaho: Sapir and Hoijer, 1967), or a mixture of both (Mohawk: Mithun, 1989). In many Amerindian languages affixes often consist of a single segment, sometimes only a glottal stop, so that a single syllable can contain three or more morphemes. This can be expected to render segmentation difficult. Even when affixes consist of full syllables, as is common in the Eskimo languages, segmentation can be rendered difficult if extensive morphophonemic changes cause a morpheme to have several phonological shapes. Positionally, we mentioned earlier that derivational affixes generally occur closer to stems than do inflections. In many polysynthetic languages, however, there is no fixed order among the derivations because processes such as nominalization or verbalization can apply multiply within a single word (Fortescue and Lennert Olsen, 1992: 115). Finally, several functions can be fused into a single affix. These properties suggest that the polysynthetic languages should be the hardest to segment into component morphemes, and that learners will have to use very different strategies than learners of isolating or agglutinative languages.

The segmentability of a language may be influenced not only by its basic morphological characteristics but also by rhythmic characteristics, particularly the degree to which the language is stress or syllable-timed. In stress-timed languages stressed syllables get disproportionately more weight, in terms of both length and intensity, than unstressed ones, while in syllable-timed languages each mora or syllable receives a weighting that is more proportional to the amount of phonetic material it contains. These stress and timing differences affect not only the relative magnitudes of regular prominences (stresses) in a language but also the regularity of spacing between them. These attributes may be important to learners because the stressed syllables of stress-timed languages offer natural segmentation points. The rhythmic foot structure of these languages may also be important because a metrical foot offers a naturally segmentable phonological chunk. We now know that babies growing up in an English-speaking environment become aware of the trochaic (strong–weak) structure of English words by the time they are nine months old (Jusczyk, Cutler, and Redanz, 1993); we still do not know, however, whether babies develop an analogous iambic preference when they are exposed to a language such as French which, although syllable-timed, has stresslike lengthening on the *final* syllables of clauses and phrases.

Researchers have only begun looking crosslinguistically at the strategies children use to acquire grammatical morphemes. As a way of encouraging further work in this area I will conclude by presenting a preliminary list of ten strategies children seem to be using based on the literature on acquisition of specific languages. Although several of these proposals owe a debt to earlier important work on strategies by Slobin (1973, 1985b) and MacWhinney (1978, 1985a; especially his ideas about rote and amalgam acquisition), as well as my own earlier work (Peters, 1983, 1985), I include and rephrase them for the sake of a more complete and coherent view of what we know now. After each strategy I have indicated the areas of acquisition I think it is relevant to. These include: influence of Prosody, Segmentation, Production, and Analysis of function.

> 1 When boundaries are hard to find, a useful strategy is to segment prosodically delimited chunks, regardless of morphological

constituency; these include whole utterances, feet, or syllables (K'iché, Mohawk, Hebrew). [Prosody, Segmentation]

2   When functors fuse phonologically and prosodically with neighboring morphemes, children are likely to include them in amalgams, especially if the sequences are frequent (such as *didja, wanna, hafta*); when functors are syllabic and are easy to segment children are less likely to include them in unsegmented amalgams. [Prosody, Segmentation]

3   Prosodically oriented learners are likely to produce protomorphemic fillers when it is easy to perceive a "slot" but harder to determine what fills it; this is likely when the functor that fills the slot consists of a full syllable that is stressless (or perhaps toneless in tone languages); children who produce protomorphemes have now been observed in Danish, English, Finnish, German, Norwegian, and Portuguese (see Peters, to appear, for discussion). [Prosody, Production]

4   When functors straddle syllable boundaries, learners tend at first to reproduce only those parts that fall within stressed syllables or metrical feet (Mohawk, K'iché). [Prosody, Production]

5   Learners may produce productive combinations of two bound morphemes earlier than productive combinations of two free morphemes when full sentences of their language tend to consist of single words with many affixes (Japanese, Turkish, West Greenlandic). [Prosody, Production]

6   The first bound morphemes that learners will produce in productive combinations are those which occur at the outer edges of phonologically defined words; these are generally inflections, which are also both more obligatory and more frequent than derivational morphemes; control moves gradually to affixes nearer the stem (e.g. Mohawk, Turkish, West Greenlandic). [Prosody, Production]

7   Learners tend to omit functors which occur only in the inner recesses of a word. [Prosody, Production]

8   Unless such functors have some degree of phonological salience, learners tend to omit grammatical morphemes for which the functions are hard to determine because of fusion or bleaching. [Analysis, Production]

9   Homonymy within a set of functors may be similar to fusion in that learners will have a hard time discovering the separate functions of all the members of the set; this may result in omission or in inappropriate production. [Analysis]

10   Learners may produce productive combinations of two bound morphemes earlier than productive combinations of two free morphemes when their language has derivational morphemes that (a) have sufficient phonological content to be easily perceivable, (b) sufficiently clear semantic roles, and (c) one-to-one mappings between form and content (Japanese, Turkish). [Prosody, Analysis, Production]

NOTES

1 I would like to thank Paul Fletcher, George Grace, Brian MacWhinney, and William O'Grady for helpful comments on an earlier draft. The transcription of the Seth data was supported in part by NSF grant BNS-8418272.

2 Because I wish this chapter to be as crosslinguistically valid as possible I will refer to lexical items such as noun(-stem)s, verb(-stem)s, or adjective(-stem)s as "open class," whether they be free or bound; similarly, I will refer interchangeably to grammatical morphemes as "closed-class morphemes" or "functors," whether they be free or bound. Furthermore, since they do not admit new members, I am including pronouns and appositions among the "closed-class" subcategories.

3 As regards the debate about how much of language is innate and how much is learned, my assumption is that it is necessary for children to make simultaneous use of (a) inborn predispositions to extract specific kinds of patterns from the language to which they are exposed, and (b) the particular sound–meaning and form–function mappings in that language. As researchers, we cannot begin to sort out what the child might have been able to *learn* and what she/he must have acquired by relying on *innate* abilities without sufficient knowledge of the forms to which a particular child is exposed. As regards grammatical morphemes, children must *learn* at least the particular sound–function mappings in their particular language.

4 This topic is dealt with at greater length in Peters and Menn (1993) and Peters (to appear).

5 I will use the abbreviation {Z} to refer to this alternation pattern.

6 I include the full set of morphophonemic alternations in the notion of "phonological sequence."

7 Daniel's first rule seems to have been to add [s] or [z] to the end of certain nonreduplicated two-syllable words including those ending in /r/ (e.g. butter, water) and those having medial coronals and ending in /i/ (e.g. daddy, dirty), regardless of whether plurality or possession was being conveyed.

8 Hebrew has a spirantization rule which converts /k/ to /x/ and /b/ to /v/ in certain environments.

9 Although it has proved to be difficult to pin down adequate definitions (see Bertinetto, 1989, for discussion of some of the issues), the terms *syllable-timed* and *stress-timed* are useful for distinguishing between languages, such as Turkish or Finnish, in which all syllables have roughly equal prosodic weight, and those, such as English or German, in which some syllables (the stressed ones) tend to be both louder and longer than others.

10 Of course it is possible for many free functors to receive contrastive stress, and this may help learners perceive them. In a stress-timed language, unstressed syllables are usually defined as those which have reduced (as opposed to full) vowels.

11 The fact that my evidence is only from production raises as yet unanswerable questions about how much a child perceives at a given stage of production. These can best be answered with a research design

that combines longitudinal collection of production data with a longitudinal set of experimental probes of the interaction of perception and production such as those of Gerken and McIntosh (1992).

12   When a word begins with a vowel Seth often geminates the consonant from the end of the preceding word, as in *open it* > [opǝnnIt], *close it* > [kwozzIt], *pull it* > [pUlllt]; this geminated consonant is represented by C.

13   A protracted period of wide phonetic variation within a very small total productive vocabulary has been reported by Labov and Labov (1978), who discuss the various kinds of learning that are taking place during this period.

14   Such chunks have been termed "associative patterns" (Braine, 1976), "amalgams" (MacWhinney, 1978) or "formulaic expressions" (Peters, 1983). Plunkett (1993) demonstrates how the use of articulatory/fluency criteria, including presence/lack of pauses separating the adult units, do a good job of indicating which such "combinations" have or have not been analyzed by the child.

15   The fact that each morpheme is written as a separate character probably helps perpetuate the perception that they are separate words.

18 Phrase Structure and Functional Categories

ANDREW RADFORD

1 Aims

This chapter is an attempt to characterize the earliest stages in the development of phrase structure in young children (aged between 20 and 30 months or so) acquiring English as their L1. The framework I will assume is that of *Government and Binding Theory* (GB), in the version outlined in Chomsky (1986a), with modifications introduced by Abney (1987) (though what is said here could equally be recast in more recent frameworks, such as that of Pollock, 1989). The database for the present study is a corpus of several hundred naturalistic recordings of the spontaneous speech of children aged one to three years: the total corpus (described in Radford, 1990: 11–13) amounts to more than 100,000 child utterances.

1.1 Early child English

It is generally assumed that children first start to form productive syntactic structures during the period of *early patterned/multiword speech* which typically lasts from around 20–24 (±20 percent) months of age (cf. e.g. Goodluck, 1991): I shall refer to this period as *Early Child English*. What I shall suggest here is that the syntactic structures found in Early Child English differ significantly from those found in adult English in two interesting and interrelated respects. Firstly, whereas adult sentences are projections of both lexical and functional heads alike, child sentence structures are projections of the four primary *lexical* heads (noun, verb, adjective, and preposition), and lack functional heads (auxiliaries, complementizers, determiners, case particles) and their projections altogether. Secondly, whereas adult structures are networks of both *thematic* and *nonthematic* sisterhood relations, their child counterparts are pure networks of thematic relations (in the sense that every set of sister constituents is thematically interrelated). Thus, all structures found in Early Child English are sets of lexical categories bound together by thematic sisterhood relations: we might therefore say that the earliest structures produced by English-acquiring children are *lexical–thematic* in nature.

We can illustrate what this means in concrete terms by considering the structure of a typical child utterance such as "Man drive car." Given the *lexical–thematic* analysis of Early Child English proposed here, this would have the simplified structure (1) below:

(1)

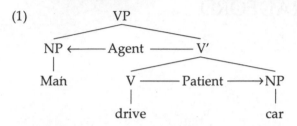

The whole structure would be a verb phrase (i.e. a *verbal small clause*, using the terminology of Radford, 1988a: 324–31): it would be a *lexical* structure in that it comprises only projections of the head lexical categories N and V. It would also be a *thematic* structure in the sense that the V *drive* theta-marks its sister NP constituent *car* (assigning it the role of Patient), the V-bar *drive car* theta-marks its sister NP constituent *man* (assigning it the role of Agent), the NP *car* is theta-marked by its sister V *drive*, and the NP *man* is theta-marked by its sister V-bar *drive car*. The twin hypotheses that the earliest structures produced by English-acquiring children contain lexical but not functional categories bound together by thematic but not nonthematic relations will be closely interrelated if we follow Abney (1987: 54ff.) in positing that the essential difference between *lexical* and *functional* categories lies in the fact that lexical categories have *thematic content* whereas functional categories do not. The hypothesis that early child sentences are purely *lexical–thematic* structures echoes earlier ideas in Radford (1986, 1987, 1988b, 1990, 1991), Abney (1987: 64), Guilfoyle and Noonan (1989), Lebeaux (1987, 1988), Kazman (1988), and Platzack (1990).

In the first part of this chapter, I shall present empirical evidence in support of the *lexical–thematic* analysis of early child speech, arguing that this provides a correct characterization of the structure both of the clausal structures produced by young children (section two), and of the corresponding nominal structures (section three). In section four I look at possible explanations for the character of Early Child English. Subsequently (in sections five to seven) I look at later stages in children's morphosyntactic development.

2   Clauses in Early Child English

If – as is implicit in (1) – the earliest verbal clauses produced by young children are lexical–thematic VPs, then we expect to find that they lack the further functional projections of VP into IP and CP found in the corresponding adult clause structures. In section 2.1 below, I argue that there is no I-system found in Early Child English; and in section 2.2, I go on to claim that there is no C-system either.

2.1   Absence of an I-system in Early Child English

Given the assumption (within the *Barriers* framework) that modals are base-generated in I in adult English, an obvious prediction made by the hypothesis that early child clauses lack functional category systems is that young children will show no evidence of having developed a category of modal I constituents. Numerous published studies have commented on the systematic absence of modals as a salient characteristic of early child speech: cf. e.g. Brown (1973), Wells (1979), Hyams (1986), and Aldridge (1989). Indeed, this pattern was reported in studies of *imitative speech* in the 1960s. For example, Brown and Fraser (1963), Brown and Bellugi (1964), and Ervin-Tripp (1964) observed that children systematically omit modals when asked to repeat model sentences containing them, as illustrated by the following examples which they provide (here and below, first names and two-figure numbers indicate the name and age – in months – of the child who produced the utterance concerned):

(2)   Adult model sentence   Child's imitation   Child
   (a)   Mr Miller will try   Miller try   Susan 24
   (b)   I will read the book   Read book   Eve 25
   (c)   I can see a cow   See cow   Eve 25
   (d)   The doggy will bite   Doggy bite   Adam 28

It seems reasonable to suppose that whereas the adult model sentences in (2) are functional–nonthematic IPs (contained within an abstract CP), their child counterparts are lexical–thematic VPs: for example, the adult model sentence in (2d) is a (CP containing an) IP of the form (3a) below, whereas the child's imitation by contrast is a VP of the form (3b). (Here and elsewhere, I omit single-bar constituents, for simplicity):

(3)   (a)   [$_{IP}$ [$_{DP}$ The doggy] [$_I$ will] [$_{VP}$ [$_V$ bite]]]]
      (b)   [$_{VP}$ [$_{NP}$ Doggy] [$_V$ bite]]

The systematic differences between the adult model sentences and their child counterparts are directly predictable from our hypothesis that early child grammars lack functional/nonthematic constituents, so that in place of adult functional IPs children use lexical VPs (moreover, they replace the functional DPs *Mr Miller/the book/a cow/the doggy* by the lexical NPs *Miller/book/cow/doggy*, and likewise have a null argument in place of the adult pronominal determiner *I*). It should be immediately apparent that (3b) is a lexical–thematic structure of essentially the same form as (1) above (save for the fact that it is headed by an intransitive verb which has no sister complement to theta-mark). The fact that children use nonmodal VPs in contexts where adults use modal IPs provides us with further evidence that the earliest clauses produced by young children are purely *lexical–thematic* structures.

Although we have concentrated on modal auxiliaries here, there is parallel evidence that children likewise make no productive use of the nonmodal auxiliaries *do/have/be* at this stage. We can illustrate this in terms of examples such as the following:

(4)   (a)   Kathryn no like celery (= "Kathryn *doesn't* like celery," Kathryn 22, from Bloom, 1970)
      (b)   Wayne taken bubble (= "Wayne *has* taken the bubble container," Daniel 21)
      (c)   Mummy doing dinner (= "Mummy *is* doing the dinner," Daniel 22)
      (d)   Hair wet (= "My hair *is* wet," Kendall 22, from Bowerman, 1973)

The adult counterpart of (4a) would require the dummy auxiliary *do* to be base-generated in I; however, the absence of *do* in the child's utterance suggests the absence of an I-system in early child clauses. Likewise, the adult counterpart of (4b), (c), and (d) would require the auxiliaries *have/be* to be base-generated in V, and then raised to I. But if early child grammars have no functional I constituents, such structures will clearly pose problems for children, both in terms of parsing and in terms of production. Moreover, all three nonmodal auxiliaries *do/have/be* might be argued to have no intrinsic thematic properties of their own (e.g. they do not indirectly assign thematic properties of their own to their subjects, and arguably do not assign any conventional theta-role such as Patient to their complements), and similarly they lack the *descriptive* semantic content which Abney (1987) takes to be a criterial property of lexical categories. If nonmodal auxiliaries are *nonthematic* constituents which superficially occupy *functional* positions in clauses, the *lexical–thematic* analysis of Early Child English will correctly predict that children will make no productive use of such items at this stage.

An additional prediction made by the claim that early child clauses are lexical VPs which lack functional I constituents is that children at this stage will make no productive use of the tense/agreement affixes +d/+s which are attached to finite nonauxiliary verbs in adult English. Empirical support for this claim comes from the fact that children typically use tenseless/agreementless forms in contexts where adults would require a finite verb inflected for tense/agreement. For example:

(5)   (a)   Baby doll *ride* truck. Horse *tumble*. Man *drive* truck. Baby *open* door. Baby *ride* truck. Pig *ride* (Allison 22, from Bloom, 1970)
      (b)   Mummy *cry*. Mummy *sit* down. Mummy *go*. Mummy *take* top off. Mummy *get* cross. Mummy *smack* Jem (Jem 23)

(c) Daddy *want* golf. Daddy *want* golf ball. Chicken *want* bread. Lady *want* bread. Roland *want* sweet. Duck *want* bread. Pump *go* in. Wayne *take* stick (Daniel 23–4)

(d) Mommy *sit*. Daddy *sit*. Andrew *walk*. Daddy *work*. Daddy *sleep*. Daddy *walk*. Boy *walk*. Man *walk*. Elliot *sleep*. Andrew *sleep* (Jonathan 24, from Braine, 1976)

Moreover, children at this stage typically reply to questions containing a verb overtly marked for tense with a sentence containing a tenseless verb: cf. the following dialogue:

(6) Adult: What *did* you draw?
    Child: Hayley *draw* boat (Hayley 20)

Likewise, when asked a question containing a verb overtly inflected for agreement, children at this stage typically reply using an uninflected, agreementless verb:

(7) (a) Adult: What *does* Ashley do?
        Child: Ashley *do* pee . . . Ashley *do* poo (Jem 23)
    (b) Adult: What *does* the pig say?
        Child: Pig *say* oink (Claire 25, from Hill, 1983)

Since tense/agreement affixes are realizations of properties of I, the fact that such children make no productive use of tense/agreement inflections provides further evidence in support of our claim that they have not yet acquired an I-system. Nonacquisition of finite verb inflections is a characteristic property of Early Child English widely reported in traditional acquisition studies (e.g. Brown and Fraser, 1963; de Villiers and de Villiers, 1973a; Brown, 1973, etc.).

It is perhaps useful to pinpoint the exact nature of the differences between auxiliariless finite clauses in adult English, and their child counterparts. Given the assumptions made here, the child's reply *Pig say oink* in (7b) would be a lexical VP with the simplified structure (8a) below, whereas its adult counterpart *The pig says oink* would be a functional (CP containing an) IP with the simplified superficial structure (8b) (where *e* denotes an empty category):

(8) (a) [$_{VP}$ [$_{NP}$ Pig] [$_V$ say] oink]
    (b) [$_{IP}$ [$_{DP}$ The pig] [$_I$ *e*] [$_{VP}$ [$_V$ says] oink]]

The differences between the two structures reflect the familiar pattern that adult clauses are *functional–nonthematic* structures, whereas their child counterparts are *lexical–thematic* structures. Thus, the overall clause has the status of a functional CP/IP containing a lexical VP complement in adult English, but of a lexical VP in Early Child English; the verb *says* carries an +s inflection which encodes properties of I in (8b), but the child's verb *say* in (8a) carries no

I inflections for the obvious reason that the child's grammar has no I-system; the adult subject *the pig* is a functional DP which superficially occupies a functional nonthematic position (as the specifier of the functional category IP) in (8a), whereas its child counterpart is a lexical NP which superficially occupies a lexical thematic position (as the specifier of the lexical category VP) in (8b).

2.2   Absence of a C-system in Early Child English

Having argued that early child clauses lack an I-system, I now turn to argue that early child clauses likewise lack the functional C-system found in adult English *ordinary clauses*. Given that complementizers are both *functional* and *nonthematic* constituents, it follows that our *lexical–thematic* analysis would predict that early child clauses will contain no C-system whatever. Some evidence which supports this conclusion comes from the fact that children's complement clauses at this stage are never introduced by complementizers like *that/for/if*: on the contrary, children's complement clauses at this stage are purely *lexical–thematic* structures, as illustrated by the bracketed clausal complements of *want* in (9) below:

(9)   (a)   Want [baby talking] (Hayley 20)
      (b)   Want [mummy come] (Jew 21)
      (c)   Want [lady get chocolate] (Daniel 23)
      (d)   Want [hat on]. Want [monkey on bed] (Daniel 23)

Children's complement clauses at this stage resemble adult *small clauses*: the complement clause is never introduced by a complementizer – a fact which is clearly consistent with the view that early child clauses entirely lack a C-system. Moreover, imitative speech data yield the same conclusion: Phinney (1981) argues that young children consistently omit complementizers on sentence repetition tasks.

    Given that a second role of the C constituent in adult speech is to act as the landingsite for preposed auxiliaries (which move into a root C, e.g. in direct questions), we should expect that children under two years of age will not show any productive examples of (subject-auxiliary) *inversion* in direct questions. In fact, early child interrogative clauses show no evidence whatever of auxiliaries preposed into C, and more generally lack auxiliaries altogether. Typical examples of auxiliariless interrogatives in early child speech are found in the transcripts of the speech of Claire at 24–5 months in Hill (1983), where we find questions such as the following:

(10)   Chair go? Kitty go? Car go? Jane go home? Mommy gone?

As Klima and Bellugi remark (1966: 201) it is characteristic of early child English at this stage that "There are no auxiliaries, and there is no form of subject–verb inversion." Once again, the absence of preposed auxiliaries is consistent with our hypothesis that early child clauses lack a syntactic C-system (given that preposed auxiliaries are positioned in C): cf. similar conclusions reached in Radford, 1986, 1987, 1988a, 1990, and echoed in Guilfoyle and Noonan, 1989.

On the assumption that children's clauses lack a C-system at this stage, if follows that they will also lack a specifier of C, and hence that young children will not show any evidence of having acquired the adult English rule of *wh-movement* which (in simple cases) moves wh-phrases out of a thematic position within VP into the nonthematic C-specifier position to the left of C. In this connection, it is interesting to note that Fukui (1986: 234) argues that the absence of syntactic wh-movement in Japanese is a direct consequence of the fact that Japanese is a language which has no C-system, since this will mean that Japanese has no C-specifier position to act as a landingsite for preposed wh-phrases. Thus, if Early Child English resembles adult Japanese in respect of lacking a C-system, then we should expect that at this stage we will not find examples of interrogatives showing clear evidence of a wh-phrase having being moved into the precomplementizer position within CP. Significantly, studies of wh-questions in child speech over the past decade have generally agreed that children under two years of age do not show any evidence of making productive use of *wh-movement* (e.g. Klima and Bellugi, 1966; Brown, 1968; Bowerman, 1973; Wells, 1985). This finding is obviously consistent with the hypothesis that early child clauses have no C-system (given the assumption that preposed wh-phrases in adult English occupy the specifier position within CP).

In contexts where they attempt to imitate an adult question containing a preposed auxiliary and a preposed wh-word, children typically omit both the auxiliary and the wh-word, as examples such as the following illustrate (the last two examples are from Brown and Fraser, 1963):

(11) Adult model sentence   Child's imitation
      Where does Daddy go?   Daddy go? (Daniel 23)
      Where shall I go?   Go? (Eve 25)
      Where does it go?   Go? (Adam 28)

A similar pattern (no preposed wh-word or preposed auxiliary) is found in child counterparts of adult wh-questions in spontaneous speech, as examples such as those in (12) illustrate:

(12) (a) Bow-wow go? (*"Where did* the bow-wow go?" Louise 15)
      (b) Mummy doing? (*"What is* mummy doing?" Daniel 21)
      (c) Car going? (*"Where is* the car going?" Jem 21)
      (d) Doing there? (*"What is* he doing there?" John 22)
      (e) Mouse doing? (*"What is* the mouse doing?" Paula 23)

The omission of the italicized preposed wh-phrases and preposed auxiliaries is obviously consistent with the assumption that children have not yet developed a syntactic C-system, and thus lack a landingsite for preposed auxiliaries and preposed wh-phrases (omission of preposed wh-expressions is also reported in the early stages of the acquisition of French by Guillaume, 1927: 241). It is also interesting to note the omission of the pronominal determiners *I/it/he* and the prenominal determiner *the* in (12) and (13).

Interestingly, *comprehension* data appear to reinforce our conclusion that children have not developed a C-system at this stage. The relevant data concern the fact that children at the lexical–thematic stage of development appear to have considerable difficulty in understanding wh-questions which show clear evidence of the preposing of a wh-phrase from a thematic complement position within VP into the nonthematic specifier position within CP. This was noted by Klima and Bellugi (1966: 201–2), who observe that children at this stage frequently fail to understand questions involving a preposed wh-word (for example, a preposed wh-object like *what* in "*What* are you doing?"). They remark (1966: 201) that "If one looks at the set of *what*-object questions which the mother asks the child in the course of the samples of speech, one finds that at stage I the child generally does not respond or responds inappropriately." Among the examples they provide (1966: 202) in support of this claim are the following, where the question is asked by the mother, and the italicized expression is the child's reply:

(13) (a)   What did you do? – *Head*
      (b)   What do you want me to do with this shoe? – *Cromer shoe*
      (c)   What are you doing? – *No*

Klima and Bellugi conclude of children at this stage that "They do not understand this construction when they hear it." Why should this be? The answer we suggest here is that early child clauses are purely lexical–thematic structures which lack a C-system, with the result that children are unable to *parse* (i.e. assign a proper syntactic and thematic analysis to) adult CP constituents (they have to rely on *pragmatic* rather than *syntactic* competence in order to attempt to assign an interpretation to adult CP structures). Of course, semantic and pragmatic clues may enable children (sporadically) to interpret sentences which they are as yet unable to parse syntactically (cf. Radford, 1990: 14–16): this may be why the children cited earlier respond appropriately to the wh-complement questions in (7) above (or indeed such questions may be "routines" for children).

3   Nominals in Early Child English

Having argued that early child clauses are lexical–thematic structures, I now turn to consider the nature of early child nominals. Before doing so, it is useful (for comparative purposes) to begin with a brief outline of the structure of adult nominals. The analysis which I shall presuppose here is the so-called *DP analysis*, under which determiners (= D) are analyzed as the head constituents of their containing nominals (slightly differing versions of the DP analysis are outlined in Fukui, 1986; Hellan, 1986; Abney, 1987, Fassi Fehri, 1988; Ritter, 1988). Under this analysis, *all* word categories (whether lexical or functional) are taken to be *projectable* into phrasal categories, so that just as N projects into NP, so too D projects into DP. Accordingly, a nominal such as *a photo of you* is analyzed as a DP (= determiner phrase) constituent with the simplified structure indicated in (14):

(14) [$_{DP}$ [$_D$ a] [$_{NP}$ [$_N$ photo] [$_{KP}$ [$_K$ of] [$_{DP}$ [$_D$ you]]]]]

Thus, the overall nominal *a photo of you* is a DP whose head is the determiner *a*; moreover, the pronoun *you* which functions as the complement of the genitive case particle (= K constituent) *of* is analyzed as a pronominal determiner (if *you* is a second person prenominal determiner in an expression such as *you idiot(s)*, it seems reasonable to suppose that it is likewise a second person pronominal determiner when used without a complement). It is interesting to note that genitive *of* which introduces the complement of the noun appears to be both *functional* and *nonthematic* in nature (in the sense that it has no intrinsic thematic content of its own), since the complement *you* would appear to be theta-marked by the noun *photo*. A structure such as (14) shows that adult English nominals can contain both *functional* elements (e.g. prenominal determiners like *a* and pronominal determiners like *you*), and *nonthematic* elements (e.g. genitive *of*).

3.1 Absence of nonthematic constituents

If – as is claimed here – the earliest structures produced by young children comprise only *lexical–thematic* constituents, then we should expect to find (*inter alia*) that early child nominals contain no nonthematic constituents. This in turn would lead us to expect that children will not make productive use of *nonthematic* nominals (i.e. nominals not theta-marked by any predicate). The most familiar type of nonthematic nominal in English are so-called "expletive" pronouns like "dummy" *it/there* in structures such as "*It* is raining," and "*There* is someone at the door." In this connection, it is interesting to note the observation made by Hyams (1986: 63) that Early Child English is characterized by "a notable lack of expletive pronouns." Her observation would appear to be borne out by data such as (15):

(15) (a) Raining (= "*It's* raining," Jenny 22)
      (b) Outside cold (= "*It's* cold outside," Hyams, 1986)

    (c)   No morning (= *"It's* not morning," Hyams, 1986)
    (d)   Mouse in window (= *"There* is a mouse in the window," Hayley 20)
    (e)   Bubble on dungaree (= *"There* is a bubble on my dungarees," Daniel 21)
    (f)   Mess on legs (= *"There* is a mess on my legs," Daniel 24)

In each of these examples, the natural adult counterpart would be a structure involving an (italicized) expletive pronoun; but the children concerned systematically avoid expletive structures, in keeping with the overall claim that children have not yet developed a mechanism for licensing *nonthematic* constituents. We might argue that the absence of *nonthematic* constituents (like expletive *it/there*) is a direct consequence of the absence of *functional* constituents in Early Child English, in that nonthematic constituents are required in adult English to satisfy functional requirements: e.g. the "dummy" *it* in "It's raining" is needed in order to satisfy the requirement in adult English that the nominative case assigned by a finite auxiliary be discharged onto an overt (pro)nominal.

    The absence of *nonthematic* constituents in early child grammars is further illustrated by the fact that children consistently omit the functional/nonthematic case particle *of* before nominal complements of nouns, as we see from examples such as the following:

(16)   (a)   [*Cup* tea] (= "a cup of tea," Stefan 17)
       (b)   [*Bottle* juice] (= "a bottle of juice," Lucy 20)
       (c)   [*Picture* Gia] (= "a picture of Gia," Gia 20, from Bloom, 1970)
       (d)   Want [*piece* bar] (= "I want a piece of the chocolate bar," Daniel 20)

Instead, the (bracketed) child nominal in each case comprises only an italicized (theta-marking) head noun and a following (theta-marked) complement noun, i.e. the child nominal is a purely *thematic* structure. For example, the nominal *piece bar* in (16d) is arguably an NP with the simplified categorial structure indicated in (17):

(17) [$_{NP}$ [$_N$ piece] [$_{NP}$ [$_N$ bar]]]

The structure conforms to the lexical–thematic schema in (1) above in that it comprises only projections of the lexical category noun, and the complement NP *bar* is theta-marked by its sister constituent *piece*. By contrast, the adult counterpart of (17) would be the *functional–nonthematic* structure (18):

(18) [$_{DP}$ [$_D$ a] [$_{NP}$ [$_N$ piece] [$_{KP}$ [$_K$ of] [$_{DP}$ [$_D$ the] [$_{NP}$ [$_N$ bar]]]]]]

This adult structure is a *functional–nonthematic* one in that it contains the functional D constituents *a* and *the*, and the functional/nonthematic case (K) particle *of* (the fact that *of* is nonthematic can be seen from the impossibility of using *of* here as a predicate, in structures like *"It is *of the bar"*). Furthermore, (18) is not the type of *lexical–thematic* structure which children use, in that the complement *the bar* is not theta-marked by its immediate sister *of*, but rather by its aunt *piece*. The fact that the child uses the *lexical–thematic* structure (17) in a context where the adult would require the *functional–nonthematic* structure (18) underlines our central hypothesis that there are no functional or non-thematic constituents in early child grammars.

3.2   Absence of a determiner system

If we compare the adult nominal (18) with its child counterpart (17), we are led to the conclusion that children use NPs in contexts where adults require DPs. Perhaps the most obvious piece of evidence in support of this claim is the fact that children use *indeterminate* nominals (i.e. nominals lacking a syntactically projected D-system) in contexts where adults would require *determinate* nominals (i.e. nominals containing a D-system). This can be illustrated by the spontaneous speech data in (19):

(19)   (a)   Hayley draw *boat*. Turn *page*. Reading *book*. Want *duck*. Want *boot* (Hayley 20)

      (b)   *Blanket* gone. *Stick* gone. *Dog* barking. Got *lorry*. *Paper* off. Want *ball* (Bethan 21)

      (c)   Open *can*. Open *box*. Eat *cookie*. Get *diaper*. Build *tower*. Hurt *knee*. Help *cow* in *table*. *Horse* tumble. *Man* drive *truck*. *Pig* ride. *Diaper* out. *Napkin* out (Allison 22, from Bloom, 1973)

      (d)   Wayne in *garden*. Want *tractor*. Want *sweet*. Want *chocolate biscuit*. Want *orange*. Want *coat*. Daddy want *golf ball*. *Lady* get *sweetie* now. Where *car*? Where *bike*? Where *tractor*? *Tractor* broken (Daniel 23)

In each of these examples, the italicized child nominal is headed by a singular count noun, and would therefore require a premodifying determiner such as *a*, *the*, *my*, etc. in adult speech; but the child's nominal is indeterminate in every case, thus suggesting that the children in question have not yet developed a determiner system.

There is a further source of evidence which we can look to in order to seek corroboration for our claim that early child nominals are indeterminate (in the sense that they lack a D-system). Recent work (e.g. Fukui, 1986; Ritter, 1988) has suggested that the genitive *'s* morpheme in English functions as a head determiner constituent, taking a preceding DP as its specifier and a following NP as its complement. Given these assumptions, a nominal such as *the president's car* would be assigned a structure along the lines of (20):

(20)   [DP [DP the president] [D's] [NP car]]

Mona Anderson (1983) has argued that concrete nominals (like *car*) do not theta-mark possessor NPs, and that the latter must therefore receive a theta-role from possessive '*s*. If this is so, then possessive '*s* (in this use) will be a functional but thematic constituent. However, given that our lexical–thematic analysis predicts that children use only constituents which are both functional and thematic, we should accordingly expect to find that when children are at the *lexical–nonthematic* stage of their development, their counterpart of adult genitive DP structures will show no evidence of acquisition of the functional '*s* morpheme. And this prediction is borne out by the fact that children at this stage do not productively attach the genitive '*s* suffix to possessor nominals, as traditional morpheme acquisition studies have shown. Citing just one work for illustrative purposes, the data in (21) below are examples (from Bloom, 1970) of uninflected possessor nominals in Kathryn's speech at 21 months:

(21)   *Mommy* haircurl(er); *mommy* cottage cheese; *mommy* milk; *mommy* hangnail; *mommy* vegetable; *mommy* pigtail; *mommy* sock; *mommy* slipper; *Kathryn* sock; *Kathryn* shoe; *Wendy* cottage cheese; *baby* cottage cheese; *cat* cottage cheese; *Jocelyn* cheek; *baby* milk; *tiger* tail; *sheep* ear (Kathryn 21)

The use of s-less possessives is widely reported as a typical characteristic of early child English in the acquisition literature: cf. e.g. Brown and Bellugi, 1964; Cazden, 1968; Bloom, 1970; Brown, 1973; Bowerman, 1973; de Villiers and de Villiers, 1973a; Braine, 1976; Hill 1983; Greenfield et al., 1985, etc. The fact that children at this point in their development have not acquired the functional determiner '*s* is consistent with our more general suggestion that such children are at a purely *lexical–thematic* stage in their development.

Additional evidence in support of the proposed analysis comes from the fact (frequently noted in the acquisition literature) that early child English is typically characterized by a lack of so-called "personal pronouns." As we noted earlier in relation to examples such as (14) above, Abney (1987) – adapting an earlier analysis by Postal (1970) – argues that personal pronouns are determiners, and hence occupy the head D position of DP (a variant of this analysis is to suppose that they are determinate nominals, and so exhibit properties of both D and N – cf. Radford, 1993). Now, if we are correct in supposing that early child grammars contain no determiner system, then we should expect to find that young children at this stage show no evidence of having acquired the morphosyntax of personal pronouns. In this connection, it is interesting to note the observation by Bloom et al. (1978) that young children at this stage typically have a *nominal* style of speech which is characterized by their avoidance of case-marked pronouns such as *I/you/he/she/we/they* etc.: cf. the parallel remark by Bowerman (1973: 109) that in the first stage of their grammatical development "Seppo and Kendall used no personal pronouns at all." We can illustrate this nominal speech style from the transcript of the speech of Allison Bloom at age 22 months provided in the appendix to Bloom (1973: 233–57), since Bloom et al. (1978: 237) report that Allison's NPs at this stage were "exclusively nominal." Of particular interest to us is the fact that Allison used nominals in contexts where adults would use pronominals. For example, in conversation with her mother, Allison uses the nominal expressions *baby*, *baby Allison*, or *Allison* to refer to herself (where an adult would use the first person pronouns *I/me/my*), as we see from the examples in (22):

(22) (a) *Baby Allison* comb hair. *Baby* eat cookies. *Baby* eat cookie. *Baby* eat.
      Baby open door. *Baby* drive truck. *Baby* ride truck. *Baby* down chair.
  (b) Help *baby*.
  (c) *Allison* cookie. Put away *Allison* bag. *Baby* cookie. *Baby* diaper. *Baby*
      back. Wiping *baby* chin (Allison 22, from Bloom, 1973)

The adult counterparts of Allison's sentences would contain (in place of the italicized nominal) the nominative pronoun *I* in (22a), the objective pronoun *me* in (22b), and the genitive pronoun *my* in (22c); but Allison's utterances in each example contain only an uninflected nominal. Now, if personal pronouns function as pronominal determiners, then the fact that children like Allison make no productive use of personal pronouns at this stage would clearly lend further empirical support to the claim that such children have not yet acquired a D-system; more specifically, the fact that children are using nominals in (what in adult terms are) pronominal contexts would suggest that they are using simple NPs in contexts where adults require DPs: and indeed, the fact that the genitive determiner *'s* is systematically omitted in examples such as (22c) lends further credence to the claim that the nominal constituents developed by young children at this stage have the status of indeterminate NPs which lack a D-system.

4 Explaining the Nature of Early Child English

The evidence adduced in sections two and three above leads to the twin conclusions that early child clauses are lexical–thematic VPs (which lack the functional/nonthematic I and C constituents found in adult ordinary clauses), and that early child nominals are lexical–thematic NPs (which lack the functional/nonthematic D and K constituents found in adult nominal arguments). It would therefore seem that both clausal and nominal constituents in early child grammars are lexical structures which are direct projections of thematic relations. However, given that the ultimate goal of linguistic theory is to attain explanatory adequacy, an important question to ask is *why* early child grammars of English should lack functional/nonthematic constituents.

There are a number of traditional explanations offered in the literature for why functors are late acquired. Many of these seem problematic in a variety of ways. For example, the suggestion by Gleitman and Wanner (1982) that functors are late acquired because of perceptual problems posed by their lack of phonological salience raises the question of why the (phonetically insubstantial and morphophonologically variable) noun plural +s suffix should be used productively from around 20 months of age. Likewise, any suggestion that functors are acquired later than contentives because of their greater morphosyntactic irregularity (e.g. the determiner *that* is acquired later than the noun *cat* because it has the irregular plural form *these*) is called into question by the fact that irregularity as such seems to pose no barrier to acquisition, since children typically regularize irregular forms, so that a noun like *man* will be given an overgeneralized plural form like *mans*. Moreover, intuitively plausible *cognitive* explanations to the effect that functors are cognitively more complex than contentives (and so cannot be acquired until the child has reached a certain level of cognitive maturity) pose the problem that there is no objective way of determining the relative cognitive complexity of different items, and no reliable language-independent means of determining the child's cognitive capacity at any given stage of development (as noted by Atkinson, 1982).

Given obvious drawbacks to traditional explanations, we might explore alternative possibilities. One alternative would be a *teleological* explanation. We might argue that IP and CP are extended functional projections of V, and likewise that DP and KP are extended functional projections of N: this would be in keeping with suggestions in Jackendoff (1977) and Emonds (1985) that IP is an extended projection of V, and in Bresnan (1986: 20) that CP is likewise an (extended) projection of V. If this were so, then we might argue that a V-system must be "in place" before an I-system or C-system can develop, and likewise that an N-system must be in place before a D-system or K-system can develop. We might then argue that it follows from this that children will develop lexical NP and VP constituents before they develop their functional superprojections IP/CP and DP/KP. However, it should be noted that the teleological analysis does not exclude the possibility of *simultaneous* acquisition of lexical projections and their functional superprojections. We might therefore expect to find that in an analytic language which has autonomous functional heads (like English), lexical heads are acquired before their functional counterparts, but in a synthetic language which has agglutinating functional heads, lexical heads and their immediate functional counterparts will be acquired together.

An alternative teleological account might go along the following lines. We might say that it follows from the Projection Principle (which requires the lexical properties of items to be satisfied at every level of syntactic structure) that the first stage in the acquisition of syntax is to build up lexical entries for items. Now, lexical properties are strictly *local* (e.g. such-and-such a verb takes an Agent NP as its specifier/subject, and a Theme NP as its complement), in the sense that they are properties which hold between a head and its dependents (i.e. those constituents which occur within the maximal projection of the head). We might therefore suppose (e.g. in relation to the acquisition of clause structure) that the first stage is for the child to identify the *argument structure* of a given verb, and how that is projected into syntax (e.g. Agent is projected as an NP specifier of VP, Theme is projected as an NP complement of VP). Only *after* this point can functional superstructure (e.g. IP) be acquired. Why? Because within the framework adopted here, subjects (in adult English) originate in the specifier position within VP, and raise to the specifier position within IP; but if the Projection Principle is to be satisfied, the trace of the raised subject (in VP-specifier position) must satisfy the lexical requirements of V, namely that the specifier (for a verb like *murder*) be an Agent NP. Clearly, this requirement cannot be met unless the child has first identified the lexical properties of predicates (verbs). What this implies is that children acquire lexical structure first (of necessity, because of the Projection Principle), and that since lexical requirements are purely *local* (i.e. VP-internal in the case of verbs), the earliest clause structures developed by children are VP structures.

We can reach a similar conclusion via a different route. Consider the kind of evidence which might lead a child to conclude that English is a language which has syntactic wh-movement. The primary evidence which would lead the child to this conclusion is the fact that wh-phrases occupy noncanonical positions: but this in turn presupposes that the child has already developed a set of lexical entries identifying canonical constituent positions. For example, a child hearing a wh-question like *What are you doing*? may "realize" (tacitly) that *what* is the complement of *doing*, but does not occupy canonical VP-complement position, and hence must have moved to its surface position from its canonical (underlying) position. However, the child can only draw this inference if he or she has first built up a lexical entry for *do*, specifying the type of Verb Phrase that it occurs in (viz. a VP with an Agent nominal canonically in the specifier position within VP, and a Patient nominal canonically in the complement position within VP). Thus, the first stage of acquisition must of necessity be to build up *lexical* structure.

A further explanation for why lexical heads are acquired before their functional counterparts in English might be in terms of parameter theory. Chomsky (1989) suggested that all parameterization in grammars may be located in their functional category systems: this is generally referred to as the *functional parameterization hypothesis*. If this is so, then it would seem reasonable to suggest that lexical category systems develop first because their properties are determined by innate (nonparameterized) principles of UG, and that functional category systems are acquired later because considerable linguistic experience is required in order for the child to set the functionality parameters which determine the range and nature of functional category systems. If (as is implicit in Fukui, 1986) Japanese has no C-system, D-system or AGR-system, then one type of functionality parameter will relate to the range of functional heads in a given language; a second type of functionality parameter will relate to the morphosyntactic mechanisms used to encode functional properties (e.g. via autonomous heads, or incorporated affixes).

A further type of explanation which we might consider is a *maturational* one, to the effect that different linguistic principles are genetically programmed to come into operation at different stages of maturation (cf. e.g. Borer and Wexler, 1987; Cinque, 1988). We might conjecture that the principles which enable children to form lexical–thematic structures come "on line" at around the age of 20 months (±20 percent), coinciding with the phenomenon of *vocabulary spurt* described in Smith (1926), Benedict (1979), McCune-Nicolich (1981b), and Barrett (chapter 13, this volume). We might also suppose that the principles which enable the child to form functional–nonthematic structures come on line at around the age of 24 months (±20 percent), coinciding with the *syntax spurt* described in Anisfeld (1984: 129–30).

5   Later Child English

Using evidence from an extensive naturalistic corpus of children acquiring English as their first language, Aldridge (1989) argues that finite auxiliaries, finite tense/agreement affixes, nominative pronouns, and auxiliary inversion are all acquired at the same stage of-development (typically shortly after children reach two years of age). Data such as the following (from Radford, 1990: 278–88) seem to reinforce her claim (I present data from only two children here, for the sake of brevity):

(23)   (a)   I'll have that one, shall I? I'm opening that. I don't know. You will save me. Would you like a sweetie? Can I have it? He's smacking her, isn't he? I'm going to have one of those dollies. He has to leave it there now. Do you want to have that one? Wait till that starts. It tastes nice. I tipped them all in there. That does. Did you want that one? Matthew has left his duck behind. Shall I close it? Isn't he beautiful? Wasn't that a shame? What's that teddy doing? What have you got? Why was he gone? (Heather 26)

(b)   I'm not on that one. I'm drinking my cup of tea there. There I am again. I don't like her. He didn't find it. We can see now. You can see yourself. He can't find them. "They're not in there," he said. She had to lie on my lap. We won't have that one. One of these broke off. And it winds up. It hasn't got a key on, to wind on. I want to sit here. He frightened the cat. I was at Nanny's. I said a lot. Have I got it? Aren't I in here? Is it a polly? Does this one open? Shall I go fetch it? Have you got it off? What are you saying? What have you got there? (Elizabeth 26)

By the age of 26 months, these two children seem to have acquired auxiliaries such as *shall/will/would/can/be/have/do*, tense and agreement affixes (cf. inflected forms such as *starts/tastes/tipped/frightened*), nominative case marking (cf. *I/we/he/she/they*), genitive *of* (cf. *one of those dollies/cup of tea*), and auxiliary inversion (cf. *Would you . . . ?/Have I . . . ?/ s it . . . ?*). Such data provide us with evidence that the children concerned have now developed the full range of *functional* projections for verbs and nouns, and are already able to project VP into IP and CP, and NP into DP and KP. Thus, it would seem that there is a certain amount of empirical evidence in support of the hypothesis of *parallel development* – viz. the hypothesis that the various different functional category systems (the I-system, the C-system, the D-system, and the K-system) develop in parallel.

However, although we have suggested that functional category systems are *acquired* from around two years of age, this is not to say that two-year-olds have *mastered* all the complexities of the morphosyntax of functional categories (cf. Radford, 1990: 24–5 for a discussion of the distinction between *acquisition* and *mastery*). On the contrary, two-year-old children who have reached the *functional* stage of development seem to go through a transitional phase in which they alternate between (what in adult terms are) grammatical structures in which functors are correctly used, and ungrammatical structures in which they are misused (or simply not used at all): in the remainder of this chapter, I shall take a close look at such transitional phenomena. I shall look at transitional phenomena in the acquisition of the I-system in section six, and the C-system in section seven.

6   Transitional Phenomena in the Acquisition of the I-system

Typical of the speech of two-year-olds who are emerging from the earlier lexical stage into the later functional stage are data such as those in (24):

(24) (a)   *I'm* pulling this. *Me* going make a castle (Holly 24)
    (b)   *She's* gone. *Her* gone school (Domenico 24)
    (c)   *I* can't do it. *Me* want to get down (Michael 24)
    (d)   *He's* kicking a beach ball. *Her* climbing up the ladder there (Jem 24)
    (e)   *I* can mend it. *Me* finding something (Adam 26)
    (f)   *I'm* having this. *Me* driving (Rebecca 26)

The relevant children seem to alternate between (what appear to be) finite structures containing an auxiliary and a nominative subject on the one hand, and nonfinite structures with no auxiliary and objective subjects on the other. The alternation between nominative and objective subjects for independent sentences gradually seems to die out: in my own corpus, 50 percent of the two-year-olds and 20 percent of the three-year-olds alternate between nominative and objective subjects. How can we account for this type of alternation between (seemingly) more advanced and less advanced structures?

Roeper and de Villiers (1991) suggest that children's clauses at this stage are sometimes lexical VPs (of the type produced at the earlier "small clause stage"), and sometimes functional IPs. This seems to amount to claiming that some form of *grammatical code switching* is going on, and that children switch between an earlier *lexical* grammar (which has not yet been fully discarded), and a later *functional* grammar (which has not yet been fully developed). They account for the alternation between nominative subjects in finite clauses and objective subjects in nonfinite clauses by positing that the subjects of IPs are assigned nominative case under government by their head finite I, whereas the subjects of nonfinite VPs are assigned objective case by a *structural* default rule which stipulates that a (specifier) NP is assigned objective case by default if it cannot receive case from elsewhere: cf. Vainikka (1992b) for a similar analysis.

Of course, a crucial assumption made by Roeper and de Villiers is that two-year-old children develop a "nonfinite objective subject" rule (whatever its precise form) whereby the subject of a nonfinite clause is assigned objective case by default. However, careful analysis of my own (substantial) corpus shows that sentences with objective subjects are not the result of a default rule assigning objective case to the subject of a nonfinite clause. There are two reasons for saying this. Firstly, there are numerous examples of nonfinite clauses with *nominative* subjects. For example:

(25) (a)   *I* teasing mummy (Holly 24)
       (b)   *I* singing. *I* done it (Angela 25)
       (c)   *We* been there (Robert 26)
       (d)   *I* been in pub. *He* gone (Alexander 26)
       (e)   *I* having this (Oliivia 27)
       (f)   *He* hiding (Katy 28)

Secondly, we find frequent examples of finite clauses with objective subjects:

(26) (a)   *Me* falled in a grave. *Me*'s painted that this afternoon. *Me* didn't paint that. *Him* don't stroke me (Adam 26)
       (b)   *Me* haven't seen Spider. *Him* came down and had porridge. *Me* can have apple? (Jem 24, 27, 28)
       (c)   *Me* can make a hen. Can *me* put lots and lots? *Him* can see fire. *Him* does go there. *Her* does go there. Because *him* is tired (Hannah, 28, 30)

Indeed, the children concerned seem to alternate between using objective and nominative subjects for finite clauses, as we see from examples like the following:

(27) (a) *I* need this one, *me* does (Adam 26)
      (b) No! *Me* can't, *I* can't (Hannah 28)
      (c) *Me* can get this off. *I* can open it (Michelle 29)

Thus, the dual claim by Roeper and de Villiers that children's nonfinite clauses always have objective subjects and conversely that their finite clauses always have nominative subjects seems to be empirically untenable.

How then are we to handle the alternation between auxiliary structures and auxiliariless structures, or between nominative subjects and objective subjects? A more promising approach is suggested by Aldridge (1989): she argues at great length that children typically acquire an I-system at around 24 months of age (at which point, we start to see evidence of productive use of finite verbs and auxiliaries, infinitival *to*, etc.). She also argues that once the I-system has been acquired, *all* independent sentences produced by two-year-olds have the status of finite IPs, headed by an overt or covert I constituent (hence, for example, the absence of *to* infinitives uses as independent sentences). The main surface difference between adult and child finite clauses in two-year-olds is that children sometimes use covert finite inflections where adults use overt inflections, and sometimes use null allomorphs of auxiliaries like *be/have/do* where adults use clitic allomorphs (so that in this latter respect, Early Child English resembles adult Black English somewhat). Part of the evidence which Aldridge adduces in support of her claim that sentences which appear to be nonfinite are best analyzed as finite clauses headed by a covert I constituent comes from the fact that seemingly nonfinite clauses are given finite tags by children – as we see from examples such as the following:

(28) (a) *I* on it, *aren't I*? (Sarah 26)
      (b) *I* on this one, *aren't I*? (Elizabeth 26)
      (c) *I* see Granny, *I do*. *I* see Timmy, *I do* (Robert 26)
      (d) Those steps, those *are* (Alistair 30)
      (e) *He* play with me, *he did*. *He* play with Laura, *he does* (Laura 32)
      (f) *I* do it, *I can* (Lisa 34)
      (g) We done those two, *haven't* we? It got water on now, *hasn't* it? We have to use something else, *won't* we? We put it just there, *won't* we? (Matthew 39)
      (h) So we have to use something else, *won't* we? (Per 41)
      (i) He make me cry, *won't* he? (Anna 44)

A second piece of evidence in support of the same conclusion comes from the fact that children often produce *replacement sequences*, in which an auxiliariless structure is expanded into an auxiliary structure:

(29) (a) I teasing Mummy. *I'm* teasing Mummy (Holly 24)
      (b) I having this. *I'm* having 'nana (Olivia 27)
      (c) We been there. *We've* been there (Robert 26)

    (d)   I not got that. I*'ve* not got that (Tony 36)
    (e)   He sleeping. He*'s* sleeping (Alistair 30)
    (f)   Daddy gone. He*'s* gone (Neil 24)
    (g)   Mummy fix this. Mummy*'ll* fix this (Holly 24)
    (h)   I get it. I *will* get it (Angela 25)
    (i)   I eat you all up. I*'ll* eat you all up (Hannah 32)
    (j)   I find it. I *can* find it, Mummy (Nancy 39)
    (k)   That dress not fit me. That dress *doesn*'t fit me (Betty 33)

In this respect, child English seems to resemble adult Black English (= BE), since in BE specific forms of *be* have null variants (so that we find null allomorphs of *are* and *is* in contexts where standard English would require the contracted allomorphs *'s* and *'re*): cf. Labov (1969), Wolfram (1971), and Fasold (1980). In Radford (1991) I argue that the essential difference between child English and adult English is that children have *null allomorphs* for those functional heads which have adult contracted or clitic allomorphs (so that "Daddy*'s* working" sometimes surfaces as "Daddy working," "We*'ve* been there" as "We been there," "He*'ll* not help me" as "He not help me," etc.). Thus, the nature of the error made in sentences such as (25), (28), and (29) is the use of a null allomorph where adults require an overt (generally unstressed monosegmental clitic) allomorph.

    Now, if all independent sentences produced by children from two years of age on are finite IPs headed by an (overt or covert) finite I constituent, then the nominative case assigned to the subject of seemingly nonfinite clauses like those in (25) above is nonproblematic, since such clauses will be IPs headed by a finite I which assigns nominative case to its subject. What then remains to be accounted for are objective subjects in sentences such as (24), (26), and (27). Of course, once we assume that all independent sentences in children who have reached the *functional* stage of development are finite IPs, then it follows that the phenomenon we are dealing with is the assignment of "the wrong case" to the subject of a finite clause. It is significant that complements are (without exception in my corpus, although sporadic exceptions are reported in the literature) assigned the appropriate case, e.g. the complement of a transitive head is uniformly assigned objective case. Case errors seem to be confined to *subjects*. As already noted, the commonest pattern of error is for children to alternate between nominative and objective subjects for finite clauses, as data such as the following illustrate:

(30) (a) *I* can't see it. *Me* haven't see Spider (Jem 26)
     (b) *I* can mend this. *Me* don't paint that (Adam 26)
     (c) *I* can open it. *Me* can get this off (Michelle 29)
     (d) *I*'m having this little one. *Me*'ll have that (Betty 30)
     (e) *I* can't. *Me* can make a hen (Hannah 32)
     (f) *I* won't do it. Can *me* have it? (James 34)
     (g) *I* can't see her. *Me* won't fall down there (Harriet 36)

Much less frequently, we find (what would seem to be) the *genitive* pronoun *my* licensed to occur as a finite clause subject (alongside nominatives, and sometimes also objectives):

(31) (a) *My* don't (Elspeth 27)
      (b) *My* don't want to (Geoffrey 30)
      (c) *My* did get my leg dry (Betty 30)
      (d) *My* want a wee (Matthew 30)

Why should it be that these case errors occur only in subject position, not in complement position (where objective pronouns are consistently used as the complements of transitive heads)? What is the nature of the errors involved here?

To see this, consider how we might account for a hypothetical alternation between forms like "*I/me/my* can do it." Given the assumptions made here, these utterances would have the simplified structure of (32) below (where SPEC = "specifier")

(32) [$_{IP}$ [$_{SPEC}$ *I/me/my*] [$_I$ can] [$_{VP}$ do it]]

In adult English, only a nominative expression is licensed to occur as the specifier of a finite head (e.g. as the subject of an auxiliary); the error made by the child is in licensing not only nominatives but also objective and genitive expressions to occur as the specifier of a finite head. Thus, the nature of the error resides in the child not having mastered the complex conditions under which a particular kind of head licenses a particular kind of specifier. We might therefore say that the error is one of *specifier-head mislicensing*, in that a head licenses too wide a range of specifiers.

We might argue that a similar mislicensing error is involved in sentences in which a child apparently fails to make the correct agreement between a finite verb or auxiliary and its specifier (= subject). For example, we sometimes find that base (uninflected) verb forms license third person singular subjects (as well as other kinds of subject), and conversely that an +s-inflected form licenses not only third person singular subjects but also other subjects:

(33) (a) I *has* pegs (Holly 24)
      (b) I *likes* it (Nancy 30)
      (c) Yes, I *does* (Laura 32)
      (d) When you *goes* to school, Robert and me play with him (Darren 39)
      (e) He *bite* me, he *do* (Tony 27)
      (f) Mummy *haven't* finished yet, has she? (Olivia 36)
      (g) Suzy goes out for a wee, Suzy *do* (Louise 44)
      (h) That one *go* there (Rebecca 26)
      (i) That *go* in car (Robert 27)

Indeed, in some examples, we find both misagreement and case misassignment – cf. examples such as the following, where both the finite auxiliary and its subject have the "wrong" form:

(34)   (a)   *Me's* painted that this afternoon. I need this one, *me* does (Adam 26)
         (b)   And me *wants* a pillow (Darren 30)

But why should it be that children make both case and agreement errors in this way?

It might be argued that case and agreement errors are interrelated, and reflect a common error pattern. Recent work (e.g. Rizzi, 1990) has suggested that nominative case assignment and subject–verb agreement are different reflexes of an abstract specifier-head agreement relationship: for example, in a sentence such as "He doesn't know," we might argue that the specifier-head relationship between the dummy auxiliary *doesn't* and its subject/specifier *he* is encoded both by the nominative case carried by the pronoun *he* and by the agreement inflection +*s* carried on *doesn't*. If this is so, then both case errors in sentences like (31) and (32) and agreement errors in sentences like (34) will be attributable to the child's failure to master the two different morphological reflexes of this abstract syntactic relationship between the head I of IP and the specifier of IP (viz. via case marking on the subject and agreement marking on the verb).

7   Transitional Phenomena in the Acquisition of the C-system

We start to find evidence that children have developed a C-system from around two years of age, as our earlier examples in (23) above illustrate. At this point, they start to make productive use of "auxiliary inversion" structures (i.e. structures in which the inverted auxiliary is positioned in the head C of CP), as in the following examples (produced by Heather at age 26 months):

(35)   *Did* you want that one? *Do* you like that one? *Can* I have it? *Can* I do that? *Can* I open that? *Shall* I close it? *Are* we going on an aeroplane now? *Isn't* I he beautiful? *Wasn't* that a shame? *Would* you like a sweetie? *Would* you like that one? What *have* you got? You open that, *shall* we? Don't get my trousers on, *will* you? I'll read you that one, *shall* I?

However, it is by no means the case that preschool children use inversion in precisely the same way as adults. A recurrent pattern in two and three-year-old English is that children (sporadically or systematically) fail to invert (some or all) auxiliaries in contexts where inversion is obligatory in adult English, particularly in direct wh-questions. This phenomenon was first described in Ursula Bellugi's early work (Bellugi, 1965; Klima and Bellugi, 1966): she reported a stage of development at which some children have inverted auxiliaries in yes–no questions, but not in wh-questions. Among the data she used to support this claim were the following:

(36) (a) *Will* you help me?
     (b) *Where* the other Joe *will* drive?

(37) (a) *Can* I have a piece of paper?
     (b) *What* he *can* ride in?

How can we account for the fact that such children do not use inverted auxiliaries in wh-questions?

Clearly, we cannot simply say that the children concerned never allow auxiliaries to be inverted (i.e. positioned in presubject C position), since yes–no questions show inversion. It would seem that inversion is blocked only in wh-questions; but why? What I shall suggest here is that this may be the result of an overgeneralization of specifier-head agreement on the part of the child. Following Kayne (1982), I shall assume that an inverted auxiliary can be moved into a verbal C position, but not into a nonverbal C position; if we posit that a complement clause C position in adult English is intrinsically a nonverbal position (as suggested by the fact, for example, that *for* is a prepositional complementizer), then it follows that there will be no auxiliary inversion in complement clauses (since a complement C is nonverbal, and hence cannot host a preposed verbal auxiliary). Following Radford (1993b) I shall also posit that C in early child clauses is *underspecified* and lacks intrinsic categorial features – and in particular is unspecified with respect to whether it is a verbal/nominal constituent. If C lacks intrinsic categorial features at this stage, then it would follow that auxiliary inversion should be possible, since this would involve movement of a verbal auxiliary into a C position which is nondistinct in respect of the relevant categorial features (since C is neither specified as intrinsically verbal nor as intrinsically nonverbal); and indeed, it is clear from sentences such as (36a) and (37a) above that auxiliary inversion does indeed take place in yes–no questions.

But how can we account for the fact that auxiliary inversion is blocked in wh-questions like (36b) and (37b)? One possibility is to posit that while the head C of CP has no intrinsic (nominal/verbal) categorial features, it inherits (or is assigned) the categorical features of its specifier, via an overextension of specifier-head agreement. More concretely, we might suppose that a sentence such as (37b) would have the skeletal structure of (38):

(38) $[_{CP}$ What $[_{C}$ e$]$ $[_{IP}$ he $[_{I}$ can$]$ ride in – $]$ $]$?

(where – marks the underlying position out of which the wh-pronoun was extracted). In (38), the specifier position within CP is filled by *what*, and the head C position of CP is empty (= *e*). Since the wh-specifier *what* is intrinsically nominal, and since (we posit) C carries no intrinsic categorical properties of its own at this stage in the child's development but rather is assigned those of its specifier (via an overextension of specifier-head agreement), it follows that the head C position of CP will inherit (or be assigned) the nominal properties of its specifier *what*. But since a verbal auxiliary like *can* cannot move into a nominal C position, it follows that auxiliary inversion will be blocked in structures such as (38). More generally, since preposed wh-phrases are always nonverbal constituents (by virtue of the fact that wh-movement cannot target VP, IP, or CP constituents), it follows that (for children who have this type of system) auxiliary inversion will never be possible in wh-questions. Of course, inversion will indeed be possible in yes–no questions, since C has no specifier whose categorial properties it can inherit, and hence remains unspecified in respect of the relevant core (i.e. nominal/verbal) categorial features, and so allows inversion (since this is movement of a verbal constituent into a categorially nondistinct position).

The essence of the account offered here is that what blocks inversion in wh-questions is overgeneralization of specifier-head agreement with CP. In fact, there is some empirical evidence for the claim that children overgeneralize specifier-head agreement within CP, from sentences such as:

(39) (a)   What's the wheels doing? (Holly 24)
      (b)   What's those (Alistair 30)
      (c)   What's you doing? (Ellen 33)
      (d)   What's they doing? What's they called now? (James 34)

(40) (a)   Where is his feet? (Jonathan 39)
      (b)   Where's me? (Michelle 29 = "Where am I?")
      (c)   Where's we going tonight? (James 34)
      (d)   Where is you? (Elspeth 39 = "Where are you?")

If we suppose that the wh-constituents *what* and *where* are in the CP-specifier position in (39) and (40), then it would appear that the inverted auxiliary *is/'s* is agreeing with the specifier of CP (if we make the not unreasonable assumption that *what/where* are third person singular pronouns) and not (as in adult English) with the subject in the specifier of IP. Given that sentences like (39/40) provide evidence for a (morphologically) overt agreement relation between the specifier and head of CP, it seems plausible to invoke a covert specifier-head agreement relationship to account for the absence of inversion in uninverted wh-questions such as (36b) and (37b).

8   Summary

What I have suggested in this chapter is the following. The earliest structures produced by young children (under two years of age) are lexical/thematic in nature, and functional/nonthematic structures typically come "on line" at around two years of age. Although many two-year-olds appear to go through a transitional stage where they seem to alternate between simple lexical structures and more complex functional structures (and thus might seem to be code switching between a lexical grammar and a functional grammar), this apparent code switching is simply an illusion. In reality, such children have reached the functional stage and have *acquired* (though not yet *mastered*) a full set of functional category systems: the errors they make are accounted for in part by the fact that they use null allomorphs of functional heads in contexts where adults would use clitic allomorphs, and in part by the fact that they have not yet mastered the morphosyntactic reflexes of the complex agreement relation which holds between functional heads and their specifiers. This position allows us to maintain the commonsense view that children operate with only *one* grammar at any one stage of development (and do not *code switch* between more and less mature grammars).

19 Empty Categories and Complex Sentences: The Case of wh-questions

JILL DE VILLIERS

Introduction

The present chapter has as its topic the acquisition of complex syntax and the special problems it presents to the language learning child. The phenomena are at the forefront of modern linguistic theory, and the subtle predictions they make deserve notice by theorists of child language. In what follows I will point to some of the phenomena that fall under the notion of "empty categories" in syntax, then describe in more detail the types of empty categories that have been proposed in modern work. Following that description, I will raise questions about the acquisition of the forms: how do children's grammars accommodate empty categories, and how do we know when they do? The bulk of the chapter will be concerned with the evidence of acquisition of one major type of empty category, namely the one left behind when a wh-question is moved to the front of a sentence: wh-trace.

Why do linguists talk about "empty categories"? The well-grounded theoretical decision to permit movement rules in syntax had as a consequence the necessity of postulating empty categories in the original sites of the moved elements. Many complex sentences in English are argued to involve movement rules and/or empty categories, both of which present special challenges to acquisition theories. But are they theoretical entities that will disappear with the next theoretical shift? Consider some of the constructions in which empty categories have been proposed, with the small (e) indicating the empty category:

(1) Mary seems (e) to be a success.
(2) Bella decided (e) to buy a car.
(3) What are you wearing (e)?
(4) What are you looking for (e)?

In each case, some crucial component (argument) of the sentence has been omitted, for example an object of a verb that is obligatorily transitive (3), or a subject (1 and 2), and some mechanism must be proposed to reconstruct its role. It cannot be the case that we simply fill in any empty slot by inference, because there are sharp grammaticality contrasts when the empty element appears in some other positions:

(5) *Jane agrees that (e) should go.
(6) *Who did you say that (e) went?
(7) *I'm looking for my hat, will you look for (e) too?

If the phenomenon of empty categories is a discourse or pragmatic phenomenon, in which certain redundant things need not be said, then why are cases (5) through (7) different? The contrast (6) provides with (1) and (2) demonstrates that an empty subject cannot appear in a finite, or tensed, complement. Clearly, at least some of these phenomena are not explainable on pragmatic or inferential grounds, but on the basis of grammatical principles.

Consider more closely the case in (3) involving the wh-question. The verb *wear* is obligatorily transitive, as shown by the ungrammaticality of a sentence such as

(8) My brother wears.

So *wear* has a requirement that the thematic role of object be filled. That lexical requirement is satisfied in the theory that the question word *what* began adjacent to the verb in the object position of the D-structure, and then moved to the front of the sentence in the S-structure. The movement leaves behind an empty element coindexed with the wh-word, and called a *wh-trace*.

Consider the contrast between (8) and (4), for an illustration of the principled nature of empty categories. Sentence (8) demonstrates that one cannot, apparently, have an empty object after a preposition. The object after prepositions must be filled: it is not a grammatical position for an empty category. Then why was (4) permissible? Sentence (4) involves a wh-question, and the assumption is that the object position is in fact occupied by the trace the wh-movement left behind, as in (3), fulfilling the requirement that prepositions need objects. But (7) shows that wh-words cannot leave traces in every possible position: in particular, not in the subject position of a clause beginning with "that."

Where does the wh-question move to? In current syntax, the topmost node in sentence structure is typically the functional category CP, whose head is the functional category C, or complementizer. In an embedded sentence, that C position would be occupied by such forms as *that*, *if*, or *for*. In main clauses, the C constituent is held to be obligatorily empty in English except in the case of questions. In yes/no questions, the C serves as the landing site for auxiliary movement (now called "I-to-C movement"):

(9) Can he come early?

and as the landing site for wh-question movement:

(10) What should I bring?

The fact that both auxiliaries and wh-questions move to the CP suggests it has further internal structure, in other words that the wh-word actually moves to the specifier position of CP and the Aux into the head of CP:

(11)

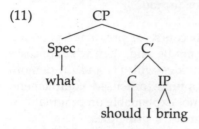

Furthermore, the movement of wh-questions is argued to be cyclic, in other words, the wh-word moves one clause at a time if it originates in an embedded position:

(12) How did you say you wanted me to move the trunk?
      With the trolley.

The "how" has originated as an adverb attached to "move" in the lowest clause, and has "cycled" through the intermediate CPs in order to meet the requirement that movement be clause bound. In each spec of CP, then, there is a trace left by the movement, and the whole chain of traces is coindexed with the moved "how":

(13) $_{CP}$[How$_i$ did you say $_{CP}$[t$_i$ you wanted me $_{CP}$[t$_i$ to move the trunk t$_i$]]]?

There are significant constraints on such long-distance movement, which will be discussed in more detail below as we discuss their acquisition.

How are wh-traces different from other empty categories? In the next section, I will describe briefly where wh-traces fall in the larger scheme of empty categories that has been developed.

The Inventory of Empty Categories

In contemporary work in the GB framework, there exists an inventory of empty categories that parallel the inventory of possible overt Noun Phrase

(NP) categories in language. Just as there are three types of nominals: lexical NPs, pronouns, and anaphors, there are corresponding empty categories governed by the same binding principles (Chomsky, 1981), principles that define whether the nominals are free or get reference by being coindexed with (bound to) another nominal:

(a) Pronouns must be free in their governing category.[1]
(b) Anaphors must be bound in their governing category.
(c) Referring expressions must be free everywhere.

These principles dictate the grammatical conditions for each of the types of noun phrase in the syntax. So, for instance, the binding principle for pronouns in (a) states that pronouns cannot occur in positions where they are coindexed with an NP in the same clause. One cannot say

(14)   Bill$_i$ shaved him$_i$

and mean that Bill shaved himself. On the other hand, one cannot have reflexive pronouns (an example of anaphors) too distant from their coindexed NP, so one cannot say

(15)   Bill$_i$ asked her to shave himself$_i$.

Finally, it is ungrammatical to have full NPs bound at all:

(16)   The child$_i$ washed the child$_i$.

These same binding principles are extended to define the conditions on the appearance of different types of empty nominals. Chomsky captured the variation among the empty categories by arguing for a fourfold categorization based on two features: +/− pronominal, and +/− anaphoric. These are shown in table 19.1.

The equivalent of the *overt* lexical NP (neither pronominal nor anaphoric) is the trace left by wh-movement, usually written as t. As discussed, it would occur in wh-questions such as the following:

(17)   What$_i$ did he buy t$_i$?

in which the "what" has moved in the syntax to the front of the sentence. Technically, it occupies the specifier position in the CP, which is the topmost maximal projection in the current syntax (see figure 19.1).[2] The trace is bound semantically to the wh-Operator, and is a *variable*, that is, it refers to the members of a set, rather than being a name.

The small pro (+p, −a) is distributed as a *pronoun* in languages that permit

Table 19.1

	+p	−p
+a	PRO	Np-trace
−a	pro	Wh-trace

Figure 19.1

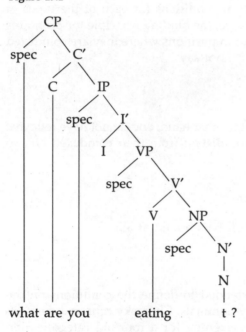

what are you   eating   t ?

it, namely free in its minimal governing category. For instance, in Italian, it would occur in a sentence such as

(18) (*pro*) more
      (he went)

Small pro does not occur in adult English, and it is hypothesized to occur only in languages that have a rich inflectional system, so that the case and number of the subject (agreement) are actually marked on the verb inflection. It is only licensed, in other words, by a feature of the agreement (AGR) category.

The trace left by NP movement (from e.g. passivization) is an *anaphor* (+a, −p), which must be bound in its governing category. For instance, there is an empty category hypothesized in the passive sentence

(19)   The cat$_i$ was chased e$_i$ by the dog

and also in the "raising verb" sentence already cited:

(1)   Mary$_i$ seems e$_i$ to be a success.

However, these three empty category types do not exhaust the possible types in English, as the form PRO must still be accounted for. PRO is hypothesized as the empty subject of infinitives in (2) from above:

(2)   Bella decided PRO to buy a car.

PRO behaves sometimes as a pronoun and sometimes as an anaphor (hence +p, +a), leading to a variety of proposals about its distribution. The theory of Control was developed to account for the distribution of PRO (Chomsky, 1981). Essentially, some verbs allow subject control of the PRO in the infinitival clause as in (2), where Bella is the subject of both clauses, while others like *persuade* allow object control:

(20)   Bill persuaded Jim$_i$ PRO$_i$ to buy a car.

In other cases, PRO behaves as a pronoun with arbitrary reference:

(21)   Bill liked the decision PRO$_{arb}$ to buy a car.

The adequacy of the above scheme has been debated in recent work, and several changes have been proposed. Rizzi (1992) expands on the notation used by Chomsky for empty categories by adding the feature +/− variable to the class of possibilities, following work by Lasnik and Saito (1992). The +/− variable feature is designed to capture other differences in the way empty categories behave, in particular, whether they behave as variables or as constants. As mentioned above, a wh-trace has the characteristics of a variable: the answer to a genuine question such as

(22)   Who came to the party?

must be a set of individuals, not a constant. Rizzi adds new categories to the scheme in table 19.1, but the full ramifications of those additions remain to be established, so they are only mentioned here.

An important principle governing the distribution of the nonpronominal empty categories and formulated variously over the past several years is known as the Empty Category Principle (here from Rizzi, 1990):

A non-pronominal empty category must be properly governed. Proper government can be satisfied either by lexical or antecedent government.

Lexical government is satisfied by e.g. a transitive verb or a preposition requiring an object; antecedent government by a coindexed governor in the same clause. The principle has application especially in explanation of the distribution of wh-traces, for example in the different behavior of adjunct and argument traces discussed below.

Notice that the empty category set is *parameterized* because (a) small pro appears only in certain languages, namely pro-drop languages with a rich inflectional system, and (b) wh-trace does not occur in languages with no overt wh-movement in the syntax (e.g. Chinese, Japanese, Turkish).

In addition, the properties of the empty categories interact with the syntax of the language (e.g. in the definition of governing category) and with the lexicon (e.g. in the class of verbs that control PRO). Having situated the nature of wh-traces within the larger scheme of empty categories, let us turn to the special problems that are presented in accounting for the acquisition of these forms.

The Acquisition Problem

Here are some of the general problems that arise in considering the acquisition problems for the child in learning about empty categories.

(a) How does the child determine what is the inventory of empty categories for her language?

For example, could the child begin with a generic empty category as a "default," then differentiate them? A very natural proposal might be for the child to begin with the category *pro*, because pro simply fulfills the requirements of lexical theta-projection, without involving any chains. But how do other empty categories then emerge? Could pro stand in place of e.g. wh-trace at the beginning (see e.g. Roeper, Rooth, Mallis, and Akiyama, 1984; de Villiers, Roeper, and Vainikka, 1990)? Alternatively, maybe the child has an undifferentiated empty category, and successively adds the features (+p, +v, +a) (see Perez-Leroux, 1993).

(b) How does the child determine the syntactic conditions under which empty categories are allowed?

For instance, how does the child learn that English lacks the rich agreement features that would license pro in subject position? How does the child recognize the passive sentence as a case involving movement?

(c) How does the child acquire constraints on empty categories such as the ECP?

Does the child automatically know the difference between adjuncts and arguments? Does the child make mistakes in this system and receive corrective feedback?

These basic questions of inventory, distribution, and constraints are general ones that will be addressed with respect to the specific case of wh-trace. First, however, consider the general difficulties faced by a researcher who wants to determine children's knowledge of empty categories. In the case of adult grammars, linguists have access to judgments and intuitions to bolster the data from production and comprehension. In the case of child language, we have limited access to intuition, so our procedures for asking about the child's grammars must be "devious," to use an expression of Chomsky's (1965). Furthermore, if the child's grammar is nonadult, can one determine which part of the network of phenomena is awry? That is, can one tell which of the following is/are true:

(a) The child's phrase structure syntax is different; for example, clauses may be adjoined rather then embedded.

(b) The inventory of empty categories is either impoverished or deviant from the adult language target; for example, may lack a feature such as "+variable."

(c) The formulation of the empty category principle is different or incomplete; for example, antecedent government may not be possible.

These questions will be addressed with respect to a particular variety of empty category, namely wh-trace, as an illustration of these challenges to analysis. Much literature has already been devoted to the "empty subject" phenomenon in child language, so that it would be impossible to include discussion of the competing proposals in that domain as well in this chapter. The debate revolves around whether the missing subjects are a performance or a competence phenomenon, and if competence, whether they are best described by discourse or grammatical rules. The interested reader is referred to Hyams (1986), Bloom (1990), Valian (1990), Rizzi (1992), Perez-Leroux (1993), Lillo-Martin (in press). The issue of control and PRO is addressed in two recent reviews with differing perspectives on the issue of whether the structures or the principles are discontinuous in acquisition (see McDaniel et al., 1990; Sherman Cohen and Lust, 1993).

How do we know that young children's wh-questions involve the category wh-trace? There are several kinds of questions that can be asked, and these will be addressed in the following sections.

Are the wh-questions a result of movement?

When young children produce a wh-question such as

(23) What can I eat?

has the wh-word actually undergone "movement"? The world's languages fall into several types, some that require wh-movement, and some that do not. Asian languages such as Chinese and Japanese do not have grammatical wh-movement, but leave the wh-word "in situ" in the sentence, occupying the place where it "belongs" in the phrase structure:

(24) Chinese: Ni xihuan shei?
           You like who?

Young English-speaking children virtually never produce such sentences – their wh-words are in the front from the beginning. Yet when one considers the learnability problem, their lack of confusion is somewhat mysterious. The input they receive from adults is ambiguous for figuring out which kind of language they are learning because the study of "motherese" reveals that it often contains questions in which the wh-word is left in place:

(25) You want what?

These questions occur with surprising frequency: one in 57 utterances in 7,000 parental utterance samples from Adam's transcripts, one in 80 in Eve's, and one in 146 in Sarah's (Brown, Cazden, and Bellugi, 1969).

But maybe if children hear *any* fronted wh-questions, that is enough information for them to figure out that the language involves syntactic wh-movement? Unfortunately, then the case is not so clear cut for a child in the reverse situation, namely learning an Asian language. Chinese speakers produce wh-words at the front of questions when they want to use emphasis, or topicalize what is being questioned, the equivalent of:

(26) *What* you want?

So both the English and the Chinese learner would have an impossible task with simple induction. Instead, both learners must figure out whether the speakers use wh-fronting (or wh-in situ) as a grammatical or a discourse device: is it the special case, dependent on certain kinds of discourse (see e.g. Pesetsky, 1987; Authier, 1993), or is it the syntactic norm?

As mentioned, the English child does not produce wh-in situ, at least at first. However, it is still possible that a wh-trace is not involved in these early productions. A separate mechanism exists in grammar for linking other kinds of "empty categories" to the NPs with which they are coreferent, as described above. It has been argued by Roeper et al. (1984) and Roeper (1988) that children's first questions might involve an empty category such as "pro" (possibly with features +p, −a) rather than a trace, though the evidence is controversial (Crain, 1991; McDaniel and McKee, 1989). In more recent syntheses, Roeper and de Villiers (1992) and Perez-Leroux (1993) speculate that the initial wh-word might also lack the variable [+v] feature. In fact, if the feature [+v] arises from having an appropriate operator in the specifier of CP, the child might lack that feature precisely until a proper movement analysis of wh-questions is achieved. So perhaps the child's grammar does not include trace until syntactic wh-movement is clearly justified for the language. As described above, the evidence about the language is murky until the child can distinguish the discourse conditions that distinguish the various types of question, and surely that rests on experience.

Do children treat the empty category in wh-questions as a variable?

The idea that the wh-trace behaves as a variable has several facets. As mentioned, the wh-operator in spec-CP is considered to be a quantificational operator, and the trace it binds is not taken to refer to a fixed individual but to a set. Takahashi (1991) and Maxfield (1991) both provide evidence of a sensitivity at age three or so to the differences between the discourse requirements of a real and an "echo" question (see also Authier, 1993). In an experimental game, Takahashi showed that three to four-year-olds would answer a real question with a fully quantified (variable) answer, but would answer an echo question with a single name, or just the information supplied by the preceding discourse. For instance, in the context of a story children were told that

The children had fruit for dessert

and were shown a picture of children eating various fruits. When asked

(27)   What did the children eat?

they answered, for example,

(28)   "Strawberry, and a banana, and a cherry"

but when asked

(29)   The children ate what?

they replied:

(30)   "Fruit."

In short, the moved wh-question, but not the in situ question, was treated as requiring a variable answer by the child. Evidence such as this is suggestive, though not conclusive, that by age three, wh-questions are derived by movement and involve a trace bound to an Operator which behaves like a quantifier. Further evidence in support of that claim is provided by an extensive comparison of wh-questions and quantifiers in Roeper and de Villiers (1991). In general, the experimental evidence reveals that children also provide exhaustive paired readings of "double" wh-questions such as:

(31)   Who brought what?

from about age three years, answering, for example,

(32)   The daddy brought the chips and the baby brought the apples

rather than, for example,

(33)   The daddy.

Supportive evidence that the older child's wh-questions are created by movement comes from a consideration of auxiliary movement. The wh-word moves into a position in the phrase structure tree known as the Specifier of the CP position (see figure 19.1). However, in questions, the auxiliary moves from its normal position as the head of IP, into this empty head of CP. Several theorists have proposed that children's grammars may be incomplete in this regard; for example, only having one position in the CP node (Roeper, 1988; Radford, 1991), or having some restriction on filling both positions at once (Weinberg, 1990). If so, that would provide an explanation for the observed delay in some children between Aux movement in yes/no questions and in wh-questions. That is, these children go through a stage in which they invert auxiliaries in yes/no questions but not in wh-questions (see Weinberg, 1991, for review). They produce sentences such as:

(34)   Can I go?
(35)   Will you do it?

at the same time as wh-questions like:

(36)   Where I can go?
(37)   What you will do?

If the child only has one grammatical site at the front of the sentence, in the wh-question there would be no "place" in the structure for the Aux to move.

A more radical alternative depends on the assumption that the CP node might not be present at the beginning of children's grammar (see Meisel, chapter one, this volume). Then the first wh-questions that children produce may in fact be formed by adjunction to the S, or to an IP, before a CP is built (see de Villiers, 1991; Vainikka, 1992). Only when the CP node is formed

long-distance interpretation in such a question as (52)? The crucial point is that the medial wh-word in (52) is in the specifier position of the medial CP, through which the lower question would have to move to obey successive cyclic movement. Hence, the "landing site" in the medial CP is blocked, and the "long-distance" reading is therefore excluded.

More precise accounts of the phenomena need to be provided, however, because there is a striking difference between *adjunct* questions and *argument* questions in this regard. Argument questions refer to arguments of the verb: subjects and objects (and possibly indirect objects for verbs such as *give*). On the other hand, adjunct questions occupy oblique roles with respect to the verb: where, how, why, when. They are not required to fulfill the verb's thematic roles. Hence, adjunct traces can only be *antecedently* governed, not *lexically* governed. This distinction turns out to be significant in comparing the long-distance movement possibilities of different questions. Consider the question:

(53)   What did he ask how to fix t?

Notice that such a question is perfectly understandable even though the trace of *what* is in the lower clause. Compare the adjunct question in (54) with the argument question in (55):

(54)   How did the man ask who to draw?
(55)   Who did the man ask how to draw?

Whereas (54) is like (52) in allowing only the short-distance interpretation, (55) allows the possibility of a long-distance reading despite the occupied medial spec of CP. Rizzi (1990) offers a full account of this difference in his formulation of the empty category principle, which allows lexical licensing of arguments, but requires antecedent licensing for adjuncts. Object wh-traces (arguments) are always properly governed because they are lexically governed by the verb, hence can be found in the lower clause even with an intervening adjunct trace in the medial COMP position:

(56)   Who$_i$ did she ask how to help t$_i$?

Adjunct wh-traces (e.g. those of how or when), however, are not lexically governed so require antecedent government. However, if another wh-word intervenes in the medial COMP, it acts as the nearest potential antecedent governor and the chain is disrupted:

(57)   *When$_i$ did she ask how to help t$_i$?

Hence, the traces of arguments and adjuncts have quite different distributional possibilities captured by the ECP. Do children know these possibilities? De Villiers, Roeper, and Vainikka (1990) looked at whether young children know

Figure 19.2   The little girl went shopping but she was very late going home. She went a short way home and ripped her dress on the wire fence. That night she told her mom, "I ripped my dress on the fence this afternoon."

these constraints on interpretation (Chomsky, 1986a). They presented children with stories followed by ambiguous questions that permitted the children a choice between a grammatical and an ungrammatical interpretation, to see if the children would systematically resist the latter. For example, take the following short story (see figure 19.2 for pictorial support like the children received):

This little girl went shopping one afternoon, but she was late getting home. She decided to take a short way home across a wire fence, but she ripped her dress. That night when she was in bed, she told her mom, "I ripped my dress this afternoon."
(58)   When did she say she ripped her dress?

Now given the story, there are two possible interpretations of (58), depending on where the listener interprets the trace to be for the wh-question "when": is it connected as an adjunct to "say," or to "rip"?:

(59)   When$_i$ did she say t$_i$ she ripped her dress?
(60)   When$_i$ did she say she ripped t$_i$ her dress?

That is, you might answer "at night" (if 59), or "that afternoon" (if 60), depending on your interpretation. The answer corresponding to (59) is referred to as a "short-distance" movement, because the wh-word moves within the first clause. The answer to (60) on the other hand, involves a long-distance movement because the wh-word moves from the lower, or embedded, clause.

De Villiers et al. (1990) showed that three to six-year-olds are quite happy to provide either answer, suggesting that they do readily permit "long-distance movement." But perhaps they are just guessing what is needed for an answer? If so, they should be just as likely to guess the long-distance answer in the case of a subtle variant of the question following the same story:

(61)   When did she say how she ripped her dress?

The long-distance interpretation "in the afternoon" should strike you as a peculiar answer now. Of course, (61) represents the case discussed above in which the medial spec of CP is occupied by the wh-complementizer *how*, so the trace of *when* in the lower clause is not properly governed according to the ECP. In fact, only rarely do three-year-old children give a long-distance answer to questions such as (61), which contains a medial wh-word. Hence, they know the subtle constraint on interpretation by about age three years.

Most importantly, de Villiers et al. (1990) tested the adjunct/argument asymmetry in children aged three to six, and found evidence that the children behaved in accordance with the ECP. That is, *not only* do children allow long-distance movement for (58), *not only* do they appropriately block it for (61), but they also show the very contrast between arguments and adjuncts that the

Table 19.2 Preschool children's long-distance interpretations of questions (percentages refer to answers interpreting the wh-question with that site)

	Argument	0 medial	
1	*Who* did the boy ask _____	to call _____ ?	
	68%	32%	
	Adjunct	0 medial	
2	*When* did she say _____	she ripped her dress _____ ?	
	50%	44%	
	Argument	Adjunct medial	
3	*Who* did the man ask _____	*how* to draw _____ ?	
	63%	30%	
	Adjunct	Argument medial	
4	*How* did the man ask _____	*who* to draw _____ ?	
	23%	8%	
	Argument	Argument medial	
5	*Who* did the girl ask _____	*what* to feed _____ ?	
	70%	2%	
	Adjunct	Adjunct medial	
6	*When* did she say _____	*how* she ripped her dress _____ ?	
	48%	6%	

Source: de Villiers, Roeper, and Vainikka, 1990

adult language respects. That is, they allowed long-distance movement of an argument over an adjunct in the medial CP (55), but not the long-distance movement of an adjunct (61) over the same barrier. Table 19.2 shows the basic results from de Villiers et al. (1990), since replicated several times for English, and in a longitudinal study (de Villiers and Roeper, in press, b). Notice that the percentages of ungrammatical long-distance readings, namely ones that violate the ECP, are very low (maximum 8 percent).[3] Recent studies (see papers in Maxfield and Plunkett, 1991) have explored children's knowledge of this constraint in German, French, Caribbean Spanish, and Greek (Leftheri, 1991), and have found strikingly similar results from young children exposed to the translations of these sentences.

Consider what a learning theory might offer as an account of how children acquire this knowledge of the conditions under which "long-distance movement" is blocked. Such a theory would have to claim that children hear questions all the time. As they do so, they observe people answering them and notice that half the time, some questions are answered one way, and half the other. Other questions (like (61)) are only answered one way, so they do likewise. But what exactly is "like (61)"? Each situation will be unique, and the child must ignore the variations in context, words, and meanings to attend only to the grammatical principles involved. For the learning theory to work, the two-year-old would have to be equipped with the ability to sift through evidence of this subtlety to arrive at the appropriate generalization. In other words, the unconscious mind of the two-year-old child would be performing an inductive analysis of the same subtlety as the conscious, trained linguist.

It is not beyond one's imagination to conceive of such a process. However, the data would have to be rich enough to distinguish the alternatives, i.e. ample evidence would be needed to successfully partition the types (52) through (61) above, and their allowable answers. The problem that immediately arises is the rarity of such sentences in the input. In hundreds of hours of recorded conversations between several young children and their caregivers, we have found a couple of dozen examples, and of course never closely contrasting pairs like those described above. The likelihood that the principles could be derived from experience alone seems rather low.

Instead, it is argued, the principles governing e.g. the movement of wh-words, or the conditions on empty categories, must be part of Universal Grammar, part of the innate equipment that the child brings to the task of language learning. On this familiar view, children don't construct "wild" grammars, that is, grammars that lie outside the family of known or possible languages.

Nevertheless, there is no guarantee that the grammar that a child constructs will be the same as that of the target language, because input data will be necessary to refine which grammar it is from the family of possibilities. Hence, the child's intermediate grammars may be interesting variants that are strikingly different from that of their parents. Such an example is provided in our work on wh-movement, and the explanation for why this particular variant is selected may provide a deep insight into children's early grammars and their inventory of empty categories.

Is the child's wh-movement entirely adultlike?

Given the data just described, why not argue that by age four or so, children have the entire grammar of wh-movement and traces established? There are several intriguing phenomena that qualify that argument and suggest that there may still be more to be mastered. Children in all the above languages show a characteristic error at three and four years of age that is similar to an option for interpretation that appears in some dialects of German (McDaniel, 1989). In German, it is possible to have questions such as:

(62) Was hat er gesagt wie er das Kuchen machen kann?
      What did he say how he the cake make can?
      [How did he say he could make the cake]

Notice that the first question word "was" [= "what" in English] is not answered; it just serves to mark the sentence as a question. It is only the medial question "wie" [= how] that needs an answer. This is thus an option in Universal Grammar, and it is an option that young children readily allow around the age of three to four years. That is, asked a question such as:

(63)   When did she say she how she ripped her dress?

young children are very prone to answer the medial "how" in English (de Villiers et al., 1990), German, French, and Spanish (see papers in Maxfield and Plunkett, 1991) in Greek (Leftheri, 1991), Black English (Seymour et al., 1991), and Mauritian Creole (Adone and Vainikka, 1990). They are especially likely to do so when the medial question is an argument such as "who" or "what" (de Villiers et al., 1990).

Simpler explanations spring to mind for this phenomenon: perhaps the children just answer the last question word they hear? Several control experiments rule out the simpler explanations (see Roeper and de Villiers, 1992). For instance, children do not answer the medial question in a yes/no question:

(64)   Did Micky tell Minnie what he bought?

nor do they answer the final "who" if it is the complementizer of a relative clause:

(65)   How did the dog climb up who barked?

(de Villiers and Roeper, 1991a, and in press, a). They thus restrict their answers to the medial embedded question of a sentence marked initially as a wh-question. Children's interpretations therefore appear to fall within the options provided by Universal Grammar, but why is partial movement such a likely "default" (Lebeaux, 1988, 1990)? Thornton (1991) discovered that children's productions also allow a "copy" of the initial wh-word when they are put in an elicited production situation and encouraged to produce complex sentences. For example, they produce questions such as:

(66)   What do you think what's in her hat?

and less frequently, cases in which the medial question is not a direct copy:

(67)   What do you think where the marble is?

Thornton's analysis also connects the phenomenon to the partial movement possibility in German, but she argues that the phenomenon is due to the child's rules for specifier-head agreement. That is, for a case of long-distance movement when there is a trace in the intermediate specifier of CP, the children's grammar insists upon an explicit complementizer to carry agreement features, and that complementizer is realized as a wh-form. In support of this claim, Thornton demonstrates that children do not produce these intermediate forms in the case of infinitival complements, only tensed complements, because only the latter trigger spec-head agreement. In their later development, children must observe that spec-head agreement is only necessary for subject extraction questions, and that the agreeing complementizer must in fact be null (Rizzi, 1990). The difficulty in reconciling this plausible account with the comprehension data lies in the fact that children *answer* the medial questions, and they do so for both infinitival and tensed questions. This fact makes it necessary to propose that the medial questions are part of a semantic chain, rather than just a morphological reflex.

Consider an alternative perspective. It is established that in some languages the initial wh-word serves as a scope marker, linked to the medial wh-word, but only one trace and one movement are involved:

(68) What$_i$ did you say [$_{CP}$ what$_i$ [you want t$_i$]][4]

German is the language where the phenomenon has been analyzed in the greatest depth and an important feature emerges: partial movement occurs only where there is no subcategorization. That is, first, partial movement occurs with verbs that do not subcategorize for a wh-word, like *denken* (think), but not *fragen* (ask), which takes indirect questions (that is, one can say "ask when..." but not "*think when...").

Second, the structure appears at the right in German, but the righthand complement must have been extraposed, as German is an SOV language with government to the left. In other words, the verb complement must have begun to the left of the verb, then been extraposed. How could the extraction be from this clause once it is moved to the right? After extraposition, the clause is no longer embedded, but adjoined, yet German speakers can interpret wh-questions as arising there. Clearly whatever explains this fact in German must be connected to the facts in English child acquisition. German permits both partial movement and long-distance movement from such clauses; so does the young child. The extraction from an "extraposed" clause has been addressed in a variety of ways, for instance Koster (1987) and Bayer (1992) introduces a notion of "domain extension" to account for the fact that this clause is accessible to movement.

Roeper and de Villiers (1992) propose that the child's complement clause is attached at a higher level than for the adult: it is not *syntactically* subcategorized by the verb though it is *thematically* governed by it. They propose that it is attached at a higher level than V, perhaps at the level of VP. As such, it is analogous to the German complement, namely not subcategorized to the right by the verb, but attached at a higher level. Thus, for the child's grammar, the empty category in the lower clause is licensed by "thematic government," a weaker version of the ECP. Roeper and de Villiers offer the suggestion that only when this complement is syntactically subcategorized does the possibility arise for the empty category to become a trace under proper licensing by the ECP, consequently permitting the formation of successive cyclic chains. Hence, the appearance of strict syntactic subcategorization should coincide with the disappearance of partial movement as an option for the child.

On behalf of this claim, Roeper and de Villiers put forward evidence from the child's spontaneous productions that suggests that all the features of syntactic subcategorization are not worked out immediately. Particular verbs set particular requirements on the form of their complements which are not necessarily respected by young children, for example (Roeper and de Villiers, 1992):

(69)   "did I seem that I was under the covers" (two times)
       "it's clear to hear" (two times)
       ". . . listening what you think"
       ". . . listening what I whistled"
       "I'm thinking why it's broken"

If these arguments are correct, and it must be admitted that they are controversial, then the Empty Category Principle may be formulated along different lines at the start, to accommodate the possibility of long-distance movement in the presence of incompletely specified complement structures. Thus, the presence of medial answers leads to a radical proposal about the nature of children's initial grammars, but they remain inside the domain of possibilities of Universal Grammar. Future work on German and other languages with this option may offer new understanding of child grammars in this regard.

Is there evidence for a null operator in child grammar?

A subtle variant on the constraint on long-distance interpretation comes from a consideration of the possibilities of another class of sentences discussed in the adult literature on wh-movement. A null operator occurs in adult language in certain sentences in which the CP position is c-commanded by an NP, and it in turn binds an empty category (not a trace), which forms a coindexed chain with that NP (Chomsky, 1976; 1981):

(70)   Sam is hard to find a job for
(71)   Sam is hard [OP$_i$ PRO to find a job for e$_i$]

Given that children show sensitivity to the presence of a medial question as a barrier to adjunct long-distance movement, questions then arise about other kinds of elements that could serve as barriers. The proposed existence of null operators raises the question: do children's grammars show sensitivity to null operators as barriers? Vainikka and Roeper (in press) tested the hypothesis that children would have access at this same age to an empty version of the wh-operator, an abstract (null) operator. How could one test whether children have a null operator in their grammars? The consequence of such a null operator filling the spec CP position is that it blocks wh-movement through that CP, just as an overt operator would:

Overt operator in medial CP:
(72)   *How$_i$ did Sam say WHERE to fix the car t$_i$?
Abstract/null operator in medial CP:
(73)   *Where$_i$ did the boy buy it OP to splash on his face t$_i$?

Notice that in both questions, the short-distance reading is available but the long-distance reading is not. Vainikka and Roeper argued that if children project a null operator in such purpose clauses, they should restrict their interpretations of questions to the short-distance readings. Remarkably, in a tightly controlled experiment, three to six-year-olds did so 98 percent of the time. The authors argue that before age three, the evidence for abstract operators in children's spontaneous speech is more slim, and they tie the appearance of the operators to the full development of the CP (see Vainikka, 1992). After age three, abundant use of purpose clauses begins, in which there is an empty category in the object position, coindexed with a moved NP. The assumption is that they also involve an empty operator to license the chain. Examples of these constructions are as follows (examples from Nina in CHILDES):

(74)   And the spaghetti for the dogs to eat (e)$_i$.
       This$_i$ is for the dog to eat (e)$_i$.
       He doesn't like nothing$_i$ to eat (e)$_i$.
       We don't have any more blocks$_i$ to make (e)$_i$.
       We could play with these and make a little horsie$_i$ to ride on (e)$_i$.

Are there other restrictions on where wh-trace can appear in children's grammars?

Other research on young children has uncovered obedience to a variety of constraints described for the adult language. However, it is not the case that constraints are automatically present from the earliest age. In some cases, they depend on lexical acquisitions, or the establishment of some other grammatical feature, before they can be fixed. The picture is thus a more complex one than the claim that children know constraints from the beginning: the course of their appearance sheds light on other significant aspects of acquisition such as case, control, and the semantics of complementation. In this section, the interaction of restrictions on wh-trace and these other aspects of syntax will be discussed, but much work in this area is ongoing and the theories may not be fully resolved.

Cases of obedience to constraints on wh-movement

In addition to the studies of wh-islands described above, children's grammars are sensitive to NP barriers, both nominalizations and relative clauses. Roeper and de Villiers (1991) showed that three to five-year-olds do not allow adjunct wh-questions to extract from nominalizations, e.g.:

(75)   *How$_i$ did the mother see his riding t$_i$?

Interestingly, they readily allowed argument extraction:

(76)   Who$_i$ did the mother show his copying t$_i$?

showing the same asymmetry in this regard as adult subjects tested in the same way. Following work by Otsu (1981), de Villiers and Roeper (in press, b) tested wh-extraction from *relative clause* environments, and showed that three to five-year-old children very consistently block adjunct extraction from inside a relative clause:

(77)   *How$_i$ did the woman who knitted t$_i$ swim?

Goodluck, Sedivy and Foley, (1989) tested whether preschool children would extract from *temporal adjunct* clauses, another barrier for wh-questions in adult English. The children did block movement from true adjunct clauses such as temporal adjuncts:

(78)   *Who did the elephant ask before helping t$_i$?

De Villiers and Plunkett (in preparation) explored children's obedience to a constraint known as "Superiority" (Chomsky, 1981) and given various accounts theoretically (see Cheng and Demirdash, 1990). It is designed to account for why certain orders of wh-questions are disallowed in sentences with more than one question; that is, certain questions seem to take priority over others in claiming the initial spec-CP slot:

(79)   Who slept where?
       *Where did who sleep?
(80)   How will she make what?
       *What will she make how?

In general, however, the phenomenon is incorporated into the theory as a consequence of the Empty Category Principle. Given children's general obedience to the ECP, do they obey Superiority? De Villiers and Plunkett set up an elicited production task in which the child had to confront a situation containing multiple unknowns, and after a couple of neutral models, persuaded children to ask what they needed to know to complete a scene being acted out with toys. On half of the trials, children were "led" by starting the sentence with the "wrong" wh-word, namely one that would result in a superiority violation. For instance, if the target were something like

(81)   Who slept where?

the children might be prompted with

(82)   "Where ... ?"

In this way they elicited 45 instances of "double" questions from 17 three to five-year-olds, and in only one (dubious) case was superiority violated. The children strongly resisted being misled and instead turned the misprompted sentences around, or rephrased them:

(83)   "Where ... ?"
       "Where did this one and that one sleep?"

One child even stopped the experimenter in midprompt and said "It's better if I start"!
   Other work has explored sensitivity to constraints using production methodology. In English, a constraint on subject extraction known as the "that-trace" filter disallows extraction from the subject position of a clause introduced by the complementizer "that":

(84)   *Who_i did the woman say that t_i came?

However, Thornton (1991) using elicited production tests found that preschool children did produce such forms. The children who did so were also prone to "copy" the wh-form:

(85)   What do you think that's in the box?
       What do you think what's in the box?

Thornton argued therefore that the production is a byproduct of the requirement for explicit spec-head agreement, as described earlier. She thus argues that the children are in fact producing these forms to preserve the ECP, not in violation of it.
   However, earlier work by Phinney (1981) using a comprehension task did not discover many violations of "that-trace" in her subjects. Her task involved comprehension of a sentence such as:

(86) Who did the pig see that swam?

If (86) is construed as having a trace following "that":

(87) Who$_i$ did the pig see that t$_i$ swam?

the sentence is a violation of the that-trace filter, but the child has an alternative of choosing a relative clause reading for the sentence:

(88) Who$_i$ did the pig see t$_i$ [that swam]

The pictured story defined different referents for the two readings, but the children only rarely chose the reading (87) that would result from a violation. The younger children were most prone to treat it as the simple sentence "Who did the pig see?" So Phinney's evidence is in keeping with the notion that English children obey the "that-trace" filter. How this could be so is still some-what mysterious. The "that-trace" effect is not universal – Greek, for example, lacks it – so it is not plausibly part of the child's default set of constraints. It must be triggered by some particular development elsewhere in the child's grammar. Leftheri (1991) in her study of wh-movement in Greek, and Perez-Leroux (1991) in her study of Spanish, found that children of three to five years readily extract the subject from sentences with an explicit complementizer, just as adults allow in those languages.

But what gives the child the clue about her language? Surprisingly, children do not seem particularly attentive to meaning contrasts conveyed by the com-plementizer "that," and they are rather late in using it as a complementizer for sentences (de Villiers and Roeper, 1992; see also Bloom, Rispoli, Gartner, and Hafitz, 1989). The trigger for "that-trace" must lie deeper than knowledge of the complementizer itself.

Apparent violations of constraints on wh-movement

There are other striking cases of disobedience to constraints that are more troubling because the adult languages all agree that the questions are viola-tions, so the solution does not rest on nonuniversality. For instance, take the phenomenon of extraction from quotations, or direct speech. The analysis of these forms is not completely certain syntactically: are they adjuncts, or do they involve some additional NP node? Nevertheless, the judgment that there is a barrier is very clear not just for English but for all the other languages tested:

(89) *How$_i$ did the boy say "Can I come t$_i$?"

Weissenborn, Roeper, and de Villiers (1991) report experiments in three languages: English, French, and German, in which young children aged three to six years were given short stories and then asked a question that tested whether they would allow extraction from inside a quotation environment. In each language the clues to the presence of the quotation were slightly different: in English, it was the presence of an inverted auxiliary:

(90) *How$_i$ did the boy say "Can the girl beat t$_i$ the drum?"

Compare:

(91) How$_i$ did the boy say the girl can beat t$_i$ the drum?

In French, the clue was the absence of the complementizer "que" (that), which is obligatory for indirect speech:

(92) *Comment$_i$ est-ce que le garcon a dit "La jeune fille va jouer t$_i$ du tambour"
      [How did the boy say __ "The young girl will beat the drum __"]

Compare:

(93) Comment est-ce que le garcon a dit que la jeune fille va jouer t$_i$ du tambour?

In German, the clue was given by difference in "verb-second" in the lower clause, an interesting contrast with the English case. In German, the auxiliary verb *kann* must be in second position with respect to some other element, in this case the NP *das madchen*, hence a trace is not possible from within the quotation:

(94) *Wie$_i$ sagt der Junge "Das Madchen kann trommeln t$_i$?
      [How does the boy say __ "The girl can beat the drum __"]

In a nonquotation environment, *kann* is in second position relative to the trace of the long-distance movement. Compare:

(95) Wie$_i$ sagt der Junge [t$_i$ kann das Madchen trommeln t$_i$?]

Children showed the same phenomenon in all three languages: they allowed extraction of the adjunct question freely from the quotation environments, in clear contradiction of the adult grammars. Once again, it may be necessary to invoke the difficulty that young children have in properly identifying the level of attachment of these clauses, which admittedly rests on rather fragile clues. No research has yet explored the age at which this is mastered; however, there is suggestive evidence that four-year-olds may not have full command of quotation. For example, a study by de Villiers and Roeper (1991a) on pronoun interpretation with children in the same age range found a significant group of children who allowed coreference in acting out the sentence

(96)   *"He$_i$ can sit here" said Micky$_i$.

The inverted verb in such a sentence requires that the complement be a quotation for an adult, but some four to five-year-old children did not regard that as a restriction on their interpretations of the pronoun reference.

Roeper and de Villiers (1992) argue that children's command of the right level at which to attach complements is not completed by age four or so, primarily because of the idiosyncratic nature of complements both within and across languages. In English, it is necessary to learn for each verb what kind of complementizer it takes, and for each verb class, what complements are allowed. Hence, there is considerable lexical learning that must proceed before some of these syntactic decisions can be made.

Furthermore, some semantic/conceptual acquisition is required to understand the meaning of complements, which usually involve verbs of mental activity or communication. For instance, de Villiers, Sherrard, and Fretwell (1992) tested three and four-year-olds on questions involving structures such as (103). Consider a typical story from their task:

This mom sneaked out late one night and bought a birthday cake for her little girl. When the little girl saw the bag from the store, she asked "What did you buy?" The mom wanted the cake to be a surprise, so she said, "Oh, just some paper towels!"
(97)   What did the mother say she bought?

The three-year-olds were strikingly prone to answer "cake," apparently ignoring the matrix clause. By four, more children answered "paper towels," sometimes adding "but she lied"! De Villiers et al. (1992) demonstrated experimentally that this changeover to consideration of the meaning added by the matrix clause occurs at exactly the point in time where the same children master traditional "false belief" tasks (Leslie, 1987; Wellman, 1990; Wimmer and Perner, 1983). That is, the three-year-old children but not the four-year-olds also failed on a task that involved taking into account another person's perspective and knowledge, suggesting that cognitive development may be interacting with the acquisition of the complement's meaning. The latter task was relatively independent of linguistic complement meaning. For example, the children were told the following story, which was also acted out in front of them:

This bunny rabbit bought a nice carrot, and he decided to put it in this RED basket to eat later. Then he went out to play. While he was out, the mother bunny rabbit took the carrot out of the red basket and grated some of it into a cake. Then she put it back, but she put it in the BLUE basket, see? Then she

went to borrow a cake pan. While she was gone, the little bunny rabbit comes back inside and he's hungry, so he decides to have some carrot to eat.
(98)   Where does the little bunny look for the carrot?

The same three-year-olds who answered "cake" to question (97) above, answered "the blue basket" given the above scenario and (98), neglecting the difference between reality and the content of the protagonist's speech or knowledge. Of course, there is a classic chicken and egg problem here: does linguistic development drive cognitive development, or vice versa? That is, the child could know the meaning of the complement, but must master the way that it changes dependent on particular matrix verbs. Presumably this is dependent upon developing the concept of how other minds could be different from one's own. Yet is it not possible that exposure to such linguistic differences could spur the child to that discovery?

   In another set of studies, extensive exploration of children's understanding of the inferences possible with factive verbs by Philip and de Villiers (1992a, b) has revealed that four-year-olds make different inferences than do adults. For instance, upon being told in the context of a story that

Jim forgot that his aunt was arriving by train, so he went to the bus station to pick her up

and when asked

(99)   Did Jim forget that his aunt was coming?

four-year-olds answer confidently "yes!" The particular feature that such a sentence manifests is the feature of being nonmonotonic increasing; that is, with most ordinary sentences the inference from one statement to the other works out fine. Compare:

(100)   Jim said that his aunt was coming by train.
(101)   Did Jim say his aunt was coming? – the answer is yes.

The sentence (100) has the property of being monotonic increasing; that is, one can make an inference from the subset of events described by (100) to the larger set described by (101). However, certain elements create environments in which the inference is not allowed:

Negation:
(102)   Jim didn't say his aunt was coming by train.
(103)   Did Jim say his aunt was coming? – unclear.
Factives:
(104)   Jim forgot his aunt was coming by train.
(105)   Did Jim forget his aunt was coming? – unclear.

Quantificational adverbs:
(106)   Jim often eats grapes with a fork.
(107)   Does Jim often eat grapes? – unclear.

Philip and de Villiers reported that children succeed at these inferences at different points in acquisition, and it is only once they succeed at these inferences that their grammars change in other ways. Szabolsci and Zwarts (1990, 1992) suggested that it was precisely this feature of "not being monotone increasing" that creates so-called "weak islands" for wh-movement in adult grammars. So, notice that negation, factive verbs, and adverbs all block long-distance interpretation of the wh-question:

(108)   *Why$_i$ did Jim forget his aunt was coming t$_i$?

[Note: the reading "because he lost his diary" is fine, but "to go to the Bar Mitzvah" is disallowed.]

(109)   *Why$_i$ did Jim not say his aunt was coming t$_i$?
(110)   *Why$_i$ did Jim often say he liked jazz t$_i$?

Philip and de Villiers (1992a, b) tested the hypothesis that children would fail to perceive the barrierhood of these elements as long as they also failed on the inference tasks, and the evidence was generally in support. They included the standard case of wh-islands (de Villiers et al., 1990) in their design, and proved that the same children who ignored the weak islands created by this semantic factor, were still strikingly obedient to the wh-island; that is, they never allowed long-distance readings for a sentence such as

(111)   Why did the mother ask what he made t?

Thus, they argue that child language data provides evidence for two factors in the barriers to wh-islands, one semantic and one syntactic, because they disassociate in acquisition.

One final result from our work also concerns a lexical difference for complement attachment, and reveals the fruitfulness of exploring interlinked phenomena in the area of complementation. The case is an intriguing one, and we do not pretend that the syntax is completely worked out. Boyd (1992) discusses the differences between the superficially similar sentences:

(112)   The boy made a decision to play.
(113)   The boy liked the decision to play.

The difference between the sentences with verbs like "make" and verbs like "like" are severalfold. There are different referents for the "empty" subject (PRO) in the infinitive, in the sense that *make the decision* allows the subject to be the same as in the matrix clause, but *like the decision* lets it be arbitrary in reference:

(114)   The boy$_i$ made the decision PRO$_i$ to play.
(115)   The boy liked the decision PRO$_{a/b}$ to play.

Long-distance wh-movement is different:

(116)   When$_i$ did the boy make the decision to play t$_i$?
(117)   *When$_i$ did the boy like the decision to play t$_i$?

Binding is different for a pronoun in the scope of the infinitive:

(118)   *The boy$_i$ made the decision to shave him$_i$.
(119)   The boy$_i$ made the decision to shave himself$_i$.
(120)   The boy$_i$ liked the decision to shave him$_i$.
(121)   *The boy$_i$ liked the decision to shave himself$_i$.

A full linguistic account of these facts is still tentative, but several reasonable proposals can be advanced. One is that the noun incorporates into a complex verb in the case of "make the decision" but not in the case of "like the decision." Consider the difference roughly as follows:

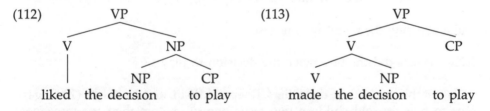

(112) VP — V (liked) — NP — NP (the decision) — CP (to play)

(113) VP — V — CP (to play); V — V (made) — NP (the decision)

As a consequence, the phrase "to play" is either a regular infinitival complement of the resulting complex verb, or not. When it is, then wh-movement is possible through the intermediate spec of CP. When it is not, then wh-movement is impossible because the CP is embedded in the complex NP, "decision to play." When PRO is controlled by the verb and coreferent with the subject, a pronoun in the lower clause cannot be coreferent with the subject without violating Principle B of the binding conditions. When PRO is arbitrary, the pronoun can corefer with the subject of the matrix verb.

Just what it means for something to become a "complex verb" is enormously complex, but the account is not completely necessary to the present purposes (see de Villiers and Roeper, in press, b). For the present, assume that the structures are quite distinct for "like the decision" and "make the decision." If children take time to learn the subcategorization frames for particular verbs, they may at first make no distinction between verbs like "make" and verbs like "like." If the default is to allow long-distance movement wherever there exists thematic government regardless of syntactic subcategorization (Roeper and de Villiers, 1992) and the verbs in question – *make, like, choose* – are complement taking verbs, the children should allow long-distance movement to occur for both types of verbs.

In the binding domain, the default assumption of children in this age range seems to be to a failure of Principle B, i.e. to treat pronouns as if they can corefer in the same way as reflexives (Wexler and Chien, 1985; Jacubowicz, 1984). Hence, for both types of verbs, the reflexive interpretation should be allowed, if not preferred. However, the following prediction relates these facts together. When children learn the difference between the structure for "make" and the structure for "like," then there should be two consequences: (1) they should disallow coreferential readings for the sentence:

(122)   *Bert$_i$ made a decision to shave him$_i$.

but allow them still for

(123)   Bert$_i$ liked the decision to shave him$_i$.

(2) They should disallow long-distance readings for the noncontrolling verb case:

(124)   *When$_i$ did the boy like the decision to play t$_i$?

while allowing them still for the case:

(125)   When$_i$ did the boy make the decision to play t$_i$?

To test this prediction, de Villiers, Roeper, Mitsui, and Hallahan (1992) gave four to five-year-old children two tests: one to explore their wh-movement across the different verb-control types, and one to test their binding of pronouns in the same structures. About half of the children allowed long-distance movement with cases such as:

(126)   *When$_i$ did the boy like the decision to play t$_i$?

and about half of the children allowed coreference for the case:

(127)   *Bert$_i$ made a decision to shave him$_i$.

Studying the two groups formed on the basis of their answers on the binding task, the evidence that emerged was in support of the predictions; namely, only children who passed the test of binding differentiated the structures in terms of their wh-movement possibilities. Thus, the acquisition of the appropriate barrier to wh-movement rested again on acquisition involving other parts of the grammar, in this case the acquisition of control into different types of complements. A similar account involving the acquisition of exceptional case marking is detailed in Roeper and de Villiers (1991).

What, then, do these cases of barrier violations have in common? Children apparently respect the barriers of medial wh-questions, empty operators, NP maximal projections, and temporal adjuncts. However, children in the same age range of four to six do not obey the barrierhood of quotation, factivity, and noncontrolling verbs. In each of these cases, other evidence can be adduced that the children fail to control some significant semantic/syntactic phenomena associated with the complement type at issue. For instance, with quotation, they are not in full control of the pronoun coreference properties that distinguish direct and indirect speech. With factives, they differ from adults in their presuppositions and their inferences. With noncontrolling verbs, they fail to respect the binding principles for pronouns. It is thus tempting to argue that these problems have a common source; the child at four years or even later has still a considerable number of subtle properties about complementation to fix. In many cases, the fixing may be delayed by idiosyncratic properties of the complement system involving lexical learning, learning that necessarily takes sufficient exposure to the language. In other cases it is possible that the development is delayed pending certain cognitive developments, say those included under the concept of "theory of mind," or the capacity to handle asymmetric inferences. The precise way in which these factors impact on the development of a mature wh-question is being actively researched.

Discussion

It is difficult to see how the child could begin with a fully worked out inventory of empty categories, given that there is some parametric variation across languages. With respect to wh-questions, the nature of the empty category in the beginning is still controversial, but it may not have precisely the features (−p, −a, +v) of wh-trace in the adult language. That determination might wait upon the right analysis of the wh-questions as involving movement, and the establishment of the landing site in spec-CP. Nevertheless, the empty category associated with wh-questions in four-year-olds' grammar does seem to have associated the quantificational properties of a true question, the requisite blocking effects on phonological phenomena such as contraction, and it appears to obey the empty category principle, a principle held to apply to nonpronominal empty categories.

However, acquiring the full grammar of questions in English and other languages is seen to interact with many other features as well as the process of lexical learning during childhood. Complexity is necessarily introduced by the problem of assigning the right analysis to the complement, which is ambiguous is multiple ways. The child must determine its level of attachment, the control features that may be transferred by the verb, the possibility of exceptional case marking, its monotonicity properties and factivity. All of these aspects require time to learn, and it is only when these features are securely fixed that a final determination of barrierhood can be made. Until that time, a weaker version of the empty category principle may be in operation, one that does not depend on strict syntactic subcategorization. This "thematic government" may be all that the child requires to license the appearance of an empty category in the embedded clause linked to a wh-question. Whether the empty category is at this point entirely equivalent to the adult wh-trace is a research question of considerable current interest.

NOTES

1 By "governing category" is meant roughly, a clause. The following is an approximation: the governing category for ∂ is the smallest category containing ∂, a governor for ∂ and a subject. A governor is a lexical head: N, V, A, P. For a more complete description, see e.g. Cook (1988).
2 See Radford and Meisel (chapters one and 18, this volume) for further descriptions of functional categories such as the CP, and descriptions of X-bar syntax.
3 The reason that the percentages sum to less than 100 percent is due to a fascinating departure from adult grammar, to be explained in more detail in the next section.
4 German typically has the expression *was*, while Slavic languages allow *how* as the scope marker (Browne, pers. comm.).

Part III Nonnormal Language Development

Introduction

The children discussed in the chapters that follow all represent special cases of language acquisition, but all rather different special cases. Nevertheless, the set of questions posed by Chapman in her review of the course of language development in Down Syndrome children could be said to guide the investigation of all types of nonnormal development of language. We ask, in relation to our group of interest, whether they evince a language deficit in comparison to normals, and if so, how does this relate to their cognitive level? Other issues center on the developmental course in these children, and whether it represents a delay, or is atypical in this group. We want to know how individually different the children are in their language development, and possibly what causes the problems we find. For most of these questions, information about normal language development is crucial.

Reliable answers to these questions depend in part on the availability of large bodies of data, and user-friendly procedures for their analysis. As in normal language development studies (see chapter five), advances in computer technology have been of considerable benefit to researchers in this field. Miller and Klee discuss general issues relating to computational approaches to language analysis, and illustrate in detail a particular approach to the analysis and interpretation of a database.

Chapters 21–3 consider specific language impairment from three distinct perspectives. Specific language impairment (SLI), while long recognized as a category of disability, has over the 20 years in which it has been intensively studied, resisted a clear and unequivocal statement of its characteristics, or its etiology. The first section of Fletcher and Ingham's chapter reviews definitions of SLI subjects in a number of studies. Differences in inclusion criteria used for subject selection (in terms of age, intellectual status, medical background) give some clues as to why its linguistic symptoms can appear so heterogeneous. Nevertheless, it is possible, at least under the headings of phonology and grammar, to make some generalizations.

In his chapter on phonological impairment Leonard points to comparisons between the phonologies of impaired children and those of normals which indicate similarities: the types of phonological processes which characterize the relationship between target and production in normal children (stopping, cluster reduction) also appear in the impaired children. However, the impaired children tend to be slower at removing some of the more immature processes (those that characterize younger normal children) from their speech. They also seem to be more likely than younger normally developing children to produce errors that are unusual. Examples are plentiful in the chapter, and in Leonard (1985): one is a lateral substituted for voiceless and voiced velar stops, and voiceless alveolar stops; another is the consistent use of a consonant to close open syllables. In reviewing models that might account for the pattern of pronunciation impairment seen in these children, Leonard favors the interactive activation model, a connectionist model developed by Stemberger (1992).

The typical study of grammatical impairment compares a group of language impaired children and a group of matched normals, and looks for differences in their linguistic performance. As Fletcher and Ingham emphasize, there may be some variability in subject selection criteria for these studies, with consequent effects on findings. Nevertheless, some generalizations have been made about identifiable areas of deficit in grammar in SLI performance. A commonly cited problem space is that of grammatical morphology. In normal language learning two broad classes of explanation are on offer for morphosyntactic categories. One relies on the parameter setting model (see Part I, Introduction and chapter one): the variation in morphosyntactic categories from language to language is handled by parameterization. Broadly speaking, the child selects the appropriate parameter setting for a particular category in her language, from a small set of possible settings, on the basis of exposure to relevant data. The other explanation appeals to strategies the child adopts in reaction to the phonetic salience, semantic function, and formal complexity of categories in the target language (see Part II, Introduction and chapter 17). The parameter setting model deals in syntactic categories, apprehended by the child through the interaction of an innate endowment with language input in some unspecified way. The strategies approach seems to rely on general pattern-seeking principles interacting with prosodically and phonetically varying exponents of syntactic categories. If SLI reflects an impairment of a language learning mechanism, which of these perspectives on normal morphosyntactic learning seems more likely to account for the SLI data? Recent crosslinguistic work by Leonard and colleagues (e.g. Leonard et al., 1992a) suggests that at least in explaining some differences between English and Italian SLI children, the phonetic salience of morphemes such as verb agreement plays a role in facilitating Italian children's learning of these forms. The work has effectively only started, and is fraught with methodological difficulties, but the crosslinguistic dimension to SLI studies pioneered by Leonard promises to be a useful testbed for explanatory accounts of grammatical impairment.

Whatever difficulties arise in describing and accounting for phonological and grammatical problems in English SLI children or those learning other languages, at least there are recognized theories and models within which data can be organized and interpreted. In recent years an additional category of language impairment has gained ground, labeled "semantic–pragmatic," or in Craig's title simply "pragmatic" (see McTear and Conti-Ramsden, 1992, for a review). These labels appear to have some face validity, in that there are older SLI children whose earlier systemic problems with phonology and grammar have largely resolved, but who continue to present with problems of language use. However, given the possible ambiguity of the term "pragmatic impairment," Craig's critical scrutiny of its actual and potential interpretations is timely.

Chapters 24–5 review the linguistic strengths and weaknesses of Down Syndrome individuals, and children with early brain damage. For different reasons we might expect both groups to be at risk, though in distinct ways. Down Syndrome is associated with a degree of cognitive limitation, and it might be supposed that linguistic development would be affected by this. Language is usually assumed for most individuals to be located in the left hemisphere, a part of which seems to be specialized for the representation of linguistic forms. Injury or insult to the region of the brain most adapted to develop language, prior to or in the early stages of acquisition, might be expected to affect language development, despite the plasticity of the immature brain. As it turns out, assumptions that these groups would have linguistic difficulties are met, though the problems are perhaps more subtle than we might have supposed.

Chapman's detailed and careful survey, involving all aspects of language in comparison with mental age normal controls, does identify a characteristic pattern of linguistic deficit in Down Syndrome individuals. She documents different rates of development in comprehension and production, and identifies different rates of development for the lexical and syntactic domains within comprehension and production. So, for example, the comprehension of syntactic structures by Down Syndrome children is advanced, relative to their expressive syntax. However, their comprehension begins to show delays relative to nonverbal cognition in adolescence. On the other hand, comprehension of vocabulary becomes advanced relative to nonverbal cognition in adolescence. Eisele and Aram conclude from their examination of the effects of early right and left hemisphere damage that despite the remarkable degree of functional recovery shown by children, a complete acquisition of language requires two fully functioning hemispheres from the outset. Delay in the emergence of early gesture, lexis, and grammar, as well as residual deficits in lexical–semantic and syntactic functions occurred in children with both left and right hemisphere damage. Eisele and Aram's documentation of the contribution of both hemispheres to the development of linguistic behavior is, they claim, an important corrective to a simplistic lateralization hypothesis.

20 Computational Approaches to the Analysis of Language Impairment

JON F. MILLER AND THOMAS KLEE

1 Introduction

The attempt to characterize the nature of language disorders in children has produced many divergent views over the past several decades. One view has held that the language production of language impaired children is developmentally delayed relative to that of children without language disorder. Another view has held that language impaired children develop a linguistic system which deviates from normal developmental patterns. To compound matters, the discipline has gone through several major shifts in emphasis over the years – mirroring the many new developments which have emerged in the fields of linguistics, psychology, and neuroscience. For example, language impairment has been seen in various eras primarily as a grammatical deficit, a semantic deficit, and a pragmatic deficit. More recently, some investigators have characterized language impairment mainly as a processing deficit while others have viewed it as a representational deficit.

It may be that all of these views contain some element of the fact that language disorder is multidimensional because it is multidetermined. Resolving any conflicting views will require careful description of disordered language performance through the life-span. Of the several problems hindering the descriptive phase of the scientific process, the definition of language disorder is central.

There is no objective, universally accepted definition for what counts as disordered language performance in children. In working towards this end, investigators have attempted to quantify various aspects of children's language production and comprehension abilities in various ways. Quantifying a child's language performance involves describing language production and comprehension numerically for the purpose of determining the various parameters by which disordered performance can be distinguished from normal developmental variation. This enterprise assumes that disordered performance is identifiable in the first place and, further, that it is amenable to objective quantification. Moreover, it assumes that the construct of language disorder has been well defined and is agreed upon by clinicians and scholars in the field, that decision criteria are well thought out and generally accepted, that developmental functions for linguistic, cognitive, social, and motor skills are well described, and that there is a universally accepted standard for determining the performance characteristics associated with language impairment. In fact, we have none of these at this time. It is clear, however, that advances have been made both in research methodology and research discoveries that will ultimately improve the description and characterization of disordered language performance.

The purpose of this chapter is to explore the potential that computational approaches might offer the analysis of language impairment. Our specific focus will be on computational methods of analyzing children's language production, although it is recognized that a full description of language disorder must eventually give equal emphasis to the many facets of language comprehension.

After examining several current models of childhood language impairment, this chapter will present an overview of computational approaches to analyzing children's language production. First, a survey of contemporary computer programs designed to facilitate language sample analysis will be presented using a hierarchical computational framework. Next, one specific computer program, Systematic Analysis of Language Transcripts (SALT) (Miller and Chapman, 1982–93), will be summarized and used to illustrate how language impairment in children might be explored from the vantage point of a reference database. Finally, we will examine how quantitative data generated by the computer might inform our views of language impairment in children.

2 Current Views of Language Disorder

Language disorders in children are associated with a wide variety of etiologies, including pre- and postnatal trauma, genetic syndromes, metabolic disorders, disease processes, and environmental deprivation. These etiologies result in impairments in sensory, cognitive, and motor performance associated with hearing impairment, mental retardation, emotional disturbance, and brain injury which adversely affect the normal development of language. In addition, there is a population of children with language disorders who suffer none of these conditions. These children have been referred to as specifically language impaired (SLI) in the literature. Past research has characterized language impaired children as comprising a single group, concluding that these children speak less frequently and less accurately, process information at a slower rate, and produce more errors than their language normal (LN) peers. In general, these children show a later onset of language skills, have a slower rate of language acquisition, and may never achieve the language skills of their peers, even as adults (Aram, Ekelman, and Nation, 1984; Schery, 1985; Weiner, 1985).

Current research on this population suggests that (1) language disorder may not be a unitary construct because there is considerable heterogeneity among children with language impairment; (2) there may be several subtypes of children in this population; and (3) different causal constructs may need to be put forth to explain each subtype. In order to address these issues we need to consider language disorder using a multidimensional model of language performance, advanced assessment technology to improve quantification of language production, and error variables as well as developmental variables in the description of linguistic performance.

Language disorder was viewed as a unitary construct in the 1970s and early 1980s, with notable exceptions (e.g. Johnston and Kamhi, 1984). In most studies of this period, single aspects of language performance (e.g. phonology, semantics, grammar, pragmatics) were studied without consideration of how they might interact with other levels. Recent arguments have been presented that research focusing on the identification of individual variables as parsimonious characterizations of disordered performance may be inadequate (e.g. Bishop, 1992a; Crystal, 1987; Johnston, 1988b; Van Kleeck and Richardson, 1988). Rarely do children exhibit unique deficits at a single level; rather, it is more typical for children to exhibit deficits at several levels of language performance simultaneously. Recent research which has investigated how deficits at one level of language performance affect other levels of performance offers initial support for this view. For example, limited phonological repertoires appear to affect children's lexical acquisition (e.g. Camarata and Schwartz, 1985). Similarly, syntactic deficits appear to alter performance on a variety of pragmatic tasks (e.g. Miller, 1978, 1981; Johnston, 1988; Johnston and Kamhi, 1984). Johnston (1988) argues that language disordered children are communicatively impaired precisely because they lack command of language form: "Without sufficient grammatical resources, they have difficulty constructing cohesive texts, repairing conversational breakdowns, and varying their speech to fit social situations" (p. 693). Clearly we need to understand not only how a *particular* linguistic level develops in children with SLI but also how deficits at one level affect other levels.

Developmental asynchronies have been observed within linguistic levels (e.g. syntax) and between processes (i.e. comprehension and production). Examples of within-level asynchrony can be found in studies that have documented simple sentence patterns developing in advance of grammatical functors and propositional embedding (Johnston and Kamhi, 1984; Liles and Watt, 1984). Asynchronies between language comprehension and production have been observed for some time in normal children (Chapman and Miller, 1975) and various disordered populations, including children with language disorders and mental retardation (Miller, 1987a, 1988; Miller, Chapman, and MacKenzie, 1981). Asynchronies observed in the language profiles of language impaired children may continue to change throughout the developmental period. Disordered language performance may look different over time as a result of continued development, adaptation, or intervention. The concept of changing profiles of language disorder complicates the problem of characterizing disordered language performance.

The language performance of children with SLI has been categorized in several different ways, primarily focusing on differences in the developmental relationship between comprehension and production abilities. Two distinct groups are identified in the DSM III-R manual: one having comprehension and production deficits and another having normal comprehension but problems with production (American Psychiatric Association, 1987). Tallal (1988) documents three distinct groups: the two recognized in DSM III-R and a third group having delayed comprehension relative to production. Rapin (1988) has suggested three categories: (1) expressive disorders with normal comprehension, (2) mixed disorders with impaired articulation, and (3) higher-order processing disorders. These categorizations focus on the independence of comprehension and production and are primarily defined by developmental variables. Recent work suggests that these categories may be too broad, viewing comprehension and production as unitary constructs which do not allow the various components of linguistic performance to be differentiated (Bates and Thal, 1991; Snow, 1991).

In summary, there is an increasing recognition that language impairment is not a unitary construct and that multidimensional models of development and disorder should prove useful in documenting different subtypes within the disorder (Fletcher, 1992a; Miller, 1987, 1991; Snow, 1991; Tallal, 1988). We will examine this issue further later in this chapter using a multidimensional measurement system on a large group of children.

3   Quantifying Children's Language Production

Progress in characterizing the causes and consequences of language impairment has been hampered by two factors: a paucity of models detailing language development and language disorder, and a lack of descriptive data delineating the onset and course of developmental progress of children with language disorders. Sophisticated models of language performance capable of describing developmental progress in language learning as well as areas of disordered performance have not been available until recently (Chapman, 1992). The importance of such models cannot be overemphasized. Models provide conceptual maps of the levels of linguistic performance and the relationships among levels in utterance comprehension and production, affording the opportunity to make predictions about specific language performance deficits given perceptual, motor, cognitive, or environmental deficiencies. To date descriptions of disordered performance have been driven by developmental models or at least developmental data. This approach has been important in deriving descriptions that do not confuse developmental progress and disordered performance or adult competence. This developmental model results in measures derived from variables documenting developmental progress which may be insufficient to characterize disordered performance.

A second factor that has limited progress has been the lack of measurement tools which can open up the way to detailed descriptions of performance and the quantification of disordered performance. It is not the lack of tests, though the ones available do not appear to be very sensitive (Aram, Morris, and Hall, 1993), nor is it the lack of effective and valid research methods for small sample research (cf. language sample analysis). Rather, it is the accessibility of research methods by large numbers of researchers and clinicians that has hampered progress in describing and defining language disorder. Researchers have been collecting samples of children's language at least since Darwin, in 1877 (cited in Bloom, 1993b), though the procedures they have used to analyze the samples have been quite varied. While samples of spontaneous speech may offer the most valid means of describing language performance, the process required to perform analyses of such data is time consuming and requires rigorous adherence to detail.

In the past, three types of computational measures have been generated from samples of children's language production for use in clinical assessment: unidimensional indices, sentence scoring measures, and profile data. Unidimensional indices evaluate single components of the child's language production system, such as mean length of utterance (MLU) and number of different words (NDW). Some of these unidimensional indices are developmental measures in that they are associated with changes in age (Klee, 1992a; Miller, 1991; Miller and Chapman, 1981). In addition, some of these indices can differentiate language impaired children from children who are developing normally (Klee, 1992a).

The second kind of quantitative measure which can be derived from a language sample is a sentence score. In this approach, selected grammatical constituents within sentences are assigned scores in accordance with their developmental complexity. Unlike unidimensional indices, sentence scoring measures attempt to represent the overall grammatical complexity of the sample with a single numerical value. Two examples of sentence scoring measures are the Developmental Sentence Score (DSS; Lee, 1974) and the Index of Productive Syntax (IPSyn; Scarborough, 1990).

A third approach to analyzing language samples is the profile analysis. Unlike either unidimensional indices or sentence scoring measures, the end-product of a profile analysis is not a single number, but rather a multidimensional profile of a child's strengths and weaknesses within a particular linguistic domain, such as grammar (e.g. LARSP; Crystal, Fletcher, and Garman, 1976/89) or phonology (e.g. PACS; Grunwell, 1985), or across several linguistic domains (e.g. BLADES; Gutfreund, Harrison, and Wells, 1989).

4   Computer Programs for Analyzing Child Language

At present, a dozen or so computer programs have been developed specifically for analyzing various aspects of children's language production. While several of these programs have a common basis, they often differ from one another in significant ways. Their commonalities and differences can be encapsulated by examining each program with respect to (1) the type of linguistic analysis offered, (2) the degree of automation offered (Baker-van den Goorbergh, 1991) and (3) the accuracy of the linguistic analysis offered. Some programs, for example, generate simple statistical measures of language production (e.g. mean utterance length; number of different words; frequency counts of word tokens) from the transcript quite accurately and automatically. Other programs have varying degrees of success at performing higher-level linguistic analysis, such as tagging words in the corpus and parsing utterances.

Leech (1991) has proposed that programs designed to analyze adult language, in both its written and spoken forms, can be categorized according to the relative contributions of the human analyst, the computer software, and the transcript. Leech observed that "There are a number of ways in which human, software and corpus resources can interact, according to how far the human analyst delegates to the computer the responsibility for analysis" (1991: 14). This interaction has produced four different models by which current language analysis programs might be considered. Leech suggests that these four models form a scale, from most human intervention to least human intervention. They include a (1) data retrieval model; (2) symbiotic model; (3) self-organizing model; and (4) discovery procedure model. The implementation of each of these models in the computational analysis of children's language is considered below, alongside contemporary computer programs which exemplify the models (see table 20.1).

At one end of Leech's scale is the data retrieval model. In this model, the computer provides the data to the human analyst in a convenient form, but the human actually performs the linguistic analysis. One example of a computer program at this level is concordancing software, which is used (e.g. in lexicography) to perform word searches of large computer corpora and display the target word along with its surrounding linguistic contexts (Rundell and Stock, 1992a, b, c). Any further analysis of the data (e.g. separating the different senses of the word) is then left to be performed by the human analyst.

Table 20.1 Corpus analysis models denoting the division of labor between the human analyst and the computer on a scale from most human intervention to least human intervention, with examples of language sample analysis programs

---

Data retrieval model
Machine provides the data in a convenient form.
Human analyzes the data.
Examples: CLAN, CLEAR, PAL, SALT2, TAS.

Symbiotic model
Machine presents the data in (partially) analyzed form.
Human iteratively improves the analytic system.
Examples: Communication Analyzer, Computerized Profiling.

Self-organizing model
Machine analyzes the data and iteratively improves its analytic system.
Human provides the parameters of the analytic system and the software.
Examples: none.

Discovery procedure model
Machine analyzes the data using its own categories of analysis, derived by clustering techniques based on data.
Human provides the software.
Examples: none.

Source: Leech (1991)

There are at least five different programs designed for child language analysis which could be considered as "data retrieval" programs: (1) Child Language Analysis programs (CLAN: MacWhinney, 1991a; see also MacWhinney, chapter five, this volume); (2) Computerised Language Error Analysis Report (CLEAR: Baker-van den Goorbergh and Baker, 1991; reviewed in Dollaghan, 1993); (3) Pye Analysis of Language – syntactic, morphological, and lexical analyses (PAL: Pye, 1988; Pye and Ingram, 1988; reviewed in Leonard, 1989); (4) Systematic Analysis of Language Transcripts – 2 (SALT2: Miller and Chapman, 1982–93); and (5) Transcript Analysis System (TAS: Gavin, Dismuke-Blakely, and Klee, 1991).

Common to each of these programs is the requirement that the human analyst designate an appropriate linguistic taxonomy, code each relevant utterance in the transcript, and summarize the codes in (developmentally or linguistically) appropriate fashion. Each of these programs allows for open-ended, user-defined coding taxonomies to be used, rather than a prespecified method of analysis. But the defining feature of each is that it is the human analyst who is responsible for performing the linguistic analysis. For example, TAS was designed so that grammatical, semantic, or pragmatic analyses, either singly or in combination, can be conducted on the transcript. CLAN and PAL were designed with this in mind as well. Once a transcript has been constructed (using either a text editor or word processing software), TAS presents each utterance in the transcript to the analyst to be coded using whichever linguistic analysis (or analyses) has been defined. In this way, TAS serves as an electronic tablet with which to collect and store linguistic codes. These codes may be retrieved and summarized at a later point in time using database management software (see Gavin, 1987, for a discussion of the use of database management software in language sample analysis). TAS, when used in conjunction with database management software, also permits concordancing, as described above.

The data retrieval model may be characterized by noting the imbalance in roles between the human analyst and the computer, with the human analyst assuming all or almost all of the burden for the linguistic analysis. In the second type of computational model (Leech, 1991) – the symbiotic model – this imbalance is shifted such that the computer takes some or all of the responsibility for linguistic analysis. Software development requires that the knowledge of the linguist be made explicit and codified in the form of computer algorithms which are then applied to the transcript of language. The computer's linguistic analysis is then checked against that of the human analyst, who provides feedback which is then incorporated into the computer program in the form of revised algorithms. This process of writing computer algorithms – followed by human correction of the computer output, followed by revising the algorithms to reflect the human's decisions – is repeated until an acceptable level of accuracy is achieved in the automatic analysis of a transcript. The best implementations of the symbiotic model currently are to be found in grammatical word tagging programs used in the analysis of adult language. These programs automatically assign grammatical tags (e.g. preposition, adjective, plural noun) to each word in the corpus. The CLAWS word-tagging program, for example, is successful at assigning grammatical tags with 96–7 percent accuracy, depending on the type of text analyzed (Garside, Leech, and Sampson, 1987).

At least two contemporary programs designed for use in child language analysis could be considered as implementations of the symbiotic model: Communication Analyzer (Finnerty, 1992) and the LARSP and DSS modules of Computerized Profiling (Long, 1987; reviewed in Klee and Sahlie, 1987; Long and Fey, 1993). In the case of the LARSP module of Computerized Profiling, for example, the computer performs a provisional syntactic analysis of the utterance, whereupon the user is required to check the analysis for accuracy and hand-correct the analysis if need be. An obvious point to be made here is that users need to be conversant with the LARSP analysis to begin with if they are to make a judgment regarding the correctness of the computer's analysis. Moreover, every utterance requires human inspection if the final analysis is to be sound. In the case of this program and others like it, a symbiotic relationship between the programmer and user exists only if the user provides feedback to the programmer about the parsing of specific sentences and the programmer alters the program to take account of the user's feedback.

Computer implementations of the symbiotic model are not dynamic; rather they are static programs. That is, the program does not *learn* from past mistakes but continues to make the same mistakes until its algorithms are manually revised. Seeing the same kind of errors time and again is, of course, particularly frustrating from the standpoint of the user. Once the user corrects the computer's provisional parse, the computer should ideally take note of the corrected analysis and revise its rules so as not to make the same mistake again. Such an approach is characteristic of Leech's (1991) third type of corpus analysis model: the self-organizing model. In this model, the balance tips a bit further towards the computer and away from the human analyst. As Leech states, "the basic idea is that the machine 'learns' to improve its language model on the basis of the data it encounters and analyses" (1991: 18). In this way, self-organizing methodologies can be thought of as dynamic programs, unlike the static programs which currently exist; they represent the next generation of computer programs in computational linguistics.

The final methodology in Leech's scale is the data discovery model. This model requires no human analysis of the data; rather, "naturally" occurring categories emerge from the corpus through the use of clustering techniques. As is the case with the self-organizing model, no programming implementations of discovery procedures yet exist.

The remainder of this chapter will focus on a description of one such computer-assisted language sample analysis: Systematic Analysis of Language Transcripts. The various components of language sample analysis will be discussed with respect to how they are implemented using the SALT program. Finally, through the use of a large-scale database, it will be shown how quantitative data can inform our knowledge of childhood language disorders.

5 SALT Computer Program

Systematic Analysis of Language Transcripts (SALT: Miller and Chapman, 1982–93) is a set of computer programs developed to quantify developmental aspects of the spoken language of typically developing children and children thought to be language impaired. The various components of the SALT program are presented in table 20.2. The development of these programs was based on a number of assumptions about language, language development, and disordered language. The first assumption was that variables documenting developmental change may not be sufficient to characterize disordered language. This suggests that disorder is more than delayed development. Recent research has crystallized this view, suggesting that there may be several distinct

Table 20.2   Components of the SALT computer program

Basic SALT programs
    SALT operating shell
    SALT editor (SED)
    SALT1 standard analyses
        Transcript summary information
        Distribution by speaker turns
        Rate and pause summary
        Word and morpheme summary
        Utterance and maze distribution tables
        Word and morpheme tables
        Code tables

Database programs
    Profiler program (with reference database)
    Build program

User-defined analyses
    SALT2 program
    Coder program

File Interface program
    SALTFile program

types of language disorder (Aram, et al., 1993). The second assumption was that language disorder represented a variety of conditions that were both independent and overlapping. The third assumption was that, in order to study language disorders in children, new variables requiring both investigation and validation as descriptors of developmental and disordered performance were needed. The final assumption was that language disorder could be quantified. These assumptions lead to the development of a measurement method that is flexible and capable of documenting developmental change as well as disordered performance at all language levels through the developmental period. We chose to focus on the analysis of spontaneous language samples as the most valid and accessible source of language performance data, using a measurement system implemented with computer technology.

The measurement system was also shaped by practical needs. First, users should be able to analyze a language sample at all language levels for a variety of variables, analysis systems, or coding taxonomies using a single transcription format. Second, users should be able to analyze samples for single or multiple variables recognizing that the variables of interest change with age, language ability, and purpose. Third, during all phases of the assessment process (i.e.

sampling, transcription, analysis, and interpretation) the process had to be reliable. Before we review SALT in detail, let us review the literature associated with each of our assumptions to clarify the driving forces which have shaped the SALT programs.

6 SALT and the Components of Language Sample Analysis

The process of conducting a language sample analysis requires four separate steps: (1) recording a representative sample of the child's speech; (2) transcribing the speech sample using a (modified) standard orthography to create a (computer-) readable text; (3) analyzing the transcription using a particular descriptive or developmental model; and (4) interpreting the linguistic analyses relative to the performance of peers in order to document the developmental status of the child's language. Each of these steps will be briefly reviewed below; additional coverage of these topics may be found in Miller (1981) and Miller and Leadholm (1992).

6.1 *Sampling*

Collecting and recording a language sample requires the examiner to decide on the sampling context; that is, whether the sample should be based on conversation, narration, picture description, or some other context. In addition, the speaking partner must be decided upon (e.g. mother, father, sibling, peer, teacher). Finally, the length of the sample must be determined (e.g. 15 minutes, three hours, 100 utterances, 500 utterances). The recording must be judged to be a valid sample of the child's usual spontaneous speech before moving on to the next step in the process. If this sample is to be compared to data from other children, then the sampling conditions must replicate the sampling conditions of the database to which it will ultimately be compared. This may require consistent training of all speaking partners to promote responsiveness to the child, and the use of consistent strategies for eliciting spontaneous language samples.

6.2 *Transcription*

Transcription is the process of transforming the acoustic signal recorded on tape into standard orthographic text. For the computer to analyze a transcript, a consistent transcription format is needed. The process of transcription involves selecting what to include and what to ignore. Many forces compete in determining the final format but the most important is the focus of the analyses: one can only analyze what one records. This issue is critical when using a computer-driven language sample analysis to *discover* characteristics of disordered performance.

Transcription is itself a form of analysis representing the transcriber's theory of language development and disorders (Miller and Leadholm, 1992; Ochs, 1979). Every decision made as to what constitutes a word or an utterance must be consistent to be replicable and interpretable. This point is discussed in some detail by Garman (1989) and Klee (1992b). The danger of computer analysis is that after the transcription is complete, the computer counts what is present in the exact form it finds it in the transcript. Unlike humans, the computer does not ignore human error in form or content when reducing the data. When interpreting the outcomes of a computer analysis, it must be remembered that the computer analyzes only what is present in the transcript.

In developing the SALT transcription format we sought to meet several goals. First, the format had to be inclusive, allowing everything the child says to be recorded, with options for denoting nonverbal behaviors that may be relevant. Second, the format had to be flexible, requiring minimal constraints. The minimum requirements are that utterances be identified by speaker and that the temporal integrity of the conversation be maintained (i.e. the order of utterances as they were produced). Beyond these, the researcher/clinician may include any level of transcription detail deemed necessary to meet the analysis goals. Third, the transcript had to be readable by humans as well as computers (see Edwards and Lampert (1993) and Miller and Leadholm (1992) for a discussion of this point). (As an aside, we have found that despite all of the progress which has been made in computer linguistic analysis, the single best evaluation of a transcript is to read it. Human information processing is simultaneous; computer analysis is linear: one variable at a time.) Fourth, the transcription format had to provide options for marking errors and intrusive behaviors (e.g. false starts, repetitions, revisions, pauses, and overlaps). Fifth, the transcription format had to provide a method for coding words, morphemes, and utterances for grammatical, semantic, and discourse features users might wish to examine. The basic problem was to develop a format that provided for a clear rendition of every morpheme, word, sentence, false start, repetition, overlap, omitted word or morpheme, unintelligible word(s) or part word, speaker identification, duration, pause, and abandoned utterance.

The Basic SALT Programs (table 20.2) include an editor which was designed for typing a transcript into a computer file and then checking it for format errors. The editor and error checking routines help control for certain aspects of transcription accuracy by ensuring that format errors do not contribute to analysis outcomes. Alternatively, transcripts may be entered into computer files through the use of word processing software or a text editor, with the restriction that the resulting file be in ASCII format.

The SALT transcription format meets all five goals outlined above. Table 20.3 illustrates an excerpt from a transcript in SALT format. Note the identifying information at the top of the transcript indicating who the speakers are, their ages, the speaking context, and other relevant information a user may want to include. Any information preceded by a + is included in the transcript analysis. A speaker identification line, beginning with a $, is the only required information line. The first initial of the name of each speaker is typically used to identify each utterance in the transcript. Most transcript conventions are transparent, but an explanation for those used in table 20.3 can be found at the bottom of the transcript.

6.3   Analysis: SALT1 standard analyses

In addition to the transcription editor, the Basic SALT Programs also contain a program (SALT1) which automatically computes a set of standard measures which quantify various aspects of the sample of language production. Table 20.2 summarizes the areas assessed by the SALT1 program. The *Word and Morpheme Summary*, for example, calculates the number of different words in the transcript (NDW), the total number of words (TNW), the number of words in mazes, the number of omitted words, type–token ratio (TTR), mean length of utterance (MLU) in both words and morphemes, Brown's stage, and age range typical of the child's MLU. All of these measures are automatically computed from the transcript without any further coding. Examining this set of standard measures serves as the starting point in investigating a transcript of language. Based on the outcome of these measures, the decision can be made whether to invest time in more comprehensive linguistic analyses which, at this point in time, must be coded by hand.

6.4   Analysis: SALT2 user-defined analyses

In addition to the set of automated, standard analyses outlined above, SALT contains two programs designed to explore the transcript in more depth. These user-defined analyses are embodied in the SALT2 and the Coder programs. These programs facilitate more detailed analysis by allowing the user to code any of a variety of linguistic elements in the transcript (e.g. morphemes, words, utterances, grammatical and semantic constituents) using coding taxonomies of the user's choosing. This strategy takes advantage of the computer's abilities for searching the transcript and sorting utterances containing specific words, morphemes, codes, or combinations thereof.

The accurate identification of many linguistic features requires the use of both linguistic and extralinguistic context, in addition to real-world knowledge. Making use of these components in performing linguistic analysis is something in which humans excel, but computer do not (yet). This situation suggests that any automated coding solution of higher-level linguistic features will be subject to frequent computational error. Rather than permit the computer to erroneously arrive at an analytical solution, our approach has been to

Table 20.3   Excerpt of a language sample in SALT transcription format

$ CHILD, EXAMI
+Name: M T
+File name: GEISS01C. CESA
+SEX: F
+DOE: 01/23/91
+DOB: 04/09/86
+CA: 4;9;14
+Examiner: MG
+Context: Conversation
+DOT: 02/08/91
+Transcriber: KAJ
–   0:00
E   TELL ME ALL THE THING/S THAT YOU/'RE DO/ING AT SCHOOL
     MONICA.
:   :02
E   TALK TO ME ON THE PHONE.
:   :03
C   WELL :03 (IT/'S) I GO HEADSTART IN X HIGHSCHOOL AND GO
     THING BUT MOMMY LET ME WALK [EU].
E   WHERE?
C   (AND H*) AND (GO HOME) GO HOME.
:   :03
E   WHAT DO YOU DO AT HEADSTART ALL DAY?
C   PAINT MOM.
:   :03
E   MHM.
E   TELL ME MORE.
:   :04
C   I PAINT.
C   I DREW THE BLUE [EU].
C   I CUT THE PLAYDOUGH AND THAT STUFF.
:   :05
C   {HUMS}.
E   <TELL ME>>
C   <I PLAY ON> THE SLIDE.
E   OH GOOD.
E   TELL ME ABOUT THE KID/S IN MISSJONI/Z CLASS.
:   :03
C   MISSJONI C*>
C   IN THE HEADSTART?
E   MHM.
C   OK.

C X, JERMIA, AND WE HAVE TWO X.
C AND JOHN AND THAT STUFF [EU].
E WELL WHAT HAPPEN/3S ALL DAY IN MISSJONI/Z CLASS?
C OK.
C SARA>
E WHAT DO THEY DO?
C AND PAGE AND ME TOO.
E DOES ANYBODY GET IN TROUBLE IN MISSJONI/Z CLASS?
C (M* Y*) YEAH DEWAYNE TIMEOUT [EU].
E DEWAYNE DOES.
C YEAH.
E AND HE GET/3S A TIMEOUT.

```
  :00 = pause within or between utterances with time noted in seconds and minutes
    X = unintelligible segment
    > = abandoned utterance
  < > = speaker overlap (both speakers talking at the same time)
 [EU] = error at the utterance level
    *  = omission
  (  ) = mazes, false starts, repetitions, revisions
```

let the user perform the actual analysis, using software designed to aid in the coding and then let the computer accurately summarize the codes.

In developing the user-defined analyses, we chose to implement a flexible coding option for two reasons. First, we wanted SALT to be used as a discovery tool, affording users the opportunity to bring their own coding schemes to the transcript. To specify an analysis, *a priori*, suggests that that analysis provides all of the information a user might wish to have (e.g. a complete developmental description of syntax or semantics). Second, we did not believe we knew enough to prescribe analytic tools to document developmental progress or disordered performance. SALT is best thought of as a tool for transcript exploration: both at a general level, in providing efficient access to a variety of features of language production, and also at a deeper level, in providing a tool for coding transcripts whereby the user can exploit the power of the computer using linguistic taxonomies of their own choosing.

The Coder program contains powerful search routines designed to locate various features of the transcript and then automatically mark them. If one were interested in studying irregular verbs, for example, one could give the computer the list of irregular verbs in English listed in the Comprehensive Grammar of the English Language (Quirk, Greenbaum, Leech, and Svartvik, 1985), instruct the program to find all of the utterances containing any of these verb forms, and either automatically insert a code marking those words as irregular verbs or review and code each instance for such properties as semantic features or time reference. These search routines allow one to use Boolean logic to construct search strings to find instances of a word, morpheme, or utterance. For example, searches can be constructed to find utterances containing

X *and* Y; X *but not* Y; X *or* Y; X *next to* Y; or X *followed by* Y. These features have been used by Johnston, Miller, Curtiss, and Tallal (in press) to develop an automated predicate coding system which identifies more than 20 different predicate types in transcripts with 95 percent accuracy, requiring human correction of only 5 percent of the data.

6.5   *Interpretation*

The SALT1 Standard Analyses generate a large number of language production measures. Putting these numbers into developmental perspective is one step required for successful interpretation. This can be done in one of two ways. First, the research literature which has made a study of these measures might be consulted and compared with the outcome of the SALT analyses. Second, SALT's Profiler program, containing data on over 250 typically developing children, might be used to judge how an individual child compares to his or her group of same-age peers. Each of these approaches will be discussed in turn.

The research database

In 1981, Miller and Chapman published a paper documenting the link between mean length of utterance in morphemes (MLU) and chronological age. MLU and age were found to be strongly correlated in a large group of typically developing children, thus allowing MLU to be predicted from age and age to be predicted from MLU in children between two and five years of age (Miller and Chapman, 1981). MLU has been used as a general developmental indicator of language performance and has been used in many research studies as a way of matching experimental and control groups (cf. Plante, Swisher, Kiernan, and Restrepo, 1993, for problems with this approach), and in clinical practice to identify developmental delay (Miller, 1981). More recently, the age range of the original research report has been extended to up to 13 years and documents a similarly high correlation between age and MLU (Miller, 1991). Another report documents the diagnostic potential of MLU. In a study of typically developing preschool children and age-matched children with SLI, age and MLU were found to be highly correlated within each group and the MLU of the SLI group was found to be significantly lower than that of the normal group (Klee, Schaffer, May, Membrino, and Mougey, 1989).

Two additional quantitative measures computed by SALT1 have been shown to be correlated with age in both typically developing children (Miller, 1991) and SLI preschoolers (Klee, 1992a): the number of different words (NDW) produced in samples controlled for number of utterances (i.e. 50 and 100 complete and intelligible utterances), and the total number of words (TNW) in samples controlled for time (i.e. 12 and 20-minute samples). MLU, NDW, and TNW are all correlated with one another (Miller, 1991), raising the possibility that MLU may be more related to advancing lexical skills than syntax or that all three measures are influenced by a common underlying cognitive construct associated with advancing language skills.

The interpretation of these general measures is central to description. At present, many interpret MLU as a general index of grammatical development although this has been the topic of some debate in the literature (Bennett-Kastor, 1988; Blake, Quartaro, and Onorati, 1993; Klee and Fitzgerald, 1985; Rondal, Ghiotto, Bredart, and Bachelet, 1987). NDW has been interpreted as a general index of semantic diversity and TNW has been interpreted as an index of overall verbal facility (Miller, 1991). Factors such as speech motor proficiency, the ability to hold the floor, understand listener utterances, formulate utterances, retrieve lexical items – all may play a role in the value TNW takes in a language sample.

These general measures constitute an initial description of language performance across levels. If one is exploring the language of children with potential language disorders, these general measures will help identify those areas of language performance that require further detailed analysis. To the researcher, these general measures may provide a way of documenting the performance of experimental and control groups. SALT provides a set of general analysis routines that allow users to explore a variety of quantitative measures in a language sample without further analysis or coding. The design of the Basic Programs was driven by the need to explore each measure to provide insight into interpretation. MLU for example can be explored further by reviewing the distribution of utterances by utterance length calculated both in words and morphemes. NDW can be explored by printing an alphabetized list of the different words and their frequencies for the child's words, the examiner's words, only those words used by both speakers, or the total set of words used by either speaker. The word list can be expanded to include bound morphemes or word codes.

SALT database programs

SALT contains two programs designed to allow comparisons of a child's transcript to either group or normative data. One program, Profiler, compares individual SALT transcripts to a selected database: either the SALT Reference Database (SALTRDB), which is furnished with the program, or local databases which can be constructed by individual users. The SALTRDB contains language production data on 252 typically developing children (i.e. children without language disorder) between the ages of three and 13 years from Madison, Wisconsin and several rural areas of northern Wisconsin. Both conversational and narrative language samples are contained in the database for each of the children. The other program, Build, is designed to build additional databases for use with the Profiler program. We will focus here on the SALT Reference Database by comparing a child of age 6;8 with the transcripts of 49 seven-year-old children in the SALTRDB.

Let us summarize with a list of general measures that we have found to be particularly informative in the clinical description of language disordered children and that form the set of Standard Measures used in the SALT Database Profiler program. Table 20.4 displays a computer printout of the first level of analysis from the Profiler. Note that analyses reflecting six categories of performance are include: (1) syntax/morphology, (2) semantics, (3) intelligibility, (4) mazes and overlaps, (5) verbal facility and rate, and (6) omissions and error codes. Measures were included in each performance category if they could be calculated directly from the transcript without any additional coding and if they demonstrated at least face validity in describing disordered performance. This was documented by clinical use over the past eight years on several thousand language impaired children (Miller, Freiberg, Rolland, and Reeves, 1992). There are no pragmatic categories included in these analyses since even the most general analyses (e.g. topic maintenance, contingency analyses) must be coded by the analyst and as yet are not conducive to automated computer analysis. The coding of certain pragmatic skills will be discussed in the User-Defined Analyses section to follow.

Note in table 20.4 that Profiler automatically compares the target transcript with age-matched peers in the same speaking condition (i.e. conversation or narration). The means of standard deviations (SD) of the comparison group are displayed for each language production measure, as are several measures of the measure's variability within the group (i.e. values ±1 SD from the group mean; the minimum and maximum values of the group). The printout also displays either one or two asterisks by each value for which the child's performance is one or two SDs above or below the group mean.

New measures: The importance of error categories

Characterizing language impairment solely in terms of developmental attainments may conceal important performance differences in language production resulting from unique cognitive, information processing, or motor skills. It has recently been argued that error categories should be included in the descriptive taxonomy for characterizing impairments of language production (Baker-van den Goorbergh, 1990; Fletcher, 1991, 1992a; Fletcher and Garman, 1988; Miller, 1987a, 1991). These include errors of omission, commission, formulation, rate, and fluency.

One such set of error categories includes false starts, repetitions, and reformulations and is thought to be related to utterance formulation load (Miller, 1987a). These have been referred to as *mazes* by Loban (1976) and represent a set of behaviors which have the potential for documenting utterance-formulation and word-finding problems. These may be as common as *um* or *er* (i.e. filled pauses) or as complex as phrase level revisions. These behaviors are quite common among normal speakers in the SALTRDB: 15–25 percent of utterances contain mazes in conversational samples and 20–35 percent of utterances contain mazes in narrative samples. Most of these mazes are filled pauses, part word, or whole word repetitions. In our experience, word and phrase level revisions are associated with word-finding or utterance-formulation problems. A great deal more research will be required to understand maze behaviors and their role in impairing the communication of children with language disorders.

Mazes are quantified by SALT1 in several ways. SALT1 computes the number of utterances with mazes, the total number of mazes, the number of mazed words, and the percentage of words in mazes divided by the total number of words. We are currently using this set of measures to explore their sensitivity for identifying word and utterance-formulation problems in normal and language disordered children. Each of these maze measures can be explored further through a series of distribution tables which document the distribution of maze length, mazes by utterance length, and the percent utterances with mazes at each utterance length. Mazes can also be explored by type, repetition, or revision. It has been argued that utterance revisions have more serious consequences for communication than repetitions and that filled pauses are minimal in consequence but phrase revisions are extremely serious (Miller, 1987; Miller and Leadholm, 1992). A frequency table is provided in SALT1, documenting the number of maze repetitions and maze revisions at the part word, word, and phrase levels. This table should prove useful in studying maze behaviors in a variety of populations.

Mazes have been used as evidence for two types of language impairment: word-finding deficits (German, 1987) and utterance-formulation deficits (MacLachlan and Chapman, 1988). Both studies found that children with language disorders produced more mazes in narrative samples than did control subjects. It is not possible to determine if these behaviors reflect a difficulty in accessing or recalling lexical items or in organizing them to formulate coherent messages.

Several studies of word retrieval have found, however, that some language disordered children have word storage deficits. That is, these children are less likely to store a word and less consistent in its retrieval (Kail, Hale, Leonard, and Nippold, 1984; Kail and Leonard, 1986; Leonard, Nippold, Kail, and Hale, 1983). In a multidimensional model of language impairment, lexical storage deficits would be associated with developmental deficits in both comprehension and production. Studies attempting to document word-finding problems using language sample data have used the following behaviors: incomplete statements, grammatical errors, pauses, repetitions, reformulations, starters, time fillers, empty words, and word substitutions (German, 1987; Schwartz and Solot, 1980). This represents a diverse set of language behaviors and the frequency and distribution of these behaviors in normal children is largely unknown. Although word-finding problems appear to be characteristic of some children with language disorders, it is doubtful that we would agree on the defining properties of this problem. It remains an empirical question whether such performance differences represent distinct subtypes of language impairment.

Table 20.4 Sample SALT database profiler analyses

TRANSCRIPT INFORMATION
File name: C:\SALT\WKSH1202.CSA
Speaker: CHILD
Name: J. A
CA: 6;8
Examiner: PA
Sample Date: 2/10/93

DATABASE INFORMATION
Database: SALTRDB
Age group: 7;0
Context: Conversation
Transcript Cut: 100 C&I Utts
No. Transcripts: 49

Measure	TRANSCRIPT	STANDARD MEASURES DATABASE						
	CHILD	Mean	SD	−1SD	+1SD	%SD	Min	Max
CA	6.67	7.09	0.18	6.91	7.28	3%	6.69	7.50
Total Utts	105	107	3.12	103.72	109.95	3%	100	113
SYNTAX/MORPHOLOGY								
# MLU (morph)	4.84*	6.34	1.26	5.09	7.60	20%	4.29	10.81
SEMANTICS								
TTR	0.41	0.44	0.04	0.39	0.48	10%	0.35	0.58
# Diff. Word Roots	163*	201	24.87	175.88	225.63	12%	156	255
# Tot M. Body Words	455*	580	116.49	463.41	696.39	20%	392	1,005
INTELLIGIBILITY								
% Intel. Utts	99%	99	1.45	97.26	100.17	1%	94	100

MAZES AND OVERLAPS

# Utts w/ Mazes	24	28	10.83	17.35	39.02	38%	7	55
# No. of Mazes	35	37	17.96	19.27	55.18	48%	7	91
# No. Maze Words	70	71	43.53	27.66	114.71	61%	9	224
# % Mz Wds/Tot Wds	13%	10	4.60	5.78	14.99	44%	2	24
Utts w/ Overlaps	4*	10	4.42	5.90	14.75	43%	1	21

VERBAL FACILITY AND RATE

No. Complete Wds	536	668	143.83	524.35	812.02	22%	422	1,100
Elapsed Time	10.08	8.19	2.16	6.04	10.35	26%	5.67	18.82
Utts/Minute	10.41*	13.67	2.66	11.01	16.33	19%	5.63	19.41
Words/Minute	53.16*	84.74	21.69	63.05	106.43	26%	34.22	140.43
Betw. Utt Pauses	30*	10	11.63	-1.55	21.71	115%	0	62
Betw. Utt Time	1.50*	0.58	0.72	-0.14	1.31	124%	0.00	3.23
W/in Utt Pauses	0	3	4.17	-0.95	7.40	129%	0	23
W/in Utt Time	0.00	0.17	0.24	-0.07	0.42	140%	0.00	1.32

OMISSIONS AND ERROR CODES

# Omitted Words	3*	1	1.30	0.08	2.69	94%	0	4
# Omitted B. Morphs	0	1	0.98	-0.21	1.76	127%	0	5
Abandoned Utts	2	4	2.50	1.85	6.84	57%	0	10
# Error Code [EO=]	1	0	0.84	-0.39	1.29	188%	0	4
# [EP=]	0	0	0.46	-0.25	0.66	223%	0	2
# [EW=]	7*	3	2.54	0.54	5.62	82%	0	9
# [EU=]	6*	2	2.31	-0.48	4.15	126%	0	10

Calculations based on complete & intelligible utterances
* At least 1SD (** for 2SDs) from the database mean

Recent analyses of the SALTRDB have turned up an additional variable which is highly correlated with age: the number of words spoken per minute. This rate variable should be useful in quantifying the verbal productivity of language impaired children. Language impaired children are frequently described as not talking very much – an observation that has not been documented in published research.

7   Testing Hypotheses about Language Disorder: Evidence from the SALT Reference Database

We will now explore characteristics of the language production of a large number of children either receiving speech and language services for language production disorders or who have been referred for the assessment of a language disorder on the basis of the Basic SALT programs. We will examine two hypotheses. The first hypothesis is that language disorder is a unitary construct, with all children exhibiting the same pattern of deficits. The second hypothesis is that language disorder is multidimensional, being characterized by different patterns of deficit in different children.

The definitions of language disorder found in the literature have been discussed earlier and each considers disordered performance to be a unitary construct. Speech–language pathologists, however, have reported several different types of language impairment (Miller, 1987, 1991). Six types of children having language disorder were identified by these clinicians:

1   developmentally delayed language
2   utterance-formulation problems
3   word-finding problems
4   rate and fluency problems
5   semantic and referencing problems
6   pragmatic/discourse problems

The measures quantifying deficits in each of these areas have been discussed in Miller (1987, 1991). Because these categories can be overlapping to some extent, it may be more accurate to discuss them as areas of deficit (Johnston, 1992). We will examine categories (1) through (4) as a test of the hypotheses above using measures from the SALT1 program. For the purpose of this analysis, categories (2) and (3) will be collapsed into a single category.

Conversation-based language samples were collected from 256 children, more than 90 percent of whom had been diagnosed as having a language disorder and were receiving language intervention. The remaining children were suspected of having a language disorder and were referred for evaluation. One hundred girls and 156 boys comprised the sample and ranged in age from two

Table 20.5 Distribution of language disordered subjects by age and sex

Age (years)	Male	Female	Total
2	2	0	2
3	4	2	6
4	8	11	19
5	23	11	34
6	17	18	35
7	28	8	36
8	24	12	36
9	12	10	22
10	8	7	15
11	10	5	15
12	5	7	12
13	9	5	14
14	6	4	10
Total	156	100	256

to 14 years. The age and sex distribution of the sample is reported in table 20.5. The conversation-based language samples were gathered using a standard protocol (Miller, 1987, 1991), transcribed into computer files using the SALT transcription format (Miller and Leadholm, 1992).

In order to explore the database for the existence of subtypes of language disordered children, three sets of language production measures were constructed. These sets of variables were chosen because they either have a history in the field or because they are robust in documenting independent domains of production strengths and weaknesses.

Variable set 1. This set of variables will document delayed development using MLU in morphemes, NDW, and TNW. These measures have been validated as indices of developmental progress for children three to 13 years of age (Miller, 1991) and demonstrate diagnostic utility in discriminating groups of normally developing and SLI preschool children (Klee, 1992a).

Variable set 2. The second set of variables will document mazes, i.e. repetitions and revisions of parts of words, words, and phrases. Mazes (Loban, 1976) have received increasing attention as indices of language deficits associated with neuropathology in adults (Garrett, 1992) and brain injury in children (Dollaghan and Campbell, 1992). Mazes as a class of behaviors have been validated as indices of utterance formulation load (Miller, 1987). Mazes are relevant descriptors for documenting both word-finding problems and utterance-formulation problems. Three maze measures were calculated for each subject: (1) the number of utterances containing mazes; (2) the total number of mazes; and (3) the percent of mazed words (calculated by dividing the number of words in mazes by the total number of words in the transcript).

Variable set 3. The third variable set will document speaking rate by calculating the number of words produced per minute, thus allowing quantification of slow or fast rates. Many clinicians have reported that children with language disorders take longer to produce a language sample with enough utterances to analyze. This variable has never been documented as a descriptor of disordered performance in the research literature but seems to have clinical face validity. At the same time, children who seem to speak very rapidly but communicate very poorly have been noted (Bishop and Rosenbloom, 1987).

An additional variable, pauses, will be evaluated to determine the degree to which they are associated with any of the three variable sets. Previously, pauses have been studied with respect to their discourse function, their relationship to mazes or speech disruptions (Dollaghan and Campbell, 1992), and their role in word-finding problems (German, 1987).

If the first hypothesis listed above is correct, then the majority of children will exhibit similar deficits as measured by the three sets of variables. If the alternative hypothesis is correct, children will exhibit several different profiles of deficit performance.

Two kinds of analyses were conducted. First, each subject's transcript was analyzed and scores were calculated for the three developmental variables (MLU, NDW, TNW), the three maze variables, the number of words per minute, and the number of pauses. Each of these measures was then compared to the relevant age group in the SALTRDB to determine if the value was within one standard deviation, or was greater than 1 SD from the mean in either direction relative to the child's chronological age peers (the direction was dependent upon the variable, i.e. mazes above +1 SD, MLU below −1 SD). One standard deviation was selected as the criterion because it reflects the statistical region used by the Madison (Wisconsin) Metropolitan School District for educational classification of suspected disordered performance. We were also interested in a liberal index where marginal performance on a number of measures could be noted. Be aware that the decision of individual school districts regarding who is disordered and who is not is typically determined by quantitative data (±1–2 SDs) as well as qualitative clinical judgments of communication impairment. (Note how circular the discussion becomes, always returning to the *definition* of language impairment!) The second analysis documented the number of children with performance above or below 1 SD for each combination of variables: developmental, mazes, rate, and pauses.

Five outcome categories of the analyses were identified: delayed development, increased mazes, slow rate, fast rate, and increased pausing. To be considered deficient in category A (see table 20.6), a subject had to exhibit performance below 1 SD on any one of the developmental measures. Deficiencies in category B meant a subject had to exhibit performance above 1 SD for any one of the maze measures. Deficiencies in the next two categories required

Table 20.6 The number and percent of subjects with performance plus or minus one standard deviation from the group mean on any of the measures of the five categories using conversational samples

Category	Number	Percent	Mean age	Age range
A: Delay	147	57.4%	7.9	2.6–14.7
B: Mazes	97	37.9%	8.2	2.6–14.8
C: Slow	98	38.3%	8.2	2.6–14.7
D: Fast	19	7.4%	7.7	4.7–11.3
E: Pauses	127	49.6%	8.5	2.6–14.8
X: Not ABCDE	20	7.8%	8.5	3.1–14.0

subjects to perform below 1 SD on words per minute to be considered as *slow* (category C) and above 1 SD on words per minute to be considered as *fast* (category D). Finally, a deficiency in category E was noted when subjects evidenced pauses either within or between utterances which were more than +1 SD higher than the SALTRDB mean. The number and percentage of subjects failing into each of the five categories is presented in table 20.6.

As can be seen in table 20.6, 147 of the 256 subjects (57.4 percent) scored at least −1 SD on one of the three developmental measures (MLU, NDW, or TNW). The age range of these subjects covered the complete range of the subject sample: 2.6 to 14.7 years with a mean of 7.9 years. Clearly, not all subjects with language disorder showed developmental delay. Miller (1991) has argued that each of these measures quantifies a different aspect of language performance: MLU – syntax, NDW – semantic diversity, and TNW – language proficiency. Each, however, correlates very highly with age in the SALTRDB.

Nearly 38 percent of the subjects demonstrated greater than +1 SD in one of the three maze categories. These measures are thought to be related to utterance-formulation or word-finding deficits. If this is representative of language impaired children in general, these deficits are reasonably frequent among children with language disorders, though clearly not all of these children exhibit disorders of this type. We interpret these data as indicating that more than one-third of these children exhibit formulation problems at the word or utterance level.

A total of 98 children (38.3 percent) produced fewer words per minute (using −1 SD as criterion) than their typically developing peers. The anecdotal observation that children with language disorders produce less talk per unit time than typically developing children is true for more than one third of these subjects. We were somewhat surprised that slow rate was distributed across the entire age range of the sample; we had expected it to be most frequent among the younger children. We expect that slow rate will be frequent among children showing delayed language performance when we examine performance across the five variable categories.

Only 19 of the 256 subjects (7.4 percent) exhibited rates above the +1 SD mark relative to their age peers. This demonstrates that some children have rate problems that run counter to the usual view that language disordered children "just don't talk very much." Anecdotally, clinicians report that these children produce very little semantic content, suggesting difficulty with specific reference. Almost 50 percent of the sample produced more within and between-utterance pauses than their age peers (i.e. greater than +1 SD). Pauses were noted if they were two seconds or longer in duration. We expect that frequent pausing may be associated with slower rates of talking and higher production of mazes.

These data were presented to examine the hypothesis that language disorder is best seen as a unitary construct. For the transcript measures evaluated here, little support is seen for such a view. Not all of the children showed deficits on any single category examined. Clearly these five categories are not exhaustive as descriptors of language disorder. There were no measures of pragmatic or discourse performance, for example. Such measures require hand-coding at this stage in measurement development. As in many previous studies, this analysis evaluated each variable as if it were independent, asking the question "Do language disordered children exhibit X?" The answer so far has always been that some do and some don't, as evidenced by the frequently contradictory outcomes of research studies evaluating single variables. The data evaluated here point out that language disorder is probably multidimensional and has yet to be described completely.

The next logical step in the investigation would involve a multivariate analysis of the dataset. When the five groups of variables are examined simultaneously, how many subjects will show a specific deficit on one variable set as opposed to showing a deficit across several variable sets? Such an analysis is beyond the scope of this chapter but it is clear that any variable evaluated in isolation will render a somewhat misleading description. The opportunity for progress seems enormous since we can now gain access to a variety of measures from a single source – the transcript. Further research will be necessary to validate specific disorder types and will require detailed simultaneous analyses of syntactic, semantic, phonological, and pragmatic performance.

8   Future Research

Computer-aided language sample analysis promises to open up many new paths of investigation in the study of childhood language disorders. Indeed, it already has. The capacity to analyze larger databases of children with and without language disorder than was once practicable is one advantage of computerization which has already been realized. We have identified four other areas which should advance the study of language development and language disorder by exploiting the transcript and the power of the computer.

1   *The development of new linguistic measures.* Thus far, computational approaches in the field of child language have involved several types of programs. There are programs that search through text files (i.e. transcripts) and count various behaviors (e.g. predefined strings of text or codes entered into the file by hand). There are programs that (attempt to) parse the utterances in the transcript. And there are programs that automate the computation of language production measures which once had to be painstakingly calculated by hand. These each marked a turning point in the analysis of child language data but in reality may offer little more than a saving in time. What is needed now is an equal expenditure of time and effort developing new linguistic measures which will shed light on the language acquisition processes of children with and without language disorder.

2   *The development of multivariate models of language disorder.* Computer software has the potential to offer simultaneous analysis of multiple aspects of language samples. Detailed study of the *relationships* among the linguistic variables observed should be of particular interest to researchers and should lead to the construction of profiles both within and across linguistic domains. This in turn may lead to the development of better models of language disorder in children. Approaching the task of description from a multivariate rather than a univariate venue will require the use of both multiple linguistic descriptors and multivariate statistical techniques (for a discussion, see Gavin, Klee, and Membrino, 1993).

3   *The longitudinal study of language impaired children.* Developmental maps as currently constituted are almost exclusively based on cross-sectional data or intensive studies of relatively few subjects. While the impact of many of these studies has been enormous in understanding developmental mechanisms and sequences, they tell us little about individual variation. Only one large-scale longitudinal study of language development currently exists which documents progress across syntactic, semantic, and pragmatic components (Wells, 1985). While longitudinal studies of normal language development are few, to date we do not have any similar longitudinal descriptive studies of large numbers of children with language disorder. While cross-sectional data offer an ideal beginning, providing opportunities to explore a range of measures across the developmental period, longitudinal data will eventually be required before models of language impairment can be advanced and tested.

4   *The development of new sampling procedures.* Finetuning the process of language sample analysis may be required in order to study specific linguistic constructions. Tailoring procedures so that specific forms and meanings can be examined in spontaneous speech will mean that the way in which language samples are typically taken (e.g. through a relatively uncontrolled conversation with a parent) will have to be supplemented by specific elicitation contexts. For instance, the child's linguistic control of various semantic themes might be explored by setting up tasks that tap temporal, spatial, or causal

knowledge. Such elicitation tasks should be able to provide deeper probes of this knowledge – and how this knowledge is mapped onto language – than do current language sampling contexts. Both Wren (1985) and Dollaghan, Campbell, and Tomlin (1990) have developed some innovative elicitation procedures which could serve as a starting point in this endeavor.

The present chapter has focused on the role computational methods have played in the analysis of language impairment. As this methodology becomes more and more linguistically sophisticated, and as larger and more diverse databases of language impaired children come to be analyzed, the field of child language stands to gain a great deal, as do the children who suffer from language impairment.

21 Phonological Impairment

LAURENCE B. LEONARD

Introduction

Part of the task of acquiring a language involves learning which speech sounds are used in the language and how these sounds are organized. For most children, this task is quite manageable; by the end of the preschool years, they produce the sounds of the ambient language accurately and contrastively, and only in the sequences permitted. However, for a significant minority of children, acquiring the speech sound system of the language is a major obstacle. The purpose of this chapter is to describe the speech sound difficulties of these children, and discuss their relevance to current accounts of phonological development.

The chapter is organized in the following fashion. First, some of the clinical classifications and terminology used in studying speech sound difficulties are introduced. Next, a summary of the characteristics of one large subgroup of children with speech sound difficulties is provided. These characteristics are then discussed in terms of the learnability problems they pose for models of phonological development. The chapter concludes with a discussion of how one such model might solve the learnability problems identified.

Some Preliminaries

Subgroups

There are many different subgroups of children who exhibit speech sound difficulties. These subgroups include children with mental retardation, children with hearing impairments, children with focal lesions of the brain, and children with autism. However, there are also children whose problems with speech sounds are not associated with such conditions. These children score at age-appropriate levels on tests of nonverbal intelligence, exhibit normal hearing, and show neither signs of frank neurological impairment nor behavioral symptoms suggestive of autism. The number of children who fall in this subgroup is not insignificant; those in the moderate to severe speech disorder range constitute approximately 2.5 percent of children in the pre-school years (Shriberg, Kwiatkowski, Best, Hengst, and Terselic-Weber, 1986). Children in this subgroup constitute the primary focus of this chapter.

The notion of phonological impairment

Early studies of children with speech sound difficulties employed the term "functional articulation disorder" to refer to the problems of these children (see McReynolds, 1988, for a representative review). In its most cautious use, this term referred only to the fact that the cause of the speech sound difficulties was unknown. However, much of the early work operated under the assumption that the deficit was one of faulty learning of articulatory gestures (see Winitz, 1969). More precisely, it was recognized that speech–motor or perceptual limitations might have been the source of the problem initially. However, it was assumed that once the child reached the point of (e.g. neuromotor) maturation at which sounds could be produced in their adult form, errors persisted due to the habits the child had formed.

In recent years, the terms "phonological disorder," "phonological disability," and "phonological impairment" have been adopted as more appropriate terms for this type of problem (Fey, 1985; Ingram, 1976; Locke, 1983b; Shriberg and Kwiatkowski, 1988).[1] The chief reason for this preference is that problems of speech sound organization are often involved in addition to, or rather than difficulties in articulatory precision. The examples in (1)–(3) illustrate this point. They come from three children with speech sound difficulties, age 3;8–4;10, studied by Leonard, Miller, and Brown (1980).

(1)   sheep → [tip]   sleep → [ʃip]

The productions in (1) reveal that the child has difficulty using [ʃ] in *sheep*. However, the errant production of [ʃip] for *sleep* suggests that the child is able to produce the sound [ʃ]. The fact that this sound was used in *sleep* but not *sheep*, however, indicates that the organization of the child's speech sound system is not appropriate.

Another example of speech sound organization problems is shown in (2):

(2)   lion → [la]   light → [da]

Here it can be seen that although [l] was not produced in the word *light*, the child used this sound in a similar phonetic context in the word *lion*. Such instances of appropriate use suggest that the child's errors were probably not attributable to the phonetic context in which [l] appeared. Instead, it appears that the problem centered on the inappropriate distinction between *lion* and *light* in the child's speech sound system.

The errors in (3) are typical of those often assumed to be due to limitations in articulatory ability, yet they, too, are not free of organizational influences:

(3) cheese → [tiz]   chip → [tIp]

It is possible that errors of this type can be traced to a difficulty with the palatoalveolar place of articulation. However, if this were the only factor, errors should be closer approximates of [ʧ]. For example, the child might have used the alveolar affricate [ts] to replace the palatoalveolar [ʧ]. Instead, the alveolar stop [t] was used. The likely reason for this choice is that [t] is a phoneme in English, whereas the closer approximate is not.

Finally, it is important to note that in the speech of children with speech sound difficulties, omission and substitution errors greatly outnumber errors that constitute within-phoneme distortions (Shriberg & Kwiatkowski, 1988). If speech sound difficulties were due principally to errors of articulatory accuracy, distortions (which appear to be near misses of the articulatory target) should represent a much higher percentage of the errors observed.

Given that errors such as those illustrated in (1)–(3) are quite common whereas distortions are not, the children discussed in this chapter will be referred to as children with phonological impairment (PI) and the general domain of difficulty will be referred to as phonology. However, it should be kept in mind that the term allows for the possibility of articulatory imprecision as well as problems of speech sound organization.

Associated problems and long-term outcome

Many children with PI also have difficulties in other areas of language, such as syntax, morphology, and the lexicon (e.g. Paul and Shriberg, 1982; Ruscello, St Louis, and Mason, 1991; Shriberg et al., 1986). In some cases, the phonological impairment probably impedes development in these other areas. For example, children who fail to use [t], [d], [s], and [z] in word-final position (e.g. *bead* → [bi], *nose* → [no]) are at a disadvantage for acquiring the noun plural -*s*, possessive '*s*, third person singular -*s*, past tense -*ed*, and contractible copula and auxiliary forms. Children who delete weak syllables in multisyllabic words (e.g. *banana* → [nana], *telephone* → [tefon]) are likely to have great difficulty using unstressed function words such as articles, uncontractible copula and auxiliary forms, and infinitival complementizers, among others. However, in other cases, a child's problems in phonology are not likely to be the direct cause of his or her difficulties in other areas of language. In such instances, a more general language disorder is likely to be present which adversely affects a range of language areas, including phonology.

Unfortunately, impairments of phonology have serious implications for future achievement. Follow-up studies of children with PI reveal significant improvement with age. However, even during adolescence and adulthood these individuals perform below the level of control groups on a range of speech, reading, spelling, and phoneme awareness tasks (e.g. Lewis and Freebairn, 1992). Residual problems are most obvious in individuals whose phonological limitations were accompanied by other language deficits during the preschool years.

Numerous studies have focused on the effects of treatment with children with PI. Although these studies have varied in their experimental rigor, improvement above the levels expected by maturation are the usual result. For example, of the 63 investigations reviewed by Sommers, Logsdon, and Wright (1992), significant treatment effects were reported in all but one.

Characteristics of the Phonology of Children with PI

In a general way, the phonological characteristics of children with PI resemble those of younger normally developing children. However, there are also some important details about these children's phonologies that make them somewhat different from those seen at any point in normal development. Some of these details have implications for theories of how children learn phonology. These similarities and differences between children with PI and normally developing children will be discussed in turn.

Some similarities between normally developing children and children with PI

Segment accuracy

Early studies of children with PI focused on these children's accuracy in producing the consonants of the ambient language. Most of these studies compared the productions of one or more children with PI with those reported in large cross-sectional studies of normally developing children. In the cross-sectional studies, each consonant of the language was assigned a particular developmental age based on the percentage of children at a particular age who used that sound accurately in a particular number of word positions.

For example, table 21.1 lists the productions obtained in a speech sample from a child with PI, age 3;4, who participated in a study reported by Leonard (1982). In table 21.2, these productions are organized according to the word-initial consonant of the target word. The consonants are listed according to the developmental ages provided by Sander (1972). The developmental age represents the age at which at least 51 percent of the normally developing children in that age group used the consonant accurately in at least two of

Table 21.1 Productions of a child with phonological impairment

Word	Child's production	Word	Child's production
away	[we]	pig	[pɪk]
baby	[bebi]	plate	[pe]
ball	[ba]	ride	[waɪ]
bed	[bɛ]	school	[ku]
boat	[bo]	shoe	[U]
chair	[te]	shovel	[to]
chicken	[tɪ]	spoon	[pun]
clock	[kak]	this	[dɪ]
cow	[kaʊ]	top	[tɔ]
daddy	[dædi]	tractor	[kaka]
duck	[gʌk]	walk	[wɔ]
fall	[wɔ]	there	[we]
fly	[paɪ]		
got	[ga]		
hide	[haɪ]		
leg	[le]		
man	[mæ]		
more	[mo]		
no	[no]		

three word position (initial, medial, final). Because the early studies did not include children younger than two years of age, consonants showing percentages well above 51 percent at 24 months were classified as "before 2."

The pattern of data shown in table 20.2 is highly representative, though, because this child is quite young, his phonological impairment would be considered less serious. The child produced all of the "before 2" consonants accurately in initial position, whereas no consonant with a developmental age of four years or higher was used with accuracy. Each of the two-year consonants was produced accurately at least once, though errors were seen in particular words. Finally, only one of the three consonants with a developmental age of three years was produced accurately.

Of course, the child's phonology was much more limited in word-final position. In this position, even many before two-year and two-year consonants were in error. For example, [m] was omitted from *man*, [p] was omitted from *top*, [t] was omitted from *plate*, [d] was omitted from *bed, hide,* and *ride,* and [g] was omitted from *leg*.

Although a few exceptions will be noted later in this chapter, the literature supports the general conclusion that children with PI are likely to show greater accuracy on consonants associated with younger ages, and limited accuracy on consonants associated with older ages. Reports of the converse – accuracy

Table 21.2 Productions of a child with phonological impairment listed according to the developmental age of the word-initial consonant of the target

Consonant	Developmental Age[a]	Productions
n	before 2	no [no]
m	before 2	man [mæ], more [mo]
p	before 2	pig [pIk], plate [pe]
b	before 2	baby [bebi], ball [ba], bed [bɛ] boat [bo]
w	before 2	walk [wɔ], where [we]
h	before 2	hide [haI]
t	2	top [tɔ], tractor [kaka]
d	2	daddy [dædi], duck [gʌk]
k	2	clock [kak], cow [kaU]
g	2	got [ga]
f	3	fall [wɔ], fly [paI]
s	3	school [ku], spoon [pun]
l	3	leg [le]
r	3	ride [waI]
ʃ	4	shoe [U] shovel [to]
ʧ	4	chair [te], chicken [tI]
ð	5	this [dI]

[a] Age at which at least 51 percent of children in age group produced the sound in at least two of three word positions (Sander, 1972).

on consonants such as [r], [ʃ], [tʃ], and [ð] and errors on those such as [m], [p], [t], and [w] – are simply not found in the literature.

In contrast to the work on consonants, few investigations have dealt with the use of vowels by children with PI. The studies that have been conducted (e.g. Hargrove, 1982; Pollock and Keiser, 1990; Stoel-Gammon and Herrington, 1990) have not produced identical results. However, there is general agreement that vowels reported to appear earlier and with greater accuracy in the speech of normally developing children (e.g. according to Wellman, Case, Mengert, and Bradbury, 1931) are also produced with greater accuracy by children with PI. Vowels that are used with only limited accuracy by children with PI are typically those that are more troublesome as well for young normally developing children.

Distinctive features

One of the obvious shortcomings of segment analyses is that each consonant or vowel is treated as if it were independent of all others. Even the early studies of segment accuracy recognized that segments share characteristics with other segments and that two segments can be more or less similar to one another based upon the number of characteristics shared. However, this notion was best captured through application of distinctive feature analyses.

The most frequently adopted distinctive feature system was that of Chomsky and Halle (1968). In this system, the similarities and differences between segments are captured through the use of features with binary (+/−) values. Thus, the similarity between [p] and [f] is represented through the shared values for a number of features: [−vocalic], [+consonantal], [+anterior], [−coronal], [−voice], and [−nasal]. Differences are limited to the fact that [p] is [−continuant] and [−strident], whereas [f] has the opposite value for these two features. Importantly, errors, too, can be described by means of distinctive features. In fact, errors on several different segments might be described in terms of a single distinctive feature pattern. For example, errors such as *pea* → [bi], *tea* → [di], and *key* → [gi] can be described as difficulty with [−voice].

An illustration of the utility of distinctive features is provided in table 21.3. The distinctive feature error patterns reflected in this table are those gleaned from the consonant segment errors shown in table 21.2.

It can be seen that the child's errors cluster around certain features. Most notably, no sounds with the feature [+ strident] were used, nor any sounds that were both [− vocalic] and [+ continuant]. The remaining segment errors were limited to particular words or word positions; for these errors, distinctive feature analysis offers no special advantages.

Comparison of the distinctive feature error patterns of children with PI and those of normally developing children reveals a great deal of similarity. For example, Menyuk (1968) reported that young normally developing children use the features [+ nasal], [+ voice], and [− coronal] earlier and more frequently

Table 21.3   Distinctive feature error patterns of child with a phonological impairment

Error pattern	Target consonants affected
[+ strident]	[f], [s], [ʃ], [ʧ]
$\begin{bmatrix} - \text{vocalic} \\ + \text{continuant} \end{bmatrix}$	[f], [s], [ʃ], [ð]

than features such as [+ continuant] and [+ strident]. The same generally holds true for children with PI.

Phonological processes

The appearance of Stampe's (1969, 1973) work brought on a significant change in the manner in which children's phonology was examined. The most notable change was the use of phonological process analysis to capture generalizations about a child's speech. Phonological processes are systematic sound changes that affect classes of sounds or sound sequences (Edwards and Shriberg, 1983). Some examples can be seen in table 21.4, which shows the segment errors of table 21.2 in terms of phonological processes.

The phonological processes that are most common in the speech of young normally developing children appear to be the most frequent in the speech of children with PI. For example, cluster reduction, gliding, final consonant deletion, and weak syllable deletion occur with relatively high percentages in normally developing children of approximately 24 months of age (Prater and Swift, 1982; Preisser, Hodson, and Paden, 1988), with the first two of these persisting for some time. These processes also appear to be among the most prevalent in the speech of children with PI (Edwards and Bernhardt, 1973; Hodson and Paden, 1981; Ingram, 1976, 1981b; Leonard, 1982; Schwartz, Leonard, Folger, and Wilcox, 1980).

Implicational laws

Several studies have examined the composition of the phonetic inventories of children with PI. The focus of some of these studies was to determine whether these inventories permit one to posit implicational laws, that is, whether the presence of particular phonetic distinctions in an inventory implies the presence of another type of distinction.

To illustrate this approach, the productions shown in table 21.1 are arranged in terms of an inventory in table 21.5. It should be noted that this is a rather generous rendering of the data, because a few of the sounds occurred only

Table 21.4 Phonological processes reflected in the speech of a child with phonological impairment

Phonological process	Examples	Exceptions
Cluster reduction	clock [kak], fly [paI] plate [pe], school [ku], spoon [pun], tractor [kaka]	——
Final consonant deletion	ball [ba], boat [bo], chair [te], chicken [tI], fall [wɔ], got [ga], hide [haI], leg [le], [mæ], more [mo], plate [pe], ride [waI], school [ku], shovel [to], this [dI], top [tɔ], walk [wɔ], where [we]	clock [kak], duck [gʌk], pig [pIk], spoon [pun]
Final devoicing	pig [pIk]	——
Liquid gliding	ride [waI]	leg [le]
Palatal fronting	chair [te], chicken [tI], shovel [to]	——
Stopping	fly [paI], shovel [to], this [dI]	——
Velar assimilation	duck [gʌk], tractor [kaka]	leg [le], pig [pIk], walk [wɔ]
Weak syllable deletion	away [we]	——

Table 21.5 Phonetic inventory of a child with phonological impairment

Labial	Alveolar	Velar	Glottal
p b	t d	k	g
m	n		
	l		
w			h
	Vowels		

once, and it is not clear whether all of them constitute true oppositions in the child's phonology. The criteria used for assuming oppositions can make a significant difference in the findings, as Ingram (1988a) had pointed out. Following this approach, the child's use of vowels as well as nonvowels suggests a distinction according to the [syllabic] feature. The presence of the glide [w] as well as true consonants such as [b] indicates a distinction according to the [consonantal] feature. Because nasals such as [n] and the liquid [l] were used as well as stops such as [d], a distinction according to [sonorant] can be assumed. Among the stops, alveolars occurred along with labials (and velars), creating a distinction according to [coronal]. The stops also showed a distinction according to [voice] given the presence of both [p] and [b], [t] and [d], and so on. Finally, the sonorant sounds can be divided, given the presence of the liquid [l] as well as the nasal [n], warranting a distinction according to [nasal].

Dinnsen, Chin, Elbert, and Powell (1990) adopted this approach in a study of the phonetic inventories of 40 children with PI. These investigators wished to determine whether the implicational laws posited for the children with PI matched those implicit in the inventories of younger normally developing children. According to the data obtained by Dinnsen et al., whenever there were distinctions of [voice] in the speech of the children with PI, there were distinctions of the features [syllabic], [consonantal], [sonorant], and [coronal]. In turn, distinctions of [continuant] (e.g. [f] as well as [p], [s] as well as [t]) occurred only when there were also the distinctions noted above. Distinctions of [nasal] were seen only when all of the above distinctions (including [continuant]) were also present. Finally, if distinctions of [strident] (e.g. [θ] as well as [s]) or [lateral] ([r] as well as [l]) were noted, the remaining distinctions were also present.[2] Dinnsen et al. (1990) concluded that these implicational laws were the same as those suggested from the inventories of young normally developing children studied by other investigators (e.g. Stoel-Gammon, 1985).

Subphonemic distinctions

For some time it has been known that not all of the changes in young children's pronunciations over time are apparent from an analysis at the level of the phoneme. In some cases, changes that more closely approximate the adult system are noted only at a subphonemic level through acoustic analysis. The same appears true for some of the productions of children with PI. For example, the productions of word-initial voiced and voiceless stops by young normally developing children sometimes differ in voice onset time (VOT) even when judges transcribe all of them as having been produced with a voiced stop (e.g. Macken and Barton, 1980). Similar findings have been reported for children with PI (Forrest and Rockman, 1988; Gierut and Dinnsen, 1986; Maxwell and Weismer, 1982; Tyler, Edwards, and Saxman, 1990). As is found with normally developing children, the voiceless targets were produced with longer VOTs.

Vowels that precede final voiced stop consonants have longer durations than those that precede final voiceless stop consonants. For some children with PI, as with young normally developing children, these same differences can be detected even when the final consonants themselves seem to have been omitted (e.g. Weismer, Dinnsen, and Elbert, 1981) or produced as a glottal stop (Smit and Bernthal, 1983). Other reported differences that are in line with developmental changes include differences in frequency and transition rate of the second formant of /r/ targets versus /w/ targets (Huer, 1989), differences in rise of the second formant in vowels preceding targets with a final velar stop versus no final consonant (Weismer, 1984), and spectral differences between the first 40 milliseconds of word-initial /t/ versus word-initial /k/ targets (Forrest, Weismer, Hodge, Dinnsen, and Elbert, 1990).

Avoidance

Another characteristic of early child phonology has been termed avoidance. Detailed observations of young normally developing children's spontaneous speech suggested that some children avoid the use of words whose adult forms contain certain sounds or syllable shapes (e.g. Ferguson, Peizer, and Weeks, 1973; Macken, 1978; Menn, 1976). This tendency was confirmed in experimental studies conducted by Schwartz and his colleagues (Leonard, Schwartz, Morris, and Chapman 1981; Schwartz and Leonard, 1982; Schwartz, Leonard, Loeb, and Swanson, 1987). In these studies, young children were presented with novel words whose phonological characteristics either resembled those of words already used by the child or bore no resemblance to the characteristics of the words that the child had attempted in the past. The findings indicated that the children produced a greater number of the novel words that conformed to their existing phonologies than novel words that were inconsistent with their phonologies. Interestingly, the children's comprehension of the two types of words did not seem to differ.

Leonard and his colleagues (Leonard, Schwartz, Chapman, Rowan, Prelock, Terrell, Weiss, and Messick, 1982) examined the same question in a study of children with PI and a comparison group of normally developing children matched for expressive vocabulary size and mean length of utterance. Both groups were found to produce more words that were consistent with existing phonologies than words that were inconsistent. Comprehension performance did not vary as a function of the phonological composition of the word for either group.

Sensitivity to ambient language

Children with PI resemble younger normally developing children in another important respect. The errors of both groups of children are influenced by the phonetic characteristics of the phonemes being acquired as well as the types of sounds in the ambient language that might serve as plausible substitutes. Children's errors in /l/ and /r/ provide a useful illustration of this point. The

Table 21.6   Common consonant substitutions of /r/ and /l/ by both normally developing children and children with phonological impairment in three languages

English		Italian		Swedish	
Target	Produced	Target	Produced	Target	Produced
r	w	r	l, n	r	h
l	w, j	l	r, n	l	j

errors shown in table 21.6 represent frequent consonant substitutions for these sounds in three different languages, (American) English, (Northern) Italian, and (Southern) Swedish (e.g. Bortolini and Leonard, 1991; Nettelbladt, 1983). The errors reflected in this table are representative of both normally developing children and children with PI within a language. However, it can be seen that there are differences across languages.

There are some good reasons why the errors look the way they do. In Italian, both /r/ (a trill) and /l/ are alveolar. The glides /w/ and /j/ occur only in a limited number of contexts, and are not even reflected in the orthography of the language. Therefore, children having difficulty with /l/ or /r/ could either use the other as a replacement, or choose another phoneme in the language that is also realized as an alveolar sound and shares many of the same features, such as /n/. In fact, the children's use of /n/ for /l/ and /r/ was context specific; /n/ replaced these sounds only when they preceded consonants such as /t/, /d/, and /ts/. It should be noted that these phonetic contexts permit the appearance of /n/. For example, the error [sɔndi] for *soldi* [sɔldi] "money" reflects the same context seen in *mondi* [mɔndi] "worlds."

Relative to English and Italian, the substitution of /h/ for /r/ in the Swedish date seems quite unusual. However, in Southern Swedish, the dialect from which these data were obtained, /r/ is realized as uvular. The replacement sound /h/ is phonemic in Swedish, and, given its glottal characteristic, may have been the most reasonable substitute for /r/. As in English, Swedish /l/ is often replaced by [j]. However, errors of [w] for /l/ are not common, as they are in English. It is no coincidence that [w] is not phonemic in Swedish; it occurs only in borrowed words.

The fact that the errors produced by children with PI are usually phonemes that are phonetically similar to the replaced sound suggests that these children are somewhat sensitive to the phonological details of the ambient language. Such findings are important because they suggest that these children's errors might be more adequately characterized as phonotactically licensed compromises than as articulatory gestures that simply miss the mark. Based on the specific selections they do and do not make, children with PI stand out first and foremost as learners of a particular phonological system – be it that of English, Italian, Swedish, or some other – and, only secondarily, as being rather poor in the process.

Some differences between normally developing children and children with PI

Although the phonological characteristics of children with PI resemble those of younger normally developing children in many respects, there are certain differences. In some cases, additional data are needed to confirm that these differences hold across a larger number of children. For example, although the feature [+ strident] seems to be among the last to appear in the speech of both normally developing children and children with PI, Menyuk (1968) observed that once segments carrying this feature appear in the speech of normally developing children, the [+ strident] feature is relatively resilient, even if other features in the target sound are in error. In contrast, children with PI seem to retain the [+ strident] feature least often. Data from children with PI reported by Leonard (1973) and McReynolds and Huston (1971) seem to support the latter observation. Additional data from young normally developing children would be helpful in determining whether this apparent difference in types of errors committed on [+ strident] target sounds is a real one.

The differences discussed below are better documented. The first seems to have a straightforward explanation. The remaining differences are more difficult to explain, and serve as a challenge for models of phonological development.

Voicing

Children with PI are not as proficient as age-matched normally developing children in their ability to produce voicing contrasts in word-initial stops (Catts and Jensen, 1983). Nevertheless, this aspect of phonology seems to be a relative strength in these children. In a comparison of children with PI and younger normally developing children with similar consonant inventory sizes, Ingram (1981b) noted that prevocalic voicing was a frequent error only in the normally developing group. Schwartz et al. (1980) found evidence of prevocalic voicing in the speech of both children with PI and younger normally developing children; however, unlike the case for the normally developing children, this type of error was never the most frequent for the children with PI.

Two investigations that measured the voicing contrast in terms of VOT have yielded similar findings. Farmer and Florance (1977) found that a group of children with PI showed VOT values for word-initial stops that approximated those seen for normally developing children of the same age. In a study of children with PI and younger normally developing children matched for both vocabulary size and consonant inventory size, Leonard, Camarata, Schwartz, Chapman, and Messick (1985) found that VOT differences between word-initial voiced and voiceless stop consonant targets were more frequent in the productions of the children with PI. However, a study conducted by Bond and Wilson (1980) had a somewhat different outcome. These investigators reported that although the pattern of VOT development shown by a group of children with PI resembled that of a group of normally developing children matched for mean length of utterance, the children with PI showed a greater tendency toward prevoicing.

More recently, Ingram (1990) examined the voicing contrast question through an analysis of the types of distinctions that were reflected in the consonant inventories of a large group of children with PI and a comparable group of younger normally developing children. Ingram found that whereas place distinctions appeared before voice distinctions in the speech of the young normally developing children, the reverse was often true for the children with PI.

These findings make it clear that children with PI show greater ability to produce voicing contrasts than younger normally developing children who are similar in many other aspects of phonological ability. A reasonable explanation for this advantage is that in these studies the children with PI have been more advanced in neuromotor development. It has been proposed that whereas short-lag (voiced) stops allow considerable variability in the coordination of oral and laryngeal movements, long-lag (voiceless) stops require a higher degree of neuromuscular coordination (Gilbert, 1977; Kewley-Port and persron, 1974). Because the children with PI have been older than the normally developing children in these studies and were seemingly normal in their physical development, it seems likely that they had attained a higher level of neuromotor development as well.

Unusual errors

Children with PI appear more likely than younger normally developing children to produce errors of an unusual nature (Leonard, 1985). Such errors are remarkable for reasons that go beyond their low frequency of occurrence. Some of these involve presumably later-developing sounds replacing presumably earlier-developing sounds. Examples include [s] for /h/ (Edwards and Bernhardt, 1973), [l] for /w/ (Lorentż, 1974), [l] for /k/, /t/, and /g/ (Weiner, 1981), [v] for /d/ and /g/ (Grunwell, 1981), and /θ/ for /f/ and /w/ (Weiner, 1981). Another example can be found in the productions of Child 1 in table 21.7. These productions constitute a representative sample of those observed in the speech of a child with PI studied by Leonard and Brown (1984). This child used [s] in word-final position of all words whose adult forms ended with sounds other than /m/, /b/, and /p/. Consequently, [s] replaced earlier sounds such as /n/, /t/, /d/, and /k/ as well as others.

Another type of unusual error is seen when the child's production constitutes an addition to the adult form. For example, Ingram's (1976) analysis of data first reported by Hinckley (1915) revealed instances of nasals added to

Table 21.7 Unusual productions of three children with phonological impairment

Child 1[a]	Child 2[b]	Child 3[c]
blue [bus]	finger [n̥ᶠga]	doll [gʌ]
bread [bɛs]	sand [n̥ᶠkan]	door [go]
cook [kus]	scarf [n̥ᶠga]	more [go]
door [dʊs]	shoe [n̥ᶠgu]	mud [gʌd]
girl [gɜs]	shop [n̥ᶠsk]	sad [gæ]
go [gas]	smoke [n̥ᶠmoUk]	sail [gæ]
light [was]	snake [n̥ᶠneI]	sock [ka]
one [wʌs]	soft [n̥ᶠd]	sword [gɔ]
snow [nos]	string [n̥ᶠtIn]	tired [gad]
two [tus]		turn [kɔ]
crib [kIp]		do [du]
cup [kʌp]		me [mi]
home [hom]		see [si]
		tie [ta]

[a] From Leonard and Brown (1984).
[b] From Grunwell (1992).
[c] From Leonard and Leonard (1985).

the initial position, such as [mbU] for *book*. Similar examples have been reported by Pollock (1983). Examples of nasals seemingly added to final position and inserted before alveolar stops (e.g. [bɜːnd] for *bird*) have been observed by Grunwell (1981) and Edwards and Bernhardt (1973), respectively. Grunwell (1981) has also reported cases of labial consonants added to initial position (e.g. [bahə] for *owl*. Some of the productions of Child 1 in table 21.8 can also be treated as instances of addition. It can be seen that [s] was used in final position of several words whose adult forms end in vowels (*blue, go, snow, two*).

Unusual productions can also take the form of consonants not found in the ambient language (or, in some cases, any natural language). Examples from English-speaking children with PI include the use of alveolar affricates (Fey, 1985), lateral fricatives (Edwards, 1980; Grunwell, 1992), ingressive lateral fricatives (Grunwell, 1981), ingressive alveolar fricatives (Ingram and Terselic, 1983), and productions involving nasal friction and/or snorts (Beebe, 1946; Edwards and Bernhardt, 1973; Hall and Tomblin, 1975). Another example can be seen in the productions of Child 2 in table 21.7. The errors of this child with PI were described by Grunwell (1992) as involving a voiceless alveolar nasal with audible nasal friction.

In some cases, unusual substitutions seem to be triggered by the appearance **of** some other type of sound in the word. For example, Willbrand and

Kleinschmidt (1978) observed a child with PI whose substitutions served to prevent nasals and stops from appearing in the same word. Thus, a word such as *mop* was produced as [bap] whereas *ten* was produced as [nɛn]. Grunwell (1981) observed children with PI who altered consonants such that they differed from the place of articulation of the consonants closest to them (e.g. [tɛŋ] for *ten*, [doʰman] for *postman*). Child 3 in table 21.7 also showed context-specific errors. This child with PI produced [k] or [g] in initial position whenever the adult form contained a nonlabial consonant in initial and final position (Leonard and Leonard, 1985).

Unsystematic application

Variability is one of the hallmarks of early child phonology, and children with PI, too, provide ample evidence of it. In some cases, careful inspection of adjacent vowels (e.g. Camarata and Gandour, 1984; Grunwell, 1981; Leonard, Devescovi, and Ossella, 1987), or the prosodic structure and syllabification of the word (Chiat, 1983, 1989) reveals that the observed variability in the speech of a child with PI is in fact systematic. However, it also appears true that children with PI are more likely than younger normally developing children to show variability even when the phonetic contexts of the words and the children's own consonant inventories provide no rationale for it. Grunwell (1981, 1992; Grunwell and Russell, 1990) has provided several different reports of cases of this type. An extreme example can be seen in Martin's (1991) study of a child with PI who used six different word-initial consonants yet showed a total lack of contrast in this position.

There is also evidence that unusual patterns are adopted less systematically by children with PI. Leonard, Schwartz, Swanson, and Loeb (1987) explored this question by presenting three types of novel words to young normally developing children and children with PI. The first type contained consonants that the child had already used appropriately in a majority of instances ("in phonology" words). The second type contained consonants that the child had apparently attempted a number of times in the past but never produced accurately ("attempted" words). These sounds had been involved in more common processes such as stopping and palatal fronting. The third type of word contained consonants that the child had neither produced not attempted in the past ("out of phonology" words). The word positions and phonetic contexts in which the sounds appeared were carefully controlled to ensure that the classification of the novel words was appropriate.

Leonard et al. expected that the greatest number of unusual productions would be observed for the out of phonology words because the children did not seem to have an available production solution for them. Consequently, one might be invented. Indeed, this was true for the normally developing children. The percentage of unusual productions for out of phonology words was more than twice that seen for either of the other word types. The findings for the children with PI were quite different. Not only did these children exhibit a higher percentage of unusual productions overall, their pattern across the three word types differed from that of the normally developing children. The percentage of unusual productions for in phonology and attempted words was as high as that observed for out of phonology words. Given that production solutions were already available for in phonology words (viz. accurate production) and attempted words (viz. use of a common and previously employed phonological process), there seems to be no clear reason why the percentage of unusual productions should have been so high for these two word types.

Phonology and the lexicon

A final difference between children with PI and younger normally developing children lies in the relationship between phonological development and lexical development. Ingram (1987) has advanced the proposal that the extent of a child's phonological disorder is a consequence of an inverse relation between the child's stage of phonological development and the size of his or her vocabulary. It is not clear if this proposal has ever been directly tested. Furthermore, in current practice, the diagnosis of a phonological impairment is usually made independently of the size of a child's lexicon. However, Ingram's proposal does center around a crucial point: children with PI are usually functioning with a much larger vocabulary than younger normally developing children who show roughly similar phonological abilities. That is, although children with PI are often slow in lexical development, their phonological development typically lags even further behind (see Shriberg et al., 1986).

It should be pointed out that phonological difficulties themselves might have an adverse effect on lexical development. Gathercole and Baddeley (1989) have reported evidence that children's performance on a test of immediate phonological memory (repeating nonwords) serves as a predictor of vocabulary ability. In a subsequent study (Gathercole and Baddeley, 1990), these investigators found that children with lexical deficits perform poorly on tests of this type. Because phonological memory serves to hold new words in store until a representation can be formed, poor memory might lead to a decay of the new material before a representation is complete. Thus, each word must be encountered additional times for an adequate representation, a process which would slow the development of new words. Of course, it must be established that the difficulties of children with PI include limitations in phonological memory. Given that a number of children with PI show only minimal or no delays in lexical development, it is not clear how many children will provide evidence of this type.

The Use of Data from Phonological Impairment to Assess Models of Phonological Development

The learnability problem

One of the empirical conditions that must be met by any satisfactory theory of language learning is the "developmental condition" (see Pinker, 1979, 1984), which requires a theory to predict the intermediate stages of development. As was seen above, children with PI do not have quite the same profile as normally developing children at any point in time. Most notably, these children's vocabulary development outpaces their phonology, and some of the production solutions they adopt in response to this limitation seem to be both unusual and quite unsystematic. Yet because these children eventually acquire the adult system, a theory of phonological learning must also be able to accommodate their particular pattern of development.

Leonard (1992) provided an examination of how alternative models of phonological development might account for the early word productions from a child with PI. It appeared that one model – the interactive activation model of Stemberger (1987, 1992) – was especially well suited for data of this type. Some of the details of this examination will be reviewed here. First, the child's productions will be presented, followed by a discussion of how the interactive activation model might account for them. Some tests are also proposed that would determine whether independent evidence for the model can be obtained and whether predictions based on the model are different from those that might be derived from other models. To pursue the latter question the general characteristics of three other models are summarized and their specific predictions based on the same data are discussed.

Early productions of a child with PI

Table 21.8 shows the initial and subsequent words of a child with PI, age 4;0, reported in Leonard (1992). The child was observed only after the subsequent words had already been acquired. The initial words were those acquired earlier according to the mother's diary, but the transcriptions appearing in table 21.8 were based on the child's productions of these words at the time of observation. For expository purposes, the words in the table are arranged according to the syllable shape (e.g. consonant + vowel) of the child's productions.

Interactive activation model

Stemberger (1987, 1992) has offered a connectionist model as a plausible account of the characteristics of child phonology. This model, the interactive activation

Table 21.8 Productions of a child with phonological impairment

Initial words	Subsequent words
baby [bebi]	doggie [gagi]
daddy [dadi]	
mommy [mami]	
bee [bi]	kiss [ki], [dis]
broke [bo]	
coat [ko]	
duck [dʌ]	
no [no]	
juice [dus]	eyes [das], [a]
shoes [dus]	
out [a]	
up [ʌ]	

model, attempts to do away with explicit procedures for deriving pronounced forms from perceived forms. In this model, information is encoded in terms of units that are organized in different levels. Production begins at the semantic level, proceeds to the word and syntactic level, then goes to the syllable level, the phoneme level, then the feature level, before reaching the motor programming system. As processing begins at each new level, partial information is passed down to the next level. Thus, a unit receives activation from sources at various levels. Finally, as the activation of lower-level units increases, the activation is passed back to higher levels and can influence the activity at these higher levels. A clear example of these feedback effects is seen when the child possesses fewer output patterns than are operative at higher levels. In these circumstances, the existing output patterns change the higher-level patterns through feedback, so that they are more in line with those at the lower level. An important aspect of this model is that if the previous productions that are fed back up to higher levels share several characteristics this leads to a "gang effect," such that the shared information is mutually reinforced.

The advantages offered by this type of model have already prompted other researchers to apply connectionist notions to the study of young children's early productions (e.g. Leonard and McGregor, 1991; Menn and Matthei, 1992). However, in order to apply this type of model to the speech of children with PI, an additional step is necessary. Specifically, a plausible source of disruption must be proposed. Leonard (1992) made the assumption that children with PI learn in the usual way but that for these children the activation that is fed back up to higher levels is disproportionately high. That is, forms actually produced burn a more lasting imprint on the child's phonology than should occur. The effect is a greater role played by higher levels in the model

Figure 21.1   (a) Initial words produced by a child with phonological impairment and composites of gang effects. (b) Composites of gang effects and subsequent words produced by child.

(a)

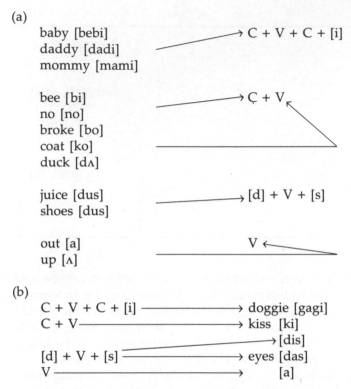

(b)

$$C + V + C + [i] \longrightarrow \text{doggie [gagi]}$$
$$C + V \longrightarrow \text{kiss [ki]}$$
$$\longrightarrow [dis]$$
$$[d] + V + [s] \longrightarrow \text{eyes [das]}$$
$$V \longrightarrow [a]$$

(e.g. word, syllable levels) than is ordinarily assumed for children who are developing normally.

Given this assumption, the interactive activation model might account for the productions in table 21.8 in a manner illustrated in figure 21.1a and 21.1b. The initial words *baby, daddy,* and *mommy* share several characteristics at the syllable, feature, and even phoneme levels. According to Stemberger's model, this leads to a gang effect such that the shared information is mutually reinforced. The shared information is presented in figure 21.1a as a composite, although in keeping with the model, this composite should be viewed as the product of a dynamic interaction rather than as a static entity. To capture the elements that are statistically favored by the gang effect, the composite is labeled C + V + C + [i], where C refers to consonant, and V refers to vowel.

The composite C + V is used not only for the words *bee* and *no*, but also for three words (*broke, coat, duck*) that contain word-final stops in the adult form but were produced with no final consonant. The assumption here, permitted by the model, is that the child had no available motor programming routine for final stops. Diverted arrows are used in figure 21.1a to reflect this. Importantly, because these words are produced as open syllables, they are operating functionally like the words *bee* and *no*. That is, the activation that is passed back up to higher levels is that of a consonant plus a vowel. Consequently, these words, too, contribute to the composite C + V.

The words *juice* and *shoes* (both produced as [dus]) share several characteristics. It can be assumed that no motor programming routines were available for initial fricatives and final voicing, and that, in their absence, the most similar routines available were activated. The shared information that was reinforced is shown in figure 21.1a as the composite [d] + V +[s].

The remaining words in the child's initial set were *out* and *up*, produced as [a] and [ʌ], respectively. Again it can be assumed that the absence of a motor programming routine for final stops led to the production of open syllables, and that activation that was fed back up the system reinforced the shared information. In figure 21.1a, the shared information is represented as the composite V.

The manner in which the model might handle the child's subsequent productions is shown in figure 21.1b. As noted earlier, an important factor is the assumption of disproportionately high activation that is fed back up the system. The result is that the gang effects will exert a powerful influence on the child's subsequent words.

The first production shown in figure 21.1b, [gagi] for *doggie*, is not handled especially well by the model. To be sure, the gang effects stemming from the child's earlier words make it highly likely that *doggie* would be produced as C + V + C + [i]. However, there is no mechanism that ensures that the two consonants will be the same, even though all of the child's earlier multisyllabic words had this characteristic. Productions such as [dagi] and [dadi] should be just as likely as [gagi] according to the model.

The child produced the word *kiss* in two different ways, as [ki] and as [dis]. The two pronunciations can be attributed to the word being subject to two influential gang effects, C + V, which permits initial velars but no final consonant, and [d] + V + [s], which requires the initial consonant to be [d] but permits final [s].

The remaining word, *eyes*, was also produced in two different ways. Again, the presence of two different pronunciations can be attributed to the word being subject to two influential gang effects, namely, [d] + V + [s], which permits final [s] but requires [d] in initial position, and V, which permits a vowel in initial position but does not permit a consonant in final position.

How does this type of model accommodate the more distinctive characteristics of children with PI, namely, an expressive vocabulary considerably in advance of phonological ability, and the use of unusual and unsystematically applied production solutions in response to this limited ability? The vocabulary–phonology discrepancy is handled in the following manner. The disproportionately high activation fed back up the system has the effect of forming deeply grooved paths of production for the child. When new words are forced into the grooves of one or another gang effect, the number of segments that are free to vary in the word is restricted.[3] This should have the effect of sharply curtailing the degree of segment analysis that is done, which should in turn slow up the process of phonemic development. Thus, as lexical development proceeds, the child's phonological system might be unable to keep pace.

Unusual productions are possible when the best-fitting gang effect happens to incorporate a segmant that is not found in the adult form, and the location of this segment is such that it appears to replace a segment with very different characteristics, or constitutes an addition to the adult form. The production of [das] for *eyes* represents such a case. Because the segments of the adult form that seem to have been replaced are sometimes produced by the child in words that are not influenced by the same gang effect, the unusual patterns appear to be applied unsystematically. For example, the word *eyes* would be considered an "in-phonology" word in the sense described earlier (after Leonard et al., 1987) because the child showed an ability to use word-initial vowels as well as word-final [s]. Consequently, a production such as [as] or [ʌs] would seem likely. However, according to the interactive activation model, gang effects can compete resulting in some of the productions taking a quite different form. In this case, the unusual production [das] appeared along with [a] .

Although the interactive activation model provides á feasible account of the relevant details of the phonology of children with PI in general and this child in particular, two additional steps seem necessary. The first would be to obtain independent evidence of the proposed source of disruption, namely disproportionately high activation that is fed back up the system. One means of testing this independently would be to determine if the child is more prone to perseverative productions than are younger normally developing children with comparable phonetic inventories.

For example, the child might be asked to imitate several times in succession a word that bears little resemblance to her other words (e.g. *phantom*). Following these imitations, the child might be asked to imitate another new word, one that bears some similarity to the first word imitated, but very little to the child's other words (e.g. *antler*). If the proposed source of disruption is accurate, the child should be more likely than the younger normally developing children to carry features of the first word imitated into her productions of the second word (e.g. produce *antler* with [f] in initial position and/or [m] in final position).

The second important test of the interactive activation model would be to ensure that predictions based on this model differ from those that would be made by alternative models. For example, if several other models can provide a plausible account of the productions in table 21.8, it would be important to establish that the interactive activation model differs from the others in its predictions concerning whether and how additional tokens of these words might have differed from those shown in the table if a larger sample had been obtained. This question is explored here.

Table 21.9 provides possible productions that might be observed given additional tokens of the words *juice, up, kiss,* and *eyes* according to the interactive activation model. The most important prediction is that additional

Table 21.9 Predictions of four models

Word	Interactive activation	Adultlike representation
juice	[dus]	[dus], [du]
up	[ʌ]	[dʌ], [ʌ]
kiss	[ki], [kis],	[ki], [kis],
	[di], [dis]	[di], [dis]
eyes	[da], [das],	[da], [das],
	[as], [a]	[as], [a]

Word	Two-lexicon	Nonlinear phonology
juice	[dus]	[dus]
up	[ʌ]	[ʌ], [ʌs]
kiss	[ki], [dis]	[ki], [kis],
		[di], [dis]
eyes	[das], [a]	[as], [a]

versions of the words *kiss* and *eyes* would be seen. That is, because the composites shown in figure 21.1 are actually possible products of gang effects, competition could result in combinations of these forms appearing in production. Thus, in addition to [ki] and [dis] as productions of *kiss*, the child could also produce [kis] and [di]. Similarly, for *eyes* the child could produce [da] and [as] in addition to [das] and [a].

Predictions based on alternative models

Predictions based on the interactive activation model are not identical to those that would be based on other models of phonological development. Some of these other models are briefly introduced here and their predictions for these same data are discussed.

Adultlike representation model

One of the most influential studies conducted in child phonology was Smith's (1973) longitudinal study of his (normally developing) son from age 2;2 to 4;0. Using the tools of classical generative phonology (Chomsky and Halle, 1986), Smith argued that the underlying forms of this child's productions were similar or identical to those of the adult system. In making his case, Smith proposed a set of realization rules for the child, rules that mapped the adult forms onto the child's produced forms.[4] For example, the rule in (4) captured the observation that the child produced nasal consonants as [n] when the nasal followed an unstressed vowel and the unstressed vowel was not preceded by [ŋ] (e.g. *bottom* → [bɔdin]):

(4)

$$[+ \text{nasal}] \rightarrow \begin{bmatrix} + \text{coronal} \\ + \text{anterior} \end{bmatrix} / X \begin{bmatrix} + \text{syllabic} \\ - \text{stress} \end{bmatrix} \_\_\_\_$$

where X ≠ /ŋ/

Generative phonology rules of this type provide a means of fully describing a child's phonological characteristics, a fact that was not lost on a number of investigators of children with PI who adopted similar procedures (e.g. Compton, 1970, 1976; Lorentz, 1976; Oller, 1973). Unfortunately, proposing such rules without qualification implies acceptance of the assumption that the child's underlying representations of mispronounced words are in fact similar to those of the adult. For example, the rule in (4) implies that *bottom* was perceived and stored in a manner that corresponded to the adult form, that is, that /m/ was represented in final position and followed an unstressed syllable, and that rules for producing the form converted /m/ to [n]. More recently, studies of children with PI have suggested that underlying forms do not always match those of adults (e.g. Dinnsen, 1984; Maxwell, 1979). In fact, closer inspection of Smith's own data suggests that some of his son's words may not have had an underlying form that corresponded to that of the adult system (e.g. Macken, 1980). For example, once the child seemingly acquired the ability to produce alveolar stops when they preceded syllabic /l/, only certain words with this context changed within a short time frame. It appeared as if the remaining words had been incorrectly stored as containing a velar rather than alveolar stop.

A model that assumes adultlike representations would account for the productions in table 21.8 in the following manner. First, the productions [mami], [dadi], [bebi], and [gagi] could be handled by proposing a rule that requires both consonants in the word to contain identical features. The productions [bo], [dʌ], and [ko] could be treated as the product of a rule that requires the deletion of final consonants. The variability seen in the words *kiss* and *eyes* would be cast in the form of optional rules. For *kiss*, deletion of the final consonant as well as the fronting of velars would be assumed to apply optionally. This also permits the possibility that both of these rules might apply, or neither might apply. Thus, one might expect that all four productions listed for *kiss* in table 21.9 could appear with additional tokens. However, this might also lead to the expectation that some of the early words, such as *juice*, would be subject to the same optional rules.

To account for the production of [das] for *eyes*, an optional rule that adds [d] to initial position must be proposed. Again, this rule must also be assumed to operate optionally on the child's earlier words. Hence, the entry [dʌ] along with [ʌ] for *up* in table 21.9.

One apparent disadvantage of the adultlike representation model is that the initial consonant addition rule is not well motivated. It provides a description for the production [das], but there is no evidence elsewhere in the child's word productions that offers a hint as to why a rule of this type should be proposed.

Two-lexicon model

The evidence that children's underlying representations for certain words were not the same as those of the adult led some investigators to propose that a word can have two different types of representation. As first noted by Ingram (1974), a representation that differs from that of the adult might be the result not only of an inadequate perception but also of the organizational principles that the child uses to systematize the data. Thus, the child might have a perceived form and a form that contains additional information that permits application of the rules that yield the surface forms. According to Ingram, the second of these types of forms appear as basic canonical shapes such as C + V and C + V + C + V.

Subsequently, Menn and her colleagues (Kiparsky and Menn, 1977; Menn, 1976, 1978, 1983) proposed a model that possesses some of these characteristics. This model became known as the two-lexicon model. According to this model, there is an input lexicon or recognition store that contains the information necessary for the child to recognize the word, rules that serve to preserve certain portions of the perceived form that map onto the output lexicon or production store, and, finally, articulatory instructions that apply to the output lexicon to yield the produced form. Data from several studies of the phonological development of normally developing children and the phonological difficulties of children with PI have been interpreted as consistent with the two-lexicon model (e.g. McGregor and Schwartz, 1992; Schwartz and Leonard, 1982; Schwartz, Leonard, Loeb, and Swanson, 1987). Using a somewhat different model, Chiat (1983) reported evidence of a separate input representation for a child with PI.

The two-lexicon model can provide a reasonable account of the data in table 21.8. The multisyllabic productions could be derived from canonical forms in the output lexicon of the form $C_1 + V + C_1 + V$ (where the equivalent subscripts refer to the fact that the two consonants are the same), along with specifications for the variable parameters for which the child has articulatory instructions, such as [+ velar], [+ coronal], and the like. Similarly, productions such as [no] and [bi] as well as those such as [bo] (for *broke*) and [ko] (for *coat*) could stem from the canonical form C + V along with relevant specifications of the variable parameters.

The productions [dus] for *juice* and [ʌ] for *up* and would also presumably derive from canonical forms such as [d] + V + [s] and V, respectively. This would lead to predictions for subsequent productions of these two words that are identical to those of the interactive activation model, as can be seen in table 21.9. However, the two models would differ in their predictions for the words

Figure 21.2   (a) Feature geometry of [d]. (b) Feature geometry of [g]. (c) Dorsal place spreading (shown by broken line).

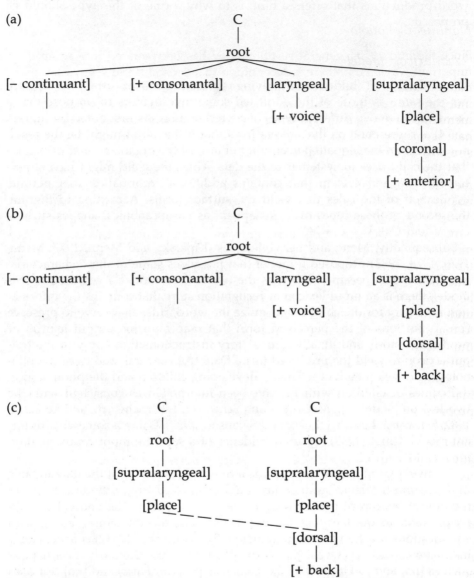

kiss, and *eyes*. In the two-lexicon model, there are only two possibilities for each of these words. For *kiss*, the canonical form C + V might be specified along with [+ velar] for the consonant and [+ high] for the vowel. Or, the canonical form [d] + V + [s] might be specified along with [+ high] for the vowel. However, there is no basis for predicting a mixture, for either one canonical form is specified or the other is. A production such as [di] should not occur. For *eyes*, the same argument applies; there would be no reason to expect a mixture of the canonical forms V and [d] + V + [s].

Nonlinear phonology

Since the mid 1970s, generative phonology has been altered in a number of important ways. First, there is recognition that prosodic and segmental information should be represented in a manner that permits both study of their independent functions and their interactions. This has led to proposals of a hierarchical representation of autonomous tiers, in which prosodic tiers dominate segmental tiers. At the level of the prosodic tier, information concerning stress assignment and syllable structure is represented.[5]

Second, at the level of the segmental tier, the features comprising each segment are organized not as unordered bundles (as in classical generative phonology) but as geometrically organized complexes such that some features are on different tiers and dominate other features. Together, these proposals offer a more realistic means of representing sound changes that operate across segments and even syllables. For example, the production [gagi] for *doggie* in table 21.8 seems to involve assimilation of place. Figure 21.2a and 21.2b provide the feature geometry of [d] and [g], respectively. The assimilation would be represented as in figure 21.2c. Only those portions of the geometry that undergo change are shown. It can be seen that the place node of [g] spreads to that of the preceding consonant slot, resulting in a change from [d] to [g]. Importantly, only the place node is involved. Given the hierarchy seen in figure 21.2, there is no reason to assume that the other nodes are affected.

Another important aspect about the segmental tier is that some features may be underspecified. That is, only those features that serve as distinctive properties in that segment or in that context are specified. As a result, some segments serve as underspecified defaults unless or until evidence from the ambient language necessitates the specification of additional features. One advantage to an assumption of underspecification is that it provides a basis for the unidirectional nature of certain sound changes. For example, [coronal] is often assumed to be a default and thus more readily replaced by features such as [labial] and [dorsal]. In fact, productions such as [gʌk] for *duck* and [bɪp] for *dip* are more common than those such as [dʌt] and [dɪt], for the same words.

Linguists differ in the degree to which they adhere to the various components of nonlinear phonology described above, and in the manner in which some of these components are characterized. However, there is some consensus on the general principles involved, and investigators have begun to apply these principles to phonological development and the study of children with PI (e.g. Bernhardt, 1992; Bernhardt and Gilbert, 1992; Chinn and Dinnsen, 1991; Gandour, 1981; Ingram, 1988b; Spencer, 1984, 1986; Stemberger and Stoel-Gammon, 1991).

A model based on nonlinear phonology offers a reasonable basis for some of the productions seen in table 21.8. Most notably, the child's use of [s] (and only [s]) in word-final position can be interpreted as the underspecified, default segment used in that position. Given that this sound is [coronal], such an interpretation is quite reasonable. The production [gagi], as mentioned earlier, is convincingly handled by means of spreading of the place node from one segment to another. Of all of the productions in table 21.8, [das] for *eyes* seems to be the most problematic for this type of model. Such a production might be described by an addition rule, but this runs counter to the major function of underspecification, which is to constrain the number and types of rules that can be applied. The motivation for a rule of addition is not apparent.

As can be seen in table 21.9, the nonlinear phonology model differs from the other three models in its predictions for *up* and *eyes*. One reason was just noted; there is no basis for expecting the addition of initial consonants. A second reason is that [ʌs] might be expected as one of the variable productions for *up*. Because [s] presumably serves as the default ([coronal]) sound for final position, it is as likely to appear in *up* as in other words requiring final consonants. This seems especially so because in this type of model, the prosodic tier and the segmental tier are autonomous, and therefore particular syllable shapes are not integrally related to particular segments as is the case for some of the other models discussed earlier.

In summary, table 21.9 makes it clear that predictions based on the interactive activation model differ from those derived from each of the three alternatives. This represents an advantage that can be added to the useful attributes of the model already discussed, namely, provision of a plausible and testable proposed source of disruption that results in lexical development well in advance of phonological development, and the ability to generate unusual and unsystematic productions. If future work confirms these impressions, this model will have passed an important litmus test. Not only will it appear reasonable as an account of the modal pattern of phonological development, it will also provide a means of accommodating the less typical but very real course of change seen in children with PI.

Summary

This chapter focused on one relatively large subgroup of children with speech sound difficulties, those whose problems with phonology seem free of complicating conditions such as hearing impairment, intellectual limitations, and frank neurological dysfunction. The speech sound difficulties of these children may be related in part to limitations in speech motor ability, but much evidence reveals that problems also exist in how these children organize sounds into a system. For this reason, "phonological impairment" seems to be the most appropriate label for these difficulties. Children with phonological impairment (PI) often have problems in other areas of language, such as syntax and morphology. Although improvement in these children's abilities occurs across time, especially with treatment, residual problems are often present as late as adolescence or even adulthood.

On most counts, the phonological characteristics of children with PI resemble those of younger children who are developing phonology normally. This holds true whether these characteristics are analyzed in terms of segments, distinctive features, phonological processes, implicational laws, subphonemic distinctions, sensitivity to details of the ambient language, or even the tendency to avoid particular sounds. However, in certain respects, children with PI differ from younger normally developing children. These children seem more likely to produce errors of an unusual nature, their patterns of production are applied less systematically, and new words enter their lexicons at a pace that seems too rapid for their limited phonological systems. These characteristics are important because together they constitute an intermediate stage of learning that should be accommodated by any successful model of phonological development. One model that seems to handle this learnability problem relatively well is the interactive activation model.

It is hoped that children with PI will be considered in future efforts to evaluate models of phonological development. Research of this type may make the dual contribution of shedding new light on the possible bases of these children's difficulties, and providing a means of choosing among two otherwise satisfactory models.

NOTES

1 The term "developmental verbal dyspraxia" has been applied to some children with serious and persisting speech sound problems. This term typically carries with it an assumption of a motor programming difficulty, possibly of a neurological origin. Unfortunately, a consistent set of criteria for making this diagnosis has not yet been established. A recent review of the work in this area can be seen in Stackhouse (1992).

2 It is interesting to note that one aspect of the inventory on table 21.5 is at variance with the implicational laws proposed by Dinnsen et al. (1990). Specifically, this child showed a distinction of [nasal] by virtue of his use of [l] as well as [n], yet he showed no evidence of a distinction according to [continuant]. However, only one word containing [l] was produced (*leg*). If a more conservative criterion for including sounds in the inventory had been adopted, no exceptions to the proposed laws would have been found.

3 Certainly some distinctive characteristics will be seen in new words that are subject to a gang effect, for specifications such as C and V permit a variety of possibilities. For example, a new word *cookie* might well be pronounced as [kuki], *tv* might be produced as [titi], and *car* might be produced as [ka]. Furthermore, certain new words might be sufficiently different in number of

syllables and stress pattern to be free of the influence of all of these gang effects. The word *banana*, for example, might be produced as [nana]. Nevertheless, the number of segments that are free to vary would be more restricted than would be the case if gang effects were not operative.

4   In Stampe's (1969, 1973) theory of Natural Phonology, it is also assumed that the child's underlying representations resemble those of the adult. Of course, in Stampe's approach, development does not involve changes in the phonological rules that are applied but rather the suppression of innate phonological processes. In the interest of space, Stampe's theory will not be examined here.

5   In fact, some of the modifications of the two-lexicon model seen in Menn (1978, 1983) were influenced by some of the same proposals in linguistics. However, because the basic character of the model did not change with these modifications, it is important to treat the two-lexicon model as separate from a model that is derived more completely from nonlinear phonology.

22 Grammatical Impairment

PAUL FLETCHER AND RICHARD INGHAM

1 Introduction

A pioneering article in this area, Morehead and Ingram (1973), set the tone for the next 20 years of research in the grammatical characteristics of specific language impairment (SLI) in children, in several ways. The language performance of the SLI group in the study was compared with a normal group judged to be their peers in *language* age; spontaneous speech data was the source of the measurements of language ability applied to both groups; and the then current model of generative grammar was the framework from which the categories of analysis were drawn. Finally, the results indicated that while the SLI children were not as successful in deploying what they knew about grammar as their normal counterparts, their grammars were not deviant in the sense that they had constructed rules which were not possible for the language they were learning. The only dimension of current research into specific language impairment not represented in the Morehead and Ingram study is an explicit comparison of the problems of English SLI children with SLI children attempting to learn another language – the so-called cross-linguistic comparison. What have we learned about grammatical impairment in English-speaking SLI children, and in similarly affected children learning languages other than English, in the 20 years or so since the Morehead and Ingram study?

As a necessary methodological preliminary to the evaluation of claims about grammatical impairment, section one of this chapter will consider the subject characteristics of SLI individuals, and the variation in definitions adopted in research to date. Section two summarizes major empirical findings on English SLIs, and considers a theoretical claim concerning the basis of their grammatical impairment. The nature of SLI in languages other than English, and the relevance of comparative linguistic studies for our understanding of SLI is reviewed in section three. Finally, in section four, we identify gaps in our knowledge of the characteristics of SLI, and indicate the main lines that future research seems likely to take.

2   Subject Characteristics

Three chapters in this section of the Handbook (this chapter, and chapters 20 and 23), deal in their different ways with nonphonological specific language impairment. This phenomenon is, in the abstract, usually defined by exclusion as a significant language deficit in an individual (usually a child, but see Gopnik and Crago, 1991) who is otherwise normal in respect of intellectual abilities and neurological status, with normal hearing and no significant medical history. In practice, however, subject selection procedures for research in SLI show considerable variation, both in terms of how the "significant language deficit" is initially defined, and with respect to the matching and background variables. Since the age, cognitive status, and linguistic status of subjects is likely to be of major significance in the evaluation of claims about the nature of SLI, we will devote some space to a more than usually detailed review of these factors and their relevance.

Table 22.1 provides details on the subjects involved in some of the research studies we consider in this chapter. The studies selected are not intended as in any way representative, but in order to illustrate the variable approaches both to subject selection and to the reporting of subject characteristics in this area. (The papers are listed in the table in historical order.) It is perhaps worth pointing out that the majority of the studies in impaired grammar acquisition have been cross-sectional studies comparing groups of normal and impaired childern. For the practical reason that language impairment is normally diagnosed quite late in the child's development, the *ab initio* detailed longitudinal study of a single child – the prototypical study in normal language development research – is not available. It is also unusual, though the reasons for this are not so obvious, to have detailed case studies of individual language impaired children from the time at which they are identified (though see Chiat and Hirson, 1987; Fletcher, 1994).

From table 22.1, a number of points emerge concerning the group studies. Authors are strikingly variable in reporting aspects of their findings (see for instance the IQ column). Numbers of subjects, especially in LI groups, tend to be small (in this set of studies the range is from six to 15). Where gender information is available in table 22.1, there are always more boys than girls, but the proportions vary. Robinson (1987), aggregating figures from ten different studies reports a sex ratio of boys to girls in the SLI population of 2.82 to 1. The ages of language impaired children included in studies vary considerably: in the papers reviewed in table 22.1 (excluding the rather special case of Gopnik and Crago) the age range is from 3;8 to 9;11. This heterogeneity on a number of fronts suggests that caution has to be observed in comparisons or generalizations across studies of the grammatical effects of SLI.

The variables most often mentioned when grammatical impairment is the focus of investigation are the SLI child's medical history/current medical status, intellectual level, and, crucially, language status. We will deal with these in turn.

2.1 Medical status

Apart from a uniform concern with hearing status, most authors give limited information on the medical history and current status of subjects included in studies. Researchers would normally rely on other professionals to have checked the hearing and neurological status of SLI children, and otherwise they tend to present with varied medical histories. Robinson (1987) reports on the relationship between various medical and physical conditions in relation to developmental language disorders. Potential causal relationships emerge in only a minority of cases. In his paper Robinson also drew attention to the higher risk of language impairment in siblings of SLI children, suggesting a genetic basis. Apart from Gopnik and Crago (1991), all the studies listed in table 22.1 include children in their subject groups who are unrelated. However, the Gopnik and Crago study of language impairment across three generations of a large British family (for details of the family see Hurst et al., 1990), familial aggregation studies (e.g. Tallal, Ross, and Curtiss, 1989; Tomblin, 1989), and studies of twins (e.g. Bishop, 1992b) are extending our knowledge of the role of genetic influence on language impairment.

Hurst et al. (1990) give details of a family of 29 individuals, 15 of whom are language impaired. Although the most salient presenting feature of the expressive language of particularly the younger affected family members is marked speech impairment, Gopnik and Crago (1991) have argued persuasively that these family members are grammatically impaired also. The size of the family, and the apparently well-defined character of the phenotype, offer the possibility that the genetic material responsible for the mutation in this family will eventually be able to be mapped and defined (Pembrey, 1992). However, as Pembrey cautions (1992: 53), mapping the gene would allow us to define a monogenic language disorder. It would not define "a 'gene for speech', and certainly not '*the* gene for speech.'"

2.2 Intellectual status

Some authors do not provide any IQ test scores for their subjects. Gopnik and Crago give no information on the intellectual status of their subjects. Fletcher (1991) relies on prior selection of his LI children into residential schools and language units (whose selection criteria in respect of IQ may differ). Morehead and Ingram (1973) selected their children from "the deviant population of children . . . seen at the Institute for Childhood Aphasia, Stanford University

Table 22.1 Subject characteristics of SLI individuals in selected studies

Study[a]	IQ[b]	Medical[c]	Other[d]
1 Morehead & Ingram, 1973 (AE)[e]			
LN = 15 (3 at each of Brown's 5 MLUm levels) CA 20–33.7 mths	No information	No information	Screened for speech and hearing pathologies
LI = 15 (3 at each Brown's 5 MLUm levels) CA 62.3–104.6 mths	No intellectual impairment	No physiological impairment	Selected from a population of language deviant children
2 Fletcher & Peters, 1984 (AE)			
LN = 20 CA = 60.86[f] mths RA[g] = 69.76 mths 68.05 mths	WISC = 73.72 mths Leiter = 71.43 mths	No significant medical history; normal hearing	Articulation normal; no oromotor problems; no oral–facial defect
LI = 9 CA = 62.33 mths RA = 48.89 mths 53.67 mths >6mth delay RDLS-E[h]	WISC = 62.29 mths Leiter = 68.5 mths	As LN group	As LN group; no speech–language therapy
3 Johnston & Kamhi, 1984 (AE)			
LN = 10 (7M, 3F)[j] CA = 36 mths MLUm[k] = 4.8	Age-appropriate Leiter = 47.2 mths	No neurological disorder; normal hearing	No speech or language impairment
LI = 10 (9M, 1F) CA = 59.35 mths MLUm = 4.81	Leiter = 61.6 mths	As LN group; no emotional disturbance	Diagnosed LI by speech pathologist in part via standardized tests of language

4 Fletcher, 1991
(BE)

LN = 12 CA = 60 mths	No information	No information	—
LI = 15 (11M, 4F) CA = 96.9 mths RA = 78.4 mths	No information	No information	From schools or units for LI children

5 Gopnik &
Crago, 1991 (BE)

LN = 6 CA 8–17 yrs	No information	No information	—
LI = 6 CA 16–74 yrs	Normal intelligence	Normal hearing	Close relatives of LN subjects

6 Leonard et al.,
1992 (AE)

LN1 = 10 CA 41–67 mths MLUw[k] 4.2–6.0	Normal intelligence	Normal hearing	Normal oral motor function
LN2 = 10 (6M, 4F) CA 35–40 mths MLUw 2.9–4.2	As LN1	As LN1	As LN1
LI = 10 (6M, 4F) CA 44–67 mths MLUw 2.7–4.2	Leiter = 107	Normal hearing; no neurological dysfunction; emotionally normal	As LN1/2 > −1SD on TOLD-P[l]

[a] See references for details.
[b] Nonverbal performance IQ.
[c] Hearing, neurological status, emotional status.
[d] Other factors: articulation; oromotor; therapy information.
[e] AE = American English speakers; BE = British English speakers.
[f] Where = used, for CA, IQ, or RA scores, indicates group mean.
[g] RA = Receptive language age as measured by standardized procedure.
[h] RDLS-E: Reynell Developmental Language Scales – Expressive.
[i] Where available, gender breakdowns for groups indicated.
[k] MLUm/MIUw = mean length of utterance in morphemes/words.
[l] Newcomer and Hammill, 1982.

School of Medicine" (1973: 212). They further claim that their SLI group did not have "sufficient intellectual . . . impairment to account for their difficulties in acquiring language."

When IQ testing is reported, the usual approach to intellectual functioning involves identifying a child as within normal limits on performance subtests of a procedure such as the Wechsler Intelligence Scale for Children (Wechsler, 1974) or on the Leiter International Performance Scale. The use of a test such as the WISC will lead to a split between verbal and nonverbal performance, with nonverbal performance within the normal range (e.g. Fletcher and Peters, 1984), or a range of scores on the Leiter International Performance Scale, similarly within the normal range. Since "the normal range" is conventionally interpreted as one standard deviation either side of the mean of the test, and since the test scores are normally distributed, about 68 percent of children will fall within these limits, indicating a potentially wide spread of intellectual abilities. Some studies report group means for SLIs on the test used: Johnston and Kamhi (1984) report a mean of 104.3 on the Leiter, while Leonard et al.'s (1992) SLI group have a mean of 107. Control children are sometimes explicitly matched to SLIs as a group, using the same test(s) as the SLIs (Curtiss and Tallal, 1991; Fletcher and Peters, 1984; Leonard et al., 1992). In other studies no information is given other than that the comparison group is "normal" (Morehead and Ingram, 1973).

In discussing the use of matching variables in experimental design, Kerlinger (1986: 289) expresses the view that unless the variable on which subjects are matched is "substantially related to the dependent variable . . . the matching is a waste of time." The use of performance IQ as a matching variable for LI and LN groups may not fit this recommendation, since it is not clear how the kinds of task typically used in these tests relate to linguistic abilities. It is not obvious that normal scores on a performance IQ test guarantee a complete cognitive infrastructure for language. We can illustrate this point, though not resolve it, by considering the use of temporal adverbials by one group of SLI.

Fletcher and Garman (1988) report that one of the features distinguishing seven-year-old from five-year-old normal children is the proportion of temporal adverbials they use (between five and seven, the proportion of adverbials increases from 0.17 to 0.30). These forms (e.g. *yesterday, on Jill's birthday, at six o'clock in the evening, on Sunday, April 5th*) are used in the adult language, in conjunction with tense and aspect selections on the verb, to specify the times at which the event described by the verb took place, and selectional restrictions operate between the tense/aspect choice and the lexical content of the adverbial (see Crystal, 1966, for details). In addition to the increase in frequency, there is also a change in semantic content of the adverbials over the period from five to seven. The proportion of what we might call "calendric" adverbials increases, from 0.00 in the case of the fives, to 0.24 of the total in the sevens. Calendric adverbials are those that, to be used appropriately, require semantic knowledge based on how the conventional system of measuring time operates, e.g. *last Monday, a week on Thursday, at six o'clock,* and so on. The SLI group in this study, all school-age children between six and nine years, pattern very like the five-year-old normals in terms of frequency of adverbials overall (0.17) and in the low number of calendric adverbials (0.04). In addition, we do find errors when an SLI child attempts calendric use, e.g. *I do go home on the weekend on Fridays and Wednesdays.*

There are at least two interpretations of this finding. One would rely on the fact that in general the SLI children patterned grammatically like the five-year-old normals rather than the seven-year-olds. Their performance on temporal adverbials could therefore be seen as in phase with the rest of their linguistic system, and so not a cause for particular concern, over and above the obvious delay they evinced. An alternative view, however, would point to the fact that the SLI children were on average much closer to the seven-year-olds in age, and hence in performance IQ. If their performance IQ predicts their general knowledge of their world, then they might be expected to know more about time and the way it is lexically coded than in fact shows up in their spontaneous speech. The question of whether we are dealing here with a grammatical deficit *per se*, in relation to temporal adverbials, or a grammatical deficit which flags a cognitive limitation, is clearly one which requires further investigation. It is instructive, however, to note Johnston's comment (Johnston, 1992: 108), in summarizing research by herself and others on SLI children's symbolic play and reasoning ability (as assessed nonverbally): "When we observe children who have normal non-verbal IQs and serious language delays, they in fact seem to be lacking the conceptual knowledge, the representational abilities, and the reasoning patterns, that would be expected for their age." While Johnston makes no explicit mention of conceptual knowledge relating to time, the Fletcher and Garman (1988) finding indicates that for at least some SLI children, this is an area for further scrutiny.

2.3 Language status

It is a truism that matching groups on more than one or at most two variables is difficult if not impossible. Since the dependent variable used in characterizing SLI is always some grammatical measure or measures, matching for language status as well as IQ is a problem. The most obvious approach would seem to be to select a group of LN children who do not differ from the LI group in age (e.g. Fletcher and Peters, 1984). While this will allow the identification of grammatical differences between the groups, these differences, it is argued, may simply reflect delay on the part of the LI subjects. If language impairment is anything other than delay, LN and LI subjects need to be of equivalent *language* age. Any grammatical deficits that are then identified in the LI group can be interpreted as impaired features. The problem is selecting an appropriate measure of language age which is not confounded with the dependent variable. Beginning with Morehead and Ingram (1973), the measure most commonly adopted (see table 22.1) has been Mean Length of Utterance, calculated either in morphemes (MLUm) or words (MLUw). Quite apart from the general problem in language acquisition studies that there is no agreed definition of what constitutes an utterance (see Fletcher and Garman, 1995), there would seem to be inherent limitations in using as a matching variable a measure of utterance length that is likely to be sensitive to grammatical properties that are the focus of inquiry. MLU is of course only relevant to language production. It is perhaps surprising that of the six studies in table 22.1, only two explicitly mention the LI or LN children's comprehension ability. It is certainly possible for comprehension and production ability to be dissociated in language development and impairment (Bates and Thal, 1991).

The main implication of the variability revealed by a consideration of the studies in table 22.1, in relation to background and matching variables, is that great care needs to be taken in attempting any general statements about the effect of language impairment on grammar. That said, we will now review some of the claims made concerning language impairment in English.

3   Grammatical Impairment in English

The investigation of grammatical impairment in English has focused on the the occurrence or nonoccurrence of elements of grammatical categories and exponents of structural types and grammatical rules, in data from spontaneous speech samples, between LI and matched LN groups. It might be instructive to recall the findings of Morehead and Ingram (1973) at this point. In writing grammars to account for the utterances of their LN and LI groups, they found virtually no differences in terms of the rules required to generate the utterances in the two corpora. It was the case, however, that the LI group showed a marked delay in the onset and acquisition of the phrase structure rules: an LI child might be delayed up to three and a half years over an LN child in the first word combinations, and could then take two years longer to reach the same stage of grammatical development as the LN child. Over and above the delay in acquisition of rules, there are quantitative differences between LI and LN groups at the same MLU-defined stage in their use of available rules. In Morehead and Ingram's study, *do*-support and NP type were cases in point. The LI group were significantly less likely to use auxiliary *do*, and significantly more likely to use NPs consisting of a simple demonstrative (as opposed to combining the demonstrative with a noun), than their LN counterparts. It is important to emphasize that in many of the studies we will review, similar findings hold: LI children's acquisition is delayed relative to normal children of the same age; the grammars they construct are very similar to normal children at the same stage of development; but LI children show a more limited ability than LNs to deploy their grammatical knowledge. It is important to emphasize that this is a quantitative difference: it is not that LI children use no agreement or tense markers or auxiliary verbs over a given

Table 22.2 Some sources of information on grammatical morphology deficits in SLI

---

plural -s
Crystal et al. (1976/90), Gopnik (1990), Leonard et al. (1992?)

3rd person singular -s
Gopnik (1990), Loeb and Leonard (1988), Leonard et al. (1991), Leonard et al. (1992a), Leonard et al. (1992b)

past tense -ed
Loeb and Leonard (1988), Leonard et al. (1992b)

aux be
Loeb and Leonard (1988), Leonard et al. (1991)

determiner the/a
Lee (1966), Leonard et al. (1992a)

infinitive particle to
Menyuk (1969), Leonard et al. (1992a)

Pronoun case-marking
Lee (1966), Menyuk (1969), Leonard et al. (1991)

---

sample, but that they use fewer of these forms than language matched normals. This immediately raises the question of whether the problem the LI children have is in building grammatical representations, or in deploying what they know about grammar under the real-time demands of production processing in conversation (Chiat and Hirson, 1987; Fletcher, 1992b; Bishop, 1993), or indeed both of these limitations.

3.1 Grammatical morphology

A recurring theme in studies of SLI in English-speaking children is summarized thus by Leonard et al. (1992a): "there is a common profile among SLI children: many are especially weak in their use of grammatical morphology." The term "grammatical morphology" here is broadly interpreted to include noun and verb inflectional morphology, pronoun case-marking, determiners, and sometimes auxiliary verbs and reduced forms of copula verbs. Table 22.2 lists sources which have produced evidence on some of these problem areas in LI individuals.

To take some examples from these studies: Crystal et al. (1976/1989) present an account of a case study in which a child aged 3;9 has the following problem areas: plural -*s*, third person singular -*s*, copula, auxiliary *be*, past tense -*ed*, and subject pronoun case-marking, as in *me want a red racing car*. Fletcher and Peters (1984), looking at somewhat older children (see table 22.1), also identify verb inflection and auxiliaries as significant discriminators between their groups. In a discriminant function analysis, the category UVF (unmarked verb form, or bare verb stem) was one of two categories that distinguished the groups, with SLIs using more bare stems than their LN counterparts. This implies that they used fewer of the grammatical resources available (tense, agreement, auxiliaries) for marking the lexical verb in English. Both of these studies use "omission in obligatory contexts" (following Brown, 1973) as the dependent measure for their inquiries. Since we know that normal children also omit morphemes from obligatory contexts, we can only conclude from the Crystal et al. study, and that by Fletcher and Peters (which used age-matched LNs) that their LI subjects are delayed in their acquisition of grammatical morphemes. The implication of the quotation above from Leonard and his colleagues is that the problem goes further. We are not simply finding a delay in LI children's grammatical morphology; the profile differences in studies that compare LIs with language-matched normals point to a specific deficit in this area.

The strongest claim concerning this deficit has been made by Gopnik, on the basis of a detailed study of language impairment in a British family. Her hypothesis is that that grammatical impairment amounts to a genetically based "feature blindness" in which

> the language errors . . . can be accounted for by the impairment of one particular language faculty – the accurate usage of syntactical–semantic features of language such as the significance of number, gender, animacy . . . tense and aspect. Grammatically consequent skills are also impaired, as in the selection of apt determiners and the omission of subject pronouns before tensed verbs. Yet other grammatical skills, such as the judgement that the sentence "he puts" is grammatical, are unimpaired.

In an experimental study that has attracted a great deal of interest because it involves members of an English family of 30 individuals across three generations, half of whom are language impaired, Gopnik and Crago (1991) seem to reinforce the findings of morphological deficit reported so frequently in nonfamilially related SLI studies. They compare six LI family members aged 16–74 years, with six family member controls on grammaticality judgment and production tasks. The judgment tests involved errors in number (e.g. *three cookie*), agreement (e.g. *the boy kiss a pretty girl*), tense (e.g. *yesterday the girl pet a dog*), and aspect (e.g. *the little girl is play with her doll*). On these tasks the SLI family members showed a marked deficit. On the production tasks also – regular past tense formation, derivational morphology, and nonsense plural formation, the LI subjects performed significantly worse than their unaffected relatives. In addition, and significantly for Gopnik and Crago's view of language impairment, their LI group's morphological deficit goes hand-in-hand with normal performance in other areas of the grammar. Their LI subjects were not significantly worse than normals in their ability to discriminate pronominals from anaphors (e.g. *he washes him* v. *he washes himself*), nor in their comprehension of gender and number marking on pronouns. Both groups were able to distinguish acceptable from unacceptable verb complementation: LI subjects were as capable as LN subjects in identifying *the girl eats a cookie to the boy*, or *the boy puts a book*, as unacceptable.

The dissociation apparent in their subjects on these tests has led Gopnik and Crago to make a rather strong claim about the basis of specific language impairment, at least in the family they have studied. They conclude that the LI subjects

> do not have the normal language learning mechanism, described by Pinker (1984), that would allow or, perhaps even compel them, to construct inflectional paradigms on the basis of regularities hypothesised from the observed linguistic evidence. This inability to construct such paradigms would result in a selective impairment of that component of the grammar that encodes abstract morphology, while sparing other linguistic abilities such as the determination of argument structures. (Gopnik and Crago 1991: 47)

Given the extensive evidence for problems similar to those in the affected family members appearing in nonrelated English-speaking SLI subjects, it might seem plausible to extend this explanation to all language impaired individuals. There are some difficulties with this, however, quite apart from the lack of comparability between the ages of subjects in the Gopnik studies and those in other studies of grammatical deficit in English (see table 22.1)

The first problem has to do with Gopnik's empirical claim. It seems as though her impaired subjects do have areas of success with "feature-related" elements. Their lack of difference from their normal relatives on pronoun/anaphor discrimination, on gender and number marking, suggests that there were at least some counterexamples to her hypothesis of "feature blindness." Secondly, the limited morphological impairment claimed by Gopnik has been questioned by other investigators of the family. Vargha-Khadem et al. (1994) confirm the affected members' morphological problems, but also point out that in comprehension testing for syntactic areas such as relative clauses, the LI group fare worse than the LNs.[1] Third, as we shall see in section three, crosslinguistic studies of nonfamilial SLI in languages other than English, where morphological problems are considerably attenuated, suggest an alternative explanation for the undoubted problems of grammatical morphology in English SLI. And finally, studies of nonfamilial SLI in English indicate that grammatical impairment may extend to other areas of the grammar.

3.2 Impairment in other areas of the grammar

How secure could we be in a generalization that the effects of language impairment on English grammar are limited to grammatical morphology, in the sense in which we have been considering it? One reason why grammatical impairment has been so strongly associated with the omission of obligatory grammatical morphemes must be methodological. In naturalistic speech samples, which have been widely used as a data source, inflectional elements occur with reasonable frequency in samples, and obligatory contexts can be identified readily. The omission of grammatical morphemes very frequently results in ungrammatical sequences, which are easily identifiable. Much of what LI children say is however grammatical, and the identification of differences between LIs and LNs depends on a comparison of *grammatical* utterances from both groups for any differences they may reveal in terms of the occurrences in the data sample of elements of a category, or exponents of a rule, or structural type. One way to interpret differences in the direction of less provision by LI children is avoidance. So, for example, Menyuk (1969) reports a less frequent use of modal auxiliaries in the LI group. We referred above to the more limited use of temporal adverbials by school-age LI children. Johnson and Kamhi (1984) also found significantly less use of adverbials in somewhat younger SLIs. One study (though see Morehead and Ingram, 1973, on the more frequent occurrence of demonstratives than demonstrative + noun sequences in LI children) has also reported a more restricted expansion of phrases in LI children's sentences than in LNs. Gavin, Klee, and Membrino (1993) found that what they term "three-element NPs" were significantly less common in the speech of SLIs (age two to four) than with age-matched normals.

An important area of grammatical organization eliminated from suspicion by Gopnik and Crago (1991) so far as the K. family is concerned, and little scrutinized by researchers into nonfamilial SLI (though see Fletcher, 1992b; Johnston and Kamhi, 1984; Van der Lely, 1994), is that of verbs and their argument structures. In a review of the grammatical problems of a group of school-age SLI children, King and Fletcher (1993) report on some infrequent errors of the omission of obligatory verb complements. Perhaps more significantly, a subset of about a third of the children studied showed particular patterns of avoidance of complement types, where the verbs they were using allowed them a choice. So, for example, where a verb (e.g. *eat*) could be either transitive or intransitive, the LI children were more likely than their normal counterparts to use the verb without an object NP. And when a verb (e.g. *move*) could be used inchoatively (as in *the truck moved*), or causatively (as in *he moved the truck*), the LI children chose the inchoative version. The selections they made resulted, as in these examples, in structures which were less complex, at least as measured by the number of verb complements.

While grammatical morphology in SLI in English has had the major share of research attention, there is evidence to suggest that grammatical impairment may show itself across a variety of domains. Before returning to the prospects for further research both in grammatical morphology and in other areas, we now turn to a review of grammatical impairment in languages other than English.

4 Grammatical Impairment in Languages Other than English

4.1 *Italian*

Crosslinguistic comparisons of SLI have a valuable contribution to make to our understanding of the etiology of specific language impairment. This is because they serve to break certain confounds that may exist in one language alone. In English, for example, there is a well known confound between grammatical morphology and lack of phonetic salience. The grammatical morphemes we discussed earlier which appear to pose particular problems for language impaired children tend to be nonsalient phonetically. Affixes such as past tense are realized as single segments which are attached to stems or as (in the case of past tense attached to a stem ending in /t/ or /d/) an unstressed syllable. Determiners and auxiliaries are liable to be unstressed. We cannot therefore be sure whether English SLIs' problems with these elements is a problem with grammatical morphology *per se* or a problem with items that lack phonetic substance.

The work of Leonard and his coworkers has demonstrated that in Italian (Leonard et al., 1987; Leonard et al., 1992b) inflectional morphology in Italian SLI children is not systematically deficient. On third person singular inflections and adjective–noun agreement, Italian SLI children aged four to five years examined by Leonard et al. (1992) did not perform significantly worse than language-matched normal children. The LIs realized third person singular agreement correctly 93 percent of the time, and also had high levels of adjective–noun agreement. Italian agreement morphemes can be argued to be phonetically more salient than English third person singular agreement morphemes. Compare Italian *lavora* (*he/she works*), with a final open vowel, with its English equivalent. The relative success of the Italian SLIs on agreement morphemes suggests that it is low-phonetic substance items, not grammatical endings *per se*, that pose problems for the English SLIs.

Another area of Italian grammar which allows us to break confounds in the evaluation of SLI children's difficulties is that of clitic object pronouns. These are reduced forms which may not appear alone; being phonetically "weak" they thus resemble English inflectional morphemes. But since they encode verb arguments they "have relatively high semantic substance" (Leonard et al., 1992: 29). In English, on the other hand, verb arguments are not encoded as preverbal clitics. This crosslinguistic difference allows one to ask whether the salient semantic status of direct object clitics – the fact that they encode a major participant in the sentence – or their nonsalient phonetic status would win out for Italian SLI children. Leonard et al. (1992) found that Italian SLI children omitted three quarters of obligatory direct object clitics, far more often than their MLU matches, while their age matches made omissions less than 10 percent of the time.

Looking at SLI from an Italian perspective, therefore, an outstanding problem for SLI children – direct object clitics – is one which does not arise in English, while a hallmark of English SLI children – third person singular agreement inflection – appears unproblematic. Intriguingly, the errors that Italian SLI children made with the past tense consisted of actuálly supplying agreement where none was required. The Italian past tense requires an auxiliary and a past participle form (e.g. *Anna ha telefonato, Anna e tornata*). If the auxiliary is *essere*, the past participle has to agree in number and gender with the subject. If the auxiliary is *avvere* no agreement is marked. The Italian SLI errors incorrectly made the past participle with an *avvere* auxiliary agree with its subject.

Leonard et al. (1987) and Leonard et al. (1992) report that adjective–noun agreement was almost impeccable in their Italian SLI subjects, while Leonard et al. (1993) found no gender agreement errors between article and noun.

Although the overall figures for article omission in Italian reported by Leonard et al. are quite high, it is important to note a certain selectivity in omission, which relates to the issue of phonetic salience. Articles ending with a consonant (*il, un*) were highly likely to be omitted, articles ending in vowels (e.g. *le, una*) were unlikely to be omitted.

4.2   German

In certain respects the characteristics of German SLI closely resemble English SLI. Using a corpus of German SLI children aged three to nine years, Clahsen (1991a) reports that articles, auxiliaries, and copula forms are very frequently omitted. Many errors, according to Clahsen, are also found with case morphology. Pronouns and articles are incorrectly case-marked. Verb inflections, as in English, are also vulnerable:[2]

Uschi hier *wohn*?
does Uschi live here
(adultlike: wohnt Uschi hier)

hund da *komm*
dog there come
(adultlike: da kommt der hund)

hier *kommen* der
here come he
(adultlike: hier kommt der)

In one important respect, however, German SLIs show a grammatical deficit not shown by English SLIs. This is in the domain of word order. Clahsen's own data showed that "verb-final patterns are dominant" for most of the children he studied. This is the correct position in German for a nonfinite verb, but for a finite verb in German declarative sentences the normal place is as the second constituent of the sentence. Since nonimperative main clauses require finiteness in order to be grammatical in German, word order in the following SLI examples is unadultlike:

dosse daun musik machen
big clown music make-INF   Klaus 2

Julia aepfel essen
Julia apples eat-INF   Julia 2

It should be noted that verb-final position with SLIs is not limited to verbs with the infinitive inflection. Many verb forms in final position are stem forms:

ich auch ein auto fahr
I too drive a car

ich ers haus bau
I first build a house

Clahsen (1991a) reports a few instances of sentence-final finite modal forms, e.g.:

aufziehn will   Julia 1
julia fische angeln will Julia 1
aber du nich darf   Petr 2

Most modals used by German SLIs are, however, in medial position.

German word order errors are of particular significance as regards theories of grammatical impairment. As we have seen, attempts to demarcate areas of specific impairment in the grammar of LI children have focused on inflectional morphology. A linguistic approach to grammatical impairment would predict that if two aspects of grammar are directly related, both should be impaired, while if they are not directly related, they need not both be impaired. In English, word order is not a function of inflectional morphology, but in German it is. Research shows word order to be unimpaired in English SLIs, but quite seriously disturbed in German SLIs. So, according to Clahsen, German SLI children's word problems can be seen as a by-product of morphological difficulties.

It is interesting, however, that the one child in Clahsen's data who did acquire the verb inflectional paradigm nevertheless did not at the same time acquire the correct placement of verbs with finite inflections. This should be the second constituent of the sentence (the so-called V2 rule). The following examples are clear V2 violations:

dann ich immer *musz* hier malen
then I still must paint here

und dann die *haben* elche
and then they have elks

das der noch *spritzt* das Wasser, ne?
that the still sprays the water, no?

ich das *mache* jetzt
I do that now   Petra 3

The examples suggest that there is no immediate relation in a German SLI child's system between the acquisition of agreement inflection and of correct placement of a finite verb.[3]

A further question one might have about the validity of Clahsen's analysis is that German SLIs' sentences were ungrammatical in more ways than morphology and word order. For example, obligatory direct object omissions were made:

ander mal holen geht
another time fetch go   Andreas 1

du dann komme
= du bekommst es dann   Jonas 2

ich aengen auf das
I'll hang (it) on that   Petra 1

ich auf tis stes
I on table put   Wolfgang

Here, German SLIs may be overgeneralizing a resource of the language. Unlike English a topicalized direct object may be omitted:

(Adult: Do you need another little man?)
Ne, brauch ich nich   Patrick

This is a perfectly adultlike alternative to *Ne, das brauch ich nicht*. The topicalized pronoun *das* can be omitted, leaving the verb in sentence-initial position (ignoring the syntactically irrelvant *ne* ("no"). The omitted direct object can thus be analyzed as a zero topic which does not violate adult grammar. But where there is a constituent in preverb position, the V2 rule disallows topicalization:

Ja? Du brauchen?   Patrick
Yes? You need?

The missing direct object here cannot be analyzed as a zero topic, and therefore does violate adult grammar.

The research reviewed has documented a range of difficulties experienced by German SLI children with the grammatical requirements of their language, but as with English, a unified account of their problems remains elusive.

4.3   Grammatical impairment in other languages

Linguistically informed research into SLI in other languages is of very recent origin, but we will mention a few studies that indicate that, crosslinguistically, SLI can take different forms.

Dromi, Leonard, and Shteiman (1993) studied Hebrew-speaking SLI children's grammatical morphology and found a rather low level of correct peformance on verb tense inflections, well below that of their chronological age peers. The only grammatical variable reported on which SLIs did significantly worse than MLU matches, however, was the accusative case marker-*et*, but even here performance was correct about 85 percent of the time. Noun–adjective agreement was usually correct, as with Italian SLI children.

However, the belief that the more morphology a language has, the better SLIs will perform on morphology, is one that should perhaps not be pushed too far. Crago, Allen, and Ningiuruvik (1993) report findings from a study of a language impaired child learning the Greenlandic language Inuktitut, which has an extremely rich system of verbal and nominal morphology. They found frequent omissions of verbal inflections marking person, number, and modality. These inflections were virtually all present in the speech of a child of the same chronological age.

Like German and Dutch, Swedish has a verb-second rule: Hansson and Nettelbladt (1991) report frequent errors whereby SLI children disregard this rule, placing two constituents before a finite verb. LN Swedish children make such errors (Platzack, 1992):

Den bara blaser
it just blows

precis Embla har pa tradet
just Embla has on the tree   Embla 23–5 months

The finite verb forms *blaser* and *har* should be in second position. What we have seen of SLI children's problems with verb morphology in German makes it unsurprising that the verb-placement rule, linked as it is to the verb form, should be problematic for Swedish SLIs.

5   Conclusions and Future Directions

It is unlikely that specific language impairment will eventually be seen as a homogeneous disorder with well-defined consequences for the grammar of those it affects. The absence of a clear etiology, and the consequent lack of clear identificatory criteria, plus the confounding influences of development and remediation in older subject groups, virtually guarantee extensive variation in any sample selected for research purposes. This can lead to apparently contradictory results. Gopnik and Crago (1991), for example, in their experimental tasks, find that their LI subjects have some problems with regular plurals. Oetting and Rice (1993) however, in a detailed study of the acquisition of plural in children with specific language impairment, conclude that "by five years of age, children with SLI demonstrate a productive and differentiated plural system." It is important when assessing these differences to remember that the Gopnik and Crago subjects ranged in age between 16 and 74 years, that is, across the three generations of the family being investigated. This family is unusual in two ways: first, because of the remarkably high incidence of a language disorder in its ranks (almost half of family members affected), and second, because half of the affected members are female. In the population of SLI at large, the sex ratio is more like three males to every one female. The possibility does arise, therefore, that the impairment described in the K. family is somewhat atypical, and hence perhaps only truly comparable with another family showing a similar incidence and sex ratio. More generally, in assessing and interpreting characterizations of grammatical impairment in SLI, it will be increasingly important to match linguistic sophistication with careful subject descriptions across all relevant variables, and where possible subject histories.

In continuing to explore grammatical impairment in English, it would be an advantage to adopt a wider perspective on the range of grammatical problems LI individuals can show. It would clearly be premature to assume that grammatical morphology constituted the alpha and omega of impairment in English. A wider perspective may however require methodological innovation in both data collection and analysis. Computational advances, for the storage and dissemination of data, and for some automatic analysis (see Miller and Klee, chapter 20, this volume) promise much. Naturalistic data will remain an important source both of information about the SLI child's grammatical system and speech production processing systems, and a source of hypotheses to be tested. But naturalistic data, however plentiful, may not always suffice.

In the study by King and Fletcher (1993), the omission of obligatory verb complements by LI children was found to be rare. This conclusion is however based on spontaneous speech samples each of which contained 63 lexical verbs. All but one of the children produced more verbs than this, but since this one child was a three-year-old normal required as a match for one of the LI individuals, and as we needed a consistent number of verbs across subjects, this was the number of verbs involved in the analysis. As we have already pointed out, speech samples of half an hour (or even 15 minutes in length) will contain numerous opportunities to identify grammatical morphemes. In a total of 63 verbs, however, it is unlikely that a particular verb will appear more than once. It is thus difficult to come to a reliable assessment of the child's mastery or otherwise of a verb's complement structure. It is not clear that extending the length of speech samples would solve this problem. As Bishop (1993) observes, "experimental studies are now needed to complement naturalistic data and provide a more efficient way of investigating the conditions which influence accuracy of production and comprehension of specific grammatical forms." It is difficult to see how children's knowledge of the grammatical requirements of verbs can be fully tapped without resorting to elicitation and experimental procedures.

Moving beyond English in the characterization of grammatical impairment has given the study of SLI a new dimension and some problems. Once a comparison is made with a language with a different morphological structure, the somewhat telegraphic character of the output of (particularly the younger) English SLIs is seen to be a consequence of their language's rather limited morphology. As with adult aphasics (see, for example, Bates, Friederici, and Wulfeck, 1987) the impaired grammar reflects the shape of the target language. One problem the comparative linguistic exercise raises relates to comparability of subjects. For the comparison of English and Italian SLI to work, the children involved must be at the same level of linguistic development. Leonard and his colleagues took great care in the design of their studies. However, ensuring that LN and LI children compared within a language are at the same level of linguistic development is not straightforward, given that we are using mean length of utterance as the matching variable. The within-language difficulties must be compounded once we move to across-language comparisons.

Grammatical impairment remains a partially explored region. Improved mapping, and a fuller understanding of the area, will require careful description on the part of its surveyors, and some ingenuity in interpreting the features they observe.

NOTES

1 Gopnik's most recent report on the family seems to acknowledge a more extensive grammatical impairment than first claimed (Gopnik, in press).

2 SLI children do use the third person singular inflection -t, but Clahsen found that it appeared almost exclusively with intransitives, and claims that it is a semantic marker of intransitivity, not an agreement marker. However, his transcripts show that where plural subjects of intransitives are overt or indicated in the gloss we do not find the -t

morpheme. Since -*t* is not overgeneralized to third person plural contexts, this suggests that, at least in terms of number, it may have an agreement function, contrary to Clahsen's claim.

3 Clahsen's position is based on normally developing German children; he concluded that it is the acquisition of agreement morphology that triggers the acquisition of verb-second. This claim has been called into question by Verrips and Weissenborn (1992) who offer evidence that verb position is acquired as a reflex of verb finiteness, well before the agreement system is acquired.

23 Pragmatic Impairments

HOLLY K. CRAIG

Pragmatics is one of the newest lines of inquiry in childhood language disorders. Its status as an emerging investigative focus necessarily means that it is in a period of transition. This transition is an exciting one. As researchers focus upon identifying the legitimate problems and methodologies for a scientific inquiry of this type, considerable debate has ensued regarding the nature and importance of developing a pragmatic theory of childhood language disorders, the priorities for an associated research agenda, and the standardization of appropriate research protocols. This debate is lively, impassioned, and fundamental to the process of an emerging paradigm (Kuhn, 1970).

It is my purpose in this chapter to identify the core issues involved in conceptualizing pragmatic impairments while giving readers the flavor of the debate in childhood language disorders, to provide selected clinical examples that demonstrate our state of understanding and of questioning at this time, and to suggest future research directions given our current knowledge. This discussion will draw heavily from some of my own previous work focusing upon children with specific language impairments (SLI). This is a population of children with language disorders for whom pragmatics seems fundamental, both in terms of characterizing the nature of their language problems and in developing specific and effective clinical management programs. As Gallagher (1990) reminds us, the very earliest definitions of language disorders were rooted in the negative social consequences associated with communication problems. As VanRiper (1939) observed, a communication disorder draws attention to itself, interferes with communication, and overall isolates the individual from his/her environment. A focus on pragmatics in SLI is intuitively attractive as it has potential to revisit these original insights. Pragmatic research on SLI mirrors all of the advantages and problems associated with defining and studying pragmatic impairments, and thus presents a clear focal point for probing key issues.

Children with SLI demonstrate significant language problems in the absence of a known etiology. The terms "language disordered," "language delayed," and "language deviant" are other terms that have been used to reference this population of children with nonorganic language problems. At this time, they are identified most frequently using Stark and Tallal's (1981) exclusion criteria, which includes: no hearing loss or history of long-term recurrent otitis media; no significant emotional or behavioral problems; no below average intelligence; no neurological problems; and no sensory or oral defects. The Stark and Tallal exclusion criteria are widely used. A notable exception, however, is the work of Bishop and colleagues who apply the term specific language impairment to a population with histories that can include significant recurrent otitis media or neurological disease (see subject descriptions of Bishop and Edmundson, 1987; then Adams and Bishop, 1989; Bishop and Adams, 1992). For the purposes of the present discussion, the term SLI will be used and will reference the less heterogeneous population identified using the Stark and Tallal exclusion criteria.

Definitions of Pragmatic Impairments

Pragmatics is the study of language usage, and "pragmatic impairments" then is the term that refers to clinically significant problems in using language. Approaches to the study of communication failures reflect two quite different theoretical perspectives about the nature of pragmatic rules. They vary specifically in their representations of the relationships among pragmatic rules and other rule systems within the language hierarchy. Prutting and Kirchner (1987) and more recently McTear and Conti-Ramsden (1992) present succinct descriptions of these approaches highlighting how each differs in terms of the hypothesized relationships among language components. Although a number of pragmatic models underly study of the discourse processes by the normal-language user, only two theoretical approaches have guided the study of pragmatic impairments. Figure 23.1 is an attempt to depict these differing organizations schematically.

Modularity: A competence-based model

In the modular approach pragmatics has been viewed simply as a conversational analog to phonology, syntax and morphology, and semantics. In the same way that one can describe phonology in terms of phonemes and phonological rules for combining or constraining their interrelationships, pragmatics is viewed as a set of pragmatic entities such as speech acts and the pragmatic rules governing their occurrence. Impairments are viewed as problems in acquiring basic constituents, such as speech acts. Modular competence-based models stand in direct opposition to recent performance-based models, especially the Competition Model which will be discussed more fully in the next section. In brief, performance-based models define problems in using

Figure 23.1 Two theoretical approaches to the study of pragmatic impairments.

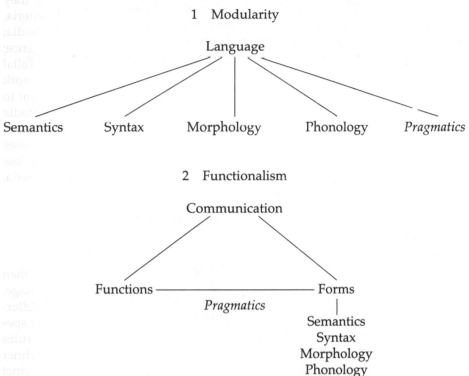

1 Modularity

Language

Semantics   Syntax   Morphology   Phonology   *Pragmatics*

2 Functionalism

Communication

Functions ──────────── Forms
Pragmatics

Semantics
Syntax
Morphology
Phonology

pragmatic entities like speech acts, in real time, whereas the competence-based approaches emphasize the role of the entities themselves.

Prutting and Kirchner (1987) labeled the modular approach the "pragmatics-as-separate" view, and McTear and Conti-Ramsden (1992) describe it as "pragmatics as a level of linguistic analysis." Johnston (1988b) has noted that this approach has been the most widely adopted when studying pragmatic impairments. It has enjoyed the longest tenure as well, introduced to childhood language disorders originally by Bloom and Lahey in 1978. Theoretically, as a conversational analog to other linguistic systems, pragmatic rules should exist in parallel with other linguistic rule systems. Emphasis, then, is placed upon distinguishing levels of meaning, particularly semantic rules (those governing sentence meanings), from pragmatic rules (those governing discourse meanings).

All of these interpretations share an emphasis on the independence of pragmatics from other linguistic systems. Modular approaches can be applied readily and comfortably to the study of pragmatic impairments because, as discussed by Craig (1983), they imply few changes to traditional research strategies in childhood language disorders and, further, any change should be relatively narrow in scope. Accordingly, from a modular perspective, a child with a

Table 23.1   A sample of Clark's responding during adult–child discourse with his mother. The child holds a toy wrench and hammer, and a toy cash register is on the floor nearby. Utterances are enclosed in quotation marks and nonverbal behaviors are in brackets.

Mother	Child
	(tapping the top of the cash register repeatedly with a toy wrench)
"makes noise"	
	"no"
"do you hear the noise?"	
	(continues tapping)
"hear it?"	
	"airplane" (puts the wrench on top of some blocks and moves them around the floor)
"airplane? what airplane?"	
	"up sky" (points to ceiling with wrench)
"up in the sky" "do you like the noise the airplane makes?"	(puts the wrench back down on top of one of the blocks)
	"huh?"
"do you like the noise the airplane makes?" "buzz-z-z-z"	(pauses and looks up at his mother)
"can you be an airplane?" "buzz-z-z-z" (puts her arms out to the side, extends them, and waves them like wings)	
	(drops toy wrench and extends arms out to side and waves them like wings)

primary pragmatic impairment would present intact or at least less impaired phonology, morphology, syntax, and semantics, but significantly deficient discourse rules. There would be an obvious discrepancy between the child's knowledge of pragmatic entities like speech acts, compared to his/her competence in other linguistic domains.

What evidence is there of pragmatic impairments when a modular approach is applied to the study of SLI? The answer overall is: very little.

Within the context of Searle's (1969, 1974, 1975) influential Speech Act Theory, the discourse functions characterizing the communications of the child with SLI have been examined extensively in terms of communicative intents. The empirical heuristic within this paradigm has been to probe the child's discourse for evidence of intact or missing functions. The presence of a full range of speech acts would imply intact pragmatic knowledge, whereas a limited repertoire and/or absence of those functions apparent for normal-language children would be interpreted as evidence of a pragmatic impairment. The presence or absence of the functions have been prioritized, rather than rules governing their occurrence, as has been more typical of the study of phonemes, morphemes, and sentence meanings.

Overall, this line of research has not revealed a critical absence of major discourse functions. Compared to normal-language age-mates and/or younger children at apparently the same language developmental stages, children with SLI evidence essentially the same major speech acts, including requesting, commenting, responding, and clarifying. They formulate these discourse functions with different and often less effective forms, but their knowledge of the functions themselves has been demonstrated repeatedly (Blank, Gessner, and Esposito, 1979; Brinton, Fujiki, Winkler, and Loeb, 1986; Gallagher and Craig, 1984; Gallagher and Darnton, 1978; Leonard, 1986; Leonard, Camarata, Rowan, and Chapman, 1982; Liles, 1985a, b, 1987; Merritt and Liles, 1987; Skarakis and Greenfield, 1982; Van Kleeck and Frankel, 1981).

The investigation of responding in this population is exemplary of how the modular approach can be applied to the study of pragmatic impairments. Responding is a major type of speech act and it is by definition dyadic, so it has been a primary focus for pragmatic studies of SLI. Considerable research reveals that children with SLI respond to prior requests and comments, but compared to age-mates their responses are likely to be unrelated to the partner's prior utterance or to be semantically inappropriate (Brinton and Fujiki, 1982; Brinton et al., 1986; Craig and Gallagher, 1986). Compared to younger children with similar mean lengths of utterance (MLU), children with SLI fail to maximize their structural skills such that the same types of responses occur regardless of the children's language structural level (Gallagher and Darnton, 1978). In addition, they may be more dependent upon discourse properties like the recency and saliency of the underlying referents (Craig and Gallagher, 1986). Considered as a whole, children with SLI respond, but in linguistically atypical ways.

Tables 23.1 and 23.2 present selected clinical examples from two children

Table 23.2 A sample of Jimmy's responding during adult–child discourse with his clinician. The two are working cooperatively on the building of a castle from a kit of building materials. Utterances are enclosed in quotation marks, nonverbal behavior are in brackets, and unintelligible words or phrases are represented by dashes.

Clinician	Child
"it's hard to find these little things, isn't it?"	
	"mhm"
	"there now we got a flag"
	(places a flag on top of a brick)
	"let's see"
	"I think I remember –"
"you think what?"	
	"I , I think I might done it, before"
"you might have what?"	
"built one of these before?"	
	"yeah, maybe"
"where at?"	
	"oh at my aunt and uncle's house"
	"she bought, he, uh, bought it Jeff, like, um, for my cousin Jeff"
"oh yeah?"	
	"Mike helped make that for me"
"did you build this castle before?"	
	"no"

diagnosed as SLI and are offered as a way to illustrate some of the key points in this discussion. Table 23.1 is from the spontaneous mother–child conversations of "Clark," a four-year-old boy with SLI. From a modular perspective, Clark's discourse includes response behaviors more often than not, indicating a knowledge of speech acts of this type. In particular, he acknowledges a prior comment ("no"), and produces a neutral clarification query ("huh?"), a special kind of listener respondent behavior. Further, he says something back to his mother after three of her six questions. Clark's utterances, however, are comprised of only one or two word phrases, indicating a clinically significant reduction in expression relative to chronological age expectations.

Within the modular paradigm, the lack of well-formedness in his responses seems due to nonpragmatic inadequacies. By implication, if he said more, the listener would be able to discern the way in which "airplane" for example, constituted an appropriate response. From this perspective, Clark's deficits appear primarily linguistic rather than pragmatic. He does not meet the test for a pragmatic impairment within this paradigm because the speech act is present in his discourse. Any interactive difficulties he experiences are best characterized as pragmatic performance problems, problems that are the result of deficits in linguistic competence. Although no clinician would ever come to these kinds of conclusions based upon a small sample of behavior like this, if findings were consistent across a variety of clinical assessment contexts and supported by other assessment data, one could conclude that Clark has a problem with linguistic rather than pragmatic knowledge. Specific interventions would be tailored accordingly, so that clinical management would focus primarily upon improving the form of his utterances. Sentence lengths should be increased, and basic subject–verb–object constructions established (e.g. "airplane" → "I hear airplane"), thereby resolving his language difficulties.

Table 23.2 presents a sample of spontaneous clinician–child conversation by "Jimmy," an 8 1/2-year-old boy with SLI. Like Clark, Jimmy's discourse includes responses, in this case to a variety of clinician questions. His sentence formulation skills are more advanced than Clark's so that his sentences reflect basic subject–object relationships and some complex syntactic structures, for example the noun phrase complement ("I think + *clause*"). They also evidence specific syntactic and morphological errors. Again, however, Jimmy does not meet the test for a pragmatic competence problem within a conversational analog paradigm because the response speech act is present. By implication, if his answers were better grammatically, his language problem would be resolved. Consequently, from a conversational analog perspective, Jimmy's intervention program would be designed to improve and further strengthen the form of his utterances.

These clinical examples also illustrate the special interpretive challenges encountered when studying pragmatic impairments. To the extent that reciprocal talk indexes responding, both Clark and Jimmy are responsive. However, most scoring taxonomies for children with normal language (for example, Dore, 1979) reflect semantic continuity as well, so that topic changes and unrelated turns are readily discernible. The communicative intents of children with SLI are less obvious. For example, is Clark's "airplane" utterance intended as a response, or as a comment about a symbolic relationship between the toys that he is manipulating? The mother interprets Clark's "airplane" utterance as a topically related response, tying it back to the notion of noise in her prior discourse ("do you like the noise the airplane makes?"). Is Jimmy's "Mike helped make that for me" an affirmative response to the prior adult utterance, or a new idea, perhaps about some previous history with a toy set like this? The partner is not sure how to interpret this utterance, queries a possibility, but the child says "no." Clearly, both Clark's and Jimmy's responses are not well formed, as the partners do a disproportionate share of the conversational work.

This line of inquiry reveals critical problems in message construction by children with SLI in the context of apparently intact speech acts. When forms and functions are examined separately, children with SLI appear to have difficulties with the ways they formulate speech acts rather than with the completeness of their speech act repertoire. From this perspective, children with SLI do not present pragmatic competence deficits. Their language deficiencies are not manifested as omissions of frequent discourse functions; instead their problems appear rooted in linguistic structure. Perhaps, however, the study of conversational constituents other than speech acts would reveal pragmatic impairments, and our failure to find pragmatic differences compared to children with normal language within the conversational analog paradigm is due to the unit of discourse analysis involved.

Presuppositions, narratives, and turns are other discourse units that have been studied for SLI. The language production of children with SLI reflects a knowledge of presuppositional principles comparable to that of children with normal language. They construct informative messages by foregrounding new information and backgrounding old information (Snyder, 1978; Rowan, Leonard, Chapman, and Weiss, 1983; Skarakis and Greenfield, 1982). The ways in which children with language problems formulate these relationships involve different and often less effective forms than those used by children who are developing language normally. Remarkably similar to the findings for dialog, children with SLI also evidence knowledge of the narrative's constituents, including episodes, abstracts, and the need for coherent ties between subcomponents. Again, however, children with SLI depend upon a fairly limited and often ineffective or erroneous set of linguistic forms during production (Liles, 1985a, b, 1987; MacLachlan and Chapman, 1988; Merritt and Liles, 1987; Sleight and Prinz, 1985). Turns have been examined to some extent by Craig and Evans (1989). The only notable difference between the turn exchange patterns of their subjects with SLI and both chronological age-mates and MLU-matched control subjects was for conversational interruptions. Although a relatively infrequent discourse behavior, interruptions were powerful in effectively gaining talking time for the normal-language subjects. Most of the children with SLI, however, failed to interrupt their adult partner in order to secure the turn at speaking. All other turn exchange features were like those for the normal-language children. Overall, talk proceeded quickly and smoothly without speaker overlaps most of the time.

Considered as a whole, research interpreted from the modular perspective fails to reveal pragmatic knowledge deficits. When presence of the discourse unit of analysis, independent of how well it is formulated, is the litmus test for impairment, then children with SLI seem pragmatically competent. They present intact pragmatic knowledge, but have communication problems presumably due to their obvious linguistic limitations. Consequently, there seems to be no pressing need to develop a pragmatic theory of SLI.

Citing these conclusions, Connell (1987) has argued that pragmatic approaches have little to contribute to clinical management of this population, as the evidence fails to support characterizations of children with language disorders as presenting pragmatic impairments. His recent research has maintained this position and focused upon interventions that target isolated morphological forms (Connell and Stone, 1992). In a like manner, Leonard and Loeb (1988) have argued in favor of studying language disorders from the perspective of government and binding theory. They propose that this reformulation (Chomsky, 1981) of the previous theory of transformational grammar has the potential to explain particular aspects of language disorders. For SLI, the domain of inquiry once more as in the past would become strictly structural.

The functionalist approach: A performance-based model

An alternative approach treats pragmatics not as a separate module, but as an interactive, competitive system. Bates, MacWhinney, and colleagues have proposed a Competition Model for conceptualizing language, its acquisition, and its disorders (Bates and MacWhinney, 1987, 1989; Bates, Thal, and MacWhinney, 1991; MacWhinney, 1987, 1991b). The Competition Model is a connectionist theory in nature. Importantly for a theory of acquisition and impairments, it is fundamentally probabilistic. Accordingly, language is viewed as a complex set of weighted form–function mappings. Two principles determine linguistic occurrences, cue validity – the importance of a cue in a particular language, for example word order in English – and cue cost – its efficiency, for example how readily it is perceived.

The Competition Model has considerable potential as a way to further our understanding of pragmatic impairments. Crucially, it distinguishes between the acquisition of form–function mappings, and the use of these mappings in real time. Rather than conceptualizing pragmatic rules as a system in parallel to other linguistic systems, pragmatics can be viewed as an additional system of patterns that establishes linkages between linguistic forms and discourse functions (see figure 23.1). Accordingly, pragmatic knowledge consists of a set of connections that are interactive in nature, specifying the dependent relations between forms and functions. McTear and Conti-Ramsden (1992) describe this in terms of "pragmatics as relating language form and language use." Prutting and Kirchner (1987) also discuss "pragmatics-as-perspective," and "pragmatics-as-cause–effect." The latter is essentially a more specific modification of the "perspective" view in which communicative effectiveness is prioritized, a factor of special relevance clinically. In my own work, I have called these functionalist approaches a "broader" interpretation of pragmatics (Craig, 1983, 1991). All of these views are less modular in character and share an emphasis on the interrelationships between language rule systems.

Potential vagueness is a possible limitation when interpreting pragmatics from a functionalist perspective. If "pragmatics" were to be interpreted as a simple substitute for the overarching "language" of prior linguistic and conversational analog models (something not presented in the figure as it does not seem viable), then this view would be too general to be useful and would contribute little in the way of new insights or predictions. The "pragmatics-as-perspective" approaches seem particularly susceptible to this type of problem. In this view, pragmatics involves study of the interactive outcomes of competence problems in other components of the language hierarchy. Accordingly, pragmatic impairments would never be more than a performance problem, and what isn't pragmatic? This view provides little direction to the study of pragmatic impairments and no clear conceptual advances from those gained by the conversational analog approach.

I have become acutely aware of the need for placing boundaries on definitions of pragmatic impairments from the study of access behaviors in a sample of children with SLI (Craig and Washington, 1993). We examined the verbal and nonverbal behaviors used by seven and eight-year-old children with SLI to join previously established dyads. Chronological age-mates and MLU-matched normal-language controls accessed the play of partners quickly and easily, using cooccurrences of verbal and nonverbal behaviors. The subjects with SLI, however, formed two subgroups. One subgroup like the normal groups was successful in accessing but did so using nonverbal behaviors only, an atypical pattern for the subjects with normal language. The findings for this successful SLI subgroup appear consistent with prevailing characterizations of children with SLI. Comparable to findings for speech acts, presuppositions, narratives, and smooth turn-exchanges, these children with SLI evidenced the same access functions as characterized the interactions of children with normal language, but accomplished them atypically.

The second subgroup appears less consistent with the prevailing picture. They failed to access, even when invited to do so by their partners. These children with SLI seemed motivated to access, and they seemed aware that they should access, but they did not do so. Access amongst normally developing children usually involves the following behaviors: physical approach, active observation of the play activity, then the taking of an unrejected verbal turn that also offers a substantive nonverbal contribution to the play activity.

Table 23.3 A sample of access behaviors by Louis, a 15-month-old boy with normally developing language skills. The partner is playing with a stuffed toy dog that was on wheels and had a cord attached for pulling. Utterances are enclosed in quotation marks and nonverbal behaviors are in brackets.

Louis	Partner
	(is sitting; pulls dog towards herself) "hi"
"hi" (stands still watching her from about four feet away)	
(walks toward her and when close stands still and continues to watch her for about one minute)	
"doggie" (bends over and pats dog on back)	
	"that's my dog" (stands and smiles)
(straightens up and smiles)	
	(pulls dog)
(pats dog)	
	(pulls dog)
(pats dog)	

Table 23.3 presents a sample of interaction observed for Louis, a 15-month-old boy with normal-language development, upon encountering a little girl of approximately the same age, playing with a stuffed toy dog at a playground. As can be seen from this sample, even this toddler has grasped the essential elements of the social task, and indeed is successful in joining the other child's play. So, does failure to access by children with SLI result from a pragmatic impairment, or from something better understood as a social-interactional deficit, a component of a social competence problem? Although

functionalism helps distinguish linguistics from pragmatics, definitions of pragmatic impairments may need to establish boundaries between social and pragmatic domains as well.

A more promising way to interpret functionalism, and one that is guiding some studies of pragmatic impairments for SLI, is to substitute "communication" for "language," and consider forms and functions relative to each other (see figure 23.1). This underscores the interpersonal foundations of language, preserves the outcome notions entailed within views of "pragmatics-as-cause–effect," while retaining the concept of pragmatic rules as a set of relationships between forms and functions, a concept common to all functionalist models. From the functionalist perspective, discourse functions influence linguistic form usage, both for acquisition and in everyday talk. This more interdependent view of language systems highlights the many integrations involved in co-ordinating a variety of linguistic options with specific discourse functions so that unsure interactive outcomes can be negotiated between interactants. As such, effective communication involves a highly complex set of linguistic and cognitive processes. Further, ineffective communications might reflect break-downs in the encoding of functions, forms, or the matching of the one to the other, but pragmatic impairments would be conceptualized only as deficits in the last of these.

What evidence is there of pragmatic impairments when a functionalist approach is applied to the study of SLI? Unfortunately, this question remains largely unanswered. A shift in theoretical paradigms like that away from a modular approach to a functionalist approach will involve the same key steps that characterize a paradigm shift in any field of inquiry. These include de-scribing the new theoretical perspective, reinterpreting facts established by the old theory, generating new facts consistent with the tenets of the proposed theory, and evaluating the resulting contributions (Kaplan, 1963; Kuhn, 1970). As discussed in the previous section, we are in the final stage of this process for the modular approach. We are just at the beginnings of this process for functionalist perspectives.

Can the pragmatic "facts" about SLI established within the modular era be reinterpreted within functionalism? The answer to this question seems clearly "yes". Two lines of research are particularly relevant. The first focuses upon the acquisition of form–function mappings by children with SLI. The second probes the kinds of constraints operating for SLI that render the use of these mappings ineffective. The major findings for each line of research are dis-cussed below.

The acquisition of form–function mappings

Functionalism implies major changes in the ways that we approach the study of pragmatic impairments. Still in its conceptual infancy, only a few studies have demonstrated the level of investigative control necessary to probe a child's knowledge of functions, forms, and the linkages between the two. An empirical heuristic within this paradigm needs to demonstrate a greater difficulty by children with SLI in matching forms to functions than that predicted by their level of structural knowledge. The child may present a full and appropriate range of discourse functions, but also high levels of redundancy from overuse of a restricted subset of forms, and/or problems with coherency resulting from the selection of poor linguistic choices to encode specific functions. One strategy is to hold a form constant and probe variations in its functions. Some of my earlier work with Tanya Gallagher was consistent with this approach. We examined the discourse of the same young boy with SLI discussed previously that we called "Clark" (Craig and Gallagher, 1986; Gallagher and Craig, 1984). First, we studied the boy's use of a single, frequently repeated utterance in his dialog with normally developing age-mates, MLU-matched younger children with normal acquisition histories, his mother, and a familiar speech–language clinician (Gallagher and Craig, 1984). We were able to conclude that his overuse of "it's gone," a memorized phrase, was an interactive access strategy, and was intended to engage his partners in a nonexistence/disappearance game that was similar in type to those often described in the childhood development literature between mothers and toddlers (Bruner, 1974; Ratner and Bruner, 1978; Snow, 1978). His interactive purpose was unclear to the partners, however, and "it's gone" was consistently ineffective as an invitation to play. From a functionalist perspective, Clark evidenced a pragmatic problem. He overused this particular phrase as though the access function could only be served by one specific form. The child's expressive skills were severely impaired, but his assessment profile revealed considerable variety in his lexicon and sentence types and an overall structural repertoire large enough to allow expression of this function in nonroutinized ways. In this sense he met the test for a pragmatic impairment within a functionalist paradigm because he demonstrated the function, a variety of forms, but a severely constrained relationship between the two. His central problem seemed to be the formation and rigid application of one specific connection between a form and interactive function so that his discourse was highly redundant and interactionally obtuse.

The Competition Model would predict that the underlying explanations can be found when the competition between cue validity and cost are determined for this child. Perhaps the form "it's gone" had special saliency for Clark as an interactive access bid because it was so successful in initiating the nonexistence/disappearance game in early play interactions with adults. In this sense, it had high cue validity, and as a single memorized phrase, it had low cue cost; hence its frequent use. Alternatively, unusual discourse constraints influenced Clark's ability to form related responses (Craig and Gallagher, 1986). Perhaps social-interactional cues have different operations for him from those for children with normal-language skills so that canonical forms for these functions are opaque to him.

Craig and Gallagher (1986) later identified one specific discourse function, acknowledgments to a prior speaker's comment, and in this case examined Clark's ability to produce related responses. For the purposes of the present discussion, this time an important function was held constant and variations in its forms examined. Whereas acknowledgments can be related using even minimal forms like "yes," "no," and "oh," Clark's structural skills, which were beyond the one word stage and included these stereotypic forms, were adequate to allow him to produce links to prior discourse in related ways. However, Clark's level of related responding appeared governed by properties of the discourse that were not operative for children with normal-language skills. These included the ratio of other-directed partner turns in play, the interactive nature of the immediately prior turns, and the frequency of shared reference in those immediately prior turns. In order to produce related responses to prior discourse, a series of discourse constraints had to be present suggestive of an unusual set of operating rules for linking forms with this function.

Conversational interruptions are another discourse function that can be accomplished using even single words and, therefore, represent a potentially revealing context for the study of form and function linkages by children with limited expression. Craig and Evans (1989) found that four of their subjects with SLI did not interrupt their partner during adult–child discourse even though chronologically younger control subjects as well as age-mates who had normal-language skills were effective at securing the speaking turn when doing so. One of the children with SLI interrupted more like the children with normal-language skills. His profile of language deficits was more circumscribed to the expressive language domain, whereas the SLI children who failed to interrupt presented receptive as well as expressive language problems. More recently, Craig and Evans (1993) have confirmed these differences with another group of ten subjects with SLI. Like the studies discussed above, there is some indication in this research that the children with SLI may present pragmatic impairments when the scope of that definition includes rules for making the linkages between forms and functions.

Consider again the clinical examples presented in tables 23.1 and 23.2. From a functionalist perspective, Clark's discourse reflects response attempts, and apparently nonroutinized forms for expressing them, but problems in integrating structures with this function. His discourse lacks coherence and some responses seem in error ("no"), or inappropriate ("airplane"). His nonverbal behavior indicates that he is attentive and from the number of turns he takes verbally and nonverbally, also appears motivated to interact. Even though Jimmy's discourse is structurally more advanced than Clark's, his dialog also lacks coherence and results in confusions for the partner. What seems striking about their talk is the lack of conversational fit across turns and between speakers. This disconnected quality is hard to characterize within a conversational analog paradigm. It is better captured from a functionalist perspective and would imply clinically that more than changing the structural components of their dialog is warranted. Rather than focusing solely upon the well-formedness of their sentences, clinical management would need to identify the range of effective and ineffective responses possible in each turn and would need to increase the saliency of linguistic response options that preserve coherence between speakers. Functions would determine which forms would be taught and in what linguistic contexts.

Why some children with SLI may have difficulties linking forms and functions is unclear at this time. The explanation may be in subtle cognitive deficits. For example, children with SLI present sequencing deficits (Curtiss and Tallal, 1991; Stark, 1967; Tallal, 1976) which may degrade input. Some need longer durations to judge sequences accurately, jeopardizing the correct synchrony between forms and functions which they experience in the environment. Some confuse sequential ordering, so that linkages between forms and functions may be mismatched. Curtiss and Tallal (1991) observe that short-term verbal memory impairments negatively impact performance outcomes for longer sentences in this population. The Competition Model, unfortunately, provides little specific direction when searching for explanatory causes of these breakdowns or distortions of form–function linkages. The notion of cue costs may be overly general for this purpose when understanding language impairment is the goal.

The use of form–function mappings in real time

A second type of performance-based problem is suggested by the Competition Model, one in which the nature of the deficit lies in processing constraints. Processing limitations would prevent effective communication even if appropriate form–function mappings had been acquired. A widely dispersed set of studies suggest that this may be the case for some children with SLI. What processing constraints characterize SLI that render the use of acquired and appropriate form–function mappings largely ineffective? A number of studies, although with fairly diverse goals, reveal processing limitations in SLI that are significant.

Processing speed is one such constraint for SLI. Memory scanning speeds rather than the encoding of items into memory storage formats, or the accessing of items in memory for processing, appear slow for children with SLI (Kirchner and Klatzky, 1985; Sininger, Klatzky, and Kirchner, 1989). Word recognition times tend to be slow (Montgomery, Scudder, and Moore, 1990), as well as perception of brief events (Tallal, Stark, and Mellits, 1985). In addition, accessing information appears significantly more difficult for children with SLI than normal-language peers. This probably includes accessing phonological (Kamhi, Catts, Mauer, Apel, and Gentry, 1988) and morphological representations (Stone and Connell, 1993). Difficulties with word-finding also characterize SLI, although underdeveloped semantics may be more the source of the problems than retrieval processes (Kail and Leonard, 1986). Recently, processing capacity concerns have been discussed as well in which children with SLI adopted performance strategies that minimized the coordination of information into complex descriptions, despite clear evidence that they had knowledge of the potential components (Johnston and Smith, 1988).

Summary

Functionalist approaches to the study of pragmatic impairments in SLI appear warranted. The conversational analog view of children with SLI as having intact pragmatic knowledge can be reinterpreted within a functionalist paradigm so that the characterization is one of pragmatic impairment. This reinterpretation allows us to ask again whether some children with SLI have acquired appropriate form–function mappings. Perhaps children like Clark and Jimmy have some forms and all functions, but have not acquired them as synchronized wholes. The Competition Model would be helpful in formulating this type of question. It may be less useful when predicting possible answers.

Future Research Directions

Primary questions for future research might include the following:

1   Are there children with SLI who demonstrate form–function mapping problems? How are these mismatches best conceptualized; as a pragmatic competence problem? As a pragmatic performance problem?
2   Are there subgroups within the population of children labeled SLI who are best conceptualized as competence-deficient, and as performance-deficient?
3   What are the cue validity and cue cost factors operative for children with SLI? How do the perceptual and cognitive skills of these children maintain or distort the typical saliency of cues?

Primary methodologies for future research might involve the following:

1   Task controls for ensuring that subjects evidence both the necessary linguistic forms and the discourse functions independent of experimental probes to see how they link the two.
2   Subject controls for ensuring that the appropriate comparisons are being made between groups. Currently, control groups are selected as age and language matches. This may be less appropriate than making comparisons to children who make the targeted form–function mapping successfully in the context of similar and different cue costs. Children with another type of language disorder or different cognitive skills may offer a richer source of interpretive insights than children who are matched for language status.

Both conversational analog approaches and functionalism offer hypotheses about the nature of the difficulties experienced by children with SLI. The conversational analog approach predicts that the core issue for SLI is probably not a pragmatic competence problem. Functionalism predicts that difficulties are due to either a pragmatic competence problem, when pragmatic rules are viewed as failure to acquire form–function mappings, or a pragmatic performance problem when constraints on effective outcomes are considered as part of the conceptualization for SLI. Interestingly, these hypotheses are amenable to direct testing fairly readily with intervention research. Inducing behavioral change in the phonological, syntactic, morphological, and semantic domains should result either in untrained improvements in interactive performances in addition to generalized gains on specific structures, or increases in sentence lengths and grammatical complexity with continued ineffective interactive outcomes. The former would support the conversational analog approach whereas the latter would be more consistent with functionalism.

Inducing behavioral change in the pragmatic domain by targeting specific form–function relationships should result in improvements in only those forms used to serve the targeted function, again supporting functionalist hypotheses. Single subject intervention research designs, in this case a multiple baseline design for the former and an alternating treatments design for the latter, would provide valuable information about the relative merits of these hypotheses. Intervention research of this type would be of considerable clinical importance, and would also inform the process of pragmatic theorizing.

In addition, an intervention-based research strategy of this type would critically depend upon the development of a functionalist approach to clinical management. The conversational analog approach to intervention has been outlined by Bloom and Lahey (1978), whereas the functionalist approach remains unspecified. Suggestions have been made by Craig (1983) and Bates et al. (1991) but at this time the specific points of similarity and dissimilarity between approaches are not well described. Both approaches prioritize natural contexts for intervention. As I have discussed elsewhere, the motivation within the conversational analog approach is to preserve naturalness and avoid distortion of operating rules about which we know little. For example, stress is placed upon ecologically valid or "functional" approaches to rehabilitation in adult aphasia (Holland, 1982). A consensus is emerging in the literature on adult aphasia that language loss after brain injury for many of these individuals is best conceptualized as a structural rather than conversational impairment. Accordingly, functional approaches to management can exploit the individual's spared discourse knowledge and efficiently work on improving structure in natural contexts. When pragmatic impairments are indeed observed in linking forms and functions, however, it would not be consistent with a functionalist paradigm to simply teach structure in everyday leisure-time and vocational contexts. I have argued elsewhere (Craig, 1983) that interventions need not preserve naturalness for the clinician, and more recently Bates et al. (1991) have described an "amplified pragmatics" which also assumes that key interactive characteristics can be preserved but need not mirror one's normal experiences. Interventions designed to test pragmatic models will need to distinguish other "functional" from "functionalist" tenets like this one for natural contexts.

A third imperative for future research on pragmatic impairments would be to define a boundary between pragmatic impairments and social-interactional problems. Functionalism has highlighted the differences between forms and functions. Future research needs to clarify the differences between communicative purposes and social goals. What roles do motivation, past social-interactional histories, and complexity of the social task play on the interactive outcomes obtained? Any definition of pragmatic impairments will remain critically incomplete until the role of social knowledge is associated with that of pragmatic and linguistic knowledge.

In summary, it is not yet clear whether children or subgroups of children with primary nonorganic language disorders present pragmatic impairments. The study of pragmatic impairments in this population requires renewed and intense inquiry into the nature of such problems and the best way to characterize them. The present discussion argues for a movement away from conversational analog approaches toward functionalism, and proposes that the Competition Model offers a promising initial driving force for this research effort.

24 Language Development in Children and Adolescents with Down Syndrome

ROBIN S. CHAPMAN

Down Syndrome is a condition brought about by an extra copy of a segment of the long arm of Chromosome 21 that is associated with characteristic physical features and cognitive delay (Kemper, 1988). Language development is an area of specific additional difficulty for many children with Down Syndrome. Its study is therefore important in its own right, for what it might suggest of typical developmental patterns, associated causes, and effective intervention strategies for children with Down Syndrome. What we learn about how language can come apart in children with language disorders is also important to the shaping of our models of normal language development. The work on language of children with Down Syndrome will carry implications for our models of normal language development as well.

Questions

Our questions about language development in children with Down Syndrome have persisted, across the last 25 years, even as our conceptualizations of language skill and our methods of assessment have altered. Studies continue to ask:

1 Is there evidence of specific language deficit in children with Down Syndrome, relative to nonverbal cognitive achievements?
2 Is there a particular pattern of language strengths and weaknesses (a "profile") characteristic of language acquired by children with Down Syndrome?
3 What is the developmental course of language acquisition? Is its course best characterized as delay, or atypical acquisition?

4   What degree of individual variation exists in development, and what are its predictors? What are the underlying causes of specific language impairment?

These questions have persisted, in part, because our conceptualization of language and cognitive skills and our assessment instruments have altered over the years. Originally, the contribution of language deficits to cognitive assessment was not recognized; nor were language deficits distinguished from speech problems. Early language assessment instruments were global in nature and shifted in content from one developmental level to another, emphasizing now production, now comprehension, now conceptual development. As assessment measures shifted to distinguish processes of comprehension and production, and to offer more precise quantification of linguistic domains, the old questions were readdressed with new measures.

Rosenberg (1982), in a careful review of previous research on language development in children with mental retardation, offered these conclusions for children with Down Syndrome a decade ago:

1   Mental age tended to predict performance on linguistic tasks better than CA.
2   Institutionalized individuals might be less advantaged in the area of language functioning than those still at home.
3   The diagnosis of Down Syndrome did not predict the pattern of linguistic performance, except in the area of articulation, and then only to a limited extent.
4   Evidence from CA comparisons of language supported a *developmental lag hypothesis*, with comprehension and production developing at similar rates.
5   Limited evidence from MLU comparisons suggested *similar language acquisition strategies*.
6   Mothers adjusted their language input appropriately to their infants' language level, although infants were less responsive to their mothers than CA-matched peers.

Inflectional morphology was identified as an area of special difficulty for children with mental retardation generally, with slower rate of acquisition than other aspects of structure, but no studies of children with Down Syndrome were available at the time.

Work since that time, reviewed by Hartley (1986), Miller (1988), Pruess, Vadasy, and Fewell (1987), Fowler (1990), and here, suggests that three of these conclusions (3, 4, and 5) can be revised. Evidence is summarized here that the diagnosis of Down Syndrome is associated with a characteristic pattern of language deficit, once cognitive status, hearing, and chronological age are taken into account. In particular, differential rates of development in comprehension and production are documented; and differential rates of development for the lexical and syntactic domains within those processes. Some differences in the details of language acquisition strategies are noted and related to discrepancies between language and cognitive domains. This account is organized by language process, and within that by linguistic domain. Evidence for the patterning of language skill in Down Syndrome is then summarized, and a related literature on auditory short-term memory is reviewed as a potential predictor of individual variability in pattern.

Language Production

Pragmatic development

Pragmatic development occurs in the social and cognitive domains as the emergence of diverse communicative goals. In the sociolinguistic domain, pragmatic development occurs as the mapping of linguistic forms to the appropriate contexts of use, relative to discourse context and speaker and listener knowledge and status. This dual view of pragmatics would lead us to expect that pragmatic development would reveal the equal or superior personal social-skill development of children with Down Syndrome when communicative intent and cognition are tapped; but limitations in those aspects of pragmatic skill (e.g. linguistic cohesion) that depend on mastery of expressive linguistic means. The current literature is consistent with that expectation.

Prelinguistic communicative signals

Children with Down Syndrome give social-communicative signals (e.g. looking, reaching, touching, pointing, showing, giving, smiling, laughing, communication routines) proportionally as often during play as their developmentally matched controls, at chronological ages of approximately 25 months and developmental levels of approximately 14 months (Fischer, 1987). These signals are less likely to be spontaneous (a greater proportion are elicited by the mother than initiated by the child, compared to control pairs) and more likely to be effective (mothers of Down Syndrome children responded contingently to their children's signals more often than did mothers of controls). Mothers' of the Down Syndrome group (who were enrolled in an early intervention program) compensate actively for their children's reduced rate of spontaneous initiation of communication.

The early emergence of communicative intents in sensorimotor stage five for children with Down Syndrome parallels normal development, although gestural means alone, rather than gesture plus vocalization or word, are more likely to be employed in comments and requests (Greenwald and Leonard, 1979). When added points are given for accompanying vocal behavior, children with Down Syndrome do more poorly than mental age-matched controls on imperative and declarative tasks (Smith and von Tezchner, 1986). Performance on declarative tasks is related to vocabulary comprehension; on imperative tasks, to expressive language.

In a study of nonverbal social interaction, indicating, and requesting among toddlers with Down Syndrome (Mundy, Sigman, Kasari, and Yirmiya, 1988), they were found to have significant strengths in nonverbal social interaction skills compared to MA controls; and significant deficits in nonverbal object requesting. Although these communicative acts were identified on the basis of nonverbal cues, they were almost all accompanied by vocalization or words. Deficits in the nonverbal object requesting were correlated with deficits in expressive language development, for the children with MAs of nine to 20 months. This pattern of difference was not present for MA-matched controls with mental retardation. Nor was frequency of social interaction negatively related to instances of object requesting, as might be expected if children with Down Syndrome preferred social interaction to object play. Caregivers were equally (and highly) responsive to communication acts from all children.

Clarification strategies of four children with Down Syndrome, mean age five years, in Brown's Stage I were found to be conversationally and communicatively responsive to adults' requests for clarification, incorporating phonetic or semantic revision more than half the time (Coggins and Stoel-Gammon, 1982). However, lack of intelligibility can interfere with pragmatic intent; young adolescents who were conversing mainly in single-word utterances were often limited in the success of their repair strategies, with signing a more reliable means than speaking (Bray and Woolnough, 1988). Lack of intelligibility does not limit communicative attempts (Leuder, 1980).

Sokolov (1992), summarizing imitations in spontaneous conversation by preschool children with Down Syndrome interacting with mothers from the CHILDES corpora, found that their rates of linguistic imitation overall were somewhat lower than the controls selected. However, the probability of imitating the mother's utterances (10 percent overall) decreased more slowly with MLU than in the normal control group. In contrast, self-repetitions declined at a similar rate with MLU. (Only children with MLUs less than three were included in this analysis). Sokolov concludes that children with Down Syndrome develop differently with respect to linguistic imitation.

In an analysis of spontaneous imitations in the course of mother–child conversation, Tager-Flusberg and Calkins (1990) found that the four children with Down Syndrome used more sentence imitations than typically developing children, but that the grammatical complexity of these imitations, as measured by IPSyn, were less than that of nonimitated spontaneous speech. This lead them to conclude that imitations were not grammatically progressive for any of the children.

A possible explanation of this finding is that the greater limitations of auditory short-term memory, or hearing loss, for children with Down Syndrome may lead to more frequent instances of partial comprehension or failure to understand than MLU matched controls. In that state, repetition of part or all of the other speaker's utterance for confirmation or clarification is a typical communication strategy.

Conversations of men with Down Syndrome and their caretakers often showed extended discourse coherence (Bennett, 1976). Social sensitivity of young adults with Down Syndrome can be discerned in nonverbal communication and postural adjustments made to acquaintances v. strangers (Leudar, 1980).

In comparison with individuals with autism or Fragile X, matched for verbal IQ, individuals with Down Syndrome show conversational profiles on a story retelling task that differ in several ways (Ferrier, Bashir, Meryash, Johnston, and Wolff, 1991). They are less fluent, in terms of sound or syllable repetition, than the group with autism; and less likely to produce utterances inappropriate on several levels. They are less likely to ask questions or request action or clarification than the group with Fragile X; and less likely to partially repeat their own utterances. They are equally as likely as either other group to maintain topic, to offer unrequested information, and to participate in the particular descriptive task primarily through speech acts of description, affirmation, and acknowledgment.

Frequency of utterances is typically higher in DS groups compared to MLU or MA matched controls (Harris, 1983; Chapman, Schwartz, and Kay-Raining Bird, 1989) when a narrative task is attempted, possibly reflecting a compensation for expressive language limitations. In comparison with mental age-matched controls, children and adolescents with Down Syndrome show poorer story recall, as indexed by gist report in story retelling; and are less likely to remember the text information associated with novel words (Chapman, Kay-Raining Bird, and Schwartz, 1991). This finding may reflect comprehension, as well as expressive language, problems.

In older children and adolescents with Down Syndrome, referential description and communication tasks reveal success as great as mental-age matched controls in conveying relevant information, at the same time that expressive language limitations are evident (Jordan and Murdoch, 1987). For example, in describing a woman reading her newspaper (as opposed to other agents, objects, and actions), a typical response from an individual with Down Syndrome might be "girl read paper"; from the control child, "It's the mother again, walking with the paper and she's reading." Both versions encode the three relevant elements. The lengthier one, in addition, employs syntax that marks each of the elements as new information pragmatically.

Knowledge of socially appropriate responses was evaluated by Loveland and Tunali (1991) during a "tea party" situation in which they introduced an account of the examiner's unhappy personal experience (e.g. a stolen wallet). Participants with Down Syndrome aged five to 20 years gave a significantly greater percentage of relevant suggestions and sympathetic comments than high functioning individuals with autism, and benefitted more from modeling of appropriate comments.

Thus, for children with Down Syndrome in the sensorimotor period, nonverbal communicative acts occur as frequently as mental-age matched controls, but their distribution differs, with less object requesting and more social interaction. As they grow older, frequency of communicative attempts is equal to (or greater than) mental-age matched peers; but its elaboration for the purpose of marking pragmatic aspects of speaker–listener knowledge is limited. Discourse aspects of pragmatic skill that are not dependent on linguistic skill – topic continuation, socially appropriate responding – appear appropriate where examined, but those dependent on linguistic skill (for example, story retelling) are limited.

Phonological development

Vocal development in the first two years

Longitudinal study of the early emergence of babbling in children with Down Syndrome has inconsistently revealed small delays relative to chronological age-matched peers. Delayed onset of canonical babbling (production of well-formed consonant–vowel syllables, e.g. "ba" or "da"), at nine months rather than seven months, has been reported (Lynch, Oller, Eilers, and Basinger, 1991) but not replicated in more detailed classification of emergence of quasivowels v. full vowels and marginal v. fully canonical syllables (Steffens, Oller, Lynch, and Urbano, 1992). Variability has been marked in these studies, which included children with mild conductive hearing loss (congenital conductive hearing loss is a factor known to be associated with delayed canonical babbling); patterns of emerging syllables were similar in the two groups. At the same time, the infants with Down Syndrome were already showing significant cognitive delays, so that, inferentially, we can identify early spontaneous vocalization as a strength relative to other developmental areas. This is consistent with other longitudinal studies finding early vocal development similar to age-matched peers (Dodd, 1972; Smith and Oller, 1981) and relatively independent of mental age.

Later phonological development

In typically developing children, the early babbling stage is thought to reveal drift toward the native language in distribution of sounds produced, and thus a continuity with later phonological development; on this basis, one might expect no later delay in the speech productions of children with Down Syndrome. However, the emergence of the lexicon allows the targets of production to be identified and articulatory errors or systematic phonological shifts to be analyzed. And indeed, substantial delays in the acquisition of stop consonant production in older children with Down Syndrome (three to six years) have been reported in longitudinal study, with evidence of phonological processes similar to normal younger (18–36 month) children (Smith and Stoel-Gammon,

1983). Final stop devoicing was a typical pattern for children with Down Syndrome across the period; final stop deletion was infrequent. Both initial cluster simplification and initial stop deaspiration declined with age.

Stoel-Gammon's earlier (1980) cross-sectional work also showed similar, but delayed, patterns of phonological error, including deletion of unstressed syllables, production of initial fricatives and affricates as stops, and substitution of glides for liquids. Bleile and Schwartz (1984) similarly reported final consonant deletion, initial cluster reduction, and stopping as the most prevalent processes in three children with Down Syndrome aged three and five.

Dodd (1976) found that phonological analysis of school-age children with Down Syndrome revealed many more errors and inconsistencies than were present in the speech of other children with mental retardation or a preschool group matched for mental age. Stoel-Gammon's review (1981) confirms both the general pattern of delay and the different characteristics to be found in the speech of younger children with Down Syndrome.

Rosin, Swift, Bless, and Vetter (1988) found significantly poorer intelligibility in their adolescents with Down Syndrome than in a control group of children with mental retardation due to other causes matched for mental age. The children also differed in percentage of consonants correctly articulated on the Goldman–Fristoe Test of Articulation (75 percent v. 94 percent) and a diadochokinetic task, requiring significantly more cuing. They did not differ on their rate or precision of consonant–vowel repetitions. MLU was also significantly lower than the mental-age matched controls with mental retardation. The intelligibility ratings, percent intelligible words, and percentage correct consonants were all significantly correlated with MLU (Spearman rank–order correlations computed from data, Rosin et al.: 57), though age may contribute to this relationship.

Phonological processes of final consonant deletion, cluster reduction, stopping, and fronting persist in adolescence (van Borsel, 1988) and early 20s (Hughes and Ratner, 1989), though overall utterance intelligibility improves in that period (Chapman, Schwartz, and Kay-Raining Bird, 1989). These findings cannot be wholly accounted for by anatomical factors such as the relatively larger tongue (lingual hyperplasia); and assessments of speech intelligibility before and after partial glossectomy for cosmetic appearances show no significant change (Margar-Bacal, Witzel, and Munro, 1987).

The persistence of phonological processes and syllable deletion contribute to the reduced intelligibility of children with Down Syndrome. The relation of these delays to hearing status is difficult to quantify, as prospective monitoring of hearing function is necessary to control for temporary hearing loss associated with otitis media in younger children. In our own work, variability in utterance intelligibility (ages five to 20 years) has been predicted by chronological age and concurrent hearing status on a screening test, but not mental age or vocabulary comprehension, accounting for 30 percent of the variance (Chapman, Schwartz, and Kay-Raining Bird, 1989).

Interestingly, Sommers and Starkey (1977), in a study of children with Down

Syndrome selected for having good or poor speech and language, and no hearing deficit, found that dichotic verbal processing of the good speakers was similar to normal children, in having a right-ear advantage; but that of the poor speakers showed no such effect. Unfortunately, no controls for the lower language level of the less intelligible group were used. Hartley (1985) also found that children with Down Syndrome and a right-ear advantage in dichotic tasks showed significantly better language comprehension than those with left-ear, or no, advantage. Again, controls for language level were lacking.

Decreases in phonological process use (cluster reduction, liquid simplification) are correlated with increases in sentence length, in six to 12-year-olds (Crosley and Dowling, 1989), indicating a link between the delays in phonology and syntax that has also been demonstrated in children with speech delay (Paul and Shriberg, 1982). Again, however, the contributions of chronological age must be taken into consideration.

Lexical development

Early words

The emergence of first words has been reported to vary widely with chronological age (eight to 45 months for two words in Berry, Gunn, Andrews, and Price, 1981; ten to 36 months for one word in Strominger, Winkler, and Cohen, 1984); the average CA is typically delayed. The first spoken 50 words produced appear similar in content and word-form categories to those reported for normally developing children (Gillham, 1990), despite differences in rate of acquisition. General nominals comprise over half the inventory; function words are rare.

The apparent variability in first word emergence is substantially reduced when nonverbal mental age is taken into account. Spoken vocabulary emerges at roughly the same mental ages in children with Down Syndrome as in typically developing children, for object words (Cardoso-Martins, Mervis, and Mervis, 1985). However, early cumulative vocabularies show a slower rate of progress than mental age controls for a majority of children with Down Syndrome (Beeghly and Cicchetti, 1986; Miller, Sedey, Miolo, Murray-Branch, and Rosin, 1992). Thus rate, but not onset, of lexical acquisition appears slower.

The finding of early delay in lexical production, however, may arise from an exclusive focus on spoken vocabulary for children who are in fact bilingual in spoken English and some form of signing. Current educational practice frequently includes the use of signs – as many as 80 percent of young children with Down Syndrome encounter signing as part of early intervention (Fristoe and Lloyd, 1978; Goodman, Wilson, and Bornstein, 1978; Kahn, 1981; Sedey, Rosin, and Miller, 1991). When signed vocabulary is included in lexical inventories for young children functioning in the second year, cognitively, the spoken vocabulary gap disappears (Miller, Sedey, Miolo, Rosin, and Murray-Branch, 1991).

This is a finding similar to that of other bilingual studies, indicating that children's initial production vocabularies overlap little, even though they may understand the words of both languages. At approximately 24–27 months, mental age, children with Down Syndrome show a dramatic increase in the number of words listed as spoken only, rather than signed only, or signed and spoken; from this point on, most new vocabulary is spoken, rather than signed (Miller, Sedey, Miolo, Rosin, and Murray-Branch, 1991).

In comparison to MLU-matched controls, Rondal (1978a) found children with Down Syndrome to use higher type–token ratios (that is, a more diverse vocabulary) in free play speech samples. Similarly, Harris (1983) reported a greater proportion of different one word utterances, and more productive use of words for outside objects, in their Down Syndrome group compared to early Stage I controls. This suggests that more diverse life experiences, or a more advanced grasp of conceptual content, contribute to a larger lexicon (relative to MLU) for the DS child. However, most other comparisons of referential, functional, or relational semantic categories failed to differ (Harris, 1983). Among young children, Mervis (1990) and her colleagues have demonstrated that vocabulary acquisition is relatively better when referents constitute good prototypes of the concept category.

Hearing and early lexicon

Young children with Down Syndrome have a high prevalence of mild to moderate hearing loss associated with otitis media (Cunningham and McArthur, 1981; Dahle and McCollister, 1986; Whiteman, Simpson, and Compton, 1986). Such losses in the first 18 months have been associated with slowed language development in otherwise typically developing children. Sedey, Miolo, Murray-Branch, and Miller (1992) investigated the relationship between hearing status and early receptive and expressive language longitudinally in children with Down Syndrome aged 16–30 months at the first visit (MAs 12–17 months). They found that 35–60 percent of the sample showed pure-tone average thresholds greater than 20 dB at a visit, with 75 percent showing raised thresholds on at least one visit of the five. However, the mean of the pure tone averages across the five visits was uncorrelated with either receptive or expressive language measures.

Later vocabulary development

Among older children and young adults with Down Syndrome, the use of nouns and verbs in picture description shows a similar shift (decrease in nouns, increase in verbs) as mental-age matched controls (Mein, 1961). Ability to designate the function of a concrete noun increases with mental age (Cornwell,

1974) and performance on word definition tasks are equivalent to mental-age matched controls (Chapman, Schwartz, and Kay-Raining Bird, 1991).

Acquisition of new production vocabulary (fast mapping) in the play context of a hiding game is as good for individuals with Down Syndrome, aged five to 20 years, as for mental-age matched controls (Chapman, Kay-Raining Bird, and Schwartz, 1990), in both immediate and delayed testing.

Use of vocabulary in narratives, however, is more restricted than mental-age matched controls. Both the total number of words and the number of different words, in 12-minute samples, are significantly smaller than those for control narratives (Chapman, Schwartz, and Kay-Raining Bird, 1991).

Syntax development

Compared to mental-age matched controls, children with Down Syndrome show deficits on grammatical closure tasks (McCarthy, 1965) and expressive syntax in free speech samples (Chapman, Schwartz, and Kay-Raining Bird, 1989; Chapman, Ross, and Seung, 1993; Miller, Miolo, Sedey, and Murray-Branch, 1993; Rosin, Bless, Swift, and Vetter, 1988). Only at the very first emergence of two-word combinations do the children with Down Syndrome appear similar in mental age to children without mental retardation (Miller, Miolo, Sedey, and Murray-Branch, 1993).

Emergence of multiword utterances

The *onset* of multiword combinations, as indicated by a rise in MLU to 1.01 or 1.05, appears to occur at mental ages similar to those of typically developing children – 20–24 months MA – as indexed by the Mental Scale of the Bayley (Miller, Miolo, Sedey, and Murray-Branch, 1993). The total group of children with Down Syndrome, followed longitudinally, shows increasing divergence of MLU from the mental-age matched controls who, by the time they reach 21 months and MLUs of 1.3, differ significantly from the group with Down Syndrome in productive syntax.

Is the expressive syntax of children with Down Syndrome, in detail, similar to that of controls matched for overall mean length of utterance? Given evidence from children with specific expressive language deficit, one might expect additional deficits in grammatical morphology. In the SLI literature, several different theories accounting for this general observation have been proposed (Leonard, 1992a): sparse morphology (a language-specific limitation in the full expression of the inflectional paradigm, e.g. regular third person present singular inflection on the verb in English); limited phonetic substance (brief and unstressed syllables carrying the morphological information); and verb agreement problems related to parameter setting in a Universal Grammar framework.

Coggins (1979) found that the two-word utterances of four children with

Down Syndrome at Brown's Stage I (aged three to six years) expressed the same basic semantic relations found in the research on typically developing children, accounting for 79 percent of the tokens. The semantic relations expressed by children in early Stage I through Stage III appeared descriptively similar to that of controls (Layton and Sharifi, 1978).

Among the studies of syntax employing MLU-matched controls is that of Rondal (1978b), in which Developmental Sentence Scoring (Lee, 1974) was carried out for free play conversational samples of mothers and children at MLU stages 1.75–2.25 and 2.50–3.00. DSS score increased with MLU, as did most of the subscale scores. A significant interaction of MLU level and group was found for the DSS score. Younger MLU controls scored lower on DSS at the lower MLU stage than children with Down Syndrome; and equivalently or higher than the Down Syndrome group at the higher MLU level. No interactions were significant for the subscales; however, children with Down Syndrome received higher scores for main verbs and grammatical sentence point scales, and lower scores for indefinite pronouns, secondary verbs, and interrogative reversals scales, than the controls. Given the way in which DSS scores are assigned, these findings would suggest the slower emergence of free grammatical morphemes (indefinite pronouns and semiauxiliaries) in the language of Down Syndrome children; and the presence of more advanced verb phrases than one would expect for the MLU of the samples. The greater grammaticality of the DS samples, as indicated by sentence point scoring, would argue against a specific deficit in inflectional grammatical morphology or verb agreement problems.

Wiegel-Crump (1981), in an analysis of free speech samples scored according to the Developmental Sentence Scoring protocol, found that DSS scores increased with mental age. However, mental age and performance was equivalent (50th–60th percentile) only for children at two years of mental age; subsequently, children with Down Syndrome scored below the 15th percentile for their mental age.

Investigators looking at restricted age ranges and generalizing beyond them have often proposed that aspects of expressive language development stop or plateau in children with Down Syndrome. The generalization that children with Down Syndrome talk only about the here-and-now (Leuder, Fraser, and Jeeves, 1981; Layton and Sharifi, 1978; Rondal, 1978a) appears true only of children with Stage I expressive syntax. Past tense marking is found in the talk of children with MLUs above 2.0 (Chapman, Schwartz, and Kay-Raining Bird, 1992), despite their expressive language delays.

Fowler (1990), in her review of more recent work on language abilities of children with Down Syndrome, concurred with Rosenberg's earlier characterization of "delayed language without deviance," but proposed an apparent limit or ceiling to syntax acquisition on the basis of observed plateauing in MLU that was unrelated to mental age. She suggested that such limits might arise from (1) a *critical period* tied to chronological aging – either the maturational events occurring around seven years associated with the apparent shift in learning the motor patterns of a second language (Fowler, 1990), or the onset of adolescence that was once thought to signal the end of the period of rapid language learning in children (Lenneberg, 1967); or (2) a restriction of the complexity of what can be learned to *simple syntax*, however long the language learning period (Fowler, 1990).

Our own cross-sectional work (Chapman, Schwartz, and Kay-Raining Bird, 1992) refutes these two hypotheses, as we found significant increases in the narratives of adolescents with Down Syndrome aged 16–20 years in comparison with younger adolescents and children aged five to 16 years. Additionally, these narratives contained instances of complex sentences at rates similar to younger preschool controls who were matched for MLU level (and therefore at younger mental ages than the DS groups). Our work suggested that the apparent plateaus found by Fowler could arise, in part, from language sampling procedures; conversational, but not narrative, samples showed such plateaus in the eight to 16 year age range in our cross-sectional sample.

Our work also confirmed that some aspects of morphosyntax are more delayed than MLU generally; free grammatical morphemes were omitted significantly more frequently by speakers with Down Syndrome than by MLU-matched controls in the narrative samples (Chapman, Schwartz, and Kay-Raining Bird, 1992). Omissions of bound morphemes also occurred at higher mean rates, but were variable enough so that significant differences did not emerge.

Similarly, in comparing the language of Dutch children with Down Syndrome aged eight to 19 years (MAs greater than 3;6 years) to that of typically developing Dutch children aged one to four years, hearing impaired, and specifically language disordered children through LARSP analysis, Bol and Kuiken (1990) found patterns of morphosyntax more severely delayed, but not atypical of the normal developmental sequence, in the Down Syndrome group. These included less frequent use of subject–predicate structures, less frequent use of pronouns, and less verb agreement. (As the developmental description was tied to age, rather than an MLU index of stage, MLU-matched comparisons could not be made).

Language Comprehension

Speech perception

In contrast to the emergence of early babbling, early speech perception skills have shown impairment relative to age-matched and developmentally matched peers. Difficulties in perceiving place of articulation distinctions signalled by rapidly changing formant transitions have been reported in children aged 13–37 months; slowing down the transitions improved performance (Eilers, Bull, Oller, and Lewis, 1985; Eilers, Moroff, and Turner, 1985). These findings suggest that acquisition of the phonology of a targeted lexicon, as opposed to early vocal development, might be selectively affected in children with Down Syndrome (Lynch and Eilers, 1991).

Auditory preferences of infants with Down Syndrome and nonhandicapped infants, studied at the developmental ages of nine and 18 months, diverge (Glenn and Cunningham, 1983) in a way that suggests the slower development of complex auditory representations. Both groups, at both ages, significantly prefer to listen to rhymes as opposed to repetitive tones; and to their mother speaking baby talk, as opposed to talk to another adult. At nine months, both groups prefer rhymes to spoken stimuli; this preference persists for children with Down Syndrome, who continue, at 18 months, to listen to rhymes more frequently, and longer, than baby talk. In contrast, the controls prefer baby talk at 18 months, and listen to it longer than rhymes. At nine months, sung nursery rhymes are preferred to a musical instrument version of the tune by both groups; infants with Down Syndrome had a much longer response duration than controls (Glenn, Cunningham, and Joyce, 1981).

Vocabulary comprehension

Comprehension vocabulary is equivalent to mental-age matched controls in the time of onset of object word comprehension (Cardoso-Martins, Mervis, and Mervis, 1985) and in later childhood comparisons with mental-age matched controls (Chapman, Schwartz, and Kay-Raining Bird, 1991). In adolescence, a number of children with Down Syndrome begin to show vocabulary comprehension superior to that of mental-age controls (Chapman, Schwartz, and Kay-Raining Bird, 1991; Rosin, Swift, Bless, and Vetter, 1988). One potential source of this disparity is the access of adolescents with Down Syndrome to a wider variety of vocational and real-world activities that may create opportunities for more diverse vocabulary exposure and learning. Thus, comprehension vocabulary is an area of potential strength.

The status of comprehension in the sensorimotor period has been traced in at least two longitudinal studies. Comprehension of object words emerged at the same mental age in six children with Down Syndrome (14.5 months) as in children developing typically (13.8 months) (Cardoso-Martins, Mervis, and Mervis, 1985), with concurrent performance on the object permanence task equally distributed in Stages 5 and 6. Additionally, the sizes of comprehension (and production) vocabularies in the DS and control Ss were similar at four different MA ranges between 13 and 21 months, suggesting no deficit in onset or acquisition of comprehension vocabulary relative to mental age, for children aged 1;6 to 3;6. However, when equated by object permanence performance, those children with Down Syndrome who had attained Stage 6 had smaller comprehension and production vocabularies than controls. (Wishart, 1988, reports that consolidation of new learning in the object permanence task is unusually prolonged in children with Down Syndrome, which may account for this finding.)

The early phase of vocabulary acquisition has been investigated in a fast-mapping paradigm in event (Chapman, Kay-Raining Bird, and Schwartz, 1990) and story (Chapman, Kay-Raining Bird, and Schwartz, 1991) contexts. The ability of Down Syndrome children aged five to 20 years to remember the nonsense object given a simple novel label in a hiding game was as good as nonverbal mental-age controls (and not relatively better than controls for the oldest groups).

When stories were presented in which the meaning of novel nouns had to be inferred from the discourse context, all subjects were far less successful in inferring a referent than in the hiding game, but no differences were found between individuals with Down Syndrome and the control group (Chapman, Kay-Raining Bird, and Schwartz, 1991). In contrast, memory for story gist, and memory for the described events associated with the novel word, was significantly poorer for the Down Syndrome group. In particular, memory for events associated with the novel words was worse than the rest of story gist recall in the Down Syndrome group, and not controls. These findings, of course, are ambiguous in their reliance on expressive verbal report and recall for an assessment of comprehension. The pattern of results, however, suggests that the comprehension demands of on-line story processing appear to limit the elaboration of the knowledge network more for individuals with Down Syndrome; and even more for the portion of the network associated with novel words.

Syntax comprehension

Syntax comprehension, in contrast, appears similar to that of mental-age matched controls in childhood; it is only among adolescents that syntax comprehension begins to lag that of mental-age matched controls (Chapman, Schwartz, and Kay-Raining Bird, 1991; Chapman, Ross, and Seung, 1993; Rosin, Swift, Bless, and Vetter, 1988).

When IQ (including vocabulary comprehension items) and chronological age are partialed out, vocabulary comprehension is unrelated to expressive language, auditory short-term memory, or hearing for adolescents and young adults with Down Syndrome (Marcell, Croen, and Sewell, 1990). The same is true of an IQ and age-matched group of young adults with mental retardation of undetermined origin. However, comprehension of grammatically difficult syntactic structures is significantly associated with sentence imitation scores, expressive vocabulary, and auditory short-term memory in both groups. The individuals with Down Syndrome perform equivalently to the control group in vocabulary comprehension, but more poorly on the latest mastered items of syntax comprehension on the Miller–Yoder Test (singular/plural, possessives, reflexives, verb inflections, and passives). For comprehension dependent on word order, in particular, individuals with Down Syndrome appear to benefit more from semantic plausibility as a cue to thematic role than MA controls (Bridges and Smith, 1984; Fowler, 1985).

Children's knowledge of the syntactic implications of verbs themselves, as opposed to lexically based plausibility or syntactic frame-based cues, has also been evaluated (Naigles, Fowler, and Helm, 1990). When comprehension of ungrammatical sentences such as "The zebra goes the lion" is assessed, such that the acting out of the sentence can rely on the sentence frame (the zebra Xs the lion, e.g. pushes) or the argument structure known to be associated with the verb (X goes to Y – the zebra goes to the lion), school-age children with Down Syndrome are less likely to show verb-based interpretations than mental-age matches. Additionally, modifications of test procedure were necessary (providing objects, repeating the test sentence), for the children with Down Syndrome often forgot the test sentence by the time they had searched for the objects with which to enact it, suggesting a far more serious comprehension deficit in real-time tasks with short-term memory demands.

Reading

A number of individuals with Down Syndrome develop reading skills when given the educational opportunity (Buckley, 1993). Estimates range from 33–86 percent of adolescents reared at home, with wide variation in educational emphasis on literacy in the differing programs studied. For example, Doherty, Fowler, and Boynton (1993) report, in a study of 33 young adult readers aged 17–25, functioning at four to eight year MAs as indicated by the Kaufman ABC, that only one third showed no word attack skill, another one third limited first-grade level word-attack skill, and the remaining one third moderate to productive (grade 2–12) skills.

In typically developing children, phoneme awareness and segmentation skills have been strongly associated with the development of reading skill; Doherty, Fowler, and Boynton (1993) report a similar association in the DS group, controlling for IQ. Further, digit span recall was associated with word attack skills, holding IQ constant. Analyses holding MA constant would be necessary to rule out the general contribution of developmental level to these relationships.

Seagoe's (1965) early diary study of an individual with Down Syndrome and an estimated six year level of mental age, indicated, however, that readers might go well beyond their early literacy levels with practice; in this case study seventh grade literacy levels were achieved in adulthood, together with writing skills more advanced than speaking ones.

Patterns Across Language Domains

The foregoing review reveals an overall pattern of language strengths and weaknesses in mean performance of children with Down Syndrome, but we can ask whether this pattern is replicated at the level of the individual child in studies that compare performance across domains. The divergence of cognition and communication skills from other skill domains is evident even in the early years of life for children with Down Syndrome. Cognitive and communication skills in the first six years of life appear to lag behind the development of personal-social and adaptive skills, as indexed by the Battelle Developmental Inventory (Tingey, Mortenson, Matheson, and Doret, 1991), even for children in exemplary early intervention programs; the overall developmental score lags increasingly from norms with age. Gesell developmental assessment of children with Down Syndrome at two and three years reveals significantly poorer performance on the language subscale at three years than on the adaptive, gross motor, fine motor, or presonal-social scales (Smith and von Tetzchner, 1986).

Early studies of performance on the Illinois Test of Psycholinguistic Abilities (Bilovsky and Share, 1965; Burr and Rohr, 1978) revealed characteristic patterns of strengths and weaknesses (compared to overall language score) for children with Down Syndrome, as compared to norms or other children with mental retardation. Bilovsky and Share (1965), studying individuals aged six to 23 years, found that above the mean (15 months or more) were tests of gestural expression, and visual decoding of meaning; below the mean (15 months) were tests of expressive grammatical morphology and an auditory digit-span task. The strength of gestural expression, and greatest deficits in expressive grammatical morphology and auditory digit-span, were confirmed by Burr and Rohr (1978). Additionally, in these studies, vocabulary comprehension appeared midway in difficulty. The comprehension or production of syntax (beyond grammatical morphemes) was essentially not assessed by the ITPA, so that performance in these areas was not part of the early picture.

A deficit in symbolic representation, as indexed by symbolic play, has been noted for some children with specific language impairment. The development of play behaviors, including symbolic play, in sensorimotor and preoperational children with Down Syndrome is, however, similar to those of MA-matched controls (Beeghly, Weiss-Perry, and Cicchetti, 1990) and shows similar developmental change in distribution and level. (The exceptions to this summary include a higher rate of simple manipulative object play in a young cohort of children with Down Syndrome averaging 23 months MA; and a lag of the older cohort, MA averaging 48 months, on the higher levels of symbolic play scales that required *verbal* expression of the play. MA matching was based on the Bayley for the younger cohort and the WPPSI or the revised PPVT in the older cohort.)

Control groups matched on MLU, in contrast, showed lower MAs and younger developmental patterns of play than the groups with Down Syndrome or their MA controls. These differences confirm the deficit in the emergence of expressive syntax for the children with Down Syndrome, relative to MA expectations, and indicate that it is not associated with a general symbolic representational deficit in play. Rather, specific deficits in symbolic play only appear when their linguistic expression is required.

Work by Miller (1988) has evaluated age-equivalent performance in nonverbal cognition, language comprehension, and language production in a longitudinal study of children with Down Syndrome aged 11–58 months initially (Miller, Rosin, Pierce, Miolo, and Sedey, 1989). Defining three months' difference in score as a discrepancy for MAs below 24 months, and six months as a discrepancy for MAs of 25 months and above, three profile types were identified: (1) MA = comprehension = production (48 percent of Ss at time 1); (2) MA = comprehension > production (50 percent of Ss at time 1); (3) MA > comprehension > production (2 percent at time 1). Over visits, this distribution shifted; two years later, 21 percent showed a flat profile, 72 percent showed a production-only deficit, and 7 percent showed a deficit in both comprehension and production. profiles were stable or changed in the direction of production deficit with increasing mental age. For children of mental ages 13–24 months, 54–61 percent showed production deficits; for children of mental ages 25–36 months, 83–100 percent showed production deficits.

Further, the size of production vocabulary (including both words and signs) at onset of multiword utterances, as reported by parents on the Early Language Inventory, appears similar in the two groups, averaging 80 or 150, for children who had reached the laxer or more stringent criteria for onset. Thus, there is no evidence for a gap between cognition and syntax, or productive lexicon and syntax, at the onset of multiword combinations. This analysis, however, omits the children who are not yet combining utterances.

These data suggest normal development of comprehension relative to MA in the first five years of life for children with Down Syndrome, and the emergence of a production deficit increasing in probability with mental age. At any one time, profile distribution indicates individual differences in existence of deficits; the direction of change in profile distribution with mental age, however, suggests that the difference is one of severity rather than type.

The comprehension of syntactic structures by children with Down Syndrome is advanced, relative to their expressive syntax; but begins to show delays relative to nonverbal cognition in adolescence (Marcell, Croen, and Sewell, 1990; Chapman, Schwartz, and Kay-Raining Bird, 1991; Chapman, Ross, and Seung, 1993). In contrast, comprehension of vocabulary, as assessed by the Peabody Picture Vocabulary Test, becomes advanced relative to nonverbal cognition in adolescence (12–20 years) (Chapman, Ross, and Seung, 1993). Thus, chronological age contributes to the prediction of vocabulary and syntax comprehension even after mental age is entered in prediction equations, for children with Down Syndrome aged five to 20 years. The two predictors account for 78 percent of the variability in vocabulary comprehension and 80 percent of the variability in syntax comprehension; an additional 4 percent of the variability, in each case, is explained by hearing screening performance (Chapman, Schwartz, and Kay-Raining Bird, 1991), for this group that included children with mild hearing impairment.

Rosin, Swift, Bless, and Vetter (1988) also report deficits in syntax comprehension, relative mental-age matched groups, for children with Down Syndrome aged ten to 17 years; but not higher performance on vocabulary comprehension than cognition. This difference appears related to the differences in the two studies in cognitive assessment.

Thus, the scattered and contradictory reports of comprehension skill (or lack of it) in children with Down Syndrome can be traced to differences in the linguistic domain tested, chronological and mental age of the subjects, the exclusion or inclusion of children with mild hearing impairment, the method used to assess mental age, and tests insensitive in the developmental range in which the children are functioning. Current literature can be summarized by saying that, overall, strengths in vocabulary comprehension, and deficits in syntax comprehension, emerge in adolescence. Individual variation is related to CA, MA, and hearing loss, for vocabulary comprehension. Comprehension, in turn, is increasingly more advanced than language production; but variation in comprehension predicts variation in production (Chapman, Schwartz, and Kay-Raining Bird, 1991). This summary suggests an important change in the assessment protocols recommended for establishing Down Syndrome phenotype–genotype relationships (Epstein et al., 1991): linguistic domains should be assessed separately in comprehension and production.

Auditory Short-term Memory as a Source of Individual Variation?

The preceding review makes clear that chronological age and levels of nonverbal cognitive development are important predictors of the level of language skill and probability of deficit. IQ itself, and associated rates of cognitive development, varies almost as much within the Down Syndrome population as within the normally developing one. To a lesser extent, hearing status accounted for variance, particularly in intelligibility of speech.

Mother–child interaction is the transactional context from which early language, cognitive, and social skills emerge. The differing characteristics that children with Down Syndrome bring to that interaction, the ways in which mothers (and others) accommodate those differences, and the effect of those modulations on further development, have been the focus of a number of studies (see reviews by Miller, 1988; Berger, 1990; Crnic, 1990; Richard, 1986). These studies have generally revealed no differences in input that would account for the patterns of deficit and strength observed (Miller, 1988).

Aside from their general delay in cognitive development, children with Down Syndrome appear to have relative strengths in visual tasks and weaknesses on auditory short-term memory tasks. This pattern differs from the performance of children without mental retardation, or with mental retardation from other causes. The specific weaknesses in the auditory tasks have been taken as evidence for (variously labeled) information processing deficits: "sequential processing," "auditory processing," "short-term memory," "auditory short-term memory," and "auditory sequential short-term memory." These become candidate causes of the language deficits observed if one believes that language production depends on the collation of a large stored database of language encountered in context (Chapman, Streim et al., 1992).

A first problem in reviewing this literature, however, is to disentangle the contribution of language skills to the tasks and matching procedures used, as this has typically been ignored. Indeed, most of the studies describing "mental age" matched controls actually matched on vocabulary comprehension, using the Peabody Picture Vocabulary Test. However, vocabulary comprehension is an area of increasing strength, with age, in the pattern of language skills shown by children with Down Syndrome (Rosin et al., 1988), and can even yield performance better than indices of cognitive performance, depending on the nonverbal assessment (Chapman, Schwartz, and Kay-Raining Bird, 1991). A second problem is to choose the label: to sort out which aspects of the complex tasks used actually covary with poorer performance, relative to appropriately selected controls, across the studies.

Sequential processing deficit?

To take the most global version first, *sequential processing* has been proposed as a source of linguistic and nonverbal task difficulties alike (Pueschel, Gallagher, Zartler, and Pezzullo, 1987; Rosin et al., 1988). Rosin and colleagues found a decrement in expressive syntax and diadokokinetic rates that they attributed to a general deficit in processing sequential information. Pueschel et al. (1987) tested the hypothesis of a global deficit in sequential processing by administering the Kaufman Assessment Battery for Children (K-ABC) to 20 children with Down Syndrome and mild to moderate retardation aged eight to 12 years. They found that the group with Down Syndrome performed less well on both the Sequential and the Simultaneous processing scales than controls matched for mental age (via the PPVT – thus suggesting the actual acceleration of vocabulary comprehension skill in this group relative to other cognitive tasks); but each group performed equivalently on the Sequential and Simultaneous scales. To the extent that the K-ABC operationalizes global differences in sequential and simultaneous processing (and some critics of the test argue it does not), there was no evidence within the Down Syndrome group for a sequential processing deficit.

If sequential processing demands are to be distinguished from simultaneous processing demands, it would seem that order errors ought to occur disproportionately for the amount of material recalled. Taking this argument seriously, investigators have asked if more order reversals in recall can be found at equivalent memory-span levels for children with Down Syndrome (Kay-Raining Bird and Chapman, in press). The answer appears to be "no" for both visual sequencing tasks (Bead Memory on the Stanford-Binet, 4th ed.) and auditory sequencing tasks (Auditory Short-term Memory on the Illinois Test of Psycholinguistic Abilities), as well as a story recall task having an inherent narrative order (Kay-Raining Bird and Chapman, in press). Thus, there does not appear to be support for a global deficit in sequential processing or memory for sequence order, as Rosin et al., (1988) proposed.

Auditory processing deficit?

In the Pueschel et al. (1987) study, children with Down Syndrome performed more poorly on K-ABC tests of number recall and word order (auditory–vocal and auditory–motor tasks, respectively) than on tests of hand movement and gestalt closure (visual–motor and visual–vocal tasks, respectively). Pueschel et al. (1987) conclude that a specific auditory processing deficit exists that cannot be attributed to the hearing impairments frequently encountered in the Down Syndrome population because children with hearing impairments were excluded from the study. Hoppman and Willen (1993) report similar findings in a replication of Pueschel's work with 23 children aged eight to 12.5 years.

Ellison and Gillis (1993) have confirmed Pueschel's finding of no difference in the two K-ABC scales of Sequential and Simultaneous Processing for 77 children with Down Syndrome aged three to 12.5 years. In addition, they compared visual and auditory sequencing subtests, confirming Pueschel's finding of a significant advantage on visual sequencing in each three year age grouping. An advantage for visual simultaneous test performance v. auditory sequencing test performance was found for the two older groups. Within the visual domain, no simultaneous v. sequential task differences were found.

Better performance on visual short-term memory tasks than auditory ones is a finding in Down Syndrome children that contrasts with the usual auditory advantage in performance shown by nonretarded individuals (Marcell and Armstrong, 1982; Marcell and Weeks, 1988; McDade and Adler, 1980). This reversal of pattern has led to a search for the causes of the auditory short-term memory deficit and the potential roles it might play in relation to language acquisition.

Auditory short-term memory deficit?

A number of investigators have reported that children with Down Syndrome have exceptional difficulty on tests of auditory short-term memory, compared to children with retardation from other causes (Bilovsky and Share, 1965; Marcell, Harvey, and Cothran, 1988; Marcell and Weeks, 1988; Rohr and Burr, 1978; Snart, O'Grady, and Das, 1982). Thus, it is a particular characteristic of the genetic syndrome, rather than low IQ.

Children with Down Syndrome also do more poorly in auditory memory tasks than typically developing mental-age or vocabulary comprehension matched controls. This result is found for a variety of auditorily presented stimuli: digits (e.g. Marcell and Armstrong, 1982; Marcell, Harvey, and Cothran,

1988; Marcell and Weeks, 1988), familiar word strings (e.g. Marcell and Weeks, 1988), letter names (Varnhagen, Das, and Varnhagen, 1987), and sentences (Marcell, Ridgeway, Powell, Sizemore, and West, 1991).

The apparent magnitude of the deficit may vary in terms of control group selection; when vocabulary comprehension is used to match control groups, especially to adolescents with Down Syndrome, the controls may actually be mismatched for nonverbal cognitive skills, performing at higher levels than the Down Syndrome group (Chapman, Schwartz, and Kay-Raining Bird, 1991).

What causes auditory STM deficits in children with Down Syndrome? The task of remembering and repeating digit or word strings has a number of components that could contribute to impaired performance: speed and accuracy of lexical access in long-term store, and the consequent availability of chunking schemas; short-term auditory memory of elements and memory for order; use of the articulatory loop in keeping items in short-term store and the consequent effect of articulation rate (Baddeley, 1990); rate and accuracy of speaking the items on recall; and attention to task.

The effect of attentional distractors on digit recall was evaluated by Marcell, Harvey, and Cothran (1988), who were unable to improve recall of auditorily presented material for adolescents with Down Syndrome through headphone and goggle presentations that minimized distracting sounds or visual stimuli.

The effect of requiring verbal repetition of the strings to be recalled was evaluated by Marcell and Weeks (1988) by task variants in which recall was demonstrated through manual placement of items or pointing. Eliminating the verbal expressive demands failed to enhance performance for any subject group.

The relation of speed and accuracy of articulation to auditory short-term memory was evaluated by Racette and Fowler (1993). When adults with Down Syndrome (aged 17–25 years) were compared with preschoolers matched on the basis of auditory short-term memory, they were slower and less accurate at repeating real words ten times; but equal in speaking rate (though still less accurate) in repeating two-syllable nonsense words. Speed contributes significantly to the prediction of auditory short-term memory even when vocabulary and accuracy contributions are entered first into regression predictions. Baddeley (1990) has argued that the rate at which the articulatory loop functions might influence the amount of material recalled – and that one can infer that rate from rate of speaking. On this view, it is speaking rate that limits the covert rehearsal of auditory information, and thus its retention.

Varnhagen, Das, and Varnhagen (1987) found evidence that individuals with Down Syndrome were less likely to use the articulatory loop in learning serial lists; this was inferred by the equality of their performance on word lists that were phonologically confusable or not confusable. Control subjects typically perform more poorly on the confusable lists, indicating the use of the articulatory loop for rehearsal.

In addition, the slowness of lexical access during listening may contribute to the limited performance by children with Down Syndrome. Varnhagen, Das, and Varnhagen (1987) demonstrated that lexical access is slower, and variation in lexical access is marginally correlated with auditory memory span, for subjects with Down Syndrome but not other individuals with mental retardation.

Auditory short-term memory and language

Does auditory short-term memory performance predict language performance when nonverbal cognitive level is partialed out? Curiously, few studies have directly examined the relation between language and memory variables within the Down Syndrome population; but the wide individual differences in language within the population require it.

A significant correlation between auditory short-term memory and sentence imitation scores has been demonstrated by Marcell, Ridgeway, Powell, Sizemore, and West (1991) in adolescents with Down Syndrome. Compared to controls with mental retardation for other reasons, who were matched for chronological age and Stanford Binet IQ, the individuals with Down Syndrome showed similar digit-span scores but much reduced sentence recall scores, failing to take advantage of the usual increase in recall that sentences offer. They were also slower to initiate sentence recall.

In a study of sentence repetition and word definition, Marcell, Sewell, and Croen (1990) found equivalent accuracy of word definition for groups with Down Syndrome and mental retardation for other reasons; but poorer sentence imitation in the Down Syndrome group. The ability to imitate sentences, in both groups, was related to sentence comprehension and auditory digit span, but not to expressive word definitions or hearing. They suggested that slower identification of incoming items (and increased effort devoted to it) might have reduced capacity for retaining the item.

Subsequent work (Marcell, Croen, and Sewell, 1991) showed a significant correlation between performance on a backward masking task in which the mask rapidly (40 msec.) followed the word to be identified and measures of hearing status (Speech Reception Thresholds, acoustic reflex score). Relationships with hearing were not found with other language or cognitive tasks. Effects of IQ and chronological age were partialed out in these analyses.

Thus, close correlations can be demonstrated among the variation in auditory memory span, sentence comprehension, and expressive syntax, although age-equivalent scoring reveals far more marked deficits in the first and last. To the extent that our sentence comprehension tasks permit Ss long processing times for response, and typically depend on lexical aspects of sentence processing, our assessment procedures may conceal the true extent of discourse comprehension deficit for individuals with Down Syndrome; and some portion of the expressive language deficit may ultimately be attributable to the consequently reduced database of more complex language encountered and understood in context. If this is so, the success of interventions based on visual representation – including signing, reading, and writing – or on specific expansions within a context – become more understandable.

ACKNOWLEDGMENTS

The writing of this chapter was supported by NIH Grant R01 HD23353 to Chapman and by Core Support Grant 5 P30 HD03352 to the Waisman Center on Mental Retardation and Human Development. The help of Hye-Kyeung Seung, Allison Sedey, Scott Schwartz, and Giuliana Miolo is gratefully acknowledged.

25 Lexical and Grammatical Development in Children with Early Hemisphere Damage: A Cross-sectional View from Birth to Adolescence

JULIE A. EISELE AND DOROTHY M. ARAM

1 Introduction

The development of language, like the development of other cognitive systems, depends not only on exposure to appropriate environmental stimuli, but on significant changes in brain development that occur during the first few years of life. The period between birth and five years of age marks the most rapid and significant period of postnatal growth. Synaptic density peaks within the first two years of life (Huttenlocher, 1990), and by five years of age the brain has nearly reached its adult values (Brody et al., 1987; Chugani and Phelps, 1986; Conel, 1939–63). It is also during this period of time that children all but master their native language. Regardless of the language being acquired, all children begin babbling at approximately six months of age, produce their first words between 11 and 13 months, and acquire most of their adult grammar by five years of age. While, ultimately, the child's knowledge of language will reflect the sounds, vocabulary, and grammar of his or her own linguistic environment, the regularity and predictability with which these somewhat arbitrary features of the linguistic environment emerge appear to be largely determined by a developmental unfolding, wherein maturational changes in brain growth and organization trigger overt changes in language behavior.

Just as the normal development of language is shaped by both maturational and neuroanatomical constraints, so too is the acquisition and/or recovery of language functions in children with early hemispheric damage. Despite the remarkable degree of neural plasticity available to the immature brain, a growing number of studies have documented delays in the language acquisition of children with preperinatal injury and subtle deficits in the linguistic abilities of older children with unilateral brain lesions (see Aram and Eisele, 1992). The presence of such deficits long after the initial recovery period suggests that lesion-induced mechanisms of neural recovery and reorganization may potentially alter the normal trajectory of language development and its final "adultlike" representation.

In this chapter we review recent empirical evidence concerning the development and recovery of language functions in children with early hemisphere damage. We limit our report to the study of children with residual, i.e. non-aphasic, language disorders that persist beyond the acute phase (see Aram, 1991, and Rapin and Allen, 1988, for current reviews of acquired and developmental childhood aphasia). We focus first on the early stages of language development from birth to five years of age, namely on the emergence of gestural, lexical, and grammatical abilities in children with preperinatal hemisphere damage. We then review what is known about the lexical and grammatical abilities of older children and adolescents with unilateral brain lesions. Although still at a relatively descriptive stage, the limited evidence available documents linguistic deficits in the performance of both left and right hemisphere injured children. Moreover, the pattern of language deficits associated with left and right hemisphere damage will be shown to differ in subtle ways, from the earliest point in the language acquisition process.

1.1   Brain and language: Evidence from acquired aphasia

Issues concerning the neural basis for language focus primarily on two questions: (1) at what level do functional units of language share meaningful neurological correlates; and (2) to what extent can these units of language be localized to various regions of the brain? To this end, the study of acquired aphasia, the breakdown of language functions secondary to brain damage, has greatly advanced our understanding of the neural basis for language. In the interest of characterizing the final "steady state" of brain and language, the majority of this research has focused on acquired aphasia in the premorbidity competent adult speaker. The study of adult aphasia has revealed the potentially selective nature of language disturbances resulting from left hemisphere damage. Instances of adult aphasia have, for example, been shown to fractionate language knowledge along both modality-specific (i.e. comprehension versus production) and domain-specific lines, selectively impairing phonological, lexical, syntactic, and semantic aspects of language performance. The tightly knit organization of language in the brain is further revealed through naming disorders which can disrupt access to certain semantic categories leaving others intact, including for example, the ability to access words which describe inanimate, but not animate objects, and the ability to name fruits and vegetables, but not animals, and vice versa (Hart and Gordon, 1992; Hart, Berndt, and Caramazza, 1985; Warrington and Shallice, 1984).

While such dissociations provide compelling evidence for a functionally modular organization of language, at least at some level of neural representation, attempts to localize various aspects of linguistic behavior to precise regions of the brain have not met with much success. It has, in fact, been argued that attempts to localize subcomponents of language to discrete anatomical regions is a logically flawed model for the study of brain–language relationships (see Caplan, 1981, for further discussion of this issue). Such claims are motivated in large part by the wide degree of variability surrounding aphasic symptoms and their underlying neural correlates (Blumstein, Baker, and Goodglass, 1977; Caplan, 1989; Caplan, Baker, and Dehaut, 1985; Schwartz, 1984), and by more recent evidence from *in vivo* studies of language processing (e.g. PET) which reveal simultaneous activation of many discrete brain regions within and across the two hemispheres (Petersen, Fox, Posner, Mintun, and Raichle, 1989).

The recent failures of localization efforts notwithstanding, the continued presence of highly selective disturbances in language processing resulting from localized (Linebarger, Schwartz, and Saffran, 1983; Warrington and Shallice, 1984) and diffuse forms of injury (Hart and Gordon, 1992; Schwartz, Marin, and Saffran, 1979) continue to imply the presence of a functionally modular organization of language, at least at some level of brain organization. As currently conceived, functional modularity may resemble a sort of connectionist network, with overlapping neural nets and "convergence zones" which link together distributed facets of language knowledge (Damasio, 1989; Goldman-Rakic, 1988; Mesulam, 1990; Petersen et al., 1989; Sejnowski, Koch, and Churchland, 1988).

1.2   Neural plasticity and specialization in the context of development

In the child, issues concerning the neural basis for language must be evaluated in light of the factor of development. In contrast to the adult aphasic, where damage disrupts a fully functional language and neural system, damage sustained early in life disrupts the normal sequence of events underlying both brain and language development. The immature brain's remarkable potential to recover from neural insult through normal and lesion-induced mechanisms of neural plasticity affords the child a substantial degree of functional recovery not available to the adult brain. Consequently, attempts to delineate biological constraints on the development and recovery of language functions following injury are faced with the task of weighing residual deficits in language ability in light of the generally exceptional degree of functional recovery evidenced by the child.

It is this resiliency of the immature brain to injury that has long complicated the debate between proponents of an invariant left hemisphere specialization for language and those which favor a somewhat weaker version of the neural specialization hypothesis. How, for example, are we to conceptualize an invariant neural substrate for language given the dramatic recovery of language functions often observed in children with left hemisphere damage? As we report below, the validity of this long-standing dichotomy between neural specialization and recovery or plasticity of function has recently been challenged on both theoretical and empirical grounds.

Issues of hemispheric dominance, developmental invariance, and their counterparts (e.g. equipotentiality, progressive lateralization) have long dominated the study of acquired childhood aphasia. Early views of brain and language such as Lenneberg's theory of equipotentiality favored a weaker version of the language lateralization hypothesis (Bay, 1975; Brown and Jaffe, 1975; Lenneberg, 1967). According to Lenneberg (1967: 151), left hemisphere dominance for language was claimed to come about through an ontogenetic specialization of the two hemispheres; contingent on maturation of the two hemispheres and exposure to a linguistic environment:

> At the beginning of language development both hemispheres seem to be equally involved; the dominance phenomenon seems to come about through a progressive decrease in involvement of the right hemisphere. If, however, the left hemisphere is not functioning properly, the physiological activities of the right hemisphere persist in their earlier function.

The right hemisphere's potential for assuming control of language following left hemisphere injury was thought to be limited to the onset of puberty, the age at which Lenneberg claimed the lateralization of language to be complete.

Lenneberg's theory of equipotentiality and similar claims for an early diffuse neural representation of language (Bay, 1975; Brown and Jaffe, 1975) were based in large part on clinical reports which noted a relative infrequency of acquired aphasia during childhood, its transitory nature, and its occurrence following right hemisphere damage. A review of more recent literature on acquired childhood aphasia provides data inconsistent with each of these claims. Acquired childhood aphasia not only occurs with greater frequency in children with left rather than right hemisphere damage, but has been documented in children as young as four years of age (Cranberg, Filley, Hart, and Alexander, 1987), and may persist in certain cases for up to two years post-onset (Van Dongen, Loonen, and Van Dongen, 1985; Van Hout, Evrard, and Lyou, 1985). A recent retrospective study by Woods and Teuber (1978) of 65 children (2–14 years) with unilateral left or right hemisphere damage reported an incidence of acquired aphasia in 73.5 percent of left hemisphere injured children, and in only 6.9 percent of right hemisphere injured children. Based on these findings, Woods and Teuber attributed the higher incidence of right hemisphere aphasia reported in earlier studies to the possibility of undetected bilateral involvement stemming from preantibiotic infections and a shift in etiology away from diffuse, systemic bacterial infections to more discrete focal lesions. Several subsequent studies have now replicated Woods and Teubers' findings concerning the relative rarity of right hemisphere aphasia in children (Carter, Hohenegger, and Satz, 1982; Hecaen, 1983). Contrary to previous claims for a relative infrequency of acquired aphasia in children, Hecaen (1983) reported a higher frequency of aphasic symptoms in children $3\frac{1}{2}$–15 years) than in adults (73 percent > 63 percent) with left hemisphere lesions, and an even higher frequency of aphasic symptoms in children with injury sustained prior to rather than after ten years of age.

In addition to the relative rarity of right hemisphere aphasia, reports of neuroanatomical (Geschwind and Levitsky, 1968; Witelson, 1977), electrophysiological (Molfese and Molfese, 1979) and behavioral (Kinsbourne and Hiscock, 1977) differences claimed to favor a left hemisphere specialization for language, led to a widespread rejection of Lenneberg's equipotentiality hypothesis (see Satz, Strauss, and Whitaker, 1990; Witelson, 1987). As Satz et al. (1990) and others (Bullock, Liederman, and Todorovic, 1987), have recently suggested, however, equipotentiality and neural specialization need not be considered contradictory, but rather complementary features of brain organization and development. An attempt to reconcile the apparent paradox surrounding an invariant neural specialization for language and the dramatic recovery of function observed following early brain damage led Bullock et al. (1987) to propose a state of "near-equipotentiality" during childhood. According to Bullock et al. (1987: 694), the dominance of the left hemisphere emerges as a result of "symmetry-breaking factors" which act in concert with normal mechanisms of interhemispheric competition and stabilization during brain development, i.e. one such symmetry-breaking factor frequently proposed is a slightly more precocious maturation of the left hemisphere (Corballis and Morgan, 1978). When, however, the natural course of interhemispheric competition is disrupted, as in the case of brain injury, lesion-induced mechanisms simply "release the previously masked functional potentials already possessed by the (non-dominant) hemisphere."

Following in a similar vein, Satz et al. (1990) suggested that equipotentiality, as originally conceived by Lashley, implied a "latent activation" of alternative (nondominant) brain regions following injury; not that of an initial bilateral representation of speech functions as claimed by Lenneberg.

Implicit in both of the above reformulations is the view that hemispheric dominance is an emergent phenomenon, contingent upon neural changes that occur in the context of normal and abnormal brain development; their advantage lies in their ability to account for a normal left hemisphere dominance for language and at the same time to account for the orderly and efficient reorganization of neural systems presumed to occur following early hemisphere damage.

In this next section we review empirical evidence bearing on the acquisition of early language milestones in toddlers and young children with pre- or perinatal damage. The results of these studies reveal significant delays in the early language development of left and right hemisphere injured children, ranging from the use of prelinguistic gestures through early grammatical development. Hemispheric differences, although present, fail to provide the empirical support necessary for a simplistic view of the language lateralization hypothesis.

2 Early Language Development in Children with Focal Lesions

2.1 Gestural development

Prior to the acquisition of formal language, gestural communication (e.g. pointing, waving, nodding) represents the child's primary form of expression. Similar to language and other forms of nonverbal communication (e.g. deferred imitation, mental imagery, symbolic play), gesture requires the ability to engage in symbolic behavior; namely, the ability to map from an abstract mental representation to a real-world referent (Piaget, 1962). The question of whether language and gesture arise from a common set of representational abilities is one which is currently widely debated (Bates, Benigni, Bretherton, Camaioni, and Volterra, 1977; see the Piaget–Chomsky debate in Piatelli-Palmerini, 1980). Proponents of the "local homology" view hold that language may be considered an outgrowth of a more general symbolic function, where certain, but not all, aspects of language and gesture are derived from a shared set of representational abilities (Bates et al., 1977). Others view the mental representation of language as modular in nature, independent from more general forms of cognitive representations (Chomksy, 1976, 1980; Gleitman, 1984; Fodor, 1983; Pinker, 1991). Empirical evidence for these two opposing views comes largely from reports of parallels and dissociations in gesture and language development (Bates, Thal, Fenson, Whitesell, and Oakes, 1989; Corrigan, 1978; Thal and Bates, 1988a), and in the breakdown of these two aspects of communication (Bellugi, Klima, and Poizner, 1988).

Below, we review what little is known about the development of gesture in children with early hemisphere damage. Although limited, this research documents the potential for significant delays in gestural development following early left, as well as early right, hemisphere damage.

A recent study by Eisele and Aram (in prep) assessed the gestural and early language development of nine left (LL) and four right (RL) hemisphere injured children, ranging in age from eight to 42 months.[1] Using the *MacArthur Communicative Development Inventory* (CDI) for Infants (Fenson, Dale, Reznick,

Thal, Bates, Hartung, Pethick, and Reilly, 1993), parents were asked to indicate their child's use of 64 communicative gestures, ranging from "early gestures" (e.g. pointing, giving, showing, nodding) to "later gestures" which included actions with common objects (e.g. eating with a spoon or fork), pretense (e.g. pretending to be a parent), and imitation (i.e. of adult actions). Parental report data revealed significant delays in the use of both "early" and "late" gestures in four of the nine LL children, and in one of the four RL children. Delays in these five children ranged from six to 23 months below age level. As reported below, gestural delays in the majority of LL children were accompanied by significant delays in the production, but not comprehension, of first words, while the reverse was true for the single RL child.

Similar findings were reported by Marchman (Marchman, Miller, and Bates, 1991) in a study of five children with focal hemisphere damage (four LL; one RL) sustained prior to six months of age. Children were assessed longitudinally at three points in time; twice after the onset of canonical babbling, but before the child produced more than four word forms (9–13 months), and once when children were producing approximately ten words, or at 22 months of age, whichever came first. Parental report of early gestures using the CDI for Infants revealed significant delays (below the 28th percentile) in the gestural development of all five children assessed at nine to 13 months of age. Delays were still present in three children (two LL; one RL) at 22 months of age. Gestural delays at this later point in development were invariably associated with expressive delays in vocabulary development, and in two children (one LL; one RL) were accompanied by delays in receptive vocabulary as well.

Gestural delays were also noted in a study of six native Italian-speaking children with hemisphere damage sustained prior to one year of age (Dall'Oglio, Bates, Volterra, Di Capua, and Pezzine, 1992). Parental report on the CDI Infant scale revealed persistent delays in one of four LL children assessed longitudinally from 28 to 34 months, and in the single RL child assessed from 13 to 24 months of age. In both cases, gestural delays were accompanied by delays in the production, but not comprehension, of first words.

Delays in gestures involving fine or gross motor coordination and their frequent association with expressive language delays are not surprising given the likely involvement of motor cortex in some of these brain injured children. Gestural and language delays could potentially be attributed to limitations in motor functioning. The hypothesis of a generalized motor deficit in these children can, however, be discredited on several counts. In the study by Eisele and Aram (in prep), delays in gestural development were not directly related to the presence or absence of motor dysfunction. Children with and without motor involvement were significantly delayed in their use of gestures, while some children with frank hemiparesis were not. Moreover, in two children (one LL; one RL) significant delays in gestural development at 20 months were associated with delays in comprehension but not production. Second, gestural delays in each of the three populations studied were associated with anterior (prerolandic) and/or posterior (postrolandic) damage which did not involve the motor cortex. Third, delays in some of the "more sophisticated" symbolic gestures, namely, delayed imitation, symbolic play, etc., which persisted into the second and third year of life, could not be explained simply on the basis of a motor deficit hypothesis.

Delays in gestural development have been interpreted as indicative of a delayed emergence of certain rudimentary forms of mental representation. Such a hypothesis would account for the association between gestural delays and delays in early word learning skills. Assuming for a moment that language and gesture do spring from a common or overlapping set of representational abilities, then we might question whether delays in gestural development anticipate delays in lexical development and vice versa. The longitudinal studies reviewed above provide evidence for and against a continuity from gesture to language development. Delays in gestural development, when present, consistently predicted delays in either the comprehension or production of first words. On the other hand, delays in lexical development were not always anticipated by delays in gestural development. For example, in two of the LL children followed by Eisele and Aram (in prep), expressive delays of from one to one and one-half years of age occurred in the context of a seemingly normal gestural development.

2.2 Phonological development – babble

Canonical babbling represents an important milestone in language development and is often considered to mark the onset of phonological development. In one of the first and few studies to investigate the effects of early hemisphere damage on phonological development, Marchman, Miller, and Bates (1991) analyzed the spontaneous speech of five children with focal hemisphere damage (four LL; one RL). Vocalizations obtained over three longitudinal 30-minute free-play sessions were analyzed according to vocalization frequency and length, consonant production, and syllable structure. Analyses at both the "zero word point" (9–13 months), and "four word point" (21–22 months) revealed that lesion children did not babble any less, nor did their vocalizations differ qualitatively from those of normal controls. At the "zero word point," however, lesion children did tend to produce a greater proportion of monosyllabic vocalizations than controls, and during all three sessions tended to produce proportionately fewer labials, but not dentals or velars, relative to normal controls. Finally, all five brain injured children produced fewer consonants during the "zero word point." This persisted in two of the four LL children, who at 22 months of age had not yet acquired an expressive vocabulary of ten words.

In another recent study, analyses of the spontaneous speech of two LL and two RL children, assessed between two and there and one-half years of age, revealed a seemingly normal pattern of phonological development (Keefe, Feldman, and Holland, 1989). Similar to normal controls, left and right hemisphere injured children were observed to produce a number of age-appropriate phonological simplifications, including cluster reduction, liquid simplification, and final consonant deletion. In one LL child, however, the prolonged use of progressive and regressive assimilations at three and one-half years of age was accompanied by a significant delay in expressive syntax as assessed by the *Sequenced Inventory of Communicative Development* (SICD), as well as by performance on a novel word learning task.

The limited evidence reviewed above suggests that phonological development may be relatively resilient to early hemisphere damage. When present, however, delays in the emergence of consonant production and the prolonged use of phonological simplification processes tended to be associated with a delayed emergence of first words.

2.3   Lexical development

Most children exhibit a striking developmental dissociation in their comprehension and production of first words during normal language development (Bates, Bretherton, and Snyder, 1988; Benedict, 1979; Fenson et al., 1993). Children begin to exhibit reliable signs of single-word comprehension between eight and ten months of age, followed by a significant "burst" in vocabulary comprehension by one year. This early period of lexical development is marked by a wide degree of individual variation. A recent normative study of vocabulary development in approximately 1,600 children (Fenson et al., 1993) revealed a mean of 57.9 words comprehended at ten months of age, with a range of between eight and 183 words. A mean of 110 words comprehended was reported at 12 months, 165.5 at 14 months, and 210.6 at 16 months of age.

A somewhat different developmental time course characterizes the production of first words. Most children do not produce their first "true" words until between 11 and 13 months, gradually reach the 50–75 word point by 16 months, and exhibit a " burst" in expressive vocabulary development somewhere between 18 and 22 months of age. The normative study by Fenson et al. (1993) reported an average of 3.6 words or "word-like sounds" at ten months, 11.9 words at 12 months, 79 words at 16 months, and 317 words at 24 months.

This developmental disparity in the onset of lexical comprehension and production during normal language development very likely reflects maturational differences in the neural substrate mediating these two modalities of lexical performance. While we are not yet able to map the onset of specific language functions to particular regions and/or pathways in the brain, changes in brain development do parallel significant changes that occur during language development. Neural events that occur at around the time most children utter their first words include a peak in metabolic activity of the frontal lobes by approximately eight to ten months of age (Chugani, Phelps, and Mazziotta, 1987), a peak in synaptic density of the middle frontal gyrus peaks at about one year of age (Huttenlocher, 1990), and a maturation of corticosubcortical fibers of the pyramidal tract, the motor system for speech, to between 50–90 percent of adult levels by one and one-half years of age (Brody et al., 1987).

To date, very little is known about the development of lexical abilities following early hemisphere damage. It is not known, for example, whether early left and/or right hemisphere damage delays lexical acquisition, while preserving the normal developmental dissociation of these two modalities, or whether these two modalities can be selectively impaired, as in the case of adult aphasia. Nor is it known whether disorders of comprehension and production following early brain injury will adhere to the sensory-motor organization of the brain, or whether, as in the adult, such disorders will result from multiple sites within and across the two hemispheres. In this next section we review the handful of studies that have investigated the development of lexical abilities in young children with hemispheric damage. The results of these studies provide critical information with regard to the questions raised above.

2.4   *Lexical comprehension*

Of all language functions, semantic representations which mediate the comprehension of individual word meanings are thought to be the most widely distributed in their neural representation (Damasio, 1989; Hart, Lesser, Fischer, Schwerdt, Bryan, and Gordon, 1991; Petersen et al., 1989). Damage to various regions in the left or right hemisphere in the adult frequently disrupts access to the semantic features associated with individual words. Right hemisphere damage, in particular, has been associated with a lack of sensitivity to subtle aspects of semantic meaning, including metaphorical or nonliteral aspects of word meaning (Brownell et al., 1984; Brownell, Simpson, Bihrle, Potter, and Gardner, 1990; Winner and Gardner, 1977). The developmental studies we report below are consistent with the adult literature and provide evidence for an early and continuous involvement of both hemispheres in mediating lexical–semantic knowledge.

Thal et al. (1991) recently reported on the lexical development of 16 children with early hemisphere damage (ten LL; six RL), assessed over a period of from 12 to 22 months of age on the CDI (Fenson et al., 1993). Significant delays in the onset of word comprehension were noted in both LL and RL children, and were slightly more pronounced in the performance of RL than LL children (RL mean score = 29.8 percent, LL mean score = 37.5 percent). Consistent with this finding, within-subject analyses revealed a greater proportion of RL than LL children scoring below both the 25th (67 percent of RL subjects, 50 percent of LL subjects) and 10th percentiles (50 percent of RL subjects, 30 percent of LL subjects).

Delays in vocabulary comprehension were slightly less evident in the population of children studied by Eisele and Aram (in prep). Three of the eight LL children (aged eight to 32 months) and one of the three RL children (aged 13 to 22 months) exhibited delays of six months or greater when assessed using the CDI Infant scale (Fenson et al., 1993).[2] Comprehension deficits did, however, tend to be slightly more prevalent following right hemisphere damage when a larger and older sample of children was assessed using a picture-pointing test of single-word comprehension. Twenty-eight children with uni-lateral left (n = 17) or right (n = 11) hemisphere damage, ranging from two to five years of age, were tested on the Peabody Picture Test of Vocabulary – Revised (PPVT–R) (Dunn and Dunn, 1981). An analysis of children's percen-tile scores revealed a slightly greater proportion of RL (36 percent) than LL (27.8 percent) children scoring one or more standard deviations below the mean (below the 16th percentile). RL children also scored slightly lower than LL children overall (RL mean score = 26.3 percent, LL mean score = 33 percent). As we report below, these findings replicate an earlier study by Eisele and Aram (1993) involving slightly older groups of left and right hemisphere injured children.

Finally, a study of novel word learning skills in two LL and two RL children (26 to 41 months) revealed a slight tendency for lesion subjects to require a greater number of teaching presentations than normal controls in their com-prehension of nonsense nouns and verbs (Keefe et al., 1989).

Taken together, these results support the presence of an early and signific-ant contribution of both hemispheres in the acquisition of word meaning. The slightly greater proportion of comprehension deficits following right hemi-sphere damage (Eisele and Aram, in prep; 1993; Thal et al., 1991), while pro-vocative, remains to be replicated in future studies.

2.5   Lexical production – first words

Disturbances of spoken output, ranging from the production of individual phonemes to the production of grammatically well-formed sentences, occur with much greater frequency in adults with left than right hemisphere dam-age. In this next section we summarize studies which have investigated the emergence of first words following early hemisphere damage. Contradictory to the adult data, the results of these studies suggest that neural systems mediating the production of first words may, during early language develop-ment, depend to a greater extent on the normal functioning of both the left and right hemisphere.

The majority of infants followed by Eisele and Aram (in prep) experienced significant delays in the onset of first words following damage to the left hemisphere. Assessed between eight and 32 months of age, six of the nine LL children exhibited delays on the CDI, which ranged from six to 24 months below age level. In contrast, only one of the four RL subjects was delayed in his production of first words, performing six months below age level at 22 months. Rather than improve with increasing age, delays in the expressive vocabularies of left and right hemisphere injured children often became more pronounced over time. When the majority of these same children were assessed between 16 months and five years of age, eight of the nine LL children and two of the four RL children scored six months or more below age level in their production of first words. Assessed at between two and three years of age, expressive vocabularies for the majority of LL and RL children clustered at the 50 word point, in sharp contrast to the mean of 317 words at two years of age reported for normally developing children (Fenson et al., 1991).

A study of expressive naming skills using the Expressive One-word Picture Vocabulary Test (EOWPVT) (Gardner, 1979) with a slightly larger and older sample of Aram's population, revealed significant delays (below the 16th percentile) in eight of the 18 LL children and six of the 11 RL children studied between 2;6–5;4 years of age (Eisele and Aram, in prep).

Expressive delays in the performance of left and right hemisphere injured children were also reported in the study by Thal et al. (1991). A cross-sectional analysis of children aged 12 to 35 months revealed significant delays in 15 of the 19 LL children (79 percent) and in five of the eight RL children (62.5 percent) on the CDI. An analysis of these children at a slightly later stage of development, between 17 and 35 months of age, revealed a greater tendency for expressive deficits following left than right hemisphere damage (LL M = 15.9 percent versus RL M = 49 percent).

Finally, left and right hemisphere injured children followed by Feldman (Feldman, Holland, Kemp, and Janosky, 1992) produced significantly fewer words and word types during a 20 minute free-play session than did normal controls. Lexical expression was severely delayed in one of the five LL children who had just begun using words at 42 months of age and in one of the four RL children, who had not yet begun producing words at 27 months of age.

Thus, while delays in the onset of first words do occur with greater frequency following early left hemisphere damage, their presence in right hemisphere injured children argues against a complete lateralization of expressive language functions during the language acquisition process.

2.6 Early grammatical development

Not surprisingly, delays in the onset of first words which persist into the second and third year of life are frequently associated with delays in early grammatical development. It is during this period of time, the point at which most children are rapidly breaking into the grammatical code of their native language, that some of the most pronounced effects of early hemisphere damage are seen.

An analysis of early morphological and grammatical development by Eisele and Aram (in prep) revealed significant delays in children with both left and right hemisphere damage. Using the CDI Toddler Scale (Fenson et al., 1993), parents were asked to describe their child's use of morphological inflections, including plural, possessive, present progressive, and regular past tense ("ed") forms. For example, parents were asked to indicate whether their child's utterances resembled the uninflected noun phrase "two shoe" or its inflected counterpart "two shoes." Grammatical development surveyed the presence of function words (e.g. "Doggie table" versus "Doggie on table"), subject–auxiliary inversion in question forms, negation, contractions, and grammatical complexity through the addition of noun complements, prepositional phrases, complementizers, etc. In addition, parents were asked to report the three longest sentences produced by their child. On each of these measures, the majority of left (67–78 percent) and right (50–75 percent) hemisphere injured children were significantly delayed, often falling up to two years below age level. Utterance length was significantly delayed in seven of the nine LL children followed between 16 months and five years of age, with delays ranging from six months to just under two years. At two years of age, five of these LL children had not yet begun to combine words. Two of the four RL children were delayed in their production of word combinations, with one child exhibiting a mild delay of six months at $2\frac{1}{2}$ years of age, and the other exhibiting a more severe delay of 20 months at 42 months of age.

In what appears to be the only other study to investigate grammatical development following early hemisphere damage, Feldman et al. (1992) reported significant delays in MLU and expressive syntax, in one of five LL children and two of four RL children studied. In these three children, expressive delays persisted through final assessments at 48, 27, and 39 months of age respectively. With the exception of one RL child, all children evidenced relatively steady improvement between $1\frac{1}{2}$ to $3\frac{1}{2}$ years of age.

2.7   *Individual dissociations in comprehension and production*

Earlier we questioned whether hemispheric damage sustained prior to the acquisition of language would selectively impair lexical development along modality-specific lines. In each of the studies by Marchman, Miller, and Bates (1991), Thal et al. (1991), and by Eisele and Aram (in prep), dissociations in lexical comprehension and production were noted to occur following left as well as right hemisphere damage. Moreover, the nature of such dissociations appeared to interact with lesion laterality from the earliest point in development. In each of these studies, children with left hemisphere damage tended to exhibit significant delays in lexical production, which often became more pronounced over time, coupled with relatively preserved comprehension vocabularies. Right hemisphere injured children, although relatively few in number, tended to exhibit the reverse pattern, namely one of spared expressive vocabularies and delayed comprehension, or one of delayed comprehension and production. The delayed expression of first words in some right hemisphere injured children, although rare, suggests that early in development the right hemisphere may exert a potentially greater role in mediating the acquisition of expressive language relative to that observed later in development. As in LL children, expressive delays in RL children frequently persisted into the second and third year of life, giving rise to delays in early grammatical development as well.

2.8 Continuities and discontinuities across development

The longitudinal studies summarized above support the existence of modality-specific and domain-specific deficits in the period of language acquisition from birth to five years of age. Delays in language development were shown to cut across discrete points in time, selectively impairing lexical but not gestural development, the production but not comprehension of first words and vice versa. Dissociations were also observed in the onset of canonical babbling and the production of first words. In the study by Marchman, Miller, and Bates (1991), for example, delays in the onset of first words at 22 months of age were not necessarily antedated by a delayed emergence of consonant production.

Continuities in language development following early hemisphere damage were most apparent in the transition from first words to the onset of grammar. In the study by Eisele and Aram (in prep), the vast majority of LL and RL children with delays in early morphosyntactic development at 16 to 36 months of age had not yet reached the "burst" in vocabulary development frequently reported. LL children exhibited a range of from one to 79 words with a mean vocabulary of 23.8 words. As a group, RL children were producing slightly more words at this time (mean = 46.5 words), with a range of from 36 to 57 words. Consistent with these data is the notion that children need to achieve a "critical mass" in vocabulary development before breaking into the early stages of grammatical development (Bates et al., 1988).

3 Later Language Development in Older Children and Adolescents with Focal Lesions

The following section summarizes later language development in children with focal brain lesions, focusing in particular on the lexical and grammatical skills of children from six years of age to early adulthood. Although most children with early focal damage have undergone a period of "catch-up" growth by this stage of development, subtle deficits in linguistic performance well be shown to persist well beyond the initial phase of recovery.

3.1 Disorders of lexical production in older children with focal lesions

Despite previous claims for a lack of "positive symptoms" in acquired child-hood aphasia (Alajouanine and Lhermitte, 1965; Guttmann, 1942), more recent reports have noted a range of adultlike symptoms in children as young as three and four years of age (Cranberg et al., 1987), including those presumed to reflect disturbances in lexical processing, i.e. anomias, semantic paraphasias, and neologisms (Van Dongen and Visch-Brink, 1988; Van Dongen et al., 1985; Van Hout et al., 1985). While these overt aphasic symptoms generally subside rather quickly in children with focal brain injury, long-standing deficits in naming and single-word comprehension have been reported in left and right hemisphere injured children.

Woods and Carey (1979) and Vargha-Khadem (Vargha-Khadem, O'Gorman, and Watters, 1985) reported significant deficits in the naming performance of left hemisphere injured children tested on the Oldfield and Wingfield Naming Test. In the population of children studied by Woods and Carey (eight to 25 years of age), naming deficits were significant when injury was sustained after, but not before, one year of age, while Vargha-Khadem et al. reported significant naming deficits in her population of LL children (six to 17 years of age), regardless of whether injury was sustained prenatally or as late as 13 years of age. Here too, however, naming deficits were more likely to occur following later rather than earlier injury. Finally, Hecaen (1983) noted a higher incidence of naming disorders following early left than right hemisphere dam-age, and the incidence was even higher in children younger than ten years of age than those between 11 and 15 years of age (64 percent > 30 percent). Included in Hecaen's study, however, were children with chronic tumors and traumatic head injury, raising the possibility of bilateral involvement in some of these children.

Early injury to the nondominant right hemisphere has also been shown to leave behind residual deficits in naming ability (Aram, Ekelman, Rose, and Whitaker, 1985; Eisele and Aram, 1993; Riva, Cazzaniga, Pataleoni, Milani, and Fedrizzi, 1986; Vargha-Khadem et al., 1985). Vargha-Khadem et al. (1985) reported significant deficits in the naming performance of right hemisphere injured children aged six to 17 years when injury was sustained between three months and five years of age, and Riva et al. (1986) reported significant deficits in the expressive vocabularies of LL and RL children ranging in age from five to 15 years. RL children studied by Aram et al. (1985) were more likely than LL children (one to eight years of age) to score one or more standard devia-tions below normal on the EOWPVT (Gardner, 1979). This same finding was replicated in a subsequent study involving a slightly larger and older (two to 14 years of age) sample of Aram's lesion population (Eisele and Aram, 1993). RL children scored lower than did LL children as a group (RL mean score = 45 percent < LL mean score = 61 percent), and individually RL children were more likely to score below the 16th percentile than were LL children. In both groups, performance tended to improve with increasing age and consequently the lower performance of RL children may have reflected their younger age (RL mean age = 5;08; LL mean age =7;05). As reported below, however, comprehension deficits in this group of RL children were much more pronounced than were deficits in their naming abilities.

In order to assess the effects of early hemisphere damage on lexical retrieval, Aram and Ekelman (1987) administered the Word-Finding Test (Wiegel-Crump and Dennis, 1984) and the Rapid Automatized Naming Test (Denckla and Rudel, 1976) to a group of LL and RL children between six and 17 years of age. The word-finding task required subjects to generate names of words belonging to a particular semantic category (e.g. food, animals, clothing) in response to semantic, rhyming, and visual cues. Semantic cues, for example, were as follows: "It's an animal; it lives around the house; it walks on four legs; it chews on bones and barks; It's a ____." Rhyming cues were of the form "It's a food; it rhymes with sewnut: it's a ____," and visual cues were provided by line drawings. On the rapid naming task, subjects were required to name, as quickly as possible, colors, numbers, objects, and letters that appeared on a printed picture board. Performance on the cued retrieval task revealed that LL children not only responded slower than age-matched controls on the semantic and visual cues, but also made significantly more errors than controls in response to rhyming cues. RL children, in contrast, typically responded faster than their controls, yet were less accurate, leading Aram et al. (1987) to suggest a speed–accuracy tradeoff. Similar to the results obtained by Aram and Ekelman (1987), left hemidecorticate children tested by Dennis (1980) had more difficulty responding to rhyming cues than to either semantic or visual cues: a finding which Dennis attributed to the isolated right hemisphere's somewhat limited access to phonological representations.

3.2 Disorders of lexical comprehension in older children with focal lesions

Consistent with the adult literature and with the studies of first language acquisition described above, disorders of lexical comprehension are frequently noted in the later language abilities of left and right hemisphere injured children. The results of several studies based on the Peabody Picture Vocabulary Test (Dunn and Dunn, 1981) have revealed significant comprehension deficits in school-aged children regardless of lesion laterality (Aram et al., 1985; Aram and Eisele, in prep; Levine, Huttenlocher, Banich, and Duda, 1987; Riva et al., 1986). In fact, more pronounced comprehension deficits were observed following early right, as opposed to left, hemisphere damage in a recent study of children aged two to 14 years (Eisele and Aram, 1993). RL children scored significantly lower on the PPVT–R than LL subjects (RL mean score = 21 percent, LL mean score = 44 percent). Moreover, within-subject analyses revealed that each and every RL child performed below age level, with no RL child scoring above the 40th percentile.

A subsequent study involving many of these same children revealed deficits in both LL and RL subjects' performance on a semantic relations task. Given a set of four printed words, subjects were asked to select two words that were (1) most opposite in meaning (antonyms), (2) most similar in meaning (synonyms), or (3) related by class-inclusion, where one word was an exemplar of the other. LL and RL groups made significantly more errors than age-matched controls overall. All groups, however, exhibited a similar pattern of performance; each making the fewest errors in their judgments of class inclusion and the greatest number of errors in their judgments of synonyms. In addition, all groups were slightly more proficient in their semantic judgments involving verbs than adjectives.

Finally, as discussed below in greater detail, RL children tested by Eisele (1992) were selectively impaired in their presuppositions of truth when such inferences required the ability to integrate lexical negation (i.e. the verb "forget") with syntactic and semantic features of the sentence.

The above results, based on a variety of task methodologies, document the potentially long-term effects early left and right hemisphere damage can have on lexical comprehension and production. In general, disorders of lexical production were more frequently associated with left hemisphere damage, while disorders of comprehension appeared just as likely to occur following left or right hemisphere damage; a pattern of performance similar to that observed in young children and adults with hemispheric damage. In some cases, the significant comprehension deficits of right hemisphere injured children may have contributed to the occasional delays in the emergence of first words, and to the expressive naming deficits of some older RL children.

3.3 Disorders of syntactic comprehension in older children with focal lesions

In contrast to the wealth of research on syntactic deficits in the adult, studies of children and adolescents with early focal hemisphere damage are just beginning to rely on the use of linguistically sensitive measures of syntactic comprehension (Dennis and Kohn, 1975; Dennis and Whitaker, 1976; Dennis, 1980; Eisele, 1992; Eisele and Aram, 1994; Eisele, Aram, and Lust, in prep; Jackson, 1991; Woods and Carey, 1979). The results of these studies not only document the presence of selective, but persistent, deficits in syntactic comprehension following early left hemisphere damage, but have recently revealed what appears to be an important role of the right hemisphere in mediating certain aspects of sentence meaning (Eisele, 1992; Eisele and Aram, in press).

Similar to the pattern of comprehension deficits observed in adult aphasics, disorders of syntactic comprehension in older children and adolescents with hemispheric damage are especially evident in noncanonical passive and relative clause structures, where a grammatically correct interpretation of sentence meaning requires the ability to represent and compute over abstract syntactic relations.

Some of the earliest research to support an early specialization of the left hemisphere for syntax came from the study of hemispherectomy children, who following long-standing seizure disorders underwent surgical removal of the left (left hemidecortication) or right (right hemidecortication) hemisphere, often during the first few months of life. In a series of articles, Dennis and her colleagues documented a superiority of the isolated left hemisphere for processing complex grammatical information (Dennis, 1980; Dennis and Kohn, 1975; Dennis and Whitaker, 1976). In an early study, Dennis and Kohn (1975) tested five left hemidecorticate (LH) and four right hemidecorticate (RH) patients (8;2–28;11 years of age) on their comprehension of affirmative and negative active and passive sentences like those below:

1 The boy pushes the girl.
2 The boy does not push the girl.
3 The girl$_i$ is pushed t$_i$ by the boy.
4 The girl$_i$ is not pushed t$_i$ by the boy.

Left and right hemidecorticate children were fairly successful in their comprehension of affirmative and negative actives like those in (1) and (2). Only right hemidecorticate children with a remaining left hemisphere, however, were consistent in their interpretation of passive sentence types. On passive affirmative and negative sentences, two of the five LH children performed at chance levels in their assignment of thematic roles. Given a sentence like that in (3), children with an isolated right hemisphere frequently selected a picture of a girl pushing a boy.

A follow-up study of one RH and two LH children (nine to ten years of age) by Dennis and Whitaker (1976) revealed deficiencies in the performance of left, but not right, hemidecorticates on a variety of linguistic tasks including grammaticality judgments, repeating stylistically permuted sentences, producing tag questions (e.g. "Jill is very smart, isn't she?"), determining sentential implications, selecting grammatically correct pronouns, and appreciating abstract syntactic relations. Left hemidecorticate children were not, however, deficient on all language tasks. Despite their failures on tasks of syntactic relations, left hemidecorticates were just as proficient as right hemidecorticates on tasks of phonemic discrimination, articulation, word meaning, and judgments of semantically anomalous sentences, e.g. "My favorite breakfast is radios with cream." Thus, despite its limited syntactic abilities, the isolated right hemisphere appears to be an adequate substrate for mediating semantic representations, as well as the production and perception of speech.

Disorders of syntactic comprehension have also been documented in children with less radical forms of left hemisphere damage. A study of 27 children and adolescents (eight to 25 years) by Woods and Carey (1979) revealed residual deficits in syntactic comprehension if injury was sustained after one year of age. LL subjects were shown to be deficient in their comprehension on the Token Test (e.g. "Touch the blue circle with the red rectangle"), a relative clause task of semantic anomalies (e.g. "The boat that built the boy went in for lunch"), and a test of logical relations (e.g. "My father's aunt is my sister"). When, however, Woods and Carey divided this group of LL children with later injuries into a group of "recovered aphasics" and "never aphasic" children, only the "recovered aphasic" group differed significantly from their controls on tests of syntactic comprehension and production.

The results of these studies, while consistent with an early left hemisphere specialization for language, leave unanswered questions concerning the role of the right hemisphere damage in mediating the acquisition and recovery of syntactic functions. Despite the noted limitations of the isolated right hemisphere in mediating syntactic functions, left hemidecorticate children followed by Dennis et al. (1976) were capable of achieving an impressive degree of linguistic ability. Consistent with these findings, the studies reported below provide some evidence to suggest that certain aspects of syntactic comprehension may depend on the presence of an intact right hemisphere from the earliest stages of development.

A recent study of syntactic comprehension by Eisele and Aram (1994) revealed comprehension deficits in a subset of the left and right hemisphere injured children tested. Using an 'act-out' task of sentence comprehension, 25 children with early left (n = 16) or right (n = 9) hemisphere damage were tested on their ability to interpret semantically reversible coordinate, passive, and relative clause structures like those below, among others:

5   The elephant hit the lion and he patted the hippo.
6   The lion licked the dog and the hippo kicked him.
7   The lion scratched the hippo and was chased by the dog.
8   The dog that licked the hippo patted the elephant.

Subjects ranged in age from 7;2 to 23;1 years of age at time of testing and lesion age ranged from the prenatal period to 15;11 years. Although neither left nor right lesion groups differed significantly from their controls overall, within-subject analyses revealed a subset of LL (n = 5) and RL (n = 3) children whose comprehension performance fell at or near chance levels. Qualitatively, lesion and control groups exhibited a similar pattern of performance. All groups made the greatest number of errors in their comprehension of relatives, followed by passives, and finally coordinates. Thus, similar to the pattern of performance observed in adult aphasics and in normal children acquiring a first language, embedded structures were more difficult to interpret than conjoined ones, noncanonical thematic role structures more difficult than canonical ones, and sentences with empty categories more difficult than those with overt referential dependencies, i.e. pronouns. Predominant error strategies on passive and relative clause structures were characterized by a linear-order assignment of thematic roles to lexical NPs, again replicating the pattern of performance observed during normal language development and in adults with left hemisphere damage. For example, given a sentence like (8), lesion subjects frequently interpreted the "hippo" as the agent of the main clause verb "patted."

The lack of significant group differences between lesion subjects and their controls replicates an earlier comprehension study (Aram and Ekelman, 1987) involving a subset of these same children tested on the Revised Token Test (McNeil and Prescott, 1978).

Relatively mild comprehension deficits were also reported in a recent study involving a slightly younger group of LL children. Jackson (1991) tested six children (5;9–13;2) with left hemisphere damage sustained between birth and five years on their ability to interpret the meaning of pronouns and reflexives in active, passive, and control structure structures like those in nine through 14, and to interpret complex control structures, relatives, and adverbials like those in 15 through 18, among others:

9   He washed Gumby.
10   The robot is washing him.
11   Gumby tells Pokey to pat him.
12   Gumby tells him that the robot will jump over the fence.
13   Gumby is patting himself.
14   Pokey tells the deer to look at himself.
15   The girl promises Gumby to go into the cage.
16   The lion tells the bear to jump over the fence.
17   The girl kicks the horse that jumps over the bear.
18   The elephant pushes the lion before jumping over the fence.

Overall, LL children were fairly successful in their act-out performance (mean score = 81 percent correct). Subjects were particularly successful in their comprehension of relative clause structures, with only two of the six children having some difficulty (67 percent correct) on object relatives, e.g. "The girl kicks the bear that the cowboy hits." Despite their relatively successful comprehension of relatives, however, a majority of subjects erred in their comprehension of object pronouns in both simple (e.g. (10)) and complex (e.g. (11–12)) sentences. When presented with sentences like (10–12), children frequently assigned a reflexive interpretation to the accusative pronoun "him." LL children also had difficulty comprehending subject control structures with the main verb "promise" (e.g. (15)), and sentences with adverbial complements as in (18). On these later sentence types, subjects appear to have adopted a linear-order assignment of thematic roles, assigning the role of agent to the NP immediately in front of the verb. For example, in a sentence like (15), subjects frequently misinterpreted the NP "Gumby" as the agent of the verb "to go." Here, too, such error strategies parallel those frequently observed in young children and in adult aphasics. In contrast to their generally successful comprehension, performance on a grammaticality judgment task by Jackson's LL subjects fell to chance levels (mean score = 49 percent correct). An analysis of subjects' responses revealed a tendency on the part of LL children to respond "yes" to both grammatical and ungrammatical sentences. This tendency towards an overacceptance or "yes" response bias is frequently observed in young children, and often implies a failure to comprehend task demands. The observed dissociation between comprehension and grammaticality judgments in these children is also consistent with the performance of adult aphasics, who despite severe comprehension failures are quite proficient in their ability to discriminate grammatical from ungrammatical sentences (Linebarger et al., 1983; Schwartz, Linebarger, Saffran, and Pate, 1987).

Finally, a recent study of pragmatic language knowledge revealed comprehension deficits in the presupposition and implication performance of LL and RL children. Critically, however, the pattern of comprehension deficits observed following left and right hemisphere damage was shown to vary in accordance with structural and semantic features of the sentence. Using a sentence–question task, Eisele (1992; Eisele, Aram, and Lust, to appear) tested 15 LL and 11 RL children on their ability to (1) judge the truth of presuppositions associated with sentences containing "factive," or "implicative," predicates and tensed embedded complements like those in (19–21), and (2) to infer the truth or falsity of implications associated with sentences containing "implicative" verbs and infinitive complements like those in (22–3):

19   Max knew that he locked the door.
20   Max remembered that he locked the door.
21   Max forgot that he locked the door.
22   Max remembered to lock the door.
23   Max forgot to lock the door.

Sentences varied according to the semantic properties of the main clause verbs (e.g. factive versus implicative), the syntax of the embedded complements (e.g. +/– tense), and according to the presence or absence of lexical and syntactic negation in the main and/or subordinate clause.

Sentences with factive verbs as in (19) presuppose the truth of their embedded complements, regardless of the presence or absence of negation. For example, in a sentence like (24), it is presupposed that Max locked the door, regardless of whether or not Max knew it:

24   Max did not know that he locked the door.

In contrast, in sentences with implicative verbs and infinitive complements as in (22) and (23), the truth of the embedded complement varies in its truth or falsity in accordance with the presence or absence of negation and the meaning of individual words in the sentence. For example, in a sentence like (22), the truth of the complement is implied, while in sentences like (23) and

(25), the presence of lexical or syntactic negation is associated with a denial of complement truth: that is, that Max did not lock the door:

25 Max did not remember to lock the door.

Thus, sentences like those in (19–25) above, require subjects to vary their inferences of truth in accordance with lexical, syntactic, and pragmatic features of the sentence.

An analysis of correct performance on these sentence types revealed hemispheric differences with respect to both the nature of the inference to be judged, e.g. presuppositions versus implications, and the presence and type of linguistic negation, e.g. lexical versus syntactic. LL children were deficient in both their presuppositions and implications of truth, although such deficits were particularly evident in sentences involving either syntactic or lexical forms of negation. For example, when presented with a sentence containing lexical negation as in (21), or syntactic negation as in (24), LL children frequently overextended the scope of negation to negate the embedded complement. LL subjects performed at chance in their presuppositions of truth on sentences with syntactic negation and below chance on sentences with the verb "forget." The performance of RL children, in contrast, revealed a more selective deficit. Unlike LL children and normal controls, RL children were more likely to err in their implications than presuppositions of truth, and were more likely to err on sentences involving lexical negation than those with syntactic negation. RL children's difficulty in interpreting inferences associated with the lexically negative verb "forget" emerged in both their implications and presuppositions of truth. Despite their generally successful presupposition performance, RL children's performance on a sentence like that in (21) fell to below chance levels (mean score = 25 percent). Given a sentence like (21), RL subjects frequently overextended the scope of lexical negation to the complement clause. RL subjects' failure to presuppose the truth of sentences with lexical negation was particularly significant given their successful comprehension of presuppositions involving syntactic negation.

3.4 Disorders of syntactic production in older children with focal lesions

Reduced verbal output, ranging from mutism to the telegraphic speech characteristic of adult agrammatics, has long been noted as a predominant feature of acquired childhood aphasia. Reports of acquired childhood aphasia have recently described adultlike features of agrammatic speech, complete with phonemic paraphasias, omissions and/or substitutions of function words and morphological inflections, in children as young as four years of age (Cranberg et al., 1987). Moreover, adultlike aphasic symptoms in young children do not necessarily require the presence of a functional or operative grammar at the time of insult. Disorders of sentence production, including stutteringlike dysfluencies, phonemic and semantic paraphasias, and rapid, jargonistic speech, have been observed in the emerging grammatical abilities of children with pre-perinatal left and right hemisphere damage (authors' personal observation).

As in the adult, disorders of expressive syntax occur more frequently and are more persistent following early left than right hemisphere damage. In one of the first studies to formally assess the syntactic characteristics of spontaneous speech following early focal hemisphere damage, Aram and colleagues (Aram, Ekelman, and Whitaker, 1986) reported on the expressive language of eight LL and eight RL children, aged one and one-half to eight years. Syntactic complexity was assessed using the Developmental Sentence Score (Lee, 1974), which divides eight grammatical categories (e.g. pronouns, embedded verbs, negatives) into eight weighted developmental levels. With regard to MLU, spontaneous speech samples revealed significant differences between LL and RL children and their respective controls. A closer analysis of syntactic complexity, however, revealed far more pronounced and consistent deficits in the spoken language of LL than RL children. LL children produced significantly fewer simple and complex sentences (both grammatical and ungrammatical), containing significantly fewer embeddings, subject–aux inversions, wh-question forms, and a range of grammatical markers including third person pronouns, tense inflections, copulas, and auxiliaries. RL children produced a significantly smaller proportion of simple, but not complex, sentences relative to age-matched controls and were also somewhat deficient in their use of grammatical markers.

Woods and Carey (1979) reported significant deficits on the sentence completion task of the Boston Diagnostic Aphasia Examination (Goodglass and Kaplan, 1983) (i.e. "Water is . . . ," "A mother has a . . .") in children with left hemisphere damage sustained after one year of age. These deficits were more pronounced if the initial injury resulted in acute aphasic symptoms. Riva et al. (1986) reported significant deficits on the Benton test of sentence repetition for LL, but not RL, children (five to 15 years). LL children (seven to 14 years) studied by Kiessling (Kiessling, Denckla, and Carlton, 1983) made significantly more errors on the Binet sentences than did RL children or sibling controls. Finally, left and right hemidecorticate children tested by Dennis (Dennis, 1980; Dennis and Whitaker, 1976) were noticeably impaired in their imitation of complex sentences, semantically, and grammatically anomalous sentences, and random word strings. Imitation deficits were particularly pronounced in those LH children who failed in their comprehension of semantically reversible passives.

Similar to the findings reported above, a recent experimental test of sentence imitation revealed significant deficits in the imitation performance of left and right hemisphere injured children. Using a matched experimental design, Eisele and Aram (1994) tested LL and RL children (seven to 23 years) on the same sentence types used in the "act-out" study described above. These sentence types are replicated below:

26 The elephant hit the lion and he patted the hippo.
27 The lion licked the dog and the hippo kicked him.
28 The lion scratched the hippo and was chased by the dog.
29 The dog that licked the hippo patted the elephant.

Despite the relatively successful comprehension performance of LL and RL groups on sentences like those in (26–29), their imitation performance fell to chance levels. Imitation deficits were particularly pronounced in the LL group, whose mean performance fell below chance (LL mean score = 44 percent; RL mean score = 64 percent). Within-subject analyses revealed a majority of LL children performing well below their age-matched controls, with half of the 16 LL children erring on 66 percent or more of sentence items.

A comparison of lesion and control subjects' imitation and comprehension performance revealed an interaction between performance modality and the structural and surface properties of the sentence. In direct contrast to their comprehension performance, LL children, similar to normal controls, had the greatest difficulty imitating coordinate and passive sentence types, and the least difficulty imitating relative clause structures. RL children had the greatest difficulty on passives, followed by coordinates and then relatives. This pattern of results suggests that comprehension in these children may be more sensitive to structural features of sentence complexity (i.e. embedding, movement), while imitation may depend to a greater degree on surface complexity, namely sentence length and the number of content words. Smith and Van Kleeck (1986) reported a similar set of findings in normal children's comprehension and imitation performance, leading them to argue for an interaction between task performance and sentence complexity defined in terms of "interpretive complexity," i.e. embedding, the number of empty categories, and "surface complexity"; i.e. sentence length, content load, etc. Consistent with this hypothesis, a far greater number of "lexical" errors (e.g. noun or verb substitutions) than "structural" errors occurred on the imitation task, particularly on coordinate structures, while a greater number of structural errors occurred in subjects' comprehension of passive and relativized structures.

Finally, LL children tested by Jackson (1991) were fairly successful in their performance on a sentence production task (91 percent) designed to elicit simple and complex structures like those in (9) through (18).

4 Preliminary conclusions on the development of language in the context of early hemisphere damage

Our review of language development following early hemisphere damage challenges a simplistic view of the language lateralization hypothesis. Rather, consistent with recent evidence from PET and other *in vivo* studies of brain functioning in the adult, the studies presented here document an important contribution of both hemispheres in mediating the development of linguistic behavior. A delayed emergence of early gesture, vocabulary, and grammar, as well as residual deficits in lexical–semantic and syntactic functions were noted in children with focal left and right hemisphere damage. From the earliest point in development, however, the nature of language deficits associated with left and right hemisphere damage appeared to differ in subtle ways. Gestural delays, although present in both LL and RL children, tended in LL children to be more strongly associated with delays in the production of first words. Despite the limited evidence available on phonological development, delays in the onset of canonical babbling tended to be relatively mild in comparison to those observed in gestural and lexical development. Left hemisphere damage was frequently associated with delays in the production of first words and word combinations, and with later deficits in syntactic production. Right hemisphere damage, in contrast, was more likely to result in a delayed comprehension of first words. The significant deficits in lexical comprehension reported by Eisele and Aram (1993) and the selective failure of RL children to comprehend presuppositions and implications of truth associated with the lexically negative verb "forget" (Eisele, 1992) argue for an important role of the right hemisphere in mediating semantic development. Finally, disorders of syntactic comprehension associated with early left and right hemisphere damage tended to be relatively mild in light of the significant deficits observed on tasks of sentence imitation.

The presence of early left or right hemisphere damage does not, however, invariably lead to persistent deficits in linguistic performance. Rather, recovery from early hemisphere damage is characterized by a wide degree of variability within and across individual children. So far, attempts to characterize this variability in terms of lesion-specific factors have not met with much success (Aram and Eisele, 1992). Despite the generally remarkable degree of functional recovery observed in children relative to adults, the factor of age at lesion onset has not emerged as a consistent predictor of linguistic recovery. The factors of lesion location and lesion size have also failed to consistently predict recovery of function, although there is some evidence to suggest that damage to subcortical structures may prove to be critical in predicting early and later linguistic ability (Eisele, Aram, and Alexander, in prep).

The studies reviewed in this chapter contribute to our understanding of the behavioral phenomenon that characterize linguistic development following early hemisphere damage. Although we are far from understanding the biological constraints that limit functional recovery in brain injured children, the data presented here strongly suggest that a complete acquisition of language requires the normal functioning of both hemispheres from the earliest point in development.

NOTES

1 Hemisphere damage in this population of children, and in all others referred to in studies by Aram and her colleagues, resulted from a single neurological event, vascular in nature. MRI and/or CT confirmed the presence of a unilateral lesion in all children and no children with ongoing seizure disorders were included as subjects. See Aram (1988) for a more detailed description of the population.

2 Differences in the pattern of CDI results obtained in studies by Thal et al. (1991) and Marchman, Miller, and Bates (1991) versus those obtained by Aram and her colleagues may have resulted from differences in the scoring system used. Thal and Marchman used percentile scores, which required comparing children older than 16 months old normative data, while Eisele and Aram (in prep) used mental age norms (at the 50th percentile) to evaluate subjects' performance.

References

Abney, S. (1987) The English noun phrase in its sentential aspect. Ph.D. dissertation, MIT.

Achenbach, T. (1978) The child behavior profile I: Boys aged 6–11. *Journal of Consulting and Clinical Psychology*, 46, 478–88.

Acredolo, L. P. (1978) Development of spatial orientation in infancy. *Developmental Psychology*, 14, 224–34.

—— (1980) Laboratory versus home: The effect of environment on the nine-month-old infant's choice of spatial reference system. *Developmental Psychology*, 15, 666–7.

Acredolo, L., and Evans, D. (1980) Developmental changes in the effects of landmarks on infant spatial behavior. *Developmental Psychology*, 16, 312–18.

Adams, C., and Bishop, D. V. M. (1989) Conversational characteristics of children with semantic–pragmatic disorder. I: Exchange structure, turntaking, repairs and cohesion. *British Journal of Disorders of Communication*, 24, 211–39.

Adone, D. and Vainikka, A. (1990) The acquisition of Wh-questions in Mauritian Creole. Paper presented at the 15th annual Boston University conference on Language Development.

Aitchison, J. (1987) *Words in the Mind: an introduction to the mental lexicon.* Oxford: Blackwell.

Akhtar, N., Dunham, F., and Dunham, P. J. (1991) Directive interactions and early vocabulary development: the role of joint attentional focus. *Journal of Child Language*, 18, 41–50.

Aksu-Koç, A. (1988) *The Acquisition of Aspect and Modality: the case of past reference in Turkish.* Cambridge: Cambridge University Press.

Aksu-Koç, A. and Slobin, D. I. (1985) The acquisition of Turkish. In D. I. Slobin (ed.), *The Crosslinguistic Study of Language Acquisition*, 1, 839–78. Hillsdale, NJ: Lawrence Erlbaum Associates.

Aksu-Koç, A. and Stutterheim, C. (1994) Temporal relations in narratives: simultaneity. In R. A. Berman and D. I. Slobin (eds), *Different Ways of Relating Events in Narrative: a crosslinguistic developmental study.* Hillsdale, NJ: Lawrence Erlbaum Associates.

Alajouanine, T. H. and Lhermitte, F. (1965) Acquired aphasia in children. *Brain*, 88(4), 653–62.

Aldridge, M. (1989) *The Acquisition of INFL.* Bloomington: Indiana University Linguistics Club Publications.

American Association of University Women (1992) *How Schools Shortchange Girls.* Washington, DC: American Association of University Women Education Foundation and the National Education Association.

American Psychiatric Association (1987) *Diagnostic and Statistical Manual of Mental Disorders, DSM III-R*, 3rd ed., rev. Washington, DC.

Amidon, A. and Carey, P. (1972) Why 5-year-olds cannot understand before and after. *Journal of Verbal Learning and Verbal Behavior*, 11, 417–23.

Ammon, M. and Slobin, D. I. (1979) A cross-linguistic study of the processing of causative sentences. *Cognition*, 7, 3–17.

Andersen, E., Dunlea, A., and Kekelis, L. (1993) The impact of input: language acquisition in the visually impaired. *First Language*, 13, 23–50.

Anderson, M. (1983) Prenominal Genitive NPs. *The Linguistic Review*, 3, 1–24.

Anderson, R., Wilson, P., and Fielding, L. (1988) Growth in reading and how children spend their time outside of school. *Reading Research Quarterly*, 23, 285–303.

Anderson, S. R. and Keenan, E. L. (1985) Deixis. In J. Haiman and T. Shopen (eds), *Language Typology and Syntactic Description*, vol. 3, *Grammatical Categories and The Lexicon*, 259–308. Cambridge: Cambridge University Press.

Andrew, R. J. (1963) The origin and evolution of the calls and facial expressions of the primates. *Behaviour*, 20, 1–109.

—— (1964) The displays of the primates. In J. Buettner-Janusch (ed.), *Evolutionary and Genetic Biology of Primates*, 2. New York: Academic Press.

Anglin, J. M. (1977) *Word, Object and Conceptual Development*. New York: Norton.

—— (1979) The child's first terms of reference. In N. Smith and M. Franklin (eds), *Symbolic Functioning in Childhood*. Hillsdale, NJ: Lawrence Erlbaum Associates.

—— (1983) Extensional aspects of the preschool child's word concepts. In T. Seiler and W. Wannenmacher (eds), *Concept Development and the Development of Word Meaning*. Berlin: Springer Verlag.

—— (1986) Semantic and conceptual knowledge underlying the child's first words. In S. A. Kuczaj and M. D. Barrett (eds), *The Development of Word Meaning*. New York: Springer Verlag.

Anisfeld, M. (1984) *Language Development From Birth to Three*. London: Lawrence Erlbaum Associates.

Antinucci, F. and Miller, R. (1976) How children talk about what happened. *Journal of Child Language*, 9, 627–43.

Applebee, A. N. (1978) *The Child's Concept of Story*. Chicago: University of Chicago Press.

Aram, D. (1988) Language sequelae of unilateral brain lesions in children. In F. Plum (ed.), *Language, Communication, and the Brain*. New York: Raven Press.

—— (1991) Acquired aphasia in children. In M. Sarno (ed.), *Acquired Aphasia*, 2nd ed. San Diego, CA: Academic Press.

Aram, D. and Eisele, J. (1992) Plasticity and recovery of higher cortical functions following early brain injury. In F. Boller and J. Grafman (eds), *Handbook of Neuropsychology: child neuropsychology*, 73–92. New York: Elsevier.

Aram, D. and Ekelman, B. L. (1987) Unilateral brain lesions in childhood: performance on the revised token test. *Brain and Language*, 32, 137–58.

Aram, D., Ekelman, B. L., and Nation, J. E. (1984) Preschoolers with language disorders: 10 years later. *Journal of Speech and Hearing Research*, 27, 232–44.

Aram, D., Ekelman, B. L., and Whitaker, H. A. (1986) Spoken syntax in children with acquired unilateral hemisphere lesions. *Brain and Language*, 27, 75–100.

—— (1987) Lexical retrieval in left and right brain lesioned children. *Brain and Language*, 31, 61–87.

Aram, D., Morris, R., and Hall, N. E. (1993) Clinical and research congruence in identifying children with specific language impairment. *Journal of Speech and Hearing Research*, 36, 580–91.

Aram, D., Ekelman, B., Rose, D., and Whitaker, H. (1985) Verbal and cognitive sequelae following unilateral lesions acquired in early childhood. *Journal of Clinical and Experimental Neuropsychology*, 3, 55–78.

Arnberg, L., (1987). *Raising Children Bilingually: the pre-school years*. Clevedon: Multilingual Matters.

Arnberg, L. and Arnberg, P. (1985) The relation between code differentiation and language mixing in bilingual three- to four-year-old children. *The Bilingual Review/La Revista Bilingüe*, 12, 20–32.

Arnberg, L. and Arnberg, P. (1992) Language awareness and language separation in the young bilingual child. In R. Harris (ed.), *Cognitive Processing in Bilinguals*, 475–500. Amsterdam: Elsevier Science Publishers.

Atkinson, M. (1979) Prerequisites for reference. In E. Ochs and B. B. Schieffelin (eds), *Developmental Pragmatics*, 229–49. London: Academic Press.

—— (1982) *Explanations in the Study of Child Language Development*. Cambridge: Cambridge University Press.

—— (1987) Mechanisms for language acquisition: parameter-setting, triggering and learning. *First Language*, 7, 3–30.

—— (1992) *Children's Syntax: an introduction to principles and parameters theory*. Oxford: Blackwell.

Atkinson-King, K. (1973) Children's Acquisition of Phonological Stress Contrasts, *Working Papers in Phonetics*, 25. Los Angeles: Phonetics Laboratory, UCLA.

Auer, J. C. P. (1988) A conversational analytic approach to code-switching and transfer. In M. Heller (ed.) *Code-Switching: anthropological and sociolinguistic perspectives*, 187–213. Berlin: Mouton.

Authier, J.-M. (1993) Nonquantificational wh and weakest crossover. *Linguistic Inquiry*, 24, 161–8.

Baddeley, A. (1990) *Human Memory: theory and practice*. Boston: Allyn and Bacon.

Baetens Beardsmore, H., (1982) *Bilingualism: basic principles*. Clevedon: Tieto Ltd.

Bain, B. and Yu, A., (1980) Cognitive consequences of raising children bilingually: "one parent, one language." *Canadian Journal of Psychology*, 34, 304–13.

Baker, C. L. (1979) Syntactic theory and the projection problem. *Linguistic Inquiry*, 10, 533–81.

—— (1989) Some observations on degree of learnability. *Behavioral and Brain Sciences*, 12, 334–5.

Baker-van den Goorbergh, L. (1990) CLEAR: computerized language-error analysis report. *Clinical Linguistics & Phonetics*, 4, 285–93.

—— (1991) Computers and the analysis of spontaneous language. Unpublished manuscript.

Baker-van den Goorbergh, L. and Baker, K. (1991) *Computerised Language Error Analysis Report (CLEAR)* [Computer software, IBM]. Leicester: Dave Rowley, Publisher.

Bakhtin, M. M. (1981) *The Dialogic Imagination*. Austin, TX: University of Texas Press.

Baldwin, D. A. and Markman, E. M. (1989) Establishing word–object relations: a first step. *Child Development*, 60, 381–98.

Ball, M. (1984) Phonological development and assessment. In N. Miller (ed.), *Bilingualism and Language Disability: assessment and remediation*, 115–31. London: Croom Helm.

Bamberg, M. G. W. (1986) A functional approach to the acquisition of anaphoric relationships. *Linguistics*, 24, 227–84.

—— (1987) *The Acquisition of Narratives: learning to use language*. Berlin: Mouton de Gruyter.

—— (1990) The German Perfekt: form and function of tense alternations. *Studies in Language*, 14, 253–90.

Bamberg, M. and Marchman, V. (1990) What holds a narrative together? The linguistic encoding of episode boundaries. *Pragmatics*, 4, 58–121.

Bandura, A. (1977) *A Social Learning Theory*. Englewood Cliffs, NJ: Prentice-Hall.

Bar-Adon, A. and Leopold, W. F. (1971) *Child Language: a book of readings*. Englewood Cliffs, NJ: Prentice-Hall.

Barnes, S., Gutfreund, M., Satterly, D., and Wells, G. (1983) Characteristics of adult speech which predict children's language development. *Journal of Child Language*, 10, 65–84.

Baron, J. and Kaiser, A. (1975) Semantic components in children's errors with pronouns. *Journal of Psycholinguistic Research*, 4, 303–17.

Baron-Cohen, S., Leslie, A. M., and Frith, U. (1985) Does the autistic child have a "theory of mind"? *Cognition*, 21, 37–46.

Barrett, M. D. (1978) Lexical development and overextension in child language. *Journal of Child Language*, 5, 205–19.

—— (1981) The communicative functions of early child language. *Linguistics*, 19, 273–305.

—— (1982) Distinguishing between prototypes: the early acquisition of the meanings of object names. In S. A. Kuczaj (ed.), Language Development, vol. 1: Syntax and Semantics. Hillsdale, NJ: Lawrence Erlbaum Associates.

—— (1983a) The early acquisition and development of the meanings of action-related words. In T. Seiler and W. Wannenmacher (eds), *Concept Development and the Development of Word Meaning*. Berlin: Springer Verlag.

—— (1983b) Scripts, prototypes, and the early acquisition of word meaning. Paper presented at the Annual Conference of the British Psychological Society Developmental Section, Oxford, September 1983.

—— (1986) Early semantic representations and early word usage. In S. A. Kuczaj and M. D. Barrett (eds), *The Development of Word Meaning*. New York: Springer Verlag.

—— (1987) Theoretical constructs in the explanation of early word meaning: event representations and prototypes. Paper presented at the Fourth International Congress for the Study of Child Language, Lund, Sweden, July 1987.

—— (1989) Early language development. In A. Slater and G. Bremner (eds), *Infant Development*. London: Lawrence Erlbaum Associates.

—— (1991) The multi-route model of early lexical development. *Anales de Psicologia*, 7, 123–36.

Barrett, M. D., Harris, M., and Chasin, J. (1991) Early lexical development and maternal speech: a comparison of children's initial and subsequent uses of words. *Journal of Child Language*, 18, 21–4.

Barton, D. P. (1980) Phoneme perception in children. In G. H. Yeni-Komshian J. F. Kavanagh, and C. A. Ferguson (eds), *Child Phonology*, vol. 2. New York: Academic Press.

Barton, M. and Tomasello, M. (1994) The rest of the family: the role of fathers and siblings in early language development. In C. Gallaway and B. Richards (eds), *Input and Interaction in Language Acquisition*, 109–34. London: Cambridge University Press.

Bates, E. and Carnevale, G. F. (1993) New directions in research on language development. *Developmental Review*, 13, 436–70.

Bates, E. and MacWhinney, B. (1982) Functionalist approaches to grammar. In E. Wanner and L. Gleitman (eds), *Language Acquisition: the state of the act*, 173–218. New York: Cambridge University Press.

—— (1987) Competition, variation, and language learning. In B. MacWhinney (ed.), *Mechanisms of Language Acquisition*. Hillsdale, NJ: Lawrence Erlbaum Associates.

—— (1989) Functionalism and the competition model. In B. MacWhinney and E. Bates (eds), *The crosslinguistic study of sentence processing*. New York: Cambridge University Press.

Bates, E. and Snyder, L. (1987) The cognitive hypothesis in language development. In I. Uzgiris and J. M. Hunt (eds), *Research with Scales of Psychological Development in Infancy*. Champaign-Urbana, Ill.: University of Illinois Press.

Bates, E. and Thal, D. (1991) Associations and dissociations in language development. In J. F. Miller (ed.), *Research on Child Language Disorders: a decade of progress*, 145–68. Austin, Tx: Pro-Ed.

Bates, E., Bretherton, I., and Snyder, L. (eds) (1988) *From First Words to Grammar: individual differences and dissociable mechanisms*. Cambridge: Cambridge University Press.

Bates, E., Camaioni, L., and Volterra, V. (1975) The acquisition of performatives prior to speech. *Merrill-Palmer Quarterly*, 21, 205–26.

—— (1979) The acquisition of performatives prior to speech. In E. Ochs and B. B. Schieffelin (eds), *Developmental Pragmatics*. New York: Academic Press.

Bates, E., Frederici, A., and Wulfeck, B. (1987) Grammatical morphology in aphasia: evidence from three languages. *Cortex*, 23, 545–74.

Bates, E., Thal, D., and Janowsky, J. S. (1992) Early language development and its neural correlates. In I. Rapin and S. Segalowitz (eds), *Handbook of Neuropsychology*, vol. 7, *Child Neurology*. Amsterdam: Elsevier.

Bates, E., Thal, D., and MacWhinney, B. (1991) A functionalist approach to language and its implications for assessment and intervention. In T. M. Gallagher (ed.), *Pragmatics of Language: clinical Practice issues*. San Diego: Singular Publishing Group, Inc.

Bates, E., Thal, D., and Marchman, V. (1991) Symbols and syntax: a Darwinian approach to language development. In N. Krasnegor, D. Rumbaugh, R. Schiefelbusch, and M. Studdert-Kennedy (eds), *Biological and Behavioral Determinants of Language Development*. Hillsdale, NJ: Lawrence Erlbaum Associates.

Bates, E., Benigni, L., Bretherton, I., Camaioni, L., and Volterra, V. (1977) From gesture to the first word. In M. Lewis, N. Lewis, and L. Rosenblum (eds), *Interaction, Conversation, and the Development of Language*. New York: Wiley.

—— (1979) *The Emergence of Symbols: cognition and communication in infancy*. New York: Academic Press.

Bates, E., Thal, D., Whitesell, K., Fenson, L., and Oakes, L. (1989) Integrating language and gesture in infancy. *Developmental Psychology*, 25(6), 1,004–19.

Bates, E., MacWhinney, B., Caselli, C., Devescovi, A., Natale, F., and Venza, V. (1984) A cross-linguistic study of the development of sentence interpretation strategies. *Child Development*, 55, 341–54.

Bates, E., Marchman, V., Thal, D., Fenson, L., Dale, P., Reznick, J. S., Reilly, J., and Hartung, J. (1994) Developmental and stylistic variation in the composition of early vocabulary. *Journal of Child Language*, 21: 1, 85–124.

Bauer, H. (1988) The ethologic model of phonetic development: I Phonetic contrast estimators. *Clinical Linguistics and Phonetics*, 2, 347–80.

Bauer, H. R. and Kent, R. D. (1987) Acoustic analysis of infant fricative and trill vocalizations. *Journal of the Acoustical Society of America*, 81, 505–11.

Bauer, P. J. and Mandler, J. M. (1989) One thing following another: effects of temporal structure on one- and two-year-olds' recall of events. *Developmental Psychology*, 25, 197–206.

Bavin, E. (1989) Some lexical and morphological changes in Walpiri. In N. Dorian (ed.), *Investigating Obsolescence: studies in language contraction*, 267–86. Cambridge: Cambridge University Press.

Bavin, E. (1992) The acquisition of Walpiri. In D. Slobin (ed.), *The Crosslinguistic Study of Language Acquisition*, 309–72. Hillsdale, NJ: Lawrence Erlbaum Associates.

Bay, E. (1975) Ontogeny of stable speech areas in the human brain. In E. Lenneberg and E. Lenneberg (eds), *Foundation of Language Development: a multi-disciplinary approach*, vol. 2, 21–9. New York: Academic Press.

Bayer, J. (1992) On the origin of sentential arguments in German and Bengali. Unpublished manuscript University of Dusseldorf.

Baylis, J. R. (1975) A quantitative, comparative study of courtship in two sympatric species of the genus, Cichlasoma, (Teleostei, Cichlidae). Unpublished doctoral dissertation, University of California, Berkeley.

Bazzanella, C. and Calleri, D. (1991) Tense coherence and grounding in children's narratives. *Text*, 11, 175–87.

Beals, D. and Tabors, P. (1993) Arboretum, bureaucratic, and carbohydrates: preschoolers' exposure to rare vocabulary at home. Paper presented at the 60th Anniversary Meeting of the Society for Research in Child Development, New Orleans.

Becker, J. A. (1990) Processes in the acquisition of pragmatic competence. In G. Conti-Ramsden and C. E. Snow (eds), *Children's Language*, vol. 7. Hillsdale, NJ: Lawrence Erlbaum Associates.

Beckwith, R., Tinker, E., and Bloom, L. (1989) The acquisition of non-basic sentences. Paper presented at the Boston University Conference on Language Development, Boston.

Beebe, H. (1946) Sigmatismus nasalis. *Journal of Speech Disorders*, 11, 35–7.

Beeghly, M. and Cicchetti, D. (1986) Early language development in children with Down syndrome: a longitudinal study. Paper presented at the *11th Annual Boston University Conference on Language Development*, Boston.

Beeghly, M., Weiss-Perry, B., and Cicchetti, D. (1990) Beyond sensorimotor functioning:

early communicative and play development of children with Down syndrome. In D. Cicchetti and M. Beeghly (eds), *Children with Down Syndrome: a developmental perspective*, 329–68. Cambridge: Cambridge University Press.

Beilin, H. (1975) *Studies in the Cognitive Basis of Language Development*. New York: Academic Press.

Bellinger, D. and Gleason, J. B. (1982) Sex differences in parental directives to young children. *Journal of Sex Roles*, 8, 1,123–9.

Bellugi, U. (1965) The development of interrogative structures in children's speech. In K. Riegel (ed.), *The Development of Language Functions*. University of Michigan Language Development Program, report no. 8, 103–38.

Bellugi, U., Klima, E. S., and Poizner, H. (1988) Sign language and the brain. In F. Plum (ed.), *Language, Communication, and the Brain*, 39–56. New York: Raven Press.

Bellugi, U., Sabo, H., and Vaid, J. (1988) Spatial deficits in children with Williams syndrome. In J. Stiles-Davis, M. Kritchevsky, and U. Bellugi (eds), *Spatial Cognition: brain bases and development*. Hillsdale, NJ: Lawrence Erlbaum Associates.

Bellugi, U., Wang, P., and Jernigan, T. (in press) Williams syndrome: An unusual neuropsychological profile. In S. Broman and J. Grafman (eds), *Cognitive Deficits in Developmental Disorders: implications for brain function*. Hillsdale, NJ: Lawrence Erlbaum Associates.

Bellugi, U., Marks, S., Bihrle, A. M., and Sabo, H. (1988) Dissociation between language and social functions in Williams syndrome. In K. Mogford and D. Bishop (eds), *Language Development in Exceptional Circumstances*, 177–89. New York: Churchill Livingstone Inc.

Bellugi, U., Bihrle, A., Jernigan, T., Trauner, D., and Doherty, S. (1990) Neuropsychological, neurological and neuroanatomical profile of Williams syndrome children. *American Journal of Medical Genetics*, 6, 115–25.

Bellugi, U., Bihrle, A., Neville, H., Jernigan, T., and Doherty, S. (1992) Language, cognition, and brain organization in a neurodevelopmental disorder. In M. Gunnar and C. Nelson (eds), *Developmental Behavioral Neuroscience*, 201–32. Hillsdale, NJ: Lawrence Erlbaum Associates.

Benedict, H. E. (1979) Early lexical development: comprehension and production. *Journal of Child Language*, 6, 183–200.

Bennett, T. L. (1976) Code-switching in Down's syndrome. *Proceedings of the Second Annual Meeting of the Berkeley Linguistic Society*, Berkeley, CA.

Bennett-Kastor, T. (1983) Noun phrases and coherence in child narrative. *Journal of Child Language*, 10, 135–49.

Bennett-Kastor, T. (1986) Cohesion and predication in child narrative. *Journal Child Language*, 13, 353–70.

Bennett-Kastor, T. (1988) *Analyzing Children's Language: methods and theory*. Oxford: Basil Blackwell.

Bentahila, A. and Davies, E. (1992) Two languages, three varieties: a look at some bilingual children's code-switching. Paper presented at the International Colloquium on Early Bilingualism, Amsterdam.

Benzaquen, S., Gagnon, R., Hunse, C., and Foreman, J. (1990) The intrauterine sound environment of the human fetus during labor. *American Journal of Obstetrics and Gynecology*, 163, 484–90.

Berger, J. (1990) Interactions between parents and their infants with Down syndrome. In D. Cicchetti and M. Beeghly (eds), *Children with Down Syndrome: a developmental perspective*, 101–46. Cambridge: Cambridge University Press.

Berger, J. and Cunningham, C. C. (1981) The development of eye contact between mothers and normal versus Down's syndrome infants. *Developmental Psychology*, 17, 678–89.

—— (1983) Development of early vocal behaviors and interactions in Down's syndrome and nonhandicapped infant–mother pairs. *Developmental Psychology*, 19, 322–31.

Bergman, C. R. (1976) Interference vs. independent development in infant bilingualism. In D. Keller, R. Teschner and S. Viera (eds), *Bilingualism in the Bicentennial and Beyond*, 86–96. New York: Bilingual Press/Editorial Bilingüe.

Berkele, G. (1983) *Die Entwicklung des Ausdrucks von Objektreferenz am Beispiel der Determinanten. Eine empirische Untersuchung zum Spracherwerb bilingualer Kinder (Französisch/Deutsch)* [The development of the expression of object reference using determiners. An empirical investigation concerning the language acquisition of bilingual children (French/German)] Unpublished thesis. Hamburg: University of Hamburg.

Berko, J. (1958) The child's learning of English morphology. *Word*, 14, 150–77.

Berkovits, R. and Wigodsky, M. (1979) On interpreting noncoreferent pronouns: a longitudinal study. *Journal of Child Language*, 6, 585–92.

Berman, R. A. (1985) The acquisition of Hebrew. In D. I. Slobin (ed.), The Crosslinguistic Study of Language Acquisition, vol. 1, 255–371. Hillsdale, NJ: Lawrence Erlbaum Associates.

—— (1988a) Word class distinctions in developing grammars. In Y. Levy, I. M. Schlesinger, and M. D. S. Braine (eds), *Categories and Processes in Language Acquisition*, 45–72. Hillsdale, NJ: Lawrence Erlbaum Associates.

Berman, R. A. (1988b) On the ability to relate events in narrative. *Discourse Processes*, 11, 469–97.

Berman, R. A. and Clark, E. V. (1989) Learning to use compounds for contrast: data from Hebrew. *First Language*, 9.3, 247–70.

Berman, R. A. and Neeman, Y. (1994) Development of linguistic forms: Hebrew. In R. A. Berman and D. I. Slobin (eds), *Different Ways of Relating Events in Narrative: a crosslinguistic developmental study*. Hillsdale, NJ: Lawrence Erlbaum Associates.

Berman, R. A. and Slobin, D. I. (1987) Five ways of learning how to talk about events: a crosslinguistic study of children's narratives. Berkeley Cognitive Science Report.

—— (eds) (1994) *Different Ways of Relating Events in Narrative: a crosslinguistic developmental study*. Hillsdale, NJ: Lawrence Erlbaum Associates.

Bernhardt, B. (1992) Developmental implications of nonlinear phonological theory. *Clinical Linguistics & Phonetics*, 16, 259–81.

Bernhardt, B. and Gilbert, J. (1992) Applying linguistic theory to speech–language pathology: the case for nonlinear phonology. *Clinical Linguistics & Phonetics*, 6, 123–45.

Bernstein Ratner, N. (1984a) Patterns of vowel modification in mother–child speech. *Journal of Child Language*, 11, 557–78.

—— (1984b) Phonological rule usage in mother–child speech. *Journal of Phonetics*, 12, 245–54.

Bernstein Ratner, N. and Pye, C. (1984) Higher pitch in BT is not universal: acoustic evidence from Quiche Mayan. *Journal of Child Language*, 1, 515–22.

Berry, P., Gunn, P., Andrews, R., and Price, C. (1981) Characteristics of Down's syndrome infants and their families. *Australian Paediatrics Journal*, 17, 40–3.

Bertenthal, B. I., Campos, J. J., and Barrett, K. C. (1984) Self-produced locomotion: an organizer of emotional, cognitive, and social development in infancy. In R. N. Emde and R. J. Harmon (eds), *Continuities and Discontinuities in Development*. New York: Plenum Publishing Corporation.

Bertinetto, P. M. (1989) Reflections on the dichotomy "stress" vs. "syllable-timing." *Revue de Phonetique Appliquée*, 91/92/93, 99–130.

Bertoncini, J., Morais, J., Bijeljac-Babic, R., McAdams, S., Peretz, I., and Mehler, J. (1989) Dichotic perception and laterality in neonates. *Brain and Language*, 37, 591–605.

Bertrand, J., Mervis, C. B., Rice, C. E., and Adamson, L. (1993) Development of joint attention by a toddler with Williams syndrome. Paper presented at the Gatlinburg Conference on Research and Theory in Mental Retardation and Developmental Disabilities. Gatlinburg, TN.

Berwick. R. (1985) *The Acquisition of Syntactic Knowledge*. Cambridge, Mass.: MIT Press.

Berwick, R. and Weinberg, A. S. (1984) *The Grammatical Basis of Linguistic Performance: language use and acquisition*. Cambridge, Mass.: MIT Press.

Best, C. (1993) Language-specific developmental changes in perception of nonnative speech contrasts: a window on early phonological development. In B. de Boysson-Bardies et al. (eds), to appear.

Bever, T. G. (1970) The cognitive basis for linguistic structures. In J. R. Hayes (ed.), *Cognition and the Development of Language*, 279–362. New York: John Wiley and Sons, Inc.

Bickerton, D. (1984) The language bioprogram hypothesis. *The Behavioral and Brain Sciences*, 7, 173–87.

—— (1990a) *Language and Species*. Chicago: University of Chicago Press.

—— (1990b) Syntactic development: the brain just does it. Unpublished manuscript, University of Hawai'i at Manoa.

Bickley, C., Lindblom, B., and Roug, L. (1986) Acoustic measures of rhythm in infants' babbling, or "All God's children got rhythm." *Proceedings of the 12th International Congress on Acoustics*.

Bihrle, A. M., Bellugi, U., Delis, M., and Marks, S. (1989) Seeing either the forest or the trees: dissociation in visuospatial processing. *Brain and Cognition*, 11, 37–49.

Bilovsky, D. and Share, J. (1965) The ITPA and Down's syndrome: an exploratory study. *American Journal of Mental Deficiency*, 70, 78–82.

Birnholz, J. C. and Benacerraf, B. R. (1983) The development of human fetal hearing. *Science*, 222, 516–18.

Bishop, D. V. M. (1992a) The underlying nature of specific language impairment. *Journal of Child Psychology and Psychiatry*, 33, 3–66.

—— (1992b) Biological basis of developmental language disorders. In P. Fletcher and D. Hall (eds), *Specific Speech and Language Disorders in Children*. London: Whurr Publishers.

—— (1993) Grammatical errors in specific language impairment: competence or performance limitations? *Applied Psycholinguistics*, in Press.

Bishop, D. V. M. and Adams, C. (1992) Comprehension problems in children with specific language impairment: literal and inferential meaning. *Journal of Speech and Hearing Research*, 35, 119–29.

Bishop, D. V. M. and Edmundson, A. (1987) Specific language impairment as a maturational lag: evidence from longitudinal data on language and motor development. *Developmental Medicine and Child Neurology*, 29, 442–59.

Bishop, D. V. M. and Rosenbloom, L. (1987) Childhood language disorders: classification and overview. In W. Yule and M. Rutter (eds), *Language Development and Disorders* (Clinics in Developmental Medicine, no. 101/102, 16–41). Oxford: Blackwell Scientific Publications.

Black, B. and Hazen, N. L. (1990) Social status and patterns of communication in acquainted and unacquainted preschool children. *Developmental Psychology*, 26, 379–87.

Blake, J. and Fink, R. (1987) Sound–meaning correspondences in babbling. *Journal of Child Language*, 14, 229–53.

Blake, J., Quartaro, G., and Onorati, S. (1993) Evaluating quantitative measures of grammatical complexity in spontaneous speech samples. *Journal of Child Language*, 20, 139–52.

Blank, M., Gessner, M., and Esposito, A. (1979) Language without communicaton: a case study. *Journal of Child Language*, 6, 329–52.

Bleile, K. and Schwartz, I. (1984) Three perspectives on the speech of children with Down's syndrome. *Journal of Communication Disorders*, 17, 87–94.

Bliss, L. S. (1989) Selected syntactic usage of language-impaired children. *Journal of Communication Disorders*, 22, 277–89.

Bloom, K. (1988) Quality of adult vocalizations affects the quality of infant vocalizations. *Journal of Child Language*, 15, 469–80.

—— (1990) Selectivity and early infant vocalization. In J. T. Enns (ed.), *The Development of Attention: research and theory*, 121–36. BV North-Holland: Elsevier Science Publishers.

Bloom, K., Russell, A., and Wassenberg, K. (1987) Turn taking affects the quality of infant vocalizations. *Journal of Child Language*, 14, 211–27.

Bloom, L. (1970) *Language Development*. Cambridge, Mass.: MIT Press.

—— (1973) *One Word at a Time*. The Hague: Mouton.

—— (1975) Language development. In F. Horowitz (ed.), *Review of Child Development Research*. Chicago: University of Chicago Press.

—— (1978) The Semantics of verbs in child language. Paper presented at the Eastern Psychological Association Meeting, New York.

—— (1993a) Transcription and coding for child language research: the parts are more than the whole. In J. A. Edwards and M. D. Lampert (eds), *Talking Data: transcription and coding in discourse research*, 149–66. Hillsdale, NJ: Lawrence Erlbaum Associates.

—— (1993b) *The Transition from Infancy to Language: acquiring the power of expression*. New York: Cambridge University Press.

—— (1994) Meaning and expression. In W. Overton (ed.), *The Nature and Ontogenesis of Meaning*. Norwood, NJ: Ablex.

Bloom, L., and Lahey, M. (1978) Language development and language disorders. New York: John Wiley and Sons.

Bloom, L. Lifter, K., and Broughton, J. (1985) The convergence of early cognition and language in the second year of life: problems in conceptualization and measurement. In M. D. Barrett (ed.), *Children's Single-Word Speech*. Chichester: Wiley.

Bloom, L., Lifter, K., and Hafitz, J. (1980) Semantics of verbs and the development of verb inflection in child language. *Language*, 56, 386–412.

Bloom, L., Lightbown, L., and Hood, L. (1975) Structure and variation in child language. *Monographs for the Society for Research in Child Development*, 40, whole no. 2.

Bloom, L., Lightbown, P., and Hood, L. (1978) Pronominal–Nominal Variation in Child Language. In L. Bloom (ed.), *Readings in Language Development*, 231–8. New York: Wiley.

Bloom, L., Rispoli, M., Gartner, B., and Hafitz, J. (1989) Acquisition of complementation. *Journal of Child Language*, 16, 101–20.

Bloom, P. (1990) Subjectless sentences in child language. *Linguistic Inquiry*, 21, 491–504.

—— (in press a) Possible names: the role of syntax–semantics mappings in the acquisition of nominals. *Lingua*.

—— (in press b) Theories of word learning: rationalist alternatives to associationism. In *Handbook of Language Acquisition*. New York: Academic Press.

Blum-Kulka, S. (1990) You don't touch lettuce with your fingers: parental politeness in family discourse. *Journal of Pragmatics*, 14, 259–88.

Blumstein, S., Baker, E., and Goodglass, H. (1977) Phonological factors in auditory comprehension in aphasia. *Neuropsychologia*, 15, 19–30.

Bodin, L. and Snow, C. E. (1994) What kind of birdie is this? Learning to use superordinates. In J. L. Sokolov and C. E. Snow (eds), *Handbook of Research in Language Development Using CHILDES*, 77–109. Hillsdale, NJ: Lawrence Erlbaum Associates.

Bol, G. and Kuiken, F. (1990) Grammatical analysis of developmental language disorders: a study of the morphosyntax of children with specific language disorders, with hearing impairment and with Down's syndrome. *Clinical Linguistics & Phonetics*, 4, 77–86.

Bolinger, D. (1977) *Meaning and Form*. London: Longman.

Bond, Z. and Wilson, H. (1980) Acquisition of the voicing contrast by language-delayed and normal-speaking children. *Journal of Speech and Hearing Research*, 23, 152–61.

Bonvillian, J. D. and Folven, R. J. (1987) The onset of signing in young children. Paper presented at the Fourth International Symposium on Sign Language Research. Lappeenranta, Finland.

Bonvillian, J. D., Orlansky, M. D., and Novack, L. L. (1983) Developmental milestones: sign language acquisition and motor development. *Child Development*, 54, 1,435–45.

Borer, H. (1984) *Parametric Syntax*. Dordrecht: Foris.

Borer, H. and Wexler, K. (1987) The maturation of syntax. In T. Roeper and E. Williams (eds), *Parameter-setting and Language Acquisition*. Dordrecht: Reidel.

Bornstein, M. H., Vibbert, M., Tal, J., and O'Donnell, K. (1992) Toddler language and play in the second year: stability, covariation and influences of parenting. *First Language*, 12, 323–38.

Bortolini, U. and Leonard, L. (1991) The speech of phonologically disordered children acquiring Italian. *Clinical Linguistics and Phonetics*, 5, 1–12.

Bosma, J. F. (1975) Anatomic and physiologic development of the speech apparatus. In D. B. Tower (ed.), *The Nervous System*, vol. 3, *Human Communication and its Disorders*, 469–81. New York: Raven Press.

Bottari, P., Cipriani, P., and Chilosi, A. M. (1991) Pre-syntactic devices in the acquisition of Italian free morphology. Pisa: University of Pisa.

Bowerman, M. (1973) Structural relationships in children's utterances: syntactic or semantic? In T. Moore (ed.), *Cognitive Development and the Acquisition of Language*. New York: Academic Press.

—— (1978) The acquisition of word meaning: an investigation into some current conflicts. In N. Waterson and C. Snow (eds), *The Development of Communication*. Chichester: Wiley.

—— (1980) The structure and origin of semantic categories in the language-learning child. In M. Foster and S. Brandes (eds), *Symbol as Sense*. New York: Academic Press.

—— (1982a) Starting to talk worse: clues to language acquisition from children's late speech errors. In Strauss, S. (ed.), *U-shaped Behavioral Growth*. New York: Academic Press.

—— (1982b) Reorganizational processes in lexical development. In E. Wanner and L. R. Gleitman (eds), *Language Acquisition: the state of the art*, 320–46. New York: Cambridge University Press.

—— (1985) What shapes children's grammar? In D. I. Slobin (ed.), *The Cross-linguistic Study of Language Acquisition*, 1,257–319. Hillsdale, NJ: Lawrence Erlbaum Associates.

—— (1987) The "no negative evidence" problem: how do children avoid constructing an overly general grammar? In J. A. Hawkins (ed.), *Explaining Language Universals*, 73–101. Oxford: Basil Blackwell.

—— (1989) Learning a semantic system: what role do cognitive predispositions play? In M. L. Rice and R. L. Schiefelbusch (eds), *The Teachability of Language*, 133–69. Baltimore: Paul H. Brooks.

Bowlby, J. (1969) *Attachment and Loss*. Vol. 1: *Attachment*. New York: Basic Books.

Boyd, J. (1992) The theory of control. Ph.D. dissertation, University of Massachusetts at Amherst.

Boysson-Bardies, B. de, Halle, P., Sagart, L., and Durand, C. (1989) A crosslinguistic investigation of vowel formants in babbling. *Journal of Child Language*, 16, 1–17.

Boysson-Bardies, B. de, Sagart, J., Halle, P., and Durand, C. (1986) Acoustic investigation of cross linguistic variability in babbling. In B. Lindblom and R. Zetterstrom (eds), *Precursors of Early Speech*, 113–27. New York: Stockton Press.

Boysson-Bardies, B. de, Schonen, S. de, Juszcyk, P., MacNeilage, P., and Morton, J. (eds), (1993) *Developmental Neurocognition: speech and face processing in the first year of life.* Dordrecht: Kluwer.

Boysson-Bardies, B. de. Vihman, M. M., Roug-Hellichius, L., Durand, C., Landberg, I., and Arao, F. (1992) Material evidence of infant selection from target language: a cross-linguistic study. In C. A. Ferguson, L. Menn, and C. Stoel-Gammon (eds), *Phonological Development: models, research, implications*, 369–91. Timonium, MD: York Press.

Bradley, L. (1992) Rhymes, rimes, and learning to read. In C. A. Ferguson, L. Menn, and C Stoel-Gammon (eds), *Phonological Development: models, research, implications*, 553–62. Timonium, MD: York Press.

Bradley, L. and Bryant, P. E. (1978) Difficulties in auditory organization as a possible cause of reading backwardness. *Nature*, 271, 746–7.

—— (1983) Categorizing sounds and learning to read – a causal connection. *Nature*, 301, 419–21.

—— (1985) *Rhyme and Reason in Reading and Spelling. IARLD Monographs*, 1. Ann Arbor. MI: University of Michigan Press.

Braine, M. D. S. (1963) The ontogeny of English phrase structure: the first phase. *Language*, 39, 3–13.

—— (1976) Children's first word combinations. *Monographs of the Society for Research in Child Development*, 41, serial no. 164.

—— (1987) What is learned in acquiring word classes – a step toward an acquisition theory. In B. MacWhinney (ed.), *Mechanisms of Language Acquisition*, 65–87. Hillsdale, NJ: Lawrence Erlbaum Associates.

Branigan, G. (1979) Some reasons why successive utterances are not. *Journal of Child Language*, 6, 411–21.

Braun, M., (1937) Beobachtungen zur Frage der Mehrsprachigkeit [Comments on the question of multilingualism] *Göttingische Gelehrte Anzeigne*, 199, 115–30.

Bray, M. and Woolnough, L. (1988) The language skills of children with Down's syndrome aged 12 to 16 years. *Child Language Teaching and Therapy*, 4, 311–24.

Bréal, M. (1897) *Essai de Semantique*. Paris: Hachette.

Bresnan, J. (1978) *Contraction and the Transformational Cycle in English*. The Indiana Linguistics Club.

Bresnan, J. W. (1986) On the Form and Functioning of Transformations. *Linguistic Inquiry*, 7, 3–40.

Bretherton, I. (1992) The origins of attachment theory: John Bowlby and Mary Ainsworth. *Developmental Psychology*, 28, 759–75.

Bretherton, I., McNew, S., and Beeghly-Smith, M. (1981) Early person knowledge expressed in gestural and verbal communication: when do infants acquire "theory of mind"? In M. Lamb and L. Sherrod (eds), *Infant Social Cognition*. Hillsdale, NJ: Lawrence Erlbaum Associates.

Bretherton, I., McNew, S., Snyder, L., and Bates, E. (1983) Individual differences at 20 months: analytic and holistic strategies in language acquisition. *Journal of Child Language*, 10, 293–320.

Bridges, A. and Smith, J. V. (1984) Syntactic comprehension in Down's syndrome children. *British Journal of Psychology*, 75, 187–96.

Brinton, B. and Fujiki, M. (1982) A comparison of request–response sequences in the discourse of normal and language-disordered children. *Journal of Speech and Hearing Disorders*, 47, 57–62.

Brinton, B., Fujiki, M., Winkler, E., and Loeb, D. (1986) Responses to requests for clarification in linguistically normal and language-impaired children. *Journal of Speech and Hearing Disorders*, 51, 370–8.

Brody, B. A., Kinney, H. C., Kloman, A. S., and Gilles, F. H. (1987) Sequence of central nervous system myelination in human infancy. I: An autopsy study of myelination. *Journal of Neuropathology and Experimental Neurology*, 46, 283–309.

Bronckart, J.-P. and Schneuwly, B. (1991) Children's production of textual organizers. In G. Piéraut-Le Bonniec and M. Dolitsky (eds), *Language Bases . . . Discourse Bases*. Amsterdam: Benjamins.

Bronckart, J.-P. and Sinclair, H. (1973) Time, tense, and aspect. *Cognition*, 2, 107–30.

Brothers, L. (1990) The social brain: a project for integrating primate behavior and neurophysiology in a new domain. *Concepts in Neuroscience*, 1, 27–51.

Browman, C. P. and Goldstein, L. (1989) Articulatory gestures as phonological units. *Phonology*, 6, 102–51.

Brown, R. (1957) Linguistic determinism and the part of speech. *Journal of Abnormal and Social Psychology*, 55, 1–5.

—— (1968) The development of wh questions in child speech. *Journal of Verbal Learning and Verbal Behaviour*, 7, 279–90.

—— (1973) *A First Language: the early stages*. London: George Allen and Unwin.

—— (1977) Introduction. In C. Snow and C. Ferguson *Talking to Children: language input and acquisition*. Cambridge: Cambridge University Press.

Brown, R. and Bellugi, U. (1964) Three processes in the child's acquisition of syntax. *Harvard Educational Review*, 34, 133–51. Reprinted in A. Bar-Adon and W. F. Leopold (1971) *Child Language: a book of readings*, 307–18.

Brown, R. and Fraser, C. (1963) The acquisition of syntax. In C. Cofer and B. Musgrave (eds), *Verbal Behaviour and Learning: problems and processes*, 158–201. New York: McGraw-Hill.

Brown, R. and Hanlon, C. (1970) Derivational complexity and order of acquisition in child speech. In J. R. Hayes (ed.), *Cognition and the Development of Language*, 11–53. New York: Wiley.

Brown, R., Cazden, C., and Bellugi, U. (1968) The child's grammar from I to III. In J. P. Hill (ed.), *Second Annual Minnesota Symposium on Child Psychology*, 28–73. Minneapolis: University of Minnesota Press.

Brown, J. R. and Dunn, J. (1992) Talk with your mother or your sibling? Developmental changes in early family conversations about feelings. *Child Development*, 63, 336–49.

Brown, J. W. and Jaffe, J. (1975) Hypothesis on cerebral dominance. *Neuropsychologia*, 13, 107–10.

Brownell, C. (1988) Combinatorial skills: converging developments over the second year. *Child Development*, 59, 675–85.

Brownell, H. H., Potter, H. H., and Michelow, D. (1984) Sensitivity to lexical denotation and connotation in brain-damaged patients: a double dissociation? *Brain and Language*, 22, 253–65.

Brownell, H. H., Simpson, T., Bihrle, A., Potter, H., and Gardner, H. (1990) Appreciation of metaphoric alternative word meanings by left and right brain-damaged patients. *Neuropsychologia*, 28(4), 375–83.

Bruner, J. (1974) Organization of early skilled action. In M. Richards (ed.), *The Integration of a Child into a Social World.* London: Cambridge University Press.

Bruner, J. S. (1983) *Child's Talk: learning to use language.* New York: W. W. Norton.

—— (1986) *Actual Minds, Possible Worlds.* Cambridge, Mass.: Harvard University Press.

Bruner, J. S. and Sherwood, V. (1976) Early rule structure: the case of "peekaboo." In R. Harré (ed.), *Life Sentences: aspects of the social role of language.* New York: John Wiley.

Bryce, J. (1987) Family time and television use. In T. Linklof (ed.), *Natural Audiences.* Norwood, NJ: Ablex.

Buckley, S. (1984) *Reading and Language Development in Children with Down's Syndrome: a guide for parents and teachers.* Portsmouth, UK: Portsmouth Polytechnic.

—— (1985) Attaining basic educational skills: reading, writing and number. In D. Lane and B. Stratford (eds), *Current Approaches to Down's Syndrome.* London: Holt, Rinehart and Winston.

—— (1993) Developing the speech and language skills of teenagers with Down's syndrome. *Down's Syndrome: Research and Practice*, 1, 63–71.

Budwig, N. (1990a) A functional approach to the acquisition of personal pronouns.

—— (1990b) The linguistic marking of nonprototypical agency: an exploration into children's use of passives. *Linguistics*, 28, 1,221–52.

Buhr, R. D. (1980) The emergence of vowels in an infant. *Journal of Speech and Hearing Research*, 23, 73–94.

Bullock, D., Liederman, J., and Todorovic, D. (1987) Reconciling stable asymmetry with recovery of function: an adaptive systems perspective on functional plasticity. *Child Development*, 58(3), 689–97.

Bullowa, M. (1979) Prelinguistic communication: a field for scientific research. In M. Bullowa (ed.), *Before Speech: the beginning of interpersonal communication.* New York: Cambridge University Press.

Burr, D. B. and Rohr, A. (1978) Patterns of psycholinguistic development in the severely mentally retarded: a hypothesis. *Social Biology*, 25, 15–22.

Bushnell, I. W. R., Sai, F., and Mullin, J. T. (1989) Neonatal recognition of the mother's face. *British Journal of Developmental Psychology*, 7, 3–15.

Bybee, J. L. (1985) *Morphology: a study of the relation between meaning and form.* Amsterdam: John Benjamins Publishing.

Bybee, J. L. and Slobin D. I. (1982) Rules and schemas in the development and use of English past tense. *Language*, 58, 265–89.

Camaioni, L., Caselli, M. C., Longobardi, E., and Volterra, V. (1991) A parent report instrument for early language assessment. *First Language*, 11, 345–59.

Camarata, S. and Gandour, J. (1984) On describing idiosyncratic phonologic systems. *Journal of Speech and Hearing Disorders*, 50, 40–5.

Camarata, S. M. and Schwartz, R. G. (1985) Production of object words and action words: evidence for a relationship between phonology and semantics. *Journal of Speech and Hearing Research*, 28, 323–30.

Camhi, J. M. (1984) *Neuroethology: nerve cells and the natural behavior of animals*. Sunderland, Mass.: Sinauer Associates Inc.

Campos, J. J. and Sternberg, C. (1981) Perception, appraisal and emotions: the onset of social referencing. In M. E. Lamb and L. R. Sherrod (eds), *Infant Social Cognition: empirical and theoretical considerations*. Hillsdale, NJ: Lawrence Erlbaum Associates.

Caplan, D. (1981) On the cerebral localization of linguistic functions: logical and empirical issues surrounding deficit analysis and functional localization. *Brain and Language*, 14, 120–37.

—— (1989) Telencephalic organization for language. Paper presented at meeting of the American Association for the Advancement of Science, San Francisco, CA.

Caplan, D., Baker, C., and Dehaut, F. (1985) Syntactic determinants of sentence comprehension in aphasia. *Cognition*, 27, 117–75.

Capute, A. J., Palmer, F. B., Shapiro, B. K., Wachtel, R. C., Schmidt, S., and Ross, A. (1986) Clinical linguistic and auditory milestone scale: prediction of cognition in infancy. *Developmental Medicine and Child Neurology*, 28, 762–71.

Cardoso-Martins, C., Mervis, C. B., ad Mervis, C. A. (1985) Early vocabulary acquisition by children with Down syndrome. *American Journal of Mental Deficiency*, 90, 177–84.

Carey, S. (1978) The child as word learner. In M. Halle, J. Bresnan, and G. A. Miller (eds), *Linguistic Theory and Psychological Reality*, 264–93. Cambridge, Mass.: MIT Press.

Carey, S. and Grant, J. (1993) Conceptual structure of adults/adolescents with Williams syndrome. Paper presented at the 60th Annual Meeting of the Society for Research in Child Development, New Orleans, LA.

Carey, S., Johnson, S., and Levine, K. (1993) Conceptual structure of adults/adolescents with Williams Syndrome. Paper presented at the 60th Annual Meeting of the Society for Research in Child Development, New Orleans.

Carr, J. (1988) Six weeks to twenty-one years old: a longitudinal study of children with Down's syndrome and their families. *Journal of Child Psychology and Psychiatry*, 29, 407–31.

Carroll, S. (1989) Language acquisition studies and a feasible theory of grammar. *Canadian Journal of Linguistics*, 34, 399–418.

Carson, D. K., Skarpness, L. R., Schultz, N. W., and McGhee, P. E. (1986) Temperamental and communicative competence as predictors of young children's humor. *Merrill-Palmer Quarterly*, 32, 415–26.

Carter, R. L., Hohenegger, M. K., and Satz, P. (1982) Aphasia and speech organization in children. *Science*, 219, 797–9.

Catts, H. and Jensen, P. (1983) Speech timing of phonologically disordered children: voicing contrasts of initial and final stop consonants. *Journal of Speech and Hearing Research*, 26, 501–10.

Caulfield, M. B., Fischel, J. E., DeBaryshe, B. D., and Whitehurst, G. J. (1989) Behavioral correlates of developmental expressive language disorder. *Journal of Abnormal Child Psychology*, 17, 187–201.

Cazden, C. (1965) Environmental assistance to the child's acquisition of grammar. Unpublished Ph.D. dissertation, Harvard University.

Cazden, C. B. (1968) The acquisition of noun and verb inflections. *Child Development*, 39, 433–48.

Chafe, W. (1976) Givenness, contrastiveness, definiteness, subjects, topics and point of view. In C. N. Li (ed.), *Subject and Topic*, 25–55. New York: Academic Press.

—— (1979) The flow of thought and the flow of language. In T. Givón (ed.), *Syntax and Semantics*, vol. 12, *Discourse and Syntax*, 159–82. New York: Academic Press.

Chall, J., Jacobs, V. A., and Baldwin, L. E. (1990) *The Reading Crisis: why poor children fall behind*. Cambridge, Mass.: Harvard University Press.

Chapman, R. S. (1978) Comprehension strategies in children: a discussion of Bransford and Nitsch's paper. In J. Kavanagh and W. Strange (eds), *Speech and Language in the Laboratory, School, and Clinic*, 308–27. Cambridge, Mass.: MIT Press.

—— (1992) *Processes in Language Acquisition and Disorders*. St Louis: Mosby-Year Book.

Chapman, R. S. and Kohn, L. L. (1978) Comprehension strategies in two and three-year olds: animate agents or probable events. *Journal of Speech and Hearing Research*, 21, 746–61.

Chapman, R. S. and Miller, J. F. (1975) Word order in early two- and three-word utterances: does production precede comprehension? *Journal of Speech and Hearing Research*, 18, 355–71.

Chapman, R. S., Kay-Raining Bird, E., and Schwartz, S. E. (1990) Fast mapping of novel words in event contexts by children with Down syndrome. *Journal of Speech and Hearing Disorders*, 55, 761–70.

—— (1991) Fast mapping in stories: deficits in Down syndrome. Paper presented at the American Speech–Language–Hearing Association meeting, Atlanta, GA.

Chapman, R. S., Ross, D. R., and Seung, H.-K. (1993) Longitudinal change in language production of children and adolescents with Down syndrome. Paper presented at the Sixth International Congress of the Study of Child Language, Trieste, Italy.

Chapman, R. S., Schwartz, S. E., and Kay-Raining Bird, E. (1989) Are children with Down syndrome language delayed? Paper presented at the American Speech–Language–Hearing Association meeting, St Louis, MO.

—— (1991) Language skills of children and adolescents with Down syndrome. I: Comprehension. *Journal of Speech and Hearing Research*, 34, 1,106–20.

—— (1992) Language production of children and adolescents with Down syndrome. Paper presented at the 9th World Congress of the International Association for the Scientific Study of Mental Deficiency, Gold Coast, Australia.

Chapman, R. S., Streim, N., Crais, E., Salmon, D., Negri, N., and Strand, E. (1992) Child talk: assumptions of a developmental process model for early language learning. In R. S. Chapman (ed.), *Processes in Language Acquisition and Disorders*, 3–19. St Louis: Mosby-Year Book.

Charney, R. (1978) The development of personal pronouns. Doctoral dissertation, University of Chicago.

Charney, R. (1979) The comprehension of "here" and "there." *Journal of Child Language*, 6, 69–80.

Chauvin, Y. (1988) Symbol acquisition in humans and neural (PDP) networks. Ph.D. thesis, University of California, San Diego.

Cheguni, H. T., Phelps, M. E., and Mazziota, J. C. (1987) Positron emission tomography study of human brain functional development. *Annals of Neurology*, 22, 487–97.

Chen, H. P. and Irwin, O. C. (1946) Infant speech: vowel and consonant types. *Journal of speech disorders*, 11, 27–9.

Cheng, L. and Demirdash, H. (1990) Superiority violations. *MIT Working Papers in Linguistics*.

Chiat, S. (1983) Why *Mikey's* right and *my key's* wrong: the significance of stress and word boundaries in a child's output system. *Cognition*, 14, 275–300.

—— (1989) The relation between prosodic structure, syllabification and segmental realization: evidence from a child with fricative stopping. *Clinical Linguistics and Phonetics*, 3, 223–42.

Chiat, S. and Hirson, A. (1987) From conceptual intention to utterance: a study of impaired language output in a child with developmental dysphasia. *The British Journal of Disorders of Communication*, 22, 37–64.

Chien, Y.-C. and Wexler, K. (1987) Children's acquisition of reflexives and pronouns. *Papers and Reports on Child Language Development*, 26, 30–9.

—— (1991) Children's knowledge of locality conditions in binding as evidence for the modularity of syntax and pragmatics. *Language Acquisition*, 1, 225–95.

Chinn, S. and Dinnsen, D. (1991) Feature geometry in disordered phonologies. *Clinical Linguistics and Phonetics*, 5, 329–37.

Chipman, H. H. and de Dardel, C. (1974) Developmental study of the comprehension and production of the pronoun "it." *Journal of Psycholinguistic Research*, 3, 91–9.

Chmura-Klekotowa, M. (1971) Neologizmy slowotworczych w mowie dzieci [Derivational neologisms in children's speech]. *Prace Filologiczne*, 21, 99–235.

Choi, S. and Bowerman, M. (1991) Learning to express motion events in English and Korean: the influence of language-specific lexicalization patterns. *Cognition*, 41, 83–121. Reprinted in B. Levin and S. Pinker (eds), *Lexical and Conceptual Semantics*. Cambridge, Mass.: Blackwell.

Chomsky, C. (1969) *The Acquisition of Syntax in Children from 5 to 10*. Cambridge, Mass.: MIT Press.

Chomsky, N. (1957) *Syntactic Structures*. The Hague: Mouton.

—— (1959) Review of B. F. Skinner's Verbal Behaviour. *Language*, 35, 16–58.

—— (1964) Formal discussion. In U. Bellugi and R. Brown (eds), *The Acquisition of Language. Monographs of the Society for Research in Child Development*, 29 (1, serial no. 92).

—— (1965) *Aspects of the Theory of Syntax*. Cambridge, Mass.: MIT Press.

—— (1972) *Language and Mind* (enlarged edition). New York: Harcourt Brace Jovanovitch.

—— (1973) Conditions on transformations. In S. Anderson and P. Kiparsky (eds), *A Festchrift for Morris Halle*. New York: Holt, Rhinehart and Winston.

—— (1976) *Reflections on Language*. London: Temple Smith.

—— (1980) *Rules and Representations*. New York: Columbia University Press.

—— (1981) *Lectures on Government and Binding*. Dordrecht: Foris.

—— (1986a) *Barriers*. Cambridge, Mass.: MIT Press.

—— (1986b) *Knowledge of Language: its nature, origin, and use*. London: Praeger.

—— (1988) *Language and Problems of Knowledge*. Cambridge, Mass.: MIT Press.

—— (1989) Some notes on economy of derivation and representation. In I. Laka and A. Mahajan (eds), *Functional Heads and Clause Structure. MIT Working Papers in Linguistics*, 10, 43–74.

Chomsky, N. and Halle, M. (1968) *The Sound Pattern of English*. New York: Harper & Row.

Chugani, H. T. and Phelps, M. E. (1986) Maturational changes in cerebral function in infants determined by FDG positron emission tomography. *Science*, 231, 840–3.

Chugani, H. T., Phelps, M. E., and Mazziotta, J. C. (1987) Positron emission tomography study of human brain functional development. *Annals of Neurology*, 22, 487–97.

Chvany, C. V. (1985) Backgrounded perfectives and plot line imperfectives. In Flier and Timberlake (eds), *The Scope of Slavic Aspect*, 247–65. Columbus: Slavica.

Cinque, G. (1988) Comments on D. Lightfoot. *Behavioural and Brain Sciences*.

Clahsen, H. (1991a) *Child Language and Developmental Dysphasia: linguistic studies of the acquisition of German*. Amsterdam: John Benjamins.

—— (1991b) Constraints on parameter setting. A grammatical analysis of some acquisition stages in German child language. *Language Acquisition*, 1, 361–91.

—— (1992) Learnability theory and the problem of development in language acquisition. In J. Weissenborn, H. Goodluck, and T. Roeper (eds), *Theoretical Issues in Language Acquisition: continuity and change in development*, 53–76. Hillsdale, NJ: Lawrence Erlbaum Associates.

Clahsen, H., Rothweiler, M., Woest, A., and Marcus, G. F. (1992) Regular and irregular inflection in the acquisition of German noun plurals. *Cognition*, 45, 225–55.

Clancy, P. (1985) The acquisition of Japanese. In D. Slobin (ed.), *The Cross-linguistic Study of Language Acquisition*. Hillsdale, NJ: Lawrence Erlbaum Associates.

—— (1986) The acquisition of communicative style in Japanese. In B. B. Schieffelin and E. Ochs (eds), *Language Socialization across Cultures*, 213–50. Cambridge: Cambridge University Press.

Clark, E. V. (1972a) On the child's acquisition of antonyms in two semantic fields. *Journal of Verbal Learning and Verbal Behavior*, 11, 750–8.

—— (1972b) Some perceptual factors in the acquisition of locative terms by young children. *Proceedings of the Chicago Linguistic Society*, 8, 431–9.

—— (1973a) What's in a word? On the child's acquisition of semantics in his first language. In T. E. Moore (ed.), *Cognitive Development and the Acquisition of Language*. New York: Academic Press.

—— (1973b) How children describe time and order. In C. A. Ferguson and D. I. Slobin (eds), *Studies of Child Language Development*, 585–606. New York: Holt, Rinehart & Winston.

—— (1975) Knowledge, context and strategy in the acquisition of meaning. In D. P. Dato (ed.), *Developmental Psycholinguistics: theory and applications. Georgetown University Round Table on Languages and Linguistics 1975*. Washington, DC: Georgetown University Press.

—— (1978a) Discovering what words can do. In D. Farkas, W. M. Jacobsen, and K. W. Todrys (eds), *Papers from the Parasession on the Lexicon*. Chicago, Ill: Chicago Linguistic Society, 34–57.

—— (1978b) From gesture to word: on the natural history of deixis in language acquisition. In J. S. Bruner and A. Garton (eds), *Human Growth and Development: Wolfson College Lectures 1976*, 85–120, Oxford: Oxford University Press.

—— (1978c) Awareness of language: some evidence from what children say and do. In A. Sinclair, R. Jarvella, and W. Levelt (eds), *The Child's Conception of Language*, 17–43, New York: Springer.

—— (1979) Building a vocabulary: words for objects, actions, and relations. In P. Fletcher and M. Garman (eds), *Language Acquisition: studies in language development*, 149–60. Cambridge: Cambridge University Press.

—— (1982) The young word-maker: a case study of innovation in the child's lexicon. In E. Wanner and L. R. Gleitman (eds), *Language Acquisition: the state of the art*, 390–425. Cambridge: Cambridge University Press.

—— (1983) Meanings and concepts. In J. H. Flavell and E. Markman (eds), *Handbook of Child Psychology*, vol. 3: *Cognitive Development*. Chichester: Wiley.

—— (1987) The principle of contrast: a constraint on language acquisition. In B. MacWhinney (ed.), *Mechanisms of Language Acquisition*. Hillsdale, NJ: Lawrence Erlbaum Associates.

—— (1990a) On the pragmatics of contrast. *Journal of Child Language*, 17, 417–31.

—— (1990b) Speaker perspective in language acquisition. *Linguistics*, 28, 1,201–20.

—— (1993) *The Lexicon in Acquisition*. Cambridge: Cambridge University Press.

Clark, E. V. and Berman, R. A. (1984) Structure and use in the acquisition of word formation. *Language*, 60, 542–90.

Clark, E. V. and Carpenter, K. L. (1989) The notion of source in language acquisition. *Language*, 65, 1–30.

Clark, E. V. and Clark, H. H. (1979) When nouns surface as verbs. *Language*, 55, 767–811.

Clark, E. V. and Cohen, S. R. (1984) Productivity and memory for newly formed words. *Journal of Child Language*, 11, 611–25.

Clark, E. V. and Garnica, O. (1974) Is he coming or going? On the acquisition of deictic verbs. *Journal of Verbal Learning and Verbal Behavior*, 13, 559–72.

Clark, E. V., and Hecht, B. F. (1982) Learning to coin agent and instrument nouns. *Cognition*, 12, 1–24.

Clark, E. V. and Sengul, C. J. (1978) Strategies in the acquisition of deixis. *Journal of Child Language*, 5, 457–75.

Clark, E. V. and Svaib, T. (1991) Speaker perspective and lexical acquisition. Child Language Seminar (annual meeting), University of Manchester.

Clark, E. V., Gelman, S. A., and Lane, N. M. (1985) Compound nouns and category structure in young children. *Child Development* 56, 84–94.

Clark, H. H. (1973) Space, time, semantics and the child. In T. E. Moore (ed.), *Cognitive Development and the Acquisition of Language*. New York: Academic Press.

Clark, H. H. and Clark, E. (1977) *Psychology and Language*. New York: Harcourt Brace Jovanovich.

Clark, H. H. and Haviland, S. E. (1976) Comprehension and the given-new contrast. In R. Freedle (ed.), *Discourse Production and Comprehension*. Hillsdale, NJ: Lawrence Eribaum Associates.

Clarke-Stewart, K. A. (1978) And daddy makes three: the father's impact on mother and young child. *Child Development*, 49, 466–78.

Clyne, M. (1987) "Don't you get bored speaking only English?" Expressions of metalinguistic awareness in a bilingual child. In R. Steele and T. Threadgold, (eds), *Language Topics: essays in honour of Michael Halliday*, 85–103. Amsterdam: John Benjamins.

Cocking, R. R. and McHale, S. (1981) A comparative study of the use of pictures and objects in assessing children's receptive and productive language. *Journal of Child Language*, 8, 1–13.

Coggins, T. (1979) Relational meaning encoded in the two-word utterances of stage 1 Down's syndrome children. *Journal of Speech and Hearing Research*, 22, 166–78.

Coggins, T. and Stoel-Gammon, C. (1982) Clarification strategies used by four Down's syndrome children for maintaining normal conversational interaction. *Education and Training of the Mentally Retarded*, 17, 65–7.

Cohen, A. and Lieberman, A. (1986) Digital signal processing of stridor and snoring in children. *International Journal of Pediatric Otorhinolaryngology*, 12, 173–85.

Cohn, J. F. and Tronick, E. Z. (1983) Three-month-old infants' reaction to simulated maternal depression. *Child Development*, 54, 185–93.

Coker, P. A. (1977) Syntactic and semantic factors in the acquisition of *before* and *after*. *Journal of Child Language*, 5, 261–77.

Collis, G. M. (1977) Visual co-orientation and maternal speech. In H. R. Schaffer (ed.), *Studies in Mother–infant Interaction*. New York: Academic Press.

Colombo, J., O'Brien, M., Mitchell, D., Roberts, K., and Horowitz, F. (1987) A lower boundary for category formation in preverbal infants. *Journal of Child Language*, 14, 383–5.

Compton, A. (1970) Generative studies of children's phonological disorders. *Journal of Speech and Hearing Disorders*, 35, 315–39.

—— (1976) Generative studies of children's phonological disorders: clinical ramifications. In D. Morehead and A. Morehead (eds), *Normal and Deficient Child Language*, 61–96. Baltimore: University Park Press.

Comrie, B. (1976a) *Aspect: an introduction to the study of verbal aspect and related problems*. Cambridge: Cambridge University Press.

—— (1976b) Tense and time reference: from meaning to interpretation in the chronological structure of a text. *Journal of Literary Semantics*, 15, 12–22.

—— (1981) *Language Universals and Linguistic Typology*. Oxford: Blackwell.

—— (1985) *Tense*. Cambridge: Cambridge University Press.

Conel, J. L. (1939–63) *The Postnatal Development of the Human Cerebral Cortex*. Cambridge, Mass.: Harvard University Press.

Connell, P. (1987) Teaching language form, meaning, and function to specific-language-impaired children. In S. Rosenberg (ed.), *Advances in Applied Psycholinguistics*, vol. 1: *First-language Development*, 40–75. New York: Cambridge University Press.

Connell, P. J. and Stone, C. A. (1992) Morpheme learning of children with specific language impairment under controlled instructional conditions. *Journal of Speech and Hearing Research*, 35, 844–52.

Conti-Ramsden, G. (1994) Language interaction with atypical language learners. In C. Gallaway and B. Richards (eds), *Input and Interaction in Language Acquisition*, 183–98. London: Cambridge University Press.

Cook, H. M. (1988) Sentential particles in Japanese conversation: a study of indexicality, Unpublished Ph.D. dissertation. University of Southern California.

Cook, V. (1988) *Chomsky's Universal Grammar*. London: Blackwell.

Corballis, M. C. and Morgan, M. J. (1978) On the biological basis of human laterality, 1: Evidence for a maturational left–right gradient. *Behavioral and Brain Sciences*, 2, 261–336.

Cornwell, A. C. (1974) Development of language, abstraction, and numerical concept formation in Down's syndrome children. *American Journal of Mental Deficiency*, 79, 179–90.

Corrigan, R. (1978) Language development as related to Stage 6 object permanence development. *Journal of Child Language*, 5, 173–89.

—— (1979) Cognitive correlates of language: differential criteria yield differential results. *Child Development*, 50, 617–31.

Cottrell, G. W. and Plunkett, K. (in press) Acquiring the mapping from meanings to sounds. *Connection Science*.

Cox, M. and Isard, S. (1990) Children's deictic and nondeictic interpretations of the spatial locatives *in front of* and *behind*. *Journal of Child Language*, 17, 481–8.

Crago, M. B. (1988) Cultural context in communicative interaction of Inuit Children. Unpublished Ph.D. dissertation. McGill University, Montreal.

Crago, M. B., Allen, S., and Ningiuruvik, L. (1993) Inflections gone askew: SLI in a morphologically complex language. Paper presented at the Sixth Congress of the International Association for the Study of Child Language, Trieste.

Craig, H. K. (1983) Applications of pragmatic language models for intervention. In T. Gallagher and C. Prutting (eds), *Pragmatic Assessment and Intervention Issues in Language*, 101–27. San Diego: College-Hill Press.

—— (1990) Peer commentary on "Clinical pragmatics: Expectations and realizations" by Tanya M. Gallagher. *Journal of Speech Language Pathologists and Audiologists*, 14, 8–10.

—— (1991) Pragmatic characteristics of the child with specific language impairment: an interactionist perspective. In T. M. Gallagher (ed.), *Pragmatics of Language: clinical practice issues*. San Diego: Singular Publishing Group, Inc.

Craig, H. K. and Evans, J. (1989) Turn exchange characteristics of SLI children's simultaneous and nonsimultaneous speech. *Journal of Speech and Hearing Disorders*, 54, 334–47.

—— (1992) Pragmatics and SLI: a comparison of expressive and expressive-receptive subgroups. Manuscript submitted for publication.

—— (1993) Pragmatics and SLI: within-group variations in discourse behaviors. *Journal of Speech and Hearing Research*, 36, 777–89.

Craig, H. K. and Gallagher, T. M. (1986) Interactive play: the frequency of related verbal responses. *Journal of Speech and Hearing Research*, 29, 375–83.

Craig, H. K. and Washington, J. A. (1993) The access behaviors of children with specific language impairment. *Journal of Speech and Hearing Research*, 36, 322–37.

Crain, S. (1982) Temporal terms: mastery by age five. *Papers and Reports on Child Language Development* 21, 33–8.

—— (1989) Why production precedes comprehension. Paper presented at the Boston University Development Conference, Boston, Mass.

—— (1992) Language acquisition in the absence of experience. *Behavioral and Brain Sciences*, 14, 597–611.

Crain, S. and McKee, C. (1986) Acquisition of structural constraints on anaphora. *Proceedings from the 16th Annual Meeting of the North Eastern Linguistic Society*, McGill University, Montreal.

Crain, S. and Thornton, R. (1991a) Levels of representation in child grammar. Paper presented at GLOW colloquium, Cambridge, UK.

Crain, S. and Thornton, R. (1991b) Recharting the course of language acquisition: studies in elicited production. In N. Krasnegor, D. Rumbaugh, R. Schiefelbusch, and M. Studdert-Kennedy (eds), *Biobehavioral foundations of language development*. Lawrence Erlbaum Associates.

Crain-Thoreson, C., and Dale, P. S. (1992) Do early talkers become early readers? Linguistic precocity, preschool language, and emergent literacy. *Developmental Psychology*, 28, 421–9.

Cranberg, L. D., Filley, C. M., Hart, E. J., and Alexander, M. P. (1987) Acquired aphasia in childhood: clinical and CT investigations. *Neurology*, 37, 1,165–72.

Crnic, K. A. (1990) Families of children with Down syndrome: ecological contexts and characteristics. In D. Cicchetti, and M. Beeghly (eds), *Children with Down Syndrome: a developmental perspective*, 399–423. Cambridge: Cambridge University Press.

Cromer, R. F. (1974) The development of language and cognition: the cognitive hypothesis. In B. Foss (ed.), *New Perspective in Child Development*. Harmondsworth: Penguin.

—— (1988) The cognitive hypothesis revisited. In F. S. Kessel (ed.), *The Development of Language and Language Researchers: essays in honour of Roger Brown*. Hillsdale, NJ: Lawrence Erlbaum Associates.

—— (1991) *Language and Thought in Normal and Handicapped Children*. Oxford: Blackwell.

Crosley, P. A. and Dowling, S. (1989) The relationship between cluster and liquid simplification and sentence length, age, and IQ in Down's syndrome children. *Journal of Communication Disorders*, 22, 151–68.

Cross, T. (1977) Mothers' speech adjustments: the contribution of selected child listener variables. In C. Snow and C. Ferguson (eds), *Talking to Children: language input and acquisition* 1–188. Cambridge: Cambridge University Press.

Cross, T. G. (1978) Mothers' speech and its association with rate of linguistic development in young children. In N. Waterson and C. Snow (eds), *The Development of Communication*. New York: Wiley.

Cruttenden, A. (1974) An experiment involving comprehension of intonation in children 7 to 10. *Journal of Child Language*, 1, 221–32.

—— (1985) Intonation comprehension in ten year olds. *Journal of Child Language*, 12, 643–61.

—— (1994) Phonetic and prosodic aspects of baby talk. In C. Gallaway and B. Richards (eds), *Input and Interaction in Language Acquisition*, 135–52. London: Cambridge University Press.

Crystal, D. (1966) Specification and English tenses. *Journal of Linguistics* 2, 1–33.

—— (1974) Review of R. Brown, "A first language: the early stages." *Journal of Child Language*, 1, 289–307.

—— (1982) *Profiling Linguistic Disability*. London: Edward Arnold.

—— (1987) Towards a "bucket" theory of language disability: taking account of interaction between linguistic levels. *Clinical Linguistics and Phonetics*, 1, 7–22.

Crystal, D., Fletcher, P., and Garman, M. (1976/1989) *The Grammatical Analysis of Language Disability: a procedure for assessment and remediation*. London: Edward Arnold (1st edition); London: Whurr Publishers (2nd edition).

Culp, R., Watkins, R., Lawrence, H., Letts, D., Kelly, D., and Rice, M. (1991) Maltreated children's language and speech development: abused, neglected, and abused and neglected. *First Language*, 11, 377–90.

Cunningham, C. and McArthur, K. (1981) Hearing loss and treatment in young Down's syndrome children. *Child Care, Health, and Development*, 7, 357–74.

Curtiss, S. and Tallal, P. (1991) On the nature of impairment in language-impaired children. In J. F. Miller (ed.), *Research on Child Language Disorders: a decade of progress*, 189–210, Austin TX: Pro-Ed.

Cutler, A. (1993) Phonological cues to open- and closed-class words in the processing of spoken sentences. *Journal of Psycholinguistic Research*, 22, 109–31.

Cziko, G. A. (1986a). Testing the language bioprogram hypothesis: a review of children's acquisition of articles. *Language*, 62, 878–98.

Cziko, G. A. (1986b) A review of the state–process and punctual–nonpunctual distinctions in children's acquisitions of verbs. *First Language*, 9, 1–31.

D'Odorico, L. (1984) Nonsegmental features in prelinguistic communications: an analysis of some types of infant cry and noncry vocalizations. *Journal of Child Language*, 11, 17–27.

D'Odorico, L., Franco, F., and Vidotto, G. (1985) Temporal characteristics in infant cry and non-cry vocalizations. *Language and Speech*, 28, 29–46.

Dahl, O. (1985) *Tense and Aspect Systems*. Oxford: Basil Blackwell.

Dahle, A. J. and McCollister, F. P. (1986) Hearing and otologic disorders in children with Down syndrome. *American Journal of Mental Deficiency*, 90, 636–42.

Dale, P. S. (1991) The validity of a parent report measure of vocabulary and syntax at 24 months. *Journal of Speech and Hearing Sciences*, 34, 565–71.

Dale, P. S., Robinson, N. M., and Crain-Thoreson, C. (1992) Linguistic precocity and the development of reading: a final report. Manuscript submitted for publication.

Dale, P. S., Bates, E., Reznick, J. S., and Morisset, C. (1989) The validity of a parent report instrument of child language at 20 months. *Journal of Child Language*, 16, 239–49.

Dall'Oglio, A. M., Bates, E., Volterra, V., Di Capua, M., and Pezzini, G. (1992) Early cognition, communication, and language in children with focal brain injury. Technical Report 9202, Project in Cognitive Neurodevelopment, University of California, San Diego.

Damasio, A. R. (1989) The brain binds entities and events by multiregional activation from convergence zones. *Neural Computation*, 1, 331–41.

Daneš, F. (1974) Functional sentence perspective and the organization of text. In F. Danes (ed.), *Papers on Functional Sentence Perspective*, 106–28. Prague: Academia.

Davis, B. L. and MacNeilage, P. F. (1990) Acquisition of correct vowel production: a quantitative case study. *Journal of Speech and Hearing Research*, 33, 16–27.

de Acedo, B. (1993) Early morphological development: the acquisition of articles in Spanish. In J. Sokolov and C. Snow (eds) (1994), *Handbook of Research in Language Development Using CHILDES*. Hillsdale, NJ: Lawrence Erlbaum Associates.

DeCasper, A. and Fifer, W. P. (1980) On human bonding: newborns prefer their mothers' voices. *Science*, 208, 1,174–6.

DeCasper, A. and Spence, M. (1986) Prenatal maternal speech influences newborns' perception of speech sounds. *Infant Bahavior and Development*, 9, 133–50.

De Houwer, A. (1983) Some aspects of the simultaneous acquisition of Dutch and English by a three-year-old child. *Nottingham Linguistic Circular*, 12, 106–29.

—— (1987a) Gender marking in a young Dutch–English bilingual child. *Proceedings of the 1987 Child Language Seminar*, 53–65. York: University of York.

—— (1987b) Two at a time: an exploration of how children acquire two languages from birth. Unpublished Ph.D. dissertation. Brussels: Vrije Universiteit Brussel.

—— (1988) Word order patterns in the speech productions of a three-year-old. *ABLA Papers*, 12, 189–206.

—— (1990) *The Acquisition of Two Languages from Birth: a case study*. New York: Cambridge University Press.

—— (1992) Portrait of a mini-bilingual: past and future perspectives. Paper presented at the Fourth NELAS Conference, Oslo.

—— (1994) The separate development hypothesis: method and implications. In G. Extra and L. Verhoeven, (eds), *The Cross-Linguistic Study of Bilingual Development*. Amsterdam: Royal Netherlands Academy of Arts and Sciences.

de Jong, E. (1986) *The Bilingual Experience: a book for parents*. Cambridge: Cambridge University Press.

De Lemos, C. (1981) Interactional processes in the child's construction of language. In W. Deutsch (ed.), *The Child's Construction of Language*. New York: Academic Press.

De Temple, J. and Beals, D. (1991) Family talk: sources of support for the development of decontenxtualized language skills. *Journal of Research in Childhood Education*, 6, 11–19.

de Villiers, J. G. (1991) Why questions? In T. Maxfield and B. Plunkett (eds), *The Acquisition of wh*. University of Massachusetts Occasional Papers in Linguistics.

de Villiers, J. G. and de Villiers, P. A. (1973a) A cross-sectional study of the acquisition of grammatical morphemes in child speech. *Journal of Psycholinguistic Research*, 2, 267–78.

de Villiers, J. G. and de Villiers, P. A. (1973b) Development of the use of word order in comprehension. *Journal of Psycholinguistic Research*, 2, 331–41.

de Villiers, J. G. and Plunkett, B. (in preparation) Children show superiority in asking wh-questions.

de Villiers, J. G. and Roeper, T. (1991a) Introduction. In T. Maxfield and B. Plunkett (eds) *The Acquisition of wh*. University of Massachusetts Occasional Papers in Linguistics.

—— (1991b) The acquisition of subordination and quotation. Paper presented at the 16th Boston University Conference on Language Development.

—— (1992) The acquisition of the CP. Paper presented at Boston University Conference on Language Development.

—— (in press, a) The emergence of bound variable structures. In E. Reuland and W. Abraham (eds), *Knowledge and Language: Orwell's problem and Plato's problem*. Reidel.

—— (in press, b) Relative clauses are barriers to wh-movement for young children. *Journal of Child Language*.

de Villiers, J. G., Phinney, M., and Avery, A. (1982) Understanding passives with non-action verbs. Paper presented at the Seventh Annual Boston University Conference on Language Development.

de Villiers, J. G., Roeper, T., and Vainikka, A. (1990) The acquisition of long distance rules. In L. Frazier and J. G. de Villiers (eds), *Language Processing and Acquisition*. Dordrecht: Kluwe.

de Villiers, J. G., Sherrard, K., and Fretwell, L. (1992) Wh-questions and theory of mind. Paper presented at the Second Roundtable on Wh-questions, University of Massachusetts, Amherst.

de Villiers, J. G., Roeper, T., Mitsui, H., and Hallahan, K. (1992) Wh-questions and control. Paper presented at the Second Roundtable on Wh-questions, University of Massachusetts, Amherst.

de Villiers, P. A. and de Villiers, J. G. (1972) Early judgments of semantic and syntactic acceptability by children. *Journal of Psycholinguistic Research*, 1, 299–310.

de Villiers, P. A. and de Villiers, J. G. (1974) On this, that, and the other: nonegocentrism in very young children. *Journal of Experimental Psychology* 18, 438–47.

de Villiers, P. A. and de Villiers, J. G. (1979) *Early Language*. London: Fontana.

Delack, J. B. and Fowlow, P. J. (1978) The ontogenesis of differential vocalization: development of prosodic contrastivity during the first year of life. In N. Waterson and C. Snow (eds), *The Development of Communication*, 93–110. New York: Wiley.

De Weck, G. (1991) La cohésion dans les narrations d'enfants. Neuchâtel: Delachaux and Niestlé.

De Weck, G. and Schneuwly, B. (in press) Anaphoric procedures in four types of texts written by children. *Discourse Processes*.

Della Corte, M., Benedict, H., and Klein, D. (1983) The relationship of pragmatic dimensions of mother's speech to the referential–expressive distinction. *Journal of Child Language*, 10, 35–43.

Demuth, C. (1986) Prompting routines in the language socialization of Basotho children. In B. B. Schieffelin and E. Ochs (eds), *Language Socialization across Cultures*. Cambridge: Cambridge University Press.

Demuth, K. (1989) Maturation and the acquisition of the Sesotho passive. *Language*, 65, 56–80.

—— (1990) Subject, topic and Sesotho passive. *Journal of Child Language*, 17, 67–84.

—— (1992) The acquisition of Sesotho. In D. I. Slobin (ed.), *The Crosslinguistic Study of Language Acquisition*, 3, 557–638. Hillsdale, NJ: Lawrence Erlbaum Associates.

Denckla, M. B. and Rudel, R. G. (1976) Rapid "automatized" naming (R. A. N.): dyslexia differentiated from other learning disabilities. *Neuropsychologia*, 14, 471–9.

Dennis, M. (1980) Capacity and strategy for syntactic comprehension after left or right hemidecortication. *Brain and Language*, 10, 287–317.

Dennis, M. and Kohn, B. (1975) Comprhension of syntax in infantile hemiplegics after cerebral hemidecortication: left hemisphere superiority. *Brain and Language*, 2, 472–82.

Dennis, M. and Whitaker, H. A. (1976) Linguistic superiority of the left over the right hemisphere. *Brain and Language*, 3, 404–33.

Derwing, B. L. and Baker, W. J. (1986) Assessing morphological development. In P. Fletcher and M. Garman (eds), *Language Acquisition*, 2nd edn, 326–8. New York: Cambridge University Press.

Desimone, R. (1991) Face-selective cells in the temporal cortex of monkeys. *Journal of Cognitive Neuroscience,* 3, 1–8.

Deuchar, M. (1988) Review of *Raising Children Bilingually: the pre-school years* by Lenore Arnberg. *Journal of Child Language,* 15, 459–68.

—— (1989) ESRC report on project "Infant bilingualism: one system or two?" Unpublished manuscript.

—— (1992) Can government and binding theory account for language acquisition? In C. Vide (ed.), *Lenguajes Naturales y Lenguajes Formales VIII,* 273–9. Barcelona: Universitat de Barcelona.

Deuchar, M. and Clark, A., (1988) Acquisition of voicing in a Spanish–English bilingual. Paper presented at the Annual Meeting of the Linguistic Society of America, New Orleans.

—— (1992) Bilingual acquisition of the voicing contrast in word-initial stop consonants in English and Spanish. Cognitive science research paper 213. Brighton: University of Sussex.

Deutsch, W. C. and Koster, J. (1982) Children's interpretation of sentence-internal anaphora. *Papers and Reports on Child Language Development* 21, 39–45.

Deutsch, W. C., Koster, C., and Koster, J. (1986) What can we learn from children's errors in understanding anaphora? *Linguistics,* 24, 203–25.

DeVos, G. A. (1967) Essential elements of caste: psychological determinants in structural theory. In G. A. DeVos & H. Wagatsuma (eds), *Japan's Invisible Race: case in culture and personality.* Berkeley: University of California Press.

Di Paolo, M. and Smith, C. S. (1978) Cognitive and linguistic factors in the acquisition of temporal and aspectual expressions. In P. French (ed.), *The Development of Meaning.* Tokyo: Bunka Hyoron.

Dinnsen, D. (1984) Methods and empirical issues in analyzing functional misarticulation. *ASHA Monographs,* 22, 5–17.

—— (1992) Variation in developing and fully developed phonetics inventories. In C. A. Ferguson, L. Menn, and C. Stoel-Gammon (eds), *Phonological Development: models, research, implications,* 191–210. Timonium, MD: York Press.

Dinnsen, D., Chin, S., Elbert, M., and Powell, T. (1990) Some constraints on functionally disordered phonologies: phonetic inventories and phonotactics. *Journal of Speech and Hearing Research,* 33, 28–37.

Disner, S. D. and Ladefoged, P. (1976) Trill seeking. *Journal of the Acoustical Society of America,* suppl. 1, 60, S45.

Dixon, W. E. and Shore, C. (1992) Confirming linguistic styles. Paper presented at the International Conference on Infant Studies, Miami Beach.

—— (1993). Short-term stability and temperamental predictors of linguistic style. Poster presented at the 60th Annual Meeting of the Society for Research in Child Development, New Orleans.

Dobbing, J. and Sands, J. (1979) Comparative aspects of the brain spurt. *Early Human Development,* 3, 79–83.

Dodd, B. (1979) Lip reading in infants: attention to speech presented in-and-out-of-synchrony. *Cognitive Psychology,* 11, 478–84.

Dodd, B. J. (1972) Comparison of babbling patterns in normal and Down-syndrome infants. *Journal of Mental Deficiency Research,* 16, 35–40.

—— (1976) A comparison of the phonological systems of mental age matched normal, severely subnormal, and Down's syndrome children. *British Journal of Communication Disorders,* 11, 35–43.

D'Odorico, L. (1984) Nonsegmental features in prelinguistic communications: an analysis of some types of infant cry and noncry vocalizations. *Journal of Child Language,* 11, 17–27.

Doherty, B., Fowler, A., and Boynton, L. (1993) Phonological prerequisites to reading in young adults with Down syndrome. Poster presented at Biennial Meeting of Society for Research in Child Development, New Orleans.

Dollaghan, C. A. (1993) Review of L. Baker-van den Goorbergh and K. Baker, CLEAR computer program. *Child Language Teaching and Therapy*, 9, 251–4.

Dollaghan, C. A. and Campbell, T. F. (1992) A procedure for classifying disruptions in spontaneous language samples. *Topics in Language Disorders*, 12(2), 56–68.

Dollaghan, C. A., Campbell, T. F., and Tomlin, R. (1990) Video narration as a language sampling context. *Journal of Speech and Hearing Disorders*, 55, 582–90.

Donahue, M. (1986) Phonological constraints on the emergence of two-word utterances. *Journal of Child Language*, 13, 209–18.

Donaldson, M. and Wales, R. J. (1970) On the acquisition of some relational terms. In J. R. Hayes (ed.), *Cognition and the Development of Language*, 235–68. New York: John Wiley and Sons.

Döpke, S. (1986) Discourse structures in bilingual families. *Journal of Multilingual and Multicultural Development*, 7, 493–507.

—— (1988) The role of parental teaching techniques in bilingual German–English families. *International Journal of the Sociology of Language*, 72, 101–12.

Dore, J. (1974) A pragmatic description of early language development. *Journal of Psycholinguistic Research*, 4, 423–30.

—— (1978) Conditions for the acquisition of speech acts. In I. Markova (ed.), *The Social Context of Language*. Chichester: Wiley.

—— (1979) Conversational and preschool language development. In P. Fletcher and M. Garman (eds), *Language Acquisition*, 337–62. Cambridge: Cambridge University Press.

—— (1985) Holophrases revisited: their "logical" development from dialog. In M. D. Barrett (ed.), *Children's Single-Word Speech*. Chichester: Wiley.

Dorian, N. (ed.) (1989) *Investigating Obsolescence: studies in language contraction and death*. Cambridge: Cambridge University Press.

Dowty, D. R. (1982) Tenses, time adverbials, and compositional semantic theory. *Linguistics and Philosophy* 5, 23–55.

—— (1986) The effects of aspectual classes on the temporal structure of discourse: semantics or pragmatics? In D. R. Dowty (ed.), *Linguistics and Philosophy*, vol. 9, *Tense and Aspect in Discourse*, 37–61.

Dresel, L. H. (1977) Palatalization in Hausa child language. Paper read at the Annual Meeting of the Linguistic Society of America.

Dromi, E. (1987) *Early Lexical Development*. Cambridge: Cambridge University Press.

Dromi, E., Leonard, L., and Shteiman, M. (1993) The grammatical morphology of Hebrew-speaking children with SLI: some competing hypotheses. *Journal of Speech and Hearing Research*, 36, 760–71.

Dry, H. (1981) Sentence aspect and the movement of narrative time. *Text*, 1, 233–40.

—— (1983) The movement of narrative time. *Journal of Literary Semantics*, 12, 19–53.

Dukette, D. and Stiles, J. (1991) Spatial pattern analysis in preschool children: evidence from a matching task using hierarchical letter stimuli. Paper presented at the biannual meeting of the Society for Research in Child Development, Seattle.

Dunn, J. (1988) *The Beginnings of Social Understanding*. Cambridge, Mass.: Harvard University Press.

Dunn, J. and Kendrick, C. (1982) *Siblings: love, envy and understanding*. Cambridge, Mass.: Harvard University Press.

Dunn, J. and Munn, P. (1987) Development of justification in disputes with mother and sibling. *Developmental Psychology*, 23, 791–8.

Dunn, L. M. and Dunn, L. M. (1981) *Peabody Picture Vocabulary Test-Revised*, Manual for Forms L. and M. Circle Pines, MN: American Guidance Service.

Dunst, C. J. (1990) Sensorimotor development of infants with Down syndrome. In D. Cicchetti and M. Beeghly (eds), *Children with Down Syndrome: a developmental perspective*, 180–230. Cambridge: Cambridge University Press.

Duranti, A. and Goodwin, C. (eds) (1992) *Rethinking Context: language as an interactive phenomenon*. New York: Cambridge University Press.

Dyson, A. (1988) Phonetic inventories of 2- and 3-year-old children. *Journal of Speech and Hearing Disorders*, 53, 89–93.

Edmonds, J. (1970) *Root and Structure-preserving Transformations*. Doctoral dissertation, MIT.

Edwards, J. A. and Lampert, M. D. (eds) (1993) *Talking Data: transcription and coding in discourse research*. Hillsdale, NJ: Lawrence Erlbaum Associates.

Edwards, M. L. (1978) Word position in fricative acquisition. Paper presented at the Boston University Conference on Language Acquisition.

—— (1979) Patterns and processes in fricative acquisition: longitudinal evidence from six English-learning children. Unpublished doctoral dissertation, Stanford University.

—— (1980) The use of "favorite sounds" by children with phonological disorders. Paper presented at the Boston University Conference on Language Development, Boston.

Edwards, M. L. and Shriberg, L. (1983) *Phonology: applications in communicative disorders*. San Diego: College-Hill Press.

Edwards, M. L. and Bernhardt, B. (1973) Phonological analyses of the speech of four children with language disorders. Unpublished paper, Stanford University.

Edwards, M. L. and Shriberg, L. (1983) *Phonology: applications in communicative disorders*. San Diego: College-Hill Press.

Ehlich, K. (1982) Anaphora and deixis: same, similar, or different? In R. Jarvella and W. Klein (eds), *Speech, Place, and Action: studies in deixis and related topics*. New York: Wiley.

Ehrich, V. (1982) Discourse organization and sentence form in child language: how children describe rooms. *Papers and Reports on Child Language Development*, 21, 55–62.

Ehrich, V. and Koster, C. (1983) Discourse organization and sentence form: the structure of room descriptions in Dutch. *Discourse Processes*, 6, 169–95.

Ehrlich, S. (1987) Aspect, foregrounding and point of view. *Text*, 7, 363–76.

—— (1988) Cohesive devices and discourse competence. *World Englishes*, 7, 111–18.

Eilers, R. E., Moroff, D. A., and Turner, R. H. (1985) Discrimination of formant transitions by Down syndrome and normally developing infants. *Human Communication Canada*, 9, 99–103.

Eilers, R. E., Bull, D. H., Oller, D. K., and Lewis, D. C. (1985) The discrimination of rapid spectral speech cues by Down syndrome and normally developing infants. In S. Harel and N. Anastasiow (eds), *The At-risk Infant: psycho/social/medical aspects*. Baltimore: Brookes.

Eimas, P. D., Siqueland, E. R., Jusczyk, P., and Vigorito, J. (1971) Speech perception in infants. *Science*, 171, 303–6.

Eisele, J. (1992) The role of negation in determining presuppositions and implications of truth: a study of early hemisphere damage. Unpublished Ph.D. dissertation, Cornell University.

Eisele, J. and Aram, D. (1993) Differential effects of early hemisphere damage on lexical comprehension and production. *Aphasiology*, 7(5), 513–23.

Eisele, J. and Aram, D. (1994) Comprehension and imitation of syntax following early hemisphere damage. *Brain and Language*, 46, 212–31.

Eisele, J. and Aram, D. (in preparation). Early lexical and grammatical development following early hemisphere damage.

Eisele, J., Aram, D., and Alexander, M. (in preparation) Language and cognition following subcortical lesions in children.

Eisele, J., Aram, D., and Lust, B. (to appear) Presuppositions and implications of truth: linguistic deficits following early brain lesions. *Brain and Language*, special issue, M. Dennis (ed.).

Eisenberg, A. R. (1985) Learning to describe past-experiences in conversation. *Discourse Processes*, 8, 177–204.

—— (1986) Teasing: verbal play in two Mexican homes. In B. B. Schieffelin and E. Ochs (eds), *Language Socialization across Cultures*. Cambridge: Cambridge University Press.

Ekman, P. and Friesen, W. V. (1969) The repertoire of nonverbal behavior: categories, origins, usage, and coding. *Semiotica*, 1, 49–98.

Elbers, L. (1982) Operating principles in repetitive babbling: a cognitive continuity approach. *Cognition*, 12, 45–63.

Ellison, D. and Gillis, B. J. (1993) Developmental changes in the cognitive functioning of children with Down syndrome. Poster presented at the 60th meeting of the Society for Research in Child Development, New Orleans.

Elman, J. L. (1990) Finding structure in time. *Cognitive Science*, 14, 179–211.

—— (1992) Learning and development in neural networks: the importance of starting small. In C. Umilta and M. Moscovitch (eds), *Attention and Performance XV: conscious and nonconscious information processing*. Hillsdale, NJ: Lawrence Erlbaum Associates.

Ely, R. and McCabe, A. (1993) Remembered voices. *Journal of child Language*, 20.

Emonds, J. E. (1970) Root and structure-preserving transformations. Doctoral dissertation, MIT.

—— (1985) *A Unified Theory of Syntactic Categories*. Dordrecht: Foris.

Emslie, H. C. and Stevenson, R. J. (1981) Pre-school children's use of the articles in definite and indefinite referring expressions. *Journal of Child language*, 8, 313–28.

Epstein, C., Korenberg, J., Anneren, G., Antonarakis, S., Ayme, S., Courchesne, E., Epstein, L., Fowler, A., Groner, Y., Huret, J., Kemper, T., Lott, I., Lubin, B., Magenis, E., Opitz, J., Patterson, D., Priest, J., Pueschel, S., Rapoport, S., Sinet, P.-M., Tanzi, R., and de la Cruz, F. (1991) Protocols to establish genotype–phenotype correlations in Down syndrome. *American Journal of Human Genetics*, 49, 207–35.

Espéret, E. (1991) The development and role of narrative schema storytelling. In G. Piéraut-Le Bonniec and M. Dolitsky (eds), *Language Bases . . . Discourse Bases*. Amsterdam: Benjamins.

Ervin-Tripp, S. M. (1964) Imitation and structural change in children's language. In E. H. Lenneberg (ed.), *New Directions in the Study of Language*, 163–89. Cambridge, Mass.: MIT Press.

Ervin-Tripp, S. (1979) Children's verbal turn-taking. In E. Ochs and B. Schieffelin (eds), *Developmental Pragmatics*. New York: Academic Press.

Evans, M. (1987) Linguistic accommodation in a bilingual family, one perspective on the language acquisition of a bilingual child being raised in a monolingual community. *Journal of Multilingual and Multicultural Development*, 8, 231–5.

Ewing, G. (1982) Word-order invariance and variability in five children's three-word utterances: a limited-scope formula analysis. In C. E. Johnson and C. L. Thew (eds), *Proceedings of the Second International Congress for the Study of Child Language*, vol. 1. Washington DC: University Press of America.

Fagot, B. A. and Hagan, R. (1991) Observations of parent reactions to sex-stereotyped behaviors: age and sex effects. *Child Development*, 62, 617–28.

Fantini, A. (1985) *Language Acquisition of a Bilingual Child, a Sociolinguistic Perspective (to age ten)*. Clevedon: Multilingual Matters.

Farmer, A. and Florance, K. (1977) Segmental duration differences: language disordered and normal children. In J. Andrews and M. Burns (eds), *Selected Papers in Language and Phonology*, vol. 2: *Language Remediation*. Evanston, Ill: Institute for Continuing Professional Education.

Farran, D. C. and Kasari, C. (1990) A longitudinal analysis of the development of synchrony in mutual gaze in mother–child dyads. *Journal of Applied Developmental Psychology*, 11, 419–30.

Farrar, J. (1990) Discourse and the acquisition of grammatical morphemes. *Journal of Child Language*, 17, 607–24.

Fasold, R. (1980) The relation between Black and White speech in the south. Mimeo. Washington DC: School of Languages and Linguistics, Georgetown University.

Fassi Fehri, A. (1988) Generalised IP structure, case, and VS word order. In A. Fassi Fehri, A. Hajji, H. Elmoujahid, and A. Jamari (eds), *Proceedings of the First International Conference of the Linguistic Society of Morocco*, 189–221. Rabat: Editions OKAD.

Fayol, M. (1985) *Le Récit et sa Construction: Une Approche de psychologie cognitive*. Neuchâtel: Delachaux and Niestlé.

—— (1991) Stories: A psycholinguistic and ontogenetic approach to the acquistion of narrative abilities. In G. Piéraut-Le Bonniec and M. Dolitsky (eds), *Language Bases . . . Discourse Bases*. Amsterdam: Benjamins.

Fayol, M., Abdi, H., and Gombert, J. E. (1989) Use of past tense verb inflections in French: developmental study of the interaction between type of process and context. *European Bulletin of Cognitive Psychology*, 9, 279–95.

Feldman, H., Goldin-Meadow, S., and Gleitman, L. R. (1978) Beyond Herodotus: the creation of language by linguistically deprived deaf children. In A. Lock (ed.), *Action, Symbol, and Gesture: the emergence of language*. New York: Academic Press.

Feldman, H. M., Holland, L., Kemp, S. S., and Janosky, J. E. (1992) Language development after unilateral brain injury. *Brain and Language*, 42, 89–102.

Felix, S. W. (1984) Maturational aspects of Universal Grammar. In A. Davies, C. Cripper, and A. Howatt (eds), *Interlanguage*, 133–61. Edinburgh: Edinburgh University Press.

—— (1987) *Cognition and Language Growth*. Dordrecht: Foris.

—— (1992) Language acquisition as a maturational process. In J. Weissenborn, H. Goodluck, and T. Roeper (eds), *Theoretical Issues in Language Acquisition: continuity and change in development*, 25–52. Hillsdale, NJ: Lawrence Erlbaum Associates.

Fenson, L., Dale, P. S., Reznick, J. S., Bates, E., and Thal, D. (in press) *Variability in Early Communicative Development. Monographs of the Society for Research in Child Development.*

Fenson, L., Dale, P. S., Reznick, J. S., Thal, D., Bates, E., Hartung, J., Pethick, S., and Reilly, J. (1993) *The MacArthur Communicative Development Inventories: user's guide and technical manual*. San Diego: Singular Publishing Group.

Ferguson, C. (1964) Baby talk in six languages. *American Anthropologist*, 66(6), 103–14.

—— (1977) Baby talk as a simplified register. In C. E. Snow and C. A. Ferguson (eds), *Talking to Children*. Cambridge: Cambridge University Press.

—— (1978a) Talking to children: a search for universals. In J. Greenberg, C. A. Ferguson, and E. A. Moravscik (eds), *Universals of Human Language*, vol. 1, (203–24). Stanford, CA: Stanford University Press.

—— (1978b) Learning to pronounce: the earliest stages of phonological development in the child. In F. D. Minifie and L. L. Lloyd (eds), *Communicative and Cognitive Abilities: early behavioral assessment*, 273–97. Baltimore: University Park Press.

—— (1982) Simplified registers and linguistic theory. In L. K. Obler and Lise Menn (eds), *Exceptional Language and Linguistics*. New York: Academic Press.

—— (1986) Discovering sound units and constructing sound systems: it's child's play. In J. Perkell and D. Klatt (eds), *Invariance and Variability in Speech Processes*, 36–51. Hillsdale, NJ: Lawrence Erlbaum Associates.

Ferguson, C. A. and Farwell, C. B. (1975) Words and sounds in early language acquisition. *Language*, 51, 419–39.

Ferguson, C., Peizer, D., and Weeks, T. (1973) Model and replica phonological grammar of a child's first words. *Lingua*, 31, 35–65.

Fernald, A. (1984) The perceptual and affective salience of mothers' speech to infants. In L. Feagans, C. Garvey, and R. Golinkoff (eds), *The Origins and Growth of Communication*. Norwood, NJ: Ablex.

—— (1985) Four-month-old infants prefer to listen to motherese. *Infant Behavior and Development*, 8, 181–95.

—— (1992a) Human maternal vocalisations to infants as biologically relevant signals: an evolutionary perspective. In Barkow, J. H., Cosmides, L., and Tooby, J. (eds), *The Adapted Mind: evolutionary psychology and the generation of culture*. New York: Oxford University Press.

—— (1992b) Meaningful melodies in mothers' speech. In H. Papousek, U. Jurgens, and M. Papousek (eds), *Origins and Development of Nonverbal Vocal Communication: evolutionary, comparative, and methodological aspects*. Cambridge: Cambridge University Press.

—— (in press a) Meaningful melodies in mothers' speech to infants. In H. Papousek, U. Jurgens, and M. Papousek (eds), *Origins and Development of Nonverbal Vocal Communication: evolutionary, comparative, and methodological aspects*. Cambridge: Cambridge University Press.

—— (in press b) Prosody in speech to children: prelinguistic and linguistic functions. *Annals of Child Development*, 8.

Fernald, A. and Kuhl, P. (1987) Acoustic determinants of infant preference for motherese speech. *Infant Behavior and Development*, 10, 279–93.

Fernald, A. and Simon, T. (1984) Expanded intonation contours in mothers' speech to newborns. *Developmental Psychology*, 20, 104–13.

Fernald, A., Taeschner, T., Dunn, J., Papousek, M., Boysson-Bardies, B. de, and Fukui, I. (1989) A cross-language study of prosodic modifications in mothers' and fathers' speech to preverbal infants. *Journal of Child Language*, 16, 477–501.

Ferrier, L. J. (1978) Some observations of error in context. In N. Waterson and C. Snow (eds), *The Development of Communication*. Chichester: Wiley.

Ferrier, L. J., Bashir, A. S., Meryash, D. L., Johnston, J., and Wolff, P. (1991) Conversational skills of individuals with Down syndrome. *Developmental Medicine and Child Neurology*, 33, 776–88.

Fey, M. (1985) Articulation and phonology: inextricable constructs in speech pathology. *Human Communication Canada*, 9, 7–16.

Field, T. M., Cohen, D., Garcia, R., and Greenberg, R. (1984) Mother–stranger face discrimination by the newborn. *Infant Behavior and Development*, 7, 19–25.

Fillmore, C. J. (1982) A descriptive framework for spatial deixis. In R. Jarvella and W. Klein (eds), *Speech, Place, and Action: studies in deixis and related topics*. New York: Wiley.

Finnerty, J. (1992) *Communication Analyzer* [Computer software, IBM]. Lexington, Mass.: Educational Software Research, Inc.

Firbas, J. (1964) On defining the theme in functional sentence analysis. *Travaux Linguistiques de Prague*, 1, 267–80.

—— (1966) Nonthematic subjects in contemporary English. *Travaux Linguistiques de Prague*, 2, 239–56.

—— (1971) On the concept of communicative dynamism in the theory of functional sentence perspective. In *Studia Minora Facultatis Philosophicae Universitatis Brunensis*, 135–44.

Fischel, J. E., Whitehurst, G., and Connors, G. (1987) Language growth in children with expressive language delay. Paper presented at the biennial meeting of the Society for Research in Child Development, Baltimore, MD.

Fischel, J. E., Whitehurst, G. J., Caulfield, M. B., and Debaryshe, B. D. (1989). Language growth in children with expressive language delay. *Pediatrics*, 82, 218–27.

Fischer, M. A. (1987) Mother–child interaction in preverbal children with Down syndrome. *Journal of Speech and Hearing Disorders*, 52, 179–90.

Fisher, C., Gleitman, H., and Gleitman, L. (1991) Relationships between verb meanings and their syntactic structures. *Cognitive Psychology*, 23, 331–92.

Fisher, C., Hall, D. G., Rakowitz, S., and Gleitman, L. R. (1994) When it is better to receive than to give: structural and conceptual cues to verb meaning. *Lingua*, 92, 333–75.

Fivush, R. and Mandler, J. (1985) Developmental changes in the understanding of temporal sequence. *Child Development*, 56, 1,437–46.

Fivush, R., Gray, J. T., and Fromhoff, F. A. (1987) Two-year-olds' talk about the past. *Cognitive Development*, 2, 393–409.

Fletcher, P. (1979) The development of the verb phrase. In P. Fletcher and M. Garman (eds), *Language Acquisition*. Cambridge: Cambridge University Press.

—— (1981) Description and explanation in the acquisition of verb forms. *Journal of Child Language*, 8, 93–108.

—— (1985) *A Child's Learning of English*. Oxford: Basil Blackwell.

—— (1991) Evidence from syntax for language impairment. In J. F. Miller (ed.), *Research on Child Language Disorders: a decade of progress*, 169–87. Austin, TX: Pro-Ed.

—— (1992a). Sub-groups in school-age language-impaired children. In P. Fletcher and D. Hall (eds), *Specific Speech and Language Disorders in Children*, 152–63. London: Whurr Publishers; San Diego: Singular Publishing Group.

—— (1992b) Lexical verbs and language impairment: a case study. *Clinical Linguistics and Phonetics*, 6, 147–54.

—— (1994) Grammar and language impairment: clinical linguistics as applied linguistics. In D. Graddol and J. Swann (eds), *Evaluating Language*. Clevedon: BAAL/Multilingual Matters.

Fletcher, P. and Garman, M. (1988) Normal language development and language impairment: language and beyond. *Clinical Linguistics and Phonetics*, 2, 97–113.

—— (1995) Transcription, segmentation and analysis: corpora from the language-impaired. In G. Leech, J. Thomas, and G. Myers (eds), *Spoken English on Computer*. London: Longman.

Fletcher, P. and Hall, D. (eds) (1992) *Specific Speech and Language Disorders in Children*. London: Whurr Publishers; San Diego: Singular Publishing Group.

Fletcher, P. and Peters, J. (1984) Characterizing language impairment in children: an exploratory study. *Language Testing*, 1, 33–49.

Fodor, J. A. (1983) *The Modularity of Mind*. Cambridge, Mass.: MIT Press.

Fodor, J. A. and Pylyshyn, Z. (1988) Connectionism and cognitive architecture: a critical analysis. *Cognition*, 28, 3–71.

Foley, W. A. and van Valin, R. D. (1985) *Functional Syntax and Universal Grammar*. Cambridge: Cambridge University Press.

Forrest, K. and Rockman, B. (1988) Acoustic and perceptual analysis of word-initial stop consonants in phonologically disordered children. *Journal of Speech and Hearing Research*, 31, 449–59.

Forrest, K., Weismer, G., Hodge, M., Dinnsen, D., and Elbert, E. (1990) Statistical analysis of word-initial /k/ and /t/ produced by normal and phonologically disordered children. *Clinical Linguistics and Phonetics*, 4, 327–40.

Fortescue, M. and Lennert Olsen, L. (1992) The acquisition of West Greenlandic. In D. I. Slobin (ed.), The Crosslinguistic Study of Language Acquisition, vol. 3, 111–219. Hillsdale, NJ: Lawrence Erlbaum Associates.

Fowler, A. (1985) Language acquisition of Down's syndrome children: production and comprehension. *Dissertation Abstracts International*, 46(1-B), 324.

—— (1990) Language abilities in children with Down syndrome: evidence for a specific syntactic delay. In D. Cicchetti and M. Beeghly (eds), *Children with Down Syndrome: a developmental perspective*, 302–28. Cambridge: Cambridge University Press.

Fox, B. and Routh, D. K. (1975) Analyzing spoken language into words, syllables, and phonemes: a developmental study. *Journal of Psycholinguistic Research*, 4, 331–42.

Fraiberg, S. (1979) Blind infants and their mothers: an examination of the sign system. In M. Bullowa (ed.), *Before Speech: the beginning of interpersonal communication*. New York: Cambridge University Press.

Fraser, C., Bellugi, U., and Brown, R. (1963) Control of grammar in imitation, comprehension, and production. *Journal of Psycholinguistic Research*, 2, 331–42.

Freedman, D. G. (1964) Smiling in blind infants and the issue of innate vs. acquired. *Journal of Child Psychology and Psychiatry*, 5, 171–84.

Freidin, R. (1992) *Foundations of Generative Syntax*. Cambridge, Mass.: MIT Press.

Fremgen, A. and Fay, D. (1980) Overextensions in production and comprehension. *Journal of Child Language*, 7, 205–12.

French, L. A. and Brown, A. (1977) Comprehension of *before* and *after* in logical and arbitrary sequences. *Journal of Child Language*, 4, 247–56.

French, L. A. and Nelson, K. (1985) *Children's Acquisition of Relational Terms: some is, ors, and buts*. New York: Springer Verlag.

Freud, S. (1924/1952) *A General Introduction to Psychoanalysis*. New York: Washington Square Press.

Friedman, S. and Stevenson, M. (1975) Developmental changes in the understanding of implied motion in two-dimensional pictures. *Child Development*, 46, 775–8.

Fristoe, M. and Lloyd, L. (1978) A survey of the use of non-speech systems with the severely communication impaired. *Mental Retardation*, 16, 99–103.

Fry, D. B. (1966) The development of the phonological system in the normal and the deaf child. In F. Smith and G. Miller (eds), *The Genesis of Language*, 187–206. Cambridge, Mass.: MIT Press.

Fukui, N. (1986) *A Theory of Category Projection and its Applications.* Ph.D. dissertation, MIT.

Furrow, D., Moore, C., Davidge, J., and Chiasson, L. (1992) Mental terms in mothers' and children's speech: similarities and relationships. *Journal of Child Language*, 19, 597–617.

Gal, S. (1979) *Language Shift: social determinants of linguistic change in bilingual austria.* New York: Academic Press.

—— (1985) Review of *The sun is feminine* by Traute Taeschner. *Language*, 61, 244–5.

Gallagher, T. (1990) Clinical pragmatics: expectations and realizations. *Journal of Speech–Language Pathology and Audiology*, 14, 3–6.

Gallagher, T. M. and Craig, H. K. (1984) Pragmatic assessmen: analysis of a highly frequent repeated utterance. *Journal of Speech and Hearing Disorders*, 49, 368–77.

Gallagher, T. M. and Darnton, B. (1978) Conversational aspects of the speech of language-disordered children: revision behaviors. *Journal of Speech and Hearing Research*, 21, 118–35.

Gallaway, C. and Richards, B. (1994) *Input and Interaction in Language Acquisition.* London: Cambridge University Press.

Gallaway, C. and Woll, B. (1994) Interaction and childhood deafness. In C. Galloway and B. Richards (eds), *Input and Interaction in Language Acquisition*, 197–218. London: Cambridge University Press.

Gandour, J. (1981) The nondeviant nature of deviant phonological systems. *Journal of Communication Disorders*, 14, 11–29.

García, E. (1983) *Early Childhood Bilingualism.* Albuquerque: University of New Mexico Press.

Gardner, M. F. (1979) *Expressive One-Word Picture Vocabulary Test Manual.* Novato, CA: Academic Therapy Publications.

Gardner, R. A., Gardner, B. T., and Drumm, P. (1989) Voiced and signed responses of cross-fostered chimpanzees. In R. A. Gardner, B. T. Gardner, and T. E. Van cantfort (eds), *Teaching Sign Language to Chimpanzees.* Albany: State University of New York Press.

Garman, M. (1989) The role of linguistics in speech therapy: assessment and interpretation. In P. Grunwell and A. James (eds), *The Functional Evaluation of Language Disorders*, 29–57. London: Croom Helm.

Garnham, A., Oakhill, J., and Johnson-Laird, P. (1982) Referential continuity and the coherence of discourse. *Cognition*, 11, 29–46.

Garnica, O. (1977) Some prosodic and paralinguistic features of speech to young children. In D. E. Snow and C. A. Ferguson (eds), *Talking to Children: language input and acquisition.* Cambridge: Cambridge University Press.

Garrett, M. (1992) Disorders of lexical selection. *Cognition*, 42, 143–80.

Garside, R., Leech, G., and Sampson, G. (eds) (1987) *The Computational Analysis of English: a corpus-based approach.* London: Longman.

Gathercole, S. and Baddeley, A. (1989) Evaluation of the role of phonological STM in the development of vocabulary in children: a longitudinal study. *Journal of Memory and Language*, 28, 200–13.

—— (1990) Phonological memory deficits in language-disordered children: is there a causal connection? *Journal of Memory and Language*, 29, 336–60.

Gathercole, S. E., Willis, C. S., Emslie, H., and Baddeley, A. D. (1992) Phonological memory and vocabulary development during the early school years: a longitudinal study. *Developmental Psychology*, 28, 887–98.

Gavin, W. J. (1987) Interactive data management software for language sample analyses. *Child Language Teaching and Therapy*, 3, 183–99.

Gavin, W. J., Dismuke-Blakely, R., and Klee, T. (1991) *Transcript Analysis System* (TAS) [Computer software, VAX/VMS version]. Laramie, WY: Child Language Laboratory, University of Wyoming.

Gavin, W. J., Klee, T., and Membrino, I. (1993) Differentiating specific language impairment from normal language development using grammatical analysis. *Clinical Linguistics and Phonetics*, 7, 191–206.

Gee, J. P. (1990) *Social Linguistics and Literacies: ideology in discourse*. London: Falmer Press.

Gee, J. P. (1992) *The Social Mind: language, ideology and social practice*. New York: Bergin and Garvey.

Gelman, S. A., Wilcox, S. A., and Clark, E. V. (1989) Conceptual and lexical hierarchies in young children. *Cognitive Development*, 4, 309–26.

Genesee, F. (1989) Early bilingual development, one language or two? *Journal of Child Language*, 16, 161–79.

Genishi, C. (1981) Code-switching in Chicano Six Year Olds. In R. Duran (ed.), *Latino Language and Communicative Behavior*, 133–52. Norwood, NJ: Ablex.

Gentner, D. (1977) Children's performance on a spatial analogies task. *Child Development*, 48, 1,034–9.

—— (1978) On relational meaning: the acquisition of verb meaning. *Child Development*, 49, 988–98.

—— (1982) Why nouns are learned before verbs: linguistic relativity versus natural partitioning. In S. Kuczaj (ed.), *Language Development*, vol. 2, *Language, Thought, and Culture*. Hillsdale, NJ: Lawrence Erlbaum Associates.

Gerhardt, J. B. and Savasir, I. (1986) The use of the simple present in the speech of two three-year-olds: normativity not subjectivity. *Language and Society*, 15, 501–36.

Gerken, L. (1994) Sentential processes in early language. In J. C. Goodman and H. C. Nusbaum (eds), *The Development of Speech Perception: transitions from speech sounds to spoken words*. Cambridge, Mass.: MIT Press.

Gerken, L. A. and McIntosh, B. J. (1992) The interplay of function morphemes and prosody in early language. Submitted for publication.

Gerken, L. A., Landau, B., and Remez, R. E. (1990) Function morphemes in young children's speech perception and production. *Developmental Psychology*, 27, 204–16.

German, D. J. (1987) Spontaneous language profiles of children with word-finding problems. *Language, Speech, and Hearing Services in Schools*, 18, 217–30.

Gernsbacher, M. A. (1988) *Cognitive processes and mechanisms in language comprehension: the structure building framework*. Paper presented at the meeting of the Western Psychological Association, San Fransicso.

—— (1990) *Language Comprehension as Structure Building*. Hillsdale, NJ: Lawrence Erlbaum Associates.

Geschwind, N. and Levitsky, W. (1968) Human brain: left–right asymmetries in temporal speech region. *Science*, 161, 186–7.

Gibbs, R. W. (1987) Linguistic factors in children's understanding of idioms. *Journal of Child Language*, 14, 569–86.

Gierut, J. and Dinnsen, D. (1986) On word-initial voicing: converging sources of evidence in phonologically disordered speech. *Language and Speech*, 29, 97–114.

Gilbert, J. (1977) A voice onset time analysis of apical stop production in 3-year-olds. *Journal of Child Language*, 4, 103–10.

Gillette, J. (1992) The acquisition of mental verbs. Unpublished manuscript, University of Pennsylvania.

Gillette, J. and Gleitman, L. R. (forthcoming) Nouns can be learned from context but verbs cannot.

Gillham, B. (1990) First words in normal and Down syndrome children: a comparison of content and word-form categories. *Child Language Teaching and Therapy*.

Ginsburg, G. P. and Kilbourne, B. K. (1988) Emergence of vocal alternation in mother–infant interchanges. *Journal of Child Language*, 15, 221–35.

Givón, T. (1983) Topic continuity in discourse: the functional domain of switch reference. In J. Haiman and P. Munro (eds), *Typological Studies in Language*, vol. 2, *Switch Reference and Universal Grammar*, 150–280. Amsterdam: Benjamins.

—— (1987) Beyond foreground and background. In R. S. Tomlin (ed.), *Coherence and Grounding in Discourse*. Amsterdam: Benjamins.

Gleason, J. B. (1975) Fathers and other strangers: men's speech to young children. In D. P. Dato (ed.), *Developmental Psycholinguistics: theory and applications*. Washington, DC: Georgetown University Press.

—— (1980) The acquisition of social speech routines and politeness formulas. In H. Giles, W. P. Robinson, and P. Smith (eds), *Language: social psychological perspectives*. Oxford: Pergamon Press.

—— (1987) Sex differences in parent–child interaction. In S. U. Philips, S. Steele, and C. Tanz (eds), *Language, Gender and Sex in Comparative Perspective*. New York: Cambridge University Press.

—— (1988) Language and socialization. In F. Kessel (ed.), *The Development of Language and Language Researchers*. Hillsdale, NJ: Lawrence Erlbaum Associates.

Gleason, J. B. and Weintraub, S. (1976) The acquisition of routines in child language. *Language in Society*, 5, 129–36.

Gleason, J. B., Ely, R., and Perlmann, R. Y. (1992) "What do you say, dear?" Children's recasts after adult prompts. Paper presented at the 5th European Conference on Developmental Psychology, Seville, Spain.

Gleason, J. B., Hay, D., and Cain, L. (1988) Social and affective determinants of language acquisition. In M. L. Rice and R. L. Schiefelbusch (eds), *The Teachability of Language*. Baltimore: Paul H. Brookes.

Gleason, J. B., Perlmann, R. Y., and Greif, E. (1984). What's the magic word: learning language through politeness routines. *Discourse Processes*, 7, 493–502.

Gleason, J. B., Perlmann, R. Y., Ely, R., and Evans, D. (1994) The babytalk register: parents' use of diminutives. In J. F. Sokolov and C. E. Snow (eds), *Handbook of Research in Language Development Using CHILDES*. Hillsdale, NJ: Lawrence Erlbaum Associates.

Gleitman, L. R. (1981) Maturational determinants of language growth. *Cognition*, 10, 103–14.

—— (1984) Biological predispositions to learn language. In P. Marler and H. S. Terrance (eds), *The Biology of Learning*, 553–84. New York: Springer-Verlag.

—— (1990) The structural sources of word meaning. *Language Acquisition*, 1(1), 3–55.

Gleitman, L. R. and Gleitman, H. (1992) A picture is worth a thousand words, but that's the problem: the role of syntax in vocabulary acquisition. *Current Directions in Psychological Science*, 1:1, 31–5.

Gleitman, L. R. and Wanner, E. (1982) Language acquisition: the state of the state of the art. In E. Wanner and L. Gleitman (eds), *Language Acquisition: the state of the art*. New York: Cambridge University Press.

—— (1988) Current issues in language learning. In M. Bornstein and M. Lamb (eds), *Developmental Psychology: an advanced textbook*, 297–356. Hillsdale, NJ: Lawrence Erlbaum Associates.

Glenn, S. and Cunningham, C. C. (1983) What do babies listen to most? A developmental study of auditory preferences in nonhandicapped infants and infants with Down's syndrome. *Developmental Psychology*, 19, 332–7.

Glenn, S., Cunningham, C. C. and Joyce, P. F. (1981) A study of auditory preferences in nonhandicapped infants and infants with Down's syndrome. *Child Development*, 52, 1,303–7.

Goffman, E. (1974) *Frame Analysis: an essay on the organization of experience*. Boston: Northeastern University Press.

Goldfield, B. (1986) Referential and expressive language: a study of two mother–child dyads. *First Language*, 6, 119–31.

—— (1987) The contributions of child and caregiver to referential and expressive language. *Applied Psycholinguistics*, 8, 267–80.

—— (1990) Pointing, naming, and talk about objects: referential behaviour in children and mothers. *First Language*, 10, 231–42.

—— (1993) Noun bias in maternal speech to one-year-olds. *Journal of Child Language*, 20, 85–100.

Goldfield, B. and Reznick, J. S. (1990) Early lexical acquisition: rate, content, and the vocabulary spurt. *Journal of Child Language*, 17, 171–83.

Goldfield, B. A. and Snow, C. (1985) Individual differences in language acquisition. In J. Gleason (ed.), *Language Development*. Columbus: Merrill Publishing Co.

Goldin-Meadow, S. and Feldman, H. (1977) The development of language-like communication without a language model. *Science*, 197, 401–3.

Goldin-Meadow, S. and Mylander, C. (1990) Beyond the input given: the child's role in the acquisition of language. *Language*, 66, 323–55.

Goldin-Meadow, S., Seligman, M. E. P., and Gelman, R. (1976) Language in the two-year-old. *Cognition*, 4, 189–202.

Goldman-Rakic, P. S. (1988) Topography of cognition: parallel distributed networks in primate association cortex. *Annual Review of Neuroscience*, 11, 137–56.

Goldsmith, J. A. (1990) *Autosegmental and Metrical Phonology*. Oxford: Basil Blackwell.

Golinkoff, R. M. and Hirsh-Pasek, K. (1981) A new approach to language comprehension. Unpublished grant proposal to National Institute of Child Health and Human Development.

Golinkoff, R. M. and Markessini, J. (1980) "Mommy sock": the child's understanding of possession as expressed in two-noun phrases. *Journal of Child Language*, 7, 119–36.

Golinkoff, R. M., Mervis, C. V., and Hirsh-Pasek, K. (1993) Early object labels: the case for lexical principles. Manuscript submitted for publication.

Golinkoff, R. M., Diznoff, J., Yasik, A., and Hirsh-Pasek, K. (1992) How children identify nouns vs. verbs. International Conference on Infant Studies.

Golinkoff, R. M., Hirsh-Pasek, K., Cauley, K. M., and Gordon, L. (1987) The eyes have it: lexical and syntactic comprehension in a new paradigm. *Journal of Child Language*, 14, 23–45.

Golinkoff, R. M., Menutti, T., Lengle, C., and Hermon, G. (1992) Is "glorpy" a noun or an adjective?: Identifying the part of speech of a novel word. International Conference on Infant Studies.

Gollin, E. S. (1981) *Development and Plasticity: behavioral and biological aspects of variation in development*, 231–53. New York: Academic Press.

Goodglass, H. and Kaplan, E. (1983) *The Assessment of Aphasia and Related Disorders*, 2nd (ed.) Philadelphia: Lea and Febiger.

Goodglass, H. and Menn, L. (1985) Is agrammatism a unitary phenomenon? In M.-L. Kean (ed.), *Agrammatism*. New York: Academic Press.

Goodluck, H. (1991) *Language Acquisition: a linguistic introduction*. Cambridge, Mass.: Blackwell.

Goodluck, H., Sedivy, J., and Foley, M. (1989) On Wh-questions and extraction from temporal adjuncts: a case for movement. *Papers and Reports on Child Language Development*, 28, 123–30.

Goodman, J. C. and Nusbaum, H. C. (eds) (1994) *The Development of Speech Perception: the transition from speech sounds to spoken words*. Cambridge, Mass.: MIT Press.

Goodman, J. C., Nusbaum, H. C., Lee, L., and Broihier, K. (1990) The effects of syntactic and discourse variables on the segmental intelligibility of speech. *The Proceedings of the 1990 International Conference on Spoken Language Processing*, 393–6. Kobe, Japan: The Acoustical Society of Japan.

Goodman, L., Wilson, P., and Bornstein, H. (1978) Results of a national survey of sign language programs in special education. *Mental Retardation*, 16, 104–6.

Goodz, N., (1989) Parental language mixing in bilingual families. *Infant Mental Health Journal*, 10, 25–44.

Goodz, N., Bilodeau, L., and Legaré, M. C. (1988) Variables influencing parental language mixing to children in bilingual families. Paper presented at the International Conference on Infant Studies, Washington.

Goodz, N., Legaré, M. C., and Bilodeau, L. (1987) The influence of bilingualism on linguistic awareness in pre-school children. Paper presented at the annual meeting of the Canadian Psychological Association, Vancouver.

—— (1990) Language acquisition in bilingual families. Poster presented at the 7th International Conference on Infant Studies, Montreal.

Goodz, N., Amsel, R., Bilodeau, L., and White, K. (1989) Child directed speech in bilingual families, a longitudinal study. Paper presented at the meeting of the World Association of Infant Psychiatry and Allied Disciplines, Lugano.

Gopnik, A. (1981) Development of non-nominal expressions in 1–2 year olds: why the first words aren't about things. In P. Dale and D. Ingram (eds), *Child Language: an international Perspective*. Baltimore: University Park Press.

—— (1982) Words and plans: early language and the development of intelligent action. *Journal of Child Language*, 9, 303–18.

—— (1984) The acquisition of "gone" and the development of the object concept. *Journal of Child Language*, 11, 273–92.

Gopnik, A. and Meltzoff, A. (1984) Semantic and cognitive development in 15- to 21-month-old children. *Journal of Child Language*, 11, 495–513.

—— (1986a) Relations between semantic and cognitive development in the one-word stage: the specificity hypothesis. *Child Development*, 57, 1,040–53.

—— (1986b) Words, plans, things and locations: interactions between semantic and cognitive development in the one-word stage. In S. A. Kuczaj and M. D. Barrett (eds), *The Development of Word Meaning*. New York: Springer Verlag.

—— (1987) The development of categorization in the second year and its relation to other cognitive and linguistic developments. *Child Development*, 58, 1,523–31.

Gopnik, M. (1989) The development of text competence. In Conte, M., Petöfi, J., and Sözer (eds), *Text and Discourse Connectedness*, Amsterdam: Benjamins.

—— (1990a) Feature-blind grammar and dysphasia. *Nature*, 344, 715.

—— (1990b) Feature-blindness: a case study. *Language Acquisition*, 1, 139–64.

Gopnik, M. (in press) Impairments of tense in a familial language disorder. *Journal of Neurolinguistics*.

Gopnik, M. and Crago, M. (1991) Familial aggregation of a developmental language disorder. *Cognition*, 39, 1–50.

Gordon, P. and Chafetz, J. (1990) Verb-based vs. class-based accounts of actionality effects in children's comprehension of passives. *Cognition*, 36, 227–54.

Goren, C. C., Sarty, M., and Wu, P. Y. K. (1975) Visual following and pattern discrimination of face-like stimuli by newborn infants. *Pediatrics*, 56, 544–9.

Gottlieb, G. (1991a) Experiential canalization of behavioral development: theory. *Developmental Psychology*, 27, 4–13.

—— (1991b) Experiential canalization of behavioral development: results. *Developmental Psychology*, 27, 35–9.

Gottlieb, G. and Krasnegor, N. A. (eds) (1985) *Measurement of Audition and Vision in the First Year of Postnatal Life: a methodological overview*. Norwood, NJ: Ablex.

Green, S. (1975) Variation of vocal pattern with social situation in the Japanese monkey (Macaca fascata): a field study. In L. A. Rosenblum (ed.), *Primate Behavior: Developments in field and laboratory research*. New York: Academic Press.

Greenberg, J. and Kuczaj, S. A. (1982) Towards a theory of substantive word-meaning acquisition. In S. A. Kuczaj (ed.), *Language Development*, vol. 1, *Syntax and Semantics*. Hillsdale, NJ: Lawrence Erlbaum Associates.

Greenberg, J. H. (1963). Some universals of grammar with particular reference to the order of meaningful elements. In J. H. Greenberg (ed.), *Universals of Language*. Cambridge, Mass.: MIT Press.

Greenfield, P. M. (1991) Language, tools and brain: the ontogeny and phylogeny of hierarchically organized sequential behavior. *Behavioral and Brain Sciences*, 14, 531–50.

Greenfield, P., Reilly, J., Leaper, C., and Baker, N. (1985) The structural and functional status of single-word utterances and their relationship to early multi-word speech. In M. Barrett (ed.), (1985) *Children's Single-word Speech*, 233–67. Chichester: John Wiley.

Greenough, W. T., Black, J. F., and Wallace, C. S. (1987) Experience and brain development. *Child Development*, 58, 539–59.

Greenwald, C. A. and Leonard, L. B. (1979) Communicative and sensorimotor development of Down's syndrome children. *American Journal of Mental Deficiency*, 84, 296–303.

Greif, E. B. (1980) Sex differences in parent–child conversations. In C. Kramarae (ed.), *The Voices and Words of Women and Men*. New York: Pergamon Press.

Greif, E. B. and Gleason, J. B. (1980) Hi, thanks, and goodbye: more routine information. *Language in Society*, 9, 159–66.

Grice, H. P. (1975) Logic and conversation. In P. Cole and J. L. Morgan (eds), *Syntax and Semantics*, vol 3. New York: Academic Press.

Grieser, D. L. and Kuhl, P. (1988) Maternal speech to infants in a tonal language: support for universal prosodic features in motherese. *Developmental Psychology*, 24, 14–20.

Grieve, R. and Hoogenraad, R. (1977) Using language if you don't have much. In R. Wales and E. Walker (eds), *New Approaches to Language Mechanisms*. Amsterdam: North Holland Publishing.

Grimshaw, J. (1981) Form, function, and the language acquisition device. In C. L. Baker and J. McCarthy (eds), *The Logical Problem of Language Acquisition*. Cambridge, Mass.: MIT Press.

—— (1990) *Argument Structure: linguistic inquiry monograph 18*. Cambridge, Mass.: MIT Press.

Grimshaw, J. and Rosen, S. T. (1990) Knowledge and obedience: the developmental status of the binding theory. *Linguistic Inquiry*, 21, 187–222.

Gropen, J., Pinker, S., Hollander, M., and Goldberg, R. (1991) Syntax and semantics in the acquisition of locative verbs. *Journal of Child Language*, 8, 115–51.

Gropen, J., Pinker, S., Hollander, M., Goldberg, R., and Wilson, R. (1989) The learnability and acquisition of the dative alternation in English. *Language*, 65, 203–57.

Grosjean, F. (1982) *Life with Two Languages, an introduction to bilingualism*. Cambridge, Mass.: Harvard University Press.

Gruendel, J. (1977) Referential extension in early language development. *Child Language*, 48, 1,567–76.

Grunwell, P. (1981) *The Nature of Phonological Disability in Children*. London: Edward Arnold.

—— (1985) *Phonological Assessment of Child Speech* (PACS). Windsor: NFER-Nelson.

—— (1992) Assessment of child phonology in the clinical context. In C. Ferguson, L. Menn, and C. Stoel-Gammon (eds), *Phonological Development: models, research, implications*, 457–83.

Grunwell, P. and Russell, J. (1990) A phonological disorder in an English-speaking child. *Clinical Linguistics and Phonetics*, 4, 29–38.

Guilfoyle, E. and Noonan, M. (1988) Functional categories and language acquisition. Unpublished manuscript, McGill University, Montreal.

—— (1989) Functional categories and language acquisition. Manuscript, McGill University, Montreal.

Guillaume, P. (1927/1973) The development of formal elements in the child's speech. In C. A. Ferguson and D. I. Slobin (eds), *Studies of Child Language Development*, 240–51. New York: Holt Rinehart and Winston.

Gumperz, J. (1982a) *Discourse Strategies*. Cambridge: Cambridge University Press.

—— (ed.) (1982b) *Language and Social Identity*. Cambridge: Cambridge University Press.

Gutfreund, M., Harrison, M., and Wells, G. (1989) *Bristol Language Development Scales*. Windsor: NFER-Nelson.

Guttman, E. (1942) Aphasia in children. *Brain*, 65, 205–19.

Haider, H. (1993) Principled variability: parametrization without parameter fixing. In G. Fanselow (ed.), *The Parametrization of Universal Grammar*, 1–16. Amsterdam: John Benjamins.

Haith, M. M., Bergman, T., and Moore, M. J. (1977) Eye contact and face scanning in early infancy. *Science*, 198, 853–5.

Hakuta, K. (1986) *Mirror of Language: the debate on bilingualism*. New York: Basic Books.

Hakuta, K. and Diaz, R. (1985) The relationship between degree of bilingualism and cognitive ability. In K. Nelson (ed.), *Children's Language*, vol. 5, 319–44. Hillsdale, NJ: Lawrence Erlbaum Associates.

Hall, P. and Tomblin, J. B. (1975) Case study: therapy procedures for remediation of a nasal lisp. *Language, Speech and Hearing Services in Schools*, 6, 29–32.

Halliday, M. A. K. (1975) *Learning How to Mean: explorations in the development of language*. London: Edward Arnold.

Halliday, M. A. K. and Hasan, R. (1976) *Cohesion in English*. London: Longman.

Hampson, J. (1989) Elements of style: maternal and child contributions to referential and expressive styles of language acquisition. Unpublished doctoral dissertation, City University of New York.

Hampson, J. and Nelson, K. (1993) Relation of maternal language to variation in rate and style of language acquisition. *Journal of Child Language*, 20: 2, 313–42.

Hansen-Strain, L. (1990) Attrition of Japanese by English-speaking children, an interim report. *Language Sciences*, 12, 367–77.

Hansson, K. and Nettelbladt, U. (1991) Swedish children with dysgrammatism. A comparison with normally developed children. *Working Papers in Logopaedics and Phoniatrics*, 7. Lund: Lund Univerisity.

Harding, C. G. and Golinkoff, R. (1979) The origins of intentional vocalizations in prelinguistic infants. *Child Development*, 50, 33–40.

Harding, E. and Reilly, P. (1987) *The Bilingual Family: a handbook for parents*. Cambridge: Cambridge University Press.

Hardy-Brown, K., Plomin, R., and DeFries, J. (1981) Genetic and environmental influences on the rate of communicative development in the first year of life. *Developmental Psychology*, 17, 704–17.

Hare, G. (1983) Development at two years. In J. V. Irwin and S. P. Wong (eds), *Phonological Development in Children: 18 to 72 months*, 55–85. Carbondale: Southern Illinois University Press.

Hare, M. and Elman, J. L. (1993) From weared to wore: a connectionist account of language change. *Proceedings of the Fifteenth Annual Cognitive Science Society Conference, Boulder*, 528–533. Hillsdale, NJ: Lawrence Erlbaum Associates.

Hargrove, P. (1982) Misarticulated vowels: a case study. *Language, Speech and Hearing Services in Schools*, 13, 86–95.

Harner, L. (1976) Children's understanding of linguistic reference to past and future. *Journal of Psycholinguistic Research*, 5, 65–84.

—— (1980) Comprehension of past and future reference revisited. *Journal of Experimental Child Psychology*, 29, 170–82.

—— (1981) Children talk about the time and aspect of actions. *Child Development*, 52, 498–506.

—— (1982) Talking about the past and future. In W. J. Friedman (ed.), *The Developmental Psychology of Time*. New York: Academic Press.

Harris, J. (1983) What does mean length of utterance mean? Evidence from a comparative study of normal and Down's syndrome children. *Journal of Mental Deficiency Research*, 33, 193–210.

Harris, M., Jones, D., and Grant, J. (1983) The nonverbal context of mothers' speech to infants. *First Language*, 4, 21–30.

—— (1984) The social interactional context of maternal speech to infants: an explanation for the event-bound nature of early word use? *First Language*, 5, 89–100.

Harris, M., Barrett, M. D., Jones, D., and Brookes, S. (1988) Linguistic input and early word meaning. *Journal of Child Language*, 15, 77–94.

Harris, M., Jones, D., Brookes, S., and Grant, J. (1986) Relations between the non-verbal context of maternal speech and rate of language development. *British Journal of Developmental Psychology*, 4, 261–8.

Harrison, G. and Piette, A. (1980) Young bilingual children's language selection. *Journal of Multilingual and Multicultural Development*, 1, 217–30.

Harrison, G., Bellin, W., and Piette, B. (1981) Bilingual mothers in Wales and the language of their children. Cardiff: University of Wales Press.

Hart, B. (1991) Input frequency and children's first words. *First Language*, 11, 289–300.

Hart, Jr., J. and Gordon, B. (1992) Neural subsystems for object knowledge. *Nature*, 359, 60–4.

Hart, Jr., J., Berndt, R. S., and Caramazza, A. (1985) Category-specific naming deficit following cerebral infarction. *Nature*, 316, 439–40.

Hart, Jr., J., Lesser, R. P., Fisher, R., Schwerdt, P., Bryan, R. N., and Gordon, B. (1991) Dominant-side intracarotid amobarbital spares comprehension of word meaning. *Archives of Neurology*, 148, 55–8.

Hartley, X. Y. (1985) Receptive language processing and ear advantage of Down's syndrome children. *Journal of Mental Deficiency Research*, 29, 197–205.

—— (1986) A summary of recent research into the development of children with Down's syndrome. *Journal of Mental Deficiency Research*, 26, 263–9.

Harvey, P. H. and Clutton-Brock, T. H. (1985) Life history variation in primates. *Evolution*, 39, 559–81.

Haugen, E. (1956) The syllable in linguistic description. In M., Halle, H. G., Lunt, H., Mclean, and C. H. Van Schooneveld (eds), *For Roman Jakobson*, 213–21. The Hague: Mouton.

Hausser, R. (1990) Principles of computational morphology, *Computational Linguistics*, 47.

Haviland, S. E. and Clark, H. H. (1974) What's new? Acquiring new information as a process in comprehension. *Journal of Verbal Learning and Verbal Behavior*, 13, 512–21.

Hayashi, M. (1989) Initial language differentiation in bilingual children with special reference to strategy choice and strategy shift – a cross-linguistic study. *Proceedings from the Second Scandinavian Child Language Symposium*, 49–57. Lund: Child Language Research Institute.

—— (1992a) A longitudinal investigation of language development in bilingual children (abstract). Unpublished Ph.D. dissertation. Risskov: University of Aarhus.

—— (1992b) Lexical development and early translation equivalents in bilingual children. Poster presented at the 1992 Child Language Seminar, Glasgow.

Hayes, D. P. (1988) Speaking and writing: distinct patterns of word choice. *Journal of Memory and Language*, 27, 572–85.

Hayes, J. R. (ed.) (1970) *Cognition and the Development of Language*. New York: John Wiley and Sons, Inc.

Haynes, L. M. and Cooper, R. L. (1986) A note on Ferguson's proposed baby-talk universals. In J. A. Fishman, A. Tabouret-Keller, M. Clyne, B. Krishnamurti, and M. Abdulaziz (eds), *The Fergusonian Impact*, vol. 1, *from phonology to society*, 127–34. Berlin: Mouton De Gruyter.

Heath, S. B. (1982) What no bedtime story means: narrative skills at home and school. *Language in Society*, 11, 49–76.

—— (1983) *Ways with Words: language, life and work in communities and classrooms*. Cambridge: Cambridge University Press.

Hecaen, H. (1976) Acquired aphasia in children and the ontogenesis of hemispheric functional specialization. *Brain and Language*, 3, 114–34.

—— (1983) Acquired aphasia in children: revisited. *Neuropsychologia*, 21(6), 581–7.

Heibeck, T. H. and Markman, E. M. (1987) Word learning in children: an examination of fast mapping. *Child Development*, 58, 1,021–34.

Hein, A. and Held, R. (1967) Dissociation of the visual placing response into elicited and guided components. *Science*, 158, 390–2.

Held, R. and Hein, A. (1963) Movement-produced stimulation in the development of visually guided behavior. *Journal of Comparative and Physiological Psychology*, 56, 872–6.

Hellan, L. (1986) The headedness of NPs in Norwegian. In P. Muysken and H. Van Riemsdijk (eds), *Features and Projections*, 89–122. Dordrecht: Foris.

Hendriks, H. (1993) Motion and location in narrative discourse: a crosslinguistic and developmental perspective. Doctoral dissertation, Rijksuniversiteit Leiden.

Hickmann, M. (1980) Creating referents in discourse: a developmental analysis of linguistic cohesion. In J. Kreiman and E. Ojeda (eds), *Papers from the Parasession on Pronouns and Anaphora*, 192–203. Chicago Linguistic Society.

—— (1982) The development of narrative skills: pragmatic and metapragmatic aspects of discourse cohesion. Doctoral dissertation, University of Chicago.

—— (1986) Psychosocial aspects of language acquisition. In P. Fletcher and M. Garman (eds), *Language Acquisition*, 2nd edn. Cambridge: Cambridge University Press.

—— (ed.) (1987a) *Social and Functional Approaches to Language and Thought*. Orlando: Academic Press.

—— (1987b) The pragmatics of reference in child language: some issues in developmental theory. In M. Hickmann (ed.), *Social and Functional Approaches to Language and Thought*. Orlando: Academic Press.

—— (1991a) The development of discourse cohesion: some functional and cross-linguistic issues. In G. Piéraut-Le Bonniec and M. Dolitsky (eds), *Language Bases . . . Discourse Bases*. Amsterdam: Benjamins.

—— (1991b) Review of *The Acquisition of Narratives: learning to use language* by M. G. W. Bamberg. *Language*, 67, 111–14.

—— (1993a) The boundaries of reported speech: some developmental speech. In J. A. Lucy (ed.), *Reflexive Language: reported speech and metapragmatics*. Cambridge: Cambridge University Press.

—— (1993b) Functional determinants in language acquisition: person, space, and time in children's discourse. Tenth World Congress of the International Association of Applied Linguistics, Vrije Universiteit Amsterdam.

Hickmann, M. and Liang, J. (1990) Clause-structure variation in Chinese narrative discourse: a developmental analysis. *Linguistics*, 28, 1,167–200.

Hickmann, M. and Schneider, P. (1993) Children's ability to restore the referential cohesion of stories. *First Language*.

Hickmann, M., Kaiser, B., and Roland, F. (1991) Semantics and pragmatics in the development of tense and aspect: a crosslinguistic study. Second European Congress of Psychology, Budapest.

Higginbotham, J. and May, R. (1987) Questions, quantifiers and crossing. *Linguistic Review*, 1, 41–80.

Higginson, R. and MacWhinney, B. (1990) *CHILDES/BIB: an annotated bibliography of child language and language disorders*. Hillsdale, NJ: Lawrence Erlbaum Associates.

Hill, J. and Hill, K. (1986) *Speaking Mexicano: dynamics of syncretic language in central Mexico*. Tuscon: University of Arizona Press.

Hill, J. A. C. (1983) *A Computational Model of Language Acquisition in the Two Year Old*. Bloomington: Indiana University Linguistics Club.

Hinckley, A. (1915) A case of retarded speech development. *Pediatric Seminary*, 22, 121–46.

Hinrichs, E. (1986) Temporal anaphora in discourses of English. *Linguistics and Philosophy*, 9, 63–82.

Hirano, M., Kurita, S., and Nakachima, T. (1983) Growth, development and aging of the human vocal folds. In D. Bless and J. H. Abbs (eds), *Vocal Fold Physiology – Contemporary Research and Clinical Issues*, 22–43. San Diego: College–Hill.

Hirschberg, J. (1980) Acoustic analysis of pathologic cries, stridors and coughing sounds in infancy. *International Journal of Pediatric Otorhinolaryngology*, 2, 287–300.

Hirsh-Pasek, K. and Golinkoff, R. M. (1991) Language comprehension: a new look at some old themes. In N. Krasnegor, D. Rumbaugh, M. Studdert-Kennedy, and R. Schiefelbusch (eds), *Biological and Behavioral Aspects of Language Acquisition*, 301–20. Hillsdale, NJ: Lawrence Erlbaum Associates.

—— (1993a) Skeletal supports for grammatical learning: what the infant brings to the language learning task. In C. K. Rovee-Collier (ed.), *Advances in Infancy Research*, vol. 10. Norwood, NJ: Ablex.

—— (1993b) *The origins of grammar as revealed in language comprehension*. Unpublished manuscript.

Hirsh-Pasek, K., Tucker, M., and Golinkoff, R. M. (in press) Dynamical systems: reinterpreting prosodic bootstrapping. In J. Morgan and K. Demuth (eds), *Signal to Syntax: bootstrapping from speech to grammar in early acquisition*. Hillsdale, NJ: Lawrence Erlbaum Associates.

Hirsh-Pasek, K., Naigles, L., Golinkoff, R. M., Gleitman, L. R., and Gleitman, H. (1988) *Syntactic Bootstrapping: evidence from comprehension*. Boston Child Language Conference.

Hirsh-Pasek, K., Kemler Nelson, D. G., Jusczyk, P. W., Cassidy, K. W., Druss, B., and Kennedy, L. (1987) Clauses are perceptual units for young infants. *Cognition*, 26, 269–86.

Hodge, M. (1989) A comparison of spectral–temporal measures across speaker age: implications for an acoustic characterization of speech maturation. Unpublished doctoral dissertation, University of Wisconsin, Madison.

Hodson, B. and Paden, E. (1981) Phonological processes which characterize unintelligible and intelligible speech in early childhood. *Journal of Speech and Hearing Disorders*, 46, 369–73.

Hoeffner, J. (1992) Are rules a thing of the past? The acquisition of verbal morphology by an attractor network. *Proceedings of the Fourteenth Annual Cognitive Science Society Conference, Bloomington, IN*, 861–6. Hillsdale, NJ: Lawrence Erlbaum Associates.

Hoek, D., Ingram, D., and Gibson, D. (1986) Some possible causes of children's early word overextensions. *Journal of Child Language*, 13, 477–94.

Hoff-Ginsberg, E. (1985) Some contributions of mothers' speech to their children's syntactic growth. *Journal of Child Language*, 12, 367–85.

—— (1991) Mother–child conversation in different social classes and communicative settings. *Child Development*, 62, 782–96.

—— (1992) How should frequency input be measured? *First Language*, 12, 233–44.

Hoffman, C. (1985) Language acquisition in two trilingual children. *Journal of Multilingual and Multicultural Development*, 6, 479–95.

Holcomb, P. J., Coffey, S. A., and Neville, H. (1992) Visual and auditory sentence processing: a developmental analysis using event-related brain potentials. *Developmental Neuropsychology*, 8, 203–41.

Holland, A. (1982) Observing functional communication of aphasic adults. *Journal of Speech and Hearing Disorders*, 47, 50–6.

Hollingshead, A. (1975) *Four factor index of social status*. Unpublished manuscript, University of Michigan.

Holmes, M. D., Ojemann, G. A., Cawthon, D. F., and Lettich, E. (1991) Neuronal activity in nondominant human lateral temporal cortex related to short term spatial memory and visuospatial recognition. Poster presented at the 21st Annual Meeting of the Society for Neuroscience, New Orleans.

Holmgren, K., Lindblom, B., Aurelius, G., Jalling, B., and Zetterstrom, R. (1986) On the phonetics of infant vocalization. In B. Lindblom and R. Zetterstrom (eds), *Precursors of Early Speech*, 51–63. New York: Stockton Press.

Holt, E. B. (1931) *Animal Drive and Learning Process*, vol. 1. New York: Holt.

Hopper, P. J. (1979a) Aspect and foregrounding in discourse. In T. Givón (ed.), *Syntax and Semantics*, vol. 12, *Discourse and Syntax*. New York: Academic Press.

—— (1979b). Some observations on the typology of focus and aspect in narrative language. *Studies in Language*, 3, 37–64.

—— (ed.) (1982) *Tense and Aspect: between syntax and semantics*. Amsterdam: Benjamins.

Hopper, P. J. and Thomson, S. A. (1980) Transitivity in grammar and discourse. *Language*, 56, 65–80.

Hoppman, M. and Willen, E. (1993) Visual and auditory processing in children with Down syndrome: individual differences. Poster presented at the 60th meeting of the Society for Research in Child Development, New Orleans.

Horgan, D. (1980) Nouns: love 'em or leave 'em. In V. Teller, and S. J. White (eds), *Studies in Child Language and Multilingualism*. *Annals of the New York Academy of Sciences*, 345, 5–25.

—— (1981) Rate of language acquisition and noun emphasis. *Journal of Psycholinguistic Research*, 10, 629–40.

Hornby, P. (1971) Surface structure and the topic–comment distinction: a developmental study. *Child Development*, 42, 1,975–88.

Howe, N. (1991) Sibling-directed internal state language, perspective talking and affective behavior. *Child Development*, 62, 1,503–12.

Howe, N. and Ross, H. (1990) Socialization, perspective-taking, and the sibling relationship. *Developmental Psychology*, 26, 160–5.

Huang, C. T. (1984) On the distance and reference of empty pronouns. *Linguistic Inquiry*, 15, 531–74.

Hudson, J. and Nelson, K. (1983) Effects of script structure on children's story recall. *Developmental Psychology*, 19, 625–35.

Huer, M. (1989) Acoustic tracking of articulation errors: [r]. *Journal of Speech and Hearing Disorders*, 54, 530–4.

Huerta-Macías, A. (1981) Codeswitching: all in the family. In R. Durán (ed.), *Latino Language and Communicative Behavior*, 153–68. Norwood: Ablex Publishers.

Huggins, A. W. F. (1980) Better spectrograms from children's speech: a research note. *Journal of Speech and Hearing Research*, 23, 19–27.

Hughes, M. and Ratner, N. (1989) Phonological processes in the speech of Down syndrome adults. Paper presented at the American Speech–Language–Hearing Association meeting, St Louis.

Humphreys, M. W. (1880) A contribution to infantile linguistics. *Transactions of the American Philological Association*, 11, 5–17.

Hurst, J., Baraister, M., Auger, E., Graham, F., and Norell, S. (1990) An extended family with a dominantly inherited speech disorder. *Child Development and Child Neurology*, 32, 352–5.

Huttenlocher, J., Haight, W., Bryk, A., Seltzer, M., and Lyons, T. (1991) Early vocabulary growth: relation to language input and gender. *Developmental Psychology*, 27, 236–48.

Huttenlocher, P. R. (1990) Morphometric study of human cerebral cortex development. *Neuropsychologia*, 28(6), 517–27.

Huxley, R. (1970) The development of the correct use of subject personal pronouns in two children. In G. B. Flores d'Arcais and W. J. M. Levelt (eds), *Advances in Psycholinguistics*. Amsterdam: North-Holland-Elsevier.

Hyams, N. (1986) *Language Acquisition and Theory of Parameters*. Dordrecht: D. Reidel.

—— (1989) The null subject parameter in language acquisition. In O. Jaeggli and K. J. Safir (eds), *The Null Subject Parameter*, 215–38. Dordrecht: Kluwer.

Hymes, D. (1972) Models of the interaction of language and social life. In J. J. Gumperez and D. Hymes (eds), *Directions in Sociolinguistics*. New York: Holt, Rinehart and Winston.

Hymes, D. and Cazden, C. (1980) Narrative thinking and story-telling rights: a folklorist's clue to a critique of education. In D. Hymes (ed.), *Language in Education: ethnolinguistic essays*. Washington, DC: Center for Applied Linguistics.

Idiazábal, I. (1984) Conciencia bilingüe del niño bilingüe [Bilingual awareness of the bilingual child]. In M. Siguan (ed.), *Adquisición precoz de una segunda lengua* [Early acquisition of a second language], 55–63. Barcelona: Publicacions i edicions de la universitat de Barcelona.

—— (1988) First verbal productions of a bilingual child learning Basque and Spanish simultaneously. Analysis of the noun phrase. Unpublished manuscript.

—— (1991) Evolución de la determinación nominal en un niño bilingüe vasco-hispanofono [The evolution of nominal determination in a Basque/Spanish bilingual child]. Paper presented at the 1st International Conference on Spanish in Contact with Other Languages, University of Southern California, Los Angeles.

Imedadze, N. and Tuite, K. (1992) The acquisition of Georgian. In D. I. Slobin (ed.), The Crosslinguistic Study of Language Acquisition, vol. 3, 39–109. Hillsdale, NJ: Lawrence Erlbaum Associates.

Ingram, D. (1974) Phonological rules in young children. *Journal of Child Language*, 1, 49–64.

—— (1976) *Phonological Disability in Children*. London: Edward Arnold.

—— (1981a) The emerging phonological system of an Italian–English bilingual child. *Journal of Italian Linguistics*, 2, 95–113.

—— (1981b) *Procedures for the Phonological Analysis of Children's Language*. Baltimore: University Park Press.

—— (1987) Categories of phonological disorders. *Proceedings of the First International Symposium on Specific Speech and Language Disorders in Children*, 88–99. Brentford, UK: Association for All Speech Impaired Children.

—— (1988a) Jakobson revisited: some evidence from the acquisition of Polish. *Lingua*, 75, 55–82.

—— (1988b) Language acquisition, learnability, and underspecification theory. Unpublished paper, University of British Columbia.

—— (1990) The acquisition of the feature [voice] in normal and phonologically delayed English children. Paper presented at the Convention of the American Speech–Language–Hearing Association, Seattle.

—— (1992) Early phonological acquisition: a cross-linguistic perspective. In C. A. Ferguson. L. Menn, and C. Stoel-Gammon (eds), *Phonological Develoment: models, research, implications*, 423–35. Timonium, MD: York Press.

Ingram, D. and Shaw, C. (1988) The comprehension of pronominal reference in children. *Canadian Journal of Linguistics*, 33, 395–407.

Ingram, D. and Terselic, B. (1983) Final ingression: a case of deviant child phonology. *Topics in Language Disorders*, 3, 45–50.

Ingram, D., Christensen, L., Veach, S., and Webster, B. (1980) The acquisition of word-initial fricatives and affricates in English by children between 2 and 6 years. In G. Yeni-Komshian, J. Kavanagh, and C. A. Ferguson (eds), *Child Phonology*, vol. 1, *production*, 169–92. New York: Academic Press.

Irwin, J. V. and Wong, S. P. (eds) (1983) *Phonological Development in Children: 18 to 72 months*. Carbondale, IL: Southern Illinois University Press.

Irwin, O. C. (1947a) Infant speech: consonant sounds according to manner of articulation. *Journal of Speech Disorders*, 12, 402–4.

—— (1947b) Infant speech: consonantal sounds according to place of articulation. *Journal of Speech Disorders*, 12, 397–401.

—— (1948) Infant speech: development of vowel sounds. *Journal of Speech and Hearing Disorders*, 13, 31–34.

Irwin, O. C. and Chen, H. P. (1946) Infant speech: vowel and consonant frequency. *Journal of Speech Disorders*, 11, 123–5.

Isaacs, S. (1930) *Intellectual Growth in Young Children*. London: Routledge and Kegan Paul.

Isaacs, S. (1933) *Social Development in Young Children*. London: Routledge and Kegan Paul.

Jackendoff, R. S. (1972) *Semantic Interpretation in Generative Grammar*. Cambridge, Mass.: MIT Press.

—— (1977) *X Syntax: a study of phrase structure*. Cambridge, Mass.: MIT Press.

Jackson, C. A. (1991) The grammatical consequences of early focal damage to the left hemisphere of the brain. Unpublished Ph.D. dissertation, University of California, Los Angeles.

Jacubowicz, C. (1984) On markedness and the binding principles. *Proceedings of the Northeastern Linguistics Society*, 14, 154–82.

Jaeggli, O. A. (1986) Passive. *Linguistic Inquiry*, 17, 587–622.

Jaeggli, O. A. and Safir, K. J. (eds) (1989) *The Null Subject Parameter*. Dordrecht: Kluwer.

Jakobson, R. (1941/1986) *Child Language, Aphasia, and Language Universals*, trans. A. Keiler. The Hague: Mouton.

—— (1971) Shifters, verbal categories, and the Russian verb. In R. Jakobson, *Selected Writings*, vol. 2, *Word and Language*.

Jakubowicz, C. (1984) On markedness and binding principles. *Proceedings from the 14th Annual Meeting of the Northeastern Linguistics Society*. University of Massachusetts, Amherst.

Jarvella, R. and Klein, W. (eds) (1982) *Speech, Place, and Action: studies in deixis and related topics*. New York: Wiley.

Jekat, S., (1985) Die Entwicklung des Wortschatzes bei bilingualen Kindern (Frz.-Dt.) in den ersten vier Lebensjahren [The development of the lexicon in bilingual children (French–German) in the first four years of life]. Unpublished Master's thesis. Hamburg: University of Hamburg.

Jernigan, T. L. and Bellugi, U. (1990) Anomalous brain morphology on magnetic resonance images in Williams Syndrome and Down Syndrome. *Archives of Neurology*, 47, 429–533.

Jernigan, T. L., Bellugi, U., Sowell, E., Doherty, S., and Hesselink, J. R. (1993) Cerebral morphological distinctions between Williams and Down syndromes. *Archives of Neurology*, 50, 186–91.

Jisa, H. (1984/85) French preschoolers' use of *et pis* ("and then"). *First Language*, 5, 169–84.

—— (1987) Sentence connectors in French children's monologue performance. *Journal of Pragmatics*, 11, 607–21.

Johnson, C. J. (1985) The emergence of present perfect verb forms: semantic influences on selective imitation. *Journal of Child Language*, 12, 325–52.

Johnson, H. L. (1975) The meaning of *before* and *after* for preschool children. *Journal of Experimental Child Psychology*, 19, 88–99.

Johnson-Laird, P. N. (1983) *Mental Models*. Cambridge, Mass.: Harvard University Press.

Johnston, J. R. (1984) Acquisition of locative meanings: behind and in front of. *Journal of Child Language*, 11, 407–22.

—— (1988a) Children's verbal representation of spatial location. In J. Stiles-Davis, M. Kritchevsky, and U. Bellugi (eds), *Spatial Cognition*. Hillsdale, NJ: Lawrence Erlbaum Associates.

—— (1988b) Specific language disorders in the child. In N. J. Lass, L. V. McReynolds, J. L. Northern, and D. E. Yoder (eds), *Handbook of Speech–Language Pathology and Audiology*, 685–715. Toronto: BC Decker.

—— (1992) Cognitive abilities of language-impaired children. In P. Fletcher and D. Hall, (eds), *Specific Speech and Language Disorders in Children*, 105–16. London: Whurr Publishers; San Diego: Singular Publishing Group.

Johnston, J. R. and Kamhi, A. (1984) Syntactic and semantic aspects of the utterances of language-impaired children: the same can be less. *Merrill-Palmer Quarterly*, 30, 65–86.

Johnston, J. R. and Schery, T. K. (1976) The use of grammatical morphemes by children with communication disorders. In D. M. Morehead and A. E. Morehead (eds), *Normal and Deficient Child Language*. Baltimore: University Park Press.

Johnston, J. R. and Slobin, D. I. (1979) The development of locative expressions in English, Italian, Serbo-Croatian and Turkish. *Journal of Child Language*, 6, 529–45.

Johnston, J. R. and Smith, L. (1988) Six ways to skin the cat: communicative strategies used by language-impaired children. Paper presented at the Symposium for Research in Child Language Disorders, University of Wisconsin, Madison.

Johnston, J. R., Miller, J. F., Curtiss, S., and Tallal, P. (in press) Acquisition of cognitive-state predicates by language-impaired children: a test of theory. *Journal of Speech and Hearing Research*.

Jordan, F. M. and Murdoch, B. E. (1987) Referential communication skills of children with Down syndrome. *Australian Journal of Human Communication Disorders*, 15, 47–59.

Jusczyk, P. W. (1992) Developing phonological categories from the speech signal. In C. A. Ferguson, L. Menn, and C. Steol-Gammon (eds), *Phonological Development: models, research, implications*, 17–64. Timonium, MD: York Press.

—— (1993) From innate capacities to language-specific ones: the first steps. In B. de Boysson-Bardies et al. (eds), *Developmental Neurocognition: speech and face processing in the first year of life*. Dordrecht: Kluwer.

Jusczyk, P. W., Cutler, A., and Redanz, N. J. (1993) Preference for the predominant stress patterns of English words. *Child Development*, 64, 675–87.

Jusczyk, P. W., Pisoni, D. B., and Mullennix, J. (in press) Some consequences of talker variability on speech perception by 2-month-old infants. *Cognition*.

Jusczyck, P. W., Friederici, A. D., Wessels, J. M. I., Svenkerud, V. Y., and Jusczyk, A. M. (in press) Infants' sensitivity to the patterns of native language words. *Journal of Phonetics*.

Jusczyk, P. W., Hirsh-Pasek, K., Kemler Nelson, D. G., Kennedy, L. J., Woodward, A., and Piwoz, J. (1992) Perception of acoustic correlates of major phrasal units by young infants. *Cognitive Psychology*, 24, 252–93.

Kagan, J. (1971) *Change and Continuity in Infancy*. New York: John Wiley and Sons.

Kahn, J. V. (1981) A comparison of sign and verbal language training with nonverbal retarded children. *Journal of Speech and Hearing Research*, 24, 113–19.

Kahn, L. and James, S. (1983) Grammatical morpheme develoment in three language-disordered children. *Journal of Childhood Communication Disorders*, 6, 85–100.

Kail, M. (1983) La coréférence des pronoms: pertinence de la stratégie des fonctions parallèles. In J.-P. Bronckart, M. Kail, and G. Noizet (eds), *Psycholinguistique de l'Enfant*. Neuchâtel: Delachaux et Niestlé.

Kail, M. and Hickmann, M. (1992) French children's ability to introduce referents in narratives as a function of mutual knowledge. *First Language*, 12, 73–94.

Kail, M. and Léveillé, M. (1977) Compréhension de la coréférence des pronoms personnels chez l'enfant et l'adulte. *L'Année Psychologigue*, 77, 79–94.

Kail, R. and Leonard, L. B. (1986) Word-finding abilities in language-impaired children. *ASHA Monographs*, 25. Rockville, MD: American Speech–Language–Hearing Association.

Kail, R., Hale, C. A., Leonard, L. B., and Nippold, M. A. (1984) Lexical storage and retrieval in language-impaired children. *Applied Psycholinguistics*, 5, 37–49.

Kamhi, A. G. (1986) The elusive first word: the importance of the naming insight for the development of referential speech. *Journal of Child Language*, 13, 155–61.

Kamhi, A. G., Catts, H. W., Mauer, D., Apel, K., and Gentry, B. F. (1988) Phonological and spatial processing abilities in language-and reading-impaired children. *Journal of Speech and Hearing Disorders*, 53, 316–27.

Kamp, H. (1979) Events, instants, and temporal reference. In R. Bäuerle, U. Egli, and A. V. Stechow (eds), *Semantics from Different Points of View*, 376–417. New York: Springer.

Kaper, W. (1976). Pronominal case errors. *Journal of Child Language*, 3, 439–41.

Kaplan, A. (1963) *The Conduct of Inquiry: methodology for behavioral science*. New York: Harper and Row.

Kardam, F. and Pfaff, C. (to appear) Issues in educational policy and language development of bilingual children in Berlin. In S. Kroon (ed.), *Multisthnische Gesellschaft und Schulen in Berlin* [Multi-ethnic society and schools in Berlin].

Karmiloff-Smith, A. (1979) *A Functional Approach to Child Language: a study of determiners and reference*. Cambridge: Cambridge University Press.

—— (1981) The grammatical marking of thematic structure in the development of language production. In W. Deutsch (ed.), *The Child's Construction of Language*, 121–47. New York: Academic Press.

—— (1985) Language and cognitive processes from a developmental perspective. *Language and Cognitive Processes*, 1: 1, 61–85.

—— (1987) Function and process in comparing language and cognition. In M. Hickmann (ed.), *Social and Functional Approaches to Language and Thought*. Orlando: Academic Press.

—— (1992) *Beyond Modularity: a developmental perspective on cognitive science*. Cambridge, Mass.: MIT Press.

Karmiloff-Smith, A. and Grant, J. (1993) Linguistic and cognitive development in Williams syndrome: a window on the normal mind. Poster presented at the 60th Annual Meeting of the Society for Research in Child Development, New Orleans.

Kaufman, D. (1987) "Who's him?": evidence for principle B in children's grammar. Paper presented at the Conference on Language Development, Boston.

Kay, D. and Anglin, J. M. (1982) Overextension and underextension in the child's expressive and receptive speech. *Journal of Child Language*, 9, 83–98.

Kay-Raining Bird, E. and Chapman, R. S. (in press) Sequential recall in individuals with Down syndrome. *Journal of Speech and Hearing Research*.

Kaye, K. (1982) *The Mental and Social Life of Babies*. Chicago: University of Chicago Press.

Kayne, R. S. (1982) Predicates and arguments, verbs and nouns. *GLOW Newsletter*, 8, 24.

Kazman, R. (1988) Null arguments and the acquisition of case and INFL. Text of paper presented at University of Boston conference on language acquisition.

Keating, P. and Buhr, R. (1978) Fundamental frequency in the speech of infants and children. *Journal of the Acoustical Society of America*, 63, 567–71.

Keefe, K. A., Feldman, H. M., and Holland, A. L. (1989) Lexical learning and language abilities in preschoolers with prenatal brain damage. *Journal of Speech and Hearing Disorders*, 54, 395–402.

Keenan, E. O. (1974) Conversational competence in children. *Journal of Child Language*, 1, 163–83.

—— (1977) Making it last: repetition in children's discourse. In S. Ervin-Tripp and C. Mitchell-Kernan (eds), *Child Discourse*, 125–38. New York: Academic Press.

Keenan, E. O. and Klein, E. (1975) Coherency in children's discourse. *Journal of Psycholinguistic Research*, 4.

Keenan, E. O. and Schieffelin, B. B. (1976) Topic as a discourse notion: a study of topic in the conversations of children and adults. In C. N. Li (ed.), *Subject and Topic*, 335–84. New York: Academic Press.

Keller-Cohen, D. (1978) Context in child language. *Annual Review of Anthropology*, 7, 453–82.

Kelly, C. A. and Dale, P. S. (1989) Cognitive skills associated with the onset of multiword utterances. *Journal of Speech and Hearing Research*, 32, 645–56.

Kelly, M. H. (1992) Using sound to solve syntactic problems: the role of phonology in grammatical category assignments. *Psychological Review*, 99, 349–64.

Kemler Nelson, D. G., Hirsh-Pasek, K., Juscyzk, P. W., and Wright Cassidy, K. (1989) How the prosodic cues in motherese might assist language learning. *Journal of Child Language*, 16, 53–68.

Kemper, S. (1984) The development of narrative skills: explanations and entailments. In S. A. Kuczaj (ed.), *Discourse Development: progress in cognitive research*. New York: Spinger.

Kemper, T. L. (1988) The neuropathology of Down syndrome. In L. Nadel (ed.), *The Psychobiology of Down Syndrome*, 269–89. Cambridge, Mass.: MIT Press.

Kent, R. D. (1984) The psychobiology of speech development: co-emergence of language and a movement system. *American Journal of Physiology*, 246, R888–94.

—— (1992a) The biology of phonological development. In C. A. Ferguson, L. Menn, and C. Stoel-Gammon (eds), *Phonological Development: models, research, implications*, 65–90. Timonium, MD: York Press.

—— (1992b) Phonological development as biology and behavior. In R. S. Chapman (ed.), *Processes in Language Acquisition and Disorders*, 67–85. St Louis: Mosby-Year Book, Inc.

—— (1992c) Sonority theory and syllable pattern as keys to sensory–motor–cognitive interactions in infant vocal development. Paper presented at the NATO Advanced Research Workshop on "Changes in Speech and Face Processing in Infancy: A Glimpse at Developmental Mechanisms of Cognition," Carry le Rouet, France.

Kent, R. D. and Bauer, H. R. (1985) Vocalizations of one-year-olds. *Journal of Child Language*, 12, 491–526.

Kent, R. D. and Murray, A. D. (1982) Acoustic features of infant vocalic utterances. *Journal of the Acoustical Society of America*, 72, 353–65.

Kent, R. D. and Read, C. (1992) *The Acoustic Analysis of Speech*. San Diego: Singular Publishing Group.

Kent, R. D., Mitchell, P. R., and Sancier, M. (1991) Evidence and role of rhythmic organization in early vocal development in human infants. In J. Fagard and P. Wolff (eds), *The Development of Timing Control and Temporal Organization in Coordinated Action*, 135–49. Amsterdam: Elsevier.

Kent, R. D., Osberger, M. J., Netsell, R., and Hustedde, C. G. (1986) Phonetic development in identical twins differing in auditory function. *Journal of Speech and Hearing Disorders*, 52, 64–75.

Kerlinger, F. (1986) *Foundations of Behavioral Research*, 3rd ed. London: Holt, Rinehart and Winston.

Kessen, W., Levine, J., and Wendrich, K. (1979) The imitation of pitch in infants. *Infant Behavior and Development*, 2, 93–100.

Kessler, C. (1984) Language acquisition in bilingual children. In N. Miller (ed.), *Bilingualism and Language Disability: assessment and remediation*, 26–54. London: Croom Helm.

Kewley-Port, D. and Preston, M. (1974) Early apical stop production: a voice onset time analysis. *Journal of Phonetics*, 2, 195–210.

Kielhöfer, B. (1987) Le bon changement de langue et le mauvais mélange de langues. Quelques observations sur la conscience normative de deux enfants bilingues [Good code-switching and bad /code-mixing. Some observations on the normative awareness of two bilingual children]. In G. Lüdi (ed.), *Devenir bilingue – parler bilingue* [Becoming bilingual – bilingual speech], 135–55. Tübingen: Max Niemeyer.

Kielhöfer, B. and Jonekeit, S., (1983) *Zweisprachige Kindererziehung* [Bringing children up bilingually]. Tübingen: Stauffenberg Verlag.

Kiessling, L. S., Denckla, M. B., and Carlton, M. (1983) Evidence for differential hemispheric function in children with hemiplegic cerebral palsy. *Developmental Medicine and Child Neurology*, 25, 727–34.

Kim, J. J., Pinker, S., Prince, A., and Prasada, S. (1991) Why no mere mortal has ever flown out to center field. *Cognitive Science*, 15, 173–218.

King, G. and Fletcher, P. (1993) Grammatical problems in school-age children with specific language impairment. *Clinical Linguistics & Phonetics*, 7, 339–52.

Kinsbourne, M. and Hiscock, M. (1977) Does cerebral dominance develop? In S. J. Segalowitz and F. A. Gruber (eds), *Language Development and Neurological Theory*, 171–91. New York: Academic Press.

Kintsch, W. (1988) The role of knowledge in discourse comprehension: a construction–integration model. *Psychological Review*, 95, 163–82.

Kiparsky, P. and Menn, L. (1977) On the acquisition of phonology. In J. Macnamara (ed.), *Language Learning and Thought*, 47–78. New York: Academic Press.

Kirchner, D. M. and Klatzky, R. L. (1985) Verbal rehearsal and memory in language-disordered children. *Journal of Speech and Hearing Research*, 28, 556–65.

Klatt, D. H. (1976) Linguistic uses of segmental duration in English: acoustic and perceptual evidence. *Journal of the Acoustical Society of America*, 59, 1,208–21.

Klausen, T. and Hayashi, M. (1990) A cross linguistic study of the development of bilingualism – reorganisation in early lexical development. *The European Journal of Intercultural Studies*, 1, 31–41.

Klausen, T., Subritzky, M., and Hayashi, M. (1992) Initial production of inflections in bilingual children. In G. Turner and D. Messer (eds), *Critical Aspects of Language Acquisition and Development*. London: Macmillan.

Klee, T. (1992a) Developmental and diagnostic characteristics of quantitative measures of children's language production. *Topics in Language Disorders*, 12(2), 28–41.

—— (1992b) Measuring children's conversational language. In S. F. Warren and J. Reichle (eds), *Causes and Effects in Communication and Language Intervention*, 315–30. Baltimore: Brookes.

Klee, T. and Fitzgerald, M. D. (1985) The relation between grammatical development and mean length of utterance in morphemes. *Journal of Child Language*, 12, 251–69.

Klee, T. and Sahlie, E. (1987) Review of S. Long, Computerized Profiling computer program. *Child Language Teaching and Therapy*, 3, 87–93.

Klee, T., Schaffer, M., May, S., Membrino, I., and Mougey, K. (1989) A comparison of the age–MLU relation in normal and specifically language-impaired preschool children. *Journal of Speech and Hearing Disorders*, 54, 226–33.

Klein, W. (in press) A frame of analysis. In R. Dietrich, W. Klein, and C. Noyau (eds), *The Acquisition of Temporality*. Amsterdam: Benjamins.

Klima, E. S. and Bellugi, U. (1966) Syntactic regularities in the speech of children. In J. Lyons and R. Wales (eds), *Psycholinguistic Papers*, 183–207. Edinburgh: Edinburgh University Press.

Klinge, S. (1990) Prepositions in bilingual language acquisition. In J. Meisel (ed.), *Two First Languages: early grammatical development in bilingual children*, 123–56. Dordrecht: Foris.

Koehn, C. (1989) Der Erwerb der Pluralmarkierungen durch bilinguale Kinder (Französisch/Deutsch). Eine empirische Untersuchung [The acquisition of plural marking by bilingual children (French/German). An empirical investigation]. Unpublished MA thesis. Hamburg: University of Hamburg.

Koehn, C. and Müller, N. (1990) Neuere Arbeitsergebnisse in der Bilingualismusforschung [Some more recent findings in research on bilingualism]. *Deutschunterricht*, 5, 49–59.

Koluchova, J. (1972) Severe deprivation in twins: a case study. *Journal of Child Psychology and Psychiatry*, 13, 107–14.

—— (1976) The further development of twins after severe deprivation: a second report. *Journal of Child Psychology and Psychiatry*, 17, 181–8.

Koster, J. (1987) *Domains and Dynasties*. Dordrecht: Kluwer.

Kuczaj, S. A. (1977) The acquisition of regular and irregular past tense forms. *Journal of Verbal Learning and Verbal Behaviour*, 16, 589–600.

—— (1978) Why do children fail to overregularize the progressive inflection? *Journal of Child Language*, 5, 167–71.

—— (1982) Young children's overextension of object words in comprehension and/or production: support for a prototype theory of early object word meaning. *First Language*, 3, 93–105.

—— (1986) Thoughts on the intensional basis of early object word extension: evidence from comprehension and production. In S. A. Kuczaj and M. D. Barrett (eds), *The Development of Word Meaning*. New York: Springer Verlag.

Kuczaj, S. A. and Barrett, M. D. (1986) *The Development of Word Meaning*. New York: Springer Verlag.

Kuczaj, S. A. and Maratsos, M. P. (1975) On the acquisition of *front, back,* and *side. Child Development*, 46, 202–10.

Kuhl, P. K. (1987) Perception of speech and sound in early infancy. In P. Salapatek and L. Cohen (eds), *Handbook of Infancy Perception*, vol. 2, 275–382. New York: Academic Press.

—— (1988) Auditory perception and the evolution of speech. *Human Evolution*, 3, 19–43.

—— (1993) Effects of linguistic experience in the first half-year of life: implication for a theory of infant speech development. In B. de Boysson-Bardies et al. (eds), *Developmental Neurocognition: speech and face processing in the first year of life*. Dordrecht: Kluwer.

Kuhl, P. K. and Meltzoff, A. N. (1982) The bimodal perception of speech in infancy. *Science*, 218, 1,138–41.

—— (1984) Intermodal representation of speech in infants. *Infant Behavior and Development*, 7, 361–81.

—— (1988) Speech as an intermodal object of perception. In A. Yonas (ed.), *The Minnesota Symposia on Child Psychology*, vol. 20, *Perceptual Development in Infancy*, 235–66. Hillsdale, NJ: Lawrence Erlbaum Associates.

Kuhn, T. S. (1970) *The Structure of Scientific Revolutions*. Chicago: The University of Chicago Press.

Kulick, D. (1992) *Language Shift and Cultural Reproduction: socialization, self, and syncretism in a Papua New Guinean village*. Cambridge: Cambridge University Press.

Kuo, Z.-Y. (1976) *The Dynamics of Behavior Development*. New York: Plenum Press.

Kwan-Tarry, A. (1992) Code-switching and code-mixing: the case of a child learning English and Chinese simultaneously. *Journal of Multilingual and Multicultural Development*, 13, 243–59.

Labov, W. (1969) Contraction, deletion, and inherent variability of the English copula. *Language*, 45, 715–62.

—— (1972) *Language in the Inner City: studies in the Black English vernacular*. Philadelphia: University of Pennsylvania Press.

—— (1984) Intensity. In D. Shiffrin (ed.), *Meaning, Form, and Use in Context: linguistic applications*, 43–70. Georgetown University Round Table on Languages and Literature. Washington, DC: Georgetown University Press.

Labov, W. and Labov, T. (1978) The phonetics of CAT and MAMA. *Language*, 54, 816–52.

Labov, W. and Waletzky, J. (1967) Narrative analysis: oral versions of personal experience. In J. Helm (ed.), *Essays on the Verbal and the Visual Arts*. Seattle and London: University of Washington Press.

Lahey, M. (1988) *Language Disorders and Language Development*. New York: Macmillan.

Lamb, M. R., Robertson, L. C., and Knight, R. T. (1990) Component mechanisms underlying the processing of hierarchically organized patterns: inferences from patients with unilateral cortical lesions. *Journal of Experimental Psychology: Learning, Memory, and Cognition*, 16, 471–83.

Lambrecht, K. (1981) Topic, antitopic, and verb agreement in non-standard French. Series *Pragmatics and Beyond*. Amsterdam: Benjamins.

Landau, B. and Gleitman, L. R. (1985) *Language and Experience: evidence from the blind child*. Cambridge, Mass.: Harvard University Press.

Lanza, E. (1988) Language strategies in the home: linguistic input and infant bilingualism. In A. Holmen, E. Hansen, J. Gimbel, and J. N. Jørgensen (eds), *Bilingualism and the Individual*, 69–84. Clevedon: Multilingual Matters.

—— (1990) Language mixing in infant bilingualism, a sociolinguistic perspective. Unpublished Ph.D. dissertation. Washington: Georgetown University.

—— (1992) Can bilingual two-year-olds code-switch? *Journal of Child Language*, 19, 633–58.

Largo, R. H., Molinair, L., Comenale Pinto, L., Weber, M., and Duc, G. (1986) Language development of term and preterm children during the first five years of life. *Developmental Medicine and Child Neurology*, 28, 333–50.

Lasnik, H. and Saito, M. (1984) On the nature of proper government. *Linguistic Inquiry*, 15: 2.

—— (1992) *Move Alpha*. Cambridge, Mass.: MIT Press.

Laufer, M. Z. (1976) Language acquisition: some acoustic and interactive aspects of infancy. Final report of project 3–4014, Grant NE-G-003–0077, National Institute of Education, US Department of Health, Education and Welfare.

—— (1980) Temporal regularity in prespeech. In T. Murry and J. Murry (eds), *Infant Communication: cry and early speech*, 284–309. San Diego: College-Hill Press.

Lave, J. and E. Wenger (1991) *Situated Learning: legitimate peripheral participation*. Cambridge: Cambridge University Press.

Laveck, B. and Laveck, G. D. (1977) Sex differences among young children with Down syndrome. *Journal of Pediatrics*, 91, 767–9.

Layton, T. and Sharifi, H. (1978) Meaning and structure of Down's syndrome and nonretarded children's spontaneous speech. *American Journal of Mental Deficiency*, 83, 439–45.

LeBarre, W. (1973) The development of mind in man in primitive cultures. In F. Richardson (ed.), *Brain and Intelligence: the ecology of child development*. Hyattsville, Md: National Educational Press.

Lebeaux, D. S. (1987) Comments on Hyams. In T. Roeper and E. Williams (eds), *Parameter Setting*, 23–39. Dordrecht: Reidel.

—— (1988) *Language Acquisition and the Form of the Grammar*. Ph.D. dissertation, University of Massachusetts, Amherst.

—— (1990) The grammatical nature of the acquisition sequence: adjoin-a and the formation of relative clauses. In L. Frazier and J. G. de Villiers (eds), *Language Processing and Acquisition*. Dordrecht: Kluwer.

Lebrun, Y. and Paradis, M. (1984) To be or not to be an early bilingual? In Y. Lebrun and M. Paradis (eds), *Early Bilingualism and Child Development*, 9–18. Amsterdam: Swets and Zeitlinger.

Lecanuet, J.-P. and Granier-Deferre, C. (1993) Speech stimuli in the fetal environment. In B. de Boysson-Bardies, S. de Schonen, P. Jusczyk, P. MacNeilage, and J. Morton (eds),

Developmental Neurocognition: speech and voice processing in the first year of life, 237–48. Dordrecht: Kluwer.

Lecours, A. R. (1975) Myelogenetic correlates of the development of speech and language. In E. Lenneberg and E. Lenneberg (eds), *Foundations of Language Development: a multidisciplinary approach*, vol. 1, 121–35. New York: Academic Press.

Lederer, A., Gleitman, H., and Gleitman, L. R. (forthcoming) The information structure for verb learning.

Lederer, A., Gleitman, L. R., and Gleitman, H. (in press) Structure of the input corpus for language learning. In M. Tomasello (ed.), *The Acquisition of Verb Meaning*. Meridian Books.

Lee, L. (1966) Developmental sentence types: a method for comparing normal and deviant syntactic development. *Journal of Speech and Hearing Disorders*, 31, 311–30.

—— (1974) *Developmental Sentence Analysis*. Evanston Il: Northwestern University Press.

Leech, G. (1991) The state of the art in corpus linguistics. In K. Aijmer and B. Altenberg (eds), *English Corpus Linguistics*, 8–29. New York: Longman.

Leemans, M. and Ramaekers, B. (1982) De volgorde van Subject–Object–Verbum in Nederlandse kindertaal [The order of Subject–Object–Verb in Dutch child language]. Unpublished Master's thesis. Leuven: Katholieke Universiteit Leuven.

Leftheri, K. (1991) Learning to interpret wh-questions in Greek. Unpublished Honors thesis, Smith College, Massachusetts.

Leiter, R. G. (1969) *The Leiter International Performance Scale*. Chicago: Stoelting.

Lemish, D. and Rice, M. L. (1986) Television as a talking picture book: a prop for language acquisition. *Journal of Child Language*, 13, 251–74.

Lenneberg, E. (1967) *Biological Foundations of Language*. New York: Wiley Press.

Leonard, L. (1973) The nature of deviant articulation. *Journal of Speech and Hearing Disorders*, 38, 156–61.

—— (1976) *Meaning in Child Language*. New York: Grune and Stratton.

—— (1982) Phonological deficits in children with developmental language impairment. *Brain and Language*, 16, 73–86.

—— (1985) Unusual and subtle phonological behavior in the speech of phonologically disordered children. *Journal of Speech and Hearing Disorders*, 50, 4–13.

—— (1986) Conversational replies of children with specific language impairment. *Journal of Speech and Hearing Research*, 29, 114–19.

—— (1989) Review of C. Pye, PAL computer program. *Child Language Teaching and Therapy*, 5, 79–86.

—— (1992a) The use of morphology by children with specific language impairment: evidence from three languages. In R. S. Chapman (ed.), *Processes in Language Acquisition and Disorders*, 186–201. St Louis: Mosby-Year Book.

—— (1992b) Models of phonological development and children with phonological disorders. In C. Ferguson, L. Menn, and C. Stoel-Gammon (eds), *Phonological Development: models, research, implications*, 495–507. Timonium, Md: York Press.

Leonard, L. and Brown, B. (1984) The nature and boundaries of phonologic categories: a case study of an unusual phonologic pattern in a language-impaired child. *Journal of Speech and Hearing Disorders*, 49, 419–28.

Leonard, L. and Leonard, J. (1985) The contribution of phonetic context to an unusual phonological pattern: a case study. *Language, Speech and Hearing Services in Schools*, 16, 110–18.

Leonard, L. and Loeb, D. (1988) Government-binding theory and some of its applications: a tutorial. *Journal of Speech and Hearing Research*, 31, 515–24.

Leonard, L. and McGregor, K. (1991) Unusual phonological patterns and their underlying representations: a case study. *Journal of Child Language*, 18, 261–71.

Leonard, L., Devescovi, A., and Ossella, T. (1987) Context-sensitive phonological patterns in children with poor intelligibility. *Child Language Teaching and Therapy*, 3, 125–32.

Leonard, L., Miller, J., and Brown, H. (1980) Consonant and syllable harmony in the speech of language-disordered children. *Journal of Speech and Hearing Disorders*, 45, 336–45.

Leonard, L., Bortolini, C., Caselli, M. and Sabbadini, L. (1993) The use of articles by Italian-speaking children with SLI. *Clinical Linguistics and Phonetics*, 7, 19–27.

Leonard, L., Camarata, S., Rowan, L., and Chapman, K. (1982) The communicative functions of lexical usage by language-impaired children. *Applied Psycholinguistics*, 3, 109–25.

Leonard, L., Nippold, M. A., Kail, R., and Hale, C. A. (1983) Picture naming in language-impaired children. *Journal of Speech and Hearing Research*, 26, 609–15.

Leonard, L., Sabbadini, L., Volterra, V., and Leonard, J. (1987) Specific language impairment in children: a cross-linguistic study. *Brain and Language*, 32, 233–52.

Leonard, L., Schwartz, R. G., Morris, B., and Chapman, K. (1981) Factors influencing early lexical acquisition: lexical orientation and phonological composition. *Child Development*, 52, 882–7.

Leonard, L., Schwartz, R. G., Swanson, L., and Loeb, D. F. (1987) Some conditions that promote unusual phonological behaviour in children. *Clinical Linguistics and Phonetics*, 1, 23–34.

Leonard, L., Bortolini, U., Caselli, M. C., McGregor, K., and Sabbadini, L. (1992) Morphological deficits in children with specific language impairment: the status of features in the underlying grammar. *Language Acquisition*, 2, 151–79.

Leonard, L., Camarata, S., Schwartz, R., Chapman, K., and Messick, C. (1985) Homonymy and the voiced–voiceless distinction in the speech of children with specific language impairment. *Journal of Speech and Hearing Research*, 28, 215–24.

Leonard, L., Schwartz, R., Chapman, K., Rowan, L., Prelock, P., Terrell, B., Weiss, A., and Messick, C. (1982) Early lexical acquisition in children with specific language impairment. *Journal of Speech and Hearing Research*, 25, 554–64.

Leopold, W. F. (1939–49) *Speech development of a bilingual child: a linguist's record* (4 vols). Evanston, Il: Northwestern University Press.

Leslie, A. (1987) Pretense and representation: the origins of "theory of mind." *Psychological Review*, 94, 412–26.

Leuder, I. (1980) Some aspects of communication in Down's syndrome. In H. Giles, W. P. Robinson, and P. M. Smith (eds), *Language: social psychological perspectives*. Oxford: Pergamon Press.

Leuder, I., Fraser, N., and Jeeves, M. (1981) Social familiarity and communication in Down syndrome. *Journal of Mental Deficiency Research*, 35, 133–42.

Leutenegger, W. (1980) Encephalization and obstetrics in primates with particular reference to human evolution. In E. Armstrong and D. Falk (eds), *Primate Brain Evolution: methods and concepts*. New York: Plenum Press.

Levin, B. (1993) *English Verb Classes and Alternations: a preliminary investigation*. Chicago, Il: University of Chicago Press.

LeVine, R. A. (1988) Human parental care: universal goals, cultural strategies, individual behaviors. In R. A. LeVine, P.

Levine, S. C., Huttenlocher, P., Banich, M. T., and Duda, E. (1987) Factors affecting cognitive functioning of hemiplegic children. *Developmental Medicine and Child Neurology*, 29, 27–35.

Levinson, S. C. (1983) *Pragmatics*. Cambridge: Cambridge University Press.

—— (1990) Figure and ground in Mayan spatial description: Tzeltal locative descriptions. Paper presented at the conference "Time, space and the lexicon," Max-Planck Institute for Psycholinguistics, Nijmegen.

Levorato, M. C. and Cacciari, C. (1992) Children's comprehension and production of idioms: the role of context and familiarity. *Journal of Child Language*, 19, 415–33.

Levy, E. (1989) Monologue as development of the text-forming function of language. In K. Nelson (ed.), *Narratives from the Crib*, 123–70. Cambridge, Mass.: Harvard University Press.

Levy, E. and Nelson, K. (in press) Words in discourse: a dialectical approach to the acquisition of meaning and use. *Journal of Child Language*.

Levy, Y. (1985) Theoretical gains from the study of bilingualism: a case report. *Language Learning*, 35, 541–54.

Lewis, B. and Freebairn, L. (1992) Residual effects of preschool phonology disorders in grade school, adolescence, and adulthood. *Journal of Speech and Hearing Research*, 35, 819–31.

Li, C. N. (ed.) (1976) *Subject and Topic*. New York: Academic Press.

Li, C. N. and Thompson, S. (1976) Subject and topic: a new typology of language. In C. N. Li (ed.), *Subject and Topic*. New York: Academic Press.

—— (1979) Third person pronouns in zero-anaphora in Chinese discourse. In T. Givón (ed.), *Syntax and Semantics*, vol. 12, *Discourse and Syntax*, 311–35. New York: Academic Press.

—— (1981) *Mandarin Chinese: a functional reference grammar*. Berkeley: University of California Press.

Li, C. N., Thompson, S. A., and McMillan Thompson, R. (1982) The discourse motivation for the perfect aspect: the Mandarin particle *le*. In P. J. Hopper (ed.), *Tense and Aspect: between syntax and semantics*. Amsterdam: Benjamins.

Li Ping, (1990) Aspect and Aktionsart in child Mandarin. Doctoral dissertation, Rijksuniversiteit Leiden.

Liberman, A. M. (1970) The grammars of speech and language. *Cognitive Psychology*, 1, 301–23.

Liberman, A. M., and Mattingly, I. M. (1985) The motor theory of speech perception revised. *Cognition*, 21, 1–36.

—— (1991) A specialization for speech perception. *Science*, 243, 489–94.

Liberman, I. Y., Shankweiler, D., Fischer, F. W., and Carter, B. (1974) Explicit syllable and phoneme segmentation in the young child. *Journal of Experimental Child Psychology*, 18, 201–12.

Lieberman, P. (1975) *On the Origins of Language*. New York: MacMillan.

—— (1977) *Speech Physiology and Acoustic Phonetics*. New York: MacMillan.

—— (1980) On the development of vowel production in young children. In G. Yeni-Komashian, J. Kavanagh, and C. Ferguson (eds), *Child Phonology*, vol. 1, *Production*, 23–42. New York: Academic Press.

Lieberman, P., Crelin, E. S., and Klatt, D. H. (1971) Phonetic ability and related anatomy of the newborn, adult human, Neanderthal Man and the chimpanzee. *American Anthropologist*, 74, 287–307.

Lieberman, P., Harris, K. S., Wolff, O., and Russel, L. H. (1971) Newborn infant cry and primate vocalizations. *Journal of Speech and Hearing Research*, 14, 718–27.

Lieven, É. V. M. (1994) Crosslinguistic and crosscultural aspects of language addressed to children. In C. Gallaway and B. Richards (eds), *Input and Interaction in Language Acquisition*, 56–73. London: Cambridge University Press.

Lieven, E. V. M., Pine, J. M., and Dresner Barnes, H. (1992) Individual differences in early vocabulary development: redefining the referential–expressive distinction. *Journal of Child Language*, 19, 287–310.

Lightfoot, D. (1989) The child's trigger experience: degree-0 learnability. *Behavioral and Brain Sciences*, 12.2, 321–34.

—— (1991) *How to Set Parameters: arguments from language change*. Cambridge, Mass.: MIT Press.

Liles, B. (1985a) Cohesion in the narratives of normal and language disordered children. *Journal of Speech and Hearing Research*, 28, 123–33.

—— (1985b) Production and comprehension of narrative discourse in normal and language disordered children. *Journal of Communication Disorders*, 18, 409–27.

—— (1987) Episode organization and cohesive conjunctives in narratives of children with and without language disorder. *Journal of Speech and Hearing Research*, 30, 185–96.

Liles, B. and Watt, J. (1984) On the meaning of "language delay." *Folia Phoniatrica*, 36, 40–8.

Lillo-Martin, D. (in press) Setting the null subject parameter: evidence from ASL and other languages. In B. Lust, G. Hermon, and J. Kornfilt (eds), *Syntactic Theory and First Language Acquisition: cross linguistic perspectives*. Hillsdale, NJ: Lawrence Erlbaum Associates.

Lindblom, B. (1992) Phonological units as adaptive emergents of lexical development. In C. A. Ferguson, L. Menn, and C. Stoel-Gammon (eds), *Phonological Development: models, research, implications*, 131–63. Timonium, Md: York Press.

Lindblom, B., MacNeilage, P., and Studdert-Kennedy, M. (1983) Self-organizing processes and the explanation of phonological universals. In B. Butterworth, B. Comrie, and O. Dahl (eds). *Explanation of Linguistic Universals*, 181–204. The Hague: Mouton.

Lindburg, D. G. (1982) Primate obstetrics: the biology of birth. *American Journal of Primatology*, Supplement 1, 193–9.

Lindholm, K. (1980) Bilingual children: some interpretations of cognitive and linguistic development. In K. Nelson (ed.), *Children's Language*, vol. 2, 215–66. New York: Gardner Press.

Linebarger, M., Schwartz, M., and Saffran, E. (1983) Sensitivity to grammatical structure in so-called agrammatic aphasics. *Cognition*, 13, 361–92.

Loban, W. (1976) *Language Development: kindergarten through grade twelve*. Research report 18. Urbana, Ill: National Council of Teachers of English.

Locke, J. (1690/1964) *An Essay Concerning Human Understanding*. Cleveland: Meridian Books.

Locke, J. L. (1983a) *Phonological Acquisition and Change*. New York: Academic Press.

—— (1983b) Clinical phonology: the explanation and treatment of speech sound disorders. *Journal of Speech and Hearing Disorders*, 48, 339–41.

—— (1985) The role of phonetic factors in parent reference. *Journal of Child Language*, 12, 215–20.

—— (1986) The linguistic significance of babbling. In B. Lindblom and R. Zetterstrom (eds), *Precursors of Early Speech*. New York: Stockton Press.

—— (1990) Structure and stimulation in the ontogeny of spoken language. *Developmental Psychobiology*, 23, 621–43.

—— (1992) Neural specializations for language: a developmental perspective. *Seminars in the Neurosciences*, 4, 425–31.

—— (1993a) The role of the face in vocal learning and the development of spoken language. In B. de Boysson-Bardies, S. de Schonen, P. Jusczyk, P. MacNeilage, and J. Morton (eds), *Developmental Neurocognition: speech and face processing in the first year of life*. Boston: Kluwer Academic Publishers.

—— (1993b) *The Child's Path to Spoken Language*. Cambridge, Mass.: Harvard University Press.

—— (in press, a) Phases in the development of linguistic capacity. In C. L. Bolis, D. C. Gajdusek, and G. McKhann (eds), *Discussions in Neuroscience*.

—— (in press, b) Gradual emergence of developmental language disorders. *Journal of Speech and Hearing Research*.

Locke, J. L. and Pearson, D. M. (1990) Linguistic significance of babbling: evidence from a tracheostomized infant. *Journal of Child Language*, 17, 1–16.

—— (1992) Vocal learning and the emergence of phonological capacity: a neurobiological approach. In C. Ferguson, L. Menn, and C. Stoel-Gammon (eds), *Phonological Development: models, research, implications*. Parkton, Md: York Press.

Locke, J. L., Bekken, K. E., Wein, D., and McMinn-Larson, L. (1991) Emergent control of manual and vocal-motor activity in reference to human language. Society for Neuroscience, New Orleans.

Loeb, D. F. and Leonard, L. (1988) Specific language impairment and parameter theory. *Clinical Linguistics & Phonetics* 2, 317–27.

Long, S. H. (1987) "Computerized profiling" of clinical language samples. *Clinical Linguistics & Phonetics*, 1, 97–105.

Long, S. H. and Fey, M. E. (1993) *Computerized Profiling* [Computer software, IBM, Apple Macintosh]. San Antonio, Texas: The Psychological Corporation.

Lorentz, J. (1974) A deviant phonological system of English. *Papers and Reports on Child Language Development, 8,* 55–64.

—— (1976) An analysis of some deviant phonological rules of English. In D. Morehead and A. Morehead (eds), *Normal and Deficient Child Language,* 29–59. Baltimore: University Park Press.

Loveland, K. A. (1984) Learning about points of view: spatial perspective and the acquisition of I/you. *Journal of Child Language, 11,* 535–56.

Loveland, K. A. and Tunali, B. (1991) Social scripts for conversational interactions in autism and Down syndrome. *Journal of Autism and Developmental Disorders, 21,* 177–86.

Lust, B. (ed.) (1986) *Studies in the Acquisition of Anaphora.* Dordrecht: Reidel.

Lynch, M. P. and Eilers, R. E. (1991) Perspectives on early language from typical development and Down syndrome. In N. W. Bray (ed.), *International Review of Research on Mental Retardation,* vol. 17, 50–90. New York: Academic Press.

Lynch, M. P., Oller, D. K., Eilers, R. E., and Basinger, D. (1991) Vocal development of infants with Down syndrome. Paper presented at the 11th Symposium for Research on Child Language Disorders, Madison, WI.

Lyons, J. (1975) Deixis as the source of reference. In E. L. Keenan (ed.), *Formal Semantics of Natural Language,* 61–83. London and New York: Cambridge University Press.

—— (1977) *Semantics.* Cambridge: Cambridge University Press.

McCabe, A. and Lipscomb, T. J. (1988) Sex differences in children's verbal aggression. *Merrill-Palmer Quarterly, 34,* 389–401.

McCabe, A. and Peterson, C. (eds) (1991a) *Developing Narrative Structure.* Hillsdale, NJ: Lawrence Erlbaum Associates.

—— (1991b) Getting the story: a longitudinal study of parental styles in eliciting personal narratives and developing narrative skill. In A. McCabe and C. Peterson (eds), *Developing Narrative Structure,* 217–53. Hillsdale, NJ: Lawrence Erlbaum Associates.

McCall, R., Eichorn, D., and Hogarty, P. (1977) Transitions in early mental development. *Monographs of the Society for Research in Child Development,* serial #171.

McCarthy, J. J. (1965) *Patterns of psycholinguistic development of mongoloid and non-mongoloid severely retarded children.* Doctoral dissertation, University of Illinois.

McCarthy, J. J. and Prince, A. S. (1990) Foot and word in prosodic morphology: the Arabic broken plural. *Natural Language and Linguistic Theory, 8,* 209–83.

McCartney, K. A. and Nelson, K. (1981) Children's use of scripts in story recall. *Discourse Processes, 4,* 59–70.

McClure, E. (1977) Aspects of code-switching in the discourse of bilingual Mexican–American children. In M. Saville-Troike (ed.), *Linguistics and Anthropology: Georgetown University round table on languages and linguistics.* Washington, DC: Georgetown University Press.

—— (1981) Formal and functional aspects of the code-switched discourse of bilingual children. In R. Durán (ed.), *Latino Language and Communicative Behavior,* 69–94. Norwood: Ablex Publishers.

Maccoby, E. E. (1992) The role of parents in the socialization of children: an historical overview. *Developmental Psychology, 28,* 1,006–17.

McCune, L. (1992) First words: a dynamic systems view. In C. A. Ferguson, L. Menn, and C. Stoel-Gammon (eds), *Phonological Development: models, research, implications,* 313–36. Timomium, Md: York Press.

McCune-Nicolich, L. (1981a) Toward symbolic functioning: structure of early pretend games and potential parallels with language. *Child Development, 52,* 785–97.

—— (1981b) The cognitive bases of relational words in the single-word period. *Journal of Child Language, 8,* 15–34.

McCune-Nicolich, L. and Bruskin, C. (1982) Combinatorial competency in play and language. In D. Pepler and K. Rubin (eds), *The play of Children: current theory and research,* 30–45. New York: Karger.

McDade, H. L. and Adler, S. (1980) Down syndrome and short-term memory impairment: a storage or retrieval deficit? *American Journal of Mental Deficiency*, 84, 561–7.

McDaniel, D. (1989) Partial and multiple wh-movement. *Natural Language and Linguistic Theory*, 7, 565–605.

McDaniel, D. and McKee, C. (1989) Which children did they show obey strong crossover? In H. Goodluck and M. Rochemont (eds), *The Psycholinguistics of Island Constraints*. Dordrecht: Kluwer.

McDaniel, D., Cairns, H., and Hsu, J. (1990) Control principles in the grammars of young children. *Language Acquisition*, 4, 297–336.

McGann, W. and Schwartz, A. (1988) Main character in children's narratives. *Linguistics*, 21, 215–33.

McGregor, K. and Schwartz, R. (1992) Converging evidence for underlying phonological representation in a child who misarticulates. *Journal of Speech and Hearing Research*, 35, 596–603.

McHenry, H. M. (1975) Biochemical interpretation of the early hominid hip. *Journal of Human Evolution*, 4, 343–55.

MacKain, K. S. (1984) Speaking without a tongue. *Journal of the National Student Speech Language Hearing Association*, 12, 46–71.

MacKain, K. S., Studdert-Kennedy, M., Spieker, S., and Stern, D. (1983) Infant intermodal speech perception is a left-hemisphere function. *Science*, 219, 1,347–9.

Macken, M. (1978) Permitted complexity in phonological development: one child's acquisition of Spanish consonants. *Lingua*, 44, 219–53.

—— (1980) The child's lexical representation. *Journal of Linguistics*, 16, 1–17.

—— (1992) Where's phonology? In C. A. Ferguson, L. Menn, and C. Stoel-Gammon (eds), *Phonological Development: models, research, implications*, 249–69. Timonium, MD: York Press.

—— (1993) Developmental changes in the acquisition of phonology. In B. de Boysson-Bardies et al. (eds), *Developmental Neurocognition: speech and face processing in the first year of life*. Dordrecht: Kluwer.

Macken, M. and Barton, D. (1980) The acquisition of the voicing contrast in English: a study of voice onset time in word-initial stop consonants. *Journal of Child Language*, 7, 41–74.

Macken, M. and Ferguson, C. A. (1983) Cognitive aspects of phonological development. In K. E. Nelson (ed.), *Children's Language*, vol. 4, 255–82. Hillsdale, NJ: Lawrence Erlbaum Associates.

MacLachlan, B. and Chapman, R. (1988) Communication breakdowns in normal and language learning-disabled children's conversation and narration. *Journal of Speech and Hearing Disorders*, 53, 2–7.

McLaughlin, B. (1984a) Early bilingualism: methodological and theoretical issues. In M. Paradis and Y. Lebrun (eds), *Early Bilingualism and Child Development*, 19–45. Lisse, Swets and Zeitlinger.

—— (1984b) *Second-Language Acquisition in Childhood*, vol. 1, *Preschool Children*, 2nd ed. Hillsdale: Lawrence Erlbaum Associates.

MacNamara, J., Baker, E., and Olson, C. L. (1976) Four-year-olds' understanding of *pretend*, *forget* and *know*: evidence for propositional operations. *Child Development*, 47, 62–70.

McNeil, M. R. and Prescott, T. E. (1978) *Revised Token Test*. Austin, TX: Pro-Ed.

MacNeilage, P. F. and Davis, B. (1990) Acquisition of speech production: frames, then content. In M. Jeannerod (ed.), *Attention and Performance*, vol. 13, *Motor Representation and Control*, 453–76. Hillsdale, NJ: Lawrence Erlbaum Associates.

McNeill, D. (1970) *The Acquisition of Language: the study of developmental psycholinguistics*. New York: Harper & Row.

McReynolds, L. (1988) Articulation disorders of unknown etiology. In N. Lass, L. McReynolds, J. Northern, and D. Yoder (eds), *Handbook of Speech–Language Pathology and Audiology*, 419–41. Toronto: BC Decker.

McReynolds, L. and Huston, K. (1971) A distinctive feature analysis of children's misarticulations. *Journal of Speech and Hearing Disorders*, 36, 155–66.

McShane, J. (1979) The development of naming. *Linguistics*, 17, 879–905.

—— (1980) *Learning to Talk*. Cambridge: Cambridge University Press.

McShane, J. and Whittaker, S. (1988) The encoding of tense and aspect by three- to five-year-old children. *Journal of Experimental Child Psychology*, 45, 52–70.

McShane, J., Whittaker, S., and Dockwell, J. (1986) Verbs and time. In S. A. Kuczaj and M. D. Barrett (eds), *The Development of Word Meaning*, 275–302. New York: Springer.

McTear, M. F. and Conti-Ramsden, G. (eds) (1992) *Pragmatic Disability in Children: studies in disorders of communication*. San Diego: Singular Publishing.

MacWhinney, B. (1975a) Rules, rote, and analogy in morphological formations by Hungarian children. *Journal of Child Language*, 2, 65–77.

—— (1975b) Pragmatic patterns in child syntax. *Papers and Reports on Child Language Development* (Dept. of Linguistics, Stanford University), 10, 153–65.

—— (1976) Hungarian research on the acquisition of morphology and syntax. *Journal of Child Language*, 3, 397–410.

—— (1977) Starting points. *Language*, 53, 152–68.

—— (1978) Processing a first language: the acquisition of morphophonology. *Monographs of the Society for Research in Child Development*, 43(1–2), serial no. 174.

—— (1985a) Hungarian language acquisition as an exemplification of a general model of grammatical development. In D. I. Slobin (ed.), *The Crosslinguistic Study of Language Acquisition*, vol. 2, 1,069–155. Hillsdale, NJ: Lawrence Erlbaum Associates.

—— (1985b) Grammatical devices for sharing points. In R. Schiefelbusch (ed.), *Communicative Competence: acquisition and intervention*. Baltimore: University Park Press.

—— (1987) The competition model. In B. MacWhinney (ed.), *Mechanisms of Language Acquisition*. Hillsdale, NJ: Lawrence Erlbaum Associates.

—— (1989) Competition and connectionism. In B. MacWhinney and E. Bates (eds), *The Crosslinguistic Study of Sentence Processing*. New York: Cambridge University Press.

—— (1991a) *The CHILDES Project: tools for Analyzing talk*. Hillsdale, NJ: Lawrence Erlbaum Associates.

—— (1991b) Connectionism as a framework for language acquisition theory. In J. Miller (ed.), *Research on Child Language Disorders: a decade of progress*. Austin, TX: Pro Ed.

—— (1993) *The CHILDES Database: Second Edition*. Dublin, OH: Discovery Systems.

—— (1994) The dinosaurs and the ring. In R. Corrigan, S. Lima, M. Noonan (eds), *The Reality of Linguistic Rules*. San Diego: Academic Press.

MacWhinney, B. and Bates, E. (1978) Sentential devices for conveying givenness and newness: a cross-cultural developmental study. *Journal of Verbal Learning and Verbal Behavior*, 17, 539–58.

—— (eds) (1989) *The Cross-linguistic Study of Sentence Processing*. Cambridge and New York: Cambridge University Press.

MacWhinney, B. Leinbach, A. J. (1991) Implementations are not conceptualizations: revising the verb learning model. *Cognition*, 29, 121–57.

MacWhinney, B. and Snow, C. (1985) The child language data exchange system. *Journal of Child Language*, 12, 271–96.

—— (1990) The child language data exchange system: an update. Journal of Child Language, 17, 457–72.

MacWhinney, B., Leinbach, J., Taraban, R., and McDonald, J. (1989) Language learning: cues or rules? *Journal of Memory and Language*, 28, 255–77.

Malatesta, C. Z. (1981) Infant emotion and the vocal affect lexicon. *Motivation and Emotion*, 5, 1–23.

Mandler, J. M. (1978) A code in the node: the use of a story schema in retrieval. *Discourse Processes*, 1, 14–35.

—— (1983) Representation. In J. H. Flavell and E. Markman (eds), *Handbook of Child Psychology*, vol. 3, *Cognitive Development*. Chichester: Wiley.

—— (1992) How to build a baby II: conceptual primitives. *Psychological Review*, 99, 587–604.

Mandler, J. M. and DeForest, M. (1979) Is there more than one way to recall a story? *Child Development*, 50, 886–9.

Mandler, J. M. and Johnson, N. S. (1977) Remembrance of things passed: story structure and recall. *Cognitive Psychology*, 9, 111–51.

Mannle, S. and Tomasello, M. (1987) Fathers, siblings, and the bridge hypothesis. In K. E. Nelson and A. van Kleeck (eds), *Children's Language*, vol. 6, 23–42. Hillsdale, NJ: Lawrence Erlbaum Associates.

Manzini, M. R. and Wexler, K. (1987) Parameters, binding theory, and learnability. *Linguistic Inquiry*, 18(3), 413–44.

Mapstone, E. R. and Harris, P. L. (1985) Is the English present progressive unique? *Journal of Child Language*, 12, 433–41.

Maratsos, M. P. (1974) Preschool children's use of definite and indefinite articles. *Child Development*, 45, 446–55.

—— (1976) *The Use of Definite and Indefinite Reference in Young Children*. Cambridge: Cambridge University Press.

Marastsos, M. P. and Abramovitch, R. (1975) How children understand full, truncated and anomalous passives. *Journal of Verbal Learning and Verbal Behavior*, 14, 145–57.

Maratsos, M. P., Fox, D. E., Becker, J. A., and Chalkley, M. A. (1985) Semantic restrictions on children's passives. *Cognition*, 19, 167–91.

Maratsos, M. P., Kuczaj, S. A., Fox, D., and Chalkley, M. A. (1979) Some empirical studies in the acquisition of transformational relations: passives, negatives and the past tense. In W. A. Collins (ed.), *Children's Language and Communications*, 1–45. The Minnesota Symposium on Child Psychology, vol. 12. Hillsdale, NJ: Lawrence Erlbaum Associates.

Marcell, M. and Armstrong, V. (1982) Auditory and visual sequential memory of Down syndrome and nonretarded children. *American Journal of Mental Deficiency*, 87, 86–95.

Marcell, M. and Weeks, S. L. (1988) Short-term memory difficulties in Down's syndrome. *Journal of Mental Deficiency Research*, 32, 153–62.

Marcell, M., Croen, P. S., and Sewell, D. H. (1990) Language comprehension in Down syndrome and other trainable mentally handicapped individuals. Paper presented at the Conference on Human Development, Richmond, VA.

Marcell, M., Croen, S., and Sewell, D. (1991) Spoken word identification by Down syndrome and other mentally handicapped adolescents. Paper presented at the Biennial Meeting of the Society for Research in Child Development, Seattle: April.

Marcell, M., Harvey, C. F., and Cothran, L. P. (1988) An attempt to improve auditory short-term memory in Down syndrome individuals through reducing distractions. *Research in Developmental Disabilities*, 9, 405–17.

Marcell, M., Sewell, D. H., and Croen, P. S. (1990) Expressive language in Down syndrome and other trainable mentally handicapped individuals. Paper presented at the Conference on Human Development, Richmond, VA: March.

Marcell, M., Ridgeway, M., Powell, A., Sizemore, T., and West, D. (1991) Sentence imitation by Down syndrome individuals. Paper presented at the Biennial Meeting of the Society for Research in Child Development, Seattle.

Marchman, V. (1993) Constraints on plasticity in a connectionist model of the English past tense. *Journal of Cognitive Neuroscience*, 5(2), 215–34.

Marchman, V. and Bates, E. (1994) Continuity in lexical and morphological development: a test of the critical mass hypothesis. *Journal of Child Language*, 21, 339–66.

Marchman, V., Miller, R., and Bates, E. A. (1991) Babble and first words in children with focal brain injury. *Applied Psycholinguistics*, 12, 1–22.

Marchman, V., Bates, E., Burkhardt, A., and Good, A. (1991) Functional constraints on the acquisition of the passive: toward a model of the competence to perform. *First Language*, 11, 65–92.

Marcon, R. A. and Coon, R. C. (1983) Communication styles of bilingual preschoolers in preferred and non-preferred languages. *Journal of Genetic Psychology*, 142, 189–202.

Marcus, G. F., Brinkmann, U., Clahsen, H., Wiese, R., Woest, A., and Pinker, S. (1993) German inflection: the exception that proves the rule. *Occasional Paper #47, Center for Cognitive Science, MIT.*

Marcus, G. F., Pinker, S., Ullman, M., Hollander, M., Rosen, T. J., and Xu, F. (1992) Over-regularization in language acquisition. *Monographs of the Society for Research in Child Development*, 57(4), serial no. 228.

Marcus, M. (1980) *A Theory of Syntactic Recognition for Natural Languages.* Cambridge, Mass.: MIT Press.

Margar-Bacal, F., Witzel, M. A., and Munro, I. (1987) Speech intelligibility after partial glossectomy in children with Down's syndrome. *Plastic and Reconstructive Surgery*, 79, 44–9.

Markman, E. M. (1987) How children constrain the possible meanings of words. In U. Neisser (ed.), *Concepts and Conceptual Development: ecological and intellectual factors in categorization*, 255–87. Cambridge: Cambridge University Press.

—— (1989) *Categorization and Naming in Children.* Cambridge, Mass.: MIT Press.

—— (1990) Constraints children place on word meanings. *Cognitive Science*, 14, 57–77.

Markman, E. M. and Wachtel, G. F. (in press) Children's use of mutual exclusivity to constrain the meaning of words. *Cognitive Psychology.*

Marler, P. (1982) Social organization, communication and graded signals: the chimpanzee and the gorilla. In P. P. G. Bateson and R. A. Hinde (eds), *Growing Points in Ethology*, 239–80. Cambridge: Cambridge University Press.

—— (1984) Song learning: innate species differences in the learning process. In P. Marler and H. S. Terrace (eds). *The Biology of Learning: report of the Dahlem workshop, Berlin, 1983*, 289–309. Berlin: Springer.

Martin, G. B. and Clark, R. D. (1982) Distress crying in neonates: species and peer specificity. *Developmental Psychology*, 18, 3–9.

Martin, J. A. M. (1981) *Voice, Speech, Language in the Child: development and disorder.* New York: Springer-Verlag.

Martin, P. and Caro, T. M. (1985) On the functions of play and its role in behavioral development. *Advances in the Study of Behaviour*, 15, 59–103.

Martin, S. (1991) Input training in phonological disorder: a case discussion. In M. Yavas (ed.), *Phonological Disorders in Children: theory, research and practice*, 152–72. London: Routledge.

Martlew, M., Connolly, K. J., and McCleod, C. (1978) Language use, role and context in a five-year-old. *Journal of Child Language*, 5, 81–99.

Masataka, N. (1992) Pitch characteristics of Japanese maternal speech to infants. *Journal of Child Language*, 19, 213–24.

Masten, A. C. (1986) Humor and competence in school-aged children. *Child Development*, 57, 461–73.

Matthei, E. (1989) Crossing boundaries: more evidence for phonological constraints on early multi-word utterances. *Journal of Child Language*, 16, 41–54.

Maxfield, T. (1991) Children answer echo questions *how*? In B Plunkett and T. Maxfield (eds), *The Acquisition of Wh. University of Massachusetts Occasional papers in Linguistics.* GSLA, Amherst.

Maxfield, T., and Plunkett, B. (eds) (1991) The acquisition of wh. *University of Massachusetts Occasional Papers in Linguistics.* Amherst: GSLA.

Maxwell, E. (1979) Competing analyses of a deviant phonology. *Glossa*, 13, 181–214.

Maxwell, E. and Weismer, G. (1982) The contribution of phonological, acoustic, and perceptual techniques to the characterization of a misarticulating child's voice contrast for stops. *Applied Psycholinguistics*, 3, 29–44.

Mazurkewicz, I. and White, L. (1984) The acquisition of the dative alternation: unlearning over-generalizations. *Cognition*, 16, 261–83.

Mehler, J., Bertoncini, J., Barriere, M., and Jassik-Gerschenfeld, D. (1978) Infant recognition of mother's voice. *Perception*, 7, 491–7.

Mehler, J., Jusczyk, P., Lambertz, G., Halsted, N., Bertoncini, J., and Amiel-Tison, C. (1988) A precursor of language acquisition in young infants. *Cognition*, 29, 143–78.

Meier, R. P. and Newport, E. L. (1990) Out of the hands of babes: on a possible sign advantage in language acquisition. *Language*, 66, 1–23.

Mein, R. (1961) A study of the oral vocabularies of SSN patients II: grammatical analysis of speech samples. *Journal of Mental Deficiency Research*, 5, 52.

Meisel, J. M. (1985) Les phases initiales du développement des notions temporelles, aspectuelles et de modes d'action. *Lingua*, 66, 321–74.

—— (1986) Word order and case marking in early child language. Evidence from simultaneous acquisition of two first languages: French and German. *Linguistics*, 24, 123–83.

—— (1989) Early differentiation of languages in bilingual children. In K. Hyltenstam and L. Obler (eds), *Bilingualism Across the Lifespan: aspects of acquisition, maturity and loss*, 13–40. Cambridge: Cambridge University Press.

—— (1990a) Code-switching and related phenomena in young bilingual children. *Papers for the Workshop on Concepts, Methodology and Data*, 143–68. Basel: ESF Network on Code-Switching and Language Contact.

—— (1990b) Grammatical development in the simultaneous acquisition of two first languages. In J. Meisel (ed.), *Two First Languages: early grammatical development in bilingual children*, 5–22. Dordrecht: Foris.

—— (1990c) INFL-ection: subjects and subject-verb agreement. In J. Meisel (ed.), *Two First Languages: early grammatical development in bilingual children*, 237–98. Dordrecht: Foris.

—— (ed.) (1992) *The Acquisition of Verb Placement: functional categories and V2 phenomena in language acquisition*. Dordrecht: Kluwer.

—— (1994) Getting FAT: finiteness, agreement and tense in early grammars. In J. M. Meisel (ed.), *Bilingual First Language Acquisition: French and German grammatical development*. Amsterdam: John Benjamins.

Meisel, J. M. and Mahlau, A. (1988) La adquisición simultanea de dos primeras lenguas. Discusión general e implicaciones para el estudio del bilingüismo en euzkadi [The simultaneous acquisition of two first languages. General discussion and implications for the study of bilingualism in the Basque country]. *Actas del II Congreso Mundial Vasco: Congreso sobre la Lengua Vasca, Tomo III* [Proceedings of the Second Basque World Congress: Congress on the Basque Language], Vitoria: Servicio de publicaciones del Gobierno Vasco.

Meisel, J. M. and Müller, N. (1992) Finiteness and verb placement in early child grammars. Evidence from simultaneous acquisition of two first languages: French and German. In J. Meisel (ed.), *The Acquisition of Verb Placement: functional categories and V2 phenomena in language acquisition*, 109–38. Dordrecht: Kluwer.

Meltzoff, A. N. (1990) Towards a developmental cognitive science: the implications of cross-modal matching and imitation for the development of representation and memory in infancy. In A. Diamond (ed.), *Annals of New York Academy of Sciences*, vol. 608, *The Development and Neural Bases of Higher Cognitive Functions*, 1–37. New York: New York Academy of Sciences.

Meltzoff, A. N. and Gopnik, A. (1993) The role of imitation in understanding persons and developing a theory of mind. In S. Baron-Cohen, H. Tager-Flusberg, and D. Cohen, *Understanding Other Minds*, 335–65. Oxford: Oxford University Press.

Meltzoff, A. N. and Moore, M. K. (1977) Imitation of facial and manual gestures by human neonates. *Science*, 198, 75–8.

Menig-Peterson, C. L. (1975) The modification of communicative behavior in preschool-aged children as a function of the listener's perspective. *Child Development*, 46, 1,015–18.

Menig-Peterson, C. L. and McCabe, A. (1978) Children's orientation of a listener to the context of their narratives. *Developmental Psychology*, 14, 582–92.

Menn, L. (1971) Phonotactic rules in beginning speech. *Lingua*, 26, 225–41.

—— (1976) Pattern, control, and contrast in beginning speech: a case study in the development of word form and word function. Doctoral dissertation, University of Illinois, Urbana.

—— (1978) Phonological units in beginning speech. In A. Bell and J. B. Hooper (eds), *Syllables and Segments*, 157–71. Amsterdam: North-Holland.

—— (1983) Development of articulatory, phonetic, and phonological capabilities. In B. Butterworth (ed.), *Language Production*, vol. 2, 3–50. London: Academic Press.

Menn, L. and Gleason, J. B. (1986) Babytalk as a stereotype and register. In J. A. Fishman, A. Tabouret-Keller, M. Clyne, B. Erishnamurti, and M. Abdulaziz (eds), *The Fergusonian Impact*, vol 1, *From Phonology to Society*, 111–25. Berlin: Mouton de Gruyter.

Menn, L. and MacWhinney, B. (1984) The repeated morph constraint: toward an explanation. *Language*, 60, 519–41.

Menn, L. and Matthei, E. (1992) The "two-lexicon" account of child phonology: looking back, looking ahead. In C. Ferguson, L. Menn, and C. Stoel-Gammon (eds), *Phonological Development: models, research, implications*, 211–47. Timonium, Md: York Press.

Menyuk, P. (1968) The role of distinctive features in children's acquisition of phonology. *Journal of Speech and Hearing Research*, 11, 138–46.

—— (1969) *Sentences Children Use*. Cambridge, Mass.: MIT Press.

Menyuk, P., Liebergott, J., and Schultz, M. (1986) Predicting phonological development. In B. Lindblom and R. Zetterstrom (eds), *Precursors of Early Speech*. New York: Stockton Press.

Merriman, W. E. and Bowman, L. (1989) The mutual exclusivity bias in children's word learning. *Monographs of the Society for Research in Child Development*, 54, serial no. 220.

Merritt, D. and Liles, B. (1987) Story grammar ability in children with and without language disorder: story generation, story retelling, and story comprehension. *Journal of Speech and Hearing Research*, 30, 539–52.

Mervis, C. B. (1983) Acquisition of a lexicon. *Contemporary Educational Psychology*, 8, 210–36.

—— (1984) Early lexical development: the contributions of mother and child. In C. Sophian (ed.), *Origins of Cognitive Skills*. Hillsdale, NJ: Lawrence Erlbaum Associates.

—— (1990) Early conceptual development of children with Down syndrome. In D. Cicchetti and M. Beeghly (eds), *Children with Down Syndrome: a developmental perspective*, 252–301. Cambridge: Cambridge University Press.

Mervis, C. B. and Bertrand, J. (1993) Early language and cognitive development: implications of research with children who have Williams syndrome or Down syndrome. Paper presented at the 60th Anniversary Meeting of the Society for Research in Child Development, New Orleans.

Mervis, C. B. and Johnson, K. F. (1991) Acquisition of the plural morpheme: a case study. *Developmental Psychology*, 27, 222–35.

Messick, C. K. (1984) Phonetic and contextual aspects of the transition to early words. Doctoral dissertation, Purdue University.

Mesulam, M. M. (1990) Large-scale neurocognitive networks and distributed processing for attention, language, and memory. *Annals of Neurology*, 28, 597–613.

Michaels, S. (1981) "Sharing time:" children's narrative styles and differential access to literacy. *Language in Society*, 10, 423–42.

—— (1991) The dismantling of narrative. In A. McCabe and C. Peterson (eds), *Developing Narrative Structure*. Hillsdale, NJ: Lawrence Erlbaum Associates.

Michaels, S. and Cazden, C. B. (1986) Teacher/child collaboration as oral preparation for literacy. In B. B. Schieffelin and P. Gilmore (eds), *The Acquisition of Literacy: ethnographic perspectives*. Norwood, NJ: Ablex.

Mikes, M. (1990) Some issues of lexical development in early bi- and trilinguals. In G. Conti-Ramsden and C. Snow (eds), *Children's Language*, vol. 7, 103–20. Hillsdale, NJ: Lawrence Erlbaum Associates.

Miller, C. J., Roussel, N., Daniloff, R., and Hoffman, P. (1991) Estimation of formant frequency in synthetic infant CV tokens. *Clinical Linguistics and Phonetics*, 5, 283–96.

Miller, G. A. (1977) *Spontaneous Apprentices: children and language*. New York: Seabury Press.

—— (1981) Comments on the symposium papers. Presented at the symposium "The development of language and of language researchers: Whatever happened to linguistic theory?"; F. Kessel and R. Brown, Chair. Biennial Meeting of the Society for Research in Child Development, Boston.

—— (1990) The place of language in a scientific psychology. *American Psychological Society*, 1, 7–14.

Miller, G. A. and Johnson-Laird, P. (1976) *Language and Perception*. Cambridge, Mass.: Harvard University Press.

Miller, J. F. (1978) Assessing children's language behavior: a developmental process approach. In R. L. Schiefelbusch (ed.), *Bases of Language Intervention*, 269–318. Baltimore: University Park Press.

—— (1981) *Assessing Language Production in Children: experimental procedures*. Baltimore: University Park Press.

—— (1987a) A grammatical characterization of language disorder. In J. A. M. Martin, P. Fletcher, P. Grunwell, and D. Hall (eds), *Proceedings of the First International Symposium on Specific Speech and Language Disorders in Children*, 100–13. London: AFASIC.

—— (1987b) Language and communication characteristics of children with Down Syndrome. In S. Pueschel, C. Tingey, J. Rynders, A. Crocker, and D. Crutcher (eds), *New Perspectives on Down Syndrome*, 233–62.

—— (1988) The developmental asynchrony of language development in children with Down syndrome. In L. Nadel (ed.), *The Psychobiology of Down Syndrome*, 167–98. Cambridge, Mass.: MIT Press.

—— (1991) Quantifying productive language disorders. In J. F. Miller (ed.), *Research on Child Language Disorders: a decade of progress*, 211–20. Austin, TX: Pro-Ed.

—— (in press, a) Lexical acquisition in children with Down Syndrome. In R. S. Chapman (ed.), *Child Talk: advances in language acquisition*. Year Book Medical Publishers In.

—— (in press, b) The development of speech and language in children with Down Syndrome. In E. McCoy and I. Lott (eds), *Clinical Care for Persons with Down Syndrome*. New York: Academic Press.

Miller, J. F. and Chapman, R. S. (1981) The relation between age and mean length of utterance in morphemes. *Journal of Speech and Hearing Research*, 24, 154–61.

—— (1982–93) *Systematic Analysis of Language Transcripts* (SALT) [Computer software, IBM, Apple Macintosh, VAX/VMS]. Madison, WI: Language Analysis Laboratory, University of Wisconsin–Madison.

Miller J. F. and Leadholm, B. J. (1992) *Language Sample Analysis: the Wisconsin guide*. Madison, WI: Bureau for Exceptional Children, Wisconsin Department of Public Instruction.

Miller J. F., Chapman, R. S., and MacKenzie, H. (1981) Individual differences in the language acquisition of mentally retarded children. Paper presented at the 2nd International Congress for the Study of Child Language, Vancouver.

Miller, J. F., Chapman, R. S., Branston, M., and Reichle, J. (1980) Language comprehension in sensorimotor stages V and VI. *Journal of Speech and Hearing Research*, 23, 284–311.

Miller, J. F., Freiberg, C., Rolland, M.-B., and Reeves, M. A. (1992) Implementing computerized language sample analysis in the public school. *Topics in Language Disorders*, 12(2), 69–82.

Miller, J. F., Miolo, G., Sedey, A., and Murray-Branch, J. (1993) The emergence of multiword combinations in children with Down syndrome. Poster presented at the Symposium for Research in Child Language Disorders, Madison, WI.

Miller, J. F., Rosin, M., Pierce, K., Miolo, G., and Sedey, A. (1989) Language profile stability in children with Down syndrome. Poster presented at the American Speech–Language–Hearing Association convention, St Louis.

Miller, J. F., Sedey, A., Miolo, G., Murray-Branch, J., and Rosin, M. (1992) Longitudinal investigation of vocabulary acquisition in children with Down syndrome. Poster presented at the Symposium for Research on Child Language Disorders, Madison, WI.

Miller, J. F., Sedey, A., Miolo, G., Rosin, M., and Murray-Branch, J. (1991) Spoken and sign vocabulary acquisition in children with Down syndrome. Poster presented at the American Speech–Language–Hearing Association convention, Atlanta.

Miller, P. (1982) *Amy, Wendy, and Beth: learning language in south Baltimore*. Austin: University of Texas Press.

Miller, P. and Sperry, L. L. (1987) The socialization of anger and aggression. *Merrill-Palmer Quarterly*, 33, 1–32.

Miller, P. J. and Sperry, L. L. (1988) Early talk about the past: the origins of conversational stories of personal experience. *Journal of Child Language*, 15, 293–315.

Miller P. J. and West, M. M. (eds), Parental behavior in diverse societies. *New Directions for Child Development*, 40. San Francisco: Jossey-Bass.

Mills, D. (1993) Differentiation of neural subsystems for open- and closed-class words during primary language acquisition. Paper presented at the annual meeting of the American Psychological Association, Chicago.

Mills, D., Coffey, S., and Neville, H. (1993) Changes in cerebral organization in infancy during primary language acquisition. In G. Dawson and K. Fischer (eds), *Human Behavior and the Developing Brain*. New York: Guilford Publications.

—— (in press) Language acquisition and cerebral specialization in 20-month-old children. *Journal of Cognitive Neuroscience*.

Milner, E. (1976) CNS maturation and language acquisition. In H. Whitaker and H. A. Whitaker (eds), *Studies in Neurolinguistics*, Vol. 1, 31–102. New York: Academic Press.

Minsky, M. L. and Papert, S. A. (1969) *Perceptrons: an introduction to computational geometry*, Cambridge, Mass.: MIT Press.

Miranda, S. B. and Fantz, R. (1974) Recognition memory in Down's syndrome and normal infants. *Child Development*, 45, 651–60.

Mitchell, P. (1988) Phonetic variation and final syllable lengthening in multisyllable babbling. Unpublished manuscript, University of Wisconsin–Madison.

Mitchell, P. R. and Kent, R. D. (1990) Phonetic variation in multisyllabic babbling. *Journal of Child Language*, 17, 247–65.

Mithun, M. (1989) The acquisition of polysynthesis. *Journal of Child Language*, 16, 285–312.

Moerk, E. (1983) *The Mother of Eve – as a first language teacher*. Norwood, NJ: Ablex.

Molfese, D. L. (1983) Event related potentials and language processes. In A. W. K. Gaillard and W. Ritter (eds), *Tutorials in ERP Research: endogenous components*, 345–68. Amsterdam: North Holland Publishing.

Molfese, D. L. and Molfese, V. J. (1979) Hemisphere and stimulus differences as reflected in the cortical responses of newborn infants to speech stimuli. *Developmental Psychology*, 15, 505–11.

Molfese, D. L. and Segalowitz, S. J. (1988) *Brain Lateralization in Children: developmental implications*. New York: Guildford Press.

Molfese, D. L., Morse, P., and Peters, C. (1990) Auditory evoked responses to names for different objects: cross-modal processing as a basis for infant language acquisition. *Developmental Psychology*, 26, 780–95.

Molfese, D. L., Golinkoff, R. M., Burger-Judisch, L., Gill, L., and Hirsh-Pasek, K. (1993) Evoked responses: discriminate nouns from verbs during a visual–auditory matching task. Unpublished manuscript.

Montgomery, J. W., Scudder, R. R., and Moore, C. A. (1990) Language-impaired children's real-time comprehension of spoken language. *Applied Psycholinguistics*, 11, 273–90.

Morehead, D. and Ingram, D. (1973) The development of base syntax in normal and linguistically deviant children. In D. Morehead and A. Morehead (eds), *Normal and Deficient Children*, 209–38. Baltimore: University Park Press.

Morgan, J. L. (1986) *From Simple Input to Complex Grammar*. Cambridge, Mass.: MIT Press.

Morgan, J. L. (in press) Perceptual bases of grammatical categories. In. J. Morgan and K. Demuth (eds), *Signal to Syntax: bootstrapping from speech to grammar in early acquisition*. Hillsdale, NJ: Lawrence Erlbaum Associates.

750   *References*

Moskowitz, A. (1970) The two-year-old stage in the acquisition of phonology. *Language*, 46, 426–41.

Moskowitz, B. A. (1975) The acquisition of fricatives: a study in phonetics and phonology. *Journal of Phonetics*, 3, 141–50.

—— (1980) Idioms in phonology acquisition and phonological change. *Journal of Phonetics*, 8, 69–83.

Mowrer, D. E. (1980) Phonological development during the first year of life. In N. J. Lass (ed.), *Speech and Language: advances in basic research and practice*, Vol. 4, 99–137. New York: Academic Press.

Moynihan, M. H. (1964) Some behavior patterns of platyrrhine monkeys I: The night monkey (Aotus triviargatus). *Smithsonian Miscellaneous Collections*, 146, 1–84.

Mulford, R. (1988) First words of the blind child. In M. D. Smith and J. L. Locke (eds), *The Emergent Lexicon: the child's development of a linguistic vocabulary*. New York: Academic Press.

Müller, N. (1990a) Developing two gender assignment systems simultaneously. In J. Meisel (ed.), *Two First Languages: early grammatical development in bilingual children*, 193–236. Dordrecht: Foris.

Müller, N. (1990b) Erwerb der Wortstellung im Französischen und Deutschen. Zur Distribution von Finitheitsmerkmalen in der Grammatik bilingualer Kinder [The acquisition of word order in French and German. On the distribution of markings of the finite/non-finite distinction in the grammar of bilingual children]. In M. Rothweiler (ed.), *Spracherwerb und Grammatik. Linguistische Untersuchungen zum Erwerb von Syntax und Morphologie* [Language acquisition and grammar. Linguistic investigations of the acquisition of syntax and morphology], 127–51. Opladen: Westdeutscher Verlag.

Müller, N. (1993) *Komplexe Satze. Der Erwerb von COMP und von Wortstellungsmustern bei Bilingualen Kindern (Französisch/Deutsch)* [Complex Sentences. The Acquisition of COMP and of Word Order Patterns by Bilingual Children (French/German)]. Tubingen: Narr.

Müller, N. (1994) Parameters cannot be reset: evidence from the development of COMP. In J. M. Meisel (ed.), *Bilingual First Language Acquisition: French and German grammatical development*. Amsterdam: John Benjamins.

Mundy, P., Sigman, M., Kasari, C., and Yirmiya, N. (1988) Nonverbal communication skills in Down syndrome children. *Child Development*, 59, 235–49.

Murry, T. and Murry, J. (eds) (1980) *Infant Communication: cry and early speech*. San Diego: College-Hill Press.

Myers-Scotton, C. (1990) Intersections between social motivations and structural processing in code-switching. *Papers for the Workshop on Constraints, Conditions and Models*, 57–82. London: ESF Network on Code-Switching and Language Contact.

Myerson, R. (1975) *A developmental study of children's knowledge of complex derived words of English*. Cambridge, Mass.: Harvard dissertation.

Nagy, W. E. and Anderson, R. C. (1984) The number of words in printed school English. *Reading Research Ouarterly*, 19, 304–30.

Nagy, W. E. and Herman, P. A. (1987) Breadth and depth of vocabulary knowledge: Implications for acquisition and instruction. In Margaret G. McKeown and Mary E. Curtis (eds), *The Nature of Vocabulary Acquisition*, 19–35. Hillsdale, NJ: Lawrence Erlbaum Associates.

Naigles, L. R. (1990) Children use syntax to learn verb meanings. *Journal of Child Language*, 17, 357–74.

Naigles, L. R. and Hoff-Ginsberg, E. (1993) Input to verb learning: verb frame diversity in mother's speech predicts children's verb use. Unpublished manuscript, Yale University.

Naigles, L. R., Fowler, A., and Helm, A. (1991) The endpoint of syntactic bootstrapping? The comprehension of ungrammatical sentences by normal-IQ and Down's syndrome schoolchildren. Paper presented at the Biennial Meeting of the Society for Research in Child Development, Seattle.

Naigles, L. R., Gleitman, H., and Gleitman, L. R. (1993) Children acquire word meaning components from syntactic evidence. In E. Dromi (ed.), *Language and Cognition: a developmental perspective*. Norwood, NJ: Ablex.

Nakazima, S. (1980) The reorganisation process of babbling. In T. Murry and J. Murry (eds), *Infant Communication: cry and early speech*, 272–83. Houston: College-Hill.

Nelson, K. (1973) *Structure and Strategy in Learning to Talk. Monographs of the Society for Research in Child Development*, 38, serial no. 149.

—— (1981) Individual differences in language development: implications for development and language. *Developmental Psychology*, 17, 170–87.

—— (1983) The conceptual basis for language. In T. Seiler and W. Wannenmacher (eds), *Concept Development and the Development of Word Meaning*. Berlin: Springer Verlag.

—— (1985) Making Sense: the acquisition of shared meaning. New York: Academic Press.

—— (ed.) (1986) *Event Knowledge: structure and function in development*. Hillsdale, NJ: Lawrence Erlbaum Associates.

—— (1988) Constraints on word learning? *Cognitive Development*, 3, 221–46.

Nelson, K. and Gruendel, J. M. (1979) At morning it's lunchtime: a scriptal view of children's dialogues. *Discourse Processes*, 2, 73–94.

—— (1981) Generalized event representations: basic building blocks of cognitive development. In M. E. Lamb and A. L. Brown (eds), *Advances in Developmental Psychology*, vol. 1, 131–58. Hillsdale, NJ: Lawrence Erlbaum Associates.

Nelson, K. and Levy, E. (1987) Development of referential cohesion in a child's monologues. In R. Steele and T. Threadgold (eds), *Language Topics: essays in honor of Michael Halliday*, vol. 1, 119–36. Amsterdam: Benjamins.

Nelson, K. and Lucariello, J. (1985) The development of meaning in first words. In M. D. Barrett (ed.), *Children's Single-Word Speech*. Chichester: Wiley.

Nelson, K., Hampson, J., and Kessler Shaw, L. (1993) Nouns in early lexicons: evidence, explanations, and implications. *Journal of Child Language*, 20, 61–84.

Nelson, K. E. (1982) Experimental gambits in the service of language acquisition theory. In S. A. Kuczaj (ed.), *Language Development*, vol. 1, *Syntax and Semantics*. Hillsdale, NJ: Lawrence Erlbaum Associates.

—— (1987) Some observations from the perspective of the rare event cognitive comparison theory of language acquisition. In K. E. Nelson and A. van Kleek (eds), *Children's Language*, vol. 6, Hillsdale, NJ: Lawrence Erlbaum Associates.

Nelson, K. E. and Bonvillian, J. (1978) Concepts and words in the two-year-old: acquisition of concept names under controlled conditions. In K. E. Nelson (ed.), *Children's Language*, vol. I. New York: Gardner Press.

Nelson, K. E., Baker, N., Denninger, M., Bonvillian, J., and Kaplan, B. (1985) "Cookie" versus "Do-it-again": imitative–referential and personal-social-syntactic-initiating styles in young children. *Linguistics*, 23: 3.

Nelson, K. E., Camarata, S., Welsh, J., Butkovsky, L., and Camarata, M. (1993) Effects of imitative and conversational recasting therapy techniques on syntactic progress in children with specific language impairment and younger language-matched children. Manuscript, Penn State University.

Nelson, K. E., Welsh, J., Camarata, S., Butkovsky, L., and Camarata, M. (1993) Available input and available language learning mechanisms for language-impaired children and younger children of matched language levels. Manuscript, Penn State University.

Nelson, L. and Bauer, H. (1991) Speech and language production at age 2: evidence for tradeoffs between linguistic and phonetic processing. *Journal of Speech and Hearing Research*, 34, 879–92.

Netsell, R. (1981) The acquisition of speech motor control: a perspective with directions for research. In R. E. Stark (ed.), *Language Behavior in Infancy and Early Childhood*, 126–56. Amsterdam: Elsevier.

Nettelbladt, U. (1983) *Developmental Studies of Dysphonology in Children*. Lund, Sweden: CWK Gleerup.

Neuman, S. B. (1991) *Literacy in the Television Age*. Norwood, NJ: Ablex.

Newcomer, P. and Hammill, D. (1982) *Test of Language Development – Primary*. Austin, TX: Pro-Ed.

Newman, J. D. (1985) The infant cry of primates: an evolutionary perspective. In B. M. Lester and C. F. Z. Boukydis (eds), *Infant Crying: theoretical and research perspectives*. New York: Plenum Press.

Newman, L. (1989) *Heather has Two Mommies*. Boston: Alyson Publications.

Newport, E., Gleitman, H., and Gleitman, L. (1977) Mother, I'd rather do it myself: some effects and noneffects of maternal speech style. In C. Snow and C. Ferguson (eds), *Talking to Children: language input and acquisition*. Cambridge: Cambridge University Press.

Nicolich, L. (1977) Beyond sensorimotor intelligence: assessment of symbolic maturity through analysis of pretend play. *Merrill-Palmer Quarterly*, 23, 89–99.

Nielsen Company (1987) *1987 Nielsen Report on Television*. Northbrook Ill: AC Nielsen Company.

Ninio, A. (1980) Ostensive definition in vocabulary teaching. *Journal of Child Language*, 7: 3, 565–74.

—— (1992) The relation of children's single word utterances to single word utterances in the input. *Journal of Child Language*, 19, 87–110.

Ninio, A. and Bruner, J. (1978) The achievements and antecedents of labelling. *Journal of Child Language*, 5, 1–15.

Nittrouer, S., Studdert-Kennedy, M., and McGowan, R. S. (1989) The emergence of phonetic segments: evidence from the spectral structure of fricative-vowel syllables spoken by children and adults. *Journal of Speech and Hearing Research*, 32, 120–32.

Noble, G. (1983) Social learning from everyday television. In M. Howe (ed.), *Learning from Television: psychological and educational research*. New York: Academic Press.

Nwokah, E. (1984) Simultaneous and sequential acquisition in Nigerian children. *First Language*, 5, 57–73.

O'Connell, B. and Gerard A. (1985) Scripts and scraps: the development of sequential understanding; *Child Development*, 56, 671–81.

O'Grady, W. (1987) *Principles of Grammar Learning*. Chicago: University of Chicago Press.

Ochs, E. (1979) Transcription as theory. In E. Ochs and B. Schieffelin (eds), *Developmental Pragmatics*. New York: Academic Press.

—— (1982) "Talking to children in Western Samoa." *Language in Society*, 11, 77–104.

—— (1985) Variation and error: a sociolinguistic study of language acquisition in Samoa. In D. Slobin (ed.), *The Crosslinguistic Study of Language Acquisition*, 783–838. Hillsdale, NJ: Lawrence Erlbaum Associates.

—— (1988) *Culture and Language Development: language acquisition and language socialization in a Samoan village*. Cambridge: Cambridge University Press.

—— (1990) Cultural universals in the acquisition of language. *Papers and Reports on Child Language Development* 29, 1–19.

—— (1993) Constructing social identity: a language socialization perspective. *Research on Language and Social Interaction*, 26, 3: 287–306.

Ochs, E. and B. B. Schieffelin (1984) Language acquisition and socialization: three developmental stories and their implications. In R. Shweder and R. Levine (eds), *Culture Theory: essays on mind, self and emotion*, 276–320. New York: Cambridge University Press.

—— (1989) Language has a heart. *Text*, 9(1), 7–25.

Oetting, J. and Rice, M. (1993) Plural acquisition of children with SLI. *Journal of Speech and Hearing Research*, 36, 1, 236–48.

Ogbu, J. V. (1990) Cultural model, identity, and literacy, In J. W. Stigler, R. A. Shweder, and G. Herdt (eds), *Cultural Psychology: essays on comparative human development*. New York: Cambridge University Press.

Ojemann, G. A. (1984) Common cortical and thalamic mechanisms for language and motor functions. *American Journal of Physiology*, 246, (Regulatory Integrative and Comparative Physiology 15), R901–3.

Oller, D. K. (1973) Regularities in abnormal child phonology. *Journal of Speech and Hearing Disorders*, 38, 36–47.

—— (1976) Infant vocalizations: a linguistic and speech scientific perspective. Miniseminar for the American Speech and Hearing Association. Houston.

—— (1978) Infant vocalizations and the development of speech. *Allied Health and Behavioral Science*, 1, 523–49.

—— (1980) The emergence of sounds of speech in infancy. In G. H. Yeni-Komshian, J. F. Kavanagh, and C. A. Ferguson (eds), *Child Phonology*, vol. 1, *Production*, New York: Academic Press.

—— (1981) Infant vocalization; exploration and reflexivity. In R. Stark (ed.), *Language Behavior in Infancy and Early Childhood*. New York: Elsevier/North Holland.

—— (1986) Metaphonology and infant vocalizations. In B. Lindblom and R. Zetterstrom (eds), *Precursors of Early Speech*, 21–35. New York: Stockton Press.

Oller, D. K. and Eilers, R. E. (1975) Phonetic expectation and transcription validity. *Phonetica*, 31, 288–304.

—— (1988) The role of audition in babbling. *Child Development*, 59, 441–9.

Oller, D. K. and Lynch, M. P. (1992) Infant vocalizations and innovation in infraphonology: toward a broader theory of development and disorders. In C. A. Ferguson, L. Menn, and C. Stoel-Gammon (eds), *Phonological Development: models, research, implications*, 509–36. Timonium, Md: York Press.

Oller, D. K. and Seibert, J. M. (1988) Babbling of prelinguistic mentally retarded children. *American Journal of Mental Retardation*, 92, 369–75.

Oller, D. K. and Smith, B. L. (1977) Effect of final-syllable position on vowel duration in infant babbling. *Journal of the Acoustical Society of America*, 62, 994–7.

Oller, D. K., Wieman, L. A., Doyle, W., and Ross, C. (1976) Infant babbling and speech. *Journal of Child Language*, 3, 1–11.

Orlansky, M. D. and Bonvillian, J. D. (1984) The role of iconicity in early sign language acquisition. *Journal of Speech and Hearing Disorders*, 49, 287–92.

Orsolini, M. (1990) Episodic structure in children's fantasy narratives: "breakthrough" to decontextualised discourse. *Language and Cognitive Processes*, 5, 53–79.

Otomo, K. (1988) Development of vowel articulation from 22 to 30 months of age: preliminary analyses. Paper presented at the Child Phonology Conference, University of Illinois, Urbana-Champain.

Otsu, Y. (1981) Universal grammar and syntactic development of young children. Ph.D. dissertation, MIT.

Ouhalla, J. (1990) Sentential negation, relativized minimality, and the aspectual status of auxiliaries. *The Linguistic Review*, 7, 183–231.

—— (1991) *Functional Categories and Parametric Variation*. London: Routledge.

Oviatt, S. L. (1980) The emerging ability to comprehend language: an experimental approach. *Child Development*, 51, 97–106.

Pan, B., Feldman, H., and Snow, C. (1993) Parental speech to low-risk and at-risk children. Manuscript, Harvard Graduate School of Education.

Papousek, H. and Papousek, M. (1975) Cognitive aspects of preverbal social interaction between human infants and adults. *Parent–Infant Interaction*, CIBA Foundation Symposium 33. New York: Elsevier.

Papousek, M. and Papousek, H. (1981) Musical elements in the infant's vocalization: their significance for communication, cognition and creativity. In L. P. Lipsitt (ed.), *Advances in Infancy Research*, Vol. 1, 164–224. Norwood, NJ: Ablex.

Parodi, T. (1990) The acquisition of word order regularities and case morphology. In J. Meisel (ed.), *Two First Languages: early grammatical development in bilingual children*, 157–92. Dordrecht: Foris.

Partee, B. (1973) Some structural analogies between tenses and pronouns in English. *The Journal of Philosophy*, 70, 601–9.

Paschell, L. (1983) Development at 18 months. In J. V. Irwin and S. P. Wong (eds), *Phonological*

Development in Children: 18 to 72 months, 27–54. Carbondale: Southern Illinois University Press.

Paul, R. (1991) Profiles of toddlers with slow expressive language development. *Topics in Language Disorders*, 11: 4, 1–13.

Paul, R. and Shriberg, L. (1982) Associations between phonology and syntax in speech-delayed children. *Journal of Speech and Hearing Research*, 22, 536–47.

Paul, R., Spangle-Looney, S., and Dahm, P. S. (1991) Communication and socialization skills at ages 2 and 3 in late-talking young children. *Journal of Speech and Hearing Research*, 4, 858–65.

Pawlby, S. J. (1977) Imitative interaction. In H. R. Schaffer (ed.), *Studies in Mother–Infant Interaction*. New York: Academic Press.

Peirce, C. S. (1931–58) Collected Papers of Charles Sanders Peirce, 8 vols, (eds) C. Hartshorne, P. Weiss, and A. Birks. Cambridge, Mass.: Harvard University Press.

Pellegrini, A. D. (1984) The effect of dramatic play on children's generation of cohesive text. *Discourse Processes*, 7, 57–67.

Pembrey, M. (1992) Genetics and language disorder. In P. Fletcher and D. Hall (eds), *Specific Speech and Language Disorders in Children*, 51–62. London: Whurr Publishers.

Perez-Leroux, A. (1991) The acquisition of long distance movement in Caribbean Spanish. In T. Maxfield and B. Plunkett (eds), *The Acquisition of Wh. University of Massachusetts Occasional Papers in Linguistics*.

—— (1993) Empty categories and the acquisition of wh-movement. Ph.D. dissertation, University of Massachusetts, Amherst.

Perez-Leroux, A. and Roeper, T. (1992) Copying wh-questions. Paper presented at the Boston University Conference on Language Development.

Perlmann, R. Y. (1984) Variations in socialization styles: family talk at the dinner table. Unpublished doctoral dissertation, Boston University.

Perlmann, R. Y. and Gleason, J. B. (1990) Patterns of prohibition in mothers' speech to children. Paper presented at the meeting of the International Association for the Study of Child Language, Budapest.

Pesetsky D. (1982) *Paths and Categories*. Ph.D. dissertation, MIT.

—— (1987) Wh-in-situ: movement and unselective binding. In E. J. Reuland and A. ter Meulen (eds), *The Representation of (In)definiteness*. Cambridge, Mass.: MIT Press.

Peters, A. M. (1977) Language learning strategies: does the whole equal the sum of the parts? *Language*, 53, 560–73.

—— (1983) *The Units of Language Acquisition*. New York: Cambridge University Press.

—— (1985) Language segmentation: operating principles for the perception and analysis of language. In D. Slobin (ed.), *The Crosslinguistic Study of Language Acquisition*, vol. 2, *Theoretical Issues*, 1,029–68. Hillsdale, NJ: Lawrence Erlbaum Associates.

—— (1986) Early syntax. In P. Fletcher and M. Garman (eds), *Language Acquisition*, 2nd edn, 307–25. New York: Cambridge University Press.

—— (1987) The role of imitation in the developing syntax of a blind child. *Text*, 7, 289–311.

—— (to appear) Language typology, prosody and the acquisition of grammatical morphemes. In D. I. Slobin (ed.), *The Crosslinguistic Study of Language Acquisition*, vol. 4. Hillsdale, NJ: Lawrence Erlbaum Associates.

Peters, A. M. and Menn, L. (1993) False starts and filler syllables: ways to learn grammatical morphemes. *Language*, 69, 743–77.

Peters, A., Fahn, R., Glover, G., Harley, H., Sawyer, M., and Shimura, A. (1990) Keeping close to the data: a two-tier computer-coding schema for the analysis of morphological development. Unpublished manuscript, University of Hawaii, Honolulu.

Petersen, S. E., Fox, P. T., Posner, M. I., Mintum, M., and Raichle, M. E. (1988) Positron emission: tomographic studies of the cortical anatomy of single-word processing. *Nature*, 331, 585–9.

Peterson, C. (1990) The who, when and where of early narratives. *Journal of Child Language*, 17, 433–55.

Peterson, C. and Dodsworth, P. (1991) A longitudinal analysis of young children's cohesion and noun specification in narratives. *Journal of Child Language*, 18, 397–415.

Peterson, C. and McCabe (1983) *Developmental Psycholinguistics: three ways of looking at children's narrative*. New York: Plenum.

—— (1992) Parental styles of narrative elicitation: effect on children's narrative structure and content. *First Language*, 12, 299–322.

Petitto, L. A. and Marentette, P. F. (1991) Babbling in the manual mode: evidence for the ontogeny of language. *Science*, 251, 1,493–6.

Pfaff, C. (1990) Mixing and linguistic convergence in migrant speech communities: linguistic constraints, social conditions and models of acquisition. *Papers for the Workshop on Constraints, Conditions and Models*, 119–53. London: ESF Network on Code-Switching and Language Contact.

—— (1991) Turkish in contact with German: language maintenance and loss among immigrant children in Berlin (West). *International Journal for the Sociology of Language*, 90, 97–129.

—— (1992) The issue of grammaticalization in early German second language. *Studies in Second Language Acquisition*, 14, 273–96.

Pfaff, C. and Savas, T. (1988) Language development in a bilingual setting: the acquisition of Turkish in Germany. Paper presented at the Fourth Turkish Linguistics Conference, Ankara.

Philip, W. and de Villiers, J. (1992a) Monotonicity and the acquisition of weak wh-islands. *The Proceedings of the Twenty-fourth Annual Child Language Forum*. Stanford/CSLI.

—— (1992b) The acquisition of weak wh-islands. Paper presented at the 17th annual Boston University Conference on Language Development.

Philips, S. U. (1983) *The Invisible Culture: communication in classroom and community on the Warm Springs Indian Reservation*. New York: Longman.

Phinney, M. (1981) *Syntactic Constraints and the Acquisition of Embedded Sentential Complements*. Ph.D. dissertation, University of Massachusetts.

Piaget, J. (1932/65) *The Morla Judgement of the Child*. New York: Free Press.

—— (1953) *The Origin of Intelligence in the Child*. London: Routledge & Kegan Paul.

—— (1955) *The Child's Construction of Reality*. London: Routledge & Kegan Paul.

—— (1959) *The Language and Thought of the Child*. London: Routledge & Kegan Paul.

—— (1962) *Play, Dreams, and Imitation*. New York: Norton.

Piaget, J. and Inhelder, B. (1956)*The Child's Conception of Space*. London: Routledge & Kegan Paul.

Piatelli-Palmerini, M. (ed.) (1980) *Language and Learning: the debate between Jean Piaget and Noam Chomsky*. Cambridge, Mass.: Harvard University Press.

Pickett, J. M. and Pollack, I. (1963) Intelligibility of excerpts from fluent speech: effects of rate of utterance and duration of excerpt. *Language and Speech*, 7, 151–64.

Piéraut-Le Bonniec, G. and Dolitsky, M. (eds) (1991) *Language Bases . . . Discourse Bases*. Amsterdam: Benjamins.

Pine, J. (1992) Functional basis of referentiality: evidence from children's spontaneous speech. *First Language*, 12, 39–55.

—— (1994) The language of primary caretakers. In C. Gallaway and B. Richards (eds), *Input and Interaction in Language Acquisition*, 15–37. Cambridge: Cambridge University Press.

Pine, J. and Lieven, E. (1990) Referential style at thirteen months: why age-defined cross-sectional measures are inappropriate for the study of strategy differences in early language development. *Journal of Child Language*, 17, 625–31.

Pinker, S. (1979) Formal models of language learning. *Cognition*, 7, 217–83.

—— (1984) *Language Learnability and Language Development*. Cambridge, Mass.: Harvard University Press.

—— (1989) *Learnability and Cognition: the acquisition of argument structure*. Cambridge, Mass.: MIT/Bradford.

—— (1991) Rules of language. *Science*, 253, 530–5.

Pinker, S. and Prince, A. (1988) On language and connectionism: analysis of a parallel distributed processing model of language acquisition. *Cognition*, 29, 73–193.

Pinker, S., Lebeaux, D. S., and Frost, L. A. (1987) Productivity and constraints in the acquisition of the passive. *Cognition*, 26, 195–267.

Pizzuto, E. and Caselli, M. (1993) The acquisition of Italian morphology: implications for models of language development. *Journal of Child Language*, 1991.

Plante, E., Swisher, L., Kiernan, B., and Restrepo, M. A. (1993) Language matches: illuminating or confounding? *Journal of Speech and Hearing Research*, 36, 772–6.

Platt, M. (1986) Social norms and lexical acquisition: a study of deictic verbs in Samoan child language. In B. B. Schieffelin and E. Ochs (eds), *Language Socialization Across Cultures*, 127–51. Cambridge: Cambridge University Press.

Platzack, C. (1990) A grammar without functional categories: a syntactic study of early Swedish child language. Manuscript, Lund University, Sweden.

—— (1992) Functional categories and early Swedish. In J. Meisel (ed.), *The Acquisition of Verb Placement*. Dordrecht: Kluwer.

Platzack, C. and Holmberg, A. (1989) The role of AGR and finiteness in Germanic VO languages. *Scandinavian Working Papers in Linguistics*, 43, 51–76.

Pléh, C., Jarovinskij, A., and Balajan, A. (1987) Sentence comprehension in Hungarian–Russian bilingual and monolingual preschool children. *Journal of Child Language*, 14, 587–603.

Plunkett, B. (1991) Inversion and early wh-questions. In T. L. Maxfield and B. Plunkett (eds), *Papers in the Acquisition of WH*, 125–53. Amherst: GLSA Publications.

Plunkett, K. (1986) Learning strategies in two Danish children's language development. *Scandinavian Journal of Psychology*, 27, 64–73.

—— (1993) Lexical segmentation and vocabulary growth in early language acquisition. *Journal of Child Language*, 20, 43–60.

Plunkett, K. and Marchman, V. (1991) U-shaped learning and frequency effects in a multi-layered perceptron: implications for child language acquisition. *Cognition*, 38, 43–102.

—— (1993) From rote learning to system building: acquiring verb morphology in children and connectionist nets. *Cognition*, 48, 21–69.

Plunkett, K. and Sinha, C. (1992) Connectionism and developmental theory. *British Journal of Development Psychology*, 10, 209–54.

Plunkett, K., Sinha, C. G., Moller, M. F., and Strandsby (1992) Symbol grounding or the emergence of symbols: Vocabulary growth in children and a connectionist net. *Connection Science*, 4, 293–312.

Polger, G. and Weng, T. (1979) *Pulmonary Function Testing in Children: techniques and standards*. Philadelphia: WB Saunders.

Pollack, I. and Pickett, J. M. (1963) The intelligibility of excerpts from conversation. *Language and Speech*, 6, 165–71.

Pollock, J.-Y. (1989) Verb movement, Universal Grammar, and the structure of IP. *Linguistic Inquiry*, 20, 365–424.

Pollock, K. (1983) Individual preference: case study of a phonologically delayed child. *Topics in Language Disorders*, 3, 10–23.

Pollock, K. and Keiser, N. (1990) An examination of vowel errors in phonologically disordered children. *Clinical Linguistics and Phonetics*, 4, 161–78.

Poole, I. (1934) Genetic development of articulation of consonant sounds in speech. *Elementary English Review*, 11, 159–61.

Poplack, S. (1980) Sometimes I'll start a sentence in Spanish Y TERMINO EN ESPANOL: toward a typology of code-switching. *Linguistics*, 18, 581–618.

—— (1981) Syntactic structure and social function of codeswitching. In R. Durán (ed.), *Latino Language and Communicative Behavior*, 169–84. Norwood: Ablex Publishers.

Porter, R. H., Makin, J. W., Davis, L. B., and Christensen, K. M. (1992) Breast-fed infants respond to olfactory cues from their own mother and unfamiliar lactating females. *Infant Behavior and Development*, 15, 85–94.

Posner, M. I. and Keele, S. W. (1970) Retention of abstract ideas. *Journal of Experimental Psychology*, 83, 304–8.

Posner, M. I., Petersen, S. E., Fox, P. T., and Raichle, M. E. (1988) Localization of cognitive operations in the human brain. *Science*, 240, 1,627–31.

Post, K. (1993) Negative evidence. In J. Sokolov and C. Snow (eds), *Handbook of Research in Language Development Using CHILDES*. Hillsdale, NJ: Lawrence Erlbaum Associates.

Postal, P. M. (1970) On so-called pronouns in English. In R. A. Jacobs and P. S. Rosenbaum (eds), *Readings in English Transformational Grammar*, 56–82. Waltham, Mass.: Ginn and Co.

Power, R. J. D. and Dal Martello, M. F. (1986) The use of the definite and indefinite articles by Italian preschool children. *Journal of Child Language*, 13, 145–54.

Prasada, S. and Pinker, S. (1993) Generalisation of regular and irregular morphological patterns. *Language and Cognitive Processes*, 8(1), 1–56.

Prater, R. and Swift, R. (1982) Phonological process development with MLU-referenced guidelines. *Journal of Communication Disorders*, 15, 395–410.

Prather, E., Hedrick, D., and Kern, C. (1975) Articulation development in children aged two to four years. *Journal of Speech and Hearing Disorders*, 40, 179–91.

Pratt, M. W., Kerig, P. K., Cowan, P. A., and Cowan, C. P. (1992) Family worlds: couple satisfaction, parenting style, and mothers' and fathers' speech to young children. *Merrill-Palmer Quarterly*, 38, 245–62.

Preece, A. (1987) The range of narrative forms conversationally produced by young children. *Journal of Child Language*, 14, 353–73.

—— (1992) Collaborators and critics: the nature and effects of peer interaction on children's conversational narratives. *Journal of Narrative and Life History*, 2, 277–92.

Preisser, D., Hodson, B., and Paden, E. (1988) Developmental phonology: 18–29 months. *Journal of Speech and Hearing Disorders*, 53, 125–30.

Priestly, T. M. S. (1977) One idiosyncratic strategy in the acquisition of phonology. *Journal of Child Language*, 4, 45–66.

Provenzo, E. F. (1991) *Video Kids: making sense of Nintendo*. Cambridge: Harvard University Press.

Pruess, J. B., Vadasy, P. F., and Fewell, R. R. (1987) Language development in children with Down syndrome: an overview of recent research. *Education and Training of the Mentally Retarded*, 22, 44–55.

Prutting, C. A. and Kirchner, D. M. (1987) A clinical appraisal of the pragmatic aspects of language. *Journal of Speech and Hearing Disorders*, 52, 105–19.

Pueschel, S., Gallagher, P., Zartler, A., and Pezzullo, J. (1987) Cognitive and learning processes in children with Down syndrome. *Research in Developmental Disabilities*, 8, 21–37.

Pye, C. (1986) One lexicon or two? An alternative interpretation of early bilingual speech. *Journal of Child Language*, 13, 591–3.

—— (1988) *Pye Analysis of Language* (PAL) [Computer software, IBM]. Lawrence, Kansas: author.

—— (1992) The acquisition of K'iche' Maya. In D. Slobin (ed.), *The Crosslinguistic Study of Language Acquisition*, vol. 3, 221–308. Hillsdale, NJ: Lawrence Erlbaum Associates.

Pye, C. and Ingram, D. (1988) Automating the analysis of child phonology. *Clinical Linguistics & Phonetics*, 2, 115–37.

Pye, C., Ingram, D., and List, H. (1987) A comparison of initial consonant acquisition in English and Quiché. In K. E. Nelson and A. van Kleek (eds), *Children's Language* vol. 6, 175–90. Hillsdale, NJ: Lawrence Erlbaum Associates.

Quasthoff, U. M. and Nikolaus, K. (1982) What makes a good story? Towards the production of conversational narratives. In A. Flammer and W. Kintsch (eds), *Discourse Processing*, 16–28. New York: North Holland.

Quay, S. (1992) Explaining language choice in early infant bilingualism. Paper presented at the Ninth Sociolinguistics Symposium, Reading, UK.

—— (1993) Bilingual evidence against the principle of contrast. Paper presented at the 67th Annual Meeting of the Linguistic Society of America, Los Angeles.

Querleu, D., Renard, X., and Crepin, G. (1981) Perception auditive et réactivité foetale aux stimulations sonores. *Journal de Gynecologie, Obstetrique et Biologie Reproduction*, 10, 307–14.

Quine, W. V. O. (1960) *Word and Object*. Cambridge, Mass.: MIT Press.

Quirk, R., Greenbaum, A., Leech, G., and Svartvik, J. (1985) *A Comprehensive Grammar of the English Language*. London: Longman.

Racette, K. and Fowler, A. (1993) Phonological bases of memory in normal preschools and young adults with Down syndrome. Poster presented at the 60th meeting of the Society for Research in Child Development, New Orleans.

Radford, A. (1986) Small children's small clauses. *Bangor Research Papers in Linguistics*, 1, 1–38.

—— (1987) The acquisition of the complementiser system. *Research Papers in Linguistics*, 2, 55–76. Bangor: University College of North Wales.

—— (1988a) *Transformational Grammar*. Cambridge: Cambridge University Press.

—— (1988b) Small children's small clauses. *Transactions of the Philological Society*, 86, 1–46 (revised and extended version of Radford, 1986).

—— (1990) *Syntactic Theory and the Acquisition of English Syntax: the nature of early child grammars of English*. Oxford: Blackwell.

—— (1991) The acquisition of the morphosyntax of finite verbs in English. In J. Meisel (ed.), *The Acquisition of Verb Placement: functional categories and V2 phenomena in language development, Studies in Theoretical Psycholinguistics*, 23–62. Dordrecht: Kluwer.

—— (1993) Head-hunting: on the trail of the nominal Janus. In G. Corbett et al. (eds), *Heads in Grammatical Theory*, 73–113. Cambridge: Cambridge University Press.

—— (1994) The syntax of questions in child English: *Journal of Child Language*.

Ramer, A. L. H. (1976) Syntactic styles in emerging language. *Journal of Child Language*, 3, 49–62.

Randall, J. (1990) Catapults and pendulums: the mechanisms of language acquisition. *Linguistics*, 38, 1,381–1406.

—— (1992) The catapult hypothesis: an approach to unlearning. In J. Weissenborn, H. Goodluck, and T. Roeper (eds), *Theoretical Issues in Language Acquisition: continuity and change in development*, 93–138. Hillsdale, NJ: Lawrence Erlbaum Associates.

Rapin, I. (1988) Disorders of higher cerebral function in preschool children. *American Journal of Diseases of Children*, 142, 1,119–24.

Rapin, I. and Allen, D. A. (1988) Syndromes in developmental dysphasia and adult aphasia. In F. Plum (ed.), *Language, Communication, and the Brain*, 57–75. New York: Raven Press.

Rasmussen, T. and Milner, B. (1977) The role of early left-brain injury in determining lateralization of cerebral speech functions. *Annals of the New York Academy of Sciences*, 299, 355–69.

Rast, M. and Meltzoff, A. (1993) Imitation from memory in young children with Down syndrome. Poster presented at the 60th meeting of the Society for Research in Child Development, New Orleans.

Ratner, N. B. (1988) Patterns of parental vocabulary selection in speech to very young children. *Journal of Child Language*, 15, 481–92.

Ratner, N. B. and Bruner, J. (1978) Games, social exchange and the acquisition of language. *Journal of Child Language*, 5, 391–401.

Ratner, N. B. and Pye, C. (1984) Higher pitch in BT is not universal: acoustic evidence from Qu'iche Mayan. *Journal of Child Language*, 11, 515–22.

Redlinger, W. (1979) Early developmental bilingualism, a review of the literature. *The Bilingual Review/La Revista Bilingüe*, 6, 11–30.

Redlinger, W. and Park, T. Z. (1980) Language mixing in young bilinguals. *Journal of Child Language*, 3, 449–55.

Reich, P. A. (1976) The early acquisition of word meaning. *Journal of Child Language*, 3, 117–23.

Reilly, J., Klima, E. S. and Bellugi, U. (1991) Once more with feeling: affect and language in atypical populations. *Development and Psychopathology*, 367–91.

Reinhart, T. (1984) Principles of Gestalt perception in the temporal organization of narrative texts. *Linguistics*, 22, 779–809.

Rescorla, L. (1976) Concept formation in word learning. Unpublished Doctoral dissertation, Yale University.

—— (1980) Overextension in early language development. *Journal of Child Language*, 7, 321–35.

—— (1981) Category development in early language. *Journal of Child Language*, 8, 225–38.

—— (1989) The language development survey: a screening tool for delayed language in toddlers. *Journal of Speech and Hearing Disorders*, 54, 587–99.

—— (1993) Outcome of toddlers with specific expressive language delay (SELD) at ages 3, 4, 5, and 6. Poster presented at the 60th annual meeting of the Society for Research in Child Development, New Orleans.

Rescorla, L. and Goossens, M. (1992) Symbolic play development in toddlers with expressive specific language impairment. *Journal of Speech and Hearing Research*, 6, 1,290–1,320.

Rescorla, L. and Schwartz, E. (1990) Outcome of toddlers with specific expressive language delay. *Applied Psycholinguistics*, 11, 393–408.

Retherford, K., Schwartz, B., and Chapman, R. (1981) Semantic roles and residual grammatical categories in mother and child speech: who tunes into whom? *Journal of Child Language*, 8, 583–608.

Reznick, J. S. and Goldfield, B. A. (1992) Rapid change in lexical development in comprehension and production. *Developmental Psychology*, 28, 406–13.

Rice, M. L. (1983) The role of television in language acquisition. *Developmental Review*, 3, 211–24.

—— (1984) Cognitive aspects of communicative development. In R. Schiefelbusch and J. Pickar (eds), *The Acquisition of Communicative Competence*. Baltimore: University Park Press.

—— (1992) "Don't talk to him; he's weird": the role of language in early social interactions. In A. Kaiser and D. Gray (eds), *Enhancing Children's Communication: the social use of language*. Baltimore: Brookes.

Rice, M. L. and Haight, P. L. (1986) "Motherese" of Mr. Rogers: a description of the dialogue of educational television programs. *Journal of Speech and Hearing Disorders*, 51, 282–7.

Rice, M. L. and Woodsmall, L. (1988) Lessons from television. Children's word learning when viewing. *Child Development*, 59, 420–9.

Rice, M. L., Huston, A. C., Truglio, R., and Wright, J. C. (1990) Words from "Sesame Street": learning vocabulary while viewing. *Developmental Psychology*, 26, 421–8.

Richard, N. (1986) Interaction between mothers and infants with Down syndrome: infant characteristics. *Topics in Early Childhood Special Education*, 6, 54–71.

Richards, M. and Light, P. (eds) (1986) *Children of Social Worlds*. Cambridge: Harvard University Press.

Rispoli, M. (1990) Lexical assignability and perspective switch: the acquisition of verb subcategorization for aspectual inflections. *Journal of Child Language*, 17, 375–92.

Ritter, E. (1988) A head-movement approach to construct-state noun phrases. *Linguistics*, 26, 909–29.

Riva, D., Cazzaniga, L., Pantaleoni, C., Milani, N., and Fedrizzi, E. (1986) Acute hemiplegia in childhood: the neuropsychological prognosis. *Journal of Pediatric Neuroscience*, 2(4), 239–50.

Rizzi, L. (1989) On the format for parameters. *Behavioral and Brain Sciences*, 12, 355–6.

—— (1990) *Relativized Minimality*. Cambridge, Mass.: MIT Press.

—— (1992) Early null subjects & root null subjects. *Geneva Generative Papers*.

Robb, M. P. and Bauer, H. R. (1991) The ethological model of phonetic development II: the closant curve. *Clinical Linguistics and Phonetics*, 5, 336–53.

Robb, M. P. and Saxman, J. H. (1985) Developmental trends in vocal fundamental frequency of young children. *Journal of Speech and Hearing Research*, 28, 421–7.

—— (1988) Acoustic observations in young children's non-cry vocalizations. *Journal of the Acoustical Society of America*, 83, 1,876–82.

—— (1990) Syllable durations of preword and early word vocalizations. *Journal of Speech and Hearing Research*, 33, 583–93.

Robb, M. P., Saxman, J. H., and Grant, A. A. (1989) Vocal fundamental frequency characteristics during the first two years of life. *Journal of the Acoustical Society of America*, 85, 1,708–17.

Roberts, K. and Horowitz, F. (1986) Basic level categorization in seven- and nine-month-old infants. *Journal of Child Language*, 13, 191–208.

Roberts, S. (1983) Comprehension and production of word order in stage I. *Child Development*, 54, 443–9.

Robertson, L. C. and Delis, D. C. (1986) "Part-whole" processing in unilateral brain-damaged patients: dysfunction of hierarchical organization. *Neuropsychologia*, 24(3), 363–70.

Robinson, N. M., Dale, P. S., and Landesman, S. (1990) Validity of Stanford-Binet IV with linguistically precocious toddlers. *Intelligence*, 14, 173–86.

Robinson, R. J. (1987) Introduction and overview. *Proceedings of the First International Symposium on Specific Speech and Language Disorders in Children*, 1–19. London: Association for All Speech-Impaired Children (AFASIC).

Roeper, T. (1973) Connecting children's language and linguistic theory. In T. Moore (ed.), *Cognitive Development and the Acquisition of Language*, 187–96. New York: Academic Press.

—— (1988) Spec as trigger: comments in the symposium on wh-movement. Paper presented at the 13th annual Boston University Conference on Language Development.

—— (1992) From the Initial State to V2. *The acquisition of verb placement: functional categories and V2 phenomena in language acquisition*, 333–70. Dordrecht: Kluwer.

Roeper, T. and de Villiers, J. (1991) Ordered decisions in the acquisition of wh-questions. In J. Weissenborn, H. Goodluck, and T. Roeper (eds), *Theoretical Issues in Language Acquisition*, 191–236. Hillsdale NJ: Lawrence Erlbaum Associates.

—— (1992) The one feature hypothesis for acquisition. Manuscript, University of Massachusetts.

—— (in press) Lexical links in the Wh-chain. In B. Lust, G. Hermon, and J. Kornfilt (eds), *Syntactic Theory and First Language Acquisition: cross linguistic perspectives*, vol. 2, *Binding, Dependencies and Learnability*. Hillsdale, NJ: Lawrence Erlbaum Associates.

Roeper, T. and Weissenborn, J. (1990) How to make parameters work: comments on Valian. In L. Frazier and J. de Villiers (eds), *Language Processing and Language Acquisition*, 147–62. Dordrecht: Kluwer.

Roeper, T. and Williams, E. (eds) (1987) *Parameter Setting*. Dordrecht: Reidel.

Roeper, T., Rooth, M., Mallis, L., and Akiyama, A. (1984) The problem of empty categories and bound variables in language acquisition. Manuscript, University of Massachusetts.

Rogoff, B. (1990) *Apprenticeship in thinking: cognitive development in social context*. New York: Oxford University Press.

Rohr, A. and Burr, D. B. (1978) Etiological differences in patterns of psycholinguistic development of children of IQ 30 to 60. *American Journal of Mental Deficiency*, 82, 549–53.

Rollins, P. (1993) Language profiles of children with specific language impairment. In J. Sokolov and C. Snow (eds), *Handbook of Research in Language Development Using CHILDES*. Hillsdale, NJ: Lawrence Erlbaum Associates.

Romaine, S. (1989) *Bilingualism*. Oxford: Basil Blackwell.

Rondal, J. (1978a) Maternal speech to normal and Down's syndrome children matched for mean length of utterance. In C. E. Meyers (ed.), *Quality of Life in Severely and Profoundly Mentally Retarded People: research foundations for improvement*. Washington, DC: American Association on Mental Deficiency.

—— (1978b) Developmental Sentence Scoring procedure and the delay-difference question in language development of Down's syndrome children. *Mental Retardation*, 16, 169–71.

—— (1980) Fathers' and mothers' speech in early language development. *Journal of Child Language*, 7, 353–69.

Rondal, J. A., Ghiotto, M., Bredart, S., and Bachelet, J.-F. (1987) Age-relation, reliability and grammatical validity of measures of utterance length. *Journal of Child Language*, 14, 433–6.

Ronjat, J. (1913) *Le développment du langage observé chez un enfant bilingue*. Paris: Champion.

Rosenberg, S. (1982) The language of the mentally retarded: development, processes, and intervention. In S. Rosenberg (ed.), *Handbook of Applied Psycholinguistics*. Hillsdale, NJ: Lawrence Erlbaum Associates.

Rosin, M. M., Swift, E., Bless, D., and Vetter, D. K. (1988) Communication profiles of adolescents with Down syndrome. *Journal of Childhood Communication Disorders*, 12, 49–64.

Ross, E. D. and Mesulam, M. M. (1979) Dominant language functions of the right hemisphere: prosody and emotional gesturing. *Archives of Neurology*, 36, 144–8.

Rothweiler, M. (1989) *Nebensatzewerb im Deutschen. Eine empirische Untersuchung zum Primarspracherwerb* [Acquisition of Subordinate Clauses in German. An Empirical investigation of Primary Language Acquisition]. Doctoral dissertation, Tubingen.

Roug, L., Landberg, I., and Lundberg, L.-J. (1989) Phonetic development in early infancy: a study of four Swedish children during the first eighteen months of life. *Journal of Child Language*, 16, 19–40.

Rowan, L., Leonard, L., Chapman, K., and Weiss, A. (1983) Performative and presuppositional skills in language-disordered and normal children. *Journal of Speech and Hearing Research*, 26, 97–106.

Rubba, J. and Klima, E. S. (1991) Preposition use in a speaker with Williams Syndrome: Some cognitive grammar proposals. *Center for Research in Language Newsletter*, 6, 1. San Diego: University of California.

Rumelhart, D. E. and McClelland, J. L. (1986) On learning the past tense of English verbs. In J. L. McClelland, D. E. Rumelhart, and the PDP Research Group (eds), *Parallel Distributed Processing: explorations in the microstructure of cognition*, vol. 2, *Psychological and Biological Models*, 216–71. Cambridge, Mass.: Bradford Books, MIT Press.

Rundell, M. and Stock. P. (1992a) The corpus revolution, part 1. *English Today*, 8(2), 9–14.

—— (1992b) The corpus revolution, part 2. *English Today*, 8(3), 21–32.

—— (1992c) The corpus revolution, part 3. *English Today*, 8(4), 45–51.

Ruscello, D., St Louis, K., and Mason, N. (1991) School-aged children with phonologic disorders: coexistence with other speech/language disorders. *Journal of Speech and Hearing Research*, 34, 236–42.

Rutter, M. (1978) Diagnosis and definition. In M. Rutter and E. Schopler (eds), *Autism: a reappraisal of concepts and treatment*. New York: Plenum.

Sachs, J. (1977) The adaptive significance of linguistic input to prelinguistic infants. In C. E. Snow and C. A. Ferguson (eds), *Talking to Children: language input and acquisition*. Cambridge: Cambridge University Press.

Sachs, J. (1979) Topic selection in parent–child discourse. *Discourse Processes*, 2, 145–53.

Sachs, J. (1983) Talking about the there and then: the emergence of displaced reference in parent–child discourse. In K. E. Nelson (ed.), *Children's Language*, vol 4. Hillsdale, NJ: Lawrence Erlbaum Associates.

Sachs, J., Bard, B., and Johnson, M. S. (1981) Language learning with restricted input: case studies of two hearing children of deaf parents. *Applied Psycholinguistics*, 2, 33–54.

Sadker, D., Sadker, M., and Thomas, D. (1981) Sex equity and special education. *The Pointer*, 26, 33–8.

Sadker, M. and Sadker, D. (1984) *Year 3: final report, promoting effectiveness in classroom instruction*. Washington, DC: National Institute of Education.

Sag, I. A. and Hankamer, J. (1984) Toward a theory of anaphoric processing. *Linguistics and Philosophy*, 7, 325–45.

Sancier, M. L. (1989) A descriptive study of sound production in cleft palate infants: patterns, productivity and contrastivity. Unpublished Master's thesis, University of Wisconsin–Madison.

Sander, E. (1972) When are speech sounds learned? *Journal of Speech and Hearing Disorders*, 37, 55–63.

Sankoff, G. (1980) *The Social Life of Language*. Philadelphia: University of Pennsylvania Press.

Sapir, E. and Hoijer, H. (1967) The phonology and morphology of the Navaho language. University of California Publications, Linguistics, no. 50. Berkeley, CA: University of California Press.

Satz, P., Strauss, E., and Whitaker, H. (1990) The ontogeny of hemispheric specialization: some old hypotheses revisited. *Brain and Language*, 38, 596–614.

Saunders, G. (1982) *Bilingual Children: guidance for the family*. Clevedon: Multilingual Matters.

—— (1988) *Bilingual Children: from birth to teens*. Clevedon: Multilingual Matters.

Sauvaire, V. and Vion, M. (1989) Expression of the given/new contract in referential communication: a study of seven- and nine-year-old children. *European Bulletin of Cognitive Psychology*, 9, 431–49.

Savage-Rumbaugh, E. S. (1990) Language acquisition in a non-human species: implications for the innateness debate. *Developmental Psychobiology*, 23, 599–620.

Scaife, M. and Bruner, J. S. (1975) The capacity for joint visual attention in the infant. *Nature*, 253, 265–6.

Scarborough, H. S. (1990) Index of productive syntax. *Applied Psycholinguistics*, 11, 1–22.

Scarborough, H. S. and Dobrich, W. (1990) Development of children with early language delay. *Journal of Speech and Hearing Research*, 33, 70–83.

Scarborough, H. S., Rescorla, L., Tager-Flusberg, H., Fowler, A., and Sudhalter, V. (1991) The relation of utterance length to grammatical complexity in normal and language-disordered groups. *Applied Psycholinguistics*, 12, 23–45.

Schaerlaekens, A. M. (1977) *De taalontwikkeling van het kind. Een oriëntatie in het Nederlandstalig onderzoek*. Groningen: Wolters-Noordhof.

Schaerlaekens, A. M. and Gillis, S. (1987) *De taalverwerving van het kind. Een hernieuwde oriëntatie in het Nederlandstalig onderzoek* [The acquisition of language by children. A renewed orientation in Dutch research]. Groningen: Wolters-Noordhoff.

Schaffer, H. R. (1984) *The Child's Entry into a Social World*. New York: Academic Press.

Schaffer, H. R., Hepburn, A., and Collis, G. (1983) Verbal and non-verbal aspects of mothers' directives. *Journal of Child Language*, 10, 337–55.

Schegloff, E. A., Jefferson, G., and Sacks, H. (1977) The preference for self-correction in the organization of repair in conversation. *Language*, 53, 361–82.

Scheibel, A. E. (1993) Dendritic structure and language development. In B. de Boysson-Bardies, S. de Schonen, P. Jusczyk, P. MacNeilage, and J. Morton (eds), *Developmental Neurocognition: speech and voice processing in the first year of life*, 51–62. Dordrecht: Kluwer.

Scherer, K. (1979) Acoustic concomitants of emotional dimensions: judging affect from synthesized tone sequences. In Weitz, S. (ed.), *Nonverbal Communication*. New York: Oxford University Press.

Schery, T. K. (1985) Correlates of language development in language-disordered children. *Journal of Speech and Hearing Disorders*, 50, 73–83.

Schieffelin, B. B. (1983) Talking like birds: sound play in a cultural perspective. In E. Ochs and B. B. Schieffelin (eds), *Acquiring Conversational Competence*. London: Routledge and Kegan Paul.

—— (1986) The acquisition of Kaluli. In D. Slobin (ed.), *The Crosslinguistic Study of Language Acquisition*, 525–594. Hillsdale, NJ: Lawrence Erlbaum Associates.

—— (1990) *The Give and Take of Everyday Life: language socialization of Kaluli children*. Cambridge: Cambridge University Press.

—— (1994) Code-switching and Language socialization: some probable relationships. In J. F.

Duchan, L. E. Hewitt, and R. M. Sonnenmeier (eds), *Pragmatics: from theory to practice*, 20–42. New York: Prentice Hall.

Schieffelin, B. B. and Ochs, E. (1986a) Language socialization. Annual Review of Anthropology, 163–246. Palo Alto: Annual Reviews, Inc.

—— (eds.) (1986b) *Language Socialization Across Cultures*. New York: Cambridge University Press.

Schiffrin, D. (1981) Tense variation in narrative. *Language*, 57, 45–62.

—— (1990) Between text and context: deixis, anaphora, and the meaning of *then*. *Text*, 10, 245–70.

Schlesinger, I. M. (1971) Production of utterances and language acquisition. In D. I. Slobin (ed.), *The Ontogenesis of Grammar*, 63–102. New York: Academic Press.

Schlyter, S. (1987) Language mixing and linguistic level in three bilingual children. *Scandinavian Working Papers on Bilingualism*, 7, 29–48.

—— (1990a) Introducing the DUFDE project. In J. Meisel (ed.), *Two First Languages: early grammatical development in bilingual children*, 73–86. Dordrecht: Foris.

—— (1990b) The acquisition of tense and aspect. In J. Meisel (ed.), *Two First Languages: early grammatical development in bilingual children*, 87–122. Dordrecht: Foris.

—— (1993) The weaker language in bilingual Swedish–French children. In K. Hyltenstam and A. Viberg (eds), *Progression and Regression in Language: sociocultural, neuropsychological and linguistic perspectives*. Cambridge: Cambridge University Press.

Schlyter, S. and Westholm, L. (1991) Interaction familiale et développement des deux langues chez des enfants bilingues [Family interaction and development of two languages in bilingual children]. In C. Russier, H. Stoffel, and D. Véronique (eds), *Interactions en langue étrangère* [Interactions in a foreign language], 193–201. Aix-en-Provence: Publications de l'Université de Provence.

Schmidt, A. (1985) *Young People's Djirbal: an example of language death from Australia*. Cambridge: Cambridge University Press.

Schramm, W., Lyle, J., and Parker, E. B. (1961) *Television in the Lives of our Children*. Stanford, CA: Stanford University Press.

Schwartz, E. R. and Solot, C. B. (1980) Response patterns characteristic of verbal expressive disorders. *Language, Speech, and Hearing Services in Schools*, 11, 139–44.

Schwartz, M. F. (1984) What the classical aphasia categories can't do for us, and why. *Brain and Language*, 21, 3–8.

Schwartz, M. F., Marin, O., and Saffran, E. (1979) Dissociations of language function in dementia: a case study. *Brain and Language*, 7, 277–306.

Schwartz, M. F., Linebarger, E., Saffran, E., and Pate, D. (1987) Syntactic transparency and sentence interpretation in aphasia. *Language and Cognitive Processes*, 2, 85–113.

Schwartz, R. and Leonard, L. (1982) Do children pick and choose: an examination of phonological selection and avoidance in early lexical acquisition. *Journal of Child Language*, 9, 319–36.

Schwartz, R. and Terrell, B. (1983) The role of input frequency in lexical acquisition. *Journal of Child Language*, 10, 57–64.

Schwartz, R., Leonard, L., Folger, M. K., and Wilcox, M. J. (1980) Early phonological behavior in normal-speaking and language disordered children: evidence for a synergistic view of linguistic disorders. *Journal of Speech and Hearing Disorders*, 45, 357–77.

Schwartz, R., Leonard, L., Loeb, D. F., and Swanson, L. (1987) Attempted sounds are sometimes not: an expanded view of phonological selection and avoidance. *Journal of Child Language*, 14, 411–18.

Scollon, R. (1976) *Conversations with a One Year Old*. Honolulu: University Press of Hawai'i.

Scollon, S. (1982) *Reality set, socialization and linguistic convergence*. Unpublished Ph.D. dissertation, University of Hawai'i.

Scott, C. (1984) Adverbial connectivity in conversations of children 6 to 12. *Journal of Child Language*, 11, 423–52.

Seagoe, M. V. (1965) Verbal development in a mongoloid. *Exceptional Children*, 31, 269–73.

Searle, J. R. (1969) *Speech Acts*. Cambridge: Cambridge University Press.

—— (1974) Chomsky's revolution in linguistics. In G. Harman (ed.), *On Noam Chomsky: critical essays*, 2–33. New York: Anchor Books.

—— (1975) Indirect speech acts. In P. Cole and J. L. Morgan (eds), *Syntax and Semantics 3: speech acts*. New York: Academic Press.

Seashore, R. H. and Eckerson, L. D. (1940) The measurement of individual differences in general English vocabularies. *Journal of Educational Psychology*, 31, 14–38.

Sedey, A., Rosin, M., and Miller, J. (1991) The use of signs among children with Down syndrome. Poster presented at the American Speech–Language–Hearing Association Convention, Atlanta.

Sedey, A., Miolo, G., Murray-Branch, J., and Miller, J. (1992) Hearing status and language development in children with Down syndrome. Poster presented at the American Speech–Language Hearing Association convention, San Antonio.

Sejnowski, T. J., Koch, C., and Churchland, P. S. (1988) Computational neuroscience. *Science*, 241, 1,299–1,306.

Sell, M. A. (1992) The development of children's knowledge structures: events, slots, and taxonomies. *Journal of Child Language*, 19(3), 659–76.

Seymour, H., Bland, L., Champion, T., de Villiers, J., and Roeper, T. (1991) The development of Wh-movement in Black English. Paper presented at the Black Speech, Hearing and Language Association, Los Angeles.

Shank, R. C. and Abelson, R. P. (1977) *Scripts, Plans, Goals, and Understanding*. Hillsdale, NJ: Lawrence Erlbaum Associates.

Shapiro, L. R. and Hudson, J. A. (1991) Tell me a make-believe story: coherence and cohesion in young children's picture elicited narratives. *Developmental Psychology*, 27, 960–74.

Shatz, M. (1978) On the development of communicative understanding: an early strategy for interpreting and responding to messages. *Cognitive Psychology*, 3, 271–301.

—— (1982) On mechanisms of language acquisition: can features of the communicative environment account for development? In L. Geitman and E. Wanner (eds), *Language Acquisition: the state of the art*. New York: Cambridge University Press.

—— (1983) Communication. *Handbook of Child Psychology*, vol. 3, *Cognitive Development*, 841–90. New York: John Wiley & Sons.

Sherman Cohen, J. and Lust, B. (1993) Children are in control. *Cognition*, 46(1), 1–51.

Shipley, E. F., Smith, C. S., and Gleitman, L. R. (1969) A study in the acquisition of language: free responses to commands. *Language*, 45, 322–42.

Shore, C. (1986) Combinatorial play: conceptual development and early multiword speech. *Developmental Psychology*, 22, 184–90.

Shore, C., O'Connell, B., and Bates, E. (1984) First sentences in language and symbolic play. *Developmental Psychology*, 20, 872–80.

Shore, C., Bates, E., Bretherton, I., Beeghly, M., and O'Connell, B. (1990) Vocal and gestural symbols: similarities and differences from 13 to 28 months. In V. Volterra and C. J. Erting (eds), *From Gesture to Language in Hearing and Deaf Children*, 79–92. New York: Springer-Verlag.

Shriberg, L. (1990) *Programs to Examine Phonetic and Phonologic Evaluation Records*. Hillsdale, NJ: Lawrence Erlbaum Associates.

Shriberg, L. and Kwiatkowski, J. (1988) A follow-up study of children with phonologic disorders of unknown origin. *Journal of Speech and Hearing Disorders*, 53, 144–55.

Shriberg, L., Kwiatkowski, J., Best, S., Hengst, J., and Terselic-Weber, B. (1986) Characteristics of children with phonologic disorders of unknown origin. *Journal of Speech and Hearing Disorders*, 51, 140–61.

Shweder, R. and Much, N. C. (1987) Determinations of meaning: discourse and moral socialization. In W. M. Kurtines and J. L. Gewirtz (eds), *Moral Development through Social Interaction*. New York: Wiley & Sons.

Silva-Corvalán, C. (1983) Tense and aspect in oral Spanish narrative: context and meaning. *Language*, 59, 760–80.

Silverstein, M. (1976) Shifters, linguistic categories, and cultural description. In K. H. Basso and H. A. Selby (eds), *Meaning in Anthropology*. Albuquerque: University of Mexico Press.

—— (1987a) The three faces of "function": preliminaries to a psychology of language. In M. Hickmann (ed.), *Social and Functional Approaches to Language and Thought*. Orlando: Academic Press.

—— (1987b) Cognitive implications of a referential hierarchy. In M. Hickmann (ed.), *Social and Functional Approaches to Language and Thought*. Orlando: Academic Press.

—— (1993) Metapragmatic discourse and metapragmatic function. In J. Lucy (ed.), *Reflexive Language: reported speech and metapragmatics*. Cambridge: Cambridge University Press, 33–58.

Simoes, M. C. P. and Stoel-Gammon, C. (1979) The acquisition of inflection in Portuguese: a study of the development of person markers on verbs. *Journal of Child Language*, 6, 53–67.

Simonsen, H. G. (1990) Barns fonologi: System og variasjon hos tre norske og et samoisk barn [Child phonology: system and variation in three Norwegian children and one Samoan child]. Doctoral dissertation, Department of Linguistics and Philosophy, University of Oslo.

Singer, D. G. and Singer, J. L. (1990) *The House of Make-believe: play and the developing imagination*. Cambridge, Mass.: Harvard University Press.

Singer, J. L. and Singer, D. G. (1981) *Television, Imagination, and Aggression: a study of preschoolers*. Hillsdale, NJ: Lawrence Erlbaum Associates.

Sininger, Y. S., Klatzky, R. L., and Kirchner, D. M. (1989) Memory scanning speech in language-disordered children. *Journal of Speech and Hearing Research*, 32, 289–97.

Skarakis, E. and Greenfield, P. (1982) The role of new and old information in the verbal expression of language-disordered children. *Journal of Speech and Hearing Research*, 25, 462–7.

Skinner, B. F. (1957) *Verbal Behavior*. Englewood Cliffs, NJ: Prentice-Hall.

Sleight, C. and Prinz, P. (1985) Use of abstracts, orientations, and codas in narration by language-disordered and nondisordered children. *Journal of Speech and Hearing Disorders*, 50, 361–71.

Slobin, D. I. (1970) Universals of grammatical development in children. In G. B. Flores d'Arcais and W. J. M. Levelt (eds), *Advances in Psycholinguistics*, 174–86. North Holland.

—— (1973) Cognitive prerequisites for the development of grammar. In C. A. Ferguson and D. I. Slobin (eds), *Studies of Child Language Development*. New York: Holt, Rinehart, and Winston.

—— (1979) *Psycholinguistics*. San Francisco: Scott Foresman and Co.

—— (1982) Universal and particular in the acquisition of language. In E. Wanner and L. Gleitman (eds), *Language Acquisition: the state of the art*. New York: Cambridge University Press.

—— (1985a) Crosslinguistic evidence for the languagemaking capacity. In D. I. Slobin (ed.), *The Crosslinguistic Study of Language Acquisition*, vol. 2, *Theoretical Issues*, 1,157–1,256. Hillsdale, NJ: Lawrence Erlbaum Associates.

—— (ed.) (1985b) *The Crosslinguistic Study of Language Acquisition*, vols. 1 & 2. Hillsdale, NJ: Lawrence Erlbaum Associates.

—— (1991) Learning to think for speaking: native language, cognition and rhetorical style. *Pragmatics*, 1, 7–25.

—— (ed.) (1992) *The Crosslinguistic Study of Language Acquisition*, vol. 3. Hillsdale, NJ: Lawrence Erlbaum Associates.

Slobin, D. I. and Bever, T. (1982) Children's use of canonical sentence schemas: a crosslinguistic study of word order and inflections. *Cognition*, 12, 229.

Smit and Bernthal, J. (1983) Voicing contrasts and their phonological implications in the speech of articulation-disordered children. *Journal of Speech and Hearing Research*, 26, 486–500.

Smit, A. B., Hand, L., Freilinger, J. J., Bernthal, J. E., and Bird, A. (1990) The Iowa–Nebraska Articulation Norms Project and its Nebraska replication. *Journal of Speech and Hearing Disorders*, 55, 779–98.

Smith, B. L. (1988) The emergent lexicon from a phonetic perspective. In M. D. Smith and J. L. Locke (eds), *The Emergent Lexicon: the child's development of a linguistic vocabulary*, 75–106. New York: Academic Press.

Smith, B. L. and Oller, D. K. (1981) A comparative study of the development of stop consonant production in normal and Down's syndrome children. *Journal of Speech and Hearing Disorders*, 48, 114–18.

Smith, B. L. and Stoel-Gammon, C. (1983) A longitudinal study of the development of stop consonant production in normal and Down's syndrome children. *Journal of Speech and Hearing Disorders*, 48, 114–18.

Smith, B. L., Brown-Sweeney, S., and Stoel-Gammon, C. (1989) A quantitative analysis of reduplicated and variegated babbling. *First Language*, 9, 175–90.

Smith, C. (1980) The acquisition of time talk: relations between child and adult grammars. *Journal of Child Language*, 7, 263–78.

—— (1983) A theory of aspectual choice. *Language*, 59, 479–501.

—— (1986) A speaker-based approach to aspect. *Linguistics and Philosophy*, 9, 97–115.

Smith, C. and Sachs, J. (1990) Cognition and the verb lexicon in early lexical development. *Applied Psycholinguistics*, 11, 409–24.

Smith, C. A. and Van Kleeck, A. (1986) Linguistic complexity and performance. *Journal of Child Language*, 13, 389–408.

Smith, L. and von Tetzchner, S. (1986) Communicative, sensorimotor, and language skills of young children with Down syndrome. *American Journal of Mental Deficiency*, 91, 57–66.

Smith, M. (1926) *An investigation of the development of the sentence and the extent of vocabulary in young children*. University of Iowa Studies in Child Welfare, 3, 5.

Smith, N. V. (1973) *The Acquisition of Phonology: a case study*. Cambridge: Cambridge University Press.

Smith-Hefner, B. (1988) The linguistic socialization of Javanese children. *Anthropological Linguistics*, 30(2), 166–98.

Smoczynska, M. (1992) Developing narrative skills: learning to introduce referents in Polish. *Polish Psychological Bulletin*, 23, 103–20.

Snart, F., O'Grady, M., and Das, J. P. (1982) Cognitive processing by subgroups of moderately mentally retarded children. *American Journal of Mental Deficiency*, 86, 465–72.

Snow, C. E. (1977) Mothers' speech research: from input to interaction. In C. E. Snow and C. A. Ferguson (eds), *Talking to Children: language input and acquisition*, 31–49. Cambridge: Cambridge University Press.

—— (1978) The conversational context of language acquistion. In R. Campbell and P. Smith (eds), *Recent Advances in the Psychology of Language: language development and mother–child interaction*. New York: Plenum Press.

—— (1985) Review of *Early Bilingualism and Child Development* edited by M. Paradis and Y. Lebrun. *Applied Psycholinguistics*, 6, 195–7.

—— (1986) Conversations with children. In P. Fletcher and M. Garman (eds), *Language Acquisition*, 2nd edn, 363–75. New York: Cambridge University Press.

—— (1989) Understanding social interaction and language acquisition: sentences are not enough. In M. Bornstein and J. Bruner (eds), *Interaction in Human Development*, 83–103. Hillsdale, NJ: Lawrence Erlbaum Associates.

—— (1991) Diverse conversational contexts for the acquisition of various language skills. In J. F. Miller (ed.), *Research on Child Language Disorders: a decade of progress*, 105–24. Austin, TX: Pro-Ed.

Snow, C. E. and Dickinson, D. (1990) Social sources of narrative skills at home and at school. *First Language*, 10, 87–104.

Snow, C. E. and Ferguson, C. (1977) *Talking to Children: language input and language acquisition*. Combridge: Cambridge University Press.

Snow, C. E. and Gilbreath, B. J. (1983) Explaining transitions. In R. Golinkoff (ed.), *The Transition from Prelinguistic to Linguistic Communication*, 281–96. Hillsdale, NJ: Lawrence Erlbaum Associates.

Snow, C. E. and Tabors, P. (1993) Home influences in the development of literacy-related language skills. Paper presented at the 60th Anniversary Meeting of The Society for Research in Child Development, New Orleans.

Snow, C. E., Perlmann, R., and Nathan, D. (1987) Why routines are different: toward a multiple-factors model of the relation between input and language acquisition. In K. Nelson and A. van Kleeck (eds), *Children's Language*, vol. 6, 65–97. Hillsdale, NJ: Lawrence Erlbaum Associates.

Snow, C. E., Perlmann, R. Y., Gleason, J. B., and Hooshyar, N. (1990) Developmental perspectives on politeness: sources of children's knowledge. *Journal of Pragmatics*, 14, 289–305.

Snow, C. E., Barnes, W. S., Chandler, J., Goodman, I. F., and Hemphill, L. (1991) *Unfulfilled expectations: home and school influences in literacy*. Cambridge, Mass.: Harvard University Press.

Snyder, L. (1978) Communicative and cognitive abilities and disabilities in the sensorimotor period. *Merrill-Palmer Quarterly*, 24, 161–80.

Snyder, L., Bates, E., and Bretherton, I. (1981) Content and context in early lexical development. *Journal of Child Language*, 8, 565–82.

Sodian, B., Taylor, C., Harris, P. L., and Perner, J. (1991) Early deception and the child's theory of mind: false trails and genuine markers. *Child Development*, 62, 468–83.

Sokolov, J. (1992) Linguistic imitation in children with Down syndrome. *American Journal of Mental Retardation*, 97, 209–21.

—— (1993) A local contingency analysis of the fine-tuning hypothesis. *Developmental Psychology*, 29, 1,008–23.

Sokolov, J. and Moreton, J. (1994) Individual differences in linguistic imitativeness. In J. Sokolov and C. Snow (eds), *Handbook of Research in Language Development using CHILDES*. Hillsdale, NJ: Lawrence Erlbaum Associates.

Sokolov, J. and Snow, C. (1994a) *Handbook of Research in Language Development using CHILDES*. Hillsdale, NJ: Lawrence Erlbaum Associates.

—— (1994b) The changing role of negative evidence in theories of language acquisition. In C. Gallaway and B. Richards (eds), *Input and Interaction in Language Acquisition*, 38–55. London: Cambridge University Press.

Solan, L. (1983) *Pronominal Reference: child language and the theory of grammar*. Dordrecht: Reidel.

Sommers, R. K. and Starkey, K. L. (1977) Dichotic verbal processing in Down's syndrome children having qualitatively different speech and language skills. *American Journal of Mental Deficiency*, 82, 44–53.

Sommers, R. K., Logsdon, B., and Wright, J. (1992) A review and critical analysis of treatment research related to articulation and phonological disorders. *Journal of Communication Disorders*, 25, 3–22.

Sorce, J. F., Emde, R. N., Campos, J. J., and Klinnert, M. D. (1985) Maternal emotional signaling: its effect on the visual cliff behavior of 1-year-olds. *Developmental Psychology*, 21, 195–200.

Sorsby, A. and Martlew, M. (1991) Representational demands in mothers' talk to preschool children in two contexts: picture book reading and a modelling task. *Journal of Child Language*, 18, 373–96.

Speas, M. (1990) *Phrase Structure in Natural Language*. Dordrecht: Kluwer.

Spencer, A. (1984) A nonlinear analysis of phonological disability. *Journal of Communication Disorders*, 17, 325–48.

—— (1986) Towards a theory of phonological development. *Lingua*, 68, 3–38.

Sridhar, S. N. (1989) Cognitive structures in language production: a cross-linguistic study. In

B. MacWhinney and E. Bates (eds), *The Cross-linguistic Study of Sentence Processing*. Cambridge: Cambridge University Press.

Sridhar, S. N. and Sridhar, K. K. (1980) The syntax and psycholinguistics of bilingual code mixing. *Studies in the Linguistic Sciences*, 10, 203–15.

Stackhouse, J. (1992) Developmental verbal dyspraxia I: A review and critique. *European Journal of Disorders of Communication*, 27, 19–34.

Stampe, D. (1969) The acquisition of phonetic representation. *Proceedings of the Fifth Regional Meeting of the Chicago Linguistic Society*, 433–44.

—— (1973) A dissertation on natural phonology. Doctoral dissertation, University of Chicago.

Stark, J. (1967) A comparison of the performance of aphasic children on three sequencint tests. *Journal of Communication Disorders*, 1, 31–4.

Stark, R. E. (1978) Features of infant sounds: the emergence of cooing. *Journal of Child Language*, 5, 379–90.

—— (1979) Prespeech segmental feature development. In P. Fletcher and M. Garman (eds), *Language Acquisition*, 15–32. New York: Cambridge University Press.

—— (1980) Stages of speech development in the first year of life. In G. Yeni-Komashian, J. Kavanagh, and C. Ferguson (eds), *Child Phonology*, vol. 1, *Production*, 73–90. New York: Academic Press.

Stark, R. E. and Tallal, P. (1981) Selection of children with specific language deficits. *Journal of Speech and Hearing Disorders*, 46, 114–33.

Stasny, E. A. and Bauer, H. R. (1990) Deviations from randomness in children's early speech. *Journal of the American Statistical Association*, 85, 46–57.

Stavans, A. (1990) Code-switching in children acquiring English, Spanish and Hebrew: a case study. Unpublished Ph.D. dissertation, University of Pittsburgh.

Steckol, K. and Leonard, L. (1979) The use of grammatical morphemes by normal and language-impaired children. *Journal of Communication Disorders*, 12, 291–301.

Steffens, M., Oller, D. K., Lynch, M., and Urbano, R. C. (1992) Vocal development in infants with Down syndrome and infants who are developing normally. *American Journal on Mental Retardation*, 97, 235–46.

Stein, N. L. (1982) The definition of a story. *Journal of Pragmatics*, 6, 487–507.

Stein, N. L. and Glenn, C. G. (1979) An analysis of story comprehension in elementary school children. In R. Freedle (ed.), *New Directions in Discourse Processing*. Norwood, NJ: Ablex.

—— (1982) Children's concepts of time: the development of a story schema. In W. Friedman (ed.), *The Developmental Psychology of Time*, 255–81. New York: Academic Press.

Stein, N. L. and Nezworski, M. T. (1978) The effects of organization and instructional set of story memory. *Discourse Processes*, 1, 177–93.

Stein, N. L. and Trabasso, T. (1981) What's in a story: critical issues in story comprehension. In R. Glaser (ed.), *Advances in the Psychology of Instruction*, 213–67. Hillsdale, NJ: Lawrence Erlbaum Associates.

Stemberger, J. (1987) Child phonology: phonological processing without phonological processes. Unpublished paper, University of Minnesota.

—— (1988) Between-word processes in child phonology. *Journal of Child Language*, 15, 39–62.

—— (1992) A connectionist view of child phonology: phonological processing without phonological processes. In C. Ferguson, L. Menn, and C. Stoel-Gammon (eds), *Phonological Development: models, research, implications*, 165–89. Timonium, Md: York Press.

Stemberger, J. and Stoel-Gammon, C. (1991) The underspecification of coronal: evidence from language acquisition and performance errors. In C. Paradis and J. Prunet (eds), *The Special Status of Coronals*. Orlando: Academic Press.

Stenning, K. and Michell, L. (1985) Learning how to tell a good story: the development of content and language in children's telling of one tale. *Discourse Processes*, 8, 261–79.

Stephany, U. (1981) Verbal grammar in modern Greek child language. In S. Dale and D. Ingram (eds), *Child Language: an international perspective*. Baltimore: University Park Press.

Stern, C. and Stern, W. (1928) *Die Kindersprache* [Child language]. Darmstadt: Wissenschaftliche Buchgesellschaft.

Stern, D. (1977) *The First Relationship: infant and mother*. London: Fontana/Open Books.

Stern, D. N. (1985) *The Interpersonal World of the Infant*. New York: Basic Books.

Stern, D. N., Spieker, S., Barnett, R. K., and MacKain, K. (1983) The prosody of maternal speech: infant age and context related changes. *Journal of Child Language*, 10, 1–15.

Stevenson, R. J. and Pickering, M. (1987) The effects of linguistic and non-linguistic knowledge on the acquisition of pronouns. In P. Griffiths (ed.), *Proceedings of the Child Language Seminar*, Department of Language, York.

Stevenson, R. J. and Pollitt, C. (1987) The acquisition of temporal terms. *Journal of Child Language*, 14, 533–45.

Stiles, J. and Thal, D. (1993) Linguistic and spatial cognitive development following early focal brain injury: patterns of deficit and recovery. In M. Johnson (ed.), *Brain Development and Cognition: a reader*, 643–64. Oxford: Blackwell Publishers.

Stockman, I, D., Woods, D. R., and Tishman, A. (1981) Listener agreement on phonetic segments in early infant vocalizations. *Journal of Psycholinguistic Research*, 10, 593–617.

Stoel-Gammon, C. (1980) Phonological analysis of four Down's syndrome children. *Applied Psycholinguistics*, 1, 31–48.

—— (1981) Speech development of infants and children with Down's syndrome. In J. K. Darby (ed.), *Speech Evaluation in Medicine*, 341–59. New York: Grune & Stratton.

—— (1983) Constraints on consonant–vowel sequences in early words. *Journal of Child Language*, 10, 455–7.

—— (1985) Phonetic inventories, 15–22 months: a longitudinal study. *Journal of Speech and Hearing Research*, 28, 505–12.

—— (1988) Prelinguistic vocalizations of hearing-impaired and normally hearing subjects: a comparison of consonantal inventories. *Journal of Speech and Hearing Disorders*, 53, 302–15.

—— (1989) Prespeech and early speech development of two late talkers. *First Language*, 9, 207–24.

Stoel-Gammon, C. and Cooper, J. (1984) Patterns of early lexical and phonological development. *Journal of Child Language*, 11, 247–71.

Stoel-Gammon, C. and Herrington, P. (1990) Vowel systems of normally developing and phonologically disordered children. *Clinical Linguistics and Phonetics*, 4, 145–60.

Stoel-Gammon, C. and Otomo, K. (1986) Babbling development of hearing-impaired and normally-hearing subjects. *Journal of Speech and Hearing Disorders*, 51, 33–41.

Stone, C. A. and Connell, P. J. (1993) Induction of a visual symbolic rule in children with specific language impairment. *Journal of Speech and Hearing Research*, 36, 599–608.

Stoneman, Z. and Brody, G. (1981) Two's company, three makes a difference – an examination of mothers' and fathers' speech to their young children. *Child Development*, 52, 705–7.

Strevens, P. (1960) Spectra of fricative noise in human speech. *Language and Speech*, 3, 32–49.

Strohner, H. and Nelson, K. E. (1974) The young child's development of sentence comprehension: influence of event probability, nonverbal context, syntactic form and strategies. *Child Development*, 45, 564–76.

Strominger, A. Z., Winkler, M. R., and Cohen, L. T. (1984) Speech and language evaluation. In S. M. Pueshel (ed.), *The Young Child with Down Syndrome*. New York: Human Sciences Press.

Stromswold, K., Pinker, S., and Kaplan, R. M. (1985) Cues for understanding the passive voice. *Papers and Reports in Child Language*, 24. Stanford, CA: Stanford University Department of Linguistics.

Studdert-Kennedy, M. (1991) Language development from an evolutionary perspective. In N. Krasnegor, D. Rumbaugh, R. Schiefelbusch, and M. Studdert-Kennedy (eds), *Language Acquisition: biological and behavioral determinants*. Hillsdale, NJ: Lawrence Erlbaum Associates.

Sugarman, S. (1983) Empirical versus logical issues in the transition from prelinguistic to linguistic communication. In R. M. Golinkoff (ed.), *The Transition from Prelinguistic to Linguistic Communication*. Hillsdale, NJ: Lawrence Erlbaum Associates.

Suppes, P., Smith, R., and Leveillé, M. (1973) The French syntax of a child's noun phrases. *Archives de Psychologie*, 42, 207–69.

Syrdal, A. and Gopal, H. (1986) A perceptual model of vowel recognition based on the auditory representation of American English vowels. *Journal of the Acoustical Society of America*, 79, 1,086–100.

Szabolcsi, A. and Zwarts, F. (1990) Islands, monotonicity, composition and heads. Paper presented at GLOW Conference, University of Leiden.

—— (1992) Unbounded dependencies and the algebraic semantics. Lecture notes of the Third European Summer School in Logic, Language and Information, Saarbrucken, 1991.

Szagun, G. (1978) On the frequency of use of tenses in English and German children's spontaneous speech. *Child Development*, 49, 898–901.

Taeschner, T. (1983) *The Sun is Feminine: a study on language Acquisition in bilingual children*. Berlin/Heidelberg: Springer.

—— (1987) Analyse de quelques interférences produites par des enfants bilingues [Analysis of some cases of interference produced by bilingual children]. In G. Lüdi (ed.) *Devenir bilingue – parler bilingue* [Becoming bilingual – bilingual speech], 243–56. Tübingen: Max Niemeyer.

Taeschner, T., Volterra, V., and Wintermantel, M. (1982) The development of basic sentence structure in bilingual and monolingual Italian and German children. *Journal of Italian Linguistics*, 2, 19–48.

Tager-Flusberg, H. (1992) Autistic children's talk about psychological states: deficits in the early acquisition of a theory of mind. *Child Development*, 63, 161–72.

Tager-Flusberg, H. and Calkins, S. (1990) Does imitation facilitate the acquisition of grammar? Evidence from a study of autistic, Down's syndrome and normal children. *Journal of Child Language*, 17, 591–606.

Takahashi, M. (1991) The acquisition of echo questions. In B. Plunkett and T. Maxfield (eds), The acquisition of wh. *University of Massachusetts Occasional Papers in Linguistics*. GSLA Amherst.

Tallal, P. (1976) Rapid auditory processing in normal and disordered language development. *Journal of Speech and Hearing Research*, 19, 561–71.

—— (1988) Developmental language disorders. In J. F. Kavanagh and T. J. Truss, Jr. (eds), *Learning Disabilities: Proceedings of the National Conference*, 181–272. Parkton, Md: York Press.

Tallal, P., Ross, R., and Curtiss, S. (1989) Familial aggregation in specific language impairment. *Journal of Speech and Hearing Disorders*, 54, 167–73.

Tallal, P., Stark, R., and Mellits, D. (1985) Identification of language-impaired children on the basis of rapid perception and production skills. *Brain and Language*, 25, 314–22.

Talmy, L. (1983) How language structures space. In H. Pick and L. Acredolo (eds), *Spatial Orientation: theory, research, and application*. New York: Plenum.

—— (1985) Lexicalization patterns: semantic structure in lexical forms. In T. Shopen (ed.), *Language Typology and Syntactic Description*, vol. 3, *Grammatical Categories and the Lexicon*. Cambridge: Cambridge University Press.

Tannen, D. (1990) Gender differences in conversational coherence: physical alignment and topical cohesion. In B. Dorval (ed.), *Conversational Organization and its Development*. Norwood, NJ: Ablex.

Tanz, C. (1974) Cognitive principles underlying children's errors in pronominal case-markings. *Journal of Child Language*, 1, 271–6.

—— (1976) Learning how "it" works. *Journal of Child Language*, 3, 225–35.

—— (1980) *Studies in the Acquisition of Deictic Terms*. Cambridge: Cambridge University Press.

Teale, W. H. and Sulzby, E. (eds) (1986) *Emergent Literacy: writing and reading*. Norwood, NJ: Ablex.

Telzrow, R. W., Campos, J. J., Shepherd, A., Bertenthal, B. I., and Atwater, S. (1987) Spatial understanding in infants with motor handicaps. In K. Jaffe (ed.), *Childhood Powered Mobility: developmental, technical and clinical perspectives*. Washington, DC: RESNA.

Templin, M. (1957) *Certain Language Skills in Children: their development and interrelationships.* Institute of Child Welfare Monograph, 26. Minneapolis: University of Minnesota Press.

Tew, B. (1975) The "Cocktail Party Syndrome" in children with hydrocephalus and spina bifida. *British Journal of Disorders of Communication*, 41, 89–101.

Thal, D. and Bates, E. (1988a) Language and gesture in late talkers. *Journal of Speech and Hearing Research*, 31, 115–23.

—— (1988b) Relationships between language and cognition: evidence from linguistically precocious children. Paper presented to the Annual Convention of the American Speech–Language–Hearing Association, Boston.

Thal, D. and Schick, K. (in preparation) Relationships between language and gesture in linguistically precocious toddlers.

Thal, D., Bates, E., and Bellugi, U. (1989) Language and cognition in two children with Williams Syndrome. *Journal of Speech and Hearing Research*, 32, 489–500.

Thal, D., Bates, E., and Fenson, L. (in preparation) Characteristics of toddlers with delayed language development.

Thal, D., Bates, E., Zappia, M. J., and Oroz, M. (1994). Ties between lexical and grammatical development: evidence from early–talkers. Tech. Rep. 9401. La Jolla: University of Catifornia, San Diego, Project in Cognitive Neurodevelopment, Center for Research in Language.

Thal, D., Cleveland, S., and Oroz, M. (in preparation) Lexical and grammatical development in normal and late-talking toddlers.

Thal, D., Tobias, S., and Morrison, D. (1991) Language and gesture in late talkers: a one year follow-up. *Journal of Speech and Hearing Research*, 34(3), 604–12.

Thal, D., Marchman, V., Stiles, J., Aram, D., Trauner, D., Nass, R., and Bates, E. (1991) Early lexical development in children with focal brain injury. *Brain and Language*, 40, 491–527.

Thelen, E. (1981) Rhythmical behavior in infancy: an ethological perspective. *Developmental Psychology*, 17, 237–57.

Thelen, E. and Smith, L. (1994) *A Dynamic Systems Approaches to the Development of Cognition and Action.* Cambridge, Mass.: MIT Press.

Thomas, D. C., Campos, J. J., Shucard, W., Ransay, D. S., and Shucard, J. (1981) Semantic comprehension in infancy: a signal detection analysis. *Child Development*, 52, 798–803.

Thomas, M. (1989) The acquisition of English articles by first- and second-language learners. *Applied Psycholinguistics*, 10, 335–55.

Thompson, S. (1987) "Subordination" and narrative event structure. In R. S. Tomlin (ed.), *Coherence and Grounding in Discourse.* Amsterdam: Benjamins.

Thomson, J. and Chapman, R. (1977) Who is "daddy" revisited: the status of two-year-olds' overextended words in use and comprehension. *Journal of Child Language*, 4, 359–75.

Thornton, R. (1990) A principle based explanation of some exceptional wh-questions. Paper presented at the 15th annual Boston University Conference on Language Development.

—— (1991) *Adventures in long distance moving: the acquisition of complex wh-questions.* Ph.D. dissertation, University of Connecticut.

Tinbergen, D. (1991) Kinderpraat [Child talk]. *De Nieuwe Taalgids*, 13, 1–16/65–86.

Tingey, C., Mortensen, L., Matheson, P., and Doret, W. (1991) Developmental attainment of infants and young children with Down syndrome. *International Journal of Disability, Development and Education*, 38, 15–26.

Todd, C. and Perlmutter, M. (1980) Reality recalled by preschool children. In M. Perlmutter (ed.), *New Directions for Child Development*, vol. 10, *Children's Memory.* San Francisco: Jossey-Bass.

Tomasello, M. (1992) *First Verbs: a case study of early grammatical development.* Cambridge: Cambridge University Press.

Tomasello, M. and Farrar, J. (1984) Cognitive bases of early language: object permanence and relational words. *Journal of Child Language*, 11, 477–93.

—— (1986a) Object permanence and relational words: a lexical training study. *Journal of Child Language*, 13, 495–505.

—— (1986b) Joint attention and early language. Child *Development*, 57, 1,454–63.

Tomasello, M. and Kruger, A. C. (1992) Joint attention on actions: acquiring verbs in osten-sive and non-ostensive contexts. *Journal of Child Language*, 19, 1–23.

Tomasello, M. and Todd, J. (1983) Joint attention and lexical acquisition style. *First Language*, 4, 197–212.

Tomasello, M., Mannle, S., and Kruger, A. (1986) The linguistic environment of one to two year old twins. *Developmental Psychology*, 22, 169–76.

Tomblin, J. B. (1989) Familial concentration of developmental language impairment. *Journal of Speech and Hearing Disorders*, 54, 287–95.

Tomlin, R. S. (1985) Foreground–background information and the syntax of subordination: evidence from English discourse. *Text*, 5, 85–122.

—— (1987) *Coherence and Grounding in Discourse*. Amsterdam: Benjamins.

Trachy, R. E., Sutton, D., and Lindeman, R. C. (1981) Primate phonation: anterior cingulate lesion effects on response rate and acoustical structure. *American Journal of Primatology*, 1, 43–55.

Trevarthen, C. (1979) Communication and co-operation in early infancy: a description of primary intersubjectivity. In M. Bullowa (ed.), *Before Speech*, 321–49. Cambridge: Cambridge University Press..

—— (1988) Universal co-operative motives: how infants begin to know the language and culture of their parents. In G. Jahoda and I. M. Lewis (eds), *Acquiring Culture: cross cultural studies in child development*. London: Croom Helm.

Trevarthen, C. and Marwick, H. (1986) Signs of motivation for speech in infants and the nature of a mother's support for development of language. In B. Lindblom and R. Zetterstrom (eds), *Precursors of Early Speech*, 279–308. New York: Stockton Press.

Tronick, E., Als, H., Adamson, L., Wise, S., and Brazleton, T. B. (1978) The infant's response to entrapment between contradictory messages in face-to-face interaction. *Journal of the American Academy of Child Psychiatry*, 17, 1–13.

Trosborg, A. (1982) Children's comprehension of "before" and "after" reinvestigated. *Journal of Child Language*, 9, 381–402.

Truscott, J. and Wexler, K. (1989) Some problems in the parametric analysis of learnability. In R. Matthews and W. Demopoulos (eds), *Learnability and Linguistic Theory*, 155–76. Dordrecht: Kluwer.

Tucker, M. L. and Hirsh-Pasek, K. (1993) A dynamic systems approach to development: applications. In L. Smith and E. Thelen (eds), *Dynamic Systems and Development: applications*. Cambridge, Mass.: MIT Press.

Turner, E. A. and Rommetveit, R. (1967) Experimental manipulation of the production of active and passive voice in children. *Language and Speech*, 10, 169–80.

Tyler, A., Edwards, M. L., and Saxman, J. (1990) Acoustic validation of phonological knowledge and its relationship to treatment. *Journal of Speech and Hearing Disorders*, 55, 251–61.

Tyler, L. (1984) Integration of information during language comprehension: a developmental study. *Papers and Reports on Child Language Development*, 23, 125–33.

Umeda, N. (1975) Vowel duration in American English. *Journal of the Acoustical Society of America*, 58, 434–45.

Umiker-Sebeok, D. J. (1979) Preschool children's intraconversational narratives. *Journal of Child Language*, 6, 91–109.

Uzgiris, I. C., Benson, J. B., Kruper, J. C., and Vasek, M. E. (1989) Contextual influences on imitative interactions between mothers and infants. In J. Lockman and N. Hazen (eds), *Action in a Social Context: perspectives on early development*. New York: Plenum.

Vainikka, A. (1992a) Subject case and the acquisition of the CP. Paper presented at the 17th annual Boston University Conference on Language Development.

—— (1992b) Case in the development of English syntax. Manuscript, University of Massachusetts.

Vainikka, A. and Roeper, T. (in press) Abstract operators in early acquisition. *The Linguistics Review*.

Valian, V. (1986) Syntactic categories in the speech of young children. *Developmental Psychology*, 22, 562–79.

—— (1988) Positive evidence, indirect negative evidence, parameter setting, and language learning. Unpublished manuscript, Hunter College.

—— (1990a) Logical and psychological constraints on the acquisition of syntax. In L. Frazier and J. de Villiers (eds), *Language Processing and Language Acquisition*, 119–45. Dordrecht: Kluwer.

—— (1990b) Null subjects: a problem for parameter-setting models of language acquisition. *Cognition*, 35, 105–22.

—— (1991) Syntactic subjects in the early speech of American and Italian children. *Cognition*, 40, 21–81.

Valian, V., Lasser, I., and Mandelbaum, D. (1992) Competing analyses of children's early questions. Paper presented at the 17th annual Boston University Conference on Language Development.

Van der Lely, H. (1994) Canonical linking rules: forward vs. reverse linking in normally developing and specifically language impaired children. *Cognition*.

Van Borsel, J. (1988) An analysis of the speech of five Down's syndrome adolescents. *Journal of Communication Disorders*, 21, 409–21.

Van Dijk, R. T. (1980) *Semantic Macrostructures*. New York: Lawrence Erlbaum Associates.

Van Dongen, H. R. and Visch-Brink, E. G. (1988) Naming in aphasic children: analysis of paraphasic errors. *Neuropsychologia*, 26, 629–32.

Van Dongen, H. R., Loonen, M. C. B., and Van Dongen, K. J. (1985) Anatomical basis for acquired fluent aphasia in children. *Annals of Neurology*, 17, 306–9.

Van Geert, P. (1991) A dynamic systems model of cognitive and language growth. *Psychological Review*, 98, 3–53.

Van Hout, A., Evrard, P., and Lyon, G. (1985) On the positive semiology of acquired aphasia in children. *Developmental Medicine and Child Neurology*, 27, 231–41.

Van Kleeck, A., and Frankel, T. (1981) Discourse devices used by language disordered children: a preliminary investigation. *Journal of Speech and Hearing Disorders*, 46, 250–7.

Van Kleeck, A. and Richardson, A. (1988) Language delay in the child. In N. J. Lass, L. V. McReynolds, J. L. Northern, and D. E. Yoder (eds), *Handbook of Speech–Language Pathology and Audiology*, 655–84. Toronto: BC Decker.

Van Lancker, D. (1991) Personal relevance and the human right hemisphere. *Brain and Cognition*, 17, 64–92.

Van Riper, C. (1939) Speech Correction: principles and methods. New York: Prentice-Hall.

Vargha-Khadem, F., O'Gorman, A. M., and Watters, G. V. (1985) Aphasia and handedness in relation to hemispheric side, age at injury and severity of cerebral lesion during childhood. *Brain*, 108, 677–96.

Vargha-Khadem, F., Watkins, K., Passingham, R., and Fletcher, P. (1994) Praxic and non-verbal cognitive deficits in a large family with a genetically transmitted speech and language disorder. Manuscript, Institute of Child Health, University of London.

Vargha-Khadem, F., Isaacs, E., Van der Werf, S., Robb, S., and Wilson, J. (1992) Development of intelligence and memory in children with hemiplegic cerebral palsy: the deleterious consequences of early seizures. *Brain*, 115, 315–29.

Varnhagen, C., Das, J., and Varnhagen, S. (1987) Auditory and visual memory span: cognitive processing by TMR individuals with Down syndrome or other etiologies. *American Journal of Mental Deficiency*, 91, 398–405.

Velleman, S. L. (1983) Children's production and perception of English voiceless fricatives. Dissertation. Austin: University of Texas.

Velten, H. V. (1943) The growth of phonemic and lexical patterns in infant language. *Language*, 19, 281–92.

Vendler, Z. (1967) Verbs and times. In Z. Vendler (ed.), *Linguistics in Philosophy*. Ithaca: Cornell University Press.

Veneziano, E. (1988) Vocal/verbal interaction and the construction of early lexical knowledge. In M. D. Smith and J. L. Locke (eds), *The Emergent Lexicon: the child's development of a linguistic vocabulary*. New York: Academic Press.

Verrips, M. and Weissenborn, J. (1992) Routes to verb placement in early German and French: the independence of finiteness and agreement. In J. Meisel (ed.), *The Acquisition of Verb Placement*. Dordrecht: Kluwer.

Vihman, M. M. (1981a) Language mixing and code-switching, conversations between a pair of bilingual siblings. Paper presented at the Second International Congress for the Study of Child Language, Vancouver.

—— (1981b) Phonology and the development of the lexicon: evidence from children's errors. *Journal of Child Language*, 8, 239–64.

—— (1981c) Phonology and the development of the lexicon: evidence from children's errors. *Journal of Child Language*, 8, 239–64.

—— (1982) The acquisition of morphology by a bilingual child, a whole-word approach. *Applied Psycholinguistics*, 3, 141–60.

—— (1985) Language differentiation by the bilingual infant. *Journal of Child Language*, 12, 297–324.

—— (1986a) Individual differences in babbling and early speech: predicting to age three. In B. Lindblom and R. Zetterstrom (eds), *Precursors of Early Speech*. New York: Stockton Press.

—— (1986b) More on language differentiation. *Journal of Child Language*, 13, 595–7.

—— (1992) Early syllables and the construction of phonology. In C. A. Ferguson, L. Menn, and C. Stoel-Gammon (eds), *Phonological Development: models, research, implications*, 393–422. Timonium, Md: York Press.

Vihman, M. M. and Miller, R. (1988) Words and babble at the threshold of language acquisition. In M. D. Smith and J. L. Locke (eds), *The Emergent Lexicon: the child's development of a linguistic vocabulary*, 151–83. New York: Academic Press.

Vihman. M. M., Ferguson, C. A., and Elbert, M. (1986) Phonological development from babbling to speech: common tendencies and individual differences. *Applied Psycholinguistics*, 7, 3–40.

Vihman, M. M., Macken, M. A., Miller, R., Simmons, H., and Miller, J. (1985) From babbling to speech: a reassessment of the continuity issue. *Language*, 61, 395–443.

Vila, I. (1984) Yo siempre hablo Catalan y Castellano: datos de una investigación en curso sobre la adquisición del lenguaje en niños bilingües familiares [I always speak Catalan and Spanish: data from an ongoing investigation into the language acquisition of children growing up bilingually within the family]. In M. Siguan (ed.), *Adquisición precoz de una segunda lengua* [Early acquisition of a second language], 31–51. Barcelona: Publicacions i edicions de la universitat de Barcelona.

Vion, M. and Colas, A. (1987) La présentation du caractère ancien ou nouveau d'une information en Français. *Archives de Psychologie*, 55, 243–64.

Volterra, V. and Taeschner, T. (1978) The acquisition and development of language by bilingual children. *Journal of Child Language*, 5, 311–26.

Vygotsky, L. S. (1978) *Mind in Society*. Cambridge, Mass.: Harvard University Press.

—— (1986) *Thought and Language*. Cambridge, Mass.: Harvard University Press.

Waddington, C. H. (1940) *Organisers and Genes*. Cambridge: Cambridge University Press.

Wales, R. (1986) Deixis. In P. Fletcher and M. Garman (eds), *Language Acquisition*, 2nd edn. Cambridge: Cambridge University Press.

Wang, P. P. and Bellugi, U. (1993) Evidence from two genetic syndromes for a dissociation between verbal and visual short-term memory. Manuscript submitted for publication.

Wang, P. P., Doherty, S., Hesselink, J. H., and Bellugi, U. (1992) Callosal morphology concurs with neurobehavioral and neuropathological findings in two neurodevelopmental disorders. *Archives of Neurology*, 49, 407–11.

Wang, P. P., Hesselink, J. H., Jernigan, T., Doherty, S., and Bellugi, U. (1992). Specific neurobehavioral profile of Williams syndrome is associated with neocerebellar hemispheric preservation. *Neurology*, 42, 1,999–2,002.

Wanner, E. and Gleitman, L. (1982) *Language Acquisition: the state of the art*. Cambridge: Cambridge University Press.

Wanner, E. and Maratsos, M. (1978) An ATN approach to comprehension. In M. Halle, J. Bresnan, and G. A. Miller (eds), *Linguistic Theory and Psychological Reality*, 119–61. Cambridge, Mass.: MIT Press.

Ward, M. (1971) *Them Children: a study in language*. New York: Holt, Rinehart and Winston.

Warden, D. (1976) The influence of context on children's uses of identifying expressions and reference. *British Journal of Psychology*, 67, 101–12.

—— (1981) Learning to identify referents. *British Journal of Psychology*, 72, 93–9.

Warren-Leubecker, A. (1982) Sex differences in speech to children. Unpublished Master's thesis, Georgia Institute of Technology, Atlanta.

Warrington, E. K. and Shallice, T. (1984) Category specific semantic impairments. *Brain*, 107, 829–54.

Washburn, S. L. (1960) Tools and human evolution. *Scientific American*, 203, 63–75.

Wasow, T. (1989) Why degree-0? *Behavioral and Brain Sciences*, 12, 361–2.

Waterson, N. (1971) Child phonology: a prosodic view. *Journal of Linguistics*, 7, 179–211.

Watson, R. (1989) Literate discourse and cognitive organization: some relations between parents' talk and 3-year-olds' thought. *Applied Psycholinguistics*, 10, 221–36.

Watson-Gegeo, K. A. and Boggs, S. T. (1977) From verbal play to talk story: the roles of routines in speech events among Hawaiian children. In S. Ervin-Tripp and C. Mitchell-Kernan (eds), *Child Discourse*. New York: Academic Press.

Watson-Gegeo, K. A. and Gegeo, D. (1986) Calling out and repeating routines in the language socialization of Basotho children. In B. B. Schieffelin and E. Ochs (eds), *Language Socialization Across Cultures*, 17–50. Cambridge: Cambridge University Press.

Waxman, S. R. and Hatch, T. (1992) Beyond the basics: preschool children label objects flexibly at multiple hierarchical levels. *Journal of Child Language*, 19, 153–66.

Waxman, S. R. and Kosowski, T. D. (1990) Constraints on learning as default assumptions: comment on Merriman and Bowman's "The mutual exclusivity bias in children's word learning." *Developmental Review*, 14, 57–77.

Webb, P. A. and Abrahamson, A. A. (1976) Stages of egocentricism in children's use of "this" and "that": a different point of view. *Journal of Child Language*, 3, 349–67.

Webster, P. E. and Plante, A. S. (1992) Effects of phonological impairment on word, syllable, and phoneme segmentation. *Language, Speech, and Hearing Services in Schools*, 23, 176–82.

Wechsler, D. (1974) *Manual of the Wechsler Intelligence Scale for Children: Revised*. New York: Psychological Corporation.

Weinberg, A. (1987) Comments on Borer and Wexler. In T. Roeper and E. Williams (eds), *Parameter Setting*, 173–87. Dordrecht: Reidel.

—— (1990) Markedness versus maturation: the case of subject-auxiliary inversion. *Language Acquisition*, 1, 165–94.

Weiner, P. (1981) Systematic sound preference as a characteristic of phonological disability. *Journal of Speech and Hearing Disorders*, 46, 281–6.

—— (1985) The value of follow-up studies. *Topics in Language Disorders*, 5, 78–92.

Weinrich, U. (1953) *Languages in Contact*. The Hague: Mouton.

Weintraub, A., Walton, G. E., and Bower, T. G. R. (1992) Forward and "backward" sounds: evidence for speech processing in the newborn. Poster presented at the meeting of the International Conference in Infant Studies, Miami.

Weir, R. (1962) *Language in the Crib*. The Hague: Mouton.

Weismer, G. (1984) Acoustic analysis strategies for the refinement of phonological analysis. *ASHA Monographs*, no. 22, 30–52.

Weismer, G., Dinnsen, D., and Elbert, M. (1981) A study of the voicing distinction associated with omitted, word-final stops. *Journal of Speech and Hearing Disorders*, 46, 320–7.

Weissenborn, J. (1992) Null subjects in early grammars: implications for parameter-setting theory. In J. Weissenborn, H. Goodluck, and T. Roeper (eds), *Theoretical Issues in Language*

Acquisition: continuity and change in development, 269–99. Hillsdale, NJ: Lawrence Erlbaum Associates.

—— (1986) Learning how to become an interlocutor: the verbal negotiation of common frames of reference and actions in dyads of 7–14 year-old children. In J. Cook-Gumperz, W. Corsaro, and J. Streek (eds), *Children's World and Children's Language*, 377–404. Berlin: Mouton de Gruyter.

Weissenborn, J. and Klein, W. (1982) *HERE and THERE: cross-linguistic studies in deixis and demonstration*. Amsterdam: Benjamins.

Weissenborn, J., Roeper, T., and de Villiers, J. G. (1991) The acquisition of wh-movement in French and German. In B. Plunkett and T. Maxfield (eds), *The Acquisition of Wh. University of Massachusetts Occasional Papers in Linguistics*. GSLA Amherst.

Weist, R. M. (1986) Tense and aspect. In P. Fletcher and M. Garman (eds), *Language Acquisition*, 2nd edn, 356–74. London and New York: Cambridge University Press.

—— (1989) Time concepts in language and thought: filling the Piagetian void from two to five years. In I. Levin and D. Zakay (eds), Time and Human Cognition: a life-span perspective. Elsevier (North Holland).

—— (1991) Spatial and temporal location in child language. *First Language*, 11, 253–67.

Weist, R. M. and Buczowska, E. (1987) The emergence of temporal adverbs in Polish. *First Language*, 7, 217–29.

Weist, R. M. and Konieczna, E. (1985) Affix processing strategies and linguistic systems. *Journal of Child Language*, 12, 27–35.

Weist, R. M. and Kruppe, B. (1977) Parent and sibling comprehension in children's speech. *Journal of Psycholinguistic Research*, 6, 49–58.

Weist, R. M., Wysocka, H., and Lyytinen, P. (1991) Temporal systems in child language: a cross-linguistic evaluation. *Journal of Child Language*, 18, 67–92.

Weist, R. M., Wysocka, H., Witkowska-Stadnik, K., Buczowska, E., and Konieczna, E. (1984) The defective tense hypothesis: on the emergence of tense and aspect in child Polish. *Journal of Child Language*, 11, 347–74.

Wellen, C. J. (1985) Effects of older siblings on the language young children hear and produce. *Journal of Speech and Hearing Disorders*, 50, 84–99.

Wellman, B., Case, I., Mengert, I., and Bradbury, D. (1931) Speech sounds of young children. *University of Iowa Studies of Child Welfare*, 5(2).

Wellman, H. (1990) *The Child's Theory of Mind*. Cambridge, Mass.: Bradford Books.

Wells, C. G. (1978) What makes for successful language development? In R. Campbell and P. Smith (eds), *Recent Advances in the Psychology of Language*. New York: Plenum.

—— (1979) Learning and using the auxiliary verb in English. In V. Lee (ed.), *Language Development*, 250–70. London: Croom Helm.

—— (1985) *Language Development in the Pre-school Years*. Cambridge: Cambridge University Press.

Werker, J. F. (1993) The ontogeny and developmental significance of language specific phonetic production. In B. de Boysson-Bardies, *Developmental Neurocognition: speech and face processing in the first year of life*. Dordrecht: Kluwer.

Werker, J. F. and McLeod, P. J. (1989) Infant preference for both male and female infant-directed talk: a developmental study of attentional and affective responsiveness. *Canadian Journal of Psychology*, 43, 230–46.

Werker, J. F. and Pegg, J. E. (1992) Infant speech perception and phonological acquisition. In C. A. Ferguson, L. Menn, and C. Stoel-Gammon (eds), *Phonological Development: models, research, implications*, 285–311. Timonium. Md: York Press.

Werker, J. F. and Tees, R. C. (1984) Cross-language speech perception: evidence for the perceptual reorganization during the first year of life. *Infant Behavior and Development*, 7, 49–63.

Wertsch, J. W. (1985) *Vygotsky and the Social Formation of the Mind*. Cambridge, Mass.: Harvard University Press.

—— (1991) *Voices of the Mind*. Cambridge, Mass.: Harvard University Press.

Wetstone, H. and Friedlander. B. (1973) The effect of word order on young children's responses to simple questions and commands. *Child Development*, 44, 734–40.

Wexler, K. (1990) On unparsable input in language acquisition. In L. Frazier and J. de Villiers (eds), *Language Processing and Language Acquisition*, 105–17. Dordrecht: Kluwer.

Wexler, K. and Chien, Y. C. (1985) The development of lexical anaphors and pronouns. *Papers and Reports on Child Language Development*, 24. Stanford, CA: Stanford University Press.

Wexler, K. and Culicover, P. W. (1980) *Formal Principles of Language Acquisition*. Cambridge, Mass.: MIT Press.

Wexler, K. and Manzini, M. R. (1987) Parameters and learnability in binding theory. In T. Roeper and E. Williams (eds), *Parameter Setting*, 41–76. Dordrecht: Reidel.

Whitaker, H. A. (1976) Disorders of speech production mechanisms. In E. C. Carterette and M. Friedman (eds), *Handbook of Perception*, vol. 7, *Language and Speech*, 429–42. New York: Academic Press.

White, L. (1982) The responsibility of grammatical theory to acquisitional data. In N. Hornstein and D. Lightfoot (eds), *Explanation in Linguistics: the Logical problem of language acquisition*, 241–71. London: Longman.

Whitehurst, G., Fischel, J., Arnold, D., and Lonigan, C. (1992) Evaluating outcomes with children with expressive language delay. In W. Warren and J. Reichle (eds), *Causes and Effects in Communication and Language Intervention*, 277–314. Baltimore: Paul Brookes.

Whiteman, B. C., Simpson, G. B., and Compton, W. C. (1986) Relationship of otitis media and language impairment in adolescents with Down syndrome. *Mental Retardation*, 25, 281–6.

Whiting, B. B. and Edwards, C. P. (1988) *Children of Different Worlds: the formation of social behavior*. Cambridge, Mass.: Harvard University Press.

Wiegel-Crump, C. A. (1981) The development of grammar in Down's syndrome children between the mental ages of 2–0 and 6–11 years. *Education and Training of the Mentally Retarded*, February, 24–30.

Wiegel-Crump, C. A. and Dennis, M. (1984) *The Word-Finding Test*, (unpublished test). Toronto: The Hospital for Sick Children.

Wigglesworth, G. (1990) Children's narrative acquisition: a study of some aspects of reference and anaphora. *First Language*, 10, 105–25.

—— (1993) Investigating children's cognitive and linguistic development through narrative. Doctoral dissertation, La Trobe University.

Wilkins, W. (1989) Why degree-0? *Behavioral and Brain Sciences*, 12, 362–3.

Willbrand, M. and Kleinschmidt, M. (1978) Substitution patterns and word constraints. *Language, Speech and Hearing Services in Schools*, 9, 155–61.

Williams, E. (1987) Introduction. In T. Roeper and E. Williams (eds), *Parameter Setting*, vii–xix. Dordrecht: Reidel.

—— (1989) Linguistic variation and learnability. *Behavioral and Brain Sciences*, 12, 363–4.

Williams, P. A., Haertel, E. H., Haertel, G. D., and Walberg, H. J. (1982) The impact of leisure-time television on school learning: a research synthesis. *American Educational Research Journal*, 19, 19–50.

Williams, T. M. (ed.) (1986) *The Impact of Television: a natural experiment in three communities*. New York: Academic Press.

Williamson, S. G. (1979) Tamil baby talk: a cross-cultural study. Unpublished Ph.D. dissertation, University of Pennsylvania.

Wilson, B. (1986) The emergence of the semantics of tense and aspect in the language of a visually impaired child. Unpublished Ph.D. dissertation, University of Hawai'i.

Wimmer, H. and Perner, J. (1983) Beliefs about beliefs: representation and constraining function of wrong beliefs in young children's understanding of deception. *Cognition*, 13, 103–28.

Winitz, H. (1969) *Articulatory Acquisition and Behavior*. New York: Appleton-Century-Croft.

Winner, E. (1988) *The Point of Words: children's understanding of metaphor and irony*. Cambridge, Mass.: Harvard University Press.

Winner, E. and Gardner, H. (1977) The comprehension of metaphors in brain-damaged patients. *Brain*, 100, 719–27.

Wishart, J. (1988) Early learning in infants and young children with Down syndrome. In L. Nadel (ed.), *The Psychobiology of Down Syndrome*. Cambridge, Mass.: MIT Press.

Witelson, S. F. (1977) Anatomical asymmetry in the temporal lobes: its documentation, phytogenesis, and relationship to functional asymmetry. *Annals of the New York Academy of Sciences*, 299, 328–54.

Witelson, S. F. (1987) Neurobiological aspects of language in children. *Child Development*, 58(3), 653–88.

Wode, H. (1981) *Learning a Second Language: an integrated view of second language acquisition*. Tübingen: Narr.

—— (1990) But grandpa always goes like this . ... Or, The ontogeny of code-switching. *Papers for the Workshop on Impact and Consequences*, 17–50. Brussels: ESF Network on Code-Switching and Language Contact.

Wölck, W. (1984) Komplementierung und Fusion: Prozesse natürlicher Zweisprachigkeit [Complementation and fusion: processes of natural bilingualism]. In E. Oksaar (ed.), *Spracherwerb – Sprachkontakt – Sprachkonflikt* [Language acquisition – language contact – language conflict], 107–28. Berlin and New York: de Gruyter.

—— (1987/88) Types of natural bilingual behavior: a review and revision. *The Bilingual Review/La Revista Bilingüe*, 14, 3–16.

Wolf, D., Moreton, J., and Camp, L. (1994) Children's acquisition of different kinds of narrative discourse: genres and lines of talk. In J. Sokolov C. Snow (eds), *Handbook of Research in Language Development Using CHILDES*. Hillsdale, NJ: Lawrence Erlbaum Associates.

Wolff, P. H. (1969) The natural history of crying and other vocalization in early infancy. In B. M. Foss (ed.), *Determinants of Infant Behaviour*, vol. 4. London: Methuen.

Wolfram, W. (1971) Black–white speech differences revisited. In W. Wolfram and N. H. Clark (eds), *Black–White Speech Relationships*, 139–61. Washington DC: Center for Applied Linguistics.

Wolfson, N. (1979) The conversational historical present alternation. *Language*, 55, 168–82.

Wong-Fillmore, L. (1979) Individual differences in second-language acquisition. In C. J. Fillmore, D. Kempler, and W. Wang (eds), *Individual Differences in Language Ability and Language Behavior*. New York: Academic Press.

Woods, B. T. and Carey, S. (1979) Language deficits after apparent clinical recovery from childhood aphasia. *Annals of Neurology*, 6, 405–9.

Woods, B. T. and Teuber, H. L. (1978) Changing patterns of childhood aphasia. *Annals of Neurology*, 3, 272–80.

Woodward, A. (1987) *In the beginning was the word: infants' early perception of word-units in the speech stream*. Honors thesis in psychology, Swarthmore College.

Wren, C. T. (1985) Collecting language samples from children with syntax problems. *Language, Speech, and Hearing Services in Schools*, 16, 83–102.

Wulfeck, B., Trauner, D., and Tallal, P. (1991) Neurologic, cognitive and linguistic features of infants after early stroke. *Pediatric Neurology*, 7, 266–9.

Wurzel, W. U. (1990) The mechanism of inflection: lexicon representations, rules, and irregularities. In W. U. Dressler et al. (eds) *Contemporary Morphology*. Berlin: de Gruyter.

Youssef, V. (1990) The early development of perfect aspect: adverbial, verbal and contextual specification. *Journal of Child Language*, 17, 295–312.

Zentella, A. C. (1990) Integrating qualitative and quantitative methods in the study of bilingual code-switching. In E. Bendix (ed.), *The Uses of Linguistics: annals of the New York Academy of Sciences*, vol. 583, 75–92. New York: New York Academy of Sciences.

Zimmer, E. Z., Fifer, W. P., Kim, Y-I., Rey, H. R., Chao, C. R., and Myers, M. M. (1993) Response of the premature fetus to stimulation by speech sounds. *Early Human Development*, 33, 207–15.

Zlatin-Laufer, M. and Horii, Y. (1977) Fundamental frequency characteristics of infant nondistress vocalization during the first 24 weeks. *Journal of Child Language*, 4, 171–84.

Zwicky, A. (1971). In a manner of speaking. *Linguistic Inquiry*, 2, 223–33.

Index